MW01077227

# The SAGE Handbook of
# Interpersonal Communication

## Fourth Edition

BRANT BURLESON, 1952–2010

*For everyone who knew him, loved him, and profited from his scholarship, we dedicate this book to Brant Burleson. Brant was our field's leading authority in the study of social support, and his contributions to our understanding of communication skills were huge. The support he gave as mentor, friend, and family member made others want to be supportive. As he said many times, he found joy in the study of communication processes. He also left a part of this joy in our hearts.*

# The SAGE Handbook of
# Interpersonal Communication

## Fourth Edition

Edited by

### Mark L. Knapp
*The University of Texas at Austin*

### John A. Daly
*The University of Texas at Austin*

Los Angeles | London | New Delhi
Singapore | Washington DC

Los Angeles | London | New Delhi
Singapore | Washington DC

FOR INFORMATION:

SAGE Publications, Inc.
2455 Teller Road
Thousand Oaks, California 91320
E-mail: order@sagepub.com

SAGE Publications Ltd.
1 Oliver's Yard
55 City Road
London EC1Y 1SP
United Kingdom

SAGE Publications India Pvt. Ltd.
B 1/I 1 Mohan Cooperative Industrial Area
Mathura Road, New Delhi 110 044
India

SAGE Publications Asia-Pacific Pte. Ltd.
33 Pekin Street #02-01
Far East Square
Singapore 048763

Acquisitions Editor:   Matthew Byrnie
Associate Editor:   Nathan Davidson
Editorial Assistant:   Elizabeth Borders
Production Editor:   Eric Garner
Copy Editor:   QuADS Prepress (P) Ltd.
Typesetter:   C&M Digitals (P) Ltd.
Proofreader:   Theresa Kay
Indexer:   Diggs Publication Services
Cover Designer:   Gail Buschman
Marketing Manager:   Liz Thornton
Permissions Editor:   Karen Ehrmann

Printed in the United States of America

*Library of Congress Cataloging-in-Publication Data*

The Sage handbook of interpersonal communication/
Mark L. Knapp, John A. Daly, editors.—4th ed.

p. cm.
Includes bibliographical references and index.

ISBN 978-1-4129-7474-5 (cloth)

1. Interpersonal communication. I. Knapp, Mark L.
II. Daly, John A. (John Augustine), 1952- III. Interpersonal
communication. IV. Title: Handbook of interpersonal
communication.

BF637.C45I645 2011
302.2—dc23          2011024470

This book is printed on acid-free paper.

11 12 13 14 15 10 9 8 7 6 5 4 3 2 1

# Contents

# Acknowledgments

In an effort to make this fourth edition of the *Handbook of Interpersonal Communication* meet the needs of our readers better, a number of significant changes were implemented. Many of these changes were recommended by the following scholars, who provided detailed reviews with specific suggestions:

Sakile Camara (California State University, Northridge)

Kathryn Greene (Rutgers)

Javette Hayes (California State University, Fullerton)

Amy Johnson (University of Oklahoma)

Maureen Keeley (Texas State University, San Marcos)

Terry Kinney (Wayne State University)

Michael Kotowski (University of Tennessee)

Mei-chen Lin (Kent State University)

Erina MacGeorge (Purdue University)

William Mullen (Liberty University)

Caroline Rankin (University of Kentucky)

Jennifer Samp (University of Georgia)

Chris Segrin (University of Arizona)

Laura Stafford (University of Kentucky)

We, and future readers of this volume, owe them a huge debt of thanks.

# PART I

# Basic Issues and Approaches

# CHAPTER 1

# Background and Current Trends in the Study of Interpersonal Communication

*Mark L. Knapp*

*John A. Daly*

This is the fourth edition of the *Handbook of Interpersonal Communication*. As in the first three editions, we have brought together a number of experts in the multifaceted field of interpersonal communication. Each author has assessed within his or her own area of the field where we have been, what we know, what we don't know, what we need to know, and where we should be going. We hope that, like the previous editions, this will be an important reference work for people interested in the study of interpersonal communication.

In response to changes in the field and detailed feedback from readers, we have made some significant changes in this edition. Authors of chapters from the previous edition have updated the theory and research related to their topics, and several have added coauthors, who

brought their own knowledge and perspectives to those chapters. In an effort to maintain chapters that were at the forefront of knowledge in the field, we specifically sought input from scholars whose experiences and time in the field were varied. We retained some of the topics from the previous edition but sought new authors with a fresh perspective (e.g., Chapter 7, on language; Chapter 16, on the workplace; Chapter 2, on quantitative methods; and Chapter 3, on qualitative methods). This edition also has four new chapters that represent new and stimulating opportunities for understanding interpersonal processes (Chapter 4 on biological/physiological responses, Chapter 11 on social networks, Chapter 17 on intercultural encounters, and Chapter 21 on interpersonal communication across the lifespan).

The organization of this *Handbook* is similar to that of the previous editions. The first four chapters (Parts I and II) introduce some of the key theoretical and methodological issues facing those who study interpersonal communication, including biological and physiological approaches for the first time. The next four chapters (Part III) focus on the components of the process—verbal and nonverbal behavior, social cognitions, and the characteristics each communicator brings to the encounter. The next seven chapters (Part IV) focus on the various processes and functions of interpersonal communication, such as emotion, social support, social networks, social influence, conflict, and computer-mediated communication. The final chapter in this group (Chapter 15) addresses the issues associated with interpersonal competence. The six chapters in Part V of the book examine interpersonal processes in important and familiar contexts—the workplace, intercultural transactions, romantic relationships, physician and patient encounters, family interaction, and interpersonal communication across the lifespan.

The rest of this introductory chapter is designed to set the stage for the book by (a) giving a brief historical perspective to the current study of interpersonal communication, (b) speculating on the trends that may have a strong influence on future studies of interpersonal communication, (c) looking closely at the referent for the term *interpersonal communication*, and (d) setting forth in capsule form some of the primary conceptual themes we see represented throughout the book.

## Historical Highlights

In more extensive historical accounts, other communication scholars have situated the study of interpersonal communication within the larger field of communication (Delia, 1987) and as a focus of study within speech communication (Rawlins, 1985). Historical perspectives can also be gleaned from a collection of "classic"

research studies in interpersonal communication (Knapp & Daly, 2010) and reviews of theoretical perspectives in interpersonal studies (Berger, 1977, 2005; Roloff & Anastasiou, 2001). We make no pretense of documenting, in the brief history we sketch here, all the important authors and streams of thought that are in some way tied to current approaches to interpersonal communication. Instead, we have selected what we think are important contributions from the wide variety of disciplines and interdisciplinary thinkers in this area. As we will note later, it was not until the 1960s that the study of interpersonal communication per se began to bloom profusely in the United States. But as the following shows, a great deal of pioneering work preceded that period.

## Early 20th Century

In the early 1900s, Georg Simmel (1908/1950) and other sociologists were making astute observations about interpersonal communication that are still debated today. These included concepts such as "reciprocal knowledge," "characteristics of the dyad," interaction "rituals," "secrecy," "lies and truth," and "types of social relationships."

## The 1920s and 1930s

Many intellectual seeds for the study of interpersonal communication were sown during the 1920s and 1930s. Speech professors were writing articles on the art of conversation (Howes, 1928; Oliver, 1932). This era also saw Elton Mayo and his colleagues at the Harvard Business School uncover the potential power of social interaction and social relationships in work settings. Their studies conducted at the Western Electric Hawthorne plant raised important questions about supervisor–employee interaction as well as the influence of peer interactions on productivity. This "human relations" movement set in motion subsequent thinking about the nature of supportive communication, openness, and the effects of showing concern for another's needs during interaction (Roethlisberger & Dickson, 1939).

The origins of group dynamics are recounted elsewhere (Cartwright & Zander, 1960; Hare, Borgatta, & Bales, 1955), but the field of interpersonal studies owes much to this line of work, which was in its infancy in the 1930s. Topics such as cooperation/competition, feedback, conflict, interaction sequences, methods for coding responses, sociometric choices (group member preferences for other group members), and social networks are all areas of shared interest for group and interpersonal scholars. The study of children's interaction during the 1930s also provided insights into systematic observation methods and identified patterns of interaction, such as cooperation and dominance (Murphy, Murphy, & Newcomb, 1937). It was the analysis of children's interaction during this period that revealed the crucial process of role taking (Piaget, 1926).

The belief that the self emerges out of the individual's interaction with significant others provided the foundation for the intellectual movement known as *symbolic interactionism* (Blumer, 1969; Mead, 1934). With the recognition that the way we respond to symbols affects the development of our selves and the nature of the society we live in, the 1930s also spawned the general semantics movement, which asked us to scrutinize closely our responses to symbols. Korzybski's *Science and Sanity* (1933) put forth the principles of general semantics, but books such as Hayakawa's *Language in Action* (1941) were responsible for disseminating such ideas to the general public. Through examples of everyday experiences, the principles of general semantics continue to play an important role in textbooks devoted to the improvement of individuals' interpersonal communication skills.

## The 1940s and 1950s

Significant pioneering work in a number of current areas of study in interpersonal communication was done in the 1950s.

Eliot Chapple (1953, 1970) believed that the matching of interaction rhythms leads to an impression of harmony, whereas mismatching of rhythms signals discord—regardless of the content. Intensity, timing, and patterns of temporal organization were all elements elicited through the use of Chapple's "standardized interview" (meaning that an interviewer's behavior was predictable) and recorded by his "interaction chronograph." According to Chapple, interaction rhythm is central to an understanding of everyday competence in interpersonal communication as well as psychopathology.

In the field of psychiatry, the shift from an intrapersonal orientation to an interpersonal one was largely due to the lectures and writings of the psychiatrist Harry Stack Sullivan (see Chapman, 1976). Sullivan believed that adult schizophrenia is rooted in problematic interpersonal relations during childhood and adolescence. Another psychiatrist, Jurgen Ruesch, teamed up with the anthropologist Gregory Bateson on a book that explicated the role of communication in mental illness as well as issues of cultural organization (Ruesch & Bateson, 1951). Ruesch later co-wrote the first book to use the term *nonverbal communication* in its title (Ruesch & Kees, 1956). Bateson's work was later to be the foundation for one of the most influential works in interpersonal communication scholarship, *Pragmatics of Human Communication* (Watzlawick, Beavin, & Jackson, 1967).

The anthropologists Ray Birdwhistell (1952) and Edward T. Hall (1959) were interested in the total process of communication, but their pioneering efforts and observations of body movement, gestures, postures, and the use of space laid the groundwork for the area of study called *nonverbal communication*—predominantly examined as interpersonal behavior.

Pioneering social psychologists also were greatly interested in interpersonal dynamics during the 1950s. Fritz Heider's book *The Psychology of Interpersonal Relations* (1958) helped launch a line of research on attribution theory that is integral to the study of interpersonal communication today. Theodore Newcomb's (1953) "co-orientation" model grew out of his interest in interpersonal perception and liking. It anticipated the need to study the behavior of both interactants rather than simply studying each individually. Charles Osgood, George Suci, and Percy Tannenbaum (1957) developed the "semantic differential" to study meaning, and it launched thousands of studies focused on attitudes, meaning, and social interaction. The scientific approach used by Hovland and his colleagues at Yale to study attitude change, source credibility, and fear appeals had a profound effect on speech and communication scholars in the 1960s (Hovland, Janis, & Kelley, 1953). In part, it changed the methodology used. Many young communication scholars in the 1960s embraced the use of experimental methods as a way of making their study of rhetorical principles more scientific. And even though the Yale studies examined persuasion in a person-to-group context, their findings were often used by communication scholars as the basis for hypotheses about persuasive effects in interpersonal contexts. In the same way, the work of the social psychologist Leon Festinger exerted a great deal of influence on communication scholars in the 1960s—primarily his work on attitude change, group pressures toward uniformity (Festinger, 1950), the influence of social networks and the effects of comparing one's attitude with that of others (Festinger, 1954), and the nature of cognitive dissonance (Festinger, 1957).

The first of the many influential books written by the sociologist Erving Goffman was *The Presentation of Self in Everyday Life* (1959). Goffman's influence on the study of interpersonal communication has been enormous, and his books have been "must reads" for several generations of graduate students (Goffman, 1963, 1971, 1981). Goffman's in-depth and provocative insights about the organization of social behavior and the important role played by seemingly mundane behaviors stimulated an interest in interpersonal life in communication and across the social sciences.

The 1950s was the decade that initiated the "communication revolution." This was reflected not only in what was studied but also in the establishment of new organizations and journals. Scholars from many academic disciplines and practitioners saw the growing importance of communication in the lives of human beings. Their interests were diverse and included cybernetics, information theory, mass communication, and interaction in government and business organizations. Some of them founded the National Society for the Study of Communication in 1950 and launched the *Journal of Communication* the next year. This organization later became the International Communication Association.

## The 1960s

In addition to the wealth of ideas and writings produced during the decades preceding the 1960s, the blossoming of interpersonal communication as an academically identifiable area of study was greatly affected by societal forces. The social turmoil accompanying the civil rights movement and the subsequent involvement of the U.S. military in Vietnam triggered in many citizens, particularly the young and idealistic, a deep-seated aversion to the manipulative and deceitful aspects of many mass media messages. An emerging concern for self-development and personal awareness gave rise to face-to-face communicative activities such as sensitivity training and consciousness raising. Attacks on the traditional public and mass communication orientations of most communication scholars at that time emphasized the importance of interpersonal communication to personal authentication. The critics proclaimed that the daily quality of individuals' lives is shaped by the integrity of their personal relationships rather than by the persuasive wiles of media messages crafted by advertising agencies and political consultants.

Given the prevailing climate in the 1960s, it is hardly surprising that a book such as *Pragmatics of Human Communication* (Watzlawick et al., 1967), which had a profound effect on the subsequent study of interpersonal communication, had nothing to say about the ways individuals can use communication to extract money or concessions from others but offered considerable advice on the ways people can think about and perform their communicative activities so as to improve their personal relationships with marital partners and close friends.

Many of the ideas in Watzlawick et al. (1967) continue to influence the way we think about human interaction in general and interpersonal communication specifically—for instance, the axiom "You cannot not communicate," the idea that all messages have a content and a relationship dimension to them, the concept of symmetrical and complementary communication relationships, and many others.

In a similar vein, Barnlund's (1968) anthology of theoretical and empirical papers, which stimulated interest in interpersonal communication among persons in university speech communication and communication departments, focused on the factors influencing the origination, development, and maintenance of interpersonal relationships. Argyle's (1969) review of research on "social interaction" and his resulting "social skills model" maintained a similar orientation.

Apart from a course in group dynamics or interviewing, communication graduate students in the early 1960s were not offered courses in interpersonal communication. On their own, they tried to reframe subjects such as language, feedback, style, intent, context, source credibility, and adaptation in the context of two-person conversations while embracing several areas of research in social psychology that also seemed to further their understanding of interpersonal transactions— for instance, social exchange theories (Homans, 1961; Thibaut & Kelley, 1959), person perception (Tagiuri, 1969), and interpersonal attraction (Byrne, 1971). During this decade, there was also a dominant and unyielding academic belief that all behavior was learned. The idea that certain types of communication behavior might have biological

underpinnings was too radical to have much traction until the 1990s, even though a growing number of studies of certain communicator traits and personality characteristics that were deemed less subject to environmental influences can be traced to the 1970s.

Referring to the field of speech communication, Delia (1987) contended that the events that transpired in the 1960s made interpersonal communication "the field's core research area" (p. 84) and that these factors have significantly influenced the field since.

## The 1970s

The study of interpersonal communication was firmly established during the 1970s. The evidence for this can be seen in pedagogy, theory, research, and the formal organization of scholarly interests.

The burgeoning number of college and university courses covering various aspects of interpersonal communication and interpersonal relations was accompanied by a spate of textbooks dealing with these topics—for example, Giffin and Patton (1971), Keltner (1970), and McCroskey, Larson, and Knapp (1971).

The formal establishment of areas of emphasis in scholarly and professional associations of the communication disciplines, such as the Interpersonal and Small Group Interaction Interest Group of the Speech Communication Association (now the National Communication Association) and the Interpersonal Communication Division of the International Communication Association, signaled increasing interest in the teaching and study of interpersonal communication processes. Convention programs dealing with aspects of interpersonal communication became the rule rather than the exception. One of these programs, held at the 1976 meeting of the International Communication Association in West Berlin, spawned two state-of-the-art papers that were later published in the association's journal, *Human Communication Research* (Bochner, 1978; Miller, 1978). Evidence that interpersonal communication had become an important dimension of graduate education was provided by the convening of two national doctoral honors seminars sponsored by the National Communication Association, one at Michigan State University and the other at Northwestern University. Since then, several additional doctoral honors seminars have included interpersonal communication as one of the core areas of study in communication.

The belief that interpersonal communication was "theory barren" prompted several new theoretical perspectives—for instance, uncertainty reduction theory (Berger & Calabrese, 1975) and the coordinated management of meaning (Pearce, 1976). Miller and Steinberg (1975) pointed out that we conduct our relationships with others on the basis of cultural rules and knowledge (the least personal), sociological rules and knowledge relative to our membership in societal subgroups (more personal), and psychological rules and knowledge relative to a single other person (the most personal). But the theory and research that was initiated in the 1970s and dominates the current study of interpersonal relationships deals with what Miller and Steinberg would call the most personal relationships. Duck (1973), Knapp (1978), Altman and Taylor (1973), and Kelley (1979) are representative of the early approaches to interpersonal communication in personal relationships.

Several specialized research areas also developed in the 1970s—for example, nonverbal communication (Knapp, 1972), deception (Knapp & Comadena, 1979; Knapp, Hart, & Dennis, 1974), relational control (Millar & Rogers, 1976; Rogers & Farace, 1975), communication competence (Wiemann, 1977), and mutual influence (Burgoon, 1978; Giles & Powesland, 1975).

## The 1980s

With the study of interpersonal communication firmly established during the 1970s, interpersonal scholars in the 1980s extended and refined some of their earlier theories, such as the coordinated management of meaning (Cronen, Pearce,

& Harris, 1982) and uncertainty reduction (Berger & Bradac, 1982). They also generated new theoretical perspectives such as dialectical theory (Baxter, 1988; Rawlins, 1983) and expectancy violations (Burgoon, 1983).

Social cognition was relatively untapped by communication scholars prior to the 1980s, but the work of scholars such as Delia, O'Keefe, and O'Keefe (1982) on constructivism and Greene (1984) on action assembly theory stimulated an interest that continues today.

During this period, a number of communication scholars viewed the study of messages per se as a distinguishing feature of their work. As a result, message taxonomies were developed for conflict strategies (Sillars, 1980), compliance-gaining strategies (Miller, Boster, Roloff, & Seibold, 1977; Wheeless, Barraclough, & Stewart, 1983); affinity-seeking strategies (Bell & Daly, 1984), and compliments (Knapp, Hopper, & Bell, 1984). Some studied particular types of messages—for example, personal idioms (Hopper, Knapp, & Scott, 1981) and memorable messages (Knapp, Stohl, & Reardon, 1981).

This was also a decade when a number of interpersonal researchers focused their attention on the difficulties associated with studying the dynamics of interaction or process. The idea that interactants sometimes reciprocate similar behavior and sometimes compensate by engaging in offsetting behavior had been around since Chapple's work in the 1950s. But communication scholars greatly expanded on this idea and provided new insights into this process of mutual influence (e.g., Burgoon & Hale, 1988; Cappella & Greene, 1982; Giles, Mulac, Bradac, & Johnson, 1987; Patterson, 1982).

With the launch of the *Journal of Social and Personal Relationships* in 1984, the study of personal relationships continued to gain momentum as a primary focus for those who chose to study interpersonal communication. The term *relationship* was becoming more of a context for studying interpersonal communication than a synonym for the *process* being studied. This perspective continued to grow over the next two decades, so that it is not uncommon for some of the current interpersonal scholars to equate the study of interpersonal communication with the study of personal relationships. Obviously, we have numerous interactions with strangers and acquaintances on a daily basis, but as yet these transactions have been given far less attention than close relationships by interpersonal researchers. Less studied but just as relevant to those who study close, personal relationships are those interpersonal exchanges among intimates that seem to be as impersonal as the exchanges with strangers.

## The 1990s

During the 1990s, interpersonal communication scholars began to embrace a variety of approaches to their investigations (e.g., quantitative and qualitative, micro and macro). The value of interpersonal narratives (Bochner & Ellis, 1992), a biological perspective (Beatty & McCroskey, 1997), computer-mediated interpersonal communication (Walther, 1992), and intercultural studies (Gudykunst et al., 1996) opened up new knowledge, issues, problems, and ways of understanding interpersonal transactions. The knowledge base for interpersonal communication was becoming so vast that like-minded scholars bonded together to form special-interest groups within the larger umbrella of interpersonal communication. These scholars published specialized volumes in their area (e.g., Cahn, 1992, on conflict; Canary & Stafford, 1994, on relational maintenance; Rawlins, 1992, on friendship), and in some cases, new journals (e.g., *Personal Relationships*) emerged as outlets for these specialized interests. Organizationally, what were once single divisions within both the National Communication Association and the International Communication Association devoted to the study of interpersonal and small-group behavior spawned numerous organizational entities that employed in their names terms such as *intrapersonal communication, family communication, social interaction, communication avoidance and apprehension*, and *small-group communication*.

The 1990s was also a time when edited volumes expanded the knowledge bases for various areas of interpersonal communication. This, in turn, helped increase the recognition that scholarship in this area received within the field of communication and across other disciplines.

Debates continued about whether or not interpersonal communication had any theories and, if so, which ones were "worthy" (Berger, 1991, 1992; Burleson, 1992). At the same time, new theories about, and approaches to the study of, interpersonal communication were emerging in areas such as nonverbal behavior (Burgoon, Stern, & Dillman, 1995), privacy (Petronio, 2000), cognition (Berger, 1997; Greene, 1997; Honeycutt, 1991), and dialectics (Baxter & Montgomery, 1996).

The so-called dark side of interpersonal communication also emerged in works during this decade (Cupach & Spitzberg, 1994; Spitzberg & Cupach, 1998). While the authors of these books did not argue that certain message types or strategies were inherently harmful or distasteful, some have interpreted it in this way. Obviously, communication messages or strategies achieve "positive" or "negative" status in a particular context. No doubt some message types or strategies may have a greater likelihood of being "dark" and some a greater likelihood of being "light." But context is the determining factor, not the type of message. Even apparently "light" messages such as compliments or expressions of social support can have detrimental effects on an interpersonal relationship in certain contexts.

## The Future

It is still too early to identify the key developments during the past 10 years, but some of the work done in the first decade of the 21st century gives us a basis for predicting the future.

Some researchers will choose to study interpersonal communication as it relates to social issues facing this society and the larger world community. It seems reasonable, for example, that we need to know more about the nature of conflict and cooperation, whether it focuses on understanding how antagonists representing different countries can effectively negotiate their differences or whether it focuses on two people trying to build and maintain a relationship. No doubt some scholars will be drawn to interpersonal issues interfacing with the preservation of the environment or the development of a healthier lifestyle. We also have much to learn about the role of interpersonal communication in other social problems such as crime prevention, alienation, incivility, or bridging gaps between socioeconomic groups. In contrast, we also have relatively little knowledge of interpersonal communication functioning as entertainment or play.

The widespread availability of technology for communicating is bound to play an important role in the way interpersonal transactions are thought of and manifested. Interactive video, virtual reality, texting, social media (e.g., Facebook), and portable video phones (among other technological changes) predict an interpersonal world that is potentially very different from the current one. There is also the possibility that the way we conduct face-to-face interaction will gradually change as our experience with mediated communication becomes more prevalent.

Interpersonal studies also have a history of being by and large culture and socioeconomic-class specific. Currently, our understanding of interpersonal communication is largely rooted in research on upper-middle-class students from Western cultures. In the future, it is reasonable to expect that more interpersonal research questions will cut across cultural, class, and international boundaries.

Interpersonal studies have only begun to explore the biological foundations of behavior. The central and guiding premise in interpersonal communication research until recently has been the assumption that virtually all of our interpersonal behavior is "learned." This assumption is likely to be increasingly challenged (Beatty, Marshall, & Rudd, 2001; Beatty & McCroskey, 2001). Because we believe that social scientists and humanists will be paying increasing attention to

questions concerning possible genetic and physiological influences on interpersonal behavior, we included a chapter on this subject for this edition. Communicator competence and the physical health of communicators following conflict or supportive interactions are only two of the many inviting areas of study within this framework.

Applied scholarship in interpersonal communication has a long tradition, and there is every reason to believe that this interest will continue. The central question seems to be this: What do we/can we/should we take from our knowledge of interpersonal communication for application to the problems of everyday life? Assessment, accountability, and policy—long the practical provinces of larger and more formal systems—may become an increasing concern for those who study interpersonal communication as well. For many years, students of public communication have taken their knowledge and helped people become better practitioners of communication. Scholars in interpersonal communication may increasingly see the value of using their knowledge to enhance the interpersonal effectiveness of people in their everyday lives. Improving communication between physicians and patients has been a special area of concern in recent years, and a number of communication scholars have conducted communication skills courses as part of the curriculum in some medical schools.

## The Handbook of What?

What is interpersonal communication? Obviously, a large number of scholars collectively identify with and use the term *interpersonal communication* to describe their own work. These scholars also recognize, however, that there is considerable variety in how they and their colleagues conceptually and operationally define this area of study. In some respects, the construct of interpersonal communication is like the phenomenon it represents—that is, dynamic and changing. Thus, attempts at specifying exactly what interpersonal communication *is* and *is not* are often frustrating and fall short of consensus. Bochner (1989) is probably correct when he suggests that the most we can expect interpersonal scholars to agree to is that they are studying "at least two communicators; intentionally orienting toward each other; as both subject and object; whose actions embody each other's perspectives both toward self and toward other" (p. 336). Cappella (1987), employing what he calls "definitional minimalism," states, "If interpersonal communication has any essential feature, it is that persons influence one another's behavior over and above that attributed to normal baselines of action" (p. 228).

Some of the key definitional issues that garner less consensus include the number of communicators involved, the physical proximity of the communicators, the nature of the interaction units used to explain an encounter, and the degree of formality and structure attending the interactants' relationship.

In an effort to distinguish interpersonal communication studies from research on group, organizational, or mass communication, researchers have commonly designated the number of communicators in interpersonal exchanges as two. However, two-person interactions may be extensions of larger networks; the parties may have membership in a larger group, and their conversation, thus, may be subject to the structures and norms of that group. In short, the assumption that the influence taking place in two-person transactions is entirely due to the behavior of those two persons is open to question. Another common research practice, also open to question, is that of gathering data about a particular two-person interaction or two-person interactions in general by asking *individuals* to provide the data.

Another assumption made by some researchers is that interpersonal communication involves "face-to-face" interaction, in which the communicators are in close physical proximity. Nevertheless, interactions mediated by telephone, computer, and other technologies are also a part of the literature on interpersonal communication. There

are interpersonal scholars, for example, whose research focuses on "long-distance relationships."

The nature of the interaction units used as a basis for describing and explaining interpersonal transactions varies considerably among those who study interpersonal communication. Miller and Steinberg (1975) have argued that the degree of "interpersonalness" in a relationship is determined by the kind of information participants use to make predictions about message exchanges. The more idiosyncratic, personal, and psychological information is considered "more interpersonal," and sociological or cultural information is considered "less interpersonal," or even "impersonal." Interactions in which communicator roles are key and sociological and cultural information is central are, however, very much a part of the literature of interpersonal communication. Furthermore, some researchers limit themselves to observable units, whereas others do not; single-message units satisfy some, whereas others require sequences of messages; many researchers are satisfied with a data snapshot at one point in time, but others argue that it is necessary to collect data over a longer period of time; naturally occurring talk is crucial to some, whereas others are satisfied with analyzing anticipated behavior or imagined interactions. Using published research as an indicator, we can see that interpersonal communication scholars still do not agree on whether it is important to examine nonverbal as well as verbal behavior or whether both parties to the interaction have to speak. Finally, it has been customary for interpersonal communication studies to focus on informal and unstructured interactions. But physician–patient interactions (see Chapter 19) and supervisor–employee interactions (Chapter 16), job interviews, and other role-oriented exchanges are clearly a part of this literature.

In the remaining pages of this chapter, we address the conceptual perspectives and themes that seem to crop up repeatedly in the contributions to this *Handbook*. Each of these perspectives and themes is characterized by multiple conceptualizations, thereby creating a corpus of issues that are likely to be of constant concern to those who study interpersonal communication.

# Conceptual Perspectives and Themes

## The Interaction Process

Most students of interpersonal communication believe that it is accurately thought of as a process—an ongoing, ever-changing event. Understanding the communication process, then, is largely a matter of understanding what happens over a given period of time.

Despite the widespread belief that interpersonal communication is best studied as a process, this is not a consistent perspective manifested in the research. Philosophically, one might argue that process, by definition, is not something we can ever "capture" in our studies. Once we have identified a unit of interaction for study, the argument goes, we no longer "have" a process. A less extreme position assumes that we can learn about process by making multiple observations at multiple points in time over a given time span. According to this view, an understanding of mutual adaptation in interpersonal communication can be achieved through the observation of moment-to-moment changes during interactive events. Kendon (1970), for example, using a filmed record, described the moment-to-moment changes in movement, eye gaze, and speech during the flow of interaction; Gottman (1979) made some important discoveries about marital interaction from analyses of sequential exchanges between husbands and wives in happy and unhappy couples; Cappella and Planalp (1981) analyzed a continuous audio record of informal conversation for moment-to-moment changes in vocalizations and pauses produced by both interactants; and other scholars have examined the sequential nature and effects of dialogue in conversation.

Studies of the process of interpersonal communication must account for a variety of temporal characteristics. From both speaker and listener perspectives, it is important to know how often a behavior occurs during a given period of time, what order or sequence characterizes the behavior under study, how long the behavior lasts when it occurs, and the rhythm, pacing, or "timing" of the behavior relative to co-occurring behaviors. Each of these temporal qualities occurs and can be analyzed at four levels: during a specific utterance, during a specific conversation, during the course of a relationship (see Chapter 18), and during the course of a lifetime (see Chapter 21). The study of time and timing in interpersonal transactions should also provide us with a much better understanding of how to distinguish behaviorally the developmental phases common to many experiences, such as accomplishing a goal for the first time, reestablishing the goal state, maintaining the goal state in the absence of a threat, and maintaining the goal state in the presence of a threat.

Persistent and guiding questions for any efforts directed at the study of interaction as a process include the following: (a) If change is a constant, how should we conceptualize and operationalize periods of stability and periods of transition? (b) How much change is change that makes a difference, and from whose perspective? (c) If we can't examine all aspects of the interaction process, how do we explain the potential changes in the system brought about by the units we choose not to examine?

## A Focus on Behavior

A strong and persistent theme throughout this volume concerns the value of describing and analyzing naturally occurring overt verbal and nonverbal behavior. This focus represents a rich tradition of systematic observations of behavior represented by pioneers such as Birdwhistell, Goffman, Scheflen, Ruesch, and Bateson. This approach contrasts with self-report questionnaires and/or scales as a method of gathering data about interpersonal communication. These inventories are easily administered to large numbers of respondents, and the data they generate are expected to provide a foundation for broad-based generalizations about interpersonal communication.

Although some research programs rely heavily on self-report data, more and more researchers are questioning the adequacy of knowledge about communication behavior based *solely* on such data. Can people accurately recall or predict some aspects of their interpersonal communication behavior—for example, their touching behavior? Have we developed a body of knowledge that is limited to what people *think* they would do? Isn't there a need to supplement or seek validation of self-reports with observations of actual interaction behavior? Is it enough to know the attitudes, opinions, and perceptions of *one* interaction partner, often removed from any interaction context? How will the preferences expressed on a questionnaire manifest themselves in the presence of another person or persons governed by various situational constraints?

To address such questions, the members of an expanding cadre of communication scholars have chosen to focus on more than manifested behavior. These efforts have provided an important supplement to our understanding of interpersonal communication and have pointed out some of the inadequacies of focusing *exclusively* on overt behavior. Even though we still have much to learn from the study of overt behavior, it is already clear that, first, what transpires during interpersonal transactions is more than mere responses to manifest signals. Communicator expectations, fantasies, plans, and the like may provide the bases for responses; behaviors *not* shown by the interaction partner may provide the bases for responses; behaviors shown in previous interactions (with and not with the current partner) may guide and direct subsequent reactions. Ironically, then, our examination of overt behavior has shown us the necessity of supplementing some of these observations with self-report data. Unlike those gathered in many past efforts, however, these self-descriptions are much more likely to be anchored by specific contexts.

In like manner, the study of behavior within the confines of a two-person transaction has made it clear that if we are to understand dyadic behavior, we need to extend our analyses beyond the dyad. We will more fully understand interpersonal behavior as we extend the boundaries of analysis to include the social networks impinging on the two communicators (see Chapter 11), the rules and constraints imposed by social and institutional cultures (see Chapter 17), the interaction history, and so forth. Second, what transpires behaviorally during interpersonal transactions is often extremely subtle and complex—involving behavioral configurations amenable to multiple interpretations, multiple intensities, and multiple degrees of consistency.

Another perspective associated with the focus on behavior is the gradual merging of verbal and nonverbal observations. Interpersonal communication scholars have probably always recognized the vital contributions of proxemic, kinesic, olfactory, vocal, and verbal signals to the understanding of interpersonal communication, but the early emphasis was clearly on verbal behavior. As the number of scholars studying nonverbal behavior increased, it gradually became a separate area of study. The study of verbal behavior and the study of nonverbal behavior appeared, for practical purposes, to be independent of one another. Researchers who studied facial expressions, eye gaze, and proxemics commonly did not spend much time analyzing co-occurring verbal behavior, and researchers who described themselves as discourse or conversation analysts did not commonly claim expertise in nonverbal phenomena. We can learn much by tapping the depths of verbal and nonverbal behaviors separately, but we will learn more about interpersonal communication when the interaction of both systems forms the basis for analysis, as is the case with some analyses of turn-taking and lying behavior.

As we learn more about analyzing verbal and nonverbal signals, there will probably be fewer studies that simply sum the frequency of several behaviors and more that address the interdependence and coordination of behaviors. When we have reached that point, our current preoccupation with the question of whether verbal or non-verbal behavior is more important should be moot. Studying the interrelationships of verbal and nonverbal behavior in social interaction will also demand more attention to how these signals are perceived. Interactants do not observe all the signals made available to them, nor do they process all that they do perceive in the same way. Some of these questions about the perception of signals require an understanding of the perceiver and the signal interpretation process, but describing the nature of the signals themselves is also an integral part of understanding the process. We have much to learn about the impacts of signals and combinations of signals that are related to their intensity, relevance, and location.

Our focus on behavior is gradually including more observations in naturally occurring contexts. In the past, many studies of interpersonal behavior attempted to discover the bases for predicting interpersonal behavior via experiments in controlled laboratory settings. Although behavior was the focus in the early experimental studies, the validity of the findings for naturally occurring interactive events was often challenged. For instance, some charged that interpersonal communication scholars did not have enough descriptive information about how normal interaction proceeds to draw conclusions about how one might manipulate it realistically. As a result, they argued, research participants were asked to react to unusual and sometimes extreme stimuli. Furthermore, critics believed that the employment in studies of interaction partners who were unable to respond (partners presented in slides or on audiotape), who were unwilling to respond ("neutral" confederates), or who responded inflexibly (partners programmed to respond only in certain ways) did not elicit typical interaction behaviors from research participants. Even the fundamental tenet of experimental research that requires some components of the interaction situation to be "kept constant" while others are manipulated seemed to run counter to the prevailing theoretical belief that constancy is not characteristic of ongoing interaction.

As a result of these and other challenges, it became increasingly apparent that we needed to find out more about the structure and operation of interpersonal behavior in naturally occurring situations. Researchers could use the data from these observations to construct laboratory conditions that would more closely approximate naturally occurring interactions.

The observation of behavior outside the laboratory context seems to have underlined the impact of context on behavior and to have given us a renewed appreciation of the difficulty of predicting behavior across different contexts. We also seem more aware of the need to measure the sequencing and quality of responses as well as their quantity.

## Context

Bateson (1978) states, "Without context, words and actions have no meaning at all" (p. 15). This assertion about the critical dependence of communication on context for the generation of meanings is likely to garner substantial agreement among interpersonal communication scholars and practitioners. Contextual information is considered crucial for "thick description" (Geertz, 1973) of communication events. An examination of retrospective contexts (all actions that precede a particular behavior that might help one to interpret that behavior) and emergent contexts (all events that follow the behavior that might help one to interpret the behavior) adds further depth to the understanding of interpersonal episodes.

Communication contexts have been considered in diverse ways: (a) as broad areas defining the field of communication (interpersonal communication, etc.), (b) as social settings (e.g., cocktail parties) and institutional settings (e.g., schools, prisons), (c) as types of relationships and roles (e.g., task, social, and family), (d) as objects or characteristics of the environment, and (e) as message variables (e.g., language style, affect displays preceding and subsequent to text). Therefore, context may encompass psychological, behavioral, and environmental perspectives.

Given the diversity of perspectives on the nature of context, the multiplicity of methods for studying context is not surprising. For contemporary schema theorists, general contextual information leads the investigator to examine patterns in linguistic organization, and linguistic and other contextual cues mobilize the search for particular schematic patterns. Ethnomethodologists describe context in terms of the reflexivity of language understanding (Leiter, 1980). Linguistic utterances are taken as prompts to the overall pattern of meaning, and that pattern operates as a context within which the utterances make sense. In contrast, for uncertainty reduction theorists, context is a source of information (Berger, 1987) and an object of uncertainty. Likewise, attribution theorists and expectancy violation theorists consider context to be a source of information for evaluating the other's behavior (see Chapter 8). A key source of difference in these perspectives is the interrelationship of context and communication. Is context so much a part of the communication process that it is distorted when considered apart from the process? Or is it one of the many external and isolated sources of influence on message selection and interpretation? Chapters 15, 16, and 19 are just a few of the contributions to this *Handbook* that highlight how communication is embedded in context.

Minimally, we need to consider the extent to which our research contexts (however conceptualized) match the contexts to which we apply our findings and the extent to which we can learn more about contexts (however conceptualized) by studying them directly. Furthermore, interpersonal communication researchers need to specify how and why context affects communication, for, as Rawlins (1987) stated, people and messages both transform and are transformed by context.

## Social Cognition

In one way or another, each chapter in this book addresses the role of human thought processes as they interface with interpersonal transactions. The study of interpersonal communication has, from the beginning, recognized the important reciprocal relationship between thought and overt behavior, but in recent years we have greatly advanced our understanding of this area—largely because some scholars in communication and social psychology have made this their sole focus of investigation. The work in this area can be subdivided into two nonexclusive categories: (1) understanding the interrelationships of social cognition and social behavior and (2) understanding the formation and organization of social cognition.

Virtually any thought about any aspect of our experience has the potential to affect behavior in any given encounter. However, the thoughts that are likely to have the most relevance for communicative events are thoughts about the nature of human interaction itself. Usually, the thoughts about self, other, and situation are the designated units for investigation. Information representing thought is usually gathered before and/or after encounters, rarely during them. In the past, some researchers ignored perceptual information from actual interactants, relying instead on the reactions of large groups of uninvolved observers as a basis for understanding the overt and covert behavior of the interactants.

Thoughts that influence behavior may be relatively abstract ("Friends are people who stick by you when the going gets tough") or concrete ("Mary is a person who would probably turn me in for taking a pencil home from the office"). Similarly, more abstract thoughts of what kind of person one is and more concrete thoughts about what kind of person one is as a communicator, or as a communicator with *this* person in *this* situation, may influence the manifested behavior. Individuals think of situations, too, in general ways and as specific communication contexts. Researchers often focus on a single unit of analysis: For example, studies of others include impression formation, attribution theory, or perspective taking; studies of communicator cognition include work on self-consciousness, self-awareness, self-monitoring, imagined interactions, and communicative apprehension. We are just beginning to undertake the more complex job of studying the influence of combined self/other/situation thoughts on behavior. If it were merely a matter of determining how thoughts influence behavior, the task would be easier but less representative of what actually seems to happen. Thoughts affect behavior, and behavior, in turn, reshapes the memory of the original thought(s) as well as the ensuing thoughts. If the process of gathering information for research purposes is thought of as a communicative process, our understanding of social cognition will continue to affect our methods of research too—as it already has (see Chapters 2–4).

As researchers worked to understand how social thoughts and social behavior are interrelated, it became clear that we needed to know more about how people form, organize, and interpret information germane to human interaction. These processes are discussed throughout this volume as attitudes, expectations, inferences, scripts, schemata, fantasies, rules, and wishful thinking. The study of how we form and organize our social thoughts has reemphasized the multilevel process involved in interpreting and/or assigning meaning to behavioral signals. Any given signal or sequence of signals may be taken at any one or a combination of at least five levels: (1) the literal message content, (2) a response to how the partner's preceding response was interpreted, (3) an indicator of how the partner should respond to a message, (4) an indicator of how one partner feels about himself or herself or the other partner as a person, and (5) whether further interaction (now or later) is desired.

## Consciousness and Intent

Throughout this book, readers will be confronted repeatedly with issues bearing on consciousness and intent. Communication scholars periodically acknowledge the importance of these issues, but a variety of perspectives continue to permeate the literature. For many, intentionality is essential for defining any type of communication (Bowers & Bradac, 1984).

From one perspective, the central question is the extent to which communicators "know what they're doing" or, in the case of recalled experiences, the extent to which they "know what they did." Consciousness is a prerequisite for communicating. Much of the research on persuasion and compliance gaining, for example, rests on the belief that communicators identify their goals, analyze their targets and situations, and select strategies that are calculated to maximize their desired outcomes. Research programs reported in a number of the chapters in this book highlight this focus on control and planned social influence, with the treatments in Chapters 6 and 12 being lengthy and explicit. In contrast, ritualistic communication acts, spontaneous displays of emotion, various actions related to the management and structure of conversation, and habitual patterns of interaction occurring in long-term relationships suggest a very low (or absent) level of awareness and planning. Again, this perspective is implicitly or explicitly manifested in a number of different chapters.

Theoretically, there seems to be agreement on some fundamental issues concerning consciousness and intent—for example, that (a) there are multiple levels and degrees of consciousness involved in communicating, (b) more than one intention can occur during a communicative act, (c) consciousness and intent can change during the act of communicating, and (d) communicators may be aware of a general goal and unaware of some specific intentions for reaching that goal (Stamp & Knapp, 1990). Nevertheless, our research often seems to assume a far less complex process. For example, the truism that we don't always "say what we mean or mean what we say" has not been much of a driving force for research in interpersonal communication to date.

The question of what is going on in the mind of a communicator is of little relevance to those who believe that attributions of intent are what really matter in human transactions. In this view, observable behavior is what counts. Planning and consciousness are assessed behaviorally, and perceptions of effort, persistence, emphasis, and situational expectations are used as representative criteria for assessing intent.

Despite the long-standing interest in the subject of intentions and the widespread belief that interaction is best conceived of as a process, relatively little work has been directed at how communicators negotiate intentions. From this perspective, neither the nature of the cognitive activity nor the perception of a person's behavior gives us the information necessary for understanding intentions in everyday communicative life. Intent from this perspective is a jointly constructed product.

## Meaning

How do we conceptualize meaning in interpersonal transactions? How is meaning created? Is meaning something that can be "located" in a particular place? Answers to these questions permeate our research—usually as undiscussed but guiding assumptions. In theory development, however, the centrality and importance of meaning require that it receive more explicit treatment. Symbolic interactionists, among others, believe that things have no meaning apart from our interaction with others. In this sense, then, the way we think about meaning in interaction is inseparable from the way we view human understanding and action.

The meanings of meaning among scholars concerned with human interaction, while diverse, are not wholly incompatible. Grossberg (1982) has uncovered three predominant perspectives among communication scholars, viewing meanings (a) as entities that can be exchanged, (b) as emergent products shared by the interactants, and (c) as the environment through which life is experienced. Littlejohn (1989) concludes his review of various theoretical contributions to communication study by identifying three major approaches to meaning: structural, interactional, and cognitive. The attempt to "locate" meaning in space and time and the attempt to specify how meaning emerges seem to be the goals shared among these different approaches.

To those who think of meaning as infused in the totality of the environment through which

life is experienced, the idea of "locating" the site of meaning must seem like a strange task indeed. Nevertheless, there are those who locate meaning in the text or message itself, those who subscribe to "finding" meaning in the process of interaction, and those who pinpoint meaning in the confines of the brain. Beliefs about how meaning emerges are, not surprisingly, dependent on beliefs about the site of meaning. For some, it is important to focus on the supposed inherent properties associated with signs and their referents; for others, it is the structure and sequencing of messages that trumpet meaning. Some combine various textual aspects with interpreter decisions, whereas for others, cultural and interactional rules pave the way to meaning. Some believe that the key to unlocking meaning is found in the negotiated process involved in the development of shared interpretations, whereas for others, it is the way information is mentally processed that brings meaning to life. Littlejohn (1989) offers a way of bridging some of these divergent perspectives. Meaning, he says, is probably best thought of as "an outcome of the interplay between the structure of the message, the use of the message in actual situated interaction, and the mental process necessary to manage information and make interpretation" (p. 381).

As the interpersonal communication literature is not shy about praising the value of shared experiences and shared understandings, we would like to underline what others have said about this notion. The concept of "sharing" itself is a construct that is subject to considerable variation. Daily discourse is replete with incongruent, ambiguous, and incomplete messages, and it is quite likely that interactants are able to coordinate their behavior effectively without much shared meaning (Cronen et al., 1982; Pearce, 1976). Bochner (1989) hints that when sharing does occur, it may not be so much a sharing of meanings associated with a specific interaction as it is a sharing of beliefs about interactions in general and our mutual contributions thereto: "The 'real' world of interpersonal communication is only partially a shared one in which a sense of sharing is the product of mechanisms of control over meanings as well as the mutual faith in a shared social world" (p. 338).

## A Perspective on Perspectives

Interpersonal communication scholarship contains both the manifest content of its research findings and a latent content of ideological assumptions (Lannamann, 1991). While we have spent considerable time in this chapter performing self-critiques of our methodology and our research findings, we have focused far less attention on an examination of our ideological assumptions. Some have argued that interpersonal scholars have been slower to engage in this process of questioning their ideological assumptions than have scholars in other subareas of communication (Leeds-Hurwitz, 1992). In fact, Bochner (1994) asserts that interpersonal communication scholars have generally ignored the moral, ideological, and narrative knowledge attendant on their subject matter.

Lannamann (1991) believes that we need an understanding of the role of ideology in interpersonal communication if we are to avoid the perils of reifying cultural practices and legitimating current social orders through our research findings. "Ideology," says Lannamann, "is effective; it frames the struggle over which meanings are naturalized as common sense" (p. 182). Fitzpatrick (1993) concurs that an examination of our ideologies is called for and that we can gain much insight into personal and social relationships by incorporating interpretive and cultural perspectives. Furthermore, an examination of our ideological assumptions will help prevent interpersonal communication studies from holding onto a single, orthodox position that constrains or stifles new ideas and innovative approaches.

Parks (1982) addresses this issue directly and demonstrates how the ideology of intimacy (i.e., individuals are on an unending quest for closeness) has defined the research agenda for many interpersonal communication scholars, thus resulting in the devaluation of other phenomena

for study. Other ideologies, many of which are only implicit in the research, also frame our research endeavors. For instance, the ideology of control (i.e., persons desire and are driven to regulate others and their environment) steers researchers to search for and label communicative behaviors as manipulative, influencing, compliance gaining, or persuading (Miller & Knapp, 1985). Baxter (1998) claimed that studies of interpersonal communication in personal relationships are dominated by assumptions. One that she contests is that "interpersonal life will be experienced as consensual, orderly, and stripped of its 'bumps and warts' if communication is effective" (p. 60). Perhaps less common historically but no less influenced by ideological assumptions, feminist studies are directed by the beliefs that gender is a pervasive category for understanding human experience in general (and interpersonal communication in particular) and that the prevailing gender assumptions of society should be challenged.

Ultimately, questions directed at our ideological assumptions will also prompt us to reflect on our assumptions about how we go about determining what we know and don't know and how we search for answers to puzzling aspects of interpersonal communication.

Poststructuralists and postmodernists have challenged the core ideological assumptions of social science. These critics maintain that the dominance of facts over meanings and values is a practical issue rather than an ontological one; research need not be restricted to prediction and control. Accordingly, a meaning-centered approach to interpersonal studies calls for breaking away from the norms that have equated distance and disengagement with objectivity, that have favored universals over particulars, that have made standardized criteria for making judgments the sole province of rationality, and that have relegated interactant history and context to the status of factors that need to be "controlled." Fitzpatrick (1993) believes in a discovery process that maintains a social dimension and, simultaneously, a "scientific" foundation. By rejecting a scientific approach completely, she argues, scholars will be unable to specify how to judge among competing claims; however, by rejecting a more interpretive approach, they may miss the broader social issues of theory and thus perpetuate social structures. Bochner (1994) suggests that other research practices—whether they aim to predict, interpret, criticize, change, or create—represent different discursive strategies that are useful modes of description for certain purposes. Thus, a singularly "correct" perspective, he argues, does not exist, because natural events and processes lend themselves to a multiplicity of descriptions depending on the individual's point of view.

# References

Altman, I., & Taylor, D. A. (1973). *Social penetration: The development of interpersonal relationships.* New York: Holt, Rinehart & Winston.

Argyle, M. (1969). *Social interaction.* New York: Lieber-Atherton.

Barnlund, D. C. (1968). *Interpersonal communication: Survey and studies.* Boston: Houghton Mifflin.

Bateson, G. (1978). *Mind and nature: A necessary unity.* New York: E. P. Dutton.

Baxter, L. A. (1988). A dialectic perspective on communication strategies in relationship development. In S. Duck (Ed.), *Handbook of personal relationships: Theory, research and interventions* (pp. 257–273). New York: Wiley.

Baxter, L. A. (1998). Locating the social in interpersonal communication. In J. S. Trent (Ed.), *Communication: Views from the helm for the 21st century* (pp. 60–64). Boston: Allyn & Bacon.

Baxter, L. A., & Montgomery, B. M. (1996). *Relating: Dialogues and dialectics.* New York: Guilford Press.

Beatty, M. J., Marshall, L. A., & Rudd, J. E. (2001). A twins study of communicative adaptability: Heritability of individual differences. *Quarterly Journal of Speech, 87,* 366–377.

Beatty, M. J., & McCroskey, J. C. (1997). It's in our nature: Verbal aggressiveness as temperamental expression. *Communication Quarterly, 45,* 446–460.

Beatty, M. J., & McCroskey, J. C. (2001). *The biology of communication: A communibiological perspective.* Cresskill, NJ: Hampton Press.

Bell, R. A., & Daly, J. A. (1984). The affinity-seeking function of communication. *Communication Monographs, 51,* 91–115.

Berger, C. R. (1977). Interpersonal communication: Theory and research. In B. D. Ruben (Ed.), *Communication yearbook 1* (pp. 217–228). New Brunswick, NJ: Transaction Publishers.

Berger, C. R. (1987). Communicating under uncertainty. In M. E. Roloff & C. R. Berger (Eds.), *Interpersonal processes: New directions in communication research* (pp. 39–62). Newbury Park, CA: Sage.

Berger, C. R. (1991). Communication theories and other curios. *Communication Monographs, 58,* 101–113.

Berger, C. R. (1992). Curiouser and curiouser curios. *Communication Monographs, 59,* 101–107.

Berger, C. R. (1997). *Planning strategic interaction: Attaining goals through communicative action.* Mahwah, NJ: Lawrence Erlbaum.

Berger, C. R. (2005). Interpersonal communication: Theoretical perspectives, future prospects. *Journal of Communication, 55,* 415–447.

Berger, C. R., & Bradac, J. J. (1982). *Language and social knowledge: Uncertainty in interpersonal relations.* London: Edward Arnold.

Berger, C. R., & Calabrese, R. J. (1975). Some explorations in initial interaction and beyond: Toward a developmental theory of interpersonal communication. *Human Communication Research, 1,* 99–112.

Birdwhistell, R. L. (1952). *Introduction to kinesics: An annotation system for analysis of body motion and gesture.* Ann Arbor, MI: U.S. Department of State, Foreign Service Institute/University Microfilms.

Blumer, H. (1969). *Symbolic interactionism: Perspective and method.* Englewood Cliffs, NJ: Prentice Hall.

Bochner, A. P. (1978). On taking ourselves seriously: An analysis of some persistent problems and promising directions in interpersonal research. *Human Communication Research, 4,* 179–191.

Bochner, A. P. (1989). Interpersonal communication. In E. Barnouw, G. Gerbner, W. Schramm, T. L. Worth, & L. Gross (Eds.), *International encyclopedia of communications* (pp. 336–340). New York: Oxford University Press.

Bochner, A. P. (1994). Perspectives on inquiry II: Theories and stories. In M. L. Knapp & G. R. Miller (Eds.), *Handbook of interpersonal communication* (2nd ed., pp. 21–41). Thousand Oaks, CA: Sage.

Bochner, A. P., & Ellis, C. (1992). Personal narrative as a social approach to interpersonal communication. *Communication Theory, 2,* 65–72.

Bowers, I. W., & Bradac, J. J. (1984). Contemporary problems in human communication theory. In

C. C. Arnold & I. W. Bowers (Eds.), *Handbook of rhetorical and communication theory* (pp. 871–893). Boston: Allyn & Bacon.

Burgoon, J. K. (1978). A communication model of personal space violations: Explication and an initial test. *Human Communication Research, 4,* 129–142.

Burgoon, J. K. (1983). Nonverbal violations of expectations. In J. M. Wiemann & R. P. Harrison (Eds.), *Nonverbal interaction* (pp. 77–111). Beverly Hills, CA: Sage.

Burgoon, J. K., & Hale, J. L. (1988). Nonverbal expectancy violations: Model elaboration and application to immediacy behaviors. *Communication Monographs, 55,* 58–79.

Burgoon, J. K., Stern, L. A., & Dillman, L. (1995). *Interpersonal adaptation: Dyadic interaction patterns.* New York: Cambridge University Press.

Burleson, B. R. (1992). Taking communication seriously. *Communication Monographs, 59,* 79–86.

Byrne, D. (1971). *The attraction paradigm.* New York: Academic Press.

Cahn, D. D. (1992). *Conflict in intimate relationships.* New York: Guilford Press.

Canary, D. J., & Stafford, L. (1994). *Communication and relational maintenance.* New York: Academic Press.

Cappella, J. N. (1987). Interpersonal communication: Definitions and fundamental questions. In C. R. Berger & S. H. Chaffee (Eds.), *Handbook of communication science* (pp. 184–238). Newbury Park, CA: Sage.

Cappella, J. N., & Greene, J. O. (1982). A discrepancy-arousal explanation of mutual influence in expressive behavior for adult and infant-adult interaction. *Communication Monographs, 49,* 89–114.

Cappella, J. N., & Planalp, S. (1981). Talk and silence sequences in informal conversations III: Interspeaker influence. *Human Communication Research, 7,* 117–132.

Cartwright, D., & Zander, A. (Eds.). (1960). *Group dynamics: Research and theory.* Evanston, IL: Row, Peterson.

Chapman, A. H. (1976). *Harry Stack Sullivan: His life and his work.* New York: Putnam.

Chapple, E. D. (1953). The standard experimental (stress) interview as used in interaction chronograph investigations. *Human Organizations, 12,* 23–32.

Chapple, E. D. (1970). *Culture and biological man: Explorations in behavioral anthropology.* New York: Holt, Rinehart & Winston.

Cronen, V., Pearce, W. B., & Harris, L. (1982). The coordinated management of meaning. In F. E. X. Dance (Ed.), *Human communication theory: Comparative essays* (pp. 61–89). New York: Harper & Row.

Cupach, W. R., & Spitzberg, B. H. (Eds.). (1994). *The dark side of interpersonal communication.* Hillsdale, NJ: Lawrence Erlbaum.

Delia, J. G. (1987). Communication research: A history. In C. R. Berger & S. H. Chaffee (Eds.), *Handbook of communication science* (pp. 20–98). Newbury Park, CA: Sage.

Delia, J. G., O'Keefe, B. J., & O'Keefe, D. J. (1982). The constructivist approach to communication. In F. E. X. Dance (Ed.), *Human communication theory: Comparative essays* (pp. 147–191). New York: Harper & Row.

Duck, S. (1973). *Personal relationships and personal constructs: A study of friendship formation.* New York: Wiley.

Festinger, L. (1950). Informal social communication. *Psychological Review, 57,* 271–282.

Festinger, L. (1954). A theory of social comparison processes. *Human Relations, 7,* 117–140.

Festinger, L. (1957). *A theory of cognitive dissonance.* Evanston, IL: Row, Peterson.

Fitzpatrick, M. A. (1993). Communication in the new world of relationships. *Journal of Communication, 43*(3), 119–126.

Geertz, C. (1973). *The interpretation of cultures: Selected essays.* New York: Basic Books.

Giffin, K., & Patton, B. R. (1971). *Fundamentals of interpersonal communication.* New York: Harper & Row.

Giles, H., Mulac, A., Bradac, J. J., & Johnson, P. (1987). Speech accommodation theory: The next decade and beyond. In M. McLaughlin (ed.), *Communication Yearbook 11* (pp. 13–48). Newbury Park, CA: Sage.

Giles, H., & Powesland, P. F. (1975). *Speech style and social evaluation.* London: Academic Press.

Goffman, E. (1959). *The presentation of self in everyday life.* Garden City, NY: Anchor.

Goffman, E. (1963). *Behavior in public places: Notes on the social organization of gatherings.* New York: Free Press.

Goffman, E. (1971). *Relations in public: Microstudies of the public order.* New York: Basic Books.

Goffman, E. (1981). *Forms of talk.* Philadelphia: University of Pennsylvania Press.

Gottman, J. M. (1979). *Marital interaction: Experimental investigations.* New York: Academic Press.

Greene, J. O. (1984). A cognitive approach to human communication: An action assembly theory. *Communication Monographs, 51,* 289–306.

Greene, J. O. (Ed.). (1997). *Message production: Advances in communication theory.* Hillsdale, NJ: Lawrence Erlbaum.

Grossberg, L. (1982). Does communication theory need intersubjectivity? Toward an immanent philosophy of interpersonal relations. In M. Burgoon (Ed.), *Communication yearbook 6* (pp. 171–205). Beverly Hills, CA: Sage.

Gudykunst, W., Matsumoto, Y., Ting-Toomey, S., Nishida, T., Kim, K. S., & Heyman, S. (1996). The influence of cultural individualism-collectivism, self construals, and individual values on communication styles across cultures. *Human Communication Research, 22,* 510–543.

Hall, E. T. (1959). *The silent language.* Garden City, NY: Doubleday.

Hare, A. P., Borgatta, E. F., & Bales, R. F. (Eds.). (1955). *Small groups: Studies in social interaction.* New York: Alfred A. Knopf.

Hayakawa, S. I. (1941). *Language in action.* New York: Harcourt Brace Jovanovich.

Heider, F. (1958). *The psychology of interpersonal relations.* New York: Wiley.

Homans, G. C. (1961). *Social behavior: Its elementary forms.* New York: Harcourt Brace Jovanovich.

Honeycutt, J. M. (1991). Imagined interactions, imagery and mindfulness/mindlessness. In R. Kunzendorf (Ed.), *Mental imagery* (pp. 121–128). New York: Plenum Press.

Hopper, R., Knapp, M. L., & Scott, L. (1981). Couples' personal idioms: An exploration of intimate talk. *Journal of Communication, 31,* 23–33.

Hovland, C., Janis, I., & Kelley, H. (1953). *Communication and persuasion: Psychological studies of opinion change.* New Haven, CT: Yale University Press.

Howes, R. F. (1928). Training in conversation. *Quarterly Journal of Speech, 14,* 253–259.

Kelley, H. H. (1979). *Personal relationships: Their structures and processes.* Hillsdale, NJ: Lawrence Erlbaum.

Keltner, J. W. (1970). Interpersonal speech-communication: Elements and structures. Belmont, CA: Wadsworth.

Kendon, A. (1970). Movement coordination in social interaction: Some examples described. *ActaPsychologica, 32,* 100–125.

Knapp, M. L. (1972). *Nonverbal communication in human interaction.* New York: Holt, Rinehart & Winston.

Knapp, M. L. (1978). *Social intercourse: From greeting to goodbye.* Boston: Allyn & Bacon.

Knapp, M. L., & Comadena, M. E. (1979). Telling it like it isn't: A review of theory and research on deceptive communication. *Human Communication Research, 5,* 270–285.

Knapp, M. L., & Daly, J. A. (Eds.). (2010). *Sage benchmarks in communication: Interpersonal communication* (Vols. 1–4). London: Sage.

Knapp, M. L., Hart, R. P., & Dennis, H. S. (1974). An exploration of deception as a communication construct. *Human Communication Research, 1,* 15–29.

Knapp, M. L., Hopper, R., & Bell, R. A. (1984). Compliments: A descriptive taxonomy. *Journal of Communication, 34,* 12–31.

Knapp, M. L., Stohl, C., & Reardon, K. (1981). Memorable messages. *Journal of Communication, 31,* 27–41.

Korzybski, A. (1933). *Science and sanity: An introduction to non-Aristotelian systems and general semantics.* Lancaster, PA: Science Press.

Lannamann, J. W. (1991). Interpersonal communication research as ideological practice. *Communication Theory, 1*(3), 179–203.

Leeds-Hurwitz, W. (1992). Forum introduction: Social approaches to interpersonal communication. *Communication Theory, 2*(3), 131–139.

Leiter, K. (1980). *A primer on ethnomethodology.* New York: Oxford University Press.

Littlejohn, S. (1989). *Theories of human communication* (3rd ed.). Belmont, CA: Wadsworth.

McCroskey, J. C., Larson, C., & Knapp, M. L. (1971). *An introduction to interpersonal communication.* Englewood Cliffs, NJ: Prentice Hall.

Mead, G. H. (1934). *Mind, self, and society.* Chicago: University of Chicago Press.

Millar, F. E., & Rogers, L. E. (1976). A relational approach to interpersonal communication. In G. R. Miller (Ed.), *Explorations in interpersonal communication* (pp. 87–103). Beverly Hills, CA: Sage.

Miller, G. R. (1978). The current status of theory and research in interpersonal communication. *Human Communication Research, 4,* 164–178.

Miller, G. R., Boster, F. J., Roloff, M. E., & Seibold, D. R. (1977). Compliance-gaining message strategies: A typology and some findings concerning effects of situational differences. *Communication Monographs, 44,* 37–51.

Miller, G. R., & Knapp, M. L. (1985). Introduction: Background and current trends in the study of interpersonal communication. In M. L. Knapp &

G. R. Miller (Eds.), *Handbook of interpersonal communication*. Beverly Hills, CA: Sage.

Miller, G. R., & Steinberg, M. (1975). *Between people: A new analysis of interpersonal communication.* Chicago: Science Research Associates.

Murphy, G., Murphy, L. B., & Newcomb, T. M. (1937). *Experimental social psychology.* New York: Harper & Row.

Newcomb, T. M. (1953). An approach to the study of communicative acts. *Psychological Review, 60,* 393–404.

Oliver, R. T. (1932). Conversation in the speech curriculum. *Quarterly Journal of Speech, 18,* 108–111.

Osgood, C. E., Suci, G. C., & Tannenbaum, P. H. (1957). *The measurement of meaning.* Urbana: University of Illinois Press.

Parks, M. (1982). Ideology in interpersonal communication: Off the couch and into the world. In M. Burgoon (Ed.), *Communication yearbook 5* (pp. 78–108). New Brunswick, NJ: Transaction Publishers.

Patterson, M. L. (1982). A sequential functional model of nonverbal behavior. *Psychological Review, 89,* 231–249.

Pearce, W. B. (1976). The coordinated management of meaning: A rules-based theory of interpersonal communication. In G. R. Miller (Ed.), *Explorations in interpersonal communication* (pp. 17–35). Beverly Hills, CA: Sage.

Petronio, S. (Ed.). (2000). *Balancing the secrets of private disclosures.* Mahwah, NJ: Lawrence Erlbaum.

Piaget, J. (1926). *Language and thought of the child* (M. Gabain, Trans.). London: Routledge & Kegan Paul.

Rawlins, W. K. (1983). Negotiating close friendships: The dialectic of conjunctive freedoms. *Human Communication Research, 9,* 255–266.

Rawlins, W. K. (1985). Stalking interpersonal communication effectiveness: Social, individual, or situational integration? In T. W. Benson (Ed.), *Speech communication in the 20th century* (pp. 109–129). Carbondale: Southern Illinois University Press.

Rawlins, W. K. (1987). Gregory Bateson and the composition of human communication. *Research in Language and Social Interaction, 20,* 53–77.

Rawlins, W. K. (1992). *Friendship matters: Communication, dialectics, and the life course.* New York: Aldine.

Roethlisberger, F. J., & Dickson, W. J. (1939). *Management and the worker.* Cambridge, MA: Harvard University Press.

Rogers, L. E., & Farace, R. V. (1975). Analysis of relational communication in dyads. New measurement procedures. *Human Communication Research, 1,* 222–239.

Roloff, M. E., & Anastasiou, L. (2001). Interpersonal communication research: An overview. In W. B. Gudykunst (Ed.), *Communication yearbook 24* (pp. 51–71). Thousand Oaks, CA: Sage.

Ruesch, J., & Bateson, G. (1951). *Communication: The social matrix of psychiatry.* New York: W. W. Norton.

Ruesch, J., & Kees, W. (1956). *Nonverbal communication: Notes on the visual perception of human relations.* Los Angeles: University of California Press.

Sillars, A. L. (1980). Attributions and communication in roommate conflicts. *Communication Monographs, 47,* 180–200.

Simmel, G. (1950). *The sociology of Georg Simmel* (K. H. Wolff, Ed. & Trans.). New York: Free Press. (Original work published 1908)

Spitzberg, B. H., & Cupach, W. R. (Eds.). (1998). *The dark side of close relationships.* Mahwah, NJ: Lawrence Erlbaum.

Stamp, G. H., & Knapp, M. L. (1990). The construct of intent in interpersonal communication. *Quarterly Journal of Speech, 76,* 282–299.

Tagiuri, R. (1969). Person perception. In G. Lindzey & E. Aronson (Eds.), *The handbook of social psychology* (Vol. 3). Reading, MA: Addison-Wesley.

Thibaut, J. W., & Kelley, H. H. (1959). *The social psychology of groups.* New York: Wiley.

Walther, J. B. (1992). Interpersonal effects in computer-mediated interaction: A relational perspective. *Communication Research, 19,* 52–90.

Watzlawick, P., Beavin, J. H., & Jackson, D. D. (1967). *Pragmatics of human communication: A study of interaction patterns, pathologies, and paradoxes.* New York: W. W. Norton.

Wheeless, L. R., Barraclough, R., & Stewart, R. (1983). Compliance-gaining and power in persuasion. In R. Bostrom (Ed.), *Communication yearbook 7* (pp. 105–145). Beverly Hills, CA: Sage.

Wiemann, J. M. (1977). Explication and test of a model of communicative competence. *Human Communication Research, 3,* 195–213.

# PART II

# Perspectives on Inquiry

# CHAPTER 2

# Quantitative Social Science Methods of Inquiry

*Timothy R. Levine*

As you are reading this chapter, it can be inferred that (a) you are interested in the topic of interpersonal communication and (b) you want to learn more about it. Why else would you be reading a chapter in the *Handbook of Interpersonal Communication*? Obviously, you want good information. No reasonable person would want to waste his or her time learning useless, misinformed, or misleading stuff. But how can you obtain this new knowledge, and when you do, how will you know if the knowledge is reliable? Will what you think you know stand the tests of replication and application? How can we sort out what is real insight and what is just high-sounding "bullshit."[1] There is no shortage of quackery out there. So how can you meaningfully judge the worth of the research findings you read? If you want to have a sound understanding of interpersonal communication, you need answers to questions such as these. This chapter is for you.

Some may hold the misconception that quantitative researchers are, of necessity, statistics nerds who have a natural affinity for math and computer programs. But statistics may be less central to really good quantitative interpersonal research than you may think. Knowing statistics, at least as it is most often taught, is only a small and relatively unimportant part of good quantitative social science methods. Anyway, statistics are just tools for getting at and understanding the real topic of interest. Knowledge of methods is necessary to critically assess the utility and plausibility of knowledge claims, but methods and statistics are not the same thing, and both are only a means to an end. In fact, too much focus on the rules and details of statistics can lead to boring work that lacks insight and even, ironically, to research findings that are erroneous or misleading. The path to enlightenment is not through ever more complex multivariate analyses, random effects models, hierarchical linear modeling, or structural equation models with correlated error terms, and others ad nauseam. With a few notable exceptions, simple statistics are almost always better (Boster, 2002; Cohen, 1990; Smith, Levine, Lachlan, & Fediuk, 2002). A good picture, plot, or graph of the data is often more informative than a statistical probability, such as $p < .05$. Thoughtful research questions coupled with sound measurement and tight research design typically reduce the need for complex inferential statistics. If finding cannot be seen with a careful "eyeball-ing" of a descriptive presentation of the data and instead is only apparent from asterisks on a print-out, there is a good chance that the finding is not very meaningful.

I challenge those skeptical of the above claims to read my work, especially my more recent work that appears in top journals.[2] The reader will never find a MANOVA (multivariate analysis of variance) or similar statistic in any of my articles. Although I can do path analysis by hand, you won't see path analysis or structural equation modeling (SEM) in many of my articles. The reader is much more likely to see a graph of my raw data than an HLM (hierarchical linear mod-eling) analysis. If I could get away with not reporting $p$ values at all, I would in many instances. This preference for simplicity and design and measurement over statistical analysis has not kept me out of leading communication journals. On the contrary, I have enjoyed much success over the years. My rejection rates are much lower when I submit to *Communication Monographs* or *Human Communication Research* than to the regional journals. I take this as evi-dence that I am doing some things right.

Robert Abelson (1995) wrote that a good social scientist, and this includes quantitative interpersonal communication scholars, needs the skills of a good detective, an ethical trail lawyer, and an engaging storyteller. A good interpersonal detective gathers, sorts, and integrates evidence to solve some social, theoretical, or communica-tive mystery. The metaphorical ethical trail law-yer uses the evidence to make a persuasive case about the facts without distorting them, and the storyteller weaves those facts and arguments into an engaging narrative.

To these three skill sets, I will add two more— "substantive feel" and quantitative-scientific lit-eracy. By substantive feel, I mean that to really understand interpersonal communication, you need to understand people, social interaction, and social context. You must be a curious and an insightful "people watcher" who wonders, "Why did a person do that?" and who can convert

observations into questions, hypotheses, or theo-ries that can be tested. But this needs to be done in a systemic, disciplined way if the new knowl-edge is going to be convincing and withstand scrutiny. This is where quantitative-scientific literacy comes in. But quantitative-scientific lit-eracy does not demand or imply statistical com-plexity (Boster, 2002).

One of the best contemporary examples of these points is observed in the work of Bob Cialdini (1980)—and the idea of "full-cycle social psychology," which can be aptly changed to "full-circle interpersonal scholarship." Read almost any of the many influential Cialdini research articles, and you can see this in practice. Notable examples include his work on norms and littering (e.g., Cialdini, Kallgren, & Reno, 1991), football studies on basking in reflected glory (Cialdini et al., 1976), and the effectiveness of various compliance-gaining strategies (e.g., Cialdini et al., 1975). Cialdini's research starts with an insightful obser-vation of human interaction. First, he identifies the principle(s) of human nature that seem to be at play. Then, he designs experiments to document the phenomenon he has observed and to distin-guish between plausible mechanisms that explain the phenomenon. Finally, he applies the under-standing that he had gained from his field experi-ments to the original observation and context. When you read Cialdini's work, it is clear not only that he is a skilled detective who tells convincing and engaging stories but also that he has both a keen substantive feel and a serious scientific mojo.

Abelson (1995) also draws a useful distinction between the record and the lore. The record is the set of all research findings on a topic, and the lore is the social understanding of those findings. The two are not the same, and they can, in prac-tice, be very different. Reading the record requires quantitative-scientific literacy and relying on the lore, which, often passed down in textbooks, litera-ture reviews, or article discussion sections, can lead to the propagation of persistent myths. A few examples are provided in the following paragraphs.

Have you ever heard of Solomon Asch's (1956) famous conformity experiments? Briefly, participants are shown a series of lines and asked which of three lines is of the same length as a comparison line. Participants make judgments either individually (control group) or in groups of eight people. When in groups, the other participants are actually research confederates, who sometimes all give the same wrong answer. Assuming that you learned about this study before, what percentage of Asch's participants always conformed? What percentage never conformed, always giving the correct answer regardless of others' incorrect answers? Which percentage is greater?

Next, have you ever heard of the tendency of people to explain their own behavior with situational causes but to attribute others' behavior to personal causes? Does research support this claim?

Now, the answers. In Asch (1956), 29 out of 123 (24%) participants never conformed, whereas only 6 out of 123 (5%) always conformed. The results are clearly presented in the original write-up. In attribution research, across 173 studies, research does not find evidence for actor–observer asymmetry in attributions (and this is not the same as the so-called fundamental attribution error; see Malle, 2006). Surprised?

The lore is fallible. Textbook presentations and literature reviews and discussion sections in articles cannot always be trusted. This, by the way, is true of methods education too. A lot of information presented in methods texts "just ain't so" (Cohen, 1990).

This chapter is about creating and understanding the research record so that you do not have to rely on the lore. It is about methods of generating new knowledge and assessing the merit of existing knowledge claims involving interpersonal communication. Whether the reader is a cutting-edge interpersonal researcher, a student taking his or her first graduate class in interpersonal communication, or a practitioner of interpersonal skills, the ideas described here are useful for both the creators and the users of new knowledge. The focus is on methods of ensuring that the knowledge claims carry with them both credentials and real utility while at the same time

being innovative, convincing, and engaging. This is not a chapter about the dry, boring, conventional, and intellectually barren approach to social science statistics that unfortunately populates the university curriculum, especially statistics textbooks. It is not about mindlessly following the conventions associated with testing data against implausible statistical distributions that provide the basis for the null hypothesis used in significance testing. It is not about conventional, philosophically illiterate takes on metatheory or the philosophy of science. Instead, it is about the disciplined thinking and the sophisticated approach to understanding that are needed to unlock the mysteries behind why people do what they do when they communicate interpersonally.

## Social Science and the Quantitative–Qualitative (False?) Dichotomy

Quantitative, social-scientific communication research involves the application of a set of social-scientific methods for testing defensible knowledge claims about human communication based on empirical data, statistical description, and/or statistical inference. The term *quantitative approach* implies a contrast between quantitative research and qualitative research. The former seeks to quantify constructs of interest, whereas the latter does not. Qualitative research is sometimes portrayed as more exploratory, being useful in generating new ideas and understandings, while quantitative research is often seen as involving formal hypothesis testing. Both quantitative and qualitative research, however, can serve either function.

Qualitative methods can be used to formally test theories (e.g., Festinger, Riecken, & Schachter, 1956), and quantitative research does not need hypotheses (Rozin, 2001). Generally, quantitative research is useful when the phenomena of interest can either be classified as present/absent or when the phenomena have measurable attributes that vary in degrees or amounts. If something can be scaled or counted, a quantitative approach can be used. The primary advantage of quantitative research is that statistical evidence can be used to enhance confidence in a knowledge claim. The second advantage is that many quantitative methodologies offer mechanisms to control nuisance variables, rule out rival explanations, and otherwise enhance confidence in knowledge claims.

More useful than the quantitative–qualitative distinction, however, is a broader distinction between social-scientific approaches and nonscience approaches such as rhetorical criticism, postmodern analysis, feminist scholarship, and critical scholarship. What makes an approach social scientific or not rests on issues other than whether or not numbers are involved. Science-based and nonscientific modes of research reflect very different understandings about the nature of knowledge, how knowledge is generated, what is useful to know, and how (or even if) we can have confidence in what we know. The quantitative–qualitative distinction need not involve these deeper philosophical differences about the nature of knowledge and knowledge generation. Nevertheless, most social scientists use quantitative methods at least some of the time, and the use of quantitative methods usually implies a social-scientific approach to knowledge generation, whereas qualitative research may or may not be social scientific in character. This said, a purely quantitative approach that shuns all qualitative inference will surely lack substantive feel. The best experimenters rely on personal experience for inspiration and talk to and observe their research participants to gain insight into their perspectives. Both qualitative and quantitative data have been extensively used in the works of master social scientists such as Musifer Sherif, Leon Festinger, Gerg Gigerenzer, and Paul Meehl, who happen to be my research heroes. My sympathies are for those not familiar with their brilliant work.

One hears from time to time that qualitative research is easier than quantitative work. After all, those wanting to do quantitative research need to take several statistics classes. Quantitative researchers need to do coding with multiple coders or spend hours in the lab running experiments. I suspect, however, that the opposite is more often true. Doing qualitative research well and effectively may be considerably more difficult than doing equally influential quantitative research. If one looks at the author studies that are published from time to time (e.g., Bunz, 2005; Hickson, Self, Johnson, Peacock, & Bodon, 2009), the most prolific authors in communication disproportionally seem to do quantitative research. The same trend is evidenced in the analysis of citation patterns (Levine, 2010b). The research in the field that is most cited is disproportionally quantitative. One (but certainly not the only) interpretation of these trends is that quantitative research may just be easier to do well.

Second, it seems fashionable in some intellectual circles to claim that one *does* both qualitative and quantitative research. Certainly, one can read and appreciate both and find both interesting, useful, and valuable. For the research consumer, being eclectic is a virtue. But for the aspiring young interpersonal researcher, perfecting one's craft in even one of these approaches is a lifelong pursuit, a goal that is unlikely to be ever fully attained even with considerable devotion. As for me, I know that I am still learning and am still perfecting my craft, even though I have been a full professor for a number of years now. There is so much to know, and life is so short. So for most young scholars, it is probably better to do one or the other reasonably well than to dabble in both. This does not mean that the two approaches cannot inform each other. But when actually doing research to create new knowledge, having only a passing familiarity with method is downright dangerous. It is so easy to be wrong, and when bogus information gets into the lore, the field suffers. Would-be researchers need to be sharper than the critics because criticizing others' knowledge claims is a whole lot easier than creating defensible new knowledge. All this suggests that doing both qualitative and quantitative research well may be too ambitious for many mere mortals.

## Philosophical Underpinnings

Most quantitative social-scientific research adopts the philosophical approach of scientific realism (Pavitt, 2001). The presumption is that there is a real world that exists beyond our perceptions and that the real world is potentially, at least partially, knowable. The goal of research is to get our understanding more closely aligned with this objective reality. The word *verisimilitude* describes this idea of closeness to reality. We want our theories and our findings to have verisimilitude, and the extent to which we can make a case that our theories and findings have verisimilitude is the bottom line in quantitative communication science.

Sometimes, quantitative social science approaches are mistakenly equated with logical positivism or operationalism, but these problematic philosophical perspectives have long (much before the current author was born) been out of favor (Meehl, 1986) and never held much sway in quantitative communication research anyway (Miller & Berger, 1999). Logical positivism was a philosophical view that held that the only meaningful knowledge is what we prove either by objective observation or by logical proof. Operationalism is a view of measurement that equates the attributes of things with their measures. For example, to an operationalist, communication apprehension (McCroskey, 1977) is a score on a communication apprehension scale (see Levine & McCroskey, 1990), not an estimate of an abstract construct. For the true operationalist, conceptual definitions are irrelevant.

The idea from Karl Popper (1959) that hypotheses and theories need to be falsifiable is both useful and widely accepted. This view holds that for ideas to be scientifically useful, they must be testable. Further still, disconfirming evidence has more logical force than supportive evidence. That is, evidence inconsistent with a hypothesis (i.e., not merely nonsignificant but significant in the wrong direction) provides stronger evidence that a hypothesis is false than findings consistent with a hypothesis provide evidence that a hypothesis is true.

I find that the ideas of Imre Lakatos (1978) expand on Popper's ideas and have much utility for understanding quantitative communication research. Very roughly, good research programs get out in front of the data. They allow the researcher to know what variables to study and lead the researcher to good new findings with verisimilitude. Degenerative research programs, in contrast, are always trying to catch up with the data. They are perpetually generating excuses for why the data were not supportive or require data spinning to create the illusion of support. Thomas Kuhn's (1996) philosophy of science, in contrast, is too relativistic and captures less well the aims of quantitative communication research.

Quantitative social-scientific research is usually *empirical*, meaning that knowledge claims are based on data and the data stem from observation. Quantitative social-scientific research also strives for *objectivity*. Complete objectivity is impossible to obtain, but methods are designed and evaluated by the extent to which the data are likely to be free from bias and the idiosyncrasies of the researcher. Finally, quantitative social-scientific research strives to be *authority free* and *self-correcting*. It is not the status of the researcher but the quality of the evidence that allows for confidence in a knowledge claim. Confidence in a finding or conclusion is enhanced though replication, and it is presumed that incorrect conclusions will ultimately be weeded out because they fail to replicate. If a finding has verisimilitude, other researchers should also be able to produce the same finding under conditions similar to the original research. For the social scientist, objective empirical observation, coupled with replication, provides the best path to verisimilitude over time. I do not myself place that much confidence in my findings until I can replicate them or, better yet, until other researchers and other labs replicate my findings.

Research predictions and knowledge claims in quantitative communication research are usually probabilistic in nature, general within some specified conditions, and contextualized to within those specified conditions. Knowledge claims are usually probabilistic in that they are often based on statistical inferences that provide estimates of how likely or unlikely the data are given some set of assumptions. Findings and conclusions are general in that they tell us what is usual or typical within a situation or context. For example, deception research tells us that people tend to be truth biased and that people are more likely to believe other people regardless of the observed person's honesty (Levine, Kim, Park, & Hughes, 2006; Levine, Park, & McCornack, 1999). Such a finding does not imply that people always believe everything they hear or that they never think others are lying; it is just that this tends to be the case on an average. Finally, knowledge claims are contextualized in that they have boundary conditions; that is, all findings have conditions (specified or unknown) under which they apply and do not apply. For example, truth bias is diminished in situations where the person whose message is being judged is thought to have a strong motive to lie (Levine, Kim, & Blair, 2010).

## Induction, Hypothetico-Deduction, and Abduction

Most quantitative social-scientific research involves the use of one or more of three types of reasoning: induction, hypothetico-deduction (HD), and abduction. With inductive reasoning, a researcher infers conclusions from data. Inductive conclusions have the basic form "Study $X$ found such and such a result, therefore this is generally the case." A problem with this type of inference making is that the *data are always both finite and contextual*. Any given research finding is the result of a specific author or set of authors, involving some finite collection of research subjects, with the data collected at a specific point in time, with some specific method, and in some specific context. One always wonders if the conclusions would hold for different authors, with different subjects, at different times, with slightly different methods, and in different contexts. Unfortunately, there is no way to know this. Random selection and nonstudent samples do not help because one cannot random select across all time, researchers, methods, contexts, and so on. Sure, the findings can be replicated; replication is good, and replication enhances confidence. But replication does not fully solve the problem of induction either. Findings can never be replicated across all possible authors, subject populations, times, situations, and so on. And even if it were possible, surely researchers have better things to do with their time than pursuing near-infinite variations of silly replications. For these reasons, purely inductive conclusions are always logically unsatisfying. They leave the thoughtful research consumer with so many unanswerable "what if" and "why?" questions. Perhaps as a consequence, research involving purely inductive reasoning is often called *dust bowl empiricism*. The "dust bowl" charge is not flattering, and it refers to atheoretical research drawing purely inductive inferences. Induction, however, is not useless. Not by far. Inductive reasoning is a great way to get ideas and to document empirical regularities. Induction only becomes problematic when a line of research stops there and when it is the only inferential and logical tool in use.

While purely inductive research is often considered low rent and the stuff for intellectual bottom feeders, the *hypothetico-deductive* (HD) approach, in contrast, is often seen as the gold standard or the elite scientific ideal. HD research starts with theory. From theory, hypotheses are logically deduced. Research is designed specifically to test the hypotheses. If the data come out as predicted, support is inferred for the hypotheses and for the theory that led to the hypotheses, otherwise the hypotheses and theory are considered unsupported and perhaps even falsified. Thus, the HD approach is all about formal apriori theory testing, and if one wants to formally test theory, the HD way is the way to go. Much has been written on the HD method, and Hemple's (1966) work is a classic reference that is worth reading.

The trouble is that formal theory testing and quantitative social science research are often considered to be one and the same. They are not. Yet most methods, texts, and classes (and graduate advisers, journal and grant reviewers, editors, etc.) tell students (and researchers) that the scientific method is about hypothesis and theory testing and that the only way science can legitimately be done is by creating and testing hypotheses, where all good hypotheses come from theory and produce $p < .05$ findings. But this cannot be so. Science is also about making new discoveries. Great discoveries such as the theory of evolution and DNA did not come from HD-style experiments. In fact, the HD method has little resemblance to most of the research published in the life sciences (Rozin, 2001). The HD method is fine and dandy for testing existing knowledge claims and theory, but it does not contain a good mechanism for generating new directions. And new findings are where the fun (and intellectual contribution) is. I do use HD when testing an existing theory, but this is not what I am trying to do in the vast majority of my published studies. A more flexible philosophical toolbox is needed.

When serving on graduate student thesis and dissertation committees, professors almost invariably ask the students questions such as "What is your theory?" and "What is your hypothesis?" but not "Do you have a hypothesis?" or "Does existing theory meaningfully apply to your question?" (Kerr, 1998). The presumption is that all good research needs hypotheses. After all, well-known and respected texts of scholars like Kerlinger and Lee (2000) say so explicitly. Recently,

I was declined funding for a *National Science Foundation* grant application. The reviewer wrote that the project was really interesting and if the study were done, the results would be very important and the reviewer would cite such a study wherever possible.[3] But, the reviewer wrote, unfortunately the project did not merit funding because it is about finding out what people do, not about testing a specific hypothesis. This is ludicrous. My dissertation advisor has frequently told me, "If you always support your hypotheses, you will never learn anything new." The corollary to this is "If your research is confined to hypothesis testing, you are less likely to come up with an important new finding." Note that the argument here is not against theory or hypothesis. The argument is opposed to hypothesis testing as the *only* approach to science.

This is where abduction comes in. *Abductive reasoning* involves reasoning from the data to the best explanation of the data given the data. Think of abduction as a compromise between dust bowl induction and formal HD theory testing. A good example is my new "a few transparent liars" model (Levine, 2010a; Levine, Shaw, & Shulman, 2010). The model is an attempt to come up with an internally consistent logical framework that accounts for several reliable findings that do not make sense from existing theory. In short, abduction is a way to move from data toward theory. Because it is based on data, it has a better chance of being right than purely deductive theory building, but unlike purely inductive approaches, the goal is bounded explanation rather than mere generalization based on instances. Abduction is not formally valid as it exploits the affirming of the consequent fallacy, but it is nevertheless very useful in generating new theory. Abduction is not for the blind-rule follower, and the abductive-reasoning practitioner will be seen by the HD snobs as overly speculative (but not dust bowl). But if you look at what the really influential social scientists actually do rather than what the textbooks say they do, their theoretical ideas are typically generated through abduction rather

than pure induction, and only after they are for-
malized are the new ideas tested via HD.

A previous version of this chapter (by a different author) claimed that the HD approach characterized most published research on interpersonal
communication. I have a different take and believe
instead that most communication research is
really induction masquerading as HD. It is a commonly held value that good research is theoretical
(and I have much sympathy with such a belief so
long as research working toward new theory is
included as theoretical). The problem is that most
research is not really theory driven. Instead, such
research is really driven by what the author of the
work finds personally interesting. Most interpersonal researchers do not start out by thinking
"How can we give theory *XYZ* a really decisive
test?" Instead, they think, "Such and such is interesting; how can I efficiently study it?" But authors
can't say that if they want to get published.
Convention disallows curiosity-based rationales.
So the front end of the paper reviews "theory."
Sometimes real theories are reviewed. Other
times, the word *theory* is just put in, as if calling
something a theory will make it so. But if a critical
reader looks carefully at the hypotheses and the
argument leading to the hypotheses, it will
become evident that even though "theory" is
given much lip service, the argument has this
basic format: "Previous studies have found such
and such, therefore we will too." Bingo, the argument is pure induction and is not HD at all! The
twin tests to apply are (1) if the rationale for the
hypotheses are based on what previous studies
have found rather than on logical derivation from
the theoretical proposition or (2) if you can take
the theory out and the logic of the research still
makes sense, without the guiding theory, it is not
really HD research but instead pseudo-HD. I
challenge the reader to apply these tests to what
they read in the published research. Inductive
arguments dressed up as HD are probably the
norm in interpersonal communication research;
this unfortunate state of affairs stems from the
misguided belief that HD is the only way to do
good science. Ironically, if editors and reviewers

were more tolerant of careful abduction, there
might be more and better theory to test and then
Professor Charles Berger would have less to complain about in his periodic theoretical rants (see
Berger, 1991, 2005).

## The Real Role of Hypotheses and Theory

The preceding should not be taken in any way as
devaluating theory. It is often said that there is
nothing more useful than a good theory. I whole-
heartedly endorse this statement. But I would also
advance a corollary that is sure to be more controversial. While a *good* theory is a truly wonderful
thing, there are few things more intellectually
damaging than a bad theory. This, of course, begs
the question, what makes a good theory good and
what makes a bad theory bad? Good theories have
lots of nice qualities. They are internally consistent, they have a large ratio of explanatory power
to parsimony, they have good heuristic value in
generating new predictions and reconciling old
anomalies, they are testable and falsifiable, and so
on. But the single most important criterion in
distinguishing valuable theory from bad theory is
verisimilitude. Good theories are, for the most
part, consistent with the data, while bad theories
get it mostly wrong. Good theories help us understand. They give us valuable insight into how the
world works. Bad theories lead to misunderstanding and illusion. Good theories make us wiser.
Bad theories make us not only more ignorant but
also more pompous and arrogant in our ignorance. Good theories further science. Bad theories
are mythologies that gather cultlike followings
and seek to brainwash new converts into following false idols. You get the idea.

Good theories are valuable for a variety of
reasons, but three of the most important are discussed here. The first and most obvious is that
good theories provide explanation. They answer
the "why" question. As interpersonal scholars
know from uncertainty reduction theory (Berger
& Calabrese, 1975), explanatory knowledge is
deeper and richer than descriptive or predicative

knowledge. Good theories enable us to understand the principles, mechanisms, and processes behind the working of some interpersonal phenomena in a way that mere data cannot. Students of interpersonal communication want to know why things happen, and if for no other reason, this makes good theory invaluable.

Second, good theories point us in the right direction. They tell us what to study and how to study it. There are a near-infinite number of variables out there that we could include in our study. Theory not only helps us prioritize, it demands that we do so.

Besides the obvious importance of explanation and direction, a third indispensable function of theory and hypotheses is that they provide the best (and maybe only) path to external validity and generality. It has already been noted that all data are inherently finite and contextualized, which leads to the problem of induction. When we do a study, we want our findings to extend beyond the particular participants, time, and situation of our study. But our data are always limited in these ways. Some researchers try to overcome this problem by addressing what might be called the "surface features" of the research method. So they collect nonstudent data, they randomly select subjects from some population, they use multiple-message designs in conjunction with random-effect statistics, or they employ some similar ploy. All this is done to enhance the generality of the findings, but none of it ever solves the problem. The data are still finite. No statistical or methodological sleight of hand can change this. Imagine some large-scale random survey of the U.S. population. The findings may be general, within confidence limits, across the population, but they are still bound by time, the way the particular questions were worded, and so on. The problem simply cannot be overcome with a methodological fix. The only real solution is theory.

While data are always finite, theory is not constrained in the same way. Although theory is not infinite, good theory specifies boundary conditions that tell us when the theory does and does not apply. So theory, not data, allows bounded generalizations. What we can do is design our studies to test the boundary conditions of a theory. The purpose of data (and method), therefore, is very often not to make generalizations but to test generalizations (Mook, 1983). Well-designed studies can do that. Research, over time, allows for the development and testing of theory, and it is theory, in turn, that provides principles of human behavior with bounded generality. The theoretical knowledge of specifying under what conditions a proposition does and does not hold provides generality in a way that mere data cannot. This is why theory is important, and it is in this way, ironically, that basic theoretical research is often more useful, in application, than much so-called applied research.

## Quantitative Basics

### Constructs and Variables

Quantitative research involves variables. *Variables* are symbols to which numerals or numbers are assigned. Variables can also be defined as observable things that vary. That is, variables take on different values. Variables are contrasted with both constants and constructs. *Constants* are things whose values are fixed; they do not vary. *Constructs* are conceptual or theoretical entities that exist in the mind of researchers, whereas variables are observable. For example, the idea of the depth of self-disclosure is a construct, while scores on the depth dimension of a self-disclosure scale constitute a variable.

Quantitative researchers are interested in constructs and, usually, how two or more constructs are related to each other. Constructs are the ideas that are the topics of study. To research constructs, they are measured, and through measurement, values are assigned. The resulting values constitute a variable, and the relationships among variables can be tested, often with statistical analyses. When the variables are found to be statistically related in some manner, then it is inferred that the constructs are likewise related in a similar manner. Thus, constructs are (albeit imperfectly) measured, and when values are assigned to represent these constructs, we call the resulting collection of values a variable. Variables are tested for statistical association or relationship, and inferences are made about how constructs are related based on the observed relationships among the corresponding variables.

When statistical analyses are used to test the relationships among variables, and some variables are conceived of as predictors or causes of other variables, the variables that are the predictor or cause variables are called *independent variables* while the variables that are predicted, the effects or outcomes, are called *dependent variables*. Dependent variables are so called because they are specified to depend on the independent variables. Often, the notation $x$ is used to refer to the independent variable and $y$ to the dependent variable. When graphing the relationship between $x$ and $y$, $x$ is plotted on the horizontal axis and $y$ on the vertical axis.

There is nothing inherent in a variable that makes it independent or dependent. Instead, the identification of a variable as independent or dependent rests on theory, hypothesis, research design, and statistical analysis. For example, if we are looking at how biological sex affects the depth of self-disclosure, then depth of self-disclosure is a dependent variable (e.g., Dindia & Allen, 1992). In contrast, if we are considering how depth of self-disclosure reduces uncertainty in computer-mediated communication (e.g., Tidwell & Walther, 2002), then depth of self-disclosure is an independent variable.

Independent variables can be further classified as active (manipulated, induced) or measured (attribute) variables. The values of an active independent variable are set by the researcher. That is, they are induced or manipulated. This is not true for measured variables where the values are not under research control. Dependent variables are always measured and

never active. As we will see later, the distinction between active and measured independent variables is the key to distinguishing experimental and quasi-experimental research from nonexperimental studies.

## The Key Concepts of Variance and Control

The extent to which a variable varies is called *variance*. The more scores differ from one another, the more they vary, and hence the greater the variance. Statistically, variance has a more precise meaning. Variance refers to the average squared amount by which scores differ from the average score. It is helpful to remember that variance is in square units (Beatty, 2002). The square root ("un-square") of variance is the *standard deviation*. Both variance and standard deviation are metrics of dispersion, and the importance of these ideas is difficult to overstate.

Variance may be the single most important concept in quantitative research. Obviously, not all people are the same. Situations, too, differ from one another. So too do messages. Quantitative research helps us know why, when, how much, and to what effect things vary. This is often done by seeing if and how the variable we are interested in varies systematically with some other variable(s) of interest. That is, most quantitative communication research seeks to predict and/or explain how some variable of interest is related to another variable(s) of interest. This involves demonstrating that the variance in a variable is systematically related to the variance in another variable.

When variables are related, that is, one predicts, causes, or is associated with another, the variables are said to covary. So we will want to know if and how variables covary. This brings us to the idea of *function*. If $x$ is an independent variable and $y$ a dependent variable and $x$ and $y$ are systematically related to each other in some way, we can say that $y$ is a function of $x$. Symbolically,

$y = f(x)$. So if we know what $x$ is and we know the function, we can predict $y$. Then, we can do a study to see if our prediction is right. The trick, of course, is knowing the function. More about this later. Nevertheless, regardless of the specific function, it is a fundamental law of quantitative research that variance is required for covariance. That which does not vary cannot covary. If there is no variance, there can be no covariance and no meaningful function to test. If there is variance, however, then there may or may not be covariance, and if there is covariance, we will want to know the function that will let us predict $y$ from our knowledge of $x$. In short, most quantitative research is about understanding variance, and understanding variance requires having variance to observe and the skills to figure out and test the function.

This can be done in two ways. First, we can try to measure naturally occurring variance and see if we find other variables that predict that variance. The second option is to try to create or induce variance. If you are not sure how this might be done, go find a working light switch. Turn it off and on. You just created variance in how much light there is. This is how experiments work, but that is getting too far ahead for the moment.

The flip side of variance is constancy. Constants are also extremely important in quantitative research because they are central to the idea of *control*. Because that which does not vary cannot covary, constants cannot be related to anything. Hence, holding something constant is a surefire way to control (rule out) its impact. What researchers try to do is to induce or assess the variance and covariance of the variables of interest while holding constant as much else as possible. Because constants never affect other things, they provide the best mechanism for the "control" of nuisance variance in research. An example from the research on the "probing effect" will be discussed later.

These principles of constancy and covariance provide the conceptual basis for experimentation. If some variable $x$ has a causal impact on some other variable $y$, then changes in $x$ will systematically produce changes in $y$. In an experiment, the researcher systematically alters the values of $x$ and observes the values of $y$. If values of $y$ systematically change when $x$ is changed but $y$ stays constant when $x$ is constant, then evidence that $x$ leads to $y$ is obtained. Other potential causes of $y$ are held constant so that they cannot have an impact on $y$ and so that the impact of $x$ can be isolated. The tighter the control over nuisance variables, the stronger the inference that is obtained from observing $y$ vary as a function of inducing variance in $x$.

So just as the light switch controls the light, inducing variance in the switch induces variance in the lighting. Conceptually, I do the same thing in my deception experiments. I think that I know some situations in which people are more or less accurate at detecting deception. So I bring the research participants into my lab and throw the switch (my independent variable) and turn it on and off to find out how accurate they are. When I can turn my dependent measure on and off (so to speak) at will, I have evidence to enable me to understand what is going on.

A fun example is the Levine et al. (2000) norms and expectations experiment. The study was actually a class project in an MA class on research design, and my coauthors were the students in that class. The previous literature (Bond et al., 1992) had shown that people who observe unexpected, odd behavior find the target person less believable than a target person who was behaving in a more expected, typical way. Bond et al. (1992) would have us believe that this is due to expectancy violations. They claim that unexpected behavior is seen as less honest. It might be, however, that we are simply less likely to believe weird-acting people and that expectations have nothing to do with it. That is, if observation of unexpected, odd behavior makes it less likely that a person is believed, it might be due to expectancy violations or due to mere oddity. So we did an experiment to ferret this out. Research participants came into our lab and had a get-to-know-the-other-person interview with a research confederate. The confederates either acted weird (e.g., obsessively picking their teeth with their fingers or following an invisible insect around the room with their eyes—this took lots of practice) or not, and the participants were forewarned ahead of time to either expect weirdness or not. We found that flipping the expectation switch made little difference. Flipping the weird behavior on and off, however, systematically raised and lowered perceived honesty. Bond's reasoning and the predictions of Burgoon's expectance violations theory (Burgoon & Hale, 1988) were wrong.

Constancy, variance, and covariance are also central in nonexperimental quantitative research. In nonexperimental research, variance is observed rather than created, and statistical analyses are used to document differences or association. Again, variance is essential because it is required for covariance.

## Relationships Among Variables

Variables can be related to each other in different ways. This was discussed briefly earlier by introducing the idea of a function. Given that the goal of quantitative communication research is usually to document and explain how variables are related, knowing conceptually about the different types of relationships between variables (i.e., the different functions) is essential.

One possibility is that no relationship exists. That is, the variables are completely unrelated, and there is no covariance. Statistics, however, cannot be used to prove a complete lack of relationship, but statistical techniques such as confidence intervals (CIs), meta-analysis, or equivalence tests can show that a relationship is neither strong nor substantial (Levine, Weber, Park, & Hullett, 2008; for an example of equivalence testing in communication research, see Muthuswamy, Levine, & Weber's 2009 study of fear appeals in Africa). Nevertheless, it is unusual for communication researchers to purposely study weak relationships.

If variables are related, the simplest possibility is that the variance in one variable causes

variance in the other. This situation is called a *direct causal relationship*. Documenting a direct causal relationship requires showing that (a) the variables covary, (b) the cause variable precedes the effect variable in time, and (c) the effect is not explainable by some other variable called a *spurious* cause. If some other variable causes both the independent and the dependent variables, then it will look like there is a direct relationship when actually there is not. The relationship is said to be spurious. A well-known example of a spurious relationship is that towns with more churches tend to have more bars. It would be a mistake, however, to conclude that church going and alcohol consumption are related based on such an association. Obviously, both are related to population size. Larger towns tend to have more of everything. Cook and Campbell (1979) offer an excellent discussion on the concept of causation.

Sometimes direct causal relationships are stringed together. So variable *x* may lead to variable *y*, and *y*, in turn, leads to *z*. This is called a *mediated* relationship, and *y* is said to mediate the relationship between and *x* and *z*. Mediated relationships are sometimes confused with *moderated* relationships. A moderated relationship exists when the effect of an independent variable on a dependent variable varies as a function of a third variable. That is, the focal relationship of interest is variable. For example, if the relationship between self-disclosure and liking is stronger for women than for men, then sex moderates the effects of self-disclosure and liking. Evidence for moderators is reflected by a statistical interaction effect. In the previous example, there is a (hypothetical) two-way interaction between self-disclosure and sex on liking. Baron and Kenny (1986) is the most cited reference on mediated and moderated relationships, but most communication researchers test mediation hypotheses with path analysis or SEM rather than with the Baron and Kenny approach. Most moderation hypotheses are tested with the interaction term in the analysis of variance (ANOVA), although moderated multiple regression (see Cohen, Cohen, West, & Aiken, 2010) has been gaining popularity.

# Research Design

## Experimental Design

For a research study to technically be "an experiment," three necessary and jointly sufficient criteria must all be met: (1) at least one independent variable must be active, (2) at least one comparison or control group must be used, and (3) participants must be randomly assigned to the experimental conditions. Studies meeting the first two criteria but not the third are called quasi experiments. Studies lacking the first two criteria are nonexperimental. Nonexperimental research will be discussed later.

*Random assignment* means that each participant has an equal probability of being in each experimental condition. The primary purpose of random assignment is to guard against *selection effects* (Campbell & Stanley, 1963). A selection effect occurs when the participants in one condition differ systematically from the participants in another condition (a) in a way that is other than for the intended active independent variable and (b) in a way that affects the dependent measure. Random assignment should not be confused with haphazard assignment, which may have subtle systematic biases. If the first person who comes to the lab is in Condition 1, the second in Condition 2, and so forth, this is haphazard, not truly random. Who knows what kind of sneaky artifacts might slip into the study. Online random number generations that can be used to randomly assign participants to conditions can be obtained at www.random.org.

Quasi experiments (i.e., studies with active independent variables but lacking random assignment) are not inherently flawed; they just lack one protection offered by a true experiment, and for this reason, researchers would not use a quasi-experimental design if a true experiment were a viable option. Furthermore, random assignment does not preclude selection effects; it just makes them less probable. Chance is lumpy (Abelson, 1995), and randomization is useful but imperfect.

Also, random assignment should not be confused with *random selection*. Random selection refers to how participants get into the study in the first place, and it means that every participant in the population from which the results will apply has an equal probability of participation. Random selection is an issue of generality or external validity, and studies of interpersonal communication seldom employ random selection.

Experiments and quasi experiments have a number of advantages over nonexperimental research. One main advantage is that better evidence for time ordering and causal order is obtained from experimental work than from nonexperimental research. Most theories and explanations specify some order among constructs/variables. Their logic says that this leads to that (and not vice versa). So let's say our theory states that $x$ leads to $y$ (i.e., $y$ is a function of $x$). Let's make $x$ an active variable, under the experimenter's control. If $x$ leads to $y$, when we flip the $x$ switch (i.e., turn it off and on), we should observe systematic variance in $y$. And if this is the case under nicely controlled circumstances, we will gain a real insight into the $y = f(x)$ relationship. Alternatively, if $x$ leads to $y$ and we turn the $y$ switch, $x$ is unaffected because "the effects" or "the cause" flows from $x$ to $y$, not from $y$ to $x$. The results of the experiments and quasi experiments give the researcher this type of evidence. This is the beauty of active independent variables. The experimenter can flip the switch at will. Causal evidence in nonexperimental work is more tenuous.

A second advantage of experimental research is greater control through research design. What one does in an experiment is flip the switch to your independent variable while holding all other potential causal variables constant. If, when we flip the $x$ switch, $y$ changes and the only difference is $x$ being on or off, then we know that the variance in $y$ is a function of $x$ and nothing else. The trick, of course, is holding everything else constant. To the extent we can do that, we have high-quality inference because we know that constants are inert. Control in real experiments, however, is never perfect, because it is impossible to be certain that everything else is really constant. Nevertheless, the better the control, the better the evidence obtained for the results. Nonexperimental work lacks control and comparison groups and has to rely on statistical rather than design-based controls, and thus concern over the impact of unknown spurious nuisance variables is typically greater in nonexperimental studies than in well-designed experiments. Furthermore, statistical control rests on the quality of the measurement, which is always imperfect.

Textbooks often say that experiments have disadvantages such as lacking realism and generality. Such assertions are not persuasive. First, such claims often conflate lab work with fieldwork. Both lab studies and field studies can be either experimental or nonexperimental. Second, while some lab studies clearly lack realism (e.g., Bond et al., 1992), so too do many nonexperimental studies. Questionnaire and interview research often asks people questions that they would not have thought about were they not in the research study (Schwarz, 1999). Third, I do not see the research lab as somehow divorced from the real world. On the contrary, people actually talk to other people in many lab studies. It is scandalous how few published studies of interpersonal communication involve people actually communicating with other people. Finally, as noted before, I see theory as the path to generality and external validity, not the surface features of the research. So if theory can be better tested with an experimental design, I would think that experimental works offer more, not less, generalizable knowledge.

I do both experimental and nonexperimental research. In deciding which way to go for a particular study, I ask myself two key questions. First, do the independent variables lend themselves to experimental induction? So, for example, if I want to find out the dimensionality of the communication apprehension scale (see Levine & McCroskey, 1990), all I need to do is collect responses to the PRCA-24 (Personal Report of Communication Apprehension-24). No experimental induction is needed. But if I want to test the effectiveness of the Joe Ayres communication apprehension treatment program (Ayres & Hopf, 1985) against a credible placebo control (Duff, Levine, Beatty, Woobright, & Park, 2007), then I need to do an experiment. The second question I ask myself is how important is causal order and control. If the variables can be experimentally induced and if I am interested in testing one process against another, then I think of doing an experiment. If I am just interested in description or looking at statistical association or if the independent variables do not lend themselves to experimental variation, then I take the nonexperimental path. The research question and theory behind it determine the method, not some fixed preference for one method over another.

A good example of what can be done with experiment design is the probing experiments I did with Steve McCornack (see Levine & McCornack, 2001). The probing effect relates to the presence of mere question asking in deception detection. The finding is that senders who are questioned are more likely to be believed than senders who are not questioned, regardless of actual honesty (Levine & McCornack, 2001). One explanation for the probing effect is offered by interpersonal deception theory (IDT; Buller & Burgoon, 1996). According to IDT, senders who are questioned with suspicious probing questions perceive suspicion. Once they recognize that the listener is suspicious, they strategically adapt their behavior to appear more honest. Listeners pick up on the honest behavior and are more likely to judge them as honest. Thus, probing questions lead to belief, because they prompt honest-appearing behavior. Steve and I suspected that the IDT explanation was bogus (see Levine & McCornack, 1996a, 1996b, for a detailed account of our reasoning). So we did a simple experiment. We videotaped senders being questioned with neural questions. Then, with a video editor, we altered the tapes. In a no-probe condition, we just spliced out the question, leaving the answer intact. In supportive and suspicious probe conditions, we replaced the neural questioning with supportive or suspicion questions. But in all the conditions, the answers and the sender behaviors were constant. What we found was that the probed sources tended to be believed more when the listener heard the probes, regardless of probe type, thus replicating the probing effect. But since sender behavior was held constant in the research design, we could show that strategic behavioral adaptation was not responsible for the effect, at least in our data. In our more recent studies, we showed that suspicion-implying probing questions can lead to lower or higher accuracy depending on the wording of the questions (Levine & Blair, 2010; Levine, Shaw, et al., 2010). Experiments such as these provide convincing evidence for and against the predictions of different theories by inducing variance in some causal variables while holding other variables constant.

## Design Basics

The simplest experiments involve a dichotomous on/off independent variable and a single dependent (outcome) variable. In a *posttest-only control group experiment*, participants are randomly assigned to one of two groups, an experimental group that gets the experimental induction or a control group that does not. Everything else is held as constant as possible. If the two groups differ on the dependent variable, that difference is attributed to the experimental induction. An alternative is a *pretest/posttest control group experiment*. Here, all participants are first measured on the dependent variable, then they are randomly assigned to one of two groups, the experimental group that gets the experimental induction or a control group that does not. Again, everything else is held as constant as possible. Finally, participants are tested a second time. If there is more change in the experimental group than in the control group, the difference is attributed to the independent variable (the induction). Posttest-only designs are sometimes also called *independent*

groups designs* or *between-groups designs*, while pretest–posttest designs are often called *repeated designs* or *within-subjects designs*.

There are pros and cons in going with a posttest only as opposed to having a pretest. There are three big advantages in pretest–posttest designs. First, every participant is his or her own control, and thus individual differences are held constant. Second, these designs are efficient in that they have more statistical power (see later in the chapter) and may require smaller samples. Third, they let the researcher look at change, which can be critical in some research areas such as persuasion. For example, if you wanted to study boomerang effects or psychological reactance in persuasion (e.g., see Dillard & Shen, 2005), you would need a pretest to show that the participants actually changed.

There are two main disadvantages in having a pretest. First, they increase the probability of nuisance variables and artifacts known as *testing effects*, *history effects*, and *maturation effects*. A testing effect occurs when the act of pretesting affects the posttest. With a pretest, we have to worry about order effects, priming, learning, and the like. A history effect occurs when an event other than induction occurs between the pretest and posttest that might affect the dependent variable. For example, my friend and colleague Joe Walther was doing a study of Israelites and Palestinians working together in online cooperative work tasks when Israel made a military incursion into the West Bank. Such events could affect his results, perhaps further polarizing his participants. Maturation is when participants change naturally over the course of the study. And in addition to all these concerns, change scores are more difficult to deal with statistically. For these reasons, posttest-only designs are much more common in interpersonal communication research.

## Designs Researchers Really Use

Describing simple experiments is a useful teaching tool for conveying the basic ideas central to social-scientific experimentation, but most experimental work in interpersonal communication involves designs that are more complex, with more than one independent variable, multiple dependent variables, multiple induction instantiations, or some combination of these. So we need to move from the simple "building-block" designs discussed so far to the designs that researchers actually use. Let us start with multiple independent variables.

Most experiments with more than one independent variable use *factorial* designs. In a factorial design, all active independent variables are *crossed* with each other. Crossing variables involves having all possible combinations of the levels of the variables. It is important not to confuse the levels of a specific independent variable with the existence of two or more different independent variables. The levels of a variable are the different experimental values that are induced. If there are just two levels, the levels might be on/off, treatment/control, high/low, male/female, and so on. Three levels could be low, moderate, or high suspicion, as in McCornack and Levine (1990). An example of four levels of a variable is systematic desensitization, the Ayres combination treatment, no treatment control, and placebo control—as in Duff et al.'s (2007) study of communication apprehension reduction treatments. Lee, Levine, and Cambra (1997) used five different grade levels of children (fourth through eighth graders) as a variable in their study of compliance resistance in children; thus, grade had five levels in their study. So each independent variable will have two or more levels; a variable with only one level would not vary at all. It would be a constant.

The simplest possible crossed design is a $2 \times 2$. In a $2 \times 2$ crossed design, there are two independent variables with two levels each. Imagine that we have two independent variables, $X1$ and $X2$, each of which can be on or off. In a $2 \times 2$ independent-groups factorial experiment, participants are randomly assigned to one of four conditions. The four conditions are $X1$ off and $X2$ off, $X1$ on with $X2$ off, $X1$ off and $X2$ on, and $X1$ on and $X2$ on. In a $2 \times 2$ repeated design, all participants are in all four conditions in some order, but the

four conditions are the same as those just mentioned. In a $2 \times 2 \times 2$, there are three independent variables, each with two levels, yielding eight different experimental combinations or cells. In a $3 \times 2 \times 2 \times 3$, there are four independent variables, the first and the last with three levels each, the other two with two levels each. See the pattern? There is a number for each independent variable included in the design, the value of the number tells the number of levels, and the product of all the numbers identifies the number of cells.

There are a number of advantages in crossed designs, and these explain their popularity. Foremost among these is the ability to test for moderation (interaction effects) in addition to main effects. Main effects are the effects of an independent variable averaged across the other independent variables. With a crossed design, research can test for the main effect for each independent variable and for the interactions among the independent variables.

When independent variables are not crossed, they might be either *nested* or *fully confounded*. Nesting is when an independent variable only occurs within some levels of another independent variable. This is not desirable, but sometimes it is unavoidable. Confounding is when the effects of one variable are indistinguishable from those of another. For examples of nesting and confounding, consider my norms and expectations experiment mentioned previously (Levine et al., 2000). Our objection to a previous experiment by Bond et al. (1992) was that it had confounded norms and expectations. Bond et al. assigned their participants to one of two conditions: unexpected weird behaviors or expected normal behaviors. Participants, for example, either saw a person talking with one arm raised vertically over the head or a person in a more normal posture. The people in odd poses were judged to be less honest than the people in normal poses, and Bond et al. inferred from this difference that behaviors that are unexpected are seen as lies because they violate expectations. However, any differences between the two groups might have been because the behavior was just weird. Maybe people evaluate norm breakers less positively. So we unconfounded the norms and expectations in our experiment by the crossing norms and expectations to create four experimental conditions: normal–expected, normal–unexpected, weird–expected, and weird–unexpected. This let us sort things out, and we discovered that it was being weird and not violating expectations that mattered. Not only did this resolve the confound in Bond et al., but it also provided a strong test of nonverbal expectancy violation theory (Burgoon & Hale, 1988).

To vary the weirdness, we decided to use four different weird behaviors. In the weird-behavior conditions, our participants interacted with someone who did one of four things: (1) followed an invisible insect flying around the room with the eyes, (2) picked his or her teeth with the fingers obsessively, (3) dropped down on the floor and stretched during the conversations, or (4) sporadically modulated his or her speech volume. Each of these odd behaviors was only enacted in the weird-behavior conditions. Such things do not happen when acting normally. So, in our design, weird behaviors were nested within the weird-behavior condition.

In addition to multiple independent variables, it is not unusual for studies to involve multiple dependent variables. Researchers with multiple dependent variables have a number of options. One option is to do separate statistical analyses for each dependent measure. The problem with this kind of analysis is that standard statistical inference presumes a single test. Multiple tests run the risk of error inflation (see Weber, 2007). There are corrections for multiple tests such as the Bonferroni test, but such corrections just trade off one type of error for another (Smith et al., 2002). Sometimes multivariate significance tests such as MANOVA are used, but this usually makes the situation worse, not better. When interpersonal communication researchers use MANOVA, they usually just report the multivariate test and then report the separate analyses for each variable (the so-called univariate tests),

which is what is interpreted. So they end up doing more instead of fewer tests, making the problem worse, not better. Another option is that researchers could use some type of factor analysis to try to reduce the number of dependent variables. Finally, researchers can use path analysis or SEM to model the relationships among the dependent variables. In my own research, I try to keep my experiments as simple as possible and avoid variable inflation in the first place. When I have multiple dependent variables, I ask myself if I have hypotheses about if and how they are interrelated. If I think they are interrelated, I do path analysis to model those relations, otherwise I do separate analyses. I stay away from MANOVA. Simple researcher designs are usually better because there is less to go wrong and the results tend to be more interpretable (Abelson, 1995; Cohen, 1990; Smith et al., 2002).

A third type of complexity is the inclusion of multiple exemplars or instantiations nested within an induction, and if these exist, the decision to use *fixed-* or *random-effects* statistical models becomes an issue. In a basic experiment, participants are randomly assigned to a treatment (active independent variable "on") or control (active independent variable "off"). In such an experiment, the independent variable is considered a "fixed" effect, and the research participants are considered a "random" effect in the analysis. For a fixed effect, the values of the variable are set by the experimenter, and the findings only apply to those levels. We would not know, for example, what would have happened had a different treatment been used; the findings only apply to the treatment–control conditions actually tested. If you think about it though, the participants in the study are also a variable. Each and every one of them is different. In this example, however, the variability in the participants is not of interest. We are just going to average across them to get an average score in the treatment and control conditions. That is, we are interested in whether or not the average participant who got the treatment is different from the average control participant. Within-condition variability is just error. It's a nuisance. So participants are treated as a random effect. We want to generalize across them. But note that there is a difference between "generalizing across" and "generalizing beyond." Statistically treating a variable as a random effect lets you generalize across nuisance variance. It does not let us generalize beyond. That requires not only appropriate statistical analysis but also random (or some other kind of representative) sampling, and even then, we still have the problem of induction. The fact that standard *t* tests and ANOVA treat the participants as a "random factor" in the analysis does not mean that the findings necessarily apply to all people everywhere who were not in the study. No statistical analysis ever magically grants generality; there are always other considerations.

Next, consider my norms and expectations experiment (Levine et al., 2000) discussed previously. We had confederates act normal or weird. In designing that study, does it make sense to use just one confederate, or might it make more sense to use more than one? What are the pros and cons? The same logic applies to weird behaviors. Is just one weird behavior best, or might several be better? In our study, we chose to have four different confederates who each enacted each of four different weird behaviors. The obvious cost is the added complexity and variable inflation. Nevertheless, we wanted to show that our findings would hold across different confederates and different behaviors. So we did multiple instantiations of our weird behavior. It added 16 cells to our design (four confederates crossed with four behaviors), but it gave us the logical equivalent of 16 mini replications, which made our claims stronger because the findings held across confederates and weird behaviors. When we did the analysis, however, we made confederates and type of weird behaviors fixed effects, not random effects. The decision to do this was easy and correct.

In interpersonal research, researchers often want to use multiple instantiations of variables to avoid the single-example/instance problem. This applies not just to confederates and behavioral studies but also to situations and messages (e.g., see McCornack, Levine, Torres, Solowczuk, & Campbell, 1992). In a very well-known and unfortunately influential article, Jackson and Jacobs (1983) advocated the use of random-effects analyses in these types of situations:

> One serious design flaw, which involves the use of a single message to represent a category of messages, occurs in nearly all of the experimental research on communication effects. The problem with such a design is that an observed difference between categories may reflect only differences between individual, idiosyncratic cases. A related error, the language-as-fixed-effect fallacy involves use of several replications of each category, but analysis of the cases as fixed effects. The consequence is that findings cannot be *generalized beyond* the sample used. *Future research should use multiple cases within each message category studied and treat cases as nested random effects* [italics added]. (p. 169)

This may sound reasonable, but it can be very bad advice. First, random effects do not allow for generality beyond the sample used any more than generalizing findings beyond other types of nonrepresentative samples. Second, random-effects analyses have a very nasty side effect. Random-effects analyses are often very low powered (Abelson, 1995; Hunter, Hamilton, & Allen, 1989). Statistical power will be discussed later, but basically the number of levels of the random factor becomes the sample size. So in my norms study, if weird-behavior example were a random effect, it would be like doing an experiment with a sample size of $N = 4$. It makes it highly probable that if your hypothesis is really right, the statistical test will yield the wrong answer. A better solution is replication and eventual meta-analysis (Abelson, 1995; Hunter et al., 1989). Nesting should only be done with care since crossing has definite advantages and random-effects analyses, in most applications, have unacceptably high error rates. Besides, the point of much theory-guided experimentation is not to make generations but to test generalization. Theory provides a better path to generality than complex statistical models that are not well understood by the researcher using them.

## Design Validity, Artifacts, and Confounds

In evaluating research, we can talk about design validity. Design validity is the extent to which the research design permits confidence in the research conclusions. In a totally invalid design, the findings have no meaning whatsoever. More typically, however, validity can be thought of as falling on a continuum from more to less confidence depending on the degree of control of rival explanations. A perfect study has never been done, but some findings are more likely to replicate than others and some designs are much "tighter" than others.

Design validity has traditionally been split into internal validity, external validity, and construct validity (Campbell & Stanley, 1963). Internal validity is the extent to which the intended independent variable, and not something else, produces the effects on the dependent variable. External validity refers to the extent to which the findings are generalized beyond the particular circumstance of the study. Construct validity refers to how well the inductions or measures capture the constructs they are supposed to induce or measure.

As Campbell and Stanley (1963) note, internal validity is the sine qua non (without which, nothing) of research. If researchers (and readers) cannot attribute the variation in the dependent variable to the independent variable(s), then the findings are meaningless, and there is no point in doing the research. Some textbooks talk about internal validity and external validity being a trade-off, but this is silly and makes no sense. If the findings are meaningless, then generality is moot.

Campbell and Stanley (1963) classify confounds as threats to construct validity, but when an induction (i.e., active independent variable) is confounded with some other variable, I find it useful to think of confounding as an issue of internal validity. A confounded induction is when more than one variable is (usually inadvertently) manipulated in such a way that the effects of the variables cannot be parsed. For example, Booth-Butterfield and Jordan (1989) were interested in comparing communication adaptation patterns in same- and mixed-race groups. They recruited groups of college students who knew each other. Some of the groups were all white, and some were all black. In the same-race conditions, intact groups of five women interacted, and the interactions were videotaped and coded. In the mixed-race interactions, two intact groups of five were combined. So the same-race groups were all of the same race and consisted of five members, with all members known to each other previously, while the mixed-race groups had 10 members, who were mixed in race, and contained both members who were previously known to each other and others who were not known to each other. So in Booth-Butterfield and Jordan's design, the racial composition of groups (the intended independent variable) is fully confounded with group size and friends-only versus friends-and-stranger composition.

Most experimental studies are confounded in some minor ways, but not all confounds present meaningful threats to internal validity. The key question is whether the confounding variable(s) involves something that might actually change the results. In Booth-Butterfield and Jordan (1989), are group size and friend–stranger group composition likely to affect communication patterns? Because the answer would seem to be yes, the internal validity is highly suspect. There are other confounds in the Booth-Butterfield and Jordan study that are of less concern, such as interaction order (same-race groups interacted first), the number of experimenters present, and the topic of discussion. So the study was really at least a six-way confound. But not all these confounds are equally problematic.

The solution to confounds is first to identify them. When the confound is recognized, then the confound can either be held constant and thus neutralized or built into the design and thus tested. Confounds can be unconfounded and thus built in by crossing them with the other independent variables. The cost of building in variables is increased complexity, so it is often best just to hold them constant. For example, Booth-Butterfield and Jordan (1989) could have used strangers only in the same-race groups and could have had equal group sizes.

Three additional strategies for dealing with unwanted variables are randomization, double blinds, and placebo and other special controls. Random assignment was discussed previously. The idea is that by randomly assigning people to conditions, or messages to people, or randomly assigning experimental orders, and so on, the nuisance variables will average out. Another strategy is double-blind procedures. In double-blind experiments, both the researcher collecting the data and the participant are kept unaware of which experimental condition subjects are in so that this knowledge cannot inadvertently affect the results. A placebo is a believable but inert treatment used to rule out psychotherapeutic effects. Examples of communication research using these strategies effectively include the Duff et al. (2007) study of communication apprehension treatment effectiveness and the Levine, Feeley, McCornack, Hughes, and Harms (2005) study of nonverbal training in lie detection.

## Quantifying Constructs

### Nonexperimental Research

Most nonexperimental quantitative research on interpersonal communication involves asking people about something (e.g., survey, questionnaire, and interview methods), observation (e.g., behavioral observation, content analysis, textual analysis, physiological measurement), or both. Experiments, too, use these methods of measurement. The key

difference is that in experiments and quasi experiments, at least one independent variable is active. In nonexperimental research, none of the variables are active. But all quantitative research has some variables that are measured, and the trick is in measuring the intended construct well.

As a general rule, if the construct of interest is overtly behavioral in nature, something that is directly observable, or both, then observation is often the preferred method. Alternatively, if the construct is internal-psychological in nature, such as a memory, opinion, attitude, emotional state, and so on, that is not directly observable, then it often makes sense to use measurement that involves asking questions of the participants. Furthermore, self-report measurement, including questionnaire and interview methods, are most useful when the participants know the answer and are willing to give the researchers the answer. Unfortunately, self-report questionnaires often ask questions that fail to meet these necessary conditions. Researchers often overestimate peoples' self-awareness or their ability to recall their own behavior (Schwarz, 1999).

## Essentials of Valid Measurement

The new knowledge generated through empirical research can be no more valid than the measures used to make the observations. Thus, measurement validity is an absolute prerequisite for obtaining valid research results and for the defensible interpretation of findings. In short, the path to verisimilitude in quantitative research always goes through measurement.

Unfortunately, past and current trends in graduate education in most of the social sciences focus more on the statistical analysis of data than on the methods of observation and measurement used to produce data. Consequently, the typical quantitative researcher publishing in the social sciences probably took several advanced graduate-level statistics classes but likely had little training in psychometrics. Perhaps as a result, measurement is often the weakest link in our empirical knowledge claims.

It is my experience that most published scales and measures are never put to rigorous test, and of those that are put to the test, most do not fare very well. Fiske and Campbell (1992) made a similar observation. Published measures that have serious validity problems may even be more the norm than the exception. Examples that readily come to mind include measures of Machiavellianism (Christie & Geis, 1970), self-construal (i.e., that aspect of self-concept in which the self is differentiated from or converges with others; Gudykunst & Lee, 2003; Singelis, 1994), verbal aggressiveness (Infante & Wigley, 1986), and argumentativeness (Infante & Rancer, 1982). Research has shown substantial measurement problems in the scales measuring each of these constructs (Bresnahan et al., 2005; Hunter, Gerbing, & Boster, 1982; Kotowski, Levine, Baker, & Bolt, 2009; Levine, Bresnahan, Park, Lapinski, Lee, et al. 2003; Levine, Bresnahan, Park, Lapinski, Wittenbaum, et al. 2003; Levine et al., 2004).

To review, constructs and their interrelationships are the things researchers are interested in knowing about. The meaning attached to a given construct is specified in a conceptual definition. Measurement, on the other hand, is the act of assigning numbers or numerals to represent attributes of people, objects, or events (Nunnally & Bernstein, 1994). That is, measurement is the process of systematically converting abstract ideas into empirical data. Measurement allows for the representation of abstractions (i.e., constructs) with observable values or scores so that speculation, hypotheses, and theories about how various constructs are related can be put to empirical test.

Obviously, we want to maximize the degree of correspondence between the conceptual definition of a construct and the construct's measure. When the correspondence between construct and measurement is low, true relationships between constructs can appear to be false and false relationships between constructs can appear to be true. The degree of correspondence between a construct and its measurement is at the heart of measurement validity.

Measurement validity generally refers to how closely the values produced by a measure reflect the construct being measured. That is, a measure is valid to the extent that there is fidelity between scores and what the scores are meant to represent. Put differently, measurement validity is the extent to which a measure assesses what it is purported to measure, and nothing else.

As with design validity, it is important to point out that validity is not binary and measures need not be either invalid or valid. Usually, validity is considered as a continuum reflecting the degree of confidence that researchers have in a measure given the specific use for which the measure is being used. Even the best measures in the social sciences are not perfect. But some measures, such as IQ scores, for example, have considerable bodies of evidence suggesting substantial correlation between the construct and observed scores with only a small amount of systematic error (see Lubinski, 2004). For other measures, such as self-construal scales, the evidence is much more consistent with major problems: a weak correlation between the construct and observed score is attributable to substantial confounding. Consequently, researchers ought not to place much confidence in the meaning of the scores on self-construal scales (Levine, Bresnahan, Park, Lapinski, Lee, et al., 2003; Levine, Bresnahan, Park, Lapinski, Wittenbaum, et al., 2003).

Just as experimental inductions can be confounded, so too can measured variables. Measurement confounding exits when scores reflect more than one construct. A good example is self-construal scales. Several of Gudykunst's self-construal items ask people about consulting others (Gudykunst & Lee, 2003). This confounds self-concept and communication style (Levine, Bresnahan, Park, Lapinski, Lee, et al., 2003).

Another important point about measurement validity is that it is an empirical issue, requiring empirical evidence of different kinds and from a variety of sources to achieve. As evidence consistent with validity amasses over time, it is possible to have more confidence that scores on the measure are indeed indicators of the construct. In the absence of a substantial amount of evidence, arguments for a scale's validity cannot be considered defensible. Lack of evidence does not mean that a measure is invalid but rather that validity is indeterminate. Further still, a scale is never proven valid because new data might arise in the future that tips the scales back toward invalidity. The definition of the construct may change over time, or responses elicited by the measure may change over time or application.

Because it makes little sense to measure something unless you know precisely what it is that you want to measure, the most reasonable place to start when thinking about a measure is with the conceptual definition of the construct that is to be measured. Once a good conceptual definition is adopted, then the measure can be created and the validation process can begin.

## Measurement Validity and Validation Strategies

There are many different aspects of measurement validity. One sees reference to face validity, content validity, construct validity, structural validity, convergent validity, divergent/discriminant validity, and so forth. Each of these is a different aspect of measurement validity—that is, how closely the scores on the measure reflect the construct that we are seeking to quantify.

Face validity is about appearance and involves critical thinking and informed judgment. Try this test. A certain self-report scale item states, "Speaking up in a work/task group is not a problem for me." What construct is this item measuring? Maybe some aspect of leadership? Communication apprehension? If you guessed independent self-construal, you would be correct.[4] If you think it a problem that such an item would be used to measure self-concept, this too would be correct, and you get the idea of face validity.

Content validity is the extent to which a measure covers the breadth of the intended construct. A good measure would cover all the different facets of the construct and not just some narrow aspect. For example, a good measure of communication apprehension would not be limited to public-speaking contexts.

Structural validity usually refers to the "factor structure" or "dimensionality" of a scale. There should be a one-to-one correspondence between the number of constructs that a researcher wants to measure and the number of factors or dimensions of the scales used (factors and dimensions are used synonymously here). This is usually tested by some kind of factor analysis. Exploratory factor analysis (which is different from principal components analysis; see Park, Dailey, & Lemus, 2002) is used when a researcher does not know how many factors there might be or which items comprise which factor. Confirmatory factor analysis, in contrast, is used to test if a scale is factoring as intended. In either case, factor analysis, when used well, tells us how many constructs are measured but not about the substantive nature of the construct.

The principle of convergent validity (Campbell & Fiske, 1959; see Fiske & Campbell, 1992, for a useful retrospective on their idea) is that measures of the same construct should converge; they should be highly intercorrelated and should function in parallel manner with different constructs. It can be thought of as validation by triangulation; that is, if you measure a construct in different ways, all the alternative methods should triangulate or converge, all pointing to the same conclusions. When this is the case, we can have more confidence in each of the individual measures.

Divergence discriminance (Campbell & Fiske, 1959) is the flip side of convergence. The principle of divergence is that measures of different constructs act differently; they are not so highly intercorrelated as to be alternative measures of the same thing, and they act differently with respect to outside constructs. Convergent and divergent validity can be established with confirmatory factor analysis (by showing that different items measuring a single construct converge while items on different scales fall on different factors) or, better yet, multitrait–multimethod (MTMM) validation (Campbell & Fiske, 1959; for communication examples, see Bresnahan et al., 2005; Kotowski et al., 2009). MTMM offers the advantage of controlling method variance by crossing constructs and methods.

Construct validity is a more general term, referring to how well scores correspond to the construct given the theory. It encompasses structural validity, convergent validity, discriminant validity, and nomological network validation (Cronbach & Meehl, 1955). Nomological networks are theoretically specified patterns of relationships among constructs–measures. Nomological network validation involves testing if a scale is associated with other measures as theoretically specified. Nomological network validation is often conflated with construct validity, but it is better seen as one (very limited) type of evidence for construct validity (Levine, Bresnahan, Park, Lapinski, Lee, et al., 2003; Nunnally & Bernstein, 1994). Full MTMM validation is usually preferred to rule out method variance confounding.

## Reliability

Obviously, we want reliable measures. The reliability of a measure is the extent to which it is free from random response errors. Reliability is important, but it can be misleading.

Reliability is important because to the extent measures are unreliable, there is more random error; and random error obscures the relationships between variables, resulting in attenuated effect sizes and reduced statistical power. Reliability can be misleading because high reliability does not mean that a measure is valid. In fact, certain types of measurement confounds can inflate reliability (Shevlin, Miles, Davies, & Walker, 2000). This is why reliability was addressed after validity. From a research consumer perspective, we will want to know about validity first and interpret reliability in light of the validity evidence.

## The Statistical Analysis of Data

The uses of statistics in research can be roughly divided into descriptive and inferential approaches. The goal of descriptive statistics is to give a simplified account of some data at hand, making the data understandable, while inferential statistics involves using the existing data to make inferences that go beyond those data. Inferential statistics can be used in two different ways: (1) to make inferences about populations based on samples and (2) for hypothesis testing using tests of statistical significance.

## Descriptive Data Analysis

Descriptive statistics are just what the label implies. The goal of descriptive data analysis is to give an understandable summary of data. For example, in one of my most recent deception detection experiments (Levine, Shaw, et al., 2010), we had $N = 128$ students watch and judge 44 videotaped interviews. Of the students interviewed, half had cheated on a task and the other half were noncheaters. All the interviewees denied having cheated. We edited the interview tapes and showed the judges either the first few questions and answers or the last few. All judges were asked if they thought that each of the interviewees were cheaters or noncheaters, and these judgments were scored for accuracy. This resulted in 5,632 accuracy scores ($N = 128$ judges' judgments of 44 message senders). So once we got these numbers, we needed to figure out what the scores were telling us. Of course, just looking at the 5,000-plus individual accuracy scores is not very informative and is more than a little overwhelming. So we needed to summarize the results and convert the mass of numbers into sensible results. Therefore, we tallied the scores in a number of different ways (see Levine, Shaw, et al., 2010, Tables 1–3). Importantly, we looked at accuracy scores for both judges and senders. That is, we looked at how accurate each judge was averaged across the 44 senders, and we also looked at the average number of times each sender was judged correctly across the 128 judges.

The first thing we did was to look at the distribution of scores (Levine, Shaw, et al., 2010, Table 3). We also looked at the means (average scores), variances, and standard deviations because the distribution was such that the means were informative. The distribution of scores can be seen by arranging all scores in order from the smallest to the largest and looking at the spread and the clumping. This is often done with a frequency distribution or graphed with a histogram or stem-and-leaf plot. When we did this with a frequency distribution, we saw immediately that judge accuracy scores were all tightly grouped; most judge scores fell within a 20% to 25% range depending on the condition. Sender scores, however, were all over the place, ranging from 7% to 100%—a 93-point spread. This difference in spread, of course, showed up as a difference in variance. The variance for the senders was 10 times as much as the variance for the judges! The other thing we noticed right away was that the judges who watched the last three interview questions obtained more accurate scores (68% on average) than those who saw the first three questions and answers (44%). In fact, there was not much overlap in the two distributions of judges. Finally, there was even more sender variance when the senders were assessed by the judges who saw the last three questions than by those who saw the first three.

So by looking at the central tendency (means), dispersion (standard deviation and variance), and distributions, we were able to make sense out of those 5,000-plus accuracy scores. We learned that judges tend to see things the same way but some senders tend to be seen much more differently than other senders. This told us that senders are where the action is. We also learned that questioning senders makes a big difference in judge accuracy by increasing sender variance. It also helped set up our next studies, with some looking at the effects of questioning and others taking a closer look at sender variance.

While means (i.e., average scores) are often informative, and certainly the most commonly reported descriptive statistic, they can be misleading when the distribution of scores around the mean is not symmetrical. Here is an example. An important question in my main area of research, deception, is how often people lie. Deception researchers often presume that people lie frequently, but if you think about this for a moment, you will realize that this is a difficult research question to answer well. Just how do you random sample lying?

The best known study on the prevalence of lying is a diary study by DePaulo, Kashy, Kirkendol, Wyer, and Epstein (1996). They found and reported that people lie between once and twice a day. Recently, we tried to replicate this finding using survey methodology (Serota, Levine, & Boster, 2010). Just like DePaulo et al. (1996), we found an average of between one and two lies per day (mean = 1.65, standard deviation = 4.45, median = 0, mode = 0, maximum value = 53). But the average here does not tell the whole story. Sixty percent of our sample reported telling no lies at all in the past 24 hours, and 75% reported telling one or fewer lies. In contrast, about half of all reported lies were told by just 5% of the sample, and almost 25% of the lies were told by the top 1%, comprising most frequent liars. We called this finding "a few prolific liars." What's more, we requested data from previous authors and collected additional data to replicate our findings. All the data had the same pattern. Most people don't lie very often, but a few people lie with astounding frequency. The average does not reflect what the average person does! Looking at the distribution of data is crucial.

Another class of descriptive statistics consists of measures of *effect size* or strength of association. These statistics tell us how large a difference is relative to variability or how strongly variables covary. Basically, measures of effect size tell us about the magnitude of effect that one variable (or set of variables) has on another. Interpersonal communication researchers have long realized the importance of reporting and interpreting effect sizes in research, and interpersonal communication is well ahead of many other social sciences in this regard.

Common measures of effect size include $d$ (the standardized mean difference), $r$ (the correlation coefficient), $R^2$ (the multiple correlation), $\beta$ (the standardized regression coefficient), and $\eta^2$ (eta squared, the ratio of the effect of sums of squares to the total). There are also others. Table 2.1 shows conversions between $d$, $r$, and $\eta^2$ for eight values of $d$. Each of these statistics tells the same story by just using a different metric.

**Table 2.1**    Examples of Conversions Between $d$, $r$, and $\eta^2$

| $d$ | $r$ | $\eta^2$ |
|:---:|:---:|:---:|
| .10 | .05 | <.01 |
| .25 | .12 | .02 |
| .50 | .24 | .06 |
| .75 | .35 | .12 |
| 1.00 | .44 | .20 |
| 1.50 | .66 | .36 |
| 2.00 | .70 | .50 |
| 2.50 | .78 | .61 |

What the reader should take from this is the idea that descriptive statistics are really useful and informative. Compared with inferential statistics, they are simple and easy to understand. They are also essential. It is very easy to get lost in raw data. It is also sometimes tempting to focus exclusively on the inferential statistics and forget that it is really the descriptive statistics that help us see the patterns and the trends in the data. But we can't just look at averages. Dispersion, distributions, and effect sizes are important too.

### Inferential Statistics Basics

The inferential statistics used in interpersonal communication research can be divided into two types: (1) CIs and (2) statistical significance testing. The goal of a CI is to estimate population values with sample data, while statistical significance is used to test statistical hypotheses. Unfortunately, in interpersonal research, significance testing is much more common than the use of CIs, even though it would be more rational if the reverse were true.

Readers are likely to be familiar with the idea of CIs, as they are frequently mentioned in media coverage of scientific opinion polling. We often hear that some opinion poll found that some percentage of people favor (or disfavor) some sentiment with a certain margin of error. The margin of error is the CI, which, by tradition, is usually set at 95%. What this means is that, presuming the sampling was done correctly, there is 95% chance that the CI includes the population value. Furthermore, CIs are informative about the precision of statistical estimates. The smaller the CI, the more precise is the estimate.

CIs can be calculated around means, but they can also be calculated around effect sizes. When provided for effect sizes, they provide the same information as a significance test. A result that is statistically significant is one where an effect size of zero is outside the 95% CI. But CIs also provide additional information, telling us how far above zero the lower limit and also the plausible upper bound of the effect is. A useful overview of CIs is provided by Cumming and Finch (2005), and Levine, Weber, Park, et al. (2008) provide a primer on how to calculate CIs around some common effect sizes.

### The (Il)Logic of Significance Testing and the Tyranny of the $p$ Value

Statistical significance testing (or, more precisely, *null hypothesis significance testing*, NHST) is a commonly used type of inferential statistics. When you read about a finding not being significant, note that a finding is $p < .05$, or see $p$ values reported in researcher articles, it is almost certain that NHST is being done. NHST is used in conjunction with popular statistical analyses such as chi-square ($\chi^2$), $t$ tests, ANOVA, correlation, and regression. Popular statistical software packages such as SPSS (now an IBM company—SPSS was acquired by IBM in October 2009) or SAS report NHST as the default when using these statistics.

Most NHST in interpersonal research is concerned either with testing for differences (between two or more means with $t$ tests or ANOVA or between frequencies using chi-square) or with looking for the linear association between variables (correlation or regression). Each of these statistical techniques involves the calculation of a test statistic (e.g., $t$, $F$, or $\chi^2$) from the data. Each of these test statistics has a theoretical probability density function, presuming that certain assumptions are met, and predicated on the null hypothesis being true. In NHST, the $p$ value tells us the probability of the results given the null. That is, the $p$ value from NHST tells us the probability of an outcome in data assuming a true null hypothesis. If the outcome of the test is sufficiently unlikely (where sufficiently unlikely means, by convention, a probability of 5% or less, i.e., $p < .05$, the "alpha level"), then it is inferred that the data are unlikely given the null hypothesis, the null hypothesis is rejected on this basis, and support is inferred for the researcher's hypothesis.

Confused? My guess is that (a) this is not what you learned in your basic statistics class and (b) this sounds like tortured logic to you.

What is taught in most statistics classes in the social sciences is that there is a null hypothesis, $H_0$, and an alternative hypothesis, $H_1$, reflecting the researchers' hypothesis, and that $H_0$ and $H_1$ are mutually exclusive. It is presented as follows:

$$H_0: \mu_1 = \mu_2$$

$$H_1: \mu_1 \neq \mu_2,$$

where $\mu_1$ and $\mu_2$ are the estimated population means from two independent samples.

Then, we calculate a $t$ test, and if the test is $p < .05$, we reject $H_0$ and accept $H_1$. This is presented as "statistics" without reference to the mathematicians who developed this method. Readers actually interested in the origins of these ideas are directed to Chapter 1 in Gigerenzer and Murray (1987) and to Sir Ronald Fisher's (1990) three books for seminal work on NHST.

The logic of NHST typically confuses those who have not been fully indoctrinated. I suspect this is so because it does not make valid logical sense. The logical problems with NHST have been known for at least 50 years (see Rozenboom, 1960) and have been repeated by many authors (e.g., Kline, 2004; Levine, Weber, Hullett, Park, & Lindsey, 2008). Trafimow (2003) and Nickerson (2000) provide some of the most insightful analyses on the meaning of $p$ values I have seen, but they are not the easiest reads. For those interested, I would suggest starting with Gigerenzer and Murray (1987), Boster (2002), and Cohen (1990) in that order, before moving on to Levine, Weber, Hullett, et al. (2008), Nickerson (2000), and Trafimow (2003) in that order.

Nevertheless, NHST is the accepted convention in social science, and there is little evidence that a more rational approach will take hold any time soon. The brainwashing of would-be quantitative communication researchers will likely continue, and continued use of NHST will surely be expected by journal editors and reviewers in the foreseeable future. My advice to researchers is to self-educate (the citations provided in the previous two paragraphs are good places to start) and to try and slip as many descriptive statistics and CIs into their papers as they can. For research consumers, I suggest relying more on the descriptive statistics that are reported than on $p$ values and findings with asterisks.

To this point, I have been pretty hard on NHST. The criticism is very well deserved. But let me make two points of qualification to this criticism. First, I report NHST in the majority of my own papers (although I try not to rely on it too much). Second, there is a difference between having a lot of problems and being worthless. Small *p* values have some evidentiary value, and there is a need to rule out chance as a plausible explanation for a finding. An example in the next section demonstrates this point well.

## The Importance and the Confusions of Statistical Power

For the past few years, when I teach my graduate methods class, I have a short research article evaluation assignment due at the end of the first week of class. The assignment is to evaluate the contribution and validity of Cohen, Nisbett, Bowdle, and Schwarz (1996) series of experiments testing the culture of honor. What I don't tell the students in my class beforehand is that it is one of my favorite articles. Students typically want to impress me by finding a lot of flaws and write papers that are highly critical of the target research. Then, they are shocked when I hand the papers back and tell them how much I admire the work they have just shredded.

The main point of the assignment is to be judicious in criticism, saving it for when it is well deserved and not dismissing interesting findings too quickly. But there is another lesson in the assignment that is directly related to the topic of this section—an important lesson about statistical power and what *p* values do and do not tell us. One of the really good aspects of the Cohen et al. (1996) experiments is the effort to triangulate through a multiple-method approach. They use self-report measures, psychological measures, and behavioral observation to test the same focused hypothesis in more than a dozen different ways. This allows for a strong evaluation of convergent validity in a way that is very unusual in social science.

Cohen et al. (1996) use a 2 × 2 independent-groups design, crossing the presence or absence of an insult with whether or not the participant is Northern or Southern. Their hypothesis is that one cell will be different from the other three: Southerners will respond with aggression to insult. They report something like 14 different

tests of the hypothesis, with sample sizes of N = 83, 146, and 173 in three studies. Although most of the findings have the same basic pattern, by my count, only 7 of the 14 tests come out with *p* < .05.

The fact that the results are mixed is typically an avenue of attack for the overly critical graduate student. The typical student argument goes like this:

(a) Cohen et al. claim support in their discussion section.

(b) Their actual findings are mixed. There is just as much nonsupport as there is support.

(c) Therefore, Cohen et al. argue far beyond their data and are guilty of overselling their conclusions. Cohen et al.'s findings fail to provide consistent evidence for their claim, and this lack of consistency in findings seriously limits the contribution of their work.

Here are my twin questions for the reader to test his or her knowledge of NHST:

(a) If the null was in fact true and there are no real differences to be found, what outcomes are anticipated from the 14 NHSTs?

(b) Alternatively, if the null is false and Cohen et al. are right, what outcomes are anticipated?

If the null is true and we do 14 tests at *p* ≤ .05, then we can use the binomial distribution to calculate the probability of various outcomes. There is about a 49% chance that all 14 tests will be nonsignificant; there is another 36% chance of getting one hit by chance, a 12% chance of getting two hits by chance, and a 3% chance of three Type I errors. That adds up, after rounding, to 100% and therefore exhausts the plausible outcomes. The chance of getting seven or more significant findings under the null hypothesis is *p* < .0000001. Thus, Cohen et al.'s findings suggest that the null is highly implausible at much less than *p* = .05.

Now, what if the null is false? This is where statistical power comes into play. Statistical power is the chance of finding a significant result if the null is false. One minus power is the chance of a Type II error. If we presume for the sake of demonstration an effect size of $d = 0.5$, then the power of their tests are in the .36 to .62 range depending on the sample size in each study. So what this means is that if their hypothesis is in fact right, they will likely get "support" on somewhere between one third and two thirds of their tests. So finding that half of the tests are significant and half are not is well within the range of what is to be expected if their hypothesis is correct and tested 14 times. Furthermore, consider this case. If power was .5, then the chances of all 14 tests being significant is $p < .0001$. So had Cohen et al.'s findings all turned out to be significant, their findings would not have been plausible at all—they would have been much too good to be true.

This is why statistical power is so important. If power is not understood, research results will be misunderstood. And, if you are doing research, and using NHST, you need all the power you can get. For brief primers on power, see O'Keefe (2007) and Levine, Weber, Park, et al. (2008). The bottom line is that statistical power combined with publication bias (the tendency for nonsignificant results to be published less often than significant results) pretty much guarantees that all literatures that rely on NHST will show mixed results, making it very difficult to make sense of the findings (Meehl, 1986). This is one of many reasons why CIs are preferred.

## Beyond ANOVA and Correlation: Multilevel Modeling, SEM, and Meta-Analysis

If you follow published original communication research, you will know that the once omnipresent ANOVA and correlation matrices are increasingly being replaced with articles reporting multilevel modeling (MLM), SEM, and meta-analysis. These techniques are gaining popularity for good reasons. Each solves problems and satisfies important statistical needs for interpersonal researchers. However, these techniques create additional problems when misunderstood or misused.

The advent of MLM is an important advance because it allows interpersonal researchers to deal with nonindependent data. Traditional inferential statistics all share a strong assumption of *independence of observation*. To introduce this idea, consider the probabilities associated with a string of coin flips. If we flip a coin, we have a 50–50 chance of getting a heads. If we flip the coin three times in a row, there is a .125 chance of getting three heads in a row ($.5^3 = .5 \times .5 \times .5 = .125$), assuming that the outcome of the first flip did not affect the probability of subsequent flips. This is what is meant by independence of observations. What if, however, getting a heads on the first flip meant that each subsequent flip was now more or less likely than .5 to be a heads? That would change the expected probabilities, and understanding the probabilities would have to take the initial outcome and the nature of the contingency into account. Subsequent flips would be nonindependent.

The degree of nonindependence can be quantified with a statistic called the *intraclass correlation* (ICC). A positive ICC means that data points in the same "class" tend to be similar while a negative ICC means that data points in the same class tend to be dissimilar relative to data points in other classes. With the coin flip example, a negative ICC would mean that a heads is more likely to be followed by a tails. More relevant to interpersonal communication, imagine that we are interested in communication traits in dating couples. If people tend to form relationships with dispositionally similar others, it would create a positive ICC, while opposites attracting would create a negative ICC. Only if the partner's traits were uncorrelated would the ICC be zero.

Nonindependence of data becomes a potential concern when data points are nested in larger categories. Individuals might be nested within couples, families, or friendship circles. Students might be nested within classes, classes within majors, majors within colleges, and so forth. Fortunately, the existence of nonindependence can be tested with the ICC, and if the ICC is meaningfully large, then the nonindependence can be modeled with MLM. The two most popular MLM techniques in interpersonal research are David Kenny's social relations model, which is more ANOVA based, and hierarchical linear modeling (HLM), which is more regression based.

Currently, SEM is more popular than MLM. SEM combines measurement modeling (confirmatory factor analysis, CFA) and path analysis (structural causal modeling), although it is advisable to do CFA and path analysis separately. Commonly used SEM software programs include AMOS, LISREL, EQS, and M-Plus.

CFA is generally superior to EFA when it is known which constructs specific items are supposed to measure, because CFA is better able to deal with correlated factors and better able to identify measurement confounds. Path analysis, on the other hand, is useful whenever one wishes to test a causal model with at least one mediated relationship. Both CFA and path analysis require researchers to specify causal models in advance. The data are tested for how well they fit the model, and models are then accepted or rejected. The biggest problem with SEM, as it is used in interpersonal research, is that it is more often used for model fitting than for model testing. When model fitting, replication with new data is advisable to avoid capitalization of chance. This replication is called *cross-validation*, and unfortunately, it is not common practice.

Meta-analysis is a set of procedures that allow researchers to cumulate findings across studies to quantitatively summarize literatures (Hunter, Schmidt, & Jackson, 1982). This is quite useful because, as we have seen, the nature of NHST makes most literatures appear to have mixed findings whether or not consistent patterns exist. To the extent to which the findings from a literature converge on a single conclusion, the findings are said to be homogeneous. When findings are homogeneous, they can be averaged as a meaningful summary of the findings. When findings are heterogeneous,

however, researchers need to try and find out why. Sometimes there exist some subsets of the findings that tend to cluster around one outcome while other subsets cluster around another point. This suggests an important moderator.

While a well-done meta-analysis can be extremely informative, a few words of caution are advisable. First, average effects can only be safely interpreted when the findings of individual studies are homogeneous. Second, the results of meta-analysis depend on the quality of the original research. If there is some artifact or bias that runs through an entire literature, meta-analysis will not catch it. Third, meta-analysis is susceptible to publication bias, and the existence of publication bias tends to inflate the average effects reported in meta-analysis (Levine, Asada, & Carpenter, 2009).

# Conclusion

This chapter offers a relatively unconventional take on the topic of quantitative methods. As students of social science, we know that nonconformity is often not appreciated. At the same time, it is hoped that this chapter gives readers new to social-scientific thinking a glimpse at what is beyond the conventional takes on the topic that populate the overpriced but underinformed texts on the topic.

The bottom line is that the validity of research findings rests on their conceptual/theoretical foundations and the qualities of the researcher design, measurement, and statistical analysis. The findings are no better than the weakest of these crucial links. So good research requires getting theory, research design, measurement, and analysis into harmony. It is hoped that this chapter helps the reader see how this might be accomplished and highlights what the research consumer might profitably look for when making sense of research reports. While method is only a means to an end, valid and thoughtful method is necessary for a fuller, richer, and more accurate understanding on interpersonal communication. Too much methodological rule following or ever more complex statistical analysis just won't get us there.

## Notes

1. "Bullshit" is an important communication construct that is highly relevant to interpersonal communication. It was formally explicated, however, not by a communication theorist but by the Princeton analytic philosopher, Professor Harry G. Frankfurt (2005).

2. Throughout this chapter, I offer numerous examples from my own research. Although it is good practice to avoid excessive self-citation, using examples from my own research makes sense when writing about methods. I know why I made the methodological decisions I did, and thus I have insights into my works that I don't have about others' studies. Furthermore, this chapter reflects my research priorities and commitments. I gained these views, to a large extent, through the practice of being a researcher, and these views are reflected in my research. Thus, it is natural that my work exemplifies well the points I am trying to make.

3. We went ahead and did the study anyway. The funding came out of our own pockets, and the result was the lead article in Volume 36 of *Human Communication Research*.

4. Items such as these are at the heart of the self-construal debate between Levine et al. (2003a, 2003b), Gudykunst and Lee (2003), and Kim and Raja (2003) and explain why self-construal scales do not factor as intended. Factor analysis is helpful in showing validity problems, but a good critical eye for face validity is an important first step.

## References

Abelson, R. P. (1995). *Statistics as principled argument.* Hillsdale, NJ: LEA.

Asch, S. E. (1956). Studies of independence and conformity: I. A minority of one against a unanimous majority. *Psychological Monographs, 70,* 1–70.

Ayres, J., & Hopf, T. S. (1985). Visualization: A means of reducing speech anxiety. *Communication Education, 34,* 318–323.

Baron, R. M., & Kenny, D. A. (1986). The moderator–mediator variable distinction in social psychological research: Conceptual, strategic, and statistical considerations. *Journal of Personality and Social Psychology, 51,* 1173–1182.

Beatty, M. J. (2002). Do we know a vector from a scalar? Why measures of association (and not their squares) are appropriate measures of effect. *Human Communication Research, 28,* 605–625.

Berger, C. R. (1991). Communication theories and other curios. *Communication Monographs, 58,* 101–113.

Berger, C. R. (2005). Interpersonal communication: Theoretical perspectives, future prospects. *Journal of Communication, 55,* 415–447.

Berger, C. R., & Calabrese, R. J. (1975). Some explorations in initial interaction and beyond: Toward a developmental theory of interpersonal communication. *Human Communication Research, 1,* 99–112.

Bond, C. F., Omar, A., Pitre, U., Lashley, B. R., Skaggs, L. M., & Kirk, C. T. (1992). Fishy-looking liars: Deception judgments from expectancy violation. *Journal of Personality and Social Psychology, 63,* 969–977.

Booth-Butterfield, M., & Jordan, F. (1989). Communication adaptation among racially homogeneous and heterogeneous groups. *Southern Communication Journal, 54,* 253–272.

Boster, F. J. (2002). On making progress in communication science. *Human Communication Research, 28,* 473–490.

Bresnahan, B. J., Levine, T. R., Shearman, S., Lee, S. Y., Park, C. Y., & Kiyomiya, T. (2005). A multi-method-multitrait validity assessment of self-construal in Japan, Korea, and the U.S. *Human Communication Research, 31,* 33–59.

Buller, D. B., & Burgoon, J. K. (1996). Interpersonal deception theory. *Communication Theory, 6,* 203–242.

Bunz, U. (2005). Publish or perish: A limited author analysis of ICA and NCA journals. *Journal of Communication, 55,* 703–720.

Burgoon, J. K., & Hale, J. L. (1988). Nonverbal expectancy violations: Model elaboration and application to immediacy behaviors. *Communication Monographs, 55,* 58–79.

Campbell, D. T., & Fiske, D. W. (1959). Convergent and discriminant validation by the multi-trait-multimethod matrix. *Psychological Bulletin, 56,* 81–105.

Campbell, D. T., & Stanley, J. C. (1963). *Experimental and quasi-experimental designs for research.* Boston: Houghton Mifflin.

Christie, R., & Geis, F. L. (1970). *Studies in Machiavellianism.* New York: Academic Press.

Cialdini, R. B. (1980). Full-cycle social psychology. *Applied Psychology Annual, 1,* 21–47.

Cialdini, R. B., Borden, R. J., Thorne, A., Walker, M. R., Freeman, S., & Sloan, L. R. (1976). Basking in reflected glory: Three (football) field studies. *Journal of Personality and Social Psychology, 34,* 366–375.

Cialdini, R. B., Kallgren, C. A., & Reno, R. R. (1991). A focus theory of normative conduct: A theoretical refinement and reevaluation of the role of norms in human behavior. *Advances in Experimental Social Psychology, 24,* 210–234.

Cialdini, R. B., Vincent, J. E., Lewis, S. K., Catalan, J., Wheeler, D., & Darby, B. E. (1975). Reciprocal concessions procedure for inducing compliance: The door-in-the-face technique. *Journal of Personality and Social Psychology, 31,* 206–215.

Cohen, D., Nisbett, R. E., Bowdle, B. F., & Schwarz, N. (1996). Insult, aggression, and the southern culture of honor: An "experimental ethnography." *Journal of Personality and Social Psychology, 70,* 945–960.

Cohen, J. (1990). Things I have learned (so far). *American Psychologist, 45,* 1304–1312.

Cohen, J., Cohen, P., West, S. G., & Aiken, L. S. (2010). *Applied multiple regression/correlation analysis for the behavioral sciences.* New York: Taylor & Francis.

Cook, T. D., & Campbell, D. T. (1979). *Quasi-experimentation.* Boston: Houghton.

Cronbach, L. J., & Meehl, P. E. (1955). Construct validity in psychological tests. *Psychological Bulletin, 52,* 281–301.

Cumming, G., & Finch, S. (2005). Confidence intervals and how to read pictures of data. *American Psychologist, 60,* 170–180.

DePaulo, B. M., Kashy, D. A., Kirkendol, S. E., Wyer, M. M., & Epstein, J. A. (1996). Lying in everyday life. *Journal of Personality and Social Psychology, 70,* 979–995.

Dillard, J. P., & Shen, L. (2005). On the nature of reactance and its role in persuasive health communication. *Communication Monographs, 72,* 144–168.

Dindia, K., & Allen, M. (1992). Sex differences in self-disclosure: A meta-analysis. *Psychological Bulletin, 112,* 106–124.

Duff, D. C., Levine, T. R., Beatty, M. J., Woobright, J., & Park, H. S. (2007). Testing public anxiety treatments against a credible placebo control. *Communication Education, 56,* 72–88.

Festinger, L., Riecken, H. W., & Schachter, S. (1956). *When prophecy fails: A social psychological study of a modern group that predicted the destruction of the world.* Minneapolis: University of Minnesota Press.

Fisher, R. A. (1990). *Statistical methods, experimental design, and scientific inference: A re-issue of statistical methods for research workers, the design of experiments, and statistical methods and scientific inference.* Oxford, UK: Oxford University Press.

Fiske, D. W., & Campbell, D. T. (1992). Citations do not solve problems. *Psychological Bulletin, 112,* 393–395.

Frankfurt, H. G. (2005). *On bullshit.* Princeton, NJ: Princeton University Press.

Gigerenzer, G., & Murray, D. J. (1987). *Cognition as intuitive statistics.* Hillsdale, NJ: Lawrence Erlbaum.

Gudykunst, W. B., & Lee, C. M. (2003). Assessing the validity of self-construal scales: A response to Levine et al. *Human Communication Research, 29,* 253–274.

Hemple, C. G. (1966). *Philosophy of natural science.* Englewood Cliffs, NJ: Prentice Hall.

Hickson, M., Self, W. R., Johnson, J. R., Peacock, C., & Bodon, J. (2009). Prolific research in communication studies: Retrospective and prospective views. *Communication Research Reports, 26,* 337–346.

Hunter, J., Gerbing, D., & Boster, F. (1982). Machiavellian beliefs and personality: Construct invalidity of the Machiavellianism dimension. *Journal of Personality and Social Psychology, 43,* 1293–1305.

Hunter, J. E., Hamilton, M. A., & Allen, M. (1989). The design and analysis of language experiments in communication. *Communication Monographs, 56,* 341–363.

Hunter, J. E., Schmidt, F. L., & Jackson, G. B. (1982). *Meta-analysis: Cumulating research findings across studies.* Beverly Hills, CA: Sage.

Infante, D. A., & Rancer, A. S. (1982). A conceptualization and measure of argumentativeness. *Journal of Personality Assessment, 46,* 72–80.

Infante, D. A., & Wigley, C. J. (1986). Verbal aggressiveness: An interpersonal model and measure. *Communication Monographs, 53,* 61–69.

Jackson, S., & Jacobs, S. (1983). Generalizing about messages: Suggestions for the design and analysis of experiments. *Human Communication Research, 9,* 169–191.

Kerlinger, F. N., & Lee, H. B. (2000). *Foundations of behavioral research.* New York: McGraw-Hill.

Kerr, N. L. (1998). HARKing: Hypothesizing after the results are known. *Personality and Social Psychology Review, 2,* 196–217.

Kim, M. S., & Raja, N. S. (2003). When validity testing lacks validity: Comments on Levine et al. (2002). *Human Communication Research, 29,* 275–290.

Kline, R. B. (2004). *Beyond significance testing: Reforming data analysis methods in behavioral research.* Washington, DC: American Psychological Association.

Kotowski, M. R., Levine, T. R., Baker, C., & Bolt, J. (2009). A multi-trait multi-method validity assessment of the verbal aggressiveness and argumentativeness scales. *Communication Monographs, 76,* 443–462.

Kuhn, T. S. (1996). *The structure of scientific revolutions* (3rd ed.). Chicago: University of Chicago Press.

Lakatos, I. (1978). *The methodology of scientific research programmes.* Cambridge, UK: Cambridge University Press.

Lee, C. R., Levine, T. R., & Cambra, R. (1997). Resisting compliance in the multi-cultural classroom. *Communication Education, 46,* 10–28.

Levine, T. R. (2010a). A few transparent liars: Explaining 54% accuracy in deception detection experiments. In C. Salmon (Ed.), *Communication yearbook 34* (pp. 40–61). Thousand Oaks, CA: Sage.

Levine, T. R. (2010b). Ranking and trends in citation patterns of communication journals. *Communication Education, 59,* 41–51.

Levine, T. R., Anders, L. N., Banas, J., Baum, K. L., Endo, K., Hu, A. D. S., et al. (2000). Norms, expectations, and deception: A norm violation model of veracity judgments. *Communication Monographs, 67,* 123–137.

Levine, T. R., Asada, K. J., & Carpenter, C. (2009). Sample size and effect size are negatively correlated in meta-analysis: Evidence and implications of a publication bias against non-significant findings. *Communication Monographs, 76,* 286–302.

Levine, T. R., Beatty, M. J., Limon, S., Hamilton, M. A., Buck, R., & Chory-Asada, R. M. (2004). The dimensionality of the verbal aggressiveness scale. *Communication Monographs, 71,* 245–268.

Levine, T. R., & Blair, J. P. (2010). *Questioning strategies, diagnostic utility, and expertise interactions in deception detection.* Manuscript submitted for publication.

Levine, T. R., Bresnahan, M., Park, H. S., Lapinski, M. K., Lee, T. S., & Lee, D. W. (2003). The (in)validity of self-construal scales revisited. *Human Communication Research, 29,* 291–308.

Levine, T. R., Bresnahan, M., Park, H. S., Lapinski, M. K., Wittenbaum, G., Shearman, S., et al. (2003). Self report measures of self-construals lack validity. *Human Communication Research, 29,* 210–252.

Levine, T. R., Feeley, T. H., McCornack, S. A., Hughes, M., & Harms, C. M. (2005). Testing the effects of nonverbal training on deception detection accuracy with the inclusion of a bogus train control group. *Western Journal of Communication, 69,* 203–217.

Levine, T. R., Kim, R. K., & Blair, J. P. (2010). (In)accuracy at detecting true and false confessions and denials: An initial test of a projected motive model of veracity judgments. *Human Communication Research, 36,* 81–101.

Levine, T. R., Kim, R. K., Park, H. S., & Hughes, M. (2006). Deception detection accuracy is a predictable linear function of message veracity base-rate: A formal test of Park and Levine's probability model. *Communication Monographs, 73,* 243–260.

Levine, T. R., & McCornack, S. A. (1996a). Can behavioral adaption explain the probing effect? *Human Communication Research, 22,* 603–612.

Levine, T. R., & McCornack, S. A. (1996b). A critical analysis of the behavioral adaptation explanation of the probing effect. *Human Communication Research, 22,* 575–589.

Levine, T. R., & McCornack, S. A. (2001). Behavioral adaption, confidence, and heuristic-based explanations of the probing effect. *Human Communication Research, 27,* 471–502.

Levine, T. R., & McCroskey, J. C. (1990). Measuring trait communication apprehension: A test of rival measurement models of the PRCA-24. *Communication Monographs, 57,* 62–72.

Levine, T. R., Park, H. S., & McCornack, S. A. (1999). Accuracy in detecting truths and lies: Documenting the "veracity effect." *Communication Monographs, 66,* 125–144.

Levine, T. R., Shaw, A., & Shulman, H. (2010). Increasing deception detection accuracy with strategic questioning. *Human Communication Research, 36,* 216–231.

Levine, T. R., Weber, R., Park, H. S., & Hullett, C. R. (2008). A communication researchers guide to null hypothesis significance testing and alternatives. *Human Communication Research, 34,* 188–209.

Levine, T. R., Weber, R., Hullett, C. R., Park, H. S., & Lindsey, L. (2008). A critical assessment of null hypothesis significance testing in quantitative communication research. *Human Communication Research, 34,* 171–187.

Lubinski, D. (2004). Introduction to the special section on cognitive abilities: 100 years after Spearman's (1904) "'General Intelligence,' Objectively Determined and Measured." *Journal of Personality and Social Psychology, 86,* 96–111.

Malle, B. F. (2006). The actor-observer asymmetry in attribution: A (surprising) meta-analysis. *Psychological Bulletin, 132,* 895–919.

McCornack, S. A., & Levine, T. R. (1990). When lovers become leery: The relationship between suspicion and accuracy in detecting deception. *Communication Monographs, 57,* 219–230.

McCornack, S. A., Levine, T. R., Torres, H. I., Solowczuk, K. A., & Campbell, D. M. (1992). When the alteration of information is viewed as deception: An empirical test of information manipulation theory. *Communication Monographs, 59,* 17–29.

McCroskey, J. C. (1977). Oral communication apprehension: A summary of recent theory and research. *Human Communication Research, 4,* 78–96.

Meehl, P. E. (1986). What social scientists don't understand. In D. W. Fiske & R. A. Shweder (Eds.), *Meta-theory in social science* (pp. 315–338). Chicago: University of Chicago Press.

Miller, G. R., & Berger, C. R. (1999). On keeping the faith in matters scientific. *Communication Studies, 50,* 221–231.

Mook, D. G. (1983). In defense of external invalidity. *American Psychologist, 38,* 379–387.

Muthuswamy, N., Levine, T. R., & Weber, R. (2009). Scaring the already scared: Some problems with HIV/AIDS fear appeals in Africa. *Journal of Communication, 59,* 317–344.

Nickerson, R. S. (2000). Null hypothesis significance testing: A review of an old and continuing controversy. *Psychological Methods, 5,* 241–301.

Nunnally, J. C., & Bernstein, I. H. (1994). *Psychometric theory.* New York: McGraw-Hill.

O'Keefe, D. J. (2007). Post hoc power, observed power, a priori power, retrospective power, prospective power, achieved power: Sorting out appropriate use of statistical power analysis. *Communication Methods and Measures, 1,* 291–299.

Park, H. S., Dailey, R., & Lemus, D. (2002). The use of exploratory factor analysis and principal components analysis in communication research. *Human Communication Research, 28,* 562–577.

Pavitt, C. (2001). *The philosophy of science and communication theory.* Huntington, NY: Nova.

Popper, K. R. (1959). *The logic of scientific discovery.* New York: Routledge.

Rozenboom, W. W. (1960). The fallacy of the null hypothesis significance test. *Psychological Bulletin, 57,* 416–428.

Rozin, P. (2001). Social psychology and science: Some lessons from Solomon Asch. *Personality and Social Psychology Review, 5,* 2–14.

Schwarz, N. (1999). Self-reports: How the questions shape the answers. *American Psychologist, 54,* 93–105.

Serota, K. B., Levine, T. R., & Boster, F. J. (2010). The prevalence of lying in America: Three studies of reported deception. *Human Communication Research, 36,* 1–24.

Shevlin, M., Miles, J. N. V., Davies, M. N. O., & Walker, S. (2000). Coefficient alpha: A useful indicator of reliability? *Personality and Individual Differences, 28,* 229–237.

Singelis, T. M. (1994). The measurement of independent and interdependent self-construals. *Personality and Social Psychological Bulletin, 20,* 580–591.

Smith, R., Levine, T. R., Lachlan, K. A., & Fediuk, T. A. (2002). The high cost of complexity in experimental design and data analysis: Type I and Type II error rates in multiway ANOVA. *Human Communication Research, 28,* 515–530.

Tidwell, L. C., & Walther, J. B. (2002). Computer-mediated communication effects on disclosure, impressions, and interpersonal evaluations. *Human Communication Research, 28,* 317–348.

Trafimow, D. (2003). Hypothesis testing and theory evaluation at the boundaries: Surprising insights from Bayes's theorem. *Psychological Review, 110,* 526–535.

Weber, R. (2007). To adjust or not to adjust in multiple testing. *Communication Methods and Measures, 1,* 281–289.

# CHAPTER 3

# Qualitative Methods in Interpersonal Communication

*Karen Tracy*

*Kristine (Fitch) Muñoz*

Our business will be to proceed somewhat differently . . . we might then gain some increased satisfaction with our commitment to the use of observation as a basis of theorizing. That is to say, a base for using close looking at the world for theorizing about it is that from close looking at the world you can find things that we couldn't, by imagination, assert were there. (Sacks, 1992, p. 420)

It is with the kinds of materials produced by long-term, mainly (though not exclusively) qualitative, highly participative, and almost obsessively fine-comb field study in confined contexts that the mega-concepts with which social science is afflicted . . . can be given the sort of sensible actuality that makes it possible to think not only realistically and concretely *about* them, but what is most important, creatively and imaginatively *with* them. (Geertz, 1973, p. 23)

We begin this introduction to qualitative methods in interpersonal communication research with quotes from two of our favorite scholars. Clifford Geertz, an anthropologist, and Harvey Sacks, a sociologist, dramatically shaped the content and style of research in communication. What both of these men enacted in their own research, and argued for explicitly in essays, was the necessity of researchers looking at, listening to, and immersing themselves in the social worlds they were seeking to understand. It is the ability to develop rich, multifaceted portraits of situated activities, relationships, practices, or cultural scenes, in fact, that is the strength of qualitative approaches to research. To be sure, there are plenty of studies using qualitative methods that fall short of this ideal, that are trite or boring or just off base. But rich and insightful analysis is the aim of communication studies using qualitative methods. And as this review will show, there are many types of engaging and interesting qualitative studies of interpersonal communication issues.

A decade or two ago, battles were being fought regarding the value of qualitative approaches for interpersonal communication research (see Bochner 1985, 1994). No longer is this the case. Being able to understand qualitative methods, and use some of them, is now an expectation for interpersonal communication students and researchers. There are multiple qualitative theoretical approaches (e.g., ethnography of communication and action-implicative discourse analysis [AIDA]) that are connected in a variety of ways to specific, concrete methods (e.g., interviews, taping and transcribing). Each of the approaches and concrete methods has advantages and limitations. Any particular approach/method may be well suited to address certain questions about communicative life but not so good for addressing others. We will explore these issues later in the chapter.

Many (but not all) qualitative approaches came into existence as a reaction to one or another perceived shortcoming of quantitative research. As a result, many qualitative approaches initially defined themselves by what they were *not*. But as qualitative methods have become accepted, and in certain areas of communication research preferred, the relationship between qualitative and quantitative research has shifted, becoming more complicated. Some qualitative researchers remain estranged from and antagonistic toward quantitative methods. Other qualitative scholars see their work as intellectually distant from quantitative approaches but are not themselves antagonistic toward it. Still others have begun to use particular quantitative approaches in a supplemental way, recognizing the complementary character of qualitative and quantitative methods.

Becoming proficient in any particular qualitative methodology requires mastering literatures, being able to work with conceptual distinctions, and knowing how to carry out observation and analytic techniques. What is not conveyed by this largely accurate description of methodology is the emotional, personal dimension of doing research. It is a given that a researcher wants to carry out the research he or she does well. Yet the doing of qualitative research raises difficult choices that scholars, whether novice or experienced, will not have anticipated before starting. Method, theory, and epistemology are tied together and implicate each other in complicated ways. One is not merely making a technical methodological choice. One is deciding what questions can and should be asked. One is deciding what is reasonable to assume about people and the world. One is deciding what he or she regards as a more (and less) important kind of knowledge.

Because we see the link between research methods and persons as so important, we begin the chapter with our own methodological stories. In the second section, we describe the building blocks for qualitative approaches: (a) the concrete data-gathering techniques of interviewing, (b) participant observation and note taking, (c) taping and transcribing of talk, and (d) written and visual text analysis. Qualitative research approaches bring together these concrete methods in particular constellations with authors, theories, sites in the world, and questions about communication. These, in turn, are tied to larger metatheoretical research frames about what is worth knowing and how to know it. The chapter's third section describes and critiques nine qualitative approaches that either are or we believe should be influential in interpersonal communication research. In explaining each approach, we identify its key scholars, the kinds of questions about interpersonal communication that have been asked or could be asked, and the concrete methodological tools used. In addition, we provide examples of studies using the approach. We conclude the chapter with a proposal regarding how numbers and statistics could contribute to interpersonal communication inquiry that is centrally interpretive and qualitative.

On a final note, interpersonal communication can be defined in different ways. We define it broadly here. Interpersonal communication studies the processes of initiating, maintaining, or severing relationships; it investigates how friendships and issues in family life are managed. Interpersonal communication includes how people use media in their homes, and how television and newspapers frame personal relationships. It investigates encounters among persons in institutional settings, both in interaction among professionals and in exchanges between lay parties and experts. Interpersonal communication sites for study range from friend, partner, and family exchanges to schools, from health care contexts to workplaces, and from online exchanges to encounters in public places.

## Research and Persons: Our Stories

### Karen Tracy

When I meet new people in academic settings, whether at conferences or at my own university, an occasion will typically start with a request for self-description: What's your area? What do you study? What field are you in? Although my answer is tailored to what will be taken for granted—I don't mention that I'm in communication at a communication conference—my response also has standard pieces. I say something like this: "I'm a *discourse analyst* who studies interaction in institutional sites." And depending on the context, I might go on to add, "I'm especially interested in how talk does face and identity work." What my self-description makes visible is the importance of methodology to my sense of self.

Throughout my academic life, I have been fascinated with methods, spending considerable time reflecting about what it means to study something well, particularly stewing about the challenges, trade-offs, or dilemmas encountered in those pursuits. My reflections have resulted in a series of essays where I either argued for an ignored method or sketched out a (partly) new approach. As my questions about communication and social

life changed, I returned to the methodological drawing board to revise or develop another approach better fitted to the questions I have found myself asking. For several of these approaches, I have coined names. This propensity to coin names, in fact, is an idiosyncrasy about which my colleagues tease me.

To narrate the story of my methodological life, I begin with my toddler years as a graduate student. From my earliest years in graduate school, I have been focused on understanding language, conversation, and talk—what I now usually call "discourse." But exactly what I have studied and how I have done so have varied enormously. My dissertation was an experimental study of conversational comprehension that involved questionnaires and complex statistics. From there, I began inching toward the world of people talking. My first two stops were the "naturalistic experiment" (Tracy, 1989), soon after revised to be the "laboratory case study" (Tracy, 1991). These two approaches advocated bringing a goodly number of people into a lab to record them conversing, rather than the more typical experimental move of giving research participants questionnaires with segments of talk (i.e., constructed messages) to be rated. Both of these methods were hybrid quantitative–qualitative approaches, but the two methods put the approaches together differently. The naturalistic experiment privileged the goal of building explanatory relationships between variables, what quantitative approaches do well; the laboratory case study highlighted the interesting complexities and context-sensitive qualities of people's talk, what case studies excel in.

My interest in how people do things with talk, to paraphrase the philosopher of language Austin's (1962) influential book, eventually led me away from quantitative methods, as well as from lab settings. My basic concern about lab settings was that whatever task or instructions you gave people they did not speak as they would in actual settings. To understand how people report delicate problems to the police, how grad students raise criticisms of a faculty mentor's research, or how an unhappy parent speaks out in a school board meeting, you need to study people calling 911 (e.g., Tracy & Tracy, 1998), participating in departmental colloquia (Tracy, 1997), and speaking to their school board (Tracy, McDaniel, & Gronbeck, 2007).

As the wisdom of studying people talking in the kinds of communication situations I wanted to understand became increasingly self-evident, I abandoned the goal of developing explanatory theories. I realized that I needed to be thinking about the goal of inquiry differently: A thick and nuanced description of interesting, complex talk situations, I decided, was a better way to go (Tracy & Baratz, 1994).

My final methodological home, one that I have been residing in during the past 15 years, is AIDA (Tracy, 1995; Tracy & Craig, 2010). We will talk more about AIDA later, but for now, it is enough to say that it is a method that tapes, transcribes, and analyzes talk. AIDA offers a way to answer interesting questions about talk and identity in a variety of types of institutional interactions. In a recently completed project (Tracy, 2010) studying one community's school board meetings, a case that includes 63 meetings, 200-plus hours of tapes, and hundreds of two- to five-minute parent speeches, I have returned to using numbers and simple statistics. In working to flesh out the meanings and patterns in this one communicative practice, I have found quantitative methods useful. In a colloquy a few years ago about the role of quantitative methods in qualitative research, I summarized my methodological history in this way:

> As I reflect on my 25-plus years of research, I see my attitude toward quantification coming—well, not full circle, but at least two thirds of one. I have changed from a quantitative, lab-based researcher to a discourse analytic, quite anti-quantitative scholar to what I am today: a discourse analyst who sees a necessary and important role for numbers and simple statistics. (Tracy, 2007, p. 33)

My newest project is investigating judges' and attorneys' talk during oral argument in state supreme courts considering appeals of marriage laws. In these courts, in highly coded ways, attorneys and judges discuss whether it is legal to restrict marriage to one man and one woman. The exchanges in these courtrooms are unlike the many more familiar discussions about this topic that occur in coffee houses, legislative hearings, or public debates. As I encounter novel challenges working with these materials, I find myself in the throes of a methodological cold; I'm feeling the need to step back and reflect about how best to study talk in technical, writing-dependent, and argumentatively lively exchanges. AIDA 2.0 perhaps?

### Kristine Muñoz

As a sophomore at University of Texas in 1977, I planned to spend my junior year studying abroad in Salamanca, Spain. I needed to do an independent study project to earn enough hours to graduate on time. A friend introduced me to his favorite teacher, Robert Hopper, after class one day. Hopper was congenial and encouraging, if noncommittal. (After a few disastrous attempts at trying to direct undergraduates' independent study ideas based on their experiences of studying abroad, I have myself been far less congenial and a good deal more direct about refusing to do so again.) The sum total of his direction for this effort was "Keep your eyes and ears open, and keep notebooks!" Another friend, then a graduate student in the program, recommended one of the very early qualitative methods books to make its way into communication studies (Bogdan & Taylor, 1975). Written by sociologists, the subtitle of this book is instructive: "A Phenomenological Approach to the Social Sciences." Off I went to Spain, clutching this sacred text as the key to my on-time graduation with a bachelor's degree.

As I struggled through the linguistic and interpersonal challenges of a home stay (with a rabidly anti-American host father), language and history classes at a school for foreigners (where Germans, already ferociously fluent in Spanish, were the majority group among the largely European students), and the romantic ups and downs predictable for a 20-year-old far from home in an exotic land, I did what Hopper recommended: I kept notebooks. Bogdan and Taylor (1975) reassured me that that was just the way fieldwork was supposed to happen: eyes and ears wide open and writing about what I saw and heard. I bracketed my own reactions in the sense that I tried to describe in detailed ways the nuances of sound, sight, smell, taste, and touch as distinct from my highly involved and complicated emotional reactions to it all. I did not for a moment pretend that I was an objective observer of scenes or that what happened around me did not involve or affect me. It was, to put it mildly, a challenging year, and I noticed for the first time that writing social science—even in a phenomenological way—was a most useful step away from intricate interpersonal moments.

Back in Austin, I wrote a paper for independent study credit, learning a little bit along the way about reviewing the literature and situating an argument within a scholarly conversation. Then, I nervously met with Robert Hopper to hear his verdict. "Well, you clearly get an A on this," he said, having confessed that he thought I would "come home with nothing but a diary." "I also propose that we rewrite it together and submit it to a conference of this organization called the International Communication Association." I was stunned. I was also very clear that the year I'd spent watching people talk (specifically, watching foreigners switch languages in the context of an experience intended to teach them Spanish), writing down what I saw and heard, asking people questions about what they did, and then writing a paper about it was the most stimulating and fulfilling experience of my life. After the first semester of the MA program at Texas the following year, I knew that I was going to do all of that (listening, eavesdropping, asking nosy questions, reading in the library, etc.) for the rest of my working life. My MA thesis was a frame analysis of

language switching among Mexican Americans in Austin. The data were tape-recorded, transcribed moments of everyday conversation in which language switching took place. A combination of that study with the field note–based work I did in Spain resulted in a publication (Fitch & Hopper, 1983) with a title—Hopper's idea—that has continued to resonate with my understanding of the social world ever since: "If you speak Spanish, they'll think you're a German." Since this was true in language schools for foreigners in Salamanca but nonsensical in Austin, Texas, among Mexican Americans, clearly, language use and the symbolism and meanings of choices between alternatives was situated, always and forever, within speech communities.

My methodological predisposition was thus largely set before I took graduate seminars in quantitative methods and rhetorical criticism, though I learned to deeply appreciate and respect both of those families of approaches. In a course that overviewed interpersonal communication research and theory, Hopper had us read two articles that are considered by many to be among the most influential in the field of communication (Philipsen, 1975, 1976): "Speaking Like a Man in Teamsterville" and "Places for Speaking in Teamsterville." That work gave a theoretical and empirical basis for the perspective on interpersonal communication as situated within the cultural contexts I had observed in Spain and in Austin (Fitch, 2009). That fundamental premise shaped everything else I read and researched in graduate school, and even more profoundly afterward. Although I have maintained reading fluency in work that used other methodological approaches (10 years as an Institutional Review Board chair contributed enormously to this goal), the methods I teach and use always approach interpersonal communication from that assumption.

In the years since then, ethnography has been challenged both by conversation analysis (CA) (Mandelbaum, 1990–1991; Moerman, 1988; Schegloff, 1987) and by postmodernist critiques of social science that included traditional approaches to ethnography (Bochner, 1994; Conquergood, 1991; Fiske, 1991; Rosaldo, 1989). My own work has responded to those currents by, in some cases, becoming more grounded in recorded and transcribed talk than in interviews and field notes based on participant observation (Fitch, 1994, 2003). In the opposite direction, I have written an autoethnography when a particular event, process, or audience made that an appropriate methodological choice (Fitch, 1998, 2005a).

## Qualitative Basics

Qualitative research is best conceived as a family of approaches whose members share commonalities but also possess distinctive differences (Silverman, 2001). There are four features common among qualitative research approaches. First is the interest that researchers have in capturing the meanings and experiences of the participants themselves. To use Kenneth Pike's (1967) terms, qualitative researchers favor an "emic" over an "etic" perspective. A second feature is a preference for naturally occurring data—although what should count as "naturally occurring" is contested among different traditions. Third, qualitative researchers tend to proceed inductively to build claims rather than working deductively to test them. Finally, rather than numbers, qualitative researchers privilege the close analysis of words and visual images. Because of this focus, to quote Flick (2007), "issues of transforming complex social situations (or other materials such as images) into texts—issues of transcribing and writing in general—are major concerns of qualitative research" (p. x). Not all of the features we enumerated apply to every approach, but the four features are prototypical qualitative research.

At the most concrete level, qualitative methods involve the use of one or more of four data-gathering practices: (1) participating in a social scene and taking notes, (2) interviewing individuals or groups, (3) collecting tapes and analyzing talk, and (4) collecting and analyzing

written, visual, or multimedia texts. We describe key choices within each of these, and then, we turn to the distinctive approaches.

## Participating in a Social Scene and Taking Notes

Participant observation is a method of social science research that may seem to be most closely related to real life itself, and for that reason, it was a mainstay of both anthropology and sociology from the early 20th century onward. This view is to some extent contradicted by the presence of a research interest on the part of the social scientist, an ever more complicated proposition both ethically and procedurally. Leaving the ethical questions aside, the procedural issues revolve around access (to a setting or group of people), rapport (with the people), and the ways in which data may be recorded from observation. The difficulty of being able to observe important interpersonal processes, such as deception of a romantic partner about cheating, is often one reason why participant observation is rarely considered as a method for researching those processes. On the other hand, the advantage of gaining access to observation of interpersonal processes is the relative naturalism of the behavior under study and the flexibility for the researcher to absorb nuances of meaning that might not have been anticipated in a research design ahead of time. Rapport with the people whose lives are the object of study is a central dilemma of direct observation: The closer the relationship between the researcher and the participant, the greater the likelihood that they will confide (or enact) socially stigmatized actions, whether temper tantrums, infidelity, or language switching. Seeing activities as sensible from the insider's point of view almost by definition compromises an observer's ability to describe them without bias. Close relationships with the people one is studying invariably put objectivity at risk; at the same time, finding an objective position is a goal only some qualitative researchers espouse.

A different issue is posed by the methods used for recording the action observed during participant observation. The traditional anthropological method of taking extensive written notes during or soon after periods of observation has generated close interest in the notes themselves, with all their inherent idiosyncrasies, as an object of inquiry (Sanjek, 1990). In a methodological development in what might be considered the opposite direction, a preference has emerged in many kinds of qualitative research for audio- and/or video-recorded materials over the written descriptions of social action that were the hallmark of ethnographic work. Technological advances in audio and video recording have carried over into intense interest in the processes of transcription and the kinds of interpretation they foster, matters to which we will shortly return.

Some form of participant observation nonetheless remains a viable option for qualitative research, its primary advantage being relative unobtrusiveness. A classic discussion of participant observation (Gold, 1958) described it as a continuum stretched between its two key terms, from completely participating in an event or community to almost—since no researcher has yet figured out how to become invisible, or literally a fly on the wall—completely observing, from the sidelines, with no pretense (or even deliberate avoidance) of participation. Although somewhat oversimplified, the model makes one dimension of participant observation clear: Each point on the continuum creates a particular kind of identity within the scene, with attendant face concerns for the researcher and relational stakes with the people she or he proposes to study. The "crisis of representation" (Clifford & Marcus, 1986; Van Maanen, 1988, 1995; Wolf, 1992) in the sociology and anthropology of the 1970s and 1980s called for those identities and relationships to be an explicit part of the observational record, a move generally referred to as reflexivity. Rather than being concerned that their research would be judged as biased, one school of qualitative researchers would be more concerned that their interpretations would be seen as claiming objectivity, a state that they would regard as not possible (Abu-Lughod, 1990; Cain, 1986).

On the other side of these questions is a large body of instruction on participant observation and written records as a method that can be systematic and structured (Lindlof & Taylor, 2002; Spradley, 1980) and valid and reliable in ways that resonate to some degree with the traditional social science meanings of those terms (Silverman, 2004). Written records include everything from highly structured checklists derived from theory, such that the goal of the observation study is a form of hypothesis testing (Miles & Huberman, 1994), to various stages of field notes, which begin as broad and unstructured and become more focused and detailed at each stage (Emerson, Fretz, & Shaw, 1995). From teaching qualitative and ethnographic methods many times, at different institutions and to different levels of learners from undergraduates to junior faculty, we would make one observation about written records of social action: It is surprisingly and pervasively difficult for social scientists to produce descriptive prose that stays entirely out of the psychological realm of thoughts, feelings, perceptions, and attitudes. Locating communication behavior within the observable realm of what is heard and seen (occasionally smelled, tasted, and touched) in writing without recourse to audio or visual records is crucial for the practice of participant observation, in and of itself, to be a useful part of research. The plethora of methods books that attempt to spell out processes of that activity that started out so close to everyday human action may attest to that difficulty, even as no single one of them seems to have solved it.

## Interviewing

Next to participant observation, interviewing, in at least some of its forms, may be the qualitative research method most closely related to an activity of everyday talk: asking people questions about the social world around them. Qualitative "interviewing," in fact, can run the gamut from posing questions to group members as part of participation observation through designing and administering highly structured question protocols meant to obtain rigorously comparable answers across interviewees.

In addition, although interviews are more commonly done with individuals, there has been increasing interest in what can be learned by bringing individuals together—most often strangers who have had a particular experience—to discuss a small set of issues. Focus groups (Morgan, 2002; Myers, 2007; Wilkerson, 2006), as this kind of group interview is labeled, may be tightly structured, with a facilitator moving through a preset question agenda, or they may involve relatively freewheeling discussion. Focus groups also vary in the number of participants (from 3 to 30-plus), whether they use stimulus materials (an editorial, cartoons, or a problematic scenario), and how the interview discourse is analyzed (notes taken, selective transcribing of what participants say, or full transcript attending to question formulations).

Part of the methodological diversity in interview practices lies along a paradigmatic divide between postpositivist and interpretivist versions of social science. The postpositivist end emphasizes a philosophy of separation between the knower and the known, with attendant concerns about objectivity and controlling bias. The interpretivist end embodies a connection between researchers and their subjects, which is included, to widely varying degrees, in the analytic approach. This divide intersects a continuum of positions on the nature of research interviews, one pole emphasizing the topical content obtainable through interviewing and the other emphasizing the interactive nature of a research interview as a speech event. Although these divergent poles intersect one another in many places rather than just one, they provide a framework for some of the central issues involved in sketching the methodological territory of interviewing. The first dimension is elaborated by Silverman (2004) and the second by Tracy and Robles (2010), each of whom review relevant research and provide examples. Table 3.1 is an

attempt to synthesize those and older resources (Fontana & Frey, 1994; Kauffman, 1992; Spradley, 1979), although the usual cautions apply: Each category covers a wide range of approaches and analytic procedures, and in the interest of showing differences, it clearly will have left unspecified some areas of overlap and similarity.

One term from Table 3.1 requires some explanation. Rapport is at the center of many instructional treatments of interviews on the postpositivist, topic-centered side of the continuum, as both a necessary precondition for obtaining accurate information and a potential threat to reliability. Platt (2002) notes that early understandings of rapport in research interviews involved an instrumental relationship in which the researcher was respectful and friendly enough to get access and cooperation but that otherwise remained noncommittal, objective, and scientific. Challenges to scientific detachment came early, with some approaches encouraging interviewers to self-disclose in order to make interviewees comfortable with doing so. That stance, in turn, was characterized either as treating the interviewee as an equal partner in constructing meaning or as being manipulative. As Table 3.1 illustrates, the broad concept of "rapport" has largely been supplanted in interpretivist interviewing with detailed consideration of the researcher's role and identity vis-à-vis the interviewee and the circumstances under which questions are asked and responded to. This consideration extends, in discourse-situated interviewing, to examination of the interaction between interviewee and interviewer as being part of the findings of the study itself rather than secondary to information gained about particular topics raised in the interview.

A prominent strand of interview-based research in interpersonal communication involves studies of relational dialectics. There are several versions of dialectical approaches, with the two most visible represented by the work of Leslie Baxter and her colleagues (e.g., Baxter & Braithwaite, 2008; Baxter & Montgomery, 1996) and William Rawlins (e.g., 1992, 2000). Each of these approaches seeks to explicate the tensions

**Table 3.1**    Approaches to Interviewing

|  | Postpositivist | Interpretivist |
|---|---|---|
| Topical content | • Questions emerge from theory/previous research and should be pretested<br>• Responses are collected in relatively structured formats that allow for systematic comparison across interviewees<br>• Reliability begins with standard order and formulation of questions and also depends on coders' agreement on assignment of responses to categories<br>• Validity is based on strong connections to previous research/theory and concerns about whether interviewees will "tell the truth," especially about socially stigmatized identities and actions | • Interviewer sets agenda so that meaning is co-constructed in the interaction<br>• Topics may shift depending on responses of interviewees, attempting to approach their orientation to the social world from the inside<br>• Reliability rests on transcripts that allow for identification and analysis of relevant features of talk<br>• Validity questions may emerge from participant observation as well as from previous work |
| Interviewer–interviewee interaction | • Divergence from interview protocol is worrisome as a threat to reliability<br>• Rapport involves establishing open channels of communication in which the interviewee speaks freely while staying on topic<br>• Precise recording of answers focuses on words as relevant to questions asked<br>• Interview setting is intended to be relaxed yet neutral | • Loose structure is favored to allow interviewees to lead the way<br>• Interaction constitutes meaning as much as topical content does<br>• In some forms, capturing interview in transcribable ways is central to analysis<br>• Context of questions is part of content: during the event of interest? outside the usual range of activity?<br>• Interviewer expects to be reflexive about nature of relationship with interviewee |

that relational partners of a particular type (e.g., romantic couples, friends, or teacher and student) confronting certain types of situations must manage as they conduct their relationship.

Dialectical studies of relationships use depth interviews to identify, explicate, and illustrate what the relational dialectics in a particular relationship and life event look like. For instance, using the retrospective interview technique (Huston, Surra, Fitzgerald, & Cate, 1981), Toller and Braithwaite (2009) interviewed 37 parents who had lost a child, some individually and some as couples, to uncover the contradictions that marital couples faced. Contradictions included whether the couple should be grieving together or were permitted to grieve alone and the couples' troubles managing the desire to both talk and avoid talking about their child's death.

Relational dialectical studies use interviews with participants, with the exact number of interviewees determined by the number of people who are in a focal category and the difficulty of accessing these people. A research report will include interview excerpts to illustrate the character and tone of the identified dialectics. Usually, these excerpts are provided without the question that triggered the interviewee response, a practice prevalent among interview studies that discourse analysts see as problematic (see Tracy & Robles, 2010). Numbers are used in only a secondary way—to enumerate the main types of interviewees (e.g., the number of men/women, the number of interviewees participating in bereavement groups) and for describing the length of interviews and the number of pages of transcript generated. Statistics are typically avoided; among some relational dialectics scholars, there is a strong critical stance toward quantitative approaches. Rawlins (2007), for instance, commented,

> Numbers and statistics are not innocent figures. In my judgment, they symbolize and typically play into worldviews where detachment, objectivity, and the reduction of human activities and feelings to countable indicators are valued over persons' embodied performances and narrations of their lived experiences. (p. 61)

## Taping and Analysis of Talk

"Discourse analysis," the name for the methodological practice of studying people and social life by video- or audiotaping talk, can be used in personal, institutional, or public settings (Tracy & Mirivel, 2009). Tapes might be created by the researcher to study a particular kind of interaction, as Mirivel (2007) did for cosmetic surgery consultations by women desiring beauty enhancement changes, or they might be created within an institution as a regular part of how it does its business, as occurs when citizens call 911 to get emergency help (e.g., Tracy & Agne, 2002). Once tapes of interaction are collected, a discourse analyst needs to decide how to transcribe them. As there are many different systems (Edwards & Lampert, 1993), and no single correct way to transcribe, this first choice has consequences. As Ochs (1979) pointed out years

ago, the choices a researcher makes about which features of talk to record and how multiple participants' turns are to be represented—for example, formatted like a play script or with two or more running columns—are theoretically implicative, shaping how parties will be seen and what kinds of research claims will be plausible.

Creating a transcript is an entextualization process whereby some features of persons and cultures are rendered visible and others are ignored. The basic challenge discourse analysts face is to select the right level of specificity—to include all the features necessary to an analysis while keeping the transcript as reader friendly as possible. How to orthographically represent speech is another issue (Bucholtz, 2007). Should a transcript represent a person's speech as it sounds to the transcriber's ear, including, for instance, unusual pronunciations of words that may cue class, education, or ethnicity; or should speech be represented with standard spelling, thereby minimizing potential negative judgments tied to nonstandard spellings but rendering invisible certain identity markers?

When researchers are taping a scene themselves, rather than using tapes created by others, they must address a number of questions (Goodwin, 1993; Modaff & Modaff, 2000): Should they video- or audiotape, and what kind of equipment should they use? How important is it to be unobtrusive, and how important is it to capture facial expressions, gestures, and the use of objects in the environment? Will it be difficult to tell who is talking without a video? If videotaping, how many cameras should there be and where should they be positioned? Which actors should the cameras foreground if not everyone can be easily seen? There are no correct answers to these questions. Rather, researchers must make a decision about what makes the most sense in their particular study, recognizing that there will be choices among competing concerns.

Within communication, researchers tend either to use a full-blown version of the conversation-analytic transcription system (Atkinson & Heritage, 1999) or to use simpler versions of this system that capture words, repetitions, vocal sounds, and repairs but generally *not* utterance prosody, speech pacing, and overlapping speech (e.g., Tracy, 2005). Table 3.2 illustrates the most common symbols used in the conversation-analytic transcription system.

Given the complexity of the CA transcription system, it is not obvious if transcribers would use the system similarly. Although qualitative researchers do not talk much about reliability, discourse analysts do assume that transcripts are reasonably accurate representations of what people have said. Roberts and Robinson (2004) assessed this assumption by giving four experienced CA transcribers, trained at different institutions, the same two and a half minutes of talk

to transcribe in CA notation. The authors then coded 15 dimensions of the transcriptions, including, for instance, whether transcribers unitized speaking turns similarly or if they indicated the same prosodic features (sounds stretching, loudness, intonation). Roberts and Robinson found a reasonable level of agreement (above 80%) for most features. In terms of coder agreement, loudness and sound stretching were unreliably used symbols, with different transcribers using different combinations. However, if one sees these speech distinctions as jointly cuing speech stress and treats the presence of one or more of the symbol sets as alternative reasonable formats, then transcribers had agreement levels of more than 89%.

**Table 3.2**  Conversation Analysis Transcription Symbols

| | |
|---|---|
| . | (period) Falling intonation |
| ? | (question mark) Rising intonation |
| , | (comma) Continuing intonation |
| - | (hyphen) Marks an abrupt cutoff |
| :: | (colon[s]) Prolonging of sound |
| never | (underlining) Stressed syllable or word |
| WORD | (all caps) Loud speech |
| °word° | (degree symbols) Quiet speech |
| >word< | (more than and less than) Quicker speech |
| <word> | (less than and more than) Slowed speech |
| hh | (series of *h*s) Aspiration or laughter |
| .hh | (*h*s preceded by dot) Inhalation |
| [ ] | (brackets) Simultaneous or overlapping speech |
| = | (equals sign) Contiguous utterances |
| (2.4) | (number in parentheses) Length of a silence |
| (.) | (period in parentheses) Micropause, 2/10 second or less |
| ( ) | (empty parentheses) Nontranscribable segment of talk |
| (word) | (word or phrase in parentheses) Transcriptionist doubt |
| ((gazing toward the ceiling)) | (double parentheses) Description of nonspeech activity |

In the past decade, the importance of the material surround for talk and the particulars of gaze, gesture, and body positioning have increasingly been recognized. Along with this recognition has come new ways of transcribing such features, as well as building photographs into transcript excerpts and journal articles (e.g., Goodwin, 2007; LeBaron & Jones, 2002). Following the creation of a transcript, whatever the level of detail selected, an analyst studies it while relistening or rewatching the taped interaction. Often, discourse analysts gather in small groups and do "data sessions" to assess the plausibility of the interpretations researchers are building into their data, as well as collectively to help fellow participants hone their noticing and argument-building skills for future discourse-analytic projects (Fitch, 2005b).

The kinds of arguments that discourse analysts may develop with their data differ by the kind of discourse analysis they see themselves as doing. In a recent book informed by Goffman's (1974) and Tannen's (1993) notions of frames, Gordon (2009), for instance, shows how the meaning of family is created through a set of particular discursive practices. Conversation analysts, discursive psychologists, action-implicative discourse analysts, and critical discourse analysts (explained below)—all have different goals in research, as do quantitative or other qualitative researchers who use discourse analysis in supplemental ways. But whatever the kind of argument a discourse scholar is working to build, he or she will try to do so in ways that avoid common problems—such as an analysis being no more than a paraphrase of the content of the talk (Antaki, Billig, Edwards, & Potter, 2002).

## Analysis of Written Documents and Visual Texts

Written documents and visual texts both are easier and can be more difficult data than the other three. Unlike the other forms of data that involve complicated choices about how to prepare them,

texts involve few or no preparation choices. They are what they are. At the same time, ways of analyzing them—especially for visual texts—are less well established. As a result, in addition to the ever-present challenge of constructing a persuasive scholarly claim, researchers working with visual texts will face novel methodological decisions.

When understanding the meaning of a category of texts is the focal goal in research, as is the case in much critical discourse analysis (CDA), a set of texts will be sampled, collected, and analyzed. A study by Lazar (2000) examining how parenthood and gender were portrayed visually and linguistically in Singaporean ads and a study by Coupland (1996) examining how dating ads in a newspaper created selves as products to be sold to readers illustrate the foci document analyzers might take. Often, discursive explication of texts is combined with simple counting of distinctive features, as illustrated in Trix and Psenka's (2003) analysis of differences in the letters of recommendations written for female and male faculty for medical school appointments.

In much qualitative research, document analysis is integrated with one of the other kinds of data. Leeds-Hurwitz's (2002) study of wedding celebrations where the bride and groom are from different cultures illustrates one such approach. In the interviews she did, participants retold their wedding stories using photo albums as central props to recount their experiences. Others have examined how talk and text are connected in particular institutional sites. A special issue focused on legal exchanges (Komter, 2006), for instance; showed how lawyers used their notes during a criminal trial (Scheffer, 2006); and explored how documents were used when attorneys first met with clients who had been accused of a crime (Halldorsdottir, 2006).

Rapley (2007) provides a nice introduction to how one would begin to study people using documents in various contexts, and Kress (2006) offers a useful overview of how to analyze different kinds of visual materials. A recent development of earlier visual methods coming out of health care studies is a technique called photovoice (Lorenz & Kolb, 2009). Photovoice sends people in a community out to take pictures of actions/events that they see as representing their lives or an issue they confront. The photo takers return and discuss their pictures, thus enabling analysis of meanings through studying the photos in connection with the group discussion.

## Distinctive Qualitative Approaches

The nine approaches we lay out here are not an exhaustive list of qualitative approaches that are used, or could be useful, in interpersonal communication research. As a set, though, they offer a good sense of the diversity within these qualitative research approaches. We have arrayed the approaches on a continuum from those that are primarily discourse analytic to those that are primarily ethnographic, with hybrid approaches that integrate some aspects of both traditions in the middle.

### Conversation Analysis

CA is the discourse-analytic approach that has been the most influential in interpersonal communication (for overviews, see Beach, 2008; Drew, 2005). Although in the 1980s, CA was a label used for any research analyzing talk, by the 1990s it had come to be firmly connected to one particular approach. Started by the sociologist Harvey Sacks, along with Emanuel Schegeloff and Gail Jefferson, CA aims to "reveal the tacit, organized reasoning procedures which inform the production of naturally occurring talk" (Hutchby & Wooffitt, 1998, p. 1).

Among discourse approaches, CA has the tightest methodological commitments, which include (a) making transcripts as detailed as possible, since an analyst can never know in advance what features of talk will be contributing to participants' meanings; (b) building research claims by avoiding the use of outside-of-talk contextual information

and instead using recipient uptake (i.e., how participants respond to a partner) as key evidence; (c) working with naturally occurring interactive talk, especially family and friend conversations, and eschewing interview talk—unless one is studying how participants do interviews (e.g., Puchta & Potter, 2004); and (d) building collections of interactional activities for close analysis. For example, Robinson (2004) analyzed explicit apologies, and Bolden (2009) analyzed "repeated-prefaced responses" (where a person who has been asked a question repeats some of the words in her or his answer). "The primary objective of CA," according to Clayman and Gill (2004), "is to elucidate generic mechanisms that recurrently organize interaction" (p. 601).

Interpersonal communication scholars have often given these general CA commitments a personal relationship twist, as can be seen in Glenn's (2003) study of laughter, Pomerantz and Mandelbaum's (2005) analysis of how relationship categories are used, and Beach's (1996) investigations of family conversations about illness. An assumption made by CA that many interpersonal scholars will find reasonable is that ordinary conversation (outside-of-institution exchanges among family members or friends) is the primordial site for understanding social life (Drew & Heritage, 1992). As the primordial site, conversation is regarded as the most important form of talk since all other types of interaction are adaptations from this first type. Other discourse scholars (e.g., Cameron, 2001; Tracy, 2005), in contrast, see no need to compare institutional exchanges with informal or intimate interaction. Discourse analysts of this second type see the study of institutional talk as valuable in its own right. They seek to understand discourse expressions that are particular to a focal institution's goals, as, for example, Agne (2007) did in his study of the Federal Bureau of Investigation's negotiations with the barricaded Branch Davidians at Waco, Texas.

In the past decade, it has become increasingly common to see CA work in the company of quantitative coding studies (Robinson, 2007).

In combination studies, CA is used to identify the important language or interaction categories occurring in a particular occasion of talk, and then, quantitative coding is used to assess whether the identified categories relate to outcomes of interest.

## Discursive Psychology

Discursive psychology (DP) draws on conversation-analytic procedures of recording and transcribing talk, often naturally occurring though sometimes including or based on interviews, to pursue a specific discourse-analytic project. Exemplified by Potter and Hepburn (2007), Edwards (2006, 2008), and their colleagues, DP applies discourse-analytic methods and concepts to the examination of processes that have long been theorized as mental and emotional states (e.g., attitude, emotion, cognition, memory, and statements of intentions) as social actions. This work is directed to some degree to the field of social psychology and its tendency to frame interactional processes as internal and individual ones. Its practitioners analyze phenomena such as the commonplace expressions "I think," "I know," and "To be honest" and claims to remember as conversational resources used to accomplish interpersonal action rather than reflections, accurate or otherwise, of internal states (Edwards & Fasulo, 2006). DP also focuses on what Edwards (2005) describes as "how psychological business— motives and intentions, prejudices, reliability of memory and perception" (p. 259) is carried out in everyday kinds of talk and text.

The specific utility of DP to interpersonal communication is, first, that it calls attention to what is ordinarily an unreflective use of psychological vocabulary to describe practices of interpersonal communication. Analytic categories such as attribution, self-disclosure, and attitudes are still available, but the emphasis is on tracking what counts as action within those categories by attending to conversational sequence. This perspective would approach the meaning of a declaration of some personal fact—"Mother always liked my older brother best"—from the utterances that precede and follow it rather than from an external definition such as self-disclosure. DP's analytical strategy proceeds inductively, from the microanalysis of one instance at a time, in the CA mode; self-disclosure, for example, can only count as that when oriented to in more or less obvious ways by conversational participants.

That said, there are some instances of DP that start from categories that do not emerge from the talk as such but pursue complexities of an interactional phenomenon often approached as self-evident and unidimensional. An example of this kind of work is Hepburn's (2004) examination of crying in phone calls to a child protection helpline. Rather than coding crying as present or absent, she develops a transcription system that allows for distinctions between levels of crying— "wobbly voice" versus "sobbing," for example— parallel to Gail Jefferson's (1979) exploration of the intricacies of conversationally situated laughter. Emotion is widely understood as relevant to interpersonal communication and relationships; DP is a systematic way of unpacking both the form and the substance of emotions in naturally occurring talk.

## Critical Discourse Analysis

CDA is a type of discourse analysis committed to showing how power inequities are being naturalized through language practices, thereby further advantaging those who already possess advantages in society. It "developed in a particular location within a particular political situation—out of a tendency of the political left and within the new social movements (feminism, ecology, etc.) toward cultural and ideological forms of political struggle from the 1960s onward" (Fairclough, 1996, p. 52). Although currently a multidisciplinary, multinational approach, CDA began in Europe among a set of linguists, with Norman Fairclough (2009), Teun van Dijk (2009), and Ruth Wodak (Wodak & Chilton, 2007) being among its most prominent spokespersons.

CDA involves a close analysis of talk or texts with the goal of illuminating how linguistic and semiotic practices are contributing to social inequities (Fairclough & Wodak, 1997). It is better conceived as a school of discourse analysis rather than as a single approach since there is significant diversity in the methodological moves of scholars who align with it (Tracy, Martinez-Guillem, Robles, & Casteline, 2001). The analysis of written documents is a particularly common focus among CDA scholars. Van Leeuwen (2007), for instance, collected teacher-training manuals, parent brochures, and ads for school programs to explore how moral evaluation and institutional legitimation were accomplished. In this study, he showed that legitimation operated through four processes—one of which was "mythopoesis"—using narratives whose outcome rewarded what was to be seen as legitimate action. But CDA scholarship also includes analyses of talk such as family dinner conversations (Kendall, 2008) and group interviews. Augoustinos, Tuffin, and Every (2005), for instance, analyzed focus group discourse to characterize how affirmative action in schools was understood.

Certain strands of CDA regularly make use of participant observation. An example is Wodak's (1996) studies of disordered discourse in therapy, doctor–patient exchanges in outpatient clinics, and school meetings. In these studies, she provides background information about how these institutional activities operate, information that had been acquired through immersion in the scene. Then, she turns to the CDA central purpose: showing how discourse particulars support the worldview and ideology of the powerful in each site.

The central context for CDA studies has been institutional sites such as government, media, health care, and immigration. Bartesaghi's (2009) study of a family therapy clinic illustrates an interpersonal communication study that makes use of multiple data-gathering procedures to illustrate how mental illness "is a socio-political construction born of the interactional pragmatics of pysch-complex diagnoses" (p. 159). Weaving an analysis of the assumptions built into the Beck Depression Inventory and a clinic intake form with talk exchanges in the first clinic meetings between teens and the parent(s), Bartesaghi shows how nonordinary these opening conversations are, requiring clients to agree to answer questions "in ways that constrain, if not violate, their conversational rights as persons able to account" (p. 171). Given that interpersonal communication's intellectual center tends to be either intimate relationships or interactional processes that cross contexts, CDA may seem a less relevant qualitative approach for scholars in the field. But as the Bartesaghi study illustrates, if one includes in interpersonal communication studies of situated institutional interactions and how persons and relationships are represented in texts, then CDA offers a valuable new way to investigate important issues. As van Dijk's (1984, 1987) studies of racism in ordinary talk showed, CDA offers a way to explore highly sensitive topics that other methods could not address.

## Action-Implicative Discourse Analysis

AIDA is centrally interested in analyzing talk to arrive at claims about communicative practices. Developed by Tracy (1995), it is the discourse realization of grounded practical theory (Craig & Tracy, 1995; Tracy & Craig, 2010)—not to be confused with grounded theory (see below). Grounded practical theory is a metatheoretical approach that conceives of the field of communication as a practical rather than a scientific enterprise. Unlike scientific disciplines in which explanation and prediction are central, a practical discipline is one concerned with contingent matters in which acting wisely depends on attending to particulars in a scene.

Grounded practical theory takes communicative practices as its central research foci. Practices include both nameable institutional ones (e.g., mediation session, parent–teacher conference) and those that are distributed across contexts (e.g., negotiation). For a focal practice, grounded practical theory aims to describe the problems and dilemmas that confront the various categories of participants, the communicative moves/strategies that realize and address problems, and the complex, often tacit ideals of good conduct ("situated ideals") that shape participants' assessments of action.

AIDA melds the analytic moves of discourse analysis—attending to situated talk and texts—with grounded practical theory's goal of facilitating reflection about how to act. Toward that end, AIDA works to provide a reconstructed account of the communicative problems, the interaction strategies, and the normative ideals of a practice. AIDA takes a rhetorical point of view on social action, seeking to distinguish between what is better and worse. In addition, although analysis of talk is central, it regularly makes use of interviews and institutional documents to develop the multilayered knowledge of a practice that makes insightful description and critique more likely. In any particular piece, an AIDA study usually focuses on a single or possibly two aims—characterizing a practice's problem, identifying discourse moves and strategies, or describing participants' situated ideals—but across reports; AIDA research works to address all levels.

An example of a fully developed AIDA study is Tracy's (2010) recent book analyzing the challenges faced by citizens and elected board members in regularly occurring school board meetings. Weaving together analyses of meeting exchanges, newspaper accounts, and participant interviews with theorizing about face and identity work, diversity, educational testing, and democracy, Tracy describes the discursive strategies that elected officials and parent-citizens use to enact "ordinary democracy." Tracy's study concludes by advancing a norm for conduct in these sites of local governance: In times of dissent, reasonable hostility, she argues, rather than civility or politeness, is the better ideal.

## Microethnography

The term *microethnography* uses ethnography to refer to an assumption that "the foundations of social organization, culture, and interaction" are located "at the microlevel of the moment-by-moment development of human activities" (Streeck & Mehus, 2005, p. 381). The method relies on a detailed transcription of videotaped interactions in which subtle visual and physical elements of communication, such as foot positions in an auto body shop (Streeck, 2009) and, in particular, gestures (Kendon, 2004; Kita, 2003; Mondada, 2007), are examined both as inseparable from the verbal phenomena of words and sounds and as revealing cultural practices. The history of microethnography is generally traced to the work of anthropologists such as Gregory Bateson, whose photographic studies of Bali suggested the power of observation and recording of visual and bodily activity in social life, and educational researchers such as Hugh Mehan, who suggested that the microdetails of classroom interaction formed cultural systems of meaning. This work contrasts with experimental and controlled observation studies of nonverbal behavior in its emphasis on concise interpretation of finely detailed moments, often captured in drawings and frame grabs, rather than on global assessments of which nonverbal cues are attended to and how they are interpreted by participants. Microethnography, similar to qualitative methods more generally, as we have described them here, works inductively from specific cases rather than by formulating and testing hypotheses from previous research and theory. The emphasis on the integration of gestures, gaze, and often manipulation of the material environment (Goodwin, 2003, 2007) with talk leads to a focus on multimodal action (Bolden, 2003).

Findings of such work contribute to interpersonal communication in their detailed attention to aspects of interpersonal interaction that are often overlooked when the primary, de facto emphasis is on spoken life. This work also provides a perspective on cognition that, like DP, locates activities such as thought and learning not within the boundaries of an individual person but within the interaction of people with one another, including their manipulation of focal objects in the environment. Nishizaka (2006), for example, traces instruction in a videotaped violin lesson in ways that show how learning involves restructuring the physical environment, a process situated within the organization of interaction between teacher and student.

## Ethnography and Ethnography of Communication

Leeds-Hurwitz (2005) notes that the term *ethnography* can be used in two ways. As a noun, it refers to a case study of cultural practices. As an adjective, it can refer to a wide variety of qualitative approaches to social action. The ethnography of communication (EOC), she notes, has been particularly influential. Starting with the work of the linguistic anthropologist Dell Hymes (1962, 1972) and brought into the field of communication studies by Philipsen's (1975, 1976) Teamsterville studies, mentioned earlier, EOC approaches communication as situated within cultural systems of norms, premises, and symbolic meanings. The unit of analysis, following Hymes, is the speech community: a group of people who share at least one valued way of speaking. Those valued ways of speaking are discovered and described within communal groups (e.g., urban Colombians) and institutional settings—courtrooms, classrooms, medical settings, organizations—by way of fieldwork. Researchers immersed to some degree in naturally occurring action conduct participant observation, interviewing of various kinds, and, very often, analysis of recorded events or interactions and/or documents.

EOC has two foci: (1) cultural case studies that examine systems of meaning pertaining to specific groups and (2) construction of theory by comparison across those case studies. Goldsmith (1989–1990), for example, examined five case studies of gossip in different cultures to propose that evaluative talk about absent others was, in every case, considered potentially dangerous to the social order and yet necessary to maintain

social control. Gossip was thus constrained in its performance, but it was constrained differently in different cultures: Participants, instrumentalities, and settings were relevant dimensions for constraint. The value of theory construction that takes place across cultural case studies is such that it builds an empirically based account of the processes of interest, taking both cultural variation and the likelihood of universal dimensions of human sociality into consideration. This perspective has been applied to a wide range of interpersonal communication phenomena, including compliance gaining (Fitch, 1994), cultural bases for the conduct of personal relationships (Covarrubias, 2002; Katriel & Philipsen, 1981), advice (Goldsmith & Fitch, 1997), construction of social identity (Carbaugh, 1995; Sequeira, 1993), and others.

## Grounded Theory

Across the social sciences, grounded theory—or the practices that constitute it (e.g., theoretical saturation, the constant comparative technique)—is the most cited qualitative method. Between 1991 and 1998, grounded theory received 2,622 citations in the *Social Science Citation Index* (Bryant & Charmaz, 2007b). The name for this approach is, in some ways, an unfortunate choice as it miscues its identity. Grounded theory is a method of doing research, not a theory, although it produces theory. Developed by the sociologists Glaser and Strauss (1967), grounded theory was a challenge to the conventional social science of the 1960s, which was only concerned with theory testing, giving no attention to how theory (i.e., a connected set of ideas) came into existence. Theory generation, Glaser and Strauss argued, should be as important in social science research as theory verification. Initially, the kind of theory that Glaser and Strauss were interested in developing was identical to positivist-inspired social science theory; that is, it involved causal explanations. But as qualitative methods gained ascendance, so too did what counted as "theory." In the 21st century, grounded theory takes a middle position between realist and postmodern epistemologies, believing that there is a real world, albeit always known through interpretation, of which there are often multiple versions. In such a world, a researcher using grounded theory is seeking to develop a compelling interpretation of some segment of social life (Bryant & Charmaz, 2007a).

Grounded theory collects data primarily through participant observation and interviews, constantly comparing what is being observed with what has been noted previously. The field and interview notes or interview transcripts are then subjected to interpretive coding procedures. A researcher puts codes (i.e., written notes) in the data about conceptual categories that appear salient. This process, often described as "categories emerging from the data," is actually one in which researchers merge their incoming interests with what they are observing in the materials. Once key categories are developed, researchers then ask questions about how categories relate to each other (axial coding); data collection and analysis proceeds until the researcher judges there to be "theoretical saturation"—that is, no new categories are emerging (Strauss & Corbin, 1990).

Grounded theory has been particularly popular within organizational communication scholars (e.g., Doerfel, Lai, & Chewing, 2010; Hoffman & Cowan, 2010) as a way to approach and study multilayered organizational scenes. Suddaby (2006) argues that grounded theory has been overused as a description of researcher methodology. Often, it is treated as a synonym for qualitative analysis when there is little attention to its particular commitments.

Although grounded theory is less commonly used as a central frame by interpersonal communication scholars, it has its practitioners. Becker and Stamp (2005), for instance, used it to study impression management in online chat rooms. More commonly, interpersonal communication researchers use grounded theory concepts as one leg of analysis, most commonly in interview studies to describe how materials are being analyzed,

as can be seen in relational dialectics research (e.g., Sahlstein, Maguire, & Timmerman, 2009).

## Narrative Analysis

Narrative analysis is a family of methods for interpreting texts. In its most common version, it is ethnographic. Riessman (2008) defines narrative analysis, in any of its forms, as committed to "extended accounts that are preserved and treated analytically as units, rather than fragmented into thematic categories" (p. 12). She distinguishes three kinds of narrative analysis. In the first, and most common, type, "thematic analysis," stories are collected through interviews, and their content is of central interest to researchers. In thematic analyses, the researcher is located outside the story, and the focal participant's story is stitched together from what is said in the interview. Although it has some similarity to grounded theory because of its focus on themes, it differs in several ways. First, thematic analysis in narrative research, unlike grounded theory, makes use of theory upfront to structure and interpret themes in the narratives. Second, thematic analysis attends to larger sequences as its basic unit; that is, stories are kept intact. Third, there is no attempt to generalize; thematic narrative analysis is case study research that is sensitive to historical specifics.

In contrast to thematic analysis that tends to focus solely on the content of the story, the other two narrative approaches take account of how a narrative was produced, attending to its unfolding structures or viewing it holistically as the performance of key identities. In these discourse-oriented narrative approaches, stories may be generated in interviews, but they are also often collected from actually occurring oral exchanges or from written texts that had been produced for purposes other than research. In these discourse-oriented narrative approaches, there is attention to features of language choice as well as interactional specifics, in addition to story content features.

Consider three examples of narrative studies in interpersonal communication research. First,

Koenig-Kellas and Trees (2006) explored how families jointly told stories about their experiences, identifying the patterned ways in which they narrated these stories, which emphasized their identification as a family unit rather than as individual persons. Second, Witteborn (2007) interviewed Palestinians in the United States to see how they expressed their collective identities, showing how they used discourse features such as pronominal shifts to "you" and the use of reported speech (enacting others' words) to accomplish an array of subtle purposes. A final example is Benoit's (1997) study of stories of success, in which she examines the talk of athletes being interviewed after successful games, Nobel Prize winners' speeches as they accept prizes, and the award acceptances from top sellers of Mary Kay Cosmetics.

Although we tend to think of stories as the possession of individuals, it is also possible to investigate institutional narratives. As Linde (2009) comments, narration is

> the link between the way an institution represents its past, and the way its members use, alter or contest that past, in order to understand the institution as a whole as well as their own place within or apart from that institution. (p. 4)

In her study of an insurance company, Linde analyzes stories that occurred in the workplace at a time of change. She argues that the stories institutional members tell show a feature that an analyst never sees when stories are gathered through interviews. That feature is that in everyday life no one storyteller ever completely owns the story he or she tells; close others have the right—and they take it regularly—to dispute or correct the teller's story.

## Autoethnography

Autoethnography locates the experiences and feelings of the author at the center of inquiry. Narratives are proposed as theoretical vehicles in their own right, with or without explicit contextualization in extant literature; although such location is possible and in some cases desirable, it is explicitly not a requirement for autoethnography's claim to producing insight and contributing to research (Ellis & Bochner, 2006). Writing, particularly writing evocative prose that brings emotion-laden realities into focus, is an explicit focus of the method; autoethnography is meant to be distinctive from other forms of ethnography in its ability to "make (the reader) cry" (Denzin, 2006). With those as characteristic goals, some have commented that autoethnography, when restricted to its evocative instances, limits itself to emotionally riveting topics, such as illness or stigmatized identity, and then only those experienced by the researcher herself (Anderson, 2006a, 2006b).

There are different views about the role of theory and generalization in autoethnography, as illustrated by the contrast of two illness-based narratives. *The Body Silent* by Robert F. Murphy (1990) is a first-person narrative by a cultural anthropologist who became paraplegic at age 48 because of a spinal tumor. His story of going from a healthy person to a disabled one is infused, from start to finish, with connections to research and theory about the mind, the lives of people with disabilities in the United States, and the interplay of individuals with society. Murphy notes, in a variety of ways (though never in so many words), that abstraction from, and intellectual examination of, his own experiences were key to dealing with his everadvancing illness, to which he succumbed in the same year the paperback version of the book was published. He also describes, however, the movingly personal reactions this work received from people, particularly people with disabilities, in stark distinction from the reactions his scholarly work in cultural anthropology had received.

Darlene Drummond's (2008) *Diary of Gastric Bypass Surgery*, on the other hand, builds a textbook around a day-by-day process of deciding to address the complications of obesity through surgery, the surgery and recovery itself, and 15 weeks after, when she incorporated diet and exercise changes into her life to maintain her 100-pound weight loss. The narrative includes many emotional and physical details and draws attention to the disproportionate occurrence of diabetes and high blood pressure among African Americans. Each chapter ends with discussion questions that encourage readers, presumably students, to connect Drummond's experiences with their own. Some include capsule summaries of interpersonal theories (uncertainty reduction, the theory of reasoned action, the elaboration likelihood model) and recommended readings to extend the insights from one person's story to communication research.

Together, Murphy's (1990) and Drummond's (2008) autoethnographic narratives show some of the range of this kind of work. Beyond the obvious connections of personal stories of illness to health communication, each could be used to illuminate more general interpersonal processes and practices, such as social support and family communication. In their clearest connection to other strands of ethnography, both books illuminate U.S. American culture from the perspective of a particular identity: the disabled person and an initially obese person who undergoes surgery.

## Summary

In this section, we overviewed nine distinctive qualitative approaches, identifying which data-gathering practice(s) they use and the kinds of questions about communication they pursued. For several of them, we described their stance toward quantitative methods. In this chapter's last section, we argue that quantitative methods, admittedly of a particular kind, could be useful to interpretive researchers. According to those who approach social science with a John Dewey–type pragmatism (Diesing, 1991), taking the goal of social science to be centrally about enabling people to better reflect on and manage problems in their communicative worlds,

quantitative methods can sometimes be useful to qualitative researchers.

## A Role for Quantitative Methods in Pragmatism-Influenced Approaches

Thus far, we have discussed qualitative methods in terms of concrete data-gathering procedures (interviews, participant observation, talk analysis, and textual analysis) and nameable methodological/theoretical approaches (the nine approaches). As we conclude the chapter, we move up a level of abstraction and consider the different epistemological (and ontological) stances animating research. Most often, the stances are contrastively defined as social constructionism (e.g., Leeds-Hurwitz, 1995; Shotter, 1993), usually presumed to go with qualitative methods, versus postpositivism (e.g., Berger & Chaffee, 1987), the presumed companion of quantitative methods. Sometimes the two categories are split in three—postpositivist, interpretive, and critical epistemologies (e.g., Cheney, 2000; Miller, 2000; Mumby, 2000)—in which interpretive and critical approaches share a social constructionist stance but differ in the importance they assign to research having an emancipatory goal.

A researcher's commitments regarding what the world is and how one gains knowledge about it are important. All too often, however, scholarly exchanges about these issues have been unproductive. Our goal is not to tackle this divide head on; rather, we seek to address one piece of it, beginning from the qualitative side of the river. It is widely assumed that if researchers are committed to an interpretive or social construction stance, they would eschew quantitative methods. We think this need not and should not be the case. A particularly productive view of how researchers might think differently about linkages between epistemology and methodology can be found in Flyvbjerg's (2001) book *Making Social Science Matter*. Drawing on Aristotle's notion of phronesis—that is, wisdom or prudential judgment—Flyvbjerg proposes that social science should recognize that its inquiry is inescapably embedded in a world that is contingent on and open to reflection and change. As he notes, the social sciences have not succeeded in predicting/explaining activities, which the natural sciences have largely done well. Conversely, the natural sciences have contributed very little to what the social sciences, if properly refashioned, could do well: fostering "the reflective analysis and discussion of values and interests, which is the prerequisite for an enlightened political, economic and cultural development" (p. 3). Flyvbjerg goes on to say,

The problem with the study of human activity is that every attempt at a context-free definition of an action, that is, a definition based on an abstraction, will not

necessarily accord with the pragmatic way an action is defined by the actors in a concrete social situation. (p. 42)

Phronetic social science is similar to grounded practical theory, the metatheoretical expression of AIDA. Both perspectives have been influenced by the pragmatist philosopher, John Dewey, and both also draw on the rhetorical idea of phronesis.

Table 3.3 shows how a pragmatism-influenced approach to social science would differ from the traditional, postpositivist view, with particular attention being given to the role for quantitative methods. In forwarding this distinction, we seek to shift the debate from one that puts quantitative and qualitative in opposite corners to one that assumes that how communicators make meaning and how communication situations are

**Table 3.3**  The Roles for Quantitative Methods in Interpersonal Communication Inquiry

| | Traditional Social Science (Postpositivist) | Pragmatism-Influenced Inquiry (Phronetic/Grounded Practical Theory) |
|---|---|---|
| How is inquiry understood? | A process of testing theories about the social communicative world, where a theory is a complex and abstract set of ideas that are linked to each other in specified ways | A context-grounded process in which researchers seek to understand what is warrantable/defensible to believe about the social world, often with a focus on practical problems |
| Grounding | • Models inquiry based on the natural sciences (especially physics)<br>• Assumes that good social science approaches conform to rules of scientific conduct laid out by philosophers<br>• Draws on the ideas of logical positivism and empiricism, with some attention to social constructionism | • Depends on the social situation/issue/problem one is seeking to understand<br>• Pursuit of multiple legitimate aims is part of the process of investigation; judgment is crucial<br>• Draws on ideas of pragmatism scholars such as Dewey and a few concepts from Aristotle |
| Favors | • Broader, abstract, and more universal claims<br>• Explanation and prediction | • Contextually grounded, less abstract concepts and claims<br>• Pursues understanding to aid reflection and (perhaps) social change |

*(Continued)*

**Table 3.3** (Continued)

|  | *Traditional Social Science* (*Postpositivist*) | *Pragmatism-Influenced Inquiry* (*Phronetic/Grounded Practical Theory*) |
|---|---|---|
| Framework's working language | • Theory testing<br>• Theoretical concepts, operational definitions, variables, hypotheses, falsifiable "rejection of the null" | • Currently less elaborated<br>• Partly draws on theory-testing language but also draws on language of interpretation, judgment, and understanding |
| Description | Devalued, often described as "atheoretical" | Valued, seen as essential to understanding the communicative world and its problems |
| Role for numbers and statistics | • Numbers are the pinnacle of precision, the marker of science<br>• Use metric variables and avoid categorical measures where possible<br>• Inferential statistics are better than descriptive ones because the goal is to be as general as possible in claim making<br>• More sophisticated inferential statistics are often better than simple ones because the world is complex | • Numbers are useful and important, but they must be tethered to words and interpretations for meaning<br>• Categorical measures are often preferred because they are closer to how people make distinctions<br>• Descriptive statistics are valuable for case studies, but "sample" and "population" don't always fit well. Thus, inferential statistics may be inappropriate<br>• Simpler statistics are often better because they are closer to the communicative situation they are seeking to understand |

structured are important to all. Where researchers differ is in what else they assume about the social world, including their roles as researchers.

## Conclusions

For researchers who want to develop rich, contextually grounded portraits of personal or professional relationships, communication practices, or interpersonal processes, there is nothing so useful as a qualitative method. Qualitative methods bring the researcher into the heart of social life; they extend the noticing, investigating, and analyzing practices of everyday encounters in a systematic manner, offering ways to connect with the communicative worlds that we as researchers are seeking to understand. To reiterate the words

of Clifford Geertz and Harvey Sacks with which we began this chapter, qualitative methods enable researchers to think creatively and imaginatively with social science concepts, and they provide the tools to find out about social scenes and communicators' sensemaking, particularly the subtleties we would not have known without careful looking and listening.

## References

Abu-Lughod, L. (1990). Can there be a feminist ethnography? *Women & Performance: Journal of Feminist Theory, 5,* 7–7.

Agne, R. (2007). Reframing practices in moral conflict: Interaction problems in the negotiation standoff of Waco. *Discourse & Society, 18,* 549–578.

Anderson, L. (2006a). Analytic autoethnography. *Journal of Contemporary Ethnography, 35,* 373–395.

Anderson, L. (2006b). On apples, oranges, and autopsies: A response to commentators. *Journal of Contemporary Ethnography, 35,* 450–465.

Antaki, C., Billig, M., Edwards, D., & Potter, J. (2002). Discourse analysis means doing analysis: A critique of six analytic shortcomings. *Discourse Analysis Online, 1,* 1–24.

Atkinson, J. M., & Heritage, J. (1999). Jefferson's transcript notation. In A. Jaworski & N. Coupland (Eds.), *The discourse reader* (pp. 158–166). London: Routledge.

Augoustinos, M., Tuffin, K., & Every, D. (2005). New racism, meritocracy and individualism: Constraining affirmative action in education. *Discourse & Society, 16,* 315–340.

Austin, J. L. (1962). *How to do things with words.* Oxford, UK: Oxford University Press.

Bartesaghi, M. (2009). Conversation and psychotherapy: How questioning reveals institutional answers. *Discourse & Society, 11,* 153–177.

Baxter, L. A., & Braithwaite, D. O. (2008). Relational dialectics theory. In L. A. Baxter & D. O. Braithwaite (Eds.), *Engaging theories in interpersonal communication: Multiple perspectives* (pp. 349–361). Thousand Oaks, CA: Sage.

Baxter, L. A., & Montgomery, B. M. (1996). *Relating: Dialogues and dialectics.* New York: Guilford Press.

Beach, W. (2008). Conversation analysis. In W. Donsbach (Ed.), *International encyclopedia of communication* (pp. 989–995). Oxford, UK: Wiley-Blackwell.

Beach, W. A. (1996). *Conversations about illness: Family preoccupations with bulimia.* Mahwah, NJ: Lawrence Erlbaum.

Becker, J. A. H., & Stamp, G. H. (2005). Impression management in chatrooms: A grounded theory model. *Communication Studies, 56,* 243–260.

Benoit, P. J. (1997). *Telling the success story: Acclaiming and disclaiming discourse.* Albany: State University of New York Press.

Berger, C. R., & Chaffee, S. H. (1987). The study of communication as a science. In C. R. Berger & S. H. Chaffee (Eds.), *Handbook of communication science* (pp. 15–19). Newbury Park: Sage.

Bochner, A. (1985). Perspectives on inquiry: Representations, conversation, and reflection. In M. Knapp & G. Miller (Eds.), *Handbook of interpersonal communication* (pp. 27–58). Beverly Hills, CA: Sage.

Bochner, A. (1994). Perspectives on inquiry II: Theories and stories. In M. Knapp & G. Miller (Eds.), *Handbook of interpersonal communication* (pp. 21–41). Thousand Oaks, CA: Sage.

Bogdan, R., & Taylor, S. J. (1975). *Introduction to qualitative research methods: A phenomenological approach to the social sciences.* New York: Wiley.

Bolden, G. (2003). Multiple modalities in collaborative turn-sequences. *Gesture, 3,* 187–211.

Bolden, G. (2009). Beyond answering: Repeat-prefaced responses in conversation. *Communication Monographs, 76,* 121–143.

Bryant, A., & Charmaz, K. (2007a). Introduction: Grounded theory research: Methods and practices. In A. Bryant & K. Charmaz (Eds.), *The Sage handbook of grounded theory* (pp. 1–27). Thousand Oaks, CA: Sage.

Bryant, A., & Charmaz, K. (2007b). Grounded theory in historical perspective: An epistemological account. In A. Bryant & K. Charmaz (Eds.), *The Sage handbook of grounded theory* (pp. 31–57). Los Angeles, CA: Sage.

Bucholtz, M. (2007). Variation in transcription. *Discourse Studies, 9,* 784–804.

Cain, M. (1986). Realism, feminism, methodology and the law. *International Journal of the Sociology of Law, 14,* 255–267.

Cameron, D. (2001). *Working with spoken discourse.* London: Sage.

Carbaugh, D. (1995). The ethnographic communication theory of Philipsen and associates. In D. P. Cushamn & B. Kovacic (Eds.), *Watershed research traditions in human communication theory* (pp. 269–297). Albany: State University of New York Press.

Cheney, G. (2000). Interpreting interpretive research: Toward perspectivism without relativism. In S. R. Corman & M. S. Poole (Eds.), *Perspectives on organization communication: Finding common ground* (pp. 17–45). New York: Guilford Press.

Clayman, S. E., & Gill, V. T. (2004). Conversation analysis. In M. Hardy & A. Bryman (Eds.), *Handbook of data analysis* (pp. 589–606). London: Sage.

Clifford, J., & Marcus, G. (Eds.). (1986). *Writing culture: The poetics and politics of ethnography.* Berkeley: University of California Press.

Conquergood, D. (1991). Rethinking ethnography: Towards a critical cultural politics. *Communication Monographs, 58,* 179–194.

Coupland, J. (1996). Dating advertisements: Discourses of the commodified self. *Discourse & Society, 7,* 187–207.

Covarrubias, P. (2002). *Culture, communication, and cooperation: Interpersonal relations and pronominal address in a Mexican organization.* Lanaham, MD: Rowman & Littlefield.

Craig, R. T., & Tracy, K. (1995). Grounded practical theory: The case of intellectual discussion. *Communication Theory, 5,* 248–272.

Denzin, N. K. (2006). Analytic autoethnography, or deja vu all over again. *Journal of Contemporary Ethnography, 35,* 419–428.

Diesing, P. (1991). *How does social science work?* Pittsburgh, PA: University of Pittsburgh Press.

van Dijk, T. (1984). *Prejudice in discourse.* Amsterdam: John Benjamins.

van Dijk, T. (1987). *Communicating racism: Ethnic prejudice in thought and talk.* Newbury Park, CA: Sage.

van Dijk, T. (2009). Critical discourse studies: A socio-cognitive approach. In R. Wodak & M. Meyer (Eds.), *Methods for critical discourse analysis* (2nd ed., pp. 62–86). London: Sage.

Doerfel, M. L., Lai, C.-H., & Chewning, L. (2010). The evolutionary role of interorganizational communication: Modeling social capital in disaster contexts. *Human Communication Research, 36,* 125–162.

Drew, P. (2005). Conversation analysis. In K. Fitch & R. Sanders (Eds.), *Handbook of language and social interaction* (pp. 71–102). Mahwah, NJ: Lawrence Erlbaum.

Drew, P., & Heritage, J. (1992). Analyzing talk at work: An introduction. In P. Drew & J. Heritage (Eds.), *Talk at work: Interaction in institutional settings* (pp. 1–65). Cambridge, UK: Cambridge University Press.

Drummond, D. K. (2008). *A diary of gastric bypass surgery: When the benefits outweigh the costs.* Albany: State University of New York Press.

Edwards, D. (2005). Discursive psychology. In K. Fitch & R. E. Sanders (Eds.), *Handbook of language and social interaction* (pp. 257–274). Mahwah, NJ: Lawrence Erlbaum.

Edwards, D. (2006). Discourse, cognition and social practices: The rich surface of language and social interaction. *Discourse Studies, 8,* 41–49.

Edwards, D. (2008). Intentionality and mens rea in police interrogations: The production of actions as crimes. *Intercultural Pragmatics, 5,* 177–199.

Edwards, D., & Fasulo, A. (2006). "To be honest": Sequential uses of honesty phrases in talk-in-interaction. *Research on Language & Social Interaction, 39,* 343–376.

Edwards, J. A., & Lampert, M. D. (Eds.). (1993). *Talking data: Transcription and coding in discourse research.* Hillsdale, NJ: Lawrence Erlbaum.

Ellis, C. S., & Bochner, A. P. (2006). Analyzing analytic autoethnography: An autopsy. *Journal of Contemporary Ethnography, 35,* 429–449.

Emerson, R., Fretz, R., & Shaw, L. (1995). *Writing ethnographic fieldnotes.* Chicago: University of Chicago Press.

Fairclough, N. (1996). A reply to Henry Widdowson's "Discourse analysis: A critical view." *Language & Literature, 5,* 49–56.

Fairclough, N. (2009). *Language and power.* London: Longman.

Fairclough, N., & Wodak, R. (1997). Critical discourse analysis. In T. A. van Dijk (Ed.), *Discourse as social interaction* (pp. 258–284). London: Sage.

Fiske, J. (1991). Writing ethnographies: Contribution to a dialogue. *Quarterly Journal of Speech, 77,* 330–335.

Fitch, K. (1994). Criteria for evidence in qualitative research. *Western Journal of Communication, 58,* 32–38.

Fitch, K. (1998). *Speaking relationally: Culture, communication, and interpersonal connection.* New York: Guilford Press.

Fitch, K. (2003). Taken-for-granteds in (an) intercultural communication context. In P. Glenn, J. Mandelbaum, & C. LeBaron (Eds.), *Studies in language and social interaction* (pp. 91–102). Mahwah, NJ: Lawrence Erlbaum.

Fitch, K. (2005a). Both sides now: Raising Colombian-Americans. In W. Leeds-Hurwitz (Ed.), *From generation to generation: Raising bicultural children* (pp. 297–318). New York: Hampton Press.

Fitch, K. (2005b). Conclusion: Behind the scenes of language and scholarly interaction. In K. Fitch & R. E. Sanders (Eds.), *Handbook of language and social interaction* (pp. 461–482). Mahwah, NJ: Lawrence Erlbaum.

Fitch, K. (2009). Culture and interpersonal relationships. In S. R. Wilson & S. Smith (Eds.), *New directions in interpersonal communication research* (pp. 245–263). Thousand Oaks, CA: Sage.

Fitch, K., & Hopper, R. (1983). "If you speak Spanish, they'll think you're a German": Language attitudes in a multilingual setting. *Journal of Multilingual & Multicultural Development, 4,* 115–128.

Flick, U. (2007). *Designing qualitative research.* Thousand Oaks, CA: Sage.

Flyvbjerg, B. (2001). *Making social science matter: Why social inquiry fails and how it can succeed again.* Cambridge, UK: Cambridge University Press.

Fontana, A., & Frey, J. (1994). Interviewing: The art of science. In N. Denzin & Y. Lincoln (Eds.), *Handbook of qualitative research* (pp. 361–376). Thousand Oaks, CA: Sage.

Geertz, C. (1973). *The interpretation of cultures.* New York: Basic Books.

Glaser, B., & Strauss, A. (1967). *The discovery of grounded theory.* Chicago: Aldine.

Glenn, P. J. (2003). Sex, laughter, and audiotape: On invoking features of context to explain laughter in interaction. In P. Glenn, C. D. LeBaron, & J. Mandelbaum (Eds.), *Studies in language and social interaction* (pp. 263–274). Mahwah, NJ: Lawrence Erlbaum.

Goffman, E. (1974). *Frame analysis: An essay on the organization of experience.* New York: Harper & Row.

Gold, R. (1958). Roles in sociological field observations. *Social Forces, 36,* 217–223.

Goldsmith, D. (1989–1990). Gossip from the native's point of view. *Research on Language and Social Interaction, 23,* 163–193.

Goldsmith, D. J., & Fitch, K. (1997). The normative context of advice as social support. *Human Communication Research, 23,* 454–476.

Goodwin, C. (1993). Recording human interaction in natural settings. *Pragmatics, 3,* 181–209.

Goodwin, C. (2007). Environmentally coupled gestures. In S. D. Duncan, J. Cassell, & E. T. Levy (Eds.), *Gesture and the dynamic dimension of language: Essays in honor of David McNeill* (pp. 195–212). Amsterdam: John Benjamins.

Gordon, C. (2009). *Making meanings, creating family: Intertextuality and framing in family interaction.* New York: Oxford University Press.

Halldorsdottir, I. (2006). Orientations to law, guidelines, and codes in lawyer and client interaction. *Research on Language and Social Interaction, 39,* 263–301.

Hepburn, A. (2004). Crying: Notes on description, transcription, and interaction. *Research on Language & Social Interaction, 37,* 251–290.

Hoffman, M. F., & Cowan, R. (2010). Be careful what you ask for: Structuration theory and work/life accommodation. *Communication Studies, 61,* 205–223.

Huston, T. L., Surra, C., Fitzgerald, N., & Cate, R. (1981). From courtship to marriage: Mate selection as an interpersonal process. In S. Duck & R. Gilmour (Eds.), *Personal relationships: Vol. 2. Developing personal relationships* (pp. 53–88). London: Academic Press.

Hutchby, I., & Wooffitt, R. (1998). *Conversation analysis: Principles, practices, and applications.* Malden, MA: Polity Press.

Hymes, D. (1962). The ethnography of speaking. In T. Gladwin & W. C. Sturtevant (Eds.), *Anthropology and human behavior* (pp. 15–53). Washington, DC: Anthropological Society of Washington.

Hymes, D. (1972). Models of the interaction of language and social life. In J. Gumperz & D. Hymes (Eds.), *Directions in sociolinguistics: The ethnography of communication* (pp. 35–71). New York: Holt, Rinehart and Winston.

Jefferson, G. (1979). A technique for inviting laughter and its subsequent acceptance declination. In G. Psathas (Ed.), *Everyday language: Studies in ethnomethodology* (pp. 346–369). New York: Irvington.

Katriel, T., & Philipsen, G. (1981). What we need is communication: "Communication" as a cultural category in some American speech. *Communication Monographs, 48,* 301–317.

Kauffman, B. J. (1992). Feminist facts: Interview strategies and political subjects in ethnography. *Communication Theory, 2,* 187–206.

Kendall, S. (2008). The balancing act: Framing gendered parental identities at dinnertime. *Language in Society, 37,* 539–568.

Kendon, A. (2004). *Gesture: Visible action as utterance.* Cambridge, UK: Cambridge University Press.

Kita, S. (Ed.). (2003). *Pointing: Where language, culture, and cognition meet.* Mahwah, NJ: Lawrence Erlbaum.

Koenig-Kellas, J., & Trees, A. (2006). Finding meaning in difficult family experiences: Sense-making and interaction processes during joint family storytelling. *Journal of Family Communication, 6,* 49–76.

Komter, M. L. (2006). Introduction. *Research on Language and Social Interaction, 39,* 195–200.

Kress, G. (2006). *Reading images: The grammar of visual design.* London: Routledge.

Lazar, M. M. (2000). Gender discourse and semiotics: The politics of parenthood representations. *Discourse & Society, 11,* 373–400.

LeBaron, C. D., & Jones, S. E. (2002). Closing up closings: Showing the relevance of the social and material surround to the completion of interaction. *Journal of Communication, 52,* 542–565.

Leeds-Hurwitz, W. (Ed.). (1995). *Social approaches to communication.* New York: Guilford Press.

Leeds-Hurwitz, W. (2002). *Wedding as text: Communicating cultural identities through ritual.* Mahwah, NJ: Lawrence Erlbaum.

Leeds-Hurwitz, W. (2005). Ethnography. In K. Fitch & R. Sanders (Eds.), *Handbook of language and social interaction* (pp. 327–353). Mahwah, NJ: Lawrence Erlbaum.

Linde, C. (2009). *Working the past: Narrative and institutional memory.* New York: Oxford University Press.

Lindlof, T. R., & Taylor, B. (2002). *Qualitative communication research methods* (2nd ed.). Thousand Oaks, CA: Sage.

Lorenz, L. S., & Kolb, B. (2009). Involving the public through participatory visual research methods. *Health Expectations, 12,* 262–274.

Mandelbaum, J. (1990–1991). Beyond mundane reason: Conversation analysis and context. *Research on Language and Social Interaction, 24,* 333–350.

Miles, M. B., & Huberman, A. M. (1994). *Qualitative data analysis: An expanded sourcebook* (Vol. 1, 2nd ed.). Thousand Oaks, CA: Sage.

Miller, K. I. (2000). Common ground from the postpositivist perspective: From "straw person" argument to collaborative coexistence. In S. R. Corman & M. S. Poole (Eds.), *Perspectives on organization communication: Finding common ground* (pp. 46–67). New York: Guilford Press.

Mirivel, J. (2007). Managing poor surgical candidacy: Communication problems for plastic surgeons. *Discourse & Communication, 1,* 309–336.

Modaff, J. V., & Modaff, D. P. (2000). Technical notes on audio recording. *Research on Language and Social Interaction, 33,* 101–118.

Moerman, M. (1988). *Talking culture: Ethnography and conversation analysis.* Philadelphia: University of Pennsylvania Press.

Mondada, L. (2007). Multimodal resources for turn-taking: Pointing and the emergence of possible next speakers. *Discourse Studies, 9,* 194–225.

Morgan, D. L. (2002). Focus group interviewing. In J. F. Gubrium & J. A. Holstein (Eds.), *Handbook of interview research: Context and method* (pp. 141–159). Thousand Oaks, CA: Sage.

Mumby, D. K. (2000). Common ground from the critical perspective: Overcoming binary oppositions. In S. R. Corman & M. S. Poole (Eds.), *Perspectives on organization communication: Finding common ground* (pp. 68–86). New York: Guilford Press.

Murphy, R. F. (1990). *The body silent.* New York: Norton.

Myers, G. (2007). Enabling talk: How the facilitator shapes a focus group. *Text & Talk, 27,* 79–105.

Nishizaka, A. (2006). What to learn: The embodied structure of the environment. *Research on Language & Social Interaction, 39,* 119–154.

Ochs, E. (1979). Transcription as theory. In E. Ochs & B. B. Schieffelin (Eds.), *Developmental pragmatics* (pp. 43–72). New York: Academic Press.

Philipsen, G. (1975). Speaking "like a man" in Teamsterville: Culture patterns of role enactment in an urban neighborhood. *Quarterly Journal of Speech, 61,* 13–22.

Philipsen, G. (1976). Places for speaking in Teamsterville. *Quarterly Journal of Speech, 62,* 15–25.

Pike, K. L. (1967). *Language in relation to a unified theory of structure of human behavior* (2nd ed.). The Hague, Netherlands: Mouton.

Platt, J. (2002). The history of the interview. In J. Gubrium & J. Holstein (Eds.), *Handbook of interview research* (pp. 33–54). Thousand Oaks, CA: Sage.

Pomerantz, A., & Mandelbaum, J. (2005). Conversation analytic approaches to the relevance and uses of relationship categories in interaction. In K. Fitch & R. Sanders (Eds.), *Handbook of language and social interaction* (pp. 149–171). Mahwah, NJ: Lawrence Erlbaum.

Potter, J., & Hepburn, A. (2007). Chairing democracy: Psychology, time, and negotiating the institution. In K. Tracy, J. McDaniel, & B. Gronbeck (Eds.), *The prettier doll: Rhetoric, discourse, and ordinary democracy* (pp. 176–202). Tuscaloosa: University of Alabama Press.

Puchta, C., & Potter, J. (2004). *Focus group practice.* London: Sage.

Rapley, M. (2007). *Doing conversation, discourse, and document analysis.* London: Sage.

Rawlins, W. K. (1992). *Friendship matters: Communication, dialectics, and the life course.* Hawthorne, NY: de Gruyter.

Rawlins, W. K. (2000). Teaching as a mode of friendship. *Communication Theory, 10,* 5–26.

Rawlins, W. K. (2007). Living scholarship: A field report. *Communication Methods and Measures, 1*, 55–63.

Riessman, C. K. (2008). *Narrative methods for the human sciences*. Thousand Oaks, CA: Sage.

Roberts, F., & Robinson, J. D. (2004). Inter-observer agreement on "first-stage" conversation analytic transcription. *Human Communication Research, 30*, 376–410.

Robinson, J. D. (2004). The sequential organization of "explicit" apologies in naturally occurring English. *Research on Language and Social Interaction, 37*, 291–330.

Robinson, J. D. (2007). The role of numbers and statistics within conversation analysis. *Communication Methods and Measures, 1*, 65–75.

Rosaldo, R. (1989). *Culture and truth: The remaking of social analysis*. Boston: Beacon Press.

Sacks, H. (1992). *Lectures on conversation* (Vol. 1). Cambridge, MA: Blackwell.

Sahlstein, E., Maguire, K. C., & Timmerman, L. (2009). Contradictions and praxis contextualized by wartime deployment: Wives' perspectives revealed through relational dialectics. *Communication Monographs, 76*, 421–442.

Sanjek, R. (Ed.). (1990). *Fieldnotes: The makings of anthropology*. Ithaca, NY: Cornell University Press.

Scheffer, T. (2006). The microformation of criminal defense: On the lawyer's notes, speech production, and a field of presence. *Research on Language and Social Interaction, 39*, 303–342.

Schegloff, E. (1987). Between macro and micro: Contexts and other connections. In J. C. Alexander, B. Giesen, R. Munch, & N. J. Selzer (Eds.), *The micro-macro link* (pp. 207–234). Berkeley: University of California Press.

Sequeira, D. L. (1993). Personal address as negotiated meaning in an American church community. *Research on Language and Social Interaction, 26*, 259–285.

Shotter, J. (1993). *Conversational realities: Constructing life through language*. Newbury Park, CA: Sage.

Silverman, D. (2001). *Interpreting qualitative data: Methods for analysing talk, text and interaction* (2nd ed.). London: Sage.

Silverman, D. (2004). *Interpreting qualitative data: Methods for analysing talk, text and interaction* (4th ed.). Thousand Oaks, CA: Sage.

Spradley, J. P. (1979). *The ethnographic interview*. New York: Holt, Rinehart and Winston.

Spradley, J. P. (1980). *Participant observation*. New York: Holt, Rinehart and Winston.

Strauss, A., & Corbin, J. (1990). *Basics of qualitative research: Grounded theory procedures and techniques*. Newbury Park, CA: Sage.

Streeck, J. (2009). *Gesturecraft: The manu-facture of meaning*. Amsterdam: John Benjamins.

Streeck, J., & Mehus, S. (2005). Microethnography: The study of practices. In K. Fitch & R. Sanders (Eds.), *Handbook of language and social interaction* (pp. 381–404). Mahwah, NJ: Lawrence Erlbaum.

Suddaby, R. (2006). From the editors: What grounded theory is not. *Academy of Management Journal, 49*, 633–642.

Tannen, D. (Ed.). (1993). *Framing in discourse*. New York: Oxford University Press.

Toller, P. W., & Braithwaite, D. O. (2009). Grieving together and apart: Bereaved parents' contradictions of marital interaction. *Journal of Applied Communication Research, 37*, 257–277.

Tracy, K. (1989). Conversational dilemmas and the naturalistic experiment. In B. Dervin, L. Grossberg, B. J. O'Keefe, & E. Wartella (Eds.), *Rethinking communication: Vol. 2. Paradigm exemplars* (pp. 411–423). Newbury Park, CA: Sage.

Tracy, K. (1991). Discourse. In B. M. Montgomery & S. Duck (Eds.), *Studying interpersonal interaction* (pp. 179–196). New York: Guilford Press.

Tracy, K. (1995). Action-implicative discourse analysis. *Journal of Language and Social Psychology, 14*, 195–215.

Tracy, K. (1997). *Colloquium: Dilemmas of academic discourse*. Norwood, NJ: Ablex.

Tracy, K. (2005). Reconstructing communicative practices: Action-implicative discourse analysis. In K. Fitch & R. Sanders (Eds.), *Handbook of language and social interaction* (pp. 301–319). Mahwah, NJ: Lawrence Erlbaum.

Tracy, K. (2007). The role (or not) for numbers and statistics in qualitative research: An introduction. *Communication Methods and Measures, 1*, 31–35.

Tracy, K. (2010). *Challenges of ordinary democracy: A case study in deliberation and dissent*. University Park: Pennsylvania State University Press.

Tracy, K., & Agne, R. R. (2002). "I just need to ask somebody some questions": Sensitivities in domestic dispute calls. In J. Cottrell (Ed.), *Language in the legal process* (pp. 75–89). Brunel, UK: Palgrave.

Tracy, K., & Baratz, S. (1994). The case for case studies of facework. In S. Ting-Toomey (Ed.), *The challenge of facework* (pp. 287–305). Albany: State University of New York Press.

Tracy, K., & Craig, R. T. (2010). Studying interaction in order to cultivate practice: Action-implicative discourse analysis. In J. Streeck (Ed.), *New adventures in language and interaction* (pp. 145–166). Amsterdam: John Benjamins.

Tracy, K., Martinez-Guillem, S., Robles, J. S., & Casteline, K. E. (in press). Critical discourse analysis and (US) communication scholarship: Recovering old connections, envisioning new ones. In C. Salmon (Ed.), *Communication yearbook 35* (pp. 204–287). Thousand Oaks, CA: Sage.

Tracy, K., McDaniel, J. P., & Gronbeck, B. E. (Eds.). (2007). *The prettier doll: Rhetoric, discourse, and ordinary democracy.* Tuscaloosa: University of Alabama.

Tracy, K., & Mirivel, J. (2009). Discourse analysis: The practice and practical value of taping, transcribing, and analyzing. In L. Frey & K. Cissna (Eds.), *Handbook of applied communication* (pp. 153–177). Mahwah, NJ: Lawrence Erlbaum.

Tracy, K., & Robles, J. (2010). Challenges of interviewers' institutional positionings: Taking account of interview content and the interaction. *Communication Methods and Measures, 4*(3), 177–200.

Tracy, K., & Tracy, S. J. (1998). Rudeness at 911: Reconceptualizing face and face-attack. *Human Communication Research, 25,* 225–251.

Trix, F., & Psenka, C. (2003). Exploring the color of glass: Letters of recommendation for female and male medical faculty. *Discourse & Society, 14,* 191–220.

Van Leeuven, T. (2007). Legitimation in discourse and communication. *Discourse & Communication, 1,* 91–112.

Van Maanen, J. (1988). *Tales of the field: On writing ethnography.* Chicago: University of Chicago Press.

Van Maanen, J. (Ed.). (1995). *Representation in ethnography.* Thousand Oaks, CA: Sage.

Wilkerson, S. (2006). Analysing interaction in focus groups. In P. Drew, G. Raymond, & D. Weinberg (Eds.), *Talk and interaction in social research methods* (pp. 50–62). London: Sage.

Witteborn, S. (2007). The expression of Palestinian identity in narratives about personal experiences: Implications for the study of narratives, identity, and social interaction. *Research on Language and Social Interaction, 40,* 145–170.

Wodak, R. (1996). *Disorders of discourse.* London: Longman.

Wodak, R., & Chilton, P. (2007). *A new agenda in critical discourse analysis* (2nd ed.). Amsterdam: John Benjamins.

Wolf, M. (1992). *A thrice-told tale: Feminism, postmodernism, and ethnographic responsibility.* Stanford, CA: Stanford University Press.

# CHAPTER 4

# Biological and Physiological Perspectives on Interpersonal Communication

*Kory Floyd*

*Tamara D. Afifi*

**M**any communication scholars are—by nurture if not by nature—skeptical of grand pronouncements about human behavior. The historical, cultural, religious, political, economic, and aesthetic influences on communication are extraordinarily rich and diverse. Any claims of a covering law, therefore—applying *without exception* to interpersonal interaction—may easily be seen as irresponsibly naive at best and vaingloriously iconoclastic at worst. Nevertheless, we elect to begin this chapter by advancing just such a pronouncement.

We contend that *all interpersonal communication acts are biological acts.* No interpersonal behavior, whether verbal or nonverbal, is possible without the direct intervention and interaction of multiple anatomical and physiological systems. Production of a spoken word, for instance, requires intricate coordination between the cerebral cortex, the spinal cord, the respiratory system, the laryngeal complex, and the muscles of

the soft palate, tongue, and lips. Decoding of the same spoken word depends on equally intricate collaboration between the tympanic membrane, the ossicles and cochlea, the spinal cord, and the cerebral cortex. Interpersonal behaviors not only make use of anatomical and physiological systems, they, in turn, act on those systems. If the spoken word is one of anger or accusation, its decoding will likely induce muscular tension, temporary immunosuppression, and the elevation of stress hormones such as glucocorticoids in the hearer. If the word instead conveys appreciation or love, it may cause the release of neurotransmitters such as dopamine or peptide hormones such as oxytocin, imparting sensations of reward to the receiver.

Our contention does not deny that many interpersonal acts are also historical, cultural, religious, political, economic, and aesthetic. Those are pervasive influences on communicative behavior, as many other chapters in this volume articulate. None of those influences can accurately be called universal, however. Many interpersonal behaviors vary among cultures, religious traditions, or historical periods, for instance, but some do not. Therefore, although those influences can be powerful, none affects interpersonal behavior without exception. To suggest that any interpersonal act can be accomplished without the influence and intervention of biology, however, is patently untenable, which elevates our observation beyond a probabilistic claim to the status of a covering law. As the celebrated astronomer Carl Sagan noted, extraordinary claims require extraordinary evidence, and we believe that the robustness of the available evidence befits the breadth and grandness of our proposition.

Our argument implies that insight into interpersonal communication is greatly advanced by understanding and exploring its biological and physiological substrates, and that is our chief goal for this chapter. We begin by explaining the theoretical assumptions of a biophysiological approach to studying human communication behavior and by countering its most commonly encountered objections. Next, we review the major physiological systems adjudicated in biophysiological behavioral research, addressing their basic anatomy, their principal outcome measures, and the methods most typically employed to assess them. We then review research identifying the correlational and causal relationships between interpersonal communication behaviors and biophysiological measures. Finally, we articulate the advantages and limitations of the biophysiological method and offer advice for interpersonal communication researchers wishing to incorporate it into their own work.

## Taking a Biophysiological Perspective: Natural Selection and Psychophysiology

Contemporary communication scholars are adept at situating their understanding of interpersonal behaviors in cultural, social, and even psychological

venues. Appreciating interpersonal communication as a biophysiological phenomenon calls for a theoretical and methodological approach that is, at once, more general and more specific than the learning-theory explanations that populate our discourse. First, it entails a conceptualization of humans as a part of—rather than separate from—the natural, physical world. From this perspective, the human species has evolved in accordance with natural selection pressures to maximize its survival and reproductive advantages, just as other animal and plant species have. A biophysiological vantage point does not eschew the reality that humans are the highest order species with respect to cognitive and communicative abilities, but it situates humans among, not apart from, other species.

Second, a biophysiological perspective calls for detailed assessments of how the body reacts to, and interacts with, social behavior. To understand interpersonal communication, we must know more than what people perceive or how they interpret another's behaviors. We must also adjudicate those experiences to which people often do not have conscious access—such as hormonal, neurological, or immunological processes—that transpire in concert with communication behavior.

Understanding the biophysiological approach therefore requires familiarity with the theoretical principles of evolution, natural selection, and evolutionary psychology as well as the methodological principles of psychophysiology. We address both in this chapter, and we identify and discuss common misperceptions that impede understanding of those principles.

## Evolution, Natural Selection, and Evolutionary Psychology

A remarkably simple concept, evolution refers to change over time in the characteristics of living organisms. Researchers generally address two types of evolution. The first, *ontogeny*, indexes change in an individual organism (e.g., a person, animal, or plant) over time. That term is synonymous with *development*. The physical growth and cognitive maturation observed when an infant grows into an adult exemplify ontogeny. The second type of evolution, *phylogeny*, references change in the characteristics of a group or species over time. For instance, changes in the average length of the giraffe's neck or the color of the moth's wings over multiple generations exemplify phylogeny. It is that type of change, specifically, that most researchers refer to when using the word *evolution* (see, e.g., Buss, 1999).

In many cases, it is simple to document that phylogenetic changes occur, albeit slowly, often over millennia. What eluded biologists for centuries, however, was an explanation for how the process of evolution proceeds. Despite references to the *theory of evolution*, there actually is no such theory. Rather, multiple perspectives—more accurately described as *theories of evolution*—detail different aspects of how evolution works. The most prominent such explanation is Darwin's (1859) *theory of evolution by means of natural selection*, a theory that was simultaneously, and independently, proposed by Alfred Russel Wallace (1858). In this section, we detail the four primary principles of Darwin's theory of natural selection (TNS). We then offer several important observations about evolutionary adaptations that clarify and constrain the application of TNS to behavior. Finally, we describe the tenets of evolutionary psychology, a Darwinian perspective on human psychosocial behavior.

## The Process of Natural Selection

According to Darwin's TNS, natural selection proceeds according to four principles: superfecundity, variation, heritability, and selection. *Superfecundity* indicates that, in any given generation, many more members of a species are born than can possibly survive and reproduce. That creates what Darwin referred to as a "struggle for existence." *Variation* acknowledges that all members of a species have different combinations of traits. Humans, for example, vary in any number of traits, including weight, height, hair and eye color, body shape, bone density, and sensory ability. According to the third principle, *heritability*, some of that variation is inherited, or transferred genetically from parents to their biological children.[1] For example, two parents with brown eyes will tend to have brown-eyed offspring, because eye color is heritable.[2]

The fourth principle in Darwin's theory is *selection*, which suggests that heritable characteristics that provide an organism survival and procreation advantages will be passed to future generations with a greater frequency than non-advantageous characteristics. That is, genetic traits that prove advantageous to an organism because they help it meet environmental challenges are *selected for*, or retained from one generation to the next, whereas characteristics that do not prove advantageous are *selected against*, or not retained. For instance, a long neck is advantageous to giraffes because it allows access to food, which is necessary for survival. Giraffes with the longest necks, therefore, have access to more food than other giraffes and are therefore more likely to survive to sexual maturity. Because they are more likely to survive to sexual maturity, they are more likely to reproduce, and because neck length is heritable, succeeding generations of giraffes will have longer average necks than did previous generations. In the nomenclature of TNS, an environmental challenge (access to food) caused a heritable trait (neck length) to be advantageous in terms of survival and procreation and therefore to be selected for.

The above example illustrates *survival of the fittest*, a phrase coined by Herbert Spencer: Those species best adapted to the demands of their environment are the most likely to survive and procreate, and as a result, the advantageous heritable characteristics are passed on to their progeny at a greater frequency than the disadvantageous ones. Importantly, traits that would prove advantageous—or *adaptive*—in one environment may be maladaptive in another. For instance, the physical properties that make many water mammals fast swimmers impede their mobility on land, causing those properties to be adaptive for evading predators in the water but maladaptive for evading predators on land.

## Evolutionary Adaptations

Natural selection pressures give rise to adaptations, which are physical or mental characteristics that enable an organism to survive and/or reproduce within its specific environment. Several clarifications regarding adaptations are relevant to our understanding of an evolutionary approach to social behavior.

*Adaptations deal with proximal and ultimate levels of causation.* The question of why a particular behavior occurs can be addressed in at least two ways. A *proximal cause* is the set of conditions that appears to facilitate the behavior in the specific place, time, and manner in which it occurred. In response to the question "Why did you eat dinner tonight?" one might answer by invoking a proximal cause: "Because I felt hungry." In contrast, an *ultimate cause* is the set of conditions that represents the original or higher order cause of a behavior and often dictates the connection between the behavior and its proximal causes. An ultimate answer to the question "Why did you eat dinner tonight?" might therefore be something like this: "Because I must eat to survive, so I have evolved the sensation of hunger to motivate regular eating." This example illustrates how a specific behavior (eating) can have both a proximal cause (hunger) and an ultimate cause (need for nutrients). Although both are valid causes, the evolutionary approach is concerned primarily with identifying the ultimate causes that provide some clue as to the environmental challenges that adaptations have evolved to meet.

*Adaptations need not operate at a conscious level.* When asked to explain their own behaviors, people commonly identify proximal causes, with little or no regard for ultimate ones. This is often

because they are simply unaware of what the ultimate causes might be or how they might be operating through observable proximal causes (Kenrick & Simpson, 1997). Evolutionary theories acknowledge that many ultimate causes operate outside people's conscious awareness, and they contend that this is not problematic. For instance, people who are asked why they got married will likely say it is because they fell in love with each other, could not imagine their lives without each other, and wanted to spend the rest of their lives together. Few are likely to say that they got married to pass on their genetic materials to future generations. TNS posits that this is, indeed, the ultimate cause of pair bonding, irrespective of people's conscious awareness. That is, the evolutionary approach does not require individuals to be aware of the ultimate causes of their behaviors for those ultimate causes to be influential.

*Adaptations need not be adaptive for modern living.* When considering modern environments, it can be difficult to identify how particular adaptations are beneficial. Why, for instance, do humans have a taste for sweet, fatty, and salty foods? How could such a preference be adaptive when overindulgence in those types of foods can lead to obesity, high cholesterol, heart disease, and even premature death? Evolutionary theories do not attempt to explain human adaptations with reference to modern living. Rather, they focus on physical and psychological traits that would have been adaptive in the societies of our ancestors, a period called the *environment of evolutionary adaptedness.* The process of evolution is usually exceedingly slow, and modern civilization is remarkably young when considered on an evolutionary timescale. Agriculture was invented only about 10,000 years ago, and civilization (let alone modern civilization) is an even more recent phenomenon. Humankind has spent more than 99% of its history in hunter–gatherer societies, and as Morris (2001) pointed out, it is unlikely that natural selection has made any noticeable modifications in the human brain in the short period of time represented by modernity. Consequently, some traits that were adaptive for our hunter–gatherer ancestors—such as the preference for sweets, which motivated adequate consumption of the sugars necessary to fuel muscle activity—may be useless or even maladaptive in modern times.

*Adaptations need not be adaptive for every person or in every instance.* The adaptive nature of a particular trait can be difficult to ascertain if, for whatever reason, that trait fails to produce the adaptive outcomes for a specific individual. The human sex drive is a useful example. That sex is physically pleasurable for most humans can be considered adaptive insofar as it motivates humans to engage in intercourse, which is necessary for reproduction of the species.[3] To be adaptive, a trait must prove advantageous in solving an evolutionary challenge (in this case, the challenge of procreation). That does not require, however, that the trait produce its adaptive result for every person. The sex drive is adaptive because the challenge of reproduction is addressed more effectively *with it* than *without it.* Moreover, an adaptation need not produce its adaptive result in every instance. Relatively speaking, only a fraction of instances of sexual intercourse result in pregnancy. That does not make the sex drive maladaptive, however; in fact, it would be quite maladaptive if intercourse routinely resulted in pregnancy. Adaptations need only provide advantages relative to their alternatives.

*Adaptations operate at the individual level.* Humans participate in a number of important groups—including their families, social networks, and professional networks—that, in various ways, help ensure their survival. Often, therefore, what is beneficial to the group is beneficial to the individual member, and vice versa. In some cases, however, individual priorities conflict with group priorities. Consider, for instance, a communal living situation in which each person's money and possessions are considered to be the collective property of all group members and everyone in the group is provided for equally. In that situation, anything that benefits the group as a whole also benefits each member individually, due to the communal sharing of resources. Suppose, however, that one member of the group were to acquire a large sum of cash of which the other group members were unaware. Would it benefit that member to contribute the money to the group? It would, because any economic benefit to the group would benefit all members. But it would benefit the individual *more* to keep the money and not disclose its existence because that member would then be overbenefited in relation to his or her fellow members.[4] During a grave financial crisis, he or she might even be able to survive while others perished. Adaptations work in much the same way, to provide advantages to the individual (or, more specifically, the individual's *genes*) rather than to any group to which he or she belongs. Therefore, when an individual's priorities conflict with a group's, evolved adaptations tend to privilege the success of the individual over that of the group.

## Evolutionary Psychology

Many of the characteristics that provide an organism survival and reproductive advantages are physical, such as strength, attractiveness, speed, and the ability to camouflage oneself. Other advantageous characteristics, however, are cognitive or psychological, such as intelligence, intuition, empathy, and the ability to deceive. Some social scientists consider cognitive and psychological phenomena such as these to have qualitatively separate origins from physical characteristics. The evolutionary perspective acknowledges, however, that cognitive and psychological characteristics derive wholly from the brain, a physical organ that is no less subject to natural selection pressures than the eyes, skin, muscles, or any other physical feature (Tooby & Cosmides, 1996). The field of *evolutionary psychology* seeks to understand how the mind—and similarly, how mental, cognitive, emotional, and psychological phenomena—has evolved to maximize survival and reproductive motives. To understand evolutionary psychology, it is helpful to attend to several specific principles, which we detail here:

*The mind has evolved to solve recurrent problems.* Evolutionary psychology provides that the human mind—via neurological development—has evolved in response to natural selection pressures to meet the long-term physical and social challenges faced by our hominid ancestors (Tooby & Cosmides, 1992). Through the millennia, our ancestors faced many recurring problems related to survival and reproduction. Recurring problems such as deciding which foods are safe to eat, calculating the distance to a predator, and selecting a healthy mate led to the adaptation of mental activities to solve such problems. Heritable food preferences that aided survival would have been passed on to offspring at higher rates than less advantageous dietary preferences. Tendencies for intelligence and adaptive ways of reasoning would have spread throughout a given population—just as any other adaptive trait—by the consistent solving of problems related to survival and reproduction. Researchers use the term *psychological adaptations* to reference those cognitive solutions to the long-standing problems faced by our ancestors (Tooby & Cosmides, 1992).

*Different problems benefit from different psychological adaptations.* According to evolutionary psychology, the human mind evolved to acquire a host of different psychological adaptations, each generated to meet recurrent reproduction and survival needs. The evolutionary psychology approach asserts that the mind is less similar to a general-purpose problem solver than it is to a Swiss Army knife, equipped with a variety of domain-specific problem-solving tools (see Mithen, 1996). When faced with the problem of choosing a mate, for instance, a preference for facial and bodily symmetry is adaptive because it advertises a mate's reproductive potential (Rhodes,

2006). When seeking food, however, the preference for symmetry yields to a preference for fats and sweets because such dietary choices conferred important nutritional advantages for our hunter–gatherer ancestors (Cosmides & Tooby, 2006).

*Psychological adaptations need not be optimal.* Adaptations need not be optimally crafted by natural selection pressures to solve the problems an organism encounters (Buss, 1999). Human behavior and reasoning are subject to mistakes, blunders, and poorly chosen decision-making strategies. How does an evolutionary paradigm, based on the principle of survival of the fittest, account for such outcomes? For instance, isn't the value humans place on appearance somewhat foolhardy when it comes to pair bonding? After all, attractive mates do not necessarily make optimal mates. The answer is that natural selection pressures do not necessarily produce *optimal* solutions to life's problems. Adaptations evolve not because they necessarily represent the best possible solution to a problem but because they represent a solution that is superior to the available alternatives. Solutions that are even marginally more effective than others will tend to be selected even if they are less than optimal. Consequently, whereas choosing a mate on the basis of appearance may seem only somewhat efficacious, completely ignoring a potential mate's appearance is more detrimental in terms of the probability of successful reproduction.

*The mind's adaptations often work tacitly, not consciously.* To reiterate the observation that adaptations need not operate at a conscious level, evolutionary psychology is primarily concerned with how the mind has evolved to solve problems rather than how people explain their own behavior. As cognitive scientists and neuroscientists have noted, there is a vast difference between our actual cognitive functioning and what we experience consciously when reasoning (Damasio, 1999; Gazzaniga, 1998). Most of the rules and antecedents governing our decision-making processes remain hidden from our conscious experience (Gazzaniga, 1998). When selecting a potential mate, few people are consciously aware of the extent to which facial symmetry, waist-to-hip ratio, and pheromonal incompability influence the sensation of attraction. Most remain similarly unaware of the effects of such characteristics on their subsequent thoughts, feelings, and actions. We certainly become aware of our feelings of attraction for someone else, but we almost always lack insight into the multitude of ways by which such judgments have been made and how they influence our behavior (Nisbett & Wilson, 1977). According to evolutionary psychology, the conscious experience of social life is merely a glimmer of the underlying mental processes at work.

The principles of natural selection and evolutionary psychology provide a rich theoretical basis for expecting social behavior to affect, and be affected by, the natural characteristics of the body. Adjudicating *how* those characteristics provide adaptive benefits also requires a compatible methodological approach—psychophysiology—which we will now describe.

## Psychophysiology

A foundational assumption of psychophysiology is that emotional, cognitive, behavioral, and social events are all reflected in physiological processes. Experiencing the emotion of fear, for instance, is associated with a cadre of hormonal reactions, nervous system activities, and muscular responses that distinguish it from other emotional experiences, such as joy or anger. Falling in love likewise initiates neural and hormonal activities that differ systematically from those associated with falling out of love. Researchers in psychophysiology train their attention on the multiple ways in which social events—including communicative behaviors—interface with the body's physiological systems and influence health, disease, and wellness (Hugdahl, 1995;

for a review, see Loving, Heffner, & Kiecolt-Glaser, 2006).

We begin this section by linking psychophysiology theoretically to natural selection and evolutionary psychology. Next, we draw important methodological distinctions in foci.

### Links to Natural Selection

Psychophysiology is linked theoretically to evolutionary psychology—and, by extension, to Darwin's TNS—via the acknowledgment that the physiological processes characterizing cognitive, emotional, behavioral, and social events can confer specific advantages for viability or fertility. That is, particular behaviors, emotions, or cognitions generated in response to perceived environmental threats may have been retained through selection pressures for the advantages they entail, but it is often *through their corresponding physiological experiences* that those advantages are conferred.

For example, from the vantage point of evolutionary psychology, the emotion of fear is adaptive for viability because it increases surveillance of threatening situations, both for the person experiencing the emotion and for those to whom he or she expresses it. Physiologically, the fear response includes multiple activities that enhance the body's ability to surveil and respond to a threat: Pupil dilation increases visual acuity, with which to assess a potential threat; increased respiration and cardiac output fuel muscular activity for fight or flight; increased cortisol suppresses nonessential systems so that energy is used more efficiently; and increased perspiration mitigates hyperthermia. According to evolutionary psychology, those physiological reactions would confer advantages in the ability to assess and respond to a threat, which would increase the chances of surviving that threat. Thus, specific physiological processes facilitate the adaptiveness of fear, and the connections between those processes and the emotional experience that initiates them are under the purview of psychophysiology.

*Foci in Psychophysiology*

The term *psychophysiology* generally characterizes research programs focusing on how social, psychological, or behavioral events influence aspects of human physiology. The obverse causal model, in which physiological events influence social, psychological, or behavioral outcomes, is investigated by the discipline of *physiological psychology* (see Andreassi, 2000). Psychophysiology comprises several subdisciplines that differ from each other with respect to which specific physiological systems are studied. A simple way to categorize those subdisciplines is to distinguish between "wet" and "dry" psychophysiology. That distinction highlights differences in the primary methods used, with the former type dealing with the chemistries of internal body fluids and the latter type dealing with processes that are measurable externally. As noted here, however, those methods typically correspond to the study of different groups of physiological systems, so although the distinction is based on methodological differences, it captures differences in research foci fairly reliably. Our brief examination of each category will include examples relevant to the study of human communication.

*Wet Psychophysiological Methods.* Methods in wet psychophysiology include those based on immunology, hematology, and endocrinology and require the collection and analysis of body fluids (see Floyd & Roberts, 2009). Immunology investigates the functions of the immune system; for instance, several studies have demonstrated the ways in which being in a distressed marriage or having caretaking responsibilities for an elderly parent impair immunocompetence. Hematology is the study of blood and blood chemistry, and psychophysiologists might focus their research, for instance, on how relational stress influences serum cholesterol or whether various forms of managing conflict have differential effects on blood glucose. Finally, endocrinology is the study of hormones, and

psychophysiologists routinely examine how hormones such as cortisol, testosterone, and oxytocin are influenced by emotions or interpersonal interactions.

*Dry Psychophysiological Methods.* Both wet and dry psychophysiology focus on the study of physiological systems; however, dry psychophysiology comprises less invasive measures, which lend themselves to a focus on different systems from those that are typically studied in wet psychophysiology. In particular, dry psychophysiology tends to focus on neural, muscular, and nervous system activities. For example, neuropsychophysiologists use various methods to "map" the neurological activity induced by particular tasks, such as recalling the memory of time spent with a loved one. Muscular movements might also be studied to document, for instance, facial muscle reactions made in response to emotionally evocative statements from a friend. Nervous system assessments include measures of cardiovascular activity, electrodermal activity, and thermoregulation. Each of those markers might be assessed to illuminate the physiological arousal induced, for instance, by attempting to deceive a coworker or reasoning with an irate customer.

## Fallacies Impeding the Understanding of Evolutionary and Biophysiological Approaches

Despite its extraordinary explanatory ability, however, the evolutionary and biophysiological approach to studying human behavior has not enjoyed widespread popularity in the communication discipline (see Beatty, McCroskey, & Floyd, 2009). One reason for this may be found in the generalized objections to the evolutionary and biophysiological approach, many of which are grounded in misunderstanding. We detail three common fallacies in this section, noting how each impedes the understanding and proper implementation of evolutionary theories and biophysiological methods.

*The Deterministic Fallacy.* On hearing that human behavior might have physiological correlates, many people—scholars and nonscholars alike—conclude that psychophysiology implies that *biology determines behavior.* This conclusion seems to suggest that people have no control over their behaviors and that environmental influences such as parenting, media, culture, and education are benign. Because that idea seems so unacceptable—and so counter to their lived experience—many are led to reject the idea that biology has anything to do with behavior.

In point of fact, the conclusion was false to begin with. To say that biology and communication are related is not to say that biology determines communicative behavior. This straw-man argument is known as the *deterministic fallacy,* and no one working in the field of contemporary psychophysiology espouses it. It is certainly true that our biology gives us the *ability* to communicate. This is evidenced most clearly among people who are biologically constrained in some way, such as those born blind or deaf. People with vision or hearing loss adopt alternative ways of communicating to compensate for the biological abilities that others may take for granted. The ability to communicate does not dictate the *manner* in which we communicate, however, any more than the ability to write dictates the words we use or the ability to sing dictates the songs we enjoy.

*The Immutability Fallacy.* Besides making environmental influences seem irrelevant, the deterministic idea would also seem to suggest that we have no control over our behavior: Our biology makes us do what it will, and we can neither control nor change it. This idea is referred to as the *immutability fallacy,* and it, too, is a misunderstanding of the psychophysiological approach. Claiming that a characteristic has a biological basis in no way implies that it cannot be controlled or changed. Communicative traits such as reticence or argumentativeness appear to be largely genetically heritable (e.g., Beatty, Heisel, Hall, Levine, & La France, 2002; Beatty, Marshall,

& Rudd, 2001), yet with education and experience, people can learn to control their propensities for argument or change their tendencies to shy away from social situations. Much as people may wish to defend their behavior by claiming, "My genes made me do it," the reality is that biological characteristics simply *predispose us* toward certain behaviors. Humans still have control over, and responsibility for, how they act and interact.

*The Naturalistic Fallacy.* A third fallacy supposes that to call something *natural* is tantamount to endorsing it morally. That is, if we claim that a certain predisposition—such as a propensity for aggression—has biological (or natural) roots, we are simultaneously claiming that it is morally acceptable—or, at best, morally innocuous. A notable example is Thornhill and Palmer's (2000) contention that, contrary to prevailing cultural and political notions, the act of rape is not an expression of power and control but is simply an evolved adaptation that works to increase men's chances of reproduction. Many people took immediate offense to Thornhill and Palmer's idea, believing that since the authors were arguing that rape was adaptive, they must therefore believe it to be morally acceptable and excusable. In fact, the authors explicitly made the opposite claim. However, they argued that as long as scientists turn a blind eye toward the sexual drives motivating men to rape, efforts to reduce instances of rape are destined to fail.

This idea, known as the *naturalistic fallacy,* is also a misunderstanding of the biological approach. Identifying the biological roots of a behavior or behavioral tendency confers absolutely no moral legitimacy on it. The misguided logic supporting the naturalistic fallacy is this: Since we have no control over our biological makeup, whatever is biologically based must be *good.* There can be little question that the sex drive is biologically based; however, some sexual acts are morally sanctioned and others are not. There simply is no logical link between the cause of a behavior and its social, cultural, or moral acceptability. When communication researchers work to understand the cause of an interpersonal behavior—even if that cause is biological—it says nothing about their moral acceptance of that behavior.

Having described the bases of evolutionary theories and psychophysiological methods, we can now consider their implications for communicative behavior. First, however, we offer a short preview of the physiological systems, outcomes, and measurement tools that are common in research on the physiological bases of communication.

# Biophysiological Systems, Outcomes, and Measurement

To appreciate the research conducted on the psychophysiology of communication, it is useful to understand the systems, outcome measures, and measurement tools commonly used in that research. In this section, we briefly address those issues for the brain and nervous system and the cardiovascular, hematological, endocrine, and immune systems.

## Brain and Nervous System

The brain is a three-pound mass of tissue and nerves that consumes approximately 20% of the body's energy. With the exception of certain reflex actions, the brain controls every bodily activity and function. Structurally, the brain consists of four major regions: the *cerebrum, diencephalon, brain stem,* and *cerebellum.* The cerebrum, composed of the frontal, parietal, occipital, and temporal lobes, governs learning and memory, language and communication, olfaction, sensory processing, and movement. The diencephalon, also known as the inner brain, contains the thalamus, the epithalamus, and the hypothalamus; the latter is an important component of the *limbic system,* which manages emotional experiences. The brain stem consists of the midbrain, the pons, and the medulla oblongata and plays an important role in consciousness,

alertness, pain sensitivity, and cardiovascular and respiratory control. Finally, the cerebellum coordinates muscle movement, regulates muscle tone, and maintains equilibrium.

The brain, along with the spinal cord and retina, comprises the central nervous system, whose function is to coordinate all bodily activity. The spinal cord serves three primary functions. First, it relays information and instructions from the brain through the spinal nerves to coordinate motor activity. Second, it relays sensory information from the sensory organs (eyes, ears, tongue, nose, and skin) to the brain for processing. Finally, it coordinates certain reflex actions (Maton et al., 1993).

Brain activity is measured through various "mapping" techniques. The least sophisticated is the electroencephalogram (EEG), which records electrical activity in regions of the brain via electrodes attached to the scalp (Abou-Khalil & Musilus, 2006). The EEG assesses neurological activity in the form of waves, including alpha waves (produced during relaxation), beta waves (produced during excitation), and delta waves (produced during sleep) (Nelson, 1980).

Other techniques make use of the brain's chemical activity rather than its electrical activity. Positron emission tomography (PET) measures the photons released when electrons in the brain collide with the positrons produced by the breakdown of molecules in radioactively labeled water injected into the participant (Muehllehner & Karp, 2006). Magnetic resonance imaging (MRI) maps the movement of hydrogen protons after they have been magnetically aligned and then had their alignment disrupted (Elster, 1986). Functional magnetic resonance imaging (fMRI) assesses changes in blood flow to particular regions of the brain by measuring the blood's magnetic properties (Matthews & Jezzard, 2004).

In the social sciences, assessments of nervous system activity have focused on outcomes such as skin temperature, galvanic skin response, and pupil dilation, all of which index general arousal. Skin temperature is measured using thermistor probes attached to the epidermis and is often used as an indirect assessment of changes in emotion or stress (e.g., Rimm-Kaufman & Kagan, 1996). Galvanic skin response is an assessment of changes in perspiration and is used to index arousal and stress (frequently as a component of a polygraph deception detector test) (Vetrugno, Liguori, Cortelli, & Montagna, 2003). Pupil dilation—an indicator of arousal, interest, and affective processing—can react to stimuli in as fast as a fifth of a second and is measured with a pupillometer (Partala & Surakka, 2003).

## Cardiovascular System

The cardiovascular system consists of the heart and the arteries, arterioles, capillaries, veins, and venules, through which blood is circulated. The heart contracts continuously to pump oxygenated blood to the body and deoxygenated blood to the lungs (where it is reoxygenated). The human heart consists of four chambers, including the right atrium, right ventricle, left atrium, and left ventricle. Deoxygenated blood returns from the body to the right atrium, where it is passed into the right ventricle and pushed through the pulmonary artery to the lungs. Newly oxygenated blood returns from the lungs to the left atrium, where it is passed to the left ventricle for circulation via the aorta, the body's largest artery.

Two cardiovascular assessments are common in social science research. The first, *pulse rate*, indexes the number of contractions the heart makes in a specified duration, such as a minute. Beats per minute is a frequently measured outcome. At rest, the heart beats approximately 70 times per minute in healthy men and 80 times per minute in healthy women, although changes in metabolic demand, ambient temperature, arousal, and emotion can alter those rates (see Borg & Linderholm, 2009). Instead of measuring beats per minute, some research assesses the interbeat interval, which is the duration of time between contractions (Lábrová et al., 2005). Pulse

rate is typically measured by the electrocardiograph (ECG), which assesses the heart's electrical activity via electrodes positioned on the epidermis (Wagner, 2001).

The second common assessment of cardiovascular activity is *blood pressure*, which indexes the force exerted against the arterial walls by the circulating blood. Measurements of blood pressure attend to two specific indices. *Systolic blood pressure* is the force of arterial exertion when the heart is contracting (i.e., when the heart is in systole), and *diastolic blood pressure* is the force of arterial exertion when the heart is resting (i.e., in diastole). Both statistics are assessed in millimeters of mercury (mm Hg). Diagnostic measurement is often done manually with a sphygmomanometer, wherein a cuff around the arm inflates to occlude the brachial artery and sounds are assessed to determine the pressures at which blood begins to flow and at which it flows without obstruction as pressure in the cuff is decreased (Bailey & Bauer, 1993). In research practice, automated monitors are often used as a means to minimize human variability in measurement (Johnson & Kerr, 2007).

## Hematological System

Hematology is the branch of medicine dealing with blood, blood chemistry, and blood disorders. Some dimensions of blood chemistry are strongly responsive to changes in an individual's perceptual and socio-emotional experiences. For example, exposure to a stressor—whether cognitive, physical, or relational—initiates the release of the hormone cortisol from the adrenal cortex and the catecholamine epinephrine from the adrenal medulla. Both substances foster the process of *gluconeogenesis*, wherein glucose levels in the blood are elevated to fuel the body's fight-or-flight response (Garrett & Grisham, 2002). Blood glucose is measurable as a static index, which is responsive to the metabolic process and is therefore influenced by events such as eating and exercise. It is also measurable in the form of *glycosylated hemoglobin* (abbreviated as $HbA_{1c}$), an index of the average level of plasma glucose over a period of 10 to 12 weeks. Social scientists have measured both outcomes as correlates of stress and stress-related behaviors (see, e.g., Floyd, Hesse, & Haynes, 2007; Halford, Cuddihy, & Mortimer, 1990).

Also of interest to social scientists are blood lipids, such as cholesterol and triglycerides, and lipoproteins, such as HDL (high-density lipoprotein, also called "good cholesterol") and LDL (low-density lipoprotein, also called "bad cholesterol"). Like glucose, lipids and lipoproteins are elevated in response to stressors (Stoney, Matthews, Mcdonald, & Johnson, 2007). Similarly, they are reactive to incidents of depression and the presence or absence of social and emotional support (Horsten, Wamala, Vingerhoets, & Orth-Gomer, 1997; Ormiston, Wolkowitz, Reus, & Manfredi, 2003).

Whereas several studies in the social sciences have examined glucose or lipids, other hematological outcomes are also influenced by social and emotional processes. Research shows, for instance, that the rate of blood coagulation is related to social support (Wirtz, Redwine, Ehlert, & Von Känel, 2009) and that blood platelet activity is associated with stress (Aschbacher et al., 2007). Some research is also examining C-reactive protein, a diagnostic marker of inflammation, which has been shown to be affected by both stress (Owen, Poulton, Hay, Mohamed-Ali, & Steptoe, 2003) and depression (Raison, Capuron, & Miller, 2006).

Measurement of hematological outcomes requires the collection and analysis of blood samples. Some measures, including lipids and $HbA_{1c}$, can be assessed using small amounts of capillary blood (typically 10–40 microliters, the size of one or two drops). Capillary blood can be drawn using a lancet, a small medical instrument with a double-edged blade or needle that punctures the capillary bed underlying the skin tissue on a fingertip, forearm, or heel. Assessments requiring larger quantities of blood necessitate venipuncture, a procedure by which blood is drawn directly from a vein (typically the median cubital vein on the anterior forearm). Venipuncture can be used to acquire quantities of blood in the range of 10 to 40 milliliters for a single draw, which is necessary when multiple hematological outcomes are to be assessed or when a single assessment requires more blood than can be drawn from a capillary puncture.

## Endocrine System

The endocrine system comprises a network of ductless glands that produce and secrete *hormones*. Hormones are chemicals that bind to cells that contain receptor sites; a given hormone will bind only to cells with receptor sites for that hormone. Once bound, hormones alter the metabolic processes of the receptor cells. Some hormones are composed of amino acid–based molecules, such as proteins, amines, or peptides. Others are steroids, which are derived from cholesterol.

Although the endocrine system contains multiple glands, social science research has tended to focus primarily on the activities of particular glands. These include the pituitary and adrenal glands and the gonads. The pituitary gland, located at the base of the brain, secretes eight different hormones, four of which are of interest to social scientists. *Oxytocin* stimulates uterine contractions and the let-down reflex in expectant mothers; it also appears to play a role in emotional bonding and attachment (Young & Wang, 2004). *Vasopressin* regulates water absorption by the kidneys and also plays a role in pair bonding (Hammock & Young, 2006). *Prolactin* stimulates milk production in lactating women and is responsive to changes in emotion in both women (Turner et al., 2002) and men (Fleming, Corter, Stallings, & Steiner, 2002). Finally, *adrenocorticotropic hormone* (ACTH) initiates the response of the hypothalamic–pituitary–adrenal (HPA) axis to stress (Aguilera, 1994).

The adrenal glands, which sit atop the kidneys, produce *cortisol*, a steroid hormone elevated in response to stress (Burke, Davis, Otte, & Mohr, 2005). The adrenal glands also produce small quantities of *androgens*, the male sex hormones, and *estrogens*, the female sex hormones (Rainey, Carr, Sasano, Suzuki, & Mason, 2002).

Levels of androgens in females and estrogens in males are regulated by the adrenal glands. Most sex hormones, however, are secreted by the gonads. Female gonads, called ovaries, produce estrogens (including *estrone, estriol,* and *estradiol*) as well as *progesterone*. These hormones produce secondary sex characteristics and regulate menstruation; they also appear to contribute to the onset and maintenance of maternal behavior (Rosenblatt, 2008). Male gonads, called testes, produce androgens (including *testosterone*), which produce secondary sex characteristics and regulate sperm production; androgens are also associated with aggression in both men (Dabbs, Frady, Carr, & Besch, 1987) and women (Dabbs, Ruback, Frady, Hopper, & Sgoutas, 1988).

Hormones are measured by taking samples of body fluids and submitting them to hormonal *assays*, which are procedures for quantifying the amount or activity of a biochemical substance. Many hormones of interest to social scientists—including cortisol, testosterone, and estrogens—can be assayed in samples of saliva. Salivary sampling is advantageous because it is simple, is relatively noninvasive, and can be done in situ as well as in a laboratory setting. Sampling saliva also requires minimal safety precautions, as saliva is not considered a biohazardous substance. Other hormones—including oxytocin, vasopressin, and prolactin—require the collection of blood samples. Venipuncture is typically required to collect such samples, and higher levels of safety precautions are necessary for the collection, handling, storage, and analysis of blood as compared with saliva. Androgens, estrogens, oxytocin, and other hormones can also be measured in urine, a procedure that is employed more frequently for diagnostic than for research use (see Floyd & Roberts, 2009).

## Immune System

The body's immune system consists of a coordination of structures and processes that protects against disease by identifying and destroying tumor cells and pathogens, whether viral, bacterial,

fungal, parasitic, or prionic (Klosterman, 2009). The immune system makes use of two separate but interrelated components: the *innate* immune response and the *adaptive* immune response. Innate immunity is a nonspecific response that humans share not only with other mammals but also with lower order organisms such as sponges. The innate immune response incorporates three processes: (1) inflammation, produced by granulocytes and cytokines; (2) antibody response, produced by complement proteins; and (3) cellular response, facilitated by leukocytes and natural killer cells. In contrast, the adaptive immune response is a pathogen-specific response that incorporates B and T lymphocytes and immunoglobulins. Unlike the innate immune response, the adaptive immune response confers immunity, protecting the organism against future threats by the same pathogen.

Immune function is measured almost exclusively through blood assays. No single measure provides a standard, global assessment of immunocompetence (see Farnè, Boni, Corallo, Gnugnoli, & Sacco, 1994). To adjudicate the strength of the immune system, researchers quantify cells, proteins, and/or functions. The most basic approach is to determine the number of one or more specific immune cells. An adequate number of different types of immune cells is necessary for the body to mount an adequate immune defense, so cell counts provide one assessment of that ability. Some studies focus on overall leukocyte counts (Bongartz, Lyncker, & Kossman, 1987). Others focus on specific types of leukocytes, such as eosinophils (Schmid-Ott et al., 2001), or lymphocytes, including T-helper cells (Kawakami et al., 1997) and T-cytotoxic cells (Scanlan, Vitaliano, Ochs, Savage, & Borson, 1998). Still others enumerate natural killer cells (Brosschot et al., 1991).

A second approach to assess immunocompetence is to quantify the production of proteins, including antibodies and cytokines. Among antibodies, three that are commonly measured are immunoglobulin A (Deinzer & Schüller, 1998), immunoglobulin G (Nakata et al., 2000), and immunoglobulin M (Glaser, Mehl, Penn,

Speicher, & Kiecolt-Glaser, 1986). Among cytokines, the most commonly measured in social science research are interleukins, including interleukin-1β (Pugh et al., 1999), interleukin-2 (Rapaport & Stein, 1994), and interleukin-6 (Goebel, Mills, Irwin, & Ziegler, 2000). In most cases, higher levels of antibody or cytokine denote a stronger immune function. Two exceptions are worth noting, however. Proinflammatory cytokines—such as interleukin-1, interleukin-6, and tumor necrosis factor alpha (TNF-α)—are elevated in response to systemic inflammation and are therefore indicative of poorer immune function (Ershler & Keller, 2000). Similarly, antibodies against latent viruses—such as Epstein-Barr virus or herpes simplex virus—are elevated in response to viral replication, which can indicate a breakdown in cellular immune response (Jenkins & Baum, 1995).

A final strategy for measuring immunocompetence is to use functional assays that measure the ability of cells to perform specific activities. Those can include the ability of natural killer cells to kill invaders (Dopp, Miller, Myers, & Fahey, 2000) or the proliferation of T lymphocytes in response to mitogens, such as concanavalin A (Pennebaker, Kiecolt-Glaser, & Glaser, 1988), phytohemagglutinin (Stowell, Kiecolt-Glaser, & Glaser, 2001), and pokeweed mitogen (Dobbin, Harth, McCain, Martin, & Cousin, 1991). In all instances, higher outcomes denote greater immunocompetence.

Having reviewed evolutionary theories, psychophysiology, and the systems, outcomes, and measures common in psychophysiological research, we turn our attention next to the broad and growing research literature on the physiological bases of interpersonal communication.

## Applications to Interpersonal Communication

Thus far, we have reviewed some of the major concepts, biological systems, and theoretical approaches used in biophysiological social science. Even though the importance of biology was emphasized years ago by interpersonal communication scholars such as Beatty and McCroskey (Beatty, McCroskey, & Heisel, 1998; McCroskey, 1997), Cappella (e.g., 1991, 1996), and others (e.g., Andersen, Garrison, & Andersen, 1979; Horvath, 1995), communication science lags behind many other social science disciplines (including psychology, sociology, family studies, and biobehavioral health) in terms of recognizing and implementing a biological approach. Several communication scholars have contended for quite some time that a focus on biology is the "wave of the future." More than 15 years ago, Knapp, Miller, and Fudge (1994) argued in the *Handbook of Interpersonal Communication* that paying greater attention to biological correlates and influences was an important direction for interpersonal communication research to take. As evidenced by several recent top-four interpersonal communication panels at the National Communication Association or the International Communication Association, Knapp et al.'s vision for interpersonal research is finally being realized. Why has it taken so long for interpersonal communication scholars to begin to recognize the importance of biology? We can identify at least eight reasons why interpersonal communication scholars have only recently incorporated biology into their empirical studies: (1) the relative newness and smallness of the communication discipline; (2) lack of knowledge about how to conduct biosocial research; (3) the belief that researchers must be biologists or neuroscientists to do physiological research; (4) lack of understanding about the importance of biology for human behavior; (5) the logical barriers of cost, technology, and time; (6) the fear that validating the role of biology in human behavior somehow diminishes the study of behavior; (7) the concern on the part of institutional review boards and funding agencies that the communication discipline is unequipped to do such research; and (8) a backlash to the misperceived deterministic approach in biosocial research.

Regardless of just how much of our communication is genuinely genetically directed, researchers have come a long way from using deterministic approaches to study biosocial processes. As Booth, Carver, and Granger (2000) noted, until relatively recently, there were significant gaps in the understanding of the connections between physiological processes and human behavior. As those authors suggested, "The nature of many physiological processes was largely unknown, and the technology necessary to operationalize physiological variables was in its infancy" (p. 1018). Many researchers who conducted physiological research turned to rather simplistic, reductionistic explanations to understand the influence of biology on behavior (Booth et al., 2000). However, the introduction of noninvasive and relatively inexpensive measures of biological markers and the breaking of interdisciplinary boundaries has dramatically increased our knowledge of physiology in human behavior (Booth et al., 2000; Gordis, Granger, Susman, & Trickett, 2006; Hellhammer, Wust, & Kudielka, 2009). Dynamic models that recognize the fluid interplay among context, behavior, and biological processes have replaced the deterministic models. Gottlieb (1991) contends that biology lays the foundation for individuals' ability to adapt to environmental challenges. However, environmental challenges simultaneously induce behavioral change that, in turn, affects biological responses such as hormone secretion and gene manifestation (Booth et al., 2000; Gottlieb, 1991). Biological processes that predict a particular behavioral response and behaviors that predict changes in biological processes may be stimulated or attenuated by environmental challenges. Consequently, interpersonal communication and the environment that surrounds those communicative behaviors play a considerable role in influencing, and being influenced by, physiological processes.

In this section, we highlight some of the physiological research in interpersonal communication while simultaneously drawing from research in other disciplines to inform our research. More specifically, we will examine biosocial research on speech anxiety and "trait-based"

communication skills, attraction, affection, touch and social support, aggression and violence, emotions, and intrapersonal communication processes such as planning and imagined interactions.

## Speech Anxiety and "Trait-Based" Communication Skills

Most of the early theorizing about biology in communication science had its roots in "trait-like" communication patterns or communication behaviors that could be considered "in-born." For example, Cappella (1991) made a convincing argument for the biological origins of automated interaction patterns, examining the physiological and neurological mechanisms that underlie emotional responsiveness in infants and neonates. Significant discussion over the role of biology in communication research surfaced in response to Beatty and McCroskey's (1997) theorizing about communibiology, or the integration of biology into communication research. Debates arose (see, e.g., Condit, 2000) over McCroskey and Beatty's arguments that many, if not most, communicative behaviors are trait driven (McCroskey, 1997). In their article in *Communication Monographs*, Beatty et al. (1998) cited evidence leading to the conclusion that roughly 80% of the variation in the "Big Three" personality dimensions (hostility/aggression, cooperativeness/sociability, and fearful avoidance) is heritable and that the remaining 20% of variation is accounted for by environmental influences. At the time, many readers were amazed at McCroskey's (1997) declaration that his plethora of research on the social conditioning of communication apprehension was not as socially engrained as he thought.

In one of the first empirical studies focusing on biology in interpersonal communication, Horvath (1995) emphasized the significant role of biology and the genetic links of communicator style through her research with twins. Horvath surveyed 62 pairs of identical (MZ) twins and 42 pairs of fraternal (DZ) twins to determine the association between temperament, which has been shown to have a genetic influence, and communicator style, which is closely related to temperament. She found that communicator style and temperament were correlated and that nearly all of the correlations for the temperament and communicator style variables were higher for identical twins than for fraternal twins, supporting the genetic link between temperament and communicator style. Beatty et al. (2002) also conducted a meta-analysis of interpersonal communication behaviors in their research on twins. They found that the traits of interpersonal affiliation, aggressiveness, and social anxiety were all between 58% and 70% heritable, meaning that 58% to 70% of the variance in those traits could be explained by genetic variation among individuals. As their analyses indicate, a significant amount of variance in traitlike communication behaviors can be attributed to genetics, even though there is considerable disagreement about the validity of twins research and the weight of the findings (see also Beatty & McCroskey, 2000; Condit, 2000). Interestingly, studies of twins have also shown that genes and the environment work together to influence people's behavior. Research has demonstrated, for example, that genetic tendencies for maladaptive communicative behaviors are stronger in chaotic families than in stable families (e.g., Price & Jaffee, 2008). Indeed, such studies have been invaluable for illustrating the interdependent nature of genes and the environment.

Much of the initial interest in a biological approach to communication research began with the research on communication apprehension or speech anxiety as a traitlike communication behavior. Beatty et al. (1998) argue that people with high communication apprehension have an overreactive behavioral inhibition system, whereas people with low communication apprehension have an underactive inhibition system. Consequently, people who have high communication apprehension avoid public speaking situations because they become too physiologically aroused. Beatty and colleagues contend that examining the biological influences underlying communication apprehension is essential for understanding its negative impact on students and for helping students overcome it (Beatty et al., 1998; Beatty & McCroskey, 2000). Communication scholars have tested Beatty and McCroskey's (2000) assumptions. For instance, Roberts, Sawyer, and Behnke (2004) examined the self-reported speech anxiety and the corresponding cortisol patterns of 31 college students enrolled in a basic speech communication course. Baseline cortisol levels were assessed one week before the students were to give a 5-minute speech in the class. Four saliva samples were taken after the speech to determine cortisol response and recovery patterns. The results showed a two- to threefold increase in cortisol after the speech, followed by a natural decline by 40 minutes. The authors also found positive associations between self-reported speech anxiety at various time points and cortisol levels. What was missing from this study, however, was a control group of students who did not give a speech, to account for the fact that it was in fact the speech that was stress inducing. However, research in other disciplines has also confirmed that people who have high communication apprehension are more likely than people with less apprehension to experience higher levels of cortisol as a result of public speaking (e.g., Blood, Blood, Frederick, Wertz, & Simpson, 1997). In fact, giving a speech in front of a set of judges has become a common laboratory stress-inducing task.

In an interesting next step in this line of research, Priem and Solomon (2009) examined whether comforting messages can minimize the physiological stress created by communication apprehension. These authors examined the state-based communication anxiety of 43 undergraduate students enrolled in introductory public speaking courses. Saliva samples and presurveys were taken two days before their scheduled speeches. The participants were then randomly assigned to one of three conditions before their speeches: distraction, reappraisal, and control. The distraction condition entailed the participants discussing anything they could that was unrelated to the speech itself with the researcher. The reappraisal condition consisted of an 8-minute positive reappraisal of the upcoming speech with the researcher and the researcher providing comforting messages. Finally, the participants in the control condition did not engage in any communication with the researcher besides completing the presurvey. Four additional saliva samples were taken from the participants before they gave their speeches, and one saliva sample was taken 5 minutes after the in-class speech. The results revealed that the students in the distraction condition had significantly lower cortisol levels prior to and during the speech than the students in the control condition. There were no significant effects for the comforting condition. However, as the authors note, it often takes cortisol 20 minutes to reach its zenith after the onset of stress and another 20 minutes to recover. As a result, the saliva samples taken 5 minutes after the speech might not have fully captured the participants' stress responses and recoveries. Nevertheless, there appear to be ways in which people can be socialized to calm their communication anxiety and subsequently control their physiological responses, even if they involve distracting cues. Today, most scholars would agree that genetics play an important role in shaping people's communicative tendencies. Some communication processes that are more traitlike probably have stronger genetic links than other communication processes. However, genes interact with one's environment and social relationships to influence behavior and the corresponding outcomes.

## Affection, Touch, and Social Support

The influence of physiological research within the area of interpersonal communication is probably the most visible in Floyd and colleagues' work on affection (see Floyd, 2006a). Floyd's work shows that the amount of affection people receive and give to others serves an important physiological stress reduction function (e.g., Floyd et al., 2007b; Floyd & Riforgiate, 2008).

Research, in general, has shown that social skills such as affection, warmth, responsiveness, and social support are important moderators of stress reaction in the HPA axis and the sympathetic nervous system (SNS) (e.g., Pendry & Adam, 2007), whereas conflict and aggression can result in dysregulated HPA and SNS systems (i.e., abnormally high or low HPA and SNS responses) (e.g., Davies, Sturge-Apple, Cicchetti, & Cummings, 2007; Granger et al., 1998).

Floyd's work (2002, 2006b) has tested one of the fundamental assumptions of affection exchange theory, that expressing and receiving affection activate neuroendocrine responses that can mobilize the body to fight against stress, as well as protecting the body from the negative effects of stress. These effects have also been shown to operate separately for expressed and received affection (Floyd et al., 2005). For example, Floyd (2006c) examined the diurnal change in cortisol in 20 healthy individuals with four saliva samples taken over the course of a normal workday. He found that the amount of affection the participants expressed to others throughout the day was positively associated with waking cortisol levels, aggregate levels, and the amount of morning-to-evening decrease in cortisol. This association remained significant after controlling for the amount of affection received by others. These cortisol patterns are important because cortisol at waking hours typically energizes the body to combat stress throughout the day and a greater reduction in cortisol as the day progresses is indicative of the body's ability to adapt to the stress, or a healthy regulation of the HPA axis (Cannon, 1914; Hellhammer et al., 2009). Later studies indicated that higher amounts of trait-based expressed affection predict lower $HbA_{1c}$ (Floyd, Hesse, et al., 2007), higher toxicity of natural killer cells (Floyd, Pauley, Hesse, Veksler, et al., 2010), higher oxytocin reactivity to stressors (Floyd, Pauley, & Hesse, 2010), and also higher numbers of antibodies to latent Epstein-Barr virus (Floyd, Boren, Veksler, & Hesse, 2010).

In a series of other experiments, Floyd has shown that expressed affection has a moderating effect on physiological stress. Floyd et al. (2007a) asked participants to report on the amount of affectionate communication in their most affectionate significant relationship. The participants then underwent a series of traditional stress tests. Floyd and colleagues discovered that a high amount of verbal affection and supportive affection in a relationship predicted lower resting heart rates and lower cortisol responses to the acute stressors. The moderating effect of affection has even been shown to occur if it is expressed in writing. Floyd et al. (2007b) found that when exposed to acute-stress tests, where cortisol levels typically become elevated, participants who expressed affection in writing to a loved one were able to downregulate or recover from the stress task faster than those in control groups, who simply thought about a loved one or sat quietly. In another study by Floyd, Mikkelson, Hesse, and Pauley (2007), participants were assigned to either an experimental group where they were asked to write about their affection for significant people in their lives for 20 minutes on three separate days or a control group where they were asked to write about innocuous topics. Total cholesterol was assessed at the beginning and at the end of the trial. The researchers found that the participants who wrote about their affection had significant declines in their total cholesterol levels compared with the control group, which experienced an increase or no change at all in cholesterol levels.

Floyd's research (e.g., Floyd et al., 2009; Floyd & Riforgiate, 2008) has also shown that receiving affection may play an even more important role in buffering the physiological effects of stress than expressing affection. Floyd and Riforgiate (2008) examined the impact of expressed and received affection in marriage. Twenty healthy adults and their spouses took four saliva samples over the course of a typical workday to assess cortisol waking levels, change in cortisol levels, and the cortisol:dehydroepiandrosterone sulfate (DHEA-s) ratio. Floyd and Riforgiate found that the amount of affection the participants received from their spouses was a much stronger predictor

of healthy hormone responses than the amount of affection they communicated to their spouses. More specifically, the researchers found that the amount of verbal, nonverbal, and supportive affection the participants received from their spouses predicted higher cortisol awakening responses, lower evening cortisol levels, a healthy diurnal change, and a lower cortisol:DHEA-s ratio, even when controlling for the amount of expressed affection to their spouses. Floyd et al. (2009) also conducted a study on kissing in marriage. Fifty-two healthy adults in married or cohabitating relationships were randomly assigned either to an experimental group where they were asked to increase the frequency of romantic kissing with their partner or to a control group where they were not told to do so over a six-week trial. The participants who engaged in more kissing with their romantic partner reported better perceived stress, relationship satisfaction, and lower serum cholesterol.

Other research has also demonstrated that touch has a positive effect on multiple stress response systems. For example, Holt-Lunstad, Birmingham, and Light (2008) found that married couples who were taught how to engage in touch therapy with their spouses in an intervention experienced enhanced oxytocin levels and lower levels of salivary alpha-amylase (sAA; a marker of arousal) and systolic blood pressure than married couples in the control group. Similarly, Ditzen et al. (2009) found that women who received affectionate touching from their spouse or cohabitating partner before being exposed to a laboratory-induced stressor exhibited significantly lower cortisol and heart rate responses to the stress test. A significant amount of research has also shown the importance of touch for shaping not only one's social bonds but also one's biological development (Hertenstein, 2002; Kuhn & Schanberg, 1998). Some of the most compelling research findings come from work on premature infants showing how tactile stimulation can dramatically improve their physical development (Kuhn & Schanberg, 1998). Touch allows human beings to develop and maintain significant social attachments as well as thrive mentally and physically.

While touch often serves a stress reduction function, its function depends on the type of touch and the context. Touch has been shown to reduce stress and help manage pain (e.g., Fishman, Turkheimer, & DeGood, 1995). For instance, Fishman et al. (1995) found that physical touch in a medical health care setting was associated with a decrease in blood pressure and pain. They also discovered, however, that the participants' responses to touch were not stable over time and that their responses were more "statelike" than traitlike. Research has found that how people respond physiologically to touch depends on the type of person touching them, the sex of the sender and the receiver, and the context in which it occurs (e.g., Drescher, Gantt, & Whitehead, 1980; Nilsen & Vrana, 1998). Being touched by a stranger may elicit feelings of discomfort and anxiety (see Edens, Larkin, & Abel, 1992). For example, Nilsen and Vrana (1998) exposed participants to professional touch (where they were touched on the wrist to have their pulse taken), social touch (an unexplained touch to the same area of the participants' wrists), and a no-touch condition. In the professional and no-touch conditions, the participants experienced decreases in heart rate and blood pressure, but in the social condition, initial increases in heart rate and blood pressure resulted. Participants experienced a greater cardiovascular decrease when a female was the one doing the touch in a professional setting. The greatest cardiovascular increases were observed in women who were touched by men in the social condition.

Although a significant amount of research has examined the effect of affection and touch on various physiological response systems, researchers have also begun to examine more fully the connection between affection/touch and neurology, or brain activity. For example, researchers have explored the impact of childhood abuse and neglect on children's brain development and functioning. Research has shown that children who are physically or sexually abused or neglected have a smaller corpus callosum (the brain tissue connecting the right and left hemispheres of the brain) (e.g., Teicher et al., 2004), irregular electrophysiological brain activity, and smaller brain hemispheres and hippocampuses (e.g., Ito et al., 1993; Stein, 1997) compared with children who are not abused or neglected. In the field of communication, Lewis (2009) tested the idea that people ($n = 16$) who are high on trait affection have greater electrical activity in the left prefrontal cortex than in the right prefrontal cortex, which was assessed through asymmetrical baseline EEG recordings. His results tended to confirm his hypothesis. In fact, the correlation between trait affection and asymmetry in the frontal cortex EEG was -.81. When his sample was dichotomized into right-brain-dominant and left-brain-dominant individuals, the correlation was much stronger for right-brain-dominant participants ($r = .76$) than for left-brain-dominant participants ($r = .48$). As Lewis notes, "The findings support the notion that individual differences in frontal EEG asymmetry have consequences for affectionate communication, as those differences emerged as a good estimate of trait affection" (p. 12).

Research has shown similar buffering effects for related concepts such as social support, communication competence, and responsiveness. Afifi, Granger, Denes, Joseph, and Aldeis (2010b) examined *patterns or groupings* of adolescents' HPA axis response (measured through cortisol) and SNS response (measured through sAA) as a function of their parents' communication skills. The sample consisted of 118 parent–adolescent dyads from divorced ($n = 61$) and nondivorced families ($n = 57$). The dyads were asked to talk about something stressful related to the parents' relationship for up to 20 minutes in a laboratory setting. Cortisol and sAA were assessed at four points: (1) immediately before the discussion after a 7-minute small-talk period, (2) immediately after the discussion, (3) 20 minutes postdiscussion, and (4) 40 minutes postdiscussion. The results revealed that the adolescents' perception of their parents' communication skills, regardless of the parents' perception of their own skills, predicted the likelihood that adolescents would overreact, show no reaction, or downregulate in response to such a discussion—but only for sAA. More specifically, adolescents who downregulated or showed no reaction to the discussion task were twice more likely than children who overreacted to have parents who they thought were socially supportive. Likewise, adolescents who did not react were two-and-a-half times more likely than adolescents who overreacted to have parents who they believed were communicatively competent. Adolescents who were considered "overreactors" also had more negative health indices, somewhat lower psychological well-being, and poorer quality relationships with their parents. Afifi, Granger, Denes, et al.'s research provides additional evidence of the important role of communication skills in personal and relational health.

Parents' communication skills, however, may also vary as a function of the environment or context. For example, in a different manuscript using the same data set, Afifi, Granger, Joseph, Aldeis, and Denes (2010) found that regardless of the parents' marital status, the adolescents and young adults whose parents were communicatively skilled (i.e., they did not feel caught up in their parents' conflict, the parents had greater social support and communication competence) were able to downregulate quickly after the discussion task. In contrast, both children whose parents were divorced and those whose parents were still married showed elevated sAA reactions to the conversation when their parents lacked these skills. Interestingly, children whose parents were still married but lacked these communication skills had a peak in their sAA response immediately after the conversation, had an erratic response pattern, and were typically unable to recover from the conversation. In contrast, children whose divorced parents lacked these communication skills showed a delayed peak response in sAA 20 minutes after the conversation and were able to recover from it. This study may echo

previous research that has found that children whose parents stay in a conflicted marriage and lack communication skills may have poorer psychological well-being than children of divorced parents because they are unable to escape from their parents' conflict (Amato & Sobolewski, 2001; Booth & Amato, 2001). Children of divorced parents may also be accustomed to conversations of the kind that took place in this study, allowing them to recover from the conversation at a more rapid pace than children from first-marriage families.

Research by Priem and Solomon (2010a) has also found that specific features of supportive messages have a similar moderating effect on physiological stress. Priem and Solomon examined how message features of supportive communication were associated with couples' ($N = 89$) physiological stress responses after receiving negative performance feedback. They discovered that person-centered messages (see Burleson, 2009) that "validate, legitimize, and encourage exploration of a distressed individual's feelings" can enhance stress recovery (Priem & Solomon, 2010a, p. 24). More sophisticated, complex messages that legitimize another person's perspective and explore that person's thoughts in an in-depth manner may have a calming effect during a stressful interaction. Priem, McLaren, and Solomon (2010) also examined couples' ($N = 91$) relational communication during hurtful exchanges. Participants engaged in two 5-minute conversations about core traits and values. In the experimental group, the participants' partners were trained as confederates and were asked to be disconfirming about the participants' traits and values. The results showed that hurtful messages that were perceived as more sincere resulted in greater physiological arousal than hurtful messages that were perceived as less sincere. Positive affect or immediacy during hurtful exchanges also helped buffer the impact of the hurt on stress. Therefore, hurtful messages seem to have the most potent effect when they are believed to be communicated with intent, and immediacy can "soften" the impact of some of the hurt.

The degree to which people are able to effectively communicate their thoughts, feelings, and affect can also have an impact on their biological stress response systems. People who are less expressive tend to experience more SNS reactivity than people who are more expressive (Buck, 1977; Buck, Miller, & Caul, 1974). Experiments have shown that people who suppress their emotions experience increased cardiovascular activity, skin conductance, and blood pressure (Buck, 1977; Buck et al., 1974, Butler et al., 2003; Richards & Gross, 1999). In fact, Butler et al. (2003) found that when people suppressed their emotions, it increased the blood pressure of both the regulators and their romantic partner. Consequently, people who are more communicatively skilled in the sense that they are able to express their emotions may be less stressed and anxious, and their partners may be less stressed and anxious as a result, than people who lack these skills.

On the whole, research has demonstrated that communication competencies, such as social support, responsiveness, and expressiveness, buffer the effect of stress on people's health (see Rosal, King, Yunsheng, & Reed, 2004). For example, Heffner, Kiecolt-Glaser, Loving, Glaser, and Malarkey (2004) examined the associations between social support satisfaction, affect, cortisol, and blood pressure in response to conflict in samples of newlyweds and older couples who had been married for an average of 42 years. They found that among the newlywed wives, when social support satisfaction from their husbands was greater, there was less negative affect and a greater ability to downregulate after a conflict. The newlyweds also had lower blood pressure after conflict when there were high levels of spousal support satisfaction. Interestingly, the older husbands, but not the older wives, experienced an increase in cortisol when their wives' social support satisfaction was lower. As Roy, Steptoe, and Kirschbaum (1998) also found in their study of 90 male firefighters, social support may provide greater cardiovascular reactivity or mobilize the body's stress response system to combat stress. However, when a stressful event

occurs, social support allows for faster recovery from the stress and can prevent the body from becoming overwhelmed by the stress (Roy et al., 1998). Research has even shown that social support in marriage can heal wounds faster, whereas exposure to chronic, daily conflict can slow healing rates by 40% (Kiecolt-Glaser et al., 2009).

There are numerous situations, however, where communication skills such as social support can increase physiological stress responses instead of ameliorate them. In particular, talking too much about one's stress may result in stress contagion effects, whereby an individual's stress spills over onto another person (Afifi, McManus, Hutchinson, & Baker, 2007). Research on social support has shown that partners' stress and coping mutually influence each other (e.g., Coyne & Smith, 1991). More specifically, verbally ruminating about stress or "extensively discussing and revisiting problems, speculating about problems, and focusing on negative feelings" (Rose, 2002, p. 1830) has been associated with depressive symptoms, anxiety, and heightened physiological responses (Afifi et al., 2007; Byrd-Craven, Geary, Rose, & Ponzi, 2008; Rose, Carlson, & Waller, 2007). Byrd-Craven, Granger, and Auer (2010) examined verbal rumination during problem-solving discussions among 88 female friends. Half of the dyads were asked to focus on a problem related to one of them or their friendship, and the other half of the sample were given a neutral task. The friends in the problem-solving group were more likely to engage in corumination. Corumination was associated with increased cortisol levels after the problem-solving task. Negative emotions or affect predicted increases in cortisol and sAA posttask. The authors argue that future research should investigate the role of dual-activation models or situations where sAA and cortisol have an additive effect and can adversely affect individuals' health.

An interesting avenue for future research would be to explore the role of culture and social support and how access to outside social support networks affects individuals' physiological stress response systems. These outside social support networks include the extended family (e.g., aunts, uncles, mother, father, grandparents, cousins), friends, community members, programs in the community, and churches. While extended social support networks are important for Caucasian partners and families, they are crucial to people in more collectivistic cultures, such as Latin Americans and African Americans. For example, Latin Americans place heavy emphasis on the family, wherein their everyday lives revolve around maintaining family relationships, doing things together as a group, and providing social support to the extended family (Corona, Lefkowitz, Sigman, & Romo, 2005). Minority groups, such as Latin and African American families, often suffer from dysregulated HPA and SNS systems compared with Caucasian families (Desantis et al., 2007). However, extended social support networks, if they are effective, may help buffer some of that stress. Future research should examine within-culture variance in social support and the extent to which social support within these cultural groups buffers stress.

## Conflict, Aggression, and Violence

While social support tends to buffer the effects of stress on people's physiological response systems and health, conflict and violence tend to result in dysregulated physiological stress responses and subsequent health problems. A number of studies have examined the links between conflict, aggression, and/or violence and physiological stress responses. On the surface, the results of research on the association between conflict and physiological stress responses seem somewhat contradictory, with some research indicating that conflict is associated with increased physiological responses (e.g., cortisol, sAA, and testosterone levels) (e.g., Pendry & Adam, 2007) and other research indicating that conflict is associated with reduced physiological responses (Luecken, Kraft, & Hagan, 2009). However, these findings often depend on how the hormone or enzyme was measured (e.g., diurnally, basal levels, or with

an acute task), the extremity of the behavior (e.g., mild conflict or violence), and whether it involves over- or underactivation of the stress response systems.

The activation of the HPA and SNS systems in response to stress is expected and normal, but health and behavioral problems can result if these systems are over- or underactivated in some way (Fortunato, Granger, Blair, & Greenberg, 2009; McEwen, 1998). The notion of "allostatic load" becomes particularly relevant with the research on conflict, aggression, and violence. Allostasis refers to the body's ability to return to a state of homeostasis or stability after physiological arousal (McEwen, 1998). When individuals endure prolonged activation of their physiological stress response systems, it produces a great deal of burden on the body, or allostatic load, reducing the body's ability to effectively fight against the stress (McEwen, 1998). According to McEwen (1998), there are four types of HPA reactivity associated with allostatic load. First, chronic hyperactivity occurs when people are exposed to multiple chronic stressors over time. Second, given that the HPA system responds to novel, challenging, and stressful situations (Wust, Federenko, van Rossum, Koper, & Hellhammer, 2005), people become less aroused by these situations over time when exposed to them repeatedly. However, some individuals may experience hyperarousal when their bodies are unable to adapt or adjust to similar, repeated stressors. Third, inability to recover from stress or dysregulated stress recovery may result when people remain aroused for longer than expected. In other words, it might take an individual longer than average to downregulate after a stressful experience. Finally, hyporeactivity, or underarousal, may occur when people are unable to become aroused at all or when the arousal response is muted. This last response may also occur when people are exposed to chronic stress, because their body has become habituated to it and no longer becomes aroused by the stressful stimuli.

Different types of conflict can have different effects on the stress response systems. Some research suggests ready habituation of the response to acute stress on repeated presentation of the stressor (see Stetler & Miller, 2005). Stress may also affect the diurnal variation of cortisol: Acute or more moderate stress may serve to exacerbate the diurnal variability of cortisol, whereas more severe and chronic stress, such as exposure to chronic conflict, violence, or aggression, may lead to a blunting of the diurnal variability and cortisol awakening response (Stetler & Miller, 2005). Chronically high and chronically low cortisol levels have been associated with psychological problems such as anxiety and depression, whereas moderate levels are more indicative of adaptive functioning (Gordis et al., 2006).

Although the research is still rather contradictory, there is mounting evidence that chronic exposure to conflict, aggression, and violence results in hyporeactivity and acute exposure to conflict is associated with hyperreactivity (Davies et al., 2007; Granger et al., 1998). Research suggests that exposure to chronic conflict can affect people's HPA and SNS systems, which can have a debilitating effect on their physical and mental health (Davies et al., 2007). For instance, Davies et al. (2007) conducted a longitudinal study with 178 kindergarten children and their continuously married parents. They discovered that the HPA system mediated the association between chronic interparental conflict and children's externalizing problems (e.g., aggression). Chronic conflict between the parents was associated with children's lower basal cortisol levels. These cortisol levels, in turn, predicted greater externalizing problems in the children over a two-year period. Davies et al.'s findings confirm McEwen's (1998) notion of hypocortisolism, that when the body is exposed to chronic stress, it may become habituated to it over time. Other research, however, has shown that conflict is associated with hyperreactivity. For example, Pendry and Adam (2007) examined adolescents' and kindergarten-age children's cortisol levels throughout the day in response to their parents' marital functioning. Poor marital functioning (i.e., low marital satisfaction and higher levels of interparental conflict) was

associated with the children's (of both ages) higher average daily levels and waking levels of cortisol. Better marital functioning, as well as the mother's warmth and involvement, however, was associated with a significant lowering of bedtime cortisol levels and steeper diurnal slopes for kindergarten children compared with adolescents. In other words, children whose parents were more supportive and less conflicted and whose mothers were responsive were able to downregulate or recover from stress at a faster pace throughout the day.

One of the reasons why biosocial research such as this is important is that exposure to a chronic stressor, such as chronic conflict, weakens the body's ability to fight against it, increasing susceptibility to disease (Miller, Chen, & Zhou, 2007). For example, considerable attention has been given to discovering the biological mechanisms through which chronic stress "gets under the skin" to negatively affect health and create health disparities among different ethnic groups (Miller et al., 2007). Researchers believe that because minorities and people with lower socioeconomic status often suffer from an accumulation of stressors, such as violence, discrimination, and racism, they are more likely to have higher mortality rates and are at greater risk for a variety of diseases, including coronary heart disease, diabetes, and respiratory diseases (Olvera, Stewart, Galindo, & Stephens, 2007). This research is important because it demonstrates the detrimental impact that dysregulation of the SNS and HPA systems can have on people's health and also shows that these effects may disproportionately affect one ethnic group more than another.

In addition to jeopardizing one's physical and mental health, chronic conflict, and the corresponding physiological stress levels, can adversely affect people's relational health. Research has shown that over- or underactivated physiological stress responses are predictive of divorce and relationship dissatisfaction (Levenson, Carstensen, & Gottman, 1994). Among the earliest and most seminal research on marital communication and its physiological correlates is the work of Gottman and his colleagues. For example, in an earlier work, Gottman and Levenson (1985) found in a sample of 19 couples screened to be high or low on marital satisfaction that higher autonomic arousal at baseline was predictive of larger declines in marital quality three years later. In a similar study measuring finger pulse amplitudes in 73 couples, Gottman and Levenson (1992) found that greater autonomic activation of wives during marital conflict was associated with marital dissolution four years later. Gottman's research with 130 newlywed couples showed that for couples where the husbands were able to keep their heart rates lower during marital conflict, largely as a function of their wives' social support or "physiological soothing," the probability of divorce six years later was lessened. Gottman argues that men often experience greater physiological arousal (e.g., faster heart rates, higher skin conductance, stronger finger pulses) during marital conflict than women and this physiological arousal is associated with husbands' greater negative affect and arousal (Levenson et al., 1994). Men are more likely to stonewall or avoid reacting emotionally or communicatively during conflict than women in response to their physiological arousal, supposedly as a way to dissipate the conflict and prevent themselves from doing or saying something they will regret (Levenson et al., 1994).

In Gottman's research (e.g., Levenson et al., 1994) as well as other research (e.g., Kiecolt-Glaser & Newton, 2001), couples with more hostile conflict patterns tended to be more physiologically aroused during and after the conflict than couples with low hostility. For instance, Kiecolt-Glaser, Bane, Glaser, and Malarkey (2003) examined neuroendocrine functioning in 90 couples during their first year of marriage (Time 1) and 10 years later (Time 2). They found that the couples who divorced by the 10th year had hormone levels that were 34% higher than the couples who were still married. The couples who were divorced or had failing marriages after 10 years also had a greater amount of conflict and negative affect in the 1st year.

Divorce may also affect how parents perceive their own communication, which could influence their physiological responses to their communication patterns. In a study where parent–adolescent pairs were asked to talk about something stressful related to the parents' relationship, Afifi, Granger, Denes, Joseph, and Aldeis (2010a) found that when divorced and nondivorced parents had a more strained relationship, they experienced an increase in their sAA after the conversation. When the parents had a less strained relationship, those who were still married did not experience any change in their sAA. However, parents who were divorced but had a less strained relationship experienced a more dramatic rise in their sAA immediately after the conversation. A similar trend was observed for the inappropriateness of the disclosures, with more inappropriate disclosures having a greater impact on divorced parents' sAA. As Afifi et al. (2007) speculate, divorced parents who have a better relationship may feel guilty when they talk badly about the other parent, which could be stress inducing. Parents who have a strained relationship may also become desensitized to their conflict over time, making them less stressed and less cognizant of their communication with their child. If this mindlessness ensues, it could perpetuate even more inappropriate disclosures.

Most of the research on conflict, aggression, and violence has examined the effect of these communication processes on people's HPA or SNS systems and potentially how these physiological stress response systems, in turn, predict physical and mental health. Other research has begun to explore the possibility that multiple stress response systems work together to combat stress and that they should be studied as such. More specifically, research has begun to explore the possibility that the HPA and SNS systems work in concert to respond to stress (see Bauer, Quas, & Boyce, 2002). Bauer et al. (2002) present two competing models to address this argument: an additive model and an interactive model. The additive model contends that when both systems operate in a similar manner, the symmetrical activation or deactivation of the two systems could potentially result in hypo-arousal (i.e., low on both the SNS and the HPA systems) or hyperarousal (i.e., high on both the SNS and the HPA systems). According to this model, children would be at the most risk when both systems are symmetrical and at the least risk when there is a moderate level of arousal across the two systems or the systems are asymmetrical (i.e., high on one and low on the other). As Bauer et al. point out, however, there is convincing evidence that the two systems are not synonymous in their responses and that the responses are sometimes in opposition. Consequently, the authors offer a second, competing explanation, that the HPA and SNS systems may be most adaptive when they are balanced or complementary. In this "interactive model," the concurrent activation or deactivation (or synchronicity) of both systems would be adaptive and would result in fewer behavioral problems, whereas asymmetries would be maladaptive. The HPA system, in general, and cortisol, in particular, may be responsible for suppressing the initial SNS-activated stress response (Bauer et al., 2002). Because unrestrained SNS activation is detrimental to the body, cortisol may be released to restrain the sAA response and to return the body to a normal resting state (Munck, Guyre, & Holbrook, 1984). With this in mind, Bauer et al. (2002) suggest that individuals exposed to chronic, intense stressors such as chronic conflict and violence may have asymmetrical HPA and SNS systems. That is, chronically stressed individuals may have stress regulation systems that are unable to properly perform their appropriate functions in coordination with each other.

Only a handful of studies have tested Bauer et al.'s (2002) arguments. These hypothesized models were tested by Gordis et al. (2006), with somewhat mixed results. In one example, Gordis and colleagues found that the interaction between sAA and cortisol accounted for 7% of the variance in children's aggressive behavior as reported by the parent or guardian. However, the scholars found that asymmetry between sAA and cortisol was associated with less aggressive behavior, whereas symmetry was associated with more aggression. In particular, Gordis and colleagues

reported that when sAA was low, low levels of cortisol were associated with more child aggression and high levels of cortisol were associated with less child aggression. When sAA was high, there was no effect for cortisol. In support of Bauer et al.'s (2002) argument, Gordis et al. (2006) found that the interaction between the two systems accounted for more variance than if the two systems were analyzed separately. Gordis et al. speculate that sAA may buffer the effects of cortisol hypo-activity. When sAA does not buffer children from cortisol, these children may become particularly aggressive.

El-Sheikh, Erath, Buckhalt, Granger, and Mize (2008) also found support for Bauer et al.'s (2002) additive model in their examination of the relationship between the HPA (as measured through cortisol) and SNS (as measured through sAA and skin conductance) systems in 8- to 9-year-olds after two laboratory challenge tasks. Their results revealed that symmetry between the HPA and SNS systems, as indicated by higher cortisol levels and higher SNS activation, was associated with greater internalizing or externalizing of problems in children. Similarly, in their study of corumination among college-age female best friends, Byrd-Craven et al. (2008) found low HPA activation and high SNS activation when the friends focused on negative affect during a problem-solving task. These authors argue that the asymmetry between the HPA and SNS systems is similar to the findings of previous research, in which this asymmetry was associated with a lower risk for internalizing problems. In short, these studies point to the importance of examining the interactive nature of the HPA and SNS systems. Using measures of both the SNS and the HPA axes is important because of the complexity of the stress response system. A multisystems approach provides researchers with a more comprehensive picture of how the body responds to stress (Bauer et al., 2002; Gordis, Granger, Susman, & Trickett, 2008).

A significant amount of research has also examined the link between testosterone and conflict, aggression, or violence. The popular lay interpretation of aggressive boys or men who cannot control their anger is that they have too much testosterone. An enormous amount of research has attempted to link testosterone with aggression and violence, with rather inconclusive results (see Booth, Granger, Mazur, & Kivlighan, 2006; Kuepper et al., 2010). As Booth and colleagues (2006; Mazur & Booth, 1998) note, there is no clear, simple correlation between testosterone and aggression. They argue that the best explanation may be that testosterone interacts with numerous psychological, physiological, and environmental factors to influence behavior (Booth et al., 2006). Booth et al. (2006) also contend that testosterone may not be significantly associated with aggression or violence per se but, rather, with behaviors that are indicative of sensation seeking, competitiveness, risk, and dominance. Behaviors such as competitiveness and dominance, which are used to gain or maintain status or power, have been shown to be associated with higher levels of testosterone (e.g., Tremblay et al., 1998). As Tremblay et al. (1998) observed in their sample of 57 teenage boys of ages 6 to 13, the association between physical aggression and testosterone was evident in cases where the boys were attempting to gain social dominance. These arguments lead one to consider whether connections such as those between violent and criminal activity and testosterone (e.g., Soler, Vinayak, & Quadagno, 2000) are really due to the core constructs, such as dominance or risk, that underlie a particular type of violence.

Research also suggests that the impact of testosterone on behavior may be moderated by other social factors. For example, Booth, Johnson, Granger, Crouter, and McHale (2003) found that in stable families with normally developing children of ages 6 to 18, there was little association between children's testosterone levels and their risk behaviors or depressive symptoms. However, these links between testosterone and risky behaviors/depression were moderated by the quality of the parent–child relationship. When the quality of this relationship was high, these associations were not as evident. When it declined, risky behaviors and depressive symptoms that were linked to testosterone increased. Numerous studies have also found that partners' behaviors are contingent on each other's testosterone levels (Cohan, Booth, & Granger, 2003; Kaiser & Powers, 2006). For example, Cohan et al. (2003) found that husbands engaged in greater social support when both they and their wives had lower testosterone levels. Wives, however, engaged in more social support when they had higher testosterone levels and their husbands had lower testosterone levels.

## Attraction and Bonding

There is also a significant amount of research on attraction in interpersonal relationships. Much of this research focuses on the role of oxytocin, and vasopressin to a lesser degree, in love, sexual bonding, attraction, and the formation of attachments. Many studies have linked the release of oxytocin with reduction of anxiety and an increase in social bonding and reproductive behaviors (Hiller, 2004). At a fundamental level, oxytocin has been shown to help muscle contractions during and after labor, facilitate the lactation process, promote calmness in new mothers, and enhance mother–infant bonding (Hiller, 2004; Kosfeld, Heinrichs, Zak, Fischbacher, & Fehr, 2005). Oxytocin is also often released through one's senses, such as touching, warmth, and smell (Hiller, 2004). For instance, mothers who touch their babies more after birth have stronger releases of oxytocin than mothers who engage in less touching (see Hiller, 2004). The release of oxytocin can reduce stress and anxiety in the SNS system, enhancing relaxation, healing, and growth (Uvnäs-Moberg, 1998). Oxytocin also helps social relationships at a larger level by promoting prosocial approach behaviors, such as trust and affiliation (Kosfeld et al., 2005), and minimizing social threats and feelings of rejection (Zwolinski, 2008). As Kosfeld et al. (2005) note, oxytocin allows humans to go beyond their natural tendency to protect and guard themselves and encourages approach and bonding behaviors. These authors found that giving participants intranasal doses of oxytocin increased their willingness to take social risks in initial interactions with others.

Oxytocin is also associated with mating and sexuality in interpersonal relationships. Males and females who show increases in oxytocin tend to be more attracted to their partner (Hiller, 2005). While oxytocin has been shown to facilitate pair bonding in animals such as rats, prairie voles, and sheep, its benefits are yet to be fully confirmed in humans (see Carter, 2003; Neumann, 2008). However, some research on attachments (see Marazziti et al., 2006) suggests that it might facilitate mate formation in human relationships as well. While most of the research on mating has examined the effect of oxytocin, research also suggests that testosterone is associated with mating behavior but that it serves a different function from oxytocin. Numerous studies have shown that men who are romantically involved have lower testosterone levels than single men, which researchers believe is due to the lower requirement for involved men to indulge in mating behavior (Gray et al., 2004; McIntyre et al., 2006). Research has also demonstrated that even if men are romantically involved, if they are sexually interested in someone else, they will have elevated testosterone levels compared with men who are involved and not sexually interested in someone other than their current partner (McIntyre et al., 2006).

The release of oxytocin in the brain also plays an important role in the sexual behavior of males and females. Oxytocin is released during sexual activity, promoting orgasms in women and ejaculation in men (Neumann, 2008). Women, in particular, may desire greater affection, touch, and foreplay leading up to sex because these aid in the release of oxytocin, which can increase sexual desire (Hiller, 2004). There is also evidence that oxytocin contributes to bonding and relaxation in the postcoital period (Neumann, 2008). People may feel a stronger desire to hold and touch one another after sex because of the release of oxytocin.

Research has also shown that oxytocin, because it inhibits the stress-induced activation of the HPA, may enhance the buffering effects of social support and affection on physiological stress responses (e.g., Ditzen et al., 2009; Heinrichs, Baumgartner, Kirschbaum, & Ehlert, 2003). For instance, Heinrichs et al. (2003) found that when men were randomly given intranasal oxytocin prior to a laboratory stress test, the presence of social support from a best friend in preparation for the stress was more effective at reducing cortisol levels compared with control groups. Ditzen et al. (2009) found similar effects for affectionate behavior during couple conflict. In their study, oxytocin taken before a conflict episode was found to facilitate approach or affectionate behaviors during the episode and reduce cortisol levels after the conflict episode. Social support and affiliative behavior seem to buffer the effect of stress on the body, but this effect may be more pronounced with elevated levels of oxytocin. In general, oxytocin seems to facilitate affiliative behaviors in a variety of interpersonal relationships as well as increase sexual arousal and postcoital bonding.

Research also shows that human odors can attract people to, or repel them away from, each other. Odorous chemicals that are emitted from the glands in the anal-genital region and in the face, hands, feet, and chest can provide potent information about a potential mate (Saxton, Lyndon, Little, & Roberts, 2008). For example, androstadienone, an odorous compound secreted from the body, has been shown to facilitate attraction, positive affect, sexual drive, and pair bonding (see Saxton et al., 2008). Compounds such as these also vary in the different phases of a woman's menstrual cycle. Women who inhaled androstadienone in laboratory experiments experienced increased autonomic functioning, positive moods, and attraction to opposite-sex mates (Jacob & McClintock, 2000). Saxton et al. (2008) found in a speed-dating laboratory experiment that when women were exposed to androstadienone, they rated men as more attractive. Human body odor provides natural, evolutionary cues for mating.

Finally, research has linked passionate love to physiological changes and neurological changes in the brain. Studies show that passionate love is associated with increases in hormones such as oxytocin and cortisol. For example, Loving, Crockett, and Paxson (2009) found that women who were currently experiencing passionate love underwent increases in their cortisol levels when asked to think about their love for their romantic partner compared with women who were asked to think about a platonic, cross-sex friendship. fMRI research has also shown that certain parts of the brain are stimulated when people are newly or passionately in love with their partners (e.g., Aron, Mashek, & Strong, 1995), providing initial evidence for the links between neurology and love.

## Emotion and Emotional Communication

Emotions play a considerable role in the potential dysregulation of physiological stress responses and in people's personal and relational health. The autonomic nervous system responds differently to different types of emotions. For example, people experience greater heart rate acceleration and skin conductance when they use more negative facial expressions, such as anger, disgust, or fear, than when they use positive facial expressions (Ekman, Levenson, & Friesen, 1983; Levenson, Ekman, Heider, & Friesen, 1992). Mutual eye gaze, which can be an indicator of various emotions and intentions such as dominance or love, is also associated with increased physiological arousal (Mazur et al., 1980).

Models of emotions and physiology also suggest that how people appraise a stressor and respond emotionally mediates the effects of the stress on people's health (Denson, Spanovic, & Miller, 2009). In the emotion literature, cortisol has been of primary interest because of its historical ties to the immune system and the health problems that ensue when people's immune systems are altered (Denson et al., 2009). As Denson et al. (2009) note in their meta-analysis on

emotion and physiology, other meta-analytic reviews of this body of literature find inconsistent support or a lack of support for the connection between emotions and cortisol. However, these authors argue that this may be due to the fact that emotions are often operationalized as positive or negative and this broad coding of valence may obscure important and subtle distinctions between specific emotions and in the appraisal of these emotions. Denson et al. developed a theoretical model of emotions and physiology that they then tested with a meta-analysis. They hypothesized that the type of stressor (e.g., imminent, threatening one's social status, requiring extended effort) determines the associated appraisals of the stressor and the corresponding emotions, which result in a particular physiological response. For instance, the authors hypothesized that the basic emotions of surprise, anticipation, and disgust would be associated with acute increases in cortisol because of the desire to eliminate an imminent threat. Likewise, Denson et al. argue, rumination should predict elevated cortisol levels due to the prolonged activation and reactivation of negative emotions, such as worry, that shroud ruminative tendencies. Similar studies have confirmed the authors' ideas (e.g., McCullough, Orsulak, Brandon, & Akers, 2007). Denson et al. (2009) also suggest that instances where a stressor is perceived as a social threat can result in extreme angry reactions or more self-conscious emotions such as shame, guilt, or embarrassment. All of these emotional responses, they argue, should result in acute increases in cortisol levels. As the authors hypothesized, global emotional states were not significantly associated with effect sizes in cortisol. However, they found that coping strategies that alter the way people appraise the stressor, which affects their emotions, could improve health.

Even though Denson et al. (2009) found no significant support for an association between global emotions and cortisol, there has been some research that links mood to physiological responses. Because they are part of a dyad, a group, and a shared environment, people's behavior and physiological responses are correlated. As Saxbe and Repetti (2010) argue, researchers know very little about how romantic partners' daily affect and physiological responses covary or coregulate. The authors examined the coregulation of spouses' mood states and cortisol four times a day for three days. Both husbands' and wives' reports of their own and their partner's cortisol scores were related. This effect, however, was weakened by the perception of marital satisfaction by the wives. That is, cortisol scores of both husbands and wives seemed to be sensitive to the wives' satisfaction. The husbands and wives' perception of their partners' negative mood was also positively associated with their own mood, which was fully moderated by marital satisfaction. Interestingly, the spouses' positive moods were uncorrelated. These findings correspond with other research that has found that distressed couples demonstrate stronger physiological associations and more reciprocity of negative affect than nondistressed couples (e.g., Levenson & Gottman, 1983). Saxbe and Repetti (2010) also found that couples' mood and cortisol were more highly correlated in the morning and evening as well as when they were at home together rather than while working outside the home. The research, in general, shows that couples' physiological stress levels are interdependent, with stronger correlations when they are together and when the relationship is experiencing stress.

Scholars have also examined psychological constructs, such as uncertainty, that can result in the appraisal of various emotions (such as worry and anxiety) that predict physiological responses. Cortisol secretion increases in new or unfamiliar circumstances where feelings of uncertainty, worry, anxiety, and aversive experiences are likely (Rydstedt, Cropley, Devereaux, & Michalianou, 2008). For example, Priem and Solomon (2010b) tested the hypothesis that relational uncertainty (or uncertainty about the status of one's relationship) would increase physiological stress responses when interacting with a dating partner. The authors conducted two studies with dating partners to test their hypothesis. In the first study, the participants

($N = 89$) engaged in a discussion about their core personality traits and values with a romantic partner. In the second study, the participants ($N = 89$) received social support from their dating partner after engaging in a series of stress-inducing tasks and being given negative performance feedback. The results of the studies showed that when people were uncertain about their partner's feelings and commitment in the relationship (partner uncertainty), it can be stress inducing when receiving hurtful messages and less stress relieving when a partner is providing social support. They also found in the first study that self-uncertainty (or doubts about one's own involvement in the relationship) was associated with *less* stress reactivity. As Priem and Solomon speculate, perhaps uncertainty regarding a partner's commitment to a relationship results in people exacerbating the negative connotations of critical messages and perceiving less support when support is offered. Partner uncertainty may also accentuate the tension during stressful interactions (Priem & Solomon, 2010b). The authors also suggest that their counterintuitive finding regarding self-uncertainty might be due to the fact that people attach less importance to their partner's reactions when they are unsure about their own commitment to the relationship, resulting in less stressful reactions when their partner is hurtful.

Another common biosocial research area is emotion regulation, or people's ability to manage their emotions and its association with physiological stress responses. Depressed and anxious individuals often have dysregulated HPA and SNS systems primarily because of their inability to effectively filter out negative emotions (Laurent & Powers, 2007). Internalizing problems has been associated with greater increases in cortiol and sAA, a more difficult time recovering from stress, and chronically elevated or chronically low cortisol or sAA levels (e.g., Gordis et al., 2006, 2008; Laurent & Powers, 2007). The dysregulation of the immune system, in turn, is believed to make depressed and anxious individuals more susceptible to infection, disease, and other health problems (Kiecolt-Glaser, 2009).

Laurent and Powers (2007) also found that temperament and attachments can influence people's ability to regulate their emotions with their partner, affecting cortisol responses. They found that women more prone to negative emotions may be less likely to soothe their partner during a conflict and that anxiety-related attachments in men may result in greater HPA activation during conflict. As a whole, Laurent and Powers demonstrated that the impact of emotions on physiology depends on a complex set of factors, including the interdependent effects of both partners' personality and attachment.

## Theory of Mind: Planning and Imagined Interactions

While the processes we have discussed thus far involved actual interactions between people, the use of physiological markers to study intrapersonal communication has also garnered attention. Beatty and Heisel's work on message planning (e.g., Beatty & Heisel, 2007; Heisel & Beatty, 2006) and Honeycutt's (e.g., 2010; Honeycutt & Bryan, 2010) work on imagined interactions highlight the effect that metacognitions have on people's physiology. Both sets of scholarship have as their theoretical framework the "theory of mind," which differentiates what people think from what people think *others* are thinking about them (Premack & Woodruff, 1978). This work demonstrates that when people have imagined interactions with others or they plan an interaction based on how they think another person will respond, it can be physiologically arousing (Heisel & Beatty, 2006; Honeycutt, 2010; Honeycutt & Bryan, 2010).

In a study of planned behavior, Heisel and Beatty (2006) had 20 participants think about a same-sex friend. Half of the participants in the experimental condition were told that the friend had refused to let them borrow a CD without providing an explanation. The researchers asked them to think about why the friend would not let them borrow the CD while electrical activity was

being recorded using an EEG. The participants in the control condition were asked only to think about a same-sex friend. The results revealed significantly greater electrical activity in the orbitofrontal and dorsolateral prefrontal parts of the brain for the participants who were engaging in metacognitions about their friend's refusal than for the control group. In another study, Beatty and Heisel (2007) used Berger's (2002) planning theory to assess whether electrical activity in the prefrontal cortex would be greater under conditions in which people are forced to adjust their messages due to message plan failure. Twenty-six participants were randomly assigned to either a control condition where there was no plan modification required or an experimental condition where plan revision was necessary because of induced plan failure. As they expected, when people's plans failed and they had to modify them, there was a greater amount of electrical activity in the dorsolateral prefrontal cortex, supporting Berger's notion that the adjusting of plans because they have failed requires more complex thought than plans that are not interrupted or that have been successful in the past.

Honeycutt's research has also shed light on the physiological responses associated with imagined interactions, as well as on what happens to people's physiological responses when they actually interact with those who were the target of their thoughts. In one study (Honeycutt, 2010) in a longstanding line of research, Honeycutt brought 123 romantic couples into the communication laboratory. The partners were separated for an initial period before the experiment began. One partner was focused on a distracting task that consisted of completing a series of scales unrelated to the study. The other partner was assessed for baseline blood pressure and heart rate. The partner who had blood pressure and heart rate assessed was then asked to imagine a conflict scenario with the other partner and role-play into a video recorder how he or she thought the partner would respond. The partners were then asked to talk about an unpleasant topic with each other. During and after the actual interaction (and during the imagined interaction for one of the partners), the partners' blood pressure, heart rate, and wrist movements were measured. Interestingly, Honeycutt found that people's heart rate and blood pressure did not significantly change during the imagined-interaction part of the experiment. However, the imagined interactions predicted heart rate after the conversations with the partners were over. More specifically, Honeycutt found that imagined interactions that were discrepant or did not go as planned or people who did not rehearse what they were going to say predicted an increase in heart rate after the conversation was over. As Honeycutt and Bryan (2010) note, these findings suggest that planning a conversation ahead of time can reduce uncertainty and anxiety, which can ultimately reduce the physiological responses.

Although this review is far from exhaustive, it has identified multiple interpersonal communication topics to which the principles of biophysiology have been applied. To conclude our chapter, we offer the following comments on the future uses of the evolutionary and biophysiological approach and some brief words of advice for researchers interested in pursuing that approach in their own work.

# Conclusions and Directions for Future Research

To conclude this chapter, we have elected to identify some advantages and disadvantages of biophysiology as an interpersonal method. We also offer four practical suggestions for interpersonal communication researchers interested in incorporating physiological measures into their work.

## Advantages and Disadvantages of Biophysiology as an Interpersonal Method

*Access to Subconscious Processes.* One substantial advantage of using physiological methods in the study of interpersonal communication is that they can index processes to which individuals are not fully attuned consciously. In a study of interpersonal conflict, for instance, researchers might be eager to know how quickly relational partners recover from the stress of a conflict episode once it has ended. Although they can make their assessments via self-report measures, such measures only index participants' conscious, subjective experiences of stress, which may have little correspondence to the stress their bodies are actually experiencing at the time. Measuring physiological markers of stress—such as elevated blood pressure or cortisol—allows researchers to ascertain how quickly the body's stress response is initiated, how quickly it peaks, and how quickly it returns to baseline relative to the conflict episode, irrespective of what participants are experiencing psychologically.

*Accuracy of Measurement.* A second advantage for interpersonal researchers is that physiological methods have minimal measurement error and are relatively immune to memory bias and social desirability effects. The relative lack of measurement error is a marked advantage with respect to the sample sizes needed for adequate statistical power. Indeed, although relatively large samples are the norm in much interpersonal communication research, interpersonal research employing physiological methods commonly includes samples as small as 20 to 30 participants (e.g., Kurup & Kurup, 2003; Marazziti & Canale, 2004; Van Niekerk, Huppert, & Herbert, 2001). Samples of that size frequently provide sufficient statistical power due to the low measurement error rate common for physiological measures. In addition, physiological outcomes are largely unaffected by participants' memories or their intention to appear socially desirable, as many of the outcomes are outside the scope of conscious control. Although physiological methods are not entirely immune from error and misinterpretation, they are less susceptible to such problems than most methods common to interpersonal communication research.

*Education and Facilities.* One obstacle for researchers interested in including physiological measures in their studies is that doing so requires a measure of education on which outcomes to include, how to measure them, and how to interpret the results. It also requires adequate facilities for collecting, storing, and potentially analyzing body fluid samples. As the necessary education and facilities are not made available to communication researchers on a widespread basis, researchers must acquire them proactively. An effective way to do so, at least initially, is to collaborate with researchers whose work already incorporates physiological measures, an option we will discuss in greater detail below.

*Resource Requirements.* A second barrier to using physiological measures is that collecting and analyzing samples is often expensive. Depending on which outcomes—and how many—are being assessed, the cost per participant in a study with physiological measures can be substantial (per-participant costs in our own experiments have ranged from approximately $150 to more than $1,000). Consequently, even researchers with the required education and facilities will need the financial resources necessary to conduct their work. Securing that funding typically requires one to seek internal or external grants, which we will discuss below.

## Advice for Communication Scholars Interested in Biophysiology

Despite these hurdles, biophysiological research is by no means beyond the reach of interpersonal communication scholars, as evidenced by several of the studies detailed in this chapter. For the benefit of researchers—and researchers in training—who wish to include physiological methods in their work, we offer the following practical suggestions:

*Conceptualize interpersonal behaviors as biological processes.* Before including physiological outcomes is warranted, researchers must consider the biological processes and consequences of the communication behaviors in which they are interested. If one studies nonverbal communication, for instance, one might consider the cardiovascular or hormonal processes involved in encoding facial expressions of various emotions. In that way, an interpersonal behavior is understood as involving measurable biological components.

*Read the literature on psychophysiological research.* Although physiological research is becoming more common in the discipline of communication, it is already voluminous in the discipline of psychophysiology, a subspecialty of psychology. Communication scholars can learn much about the outcomes and measurement methods relevant to their interests by perusing the literature.

*Collaborate with psychophysiological researchers.* Researchers new to the field of biophysiology can often learn its methods and acquire access to the required facilities by collaborating with psychophysiological researchers at their colleges or universities. Such scholars are typically found in medical and nursing schools as well as departments of clinical or counseling psychology, kinesiology, and exercise science. They can often help with designing and conducting studies and with analyzing and interpreting the results.

*Seek grant funding.* Finally, communication scholars should seek funding from internal and external grants to support the inclusion of biophysiological measures. It is often best to start with an internal "seed" grant that will provide sufficient funding to conduct a small pilot study. If the results of the pilot are encouraging, researchers can use them as initial data in a larger grant application to an external agency. Most colleges and universities have staff members trained to assist researchers in identifying and applying for grants, and their services can be invaluable.

Besides being a historical, cultural, religious, political, economic, and aesthetic act, interpersonal communication is also a biological act. By examining its evolutionary and physiological underpinnings, researchers can shed new light on interpersonal communication processes and their significance.

## Notes

1. This is true, at least, for sexually reproducing species (see Bjorklund & Pellegrini, 2002). It should be noted that Darwin did not actually know about genetics when he proposed TNS. Rather, he merely offered that particular traits were passed from generation to generation; the discovery of genes and genetic transmission was made subsequent to Darwin's work.

2. Not all of a person's physical characteristics are inherited. If a woman loses her hearing due to an injury, that will not make her more likely to give birth to children who are deaf.

3. Advances in reproductive technology, including in vitro fertilization, have eliminated intercourse as an absolute precursor to reproduction. Such technology was unavailable to our hunter–gatherer ancestors, however, for whom the adaptive nature of the human sex drive would have been selected.

4. That type of benefit does require that the others in the group be unaware of this member's good fortune. As Cosmides and Tooby (1989, 1992) have noted, humans have evolved a type of *cheating detection mechanism* by which they notice, remember, and respond to perceived cheating on the part of others, for the protection of their own interests.

## References

Abou-Khalil, B., & Musilus, K. E. (2006). *Atlas of EEG & seizure semiology.* Amsterdam: Elsevier.

Afifi, T. D., Granger, D., Denes, A., Joseph, A., & Aldeis, D. (2010a). *Interparental conflict and parents' inappropriate disclosures: Relations to parents' and children's salivary α-amylase and cortisol.* Manuscript submitted for publication.

Afifi, T. D., Granger, D., Denes, A., Joseph, A., & Aldeis, D. (2010b). *Parents' communication skills and adolescents' salivary α-amylase and cortisol response patterns.* Manuscript submitted for publication.

Afifi, T. D., Granger, D., Joseph, A., Aldeis, D., & Denes, A. (2010). *The influence of divorce and parents' communication skills on adolescents' and young adults' stress reactivity and recovery.* Manuscript submitted for publication.

Afifi, T. D., McManus, T., Hutchinson, S., & Baker, B. (2007). Parental divorce disclosures, the factors that prompt them, and their impact on parents' and adolescents' well-being. *Communication Monographs, 74,* 78–103.

Aguilera, G. (1994). Regulation of pituitary ACTH secretion during chronic stress. *Frontiers in Neuroendocrinology, 15,* 321–350.

Amato, P. R., & Sobolewski, J. M. (2001). The effects of divorce and marital discord on adult children's psychological well-being. *American Sociological Review, 66,* 900–921.

Andersen, P. A., Garrison, J. P., & Andersen, J. F. (1979). Implications of a neurophysical approach for the study of nonverbal communication. *Human Communication Research, 6,* 74–89.

Andreassi, J. L. (2000). *Psychophysiology: Human behavior and physiological response* (4th ed.). Mahwah, NJ: Lawrence Erlbaum.

Aron, A., Mashek, D., & Strong, G. (1995). Reward, motivation and emotion systems associated with early-stage intense romantic love. *Journal of Neurophysiology, 94,* 327–337.

Aschbacher, K., von Känel, R., Mills, P. J., Hong, S., Roepke, S. K., Mausbach, B. T., et al. (2007). Combination of caregiving stress and hormone replacement therapy is associated with prolonged platelet activation to acute stress among postmenopausal women. *Psychosomatic Medicine, 69,* 910–917.

Bailey, R. H., & Bauer, J. H. (1993). A review of common errors in the indirect measurement of blood pressure: Sphygmomanometry. *Archives of Internal Medicine, 153,* 2741–2748.

Bauer, A. M., Quas, J. A., & Boyce, W. T. (2002). Associations between physiological reactivity and children's behavior: Advantages of a multisystem approach. *Journal of Developmental Behavior and Pediatrics, 23,* 102–133.

Beatty, M. J., & Heisel, A. D. (2007). Spectrum analysis of cortical activity during verbal planning: Physical evidence for the formation of social interaction routines. *Human Communication Research, 33,* 48–63.

Beatty, M. J., Heisel, A. D., Hall, A. E., Levine, T. R., & La France, G. H. (2002). What can we learn from the study of twins about genetic and environmental influences on interpersonal affiliation, aggressiveness, and social anxiety? A meta-analytic study. *Communication Monographs, 69,* 1–18.

Beatty, M. J., Marshall, L. A., & Rudd, J. E. (2001). A twins study of communicative adaptability: Heritability of individual differences. *Quarterly Journal of Speech, 87,* 366–377.

Beatty, M. J., & McCroskey, J. C. (1997). It's in our nature: Verbal aggressiveness as temperamental expression. *Communication Quarterly, 45,* 446–460.

Beatty, M. J., & McCroskey, J. C. (2000). Theory, scientific evidence, and the communibiological paradigm: Reflections on misguided criticism. *Communication Education, 49,* 36–44.

Beatty, M. J., McCroskey, J. C., & Floyd, K. (Eds.). (2009). *Biological dimensions of communication: Perspectives, research, and methods.* Cresskill, NJ: Hampton Press.

Beatty, M. J., McCroskey, J. C., & Heisel, A. D. (1998). Communication apprehension as temperamental expression: A communibiological paradigm. *Communication Monographs, 65,* 197–219.

Berger, C. R. (2002). Goals and knowledge structures in social interaction. In M. L. Knapp & J. A. Daly (Eds.), *Handbook of interpersonal communication* (3rd ed., pp. 181–212). Thousand Oaks, CA: Sage.

Bjorklund, D., & Pellegrini, A. D. (2002). *Origins of human nature: Evolutionary developmental psychology.* Washington, DC: American Psychological Association.

Blood, G., Blood, I., Frederick, S., Wertz, H., & Simpson, K. (1997). Cortisol responses in adults who stutter: Coping preferences and apprehension about communication. *Perceptual and Motor Skills, 84,* 883–889.

Bongartz, W., Lyncker, I., & Kossman, K. T. (1987). The influence of hypnosis on white blood cell count and urinary levels of catecholamines and vanillyl mandelic acid. *Hypnos, 14,* 52–61.

Booth, A., & Amato, P. R. (2001). Parental predivorce relations and offspring postdivorce well-being. *Journal of Marriage and the Family, 63,* 197–212.

Booth, A., Carver, K., & Granger, D. (2000). Biosocial perspectives on the family. *Journal of Marriage and the Family, 62,* 1018–1034.

Booth, A., Granger, D. A., Mazur, A., & Kivlighan, K. T. (2006). Testosterone and social behavior. *Social Forces, 85,* 167–191.

Booth, A., Johnson, D. R., Granger, D. A., Crouter, A. C., & McHale, S. (2003). Testosterone and child and adolescent adjustment: The moderating role of parent–child relationships. *Developmental Psychology, 39,* 85–98.

Borg, G., & Linderholm, H. (2009). Perceived exertion and pulse rate during graded exercise in various age groups. *Acta Medica Scandinavica, 181,* 194–206.

Brosschot, J. F., Smelt, D., de Smet, M., Heijen, C. J., Olff, M., Ballieux, R. E., et al. (1991). Effects of experimental psychological stress on T-lymphocytes and NK cells in man: An exploratory study. *Journal of Psychophysiology, 5,* 59–67.

Buck, R. (1977). Nonverbal communication of affect in preschool children: Relationships with personality and skin conductance. *Journal of Personality and Social Psychology, 35,* 225–236.

Buck, R., Miller, R., & Caul, W. (1974). Sex, personality, and physiological variables in the communication of affect via facial expression. *Journal of Personality and Social Psychology, 30,* 587–596.

Burke, H. M., Davis, M. C., Otte, C., & Mohr, D. C. (2005). Depression and cortisol responses to psychological stress: A meta-analysis. *Psychoneuroendocrinology, 30,* 846–856.

Burleson, B. (2009). Explaining recipient responses to supportive messages. In S. Smith & S. R. Wilson (Eds.), *New directions in interpersonal communication research* (pp. 159–179). Thousand Oaks: Sage.

Buss, D. M. (1999). *Evolutionary psychology: The new science of the mind.* Needham Heights, MA: Allyn & Bacon.

Butler, E., Egloff, B., Wilheim, F., Smith, N., Erickson, E., & Gross, J. (2003). The social consequences of expressive suppression. *Emotion, 3,* 48–67.

Byrd-Craven, J., Geary, D. C., Rose, A. J., & Ponzi, D. (2008). Co-ruminating increases stress hormone levels in women. *Hormones and Behavior, 53,* 489–492.

Byrd-Craven, J., Granger, D., & Auer, B. (2010). *Stress reactivity to co-rumination in young women's friendships: Cortisol, alpha-amylase, and negative affect focus.* Manuscript submitted for publication.

Cannon, W. B. (1914). The interrelations of emotions as suggested by recent physiological research. *American Journal of Psychology, 25,* 256–282.

Cappella, J. (1991). The biological origins of automated patterns of human interaction. *Communication Theory, 1,* 4–35.

Cappella, J. (1996). Why biological explanation? *Journal of Communication, 46,* 4–7.

Carter, C. S. (2003). Developmental consequences of oxytocin. *Physiology & Behavior, 79,* 383–397.

Cohan, C. L., Booth, A., & Granger, D. A. (2003). Gender moderates the relationship between testosterone and marital interaction. *Journal of Family Psychology, 17,* 29–40.

Condit, C. M. (2000). Culture and biology in human communication: Toward a multi-causal model. *Communication Education, 49,* 7–24.

Corona, R., Lefkowitz, E., Sigman, M., & Romo, L. (2005). Latino adolescents' adjustment, maternal depressive symptoms, and the mother–adolescent relationship. *Family Relations, 54,* 386–399.

Cosmides, L. L., & Tooby, J. (1989). Evolutionary psychology and the generation of culture. Part II. Case study: A computational theory of social exchange. *Ethology and Sociobiology, 10,* 51–97.

Cosmides, L. L., & Tooby, J. (1992). Cognitive adaptations for social exchange. In J. Barkow, L. Cosmides, & J. Tooby (Eds.), *The adapted mind* (pp. 163–228). New York: Oxford University Press.

Cosmides, L., & Tooby, J. (2006). *Evolutionary psychology: A primer.* Retrieved May 10, 2010, from www .psych.ucsb.edu/research/cep/primer.html

Coyne, J. C., & Smith, D. A. F. (1991). Couples coping with a myocardial infarction: A contextual perspective on wives' distress. *Journal of Personality and Social Psychology, 61,* 404–412.

Dabbs, J. M., Frady, R. L., Carr, T. S., & Besch, N. F. (1987). Saliva testosterone and criminal violence in young adult prison inmates. *Psychosomatic Medicine, 49,* 174–182.

Dabbs, J. M., Ruback, R. B., Frady, R. L., Hopper, C. H., & Sgoutas D. S. (1988). Saliva testosterone and criminal violence among women. *Personality and Individual Differences, 9,* 269–275.

Damasio, A. (1999). *The feeling of what happens: Body and emotions in the making of consciousness.* New York: Harcourt.

Darwin, C. (1859). *On the origin of species.* London: Murray.

Davies, P. T., Sturge-Apple, M. L., Cicchetti, D., & Cummings, E. M. (2007). The role of child adrenocortical functioning in pathways between interparental conflict and child maladjustment. *Developmental Psychology, 43,* 918–930.

Deinzer, R., & Schüller, N. (1998). Dynamics of stress-related decrease of salivary immunoglobulin A (sIgA): Relationship to symptoms of the common cold and studying behavior. *Behavioral Medicine, 23,* 161–169.

Denson, T. F., Spanovic, M., & Miller, N. (2009). Cognitive appraisals and emotions predict cortisol and immune responses: A meta-analysis of acute laboratory social stressors and emotion inductions. *Psychological Bulletin, 135,* 823–853.

Desantis, A., Adam, E., Doane, L., Mineka, S., Zinbarg, R., & Craske, M. (2007). Racial/ethnic differences in cortisol diurnal rhythms in a community sample of adolescents. *Journal of Adolescent Health, 41,* 3–13.

Ditzen, B., Schaer, M., Gabriel, B., Bodenmann, G., Ehlert, U., & Henrichs, M. (2009). Intranasal oxytocin increases positive communication and reduces cortisol levels during couple conflict. *Biological Psychiatry, 65,* 728–731.

Dobbin, J. P., Harth, M., McCain, G. A., Martin, R. A., & Cousin, K. (1991). Cytokine production and lymphocyte transformation during stress. *Brain, Behavior, and Immunity, 5,* 290–295.

Dopp, J. M., Miller, G. E., Myers, H. F., & Fahey, J. L. (2000). Increased natural killer-cell mobilization and cytotoxicity during marital conflict. *Brain, Behavior, and Immunity, 14,* 10–26.

Drescher, V., Gantt, W., & Whitehead, W. (1980). Heart rate response to touch. *Psychosomatic Medicine, 42,* 559–565.

Edens, J., Larkin, K., & Abel, L. (1992). The effect of social support and physical touch on cardiovascular reactions to mental stress. *Journal of Psychosomatic Research, 36,* 371–382.

Ekman, P., Levenson, R. W., & Friesen, W. V. (1983). Automatic nervous system distinguishes among emotions. *Science, 221,* 1208–1210.

El-Sheikh, M., Erath, S. A., Buckhalt, J. A., Granger, D. A., & Mize, J. (2008). Cortisol and children's adjustment: The moderating role of sympathetic nervous system activity. *Journal of Abnormal Child Psychology, 36,* 601–611.

Elster, A. D. (1986). *Magnetic resonance imaging.* Philadelphia: J. P. Lippincott.

Ershler, W. B., & Keller, E. T. (2000). Age-associated increased interleukin-6 gene expression, late-life diseases, and frailty. *Annual Review of Medicine,* *51,* 245–270.

Farnè, M. A., Boni, P., Corallo, A., Gnugnoli, D., & Sacco, F. L. (1994). Personality variables as moderators of hassles and objective indications of distress (sIgA). *Stress Medicine, 10,* 15–20.

Fishman, E., Turkheimer, E., & DeGood, D. (1995). Touch relieves stress and pain. *Journal of Behavioral Medicine, 18,* 69–79.

Fleming, A. S., Corter, C., Stallings, J., & Steiner, M. (2002). Testosterone and prolactin are associated with emotional responses to infant cries in new fathers. *Hormones and Behavior, 42,* 399–413.

Floyd, K. (2002). Human affection exchange: V. Attributes of the highly affectionate. *Communication Quarterly, 50,* 135–152.

Floyd, K. (2006a). *Communicating affection: Interpersonal behavior and social context.* Cambridge, UK: Cambridge University Press.

Floyd, K. (2006b). An evolutionary approach to understanding nonverbal communication. In V. Manusov & M. L. Patterson (Eds.), *The Sage handbook of nonverbal communication* (pp. 139–158). Thousand Oaks, CA: Sage.

Floyd, K. (2006c). Human affection exchange XII. Affectionate communication is associated with diurnal variation in salivary free cortisol. *Western Journal of Communication, 70,* 47–63.

Floyd, K., Boren, J. P., Hannawa, A. F., Hesse, C., McEwan, B., & Veksler, A. E. (2009). Kissing in marital and cohabiting relationships: Effects on blood lipids, stress, and relationship satisfaction. *Western Journal of Communication, 73,* 113–133.

Floyd, K., Boren, J. P., Veksler, A. E., & Hesse, C. (2010). *Affectionate communication can suppress immunity: Trait affection predicts antibody titers to latent Epstein-Barr virus.* Manuscript submitted for publication.

Floyd, K., Hess, J. A., Mizco, L. A., Halone, K. K., Mikkelson, A. C., & Tusing, K. J. (2005). Human affection exchange: VIII. Further evidence of the benefits of expressed affection. *Communication Quarterly, 53,* 285–303.

Floyd, K., Hesse, C., & Haynes, M. T. (2007). Human affection exchange: XV. Metabolic and cardiovascular correlates of trait expressed affection. *Communication Quarterly, 55,* 79–94.

Floyd, K., Mikkelson, A. C., Hesse, C., & Pauley, P. M. (2007). Affectionate writing reduces total cholesterol: Two randomized, controlled studies. *Human Communication Research, 33,* 119–142.

Floyd, K., Mikkelson, A. C., Tafoya, M. A., Farinelli, L., La Valley, A. G., Judd, J., et al. (2007a). Human affection exchange: XIII. Affectionate communication accelerates neuroendocrine stress recovery. *Health Communication, 22,* 123–132.

Floyd, K., Mikkelson, A. C., Tafoya, M. A., Farinelli, L., La Valley, A. G., Judd, J., et al. (2007b). Human affection exchange: XIV. Relational affection predicts resting heart rate and free cortisol secretion during acute stress. *Behavioral Medicine, 32,* 151–156.

Floyd, K., Pauley, P. M., & Hesse, C. (2010). State and trait affectionate communication buffer adults' stress reactions. *Communication Monographs, 77*(4), 1479–5787.

Floyd, K., Pauley, P. M., Hesse, C., Veksler, A. E., Eden, J., & Mikkelson, A. C. (2010). *Affectionate communication predicts natural killer cell strength in healthy adults.* Manuscript submitted for publication.

Floyd, K., & Riforgiate, S. (2008). Affectionate communication received from spouses predicts stress hormone levels in healthy adults. *Communication Monographs, 75,* 351–368.

Floyd, K., & Roberts, J. B. (2009). Principles of endocrine system measurement in communication research. In M. J. Beatty, J. C. McCroskey, & K. Floyd (Eds.), *Biological dimensions of communication: Perspectives, methods, and research* (pp. 249–264). Cresskill, NJ: Hampton Press.

Fortunato, C. K., Granger, D., Blair, C., & Greenberg, M. T. (2009). *Patterns of adrenocortical reactivity and recovery across infancy: Allostasis, infant behavior, and parenting quality.* Manuscript submitted for publication.

Garrett, R. H., & Grisham, C. M. (2002). *Principles of biochemistry with a human focus.* Florence, KY: Brooks/Cole.

Gazzaniga, M. S. (1998). *The mind's past.* Berkeley: University of California Press.

Glaser, R., Mehl, V. S., Penn, G., Speicher, C. E., & Kiecolt-Glaser, J. K. (1986). Stress-associated changes in plasma immunoglobulin levels. *International Journal of Psychosomatics, 33,* 41–42.

Goebel, M. U., Mills, P. J., Irwin, M. R., & Ziegler, M. G. (2000). Interleukin-6 and tumor necrosis factor-a production after acute psychological stress, exercise, and infused isoproterenol: Differential effects and pathways. *Psychosomatic Medicine, 62,* 591–598.

Gordis, E. G., Granger, D., Susman, E. J., & Trickett, P. K. (2006). Asymmetry between salivary cortisol and alpha-amylase reactivity to stress: Relation to aggressive behavior in adolescents. *Psychoneuroendocrinology, 31,* 976–987.

Gordis, E. G., Granger, D., Susman, E. J., & Trickett, P. K. (2008). Salivary alpha amylase-cortisol asymmetry in maltreated youth. *Hormones and Behavior, 53,* 96–103.

Gottlieb, G. (1991). Experiential canalization of behavioral development: Theory. *Developmental Psychology, 27,* 4–13.

Gottman, J. M., & Levenson, R. W. (1985). A valid procedure for obtaining self-report of affect in marital interaction. *Journal of Consulting and Clinical Psychology, 53,* 151–160.

Gottman, J. M., & Levenson, R. W. (1992). Marital processes predictive of later dissolution: Behavior, physiology, and health. *Journal of Personality and Social Psychology, 63,* 221–233.

Granger, D. A., Serbin, L. A., Schwartzman, A. E., Lehoux, P., Cooperman, J., & Ikeda, S. (1998). Children's salivary cortisol, internalising behaviour problems, and family environment: Results from the Concordia Longitudinal Risk Project. *International Journal of Behavioral Development, 22,* 707–728.

Gray, P. B., Chapman, J. F., Burnham, T. C., McIntyre, M. H., Lipson, S. F., & Ellison, P. T. (2004). Human male pair bonding and testosterone. *Human Nature, 15,* 119–131.

Halford, W. K., Cuddihy, S., & Mortimer, R. H. (1990). Psychological stress and blood glucose regulation in Type I diabetic patients. *Health Psychology, 9,* 516–528.

Hammock, E. A. D., & Young, L. J. (2006). Oxytocin, vasopressin and pair bonding: Implications for autism. *Philosophical Transactions of the Royal Society of London Series B: Biological Sciences, 361,* 2187–2198.

Heffner, K. L., Kiecolt-Glaser, J. K., Loving, T. J., Glaser, R., & Malarkey, W. B. (2004). Spousal support satisfaction as a modifier of physiological responses to marital conflict in younger and older couples. *Journal of Behavioral Medicine, 27,* 233–254.

Heinrichs, M., Baumgartner, T., Kirschbaum, C., & Ehlert, U. (2003). Social support and oxytocin interact to suppress cortisol and subjective responses to psychosocial stress. *Biological Psychiatry, 54,* 1389–1398.

Heisel, A. D., & Beatty, M. J. (2006). Are cognitive representations of friends' requests refusals implemented

in the orbitofrontal and dorsolateral prefrontal cortices? A comparative neuroscience approach to "theory of mind" in relationships. *Journal of Social and Personal Relationships, 23,* 249–265.

Hellhammer, D. H., Wust, S., & Kudielka, B. M. (2009). Salivary cortisol as a biomarker in stress research. *Psychoneuroendocrinology, 34,* 163–171.

Hertenstein, M. (2002). Touch: Its communicative functions in infancy. *Human Development, 45,* 70–94.

Hiller, J. (2004). Speculations on the links between feelings, emotions, and sexual behavior: Are vasopressin and oxytocin involved? *Sexual and Relationship Therapy, 19,* 1468–1479.

Hiller, J. (2005). Gender differences in sexual motivation. *Journal of Men's Health & Gender, 2,* 339–345.

Holt-Lunstad, J., Birmingham, W. A., & Light, K. C. (2008). Influence of a "warm touch" support enhancement intervention among married couples on ambulatory blood pressure, oxytocin, alpha amylase, and cortisol. *Psychosomatic Medicine, 70,* 976–985.

Honeycutt, J. M. (2010). Physiology and imagined interactions. In J. M. Honeycutt (Ed.), *Imagine that: Studies in imagined interaction* (pp. 43–64). Cresskill, NJ: Hampton Press.

Honeycutt, J. M., & Bryan, S. P. (2010). *Scripts and communication for relationships.* New York: Peter Lang.

Horsten, M., Wamala, S. P., Vingerhoets, A., & Orth-Gomer, K. (1997). Depressive symptoms, social support, and lipid profile in healthy middle-aged women. *Psychosomatic Medicine, 59,* 521–528.

Horvath, C. W. (1995). Biological origins of communicator style. *Communication Quarterly, 43,* 394–407.

Hugdahl, K. (1995). *Psychophysiology: The mind-body perspective.* Cambridge, MA: Harvard University Press.

Ito, I., Teicher, M. H., Glod, C. A., Harper, D., Magnus, E., & Gelbard, H. (1993). Increased prevalence of electrophysiological abnormalities in children with physical, psychological, and sexual abuse. *Journal of Neuropsychiatry and Clinical Neuroscience, 5,* 401–408.

Jacob, S., & McClintock, M. (2000). Psychological state and mood effects of steroidal chemosignals in women and men. *Hormones and Behavior, 37,* 57–78.

Jenkins, F. J., & Baum, A. (1995). Stress and reactivation of latent herpes simplex virus: A fusion of behavioral medicine and molecular biology. *Annals of Behavioral Medicine, 17,* 116–123.

Johnson, C. J. H., & Kerr, J. H. (2007). Automatic blood pressure monitors: A clinical evaluation in five models in adults. *Anaesthesia, 40,* 471–478.

Kaiser, H., & Powers, S. (2006). Testosterone and conflict tactics within late-adolescent couples: A dyadic predictive model. *Journal of Social and Personal Relationships, 23,* 231–248.

Kawakami, N., Tanigawa, T., Araki, S., Nakata, A., Sakurai, S., Yokoyama, K., et al. (1997). Effects of job strain on helper-inducer (CD4+CD29+) and suppressor-inducer (CD4+CD45RA+) T cells in Japanese blue-collar workers. *Psychotherapy and Psychosomatics, 66,* 192–198.

Kenrick, D. T., & Simpson, J. A. (1997). Why social psychology and evolutionary psychology need each other. In J. A. Simpson & D. T. Kenrick (Eds.), *Evolutionary social psychology* (pp. 1–20). Mahwah, NJ: Lawrence Erlbaum.

Kiecolt-Glaser, J. K. (2009). Psychology's gateway to the biomedical future. *Psychoneuroimmunology, 4,* 367–369.

Kiecolt-Glaser, J. K., Bane, C., Glaser, R., & Malarkey, W. B. (2003). Love, marriage, and divorce: Newlyweds' stress hormones foreshadow relationship changes. *Journal of Consulting and Clinical Psychology, 71,* 176–188.

Kiecolt-Glaser, J. K., Loving, T., Stowell, J. R., Malarkey, W. B., Lemeshow, S., Dickinson, S. L., et al. (2009). Hostile marital interactions, proinflammatory cytokine production, and wound healing. *Archives of General Psychiatry, 62,* 1377–1384.

Kiecolt-Glaser, J. K., & Newton, T. (2001). Marriage and health: His and hers. *Psychological Bulletin, 127,* 472–503.

Klosterman, L. (2009). *Immune system.* Tarrytown, NY: Marshall Cavendish Benchmark.

Knapp, M., Miller, G. R., & Fudge, K. (1994). Background and current trends in the study of interpersonal communication. In M. L. Knapp & G. R. Miller (Eds.), *Handbook of interpersonal communication* (2nd ed., pp. 3–20). Thousand Oaks, CA: Sage.

Kosfeld, M., Heinrichs, M., Zak, P. J., Fischbacher, U., & Fehr, E. (2005). Oxytocin increases trust in humans. *Nature, 435,* 673–676.

Kuepper, Y., Alexander, N., Oxinsky, R., Mueller, E., Schmitz, A., Netter, P., et al. (2010). Aggression-interactions of serotonin and testosterone in healthy men and women. *Behavioral Brain Research, 206,* 93–100.

Kuhn, C., & Schanberg, S. (1998). Responses to maternal separation: Mechanisms and mediators. *International Journal of Developmental Neuroscience, 16,* 261–270.

Kurup, R. K., & Kurup, P. A. (2003). Hypothalamic digoxin, hemispheric dominance, and neurobiology of love and affection. *International Journal of Neuroscience, 113,* 721–729.

Lábrová, R., Honzíková, N., Maděrová, E., Vysočanová, P., Novákova, Z., Závodná, E., et al. (2005). Age-dependent relationship between the carotid intima-media thickness, baroreflex sensitivity, and the inter-beat interval in normotensive and hypertensive subjects. *Physiological Research, 54,* 593–600.

Laurent, H. K., & Powers, S. I. (2007). Emotion regulation in emerging adult couples: Temperament, attachment, and HPA response to conflict. *Biological Psychology, 76,* 61–71.

Levenson, R. W., Carstensen, L. L., & Gottman, J. M. (1994). The influence of age and gender on affect, physiology, and their interrelations: A study of long-term marriage. *Journal of Personality and Social Psychology, 67,* 56–68.

Levenson, R. W., Ekman, P., Heider, K., & Friesen, W. (1992). Emotion and autonomic nervous system activity in the Minangkabau of West Sumatra. *Journal of Personality and Social Psychology, 62,* 972–988.

Levenson, R. W., & Gottman, J. M. (1983). Marital interaction: Physiological linkage and affection exchange. *Journal of Personality and Social Psychology, 45,* 587–597.

Lewis, R. J. (2009, May). *Trait affection and asymmetry in the prefrontal cortex: Toward a neurological profile of affectionate communicators.* Paper presented at the annual meeting of the International Communication Association, Chicago.

Loving, T. J., Crockett, E. E., & Paxson, A. A. (2009). Passionate love and relationship thinkers: Experimental evidence for acute cortisol elevations in women. *Psychoneuroendocrinology, 34,* 939–946.

Loving, T. J., Heffner, K. L., & Kiecolt-Glaser, J. K. (2006). I've got you under my skin: Physiology and interpersonal relationships. In A. L. Vangelisti & D. Perlman (Eds.), *The Cambridge handbook of personal relationships* (pp. 385–408). New York: Cambridge University Press.

Luecken, L. J., Kraft, A., & Hagan, M. J. (2009). Negative relationships in the family-of-origin predict attenuated cortisol in emerging adults. *Hormones and Behavior, 55,* 412–417.

Marazziti, D., & Canale, D. (2004). Hormonal changes when falling in love. *Psychoneuroendocrinology, 29,* 931–936.

Marazziti, D., Dell-Osso, B., Baroni, S., Mungai, F., Catena, M., Rucci, P., et al. (2006). A relationship between oxytocin and anxiety of romantic attachment. *Clinical Practice and Epidemiology in Mental Health, 2,* 2–28.

Maton, A., Hopkins, J., McLaughlin, C. W., Johnson, S., Warner, M. Q., LaHart, D., et al. (1993). *Human biology and health.* Englewood Cliffs, NJ: Prentice Hall.

Matthews, P. M., & Jezzard, P. (2004). Functional magnetic resonance imaging. *Journal of Neurology, Neurosurgery, & Psychiatry With Practical Neurology, 75,* 6–12.

Mazur, A., & Booth, A. (1998). Testosterone and dominance in men. *Behavioral and Brain Sciences, 21,* 353–363.

Mazur, A., Rosa, E., Faupel, M., Heller, J., Leen, R., & Thurman, B. (1980). Physiological aspects of communication via mutual eye gaze. *American Journal of Sociology, 86,* 50–74.

McCroskey, J. C. (1997, November). *Why we communicate the ways we do: A communibiological perspective.* Carroll C. Arnold Distinguished Lecture, presented at the annual convention of the National Communication Association, Chicago.

McCullough, M., Orsulak, P., Brandon, A., & Akers, L. (2007). Rumination, fear, and cortisol: An in vivo study of interpersonal transgressions. *Health Psychology, 26,* 126–132.

McEwen, B. S. (1998). Protective and damaging effects of stress mediators. *New England Journal of Medicine, 338,* 171–179.

McIntyre, M., Ganestad, S. W., Gray, P. B., Chapman, J. F., Burnham, T. C., O'Rourke, M. T., et al. (2006). Romantic involvement often reduces men's testosterone levels—but not always: The moderating role of extrapair sexual interest. *Journal of Personality and Social Psychology, 91,* 642–651.

Miller, G., Chen, E., & Zhou, E. (2007). If it goes up, must it come down? Chronic stress and the hypothalamic–pituitary–adrenocortical axis in humans. *Psychological Bulletin, 133,* 25–45.

Mithen, S. (1996). *The prehistory of the mind: The cognitive origins of art and science.* London: Thames & Hudson.

Morris, R. (2001). *The evolutionists: The struggle for Darwin's soul.* New York: Freeman.

Muehllehner, G., & Karp, J. S. (2006). Positron emission tomography. *Physics in Medicine & Biology, 51,* 117–137.

Munck, A., Guyre, P. M., & Holbrook, N. J. (1984). Physiological functions of glucocorticoids in stress and their relation to pharmacological actions. *Endocrinology Review, 5,* 25–44.

Nakata, A., Araki, S., Tanigawa, T., Niki, A., Sakurai, S., Kawakami, N., et al. (2000). Decrease of suppressor-inducer (CD4+CD45RA+) T lymphocytes and increase of serum immunoglobulin G due to perceived job stress in Japanese nuclear electric power plant workers. *Journal of Occupational and Environmental Medicine, 42,* 143–150.

Nelson, P. P. (1980). The neural basis of EEG waves. *Kybernetes, 9,* 217–222.

Neumann, I. D. (2008). Brain oxytocin: A key regulator of emotional and social behaviors in both females and males. *Journal of Neuroendocrinology, 20,* 858–865.

Nilsen, W., & Vrana, S. (1998). Some touching situations: The relationship between gender and contextual variables in cardiovascular responses to human touch. *Annals of Behavioral Medicine, 20,* 270–276.

Nisbett, R. E., & Wilson, T. D. (1977). Telling more than we can know: Verbal reports on mental processes. *Psychological Review, 84,* 231–259.

Olvera, A., Stewart, S., Galindo, L., & Stephens, J. (2007). Diabetes, depression, and metabolic control in Latinas. *Cultural Diversity and Ethnic Minority Psychology, 13,* 225–231.

Ormiston, T., Wolkowitz, O. M., Reus, V. I., & Manfredi, F. (2003). Behavioral implications of lowering cholesterol levels: A double-blind pilot study. *Psychosomatics, 44,* 412–414.

Owen, N., Poulton, T., Hay, F. C., Mohamed-Ali, V., & Steptoe, A. (2003). Socioeconomic status, C-reactive protein, immune factors, and responses to acute mental stress. *Brain, Behavior, and Immunity, 17,* 286–295.

Partala, T., & Surakka, V. (2003). Pupil size variation as an indication of affective processing. *International Journal of Human-Computer Studies, 59,* 185–198.

Pendry, P., & Adam, E. K. (2007). Associations between parents' marital functioning, maternal parenting quality, maternal emotion and child cortisol levels. *International Journal of Behavioral Development, 31,* 218–231.

Pennebaker, J. W., Kiecolt-Glaser, J. K., & Glaser, R. (1988). Disclosure of traumas and immune function: Health implications for psychotherapy. *Journal of Consulting and Clinical Psychology, 56,* 239–245.

Premack, D., & Woodruff, G. (1978). Does the chimpanzee have a theory of mind? *Behavioral and Brain Sciences, 4,* 515–526.

Price, T. S., & Jaffee, S. R. (2008). Effects of the family environment: Gene-environment interaction and passive gene–environment correlation. *Developmental Psychology, 44,* 305–315.

Priem, J., McLaren, R. M., & Solomon, D. H. (2010). Relational messages, perceptions of hurt, and biological stress reactions to a disconfirming interaction. *Communication Research, 37,* 48–72.

Priem, J., & Solomon, D. H. (2009). Comforting apprehensive communication: The effects of reappraisal and distraction on cortisol levels among students in a public speaking class. *Communication Quarterly, 57,* 259–281.

Priem, J., & Solomon, D. H. (2010a). *The illocutionary force of supportive communication: The effects of message features on physiological stress recovery.* Manuscript submitted for publication.

Priem, J., & Solomon, D. H. (2010b). *Relational uncertainty and physiological stress responses: Reactions to hurtful and supportive messages from a dating partner.* Manuscript submitted for publication.

Pugh, C. R., Nguyen, K. T., Gonyea, J. L., Fleshner, M., Watkins, L. R., Maler, S. F., et al. (1999). Role of interleukin-1 beta in impairment of contextual fear conditioning caused by social isolation. *Behavioural Brain Research, 106,* 109–118.

Rainey, W. E., Carr, B. R., Sasano, H., Suzuki, T., & Mason, J. I. (2002). Dissecting human adrenal androgen production. *Trends in Endocrinology and Metabolism, 13,* 234–239.

Raison, C. L., Capuron, L., & Miller, A. H. (2006). Cytokines sing the blues: Inflammation and the pathogenesis of depression. *Trends in Immunology, 27,* 24–31.

Rapaport, M. H., & Stein, M. B. (1994). Serum interleukin-2 and soluble interleukin-2 receptor levels in generalized social phobia. *Anxiety, 1,* 50–53.

Rhodes, G. (2006). The evolutionary psychology of facial beauty. *Annual Review of Psychology, 57,* 119–226.

Richards, J., & Gross, J. (1999). Composure at any cost? The cognitive consequences of emotion suppression. *Personality and Social Psychological Bulletin, 25,* 1033–1044.

Rimm-Kaufman, S. E., & Kagan, J. (1996). The psychological significance of changes in skin temperature. *Motivation and Emotion, 20,* 63–78.

Roberts, J. B., Sawyer, C. R., & Behnke, R. R. (2004). A neurological representation of speech state anxiety: Mapping salivary cortisol levels of public speakers. *Western Journal of Communication, 68,* 219–231.

Rosal, M. C., King, J., Yunsheng, M., & Reed, G. (2004). Stress, social support, and cortisol: Inverse associations? *Behavioral Medicine, 30,* 11–21.

Rose, A. (2002). Co-rumination in the friendships of boys and girls. *Child Development, 73,* 1830–1843.

Rose, A. J., Carlson, W., & Waller, E. M. (2007). Prospective associations of co-rumination with friendship and emotional adjustment: Considering the socioemotional trade-offs of co-rumination. *Developmental Psychology, 43,* 1019–1031.

Rosenblatt, J. S. (2008). Psychobiology of maternal behavior: Contribution to the clinical understanding of maternal behavior among humans. *Acta Paediatrica, 83,* 3–8.

Roy, M. P., Steptoe, A., & Kirschbaum, C. (1998). Life events and social support as moderators of individual differences in cardiovascular and cortisol reactivity. *Journal of Personality and Social Psychology, 75,* 1273–1281.

Rydstedt, L., Cropley, M., Devereaux, J., & Michalianou, G. (2008). The relationship between long-term job strain and morning and evening saliva cortisol secretion among white-collar workers. *Journal of Occupational Health Psychology, 13,* 105–113.

Saxbe, D., & Repetti, R. L. (2010). For better or worse? Coregulation of couples' cortisol levels and mood states. *Journal of Personality and Social Psychology, 98,* 92–103.

Saxton, T., Lyndon, A., Little, A., & Roberts, S. (2008). Evidence that androstadienone, a putative human chemosignal, modulates women's attributions of men's attractiveness. *Hormones and Behavior, 54,* 597–601.

Scanlan, J. M., Vitaliano, P. P., Ochs, S., Savage, M. V., & Borson, S. (1998). CD4 and CD8 counts are associated with interactions of gender and psychosocial stress. *Psychosomatic Medicine, 60,* 644–653.

Schmid-Ott, G., Jaeger, B., Adamek, C., Koch, H., Lamprecht, F., Kapp, A., et al. (2001). Levels of circulating CD8+ T lymphocytes, natural killer cells, and eosinophils increase upon acute psychosocial stress in patients with atopic dermatitis. *Journal of Allergy and Clinical Immunology, 107,* 171–177.

Soler, H., Vinayak, P., & Quadagno, D. (2000). Biosocial aspects of domestic violence. *Psychoneuroendocrinology, 25,* 721–739.

Stein, M. (1997). Hippocampal volume in women victimized by childhood sexual abuse. *Psychological Medicine, 27,* 951–959.

Stetler, C., & Miller, G. (2005). Blunted cortisol response to awakening in mild to moderate depression: Regulatory influences of sleep patterns and social contacts. *Journal of Abnormal Psychology, 114,* 697–705.

Stoney, C. M., Matthews, K. A., Mcdonald, R. H., & Johnson, C. A. (2007). Sex differences in lipid, lipoprotein, cardiovascular, and neuroendocrine responses to acute stress. *Psychophysiology, 25,* 645–656.

Stowell, J. R., Kiecolt-Glaser, J. K., & Glaser, R. (2001). Perceived stress and cellular immunity: When coping counts. *Journal of Behavioral Medicine, 24,* 323–339.

Teicher, M. H., Dumont, N. L., Ito, Y., Vaituzis, C., Giedd, J., & Andersen, S. (2004). Childhood neglect is associated with reduced corpus callosum area. *Biological Psychiatry, 56,* 80–85.

Thornhill, R., & Palmer, C. T. (2000). *A natural history of rape: Biological bases of sexual coercion.* Cambridge: MIT Press.

Tooby, J., & Cosmides, L. (1992). Psychological foundations of culture. In J. Barkow, L. Cosmides, & J. Tooby (Eds.), *The adapted mind* (pp. 19–36). New York: Oxford University Press.

Tooby, J., & Cosmides, L. (1996). Friendship and the banker's paradox: Other pathways to the evolution of adaptations for altruism. *Proceedings of the British Academy, 88,* 119–143.

Tremblay, R. E., Schaal, B., Boulerice, B., Arseneault, L., Soussignan, R. G., Paquette, D., et al. (1998). Testosterone, physical aggression, dominance, and physical development in early adolescence. *International Journal of Behavioral Development, 22,* 753–777.

Turner, R. A., Altemus, M., Yip, D. N., Kupferman, E., Fletcher, D., Bostrom, A., et al. (2002). Effects on emotion of oxytocin, prolactin, and ACTH in women. *Stress, 5,* 269–276.

Uvnäs-Moberg, K. (1998). Oxytocin may mediate the benefits of positive social interaction and emotions. *Psychoneuroendocrinology, 23,* 819–835.

Van Niekerk, J. K., Huppert, F. A., & Herbert, J. (2001). Salivary cortisol and DHEA: Association with measures of cognition and well-being in normal older men, and effects of three months of DHEA supplementation. *Psychoneuroendocrinology, 26,* 591–612.

Vetrugno, R., Liguori, R., Cortelli, P., & Montagna, P. (2003). Sympathetic skin response. *Clinical Autonomic Research, 13,* 256–270.

Wagner, G. S. (2001). *Marriott's practical electroencephalography* (10th ed.). Philadelphia: Lippincott Williams & Wilkins.

Wallace, A. R. (1858). On the tendency of varieties to depart indefinitely from the original type. *Journal of the Proceedings of the Linnean Society (Zoology), 3,* 53–62.

Wirtz, P. H., Redwine, L. S., Ehlert, U., & Von Känel, R. (2009). Independent association between lower level of social support and higher coagulation activity before and after acute psychosocial stress. *Psychosomatic Medicine, 71,* 30–37.

Wust, S., Federenko, I. S., van Rossum, E. F., Koper, J. W., & Hellhammer, D. H. (2005). Habituation of cortisol responses to repeated psychosocial stress: Further characterization an impact of genetic factors. *Psychoneuroendocrinology, 30,* 199–211.

Young, L. J., & Wang, Z. (2004). The neurobiology of pair bonding. *Nature Neuroscience, 7,* 1048–1054.

Zwolinski, J. (2008). Biopsychosocial responses to social rejection in targets of relational aggression. *Biological Psychology, 79,* 260–267.

# PART III

# Fundamental Units

# Personality and Interpersonal Communication

*John A. Daly*

The idea that people differ from one another in systematic ways has a long history. Aristotle organized the notion of character in Nichomachean ethics; Galen proposed a theory of humors. Beginning in medieval times, classification schemes for people abounded. Scholars today, in various academic disciplines, continue this tradition. In the field of communication, research on personality dispositions has a long and distinguished history. Indeed, some of the earliest empirical studies of communication revolved around individual differences in people's proclivities to be comfortable when speaking in front of others.

Given the enormous number of studies on topics related to individual differences in communication, in this chapter I highlight only major trends and limit my summaries to work done on only some of the major dispositional differences associated with communication. Although one could focus on a variety of dispositional characteristics, including abilities (e.g., intelligence), physical characteristics (e.g., stigmas, physical appearance), interests (e.g., vocational preferences), and so on, in this review, discussion is limited mostly to psychological dispositions that affect interpersonal communication. I first briefly review studies on the development of individual differences and then examine the controversial issue of the role of individual differences in predicting behavioral tendencies. After that, I offer a catalog of various personality dispositions that affect social interaction.

## How Do Individual Differences Emerge?

Significant attention has focused on the apparent heritability of certain personality dispositions. Across characteristics, heritability has been estimated to range from 30% to 50% (Plomin, DeFries, & McClearn, 1990). Clear evidence exists that many communication-related personality constructs have some degree of genetic or biochemical components. For instance, sociability and social phobias have been found to be strongly influenced by genetic inheritance (Bouchard & McGue, 1990; Rapee & Spence, 2004), as have any number of other interpersonal dispositions such as loneliness (McGuire & Clifford, 2000) and depression (Kendler & Prescott, 1999). Some research suggests that there

131

are genetic propensities for behaviors and attitudes related to personality constructs. Jerskey et al. (2010) make a strong case that marriage, and the risk of divorce, is associated with genetic predispositions. Scarr and Weinberg (1981) found that the genetic transmission of verbal ability is partially responsible for the inheritance of authoritarianism. Olson, Vernon, Harris, and Jang (2001) found that a number of communication-related behaviors (e.g., enjoying big parties, enjoying public speaking, being assertive) have significant heritability. A few communication scholars have considered genetic predispositions toward communication-related variables such as communication apprehension (Beatty, McCroskey, & Heisel, 1998) and verbal aggressiveness (Beatty & McCroskey, 1997).

The study of genetics in personality uses many different investigative techniques. Most studies compare monozygotic and dizygotic twins' correlations on various personality dimensions. When monozygotic twins have a significantly higher correlation on a trait than dizygotic twins, the assumption is that genetic influences are present. In communication, Beatty, Marshall, and Rudd (2001) found strong evidence using this method for the heritability of social composure and wit, modest heritability for social confirmation, and no heritability for articulation ability and disclosure appropriateness. Beatty, Heisel, Hall, Levine, and La France (2002), in a meta-analysis, determined that interpersonal affiliation, aggressiveness, and social anxiety are substantially heritable. Similarly, Bleidorn et al. (2010) found a significant genetic association for communal and agency orientation. The challenge with this method is, of course, that monozygotic twins are often treated differently than dizygotic ones.

Other studies examine the similarity of adult twins who were raised apart from one another beginning at early childhood. Researchers using this approach find more than a chance resemblance between twins on various personality measures, suggesting the role of genetics. Even more convincing are adoption studies, where children raised by adoptive parents resemble more closely their birth parents, with whom they have no relationship, than their adoptive parents, who raised them. These studies find strong evidence for the heritability of traits such as sociability (Daniels & Plomin, 1985).

Scholars have also tied specific genes to personality dispositions (Luo, Kranzler, Zou, Wang, & Gelernter, 2007) and to the act of speaking (e.g., the *FoxP2* gene). Sociability is linked to hormonal differences in testosterone (Dabbs, Strong, & Milun, 1997) as well as differential processing in the amygdala (Haas et al., 2009), and extraversion has been tied to the reactivity of the mesolimbic dopaminergic system (Depue, Luciana, Arbisi, Collins, & Leon, 1994).

There are other explanations for the development of various personality variables. Genetics may predispose a person to certain traits, but environmental factors exacerbate or ameliorate the development of those traits. For instance, in the case of social-communicative anxiety, evidence exists that people's anxiety may be shaped by the sorts of reinforcements that they received for communicating as children, the level of social skills they were taught, and the adequacy of the models of communication to which they were exposed as they moved through childhood (Daly & Friedrich, 1981).

## Are Individual Differences Important?

Questions about the validity of individual differences revolve around a very basic concern: Is personality a useful explanatory concept? In seeking an answer to this, scholars have undertaken a plethora of research and theorizing over the past 50 years. Perhaps, the major starting point was a critique by Mischel (1968), who pointed out that presumably, for a trait to have validity, behaviors typically associated with that trait ought to have cross-situational consistency. In looking at a number of traits, Mischel and others found an average correlation across situations of only about .30 or .40 (Funder & Colvin, 1991).

Mischel's (1968) critique resulted in a bevy of responses arguing for the validity of traits. Personality scholars demonstrated considerable evidence for the longitudinal consistency of many personality traits, including ones related to communication (e.g., Jaap, Dennissen, Asendorpf, & Van Aken, 2008; Nave, Sherman, Funder, Hampson, & Goldberg, 2010). Another response suggested that personality constructs represent general predispositions, and consequently, the correlation between any two very specific individual actions should be small. But the correlation among many behaviors, aggregated over time, context, and behavioral manifestations, ought to be high. Epstein (1979), for instance, using classical notions of reliability, found that an aggregate of several behaviors correlated quite nicely with an aggregate of other behaviors all presumed to represent some disposition. Furthermore, general dispositions ought to predict patterns of behavior substantially but be associated only weakly with individual behaviors (Daly, 1978). For example, the correlation between communication apprehension and any self-reported single behavior at one time is, as one would expect, quite small. Alternatively, the correlation between the personality variable and a summation of various behaviors across time was quite large. This notion of matching dispositional generality to behavioral breadth is critical in many formulations. Paunonen and Ashton (2001) found that very specific personality facets predicted very specific behaviors as well as or better than broader dispositions. Smith, Nezlek, Webster, and Paddock (2007) found that specific personality dimensions tied to sexuality (the "Sexy Seven," Schmitt & Buss, 2000) were more strongly associated with daily sexual interactions than more general personality constructs. Measures of traits must match the specificity of the assessed behavior. A third approach highlighted the fact that the magnitude of the relationship between behaviors and personality constructs is not that different from the magnitude of the situational effects found in traditional experiments (Funder & Ozer, 1983). Finally, scholars examined how personality changes over the life span (Lodi-Smith, Geise, Roberts, & Robins, 2009)

and suggest that high levels of intra-individual variability in behaviors associated with a trait may actually be a measure of maladaptiveness (Erickson, Newman, & Pincus, 2009).

Another approach ties personality to situations. One strand of scholarship, drawn from Lewin's (1935) suggestion of behavior being a function of the person and the situation, argues that any personality variable is relevant only in some situations. This person-by-situation-interaction approach (Koestner, Bernieri, & Zuckerman, 1989; Magnusson & Endler, 1977), later conceptualized, in a somewhat different way, as conditional, if-then traits by Mischel, 1999, or as behavioral signatures (Sherman, Nave, & Funder, 2010) supposes that traits vary in their relevance to an individual depending on the situation that person is in. For example, a highly anxious individual might do well in relaxed settings, whereas a less anxious person might do better in situations that raise his or her anxiety. Extraverted leadership enhances group performance when team members are passive but actually reduces team effectiveness when people are proactive (Grant, Gino, & Hofmann, 2011). Reis, Capobianco, and Tsai (2002) argue that personality affects romantic relationships most strongly when one partner feels vulnerable or when partners have competing aims. Other research suggests that personality correlates with behavior in meaningful ways only in some contexts. For example, personality characteristics are most strongly related to performance in jobs with high autonomy (Barrick & Mount, 1993) and to behaviors in settings where social norms are less apparent (Buss, 1989).

An alternative strand of scholarship proposes that individual differences shape the situational choices people make. This is a long-standing argument (Allport, 1937). Emmons, Diener, and Larson (1986), for example, demonstrated that extraverts gravitate toward situations that involve assertiveness, sociability, and intimacy. Daly and McCroskey (1975) found that highly communicatively apprehensive individuals choose professions that require less social interaction than do their counterparts low in apprehension.

Closely related to situational choice models is the observation that traits may be differentially relevant to individuals. For Person A, shyness may be a very relevant construct; for Person B, it may be quite irrelevant. People vary, in other words, in the extent to which dispositions influence them. Allport (1937) suggested that some traits are cardinal (most influential), some central, and others peripheral to any one individual. Since Allport developed his formulation, extensive research suggests that relevance is, or at least should be, an important consideration in studies. Bem and Allen (1974) argue that individuals differ on how consistently their behaviors are tied to any particular trait, and Baumeister and Tice (1988) offer a similar argument for the concept of "traitedness." Finally, the nature of the dependent measure used in studies matters. Some traits, for instance, are more observable than others. Not surprisingly, Funder and Colvin (1988) have found that self–peer correlations are higher with traits that are more visible.

Mischel's (1968) critique forced scholars to productively grapple with the issue of the validity of personality in understanding behavior. The conclusion, after many years, is that personality clearly reflects and affects behavior. In the sections that follow, I describe various traits relevant to interpersonal communication and provide some examples of research using them. I begin by looking at some integrative models of personality that attempt to organize traits. From there, I review many of the dispositions one encounters in communication scholarship. They are clustered, for purposes of structure, into five groups: (1) demographic correlates, (2) cognitive dispositions, (3) social-personal dispositions, (4) communicative dispositions, and (5) relational dispositions.

## Organizing the Traits

### Integrative Models

Scholars in communication, psychology, and related fields have proffered an enormous number of individual differences. Seeking parsimony, in the past 60 years many attempts have been made to cluster dispositions. The primary framework, drawing from lexical analyses of the vocabulary of the English language, is "the Big Five" (Goldberg, 1993). The five dimensions are (1) neuroticism (anxiety, angry hostility, depression, self-consciousness, impulsiveness, vulnerability), (2) extraversion (warmth, gregariousness, assertiveness, activeness, excitement seeking, positive affect), (3) intellect or openness to experience (experience seeking, education, reading widely, memory), (4) agreeableness (trustingness, straightforwardness, altruism, compliance, modesty, tender mindedness), and (5) conscientiousness (competence, order, dutifulness, achievement striving, self-discipline, deliberateness). Some scholars argue that the Big Five formulation incorporates virtually all personality constructs and represents universal superordinate traits. A few go further and suggest a general factor of personality (van der Linden, Nijenhuis, & Bakker, 2010). Other scholars argue that the Big Five exclude some important dimensions (e.g., religiosity, manipulativeness, humorousness, honesty), resulting in debates about whether there are, for instance, Big Six instead (Saucier, 2009), including conscientious, honesty/humility, agreeableness, extraversion, emotionality, and openness.

Although the Big Five taxonomy is used in numerous psychological studies of relationships (e.g., Malouff, Thorsteinsson, Schutte, Bhullar, & Rooke, 2010), relatively little research regarding the Big Five has been published in communication journals. This is disappointing, since communication-related correlates of the Big Five have often been discovered in other disciplines. Consider the extraversion dimension as an example. Compared with introverts, extraverts engage in more social activities (Watson & Clark, 1997); have more friends (Selfhout et al., 2010); are more cooperative in groups as well as more likely to raise issues in those groups (LePine & Van Dyne, 2001); are more socially active (Lucas, Le, & Dyrenforth, 2008); are more likely to engage in conversations with a positive focus (Zellars & Perrewe, 2001), experience higher levels of general positive affect (Cote & Moskowitz, 1998), and are viewed as more attractive (Meier, Robinson, Carter, Hinsz, 2010); engage in more agreeable behavior (Cote & Moskowitz, 1998); play greater leadership roles (Chan & Drasgow, 2001); engage in sexual activities more often, in more different ways, and with more partners (Wright & Reise, 1997); are more satisfied in their relationships (Dyrenforth, Kashy, Donnellan, & Lucas, 2010) and less likely to experience negative feelings in their marriages (Belsky & Hsieh, 1998); perceive typical social interactions to be more enjoyable (Barrett & Pietromonaco, 1997); have more friends and lower speech anxiety (Watson & Clark, 1997); are somewhat happier (DeNeve & Cooper, 1998); and have higher status among their peers (Anderson, John, Keltner, & Kring, 2001). Dewaele and Furnham (2000) found extraversion positively associated with speech rate and inversely related to length of utterance. Extraverts also relate stories differently (Thorne, Korobov, & Morgan, 2007).

Other dimensions of the Big Five also have communication correlates. For instance, neuroticism is linked to negative marital outcomes (Ben-Ari & Lavee, 2005) such as extramarital affairs (Buss & Shackelford, 1997), less adaptive parenting (Belsky, Crnic, & Woodworth, 1995), more complaining (Buss, 1991), and negativity (Caughlin, Huston, & Houts, 2000). Neurotic partners use more avoidance and distancing tactics in conflict (Bouchard, 2003). Agreeableness, a third component of the Big Five, is positively correlated with engaging in positive conversations (Zellars & Perrewe, 2001), being seen as attractive (Meier et al., 2010), being chosen as a friend more often (Selfhout et al., 2010), marital satisfaction (Dyrenforth et al., 2010), cooperativeness (LePine & Van Dyne, 2001), and an ability to control anger and frustration in conflict settings (Graziano, Jensen-Campbell, & Hair, 1996). Conscientiousness, a fourth factor, is, for example, positively related to relational satisfaction (Dyrenforth et al., 2010) and the use of

more words with achievement connotations in blogs (Yarkoni, 2010) and inversely related to the number of sexual partners a person has and the person's likelihood of using condoms (Bogg & Roberts, 2004).

An alternative structural formulation of traits equally tied to interpersonal behavior is the interpersonal circumplex model (Leary, 1957). Using two primary dimensions—(1) affiliation, communion, or love (warmth) and (2) control, status, or agency (dominance)—scholars suggest that certain traits (e.g., gregariousness) are complementary to some other traits (e.g., aloofness) and closely related to still others (e.g., assuredness and warmth) (Wiggins & Trobst, 1997). Hopwood et al. (in press) proposed a circumplex model of interpersonal sensitivities (reflecting sensitivities to control, attention seeking, affection, dependence, passivity, timidity, remoteness, and antagonism). Another schematic approach to personality organizes traits in terms of approach and avoidant temperaments (Elliot & Thrash, 2002). The approach dimension reflects variables such as extraversion and positive emotionality, while the avoidance dimension incorporates traits such as neuroticism and negative emotionality. An excellent review of this conceptualization is available (Simpson, Winterheld, & Chen, 2006).

The presumption of integrative frameworks is that the panoply of unorganized traits hinders the development of theory. What's necessary is an organizing scheme that offers a heuristic framework for understanding personality. Although neither the Big Five nor circumplex models can, at this point, adequately meet a sufficiency criterion, both represent interesting and useful frames.

In communication scholarship, little attention is paid to integrative models of personality. Instead, individual variables are the focus of attention. In the following subsections, I briefly review, in catalog form, a number of personality variables that communication scholars have studied. The list is not exhaustive; given the space limitations, I ignore many dispositions noted in the communication journals. I start with demographic variables and move from those to more cognitively oriented dispositions. From there, I turn to communication-related personality dispositions that focus more on social and relationship issues.

## Demographic Correlates

Surprisingly little research examines the demographic correlates of interpersonal communication. We have an extraordinary psychology of interpersonal communication but a sparse sociology of the phenomenon (Vangelisti & Daly, 1988). The most often explored variables are cross-cultural differences (see Chapter 17, by Oetzel & Ting-Toomey, this volume), differences across the life span (see Chapter 21, by Nussbaum, Pechionni, & Wright, this volume), and sex. Other issues such as race (e.g., Kurdek, 2008), ethnicity (Collier, 1996), birth order (Pollet & Nettle, 2009), epidemiological status (Schaller & Murray, 2008), poverty (Hart, Atkins, & Matsuba, 2008), and social class (Haslett, 1990) have received far less attention.

### Sex and Gender Differences

There are sex-related differences in personality traits. Why women and men might differ in traitlike behaviors is an interesting and provocative question. One explanation is tied to innate differences that may have evolutionary roots. The notion is that men and women have faced different adaptive challenges throughout history. Consequently, women tend to seek attributes in prospective mates that are different from those sought by men (Stewart, Stinnett, & Rosenfeld, 2000). For example, men see more sexuality in women than women believe they are communicating (La France, Henningsen, Oates, & Shaw, 2009). Each gender also varies in their criteria for mates (e.g., income and attractiveness) as well as in their preferences about types of infidelity (Buss et al., 1999), jealousy (Buss & Schmitt, 1993), and differential expectations for short- and long-term relationships (Stewart et al., 2000).

A second explanation focuses on socialization and norms. Women and men are taught from childhood how to behave and react, and this is reflected in the behaviors that are seen as socially desirable for each gender. When it comes to emotions and communication, there are two basic accounts for the observed differences in men's and women's communication. One, labeled the *different cultures* account, suggests that men and women really live in different emotional cultures; the other, called the *skill specialization* account, suggests that although men and women live in the same emotional culture, men have not learned the social skills that women often have (Kunkel & Burleson, 1999; Vangelisti & Daly, 1997).

Men and women differ in their use of language. Mulac, Bradac, and Gibbons (2001) summarize much of the research on language differences, noting that men tend to exceed women in (a) references to quantity ("6 feet, 4 inches tall"), (b) judgmental adjectives ("good," "dumb"), (c) elliptical sentences ("Great picture"), (d) directives ("Write that down"), (e) locatives ("in the background"), and (f) "I" references ("I think . . ."). Women, more than men, have been found to use (a) intensive adverbs ("really," "so"), (b) references to emotions ("happy," "hurt"), (c) dependent clauses ("where the shadows are"), (d) sentence initial adverbials ("Actually, it's . . . "), (e) uncertainty verbs ("It seems to be . . ."), (f) oppositions ("It's peaceful yet full of movement"), (g) negations ("It's not a . . ."), (h) hedges ("kind of"), and (i) questions ("What's that?"). Although findings are mixed, studies have also found that women are more likely than men to use (a) personal pronouns ("we," "she") and (b) tag questions ("That's not right, is it?"). It is important to remember, however, that these differences are modest (Ng & Bradac, 1993), and for each type of language difference there are greater complexities. For instance, when it comes to tag questions, women use forms that enhance interaction, whereas men use forms that seek validation (Cameron, McAlinden, & O'Leary, 1988).

There are also sex differences in broader communicative behaviors. For example, compared with men, women are more tentative during disagreements with men (Carli, 1990), especially when topics are typically masculine (Palomares, 2009); they are less assertive (Costa, Terracciano, & McCrae, 2001) and less hostile (Scherwitz, Perkins, Chesney, & Hughes, 1991) and more sensitive to avoidance of conflict (Afifi, McManus, Steuber, & Coho, 2009); they are more likely to be interrupted by men (Smith-Lovin & Brody, 1989), less visually dominant in settings where power is ambiguous (Brown, Dovidio, & Ellyson, 1990), and more democratic as leaders (Eagly & Johnson, 1990); they are more nonverbally involved during social interactions, smile and gaze at their interaction partners more often, and are more expressive (Riggio, 1986) and more easily persuaded, at least in some circumstances (Eagly & Carli, 1981). There are no differences in the need for power (Winter, 1988). In terms of emotions, women are more sensitive to emotions and better at distinguishing facial expressions (except, perhaps, those indicating anger; McClure, 2000), more emotionally aware and better able to describe emotional experiences (Barrett, Lane, Sechrest, & Schwartz, 2000), and more likely to express their emotions than men (Kring & Gordon, 1998). Women have an easier time expressing gratitude than men (Kashdan, Mishra, Breen, & Froh, 2009). Women are almost two times more likely than men to suffer from depression (Nolen-Hoeksema, 2001) and engage in more rumination (Fast & Funder, 2010). More positively, women are more gregarious, warm (Costa et al., 2001), trusting, and nurturing than men (Feingold, 1994) and less narcissistic (Fast & Funder, 2010). In terms of the Big Five, women score higher on extraversion, neuroticism, agreeableness, and conscientiousness (Schmitt, Realo, Voracek, & Allik, 2008).

Males and females also differ in the ways in which they approach relationships. Women's sense of self is more relationally interdependent than is men's (Cross & Madson, 1997). Women's friendships are marked by more disclosure than men's (Taylor & Belgave, 1986), and women receive greater disclosure than men from both other women and men (Helgeson, Shaver, & Dyer, 1987). Women are better than men at interpreting their spouses' emotional messages (Noller & Fitzpatrick, 1990) and when distressed can more accurately decode their husbands' negative messages (Notarius, Benson, Sloane, Vanzetti, & Hornyak, 1989). Men and women differ in their preferred love styles (Morrow, Clark, & Brock, 1995). Women spend more time thinking about their relationships (Ross & Holmberg, 1990), are more upset about arguments with their spouses (Almeida & Kessler, 1998), are more likely to engage in conflict talk (men are more likely to be avoidant and conciliatory [Gottman & Levenson, 1988]), and have more vivid and specific recall of marital disagreements (Ross & Holmberg, 1990). They are more likely to enunciate their unhappiness with their marriages (Hagestad & Smyer, 1982) and are more likely to initiate the end of a marriage (Cross & Madson, 1997). Women are more willing to provide emotional support to others than are men (Trobst, Collins, & Embree, 1994) and are more effective at comforting and offering social support (see Chapter 10, by MacGeorge, Feng, & Burleson, this volume). When offering support, women offer more emotion-focused responses, whereas men provide more problem-solving responses (Barbee, Gulley, & Cunningham, 1990). Women are also less argumentative and verbally less aggressive than men (Nicotera & Rancer, 1994) and demonstrate greater emotional intelligence (Ciarrochi, Chan, & Caputi, 2000).

Other research finds that men and women differ little on many communication-related variables. Dindia and Allen's (1992) meta-analysis of sex differences in disclosure found very few differences due to gender. Canary and Hause (1993) looked at the bulk of studies that have included sex differences and communication as part of their focus and found that there were minimal differences. Indeed, many of the differences observed in research may change as a function of the times. Twenge (2001) found, for instance, that although historically men have been more assertive than women, that difference has become progressively smaller over the years. Some scholars have argued that sex differences mask differences in other variables, such as status and roles. For instance, Moskowitz, Suh, and Desaulniers (1994) found that men's and women's dominant/submissive behaviors were tied more to their roles as supervisors or supervisees than to sex.

In the past few decades of the 20th century, scholars began to distinguish between sex (male vs. female) and gender (masculine vs. feminine). The observation was that people vary not only in terms of biological sex but also in the ways they approach issues psychologically. Bem (1974) suggested two independent dimensions, masculinity and femininity, which were later reconceptualized as instrumentality and expressiveness, respectively. The category that was most intriguing to scholars was the notion of androgyny—the state of being high in both masculinity and femininity. Androgynous individuals are socially more competent (Ickes, 1985), although high femininity for both partners is the strongest predictor of relational satisfaction (Lamke, 1989).

In recent years, there has been a substantial increase in studies of same-sex relationships. There are few differences between same-sex and mixed-sex relationships in terms of commitment, relational satisfaction, and quality (Kurdek, 2004), although there are differences in, for example, the amount and sources of social support (Blair & Holmberg, 2008) and the sorts of friendships people have (Galupo, 2009). There are also meaningful differences between gay and lesbian couples in how they meet as well as maintain their romantic relationships (Diamond, 2006).

## Cognitive Dispositions

### Locus of Control

Rotter's (1966) concept of locus of control concerns an individual's beliefs about his or her control over the environment. At one end of the continuum are individuals with an internal locus of control; "internals" believe that they have mastery over what happens to them. They are the "origins" of their actions. At the other end of the continuum are "externals," who believe that they have little control over their fates, that they are "pawns." They sense that their lives are shaped by chance, luck, and other variables over which they have no control. Communicatively, internals are more attuned to information that bears on their lives (Rotter, 1966) and are less likely than externals to experience negative stressors (Thoits, 1995). Internals are more attentive listeners, more socially skilled in conversations, more sensitive to social cues (Lefcourt, Martin, & Fick, 1985), more open to change (Chen & Wang, 2007), and less likely to withdraw in conflict situations (Canary, Cunningham, & Cody, 1988).

In marital and romantic relationship settings, internals are more achievement focused and task oriented, especially when it comes to marital problem solving. Internality is positively related to marital quality (Myers & Booth, 1999) and inversely related to marital commitment (Scanzoni & Arnett, 1987) and verbal aggression (Winkler & Doherty, 1983). Internals find romance and love less mysterious and approach relationships in less idealistic ways (Dion & Dion, 1973). Since Rotter's (1966) initial conceptualization, arguments have been made that locus of control is better understood in various contexts. Consequently, scholars have suggested a number of situation-specific control motivations, such as health (Wallston & Wallston, 1981), political affairs, and marriage (Miller, Lefcourt, & Ware, 1983), as well as specific sorts of interactions, such as conflict (Canary et al., 1988).

### Cognitive Complexity

In communication scholarship, cognitive complexity has been defined in terms of the number of different constructs an individual uses to describe others (differentiation), the degree to which those constructs cohere (integration), and the level of abstraction of the constructs (abstractiveness). The bulk of the research demonstrates positive consequences for complexity. Cognitively more complex individuals offer more person-centered responses when it comes to comforting (Burleson, 1994), emotional support (Samter, 2002), persuading (O'Keefe & Shepherd, 1989), or the use of regulative messages (Adams & Shepherd, 1996). The reason for this appears to be that cognitively complex individuals are better able to perform a variety of tasks related to successful communication, such as recognizing affect (Burleson, 1994), decoding nonverbal behaviors (Woods, 1996), integrating information (O'Keefe, Delia, & O'Keefe, 1977), and engaging in role taking or perspective taking (Kline, Pelias, & Delia, 1991). The messages that are produced by cognitively complex individuals are, consequently, more impactful or effective than those produced by their less complex counterparts. People who have more complex representations of their partners are happier in the romantic relationships, perhaps because they tend to handle conflicts in the relationships more effectively (Karney & Gauer, 2010). The capability to think complexly is also linked to more negative communicative behaviors. For instance, Bacue and Samter (2001) found that people high in cognitive complexity can create messages that were more effective at making romantic partners feel guilty than were people who were less complex. Burleson (1998) offers a very thorough and integrative review of the entire complexity literature as it relates to interpersonal communication.

## Authoritarianism and Dogmatism

In the early years of the empirical study of communication, authoritarianism (Adorno, Frenkel-Brunswik, Levinson, & Sanford, 1950) and dogmatism (Rokeach, 1960) were of special importance to researchers. In many ways, the two constructs (as well as a third, labeled *tolerance for ambiguity*) tap into the same broad idea: Some people are more rigid than others, and this

rigidity affects both how they communicate and how they respond to communication. For instance, authoritarians choose not to accept information that may change their attitudes (Dillehay, 1978); dogmatic individuals are more responsive to source cues when it comes to persuasion (DeBono & Klein, 1993), and they have smaller verbal working memory spans (Brown, 2007). Steinfatt (1987) offers an excellent and thorough summary of the research on these variables.

## Emotional Intelligence

In the past decade, researchers have paid significant attention to a construct labeled *emotional intelligence*. Although many consider this a relatively new construct, Thorndike (1920) presaged the concept early in the 20th century, when he discussed social intelligence as one of three kinds of intelligence. In the popular literature, Goleman (1995) suggests that the construct has five components: (1) self-awareness, (2) managing emotions, (3) motivating oneself, (4) empathy, and (5) handling relationships. In academic work, Salovey and Mayer (1990) defined emotional intelligence as the ability of people "to monitor their own and others' emotions, discriminate among them, and use the information to guide [their] thinking and actions" (p. 189). Mayer and Salovey (1997) argued that emotional intelligence is best construed as an ability. The notion underlying the construct is that emotional intelligence is very different from intelligence as it is typically narrowly defined, with a focus on academic achievement and capability.

The research on emotional intelligence has been conceptually mixed. Davies, Stankov, and Roberts (1998) found that the variables typically falling under the rubric of emotional intelligence are well described by existing measures of traits (apart from the ability to perceive emotions). Nonetheless, some sort of emotional intelligence does seem to exist, and it affects interpersonal exchanges. For example, the ability of children to recognize different emotions successfully at the age of five is positively correlated with their level of social skills (e.g., assertiveness and cooperativeness) and academic performance at the age of nine (Izard et al., 2001). Empathic accuracy (Ickes, 1997), a presumed component, is positively correlated with adjustment of teenagers in school (Gleason, Jensen-Campbell, & Ickes, 2009). Emotional accuracy depends on a person's ability to use auditory and verbal information about the person being perceived (Zaki, Bolger, & Ochsner, 2009). In the case of adults, people who are better at recognizing emotions are also higher in empathy (Mayer, DiPaulo, & Salovey, 1990), and individuals who are more socially perceptive are more sociable, less socially anxious (Schroeder & Ketrow, 1997), and seen as more socially skilled by friends (Costanzo & Archer, 1989). There is a positive correlation (albeit small) between one's ability to communicate emotional information nonverbally and to detect emotional information in others (Elfenbein & Eisenfraft, 2010). Emotional intelligence is positively associated with life satisfaction, empathy, self-esteem, relational quality, the ability to manage one's moods (Ciarrochi et al., 2000), and health (Martins, Ramalho, & Morin, 2010), as well as with extraversion, independence, and self-control; it is inversely associated with anxiety (Newsome, Day, & Catano, 2000). It is also positively related to emotional stability, optimism, stress tolerance, self-regard (Bar-On, 1997), social interaction effectiveness (Lopes et al., 2004), as well as the effective use of humor (Yip & Martin, 2006). Other scholars argue for constructs that are different from emotional intelligence but nonetheless are important for social effectiveness. For instance, Heggestad and Morrison (2008) inductively derive a four-dimensional model of social effectiveness (social potency, social appropriateness, social Emotional expression, and social reputation).

Other, more cognitive variables, such as intelligence, the need for cognition, private and public self-consciousness, and needs for achievement, affiliation, and power, are clearly important to scholars in interpersonal communication. Space limitations, however, prevent discussion of them in this chapter.

# Social-Personal Dispositions

## Loneliness

The defining characteristic of loneliness is an unpleasant or unacceptable discrepancy between what individuals want in terms of relationships and what they believe they have. Thus, one person might be lonely and yet report having numerous friends, whereas another may have very few friends and yet describe himself or herself as not at all lonely. The quantity of relationships per se is not necessarily related to loneliness. Furthermore, emotional loneliness (the absence of close emotional attachments leading to feelings of aloneness regardless of the companionship of others) is often distinguished from social loneliness (the absence of an engaging social network, resulting in feelings of boredom and marginality).

Lonely people report lower self-esteem (Wittenberg & Reis, 1986) and feel less satisfied in their romantic relationships (Flora & Segrin, 1998). They are less optimistic, lower in social support and agreeableness, and more anxious and angry (Cacioppo et al., 2006). Behaviorally, lonely individuals are less self-disclosive (Solano, Batten, & Parish, 1982), less expressive (Segrin, 1996), more socially passive (Vitkus & Horowitz, 1987), more avoidant in terms of their social reaction style (Eronen & Nurmi, 1999), particularly sensitive to rejection (Stokes, 1987), more jealous (Rotenberg, Shewchuk, & Kimberly, 2001), less socially skilled (Solano & Koester, 1989), and less empathic and less responsive to the needs, concerns, and feelings of others (Jones, Hobbs, & Hockenbury, 1982). Lonely people rate the social situations they are in less positively (Duck, Pond,

& Latham, 1994) and are less skilled in planning social encounters (Berger & Bell, 1988). Lonely people attribute their interpersonal failures to internal and stable causes and their successes in interpersonal activities to external and unstable causes (Anderson, Miller, Riger, Dill, & Sedikides, 1994). They believe that others have negative feelings toward them (Jones et al., 1982), and they feel less socially competent than do people who are not lonely (Spitzberg & Canary, 1985). Loneliness is correlated, in expected ways, with a variety of communication-oriented dispositions, such as communication apprehension (Bell & Daly, 1985). Demographically, men report higher levels of loneliness than women (Schultz & Moore, 1986). Lonely men are more aggressive than other men, especially toward women (Check, Perlman, & Malamuth, 1985). Loneliness has numerous negative health-related consequences (Orth-Gomer, 2009).

## Depression

Depression affects and is affected by communication. Theories of depression suggest that people who are depressed seek out others for personal reassurance. Paradoxically, they then often reject that reassurance, doubting the sincerity of the people who offer it and seeing it, instead, as pity (Coyne, 1976). This pattern creates a depressive spiral. Central to Coyne's (1976) theory is the notion of reassurance seeking. Joiner and Metalsky (2001) offer a measure of people's tendencies to seek reassurance and find that their proclivity to seek excessive reassurance is associated with a greater likelihood of being depressed, becoming depressed, and experiencing depression after stressful events.

Depression is correlated with less secure attachment and greater fearful avoidant attachment (Roberts, Gotlib, & Kassel, 1996), greater femininity (Cheng, 1999), greater shyness (Bruch, Rivet, & Laurenti, 2000), lower self-esteem (Tarlow & Haaga, 1996), more self-focused attention (Fast & Funder, 2010), less optimism (Vikers &

Vogeltanz, 2000), and more sensitivity to criticism (Gilbert & Miles, 2000). Depressed people, when making social comparisons, are less likely to make downward comparisons that would make them feel better about themselves (Giordano, Wood, & Michela, 2000). They believe that they themselves and their interaction partners are colder (Thompson, Whiffen, & Blain, 1995) and less socially competent than nondepressed individuals (Segrin & Abramson, 1994), although the evidence for actual behavioral differences is limited (Segrin, 1990). They also are seen as less socially competent (Dykman, Horowitz, Abramson, & Usher, 1991), yet they are more likely to seek out social information about themselves (Hildebrand-Saints & Weary, 1989).

The consequences of these sorts of behaviors and feelings are predictable. Depressed individuals describe their interactions as less satisfying (Nezlek, Imbrie, & Shean, 1994), feel they are more rejected by others (even though, in reality, they are not; Dobson, 1989), and, over time, people around depressed individuals, such as roommates, withdraw and become more negative about those with depression (Hokanson & Butler, 1992). Depressed individuals have a pessimistic attributional style; they make internal, stable, and global attributions about negative events (Day & Maltby, 2000). Interestingly, they are better than nondepressed people at detecting deception (Lane & DePaulo, 1999), even though they are slower (Cooley & Nowicki, 1989) and less accurate at reading many nonverbal cues (Persad & Polivy, 1993) and are not as effective at solving interpersonal problems (Gotlib & Asarnow, 1979). Depressed people's partners change their communication behaviors after assigning a label of depression to those people and, over time, often end up engaging in inconsistent behavior toward them (Duggan & Le Poire, 2006).

Relationally, marriages of depressed people are characterized by negativity and conflict (Beach, Whisman, & O'Leary, 1994). The disposition is associated with marital problems (Dew

& Bromet, 1991) and divorce (Bruce, 1998). In family settings, depression affects the ways in which parents communicate with their children (Cummings & Davies, 1994). Depressed mothers communicate toward their children in more negative ways than do nondepressed mothers (Messer & Gross, 1995), and those sorts of messages lead to children's externalizing problems (Cummings & Davies, 1994) and their being more irritable (Hops et al., 1987) and even more depressive themselves (Davies, Dumenci, & Windle, 1999). Importantly, recent research has explored dispositional optimism (Assad, Donnellan, & Conger, 2007) and found it invaluable for successful romantic relationships.

## Self-Esteem

One of the most influential models of the self that is tied directly to communication is Cooley's (1902) theory of the "looking-glass self," which led, over time, to symbolic interaction theory. The premise is that we construct our self-images from how we internalize what we believe others think of us. Consequently, self-esteem is affected by the interactions people have with valued others, such as family members (Kernis, Brown, & Brody, 2000). There are multiple sorts of self-esteem. Rubin and Hewstone (1998) suggest three continua: (1) global versus specific esteem, (2) trait versus state esteem, and (3) personal versus social esteem. Others suggest that people have three domains of self—actual, ideal, and ought (Higgins, 1987). Still others have proposed domain-specific sorts of esteem (Marsh, 1989). Notably, research has revealed that extremely positive self-esteem may actually be dangerous (Baumeister, Campbell, Krueger, & Vohs, 2003).

Self-esteem is clearly related to a variety of communication-related outcomes. Indeed, most measures of self-esteem include numerous items tied to interpersonal settings (Zeigler-Hill, 2010). People lower in self-esteem are shyer (McCroskey, Daly, Richmond, & Falcione, 1977),

less likely to believe that they have a voice in decisions (Brockner et al., 1998), less likely to ask questions in classrooms (Daly, Kreiser, & Roghaar, 1994), more lonely (Brage, Meredith, & Woodward, 1993) and depressed (Orth, Robins, & Roberts, 2008), more verbally aggressive (Rancer, Kosberg, & Silvestri, 1992), less likely to report marital satisfaction (Larson, Anderson, Holman, & Niemann, 1998), and more likely to experience relational jealousy (White & Mullen, 1989). They experience more distress when their romantic relationships break up (Waller & MacDonald, 2010). Self-esteem, parenthetically, also affects the ways in which jealousy is expressed (Buunk, 1995). Research on persuasion suggests that there is a quadratic relationship between esteem and persuasibility (Rhodes & Wood, 1992), although individuals with low self-esteem may be more susceptible to inoculation manipulations (Pfau, Van Bockern, & Kang, 1992).

There is evidence for sex differences in self-esteem. Males generally have slightly more positive self-esteem than do females (Kling, Hyde, Showers, & Buswell, 1999; compare Deaux & La France, 1998), although women have stronger self-esteem in areas such as reading and relationships with same-sex friends. (Men have higher domain-specific self-esteem in areas such as physical abilities, math, and appearance [Marsh, 1989].) Women's self-esteem is positively related to their memory for information about people, whereas men's self-esteem is positively associated with individualism (Josephs, Markus, & Tafarodi, 1992).

An important distinction was made by McGuire and McGuire (1981), who suggested that self-esteem and self-concept differ conceptually. Self-esteem is evaluative. Self-concept, on the other hand, is determined by what makes a person feel distinctive from others. A boy raised with many female siblings will, when asked to describe himself, quickly offer his sex as a descriptor; his sisters, asked for self-descriptions, will not mention their sex, since it fails to distinguish them in their environment.

## Narcissism

Extreme self-esteem might reach the point of narcissism. Narcissistic people are more popular at first meetings (Back, Schmukle, & Egloff, 2010), deny negative feedback (Smalley & Stake, 1996), engage in greater self-enhancement (Campbell, Reeder, Sedikides, & Elliot, 2000), use more self-referents (Fast & Funder, 2010), are more extraverted and less agreeable, and use more sexual language (Holtzman, Vazire, & Mehl, 2010). They are more likely to derogate people who critique them (Horton & Sedikides, 2009) and more likely to engage in infidelity (Buss & Shackelford, 1997). Arguing that people vary in the degree to which they need to be at the center of attention in social interactions, Vangelisti, Knapp, and Daly (1990) offer a communication-related version of narcissism under the rubric of "conversational narcissism."

## Humor

The notion that people vary systematically in their sense of humor has a long history. Empirical research suggest that an inverse relationship exists between sense of humor and neuroticism (Kohler & Ruch, 1996) and health, although the latter finding is not consistent across studies (Martin, 2001). Bippus (2000) and Booth-Butterfield and Booth-Butterfield (1991) describe measures of an individual's propensity to use humor. There are multiple styles of humor (Galloway, 2010), including affiliative, self-enhancing, aggressive, and self-defeating styles, which are related in various ways to optimism as well as many of the components of the Big Five (Veselka, Schermer, Martin, & Vernon, 2010).

## Machiavellianism

Christie and Geis (1970) proposed that people differ in the degree to which they enjoy manipulating others. Highly Machiavellian individuals prefer face-to-face interactions because such settings provide them with the most information they can use in taking advantage of others. Machiavellianism is positively related to communication flexibility (Martin, Anderson, & Thweatt, 1998), interaction planning (Allen, 1990), helping (Wolfson, 1981), self-monitoring (Riggio & Friedman, 1982), persuasibility (Burgoon, Lombardi, Burch, & Shelby, 1979; Burgoon, Miller, & Tubbs, 1972), group interaction (Bochner & Bochner, 1972) and effectiveness (Jones & White, 1983), and managerial success (Gable & Topol, 1991), although it also is associated with dysfunctional workplace behaviors such as bullying (Kiazad, Restubog, Zagenczyk, Kiewitz, & Tang, 2010). Conceptually, Machiavellianism was considered a unidimensional construct until Kessler et al. (2010) argued for three dimensions—power, manipulativeness, and harsh management practices. Recent research on people's dispositional beliefs about their ability to influence others (Chen, Langner, & Mendoza-Denton, 2009) offers an interesting adjunct to personality variables tied to influence.

## Empathy

Measures of empathy (Davis, 1983) assess components such as sympathy, personal distress, and perspective taking. Empathy is positively related to social intelligence, extraversion, affective communication (Davies et al., 1998), conversational sensitivity (Daly, Vangelisti, & Daughton, 1987), a communal orientation in relationships (Feeney & Collins, 2001), and willingness to offer social support (Trobst et al., 1994). Over the past few years, researchers have directed increasing attention toward understanding how, why, and when people forgive others for transgressions. Berry, Worthington, Parrott, O'Connor, and Wade (2001) found that dispositional forgiveness is positively correlated with agreeableness, extraversion, conscientiousness, emotional stability, and religiosity or spirituality and inversely related to trait anger, neuroticism, and hostility. It is also inversely related to rumination about relationship problems (Pronk, Karremans, Overbeek, Vermulst, & Wigboldus, 2010).

## Self-Monitoring

Snyder (1987) introduced the construct of self-monitoring, which taps people's willingness to adapt to others in social settings. Individuals high in self-monitoring are attentive to what others do and are skilled at tailoring their images in ways that best serve their goals. Compared with low self-monitors, they are more active and talkative in groups (Dabbs, Evans, Hopper, & Purvis, 1980), more expressively friendly, more outgoing, and less worried, anxious, and nervous (Lippa, 1978). They are better able to detect others' intentions (Jones & Baumeister, 1976) and remember more information about others (Berscheid, Graziano, Monson, & Dermer, 1976). They are also more conversationally sensitive (Daly et al., 1987). High self-monitors are likely to manipulate information in order to present better images of themselves to others (Fandt & Ferris, 1990) and are better able to feign interest in people verbally (Leck & Simpson, 1999). And they mimic the behaviors of others better (Estow, Jamieson, & Yates, 2007). In romantic relationships, high self-monitors report experiencing feelings of intimacy sooner, are more likely to date many different people, and feel less committed to their partners than do low self-monitors (Snyder & Simpson, 1984). They are more likely to emerge as leaders in work groups (Zaccaro, Foti, & Kenny, 1991), where social interaction is critical (Garland & Beard, 1979) and are more likely to be promoted in organizations (Kilduff & Day, 1994). They are more prone to resolve conflict through collaboration and compromise (Baron, 1989). Low self-monitors have a desire to be themselves in spite of the requirements of the situation. They keep the same friends regardless of activities, whereas high self-monitors choose different friends for different activities (Snyder, Gangestad, & Simpson, 1983).

The picture of low self-monitors is not necessarily bleak. They are less likely to misrepresent themselves in online dating sites (Hall, Park, Song, & Cody, 2010). They may develop deeper, more trusting relationships with others than do high self-monitors (Gangestad & Snyder, 2000) and anticipate greater distress were their relationships to end (Oyamot, Fuglestad, & Synder, 2010). Tennen's (2006) special section in the *Journal of Personality* offers excellent reviews. Recent work has suggested corollary personality constructs such as political skills (Momm, Blickle, & Liu, 2010).

# Communicative Dispositions

## Argumentativeness and Verbal Aggressiveness

An extensive amount of scholarship has accumulated on argumentativeness and verbal aggressiveness. Argumentativeness is constructive. It involves an individual's willingness to attack another's arguments while defending his or her own position (Infante & Rancer, 1982). Compared with people low in argumentativeness, highly argumentative individuals are more willing to participate in decision-making tasks (Anderson, Martin, & Infante, 1998) and are perceived as being more influential in decision making (Schultz, 1982) as well as more interesting, dynamic, competent, and credible (Infante, 1981). They are more willing to dispute others' statements, having a sense that arguing is a good, enjoyable, and useful activity (Rancer, Kosberg, & Baukus, 1992). They are more resistant to persuasive attempts (Kazoleas, 1993). Consequently, they are less likely to withdraw from conflict situations (Caughlin & Vangelisti, 2000). Rancer (1998) provides an excellent review of this construct.

Verbal aggressiveness differs from argumentativeness. Verbally aggressive individuals attack the self-concepts of others, attempting to cause psychological pain (Infante & Wigley, 1986). They attack and tease others regarding their character, competence, and physical appearance and also make verbal and nonverbal threats. People who are especially aggressive have lower communication skills (Infante, Trebing, Shepherd, & Seeds, 1984), report a stronger dislike for others (Infante, Riddle, Horvath, & Tumlin, 1992), are less satisfied with the interaction of the work groups to which they belong (Anderson & Martin, 1999), have lower levels of argumentative skills (Infante, 1995), engage in more physical aggression (Kassing, Pearce, & Infante, 2000), and are more likely to engage in spousal abuse (Sabourin, Infante, & Rudd, 1993). In addition, they are less open, more defensive, less willing to acknowledge their mistakes (Rancer, Kosberg, & Baukus, 1992), less flexible (Martin, Anderson, & Thweatt, 1998), less responsive (Myers, 1998), and less likely to offer verbal praise (Wigley, Pohl, & Watt, 1989). Consequently, people prefer not having them as teachers (Myers & Knox, 2000), as managers or subordinates (Infante & Gorden, 1985), or as roommates (Martin & Anderson, 1995). Verbally aggressive individuals are less likely to be selected to serve on juries (Wigley, 1999). In family settings, verbal aggressiveness is inversely correlated with the number of positive-affect messages parents offer to children (Bayer & Cegala, 1992). This disposition affects the degree of trust and satisfaction siblings feel for one another (Martin, Anderson, Burant, & Weber, 1997). Wigley (1998) presents a useful summary of the research on verbal aggressiveness. Methodologically, strong arguments have been made that the aggressiveness scale incorporates two very different dimensions: aggressiveness and verbal benevolence (Kotowski, Levine, Baker, & Bolt, 2009). The behavioral validity of the scales has also been challenged (Kotowski et al., 2009).

## Communication Apprehension

The most studied individual difference in the field of interpersonal communication has been communication apprehension. The earliest research

in the field focused on stage fright, and that work continues to this day (Bodie, 2010). However, the majority of work in recent decades has been more interpersonally oriented. Under a variety of labels—such as *reticence* and, more broadly, *social-communicative anxiety, shyness,* and *social anxiety*—the construct taps into the propensity of people to enjoy and seek out opportunities to communicate (approach) or instead to find communication opportunities punishing (avoid). Although there are numerous conceptual differences among the various constructs, for the purposes of this review, we will assume that they all tap into the same basic predisposition.

Space limitations preclude a full recitation of the profound effects of the disposition here (for a much fuller rendition, see Daly, Caughlin, & Stafford, 2009). Behaviorally, people with high levels of communication apprehension are less likely to talk in social settings (Garcia, Sinson, Ickes, Bissonnette, & Briggs, 1991). When shy people are forced to communicate, they involve others (e.g., bringing a friend, letting a friend do the talking [Bradshaw, 1998]), engage in less eye contact (Garcia et al., 1991), and are more self-protective and less disclosive (Meleshko & Alden, 1993). Shy people are less likely to seek health-related advice (Kowalski & Brown, 1994) and are less likely to be successful in positions that require communication, such as sales (Barrick & Mount, 1991). They view their teachers as less immediate and less assertive/responsive (Allen, Long, O'Mara, & Judd, 2008). Perceptually, they are seen less positively by others (Daly, McCroskey, & Richmond, 1977) in a variety of settings, such as interviews (Daly, Richmond, & Leth, 1979) and social interactions (Jones & Carpenter, 1986), especially in initial exchanges (Alden & Wallace, 1995). Interestingly, they are more astute observers of the facial moves of others (Beaton, Schmidt, Schulkin, & Hall, 2010).

In terms of personality correlates, apprehensive individuals are less assertive (Leary, 1983), less argumentative (Infante & Rancer, 1982), less conversationally sensitive (Daly et al., 1987), more embarrassable (Maltby & Day, 2000), and they have a less independent and more interdependent self-construal (Kim, Aune, Hunter, Kim, & Kim, 2001). They have lower self-esteem (McCroskey et al., 1977) and are more likely to have insecure (fearful or dismissive) attachment styles (Duggan & Brennan, 1994), to experience greater sociotropy (Bruch, Rivet, Heimberg, Hunt, & McIntosh, 1999), to believe that they don't match up to what they "ought" to be, and to become more depressed (Bruch et al., 1999). Not surprisingly, shy individuals suffer from more social isolation and more emotional and psychosomatic health problems than do nonshy people (Schmidt & Fox, 1995). Interestingly, people high in social anxiety may be less influenced by what peers say than others (Wright, London, & Waechter, 2009).

Developmentally, shy individuals do not participate as much in classroom interactions (Comadena & Prusank, 1988) and do less well in school, perhaps because of their unwillingness to engage in social exchanges (McCroskey, Andersen, Richmond, & Wheeless, 1981). Communication apprehension is inversely related to academic achievement (e.g., Messman & Jones-Corley, 2001) and cognitive performance (Bourhis & Allen, 1992). Apprehensive individuals are more likely to select occupations that do not require communication (Daly & McCroskey, 1975) and are less willing to seek advancement in work situations (McCroskey & Richmond, 1979). Relationally, shyness affects dating (Jones & Carpenter, 1986) and the decision to marry (Kerr, Lambert, & Bem, 1996).

The most common clinical treatments for the anxiety are systematic desensitization, cognitive restructuring, and visualization. Pharmacological solutions have also become available. Drugs such as monoamine oxidase inhibitors, high-potency benzodiazepenes, and selective serotonin reuptake inhibitors have been linked to the reduction of anxiety, as have various beta-blockers. The only medication approved by the U.S. Food and Drug Administration for this purpose is paroxetine (Paxil). A recent volume edited by

Daly et al. (2009) contains extensive summaries of the treatment literature. It's important to note that situational variables can affect the impact of shyness. Shy people are less comfortable in formal settings (Russell, Cutrona, & Jones, 1986), in settings where they feel particularly conspicuous (Daly, Vangelisti, & Lawrence, 1989), in novel settings (Watson & Cheek, 1986), and in mixed-sex interactions (Turner, Beidel, & Larkin, 1986).

The construct of communication apprehension has produced a number of close relatives, such as dating anxiety (Powers & Love, 2000), informational reception apprehension (Wheeless, Preiss, & Gale, 1997), singing apprehension (Andersen, Andersen, & Garrison, 1978), and intercultural communication apprehension (Neuliep & Ryan, 1998).

## Conflict

People vary in how they approach conflict. The most popular typology of conflict predispositions was developed by Kilman and Thomas (1977). It suggests that underlying the dimensions of assertiveness and cooperativeness are five styles: (1) avoiding, (2) accommodating, (3) confronting, (4) compromising, and (5) collaborating. Research has suggested the empirical validity of these five styles (Rahim & Magner, 1995) and has tied the styles to varying forms of family interactions (Dumlao & Botta, 2000). Christensen (1988) proposed six conflict strategies (reason, assertion, partner support, coercion, manipulation, and avoidance) that have been used in relationship research (Noller, Feeney, Bonnell, & Callan, 1994). Hample and Dallinger (1995) suggested that people vary in how they respond to conflict. Some people take conflict far more personally than others. Their measure, tapping six dimensions (direct personalization, persecution feelings, stress reactions, positive relational effects, negative relational effects, like/dislike valence), is positively correlated with argument avoidance. Roloff offers a good overview of conflict predispositions in Chapter 13 (this volume).

## Communicative and Social Competence and Skill

A large body of literature focuses on communication competence as a disposition. Chapter 15 by Spitzburg and Cupach (this volume) summarizes that work quite well. There are also a variety of communication-oriented variables that are indirect measures of social-communicative competence. Interaction involvement (Cegala, 1981), for instance, assesses the proclivity of individuals to interact in face-sensitive ways. The Interaction Involvement Scale is composed of three factors: responsiveness, perceptiveness, and attentiveness. The measure successfully discriminates between successful and unsuccessful interactants; it is negatively correlated with variables such as self-consciousness and communication apprehension and positively correlated with self-reported communication competence. Conversational sensitivity (Daly et al., 1987) is a seven-factor construct tapping an individual's ability to assess and respond to various communicative challenges. The seven factors are (1) detecting meaning, (2) conversational memory, (3) conversational alternatives, (4) conversational imagination, (5) conversation enjoyment, (6) interpretation, and (7) perceiving affinity. Sensitivity is positively related to the ability to draw high-level inferences when listening to social exchanges, to parsing ability, and to the tendency to emphasize conversation in memory. O'Keefe and Lambert (1995) argue that there are broad individual differences in the ways in which people produce messages. Her model suggests that at the lowest levels, individuals are direct and often insensitive to situational contingencies. At the highest level, people are rhetorically sophisticated in understanding that communication actually creates the situation. Suggesting three levels, Hart, Carlson, and Eadie (1980) propose a construct called rhetorical sensitivity, which taps into a similar idea

(although the reliability of the measure has been called into question). Assertiveness as a communication disposition has a long history (Ames & Flynn, 2007; Richmond & Martin, 1998). In 1978, Wheeless and Grotz proposed a dispositional tendency to disclose, which has received far less attention than it merits (Wigley, 1995). Finally, a construct labeled *communicator style* (Ivanov & Werner, 2010; Norton, 1978; de Vries, Bakker-Pieper, Siberg, van Gameren, & Vlug, 2009) has a variety of dimensions, such as attentiveness, preciseness, threateningness, friendliness, relaxation, dramaticism, impression-leaving, openness, contentiousness, animation, and image conscientiousness.

# Relational Dispositions

## Attachment

One of the most important relational dispositions studied in the past 30 years has been attachment style. Drawing from work by Bowlby (1982), scholars argue that there are individual differences in people's beliefs about their senses of self and other. People's early interactions with caregivers shape how they construe themselves and others as well as their expectations about the amount and types of support they might receive from others. Attachment has major impacts on a variety of interpersonal issues in marriage, parenting, and other family relationships. Vangelisti offers a splendid review of the construct in Chapter 18 (this volume).

## Rejection Sensitivity

Rejection sensitivity is an interpersonal disposition reflecting a tendency to anxiously expect, perceive, and intensely react to rejection. People who are particularly sensitive to rejection are more likely to experience depression after a romantic breakup, be hostile and nonsupportive toward their partners when they feel rejected, feel more rejected when they engage in ambiguous conversations, see insensitive behavior on the part of a new partner as having more harmful intent, feel that their partners are more likely to leave the relationship, feel less satisfied in their relationships, and (in the case of men) feel more jealousy and be more controlling (Romero-Canyas, Downey, Berenson, Ayduk, & Kang, 2010). Given the strong tendency of these individuals to focus on possible rejection, it is not surprising that their romantic relationships are likely to end sooner (Downey, Freitas, Michaelis, & Khouri, 1998). Rejection sensitivity is positively correlated with neuroticism, social avoidance, social distress, interpersonal sensitivity, and insecure attachment. It is inversely related to extraversion, self-esteem, and secure attachment (Downey & Feldman, 1996). In recent years, rejection sensitivity has been broadened to suggest multiple sources of potential rejection (e.g., friends) for different age groups (Chow, Au, & Chiu, 2008). At a more focused level, Gilbert and Miles (2000) introduce an interesting concept of people's sensitivity to "put-downs"; they find that it correlates in predictable ways with a variety of other personality constructs.

## Other Dispositions

Numerous additional individual differences have been tied to communication-related variables, but space constraints allow no more than a mention of them here. Positive and negative affect constitute a very general predisposition. Positive affect is marked by enthusiasm, favorable expectations, and general optimism (Watson, Clark, & Tellegen, 1988). Sensation seeking is inversely correlated with people's willingness to seek information about alternatives to drugs or ways of resisting peer influence about drug use (Stephenson & Palmgreen, 2001). Social desirability (Crowne & Marlowe, 1964) emphasizes how willing individuals are to act in ways they imagine are socially correct. Sociotropy (Robins et al., 1994) is a construct that references people's

excessive concern for obtaining and maintaining the approval and support of others. It is a component of interpersonal dependency and is related to variables such as jealousy and ill health (Bornstein, 1998). Belongingness has been proposed as a vital interpersonal disposition reflecting the basic human need not to be excluded (DeWall, Deckman, Pond, & Bonser, in press; Gailliot & Baumeister, 2007). Authenticity has recently been conceptualized as a personality dimension associated with behaviors such as defensiveness (Lakey, Kernis, Heppner, & Lance, 2008) and relational satisfaction (Brunell et al., 2010). Heroism (Schlenker, Weigold, & Schlenker, 2008) has also been offered as a construct related to communication. Reciprocation wariness—the fear of being exploited in relationships (Cotterell, Eisenberger, & Speicher, 1992)—is another construct, as is Mills and Clark's (1994) suggestion that people differ in their orientations to relationships—communal and exchange. Studies of dispositional embarrassability (Maltby & Day, 2000) hint at some interesting communication-related outcomes. Recent research has proposed individual differences in forgiveness and vengefulness (Balliet, 2010). In addition, there are measures of love ways (Hecht, Marston, & Larkey, 1994) and love styles (Hendricks & Hendricks, 1986) as well as envy (Smith, Parrott, Diener, Hoyle, & Kim, 1999) and intimacy motivation (McAdams, 1992). The concept of intimacy motivation follows from work on social motives such as achievement motivation and power motivation (McClelland, 1986).

## Summary

This review of the literature on personality and interpersonal communication makes apparent some useful future directions for communication scholarship. First, the discipline very much needs an integrative model of personality variables tied to communication, something akin to the Big Five and the drop the circumplex models found in psychology. Communication scholars need some way of conceptually organizing the variables they find important. More broadly, theorizing about traits is notably weak in the discipline. For example, many researchers define traits and their effects by the traits themselves. "Shy people don't talk as much as nonshy individuals" is a definition claim, not an explanatory claim. Why shy people do not talk, what communicatively competent people do to be competent, and so on, are important and largely unanswered questions. In many of the literatures reviewed here, critical constructs are poorly defined. A good example would be how one might operationalize a construct such as "adaptability" or "flexibility" beyond a self-report questionnaire or descriptive definition (e.g., How would you teach a person to be flexible?).

Second, measurement techniques need improvement. The vast majority of variables studied by communication scholars use self-report methods that are open to numerous challenges, such as their obvious susceptibility to social desirability effects. In a few instances, notably in the area of cognitive complexity (which uses sorting tasks) and in work on motives (which uses the Tapas acupressure technique [TAT]), measurement techniques are more opaque. In other areas of communication-oriented personality work, scholars would be wise to probe new methods.

Third, scholars must remember that it is important to be cautious when examining single traits. People are, for lack of a better phrase, composed of a multitude of traits, and these traits certainly interact. For example, people low in communication apprehension may behave very differently from one another, depending on their degree of conscientiousness. Or an argumentative person with high self-esteem may act very differently than an equally argumentative person with low self-esteem. Swickert, Hittner, and Foster (2010) offer an intriguing look at how three of the Big Five dimensions (extraversion, neuroticism, and openness to experience) interact to affect social support. Looking at how different traits combine to create behavioral predispositions is an important future approach for scholarship.

Fourth, work in personality and communication should consider the dyadic nature of many relationships. One person's dispositions can, and do, affect the behavior of the other person. Some studies have explored the joint impact of two interactants' traits (e.g., a competent communicator trying to interact with an incompetent one and a very extraverted individual working with a very shy one), but much more remains to be done. Fitzpatrick's (1998) couple types (traditional, independent, and separate) is a good example of the notion of relational jointness (Givertz, Segrin, & Hanzal, 2009). Findings suggest, for instance, that romantic partners who are similar on some traits are happier than partners who are dissimilar (Barelds & Barelds-Dijkstra, 2007). Markey and Markey (2007) find that satisfied couples were matched on warmth but different on dominance. Le Poire, Shepard, and Duggan (1999) demonstrated the impact of one partner's sort of attachment on the behavior of the other partner, who is similar or different in attachment style. Nonetheless, the amount of variability in relationship satisfaction predicted by similarity in traits may be quite small (Dyrenforth et al., 2010). Other work has found that when spouses agree on the personality traits each other have, they are happier (Letzring & Noftle, 2010).

Fifth, communication scholars can certainly expand their consideration of traits. The relative paucity of research on the Big Five and the circumplex models of personality in the communication literature is notable. In addition, very little research by communication scholars has examined personality disorders and their role in interpersonal communication. Some people have borderline personality disorders (Ayduk et al., 2008), some are psychopaths (Ermer & Kiehl, 2010), and others have serious personality problems (King & Terrance, 2006) or social problems, such as social anhedonia (Silvia & Kwapil, in press). Research on more pathological-related variables might spawn interest in more clinical approaches to communication.

Sixth, scholars may need to broaden the notion of "trait." Some have suggested that there are traits that go beyond the individual. McLeod and

Chaffee (1972), for example, suggest that there are four sorts of family communication patterns based on two dimensions: socio-orientation and concept orientation. Children of sociocentric parents are more susceptible to persuasion and more responsive to source-related variables such as credibility, whereas children of concept-oriented parents are less open to persuasion and, if swayed, are convinced by variables such as the strength of arguments. Concept-oriented parents produce children who are more politically involved. Ritchie and Fitzpatrick (1990) revised the McLeod and Chaffee measure using conformity orientation and conversation orientation as dimensions. Self-reported conversation orientation (i.e., a person reports that his or her family is conversation oriented) is positively related to self-esteem, self-disclosive tendencies, and sociability, whereas self-reported conformity orientation is inversely associated with self-esteem and positively correlated with shyness and self-monitoring (Huang, 1999). Other family- and relationship-oriented personality variables include parenting style, which represents two underlying dimensions (demandingness and warmth or responsiveness) that yield four styles (authoritative, authoritarian, permissive, and neglectful; Stephenson, Quick, & Hirsch, 2010). Authoritative parenting has been found generally to be the best of the four styles (Gray & Steinberg, 1999), and all have been connected, in different ways, to parent–child interaction (Gauvain & Huard, 1999). Early research found, for instance, that authoritarian and controlling parents have children who are less socially competent than those whose parents are authoritative (Baumrind, 1967).

Perhaps most important is the "so what" question. Just because we find that certain sorts of people behave differently than others in interpersonal settings, why is that important? Considering that traits are basic to a person, and considering that they are very difficult to change, what's the value of studying them? One answer is that, given enough knowledge, we can aid people of varying dispositions to be more successful. In educational settings, personality differences are often chosen as a way of segmenting student populations. Alternative kinds of instructional methods are used with different sorts of students. Just as important, in some strands of research on personality, scholars have offered more clinically based responses. There are successful therapies for social anxieties such as communication apprehension. Various methods exist to alleviate depression. Communication competence can be improved with training. Indeed, it would be well worth the time of some students of communication to take a more clinical role when it comes to their studies. Finally, individual differences deepen our understanding of the phenomenon of interpersonal communication. Science is about making distinctions that matter. Clearly, the study of personality in communication has demonstrated that differences do matter. The study of personality has long played an important role in scholarship in interpersonal communication. It has survived so long because it offers an intellectually interesting avenue of research that is grounded in the realities of people's lives.

# References

Adams, C., & Shepherd, G. J. (1996). Managing volunteer performance: Face support and situational features as predictors of volunteers' evaluations of regulative messages. *Management Communication Quarterly, 9,* 363–388.

Adorno, T. W., Frenkel-Brunswik, E., Levinson, D. J., & Sanford, R. N. (1950). *The authoritarian personality.* New York: Harper & Row.

Afifi, T. D., McManus, T., Steuber, K., & Coho, A. (2009). Verbal avoidance and dissatisfaction in intimate conflict situations. *Human Communication Research, 35,* 357–383.

Alden, L. E., & Wallace, S. T. (1995). Social phobia and social appraisal in successful and unsuccessful social interactions. *Behavior Research and Therapy, 33,* 497–505.

Allen, J. L., Long, K. M., O'Mara, J., & Judd, B. (2008). Students' predispositions and orientations toward communication and perceptions of instructor reciprocity and learning. *Communication Education, 57,* 20–40.

Allen, T. H. (1990). An investigation of Machiavellianism and imagined interaction. *Communication Research Reports, 7,* 116–120.

Allport, G. W. (1937). *Personality: A psychological interpretation.* New York: Holt.

Almeida, D. M., & Kessler, R. C. (1998). Everyday stressors and gender differences in daily distress. *Journal of Personality and Social Psychology, 75,* 670–680.

Ames, D. R., & Flynn, F. (2007). What breaks a leader: The curvilinear relation between assertiveness and leadership. *Journal of Personality and Social Psychology, 92,* 307–324.

Anderson, C., John, O. P., Keltner, D., & Kring, A. M. (2001). Who attains social status? Effects of personality and physical attractiveness in social groups. *Journal of Personality and Social Psychology, 81,* 116–132.

Anderson, C. A., Miller, R. S., Riger, A. L., Dill, J. C., & Sedikides, C. (1994). Behavioral and characterological attributional styles as predictors of depression and loneliness: Review, refinement, and test. *Journal of Personality and Social Psychology, 66,* 549–558.

Anderson, C. M., & Martin, M. M. (1999). The relationship of argumentativeness and verbal aggression to cohesion, consensus, and satisfaction in small groups. *Communication Reports, 12,* 21–31.

Anderson, C. M., Martin, M. M., & Infante, D. A. (1998). Decision-making collaboration scale: Tests of validity. *Communication Research Reports, 15,* 245–255.

Andersen, P. A., Andersen, J. F., & Garrison, J. P. (1978). Singing apprehension and talking apprehension: The development of two constructs. *Sign Language Studies, 19,* 155–186.

Assad, K., Donnellan, M. B., & Conger, R. (2007). Optimism: An enduring resource for romantic relationships. *Journal of Personality and Social Psychology, 93,* 285–297.

Ayduk, O., Zayas, V., Downey, G., Cole, A., Shoda, Y., & Mischel, W. (2008). Rejection sensitivity and executive control: Joint predictors of borderline personality features. *Journal of Research in Personality, 42,* 151–168.

Back, M., Schmukle, S., & Egloff, B. (2010). Why are narcissists so charming at first sight? *Journal of Personality and Social Psychology, 98,* 132–145.

Bacue, A. E., & Samter, W. (2001, July). *The dark side of cognitive complexity II: The production of guilt-inducing messages.* Paper presented at the Conference of the International Network on Personal Relationships, Prescott, AZ.

Balliet, D. (2010). Conscientiousness and forgivingness: A meta-analysis. *Personality and Individual Differences, 48,* 259–263.

Barbee, A. P., Gulley, M. R., & Cunningham, M. R. (1990). Social support seeking in personal relationships. *Journal of Social and Personal Relationships, 7,* 531–540.

Barelds, D., & Barelds-Dijkstra, P. (2007). Love at first sight or friends first? Ties among partner personality, trait similarity, relationship onset, relationship quality, and love. *Journal of Social and Personal Relationships, 24,* 479–496.

Bar-On, R. (1997). *Emotional quotient inventory: Technical manual.* Toronto, Ontario, Canada: Multi-Health Systems.

Baron, R. A. (1989). Personality and organizational conflict: Effects of the Type S behavior pattern and self-monitoring. *Organizational Behavior and Human Performance, 44,* 196–281.

Barrett, L. F., Lane, R. D., Sechrest, L., & Schwartz, G. E. (2000). Sex differences in emotional awareness. *Personality and Social Psychology Bulletin, 26,* 1027–1035.

Barrett, L. F., & Pietromonaco, P. R. (1997). Accuracy of the five-factor model in predicting perceptions of daily social interactions. *Personality and Social Psychology Bulletin, 23,* 1173–1187.

Barrick, M. R., & Mount, M. K. (1991). The Big Five personality dimensions and job performance: A meta-analysis. *Personnel Psychology, 44,* 1–26.

Barrick, M. R., & Mount, M. K. (1993). Autonomy as a moderator of the relationship between the Big Five personality dimensions and job performance. *Journal of Applied Psychology, 78,* 111–118.

Baumeister, R. F., Campbell, J. D., Krueger, J. I., & Vohs, K. D. (2003). Does high self-esteem cause better performance interpersonal success, happiness, or healthier lifestyles? *Psychological Science in the Public Interest, 4,* 1–44.

Baumeister, R. F., & Tice, D. M. (1988). Metatraits. *Journal of Personality, 56,* 571–598.

Baumrind, D. (1967). Child-care practices anteceding three patterns of preschool behavior. *Genetic Psychology Monographs, 75,* 43–88.

Bayer, C. L., & Cegala, D. J. (1992). Trait verbal aggressiveness and argumentativeness: Relations with parenting style. *Western Journal of Communication, 56,* 301–310.

Beach, S. R. H., Whisman, M. A., & O'Leary, K. D. (1994). Marital therapy for depression: Theoretical foundation, current status, and future directions. *Behavior Therapy, 25,* 345–371.

Beaton, E. A., Schmidt, L., Schulkin, J., & Hall, G. (2010). Neural correlates of implicit processing of facial emotions in shy adults. *Personality and Individual Differences, 49,* 755–761.

Beatty, M. J., Heisel, A. D., Hall, A. E., Levine, T. R., & La France, B. H. (2002). What can we learn from the study of twins about genetic and environmental influences on interpersonal affiliation, aggressiveness, and social anxiety? *Communication Monographs, 69,* 1–19.

Beatty, M. J., Marshall, L. A., & Rudd, J. E. (2001). A twin study of communication adaptability: Heritability of individual differences. *Quarterly Journal of Speech, 87,* 366–377.

Beatty, M. J., & McCroskey, J. C. (1997). It's in our nature: Verbal aggressiveness as temperamental expression. *Communication Quarterly, 45,* 446–460.

Beatty, M. J., McCroskey, J. C., & Heisel, A. D. (1998). Communication apprehension as temperamental expression: A communibiological paradigm. *Communication Monographs, 65,* 197–219.

Bell, R. A., & Daly, J. A. (1985). Some communicator correlates of loneliness. *Southern Speech Communication Journal, 50,* 121–142.

Belsky, J., Crnic, K., & Woodworth, S. (1995). Personality and parenting: Exploring the mediational role of transient mood and daily hassles. *Journal of Personality, 63,* 905–931.

Belsky, J., & Hsieh, K. (1998). Patterns of marital change during early childhood years: Parent personality, co-parenting, and division-of-labor correlates. *Journal of Family Psychology, 12,* 511–528.

Bem, D. J., & Allen, A. (1974). On predicting some of the people some of the time: The search for cross-situational consistencies in behavior. *Psychological Review, 81,* 506–520.

Bem, S. L. (1974). The measurement of psychological androgyny. *Journal of Consulting and Clinical Psychology, 42,* 155–162.

Ben-Ari, A., & Lavee, Y. (2005). Dyadic characteristics of individual attributes: Attachment, neuroticism, and their relations to marital quality and closeness. *American Journal of Orthopsychiatry, 75,* 621–631.

Berger, C. R., & Bell, R. A. (1988). Plans and the initiation of social relationships. *Human Communication Research, 15,* 217–235.

Berry, J. W., Worthington, E. L., Parrott, L., O'Connor, L. E., & Wade, N. G. (2001). Dispositional forgivingness: Development and construct validity of the transgression narrative test of forgivingness. *Personality and Social Psychology Bulletin, 27,* 1277–1290.

Berscheid, E., Graziano, W. G., Monson, T., & Dermer, M. (1976). Outcome dependency: Attention, attribution, and attraction. *Journal of Personality and Social Psychology, 34,* 978–989.

Bippus, A. M. (2000). Humor usage in comforting episodes: Factors predicting outcomes. *Western Journal of Communication, 64,* 359–384.

Blair, K. L., & Holmberg, D. (2008). Perceived social network support and well-being in same-sex versus mixed-sex romantic relationships. *Journal of Social and Personal Relationships, 25,* 769–791.

Bleidorn, W., Kandler, C., Riemann, R., Angleitner, A., Hulsheger, U., & Spinath, F. (2010). Nature and nurture of the interplay between personality traits and major life goals. *Journal of Personality and Social Psychology, 99,* 366–379.

Bochner, A. P., & Bochner, B. (1972). A multivariate investigation of Machiavellianism and task structure in four-man groups. *Speech Monographs, 39,* 277–285.

Bodie, G. D. (2010). A racing heart, rattling knees, and ruminative thoughts: Defining, explaining, and treating public speaking anxiety. *Communication Education, 59,* 70–105.

Bogg, T., & Roberts, R. W. (2004). Conscientiousness and health related behaviors: A meta-analysis of the leading behavioral contributors to mortality. *Psychological Bulletin, 130,* 887–919.

Booth-Butterfield, S., & Booth-Butterfield, M. (1991). Individual differences in the communication of humorous messages. *Southern Journal of Speech Communication, 56,* 205–219.

Bornstein, R. F. (1998). Interpersonal dependency and physical illness: A meta-analytic review of retrospective and prospective studies. *Journal of Research in Personality, 32,* 480–497.

Bouchard, G. (2003). Cognitive appraisals, neuroticism, and openness as correlates of coping strategies: An integrative model of adaptation to marital difficulties. *Canadian Journal of Behavioural Science, 35,* 1–12.

Bouchard, T. J., Jr., & McGue, M. (1990). Genetic and rearing environmental influences on adult personality: An analysis of adopted twins reared apart. *Journal of Personality, 58,* 263–292.

Bourhis, J., & Allen, M. (1992). Meta-analysis of the relationship between communication apprehension and cognitive performance. *Communication Education, 41,* 68–76.

Bowlby, J. (1982). *Attachment and loss: Vol 1. Attachment* (2nd ed.). London: Hogarth Press.

Bradshaw, S. D. (1998). I'll go if you will: Do shy persons utilize social surrogates? *Journal of Social and Personal Relationships, 15,* 651–669.

Brage, D., Meredith, W., & Woodward, J. (1993). Correlates of loneliness among midwestern adolescents. *Adolescence, 28,* 685–693.

Brockner, J., Heuer, L., Siegel, P. A., Wiesenfeld, B., Christopher, M., Grover, S., et al. (1998). The moderating effect of self-esteem in reaction to voice: Converging evidence from five studies. *Journal of Personality and Social Psychology, 75,* 394–407.

Brown, A. M. (2007). A cognitive approach to dogmatism: An investigation into the relationship of verbal working memory and dogmatism. *Journal of Research in Personality, 41,* 946–952.

Brown, C. E., Dovidio, J. F., & Ellyson, S. L. (1990). Reducing sex differences in visual displays of dominance: Knowledge is power. *Personality and Social Psychology Bulletin, 16,* 358–368.

Bruce, M. L. (1998). Divorce and psychopathology. In B. P. Dohrenwend (Ed.), *Adversity, stress, and psychopathology* (pp. 219–234). New York: Oxford University Press.

Bruch, M. A., Rivet, K. M., Heimberg, R. G., Hunt, A., & McIntosh, B. (1999). Shyness and sociotropy: Additive and interactive relations in predicting interpersonal concerns. *Journal of Personality, 67,* 381–406.

Bruch, M. A., Rivet, K. M., & Laurenti, H. J. (2000). Type of self-discrepancy and relationships to components of the tripartite model of emotional distress. *Personality and Individual Differences, 29,* 37–44.

Brunell, A., Kernis, M., Goldman, B., Heppner, W., Davis, P., Cascio, E., et al. (2010). Dispositional authenticity and romantic relationship functioning. *Personality and Individual Differences, 48,* 900–905.

Burgoon, M., Lombardi, D., Burch, S., & Shelby, J. (1979). Machiavellianism and type of persuasive message as predictors of attitude change. *Journal of Psychology, 101,* 123–127.

Burgoon, M., Miller, G. R., & Tubbs, S. L. (1972). Machiavellianism, justification, and attitude change following counter-attitudinal advocacy. *Journal of Personality and Social Psychology, 22,* 366–371.

Burleson, B. R. (1994). Comforting messages: Significance, approaches, and effects. In B. R. Burleson, T. L. Albrecht, & I. G. Sarason (Eds.), *The communication of social support: Messages, interactions, relationships, and community* (pp. 3–28). Thousand Oaks, CA: Sage.

Burleson, B. R. (1998). Cognitive complexity. In J. C. McCroskey, J. A. Daly, M. M. Martin, & M. J. Beatty (Eds.), *Communication and personality: Trait perspectives* (pp. 233–286). Cresskill, NJ: Hampton Press.

Buss, A. H. (1989). Personality as traits. *American Psychologist, 44,* 1378–1388.

Buss, D. M. (1991). Conflict in married couples: Personality predictors of anger and upset. *Journal of Personality, 59,* 663–688.

Buss, D. M., & Schmitt, D. P. (1993). Sexual strategies theory: A contextual evolutionary analysis of human mating. *Psychological Review, 100,* 204–232.

Buss, D. M., & Shackelford, T. K. (1997). Susceptibility to infidelity in the first year of marriage. *Journal of Research in Personality, 31,* 193–221.

Buss, D. M., Shackelford, T. K., Kirkpatrick, L. A., Choe, J. C., Lim, H. K., Hasegawa, M., et al. (1999). Jealousy and the nature of beliefs about infidelity: Tests of competing hypotheses about sex differences in the United States, Korea, and Japan. *Personal Relationships, 6,* 125–150.

Buunk, B. P. (1995). Sex, self-esteem, dependency, and extradyadic sexual experience as related to jealousy responses. *Journal of Social and Personal Relationships, 12,* 147–153.

Cacioppo, J. T., Hawkley, L. C., Ernst, J. M., Burleson, M., Berntson, G. G., Nouriani, B. B., et al. (2006). Loneliness within a nomological net: An evolutionary perspective. *Journal of Research in Personality, 40,* 1054–1085.

Cameron, D., McAlinden, F., & O'Leary, K. (1988). Lakoff in context: The social and linguistic functions of tag questions. In J. Coates & D. Cameron (Eds.), *Women in their speech communities: New perspectives on language and sex* (pp. 74–93). London: Longman.

Campbell, W. K., Reeder, G. D., Sedikides, C., & Elliot, A. J. (2000). Narcissism and comparative self-enhancement strategies. *Journal of Research in Personality, 34,* 329–347.

Canary, D. J., Cunningham, E. M., & Cody, M. J. (1988). Goal types, gender, and locus of control in managing interpersonal conflict. *Communication Research, 15,* 426–446.

Canary, D. J., & Hause, K. S. (1993). Is there any reason to research sex differences in communication? *Communication Quarterly, 41,* 129–144.

Carli, L. L. (1990). Gender, language and influence. *Journal of Personality and Social Psychology, 59,* 941–951.

Caughlin, J. P., Huston, T. L., & Houts, R. M. (2000). How does personality matter in marriage? An examination of trait anxiety, interpersonal negativity, and marital satisfaction. *Journal of Personality and Social Psychology, 78,* 326–336.

Caughlin, J. P., & Vangelisti, A. L. (2000). An individual difference explanation of why married couples engage in the demand/withdraw pattern of conflict. *Journal of Social and Personal Relationships, 17,* 523–551.

Cegala, D. J. (1981). Interaction involvement: A cognitive dimension of communication competence. *Communication Education, 30,* 109–121.

Chan, K., & Drasgow, F. (2001). Toward a theory of individual differences and leadership: Understanding the motivation to lead. *Journal of Applied Psychology, 86,* 481–498.

Check, J. V. P., Perlman, D., & Malamuth, N. M. (1985). Loneliness and aggressive behavior. *Journal of Social and Personal Relationships, 2,* 243–252.

Chen, J., & Wang, L. (2007). Locus of control and the three components of commitment to change. *Personality and Individual Differences, 42,* 503–512.

Chen, S., Langner, C. A., & Mendoza-Denton, R. (2009). When dispositional and role power fit: Implications for self-expression and self-other congruence. *Journal of Personality and Social Psychology, 96,* 710–727.

Cheng, C. (1999). Gender-role differences in susceptibility to the influence of support availability on depression. *Journal of Personality, 67,* 439–467.

Chow, D., Au, E., & Chiu, C. (2008). Predicting the psychological health of older adults: Interaction of age-based rejection sensitivity and discriminative facility. *Journal of Research in Personality, 42,* 169–182.

Christensen, A. (1988). Dysfunctional interaction patterns in couples. In P. Noller & M. A. Fitzpatrick (Eds.), *Perspectives on marital interaction* (pp. 31–52). Clevedon, UK: Multilingual Matters.

Christie, R., & Geis, F. L. (1970). *Studies in Machiavellianism.* New York: Academic Press.

Ciarrochi, J. V., Chan, A. Y. C., & Caputi, P. (2000). A critical evaluation of the emotional intelligence construct. *Personality and Individual Differences, 28,* 539–561.

Collier, M. J. (1996). Communication competence problematics in ethnic friendships. *Communication Monographs, 63,* 314–336.

Comadena, M. E., & Prusank, D. T. (1988). Communication apprehension and academic achievement among elementary and middle school children. *Communication Education, 37,* 270–277.

Cooley, C. H. (1902). *Human nature and the social order.* New York: Scribner's.

Cooley, E. L., & Nowicki, S. (1989). Discrimination of facial expressions of emotion by depressed subjects. *Genetic, Social, and General Psychology Monographs, 115,* 451–465.

Costa, P. T., Terracciano, A., & McCrae, R. R. (2001). Gender differences in personality traits across cultures: Robust and surprising findings. *Journal of Personality and Social Psychology, 81,* 322–331.

Costanzo, M., & Archer, D. (1989). Interpreting the expressive behavior of others: The interpersonal perception task. *Journal of Nonverbal Behavior, 13,* 225–245.

Cote, S., & Moskowitz, D. S. (1998). On the dynamic covariation between interpersonal behavior and affect: Prediction from neuroticism, extraversion, and agreeableness. *Journal of Personality and Social Psychology, 75,* 1032–1046.

Cotterell, N., Eisenberger, R., & Speicher, H. (1992). Inhibiting effects of reciprocation wariness on interpersonal relationships. *Journal of Personality and Social Psychology, 62,* 658–668.

Coyne, J. C. (1976). Toward an interactional description of depression. *Psychiatry, 39,* 28–40.

Cross, S. E., & Madson, L. (1997). Models of the self: Self-construals and gender. *Psychological Bulletin, 122,* 5–37.

Crowne, D. P., & Marlowe, D. (1964). A znew scale of social desirability independent of psychopathology. *Journal of Consulting Psychology, 24,* 349–354.

Cummings, E. M., & Davies, P. T. (1994). Maternal depression and child development. *Journal of Child Psychology and Psychiatry, 35,* 73–112.

Dabbs, J. M., Jr., Evans, M. S., Hopper, C. H., & Purvis, J. A. (1980). Self-monitors in conversation: What do they monitor? *Journal of Personality and Social Psychology, 39,* 278–284.

Dabbs, J. M., Jr., Strong, R., & Milun, R. (1997). Exploring the mind of testosterone: A beeper study. *Journal of Research in Personality, 31,* 577–587.

Daly, J. A. (1978). Communication apprehension and behavior: Applying a multiple act criteria. *Human Communication Research, 4,* 208–216.

Daly, J. A., Caughlin, J., & Stafford, L. (2009). Correlates and consequences of social-communicative anxiety. In J. A. Daly, J. C. McCroskey, J. Ayres, T. Hopf, D. Ayres, & T. Wongorasert (Eds.), *Avoiding communication* (pp. 23–52). New York: Hampton Press.

Daly, J. A., & Friedrich, G. (1981). The development of communication apprehension: A retrospective analysis of some contributory correlates. *Communication Quarterly, 29,* 243–255.

Daly, J. A., Kreiser, P. O., & Roghaar, L. A. (1994). Question-asking comfort: Explorations of the demography of communication in the eighth grade classroom. *Communication Education, 43,* 27–41.

Daly, J. A., & McCroskey, J. C. (1975). Occupational desirability and choice as a function of communication apprehension. *Journal of Counseling Psychology, 22,* 309–313.

Daly, J. A., McCroskey, J. C., Ayres, J., Hopf, T., Ayres, D., & Wongprasert, T. (Eds.). (2009). *Avoiding communication: Shyness, reticence, and communication apprehension* (3rd ed.). Cresskill, NJ: Hampton Press.

Daly, J. A., McCroskey, J. C., & Richmond, V. P. (1977). The relationship between vocal activity and perceptions of communicators in small group interaction. *Western Speech Communication Journal, 41,* 175–187.

Daly, J. A., Richmond, V. P., & Leth, S. (1979). Social-communicative anxiety and the personnel selection process: Testing the similarity effect in selection decisions. *Human Communication Research, 6,* 18–32.

Daly, J. A., Vangelisti, A., & Daughton, S. (1987). The nature and structure of conversational sensitivity. *Human Communication Research, 14,* 167–202.

Daly, J. A., Vangelisti, A. L., & Lawrence, S. (1989). Public speaking anxiety and self-focused attention. *Personality and Individual Differences, 10,* 903–913.

Daniels, D., & Plomin, R. (1985). Origins of individual differences in infant shyness. *Developmental Psychology, 21,* 118–121.

Davies, M., Stankov, L., & Roberts, R. D. (1998). Emotional intelligence: In search of an elusive construct. *Journal of Personality and Social Psychology, 75,* 989–1015.

Davies, P. T., Dumenci, L., & Windle, M. (1999). The interplay between maternal depressive symptoms and marital distress in the prediction of adolescent adjustment. *Journal of Marriage and Family, 61,* 238–254.

Davis, M. H. (1983). Measuring individual differences in empathy: Evidence for a multidimensional approach. *Journal of Personality and Social Psychology, 44,* 113–126.

Day, L., & Maltby, J. (2000). Can Kinderman and Bentalls' suggestions for a personal and situational attributions questionnaire be used to examine all aspects of attributional style? *Personality and Individual Differences, 29,* 1047–1055.

Deaux, K., & La France, M. (1998). Gender. In D. T. Gilbert, S. T. Fiske, & G. Lindzey (Eds.), *Handbook of social psychology* (4th ed., pp. 788–827). New York: McGraw-Hill.

DeBono, K., & Klein, C. (1993). Source expertise and persuasion: The moderating role of recipient dogmatism. *Personality and Social Psychology Bulletin, 19,* 167–173.

DeNeve, K. M., & Cooper, H. (1998). The happy personality: A meta-analysis of 137 personality traits and subjective well-being. *Psychological Bulletin, 124,* 197–229.

Depue, R. A., Luciana, M., Arbisi, P., Collins, P., & Leon, A. (1994). Dopamine and the structure of personality: Relation of agonist-induced dopamine activity to positive emotionality. *Journal of Personality and Social Psychology, 67,* 485–498.

Dew, M. A., & Bromet, E. J. (1991). Effects of depression on social support in a community sample of women. In J. Eckenrode (Ed.), *The social context of coping* (pp. 189–219). New York: Plenum Press.

Dewaele, J., & Furnham, A. (2000). Personality and speech production: A pilot study of second language learners. *Personality and Individual Differences, 28,* 355–365.

DeWall, C. N., Deckman, T., Pond, R. S., & Bonser, I. (in press). Belongingness as a core personality trait: How social exclusion influences social functioning and personality expression. *Journal of Personality.*

Diamond, L. M. (2006). The intimate same-sex relationships of sexual minorities. In A. Vangelisti & D. Perlman (Eds.), *The Cambridge handbook of personal relationships* (pp. 293–313). New York: Cambridge University Press.

Dillehay, R. (1978). Authoritarianism. In H. London & J. E. Exner (Eds.), *Dimensions of personality* (pp. 85–127). New York: Wiley.

Dindia, K., & Allen, M. (1992). Sex differences in self-disclosure: A meta-analysis. *Psychological Bulletin, 112,* 106–124.

Dion, K. L., & Dion, K. K. (1973). Correlates of romantic love. *Journal of Consulting and Clinical Psychology, 41,* 51–56.

Dobson, K. S. (1989). Real and perceived responses to subclinically anxious and depressed targets. *Cognitive Therapy and Research, 13,* 37–47.

Downey, G., Freitas, A. L., Michaelis, B., & Khouri, H. (1998). The self-fulfilling prophecy in close relationships: Rejection sensitivity and rejection by romantic partners. *Journal of Personality and Social Psychology, 75,* 545–560.

Duck, S., Pond, K., & Latham, G. (1994). Loneliness and the evaluation of relational events. *Journal of Social and Personal Relationships, 11,* 253–276.

Duggan, A. P., & Le Poire, B. (2006). One down, two involved: An application and extension of inconsistent nurturing as control theory to couples including one depressed individual. *Communication Monographs, 73,* 379–405.

Duggan, E. S., & Brennan, K. A. (1994). Social avoidance and its relation to Bartholomew's adult attachment typology. *Journal of Social and Personal Relationships, 11,* 147–153.

Dumlao, R., & Botta, R. A. (2000). Family communication patterns and the conflict styles young adults use with their fathers. *Communication Quarterly, 48,* 174–189.

Dykman, B. M., Horowitz, L., Abramson, L. Y., & Usher, M. (1991). Schematic and situational determinants of depressed and non-depressed students' interpretation of feedback. *Journal of Abnormal Psychology, 100,* 45–55.

Dyrenforth, P., Kashy, D., Donnellan, M. B., & Lucas, R. (2010). Predicting relationship and life satisfaction from personality in nationally representative samples from three countries. *Journal of Personality and Social Psychology, 99,* 690–702.

Eagly, A. H., & Carli, L. L. (1981). Sex of researchers and sex-typed communications as determinants of sex differences in influenceability: A meta-analysis of social influence studies. *Psychological Bulletin, 90,* 1–20.

Eagly, A. H., & Johnson, B. T. (1990). Gender and leadership style: A meta-analysis. *Psychological Bulletin, 108,* 233–256.

Elfenbein, A., & Eisenfraft, N. (2010). The relationship between displaying and perceiving nonverbal cues in affect. *Journal of Personality and Social Psychology, 98,* 301–318.

Elliot, A. J., & Thrash, T. M. (2002). Approach-avoidance motivation in personality: Approach and avoidance temperaments and goals. *Journal of Personality and Social Psychology, 82,* 804–818.

Emmons, R. A., Diener, E., & Larson, R. J. (1986). Choice and avoidance of everyday situations and affect congruence: Two models of reciprocal interactionism. *Journal of Personality and Social Psychology, 51,* 815–826.

Epstein, S. (1979). The stability of behavior: I. On predicting most of the people most of the time. *Journal of Personality and Social Psychology, 37,* 1097–1126.

Erickson, T. M., Newman, M., & Pincus, A. (2009). Predicting unpredictability. *Journal of Personality and Social Psychology, 97,* 893–912.

Ermer, E., & Kiehl, K. (2010). Psychopaths are impaired in social exchange and precautionary reasoning. *Psychological Science, 21,* 399–1405.

Eronen, S., & Nurmi, J. (1999). Social reaction styles, interpersonal behaviours and person perception: A multi-informant approach. *Journal of Social and Personal Relationships, 16,* 315–333.

Estow, S., Jamieson, J. P., & Yates, J. R. (2007). Self-monitoring and mimicry of positive and negative social behaviors. *Journal of Research in Personality, 41,* 425–433.

Fandt, P. M., & Ferris, G. R. (1990). The management of information and impressions: When employees behave opportunistically. *Organizational Behavior and Human Performance, 45,* 140–158.

Fast, L. A., & Funder, D. C. (2010). Gender differences in the correlates of self-referent word use: Authority, entitlement, and depressive symptoms. *Journal of Personality, 78,* 313–338.

Feeney, B. C., & Collins, N. L. (2001). Predictors of caregiving in adult intimate relationships: An attachment theoretical perspective. *Journal of Personality and Social Psychology, 80,* 972–994.

Feingold, A. (1994). Gender differences in personality: A meta-analysis. *Psychological Bulletin, 116,* 429–456.

Fitzpatrick, M. A. (1998). *Between husbands and wives: Communication in marriage.* Thousand Oaks, CA: Sage.

Flora, J., & Segrin, C. (1998). Joint leisure time in friend and romantic relationships: The role of activity type, social skills, and positivity. *Journal of Social and Personal Relationships, 15,* 711–718.

Funder, D. C., & Colvin, C. R. (1988). Friends and strangers: Acquaintanceship, agreement, and accuracy of personality judgments. *Journal of Personality and Social Psychology, 55,* 149–158.

Funder, D. C., & Colvin, C. R. (1991). Explorations in behavioral consistency: Properties of persons, situations, and behaviors. *Journal of Personality and Social Psychology, 60,* 773–794.

Funder, D. C., & Ozer, D. J. (1983). Behavior as a function of the situation. *Journal of Personality and Social Psychology, 44,* 107–112.

Gable, M., & Topol, M. T. (1991). Machiavellian managers: Do they perform better? *Journal of Business and Psychology, 5,* 355–365.

Gailliot, M. T., & Baumeister, R. F. (2007). Self-esteem, belongingness, and worldview validation: Does belongingness exert a unique influence upon self-esteem? *Journal of Research in Personality, 41,* 327–345.

Galloway, G. (2010). Individual differences in personal humor styles: Identification of prominent patterns and their associates. *Personality and Individual Differences, 48,* 563–567.

Galupo, M. P. (2009). Cross-category friendship patterns: Comparison of heterosexual and sexual minority adults. *Journal of Social and Personal Relationships, 26,* 811–831.

Gangestad, S. W., & Snyder, M. (2000). Self-monitoring: Appraisal and reappraisal. *Psychological Bulletin, 126,* 530–555.

Garcia, S., Sinson, L., Ickes, W. J., Bissonnette, V., & Briggs, S. R. (1991). Shyness and physical attractiveness in mixed-sex dyads. *Journal of Personality and Social Psychology, 61,* 35–49.

Garland, J., & Beard, J. F. (1979). Relationship between self-monitoring and leader emergence across two task situations. *Journal of Applied Psychology, 64,* 72–76.

Gauvain, M., & Huard, R. D. (1999). Family interaction, parenting style, and the development of planning: A longitudinal analysis using archival data. *Journal of Family Psychology, 13,* 75–92.

Gilbert, P., & Miles, J. N. V. (2000). Sensitivity to social put-down: Its relationship to perceptions of social rank, shame, social anxiety, depression, anger, and self-other blame. *Personality and Individual Differences, 29,* 757–774.

Giordano, C., Wood, J. V., & Michela, J. L. (2000). Depressive personality styles, dysphoria, and social comparisons in everyday life. *Journal of Personality and Social Psychology, 79,* 438–451.

Givertz, M., Segrin, C., & Hanzal, A. (2009). The association between satisfaction and commitment differs across marital couple type. *Communication Research, 36,* 561–584.

Gleason, K. A., Jensen-Campbell, L. A., & Ickes, W. (2009). The role of empathic accuracy in adolescents' peer relations and adjustment. *Personality and Social Psychology Bulletin, 35,* 997–1011.

Goldberg, L. R. (1993). The structure of phenotypic personality traits. *American Psychologist, 48,* 26–34.

Goleman, D. (1995). *Emotional intelligence: Why it can matter more than IQ.* New York: Bantam.

Gotlib, I. H., & Asarnow, R. F. (1979). Interpersonal and impersonal problem-solving skills in mildly and clinically depressed university students. *Journal of Consulting and Clinical Psychology, 47,* 86–95.

Gottman, J. M., & Levenson, R. W. (1988). The social psychophysiology of marriage. In P. Noller & M. A. Fitzpatrick (Eds.), *Perspectives on marital interaction* (pp. 182–200). Clevedon, UK: Multilingual Matters.

Grant, A. M., Gino, F., & Hofmann, D. A. (2011). Reversing the extraverted leadership advantage: The role of employee productivity. *Academy of Management Journal, 54*(3).

Gray, M. R., & Steinberg, L. (1999). Unpacking authoritative parenting: Reassessing a multidimensional construct. *Journal of Marriage and Family, 61,* 574–587.

Graziano, W. G., Jensen-Campbell, L. A., & Hair, E. C. (1996). Perceiving interpersonal conflict and reacting to it: The case for agreeableness. *Journal of Personality and Social Psychology, 70,* 820–835.

Haas, B., Mills, D., Yam, A., Hoeft, F., Bellugi, U., & Reiss, A. (2009). Genetic influences on sociability. *Journal of Neuroscience, 29,* 1132–1139.

Hagestad, G. O., & Smyer, M. A. (1982). Dissolving long-term relationships: Patterns of divorcing in middle age. In S. Duck (Ed.), *Personal relationships 4: Dissolving relationships* (pp. 115–188). New York: Academic Press.

Hall, J., Park, N., Song, H., & Cody, M. (2010). Strategic misrepresentation in online dating. *Journal of Social and Personal Relationships, 27,* 117–135.

Hample, D., & Dallinger, J. M. (1995). A Lewinian perspective on taking conflict personally: Revision, refinement, and validation of the instrument. *Communication Quarterly, 43,* 297–319.

Hart, D., Atkins, R., & Matsuba, M. K. (2008). The association of neighborhood poverty with personality change in childhood. *Journal of Personality and Social Psychology, 94,* 1048–1061.

Hart, R. P., Carlson, R. E., & Eadie, W. F. (1980). Attitudes towards communication and the assessment of rhetorical sensitivity. *Communication Monographs, 47,* 1–22.

Haslett, B. (1990). Social class, social status and communicative behavior. In H. Giles & W. P. Robinson (Eds.), *Handbook of language and social psychology* (pp. 329–344). New York: Wiley.

Hecht, M. L., Marston, P. J., & Larkey, L. K. (1994). Love ways and relationship quality in heterosexual relationships. *Journal of Social and Personal Relationships, 11,* 25–43.

Heggestad, E., & Morrison, M. J. (2008). An inductive exploration of the social effectiveness construct space. *Journal of Personality, 76,* 839–874.

Helgeson, V. S., Shaver, P., & Dyer, M. (1987). Prototypes of intimacy and distance in same-sex and opposite-sex relationships. *Journal of Social and Personal Relationships, 4,* 195–233.

Hendricks, C., & Hendricks, S. (1986). A theory and method of love. *Journal of Personality and Social Psychology, 50,* 392–402.

Higgins, E. T. (1987). Self-discrepancy: A theory relating self and affect. *Psychological Review, 94,* 319–340.

Hildebrand-Saints, L., & Weary, G. (1989). Depression and social information gathering. *Personality and Social Psychology Bulletin, 15,* 150–160.

Hokanson, J. E., & Butler, A. C. (1992). Cluster analysis of depressed college students' social behaviors. *Journal of Personality and Social Psychology, 62,* 273–280.

Holtzman, N. S., Vazire, S., & Mehl, M. (2010). Sounds like a narcissist: Behavioral manifestations of narcissism in everyday life. *Journal of Research in Personality, 44,* 478–484.

Hops, H., Biglan, A., Sherman, L., Arthur, J., Friedman, L., & Osteen, R. (1987). Home observations of family interactions of depressed women. *Journal of Consulting and Clinical Psychology, 55,* 341–346.

Hopwood, C. J., Ansell, E. B., Pincus, A. L., Wright, A., Lukowitsky, M., & Roche, M. (in press). The circumplex structure of interpersonal sensitivities. *Journal of Personality.*

Horton, R. S., & Sedikides, C. (2009). Narcissistic responding to ego threat: When the status of the evaluator matters. *Journal of Personality, 77,* 1493–1526.

Huang, L. (1999). Family communication patterns and personality characteristics. *Communication Quarterly, 47,* 230–243.

Ickes, W. J. (1985). Sex role influences in dyadic interaction: A theoretical model. In W. J. Ickes (Ed.), *Compatible and incompatible relationships* (pp. 187–208). New York: Springer-Verlag.

Ickes, W. J. (Ed.). (1997). *Empathic accuracy.* New York: Guilford Press.

Infante, D. A. (1981). Trait argumentativeness as a predictor of communicative behavior in situations requiring argument. *Central States Speech Journal, 32,* 265–277.

Infante, D. A. (1995). Teaching students to understand and control verbal aggression. *Communication Education, 44,* 51–63.

Infante, D. A., & Gorden, W. I. (1985). Superiors' argumentativeness and verbal aggressiveness as predictors of subordinates' satisfaction. *Human Communication Research, 12,* 117–125.

Infante, D. A., & Rancer, A. S. (1982). A conceptualization and measure of argumentativeness. *Journal of Personality Assessment, 45,* 72–80.

Infante, D. A., Riddle, B. L., Horvath, C. L., & Tumlin, S. A. (1992). Verbal aggressiveness: Messages and reasons. *Communication Quarterly, 40,* 116–126.

Infante, D. A., Trebing, J. D., Shepherd, P. E., & Seeds, D. E. (1984). The relationship of argumentativeness to verbal aggression. *Southern Speech Communication Journal, 50,* 67–77.

Infante, D. A., & Wigley, C. J. (1986). Verbal aggressiveness: An interpersonal model and measure. *Communication Monographs, 53,* 61–69.

Ivanov, M., & Werner, P. (2010). Behavioral communication: Individual differences in communication style. *Personality and Individual Differences, 49,* 19–23.

Izard, C. E., Fine, S., Schultz, D., Mostow, A., Ackerman, B., & Youngstrom, E. (2001). Emotion knowledge as a predictor of social behavior and academic competence in children at risk. *Psychological Science, 12,* 18–23.

Jaap, J. A., Dennissen, J., Asendorpf, J., & Van Aken, M. (2008). Childhood personality predicts long-term trajectories of shyness and aggressiveness in the context of demographic transitions in emerging adulthood. *Journal of Personality, 76,* 67–99.

Jerskey, B., Panizzon, M., Jacobson, K., Neale, M., Grant, M., Schultz, M., et al. (2010). Marriage and divorce: A genetic perspective. *Personality and Individual Differences, 49,* 473–478.

Joiner, T. E., & Metalsky, G. I. (2001). Excessive reassurance seeking: Delineating a risk factor involved in the development of depressive symptoms. *Psychological Science, 12,* 371–378.

Jones, E. E., & Baumeister, R. F. (1976). The self-monitor looks at the ingratiator. *Journal of Personality, 44,* 654–674.

Jones, R. E., & White, C. S. (1983). Relationship between Machiavellianism, task orientation, and team effectiveness. *Psychological Reports, 53,* 859–866.

Jones, W. H., & Carpenter, B. N. (1986). Shyness, social behavior, and relationships. In W. H. Jones, J. M. Cheek, & S. R. Briggs (Eds.), *Shyness: Perspectives on treatment and research* (pp. 227–238). New York: Plenum Press.

Jones, W. H., Hobbs, S. A., & Hockenbury, D. (1982). Loneliness and social skills deficits. *Journal of Personality and Social Psychology, 42,* 682–689.

Josephs, R. A., Markus, H. R., & Tafarodi, R. W. (1992). Gender and self-esteem. *Journal of Personality and Social Psychology, 63,* 391–402.

Karney, B., & Gauer, B. (2010). Cognitive complexity and marital interaction in newlywed couples. *Personal Relationships, 17,* 181–200.

Kashdan, T. B., Mishra, A., Breen, W. E., & Froh, J. J. (2009). Gender differences in gratitude: Examining appraisals, narratives, the willingness to express emotions, and changes in psychological needs. *Journal of Personality, 77,* 691–730.

Kassing, J. W., Pearce, K. J., & Infante, D. A. (2000). Corporal punishment and communication in father-son dyads. *Communication Research Reports, 17,* 237–249.

Kazoleas, D. (1993). The impact of argumentativeness on resistance to persuasion. *Human Communication Research, 20,* 118–137.

Kendler, K. S., & Prescott, C. A. (1999). A population-based twin study of depression in men and women. *Archives of General Psychiatry, 56,* 39–44.

Kernis, M. H., Brown, A. C., & Brody, G. H. (2000). Fragile self-esteem in children and its associations with perceived patterns of parent-child communication. *Journal of Personality, 68,* 225–252.

Kerr, M., Lambert, W. W., & Bem, D. J. (1996). Life course sequelae of childhood shyness in Sweden: Comparison with the United States. *Developmental Psychology, 32,* 1100–1105.

Kessler, S. R., Bandelli, A. C., Spector, P. E., Borman, W. C., Nelson, C. E., & Penney, L. M. (2010). Re-examining Machiavelli: A three-dimensional model of Machiavellianism in the workplace. *Journal of Applied Social Psychology, 40,* 1868–1896.

Kiazad, K., Restubog, S. L. D., Zagenczyk, T. J., Kiewitz, C., & Tang, R. L. (2010). In pursuit of power: The role of authoritarian leadership in the relationship between supervisors' Machiavellianism and subordinates' perceptions of abusive supervisory behavior. *Journal of Research in Personality, 44,* 512–519.

Kilduff, M., & Day, D. (1994). Do chameleons get ahead? The effects of self-monitoring on managerial careers. *Academy of Management Journal, 37,* 1047–1060.

Kilman, R., & Thomas, K. (1977). Developing a forced-choice measure of conflict-handling behavior: The "Mode" instrument. *Educational and Psychological Measurement, 37,* 309–325.

Kim, M.-S., Aune, K. S., Hunter, J. E., Kim, H.-J., & Kim, J. S. (2001). The effect of culture and self-construals on predispositions toward verbal communication. *Human Communication Research, 27,* 382–408.

King, A. R., & Terrance, C. (2006). Relationships between personality disorder attributes and friendship qualities among college students. *Journal of Social and Personal Relationships, 23,* 5–20.

Kline, S. L., Pelias, R., & Delia, J. G. (1991). The predictive validity of cognitive complexity measures on communication relevant abilities. *International Journal of Personal Construct Psychology, 4,* 347–357.

Kling, K. C., Hyde, J. S., Showers, C. J., & Buswell, B. N. (1999). Gender differences in self-esteem: A meta analysis. *Psychological Bulletin, 125,* 470–500.

Koestner, R., Bernieri, F., & Zuckerman, M. (1989). Trait-specific versus person-specific moderators of cross-situational consistency. *Journal of Personality, 57,* 1–16.

Kohler, G., & Ruch, W. (1996). Sources of variance in current sense of humor inventories: How much substance, how much method variance? *Humor: International Journal of Humor Research, 9,* 363–397.

Kotowski, M. R., Levine, T. R., Baker, C. R., & Bolt, J. M. (2009). A multitrait–multimethod validity assessment of the verbal aggressiveness and argumentativeness scales, *Communication Monographs, 76,* 443–462.

Kowalski, R. M., & Brown, K. J. (1994). Psychosocial barriers to cervical cancer screening: Concerns with self-presentation and social evaluation. *Journal of Applied Social Psychology, 24,* 941–958.

Kring, A. M., & Gordon, A. H. (1998). Sex differences in emotion: Expression, experience, and physiology. *Journal of Personality and Social Psychology, 74,* 686–703.

Kunkel, A. W., & Burleson, B. R. (1999). Assessing explanations for sex differences in emotional support: A test of the different cultures and skills specialization accounts. *Human Communication Research, 25,* 307–340.

Kurdek, L. A. (2004). Are gay and lesbian cohabiting couples really different from heterosexual married couples? *Journal of Marriage and the Family, 66,* 880–900.

Kurdek, L. A. (2008). Differences between partners from black and white heterosexual dating couples in a path model of relationship commitment. *Journal of Social and Personal Relationships, 25,* 51–70.

La France, B. H., Henningsen, D. D., Oates, A., & Shaw, C. M. (2009). Social–sexual interactions? Meta-analyses of sex differences in perceptions of flirtatiousness, seductiveness, and promiscuousness. *Communication Monographs, 76,* 263–285.

Lakey, C. E., Kernis, M. H., Heppner, W., & Lance, C. (2008). Individual differences in authenticity and mindfulness as predictors of verbal defensiveness. *Journal of Research in Personality, 42,* 230–238.

Lamke, L. (1989). Marital adjustment among rural couples: The role of expressiveness. *Sex Roles, 21,* 579–590.

Lane, J. D., & DePaulo, B. M. (1999). Completing Coyne's cycle: Dysphorics' ability to detect deception. *Journal of Research in Personality, 33,* 311–329.

Larson, J. H., Anderson, S. M., Holman, T. B., & Niemann, B. K. (1998). A longitudinal study of the effects of premarital communication, relationship stability, and self-esteem on sexual satisfaction in the first year of marriage. *Journal of Sex and Marital Therapy, 24,* 193–206.

Leary, M. R. (1983). Social anxiousness: The construct and its measurement. *Journal of Personality Assessment, 47,* 66–75.

Leary, T. (1957). *The interpersonal diagnosis of personality.* New York: Ronald Press.

Leck, K., & Simpson, J. A. (1999). Feigning romantic interest: The role of self-monitoring. *Journal of Research in Personality, 33,* 69–91.

Lefcourt, H. M., Martin, R. A., & Fick, C. M. (1985). Locus of control for affiliation and behavior in social interactions. *Journal of Personality and Social Psychology, 48,* 755–759.

LePine, J. A., & Van Dyne, L. (2001). Voice and cooperative behavior as contrasting forms of contextual performance: Evidence of differential relationships with Big Five personality characteristics and cognitive ability. *Journal of Applied Psychology, 86,* 326–336.

Le Poire, B. A., Shepard, C., & Duggan, A. (1999). Nonverbal involvement, expressiveness, and pleasantness as predicted by parental and partner attachment style. *Communication Monographs, 66,* 293–311.

Letzring, T. D., & Noftle, E. (2010). Predicting relationship quality from self-verification of broad personality traits among romantic couples. *Journal of Research in Personality, 44,* 353–362.

Lewin, K. (1935). *Dynamic theory of personality.* New York: McGraw-Hill.

van der Linden, D., Nijenhuis, J., & Bakker, A. (2010). The general factor of personality. *Journal of Research in Personality, 44,* 315–327.

Lippa, R. (1978). Expressive control, expressive consistency, and the correspondence between expressive behavior and personality. *Journal of Personality, 46,* 438–461.

Lodi-Smith, J., Geise, A. C, Roberts, B. W., & Robins, R. W. (2009). Narrating personality change. *Journal of Personality and Social Psychology, 96,* 679–689.

Lopes, P. N., Brackett, M. A., Nezlek, J. B., Schutz, A., Sellin, I., & Salovey, P. (2004). Emotional intelligence and social interaction. *Personality and Social Psychology Bulletin, 30,* 1018–1034.

Lucas, R. E., Le, K., & Dyrenforth, P. S. (2008). Explaining the extraversion/positive affect relation: Sociability cannot account for extraverts' greater happiness. *Journal of Personality, 76,* 385–414.

Luo, X., Kranzler, H. R., Zuo, L., Zhang, H., Wang, S., & Gelernter, J. (2007). CHRM2 variation predisposes to personality traits of agreeableness and conscientiousness. *Human Molecular Genetics, 16,* 1557–1568.

Magnusson, D., & Endler, N. S. (1977). *Personality at the crossroads: Current issues in interactional psychology.* Hillsdale, NJ: Lawrence Erlbaum.

Malouff, J. M., Thorsteinsson, E. B., Schutte, N. S., Bhullar, N., & Rooke, S. E. (2010). The five-factor model of personality and relationship satisfaction of intimate partners: A meta-analysis. *Journal of Research in Personality, 44,* 124–127.

Maltby, J., & Day, L. (2000). The reliability and validity of a susceptibility to embarrassment scale among adults. *Personality and Individual Differences, 29,* 749–756.

Markey, P. M., & Markey, C. N. (2007). Romantic ideas, obtainment, and relationship experiences. *Journal of Social and Personal Relationships, 24,* 517–533.

Marsh, H. W. (1989). Age and sex effects in multiple dimensions of self-concept. Preadolescence to early adulthood. *Journal of Educational Psychology, 81,* 417–430.

Martin, M. M., & Anderson, C. M. (1995). Roommate similarity: Are roommates who are similar in the communication traits more satisfied? *Communication Research Reports, 12,* 46–52.

Martin, M. M., Anderson, C. M., Burant, P. A., & Weber, K. (1997). Verbal aggression in sibling relationships. *Communication Quarterly, 45,* 304–317.

Martin, M. M., Anderson, C. M., & Thweatt, K. S. (1998). Aggressive communication traits and their relationships with the cognitive flexibility scale and the communication flexibility scale. *Journal of Social Behavior and Personality, 13,* 531–540.

Martin, R. A. (2001). Humor, laughter, and physical health: Methodological issues and research findings. *Psychological Bulletin, 127,* 504–519.

Martins, A., Ramalho, N., & Morin, E. (2010). A comprehensive meta-analysis of the relationship between emotional intelligence and health. *Personality and Individual Differences, 49,* 554–564.

Mayer, J. D., DiPaulo, M., & Salovey, P. (1990). Perceiving affective content in ambiguous visual stimuli: A component of emotional intelligence. *Journal of Personality Assessment, 54,* 772–781.

Mayer, J. D., & Salovey, P. (1997). What is emotional intelligence? In P. Salovey & D. J. Sluyter (Eds.), *Emotional development and emotional intelligence: Educational implications* (pp. 3–34). New York: Basic Books.

McAdams, D. P. (1992). The intimacy motive. In C. P. Smith (Ed.), *Motivation and personality: Handbook of thematic content analysis* (pp. 224–228). New York: Cambridge University Press.

McClelland, D. C. (1986). *Human motivation.* New York: Cambridge University Press.

McClure, E. B. (2000). A meta-analytic review of sex differences in facial expression processing and their development in infants, children, and adolescents. *Psychological Bulletin, 126,* 424–453.

McCroskey, J. C., Andersen, J., Richmond, V. P., & Wheeless, L. R. (1981). Communication apprehension of elementary and secondary students and teachers. *Communication Education, 30,* 122–132.

McCroskey, J. C., Daly, J. A., Richmond, V. P., & Falcione, R. L. (1977). Studies of the relationship between communication apprehension and self-esteem. *Human Communication Research, 3,* 269–277.

McCroskey, J. C., & Richmond, V. P. (1979). The impact of communication apprehension on individuals in organizations. *Communication Quarterly, 27,* 55–61.

McGuire, S., & Clifford, J. (2000). Genetic and environmental contributions to loneliness in children. *Psychological Science, 11,* 487–491.

McGuire, W. J., & McGuire, C. V. (1981). The spontaneous self-concept as affected by personal distinctiveness. In M. Lynch, A. A. Norem-Hebeisen, & K. J. Gergen (Eds.), *Self-concept: Advances in theory and research* (pp. 147–171). Cambridge, UK: Cambridge University Press.

McLeod, J. M., & Chaffee, S. H. (1972). The construction of social reality. In J. T. Tedeschi (Ed.), *The social influence process* (pp. 50–99). Chicago: Aldine.

Meier, B. P., Robinson, M., Carter, M. S., Hinsz, V. B. (2010). Are sociable people more beautiful? A zero-acquaintance analysis of agreeableness, extraversion, and attractiveness. *Journal of Research in Personality, 44,* 293–296.

Meleshko, K. G. A., & Alden, L. E. (1993). Anxiety and self-disclosure: Toward a motivational model. *Journal of Personality and Social Psychology, 64,* 1000–1009.

Messer, A. C., & Gross, A. M. (1995). Childhood depression and family interaction. *Journal of Clinical Child Psychology, 24,* 77–88.

Messman, S., & Jones-Corley, J. (2001). Effects of communication environment, immediacy, and communication apprehension on cognitive and affective learning. *Communication Monographs, 68,* 184–200.

Miller, P. C., Lefcourt, H. M., & Ware, E. E. (1983). The construction and development of the Miller Marital Locus of Control Scale. *Canadian Journal of Behavioral Science, 15,* 266–279.

Mills, J., & Clark, M. S. (1994). Communal and exchange relationships: New research and old controversies. In R. Gilmour & R. Erber (Eds.), *Theoretical approaches to personal relationships* (pp. 29–42). Hillsdale, NJ: Lawrence Erlbaum.

Mischel, W. (1968). *Personality and assessment.* New York: Wiley.

Mischel, W. (1999). Personality coherence and dispositions in a cognitive-affective personality system (CAPS) approach. In D. Cervone & Y. Shoda (Eds.), *The coherence of personality: Social-cognitive bases of consistency, variability, and organization* (pp. 37–60). New York: Guilford Press.

Momm, T., Blickle, G., & Liu, Y. (2010). Political skill and emotional cue learning. *Personality and Individual Differences, 49,* 396–401.

Morrow, G. D., Clark, E. M., & Brock, K. F. (1995). Individual and partner love styles: Implications for the quality of romantic involvement. *Journal of Social and Personal Relationships, 12,* 363–387.

Moskowitz, D. S., Suh, E. J., & Desaulniers, J. (1994). Situational influences on gender differences in agency and communion. *Journal of Personality and Social Psychology, 66,* 753–761.

Mulac, A., Bradac, J. J., & Gibbons, P. (2001). Empirical support for the gender-as-culture hypothesis. *Human Communication Research, 27,* 121–152.

Myers, S. A. (1998). Instructor socio-communicative style, argumentativeness, and verbal aggressiveness in the classroom. *Communication Research Reports, 15,* 141–150.

Myers, S. A., & Knox, R. L. (2000). Perceived instructor argumentativeness and verbal aggressiveness and student outcomes. *Communication Research Reports, 17,* 299–309.

Myers, S. M., & Booth, A. (1999). Marital strains and marital quality: The role of high and low locus of control. *Journal of Marriage and Family, 61,* 423–436.

Nave, C., Sherman, R., Funder, D., Hampson, S., & Goldberg, L. (2010). On the contextual independence of personality. *Social Psychological and Personality Science, 1,* 327–334.

Neuliep, J. W., & Ryan, D. J. (1998). The influence of intercultural communication apprehension and socio-communicative orientation on uncertainty reduction during initial cross-cultural interaction. *Communication Quarterly, 46,* 88–99.

Newsome, S., Day, A. L., & Catano, V. M. (2000). Assessing the predictive value of emotional intelligence. *Personality and Individual Differences, 29,* 1005–1016.

Nezlek, J. B., Imbrie, M., & Shean, G. D. (1994). Depression and everyday social interaction. *Journal of Personality and Social Psychology, 67,* 1101–1111.

Ng, S. H., & Bradac, J. J. (1993). *Power in language: Verbal communication and social influence.* Newbury Park, CA: Sage.

Nicotera, A. M., & Rancer, A. S. (1994). The influence of sex on self-perceptions and social stereotyping of aggressive communication predispositions. *Western Journal of Communication, 58,* 283–307.

Nolen-Hoeksema, S. (2001). Gender differences in depression. *Current Directions in Psychological Science, 10,* 173–176.

Noller, P., Feeney, J. A., Bonnell, D., & Callan, V. J. (1994). A longitudinal study of conflict in early marriage. *Journal of Social and Personal Relationships, 11,* 233–252.

Noller, P., & Fitzpatrick, M. A. (1990). Marital communication in the eighties. *Journal of Marriage and the Family, 52,* 832–843.

Norton, R. W. (1978). Foundations of a communicator style construct. *Human Communication Research, 4,* 99–112.

Notarius, C. I., Benson, S., Sloanc, D., Vanzetti, N., & Hornyak, L. (1989). Exploring the interface between perception and behavior: An analysis of marital interactions in distressed and non-distressed couples. *Behavioral Assessment, 11,* 39–64.

O'Keefe, B. J., Delia, J. G., & O'Keefe, D. J. (1977). Construct individuality, cognitive complexity, and the formation and remembering of interpersonal impressions. *Social Behavior and Personality, 5,* 229–240.

O'Keefe, B. J., & Lambert, B. L. (1995). Managing the flow of ideas: A local management approach to message design. In B. R. Burleson (Ed.), *Communication yearbook 18* (pp. 54–82). Thousand Oaks, CA: Sage.

O'Keefe, B. J., & Shepherd, G. J. (1989). The communication of identity during face-to-face persuasive interactions: Effects of perceiver's construct differentiation and target's message strategies. *Communication Research, 16,* 375–404.

Olson, J. M., Vernon, P. A., Harris, J. A., & Jang, K. L. (2001). The heritability of attitudes: A study of twins. *Journal of Personality and Social Psychology, 80,* 845–861.

Orth-Gomer, K. (2009). Are social relations less health protective in women than in men? Social relations, gender, and cardiovascular heath. *Journal of Social and Personal Relationships, 26,* 63–71.

Orth, U., Robins, R., & Roberts, B. (2008). Low self-esteem prospectively predicts depression in adolescence and young adulthood. *Journal of Personality and Social Psychology, 95,* 695–708.

Oyamot, C. M., Fuglestad, P. T., & Synder, M. L. (2010). Balance of power and influence in relationships: The role of self-monitoring. *Journal of Social and Personal Relationships, 27,* 23–46.

Palomares, N. (2009). Women are sort of more tentative than men, aren't they? How men and women use tentative language differently, similarly, and counterstereotypically as a function of gender salience. *Communication Research, 36,* 538–560.

Paunonen, S. V., & Ashton, M. C. (2001). Big Five factors and facets and the prediction of behavior. *Journal of Personality and Social Psychology, 81,* 524–539.

Persad, S. M., & Polivy, J. (1993). Differences between depressed and nondepressed individuals in the recognition of and response to facial emotional cues. *Journal of Abnormal Psychology, 102,* 358–368.

Pfau, M., Van Bockern, S., & Kang, J. G. (1992). Use of inoculation to promote resistance to smoking initiation among adolescents. *Communication Monographs, 59,* 213–230.

Plomin, R., DeFries, J. C., & McClearn, G. E. (1990). *Behavioral genetics: A primer.* New York: Freeman.

Pollet, T. V., & Nettle, D. (2009), Birth order and family relationships in adult life: Firstborns report better sibling relationships than laterborns. *Journal of Social and Personal Relationships, 26,* 1029–1046.

Powers, W. G., & Love, D. E. (2000). Communication apprehension in the dating partner context. *Communication Research Reports, 17,* 221–228.

Pronk, T., Karremans, J., Overbeek, G., Vermulst, A., & Wigboldus, D. (2010). What it takes to forgive. *Journal of Personality and Social Psychology, 98,* 119–131.

Rahim, M., & Magner, N. (1995). Confirmatory factor analysis of the styles of handling interpersonal conflict: First-order factor model and its invariance across groups. *Journal of Applied Psychology, 80,* 122–132.

Rancer, A. S. (1998). Argumentativeness. In J. C. McCroskey, J. A. Daly, M. M. Martin, & M. J. Beatty (Eds.), *Communication and personality: Trait perspectives* (pp. 149–170). Cresskill, NJ: Hampton Press.

Rancer, A. S., Kosberg, R. L., & Baukus, R. A. (1992). Beliefs about arguing as predictors of trait argumentativeness: Implications for training in argument and conflict management. *Communication Education, 41,* 375–387.

Rancer, A. S., Kosberg, R. L., & Silvestri, V. N. (1992). The relationship between self-esteem and aggressive communication predispositions. *Communication Research Reports, 9,* 23–32.

Rapee, R., & Spence, S. H. (2004). The etiology of social phobia: Empirical evidence and an initial model. *Clinical Psychology Review, 24,* 737–767.

Reis, H. T., Capobianco, A., & Tsai, F. F. (2002). Finding the person in personal relationships. *Journal of Personality, 70,* 813–850.

Rhodes, N., & Wood, W. (1992). Self-esteem and intelligence affect influenceability: The mediating role of message reception. *Psychological Bulletin, 111,* 156–171.

Richmond, V. P., & Martin, M. M. (1998). Sociocommunicative style and sociocommunicative orientation. In J. C. McCroskey, J. A. Daly, M. M. Martin, & M. J. Beatty (Eds.), *Communication and personality: Trait perspectives* (pp. 133–147). Cresskill, NJ: Hampton.

Riggio, R. E. (1986). Assessment of basic social skills. *Journal of Personality and Social Psychology, 51,* 649–660.

Riggio, R. E., & Friedman, H. S. (1982). The interrelationships of self-monitoring factors, personality traits, and nonverbal social skills. *Journal of Nonverbal Behavior, 7,* 33–45.

Ritchie, L. D., & Fitzpatrick, M. A. (1990). Family communication patterns: Measuring intrapersonal perceptions of interpersonal relationships. *Communication Research, 17,* 523–544.

Roberts, J. E., Gotlib, I. H., & Kassel, J. D. (1996). Adult attachment security and symptoms of depression: The mediating role of dysfunctional attitudes and low self-esteem. *Journal of Personality and Social Psychology, 70,* 310–320.

Robins, C. J., Ladd, J., Welkowitz, J., Blaney, P. H., Diaz, R., & Kutcher, G. (1994). The Personal Style Inventory: Preliminary validation studies of a new measure of sociotropy and autonomy. *Journal of Psychopathology and Behavioral Assessment, 16,* 277–300.

Rokeach, M. (1960). *The open and closed mind: Investigations into the nature of belief systems and personality systems.* New York: Basic Books.

Romero-Canyas, R., Downey, G., Berenson, K., Ayduk, O., & Kang, N. (2010). Rejection sensitivity and the rejection–hostility link in romantic relationships. *Journal of Personality, 78,* 119–148.

Ross, M., & Holmberg, D. (1990). Recounting the past: Gender differences in the recall of events in the history of a close relationship. In J. M. Olson & M. P. Zanna (Eds.), *The Ontario symposium: Vol. 6. Self-inference processes* (pp. 135–152). Hillsdale, NJ: Lawrence Erlbaum.

Rotenberg, K. J., Shewchuk, V., & Kimberly, T. (2001). Loneliness, sex, romantic jealousy, and powerlessness. *Journal of Social and Personal Relationships, 18,* 55–79.

Rotter, J. B. (1966). Generalized expectancies for internal and external control of reinforcement. *Psychological Monographs, 80,* 1–28.

Rubin, M., & Hewstone, M. (1998). Social identity theory's self-esteem hypothesis: A review and some suggestions for clarification. *Personality and Social Psychology Review, 2,* 40–62.

Russell, D. W., Cutrona, C. E., & Jones, W. H. (1986). A trait-situational analysis of shyness. In W. H. Jones, J. M. Cheek, & S. R. Briggs (Eds.), *Shyness: Perspectives on research and treatment* (pp. 239–249). New York: Plenum Press.

Sabourin, T. C., Infante, D. A., & Rudd, J. E. (1993). Verbal aggression in marriages: A comparison of violent, distressed but nonviolent, and nondistressed couples. *Human Communication Research, 20,* 245–267.

Salovey, P., & Mayer, J. D. (1990). Emotional intelligence. *Imagination, Cognition, and Personality, 9,* 185–211.

Samter, W. (2002). How gender and cognitive complexity influence the provision of emotional support: A study of indirect effects. *Communication Reports, 15,* 5–16.

Saucier, G. (2009). Recurrent personality dimensions in inclusive lexical studies: Indications for a Big Six structure. *Journal of Personality, 77,* 1577–1614.

Scanzoni, J., & Arnett, C. (1987). Enlarging the understanding of marital commitment via religious, gender role preferences, and locus of marital control. *Journal of Family Studies, 8,* 136–156.

Scarr, S., & Weinberg, R. A. (1981). The transmission of authoritarianism in families: Genetic resemblance in social-political attitudes. In S. Scarr (Ed.), *Race, social class, and individual differences in I.Q.* (pp. 399–427). Hillsdale, NJ: Lawrence Erlbaum.

Schaller, M., & Murray, D. (2008). Pathogens, personality, and culture: Disease prevalence predicts worldwide variability in sociosexuality, extraversion, and openness to experience. *Journal of Personality and Social Psychology, 95,* 212–221.

Scherwitz, L., Perkins, L., Chesney, M., & Hughes, G. (1991). Cook-Medley Hostility Scale and subsets: Relationship to demographic and psychosocial characteristics in young adults in the CARDIA study. *Psychosomatic Medicine, 53,* 36–49.

Schlenker, B., Weigold, M., & Schlenker, K. (2008). What makes a hero? The impact of integrity on admiration and interpersonal judgment. *Journal of Personality, 76,* 323–356.

Schmidt, L. A., & Fox, N. A. (1995). Individual differences in young adults' shyness and sociability: Personality and health correlates. *Personality and Individual Differences, 19,* 455–462.

Schmitt, D. P., & Buss, D. M. (2000). Sexual dimensions of person descriptions: Beyond or subsumed by the Big Five? *Journal of Research in Personality, 34,* 141–177.

Schmitt, D. P., Realo, A., Voracek, M., & Allik, J. (2008). Why can't a man be more like a woman? Sex differences in Big Five personality traits across 55 cultures. *Journal of Personality and Social Psychology, 94,* 168–182.

Schroeder, J. E., & Ketrow, S. M. (1997). Social anxiety and performance in an interpersonal perception task. *Psychological Reports, 81,* 991–996.

Schultz, B. (1982). Argumentativeness: Its effect in group decision-making and its role in leadership perceptions. *Communication Quarterly, 30,* 368–375.

Schultz, N. R., & Moore, D. (1986). The loneliness experience of college students: Sex differences. *Personality and Social Psychology Bulletin, 12,* 111–119.

Segrin, C. (1990). A meta-analytic review of social skill deficits associated with depression. *Communication Monographs, 57,* 292–308.

Segrin, C. (1996). The relationship between social skills deficits and psychosocial problems: A test of the vulnerability model. *Communication Research, 23,* 425–450.

Segrin, C., & Abramson, L. Y. (1994). Negative reactions to depressive behaviors: A communication theories analysis. *Journal of Abnormal Psychology, 103,* 655–668.

Selfhout, M., Burk, W., Branje, S., Denissen, J., Van Aken, M., & Meeus, W. (2010). Emerging late adolescent friendship networks and Big Five personality traits: A social network approach. *Journal of Personality, 78,* 509–538.

Sherman, R. A, Nave, C. S., & Funder, D. C. (2010). Situational similarity and personality predict behavioral consistency. *Journal of Personality and Social Psychology, 99,* 330–343.

Silvia , P. J., & Kwapil, T. R. (in press). Aberrant asociality: How individual differences in social anhedonia illuminate the need to belong. *Journal of Personality.*

Simpson, J. A., Winterheld, H. A., & Chen, J. Y. (2006). Personality and relationships: A temperament perspective. In A. Vangelisti & D. Perlman (Eds.), *The Cambridge handbook of personal relationships* (pp. 231–250). New York: Cambridge University Press.

Smalley, R. L., & Stake, J. E. (1996). Evaluating sources of ego-threatening feedback: Self-esteem and narcissism effects. *Journal of Research in Personality, 30,* 483–495.

Smith, C. V., Nezlek, J. B., Webster, G. D., & Paddock, E. L. (2007). Relationships between daily sexual interactions and domain-specific and general models of personality traits. *Journal of Social and Personal Relationships, 24,* 497–515.

Smith, R. H., Parrott, W. G., Diener, E. F., Hoyle, R. H., & Kim, S. H. (1999). Dispositional envy. *Personality and Social Psychology Bulletin, 25,* 1007–1020.

Smith-Lovin, L., & Brody, C. (1989). Interruptions in group discussions: The effects of gender and group composition. *American Sociological Review, 54,* 424–435.

Snyder, M. (1987). *Public appearances, private realties: The psychology of self-monitoring.* New York: Freeman.

Snyder, M., Gangestad, S. W., & Simpson, J. A. (1983). Choosing friends as activity partners: The role of self-monitoring. *Journal of Personality and Social Psychology, 45,* 1061–1072.

Snyder, M., & Simpson, J. A. (1984). Self-monitoring and dating relationships. *Journal of Personality and Social Psychology, 47,* 1281–1291.

Solano, C. H., Batten, P. G., & Parish, E. A. (1982). Loneliness and the patterns of self-disclosure. *Journal of Personality and Social Psychology, 43,* 524–531.

Solano, C. H., & Koester, N. H. (1989). Loneliness and communication problems: Subjective anxiety or objective skills? *Personality and Social Psychology Bulletin, 15,* 126–133.

Spitzberg, B. H., & Canary, D. (1985). Loneliness and relationally competent communication. *Journal of Social and Personal Relationships, 2,* 387–402.

Steinfatt, T. M. (1987). Personality and communication: Classical approaches. In J. C. McCroskey & J. A. Daly (Eds.), *Personality and interpersonal communication* (pp. 42–126). Newbury Park: Sage.

Stephenson, M. T., & Palmgreen, P. (2001). Sensation seeking, perceived message sensation value, personal involvement, and processing of anti-marijuana PSAs. *Communication Monographs, 68,* 49–71.

Stephenson, M. T., Quick, B. L., & Hirsch, H. A. (2010). Evidence in support of a strategy to target authoritarian and permissive parents in antidrug media campaigns. *Communication Research, 37,* 73–104.

Stewart, S., Stinnett, H., & Rosenfeld, L. B. (2000). Sex differences in desired characteristics of short-term and long-term relationship partners. *Journal of Social and Personal Relationships, 17,* 843–853.

Stokes, J. P. (1987). The relation of loneliness and self-disclosure. In V. J. Derlega & J. H. Berg (Eds.), *Self-disclosure: Theory, research, and therapy* (pp. 175–201). New York: Plenum Press.

Swickert, R., Hittner, J., & Foster, A. (2010). Big Five traits interact to predict perceived social support. *Personality and Individual Differences, 48,* 736–741.

Tarlow, E. M., & Haaga, D. A. F. (1996). Negative self-concept: Specificity to depressive symptoms and relation to positive and negative affectivity. *Journal of Research in Personality, 30,* 120–127.

Taylor, D. A., & Belgave, F. Z. (1986). The effects of perceived intimacy and valence on self-disclosure reciprocity. *Personality and Social Psychology Bulletin, 12,* 247–255.

Tennen, H. (2006). Self-monitoring [Special section]. *Journal of Personality, 74,* 633–778.

Thoits, P. A. (1995). Stress, coping, and social support processes: Where are we? What next? [Extra issue]. *Journal of Health and Social Behavior, 35,* 53–79.

Thompson, J. M., Whiffen, V. E., & Blain, M. D. (1995). Depressive symptoms, sex, and perceptions of intimate relationships. *Journal of Social and Personal Relationships, 12,* 49–66.

Thorndike, E. L. (1920). Intelligence and its uses. *Harper's Magazine, 140,* 227–235.

Thorne, A., Korobov, N., & Morgan, E. M. (2007). Channeling identity: A study of storytelling in conversations between introverted and extraverted friends. *Journal of Research in Personality, 41,* 1008–1031.

Trobst, K. K., Collins, R. L., & Embree, J. M. (1994). The role of emotion in social support provision: Gender, empathy, and expressions of distress. *Journal of Social and Personal Relationships, 11,* 45–62.

Turner, S. M., Beidel, D. C., & Larkin, K. T. (1986). Situational determinants of social anxiety in clinic and nonclinic samples: Physiological and cognitive correlates. *Behavioral Research and Therapy, 24*, 56–64.

Twenge, J. M. (2001). Changes in women's assertiveness in response to status and role: A cross-temporal meta-analysis, 1931–1993. *Journal of Personality and Social Psychology, 81*, 133–145.

Vangelisti, A. L., & Daly, J. A. (1988). Correlates of speaking skills in the United States: A national assessment. *Communication Education, 38*, 132–44.

Vangelisti, A. L., & Daly, J. A. (1997). Gender differences in standards for romantic relationships. *Personal Relationships, 4*, 203–219.

Vangelisti, A. L., Knapp, M. L., & Daly, J. A. (1990). Conversational narcissism. *Communication Monographs, 57*, 251–274.

Veselka, L., Schermer, J., Martin, R., & Vernon, P. (2010). Relations between humor styles and the dark triad traits of personality. *Personality and Individual Differences, 48*, 772–774.

Vikers, K. S., & Vogeltanz, N. D. (2000). Dispositional optimism as a predictor of depressive symptoms over time. *Personality and Individual Differences, 28*, 259–272.

Vitkus, J., & Horowitz, L. M. (1987). Poor social performance of lonely people: Lacking a skill or adopting a role? *Journal of Personality and Social Psychology, 52*, 1266–1273.

de Vries, R. E., Bakker-Pieper, A., Siberg, R. A., van Gameren, K., & Vlug, M. (2009). The content and dimensionality of communication styles. *Communication Research, 36*, 178–206.

Waller, K. L., & MacDonald, T. K. (2010). Trait self-esteem moderates the effect of initiator status on emotional and cognitive responses to romantic relationship dissolution. *Journal of Personality, 78*, 1271–1300.

Wallston, K. A., & Wallston, B. S. (1981). Health locus of control scales. In H. M. Lefcourt (Ed.), *Research with the locus of control construct* (Vol. 1, pp. 189–243). New York: Academic Press.

Watson, A. K., & Cheek, J. M. (1986). Shyness situations: Perspectives of a diverse sample of shy females. *Psychological Reports, 59*, 1040–1042.

Watson, D., & Clark, L. A. (1997). Extraversion and its positive emotional core. In R. Hogan, J. Johnson, & S. R. Briggs (Eds.), *Handbook of personality psychology* (pp. 751–793). San Diego, CA: Academic Press.

Watson, D., Clark, L. A., & Tellegen, A. (1988). Development and validation of brief measures of positive and negative affect: The PANAS Scales. *Journal of Personality and Social Psychology, 54*, 1063–1070.

Wheeless, L. R., & Grotz, J. (1976). Conceptualization and measurement of reported self-disclosure. *Human Communication Research, 2*, 338–346.

Wheeless, L. R., Preiss, R. W., & Gale, B. M. (1997). Receiver apprehension, informational receptivity, and cognitive processing. In J. A. Daly, J. C. McCroskey, J. Ayres, T. Hopf, & D. M. Ayres (Eds.), *Avoiding communication: Shyness, reticence, and communication apprehension* (2nd ed., pp. 151–187). Cresskill, NJ: Hampton Press.

White, G. L., & Mullen, P. E. (1989). *Jealousy: Theory, research, and clinical strategies.* New York: Guilford Press.

Wiggins, J. S., & Trobst, K. K. (1997). When is a circumplex an "interpersonal circumplex"? The case of supportive actions. In R. Plutchik & H. Conte (Eds.), *Circumplex models of personality and emotions* (pp. 57–80). Washington, DC: American Psychological Association.

Wigley, C. J. (1995). Disclosiveness, willingness to communicate, and communication apprehension as predictors of jury selection in felony trials. *Communication Quarterly, 43*, 342–352.

Wigley, C. J. (1998). Verbal aggressiveness. In J. C. McCroskey, J. A. Daly, M. M. Martin, & M. J. Beatty (Eds.), *Communication and personality: Trait perspectives* (pp. 191–214). Cresskill, NJ: Hampton Press.

Wigley, C. J. (1999). Verbal aggressiveness and communicator style characteristics of summoned jurors as predictors of actual jury selection. *Communication Monographs, 66*, 266–275.

Wigley, C. J., Pohl, G. H., & Watt, M. G. S. (1989). Conversational sensitivity as a correlate of trait verbal aggressiveness and the predisposition to verbally praise others. *Communication Reports, 2*, 92–95.

Winkler, I., & Doherty, W. J. (1983). Communication styles and marital satisfaction in Israeli and American couples. *Family Process, 22*, 221–228.

Winter, D. G. (1988). The power motive in women—and men. *Journal of Personality and Social Psychology, 54*, 510–519.

Wittenberg, M. T., & Reis, H. T. (1986). Loneliness, social skills, and social perception. *Personality and Social Psychology Bulletin, 12*, 121–130.

Wolfson, S. L. (1981). Effects of Machiavellianism and communication on helping behavior during an emergency. *British Journal of Social Psychology, 20,* 189–195.

Woods, E. (1996). Association of nonverbal decoding ability with indices of person-centered communicative ability. *Communication Reports, 9,* 13–22.

Wright, D. B., London, K., & Waechter, M. (2009). Social anxiety moderates memory conformity in adolescents. *Applied Cognitive Psychology, 24,* 1034–1045.

Wright, T. M., & Reise, S. P. (1997). Personality and unrestricted sexual behavior: Correlations of sociosexuality in Caucasian and Asian college students. *Journal of Research in Personality, 31,* 166–192.

Yarkoni, T. (2010). Personality in 100,000 words: A large-scale analysis of personality and word use among bloggers. *Journal of Research in Personality, 44,* 363–373.

Yip, J. A., & Martin, R. A. (2006). Sense of humor, emotional intelligence, and social competence. *Journal of Research in Personality, 40,* 1202–1208.

Zaccaro, S. J., Foti, R. J., & Kenny, D. A. (1991). Self-monitoring and trait-based variance in leadership: An investigation of leader flexibility across multiple group situations. *Journal of Applied Psychology, 76,* 308–315.

Zaki, J., Bolger, N., & Ochsner, K. (2009). Unpacking the informational bases of empathic accuracy. Emotion, 9, 478–487.

Zeigler-Hill, V. (2010). The interpersonal nature of self-esteem: Do different measures of self-esteem possess similar interpersonal content? *Journal of Research in Personality, 44,* 22–30.

Zellars, K. L., & Perrewe, P. L. (2001). Affective personality and the content of emotional social support: Coping in organizations. *Journal of Applied Psychology, 86,* 459–467.

# CHAPTER 6

# Knowledge Structures and Social Interaction

*Charles R. Berger*

*Nicholas A. Palomares*

**A**lthough interpersonal communication is studied in a wide variety of seemingly diverse contexts, including organizations, families, romantic relationships, education, and health, many of which are accorded separate treatment in this *Handbook*'s chapters, our view is that certain fundamental processes make interpersonal communication possible across the entire spectrum of these specific contexts as well as others. We recognize that at the margins there may be variations among contexts that must be taken into account to understand how communication functions within them; however, our approach is to seek to illuminate the significant commonalities among them. Failing to understand the general processes that cut across ostensibly unique communication contexts while, at the same time, dwelling on what may be superficial differences among them, dooms us to incomplete explanations. Our central contention is that regardless of context, interpersonal communication is fundamentally purposive. Our aim in this chapter is to trace the implications of this fundamental postulate for understanding how individuals process and produce messages during social interactions.

The idea that living organisms, including humans, are fundamentally goal-pursuing creatures has been advanced by philosophers and students of language. Some philosophers have argued that humans' ability to think in complex ways evolved from the necessity of achieving goals for the sake of survival (Bogdan, 1994, 1997). Well-developed cognitive skills, such as the ability to plan, simulate, and recall, facilitate goal achievement. Recurring need states, such as hunger and thirst, that give rise to vital survival goals, such as obtaining food and water, are more easily satisfied if humans can recall the successful procedures they have used in the past to reach these goals. Moreover, humans' capacity to make inferences about others' intentions also facilitates goal achievement by allowing organisms to anticipate the actions of those who might interfere with their goal-directed actions (Bogdan, 2000). Being able to anticipate and recognize potential roadblocks to goal attainment and the ability to overcome them are crucial to success in many spheres of life. Although the capacity to think and reason plays a critical role in successful goal achievement, philosophers have observed that language is an instrument, a tool for getting things done (Austin, 1962; Wittgenstein, 1953). This view has been echoed by Clark (1994), who argued,

> People engage in discourse not simply to use language, but to accomplish things. They want to buy shoes or get a lost address or arrange a dinner party or trade gossip or teach a child improper fractions. Language is simply a tool for achieving these aims. (p. 1018)

To these observations we would add that when people engage in social interaction with each other, they do so for the purpose of achieving goals, and social interaction between people is a tool for achieving them. Some might object to this view on the grounds that sometimes people converse with each other "just to talk" or merely "to pass the time of day." In our view, although it is possible to use language to label such social interactions as "pointless," merely saying that they are pointless does not make it so. "Passing the time of day" or "just talking" may be just another way of saying "relieving boredom," "alleviating stress," or "coping with loneliness," all of which are relatively well-defined goals. Because the act of speaking to another person is both time-consuming and resource demanding and, if carried out over a prolonged period of time, physically exhausting—after all, people do "grow tired" of talking—we assume that as a communicative resource, social interaction is dedicated to the satisfaction of goals.

In our view, goals are cognitive representations of desired end states for which people strive (Dijksterhuis, Chartrand, & Aarts, 2007; Dillard, 1997). People may desire to achieve highly abstract end states such as happiness, fame, fortune, and eternal life, or their current pursuits may be

directed at the attainment of concrete and mundane goals such as getting up, taking a shower, brushing their teeth, and getting dressed. Scholars frequently assume that goals are hierarchically represented in long-term memory, with abstract goals at the tops of the hierarchies and less abstract goals nested under them (Dillard, 1990, 1997; Lichtenstein & Brewer, 1980). The goals in the hierarchy have an enabling relationship with each other such that the achievement of lower level goals enables the realization of higher level goals. Successfully achieving the goals of getting up, taking a shower, brushing one's teeth, and getting dressed may facilitate higher level goals such as going to work or going to class. The quality of social actors' performance in these work and academic settings may hinge, in turn, on the successful attainment of communication goals such as being persuasive with coworkers or professors. Associated with communication goals such as these may be specific plans or scripts that contain concrete actions for accomplishing them. The satisfaction of these communication goals may, in turn, lead to even higher level goals such as a job promotion or a college degree, which, in turn, may enable an even more abstract goal such as becoming wealthy.

Successful goal pursuit in social situations usually not only involves a focal goal or goals but also requires the satisfaction of certain constraints. Constraints are behavioral influences that guide action during progress toward goal achievement (Kellermann, 2004). Such constraints might involve the degree to which social actors are able to be assertive or dominant in trying to achieve their focal goal or goals. For example, loose constraints might allow social actors to pursue the goal of gaining compliance from others by using promises of rewards for compliance, coercive threats for noncompliance, or both. Tight constraints, in contrast, might limit behavioral choice to just one of the two means of gaining compliance. Such constraints are frequently germane to the level of politeness with which goals can be pursued in social commerce (Brown & Levinson, 1987). Some theorists have called constraints secondary goals (Dillard, 1990, 1997), and others have labeled them metagoals, such as social appropriateness and efficiency (Berger & Kellermann, 1994). Setting these terminological differences aside, a number of social interaction theorists have argued that social actors may heed multiple constraints simultaneously in their pursuit of a focal goal or goals while interacting with others (Dillard, 1997; O'Keefe, 1988; O'Keefe & Shepard, 1987; Tracy & Coupland, 1990; Tracy & Moran, 1983). As these constraints or secondary goals proliferate, interactions become more complex, and social actors are placed under increasing levels of cognitive load as they attempt to satisfy these multiple concerns simultaneously (Greene, 1997). Engaging in such complex interactions for an extended period of time may prove to be both physically and mentally taxing to the point that social actors terminate the exhausting encounters.

Because goal hierarchies may contain several levels, it is difficult for individuals to focus on all of these hierarchical levels at once. For example, although food consumption is vital for satisfying the goal of survival, when people who are currently eating a meal are asked why they are doing so, they are very likely to reply that they are eating to satisfy the goal of alleviating their hunger, not the goal of avoiding death. However, even though people may not be consciously aware of specific goals, it would be a mistake to assume that these preconscious goals do not exert an influence on communication and action. Questions related to the preconscious processing of goals will be taken up in greater detail in the sections that follow.

Whereas social interaction is a tool for attaining goals, merely considering how individuals identify goals or how social actors' goals arise tells only part of the story. Knowing what one's goals are and the goals that others are pursuing in social situations is not sufficient for goal attainment. Successful goal pursuit also depends on the knowledge available to social actors. It is easy to imagine different people pursuing the same, well-defined goal, for example, persuading their close friend to lend them a sum of money for a few days but having widely varying degrees of success in achieving their loan acquisition goal. On the one hand, some borrowers might receive a sum of money that is more than they requested, while others might come away from the loan request encounter empty-handed. Part of the variability in their success may be attributed to their knowledge concerning how to communicate their loan request to their friend. These repositories of relevant knowledge are represented hierarchically in long-term memory. Knowledge structures such as plans and scripts represent the actions necessary to achieve goals. In terms of the loan request, the more abstract action of "being pleasant" might be associated with the goal of putting the target of the request in a good mood to enhance the chances of obtaining the loan. "Being pleasant," in turn, could be associated with more concrete, lower-order actions in the hierarchy, such as smiling, joking, complimenting, and speaking with moderate vocal intensity and a pleasant intonation.

Knowledge structures that represent action hierarchies can be differentiated with respect to their flexibility and the degree to which social actors are consciously aware of them. On the one hand, plans are, initially, consciously thought-out action sequences for attaining goals (Berger, 1997; Schank & Abelson, 1977; Wilensky, 1983). Plans can anticipate potential roadblocks and include actions for overcoming these obstacles should they arise. Including these contingent actions gives plans their flexibility and allows for goal attainment through alternative action sequences. On the other hand, scripts are rigidified action sequences that can be run off at low levels of conscious awareness. If the same plan is used repeatedly to achieve a particular goal or set of goals, it becomes a script. One would not speak of the plan to travel from San Francisco to New York, as if there is only one way in which to accomplish this goal. However, if one were to commute from San Francisco to New York on a weekly basis, one might follow the same script in doing so. Such a commuter might take the same flights both ways and the same ground transportation to get to and from airports. This travel routine or script could be fulfilled with little conscious thought. Successfully attaining goals depends on both the availability and the quality of the knowledge that is organized by plans and scripts; however, when such knowledge is not available to communicators and they wish to achieve goals, the ability to generate plans or to engage in planning becomes vital to their success.

The fact that some goals recur with great regularity in everyday life and that individuals develop scripts to attain these goals suggests that goals and the actions necessary to reach them are integrated into knowledge structures. Integrating goal–plan knowledge allows social actors to initiate actions quickly during the give and take of social interactions with others. Thus, during a conversation, one person might sense that the other person is bored and initiate a sequence of actions with the goal of alleviating the conversational partner's boredom. Or, in the midst of job interviews, interviewees might become aware that interviewers are not responding positively to them and quickly try to initiate actions that will increase the positivity of their self-presentations and thus garner favorable responses from interviewers. These kinds of rapid adjustments during social encounters require that when goals such as these arise, plans or scripts are readily available to guide actions. Moreover, they illustrate the notion that activating goals by itself cannot ensure interaction success; plans to guide actions are crucial in this process. Of course, occasions may arise when individuals are unable to access the knowledge that enables them to cope with rapidly changing circumstances, which leaves them in a state of uncertainty about what they should do or say next. This kind of uncertainty is the primary reason that individuals cite for their speechlessness when they recall instances of being at a loss for words during recent conversations with others (Berger, 2004).

Although knowledge concerning goals, plans, and scripts is vital for the skillful conduct of social interaction, there are other kinds of knowledge that are crucial for social interaction success.

As Table 6.1 shows, in addition to goal-related knowledge and the procedural knowledge embodied in plans and scripts, social actors must have funds of knowledge about the roles that people play, their personalities, their emotional states, and the social interaction context to understand fully the current states of co-interlocutors and the strategies that might be used to achieve desired goals. Table 6.1 also indicates that these types of knowledge can be general in character, for example, how professors, introverts, those experiencing anger, and persons in formal social contexts typically behave, or highly specific, that is, how Professor Farquar, an introverted close friend, an angry family member, or a romantic partner in a formal context behave. We assume that much of this knowledge is acquired experientially or tacitly by observing and interacting with other people rather than through formal instruction (Sommerville, Woodward, & Needham, 2005). For example, general knowledge about the roles people play results from identifying common attributes and behaviors of individuals who play the same role, for example, teachers or doctors. Once established, these general role expectations can serve as evaluative standards and may be in play when people make evaluative statements such as "Professor Schlock is a terrible lecturer" or "Dr. Willoughby is so wonderful." This general knowledge is different from the specific knowledge one acquires about a role incumbent, for example, a professor with whom a student has taken four small seminars. Such extensive experience may enable the student to differentiate this specific professor from professors "in general." This kind of specific knowledge about a professor may lead a student to say, for good or ill, "Professor Watson is not like any other professor I have ever experienced." Specific knowledge, then, is acquired through repeated interactions with particular individuals and may be indicated by statements such as "I know this person very well." Of course, specific knowledge may be somewhat fragile because individuals, and the social systems within which they operate, are dynamic and ever changing. If social actors

**Table 6.1**  Types of Social Interaction Knowledge

| | Specificity Level | |
|---|---|---|
| *Knowledge Type* | *General* | *Specific* |
| Goal related | Knowledge concerning the goals people in general typically pursue in a given context | Knowledge concerning the goals specific individuals pursue in a given context |
| Procedural | Knowledge of action sequences that will bring about desired end states among people in general | Knowledge of action sequences that will bring about the desired end states with specific individuals |
| Role | Role expectations for people in general | Role expectations for specific role incumbents |
| Person | General personality and dispositional prototypes and the behaviors associated with them | Knowledge of dispositional attributes unique to specific individuals |
| Emotion | Knowledge of emotional states and their blends, knowledge of emotion–behavior associations | Knowledge concerning how particular individuals express specific emotions |
| Contextual | Knowledge of contextual features that affect the behavior of people in general | Knowledge of situational features that influence the behavior of specific individuals |

fail to update their knowledge bases about specific others and predicate their current goals and plans on outdated knowledge, they may experience unpleasant surprises and failures in reaching their goals with the particular individuals.

Because of the fundamental roles that goal–plan knowledge structures play in everyday life, it is not surprising that these concepts have received considerable attention in a wide variety of academic disciplines. Artificial intelligence researchers; developmental, cognitive, and social psychologists; neuroscientists; education researchers; socio- and psycholinguists; and communication researchers have found these theoretical constructs to be of considerable use in their work. The interdisciplinary nature of this research will become apparent in subsequent sections of this chapter. Much of the theory and research concerning goals and plans has been organized

around two distinct but related areas. The first of these areas concerns the ways in which inferences concerning others' goals and plans influence our understanding of others' actions, including their utterances. Some have argued that humans understand each other's utterances and actions by inferring the goals they are pursuing and the plans they are using to do so (Green, 1996). Artificial intelligence researchers have developed computer understanding systems that are premised on this assumption (Ardissono, Boella, & Lesmo, 2000; Carberry, 1990, 2001; Schmidt, 1976). The second of these areas is concerned with action production, including the production of messages. The principle idea motivating work in this area is that knowledge structures such as plans and scripts guide people's goal-directed actions (Berger, 1997). Again, this assumption has been part and parcel of artificial intelligence research in areas such as computer robotics (Koenig, Smirnov, & Tovey, 2003; Mudgal, Tovey, & Koenig, 2004).

These two areas, goal–plan recognition and action–discourse production, will be the respective foci in the following two sections of this chapter. Because much of the work in these two areas has employed the individual processor as the unit of analysis, we recognize the necessity of "socializing" our framework to account for the unique effects of social interaction on these processes. Individuals may indeed enter the crucible of social interaction armed with particular goals and plans; however, these interactions may become highly dynamic, subject to change without notice, and, thus, nonroutine, making it necessary to modify both goals and plans as these somewhat unpredictable encounters unfold. In at least some instances, not altering inferences about others' goals and plans as well as one's own goals and plans as interactions progress might well result in goal failure. These issues are considered throughout this discussion. This chapter's overarching purpose, then, is to demonstrate the usefulness of the goal and plan concepts as explanatory tools as well as their utility in provoking theory development and research in the study of social interaction.

## Knowledge Structures and Message Processing

Knowledge structures that embody the goal and plan constructs have enjoyed considerable popularity among researchers interested in understanding the processes that make discourse and text comprehensible to social actors. As individuals interact with each other face-to-face and hear what is being said and while they observe each other's actions, their knowledge of the goals that people typically pursue during social interactions and the plans they use to pursue them enables them to achieve an understanding of each other's utterances and actions. Of course, knowledge about the situation within which the interaction

is taking place also helps social actors understand each other's actions. There are countless everyday communication contexts, such as classrooms, supermarkets, department stores, and professors' offices, in which the context itself provides significant information about how individuals are likely to act and what they are likely to say in them. For example, with no explicit guidance of any kind, college students can enter lecture halls in which they have never been and know where they should seat themselves. They also know where lecturers will position themselves in the halls when they arrive. Situation knowledge, then, is intimately linked with goal–plan knowledge structures. There are, of course, non–face-to-face social interaction contexts, such as text-based, computer-mediated communication and telephone conversations, in which social actors have no access to visual information regarding their interaction partners (Walther & Parks, 2002). However, even within these less cue-rich contexts, knowledge structures enable message comprehension processes.

This section deals with how social actors employ knowledge structures in the service of understanding each other's verbal and nonverbal messages. It begins with the fundamental problem of how social actors determine each other's goals and then explores how the activation of knowledge structures influences the ways in which social actors understand each other's discourse and actions. As will become apparent, once activated, knowledge structures can exert profound effects on how discourse and actions are comprehended and interpreted.

Because goals are mental representations, inferring someone else's goal can be a tricky business, akin to mind reading. Of course, there is nothing supernatural about inferring goals, and social actors do not actually read others' cognitions. People generate inferences about interlocutors' goals by using contextual cues in social interaction and knowledge structures. People seem to be able to infer others' goals, at least at some level, from birth, probably because of an innate inclination to infer goal directedness in behavior (Bogdan, 1997; Rosset, 2008). Indeed, 6- to 8-month-old infants can infer goals to biomechanically impossible and, thus, never before experienced human action: For example, when shown a video recording of a person reaching for an object blocked by boxes that make moving them necessary to grab the object in a realistic manner, infants interpreted the action as goal directed even if the hand movement was not physically possible (e.g., the arm and hand contorted to snake around the boxes without moving them; Southgate, Johnson, & Csibra, 2008; see also Csibra, 2008). What is more, 5- to 10-month-old chimpanzees infer goal directedness in humans (Uller, 2004). Evidence also suggests that infants attribute communicative intent to social agents prior to understanding the content of the intention (Csibra, 2010). Overall, strong support exists for the notion that people infer others' goals during social interaction and that at least a rudimentary foundation for goal detection is present at birth. Thus, it is not surprising that adults can infer goals with or without conscious awareness (Hassin, Aarts, & Ferguson, 2005) and that neural correlates for implicit and explicit goal inferences exist (Van der Cruyssen, Van Duynslaeger, Cortoos, & Van Overwalle, 2009). Furthermore, the psychological process of inferring goals seems to be identical for infants and adults (Reid et al., 2009). If goal detection is a common endeavor that people undertake for most of their lives, then the question becomes what the process is that allows people to infer others' goals.

The knowledge structures employed during social interaction affect the inferences that a goal detector generates. These knowledge structures provide cues to the goals others may be pursuing (Baker, Saxe, & Tenenbaum, 2009; Magliano, Skowronski, Britt, Güss, & Forsythe, 2008; Payne, Lambert, & Jacoby, 2002). What people observe during social interaction triggers certain knowledge structures, these knowledge structures subsequently activate particular goals (Shah, 2003), and these goals are likely inferred compared with other, less accessible goals (Fitzsimons & Bargh,

2003; Palomares, 2008). Knowledge structures, in other words, play a key role in the goal inference process because the various knowledge structures are cognitively linked to or associated with goals. One set of activated knowledge structures can lead to a goal inference that is unique compared with an inference based on a different set of activated knowledge structures (Dewhurst, Holmes, Swannell, & Barry, 2008). Unlike the innate inclination to infer goal directedness in behavior, the associations between goals and knowledge structures are primarily acquired through experience (Csibra, 2010; Sommerville et al., 2005; Woodward, Sommerville, & Guajardo, 2001). Goals and knowledge structures become linked by frequent and consistent coactivation in particular interactions (Bargh & Barndollar, 1996; Bargh & Gollwitzer, 1994; Chartrand & Bargh, 1996; Fitzsimons, Shah, Chartrand, & Bargh, 2005). Two people confronted with the same set of stimuli, therefore, can generate two distinct goal inferences given different past experiences (Kawada, Oettingen, Gollwitzer, & Bargh, 2004, Experiment 1). Yet because of the routinization of social interaction and similar knowledge structures among people in identical or comparable speech communities (Aarts & Dijksterhuis, 2000; Berger, 2005, 2007; Coulmas, 1981), people demonstrate high levels of agreement in their goal inferences, sometimes in excess of 88% (Albright, Cohen, Malloy, Christ, & Bromgard, 2004; Palomares, 2008).

Considering that knowledge structures are chief determinants of goal inferences, one conclusion is that inferences depend on the contextual and behavioral factors perceived in an interaction because these factors activate the corresponding knowledge structures that represent them (Baker et al., 2009; Dik & Aarts, 2008; Palomares, 2008; Payne et al., 2002). For example, the social setting, such as a medical visit to a physician, can be diagnostic of the goal a patient is pursuing, as is the patient's behavior in the social setting, such as the questions the patient asks the doctor or the assertions the patient or doctor makes. In a study that investigated the role these factors play in activating knowledge structures, after reading a scenario about a job fair, participants' goal inferences converged, resulting in relatively high agreement, if the job fair context and the pursuer's tactic or speech act (e.g., reveal) were both strongly and solely linked to a single goal (e.g., to give information; Palomares, 2008). In contrast, participants agreed in their inferences to a lesser extent when the job fair context and tactic (e.g., thank) were linked to distinct or disparate goals (e.g., to give information and to get something, respectively) or when the job fair context was linked to one goal (e.g., to give information) but the tactic (e.g., cooperate) was linked to three goals (e.g., to give information, to get something, and to provide assistance). Agreement was also relatively low when the context was ambiguous and, thus, no goal linkages were accessible. Overall, agreement was higher when the context and tactic "pointed to" a similar goal than when they suggested a diverse set of multiple goals or no clear goal. These data provided initial evidence for a theoretical framework on goal detection that explains the role of knowledge structures in producing goal inferences.

This framework is rooted in the rationale that the mental associations between goals and knowledge structures affect detectors' goal inferences (Palomares, 2008). The cognitive representations of contexts and tactics are associated with goals, and these linkages can influence which goal is inferred by elevating the accessibility of potentially inferred goals (Dik & Aarts, 2008; Schank & Abelson, 1977; Wilensky, 1983). Goals with greater accessibility are more likely inferred relative to other, less accessible goals (Fitzsimons & Bargh, 2003). A central tenet of the framework is the integration principle, which states that detectors will integrate the goal linkages from multiple factors (e.g., context, tactics, relational type) to generate an inference only when none of those factors individually and strongly indicates the pursuer's goal (Palomares, 2009a). In other words, when one factor alone provides adequate cues to the pursuer's goal, then other factors are less useful and not completely integrated to infer a goal.

Research on the integration principle has focused on the accuracy of goal inferences based on the social context in which an interaction occurs and the tactics pursuers employ to achieve a goal. Applying the integration principle to the social context and pursuers' tactics yields the following rationale: Pursuer's tactics facilitate goal detection accuracy only when the context provides no useful links to the pursuer's goal. Several tests of the integration principle, as applied to the context and the pursuer's tactics, have garnered support (Palomares, 2008, 2009a, 2009b). For example, because initial interactions between two strangers are strongly linked to the goal of obtaining personal information but not to the goal of obtaining reasons for having a certain political or religious affiliation, when the pursuer's goal was to obtain reasons for an affiliation, the pursuer's tactics were integrated; specifically, as a pursuer sought to obtain reasons for having a certain affiliation in an increasingly efficient manner (e.g., directly, expediently, and effortlessly), the more accurate the detector was in inferring that goal (Palomares, 2009a). In contrast, when the pursuer's goal was to obtain personal information, the pursuer's tactics were not integrated because the context and its linkage to the pursuer's goal primarily determined inferences; that is, efficiency did not affect accuracy in this condition. Thus, tactics were incorporated into the inference restriction process only if the context did not already "reveal" the pursuer's goal.

Other research extended the generalizability of these findings pertaining to the integration principle by demonstrating identical processes in stranger and close-friends dyads with a set of goals more diverse than information seeking (e.g., convincing, relaxing, avoiding awkwardness; Palomares, 2009b). More recent work also looked at moderators of the integration principle, finding that detectors' cognitive busyness (or mental load) and the extent of congruency between interlocutors' goals can alter the degree to which tactics are integrated in the inference process (Palomares, in press). Under certain conditions, a pursuer's tactics can be rendered useful for a detector's attempt to infer the pursuer's goal accurately, thereby encouraging the detector to integrate the tactics even though the context itself provides adequate diagnosticity to the pursuer's goal. For example, when the pursuer seeks to obtain personal information and the detector seeks to reveal personal information in an initial interaction, the detector tends to integrate the pursuer's tactics because the detector's goal activates another goal to potentially infer; thus, the tactics become useful for inferring the pursuer's goal. Similarly, busyness also can render the tactics useful for a detector when the pursuer seeks to obtain personal information and the detector seeks to conceal personal information. Overall, this theoretical framework for goal detection and the integration principle seem to be an accurate depiction of how people infer others' goals.

Whereas the integration principle focuses on what goal is inferred and its accuracy, work on goal detection has also examined the certainty with which detectors make their inferences. The cognitive process of assessing the extent to which someone is confident and trusts that his or her goal inference is valid is different from the process of inferring a goal (Palomares, 2008). The integration principle, in other words, does not explain inference certainty. Certainty in an inferred goal depends on the amount of inference-consistent data a detector perceives during the course of an interaction. An inference will be tentative when inference-relevant data are sparse and not consistent with the inference, whereas definitive inferences emerge when data are plentiful and confirm an inference. Such inference-relevant data are found in pursuers' communicative behavior, primarily their verbal tactics. Thus, in general, the more efficient someone is when pursuing a goal, the more certainty a detector will have in a goal inference. Research pertinent to this understanding of inference certainty has generally revealed support for this proposition (Palomares, 2008, in press), though not without an exception (Palomares, 2009b).

This work on goal inferences has almost exclusively emphasized how people understand and infer a single goal of an interaction partner. Yet a similar and broader process is how people infer others' plans and goal hierarchies. Although there is some evidence suggesting that people tend to infer a single, primary goal as opposed to multiple goals (Palomares, 2008), sometimes people infer others' plans and goal hierarchies. Plan inferences are different from goal inferences because they involve a goal and actions to achieve the goal. For example, a husband might infer that his wife is trying to obtain the goal of comforting him by the actions of listening and making comments that legitimize his feelings. Similarly, people might infer multiple goals organized hierarchically, with subordinate goals serving or facilitating the achievement of a superordinate goal (e.g., to initiate a relationship and provide information to persuade someone). People not only infer others' goals in isolation, but they also infer the actions set forth to achieve a goal as organized in plans and the interrelations among multiple, hierarchically structured goals.

Although research has only begun to scratch the surface of understanding how people infer each other's multiple goals and plans, some evidence indicates that people can infer goals in hierarchies and that people infer others' plans. For example, people "inverse plan" by working backward from someone's actions or sequences of actions to understand the goals driving the action (Baker et al., 2009). Also, experts arrange knowledge pertinent to their domain of expertise hierarchically, whereas beginners and intermediates organize knowledge temporal-causally (Caillies & Denhière, 2001; Caillies, Denhière, & Kintsch, 2002). Consistent with these organizational differences, experts tend to infer goals hierarchically, whereas beginners and intermediates do not. Thus, people interpret others' actions in terms of goals in a manner consistent with the way in which their knowledge structures are arranged. Thus, knowledge structures also seem to play an important role in goal hierarchy and plan inferences. Other research found that individuals who tend to take others' perspective are more likely to infer goals hierarchically compared with nonperspective takers because perspective taking creates overlap between an observer's and an actor's mental representations of the behavior (Lozano, Hard, & Tversky, 2006). Perceivers, in other words, map others' actions onto their own actions, which facilitates understanding.

Another form of goal detection occurs when people project their own goal onto someone else. This form of inferring a goal emerges when someone thinks that another person is trying to achieve the same objective (Kawada et al., 2004). For example, a father who seeks to spend time with his daughter might infer that the daughter also desires to spend time with him. Perceived similarity with a target promotes goal projection (Ames, 2004): Goal projection was greater when people observed themselves to be similar to a target person. In related research, participants who strongly desired casual sex with others were more likely to perceive targets to have similar sexual intent (Lenton, Bryan, Hastie, & Fischer, 2009). Whether a target actually has the projected goal has not been entirely discussed in the literature. The question, in other words, is whether goal projection requires that the target does not actually share the projected goal; instances where a target actually has the projected goal arguably could be labeled projection or merely an accurate inference. In contrast, goal projection is less questionable when the target does not actually have the projected goal. Although goal projection happens in conversation, there might be a limited set of circumstances that actually yield goal projection in social interaction. Of course, the target goal prerequisites for goal projection, while intellectually relevant for theory and research, might be inconsequential for social actors involved in the unfolding of social interactions, but debating this point should be done in the context of empirically based evidence.

The idea that goal–plan knowledge structures influence what people recall from goal-directed action and interaction sequences and thus influence how people comprehend and interpret these sequences has received substantial support from many studies. For example, individuals who watched videotape presentations of a lone individual setting up a movie projector or writing a letter and preparing to send it showed better recall for more abstract actions in goal–plan hierarchies than they did for more specific actions in the hierarchies (Lichtenstein & Brewer, 1980). For instance, participants were more likely to recall the action of "putting a sealed envelope on the table" than they were to recall enabling subordinate actions such as "putting a stamp on the envelope" or "licking the envelope." The same recall effects were found when the actions shown on the videotape were presented in the form of written descriptions, suggesting that the same goal–plan knowledge structure was used to process the action sequence regardless of the communication mode in which it was presented. Individuals' recall of the events they saw or read was influenced by the actions' location in goal–plan hierarchies.

Goal and plan constructs have also been employed to explain how story readers are able to understand characters' actions. For example, some have argued that knowledge germane to action and story understanding is organized into source–goal–plan (SGP) units. For example, John was hungry (source); he wanted a pizza (goal); so he went to the ATM to get money to buy one (plan). This work demonstrated that information structured into SGP units is better remembered than information that is related merely by repeating concepts (Abbott & Black, 1986). Other researchers have suggested that stories are organized as goal–plan–outcome episodes that are linked by a causal structure (Trabasso & Nickels, 1992; Trabasso & Wiley, 2005). Within this perspective, when characters in a story experience failure in response to pursuing goals, for example, when the romantic advances of potential paramours are rejected, characters experiencing the failure may generate subordinate goal–plan–outcome episodes to achieve their superordinate goal, for example, rendering compliments to potential paramours to put them in a more favorable mood and thus increase the likelihood that subsequent romantic advances will be reciprocated. Not only fairy tales but also a great deal of film entertainment fare consists of these causally related sequences of goal–plan–outcome episodes and subepisodes that are driven by recurring goal failure. The activation of relevant goal–plan knowledge structures, while being exposed to stories, enables viewers and readers to understand actions of characters in a story and their responses to each other. Just as narrative understanding hinges on the ability of readers to track characters' actions through time and space and to understand how goal–plan–outcome episodes are causally linked with each other (Graesser, Millis, & Zwaan, 1997; Zwaan & Radvansky, 1998), individuals involved in social interactions, whether they be mediated or face-to-face, must employ the same tools to comprehend each other's actions and utterances. In fact, the research on goal–plan detection demonstrates parallel processes for the generation of goal inferences for written scenarios and stories as well as actual conversations between interlocutors (Palomares, 2008, 2009b).

Although goal–plan knowledge structures facilitate text and discourse comprehension, they can also produce false memories. When students read and later recalled stories that were based on familiar scripts such as doing laundry at a laundromat or going to the doctor, their recollections sometimes included actions that were part of the typical script for attaining the goal but were not included in the story they read (Bower, Black, & Turner, 1979). Thus, after reading the laundromat story, a person might recall the story character putting money into a washing machine, a typical action that would be part of a laundromat script, when, in fact, the story the person read included no such action. These intrusions into story recall indicate that when individuals engage in recall, they consult relevant knowledge structures to guide their recollection of story events. In doing so, events that are part of the knowledge structure but were not part of the story may be falsely recalled. Additional studies have shown that story titles can significantly influence recall

of story content, even when the story content is the same. For example, participants heard the same audiotaped account that was titled either "Wedding Day" or "Soccer Cup Final." After completing a distractor task, participants were asked to indicate whether specific words were actually mentioned in the audiotaped story. The word lists included those that were relevant to both titles but had not actually appeared in the story. The clear result was that participants who read the "Wedding Day" title version were more likely to falsely recognize words related to weddings in the word list, while "Soccer Cup Final" participants showed more false recognitions of words related to soccer (Dewhurst et al., 2008). Presumably, the false recognition of both groups occurred because the two titles activated different knowledge structures, which in turn served to distort their memory of the story.

Knowledge structures are generated through experience, and because individuals have varying amounts of experience in different knowledge-related domains, there may be considerable variation among people with respect to the degree to which their knowledge structures for a particular domain are highly articulated. The effects of this kind of knowledge variation among people on memory was dramatically demonstrated in experiments in which individuals with varying levels of baseball expertise, as assessed by a baseball knowledge test, listened to a tape-recorded account of a half-inning of a fictitious baseball game and then recalled as much of the description as they could (Spilich, Vesonder, Chiesi, & Voss, 1979). Results showed that compared with individuals with low baseball domain knowledge, those with high levels of knowledge not only recalled more actions from the description, but they also recalled more plays that resulted in scoring runs, one of the primary goals of the game. In contrast, listeners with low knowledge tended to recall more features of the description that were irrelevant to the game, for example, background information such as the weather. Individuals with high baseball knowledge were also found to show better recall for sequences of actions and the relationships between game actions and the goal structure of baseball (Chiesi, Spilich, & Voss, 1979). Finally, when asked to generate descriptions of a half-inning of a fictitious baseball game, individuals with greater knowledge of baseball generated descriptions that contained more actions related to critical game actions as well as changes in the state of play in the game, while participants with a low knowledge of baseball included more irrelevant actions in their descriptions (Voss, Vesonder, & Spilich, 1980). Because games such as baseball involve the pursuit of various goals, for example, scoring runs or retiring batters, by using a variety of plans, for example, scoring runs by advancing a player to second base by bunting or preventing scoring by using a pitcher who throws with the opposite hand from the batter's to lower the probability of the batter making a hit, and because high-knowledge-domain individuals recalled more critical plays from the game descriptions and included more game-state changes in their own fictitious game descriptions, it seems reasonable to assume that differences in the domain-related knowledge structures of high- and low-knowledge individuals are partially responsible for these results. In this series of studies, baseball-related domain knowledge was not assessed by asking questions regarding baseball trivia but by asking respondents to answer questions about specific baseball strategies and tactics—that is, questions concerning their knowledge of various goals and plans for winning baseball games.

When people recall previous interactions or sequences of actions that they have observed, their recollections will not only be selective depending on their domain-related knowledge levels, as the baseball studies clearly demonstrate, their recollections will also consist of an admixture of actions and events that actually took place and actions that did not take place but that are included in a relevant knowledge structure. The relevance of these kinds of memory distortions to interpersonal communication is quite evident in interpersonal conflict episodes involving people

in close personal relationships. Couples who have mutually experienced the "same" sequence of events may have radically different recollections of them, and when they jointly talk about these events, they may experience substantial conflict over whose recollection is "correct." Exchanges such as "You said/did . . ."/"No, I did not!" characterize such disagreements (Sillars, 2010). Couples who have lived together for many years may engage in serial arguments about precisely what happened during jointly experienced episodes that occurred in the remote past. These continuing arguments may never be fully resolved. However, on the positive side of the ledger, convergence between couples' recollections of past events may serve both to validate their individual views of the world and to foster feelings of solidarity between them. The moral here may be that it is critical to get to know potential long-term partners' knowledge structures before attempting to engage in long-term relationships with them; however, attempting such a feat may require a significant amount of time and effort, given that knowledge structures can be both large and complex.

Much has been written about the concept of communication competence (see Wilson & Sabee, 2003, for a review). Although there is a great deal of debate about the nature of "communication competence," we contend that knowledge structures provide an important avenue for understanding skilled social interaction performance. One implication of the work discussed above is that extensive experience in a specific domain will likely result in individuals developing more elaborate knowledge structures that will, in turn, influence how they perceive and experience events in that domain. That is, having observed domain-relevant actions, experts will come away with very different interpretations of what has transpired compared with novices, who have less elaborate knowledge structures for processing information in the same domain. As previously discussed, experts tend to infer multiple goals hierarchically to a greater degree than do novices (Caillies & Denhière, 2001; Caillies et al., 2002).

It is not that novices lack any understanding of the events they have observed, but the depth of their understanding is limited compared with that of experts. As the baseball studies demonstrate, a sophisticated understanding of baseball requires that perceivers are able to relate game actions to the changing goals of the game. Similarly, sophisticated social actors must be able to do the same in relevant social interaction domains. To know what goals are being pursued and what actions are being deployed to do so in a given social situation is not enough; perceivers must also see the relationship between the two and understand how particular actions change as goal states change over time.

Consistent with this line of reasoning, skilled message processing can affect what goal inferences people make, which can affect memory and learning. While watching a video presentation of an object assembly task, perceivers took one of three perspectives: (1) their own perspective, (2) the perspective of the actor performing the task, or (3) another observer's perspective (Lozano et al., 2006). Participants subsequently conducted the task on their own. Participants taking the actor's perspective performed the task more effectively than those who did not take the actor's perspective. This learning benefit arguably occurred because of the way participants organized the actor's goals: Those taking the actor's perspective arranged the actor's goals more hierarchically than those who took either another observer's or their own perspective. Skilled message processors will use this perspective-taking benefit to their advantage. Goal inferences also altered participants' memory for texts (Dewhurst et al., 2008). When a title of a narrative strongly implied a particular goal, the text was processed in a goal-consistent way. Furthermore, participants falsely recognized words that did not actually appear in the text but were consistent with the goal inference implied in the titles. Apparently, goal inferences can modify what people remember and learn. Thus, an advanced message processor will pay heed to the goal or goals someone is pursuing and might realize that an inaccurate

inference can adversely affect their recall of events and ability to perform actions in the future.

Knowledge structures and message-processing skills also have implications for communication effectiveness, as demonstrated across a substantial amount of research. Because individuals who can generate relatively effective plans to achieve their goals tend to be mindful of their partner's goals (Waldron, 1990, 1997), skilled message processing will enhance one's ability to produce effective message plans. In a similar vein, when interaction partners who were not completely aware of each other's goals tried to construct joint, two-person plans, unstated goals produced errors that threatened the effective implementation of the plans (Larocque & Oatley, 2006). Furthermore, they tended to blame their partner for those errors, which created anger, especially if the relationship was not particularly important to them. A case study of a family with an autistic child revealed that having a good understanding of everyone's goals in the family yielded a more effective treatment program for the child (Paul & Frea, 2002). These findings suggest that understanding another's goal or goals can be central to engaging in felicitous interactions; novice message processors, such as children, might be too egocentric to develop sophisticated plans that address the goals of all involved parties. Though, there are clearly times when a misunderstood goal produces no negative consequences, such as when someone seeks information for a benevolent purpose that is never apparent to the information provider. The times when failed goal understanding yields undesirable effects might be fewer in comparison with the times when the effects are trivial; yet because research has been remiss in this arena, most of what is known is speculative.

Faulty message processing can also yield problems for conflict resolution. When school-age siblings did not establish mutual understanding during conflicts—and a large part of this understanding concerns an awareness of each other's goals—the conflict escalated and sometimes led to both verbally and physically aggressive behavior

(Perlman & Ross, 2005). Likewise, mutually beneficial conflict resolution among siblings was characterized by their trying to understand each other's yet-to-be-obtained goals and integrating those goals into plans (Ross, Ross, Stein, & Trabasso, 2006). A capable message processor, therefore, will likely seek to develop a shared awareness of everyone's goals in order to avoid exacerbating a conflict, as when a parent steps in to mediate a sibling conflict so the children accurately know each other's goals and avoid intensifying an argument. Research focused on developing a measure of dysfunctional relationship beliefs contended that individuals who expect a relational partner to read their minds are setting themselves up for disappointment and conflict because it is unrealistic for a partner to have an excellent, near-perfect grasp of someone's mind state, including goals (Eidelson & Epstein, 1982). Yet if people are able to have a general and relatively accurate understanding of their partner's mind state and maintain realistic expectations about what their partner will be able to know and infer about them, then the communication and the relationship will likely be more effective and satisfying. However, there may be cultural variations in the degree to which people are expected to apprehend others' mental states and anticipate others' needs. For example, Koreans place a high value on *nun chi* (눈치) or the ability to "read" others and discern their mental states and needs quickly and accurately. Thus, anticipating and providing help to another person without being asked to do so is an indicator of the helper's well-developed *nun chi*. In contrast, having to be explicitly asked to provide assistance by another rather than anticipating their needs nonverbally may be grounds for declaring "Nun chi o'ps o' yo" (눈치 없어요), or "That person lacks *nun chi*." This assertion is tantamount to saying that the person lacks social discernment.

Superior message processing also has potentially desirable outcomes for how people rate others in terms of communication competence. The more people thought that their close relational partner was aware of and sensitive to their goals, the more communicatively competent they perceived their partner to be (Lakey & Canary, 2002). Also, the extent to which people inferred their partner's goal accurately was positively correlated with the extent to which they judged the partner to be competent (Palomares, 2009a). The certainty of a goal inference, however, seems to moderate this outcome, as the correlation only occurred for inferences with high certainty but not for moderate or low levels of inference certainty (Palomares, in press). Thus, to have an accurate understanding of an interaction partner's goal is conducive to positive judgments about the partner, but only if there is trust and confidence in that understanding. Admittedly, communication competence is a multifaceted construct and there is no argument for the primacy of message-processing skills in its determination, but such skills play at least a partial role in promoting competent interpersonal communication.

# Knowledge Structures and Message Production

Having considered the role that knowledge structures play in the processing of text and discourse, we now turn to the question of the role knowledge structures play in message production processes. Much of the research concerning message production processes has focused on speech production, but there has been considerable interest in written message production as well (Berger, 2010). In this section, we will provide a brief overview of the message production process and then examine the functions that knowledge structures have in that process.

## Language Production Processes

The commonplace assumption that speaking is simply the reverse of listening is belied by the fact that it may take up to five times longer for speakers to generate words in their native languages than to recognize the same words when presented with them (Griffin & Ferreira, 2006). Intention is a prerequisite for speaking and writing, whereas word recognition is frequently automatic when listening or reading. Although this differential in retrieval time between word recognition and word retrieval for message production may be due to different lexical retrieval processes, it is also possible that message production entails choosing among more alternatives than is the case for message comprehension. This differential between comprehension and production is observed in the early stages of language acquisition; young children can comprehend and conceptualize more than they can express in words.

Typically, normal adults speak at the rate of 120 to 180 words per minute (Maclay & Osgood, 1959), and speech production is accomplished with minimal error. Even though adult speakers know tens of thousands of words (Oldfield, 1963), lexical selection errors are extremely rare in normal speech, with error estimates ranging from 0.25 (Deese, 1984) through 0.41 (Garnham, Shillcock, Brown, Mill, & Cutler, 1982) to 2.3 (Shallice & Butterworth, 1977) per 1,000 words uttered. Even when speakers accelerate their speech rate to a very rapid 420 words per minute, their speech remains relatively error free (Deese, 1984). In fact, slips of the tongue are so rare in everyday speech that methods have been developed to elicit them in the laboratory (Motley, Baars, & Camden, 1983). Thus, in spite of the fact that lexical retrieval in the service of speech production characteristically takes substantially longer than word recognition, speech production is a highly developed skill among adults (Greene, 1997, 2003).

A number of speech production models have been proposed that differ with respect to details (e.g., Bock & Levelt, 1994; Levelt, 1989; Levelt, Roelofs, & Meyer, 1999; MacKay, 1987); however, in general terms most models posit similar steps through which speech producers must pass to realize their intentions in articulation (Ferreira & Englehardt, 2006; Griffin & Ferreira, 2006). Much of the evidence for these production steps or stages has been obtained from analyses of speech

production errors such as slips of the tongue, tip-of-the-tongue phenomena, and speech-onset latencies and pauses; studies of speech-related pathologies; and brain-imagining studies.

Language production models typically begin with a conceptualization stage, a process during which messages are composed of abstract semantic propositions and pragmatic features or lexical concepts. This initial stage is generally postulated to be prelinguistic and is conceived of as the interface between thought and language. In the next step, or formulation stage, which involves lexical selection and grammatical encoding, the abstract propositions and concepts of the conceptualization stage are represented as lemmas or lexical entries selected to represent the abstract message. At this stage, lemmas are assigned a functional role in the projected utterance, but they must subsequently be processed and assigned a positional order. Once this positional order is determined, phonological encoding occurs, which, in turn, leads to articulation. Among a number of controversies with respect to these models are issues such as the number of steps involved in grammatical encoding (one vs. two) and the degree to which the outputs of these stages feed back and constrain one another (Ferreira & Englehardt, 2006). However, all of these models begin with a conceptual message that is ultimately realized in phonological encoding, which finally leads to articulation.

Given the differing natures of the conceptualization and formulation stages, conceptual messages are almost never fully realized in the output of the formulation processes. That is, there is almost always some slippage of meaning between conceptual messages, on the one hand, and the way they are lexicalized and grammatically formulated, on the other. Indeed, to avoid the aforementioned processing costs associated with lexical retrieval and grammatical formulation, language producers do not fully specify conceptual messages at the formulation stage; rather, they specify them only to a level sufficient to ensure their comprehensibility. These production shortcuts shift some of the processing burden to the persons who receive their messages. Thus, for example, in requesting salt at the dinner table, in some circumstances, production economy might be achieved by simply uttering "salt," which might be sufficient to achieve the desired result. In addition to underspecifying conceptual messages, another way to minimize language production costs is to employ preformulated or formulaic utterances such as "My main point is . . .," "In my opinion . . .," "I get your point," and "This one is nice, but . . ." Everyday conversations are saturated with such conversational gambits. Estimates are that up to 70% of utterances made during conversations are formulaic (Altenberg, 1990), suggesting that language producers routinely reduce message production costs by using these tactics (Coulmas, 1981; Smith, 2000; Wray & Perkins, 2000). Moreover, because social actors must satisfy recurring goals in their everyday interactions, formulaic utterances make routine social commerce more efficient; goals are accomplished with less communicative effort. To be successful in conversation, social actors must keep track of their own and their partners' utterances, goals, and plans, thus placing them under considerable memory load. Formulaic utterances help relieve this conversational cognitive load (Wray & Perkins, 2000). Those employed in occupations that involve routine service encounters, for example, fast-food restaurants and department stores, may be taught detailed scripts for dealing with customers, which they are required to follow (Ford, 1999; Leidner, 1993). Routinization not only ensures continuity of performance during service encounters, it reduces service providers' cognitive load.

## From Knowledge Structures to Messages

Some language production models have used concepts such as grammatical plans and phonetic plans to account for the ways in which message content and its phonological renderings are organized such that the message receivers can comprehend the sources' messages (Levelt, 1989). The idea that plans underwrite message production has been demonstrated in studies similar to those presented in the discussion of message processing. As described previously, when asked to generate descriptions of a half-inning of a fictitious baseball game, individuals with high baseball knowledge levels generated descriptions with more actions related to critical game actions and changes in the state of play in the game, whereas participants with low baseball knowledge included more irrelevant actions in their descriptions (Voss et al., 1980). In a similar study, in which participants also wrote fictitious narrative accounts of a half-inning of a baseball game, those written by individuals with a high baseball domain knowledge contained more game actions and fewer irrelevant nongame actions than did those written by individuals with low baseball domain knowledge (Kellogg, 2001). High levels of domain knowledge and general verbal ability each independently contributed to enhanced ratings of overall writing quality. The results of these message production studies mirror those obtained in the baseball game memory studies discussed earlier and suggest that knowledge structures may play a similar role in both message processing and production.

## Message Plans and Plan Complexity

Consistent with the general notion of knowledge structures discussed earlier, message plans are hierarchical cognitive representations of the actions necessary to attain goals with more abstract actions at higher levels of the hierarchy and successively more concrete actions nested below them (Berger, 1995, 1997). A plan to gain another's compliance might contain abstract actions such as "offer reward" or "threaten punishment," with more specific actions such as "give verbal praise" or "ground for one day" nested below them. Each of these actions could be defined, in turn, by highly specific utterances and actions, for example, "Nice job!" or "Don't do that again." Message plans can be made more complex by including more detailed actions in them, including contingencies that anticipate potential points of plan failure, or including both. For example, a plan to gain compliance by offering rewards might include alternative rewards such as various sums of money or various types of verbal praise in the event that one of the offered rewards fails. Having such contingent actions available in message plans is especially critical to success in communication situations involving bargaining and negotiation as well as conflict (Ellis, 2010; Roloff & Li, 2010; Sillars, 2010). Research has demonstrated that the complexity of plans generated by children for attaining goals, for example, planning a vacation trip, increases significantly with their age (Kreitler & Kreitler, 1987).

Message plans that are implemented in social action may fail to bring about desired goals. Although readily available plan contingencies can potentially enhance communicative success by anticipating points at which plans might fail, there are processing costs associated with increasingly complex plans containing numerous contingencies. Considerable research has shown that beyond a certain point, inducing individuals to include more contingencies in their message plans reduces their verbal fluency when they experience failure and are forced to choose alternative actions or plans (Berger, Karol, & Jordan, 1989; Knowlton & Berger, 1997). Individuals who planned one or six alternative persuasive arguments or alternative walk routes before presenting the arguments or walk routes in a subsequent interaction were significantly less verbally fluent when asked to provide alternative arguments or walk routes than were individuals who initially planned three arguments or walk routes (Knowlton & Berger, 1997). Those who planned just one alternative and then experienced failure took considerable time to generate a new alternative, which reduced their verbal fluency. Similarly, those who generated six alternatives took about the same amount of time to retrieve another alternative because of the large number

of alternatives from which they had to choose. In contrast, not only did those who generated three alternatives have alternatives available from which to choose, but the remaining number was small enough so that they could decide more quickly which alternative to deploy, thus disrupting their verbal fluency less (Knowlton & Berger, 1997). These results suggest that too few or too many contingent actions tend to undermine the fluidity of communicative performance when plan failure occurs and that there is an optimal number of contingencies that should be generated for the actions embodied in message plans, at least in terms of sustaining verbal fluency in the face of plan failure. Because reductions in verbal fluency have been shown to reduce audience members' judgments of speakers' credibility (Burgoon, Birk, & Pfau, 1990; Miller & Hewgill, 1964), avoiding verbal disfluencies associated with nonoptimal contingency planning represents an important practical message-planning consideration.

## The Hierarchy Principle

The hierarchical organization of message plans raises the issue of the levels at which message plans are altered when actions fail to bring about desired goal states. Consistent with the idea that message producers try to minimize message production costs, when failures occur, the least effortful way in which to modify message plans is to alter their low-level, concrete actions rather than the high-level abstract actions. It is less cognitively demanding to increase the amount of a monetary offer for compliance than it is to change from the abstract-act–type "reward" to "punishment." Doing the latter requires message producers to expend scarce cognitive resources in order to specify the lower level actions to realize the new abstract-action category (Berger, 1997). Research has generally supported this principle. In one study, message producers whose geographic directions were misunderstood and who were asked to provide the directions again significantly increased their vocal intensity, a low-level message plan feature, but did not alter the walk route provided in the directions, a higher level message plan feature (Berger & diBattista, 1993). Providing the same directions in a louder voice presumably required less cognitive effort than generating an entirely different walk route.

Other research has provided support for the proposition that higher level message plan alterations demand more cognitive effort than do low-level modifications. After confederates were provided geographic directions, the confederates told direction givers that they could not understand the directions because they spoke too quickly, because they did not include enough landmarks in the directions, or because the walk route they provided was not clear (Berger, Knowlton, & Abrahams, 1996). The confederates in each of these three conditions asked the direction givers to provide their directions again by slowing down, including more landmarks, or using another walk route, respectively. The amount of time it took for the direction givers to begin the second rendition of their directions, or speech onset latency, was recorded. Several experiments, some of which were done under field conditions in public places, produced highly similar results. The direction givers who were asked to speak more slowly took significantly less time to begin the second rendition of their directions than did those who were asked to provide landmarks. The direction givers who were asked to provide more landmarks were significantly faster than those who were asked to provide a new route. Assuming that altering speech rate is a low-level message plan alteration while changing the route is a high-level change, with landmarks in between these extremes, these experiments show that higher level message plan alterations are indeed more cognitively demanding than are low-level alterations.

These findings may explain why the default option for message producers in the event of goal failure is to repeat what they have said but say it in a louder voice (Berger & diBattista, 1993). Although this strategy for dealing with understanding failures demands few cognitive resources and relatively less effort, it is doubtful

that a majority of understanding failures arise from failure to hear what message producers have uttered. Even those who routinely deal with understanding failures as part of their job, such as teachers of English as a second language (ESL), report that they have difficulty controlling their tendency to speak with greater vocal intensity when their students fail to understand them. This tendency stems from the fact that although almost any feature of speech, for example, speech rate, vocal intensity, vocal intonation, vocalized pausing, and so on, can be brought under conscious control, when message producers choose to focus on controlling one of these features, they have insufficient attentional capacity to control those that are outside their attentional focus (Levelt, 1989). Thus, ESL teachers, who are usually intent on correcting their students' grammar and usage errors and monitoring the degree to which their students understand them when they speak, do not have the capacity necessary to control consciously their vocal intensity. Consequently, when they sense that their students have not understood them, they revert to the default, higher vocal intensity value for overcoming their students' lack of understanding.

## Automaticity in Goal Pursuit

The fact that message producers have limited capacity to attend to various aspects of message production raises the issue of the degree to which social actors pursue consciously activated goals. Some philosophical accounts of goal-directed action assume that social actors pursue goals on the basis of consciously formed intentions to do so. For example, Goldman's (1970) desire–belief model of action posits that when individuals desire to achieve a goal and believe that they can do so by executing a series of actions, they intend to pursue the goal. Presumably, under this view, people are aware of both their desire and their belief concerning their ability to attain the goal in forming their intention. Similarly, other philosophers of human action have argued that when individuals formulate action plans to achieve goals, their plans constitute "intentions writ large" (Bratman, 1987). That is, their planned actions represent commitments to action. Thus, while eating breakfast, someone might make plans for accomplishing a series of errands during the remainder of the day. In this view, these errand plans would constitute intentions that entail commitments to action. Again, it is assumed that this plan formulation process is a conscious one.

In contrast to this deliberative approach to planning and goal pursuit, over the past 20 years the view of goal-directed, intentional social action as a strictly conscious process has been challenged (Bargh, 1990, 1997; Bargh & Barndollar, 1996; Bargh & Gollwitzer, 1994). A considerable body of research has accumulated and indicates that goals can be activated, pursued, and attained outside conscious awareness. In many studies conducted to evaluate unconscious goal pursuit, individuals' goals are primed or activated by presenting them with either supraliminal or subliminal stimuli (Bargh & Chartrand, 2000). For example, an achievement goal might be primed by having individuals form complete sentences from sets of words, some of which are related to achievement (supraliminal priming), or exposing individuals to achievement-related words that are flashed on a computer screen for such a short duration (17 milliseconds) that they cannot be identified (subliminal). The performance of individuals who have been primed is then contrasted with that of individuals who have not been primed on a subsequent and seemingly unrelated task to see whether the primed goal was activated and produced effects on task performance. Thus, individuals who have been primed with an achievement goal should perform better and persist longer on the task than those who have not been so primed. Evidence supports such achievement-related priming effects (Bargh, Gollwitzer, Lee-Chai, Barndollar, & Troetschel, 2001). Automaticity researchers assume that representations of goals reside in memory and priming procedures serve to activate

them; that is, priming procedures do not act to create new goals.

More directly germane to social interaction contexts, a goal may become contagious simply by observing another person's goal-directed behavior and inferring the goal (Aarts, Gollwitzer, & Hassin, 2004; Dik & Aarts, 2007). Learning that a friend is about to embark on an expensive trip to a foreign destination might unconsciously activate the goal of saving money in the perceiver, so that the perceiver can take a similar trip; however, if the goal implied by the person's behavior is a socially undesirable one, such goal activation may not occur. Moreover, goals coactivated with negative affect are less likely to be pursued than are goals activated in the absence of negative affect (Aarts, Custers, & Holland, 2007), and goals coactivated with positive affect increase readiness for goal pursuit (Aarts, Custers, & Veltkamp, 2008). Thus, there are conditions under which preconscious activation of goals does not necessarily produce effects on behavior, even when the goals are implied by others' behaviors.

Because goals are cognitively represented in associational networks, concepts that are related to them can become activated when goals are activated. Conversely, when concepts that are associated with goals are preconsciously activated, the associated goals may also become active. Evidence supports both of these possibilities. In the first instance, active goals automatically brought to mind individuals who would be instrumental in satisfying the activated goals, and activated goals induced individuals to evaluate instrumental others more positively, draw closer to them, and approach them more readily, compared with noninstrumental others (Fitzsimons & Shah, 2008). Thus, even though a goal may be activated outside conscious awareness, its activation will tend to make people who might be helpful in achieving the goal more accessible to the social actor's consciousness, for example, a friend who might be instrumental in satisfying the goal of having a good time. In the second case, if a concept such as "parents" is associated with the goal "academic achievement," then priming the concept "parents," even subliminally, is likely to activate the achievement goal and enhance performance. Effects such as these have been found in a number of experiments (Shah, 2003). There are circumstances under which social actors' goals are activated preconsciously but enter conscious thought as goals are being pursued or after they have been pursued. Specifically, when individuals encounter difficulties in attaining preconsciously activated goals, they are more likely to become aware that they are or have been pursuing these goals (Bongers, Dijksterhuis, & Spears, 2010).

Although a substantial body of research supports the view that goals can be activated, pursued, and attained outside conscious awareness and that preconsciously primed goals produce effects that are similar to those observed when goals arise consciously, it would be a mistake to minimize the significance of consciously initiated goal pursuit in social interactions. For example, considerable evidence supports the idea that consciously formed implementation plans to achieve consciously activated goals can protect social actors from being diverted from pursuing their goals (Gollwitzer, 1999; Gollwitzer, Bayer, & McCulloch, 2005; Gollwitzer & Brandstätter, 1997; Gollwitzer, Gawrilow, & Oettingen, 2010). Implementation plans consist of if-then statements that specify a set of circumstances in the "if" clause, for example, "If I am speaking with Fred" or "If I am taking a test" and a set of behaviors or emotion-related states in the "then" clause, for example, "then I will smile as much as I can" or "then I will try as hard as I can." Individuals who form implementation plans perform better when the circumstances stipulated in the implementation plan arise than do those who have not previously formed implementation plans. Moreover, those who form implementation plans outperform even those who vow to try as hard as possible to achieve the focal goal before undertaking efforts to do so (Gollwitzer & Sheeran, 2006). Although there is little question that implementation plans facilitate goal pursuit by keeping

goal strivers "on track," the implementation plan concept presupposes a plan to be implemented when the appropriate circumstances arise. Thus, for example, a person might follow the implementation plan "If I see Martha, then I will try to convince her to buy my car." However, this implementation plan begs the question of whether the persuasion plan that guides the person's actions will necessarily be an effective one when Martha is encountered and the persuasion plan implemented. An implementation plan might be ill specified and thus fail to produce the intended outcome because there are multiple means to persuade Martha. Even if an implementation plan has been previously generated, implementing an ineffective plan, even at the specified time, might not necessarily result in success at achieving the goal. Thus, merely remembering to enact a plan at an opportune time, as specified in an implementation intention, does not speak to the efficacy of the plan itself.

The idea that goal pursuit can be protected by formulating implementation plans raises the broader question about the preconscious activation of goal pursuit in everyday social interaction. In the course of pursuing their goals during social interactions, social actors are exposed to a wide variety of stimuli that could serve to prime goals that might facilitate or interfere with the pursuit of consciously activated interaction goals or other preconsciously activated goals. If preconscious priming is a ubiquitous phenomenon in everyday social life, how is it possible for individuals to achieve their goals without being distracted from doing so by competing goals that are automatically activated by stimuli in the surrounding environment? People consciously formulate plans, pursue them, and successfully achieve goals, even in the absence of explicitly formed implementation plans and in spite of the potential distractions that could arise from preconscious goal priming. Imagine a conversation between two people who are both being automatically primed by the multitude of stimuli available in the immediate environment.

At the extreme, moment-to-moment preconscious activation of various goals might lead to a conversation marked by rapid topic changes and failure to acknowledge the immediately previous utterances of conversational partners and numerous nonsecateurs, thus giving rise to conversational chaos. Because such conversations are fortunately quite rare, although sometimes they may be observed at various meetings, there must be mechanisms that keep conversations on the topic, coordinated, and focused on the goal to the point that they remain coherent in spite of preconscious goal activation. A few such mechanisms have received some research attention.

In addition to implementation plans, at least two psychological mechanisms have been suggested for inhibiting the spontaneous activation of potentially competing goals. First, some have argued that once one has devoted scarce cognitive resources to pursuing a particular goal, insufficient resources remain to activate competing goals, although the activation of some alternative goals may facilitate the attainment of a focal goal (Shah & Kruglanski, 2002). Second, retrieval-induced forgetting has been suggested as another mechanism that may shield goal pursuit (McCulloch, Aarts, Fugita, & Bargh, 2008). In this case, retrieving a particular goal from memory tends to inhibit the recall of potentially competing goals. Although evidence supports the operation of both of these inhibitory psychological mechanisms, a significant limitation of the research reported in this area is that it typically involves research participants sitting at computers individually pursuing goals such as solving anagram problems, a far cry from the complexities involved in goal pursuit during ongoing social interaction.

In addition to the psychological mechanisms that may act to keep goal pursuit on track as social actors pursue their goals, there are a number of social processes that help ward off competing goals. First, as conversations progress, the act of engaging in communicative exchanges may itself exert a socially derived momentum in the direction of goal attainment. This notion of conversational momentum is reflected in everyday talk, as when individuals are heard to say, "I know where this conversation is going" before the outcome of the conversation is necessarily apparent. Because reciprocity is the rule in social interaction (Burgoon, Stern, & Dillman, 1995; Gouldner, 1960), social actors become entrained in goal pursuit and thus mutually shield the goals they are pursuing from potentially sidetracking goals. Second, because social interactants generally observe conversational maxims such as quality, quantity, relevance, and manner (Grice, 1975), following these maxims may serve to nullify the potentially distracting effects of preconscious goal activation. For example, fulfilling the maxim that one's utterances be relevant to those of fellow interlocutors serves to keep conversations focused on particular goals. Social actors cannot simply respond willy-nilly to each other's utterances. Surely, interactions can be derailed by preconscious goal activation and drifting away from the topic, but even in these cases, social actors may serve to remind each other of their focal goals. Common utterances such as "Let's get back to the main point" or "Let's get on with it" and discourse markers such as "Anyway . . ." indicate that social actors are able to recognize the emergence of conversational irrelevancies that may arise from preconscious goal activation and thus preserve their goals and follow their plans even in the face of these momentary conversational detours. Even in mass media contexts that involve political communication and advertising, "Stay on message" is a commonly heard admonition. Finally, as we pointed out previously, although attention is limited, it is also flexible and can be focused on different plan hierarchy levels. Thus, it comes as little surprise that when message plan hierarchies are implemented in action and discourse, social actors are highly conscious of only a limited portion of the hierarchy while the remainder of the hierarchy is run off nonconsciously. This fact may explain why individuals are characteristically surprised by the sound of their voice and their appearance when they hear and see themselves on video recordings. Message producers are characteristically preoccupied with what they are saying rather than the style with which they are uttering it.

## Message Production Skills

Just as there is considerable variability among social actors with respect to their ability to discern others goals, intentions, and plans, as they devise messages to attain goals and realize their intentions, social actors vary with respect to the skill with which they perform. Within specific communication contexts, some people seem to achieve their goals quickly and with little effort, while others struggle and may fail to attain similar goals. We suspect that message production expertise is fairly domain specific (Hogarth, 2001, 2005; Wilson & Sabee, 2003). That is, even when the domain is restricted to one involving goals related to gaining compliance from others (Wilson, 2010), for instance, one can easily think of individuals who are very adept at gaining compliance in one context, for example, being a highly effective manager in an organization, but at the same time utterly ineffective at gaining compliance in other contexts, for example, inducing their teenage children to do their homework or study for upcoming examinations. In fact, in this particular case, there may be some negative transfer from the job-related compliance-gaining context to the family-related compliance-gaining context; that is, plans that work quite well with adult employees may be abjectly ineffective when implemented with teenage children.

In considering message production skills and their relationship with communication effectiveness, it is important to distinguish between performance skills and skills that influence the quality of message content (Berger, 1997). The division of labor between speech writers, screen writers, and playwrights, on the one hand, and public figures and actors, on the other, nicely illustrates this distinction. Speech writers, screen writers, and playwrights are message planners whose expertise is generally confined to creating messages to be performed by those with high levels of performance skills, that is, politicians and actors. Indeed, ghostwriters may create entire texts for those with attenuated writing skills. Parenthetically, we wish to make it clear to the reader that this chapter was not penned by such phantom authors. Of course, in everyday social commerce, most social actors do not have the luxury of having professionals provide them with lines to utter and nonverbal behaviors to enact, although there is considerable research concerning the potential beneficial effects on subsequent performance of imagining interactions before engaging in them (Honeycutt, 2003; Honeycutt & Bryan, 2010). Nonetheless, given this distinction, it is possible for individuals who have knowledge structures that embody highly effective plans for achieving goals to fail in their attempts to do so because they are unable to realize their goals in performance. Likewise, others may experience goal failure even though they have highly honed performance skills but act out plans with relatively low effectiveness levels.

As noted earlier, children's plans become more complex and sophisticated as their age increases (Kreitler & Kreitler, 1987). Additional evidence suggests that reconsidering plans tends to increase their efficiency (Battmann, 1989; Pea & Hawkins, 1987). In the latter study, elementary school children were given a diagram of their classroom and asked to draw the most efficient walk route for accomplishing a number of classroom clean-up tasks. After completing the first walk route, they were given the opportunity to change it in order to complete the clean-up tasks more quickly. Results revealed that, in general, the second renditions of the walk routes were more efficient than were the first versions. Moreover, consistent with the hierarchy principle discussed earlier, in their second renditions, children tended to alter lower level plan elements rather than more abstract plan features (Pea & Hawkins, 1987). These studies suggest that practice at devising plans can improve their efficiency and that at least through childhood accreting experience promotes the development of more sophisticated and detailed plans.

Research has examined the relationship between the judged effectiveness of plans and measures related to social functioning. In two studies, college students were asked to write plans for asking someone to whom they were highly attracted at a party out for a subsequent date. They also completed a measure tapping their feelings of loneliness. The unedited, date-request plans were then given to male and female student judges, who were asked to read each plan and then judge its potential effectiveness in achieving the date-request goal; however, judges were given no specific instructions concerning the attributes of an effective date-request plan (Berger & Bell, 1988; Berger & diBattista, 1992). Both studies also asked participants to indicate whether they usually initiated date requests, whether others usually approached them and requested dates, or whether these two situations occurred about equally frequently. In both studies, men overwhelmingly reported being date-request initiators, while women overwhelmingly reported being date-request receivers. Correlations between date-request plan effectiveness and loneliness revealed that among men, those whose date request plans were judged more effective reported lower levels of loneliness. In contrast, among women, plan effectiveness and loneliness were uncorrelated, presumably because they generally did not ask men for dates. Date-request plans judged to be potentially effective were longer and more complex than those judged to be potentially less effective, and plans that included the action category "seek similarities" were judged to be more effective (Berger & Bell, 1988).

Related research has shown that college students have first-date scripts; that is, they tend to agree on the events that occur on a typical first date. However, when these first-date script events were randomly ordered and then presented to students who were asked to put them in their proper sequence, those students with more dating experience, or dating experts, were able to put the events into their typical order more quickly than were dating novices, although both experts and novices placed the events in a similar order (Pryor & Merluzzi, 1985). Although the first-date scripts of experts and novices are organized similarly, dating experts apparently have more rapid access to their scripts than do novices.

The degree to which individuals are able to order actions that are part of scripts has been used as an indicator of various cognitive disorders in children. For example, when presented with the task of sequencing actions to achieve familiar and unfamiliar goals, children diagnosed with attention deficit hyperactivity disorder (ADHD) made more sequencing errors than did children classified as normal (Braun et al., 2004). Moreover, individuals with frontal lobe and parietal lobe brain lesions tended to make more sequencing errors when they verbally described everyday, scripted action sequences associated with activities such as getting up in the morning (Godbout, Cloutier, Bouchard, Braun, & Gagnon, 2004). Other research has shown that when individuals encounter plan failures and must generate actions to surmount these failures, electrical activity in the brain's dorsolateral prefrontal cortex tends to increase (Beatty & Heisel, 2007). The dorsolateral prefrontal cortex is part of a larger system, involving at least four other areas of the brain, that not only consolidates mental representations of goal states but also tracks and coordinates the temporal sequencing of action and integrates information from short-term memory that might be of potential use in ongoing planning. Insults to this system are likely to attenuate message-planning skills, especially those related to sequencing. One may know the actions necessary to achieve a particular goal but be unable to execute them in their proper sequence (Lashley, 1951).

It would be a mistake to assume that individuals only plan in advance of acting and then employ a plan to guide their actions while involved in communication. Social interaction is frequently a somewhat uncertain activity that may produce unanticipated contingences that must be addressed on the fly. Even highly scripted, routine interactions may provide surprises, as when in the midst of a routine service encounter involving complete strangers at a restaurant, a customer asks a server for a date. In cases such as these, individuals must abandon the "usual script" and improvise a response in a relatively short amount of time. Substantial research shows that individuals plan while interacting to deal with such contingencies; moreover, the quality of the plans they generate online influences the outcomes of their interactions.

In a series of studies, individuals who participated in interactions in which they tried to achieve specific goals were given the opportunity to review a videotape of the just completed conversation and indicate, whenever possible, what they were thinking during the interaction (Waldron, 1990, 1997). Analyses of thought lists generated by this procedure revealed that close to 50% of the recalled items concerned the goals being pursued in the interaction and the plans being used to achieve them (Waldron, 1990). Other studies in this series demonstrated that individuals who were judged to be more effective in achieving their goals during their conversations tended to (a) take into account their co-interlocutor's goals in their message plans, (b) plan at more concrete levels, (c) look further ahead in the conversation, and (d) devise more complex plans than did those judged to be less effective at reaching their goals during the interaction (Waldron, 1990, 1997; Waldron & Applegate, 1994; Waldron, Caughlin, & Jackson, 1995; Waldron & Lavitt, 2000). A study that examined the complexity with which people perceive others and the complexity of their action plans as predictors of communication effectiveness found that while cognitive complexity and plan complexity were significantly and positively related, only plan complexity was significantly and positively related to communication effectiveness during the interaction (Waldron & Applegate, 1994). Cognitively complex individuals tend to generate more complex message plans than do their cognitively simple counterparts, but it is the complexity of message plans that determines

communication effectiveness rather than cognitive complexity with respect to the construal of other people.

Although much of everyday social commerce consists of social interaction routines that are at once strategic, in that they are goal directed but frequently activated outside conscious awareness (Kellermann, 1992), there are significant variations in the degree to which social actors are adept at deploying these routines to reach their goals. Observed differences in communication skills not only may arise from the accuracy of inferences about others' goals and plans but may also result from the degree to which knowledge structures are articulated and the degree to which actions can be sequenced properly. But even when these prerequisites are satisfied, timing problems may interfere with effective goal pursuit, and as pointed out earlier, attenuated performance skills may undermine even the best laid message plans. Having to juggle all of these parameters simultaneously makes highly skilled social interaction difficult to achieve. For this reason, most social actors do not try to perform optimally when they interact with each other but are content with the more modest achievement of attaining their goals within the bounds of normal social propriety and efficiency.

## Conclusion

In this chapter, we have examined the role knowledge structures that organize social actors' goals, plans, and scripts play in the processing and production of messages when people engage in social interaction with each other. The division between processing and production reflects the traditional separation of perception and action production, although we have argued that knowledge structures play a critical role in both of these processes. However, we would be remiss if we overlooked the developing trend among some neuroscientists to argue that rather than being separate processes, perception and action production are intimately intertwined in terms of brain functioning. This idea is embodied in common coding theory that asserts that the same mental representations are involved in observing actions and performing them (Eskenazi, Grosjean, Humphreys, & Knoblich, 2009). In support of this theoretical stance, its advocates point to evidence suggesting that human and primate brains have mirror neurons that are activated both when individuals perceive and when they act, thus raising questions about the traditional distinction between neurons responsible for processing perceptual inputs and motor neurons responsible for the production of action, including speech and nonverbal behaviors.

There is suggestive evidence for such "dual-use" neurons in speech perception and production. For example, as people listen to words being uttered one at a time and the level of activity of the motor neurons that control their tongue movements is measured, the level of activity of these motor neurons mimics the specific words to which they are listening. That is, when people hear the words that require more tongue movements, they show higher levels of neural activity in their tongue muscles, even though they do not utter the words to which they are listening (Fadiga, Craighero, Buccino, & Rizzolatti, 2002). Apparently, neural activity germane to speech production mimics what others are saying. Automatic mimicry and anticipatory neural activity in motor neurons may explain why social interaction can be carried out relatively smoothly, even though social actors may speak rapidly and quickly switch conversational roles from speaker to listener (Gallese, 2009; Greene, 2003; Pezullo & Castelfranchi, 2009). Moreover, neurologically based mimicry could explain why individuals sometimes use the same words and phrases that their co-interlocutors have just uttered when it is their turn to speak in a conversation. While they listen to their conversational partners, social actors neurologically rehearse what it is they have heard. As pointed out previously, reciprocity with respect to dialect, accent, speech rate, vocal intensity, vocal intonation, and other nonverbal parameters is the rule rather than the exception

when humans interact with each other (Burgoon et al., 1995; Soliz & Giles, 2010). The activity of mirror neurons may be responsible for the pervasiveness of reciprocity in interpersonal communication. However, we would caution that human social actors are not mere parrots. Social actors do not simply repeat what it is they have just heard. Consequently, although there may be strong, neurologically based proclivities toward motor mimicry, there also must be preconscious and conscious mechanisms that intervene to override this neurologically driven tendency to rehearse others' speech, so that unique message content can be formulated in response to others' utterances. It may be that motor mimicry in speech production is an ongoing, default process but is generally modulated by the action of other neurological systems to produce unique messages.

This emerging view of the neurologically based relationships between perceptual and motor processes has implications for the way in which interpersonal communication competence or interpersonal communication skill is conceived (Wilson & Sabee, 2003). In our view, social interaction skill can be conceptualized at two distinct but related levels. The most fundamental of these is related to the production of fluent speech and associated nonverbal behaviors as well as the perceptual processes aligned with these motor acts. These Level 1 skills are strongly determined by neurological processes that, if compromised by damage to critical neural circuits, can result in debilitation of fundamental interpersonal communication capabilities, as manifested in autism and related neurological disorders. In the extreme, these disorders can render the accomplishment of even routine social interaction extremely difficult. However, even if these fundamental Level 1 skills are granted, there can be wide variation in the degree to which social actors are successful in achieving their interaction goals. These variations in Level 2 skills are the product of the degree to which knowledge structures, which are built mainly thorough experience, are articulated—that is, the degree to which social actors have detailed funds of knowledge about the goals that individuals pursue and the plans they use to achieve them within a specific domain. Although it may be extremely difficult to overcome skill deficits emanating from problems occurring at Level 1, Level 2 skills can be acquired with sufficient practice. Recall that given normal Level 1 functioning, almost any aspect of speech production can be brought under conscious control, at least temporarily (Levelt, 1989). This ability to monitor and alter one's own communicative output allows social actors to modify and shape their verbal and nonverbal messages to achieve their goals. By observing the results of these messages, social actors can determine combinations of words and actions that produce desired outcomes and repeat these performances when similar circumstances arise. Thus, given normally functioning Level 1 skills, there is very good reason to be optimistic about the ability of most social actors to hone their Level 2 social interaction skills to a high level with appropriate, focused practice, making it possible for most individuals to become social interaction experts within specific social domains.

As cautioned previously, however, although Level 2 skills may be highly trainable, they may not necessarily be highly general; that is, interpersonal communication expertise within a particular domain or context may not necessarily transfer to other, seemingly similar, contexts. Persuading customers to buy used cars and persuading junior high school students to study for upcoming examinations are surely both exercises in social influence (Dillard, 2010; Wilson, 2010), but success within each of these contexts may hinge on substantially different knowledge structures, just as teaching college undergraduates and teaching elementary school pupils both involve activities related to "teaching" but, one would hope, radically different approaches to it. A university professor who is widely known as a gifted teacher might well be, at the same time, an abject failure as a teacher when faced with a classroom populated by fourth-grade elementary school pupils. Given these contextual variations, attempts to teach individuals a well-defined set of highly generalized "interpersonal communication skills" may be an exercise in futility. For better or worse, then, the communication skill devil may well reside in the details.

# References

Aarts, H., Custers, R., & Holland, R. W. (2007). The nonconscious cessation of goal pursuit: When goals and negative affect are coactivated. *Journal of Personality and Social Psychology, 92,* 165–178.

Aarts, H., Custers, R., & Veltkamp, M. (2008). Goal priming and the affective-motivational route to nonconscious goal pursuit. *Social Cognition, 26,* 555–577.

Aarts, H., & Dijksterhuis, A. (2000). Habit as knowledge structures: Automaticity in goal-directed behavior. *Journal of Personality and Social Psychology, 78,* 53–63.

Aarts, H., Gollwitzer, P. M., & Hassin, R. R. (2004). Goal contagion: Perceiving is for pursuing. *Journal of Personality and Social Psychology, 87,* 23–37.

Abbott, V. A., & Black, J. B. (1986). Goal-related inferences in comprehension. In J. A. Galambos, R. P. Abelson, & J. B. Black (Eds.), *Knowledge structures* (pp. 123–142). Hillsdale, NJ: Lawrence Erlbaum.

Albright, L., Cohen, A. I., Malloy, T. E., Christ, T., & Bromgard, G. (2004). Judgments of communicative intent in conversation. *Journal of Experimental Social Psychology, 40,* 290–302.

Altenberg, B. (1990). Speech as linear composition. In G. Caie, K. Haastrup, A. L. Jakobsen, J. E. Nielsen, J. Sevaldsen, H. Sprecht, et al. (Eds.), *Proceedings from the fourth Nordic conference for English studies* (Vol. 1., pp. 133–143). Copenhagen, Denmark: University of Copenhagen, Department of English.

Ames, D. R. (2004). Inside the mind-reader's toolkit: Projection and stereotyping in mental state inference. *Journal of Personality and Social Psychology, 87,* 340–353.

Ardissono, L., Boella, G., & Lesmo, L. (2000). A plan-based agent for interpreting natural language dialogue. *International Journal of Human-Computer Studies, 52,* 583–635.

Austin, J. L. (1962). *How to do things with words.* Oxford, UK: Oxford University Press.

Baker, C. L., Saxe, R., & Tenenbaum, J. B. (2009). Action understanding as inverse planning. *Cognition, 113,* 329–349.

Bargh, J. A. (1990). Auto motives: Preconscious determinants of social interaction. In R. M. Sorrentino & E. T. Higgins (Eds.), *Handbook of motivation and cognition: Foundations of social behavior* (Vol. 2, pp. 93–130). New York: Guilford Press.

Bargh, J. A. (1997). The automaticity of everyday life. In R. S. Wyer Jr. (Ed.), *The automaticity of everyday life: Advances in social cognition* (Vol. 10, pp. 1–61). Mahwah, NJ: Lawrence Erlbaum.

Bargh, J. A., & Barndollar, K. (1996). Automaticity in action: The unconscious as repository of chronic goals and motives. In P. M. Gollwitzer & J. A. Bargh (Eds.), *The psychology of action: Linking cognition and motivation to behavior* (pp. 457–481). New York: Guilford Press.

Bargh, J. A., & Chartrand, T. L. (2000). The mind in the middle: A practical guide to priming and automaticity research. In H. T. Reis & C. M. Judd (Eds.), *Handbook of research methods in social and personality psychology* (pp. 253–285). New York: Cambridge University Press.

Bargh, J. A., & Gollwitzer, P. M. (1994). Environmental control of goal-directed action: Automatic and strategic contingencies between situations and behavior. In W. D. Spaulding (Ed.), *Nebraska symposium on motivation: Integrative views of motivation, cognition, and emotion* (Vol. 41, pp. 71–124). Lincoln: University of Nebraska Press.

Bargh, J. A., Gollwitzer, P. M., Lee-Chai, A., Barndollar, K., & Troetschel, R. (2001). The automated will: Nonconscious activation and pursuit of behavioral goals. *Journal of Personality and Social Psychology, 81,* 1014–1027.

Battmann, W. (1989). Planning as a method of stress prevention: Will it pay off? In C. D. Spielberger, J. G. Sarason, & J. Strelau (Eds.), *Stress and anxiety* (Vol. 12, pp. 259–275). New York: Hemisphere.

Beatty, M. J., & Heisel, A. D. (2007). Spectrum analysis of cortical activity during verbal planning: Physical evidence for the formation of social interaction routines. *Human Communication Research, 33,* 48–63.

Berger, C. R. (1995). A plan-based approach to strategic communication. In D. E. Hewes (Ed.), *Cognitive bases of interpersonal communication* (pp. 141–179). Hillsdale, NJ: Lawrence Erlbaum.

Berger, C. R. (1997). *Planning strategic interaction: Attaining goals through communicative action.* Mahwah, NJ: Lawrence Erlbaum.

Berger, C. R. (2004). Speechlessness: Causal attributions, emotional features and social consequences. *Journal of Language and Social Psychology, 23,* 147–179.

Berger, C. R. (2005). Interpersonal communication: Theoretical perspectives, future prospects. *Journal of Communication, 55,* 415–447.

Berger, C. R. (2007). Communication: A goal-directed, plan-guided process. In D. R. Roskos-Ewoldsen & J. L. Monahan (Eds.), *Communication and social cognition: Theories and methods* (pp. 47–70). Mahwah, NJ: Lawrence Erlbaum.

Berger, C. R. (2010). Message production processes. In C. R. Berger, M. E. Roloff, & D. R. Roskos-Ewoldsen (Eds.), *Handbook of communication science* (2nd ed., pp. 111–127). Thousand Oaks, CA: Sage.

Berger, C. R., & Bell, R. A. (1988). Plans and the initiation of social relationships. *Human Communication Research, 15,* 217–235.

Berger, C. R., & diBattista, P. (1992). Information seeking and plan elaboration: What do you need to know to know what to do? *Communication Monographs, 59,* 368–387.

Berger, C. R., & diBattista, P. (1993). Communication failure and plan adaptation: If at first you don't succeed, say it louder and slower. *Communication Monographs, 60,* 220–238.

Berger, C. R., Karol, S. H., & Jordan, J. M. (1989). When a lot of knowledge is a dangerous thing: The debilitating effects of plan complexity on verbal fluency. *Human Communication Research, 16,* 91–119.

Berger, C. R., & Kellermann, K. (1994). Acquiring social information. In J. A. Daly & J. M. Wiemann (Eds.), *Strategic interpersonal communication* (pp. 1–31). Hillsdale, NJ: Lawrence Erlbaum.

Berger, C. R., Knowlton, S. W., & Abrahams, M. F. (1996). The hierarchy principle in strategic communication. *Communication Theory, 6,* 111–142.

Bock, K., & Levelt, W. J. M. (1994). Language production: Grammatical encoding. In M. A. Gernsbacher (Ed.), *Handbook of psycholinguistics* (pp. 945–984). San Diego, CA: Academic Press.

Bogdan, R. J. (1994). *Grounds for cognition: How goal-guided behavior shapes the mind.* Hillsdale, NJ: Lawrence Erlbaum.

Bogdan, R. J. (1997). *Interpreting minds: Evolution of a practice.* Cambridge: MIT Press.

Bogdan, R. J. (2000). *Minding minds: Evolving a reflexive mind by interpreting others.* Cambridge: MIT Press.

Bongers, K. C. A., Dijksterhuis, A., & Spears, R. (2010). On the role of consciousness in goal pursuit. *Social Cognition, 28,* 262–272.

Bower, G. H., Black, J. B., & Turner, T. J. (1979). Scripts in memory for text. C*ognitive Psychology, 3,* 193–209.

Bratman, M. (1987). *Intentions, plans and practical reason.* Cambridge, MA: Harvard University Press.

Braun, C. M. J., Godbout, L., Desbiens, C., Daigneault, S., Lussier, F., & Hamel-Hébert, I. (2004). Mental genesis of scripts in adolescents with attention deficit/hyperactivity disorder. *Child Neuropsychology, 10,* 280–296.

Brown, P., & Levinson, S. (1987). *Politeness: Some universals in language.* Cambridge, UK: Cambridge University Press.

Burgoon, J. K., Birk, T., & Pfau, M. (1990). Nonverbal behaviors, persuasion and credibility. *Human Communication Research, 17,* 140–169.

Burgoon, J. K., Stern, L. A., & Dillman, L. (1995). *Interpersonal adaptation: Dyadic interaction patterns.* New York: Cambridge University Press.

Caillies, S., & Denhière, G. (2001). The interaction between textual structures and prior knowledge: Hypotheses, data and simulations. *European Journal of Psychology of Education, 16,* 17–31.

Caillies, S., Denhière, G., & Kintsch, W. (2002). The effect of prior knowledge on understanding from text: Evidence from primed recognition. *European Journal of Cognitive Psychology, 14,* 267–286.

Carberry, S. (1990). *Plan recognition in natural language dialogue.* Cambridge: MIT Press.

Carberry, S. (2001). Techniques for plan recognition. *User Modeling and User-Adapted Interaction, 11,* 31–48.

Chartrand, T. L., & Bargh, J. A. (1996). Automatic activation of impression formation and memorization goals: Nonconscious goal priming reproduces effects of explicit task instructions. *Journal of Personality and Social Psychology, 71,* 464–478.

Chiesi, H. L., Spilich, G. J., & Voss, J. F. (1979). Acquisition of domain-related information in relation to high and low domain knowledge. *Journal of Verbal Learning and Verbal Behavior, 18,* 257–273.

Clark, H. H. (1994). Discourse in production. In M. A. Gernsbacher (Ed.), *Handbook of psycholinguistics* (pp. 985–1021). San Diego, CA: Academic Press.

Coulmas, F. (1981). Introduction: Conversational routine. In F. Coulmas (Ed.), *Conversational routine: Explorations in standardized communication situations and prepatterned speech* (pp. 1–17). The Hague, Netherlands: Mouton.

Csibra, G. (2008). Goal attribution to inanimate agents by 6.5-month-old infants. *Cognition, 107,* 705–717.

Csibra, G. (2010). Recognizing communicative intentions in infancy. *Mind and Language, 25,* 141–168.

Deese, J. (1984). *Thought into speech: The psychology of language.* Englewood Cliffs, NJ: Prentice Hall.

Dewhurst, S. A., Holmes, S. J., Swannell, E. R., & Barry, C. (2008). Beyond the text: Illusions of recollection caused by script-based inferences. *European Journal of Cognitive Psychology, 20,* 367–386.

Dijksterhuis, A., Chartrand, T. L., & Aarts, H. (2007). Effects of priming and perception on social behavior and goal pursuit. In J. A. Bargh (Ed.), *Social psychology and the unconscious: The automaticity of higher mental processes* (pp. 51–131). New York: Psychology Press.

Dik, G., & Aarts, H. (2007). Behavioral cues to others' motivation and goal pursuits: The perception of effort facilitates goal inference and contagion. *Journal of Experimental Social Psychology, 43,* 727–737.

Dik, G., & Aarts, H. (2008). I want to know what you want: How effort perception facilitates the motivation to infer another's goal. *Social Cognition, 26,* 737–754.

Dillard, J. P. (1990). The nature and substance of goals in tactical interaction. In M. J. Cody & M. L. McLaughlin (Eds.), *The psychology of tactical communication* (pp. 70–90). Clevedon, UK: Multilingual Matters.

Dillard, J. P. (1997). Explicating the goal construct: Tools for theorists. In J. O. Greene (Ed.), *Message production: Advances in communication theory* (pp. 47–60). Mahwah, NJ: Lawrence Erlbaum.

Dillard, J. P. (2010). Persuasion. In C. R. Berger, M. E. Roloff, & D. R. Roskos-Ewoldsen (Eds.), *Handbook of communication science* (2nd ed., pp. 203–218). Thousand Oaks, CA: Sage.

Eidelson, R. J., & Epstein, N. (1982). Cognition and relationship maladjustment: Development of a measure of dysfunctional relationship beliefs. *Journals of Consulting and Clinical Psychology, 50,* 715–720.

Ellis, D. G. (2010). Intergroup conflict. In C. R. Berger, M. E. Roloff, & D. R. Roskos-Ewoldsen (Eds.), *Handbook of communication science* (2nd ed., pp. 291–308). Thousand Oaks, CA: Sage.

Eskenazi, T., Grosjean, M., Humphreys, G. W., & Knoblich, G. (2009). The role of motor simulation in action perception: A neuropsychological case study. *Psychological Research, 73,* 477–485.

Fadiga, L., Craighero, L., Buccino, G., & Rizzolatti, G. (2002). Speech listening specifically modulates the excitability of tongue muscles: A TMS study. *European Journal of Neuroscience, 15,* 399–402.

Ferreira, F., & Englehardt, P. E. (2006). Syntax and production. In M. J. Traxler & M. A. Gernsbacher (Eds.), *Handbook of psycholinguistics* (2nd ed., pp. 61–91). Amsterdam: Elsevier.

Fitzsimons, G. M., & Bargh, J. A. (2003). Thinking of you: Nonconscious pursuit of interpersonal goals associated with relationship partners. *Journal of Personality & Social Psychology, 84,* 148–163.

Fitzsimons, G. M., & Shah, J. Y. (2008). How goal instrumentality shapes relationship evaluations. *Journal of Personality and Social Psychology, 95,* 319–337.

Fitzsimons, G. M., Shah, J., Chartrand, T. L., & Bargh, J. A. (2005). Goals and labors, friends and neighbors: Self-regulation and interpersonal relationships. In M. W. Baldwin (Ed.), *Interpersonal cognition* (pp. 103–125). New York: Guilford Press.

Ford, W. S. Z. (1999). Communication and customer service. In M. E. Roloff (Ed.), *Communication yearbook 22* (pp. 341–375). Thousand Oaks, CA: Sage.

Gallese, V. (2009). Motor abstraction: A neuroscientific account of how action goals and intentions are mapped and understood. *Psychological Research, 73,* 486–498.

Garnham, A., Shillcock, R. C., Brown, G. D., Mill, A. I. D., & Cutler, A. (1982). Slips of the tongue in the London-Lund corpus of spontaneous conversation. In A. Cutler (Ed.), *Slips of the tongue and language production* (pp. 251–263). Berlin, Germany: Mouton.

Godbout, L., Cloutier, P., Bouchard, C., Braun, C. M. J., & Gagnon, S. (2004). Script generation following frontal and parietal lesions. *Journal of Clinical and Experimental Neuropsychology, 26,* 857–873.

Goldman, A. I. (1970). *A theory of human action.* New York: Prentice Hall.

Gollwitzer, P. M. (1999). Implementation intentions: Strong effects of simple plans. *American Psychologist, 54,* 493–503.

Gollwitzer, P. M., Bayer, U. C., & McCulloch, C. (2005). The control of the unwanted. In R. Hassin, J. Uleman, & J. A. Bargh (Eds.), *The new unconscious* (pp. 485–515). Oxford, UK: Oxford University Press.

Gollwitzer, P. M., & Brandstätter, V. (1997). Implementation intentions and effective goal pursuit. *Journal of Personality and Social Psychology, 73,* 186–199.

Gollwitzer, P. M., Gawrilow, C., & Oettingen, G. (2010). The power of planning: Effective self-regulation of goal striving. In R. Hassin, K. Ochsner, & Y. Trope (Eds.), *Self-control in society, mind, and brain* (pp. 279–296). Oxford, UK: Oxford University Press.

Gollwitzer, P. M., & Sheeran, P. (2006). Implementation intentions and goal achievement: A meta-analysis of effects and processes. *Advances in Experimental Social Psychology, 38,* 69–119.

Gouldner, A. W. (1960). The norm of reciprocity: A preliminary statement. *American Sociological Review, 25,* 161–178.

Graesser, A. C., Millis, K. K., & Zwaan, R. A. (1997). Discourse comprehension. *Annual Review of Psychology, 48,* 163–189.

Green, G. M. (1996). *Pragmatics and natural language understanding* (2nd ed.). Hillsdale, NJ: Lawrence Erlbaum.

Greene, J. O. (1997). A second generation action assembly theory. In J. O. Greene (Ed.), *Message production: Advances in communication theory* (pp. 151–170). Mahwah, NJ: Lawrence Erlbaum.

Greene, J. O. (2003). Models of adult communication skill acquisition: Practice and the course of performance improvement. In J. O. Greene & B. R. Burleson (Eds.), *Handbook of communication and social skills* (pp. 51–91). Mahwah, NJ: Lawrence Erlbaum.

Grice, H. P. (1975). Logic and conversation. In P. Cole & J. L. Morgan (Eds.), *Syntax and semantics 3: Speech acts* (pp. 41–58). New York: Academic Press.

Griffin, Z. M., & Ferreira, V. S. (2006). Properties of spoken language production. In M. J. Traxler & M. A. Gernsbacher (Eds.), *Handbook of psycholinguistics* (2nd ed., pp. 21–60). Amsterdam: Elsevier.

Hassin, R. R., Aarts, H., & Ferguson, M. J. (2005). Automatic goal inferences. *Journal of Experimental Social Psychology, 41,* 129–140.

Hogarth, R. M. (2001). *Educating intuition.* Chicago: University of Chicago Press.

Hogarth, R. M. (2005). Deciding analytically or trusting your intuition: The advantages and disadvantages of analytic and intuitive thought. In T. Betsch & S. Haberstroh (Eds.), *The routines of decision making* (pp. 67–82). Mahwah, NJ: Erlbaum.

Honeycutt, J. M. (2003). *Imagined interactions: Daydreaming about communication.* Cresskill, NJ: Hampton Press.

Honeycutt, J. M., & Bryan, S. P. (2010). *Scripts and communication for relationships.* New York: Peter Lang.

Kawada, C. L. K., Oettingen, G., Gollwitzer, P. M., & Bargh, J. A. (2004). The projection of implicit and explicit goals. *Journal of Personal & Social Psychology, 86,* 545–559.

Kellermann, K. (1992). Communication: Inherently strategic and primarily automatic. *Communication Monographs, 59,* 288–300.

Kellermann, K. (2004). A goal-directed approach to gaining compliance: Relating differences among goals to differences in behaviors. *Communication Research, 31,* 397–445.

Kellogg, R. T. (2001). Long-term working memory in text production. *Memory and Cognition, 29,* 43–52.

Knowlton, S. W., & Berger, C. R. (1997). Message planning, communication failure, and cognitive load: Further explorations of the hierarchy principle. *Human Communication Research, 24,* 4–30.

Koenig, S., Smirnov, Y., & Tovey, C. (2003). Performance bounds for planning in unknown terrain. *Artificial Intelligence Journal, 147,* 253–279.

Kreitler, S., & Kreitler, H. (1987). Plans and planning: Their motivational and cognitive antecedents. In S. L. Friedman, E. K. Skolnick, & R. R. Cocking (Eds.), *Blueprints for thinking: The role of planning in cognitive development* (pp. 110–178). New York: Cambridge University Press.

Lakey, S. G., & Canary, D. J. (2002). Actor goal achievement and sensitivity to partner as critical factors in understanding interpersonal communication competence and conflict strategies. *Communication Monographs, 69,* 217–235.

Larocque, L., & Oatley, K. (2006). Joint plans, emotions, and relationships: A diary study of errors. *Journal of Cultural and Evolutionary Psychology, 3–4,* 245–265.

Lashley, K. S. (1951). The problem of serial order in behavior. In L. A. Jeffress (Ed.), *Cerebral mechanism in behavior* (pp. 112–146). New York: Wiley.

Leidner, R. (1993). *Fast food fast talk: Service work and the routinization of everyday life.* Berkeley: University of California Press.

Lenton, A. P., Bryan, A., Hastie, R., & Fischer, O. (2009). We want the same thing: Projection in judgments of sexual intent. *Personality and Social Psychology Bulletin, 33,* 975–988.

Levelt, W. J. M. (1989). *Speaking: From intention to articulation.* Cambridge: MIT Press.

Levelt, W. J. M., Roelofs, A., & Meyer, A. S. (1999). A theory of lexical access in speech production. *Behavioral and Brain Science, 22,* 1–45.

Lichtenstein, E. H., & Brewer, W. F. (1980). Memory for goal directed events. *Cognitive Psychology, 12,* 412–445.

Lozano, S. C., Hard, B. M., & Tversky, B. (2006). Perspective taking promotes action understanding and learning. *Journal of Experimental Psychology: Human Perception and Performance, 32,* 1405–1421.

MacKay, D. G. (1987). *The organization of perception and action: A theory for language and other cognitive skills.* New York: Springer-Verlag.

Maclay, H., & Osgood, C. E. (1959). Hesitation phenomena in spontaneous English speech. *Word, 15,* 19–44.

Magliano, J. P., Skowronski, J. J., Britt, M. A., Güss, C. D., & Forsythe, C. (2008). What do you want? How perceivers use cues to make goal inferences about others. *Cognition, 106,* 594–632.

McCulloch, K. C., Aarts, H., Fugita, K., & Bargh, J. A. (2008). Inhibition in goal systems: A retrieval-induced forgetting account. *Journal of Experimental Social Psychology, 44,* 857–865.

Miller, G. R., & Hewgill, M. A. (1964). The effect of variations in nonfluency on audience ratings of source credibility. *Quarterly Journal of Speech, 50,* 36–44.

Motley, M. T., Baars, B. J., & Camden, C. T. (1983). Experimental verbal slip studies: A review and editing model of language encoding. *Communication Monographs, 50,* 79–101.

Mudgal, A., Tovey, C., & Koenig, S. (2004, January). *Analysis of greedy robot-navigation methods.* Paper presented at the Eighth International Symposium on Artificial Intelligence and Mathematics (AMAI), Fort Lauderdale, FL.

O'Keefe, B. J. (1988). The logic of message design: Individual differences in reasoning about communication. *Communication Monographs, 55,* 80–103.

O'Keefe, B. J., & Shepard, G. J. (1987). The pursuit of multiple objectives in face-to-face persuasive interactions: Effects of construct differentiation on message organization. *Communication Monographs, 54,* 396–419.

Oldfield, R. C. (1963). Individual vocabulary and semantic currency: A preliminary study. *British Journal of Social and Clinical Psychology, 2,* 122–130.

Palomares, N. A. (2008). Toward a theory of goal detection in social interaction: Effects of contextual ambiguity and tactical functionality on goal inferences and inference certainty. *Communication Research, 35,* 109–148.

Palomares, N. A. (2009a). Did you see it coming? Effects of the specificity and efficiency of goal pursuit on the accuracy and onset of goal detection in social interaction. *Communication Research, 36,* 475–509.

Palomares, N. A. (2009b). It's not just your goal, but also who you know: How the cognitive associations among goals and relationships influence goal detection in social interaction. *Human Communication Research, 35,* 534–560.

Palomares, N. A. (in press). The dynamics of goal congruency and cognitive busyness in goal detection. *Communication Research.*

Paul, A. S., & Frea, W. D. (2002). The importance of understanding the goals of the family. *Journal of Positive Behavior Interventions, 4,* 61–63.

Payne, B. K., Lambert, A. J., & Jacoby, L. L. (2002). Best laid plans: Effects of goals on accessibility bias and cognitive control in race-based misperceptions of weapons. *Journal of Experimental Social Psychology, 38,* 384–396.

Pea, R. D., & Hawkins, J. (1987). Planning in a chore-scheduling task. In S. L. Friedman, E. K. Skolnick, & R. R. Cocking (Eds.), *Blueprints for thinking: The role of planning in cognitive development* (pp. 273–302). New York: Cambridge University Press.

Perlman, M., & Ross, H. S. (2005). If-then contingencies in children's sibling conflicts. *Merrill-Palmer Quarterly, 51,* 42–66.

Pezullo, G., & Castelfranchi, C. (2009). Intentional action: From anticipation to goal-directed behavior. *Psychological Research, 73,* 437–440.

Pryor, J. B., & Merluzzi, T. V. (1985). The role of expertise in processing social interaction scripts. *Journal of Experimental Social Psychology, 21,* 362–379.

Reid, V. M., Hoehl, S., Grigutsch, M., Groendahl, A., Parise, E., & Striano, T. (2009). The neural correlates of infant and adult goal prediction: Evidence for semantic processing systems. *Developmental Psychology, 45,* 620–629.

Roloff, M. E., & Li, S. (2010). Bargaining and negotiation. In C. R. Berger, M. E. Roloff, & D. R. Roskos-Ewoldsen (Eds.), *Handbook of communication science* (2nd ed., pp. 309–325). Thousand Oaks, CA: Sage.

Ross, H., Ross, M., Stein, N., & Trabasso, T. (2006). How siblings resolve their conflicts: The importance of first offers, planning, and limited oppositions. *Child Development, 77,* 1730–1745.

Rosset, E. (2008). It's no accident: Our bias for intentional explanations. *Cognitions, 108,* 771–780.

Schank, R. C., & Abelson, R. P. (1977). *Scripts, plans, goals and understanding: An inquiry into human knowledge structures.* Hillsdale, NJ: Lawrence Erlbaum.

Schmidt, C. F. (1976). Understanding human action: Recognizing the plans and motives of other persons. In J. S. Carroll & J. W. Payne (Eds.), *Cognition and social behavior* (pp. 47–67). Hillsdale, NJ: Lawrence Erlbaum.

Shah, J. (2003). Automatic for the people: How representations of significant others implicitly affect goal pursuit. *Journal of Personality & Social Psychology, 84,* 661–681.

Shah, J. Y., & Kruglanski, A. W. (2002). Priming against your will: How accessible alternatives affect goal pursuit. *Journal of Experimental Social Psychology, 38,* 368–383.

Shallice, T., & Butterworth, B. (1977). Short-term impairment in spontaneous speech. *Neuropsychologia, 15,* 729–735.

Sillars, A. L. (2010). Interpersonal conflict. In C. R. Berger, M. E. Roloff, & D. R. Roskos-Ewoldsen (Eds.), *Handbook of communication science* (2nd ed., pp. 273–289). Thousand Oaks, CA: Sage.

Smith, M. (2000). Conceptual structures in language production. In L. Wheeldon (Ed.), *Aspects of language production* (pp. 331–374). Hove, UK: Psychology Press.

Soliz, J., & Giles, H. (2010). Language and communication. In C. R. Berger, M. E. Roloff, & D. R. Roskos-Ewoldsen (Eds.), *Handbook of communication science* (2nd ed, pp. 75–91). Thousand Oaks, CA: Sage.

Sommerville, J. A., Woodward, A. L., & Needham, A. (2005). Action experience alters 3-month-old infants' perception of others' actions. *Cognition, 96,* B1–B11.

Southgate, V., Johnson, M. H., & Csibra, G. (2008). Infants attribute goals even to biomechanically impossible actions. *Cognition, 107,* 1059–1069.

Spilich, G. J., Vesonder, G. T., Chiesi, H. L., & Voss, J. F. (1979). Text processing of domain-related knowledge for individuals with high and low domain knowledge. *Journal of Verbal Learning and Verbal Behavior, 18*, 275–290.

Trabasso, T., & Nickels, M. (1992). The development of goal plans of action in the narration of picture stories. *Discourse Processes, 15*, 249–275.

Trabasso, T., & Wiley, J. (2005). Goal plans of action and inferences during comprehension of narratives. *Discourse Processes, 39*, 129–164.

Tracy, K, & Coupland, N. (Eds.). (1990). *Multiple goals in discourse.* Clevedon, UK: Multilingual Matters.

Tracy, K., & Moran, J. P. (1983). Conversational relevance in multiple-goal settings. In R. T. Crain & K. Tracy (Eds.), *Conversational coherence: Form, structure, and strategy* (pp. 116–135). Beverly Hills, CA: Sage.

Uller, C. (2004). Disposition to recognize goals in infant chimpanzees. *Animal Cognition, 7*, 154–161.

Van der Cruyssen, L., Van Duynslaeger, M., Cortoos, A., & Van Overwalle, F. (2009). ERP time course and brain areas of spontaneous and intentional goal inferences. *Social Neuroscience, 4*, 165–184.

Voss, J. F., Vesonder, G. T., & Spilich, G. J. (1980). Text generation and recall by high-knowledge and low-knowledge individuals. *Journal of Verbal Learning and Verbal Behavior, 19*, 651–667.

Waldron, V. R. (1990). Constrained rationality: Situational influences on information acquisition plans and tactics. *Communication Monographs, 57*, 184–201.

Waldron, V. R. (1997). Toward a theory of interactive conversational planning. In J. O. Greene (Ed.), *Message production: Advances in communication theory* (pp. 195–220). Mahwah, NJ: Lawrence Erlbaum.

Waldron, V. R., & Applegate, J. L. (1994). Interpersonal construct differentiation and conversational planning: An examination of two cognitive accounts for the production of competent verbal disagreement tactics. *Human Communication Research, 21*, 3–35.

Waldron, V. R., Caughlin, J., & Jackson, D. (1995). Talking specifics: Facilitating effects of planning on AIDS talk in peer dyads. *Health Communication, 7*, 249–266.

Waldron, V. R., & Lavitt, M. (2000). Welfare to work: Assessing communication competencies and client outcomes in a job-training program. *Southern Communication Journal, 66*, 1–15.

Walther, J. B., & Parks, M. R. (2002). Cues filtered out, cues filtered in: Computer-mediated communication and relationships. In M. L. Knapp & J. A. Daly (Eds.), *Handbook of interpersonal communication* (3rd ed., pp. 529–563). Thousand Oaks, CA: Sage.

Wilensky, R. (1983). *Planning and understanding: A computational approach to human reasoning.* London: Addison-Wesley.

Wilson, S. R. (2010). Seeking and resisting compliance. In C. R. Berger, M. E. Roloff, & D. R. Roskos-Ewoldsen (Eds.), *Handbook of communication science* (2nd ed., pp. 219–235). Thousand Oaks, CA: Sage.

Wilson, S. R., & Sabee, C. M. (2003). Explicating communication competence as a theoretical term. In J. O. Greene & B. R. Burleson (Eds.), *Handbook of communication and social interaction skills* (pp. 3–50). Mahwah, NJ: Lawrence Erlbaum.

Wittgenstein, L. (1953). *Philosophical investigations.* Oxford, UK: Basil Blackwell.

Woodward, A. L., Sommerville, J. A., & Guajardo, J. J. (2001). How infants make sense of intentional action. In B. F. Malle, L. J. Moses, & D. A. Baldwin (Eds.), *Intentions and intentionality: Foundations of social cognition* (pp. 149–169). Cambridge: MIT Press.

Wray, A., & Perkins, M. K. (2000). The functions of formulaic language: An integrated model. *Language and Communication, 20*, 1–28.

Zwaan, R. A., & Radvansky, G. A. (1998). Situation models in language comprehension and memory. *Psychological Bulletin, 123*, 162–185.

# CHAPTER 7

# Language and Interpersonal Communication

*Matthew S. McGlone*

*Howard Giles*

A ll animals communicate, but humans do so with unparalleled precision, flexibility, and creativity. These strengths derive largely from humans' unique ability to use language. The versatility of language as a medium of communication was eloquently expressed by the renowned French grammarians Arnauld and Lancelot (1660), who praised

> this marvelous invention of composing out of 25 or 30 sounds that infinite variety of expressions which, tho' they have no natural resemblance to the operations of the mind, are yet the means of unfolding all its secrets, and of disclosing unto those, who cannot see into our hearts and minds, the variety of our thoughts, and all the various stirrings of our soul. (p. 22)

Yet despite communication's status as a paradigmatic function of language, communication has not traditionally been a major focus of research in linguistics, nor has language in

interpersonal communication scholarship (Jacobs, 1994). Linguists conceive of language as a set of principles that specify the relations between a sequence of symbols and a sequence of meanings and typically devote their attention to the composition of these abstract structures rather than their communicative function per se (e.g., Chomsky, 1965). In contrast, communication scholars may acknowledge that the meanings of verbal messages derive from linguistic principles (e.g., O'Keefe, 1997) but don't often articulate the connections between them.

Linguists and communication scholars alike are fond of saying that language and communication are not the same thing. Humans can and do communicate without language, and nonhuman species that don't use language are capable of communicating adequately for their purposes. However, it would be a serious mistake to minimize the differences between linguistic and nonlinguistic communication. Although not all instances of language use are adaptively significant, it is not idle hyperbole to say that human societies are predicated on the capacity for linguistic communication and without this capacity human social interaction would be radically different.

Communication systems of all kinds operate on the same principle: Signals transmit messages from a source to a destination. A foraging honeybee communicates the direction and distance of a source of nectar to its fellow hive dwellers by engaging in an elaborate waggle dance (von Frisch, 1967). The vervet monkeys of East Africa have three distinctive vocal alarm calls that signal the presence of their three main predators— leopards, eagles, and snakes. On hearing one of these calls, a vervet will respond appropriately— climbing a tree in response to the leopard call, scanning the ground when the snake call is sounded, or seeking shelter after hearing an eagle call (Seyfarth, Cheney, & Marler, 1980). Both of these systems represent the species' adaptation to the exigencies of a particular ecological niche in which communication facilitates survival. Language can be thought of as a similar sort of adaptation.

Signals in communication systems may be *signs* or *symbols*. Signs are signals that are causally related to the message they convey. We say that a smile is a sign that someone is happy because we know that happiness is a (if not the only) cause of smiling. Symbols, on the other hand, are the products of social conventions. Because of an implicit agreement among speakers of English, the sound pattern we recognize as the word *pig* denotes the familiar category of broad-snouted barnyard animals. There is no intrinsic reason that *pig*, rather than some other sound pattern, should denote this concept, and in languages other than English, very different sound patterns represent the concept. Verbal communication often involves both signs and symbols. A quivering voice that tells us a speaker is experiencing distress is a sign—that is, a direct product of the distress it signals. But it is the symbolic content of a person's verbal communication that can tell us precisely what is stressing her out.

Language is just one of the symbol systems humans use to communicate. The "high-five" gesture conveys (in Western cultures) a message of success or approval, wearing a cross publicly proclaims the wearer's religious beliefs, and a facial grimace in response to the question "Do you like my new dress?" expresses one's negative aesthetic appraisal. Notwithstanding the utility of such symbolic displays, language endows human communication with three properties that distinguish it from these displays and from communication forms observed in other species (Hockett, 1960; Krauss & Chiu, 1997). The first is semanticity—that is, the associative ties between signals and features of the world, ties that constitute the signals' meanings (Saussure, 1916). Although pleasured pussycats often purr and we recognize purring as a sign of their pleasure, purring cannot be said to stand for pleasure in the same way as the word *pleasure* does. Second, language is generative, in that all natural languages are capable of generating an infinite number of meaningful messages from a finite number of linguistic signals. Languages permit symbols to be combined and recombined in ways that yield novel meanings, and any competent language user regularly produces utterances that have never been uttered before but are immediately comprehensible to other competent language users (Chomsky, 1965). In contrast, a vervet's system of alarm calls is limited to a fixed set of messages and lacks the ability to generate novel ones; thus, a vervet has no way to specifically signal the presence of predators other than eagles, leopards, or snakes. Third, language encodes displacement, making it possible to communicate about things that are spatially or temporally remote, or perhaps exist only in one's mind (MacWhinney, 2008). Bertrand Russell once famously remarked, "No matter how eloquently a dog may bark, he cannot tell you that his father was poor but honest." This point may be banal, but it does describe a profound difference in the expressive capacity of language and other communication modalities. Vervets can signal the presence of a predatory leopard, but even the most articulate vervet cannot refer to the leopard that attacked last week; its communication is limited to what is immediately present (Seyfarth et al., 1980). Perhaps more than any other feature, it is the capacity of language to convey displacement that distinguishes it from other communication modalities (Hockett, 1960; Jackendoff, 2002).

The ability to generate an unlimited number of meaningful, novel messages not bound to the here and now, combined with humans' cognitive capacity to exploit these signal properties, is what enables language to be such an effective tool of interpersonal communication. This assessment presumes that language's potential for communicative action (informing, influencing, insulting, etc.) derives from an intimate relationship between language and thought. Let us now consider the connections among language, thought, and action in more detail.

## Language and Thought

The special place of language in human cognition is reflected in psychologist Roger Brown's (1968) denial of language in nonhuman species:

> I grant a mind to every human being, to each a full stock of feelings, thoughts, motives, and meanings. I hope they grant as much to me. How much of this mentality that we allow one another ought we to allow the monkey, the sparrow, the goldfish, the ant? Hadn't we better reserve something for ourselves alone, perhaps consciousness or self-consciousness, possibly linguistic reference? Most people are determined to hold the line against animals . . . man alone can use language to make reference. There is a qualitative difference of mentality separating us from animals. (p. 155)

Ivan Pavlov (1941), the discoverer of the conditioned reflex, expressed a similar point of view: "It is nothing other than words which has made us human" (p. 179).

Brown and Pavlov clearly imply a deep connection between language and human thought. Such a connection can operate in at least two different ways. The first is not particularly controversial: Our brains have evolved in such a way as to make language possible, if not inevitable, in every human being (e.g., Bickerton, 2009). The second has excited both interest and controversy: The human mind is special not because it makes language possible. Instead, it is language itself that shapes the mind. Language sets us apart from other animal species not only because it reflects the complexity and richness of human thought but because it makes certain forms of thought possible. This claim can be extended even further to entail differences among languages. The particular language that we speak may not merely reflect thought but will also directly control how we think and what we can think about (e.g., Casasanto, 2008).

In the early 20th century, the relationship between language and thought was treated as one of identity by John Watson, the founder of radical behaviorism in psychology. For Watson, unobservable events and processes such as thinking were not proper objects of scientific study. How, then, could one reconcile a science of psychology with the undeniable fact of human thought? Watson's solution was simple: Thought is nothing more than speech. As children, we think aloud by speaking. Gradually, the overt thinking-aloud speech of children becomes covert, and for Watson (1913), this covert speech was thought: "Thought processes are really motor habits in the larynx" (p. 174). Covert speech could not, of course, be directly observed, but its existence could be inferred from electromyographic records of muscle activity in the speech organs. When electronic sensors are placed on a person's throat while she is asked to think, motor movements are often detected (Jacobsen, 1932). Moreover, when nonhearing people who use American Sign Language are asked to think, motor movements are detected in the muscles that control hand and finger movements (Max, 1937). At the very least, then, thinking is accompanied by language-associated muscle activity. But is this activity a necessary component of thought? To answer this question, Smith, Brown, Tomas, and Goodman (1947) used a curare-like drug that completely paralyzes the striate (voluntary) muscles of the body. The only muscle tissues that are not affected are smooth muscles such as the heart and digestive system. Smith himself ingested the drug, breathed via artificial respiration, and while in this state was given word problems (verbal analogies) to think about. When the drug wore off, he could describe the problems that he had been given and also reported that he had been able to think clearly while completely paralyzed. Thus, muscle movements in humans' speech apparatus are clearly not necessary for thought, even verbal thought.

Even though people can think without implicit speech, language could still be necessary for thought, and different languages may lead people to think differently. At roughly the same time Watson was launching radical behaviorism, cultural anthropologists and linguists like Edward Sapir were making contact with languages strikingly different from those they had studied before, such as the Hopi and Navajo languages spoken by Native American tribes in the Southwest. These languages differed from Indo-European languages in such fundamental ways that they seemed to reflect completely different means of conceptualizing the world. For example, Sapir's student Benjamin Lee Whorf studied the Nootka language spoken by the native people of Vancouver Island in British Columbia and found that nouns and verbs are not distinguished as they are in English. Based on this observation, Whorf (1956) suggested that Nootka speakers did not partition nature into classes of "things" and "actions" the way English speakers do because the grammar of the Nootka language does not differentiate between them. The general idea underlying this claim has come to be known as the "Sapir-Whorf hypothesis of linguistic relativity": People who speak different languages

think differently because of the difference between the languages. In Sapir's (1949) words,

> Human beings do not live in the objective world alone, nor alone in social activity as ordinarily understood, but are very much at the mercy of the particular language which has become the medium of expression for their society. It is quite an illusion to imagine that one adjusts to reality essentially without the use of language and that language is merely an incidental means of solving specific problems of communication or reflection. The fact of the matter is that the "real world" is to a large extent unconsciously built upon the language habits of the group . . . we see and hear and otherwise experience very largely as we do because the language habits of our community predispose certain choices of interpretation. (p. 162)

This strong version of the linguistic relativity position was widely embraced in the 1950s and 1960s, drawing empirical support initially from Brown and Lenneberg's (1954) studies of color codability and memory. They observed that colors that were the easiest to code, as indicated by high coder agreement and the need for relatively few terms, were also the easiest to recall; consequently, the availability of color terms in the mental lexicon appeared to affect the ease with which color could be remembered. Some research exploring cultural differences in color codability and subsequent memory were also consistent with Brown and Lenneberg's conclusions (Lantz & Stefflre, 1964; Stefflre, Castillo Vales, & Morley, 1966). However, Heider (1972) challenged these conclusions in a study demonstrating that Dani speakers in New Guinea, who possess only 2 basic color terms (corresponding to *light* and *dark*) compared with 11 in English, behaved in cognitive tasks as though their color categories resembled the English system. She also found that Dani speakers' judgments of similarity between colors accorded better with English basic color terms than their own. Moreoever, when asked to learn new color categories, the Dani found the task easier when the categories were grouped around English focal colors. The implication of these findings is that the perception of color—and which colors are considered focal—is determined by the biology of human color perception and not by the language one speaks (Berlin & Kay, 1969; Heider & Olivier, 1972).

Heider's findings, coupled with revelations that the linguistic evidence Whorf reported was either exaggerated or fabricated (in particular, see Pullum's 1991 account of what he calls Whorf's "Great Eskimo Vocabulary Hoax"), ushered in a period of extreme skepticism concerning linguistic relativity (Brown, 1968; Clark & Clark, 1977; Devitt & Sterelny, 1987; Glucksberg, 1988; Pinker, 1994). Doubts about linguistic relativity also dovetailed with zeitgeists in various fields studying language use. In linguistics, Chomsky's influence trained the field's focus on the "universals" of linguistic grammar—that is, similarities among languages, not differences. In addition, his strong position that language is separate from other cognitive faculties also discouraged any search for a relation between language and cognition (Chomsky, 1992). In cognitive psychology, there was a strong sense that concepts come first and that language merely names them—nouns name persons, places, or things; verbs name actions and events; adjectives name modifying concepts; and so on (e.g., Miller & Johnson-Laird, 1976). In the study of child development, Piaget (1977) and his students favored the same path of causality—from thought to language.

After years of neglect, however, the language–thought interface has become an active area of research once more (Casasanto, 2008; Deutscher, 2010; Gentner & Goldin-Meadow, 2003; Gumperz & Levinson, 1996). This resurgence can be attributed in large measure to groundbreaking work by Bowerman (e.g., Bowerman & Choi, 2001), Langacker (1999), Lucy (1994), and Talmy (1985) demonstrating important differences in how languages carve up the world. For example, English

and Korean offer their speakers very different ways of talking about joining objects. In English, placing a CD in its case or an apple in a bowl is described as putting one object *in* another. However, Korean makes a distinction according to the fit between the objects: A CD placed in a tight-fitting case is described by the verb *kkita*, whereas an apple placed in a loose-fitting bowl is described by *nehta*. In Korean, the notion of "fit" is more important than the notion of containment. Unlike English speakers, who say that a ring is placed *on* a finger and that a finger is placed *in* a ring, Korean speakers use *kkita* to describe both situations since both involve a tight-fitting relation between the objects (Bowerman & Choi, 2001). This and other demonstrations of variability in the way languages partition the world have profound implications. If semantics can vary cross-linguistically, then one cannot maintain, as many cognitive scientists have over the years, that conceptual structure is universal and that semantic structure merely reflects conceptual structure. Either conceptual structure differs across cultures and languages (and a language's semantic structure merely reflects these differences) or the semantic structure of a language can influence the conceptual structure of its speakers, as Sapir and Whorf argued, albeit from questionable field observations (Imai & Saalbach, 2010). Thus, new (and more solid) evidence of differences between languages and their cognitive consequences are renewing interest in a time-honored linguistic question that had fallen out of favor for years.

Linguistic relativity nonetheless remains a controversial issue in language studies. However, debates about whether differences between languages make their speakers think in different ways should not cast doubt on the proposition that language can influence thinking (Hunt & Agnoli, 1991). There is considerable evidence that language use affects a variety of cognitive processes. For example, the phonological properties of language used to rehearse stimulus materials can affect performance on verbal memory (Ellis & Daniel, 1971; Hoosain & Salili, 1987;

Neveh-Benjamin & Ayres, 1986); linguistic labeling of visual stimuli can affect memory of their visual form (Loftus, 1996; Schooler & Engstler-Schooler, 1990) and appraisals of their aesthetic qualities (McGlone, Kobrynowicz, & Alexander, 2005; Yamada, 2009); linguistic framing of decision and problem-solving scenarios can affect the way in which the scenarios are represented and options are chosen or solutions are discovered (Glucksberg & Weisberg, 1963; Kahneman & Tversky, 1984; McGlone, Bortfeld, & Kobrynowicz, 2007); and prosodic and semantic features of speech and text can affect the cognitive fluency with which propositions are evaluated and judged to be credible, desirable, and so on (Alter & Oppenheimer, 2008; McGlone & Tofighbakhsh, 2000; Schwarz, 2006).

The influence of language on thinking is perhaps most pronounced in the domain of social interaction. Although color perception derives from a physiological process that renders it largely immune from linguistic influence (Berlin & Kay, 1969), there is no analogous process underlying person perception (Holtgraves, 2002). Moreover, perceiving others and thinking about them is highly uncertain and ambiguous; people are more likely to disagree regarding their perceptions of another person than they are about perceptions of color. It is within this ambiguity that language can exert its influence in a number of ways. First, the specific dimensions we use to perceive others and communicate these perceptions may be constrained by our language (Hoffman, Lau, & Johnson, 1986). For example, Janice's behavior might be described as *cordial* by some and *cold* by others, but any description will be constrained by the available descriptors in one's language. In much the same way, basic attributional processes may be constrained by the perceiver's language. A language that provides a wealth of dispositional terms (such as English) may increase the likelihood that those dispositional terms will be used, and hence dispositional attributions (e.g., *Matt lost his wallet because he's careless*) will be preferred to situational

attributions (e.g., *Matt lost his wallet because he was distracted*). The most common attributional phenomenon associated with language is implicit causality—that is, the causal inferences we associate with certain verbs (Brown & Fish, 1983; Crinean & Garnham, 2006; Semin & Fiedler, 1992). For example, the sentences *Paula assists Alan* and *Paula likes Alan* both assign Paula and Alan to grammatical subject and object roles, but we nonetheless infer that Paula is the causal locus in the first sentence and Alan is the causal locus in the second. Although this phenomenon may not reflect linguistic determinism in a strict sense, there is an asymmetry in the causal locus of many verbs that may bias the attributions we infer from even simple statements.

Second, person perception is as much an interpersonal process as it is an intrapersonal one. We discuss our person perceptions with other people, receive feedback about our perceptions, and sometimes alter them in light of this feedback. In such cases, it is the use of language rather than any property of language per se that influences person perception. This influence can occur via several mechanisms. Schemas associated with the particular words used to describe a person may be activated and may influence the manner in which information about others is processed (Bransford & Johnson, 1972). The mere act of describing someone creates a verbal representation that can influence and sometimes distort recollections of that person's appearance, words, or actions later on (Schooler & Engstler-Schooler, 1990). The words people choose may subtly convey their attitudes toward the objects of their talk. They may describe their successes (or those of their in-group) with interpretive action verbs or adjectives as a means of suggesting that such actions are the usual state of affairs. Alternatively, they may describe their failures in more concrete terms to imply that such events are aberrations from the norm (Ruscher, 2001; Semin & Fiedler, 1991; Wigboldus & Douglas, 2007).

Third, the way people talk about others is constrained by pragmatic principles—that is, rules for determining the meaning of an utterance in context—which in turn can have an impact on the way we think and reason about others. These principles reflect our implicit understanding that language is used not merely to communicate information but to perform meaningful actions in the world that have consequences for the speaker, addressee, and the other people they encounter.

## Language as Action: Speech Act Theory

Prior to the 20th century, language scholars had generally assumed that the principal use of language is to communicate information. The narrowness of this view was recognized by Wittgenstein (1953), who emphasized the variety of uses to which language is put besides information transfer. Austin (1962) developed this aspect of Wittgenstein's thinking in his theory of performatives, which ultimately led to the theory of speech acts (Searle, 1969, 1979).

Statements that describe states of affairs and that can be judged true or false—that is, the kinds of statements that had previously dominated philosophical discussions of language—were termed *constatives* by Austin (1962). He contrasted this class with *performatives:* statements that accomplish something by virtue of being uttered. For Austin, to utter a performative is to do something, and doing something is neither true nor false. *Shut the door*, for example, can be used to perform the act of requesting; it may be effective or ineffective in this respect, but it is neither true nor false. Having distinguished performatives from constatives, Austin argued that all utterances are performatives of one kind or another, effectively abolishing the distinction. To utter a constative, he argued, is to perform the act of describing or asserting something.

Performatives can be explicit or implicit. The statements *I'll bet you ten dollars UT will beat Texas A&M* and *I hereby declare you man and wife,* when uttered by a responsible person under the appropriate circumstances, are examples of explicit performatives. By uttering them, the speaker performs an act (making a wager, uniting a couple in matrimony), and the speaker's intention to perform that act is explicit. A statement such as *It's rather hot in here*, when intended as an indirect request for someone to open a window, also performs an act, but the speaker's intention to perform it is implicit and must be inferred by the addressee.

A "speech act" has four components: (1) the utterance act itself (i.e., the vocal behavior of generating the utterance); (2) the locution of the utterance (its literal meaning); (3) the illocution of the utterance (the meaning intended by the speaker); (4) and the perlocution of the utterance (its effect on the addressee). For example, speaking the words *It's rather hot in here* would be an utterance act. The locution has the form of a declarative sentence to the effect that the temperature in the current context is above some comfortable norm. If the speaker's intention is to communicate information about the temperature there and then, the locution and the illocution of the utterance coincide. In certain contexts, however, the speaker might use this locution with the illocutionary force of a request; that is, the speaker might intend the statement to be taken as a request for the addressee to turn on or turn up the air conditioner perhaps. If the addressee then turned it on, the utterance would have had its intended perlocutionary effect, and illocution and perlocution would then agree. To comprehend an utterance, therefore, it is not enough to know under what conditions it would be true or false. The speaker's intention in using the utterance must also be known. Although the attribution of some intention to a speaker is normally straightforward, the process is not infallible. Probably more communication failures result from mistaking a speaker's intentions than from any source of error in linguistic interactions.

Various classifications of illocutions have been proposed. According to Searle (1979), language is used in five general ways, so there are five general categories of illocutions:

> We tell people how things are (assertives), we try to get them to do things (directives), we commit ourselves to doing things (commissives), we express our feelings and attitudes (expressives), and we bring about changes in the world through our utterances (declarations). (p. viii)

Bach and Harnish (1979) proposed a different classification, as did Austin (1962). Lack of agreement has posed serious difficulties for language scholars hoping to work with a definitive classification of language uses. However, theorists in this tradition generally agree that the central question for a theory of language-use-as-action should be as follows: How are speakers' intentions communicated to listeners? This question has two parts. First, how do speakers decide how to express a given intention? Second, how do listeners discover what a speaker's intention is?

A speaker who wants to request that an addressee take out the trash has several ways to do so. For example, the speaker can request it directly by saying *Please take out the trash* or indirectly by saying *The trash can is overflowing*. Whatever the choice, however, the felicitous performance of this speech act presupposes certain conditions: For example, there must be an obvious referent of the term *trash* in this context, and there must be an addressee who understands English and who is capable of removing the trash from this context. If the indirect way is chosen, the request will not be effective unless the addressee correctly infers the speaker's intention. How an addressee does this is not obvious: *The trash can is overflowing* could be interpreted as a statement of fact (an assertive) or an expression of annoyance (an expressive), as well as an indirect request for action (a directive). In fact, it is not even obvious how the addressee recognizes the speaker's intentions when the direct way is chosen, since *Please take out the trash* could be intended as a rebuke as well as a request for action, or could even be intended as a secret signal in some prearranged code.

Speech act theory is an attempt to state rules governing how a speaker chooses utterances to express particular intentions in particular contexts, rules that addressees also can use to attribute particular intentions to speakers in particular contexts. The rules should make explicit the conditions governing well-formed speech acts. The simple way to convey the nature of speech act theory is by example. Consider Searle's (1969) analysis of the seven conditions (often referred to as the felicity conditions) that must be satisfied for a speaker to make a promise (a commissive):

1. A speaker utters a sentence in the presence of the addressee.

2. A proposition is expressed in that utterance, which can be taken to predicate a future action by the speaker.

3. The addressee would prefer that the speaker take this action rather than not, and the speaker believes that this is so. (Otherwise it might be a threat instead of a promise.)

4. Neither the speaker nor the addressee expects that the promised action would normally have been taken without this promise. (It is seldom appropriate to promise to continue breathing, for example.)

5. The speaker sincerely intends to perform the promised action.

6. By promising, the speaker takes on an obligation to carry out the promised action.

7. The speaker intends to inform the addressee that the speaker is taking on that obligation.

If these felicity conditions are met (as well as some others that need not concern us here), a well-formed promise is made.

It should be obvious that speech act theory assumes that far more than linguistic knowledge is required to use language successfully. Speakers and addressees must both know and be able to follow relatively complex rules governing social-verbal discourse, and they must be able to draw on conceptual and interpersonal knowledge to choose appropriate forms of utterance and to interpret indirect speech acts correctly. These assumptions are of considerable importance for the study of interpersonal communication.

## The Cooperative Principle

Grice (1975) observed that linguistic competence and contextual knowledge are necessary but not sufficient for understanding language. Understanding also depends on a general communicative principle that is tacitly accepted by all participants. Although they have considerable latitude in deciding what to say at any point in a conversational exchange, there are constraints that must be respected. A conversation has a purpose or direction that organizes successive contributions, and participants implicitly agree to cooperate in achieving that purpose or advancing in that direction, otherwise they would not participate. Grice proposed that participants observe the "cooperative principle" when making their contributions to the ongoing conversation. This principle states that people will do what is required to further the purpose of their conversation: "Make your conversational contribution such as is required, at the stage at which it occurs, by the accepted purpose or direction of the talk exchange in which you are engaged" (p. 45). This directive is accomplished by following certain conversational "maxims":

1. Maxims of Quantity
   - Make your contribution as informative as is required (for the current exchange).
   - Do not make your contribution more informative than is required.

2. Maxims of Quality
   - Try to make your contribution one that is true.
   - Do not say what you believe to be false.
   - Do not say that for which you lack adequate evidence.

3. Maxim of Relation
   - Be relevant.

4. Maxims of Manner
   - Be perspicuous.
   - Avoid obscurity of expression.
   - Avoid ambiguity.
   - Be brief (avoid unnecessary prolixity).
   - Be orderly.

Grice's maxims are neither prescriptive nor descriptive of what actually happens in conversations. Rather, they express assumptions that an addressee can bring to bear, assumptions that any interpretation of a speaker's utterance should attempt to preserve. If someone seems to violate them during conversation, either the implicitly conversational contract has been broken because the speaker wishes to withdraw or the speaker expects the addressee to understand why the maxims were violated.

For example, consider a scenario in which John tells Anita, *I took out the trash last night.* If Anita already knows this and knows that John knows she knows it, then John has violated a maxim of quantity. Since John does not seem to be breaking off the conversation, Anita concludes that he means something more than he said. The violation triggers a search for an additional interpretation, and Anita decides that John's "hidden" message is that he wants her to handle that chore tonight. In this example, one might say that *I took out the trash last night* implies or suggests or means *You take the trash out tonight.* But *implies* has a logical sense that is too strong, *suggests* seems too weak, and *means* has too many other senses. Grice introduced the verb *implicate* and the noun *implicature* to cover this kind of relation. Grice's notion of conversational implicature provides a pragmatic solution for what had previously seemed to be a semantic problem.

On the Gricean account, speakers conversationally implicate proposition *P* when saying proposition *Q* by "flouting" a maxim, that is, by causing the addressee to reason as follows: The speaker is obeying the maxims, but for this to be true something must be communicated that is not what is being said (*Q*), and the likely candidate for this is *P*. Grice maintained that this reasoning underlies our ability to interpret the varieties of indirect speech acts in which the locution (literal meaning) and illocution (intended meaning) of an utterance are different. Requests, for example, are commonly made indirectly (Ervin-Tripp, 1976). It is rare that we say to someone, *Will you help me?*—preferring instead to make the request indirectly by querying their ability (*Could you help me?*) or inclination (*Would you be willing to help me?*) to provide assistance. Figures of speech (metaphors, irony, idioms, etc.) also abound in everyday discourse that require addressees to go beyond a literal meaning (e.g., *Your mother is a saint*) to determine the speaker's intended meaning (e.g., *Your mother is a kind person*). Grice and other pragmatic theorists assumed that when the locution and illocution of a message are distinct, a multistage process is required to understand it (Bach & Harnish, 1979; Clark & Clark, 1977; Gordon & Lakoff, 1975). For example, Searle (1979) assumed that before one interprets *Your mother is a saint* metaphorically, one must first contemplate and reject the possibility that the speaker intended to convey, *Your mother is a canonized, holy figure.* This assumption implies a model of metaphor understanding comprising three stages (McGlone & Manfredi, 2002). First, a literal interpretation of the utterance is derived. Second, the appropriateness of this interpretation is assessed against the context of the utterance. Third, if the literal meaning is deemed defective in context, then an alternative interpretation is derived. For Searle (as for Aristotle), the alternative entailed converting the categorically false metaphor into a simile (*Your mother is like a saint*) and then determining the salient common features of *your mother* and *saint* that the simile is intended to highlight (kindness, generosity, morality, piety, etc.).

Despite their simplicity and elegance, however, multistage models of indirect speech act processing have not fared well empirically. Studies of metaphor comprehension have generally found that people require no more time to understand metaphors than to understand comparable literal messages when adequate discourse context is provided; thus, it is not clear that a nonliteral interpretation requires two more processing stages than a literal one (McGlone, Cacciari, & Glucksberg, 1994; Ortony, Schallert, Reynolds, & Antos, 1978). Moreover, the assumption that a nonliteral interpretation is derived only after a literal interpretation has been deemed defective does not hold up either (McGlone, 2007). When Rolling Stones' lead singer Mick Jagger intoned *I'll never be your beast of burden*, the literal meaning of his claim was not defective at all (it's true he never was nor will be a camel), but listeners nonetheless reject it in favor of a nonliteral one. In the case of indirect requests, it appears that people generate the literal and nonliteral interpretations in parallel rather than serially. Like metaphors, indirect requests (*Must you open the window?*) take no longer to understand than direct requests (*Do not open the window*) when encountered in a plausible discourse context (Gibbs, 1979, 1983), which suggests that their nonliteral meanings are not derived in processing stages downstream from literal meanings. Clark (1979) explored this issue in more depth by analyzing replies to various forms of indirect request. Indirect requests were posed to merchants over the telephone for information about when the store closed (e.g., *Can you tell me what time you close tonight?*) or the price of a particular item. As one would expect, people always recognized the indirect meanings of these utterances. However, the replies frequently addressed both the literal and the nonliteral meaning of the requests. For example, in response to *Can you tell me what time you close tonight?*, people frequently responded with utterances such as *Sure, we close at 8 p.m.* The inclusion of *sure* in this utterance speaks to the literal meaning of the request, indicating that the literal meaning had been derived in parallel with the nonliteral meaning.

Other aspects of Grice's theory have also drawn criticism. Many scholars have taken issue with the stipulation that there are four (and only four) maxims. Some argue that additional maxims exist (e.g., Leech, 1983), while others argue that four is too many. In particular, Sperber and Wilson (1986) claim that there is really only one conversational maxim (be relevant) and that the other maxims are simply instances of this more general requirement. Krauss and Fussell (1996) observed that no matter how many maxims there actually are, they may not be invariant across social contexts. What counts as a maxim violation may well vary as a function of the characteristics of the speaker. Politicians, for example, can be quite skilled at violating the relevance maxim, so much so that the violation may not typically be noticed. And even if it is noticed, it may be written off as an attempt to avoid answering a question (and so no implicature will be generated; Bavelas, Black, Bryson, & Mullett, 1988; Bull & Mayer, 1993). Maxims may differ not only from speaker to speaker but also from culture to culture. For example, Keenan (1976) observed that Malagasy speakers (natives of Madagascar) routinely withhold information from one another, an action that is in clear violation of the quantity maxim. This withholding norm, she argues, is attributable to the perception of private information as a valuable commodity in a highly public, village-oriented society and a general apprehension among villagers about devaluing the information's currency by sharing it with others. As a consequence of this norm, violations of the quantity maxim do not appear to result in conversational implicatures among Malagasy speakers. Thus, it is possible that the maxims Grice delineated are relevant only in certain cultures, most likely those in the Western hemisphere (Fitch & Sanders, 1994; Holtgraves, 2002; Levinson, 2000).

# Language in Interpersonal Interaction

Speech act theory offers a useful approach for understanding at a very basic level how people use language in the service of social action. However, most of the research within this tradition has focused on illocution rather than perlocution— that is, on the meanings speakers intend to convey rather than the effects their words have on addressees. Yet when speakers make requests, promises, and apologies, the directives, commissives, and expressives they perform have effects on their addressees that can influence both the tenor of their immediate interactions and the trajectory of their relationships. Speakers are (typically) aware of the interpersonal implications of their speech acts and formulate their utterances accordingly. In this section, we explore the interpersonal considerations that guide speakers' utterance design.

## Politeness and Face Management

Politeness in the study of language use does not refer to rules of social etiquette, such as which fork to use with which meal course, but rather the numerous strategies speakers use to avoid the equally numerous ways in which addressees might be affronted by their words. In their highly influential analysis of politeness, Brown and Levinson (1987) document how people all over the world use it to grease the gears of social interaction. The starting point for their analysis is the sociologist Erving Goffman's observation that when people interact they are constantly concerned about maintaining a vague but vital commodity known as "face" (as in the expression *save face*). Goffman (1967) defined face as the "positive social value a person effectively claims for himself by the line others assume he has taken during a particular contact" (p. 5). In other words, face is the public persona people desire to display in their interactions with others. Brown and Levinson (1987) divide face into distinct desires to be held in positive regard by others ("positive" face) and to have one's actions be unimpeded by others ("negative" face). This distinction represents a fundamental duality that manifests itself in many different guises in social interaction: Connection versus autonomy (Holtgraves, 2002), communion versus agency (Bakan, 1966), intimacy versus power (MacMartin, Wood, & Kroger, 2001), and communal sharing versus authority ranking (Haslam, 2004).

Following Goffman, Brown and Levinson (1987) argue that participants in a conversation engage in "facework" to maintain their own face as well as the face of their partners. This turns out to be challenging, however, because so many kinds of conversational exchange pose a threat to the face of the addressee, the speaker, or both. The mere act of starting a conversation imposes demands on the addressee's time and attention, potentially threatening that person's negative face. Commands (e.g., *Give me a dollar*) are rarely issued because they threaten the addressee's autonomy (and thus her negative face), but requests (e.g., *May I borrow a dollar?*) are also threatening because they put the addressee in a position where if she refuses, she might come across as stingy or unfriendly (thereby compromising her positive face). Apologies and promises threaten the speaker's positive and negative face respectively, because the former entails casting oneself in a negative light and the latter committing oneself to future action. Complaints, criticisms, and disagreements potentially threaten the face of both speakers and addressees, particularly when one's speech style is called into question (see Marlow & Giles, 2010). Given the plethora of possibilities for face threat that can occur in even seemingly innocuous conversational exchanges, Pinker (2007) observed that it is no surprise that when we address a stranger the first thing we say is *Excuse me!* But despite the numerous ways in which speakers and addressees may threaten each other's face, we have to get on with the business of interaction, which sometimes requires us to command, request, apologize, criticize, and so on. The solution we employ for mitigating face threat is politeness—that is, we strategically employ words and phrases that reaffirm our positive regard for our addressees and acknowledge their autonomy.

This solution comes at a cost, however, by compromising the clarity and efficiency of our communication with others. The typology of five politeness "superstrategies" that Brown and

Levinson (1987) posit reflects the tension between interlocutors' goal to communicate clearly and efficiently, on the one hand, and to preserve face, on the other. To illustrate, consider a scenario in which Angelina, who recently auditioned for the lead role in a film, asks the director Steven whether she got the part, after he has decided to cast a different actress. Steven might convey the news to Angelina by (1) stating the news baldly "on record," with no politeness to soften the blow (e.g., *You didn't get the part*); (2) displaying "positive" politeness (thereby preserving positive face) by indicating positive regard for and solidarity with Angelina (e.g., *You're a great actress and I'm sure we would work well together, but you didn't get the part*); (3) displaying "negative" politeness (thereby preserving negative face) by acknowledging her autonomy and being self-effacing (e.g., *I know you gave it your all in the audition. It was a tough decision and I may be making a big mistake, but you didn't get the part*); (4) stating the news "off the record" via an implicature produced by violating a conversational maxim (e.g., *Perhaps a different role would better suit your talents*); or (5) in ostensibly the most polite case, withholding the news entirely (e.g., *I haven't cast the part yet but will let you know soon*). Which superstrategy will Steven use? Brown and Levinson contend that it depends on the nature and context of the social relationship between the speaker and addressee. Specifically, they propose that speakers will be more polite when (a) the relative power of the addressee over the speaker increases, (b) the social distance between the addressee and the speaker increases, and (c) the degree of imposition on the addressee increases. Thus, politeness theory predicts that Steven is likely to use a more polite superstrategy (a) when turning down a high-status instead of a low-status actress, (b) when rejecting a stranger or casual acquaintance rather than a friend, and (c) when he expects the news to be a hard blow rather than merely a disappointment (because the worse the news, the more of an imposition it is).

Politeness plays a particularly important role in the formulation of requests, because they challenge the addressee's autonomy by assuming that person's willingness to comply. The subtext of a request is that the speaker is ordering the addressee around, something you don't do to a superior or a stranger and may not even feel comfortable doing with a peer or a close friend. Consequently, requests are typically accompanied by various forms of linguistic obsequiousness, such as hedging (*If possible, could you turn the music down?*), apologizing (*Sorry to bother you, but could you turn the music down?*), acknowledging the imposition (*I know you're enjoying it, but could you turn the music down?*), minimizing the imposition (*Could you turn the music down just a little bit?*), expressing pessimism about compliance (*I don't suppose you could turn the music down*), casting the request as anomalous and done with reluctance (*I normally wouldn't ask, but could you turn the music down?*), or casting compliance as a good deed worthy of reciprocity (*Could you do me a favor by turning the music down?*). Although these strategies are occasionally written off as "sucking up," there is solid evidence that their inclusion in a request can affect its perceived politeness, which, in turn, affects the likelihood that the addressee will comply with it. In general, requests that make it easy for the addressee to decline are judged to be more polite (e.g., Clark & Schunk, 1980). However, this general rule depends on other factors, such as the size of the request (i.e., the burden complying imposes on the requestee). Brown and Levinson (1987) note that when making small requests or requesting things that the requester is entitled to request, the use of excessively polite forms may be seen as sarcastic (e.g., *I don't mean to bother you, miss, but would it be possible for us to order our food sometime soon?*). Consistent with this analysis, Holtgraves and Yang (1990) found that people judged direct requests more likely to be used for small requests than for large ones.

Several investigators have tested the predictions Brown and Levinson's (1987) model makes about the factors that influence the use of politeness superstrategies and the formulation of requests (Francik & Clark, 1985; Gibbs, 1986;

Holtgraves, 1986; Holtgraves & Yang, 1990). In general, their model predicts that requests will become increasingly indirect with increases in the size/imposition of the request, the power of the speaker over the addressee, and the social distance between the speaker and the addressee. Holtgraves and Yang (1990) used a set of vignettes to manipulate the social distance between the communicators, the power of the addressee relative to the speaker, and the politeness of the request. When participants were of equal power, direct (hence face threatening) request forms were judged both more likely and more polite when the interactants had a close, as opposed to distant, relationship. Relative power influenced perceptions of politeness, but only when the relationship was distant. Overall, Holtgraves and Yang's results support the view that social relationship factors can influence perceptions of request politeness, although they also suggest that Brown and Levinson's (1987) additive model may need refinement.

The generality of politeness theory across different cultures has been demonstrated in anthropological (Baxter, 1984; Brown & Gilman, 1989; Smith-Hefner, 1988) as well as social psychological studies (Holtgraves & Yang, 1990, 1992). For example, Holtgraves and Yang used vignettes in which a speaker made a request to a target. They manipulated the power of the target over the speaker, the social distance between the target and the speaker, and the size of the request. American and Korean participants rated the likelihood that different politeness strategies would be used in these vignettes (Holtgraves & Yang, 1990) or indicated exactly what they would say to make the request (Holtgraves & Yang, 1992). Overall, the results validated the effect of power and size of imposition on politeness and provided mixed support for the distance variable. These findings provide some evidence for the linguistic universality of politeness theory: Although Americans and Koreans weighed power and distance differently in their politeness strategy usage patterns, politeness theory provided a valid explanation of strategy usage in both cultures.

Empirical studies of the predictions that Brown and Levinson's (1987) model makes about the perceived politeness of various speech acts have produced mixed results. Brown and Gilman (1989) examined the dialogue of Shakespeare's plays and found that politeness generally increased with the addressee's status and the extent to which a particular speech act threatened face. Social distance did not influence perceived politeness, but interpersonal affect did, in that speakers spoke more politely to addressees they liked than those they did not. Slugoski and Turnbull (1988) documented a similar effect of interpersonal affect in their examination of compliments and insults. Although politeness theory generally assumes that speakers' utterances are designed to maintain the face of their coparticipants, these authors point out that it is sometimes the case that a speaker intends an utterance to be insulting, critical, or scornful. The focus on face-saving rather than face-threatening behavior, they suggest, is due to Brown and Levinson's (1987) emphasis on interpersonal relationships that are either affectively positive or neutral. To the degree that people like each other, we might expect them to be more concerned with face saving and, hence, more polite. However, interactants who dislike each other are likely to have little concern with others' face maintenance and, indeed, may intentionally threaten it. Slugoski and Turnbull (1988) examined the role of liking and social distance on the perception of speakers' intentions using vignettes in which these two factors were varied orthogonally. Each vignette ended with a remark that was literally either a compliment or an insult. Participants first indicated what they thought the speaker meant by the utterance and then rated how insulting or complimentary the remark was, how well the two participants knew each other, and how much they liked each other. Interestingly, social distance did not affect the interpretation of insults; however, the affective tone of the relationship strongly influenced the literalness of the interpretation: Literal insults were more likely to be taken nonliterally when

the addressee was liked, whereas literal compliments were judged more likely to be intended nonliterally when the addressee was disliked. Slugoski and Turnbull propose that the affective relationship of speaker and addressee be added to Brown and Levinson's (1987) model; however, as they note, it is not clear that affect has a linear relationship to indirectness. For instance, some of the most face-threatening remarks are made within the context of family arguments (e.g., *When are you going to grow up and learn to be responsible, son?*; Vangelisti, Maguire, Alexander, & Clark, 2007).

Other scholars have called for more extensive revisions of Brown and Levinson's (1987) model in light of significant weaknesses that they have documented. Lim and Bowers (1991) provide evidence for three rather than two types of face desires (solidarity/positive regard, autonomy, and tact), each of which has its own set of mitigating linguistic devices. Dillard, Wilson, Tusing, and Kinney (1997) argued that the five politeness superstrategies are neither ordered in terms of perceived politeness nor are they mutually exclusive, contra Brown and Levinson's (1987) original formulation. They offer an alternative model for classifying requests based on three message features (the explicitness of the request, the dominance of the speaker over the hearer, and the argument or rationale the speaker offers for the request) and demonstrate its value in predicting perceived politeness. Schegloff (1988) observed that politeness theory assumes that the sequential context of utterances, not just adjacency, is necessary for message interpretation. This means that interaction unfolds based on the larger relational and conversational context rather than simply the conversational move that just occurred. Unfortunately, concerns about the conceptualization of face threat have limited its utility for explaining how request interactions unfold. Craig, Tracy, and Spisak (1986) noted that the theory fails to distinguish between face threats to the speaker and the addressee. The theory also assumes that a given speech act will threaten either positive or negative face (Wilson,

Aleman, & Leatham, 1998), although it is clear that a single message can create more than one type of face threat (Johnson, Roloff, & Riffee, 2004; McGlone & Batchelor, 2003) and may even support some face needs while threatening others (Cupach & Metts, 1994; Erbert & Floyd, 2004; McGlone, Beck, & Pfiester, 2006). In an attempt to address these sorts of concerns, Wilson et al. (1998) proposed a significant modification of Brown and Levinson's (1987) model. They proposed that requesters identify potential face threats based on constitutive rules for seeking compliance and specific influence goals. For example, a request inherently threatens an addressee's negative face, but the degree of threat and potential for other face threats differ depending on influence goals. Wilson et al. (1998) argue that (a) favor requesters perceive threats to their partner's negative and their own positive face, (b) those who enforce obligations expect threats to their partner's negative and positive face, and (c) advice providers anticipated threats to their own and their partner's positive face. In a similar vein, Wilson and Kunkel (2000) found that the justifications that requesters use differed depending on the type of face threat and influence goal.

Politeness theory has been a generative research tool for studying the interplay of linguistic, social, and cognitive processes involved in interpersonal interaction. It has been hampered, however, by a variety of methodological problems, not the least of which is its exclusive reliance on speech acts as the unit of analysis (Holtgraves, 2002). The idea that speech acts are useful categories of analysis for naturally occurring speech, discourse, and conversation has been seriously questioned (Geis, 1995; Jacobs & Jackson, 1983; Levinson, 1981; Schegloff, 1988). Critics charge that speech act categories are simply too rigid to capture the fluid context dependence of most conversational turns and that politeness unfolds over a set of moves, not on an utterance-by-utterance basis (Bavelas & Chovil, 1997; Ellis, 1992). Politeness and other complex dialogical phenomena are better served, these critics argue, by discourse analysis.

## Discourse: Conversation as a Joint Project

The term *discourse* refers to the extended activities that are carried out via language; as Clark (1994) puts it, discourse is "language use in the large" (p. 985). The term derives from the Latin word for dialogue (*discursus*, literally "running back or forth"), but in communication scholarship, it is used to describe any circumscribed set of linguistic utterances used for a coherent purpose. Some discourses are highly deliberate and planned (essays, lectures, letters, novels, film and play dialogue, etc.), but many are extemporaneous, including everyday conversations. Those of the latter type (our focus here) are not created by speakers acting autonomously but rather are the emergent products of speakers working as an ensemble to accomplish one or more goals together (Atkinson & Heritage, 1984; Clark & Clark, 1977; Sacks, Schegloff, & Jefferson, 1974).

To illustrate, consider the segment below (taken from Turnbull, 2003) of a face-to-face conversation between two young women whom we'll call (A)my and (B)elinda. In this transcription, the ∧ (caret) symbol signifies a rising intonation contour (usually indicative of a question); spaced periods and spaced dashes indicate short and long pauses, respectively; colons indicate stretched vowels; and adjacent pairs of phrases bounded by brackets indicate overlapping speech.

1. A: *oh yesterday I had road rage*
2. B: (laughs) *you did*
3. A: *yes this gu:y . this old man . this old fart was only going forty the who:le . [all the way]*
4. B: *[I hate that]*
5. A: *and I couldn't do anything about it . so I had road rage .*
6. B: *did you – act on your road rage* ∧
7. A: *[no]*
8. B: *[you] didn't like pull out a pistol or*

9. A: *no . though I was quite tempted –*

10. B: *I hate that that's so frustrating eh ∧*

11. A: *yes and I was late enough as it was I was coming home from voice lessons and that [sucker was]*

12. B: *[it's always] when you're late*

13. A: *oh I know it's always when you're late you get all the red lights . you always get that forty person in front of you*

14. B: *yup yup yup*

Amy initiated this exchange to accomplish one major goal—to share her driving experience from the previous day with Belinda. As simple and straightforward as the conversation may be, it nonetheless illustrates three elements that make a discourse what Clark (1996) calls a "joint project." The first is personnel, of which this discourse has two. The personnel change their participation roles—from speaker to addressee and vice versa—from one conversational turn to the next. When there are more than two personnel, participation roles proliferate. One distinction is between participants (or "ratified participants"; Goffman, 1976) and overhearers. Participants mutually believe that they are engaged in a joint action at the moment, whereas overhearers do not. Participants may be speakers, addressees, or side participants. Speakers direct their utterances to addressees in a conversational turn; side participants may step in as speakers or addressees in subsequent turns. Overhearers may be bystanders, who have access to what the speakers are saying and whose presence is fully recognized by the participants. Alternatively, they may be eavesdroppers, who have access to what speakers are saying but their presence is not fully recognized. For example, Amy's mother might eavesdrop on the women's conversation from another room.

Second, participants in the discourse exploit their common ground—that is, the sum of their mutual knowledge, beliefs, and assumptions—to achieve the goals of their joint project (Clark & Carlson, 1982). Their communal common ground represents all the knowledge, beliefs, and assumptions they take to be universally held in the community to which they mutually belong (Fussell & Krauss, 1992). By virtue of being both native Canadians and students at the University of British Columbia (UBC) in Vancouver, Amy and Belinda might mutually assume that the other is familiar with various aspects of Western Canada's culture, customs, and climate, as well as the location of familiar landmarks in the city (Canada Place, the Gas Town Steam Clock, etc.) and UBC campus (student union, library, etc.). Amy and Belinda also have a personal common ground representing all the mutual knowledge, beliefs, and assumptions they have inferred from personal experience with each other (Bangerter & Clark, 2003). Some of these experiences are perceptual. When Amy and Belinda view or hear something together—an event as simple as hearing thunder in the distance or as complex as watching a UBC Thunderbirds hockey home game—they can assume that event is part of their personal common ground. Other joint experiences are conversational, as when Amy relates to her friend her recent emotional experience (*Oh, yesterday I had road rage*) and the ostensible cause of this feeling (*This old fart was only going forty*).

Third, participants make contributions to the discourse that serve joint project goals. When the goal is sharing past experiences, adding to the common ground the participants share is a project goal in and of itself. For Amy to add the details of her road rage experience to her common ground with Belinda, the two must satisfy a "grounding criterion": They must reach the mutual belief that Belinda understands what Amy meant to a degree sufficient for their purposes. A contribution is what emerges from satisfaction of the grounding criterion (Clark & Krych, 2004; Clark & Wilkes-Gibbs, 1986). Contributions typically consist of presentation and acceptance phases. In the former, the speaker makes the utterance, and in the latter, the addressee offers "positive evidence" that she understood it adequately for the joint project;

if she believes that she didn't understand it, then she will offer "negative evidence," prompting the speaker to clarify (Schober, 2005). Positive evidence may come in the form of a back-channel response (Yngve, 1970), as when Belinda acknowledges understanding Amy's assertion in turn (1), *oh yesterday I had road rage*, with *you did*, in effect signaling Amy to proceed with her account. Other acknowledgments such as *yes, yeah, uh huh*, head nods, and smiles all may constitute back-channel responses as well. A second form of positive evidence is a relevant subsequent contribution (Clark, 1996), as when Belinda responds to Amy's assertion in turn (5), *so I had road rage*, with the question *did you – act on your road rage^*. Here, Belinda implicitly signals that she understands what road rage is sufficiently for Amy to move from a description of its cause (*this old fart was only going forty*) to its effect on her behavior (fortunately not pistol-drawing; horn-honking perhaps).

Conversations, like any joint project, require coordination. In particular, the participants must determine the transition points between conversation segments, which do not exist unless and until participants coordinate their contributions to make them happen. Participants accomplish this coordination locally, from turn to turn (Sacks et al., 1974). One common strategy for coordinating transitions extensively studied by conversation analysts is the "adjacency pair" (Schegloff, 1968). Adjacency pairs consist of a summons by one participant and a response to the summons by another. For example, in turn (8) of the "road rage" example, Belinda proposes that Amy describe how the road rage affected her behavior; in turn (9), Amy takes up the proposal by suggesting that she was tempted to do something drastic. Amy and Belinda use these two turns to agree on the content, participants, and roles of the joint action Belinda initiated (i.e., determining the consequences of Amy's road rage). They would have failed to reach that agreement if, for example, Amy had replied *What do you mean? I don't own a pistol* (thereby failing to coordinate content) or *Are you talking to me?*

(failing to coordinate participants). Besides exchanges of information, adjacency pairs are also used to coordinate greetings (e.g., summons: *Hello*/response: *Hi Mark. How's it going?*), good-byes (*Bye/See you later*), orders (*Be quiet/Yes ma'am*), offers (*You want fries with that?/Please*), and apologies (*Really sorry, man/No worries, dude*). They can also be used to set the stage for a new topic in the conversation sequence, a function known as pre-sequencing (Auer, 1984; Jefferson, 1975; Schegloff, 1988). Perhaps the most familiar variety of a pre-sequencing adjacency pair is the pre-question/response (*May I ask you a question?/Sure. What's up?*). Other varieties include the pre-invitation (*Are you free this afternoon?/I am. Why do you ask?*), the pre-narrative (*Have you seen Howie's new car?/I haven't. What kind did he get?*), and the pre-request (*Do you have Dos Equis?/Nope, just Bud and Bud Lite*). Each pre-sequence prepares the way for participants to engage in another joint action (a Q-and-A session, an invitation to get coffee, discussing a friend's new car, ordering a beer, etc.).

Conversations are coordinated, but they are also opportunistic in that the discursive paths participants take depend on the opportunities that become available within each joint action. For example, when one participant poses a pre-narrative question (e.g., *Have you seen Howie's new car?*) to another, an affirmative response (e.g., *I did. It's snazzy for a hybrid!*) will lead the discourse down a different path from a negative one (e.g., *I haven't. What kind did he get?*). Adjacency pairs are just one type of discourse marker people use to signal the opportunities they plan to take. Another common marker is *well*, a term speakers often use to signal a shift in spatial (e.g., *Well, if you make a right at the next light, it's just two doors down on the left*), temporal (e.g., *Well, when I was in grad school, no one was doing SEM*), or interpersonal (e.g., *Well, if I were you, I'd have a doctor take a look at that mole*) perspective (Cuenca, 2008; Schober, 1998). Other markers indicate conversation boundaries such as the start of a new topic (e.g., *so, then*), the start of a digression (*by the way, oh*), or return from a digression (*anyway, at any rate*) (Bolden, 2006; Fox Tree, 2000).

The structure of conversation emerges turn by turn as people coordinate each new action in their joint project. Participants coordinate the content and roles of each action in the project, relying on their common ground to achieve this coordination and adding to their personal common ground as actions are completed. New actions are initiated opportunistically and are heralded by adjacency pairs and other discourse markers. In this manner, conversations that are locally managed from moment to moment unfold to become the "language in the large" we recognize as discourse (Clark, 1996; Sacks et al., 1974). In contemplating the commonalities of conversational structure, however, it is important that we not lose sight of the fact that all conversations are unique. What makes any conversation distinctive is its interpersonal mix, consisting of participants who may have considerable communal and even personal common ground but are nonetheless individuals with different dispositional (sex, ethnicity, socioeconomic status [SES], etc.) and situational (emotional state, familiarity with other participants, interest in the conversation topic, etc.) profiles. Politeness theory and the study of discourse structure tell us how participants generally maintain a civil and coherent conversation, but they offer little insight into how people convey their individual and group identities through language use, which in turn have a profound impact on their interpersonal interactions. We turn from conversational facework and ensemble work to "identity work" in subsequent sections.

## Language Attitudes

How people talk conveys a great deal about who they are. This is true even if we discount the specific words they are saying. Some voice qualities reflect the structure and condition of the vocal tract and provide information about the speaker's age, sex, and size (Cohen, Crystal, House, &

Neuberg, 1980; Gradol & Swann, 1983; Lass & Davis, 1976; Lass, Hughes, Bowyer, Waters, & Bourne, 1976). Others reflect a speaker's emotional states (e.g., anxiety; Cosmides, 1983), and hearers can identify these states from voice cues with reasonable accuracy (e.g., Krauss, Apple, Morency, Wenzel, & Winton, 1981). Still others reflect the geographical and social background of the speaker. Speakers learn the language and dialect of the community in which they were raised, and there are relatively stable vocal qualities associated with regional and intraregional status dialects that in turn may be associated with SES, ethnicity, and other social characteristics (Scherer & Giles, 1979). Thus, it might be said that speakers' identities are encoded in their voices. And people hearing their speech can, without training, do a remarkable job of decoding this identifying information. For example, Ellis (1967) asked undergraduates to judge speakers' SES after listening to recordings of them reading a standard passage. The correlation between judged and actual SES (as measured by the Index of Status Characteristics) was +0.80. Even when the speech samples consisted merely of people counting from 1 to 10, the correlation between judged and actual SES was +0.65.

There is abundant evidence that people not only recognize social variation in speech (i.e., accents, dialects, and styles) but also form impressions of and attitudes toward others based on these variations (Scherer & Giles, 1979). The study of "language attitudes" has been an active area of sociolinguistic inquiry since the 1960s. Although a variety of methods (ethnographies, surveys, policy analyses, etc.; for a review, see Giles & Marlow, in press) have been used to study language attitudes, the most popular has been the matched-guise technique developed by Lambert, Hodgson, Gardner, and Fillenbaum (1960). The studies employing this technique present the listeners with audiorecordings of prose passages read by bilingual and bidialectal individuals who can authentically adopt various guises of the language varieties under study. By using the same speaker to evoke these guises, prosodic, paralinguistic, and other extraneous variables (e.g., affect) that differ across speakers are held constant, and researchers are thereby able to attribute response differences chiefly to the guises being compared. Listeners typically rate the recorded speakers on a variety of subjective attributes (confidence, intelligence, kindness, etc.) found to represent the multidimensionality of raters' trait schemas (Cuddy, Fiske, & Glick, 2008; Mulac, Hanley, & Prigge, 1974; Zahn & Hopper, 1985).

In their initial study of the phenomenon, Lambert et al. (1960) compared the evaluative reactions of undergraduates in Montreal to English and French versions of a short philosophical passage read by four bilingual speakers. Each listener heard all eight recordings but was not told that he or she would hear each voice twice; in addition, the recordings were presented in an order that maximized the interval between successive presentations of the English and French guises of each speaker. Under these circumstances, the listeners believed that they were hearing eight different speakers. The listeners rated each of the recordings on scales reflecting a variety of speaker personality and physical traits. Results indicated that the listeners, who themselves were bilingual, assigned higher ratings overall to speakers' English guises than their French guises, regardless of whether their own primary language was English or French. That even the native French speakers accorded more negative attributions to French than English guises suggests a sense of "linguistic insecurity" among this group. Lambert et al. attribute the English advantage to the higher representation of English speakers in positions of social and economic power in Montreal. Consistent with this claim, they found that when listeners were asked to guess the occupations of the speakers, they assigned higher status jobs to English than to French guises (e.g., lawyer vs. store employee). In a second study, Lambert, Anisfeld, and Yeni-Komshian (1965) had Jewish and Arab adolescents in Israel listen to passages recorded by bilingual and bidialectical speakers in Arabic and two Hebrew dialects (Ashkenazic and Yemenite). The Jewish respondents generally rated the Jewish guises more positively than the Arab guises, and the Arab respondents rated the Arab guises more positively than Jewish guises, indicating a general pattern of in-group favoritism (Tajfel, 1981). Interestingly, when the Jewish respondents completed measures assessing their general attitudes toward the Jewish and Arab groups under study, these measures did not correlate well with their ratings of the spoken passages; thus, it appears that different types of attitudes were assessed by the general and language attitude measures and that respondents had relatively little awareness that their ratings of the guises revealed anything about their attitudes toward the groups these guises represented.

Over the years, research using the matched-guise technique and other elicitation procedures has demonstrated several robust tendencies in the way people form and report language attitudes. First, listeners readily form and assert language attitudes after minimal exposure to the speech varieties being compared, suggesting that these attitudes derive from schemas about the relationships among language, dialect, ethnicity, and social class acquired relatively early in life (Bradac & Giles, 1991; Floccia, Butler, Girard, & Goslin, 2009; Giles & Niedzielski, 1998; Labov, 1976). Nazzi, Jusczyk, and Johnson (2000) observed that children as young as five months old are already sensitive to dialectical variations; by the age of five, accents are as potent in children's social appraisals as sex and skin color (Kinzler, Dupoux, & Spelke, 2007). Second, the research generally indicates that standard language varieties (British Received Pronunciation, Castilian Spanish, General American English, etc.) are evaluated more favorably than nonstandard ones associated with lower SES strata, such as regional accents (e.g., Southern American English), social group accents (African American Vernacular English), or nonnative accents (Giles & Billings, 2004; Giles & Edwards, 2010; Gluszek & Dvidio, 2010). Speakers of nonstandard varieties are not only perceived to be at a disadvantage in terms of traits such as competence (intelligence, confidence, etc.) and dynamism (enthusiastic, lively, etc.; e.g., Lippi-Green, 1997) but are also judged to be less comprehensible (Giles, 1973), less persuasive (Giles, Williams, Mackie, & Rosselli, 1995), less suitable for employment in high-status jobs (Giles, Wilson, & Conway, 1981), less effective as teachers (Gill, 1994), and more likely to be guilty when under suspicion of committing a crime (Dixon & Mahoney, 2004) than standard variety speakers. On the other hand, those who speak nonstandard varieties are often seen as more friendly (Luhman, 1990), and male non-standard speakers are perceived as more masculine (Giles & Marsh, 1979) and more competent at manual labor (Giles, Henwood, Coupland, Harriman, & Coupland, 1992). Third, speech evaluations are moderated by the verbal (e.g., the subject of the stimulus passage) and social (e.g., the prestige of the speaker) context in which they occur (Giles & Johnson, 1986; Ryan & Carranza, 1975). Finally, speakers may be evaluated on a range of speech characteristics other than language or dialect, including fluency, lexical diversity, pitch, pausing, powerful/powerless speech, and self-disclosure (Bradac, 1990).

Various models have been proposed over the years for describing the process by which language attitudes are derived and generate behavioral outcomes (for a review, see Giles & Edwards, 2010). Each model has its distinctive features, but all generally afford significant roles to the context (e.g., the sociocultural milieu, the immediate setting) in which evaluations are made and the characteristics of the speakers (e.g., the accent strength) and hearers (e.g., stereotype ideation) involved and posit an interplay of cognitive processes (e.g., social categorization) and affective states (e.g., fear) that ultimately determines the behavioral outcomes (e.g., avoidance/aggressive reactions). Current thinking among language attitudes theorists also attributes a significant mediational role to sensemaking—that is, the ways in which people comprehend and construe their interactions and relationships with others (e.g., Dillard, Solomon, & Palmer, 1999). In their integrative model of language attitudes, Giles and Marlow (in press) argue that attributions of speaker motivation (e.g., *She's trying to help me* vs. *She's just criticizing me*) and other sensemaking processes influence not only the immediate formulation of language attitudes but also the manner in which listeners subsequently communicate with the speaker and the speaker replies thereafter, and so on. As these theorists note, research in this area has not traditionally entertained the idea that language attitudes are collaboratively constructed, as opposed to being responses to a static stimulus elicited in a social vacuum. But the way people speak is not static. Just as there can be social variation in language (i.e., linguistic differences between people), there is also stylistic variation (linguistic differences within a person). Speakers may vary numerous properties of their speech (pronunciation, speech rate, volume, etc.) and, if bilingual or bidialectical, may switch language varieties altogether. The interpersonal circumstances under which stylistic variation occurs are the subject of another important area of linguistic inquiry known as communication accommodation.

## Communication Accommodation

Since scholars began studying social aspects of language, one of the fundamental edicts arising was that many of a speaker's language forms are a function of the social context in which it is spoken (see Fishman, 1971). For instance, Labov (2006) showed, in 1966, that as the formality of a situation increased—from conversing about a colloquial topic to reading isolated words—New Yorkers' pronunciations took on more prestigious patterns. Speech accommodation theory (now communication accommodation theory [CAT]) emerged some 40 years ago as an attempt to give the much needed theoretical bite to that and related phenomena. Indeed, given that Labov orchestrated the very contexts in which language was elicited from his informants, Giles (1973) argued that these seminal findings might have been due to his interviewees' accommodating (or being influenced by) this commanding researcher's own changes in speech style and thereby meeting the very demands of the settings he changed for them; after all, was Labov himself contextually immune?

CAT is a framework for explaining why people adapt their communication toward and away from others, and it also explores the social consequences of doing so (see Giles, Coupland, & Coupland, 1991; Giles & Ogay, 2006). Although other useful theories have emerged over the years (for a comparison, see Shepard, Giles, & Le Poire, 2001), they have not had the interpretive depth to provide explanations for language adaptations in both micro- and macrosocietal settings or for the attributional, evaluative, and behavioral consequences of being the recipient of various accommodative moves. As such, it has been an ingredient in the mainstay diet of communication theory texts over the years (e.g., Baxter & Braithwaite, 2008; Littlejohn, 2002) as well as being featured prominently in other disciplines such as sociolinguistics (e.g., Coupland & Jaworski, 2009). Indeed, Griffin (2009, chap. 30) argued that CAT "has morphed into a communication theory of enormous scope . . . [it] . . . can be beneficially applied to any situation where people from different groups or cultures come into contact" (pp. 397–398).

Spawning, then, a robust empirical literature across many very different languages and cultures, modes of communication (e.g., conversations, voice mail, electronic) and its variable dynamics (e.g., verbal, nonverbal, and discursive), diverse qualitative and quantitative methodologies, and applied social contexts (e.g., health, organizational, intercultural), CAT has been revised and elaborated in propositional terms a number of times (e.g., Giles, Mulac, Bradac, & Johnson, 1987; Street & Giles, 1982) in ways that can be historically conceptualized—and uniquely so herein—as five developmental phases (for a detailed history of CAT, see Gallois, Ogay, & Giles, 2005).

The first "foundational phase" derived from Giles observing people (as well as himself) shifting their dialects—and bilinguals switching their languages—on a regular basis (see Giles, Taylor, & Bourhis, 1973). Speakers often shift toward higher and sometimes even lower status accents, moves called "upward" and "downward" *convergence*, respectively. Subsequently, recipients might, or might not, reciprocate these shifts to varying degrees, the latter sometimes steadfastly maintaining their linguistic integrity; these phenomena are called "symmetrical" and "asymmetrical convergence," respectively (see Gallois & Giles, 1998). The driving force behind such adjustments is similarity attraction principles that suggested that decreasing the social distance between interactants promotes mutual liking; this has been confirmed by research as well (see Giles et al., 1991). CAT proposes that the more you affiliate with or wish to gain the respect of an influential other, the more you converge toward that other; relative social power, thereby, became integral to the theory. As such, it was invoked in the language and gender literature to explain why females accommodated their language and nonverbal styles to males rather than the other way around (Mulac, Wiemann, Widenmann, & Gibson, 1988).

Someone, however, *not* converging toward another could signal the attribution that this person does not value the approval or respect of the other. Predictably, nonconvergence would be unfavorably evaluated by recipients, assuming that they were not attributed with the communicative repertoire to accomplish this (see Simard, Taylor, & Giles, 1976). Subsequently, CAT addressed notions of optimal magnitudes and rates of convergence in that social costs could be incurred by completely converging toward the communicative style of another (e.g., deliberately mimicking them in a potentially patronizing manner), and also doing this too swiftly (Giles & Smith, 1979).

While other motives for it have been discussed, the second, "intergroup/contextual phase" focused on *divergence* as a form of social differentiation, drawing on social identity theory (see Giles, 1978; Giles, Bourhis, & Taylor, 1977; see also many of the chapters in Harwood &

Giles, 2005). In interethnic situations, for example, diverging speakers are those who accentuate their in-group language style, do so when they construe their social category membership as situationally salient, and feel their group is accorded an illegitimately low status (Giles & Johnson, 1987). An example would be an African American adopting more Black Vernacular English when encountering an aloof (and possibly prejudicial) white speaker. The larger scale social conditions necessary to trigger communicative differentiations (e.g., a high group vitality) led to the development of ethnolinguistic identity theory (Giles & Johnson, 1981)—which, in turn, inspired the intergroup model of second-language acquisition (Giles & Byrne, 1982). The latter framework had theoretical appeal as it construed the learning of a second (or foreign) language to varying degrees of native-like proficiency as being an accommodative move. Interestingly, it framed so-called failure or even a cognitive inability to learn the language of a host, dominant culture in more "positive, healthy" terms as nonaccommodative in that it heralded a desire not to assimilate and lose a unique way of communicating but, tenaciously and successfully, to preserve and maintain, say, an immigrant group's culture (for a more recent analysis of acculturation and language use in CAT terms, see Giles, Bonilla, & Speer, in press).

Clearly, such a perspective could contribute to language-planning policies and intergroup contact programs and in educating people about how to speak a second language effectively and also in fostering dominant groups' tolerance of comparative cultures they found thriving, increasing in group vitality, and even threatening. Ultimately, satellite models in other intergroup contexts emerged, such as language use between speakers of different age groups (Williams & Nussbaum, 2001), among people with different physical abilities (Fox, Giles, Orne, & Bourhis, 2000), and in police–civilian interactions (for an accommodative model of racial profiling between white officers and civilians of color, see Giles, Choi, & Dixon, 2010). In all these cases, theoretical attention was afforded to how and why *nonac*commodative language forms were fundamental to understanding when individuals define an interaction more in intergroup than in interpersonal terms (i.e., when I engage Janine as a celebrated professor vs. chatting with her as a close friend)—and the communicative implications of this (see Giles, Reid, & Harwood, 2010).

A particularly accommodative variant of the foregoing is the so-called communicative-predicament-of-aging model (Ryan, Giles, Bartolucci, & Henwood, 1986), which has been influential in communication and aging research. This theory posits that young people tend to overaccommodate their elders by means of patronizing talk that those socially and cognitively alert find demeaning, whereas older folk tend to underaccommodate younger people by talking excessively about their own problems (see Giles & Gasiorek, 2010). Not only can these accommodative mis-moves lead to intergenerational dissatisfaction and avoidance, but they can, for older people, contribute to the social (and communicative) constructions of aging, fermenting lowered self-worth, depleting life satisfaction, and even accelerating demise (Giles, 1999). Indeed, cross-cultural research—even across Asia—has tended (albeit with caveats) to support such a model (e.g., Ota, Giles, & Somera, 2007).

The third, and relatively more cognitive, development can be termed a *subjectivist phase* that saw CAT embrace a quite complex propositional structure aimed at comprehensively elucidating both the antecedent conditions under which accommodative/nonaccommodative acts surfaced as well as the social consequences arising from them. It also resulted in a schematic model of the interactional processes involved in accommodative moves (for the most recent formulation, see Giles, Willemyns, Gallois, & Anderson, 2007). The prime insight here was that speakers accommodate not to where others *are* in any objectively measurable sense but rather to where they are *believed* (or biasedly heard) to be communicatively (Thakerar, Giles, & Cheshire, 1982). An example would be slowing down one's speech rate for an elderly person who is stereotyped as somewhat incompetent (and erroneously so) simply because of his advanced age. In parallel and drawing on self-categorization theory (Turner, Hogg, Oakes, Reicher, & Wetherell, 1987), people sometimes diverge from a contrastive out-group member and toward the linguistic *prototype* of what they construe as being a typical-sounding in-group member (see Gallois & Callan, 1988). Speakers have, of course, widely different prototypes of what, say, a *true* "American" should sound like, and hence, their divergences will vary accordingly. Indeed, miscarried convergences and divergences—albeit with positive intent—are very potent forms of miscommunication (see Platt & Weber, 1984).

The fourth "communicative breadth" phase (see Coupland, Coupland, Giles, & Henwood, 1988; Giles & Wadleigh, 2008) saw CAT really blossom as a general theory in its moving beyond the adaptive use of accents, slangs, and languages to embracing different discourse styles and nonverbal practices (e.g., gait and dress styles). Convergence and divergence were conceived of as but a *couple* of the many ways in which people accommodate or not (called "approximation strategies"). Attention now was also paid to "interpretability strategies," where communicators took into account the shared knowledge each had on the conversational topic on hand as well as their communicative needs and relative social statuses (called "discourse management" and "interpersonal control strategies" respectively). These developments led to an acknowledgment of speakers being able to blend convergence and divergence *simultaneously,* but at different communicative levels, to fulfill complementary identity and social needs. In this sense, a speaker may diverge from another not only to maintain his status position but also to facilitate the message's intent and directives by simplifying grammar and avoiding jargon terms, thereby directly drawing on the listener's presumed and, in this case, limited knowledge base (see grounding theory in Clark & Krych, 2004).

The last set of CAT advances to date suggests a "mediating mechanism phase." Admittedly,

and as alluded to above, prior attention had been paid to how attribution processes intervene in evaluating accommodative/nonaccommodative others (e.g., an American sojourner's inability to speak or even pronounce the Welsh language could diminish any negative reactions associated with nonconvergence by Welsh people). Building on this, theory is being directed toward how accommodations socially trigger varying emotions such as irritation, pride, and joy—which, in turn, dictate evaluative and behavioral reactions from others. For instance, studies across many cultures have shown that expressed willingness to comply with the demands of police officers is not determined directly by how accommodative you find them but, rather, more indirectly by how this instills trust in officers, which itself then facilitates compliance (e.g., Barker et al., 2008). Similarly, it has been shown that an officer's nonaccommodative stance toward a civilian does not directly trigger negative evaluations of his competence but rather is mediated by the negative affect (e.g., frustration and anger) that it instills (Myers, Giles, Reid, & Nabi, 2008). At the present time (see Giles et al., 2007), CAT principles are devised in terms of accommodation and nonaccommodation that have direct effects. An exciting challenge for the future is to invest more empirical energy and theoretical ingenuity into charting the ways in which accommodation is moderated and mediated.

These five CAT phases are not mutually exclusive or successively contained developments. Instead, they are interdependent, and refinements can be seen as evolving in all of them currently. For instance, CAT has recently been drawn on to account for the language of electronic communications, such as in e-mail, text messages, and voice mail (e.g., Buzzanell, Burrell, Stafford, & Berkowitz, 1996; Herring & Paolillo, 2006), and it has also been invoked to understand family communication processes (see Harwood, Soliz, & Lin, 2006)—that is, outgrowths of the second and fourth phases, respectively. Besides the prospective challenges already aired, among the likely others holding promise are the following: (a) contextually determining which language and nonverbal features relative to potential others are implicated in accommodative/nonaccommodative moves; (b) exploring the role of intent (attributed and actual) and automatic processes in accommodative practices; (c) analytically linking up with the growing number of studies in social psychology on mimicry and the chameleon effect (for an overview, see Chartrand & van Baaren, 2009) that seem to be very closely underpinned by CAT principles; (d) developing a deeper theoretical understanding of *under*accommodative strategies, which seem, reportedly, to greatly outnumber, and are more negatively evaluated than, their overaccommodative counterparts (Gasiorek, 2010); and (e) investigating when accommodation can reflexively create, sustain, and redefine larger social realities, such as identities, relational goals, and family coherence and satisfaction.

## Language in Relational Communication

The interdependence between people that constitutes a personal or social relationship derives in significant ways from their language use (Cappella, 1988; Duck & Pittman, 1993). Moreover, the context of conversation, in which participants must coordinate their roles and contributions to the "joint project" of discourse moment by moment (Clark, 1996), is a window through which this interdependence can be richly observed. Relationship partners may work together to relate a joint account of a common experience or be at odds by imposing abrupt topic changes on one another. Certain words or phrases they use may seem innocuous or banal to outsiders, but for the partners themselves they serve as idioms for discretely discussing confidential, intimate, and/or touchy subjects (Bell & Healey, 1992). One partner may presume to speak for another when discussing certain topics with a third party, while other topics seem to render both partners at a loss for words. These and other discourse events

suggest a specialized set of interaction rules and codes for relational communication (Sillars, Shellen, McIntosh, & Pomegranate, 1997; Watzlawick, Beavin, & Jackson, 1967).

Relationships affect language use. To be more precise, various language forms have been shown to indicate speakers' beliefs about their relationship status with others and also their evaluations of relational dynamics. Considered together, speakers' relational beliefs and evaluations constitute a significant component of their attitude toward a relationship (Fishbein & Ajzen, 1975). The language forms that convey these beliefs and evaluations may be explicit or implicit. The most common explicit form for encoding relational beliefs is the relational label. There are two general types of relational labels: (1) kinship terms (*mother, sister, uncle*, etc.), with rigid meanings in a closed semantic system of familial relations (Pasternak, Ember, & Ember, 1997), and (2) "kithship" terms, which label "fuzzy-set" relationship categories (*friend, girlfriend, homie*, etc.) without precise definitions (Rosch & Mervis, 1975). These labels encode more than mere role expectations for members in the relationship. For example, Knapp, Ellis, and Williams (1980) found that terms denoting sexual relationships (*mate, spouse, lover*) and terms denoting relationships in the nuclear family (*mother, daughter, sister*) were rated higher in intimacy than terms such as *neighbor, associate*, and *colleague*. Other relational labels clearly and primarily denote differences in power as well as role (*employee* vs. *boss, student* vs. *teacher, apprentice* vs. *master*), although such labels may imply degrees of intimacy as well (Ellis, 1992). Explicit evaluations (e.g., *We have a strong friendship*) also appear in relational discourse, but their incidence and composition are limited by two factors. First, there is a limited lexicon for relational talk, in contrast to the numerous terms available for describing individual moods, states, and traits (Berger & Bradac, 1982). As a result, relational evaluations commonly include more references to the traits and states of the individual partners than to those of the relationship itself

(Pennebaker, Mehl, & Niederhoffer, 2003). Second, there appears to be a widespread norm prohibiting the communication of explicit evaluations among mere acquaintances; as Bradac (1983) observed, "acquaintances evaluate the performance of the local baseball team instead of evaluating each other" (p. 149). There is some evidence that the willingness to exchange relational evaluations increases with relational intimacy (Altman & Taylor, 1973). Thus, friends and lovers should be more likely to explicitly evaluate one another than acquaintances. In the case of family relationships, however, parents typically have more freedom to voice explicit evaluations of their children than vice versa, an asymmetry reflecting power differences in family systems (Knapp & Vangelisti, 2004).

Speakers also "leak" relational beliefs and evaluations in implicit language forms. This leakage may occur when speakers are talking about their relationships or when they are discussing nonrelational matters with relationship partners. In their articulation of the "interactional" view of interpersonal communication, Watzlawick et al. (1967) drew a distinction between the explicit, literal meaning of a discourse message and an implicit meaning that often reflects relational dynamics (Bell & Healey, 1992; Danziger, 1976; Sillars et al., 1997; Wilmot & Shellen, 1990). Interpersonal scholars have since identified a variety of linguistic devices that encode these implicit meanings. First, certain lexical and syntactic forms provide information about a speaker's position of power in a relationship (O'Barr, 1982). In particular, hedges (e.g., *I guess*), tag questions (e.g., *That's the place, isn't it?*), vocalized pauses (e.g., *um*), and filler expressions (e.g., *like*) are associated with low power; high-power speech is characterized largely by the absence of these markers (Areni & Sparks, 2005; Bradac & Mulac, 1984; Ng & Bradac, 1993). Second, linguistic immediacy (Wiener & Mehrabian, 1968) and intensity (Bowers, 1963, 2006) signal a speaker's affective orientation toward a relational partner or topic that comes up in conversation with a partner. Low immediacy, in the form of low referential

specificity (e.g., *that person*) or probability (e.g., *I may talk with him later*), is generally indicative of more negative evaluations than high-immediacy cues such as specific reference (e.g., *my boss*) or high-probability language (e.g., *I will talk with him later*). In contrast, language intensity varies with the strength of the speaker's evaluation regardless of its valence. With more extreme evaluations, speakers become increasingly likely to use intensifying modifiers (e.g., *very, extremely*) and metaphorical language about affectively charged topics such as sex and death (Bowers, 1963). Thus, when hearing a speaker use highly immediate and intense language to describe a relational partner, a reasonable inference would be that the speaker is positively disposed; but a speaker who uses language of low immediacy but comparable intensity to describe a partner may be more likely to have a negative evaluation (McEwen & Greenberg, 1970).

Another ostensibly implicit language form that has received significant attention in recent years is pronoun usage. Some researchers have argued that first-person plural pronouns (*we, us, our*) are markers of shared identity, affiliation, and interdependence (e.g., Ellis, 1992). Consistent with this claim, studies have shown that people increase their use of first-person plural pronouns after a large-scale collective trauma (Stone & Pennebaker, 2002) or after a home football team victory (Cialdini et al., 1976). Highly committed partners use *we* pronouns more frequently when writing about their romantic relationship than do less committed ones (Agnew, Van Lange, Rusbult, & Langston, 1998). However, in the small group of studies that have examined language use during interactions between romantic partners, *we* use frequency has shown no association with relationship satisfaction (Ellis & Hamilton, 1985; Fitzpatrick, 1988; Sillars et al., 1997; Simmons Gordon, & Chambless, 2005; Williams-Baucom, Atkins, Sevier, Eldridge, & Christensen, 2010) and only a marginal association with relational interdependence (Knobloch & Solomon, 2003). Findings regarding the use of first-person-singular pronouns (*I, me, my*) have also been mixed. Sillars et al. (1997) found that couples who used fewer first-person-singular pronouns tended to have higher relationship satisfaction than those who used them more frequently. However, Simmons et al. (2005) found *I* use to be marginally positively associated with relationship satisfaction and *me* to be positively associated with negative behaviors during problem-solving discussions. Use of *I*, these researchers argue, reflects self-disclosure and perspective taking, whereas use of *me* reflects feelings of passivity and victimization, which are characteristic of less satisfying relationships. In a subsequent investigation of marital problem-solving discussions, Williams-Baucom et al. (2010) found the association between *I* use and relationship satisfaction to be moderated by marital distress: *I* use among distressed couples was positive associated with relationship satisfaction (consistent with Simmons et al., 2005), but among nondistressed couples, it was negatively associated with relationship satisfaction (consistent with Sillars et al., 1997), suggesting that the pronoun's function may reflect different thought patterns (autonomy among the former and insecurity among the latter, perhaps) in these different groups. Finally, usage of second-person pronouns (*you, your*) by couples in problem-solving discussions has been shown to be negatively correlated with relationship satisfaction (Sillars et al., 1997) and positively correlated with negative relationship behaviors (Simmons et al., 2005; Williams-Baucom et al., 2010), a pattern that may reflect excessive other-focused attention (Ickes, Reidhead, & Patterson, 1986).

Language use does not merely reflect relational dynamics but also affects them in significant ways. One impact derives from using language to communicate relational beliefs and evaluations, either explicitly or implicitly: When one partner conveys them to the other, the receiving partner may create corresponding beliefs and evaluations. And given the numerous relational themes that partners encode in their messages to one another, this impact can be significant. In their magisterial analysis of the topoi

(i.e., general themes) of relational communication, Burgoon and Hale (1984) report evidence for as many as 12 distinct relational message dimensions, including dominance versus submission, emotional arousal versus nonarousal, task versus social orientation, and intimacy versus nonintimacy. The dominance-versus-submission theme has received the most attention in the interpersonal communication literature and will be our focus here. Reid and Ng's (1999) influential framework for investigating dominance or "control" messages in communication purports that language serves three distinct control functions. One is reflecting and creating control. Language use can reflect interpersonal power differentials that arise from role relationships (boss vs. employee, parent vs. child, teacher vs. student, etc.), in the form of the powerful-versus-powerless speech styles discussed earlier (Bradac & Mulac, 1984). These speech styles not only reflect power differences but can also create them. Thus, Holtgraves and Lasky (1999) found that when speakers use a powerless style they are less persuasive than when they use a powerful style; speakers who use powerless styles are also perceived as less competent and credible than powerful speakers (Newcombe & Arnkoff, 1979).

A second control function of language is to conceal or "depoliticize" control so that it is less obvious as an attempt to impose interpersonal influence. One common concealment strategy is agency manipulation, in which the speaker casts a contentious action (e.g., a boss decides not to grant a raise to his employee) in terms that omit (e.g., *It was decided not to give you a raise*) or deceptively distribute (e.g., *We decided not to give you a raise*) the agency for this action (Fowler, Hodge, Kress, & Trew, 1979; McGlone & Pfiester, 2009). Another strategy, common in managerial discourse, is the use of family (e.g., *parent company*) and sports (e.g., *sales team*) metaphors to frame administrative decisions in an effort to promote or preserve employee loyalty and trust (McGlone et al., 2007). A third (and related) language control function is to routinize control by making power differentials seem natural, or at least customary. Nominalization is a particularly subtle yet effective device used for this purpose (McGlone, 2010; Ng & Bradac, 1993). Speakers nominalize the description of a control attempt to transform it from a control action conducted by one or more individuals (e.g., *I will assign a failing grade to any student who is absent for three or more classes*) into a routine event or regulation with no named participants (*Three or more class absences will result in automatic failure*). Another form of control routinization in multilingual settings is the use of the dominant group's language as a default tongue for intergroup interactions (Noels, Giles, & Le Poire, 2003). A variety of other language control devices are reviewed by Giles and Wiemann (1987).

In sum, language is both a dependent and an independent variable in relational communication (Giles & Hewstone, 1982), in that it can be an index of relationship status as well as an instrument of control. In serving both of these functions, it constitutes a window through which interpersonal scholars can observe the dynamics of relational interdependence (Duck, Pond, & Hendrick, 1989; Sillars et al., 1997; Wilmot & Shellen, 1990). Bradac (1983) even suggested that relationships can be conceived of as chiefly language games that change as language changes. However, most interpersonal scholars (Bradac included) are inclined to view relational ideation and language use patterns as distinct phenomena that are intimately connected and may exert mutual influence in certain ways and contexts.

## Conclusion

We began this chapter with Arnauld and Lancelot's (1660) eloquent passage celebrating the "marvelous invention" of language and have subsequently documented a selected set of the marvels illuminated by linguistic communication research. As deserving as language is of lavish praise, however, a couple of major mistakes in the famed grammarians' homage must be acknowledged. First, language was not invented. Such a versatile communication medium may seem the masterwork of a great inventor, but language has developed through natural forces that are changing its complex structure all the time, even today (Bickerton, 2009). Behind these forces have always been people, of course. Nevertheless, language change is, like a beaten path or a traffic jam, something that is brought about by people's actions but not purposefully created by them (Crystal, 2007). Changes in language do not derive from linguists' concern with its overall design but rather emerge piecemeal from laypeople's local and immediate concerns, such as keeping a conversation on track, preserving decorum in social interaction, and maintaining control in relationships. Moreover, one need not be an Edison to be a linguistic innovator. Any competent language user regularly produces utterances that have never been uttered before and typically without thinking twice about it. Not all (or even many) of these new linguistic permutations pioneer novel forms of expression, and the ones that do are more likely to be taken for granted than celebrated. In this respect, the illusory ease with which language advances obscures the interpersonal mechanisms of its advancement (Scott-Phillips, 2007).

Second, the idea that linguistic communication is achieved by one party encoding thoughts into sounds (or text) and another decoding these signals is not a fact, but a hypothesis, albeit one so ingrained in Western thought that it is hard to contemplate it as merely conjecture (Sperber & Wilson, 1986). The main merit of the hypothesis is that it accurately describes the outcome, in that utterances do succeed in conveying thoughts (Littlejohn, 2002). However, its principal defect is that it is mediationally inadequate, because it ignores the intervening variables between encoding and decoding that enable language to perform meaningful action in the social world. These intervening, interpersonal factors have been the subject of this chapter: the language–thought interface, speech acts and the cooperative principle, facework and politeness, conversational common ground and coordination activities, language attitudes, communication accommodation strategies, and the nature of the relationship between interlocutors. Research exploring these factors has both refined our understanding of language's critical role in interpersonal communication and advanced our appreciation of how the interpersonal context stimulates language's adaptive and generative character.

# References

Agnew, C. R., Van Lange, P. A. M., Rusbult, C. E., & Langston, C. A. (1998). Cognitive interdependence: Commitment and the mental representation of close relationships. *Journal of Personality and Social Psychology, 74,* 939–954.

Alter, A. L., & Oppenheimer, D. M. (2008). Easy on the mind, easy on the wallet: Effects of fluency on valuation judgments. *Psychonomic Bulletin and Review, 15,* 985–990.

Altman, I., & Taylor, D. (1973). *Social penetration: The development of interpersonal relationships.* New York: Holt, Rinehart & Winston.

Areni, C. S., & Sparks, J. R. (2005). Language power and persuasion. *Psychology and Marketing, 22,* 507–525.

Arnauld, A., & Lancelot, C. (1660). *Grammaire generale et raisonnee, ou la grammaire de Port-Royal. Reimpression des editions de Paris, 1660 et 1662.* [General and rational grammar, or grammar of Port Royal. Reprint of the Paris editions, 1660 and 1662.] Geneva, Switzerland: Slatkinem.

Atkinson, J. M., & Heritage, J. (1984). *Structures of social action: Studies in conversational analysis.* Cambridge, UK: Cambridge University Press.

Auer, J. C. P. (1984). Referential problems in conversation. *Journal of Pragmatics, 8,* 627–648.

Austin, J. L. (1962). *How to do things with words.* Oxford, UK: Clarendon Press.

Bach, K., & Harnish, R. (1979). *Linguistic communication and speech acts.* Cambridge: MIT Press.

Bakan, D. (1966). *The duality of human existence.* Chicago: Rand McNally.

Bangerter, A., & Clark, H. H. (2003). Navigating joint projects with dialogue. *Cognitive Science, 27,* 195–225.

Barker, V., Giles, H., Hajek, C., Ota, H., Noels, K., Lim, T-S., et al. (2008). Police-civilian interaction, compliance, accommodation, and trust in an intergroup context: International data. *Journal of International and Intercultural Communication, 1,* 93–112.

Bavelas, J. B., Black, A., Bryson, L., & Mullett, J. (1988). Political equivocation: A situational explanation. *Journal of Language and Social Psychology, 7,* 137–145.

Bavelas, J. B., & Chovil, N. (1997). Faces in dialogue. In J. A. Russell & J. M. Fernandez-Dols (Eds.), *The psychology of facial expression* (pp. 334–346). Cambridge, UK: Cambridge University Press.

Baxter, L. A. (1984). Compliance-gaining as politeness. *Human Communication Research, 10,* 427–456.

Baxter, L. A., & Braithwaite, D. O. (2008). *Engaging theories in interpersonal communication: Multiple perspectives.* Thousand Oaks, CA: Sage.

Bell, R. A., & Healey, J. G. (1992). Idiomatic communication and interpersonal solidarity in friends' relational cultures. *Human Communication Research, 18,* 307–335.

Berger, C. R., & Bradac, J. J. (1982). *Language and social knowledge: Uncertainty in interpersonal relations.* London: Edward Arnold.

Berlin, B., & Kay, P. (1969). *Basic color terms: Their universality and evolution.* Berkeley: University of California Press.

Bickerton, D. (2009). *Adam's tongue: How humans made language, how language made humans.* New York: Farrar, Straus, & Giroux.

Bolden, G. (2006). Little words that matter: Discourse markers "oh" and "so" and the doing of other-attentiveness in social interaction. *Journal of Communication, 56,* 661–688.

Bowerman, M., & Choi, S. (2001). Shaping meanings for language: Universal and language-specific in the acquisition of semantic categories. In M. Bowerman & S. C. Levinson (Eds.), *Language acquisition and conceptual development* (pp. 475–511). Cambridge, UK: Cambridge University Press.

Bowers, J. W. (1963). Language intensity, social introversion, and attitude change. *Speech Monographs, 30,* 345–352.

Bowers, J. W. (2006). Old eyes take a new look at Bradac's favorite variables. *Journal of Language and Social Psychology, 25,* 7–24.

Bradac, J. J. (1983). The language of lovers, flovers, and friends: Communicating in social and personal relationships. *Journal of Language and Social Psychology, 2,* 141–162.

Bradac, J. J. (1990). Language attitudes and impression formation. In H. Giles & W. P. Robinson (Eds.), *The handbook of language and social psychology* (pp. 387–412). Chichester, UK: Wiley.

Bradac, J. J., & Giles, H. (1991). Social and educational consequences of language attitudes. *Moderna Språk, 85,* 1–11.

Bradac, J. J., & Mulac, A. (1984). A molecular view of powerful and powerless speech styles: Attributional consequences of specific language features and communicator intentions. *Communication Monographs, 51,* 307–319.

Bransford, J. D., & Johnson, M. K. (1972). Contextual prerequisites for understanding: Some investigations of comprehension and recall. *Journal of Verbal Learning and Verbal Behavior, 11,* 717–726.

Brown, P., & Levinson, S. C. (1987). *Politeness: Some universals in language usage.* Cambridge, UK: Cambridge University Press.

Brown, R. (1968). *Words and things.* New York: Free Press.

Brown, R., & Fish, D. (1983). The psychological causality implicit in language. *Cognition, 14,* 237–273.

Brown, R., & Gilman, A. (1989). Politeness theory and Shakespeare's four major tragedies. *Language in Society, 18,* 159–212.

Brown, R., & Lenneberg, E. (1954). A study in language and cognition. *Journal of Abnormal and Social Psychology, 49,* 454–462.

Bull, P. E., & Mayer, K. (1993). How not to answer questions in political interviews. *Political Psychology, 14,* 651–666.

Burgoon, J. K., & Hale, J. L. (1984). The fundamental topoi of relational messages. *Communication Monographs, 51,* 193–214.

Buzzanell, P. M., Burrell, N. A., Stafford, S. R., & Berkowitz, S. (1996). When I call you up and you're not there: Application of communication accommodation theory to telephone answering machine messages. *Western Journal of Communication, 60,* 310–336.

Cappella, J. N. (1988). Personal relationships, social relationships, and patterns of interaction. In S. Duck (Ed.), *Handbook of personal relationships* (pp. 325–342). New York: Wiley.

Casasanto, D. (2008). Who's afraid of the Big Bad Whorf? Cross-linguistic differences in temporal language and thought. In P. Indefrey & M. Gullberg (Eds.), *Time to speak: Cognitive and neural prerequisites of time in language* (pp. 63–79). Oxford, UK: Wiley-Blackwell.

Chartrand, T. L., & van Baaren, R. (2009). Human mimicry. *Advances in Experimental Social Psychology, 41,* 219–274.

Chomsky, N. (1965). *Aspects of the theory of syntax.* Cambridge: MIT Press.

Chomsky, N. (1992). *Language and thought.* Wakefield, RI: Moyer Bell.

Cialdini, R. B., Borden, R. J., Thorne, A., Walker, M. R., Freeman, S., Sloan, L. R., et al. (1976). Basking in reflected glory: Three (football) field studies. *Journal of Personality and Social Psychology, 34,* 366–375.

Clark, H. H. (1979). Responding to indirect speech acts. *Cognitive Psychology, 11,* 430–477.

Clark, H. H. (1994). Discourse in production. In M. A. Gernsbacher (Ed.), *Handbook of psycholinguistics* (pp. 985–1021). San Diego, CA: Academic Press.

Clark, H. H. (1996). *Using language.* Cambridge, UK: Cambridge University Press.

Clark, H. H., & Carlson, T. B. (1982). Hearers and speech acts. *Language, 58,* 332–373.

Clark, H. H., & Clark, E. V. (1977). *Psychology and language: An introduction to psycholinguistics.* New York: Harcourt Brace Jovanovich.

Clark, H. H., & Krych, M. A. (2004). Speaking while monitoring addressees for understanding. *Journal of Memory and Language, 50,* 62–81.

Clark, H. H., & Schunk, D. H. (1980). Polite responses to polite requests. *Cognition, 8,* 111–143.

Clark, H. H., & Wilkes-Gibbs, D. (1986). Referring as a collaborative process. *Cognition, 22,* 1–39.

Cohen, J. R., Crystal, T. H., House, A. S., & Neuberg, E. P. (1980). Weighty voices and shaky evidence: A critique. *Journal of the Acoustical Society of America, 68,* 1884–1885.

Cosmides, L. (1983). Invariances in the acoustic expression of emotion in speech. *Journal of Experimental Psychology: Perception and Performance, 9,* 864–881.

Coupland, N., Coupland, J., Giles, H., & Henwood, K. (1988). Accommodating the elderly: Invoking and extending a theory. *Language in Society, 17,* 1–41.

Coupland, N., & Jaworski, A. (Eds.). (2009). *The new reader in sociolinguistics.* Basingstoke, UK: Macmillan.

Craig, R. T., Tracy, K., & Spisak, F. (1986). The discourse of requests: Assessment of a politeness approach. *Human Communication Research, 12,* 437–468.

Crinean, M., & Garnham, A. (2006). Implicit casuality, implicit consequentiality, and semantic roles. *Language and Cognitive Processes, 21,* 636–648.

Crystal, D. (2007). *How language works.* New York: Avery.

Cuddy, A. J. C., Fiske, S. T., & Glick, P. (2008). Competence and warmth as universal trait dimensions of interpersonal and intergroup perceptions: The stereotype content model and the BIAS map. In M. P. Zanna (Ed.), *Advances in experimental psychology* (Vol. 40, pp. 61–149). New York: Academic Press.

Cuenca, M. J. (2008). Pragmatic markers in contrast: The case of well. *Journal of Pragmatics, 40,* 1373–1391.

Cupach, W. R., & Metts, S. (1994). *Facework.* Thousand Oaks, CA: Sage.

Danziger, K. (1976). *Interpersonal communication.* New York: Pergamon Press.

Deutscher, G. (2010). *Through the language glass.* New York: Heinemann.

Devitt, M., & Sterelny, K. (1987). *Language and reality.* Oxford, UK: Blackwell.

Dillard, J. P., Solomon, D. H., & Palmer, M. T. (1999). Structuring the concept of relational judgments. *Communication Research, 23,* 703–723.

Dillard, J. P., Wilson, S. R., Tusing, K. J., & Kinney, T. A. (1997). Politeness judgments in personal relationships. *Journal of Language and Social Psychology, 16,* 297–325.

Dixon, J. A., & Mahoney, B. (2004). The effects of accent evaluation and evidence on perceptions of a suspect's guilt and criminality. *Journal of Social Psychology, 144,* 63–74.

Duck, S., & Pittman, G. (1993). Social and personal relationships. In M. L. Knapp & G. R. Miller (Eds.), *Handbook of interpersonal communication* (pp. 676–695). Thousand Oaks, CA: Sage.

Duck, S., Pond, K., & Hendrick, C. (1989). Friends, Romans, countrymen, lend me your retrospections: Rhetoric and reality in personal relationships. In C. Hendrick (Ed.), *Review of personality and social psychology: Vol. 10. Close relationships* (pp. 17–38). Thousand Oaks, CA: Sage.

Ellis, D. G. (1992). *From language to communication.* Hillsdale, NJ: Lawrence Erlbaum.

Ellis, D. G., & Hamilton, M. (1985). Syntactic and pragmatic code choice in interpersonal communication. *Communication Monographs, 52,* 264–278.

Ellis, D. S. (1967). Speech and social status in America. *Social Forces, 45,* 431–437.

Ellis, H. C., & Daniel, T. C. (1971). Verbal processes in long-term stimulus recognition memory. *Journal of Experimental Psychology, 90,* 18–26.

Erbert, L. A., & Floyd, K. (2004). Affectionate expressions as face-threatening acts: Receiver assessments. *Communication Studies, 55,* 254–270.

Ervin-Tripp, S. M. (1976). Is Sybil there? The structure of some American English directives. *Language in Society, 5,* 25–66.

Fishbein, M., & Ajzen, I. (1975). *Belief, attitude, intention, and behavior: An introduction to theory and research.* Reading, MA: Addison-Wesley.

Fishman, J. A. (1971). *Sociolinguistics: A brief introduction.* Rowley, MA: Newbury House.

Fitch, K. L., & Sanders, R. E. (1994). Culture, communication, and preferences for directness in expressions of directives. *Communication Theory, 4,* 219–245.

Fitzpatrick, M. A. (1988). *Between husbands and wives: Communication in marriage.* Newbury Park, CA: Sage.

Floccia, C., Butler, J., Girard, F., & Goslin, J. (2009). Categorization of regional and foreign accents in 5- to 7-year-old British children. *International Journal of Behavioral Development, 33,* 336–375.

Fowler, R., Hodge, B., Kress, G., & Trew, T. (1979). *Language and control.* London: Routledge & Kegan Paul.

Fox, S., Giles, H., Orne, M., & Bourhis, R. Y. (2000). Interability communication: Theoretical perspectives. In D. Braithwaite & T. Thompson (Eds.), *Handbook of communication and disability* (pp. 193–222). Mahwah, NJ: Lawrence Erlbaum.

Fox Tree, J. (2000). Coordinating spontaneous talk. In L. Wheeldon (Ed.), *Aspects of language production* (pp. 375–406). New York: Psychology Press.

Francik, E. P., & Clark, H. H. (1985). How to make requests that overcome obstacles to compliance. *Journal of Memory and Language, 24,* 560–568.

von Frisch, K. (1967). *The dance language and orientation of bees.* Cambridge, MA: Belknap Press of Harvard University Press.

Fussell, S. R., & Krauss, R. M. (1992). Coordination of knowledge in communication: Effects of speakers' assumptions about what others know. *Journal of Personality and Social Psychology, 62,* 378–391.

Gallois, C., & Callan, V. J. (1988). Communication accommodation and the prototypical speaker: Predicting evaluations of status and solidarity. *Language and Communication, 8,* 271–284.

Gallois, C., & Giles, H. (1998). Accommodating mutual influence in intergroup encounters. In M. Palmer (Ed.), *Mutual influence in interpersonal communication: Theory and research in cognition, affect, and behavior* (pp. 135–162). New York: Ablex.

Gallois, C., Ogay, T., & Giles, H. (2005). Communication accommodation theory: A look back and a look ahead. In W. Gudykunst (Ed.), *Theorizing about intercultural communication* (pp. 121–148). Thousand Oaks, CA: Sage.

Gasiorek, J. (2010). *Forms of nonaccommodation.* Unpublished master's thesis, University of California, Santa Barbara.

Geis, M. (1995). *Speech acts and conversational interaction.* Cambridge, UK: Cambridge University Press.

Gentner, D., & Goldin-Meadow, S. (Eds.). (2003). *Language in mind: Advances in the study of language and thought.* Cambridge: MIT Press.

Gibbs, R. W. (1979). Contextual effects in understanding indirect requests. *Discourse Processes, 2,* 1–10.

Gibbs, R. W. (1983). Do people always process the literal meanings of indirect requests? *Journal of Experimental Psychology: Learning, Memory and Cognition, 9,* 524–533.

Gibbs, R. W. (1986). What makes some indirect speech acts conventional? *Journal of Memory and Language, 25,* 181–196.

Giles, H. (1973). Accent mobility: A model and some data. *Anthropological Linguistics, 15,* 87–105.

Giles, H. (1978). Linguistic differentiation between ethnic groups. In H. Tajfel (Ed.), *Differentiation between social groups* (pp. 361–393). London: Academic Press.

Giles, H. (1999). Managing dilemmas in the "silent revolution": A call to arms! *Journal of Communication, 49,* 170–182.

Giles, H., & Billings, A. (2004). Language attitudes. In A. Davies & E. Elder (Eds.), *Handbook of applied linguistics* (pp. 187–209). Oxford, UK: Blackwell.

Giles, H., Bonilla, D., & Speer, R. B. (in press). Parameters of acculturation: Group vitality, communication accommodation, and intergroup contact. In J. Jackson (Ed.), *Routledge handbook of intercultural communication.* London: Routledge.

Giles, H., Bourhis, R. Y., & Taylor, D. M. (1977). Towards a theory of language in ethnic group relations. In H. Giles (Ed.), *Language, ethnicity and intergroup relations* (pp. 307–348). London: Academic Press.

Giles, H., & Byrne, J. L. (1982). An intergroup model of second language acquisition. *Journal of Multilingual and Multicultural Development, 3,* 17–40.

Giles, H., Choi, C. W., & Dixon, T. L. (2010). Police-civilian encounters. In H. Giles, S. A. Reid, & J. Harwood (Eds.), *The dynamics of intergroup communication* (pp. 65–76). New York: Peter Lang.

Giles, H., Coupland, J., & Coupland, N. (Eds.). (1991). *The contexts of accommodation.* New York: Cambridge University Press.

Giles, H., & Edwards, J. R. (2010). Attitudes to language: Past, present, and future. In K. Malmkjaer (Ed.), *The Routledge linguistics encyclopedia* (3rd ed., pp. 35–40). London: Routledge.

Giles, H., & Gasiorek, J. (2010). Intergenerational communication practices. In K. W. Schaie & S. Willis (Eds.), *Handbook of the psychology of aging* (7th ed., pp. 231–245). New York: Elsevier.

Giles, H., Henwood, K., Coupland, N., Harriman, J., & Coupland, J. (1992). Language attitudes and cognitive mediation. *Human Communication Research, 18,* 500–527.

Giles, H., & Hewstone, M. (1982). Cognitive structures, speech, and social situations: Two integrative models. *Language Sciences, 4,* 187–219.

Giles, H., & Johnson, P. (1981). The role of language in ethnic group relations. In J. C. Turner & H. Giles (Eds.), *Intergroup behavior* (pp. 199–243). Oxford, UK: Blackwell.

Giles, H., & Johnson, P. (1986). Perceived threat, ethnic commitment, and inter-ethnic language behavior. In Y. Kim (Ed.), *Interethnic communication: Recent research* (pp. 91–116). Newbury Park, CA: Sage.

Giles, H., & Johnson, P. (1987). Ethnolinguistic identity theory: A social psychological approach to language maintenance. *International Journal of the Sociology of Language, 68,* 69–99.

Giles, H., & Marlow, M. L. (in press). Theorizing language attitudes: Existing frameworks, an integrative model, and new directions. *Communication Yearbook 35.*

Giles, H., & Marsh, P. (1979). Perceived masculinity and accented speech. *Language Sciences, 1,* 301–315.

Giles, H., Mulac, A., Bradac, J. J., & Johnson, P. (1987). Speech accommodation theory: The first decade and beyond. In M. McLaughlin (Ed.), *Communication Yearbook 10,* 13–48. Newbury Park, CA: Sage.

Giles, H., & Niedzielski, N. (1998). Italian is beautiful, German is ugly. In L. Bauer & P. Trudgill (Eds.), *Language myths* (pp. 85–93). London: Penguin.

Giles, H., & Ogay, T. (2006). Communication accommodation theory. In B. Whaley & W. Samter (Eds.), *Explaining communication: Contemporary theories and exemplars* (pp. 293–310). Mahwah, NJ: Lawrence Erlbaum.

Giles, H., Reid, S. A., & Harwood, J. (Eds.). (2010). *The dynamics of intergroup communication.* New York: Peter Lang.

Giles, H., & Smith, P. M. (1979). Accommodation theory: Optimal levels of convergence. In H. Giles

& R. N. St. Clair (Eds.), *Language and social psychology* (pp. 45–65). Oxford, UK: Blackwell.

Giles, H., Taylor, D. M., & Bourhis, R. Y. (1973). Towards a theory of interpersonal accommodation through speech: Some Canadian data. *Language in Society, 2,* 177–192.

Giles, H., & Wadleigh, P. M. (2008). Accommodating nonverbally. In L. K. Guerrero & M. L. Hecht (Eds.), *The nonverbal communication reader: Classic and contemporary readings* (3rd ed., pp. 491–502). Prospect Heights, IL: Waveland Press.

Giles, H., & Wiemann, J. M. (1987). Language, social comparison, and power. In C. R. Berger & S. H. Chaffee (Eds.), *Handbook of communication science* (pp. 350–384). Newbury Park, CA: Sage.

Giles, H., Willemyns, M., Gallois, C., & Anderson, M. C. (2007). Accommodating a new frontier: The context of law enforcement. In K. Fiedler (Ed.), *Social communication* (pp. 129–162). New York: Psychology Press.

Giles, H., Williams, A., Mackie, D. M., & Rosselli, F. (1995). Reactions to Anglo- and Hispanic-American accented speakers: Affect, identity, persuasion, and the English-only controversy. *Language and Communication, 14,* 102–123.

Giles, H., Wilson, P., & Conway, A. (1981). Accent and lexical diversity as determinants of impression formation and employment selection. *Language Sciences, 3,* 92–103.

Gill, M. M. (1994). Accent and stereotypes: Their effect on perceptions of teacher and lecture comprehension. *Journal of Applied Communication Research, 22,* 348–361.

Glucksberg, S. (1988). Language and thought. In R. S. Sternberg & E. E. Smith (Eds.), *The psychology of human thought* (pp. 214–241). New York: Cambridge University Press.

Glucksberg, S., & Weisberg, R. W. (1963). Verbal behavior and problem solving: Some effects of labeling in a functional fixedness problem. *Journal of Experimental Psychology, 71,* 659–664.

Gluszek, A., & Dovidio, J. F. (2010). The way they speak: Stigma of non-native accents in communication. *Personality and Social Psychology Review, 14,* 214–237.

Goffman, E. (1967). *Interaction ritual: Essays on face to face behavior.* Garden City, NY: Anchor Books.

Goffman, E. (1976). Replies and responses. *Language in Society, 5,* 257–313.

Gordon, D., & Lakoff, G. (1975). Conversational postulates. In P. Cole & J. L. Morgan (Eds.), *Syntax and semantics: Vol. 3. Speech acts* (pp. 83–106). New York: Academic Press.

Gradol, D., & Swann, J. (1983). Speaking fundamental frequency: Some physical and social correlates. *Language and Speech, 26,* 351–366.

Grice, H. P. (1975). Logic and conversation. In P. Cole & J. L. Morgan (Eds.), *Syntax and semantics: Vol. 3. Speech acts* (pp. 41–58). New York: Academic Press.

Griffin, E. (2009). Communication accommodation theory of Howard Giles. In *A first look at communication theory* (7th ed., pp. 387–399). Boston: McGraw-Hill Higher Education.

Gumperz, J. J., & Levinson, S. C. (Eds.). (1996). *Rethinking linguistic relativity.* New York: Cambridge University Press.

Harwood, J., & Giles, H. (Eds.). (2005). *Intergroup communication: Multiple perspectives.* New York: Peter Lang.

Harwood, J., Soliz, J., & Lin, M-C. (2006). Communication accommodation theory: An intergroup approach to family relationships. In D. O. Braithwaite & L. A. Baxter (Eds.), *Engaging theories in family communication: Multiple perspectives* (pp. 19–34). Thousand Oaks: Sage.

Haslam, N. (2004). *Relational models theory: A contemporary overview.* Mahwah, NJ: Lawrence Erlbaum.

Heider, E. R. (1972). Universals in color naming and memory. *Journal of Experimental Psychology, 93,* 10–20.

Heider, E. R., & Olivier, D. C. (1972). The structure of the color space in naming and memory for two languages. *Cognitive Psychology, 3,* 337–354.

Herring, S. C., & Paolillo, J. C. (2006). Gender and genre variation in weblogs. *Journal of Sociolinguistics, 10,* 439–459.

Hockett, C. F. (1960). The origin of speech. *Scientific American, 203,* 89–96.

Hoffman, C., Lau, I., & Johnson, D. R. (1986). The linguistic relativity of person cognition: An English-Chinese comparison. *Journal of Personality and Social Psychology, 51,* 1097–1105.

Holtgraves, T. M. (1986). Language structure in social interaction: Perceptions of direct and indirect speech acts and interactants who use them. *Journal of Personality and Social Psychology, 51,* 305–314.

Holtgraves, T. M. (2002). *Language as social action: Social psychology and language use.* Mahwah, NJ: Lawrence Erlbaum.

Holtgraves, T. M., & Lasky, B. (1999). Linguistic power and persuasion. *Journal of Language and Social Psychology, 18,* 196–205.

Holtgraves, T. M., & Yang, J. N. (1990). Politeness as universal: Cross-cultural perceptions of request strategies and inferences based on their use. *Journal of Personality and Social Psychology, 59,* 719–729.

Holtgraves, T. M., & Yang, J. N. (1992). Interpersonal underpinnings of request strategies: General principles and differences due to culture and gender. *Journal of Personality and Social Psychology, 62,* 246–256.

Hoosain, R., & Salili, F. (1987). Language differences in pronunciation speed for numbers, digit span, and mathematical ability. *Psychologia, 30,* 34–38.

Hunt, E., & Agnoli, F. (1991). The Whorfian hypothesis: A cognitive psychology perspective. *Psychological Review, 98,* 377–389.

Ickes, W., Reidhead, S., & Patterson, M. (1986). Machiavellianism and self-monitoring: As different as "me" and "you." *Social Cognition, 4,* 58–74.

Imai, M., & Saalbach, H. (2010). Categories in mind and categories in language: Do classifier categories influence conceptual structures? In B. C. Malt & P. Wolff (Eds.), *Words and the mind: How words capture human experience* (pp. 138–164). Oxford, UK: Oxford University Press.

Jackendoff, R. (2002). *Foundations of language: Brain, meaning, grammar, and evolution.* New York: Oxford University Press.

Jacobs, S. (1994). Language and interpersonal communication. In M. L. Knapp & G. Miller (Eds.), *Handbook of interpersonal communication* (pp. 199–228). Newbury Park, CA: Sage.

Jacobs, S., & Jackson, S. (1983). Speech act structure in conversation: Rational aspects of pragmatic coherence. In R. T. Craig & K. Tracy (Eds.), *Conversational coherence* (pp. 47–66). Beverly Hills, CA: Sage.

Jacobsen, E. (1932). The electrophysiology of mental activities. *American Journal of Psychology, 44,* 677–694.

Jefferson, G. (1975). Side sequences. In D. N. Sudnow (Ed.), *Studies in social interaction* (pp. 294–338). New York: Free Press.

Johnson, D. I., Roloff, M. E., & Riffee, M. A. (2004). Politeness theory and refusals of requests: Face threat as a function of expressed obstacles. *Communication Studies, 55,* 227–238.

Kahneman, D., & Tversky, A. (1984). Choices, values, and frames. *American Psychologist, 39,* 341–350.

Keenan, E. O. (1976). The universality of conversational implicature. *Language in Society, 5,* 67–80.

Kinzler, K. D., Dupoux, E., & Spelke, E. S. (2007). The native language of social cognition. *Proceedings of the National Academy of the United States of America, 104,* 12577–12580.

Knapp, M. L., Ellis, E. G., & Williams, B. A. (1980). Perceptions of communication behavior associated with relational terms. *Communication Monographs, 47,* 262–278.

Knapp, M. L., & Vangelisti, A. L. (2004). *Interpersonal communication and human relationships* (5th ed.). Boston: Pearson.

Knobloch, L. K., & Solomon, D. H. (2003). Manifestations of relationship conceptualizations in conversation. *Human Communication Research, 29,* 482–515.

Krauss, R. M., Apple, W., Morency, N., Wenzel, C., & Winton, W. (1981). Verbal, vocal, and visible factors in judgments of another's affect. *Journal of Personality and Social Psychology, 40,* 312–320.

Krauss, R. M., & Chiu, C. Y. (1997). Language and social behavior. In D. Gilbert, S. Fiske, & G. Lindzey (Eds.), *Handbook of social psychology* (Vol. 2, pp. 41–88). Boston: McGraw-Hill.

Krauss, R. M., & Fussell, S. R. (1996). Social psychological approaches to the study of communication. In E. T. Higgins & A. Kruglanski (Eds.), *Social psychology: Handbook of basic principles* (pp. 655–701). New York: Guilford Press.

Labov, W. (1976). *Language in the inner city.* Philadelphia: University of Pennsylvania Press.

Labov, W. (2006). *The social stratification of English in New York City* (2nd ed.). New York: Cambridge University Press.

Lambert, W. E., Anisfeld, M., & Yeni-Komshian, G. (1965). Evaluational reactions of Jewish and Arab adolescents to dialect and language variations. *Journal of Personality and Social Psychology, 2,* 84–90.

Lambert, W. E., Hodgson, E. R., & Gardner, R. C., & Fillenbaum, S. (1960). Evaluation reactions to spoken languages. *Journal of Abnormal and Social Psychology, 60,* 44–51.

Langacker, R. W. (1999). *Grammar and conceptualization.* Berlin: Mouton de Gruyter.

Lantz, D., & Stefflre, V. (1964). Language and cognition revisited. *Journal of Abnormal and Social Psychology, 69,* 472–481.

Lass, N. J., & Davis, M. (1976). An investigation of speaker height and weight identification. *Journal of the Acoustical Society of America, 60,* 700–704.

Lass, N. J., Hughes, K. R., Bowyer, M. D., Waters, L. T., & Bourne, V. T. (1976). Speaker sex identification from voiced, whispered and filtered isolated vowels. *Journal of the Acoustical Society of America, 59,* 675–678.

Leech, G. (1983). *Principles of pragmatics.* London: Longman.

Levinson, S. C. (1981). Some pre-observations on the modeling of dialogue. *Discourse Processes, 4,* 93–116.

Levinson, S. C. (2000). *Presumptive meanings: The theory of generalized conversational implicature.* Cambridge: MIT Press.

Lim, T., & Bowers, J. W. (1991). Facework: Solidarity, approbation and tact. *Human Communication Research, 17,* 415–450.

Lippi-Green, R. (1997). *English with an accent: Language, ideology, and discrimination in the United States.* New York: Routledge.

Littlejohn, S. W. (2002). *Theories of human communication* (7th ed.). Belmont, CA: Wadsworth.

Loftus, E. (1996). *Eyewitness testimony.* Cambridge, MA: Harvard University Press.

Lucy, J. A. (1994). *Grammatical categories and cognition.* Cambridge, UK: Cambridge University Press.

Luhman, R. (1990). Appalachian English stereotypes: language attitudes in Kentucky. *Language in Society, 19,* 331–348.

MacMartin, C., Wood, L. A., & Kroger, R. O. (2001). Facework. In H. Giles & W. P. Robinson (Eds.), *The new handbook of language and social psychology* (pp. 221–237). Chichester, UK: Wiley.

MacWhinney, B. (2008). Cognitive precursors to language. In D. K. Oller & U. Griebel (Eds.), *Evolution of communicative flexibility* (pp. 193–214). Cambridge: MIT Press.

Marlow, M., & Giles, H. (2010). "We won't get ahead speaking like that!": Expressing and managing language criticism in Hawai'i. *Journal of Multilingual and Multicultural Communication, 31,* 237–251.

Max, L. W. (1937). An experimental study of the motor theory of consciousness: IV. Action curve responses in the deaf during awakening, kinesthetic imagery and abstract thinking. *Journal of Comparative Psychology, 24,* 301–334.

McEwen, W. J., & Greenberg, B. S. (1970). Effects of message intensity on receiver evaluation of source, message, and topic. *Journal of Communication, 20,* 340–350.

McGlone, M. S. (2007). What is the explanatory value of a conceptual metaphor? *Language and Communication, 27,* 109–126.

McGlone, M. S. (2010). Deception by selective quotation. In M. S. McGlone & M. L. Knapp (Eds.), *The interplay of truth and deception* (pp. 54–65). New York: Routledge.

McGlone, M. S., & Batchelor, J. (2003). Looking out for number one: Euphemism and face. *Journal of Communication, 53,* 251–264.

McGlone, M. S., Beck, G. A., & Pfiester, R. A. (2006). Contamination and camouflage in euphemisms. *Communication Monographs, 73,* 261–282.

McGlone, M. S., Bortfeld, H., & Kobrynowicz, D. (2007). Laying it on thin: Analogical cue frequency in the manipulation of choice. *Personality and Social Psychology Bulletin, 33,* 721–731.

McGlone, M. S., Cacciari, C., & Glucksberg, S. (1994). Semantic productivity and idiom comprehension. *Discourse Processes, 17,* 167–190.

McGlone, M. S., Kobrynowicz, D., & Alexander, R. B. (2005). A certain je ne sais quoi: Verbalization bias in evaluation. *Human Communication Research, 31,* 241–267.

McGlone, M. S., & Manfredi, D. A. (2002). Topic–vehicle interaction in metaphor comprehension. *Memory and Cognition, 29,* 1209–1219.

McGlone, M. S., & Pfiester, R. A. (2009). Does time fly when you're having fun, or do you? Affect, agency, and embodiment in temporal communication. *Journal of Language and Social Psychology, 28,* 3–31.

McGlone, M. S., & Tofighbakhsh, J. (2000). Birds of a feather flock conjointly (?): Rhyme as reason in aphorisms. *Psychological Science, 11,* 424–428.

Miller, G. A., & Johnson-Laird, P. N. (1976). *Language and perception.* Cambridge, MA: Harvard University Press.

Mulac, A., Hanley, T. D., & Prigge, D. Y. (1974). Effects of phonological speech foreignness upon three dimensions of attitude of selected listeners. *Quarterly Journal of Speech, 60,* 411–420.

Mulac, A., Wiemann, J. M., Widenmann, S. J., & Gibson, T. W. (1988). Male/female language differences and effects in same-sex and mixed-sex dyads: The gender-linked language effect. *Communication Monographs, 55,* 315–335.

Myers, P., Giles, H., Reid, S. A., & Nabi, R. L. (2008). Law enforcement encounters: The effects of officer accommodativeness and crime severity on interpersonal attributions are mediated by intergroup sensitivity. *Communication Studies, 59,* 1–15.

Nazzi, T., Jusczyk, P., & Johnson, E. (2000). Language discrimination by English-learning 5-month-olds: Effects of rhythm and familiarity. *Journal of Memory and Language, 43,* 1–19.

Neveh-Benjamin, M., & Ayres, T. J. (1986). Digit span, reading rate, and linguistic relativity. *Quarterly Journal of Experimental Psychology, 38A,* 739–751.

Newcombe, N., & Arnkoff, D. B. (1979). Effects of speech style and sex of speaker on person perception. *Journal of Personality and Social Psychology, 37,* 1293–1303.

Ng, S. H., & Bradac, J. J. (1993). *Power in language.* Newbury Park, CA: Sage.

Noels, K. A., Giles, H., & Le Poire, B. (2003). Language and communication processes. In M. A. Hogg & J. Cooper (Eds.), *The SAGE handbook of social psychology* (pp. 232–257). London: Sage.

O'Barr, W. M. (1982). *Linguistic evidence.* New York: Academic Press.

O'Keefe, B. J. (1997). Variation, adaptation, and functional explanation in the study of message design. In G. Phillipsen & T. L. Albrecht (Eds.), *Developing communication theories* (pp. 85–118). Albany: State University of New York Press.

Ortony, A., Schallert, D. L., Reynolds, R. E., & Antos, S. J. (1978). Interpreting metaphors and idioms: Some effects of context on comprehension. *Journal of Verbal Learning and Verbal Behavior, 17,* 465–477.

Ota, H., Giles, H., & Somera, L-B. (2007). Beliefs about intra- and intergenerational communication in Japan, the Philippines, and the United States: Implications for older adults' subjective well-being. *Communication Studies, 58,* 173–188.

Pasternak, B., Ember, M., & Ember, C. (1997). *Sex, gender, and kinship: A cross-cultural perspective.* Upper Saddle River, NJ: Prentice Hall.

Pavlov, I. P. (1941). *Lectures on conditioned reflexes* (Conditioned Reflexes and Psychiatry, Vol. 2, W. H. Gantt, Trans. & Ed.). New York: International.

Pennebaker, J. W., Mehl, M. R., & Niederhoffer, K. G. (2003). Psychological aspects of natural language use: Our words, our selves. *Annual Review of Psychology, 54,* 547–577.

Piaget, J. (1977). *The grasp of consciousness: Action and concept in the young child.* London: Routledge & Kegan Paul.

Pinker, S. (1994). *The language instinct.* New York: Morrow.

Pinker, S. (2007). *The stuff of thought: Language as a window into human nature.* New York: Penguin.

Platt, J., & Weber, H. (1984). Speech convergence miscarried: An investigation into inappropriate accommodation strategies. *International Journal of the Sociology of Language, 46,* 131–146.

Pullum, G. K. (1991). *The great Eskimo vocabulary hoax.* Chicago: University of Chicago Press.

Reid, S. A., & Ng, S. H. (1999). Language, power, and intergroup relations. *Journal of Social Issues, 55,* 119–139.

Rosch, E., & Mervis, C. (1975). Family resemblances: Studies in the internal structure of categories. *Cognitive Psychology, 7,* 573–605.

Ruscher, J. B. (2001). *Prejudiced communication: A social psychological perspective.* New York: Guilford Press.

Ryan, E. B., & Carranza, M. A. (1975). Evaluative reactions of adolescents towards speakers of standard English and Mexican American accented English. *Journal of Personality and Social Psychology, 31,* 855–863.

Ryan, E. B., Giles, H., Bartolucci, G., & Henwood, K. (1986). Psycholinguistic and social psychological components of communication by and with older adults. *Language and Communication, 6,* 1–24.

Sacks, H., Schegloff, E. A., & Jefferson, G. (1974). A simplest systematic for the organization of turn-taking in conversation. *Language, 50,* 696–735.

Sapir, E. (1949). *Selected writings in language, culture, and personality* (D. Mandelbaum, Ed.). Berkeley: University of California Press.

Saussure, F. (1916). *Cours de linguistique générale* [Course in general linguistics]. Lausanne Paris: Payot.

Schegloff, E. A. (1968). Sequencing in conversational openings. *American Anthropologist, 70,* 1075–1095.

Schegloff, E. A. (1988). Presequences and indirection: Applying speech act theory to ordinary conversation. *Journal of Pragmatics, 12,* 55–62.

Scherer, K. R., & Giles, H. (Eds.). (1979). *Social markers in speech.* Cambridge, UK: Cambridge University Press.

Schober, M. F. (1998). Different kinds of conversational perspective-taking. In S. Fussell & R. Kreuz (Eds.), *Social and cognitive approaches to interpersonal communication* (pp. 145–174). Mahwah, NJ: Lawrence Erlbaum.

Schober, M. F. (2005). Conceptual alignment in conversation. In B. F. Malle & S. D. Hodges (Eds.),

*Other minds: How humans bridge the divide between self and others* (pp. 239–252). New York: Guilford Press.

Schooler, J. W., & Engstler-Schooler, T. Y. (1990). Visual overshadowing of visual memories: Some things are better left unsaid. *Cognitive Psychology, 22,* 36–71.

Schwarz, N. (2006). On judgments of truth and beauty. *Daedalus, 135,* 136–138.

Scott-Phillips, T. C. (2007). The social evolution of language, and the language of social evolution. *Evolutionary Psychology, 5,* 740–753.

Searle, J. (1969). *Speech acts.* London: Cambridge University Press.

Searle, J. (1979). *Expression and meaning: Studies in the theory of speech acts.* London: Cambridge University Press.

Semin, G. R., & Fiedler, K. (1991). The linguistic category model, its bases, applications, and range. In W. Stroebe & M. Hewstone (Eds.), *European review of social psychology* (Vol. 2, pp. 1–30). London: Wiley.

Semin, G. R., & Fiedler, K. (1992). The inferential properties of interpersonal verbs. In G. R. Semin & K. Fiedler (Eds.), *Language, interaction, and social cognition* (pp. 58–78). Newbury Park, CA: Sage.

Seyfarth, R. M., Cheney, D. L., & Marler, P. (1980). Vervet monkey alarm calls: Semantic communication in a free-ranging primate. *Animal Behavior, 8,* 1070–1094.

Shepard, C. A., Giles, H., & Le Poire, B. A. (2001). Communication accommodation theory. In W. P. Robinson & H. Giles (Eds.), *The new handbook of language and social psychology* (pp. 33–56). Chichester, UK: Wiley.

Sillars, A., Shellen, W., McIntosh, A., & Pomegranate, M. (1997). Relational characteristics of language: Elaboration and differentiation in marital conversations. *Western Journal of Communication, 61,* 403–422.

Simard, L., Taylor, D. M., & Giles, H. (1976). Attribution processes and interpersonal accommodation in a bilingual setting. *Language and Speech, 19,* 374–387.

Simmons, R. A., Gordon, P. C., & Chambless, D. L. (2005). Pronouns in marital interaction: What do "you" and "I" say about marital health? *Psychological Science, 16,* 932–936.

Slugoski, B. R., & Turnbull, W. (1988). Cruel to be kind and kind to be cruel: Sarcasm, banter and social

relations. *Journal of Language and Social Psychology, 7,* 101–121.

Smith, S. M., Brown, H. O., Tomas, J. E. P., & Goodman, L. S. (1947). The lack of cerebral effects of d-tubocurarine. *Anesthesiology, 8,* 1–14.

Smith-Hefner, N. J. (1988). Women and politeness: The Javanese example. *Language in Society, 17,* 535–554.

Sperber, D., & Wilson, D. (1986). *Relevance: Communication and cognition.* Cambridge, MA: Harvard University Press.

Stefflre, V., Castillo Vales, V., & Morley, L. (1966). Language and cognition in the Yucutan: A cross-cultural replication. *Journal of Personality and Social Psychology, 4,* 112–115.

Stone, L. D., & Pennebaker, J. W. (2002). Trauma in real time: Talking and avoiding online conversations about the death of Princess Diana. *Basic and Applied Social Psychology, 24,* 172–182.

Street, R. L., & Giles, H. (1982). Speech accommodation theory: A social cognitive model of speech behavior. In M. Roloff & C. R. Berger (Eds.), *Social cognition and communication* (pp. 193–226). Beverly Hills, CA: Sage.

Tajfel, H. (1981). *Human groups and social categories.* Cambridge, UK: Cambridge University Press.

Talmy, I. (1985). Lexicalization patterns: Semantic structure in lexical forms. In T. Shopen (Ed.), *Language typology and syntactic description: Vol. 3. Grammatical categories and the lexicon* (pp. 57–149). Cambridge, UK: Cambridge University Press.

Thakerar, J. N., Giles, H., & Cheshire, J. (1982). Psychological and linguistic parameters of speech accommodation theory. In C. Fraser & K. R. Scherer (Eds.), *Advances in the social psychology of language* (pp. 205–255). Cambridge, UK: Cambridge University Press.

Turnbull, W. (2003). *Language in action: Psychological models of conversation.* New York: Psychology Press.

Turner, J. C., Hogg, M. A., Oakes, P. J., Reicher, S. D., & Wetherell, M. S. (1987). *Rediscovering the social group: A self-categorization theory.* Oxford, UK: Blackwell.

Vangelisti, A. L., Maguire, K. C., Alexander, A. L., & Clark, G. (2007). Hurtful family environments: Links with individual, relationship, and perceptual variables. *Communication Monographs, 74,* 357–385.

Watson, J. B. (1913). *Behaviorism: An introduction to comparative psychology.* New York: Henry Holt.

Watzlawick, P., Beavin, J. H., & Jackson, D. D. (1967). *Pragmatics of human communication: A study of interactional patterns, pathologies, and paradoxes.* New York: W. W. Norton.

Whorf, B. L. (1956). *Language, thought, and reality: Selected writings of Benjamin Lee Whorf* (J. B. Carroll, Ed.). Cambridge: MIT Press.

Wiener, M., & Mehrabian, A. (1968). *Language within language: Immediacy, a channel in verbal communication.* New York: Appleton-Century-Crofts.

Wigboldus, D., & Douglas, K. (2007). Language, stereotypes, and intergroup relations. In K. Fiedler (Ed.), *Social communication* (pp. 79–106). New York: Psychology Press.

Williams, J. A., & Nussbaum, J. F. (2001). *Intergenerational communication across the lifespan.* Mahwah, NJ: Lawrence Erlbaum.

Williams-Baucom, K. J., Atkins, D. C., Sevier, M., Eldridge, K. A., & Christensen, A. (2010). "You" and "I" need to talk about "us": Linguistic patterns in marital interactions. *Personal Relationships, 17,* 41–56.

Wilmot, W. W., & Shellen, W. N. (1990). Language in friendship. In H. Giles & W. P. Robinson (Eds.), *Handbook of language and social psychology* (pp. 413–431). New York: Wiley.

Wilson, S. R., Aleman, C. G., & Leatham, G. B. (1998). Identity implications of influence goals: A revised analysis of face-threatening acts and application to seeking compliance with same-sex friends. *Human Communication Research, 25,* 64–96.

Wilson, S. R., & Kunkel, A. W. (2000). Identity implications of influence goals: Similarities in perceived face threats and facework across sex and close relationships. *Journal of Language and Social Psychology, 19,* 195–221.

Wittgenstein, L. (1953). *Philosophical investigations.* Oxford, UK: Blackwell.

Yamada, A. (2009). Appreciating art verbally: Verbalization can make a work of art be both undeservedly loved and unjustly maligned. *Journal of Experimental Social Psychology, 45,* 1140–1143.

Yngve, V. H. (1970). On getting a word in edgewise. In *Papers from the sixth regional meeting of the Chicago Linguistics Society,* Chicago (pp. 567–578).

Zahn, C. J., & Hopper, R. (1985). Measuring language attitudes: The speech evaluation instrument. *Journal of Language and Social Psychology, 4,* 113–123.

# CHAPTER 8

# Nonverbal Signals

*Judee K. Burgoon*

*Laura K. Guerrero*

*Valerie Manusov*

Long before people invented linguistic systems for communicating, humans were exchanging messages nonverbally. So great has been the sweep and power of nonverbal communication that it has continually captivated philosophers and theologians, artists and writers, rhetoricians and scientists, all hoping to penetrate its mysteries and expound its principles. Today, it is a topic of intense interest not only in communication, psychology, linguistics, anthropology, and other social science fields but also in computer science and engineering, ethology, evolutionary biology, and other hard sciences. Although a single overview chapter can do little justice to such a vast, interdisciplinary body of knowledge, our hope is that it will at least acquaint the reader with some of the more central concepts, principles, and findings relevant to interpersonal communication.

## What Is Nonverbal Communication?

Nonverbal communication involves a wide variety of cues. As we will discuss in more detail in this chapter, it includes gestures, facial expressions, body movement, gaze, and dress when they are used as messages between people. It also encompasses use of the voice, touch, distancing, time, and physical objects as messages. To determine when something counts as a message is more complex than it may seem, however, but that decision is central to how different scholars choose to define what counts—or does not count—as nonverbal communication.

## Perspectives on What Counts as Nonverbal Communication

The place where meaning resides is at the heart of what are sometimes called "orientations" to communication. Scholars have advanced orientations that focus on the sender (Motley, 1990), the receiver (Andersen, 1991), and the interaction between the sender and receiver (Stamp & Knapp, 1990). This chapter is guided by two complementary orientations—the process-oriented perspective and the message orientation—that focus in part on distinguishing nonverbal *communication* from nonverbal *behavior* (see also Bavelas, 1990).

The process-based perspective (Guerrero & Floyd, 2006) is based on the idea that messages are worthy of study if they are likely to affect how people perceive and interact with one another in the short or long term. According to Guerrero and Floyd, three forms of message exchange are especially good examples of communication: (1) *successful communication* (intentional encoding and accurate decoding), (2) *miscommunication* (intentional encoding but inaccurate decoding), and (3) *accidental communication* (unintentional actions that are decoded accurately, often because they have shared social meanings). Two other forms of message exchange warrant study to the extent that they influence the process of communication. *Attempted communication* occurs when a message is encoded intentionally but not received (e.g., a husband misses the "warning look" his wife gives him when he starts to tell an embarrassing story in front of company, causing an argument to ensue later). *Misinterpretation* (unintentional encoding and inaccurate decoding) can also influence interaction; for instance, a sender might smile spontaneously in response to internal thoughts, and a receiver might misinterpret the smile as showing interest and approach the sender, leading to an awkward encounter.

A complementary approach, the *message orientation* (Burgoon, 1994), focuses on behaviors that could reasonably constitute a message. More specifically, nonverbal communication is defined as *those behaviors other than words themselves that form a socially shared coding system* (i.e., they are typically sent with intent, typically interpreted as intentional, used with regularity among members of a speech community, or have consensually recognizable interpretations). This orientation emphasizes socially shared rather than idiosyncratic behavior patterns. It also includes habitual communication practices that are displayed without much conscious awareness, as long as they are used regularly to form messages and are interpreted as such. For example, an "unintended"

frown can be regarded as a message because the behavior is one that people typically display and interpret as a signal of displeasure. If we accept the argument that much of our daily nonverbal communication is well practiced and operates in a semiautomatic, unmonitored fashion, then it becomes more productive to identify the "lexicon" of nonverbal communication than to divine the intent of each behavioral enactment. This approach rules out incidental behavior that both sender and receiver regard as unintentional.

Several assumptions are implicit in the process and message orientations. First, nonverbal communication has underlying rules that make it possible to form "grammatical" messages; we recognize when nonverbal messages are odd or "ill formed." Second, meanings are context dependent; one must know the context to determine, say, whether a squint is an expression of skepticism or a reaction to an overbright sun. Third, nonverbal communication includes both *biologically shared signals* (also called signs, symptoms, indicative behavior, expressive behavior, rituals, or spontaneous nonverbal expressions) and symbolic or *socially shared signals* (see, e.g., Buck & VanLear, 2002). The former are innate behaviors, such as howling or smiling, that are produced involuntarily and automatically and often understood across cultures, whereas the latter are context-specific behaviors such as the "AOK" sign (meaning all is well) or wearing black at a funeral, which are deliberate, often planned behaviors that lack universal meaning. Abundant research suggests that both biology and culture are major determinants of nonverbal communication (see Burgoon, Guerrero, & Floyd, 2010, for a summary of this literature).

## Nonverbal Communication Codes

Another way to define nonverbal communication is according to the codes that constitute it. Codes are the systematic means through which meanings are created (encoded), transmitted, perceived, and interpreted (decoded). Language is one such coding system. In the nonverbal realm, seven or eight coding systems are commonly recognized. These include the following:

1. *Kinesics:* The root of this term is kinesis, or movement, so kinesics refers to the display and interpretation of body movements such as posture (e.g., seated, standing, or asymmetrical), gait (e.g., slow, loping, stiff, or scampering), hand gestures, facial expressions, head movements, and eye gaze (although some prefer to give this its own category, viz., oculesics).

2. *Vocalics:* Also known as paralanguage or prosody, *vocalics* refers to all features of the voice other than the words themselves when used for communication. Loudness, pitch, tempo, intonation patterns, pauses, nonfluencies, and dialect are among the features included in vocalics.

3. *Physical appearance:* This code includes all aspects of one's appearance—attire, hair style, grooming, and accessories—that can be used as messages. Sometimes included here are other features of appearance—physiognomy, body type, height, skin color, complexion, and hair color—from which people also draw inferences.

4. *Proxemics:* This category consists of communicative distancing and spacing behavior, such as conversational distance, territoriality patterns, and arrangement of furnishings to affect spacing among people.

5. *Haptics:* This term refers to the use of touch as communication and includes numerous forms of touch (e.g., pats, caresses, slaps, kisses, kicks), their intensity, their location, and the body part performing the touch (e.g., hands, lips, head, shoulder, or foot).

6. *Chronemics:* This code refers to the ways in which time is organized, used, and perceived as communication. Features such as wait time, lead time, duration of events, promptness, and polychronic (doing many things at a time) or monochronic (doing one thing at a time) orientations all convey messages.

7. *Environment and artifacts:* Nonverbal elements such as how people arrange built environments, landscape natural ones, and design or arrange various objects within an environment all have message potential from their designers or occupants to their users and onlookers. Selection of objects can also serve as a message, as in what one's choice of computer, automobile, or home decor says about one's personality.

8. *Olfactics:* This last code refers to the use and interpretations of scents and odors as communication. Naturally arising body odors and pheromones as well as fragrances, perfumes, and other body products that appeal to the sense of smell all fall under this understudied code.

These eight categories are not the only way to divide up nonverbal codes. Sometimes they are discussed in terms of the *modalities through which messages are transmitted*, such as the body codes (kinesics, vocalics, physical appearance, and olfactics), the contact codes (proxemics and haptics), and the spatiotemporal codes (chronemics, environmental cues, and artifacts). Others conceptualize nonverbal codes according to their degree of symbolic capacity, their bandwidth (Are there single or multiple signals that the code can transmit?), and whether transmission can be parallel or must be serial. Some of these latter considerations become relevant when interpersonal communication is mediated. For example, communicators can use emoticons (☺), capitals (I REALLY appreciate it), punctuation (!!!!!), and spelling (I'm soooooo sorry) to add nonverbal elements into an e-mail or text message, but the modality still limits the type of nonverbal message they can send as well as how interactive the exchange is. The fact that people often feel compelled to add nonverbal elements to forms of mediated communication that are primarily text based attests to the important role that nonverbal messages play in the total communication process.

# Why Is Nonverbal Communication Important?

Nonverbal signals are ubiquitous in interpersonal exchanges, and they have always laid claim to communicative primacy: They came first in our evolutionary development as a species, they are our first form of communication in our onto-logical development as individuals, and they are the first signals to which we respond in our initial encounters with others. Talk show hosts, best-selling authors, and newscasters embrace the idea that nonverbal communication is essential, although they sometimes exaggerate its impor-tance or make it sound easier to master than it actually is. Their basic message, however, is right: Nonverbal messages constitute a large part of the communication system, and skill in encoding and decoding nonverbal messages is indeed one key to building and maintaining a satisfying life.

## The Role Nonverbal Messages Play in the Total Communication Process

There are many ways to see the unique contribu-tion that nonverbal cues make to the communi-cation process. One has to do with their importance relative to what people say (Mehrabian & Ferris, 1967; Mehrabian & Wiener, 1967). Numerous investigations have found, for example, that adults tend to place greater reliance on nonverbal than verbal cues under varied circumstances such as job interviews, assessments of leadership, therapeutic sessions, emotional expressions, and judgments of first impressions. Nonverbal cues are especially likely to be believed when they con-flict with a verbal message. The research findings can be framed as a series of propositions (gen-eral, empirically based conclusions) regarding reliance on nonverbal as compared with verbal

information (for a review of supporting research, see Burgoon, 1985):

1. *Adults generally rely more on nonverbal than verbal cues in determining social mean-ing.* This general principle must be quali-fied by the propositions that follow.

2. *Children rely more on verbal than nonverbal cues.* Although children begin life relying on nonverbal signals to communicate with caregivers, when they begin to acquire lan-guage, they go through a stage of being highly literal. For example, they do not interpret sarcasm well. Sometime prior to puberty, however, they return to greater belief in nonverbal signals.

3. *The more nonverbal cues are at odds with verbal ones, the more adults rely on the non-verbal cues.* As verbal and nonverbal mes-sages become more congruent with one another, verbal content takes on greater weight in contributing to meaning.

4. *Channel reliance depends on what commu-nication function is at stake.* Verbal cues are more important for factual, abstract, and persuasive communications, whereas non-verbal cues are more important for mes-sages related to impressions, relationships, and affective states. For connotative and emotional meanings or metamessages about the state of an interpersonal relation-ship, people depend largely on nonverbal signals, making nonverbal behavior espe-cially important in interpersonal contexts.

5. *When content across channels is congruent, the information from all contributing chan-nels tends to be averaged together equally; when content is incongruent, channels and cues may be weighted differentially.* Sometimes a single cue or channel will be discounted if two or more other cues are consistent with each other. For example, forward lean and close proximity may be suf-ficient to convey conversational involvement

even if a person avoids direct gaze. Sometimes people believe the most extreme or negative cue. But nonverbal cues still tend to be believed over verbal ones, even if the verbal message is more extreme.

6. *Individuals have consistent biases in channel reliance.* Some consistently depend on verbal information, some consistently depend on nonverbal information, and some are situationally adaptable. Although individuals have their personal predilections for which channels of information they attend to most often, the prevailing pattern is still one of relying more frequently and for more purposes on the nonverbal codes.

A variety of reasons have been offered for the substantial dependence on nonverbal channels in interpreting and expressing interpersonal messages. Beyond the strong primacy of nonverbal cues that is deeply ingrained, people believe strongly in the veridicality and spontaneity of nonverbal cues, leading them to perceive (rightly or wrongly) that nonverbal cues speak "the truth." Another reason is that nonverbal cues may reveal psychological and emotional information about the interactants that creates a deeper context for understanding another person's total communication. The division of labor between verbal and nonverbal cues, with the nonverbal codes being especially suited to handle interpersonal business while the verbal channel is simultaneously occupied with transmitting other information, enables nonverbal cues to play a significant role in clarifying verbal content. No matter the reason, it is clear that nonverbal signals are critical to understanding interpersonal communication.

## The Importance of Nonverbal Communication Skills

Bestsellers on interpersonal relationships often advertise that they have the secret to relationship success. Skillful nonverbal communication is one

such key. For example, college students who were better at identifying affective meanings from facial expressions and tone of voice reported experiencing better personal relationships, whereas decoding errors marked relationships that were less well off (Carton, Kessler, & Pape, 1999). The same can be said for individual well-being and mental health. A review of research on the relationship between depression and social skills found support for social skills deficits making people vulnerable to and causing depression and depression in turn causing poor skills, leading to a vicious cycle (Segrin, 2000). Clearly, nonverbal skills matter. Indeed, the capacity to transmit and acquire information accurately is one of the fundamental requirements of social life. Yet not all humans are equipped with such skills. Some individuals are naturally more gifted or are more amendable to learning nonverbal skills than others.

Nonverbal skills go by many names: nonverbal sensitivity, interpersonal sensitivity, inferential accuracy, communication competence, social skills, emotional intelligence, and empathy, among others (see Bernieri, 2001; Burgoon & Bacue, 2003; Hall, Murphy, & Schmid Mast, 2006). Most of these skills can be divided into ones that relate to *encoding*—the ability to produce and control competent nonverbal expressions—and ones that relate to *decoding*—the ability to perceive, recall, and understand nonverbal expressions (Riggio, 1992). Others include both sending and receiving abilities. For example, the highly popularized work on *emotional intelligence*, defined by its originators as "the ability to perceive emotions, to access and generate emotions so as to assist thought, to understand emotions and emotional knowledge, and to reflectively regulate emotions so as to promote emotional and intellectual growth" (Mayer & Salovey, 1997, p. 5), emphasizes four components: (1) *attention*, which refers to the perception of cues, (2) *clarity*, which refers to the ability to make fine-grained discriminations, (3) *knowledge*, which refers to cognitive understanding and assimilation of emotions, and (4) *reflective regulation*, which pertains to the ability to control own and others' emotional states.

Plentiful research has examined nonverbal encoding and decoding skills (for summaries see Burgoon & Bacue, 2003; Guerrero, Jones, & Boburka, 2006; Hall, Andrzejewski, & Yopchick, 2009). The conclusions that emerge are these:

1. *Encoding and decoding ability are correlated.* Those who are better senders tend to be better receivers and vice versa, but the relationship is a modest one.

2. *Encoding skills are related to one another, as are decoding skills.* Vocal encoding skill tends to correlate with visual encoding skill; the same is often, though not always, true of decoding skills. Those who are skilled at decoding messages of liking and disliking also tend to be skilled at judging ambivalent and deceptive messages.

3. *Encoding and decoding ability correlate with personality traits and values.* Encoding skill is greater among those who are more expressive, extraverted, nonreticent, high in self-esteem, outgoing, high in self-monitoring, socially anxious but not depressed, nondogmatic, persuasive, and physically attractive. Such individuals have expressions that are easier to decode because they include a higher rate of "meaningful" gestural, head, and eye movements that are more noticeable and vivid. Decoding skill is also associated with more favorable or adaptive psychosocial functioning. More skilled and interpersonally sensitive individuals are more gregarious, sociable, nondogmatic, and low on Machiavellianism, among others.

4. *Decoding ability increases with practice and training but is curvilinearly related to age.* Maturation, increased social development, and practice all contribute to improved accuracy in interpreting nonverbal expressions (and can even eliminate the female

advantage over several trials), up to a point. People get better at decoding emotional expressions as they move from childhood to adulthood, reaching a plateau at about age 25 to 30 (Nowicki & Duke, 1994). But elderly people lose some of their ability to detect emotions accurately, perhaps due to reductions in perceptual acuity, ability to concentrate, and memory. Thus, the experiential gain due to longevity is offset by decrements in relevant cognitive and perceptual skills. Additionally, research on deception suggests that highly experienced decoders (e.g., customs agents, police investigators, and interrogators) are no better than novices and may actually do more poorly than them, perhaps because they become overly suspicious. Here again, experience isn't necessarily the best teacher.

5. *Encoding ability increases with age.* As expected, individuals also learn to encode nonverbal messages more effectively as they move from childhood to adulthood (Custrini & Feldman, 1989). Effective encoding entails knowing when to spontaneously express one's true feelings as well as when to manage expressions to send appropriate messages. For example, individuals may not wish to show the true extent of their strong feelings for someone on a first date. Research suggests that children learn how to express emotions effectively before learning how to regulate them, with the ability to manage nonverbal expressions generally increasing and then leveling off by middle adulthood.

6. *Women are generally better than men at encoding and decoding nonverbal messages.* This encoding superiority exists regardless of age but may be limited to visual cues, nondeceptive messages, and positive (rather than negative) emotions. Some research also suggests that although women are better at encoding positive emotions, men are

slightly better at controlling or regulating certain emotional expressions. In a seminal meta-analysis by Hall (1979), 71% of the studies favored women as better senders than men, and 84% favored women as more accurate interpreters than men (although it should be noted that the magnitude of the encoding and decoding advantage is small). More recent work reconfirmed that women have more accurate recall of nonverbal behaviors, whether it be observing a videotaped interview or recalling an actual interaction partner (Hall et al., 2006), and that women are generally better at decoding emotions than are men (for reviews, see Guerrero & Reiter, 1998; Hall, Carter, & Horgan, 2000). Among the reasons suggested for why women often exceed men in encoding and decoding ability are greater expressiveness, more practice in social roles that place an advantage on good interpretive skills, socialization to being more accommodating and attentive to the intentional gist of others' communication, innate differences, cognitive processing differences, and differences in brain configurations that foster better processing of nonverbal cues.

## Functions of Nonverbal Communication

Nonverbal communication is also important because it helps people reach a variety of interpersonal goals, such as making a good impression on others, developing new relationships, and detecting others' deception. Early research, however, was limited in its ability to shed light on nonverbal communication in interpersonal interaction because it tended to isolate behaviors based on code (e.g., facial expressions, or voice) rather than focusing on interrelated, patterned constellations of cues that fulfill various communication purposes or functions. The importance of nonverbal signals becomes more apparent

when they are examined collectively. Thus, although it is necessary to isolate them for purposes of studying the structure of nonverbal communication, it is more sensible and interesting to look at how they work together to achieve any particular interpersonal objective.

Next, we review 5 of the 10 nonverbal communication functions for which there are substantial programs of research, theories, and empirical evidence pertinent to an interactional approach: (1) identification and identity management, (2) impression formation, (3) emotional expression and management, (4) relational communication and relationship management, and (5) deception. For material related to the function of message production and processing, consult Berger (2009) and Roskos-Ewoldsen and Roskos-Ewoldsen (2009). Material related to social influence is available in Chapter 12 of this volume, by Dillard and Knobloch, and in Burgoon, Segrin, and Dunbar (2002). Material related to structuring interaction, conversation management, and impression management can be found in Burgoon et al. (2010), Patterson (1983), Manusov and Patterson (2006), and Street and Cappella (1985).

## Identification and Identity Management

When communicators come together, the very first thing they must do is identify one another: Do I know this person? Is this person friend or foe? Because humans come equipped with the capacity to make such split-second assessments, these types of questions are typically asked and answered in milliseconds and often without conscious awareness. These are the processes related to identification, person perception, and impression formation.

One's self-identity is an amalgam of sociocultural and demographic characteristics such as nationality, gender, age, education, occupation, and religion, as well as personality. Manifest indications of one's cultural, social, demographic, and personal characteristics serve as "identity badges," enabling individuals to project their own identification with various personal and social categories while simultaneously enabling observers to use the same cues as an instant means of classification. As many philosophers of identity have noted, identities are not something we "have" but something we "do," and that "doing" is expressed partly through how we communicate. The concept of performing identities also implies, first, that there is not a single "inner self" but rather multiple selves and, second, that there is some fluidity to our identities. Thus, although identities are commonly thought of as unconscious, internalized, consistent, and highly stable over a given period of time, they are also malleable and emerge partly out of how we appear and act. In turn, individuals rely on their own nonverbal enactments as an affirmation or self-verification of their identities (see Swann, 1987).

Of course, we have features that are completely unique to us and that serve to differentiate us from all others. One of the burgeoning areas of research in computer science and engineering is biometrics, the automatic identification of individuals from anatomical or behavioral features (Boulgouris, Plataniotis, & Micheli-Tzanakou, 2010). When unchanging (and usually unalterable) physical features such as fingerprints, palm prints, irises, retinas, vasculature of the eye, physiognomy, height, or birthmarks are used to identify a person, it is called *hard biometrics*. When behavioral features such as gait or voice quality are used, it is called *soft biometrics*. The former are expected to yield nearly 100% accurate identification of a person, whereas the latter are more probabilistic. It is the latter that most rightly qualify as nonverbal signals in that they are subject to some variability and to some extent are under an individual's voluntary control, which means they can be selected and manipulated as communication signals. For example, a person who typically walks with a lumbering gait can speed up or slow down or walk emphatically or lackadaisically.

Before considering how individuals project their self-identities through nonverbal signals, a note of clarification is needed. Although the lines may be blurred between identity management and the process of impression management, we are making a subtle distinction between the two. (Consult Metts & Grohskopf, 2003, for a review of the impression management literature.) Identity management refers to presentation of the "phenomenological" self, or one's self-perceived "true" self, whereas impression management refers to the strategic presentation of the image for the benefit of an audience (Jones & Pittman, 1982). We focus here on identities rather than impressions, although people certainly use nonverbal cues as part of strategic self-presentation.

Because identity presentations may emanate from biological forces, acculturation, and learning processes, they may be more "indicative" (unintentionally revelatory) than "communicative." Nevertheless, because individuals may also deliberately emphasize or deemphasize features of their identity (e.g., having plastic surgery, wearing native dress, or suppressing a dialect), it is useful to analyze how nonverbal cues convey social identities, especially as they are adapted in particular interpersonal relationships.

The available information on sociocultural, demographic, and personality differences far exceeds the space that can be devoted to it here. What follows are just three of the major factors that can serve as grist for projecting one's identity. At the same time, they are the basis for observers forming perceptions and impressions. That is, in addition to being used by senders to express who they are, they are also used by receivers to identify, categorize, and form judgments about the sender. Thus, this information is equally relevant to the function of impression formation.

## Sociocultural Differences

Cultures and cocultures differ, sometimes radically, in how they perceive, interpret, and use kinesic, vocalic, spatial, tactile, appearance, chronemic, and artifactual displays as messages (for summaries, see Burgoon et al., 2010; Hall, 1977;

Kitayama, 2002). As one illustration, an oft-cited though overly simplistic distinction is between "contact" and "noncontact" cultures, with the former preferring closer interaction distances, more frequent use of touch, higher rates of gaze, and more gestural animation. This distinction reveals that people's habitual interpersonal interaction styles differ depending on their cultural heritage. Even where cultures have similar behavioral patterns, cultural display rules may modify the exhibited pattern and the circumstances of a behavior's performance (Matsumoto, 2006). Poggi (2002) went so far as to articulate the rules for Italian gestures, touches, and gaze through the formation of a "gestionary" that presents a lexicon of various expressions and their forms and meanings.

These cultural differences become one vehicle for self-identification. According to *social identity theory* (Tajfel & Turner, 1986), individuals have not one but multiple social identities that form ever-enlarging circles of social groups to which an individual belongs. By adhering to cultural or group norms, one may signal membership, thereby invoking all the characteristics and expectations stereotypically associated with that group (regardless of whether that is the sender's intent or not). By violating a culture's norms (e.g., wearing Western dress in a Muslim culture), one may likewise send a message of distancing oneself from that culture and repudiating that identity. In particular, people may establish their identities as members of sociocultural in-groups or out-groups through their vocalizations, gestures, postures, facial expressions, conversational distancing, touch, and physical appearance. By establishing a common communication style, group members signal their identification with one another while distinguishing themselves from out-group members.

Extensive research on in-group/out-group relations (see, e.g., Brewer & Hewstone, 2004; Markus & Kitayama, 1991; Tropp & Wright, 2001) speaks of the importance of self-identity in relation to one's in-group or out-group status. One theory that addresses the process whereby people signal their in-group or out-group status explicitly is *communication accommodation theory*

(Gallois, Ogay, & Giles, 2005; Giles, Coupland, & Coupland, 1991), which postulates that people converge their speech and vocalic patterns toward those of in-group members and diverge from those of out-group members. These outward manifestations of association solidify identification with primary groups.

## Gender and Sex Differences

A central ingredient of a person's self-image is her or his sexual or gender identity as female or male, feminine or masculine. A staple principle of gender theories is that gender is "performative": Through stylized bodily appearance and repetitive acts, people manifest their gendered self (Bell & Blaeuer, 2006). The nonverbal literature is rife with evidence of the means through which people perform their gender and possible explanations for differences in female/feminine versus male/masculine nonverbal displays (see, e.g., Brody & Hall, 2010; Dow & Wood, 2006; Hall et al., 2000). Some of these are rooted in primary (genetic) and secondary (physiological and anatomical) features associated with sexual functioning. Other biological differences between males and females likewise produce observable nonverbal differences in physical characteristics such as appearance and voice that may influence entire patterns of responding.

Biobehavioral predispositions, in interaction with environmental influences and social learning processes, affect a whole range of nonverbal encoding and decoding patterns. When these sex-linked differences take a behavioral form, they become part of what Birdwhistell (1970) labeled *tertiary gender displays*. Some feminine and masculine behavioral patterns may stem from biological or cultural needs to distinguish the sexes and promote sexual attraction. Provocative walking and standing postures, grooming and adornment practices that emphasize female or male physical attributes, and vocal qualities that connote strength or weakness may fit into this category. Other behavioral differences such as sitting with crossed ankles or legs may be due to socially prescribed gender-linked expectations for masculine and feminine behavior. The complexity and variety of affective, cognitive, motivational, learning, and situational factors governing behavioral displays means that in many cases men and women are more similar than different. Gender displays are therefore at best probabilistic rather than fixed constellations of behavior. Among the many differences that have been confirmed empirically are these:

1. *Kinesically,* compared with men, women smile more, are more expressive facially, gaze more while speaking and listening, and display less visual dominance (a lower ratio of looking while speaking to looking while listening), more "submissive" postures and gestures (e.g., the head tilt, open palm display, closed arm and leg positions, and moderate postural tension), positive emotions, and less anger.

2. *Vocally,* women speak with higher pitched voices, are more expressive vocally, use more rising intonations (as in questions), talk less, listen more, are more hesitant, and are interrupted more often than men.

3. *Proxemically,* men are more likely to dictate spacing and distancing patterns, whereas women are approached more closely, tolerate more spatial intrusion, give way to others more frequently, take up less physical space, adopt closer conversational distances with both sexes, prefer side-by-side seating, and respond more favorably than men to crowded situations.

4. *Haptically,* women give and receive touch and seek physical contact more often than men. (One exception is that men initiate more touch during the beginning stages of dating relationships.)

5. *Interactionally,* women accommodate more to the interaction pattern of their partners than men do.

One controversial aspect of these basic feminine and masculine display patterns is the extent to which they reflect differences in power. Henley (2001) advanced the provocative "body politics" theory that men's nonverbal behavior is characterized by dominance and women's by submissiveness. Several studies and meta-analyses have challenged these findings as well as whether the observed male–female differences should be attributed to dominance (see, e.g., Halberstadt & Saitta, 1987; Staley & Cohen, 1988). One alternative explanation that is consistent with Eagly and Koenig's (2006) *social role theory* is that women are socialized to be more nonverbally sensitive and responsive than men. Many "dominance" findings can be reinterpreted within this frame, inasmuch as they also convey supportiveness, nonaggressiveness, and positive affect.

## Personality Differences

Researchers have demonstrated reliable associations between nonverbal communication and certain personality traits (for reviews, see Gifford, 2006; Hall et al., 2009). For example, nonverbal profiles have been presented for traits such as extraversion–introversion, Machiavellianism, anxiety, authoritarianism, and the need for affiliation; disorders such as schizophrenia, paranoia, depression, and hysteria; and communication predispositions such as communication apprehension, attachment style, unwillingness to communicate, self-monitoring, social skills, and touch avoidance. Many of these associations, however, have been assumed rather than tested using behavioral data.

The nonverbal codes and cues most often implicated in the manifestation of personality and psychological states are vocalics (talk time, loudness, speech errors, pitch, voice quality, and vocal characterizers such as crying or laughing, silences, interruptions, and response latencies), kinesics (the amount of eye contact, head orientation and nods, leg movements, object adaptors, coordination of movement, the amount of gesticulation, postural relaxation, and the amount of physical movement), proxemics (conversational distance), haptics (the amount of touch), and physical appearance (personal grooming and colorfulness of clothing). Nonverbal behavior patterns such as gaze, loudness, speaking tempo, laughter, smiling, expressiveness, nervous mannerisms, conventionality of appearance, and general interpersonal style show impressive cross-situational consistency in interpersonal situations (Funder & Colvin, 1991; Gallaher, 1992).

Other soft biometrics that supply "identifying information" regarding age, race, education, occupation, and social status are also nonverbal in nature. As Sherlock Holmes was quick to demonstrate, detectives often rely on combinations of seemingly inconsequential nonverbal cues to identify their quarry. This is because nonverbal demeanor is so often an "embodiment" of the person.

## Impression Formation

The function of identification and identity management is grounded in an encoder perspective—examining how communicators manifest "who they are" through nonverbal signals; impression formation, on the other hand, is grounded in a decoder perspective—showing how receivers use the same signals to form judgments of other communicators. When people first meet or talk, they often categorize one another rapidly on characteristics such as gender, age, socioeconomic status, political affiliation, nationality, personality, and geographic residence. Indeed, researchers have found recently that voters make judgments of political candidates, for example, within milliseconds, based largely on their appearance (Olivola & Todorov, 2010). In the earliest stages of meeting someone, people begin to draw inferences about the other's political, social, and religious attitudes, personality traits, and global qualities such as attractiveness, likability, and credibility. This largely subconscious but instantaneous process of impression

formation is highly stereotypic and fraught with misjudgments, but people rely on it nevertheless. Given that initial verbal exchanges are so often constrained by convention, nonverbal cues, especially a stable physical appearance and kinesic and vocalic behaviors, take on particular importance in shaping interpersonal expectations and in generating a frame for interpreting subsequent behavior.

The extensive research on impression formation falls under headings such as social cognition, first impressions, and interpersonal perception. Five key questions underlie the relationship between nonverbal signals and impression formation in interpersonal interaction: (1) How accurate and consensual are judgments made from nonverbal cues or channels? (2) What causes judgments to be biased? (3) Which nonverbal cues are the most implicated in impression formation? (4) Do first impressions persist when people are allowed to interact? (5) What attributions are associated with nonverbal communication–based impressions?

### Accuracy and Consistency of Judgments

The twin factors of accuracy and consensus in judgments relate to people's ability to make judgments of communicators that are, at minimum, consistent across multiple judges and, at maximum, accurate reflections of a person's "true" characteristics. Although it is possible to marshal considerable evidence of receiver agreement outstripping accuracy (i.e., observers share the same perceptions but those perceptions are often erroneous; see Gifford, 2006), researchers have documented that people's hunches can also be remarkably accurate (Smith, Archer, & Costanzo, 1991) and can be made based on "thin slices" of behavior that are only seconds in length—perhaps as short as the blink of an eye (Gray & Ambady, 2006).

For example, naive raters can predict student and principal evaluations of teaching effectiveness after watching three 10-second silent video tapes of a teacher's behavior in the classroom (Ambady & Rosenthal, 1993). They also rate employees with outstanding sales records as warmer and more supportive than employees with average sales records after listening to short audio clips of their voices, and they judge high-performing managers as more likeable, trustworthy, competent, persuasive, and willing to help others based on 10-second recordings of their voices (Ambady, Krabbenhoft, & Hogan, 2006). Notwithstanding these findings, accuracy tends to be highest for judgments such as sex, age, occupation, and social status that are derivable from external and emblematic appearance and vocal cues (Burgoon et al., 2010).

Judgments of attitudes, values, and personality traits are much more variable and subject to stereotyping. Impressions founded on combinations of cues, especially the dynamic ones available during interpersonal interaction, may be more accurate because the interrelationships among concurrent cues and their congruence with the context can be judged. As Smith et al. (1991) noted,

> It now appears that multiple, redundant, interpretable cues are "diffused" throughout an interaction. . . . As a result, there are *many* paths to a correct inference, and perceivers will (quite correctly) cite as significant a disconcertingly wide variety of nonverbal cues. (p. 16)

## Biases in Impression Formation

Relevant here is the extent to which the nature of the nonverbal behavior itself influences judgments. Two biases of special import are based on the *visual primacy effect*: (1) the previously noted strong orientation, at least in Western cultures, toward visual cues that may cause overreliance on visual information to the neglect of relevant auditory information and (2) the "what is beautiful is good" stereotype, wherein beautiful people are more likely to be credited (sometimes incorrectly) with an array of positive attributes such as

honesty, intelligence, persuasiveness, poise, sociability, warmth, power, and employment success than unattractive individuals (Hatfield & Sprecher, 1986; Kitayama & Ishii, 2002; Knapp & Hall, 2010).

In the workplace, research also suggests that physical appearance only goes so far in helping applicants secure jobs. For example, Heilman and Saruwatari (1979) found that physical attractiveness was an asset to men who were seeking both managerial and clerical positions but only to women who were applying for clerical positions. Physical attractiveness is also more of an asset when people are interviewing for jobs that require interpersonal skills, such as positions in sales or counseling, as opposed to jobs where people spend much of their time alone behind a desk, such as accounting or engineering (Cash & Kilcullen, 1985). Research further shows that people hold some negative biases toward physically attractive people as potentially unapproachable, snobbish, materialistic, vain, and undesirable as long-term partners. This bias has been termed the "what is beautiful is self-centered" stereotype (Cash & Janda, 1984).

## Specific Nonverbal Cues Relevant to Impression Formation

Regarding the importance of specific nonverbal channels and cues in forming impressions, physical appearance, kinesic and vocalic demeanor, and proxemic patterns are the most immediately available sources of information. In keeping with the visual primacy and beauty biases, the visual channel appears to be more important than the auditory channel in forming impressions of attractiveness (Zuckerman, Miyake, & Hodgins, 1991). Beyond static appearance cues, communication style factors such as expressivity, smiling, gaze, nonverbal immediacy and involvement, positivity of facial expressions, and apparent spontaneity contribute to perceived attractiveness (e.g., Burgoon, 1993; Manusov, 1991; Reis et al., 1990; Remland & Jones, 1989).

For other judgments, facial and vocal cues related to maturity or babyfaceness (called neoteny), vocal loudness, pitch, pitch variety, tempo, delivery style, fluency, physical height and weight, gait, and self-touch have been shown to be reliable and consistent predictors of personality and social perceptions of power, warmth, and credibility (e.g., Barge, Schlueter, & Pritchard, 1989; Burgoon, Newton, Walther, & Baesler, 1989; Zebrowitz, 1997). One reason why these biases persist is that they have adaptive evolutionary value. By overgeneralizing from the characteristics of babies, family members and the like provide nurturing, acceptance, and patience to other unfamiliar adults, a cost that outweighs the disadvantage of sometimes misperceiving adult characteristics due to the look of a face.

During employment interviews, nonverbal behaviors reflecting expressiveness, friendliness, and confidence can give qualified interviewees an edge, although they will not overcome the lack of qualifications. Interviewees who are trained to use steady eye contact, smiling, animated voices, expressive gestures, and speech fluency are rated higher by interviewers on a number of attributes, such as self-confidence and motivation, than those who are trained to display the opposite behaviors (McGovern & Ideus, 1978). Interviewees are also more likely to be recommended for or offered positions when they exhibit nonverbal immediacy cues, such as smiling, eye contact, direct body orientation, and head nods (e.g., Forbes & Jackson, 1980; Wright & Multon, 1995), and cues related to composure and confidence, such as eye contact, expansive gestures, vocal confidence, speech fluency, relaxation, and lack of nervous movement (Burgoon & Le Poire, 1999).

## Persistence of Initial Judgments

The question of persistence of first impressions is especially relevant to interpersonal communication. If first impressions are transitory, then they should be of minimal importance once people begin to interact and become acquainted. If they have a lasting impact, they may serve as a template through which all subsequent information is filtered and assimilated. Supporting the latter position, Kenny, Horner, Kashy, and Chu (1992) found that consensus existing at "zero acquaintance" persisted after interaction, and Burgoon and Le Poire (1993) found that induced pre-interaction expectancies about a target's communication style persisted even when the target's actual nonverbal communication was contradictory. These findings match other evidence on the persistence of expectancy effects. But cues differ in their persistence. As noted previously, in ongoing relationships, static or slow signals such as physical attractiveness diminish in importance, while dynamic cues rise in prominence. Cues that are novel, unexpected, or extreme may also have greater impact.

## Attributions Associated With Impressions

The final question regarding attributions associated with nonverbal impressions also has special import for interpersonal communication to the extent that the nonverbal behaviors are attributed to be intentional and to have message value. In a program of research addressing this question, Manusov and her colleagues found that many nonverbal behaviors such as immediacy changes, gaze, smiling, facial expressions, silences, tone of voice, and mirroring of another's behavior were interpreted as intentional (for a review, see Manusov, 2007). Negative behaviors were attributed to situational factors rather than target intent where such situational attributions could be made; otherwise, they were assumed to be purposeful acts and were evaluated more negatively on competence and social evaluation. Thus, many of the dynamic nonverbal behaviors responsible for engendering impressions are assumed to be other-directed behaviors with intentional message value.

## Expectancy Violations Theory

One communication theory in particular offers a useful typology for classifying impression formation processes. *Expectancy violations theory* (Burgoon, 1993) originated as an attempt to explain the effects of proxemic violations; yet the theory offers a series of assumptions and propositions predicting when nonverbal behaviors will produce positive outcomes, such as heightened credibility and attraction, or negative outcomes.

When the meanings attributed to a person's nonverbal cues are unequivocal and/or congruent (in the case of multiple meanings), a social meaning model prevails such that the interpretations and evaluations associated with the behaviors are predicted to influence outcomes directly. For example, high conversational involvement carries positive connotations, is evaluated positively (considered desirable), and should therefore evoke desirable evaluations of the communicator. When meanings are ambiguous or conflicting, *communicator reward valence* is posited to moderate the *cognitive-affective assessment* process. Communicator valence is a summary term for all the combined communicator characteristics that, on balance, cause the communicator to be regarded positively or negatively. The interpretation and evaluation process results in a net valence for the nonverbal act. Positively valenced acts are posited to produce positive outcomes and negatively valenced acts, negative outcomes for the actor. Violations of expectations are hypothesized to intensify this process by causing an attentional shift to the source of the violation and the behaviors themselves, thus making communicator and message characteristics more salient.

Research to date on this theory (for a review, see Floyd, Ramirez, & Burgoon, 2008) has produced the following conclusions, cast here in impression formation terms:

1. *Positive-valence communicators are perceived as more credible and attractive when they (a) engage in violations of far or close distance and (b) use some forms of affiliative touch.* The touch findings may be qualified by gender and type of relationship.

2. *Negative-valence communicators reduce credibility and attraction by engaging in proxemic and haptic violations.* Some forms of touch may also be used by negative-valence communicators but are riskier, especially if initiated by males.

3. *Both positive-valence and negative-valence communicators are seen as having higher credibility and attractiveness when engaging in (a) high degrees of gaze, (b) moderately high immediacy, and (c) conversational involvement.* These all qualify as positive expectancy violations.

4. *Negative violations in the form of (a) gaze aversion, (b) nonimmediacy, and (c) detachment lower judgments of credibility and attraction.*

For another perspective that makes some similar predictions based on expectations and their violations in task-oriented groups, see expectation states theory (Ridgeway, Berger, & Smith, 1985).

# Emotional Expression and Management

Expressing and managing emotions is among the most essential and primitive functions of nonverbal communication. Indeed, it is perhaps one mark of the extent to which nonverbal scholarship has matured that nonverbal communication is no longer simplistically and exclusively equated with expressive behavior. That said, nonverbal codes are primary vehicles for expressing emotions and affective states as well as for managing emotional experiences. Indeed, "people express feelings through their communicative conduct in incredibly rich and diverse ways; understanding the processes through which they do so requires an appreciation of the biology, psychology, and sociology of emotion" (Burleson & Planalp, 2000, p. 244). As this quote suggests, nonverbal expressions of emotion are influenced by both innate forces and socialization.

Moreover, nonverbal expressions of emotion are typically multimodal, in that they usually involve several different nonverbal codes, and interpersonal, in that they often result from and have consequences for interpersonal interaction. Because an entire chapter in this volume (see Chapter 10) is devoted to emotion, this chapter focuses on the above issues as they relate to the nonverbal *expression* (or external manifestation) of emotion. (For more on the interpersonal implications of *experienced* affect, see Chapter 9, by Metts and Planalp, this volume.)

Within the nonverbal literature, the terms *emotion, affect,* and *arousal* are sometimes used interchangeably. Emotion scholars, however, differentiate between these concepts. *Emotion* refers to a discrete, relatively transitory state that entails both an affective response and some degree of physiological activation or arousal. Indeed, some scholars (e.g., Russell, 1980) define emotions based on where they fall on an affective-valence dimension (pleasant to unpleasant) and an activity dimension (aroused to relaxed). *Affect* is a broader concept than emotion as it refers to any subjective experience that is hedonically toned on a good–bad or positive–negative continuum. Many scholars believe that affect is the most fundamental component of emotional experience; at a minimum, emotion requires having a positive or negative affective reaction to a stimulus (Frijda, 1993). Finally, *arousal,* which refers to physiological, cognitive, and/or behavioral activation, is also a central defining property of different emotions. Yet arousal is also related to states such as watchful readiness or boredom, which are not considered emotions by most scholars. Thus, all emotions have an arousal dimension associated with them; however, not all arousal is emotional. Arousal can also take two forms, one related to an orientation or alertness response that entails cognitive activation but limited physical activation and the second to a defensive response that entails intense physiological reactivity (Le Poire & Burgoon, 1996). Both range from pleasant to aversive and impair performance as they become increasingly intense and negative.

## The Nature of Emotional Expression

There is a long tradition of research on the expressive function of nonverbal communication. Among the primary issues addressed in this corpus of work are the origins and development of nonverbal emotional displays, the relationship between internal states and their external manifestations, and the manner in which meaning is assigned to overt behaviors. Due to space limitations, we focus here on the broad theoretical developments pertinent to the expression of emotion by concentrating, first, on perspectives related to the general debate on whether emotions and their expressions are innate or learned (i.e., the nature–nurture debate) and, second, on the debate over whether facial displays are best conceptualized as emotional expressions or are social expressions that have little to do with emotion.

*Nature Versus Nurture.* Many early theorists were influenced by Darwin's (1872/1998) seminal book *The Expression of Emotion in Man and Animals.* Darwin claimed that many emotional expressions are largely a function of evolution and are therefore innate. As he put it, "Actions, which were at first voluntary, soon became habitual, and at last hereditary, and may then be performed even in opposition to the will" (p. 356). Darwin's work laid the foundation for the *universalistic perspective,* which is guided by four complementary assumptions: (1) emotional expressions arise from inborn neurological programs and feedback mechanisms that produce and/or elicit facial displays of emotion; (2) emotional displays are manifestations of experiences common to all humans, such as the need to ward off danger or withdraw from pain; (3) there is a close (if not identical) correspondence between external displays and internal experiences of emotion, such that expressions are seen as readouts of an individual's true feelings; and (4) certain primary affect displays are produced and understood the same way by all members of a species, including humans from different cultures (Izard, 1977; Plutchik, 1984; Tomkins, 1984).

Considerable evidence has accumulated for the universalistic perspective. Physiological studies, including research on the facial feedback hypothesis, have demonstrated that voluntarily posing a given emotion in the face can actually elicit the felt experience, thereby linking internal experiences closely to their external manifestations (Buck, 1984; Levenson, Ekman, & Friesen, 1990). Relatedly, studies examining the configurations associated with emotional expressions (e.g., diagonal lines, angularity, or roundness) have shown that the same configural properties convey meanings of threat, anger, warmth, happiness, and so on (Aronoff, Barclay, & Stevenson, 1988; Aronoff, Woike, & Hyman, 1992). These "configural properties" point to an evolutionary process whereby humans have become hardwired to express emotion through nonverbal communication (Andersen & Guerrero, 1998; Dillard, 1998).

Cross-cultural research showing a high degree of similarity of emotional expression across cultures (e.g., Ekman, 1993; Sauter, Eisner, Ekman, & Scott, 2010; Scherer & Wallbott, 1994) also supports the likelihood that such behavior is at least partially biologically based. This research has identified basic or primary emotions that are encoded and decoded through the face the same way across cultures, with happiness, sadness, anger, fear, surprise, and disgust on most lists of basic emotions (Izard, 1977; Tomkins, 1963). Research in child development has shown that infants and toddlers follow the same stages of emotional development and exhibit the same expressions at each successive stage, thereby offering further indirect support for a biological explanation. More definitive evidence comes from studies of blind, deaf, and limbless children, who, lacking the ability to learn emotional displays through sensory experience, still exhibit universally recognized expressions (e.g., Eibl-Eibesfeldt, 1973; Galati, Scherer, & Ricci-Bitti, 1997).

Those adopting a *cultural-relativist perspective* (e.g., Birdwhistell, 1970; Mead, 1975), however, assert that individuals learn to express emotion in the same way that they learn a language. Therefore, any pancultural similarities are regarded as superficial and as regulated by cultural practices. In contrast to the universalistic view that emotional reactions are concrete components of a physiological system, those adopting a cultural-relativist position see emotions as social phenomena that are constituted in relationships. The basic assumption guiding the cultural-relativist position is that because "emotions are interpreted, experienced, and expressed differently depending on the social and cultural context in which they occur, they clearly cannot be universal" (Manstead & Fischer, 2002, p. 3).

Cultural relativists cite cross-cultural variability and the strong influence of socialization practices on nonverbal expressions to bolster their position. Manstead and Fischer (2002) noted "a steady stream of publications by cultural anthropologists and ethnographers" showing that "the emotional lives of peoples from other cultures [are] different from that in the West" (p. 2). This research demonstrated that people from non-Western cultures do not always experience or express so-called basic emotions such as anger or sadness (Levy, 1973) and that some of the emotions central to their experience are not found in Western cultures. Much of the early research supporting the cultural-relativist position was qualitative in nature, whereas the universalistic perspective was supported primarily by quantitative data; thus, the two perspectives initially differed not only in philosophy but also in methodology. More recent empirical work produced findings consistent with the cultural-relativist position, showing cross-cultural differences in a variety of emotion-related processes, including (a) the channels people from different cultures attend to when processing emotion (Kitayama & Ishii, 2002); (b) how individualism and collectivism promote emotional experience and expression (Markus & Kitayama, 1991); and (c) the degree of (un)pleasantness experienced in connection with various emotions (Mesquita & Karasawa, 2002).

As a sort of compromise between the universalistic and cultural-relativist positions, Ekman (1973) advanced *neurocultural theory*, which holds that although all humans are endowed with the same innate neuromuscular programs, sociocultural factors filter what stimuli will elicit different emotions and promote cultural display rules, which dictate when, how, and with what meaning and consequences emotional displays will occur. This theory is in accordance with the universalistic perspective in that people are theorized to be hardwired with an innate affect program that includes physiological changes and facial displays related to basic emotions. It departs from the traditional universalistic perspective, however, because, rather than being a reflection of internal states alone, facial displays of emotions are also theorized to reflect cultural display rules.

These display rules, which people learn from interacting with others in their culture, help individuals regulate their internal experience and communicate emotions in socially appropriate ways. Five primary display rules involve (1) *simulation*, which occurs when people show emotion(s) that they are not feeling; (2) *inhibition*, the opposite of simulation, which occurs when people hide emotion(s) by acting like they are not feeling anything; (3) *intensification*, which calls for expressing an amplified version of an experienced emotion; (4) *miniaturization*, the opposite of intensification, in which the expression of a felt emotion is downplayed; and (5) *masking*, which is the attempt to show a different emotion than what one is experiencing.

Most contemporary research in this area from the 1990s onward has focused on the extent to which both universality and cultural relativism characterize emotional displays (e.g., Scherer & Wallbott, 1994). Substantial evidence suggests that there is cross-cultural similarity in the facial displays, physiological responses, and interpretations associated with basic emotions such as happiness, sadness, and anger (e.g., Ekman, 1993; Scherer & Wallbott, 1994). Indeed, based on a meta-analysis of the emotion literature, van Hemert, Poortinga, and van de Vijver (2007) contended that the size of cross-cultural differences in emotion has often been "overestimated," with cross-cultural differences accounting for very little variability once method-related variables are controlled. To the extent that emotional

expressions are part of the human genetic code, they form an elemental universal language that can supplant or augment more ambiguous messages and cross cultural barriers.

Nevertheless, significant differences exist in the form and intensity of emotional displays across cultures and social groups, leading Russell (1994; Fridlund & Russell, 2006) to claim that there is *minimal universality*. In relation to encoding, people tend to express more emotion if they are from a country characterized by values related to democracy, human rights, and individualism (van Hemert et al., 2007). Collectivist cultures may display more emotions that promote group cohesion and harmony than do individualistic cultures, whereas cultures with significant power differences may display more emotions that preserve such differences (Matsumoto, 2006). In relation to decoding, people have an *in-group advantage* such that accuracy is highest when people interpret the facial expressions of individuals from their own culture (Dovidio, Hebl, Richeson, & Shelton, 2006; Elfenbein & Ambady, 2002, 2003). Cultural differences are also evident in studies demonstrating that people have *nonverbal accents*. For example, Marsh, Elfenbein, and Ambady (2007) demonstrated that people could differentiate photos of Americans and Australians when they were smiling but not when they had neutral expressions, suggesting that the smiles contained an identifiable cultural "accent" that the neutral expressions lacked.

*Emotional Versus Social Signals.* Scholars have also debated the extent to which facial displays and other expressive behaviors are manifestations of underlying emotions versus broader social functions. For example, *the behavioral ecology approach* holds that facial expressions evolved to serve social rather than emotional motives and that they lack isomorphism with internal emotional states (Fridlund & Duchaine, 1996; Fridlund & Russell, 2006). Behavioral ecologists suggest that it is overly simplistic to equate facial expression with emotion only; facial expressions are also theorized to reflect people's thoughts, intentions, and physical states within the broader interpersonal context. Emotions are but one part of this social landscape. Based on this reasoning, Fridlund and Duchaine (1996) contend that facial displays are best understood in terms of social meanings rather than the emotions they might be expressing. For example, a felt smile is best conceptualized as a signal of affiliation, a so-called sad face as an elicitor of support, and a so-called angry face as a precursor to a possible attack.

Instead of seeing a false smile as simulating happiness (and therefore employing a display rule), Fridlund and Duchaine (1996) argued that false smiles are better understood as messages of appeasement, just as faces that leak anger can be regarded as showing conflict about whether to attack or not, instead of simply reflecting a cultural display rule about inhibiting or minimizing displays of anger. In fact, Fridlund and Duchaine challenge the concept of display rules by arguing that people's expressions reflect authentic social motivations rather than false or altered manifestations of people's true internal stages. From this perspective, a false smile represents social motivations such as being socially polite rather than a cultural rule about acting happy when one feels otherwise.

Other scholars have adopted a *functional perspective* for understanding expressive behavior (e.g., Barrett, 1993, 1998; Baxter, 1992; Buck, 1984). According to this perspective, rather than competing, social and emotional responses are complementary in that they both help people reach intrapersonal and interpersonal goals. Among other ideas, Barrett's (1993) functional perspective holds that "emotion-relevant movements" function to accomplish both intra-individual regulation (of physiology and behavior) and social regulation. At the individual level, emotion helps people regulate their own internal thoughts and feelings (e.g., to become more focused, motivated, or creative) as well as their own behavior (e.g., to continue or discontinue an activity). At the social level, emotion helps people manage the reactions of others (e.g., to encourage participation).

## Emotional Expressions as Multimodal

Scholars embracing functional perspectives have also noted that facial expressions are not the exclusive site for communicating emotions (Barrett, 1993). Emotional expressions emanate from multiple modalities (e.g., body, voice, or touch), and those focusing on the face alone can lead receivers to reach erroneous conclusions. Planalp, DeFrancisco, and Rutherford (1996) found that among people who know one another, reliance is much greater on nonverbal than on verbal cues when decoding emotions. Also, people typically take four to eight nonverbal cues into account, usually from the face, voice, and body, when judging the emotions another person is experiencing.

*Facial Cues.* The face signals specific emotional states, with various regions of the face salient to sending and interpreting different emotions (for a summary, see Burgoon et al., 2010). The authenticity of emotions is conveyed through timing and duration (Schmidt, Cohn, & Tian, 2003). "Real" emotions typically last from half a second to four seconds; expressions of shorter or longer duration than this range are often false or mock expressions. This may be one basis for considering some expressions as insincere or suspicious. The short duration of facial displays of emotion also led Haggard and Isaacs (1966) to study *micromomentary facial expressions*, which can be as short as one fifth of a second. Some scholars believe that these quick expressions are the truest reflection of internal feelings. The problem, however, is that in actual interpersonal interactions, micromomentary expressions are almost impossible to notice, much less decode accurately (Kaiser & Wehrle, 2001).

*Vocal Cues.* The extensive emphasis that early emotion research placed on the face overlooked the extremely important place of vocal cues in emotional expression, which was perhaps best articulated in Scherer's (1986) component process model of emotion. Acoustic features such as amplitude, fundamental frequency (pitch), tempo, intonation pattern, and stress contours differentiate specific emotions and are correlated with the intensity and valence of emotions (Banse & Scherer, 1996; see Burgoon et al., 2010, for more on the vocal qualities that characterize different emotions). Scholars have suggested that, like facial cues, vocal emotional cues such as screaming, panting, and groaning evolved as a mode of instantaneous communication that helps humans survive (Juslin & Laukka, 2003). There is also evidence for the universality of vocalic cues of emotion, both from studies that have found similar vocal patterns distinguishing various emotions across cultures (Scherer & Wallbott, 1994) and in studies demonstrating that all children, regardless of country of origin and whether they are deaf or hearing, produce laughter at about the same time (Owren & Bachorowski, 2003).

*Body Cues.* Some body cues also qualify for universal status as indicators of emotion. For example, Tracy and Matsumoto (2008) found that Olympic and Paralympic athletes displayed shame and pride through similar body cues (e.g., raised arms and hands, back head tilts, and expanded chests for pride and slumped shoulders and narrowed chests for shame) regardless of their country of origin. Defensiveness cues, such as folding one's arm across one's chest, and anxiety cues, such as twisting one's hands or shifting one's weight back and forth, may also be encoded and decoded similarly across cultures. As for facial and vocal cues, different body cues appear to align with the basic emotions. To test this proposition, Coulson (2004) had people decode the emotions of computer-generated mannequins that were posed in different positions. They found distinct profiles of body cues associated with perceptions of happiness, anger, and sadness.

*Activity Cues.* Compared with facial and vocal cues, body, tactile, and other activity cues have received less systematic attention even though they are intuitively relevant to emotional expression.

Activity cues range from solitary activities such as going for a run to interpersonal ones such as kissing or slapping (Planalp, 2008). Different types of touch appear to have specific attributes that people associate with emotion. Hertenstein, Keltner, App, Bulleit, and Jaskolka (2006) had participants from the United States and Spain try to identify the emotion of a person who touched them from behind a curtain. Each of the six basic emotions was associated with a different pattern of touch characteristics (e.g., sadness was related to stroking, squeezing, and lifting).

## Emotional Expressions as Interpersonal

As noted previously, nonverbal expressions of emotions are usually embedded within a larger interpersonal context. Indeed, emotions are critical to managing relationships (Kitayama, Markus, & Matsumoto, 1995). Moreover, being able to decode, encode, and synchronize emotional expressions effectively can lead to happier relationships (e.g., Burleson & Denton, 1997; Gottman & Porterfield, 1981).

*Decoding Ability.* The degree to which people decode emotional expressions accurately is highly variable (Elfenbein & Ambady, 2002). People have difficulty decoding some facial displays and many vocal displays of emotion accurately. In conflict situations, people have a tendency to overestimate the extent to which their partner is expressing negative versus positive affect, which can lead to spirals of aggressive behavior (Gaelick, Bodenhausen, & Wyer, 1985).

Importantly, Motley and Camden (1988) found that spontaneously expressed emotions, which often occur in interpersonal interactions, are much more ambiguous and difficult to decode than the posed expressions so often studied in the emotion literature. In addition, during interpersonal interactions, people use a greater frequency of "affect blends"—combinations of emotions displayed simultaneously—and are likely to manipulate emotional expressions to reach relational goals (e.g., conveying more affection than is felt), making it even more challenging to decipher their true emotional state. Fortunately, there is some evidence that people are more facially expressive with friends than with strangers, which makes their emotional states easier to identify (Wagner & Smith, 1991). Intense emotions also tend to be decoded more easily and accurately than less intense emotions (Hess, Blairy, & Kleck, 1997), making it less likely that people will miss each other's strongest emotions.

*Encoding Ability.* Encoding ability has been described in terms of two skills: (1) the ability to spontaneously express emotions in order to elicit support and understanding from others and (2) the ability to manage or regulate emotional expressions in socially appropriate ways. Both skills are important in interpersonal interaction. Individuals who can communicate positive emotions effectively tend be liked by others and have more satisfying relationships than those who have trouble communicating their emotions (Burgoon & Bacue, 2003; Floyd, 2006). Kemper (1984) highlighted some of the ways in which encoding skill can promote positive relationships by binding people together. For example, when facing threats or crises, people may engage in approach behaviors or display distress, which should prompt reciprocal closeness and comforting from others, thereby alleviating fears and anxieties. When elated, people may express happiness and seek greater involvement to intensify the experience. Thus, people may fulfill basic needs such as security and affiliation by regulating their expression of emotions.

*Synchrony in Emotional Displays.* In addition to being skilled at encoding and decoding emotions, effective communicators are able to coordinate or synchronize their emotional displays in ways that promote a positive, prosocial environment. Unfortunately, however, some research suggests that people more readily reciprocate negative emotional expressions than positive ones, which can lead to depressed individuals bringing others "down" or angry individuals getting others "riled up." Scholars have described several related processes by which partners influence each other's emotional experience and expression, including the interpersonal facial feedback hypothesis, the emotional contagion effect, and motor mimicry.

Cappella (1993) proposed the *interpersonal facial feedback hypothesis* as an extension of the original facial feedback hypothesis, which showed that when people put on facial expressions for even a few seconds, they start to experience the physiological changes associated with that emotion (e.g., increased heart rate and warm temperature if making an angry face). According to the interpersonal facial feedback hypothesis, people also experience physiological changes when they respond to a partner's emotional expression. So feigning sympathy and concern could actually lead a person to start feeling some of those emotions.

Hatfield, Cacioppo, and Rapson (1994) coined the term *emotional contagion* to refer to the similar phenomenon of "catching" other people's emotions. Hatfield and her colleagues proposed that one way in which emotional contagion occurs is that people automatically synchronize to the nonverbal expressions of those around them. Similar to the logic in the interpersonal facial feedback hypothesis, changes in facial expressions and body movements are then theorized to trigger physiological changes that create a mood contagion loop, with bodily changes sending a signal to the brain to feel whichever emotion is consistent with one's nonverbal expressions.

*Motor mimicry* describes a similar process that can lead to synchrony between two or more people in both emotional experience and expression. This process occurs when people react to something that happens to another person and then experience some of that person's emotions (Bavelas, Black, Lemery, & Mullett, 1986). For example, when a father sees a daughter fall down and skin her knee, he might automatically wince in response. All of these processes highlight the link between biology and expressive behavior while also demonstrating the highly interpersonal nature of emotional expression.

# Relational Communication and Relationship Management

Relational communication is a subset of interpersonal communication that focuses on how people encode and decode messages that define the nature of their interpersonal relationship. These messages help people manage their relationships by accomplishing functions such as initiating interaction and sustaining closeness. Relational messages also reflect how interactants feel about each other, about the relationship itself, or about themselves within the context of the relationship. It has been said that every communication has a "content" or "report" aspect and a "relational" or "command" aspect (Watzlawick, Beavin, & Jackson, 1967). Nonverbal relational communication can be seen to serve this latter metacommunicative function in that it tells one how to interpret other concurrent messages within the context of the relational definition that exists. But it can also be seen as the "content" of messages about the relationship itself. That is, relational communication should not be viewed as merely augmenting other messages but as making meaningful statements in its own right. Relational messages are not exclusively nonverbal, but a division of labor exists between the verbal and nonverbal channels such that the nonverbal channels do a disproportionate share of the relational "work."

## Dimensions of Relational Communication

Based on a review of ethological, anthropological, sociological, psychological, and communication literature, Burgoon and Hale (1984) proposed seven distinctive major themes of relational messages: (1) intimacy, which

comprises several subthemes related to affection, involvement, inclusion, trust, and depth; (2) emotional arousal/activation; (3) composure; (4) dominance; (5) similarity; (6) formality; and (7) task or social orientation. Of these, messages related to intimacy and dominance have received the most scholarly attention because they reflect the "horizontal" and "vertical" dimensions of relationships. The major findings related to these two central dimensions are discussed next.

*Messages of Intimacy and Affection.* Both quantitative and qualitative studies suggest that intimacy or closeness is largely communicated by nonverbal behavior, such as physical closeness, touches, lingering gazes, synchronized interactions, and prolonged time spent together (Ben-Ari & Lavee, 2007; Bernieri & Rosenthal, 1991; Prager, 2000; Register & Henley, 1992). Intimacy can be understood as the combining of two major ingredients: nonverbal involvement and the expression of positive affect. Involvement alone neither implies nor includes positivity. Instead, it comprises at least five classes of behavior: (1) *immediacy* (proximity, direct body orientation, forward lean, postural openness, gaze, and touch, which signal approach and inclusion), (2) *expressiveness* (facial, gestural, postural, and vocal displays of animation and activity), (3) *altercentrism* (kinesic and auditory cues that one is attentive to and oriented toward the other rather than the self), (4) *conversational management* (self-synchrony, fluency, coordinated movement, interactional synchrony, and short-response latencies, which create a well-paced, smooth interaction), and (5) *social composure* (e.g., postural and vocal cues of relaxation and lack of anxiety) (Coker & Burgoon, 1987). When these types of involvement behaviors are accompanied by *positive affect* (smiling, nodding, vocal pleasantness, relaxed laughter), which is often the case, the overall package of nonverbal behavior reflects greater intimacy. Prager (2000) referred to this combination of behaviors as *positive involvement.*

Other cues that communicate intimacy include affectionate touch, soft voices, postural openness, motor mimicry and mirroring (exhibiting the same behavior as another), wearing similar apparel and identification symbols (such as a tattoo that includes someone's name), punctuality, monochronic use of time, and sharing territories and possessions. Of these, touch is especially reflective of intimacy (Thayer, 1986). Mutual touch to areas of the body considered private or vulnerable are especially likely to convey intimacy, with face touch and putting an arm around someone's waist judged as more intimate than touches to the shoulder or arm (Burgoon, 1991; Lee & Guerrero, 2001) and crisscross hugs (i.e., arms around each other's waist and shoulders) rated as especially affectionate (Floyd, 1999). These types of touch all qualify as *body contact tie signs* (Morris, 1977), which communicate closeness to a partner while also signaling to others that the two people are a bonded pair. Other forms of tie signs involve objects, such as wearing wedding rings or best-friend bracelets, and mutual-grooming behaviors, such as a mother wiping a smudge off her child's face (Nelson, 2007).

Research on affectionate communication is also central to understanding relational messages related to intimacy. Floyd (2006) advanced *affection exchange theory* to explain how, why, and with what consequences people communicate affection to one another. This theory is grounded in assumptions from evolutionary psychology, including the idea that affectionate communication helps people reach goals related to survival and procreation. Five specific propositions are at the heart of affection exchange theory.

1. *Humans are born with the capacity and the need to feel affection.* This proposition implies that affection is a basic human need, which if left unfulfilled has negative consequences for an individual's social development and physical health.

2. *The experience and communication of affection are distinct but related experiences.* The experience of affection involves having internal feelings of fondness and positive

regard for someone. Affectionate communication occurs when people encode messages that reflect these feelings. Floyd and Morman (1998) conceptualized and operationalized affectionate communication in terms of a tripartite model of affectionate behavior that includes (a) *direct verbal behavior,* such as saying "I love you"; (b) *direct nonverbal behavior,* which includes hugs, holding hands, and other behaviors that communicate affection unambiguously to others; and (c) *indirect nonverbal behavior,* such as being supportive, which communicates affection in certain contexts.

3. *Communicating affection is adaptive because it increases one's ability to reach goals related to viability (survival) and fertility (procreation).* According to affection exchange theory, people are motivated to communicate affection to those with whom they are genetically related or sexually attracted. This maximizes their chances of preserving their genetic line by providing support and resources to relatives with whom they share genes and to potential mates with whom they could have offspring. Affectionate communication is related to survival in another way: A host of positive psychological and physical benefits are associated with giving and receiving affection, including more relational satisfaction, higher self-esteem, and less depression as well as healthier hormone levels, blood pressure, heart rate, and blood sugar levels (Floyd, Hesse, & Haynes, 2007; Floyd, Mikkelson, et al., 2007; Floyd & Riforgiate, 2008).

4. *Humans have different optimal tolerance levels for affection and affectionate communication.* Some individuals have a greater need for affection and affectionate communication than others, and the amount of expressed affection that people desire varies based on individual personality traits, culture, and the situation, among other

factors. For example, some people enjoy public displays of affection, whereas others are embarrassed by them.

5. *When affectionate communication exceeds or falls short of one's optimal tolerance level, aversive reactions are likely.* Thus, while not receiving enough affection can be distressing, so can receiving too much affection from the wrong person at the wrong time. For example, Floyd (2006) notes that affectionate displays from strangers usually violate norms and lead to negative emotional and psychological responses. The same is likely true for disliked others and for affectionate displays that occur in certain contexts where it would be considered inappropriate (e.g., in church or at the workplace).

*Messages of Dominance and Power.* In addition to intimacy and affection, the other major dimension defining relational communication is dominance. Whereas psychologists have often defined dominance as a personality trait, communication researchers tend to conceptualize dominance as an interaction style that fosters social influence (Burgoon & Dunbar, 2000). Scholars have also distinguished between two divergent means of gaining power and influence: intimidation and threat versus socially skilled communication (Guerrero & Floyd, 2006). Intimidation and threat are conveyed through nonverbal behaviors that emphasize superior size and strength or the ability to punish others. Any actions that showcase or enlarge one's physical size (e.g., large territories, use of gatekeepers, deeper pitch, erect posture, a "firm" stance) or imply danger (threat stares, threatening gestures, loud voices, spatial invasions) function as threat signals. Although these types of behavior can be successful in securing compliance and maintaining power, they will not have long-lasting effects if people are complying out of fear rather than respect or agreement. When people wield dominance by engaging in socially skilled communication,

however, the effects are likely to be more enduring (Guerrero & Floyd, 2006).

Several types of dominant nonverbal behaviors reflect social skill rather than intimidation (Burgoon, Johnson, & Koch, 1998; Guerrero & Floyd, 2006). Many of these behaviors convey messages related to either poise or panache. Poise is communicated through nonverbal behaviors such as asymmetrical leg and arm positions, fluent speech, facial pleasantness, low levels of random movement, and speaking moderately loudly and fast. Individuals who have panache possess an expressive, dynamic, and energetic style of communication that commands attention and is memorable. Behaviors related to panache include direct gaze and body orientation, vocal and kinesic expressiveness, and forward lean.

Dominance can also be thought of in relation to power and status. *Power* is the ability to influence others, often by controlling valued resources. *Status* involves holding a valued position within a social or organizational hierarchy. In interpersonal relationships, the *principle of least interest* sometimes defines a partner's status in a relationship, with the partner who is the most in love having the least power and status because he or she is more dependent (Sprecher & Felmlee, 1997). Nonverbal cues are associated with dominance, power, and status in accordance with several principles of power (described next). *These principles should be seen as reflecting dominant, as opposed to submissive, behavior patterns,* and most have analogs in other species, suggesting that they may be universal forms of display. The principles are applicable to both organizational and interpersonal relationships (Burgoon et al., 2002) and are as follows:

1. *Access:* Powerful people are given more access to space and larger territories. This principle is evident in large organizations as well as in families. People with more power and status have larger, more private territories that are furnished more luxuriously. In organizations, the spaces of powerful people are often protected by territorial

markers and gatekeepers, such as having an inner office with locked doors and an administrative assistant. People also tend to respect the personal space of superiors and will therefore avoid entering their personal space or getting too close unless they are invited. In addition to these proxemic perks, powerful individuals also take up more kinesic space. They sit in more open, relaxed positions and use more expansive positions.

2. *Centrality:* Powerful people often occupy central positions. Managers, parents, and group leaders are usually in central positions, such as at the head of the table or in the front of a room, to maximize their visual access. Centrality of position also allows less powerful individuals to look at and listen to more powerful individuals. In organizations, office placement sometimes reflects this principle of centrality. Lower level employees may be clustered together, whereas superiors have their own areas away from subordinates and closer to the "center of power."

3. *Elevation:* This principle is so evident that it has been incorporated into phrases such as "looking down" at someone or aspiring to be "at someone's level." Sitting in an elevated position, such as on a throne or a judge's bench, conveys power, while kneeling and bowing convey respect and sometimes submissiveness. Penthouse offices and high-rise buildings are status symbols that showcase the importance people place on vertical height. Being tall is also associated with power, higher salaries, and perhaps even behavior. In a study of communication in virtual environments, Yee and Bailenson (2007) found that participants acted more confident when they were represented by a tall character than a short character.

4. *Initiation:* Powerful people make the first moves in interaction. They are the first to approach, the first to speak, the first to determine if and how greeting touches will

occur, and so forth. Through their actions, they set the tone for the interaction.

5. *Precedence:* Powerful people "go first" literally and figuratively. Royalty, heads of state, and high-ranking military officers exhibit this principle when they are the first to walk down a red carpet or enter a room. The concepts of "leader" and "follower" reify this principle.

6. *Prerogative to violate nonverbal norms:* Within organizations, those seeking power are best served by staying within the nonverbal norms. However, those who have achieved power or status can violate those norms without being censured. In fact, research on expectancy violations theory (Burgoon & Hubbard, 2005) suggests that individuals with high status or power are often perceived more favorably after they have violated norms. They can show up late, dress casually, enter an office without knocking, interrupt others, leave a meeting early (or not show up at all), look away when others are talking, and so forth. Such behaviors reinforce their power positions while also signaling that they have important things to do. In close relationships, individuals who are "less in love" can violate norms with less penalty than can those who are "more in love," and parents can break rules that children cannot.

7. *Interactional control:* In addition to having the prerogative to violate norms, individuals who are high in status or power are perceived as having the authority to control the interactions in which they participate. Compared with more submissive or subordinate individuals, they talk, interpret, initiate topics, and switch topics more. Observers assume that individuals who engage in these types of behaviors are in leadership positions. In interpersonal relationships, individuals who exercise interactional control often have more decision-making power.

Another important issue in relationships is relative power. Dunbar (2004; Dunbar & Burgoon, 2005) developed *dyadic power theory* to explicate how relative power associates with dominance displays. Relative power refers to the degree of power partners have in relation to one another and can range from one person having all the power (and the other partner having none) to partners having equal power. Dunbar predicted a curvilinear association between relative power and dominance displays, such that people with low or high levels of relative power were hypothesized to engage in less dominant communication than people with equal or near-equal levels of power. Her thinking was that those low in power would be submissive, those high in power would not need to display it, and those equal in power would use dominance during interactions involving negotiation and decision making. A study by Dunbar and Burgoon (2005) generally supported this hypothesis, although it also showed that those low in relative power tended to interrupt more, possibly in a bid to obtain more power. An earlier study by Felmlee (1994) produced similar results, with people using more dominant behavior in equalitarian relationships than in nonequalitarian relationships, but other studies (e.g., Aida & Falbo, 1991; Dunbar, 2003) have found that dyads characterized by equal power actually display less dominance. Thus, the jury is still out on how relative power is associated with dominance displays.

## Relationship Management

Apart from examining relational messages such as intimacy and dominance, another strand of research related to this function investigates how nonverbal cues help people develop and manage their relationships. Most of this scholarship has focused on the initiation and escalation phases of romantic relationships, including courtship, or the role that nonverbal communication plays in relational maintenance and conflict management.

*Attraction.* Much of the work on nonverbal signals as agents of relationship initiation has focused on attraction. Facial features and expressions play a particularly potent role in attractiveness (Zebrowitz, 1997). According to Cunningham, Barbee, and Philhower's (2002) *multiple-fitness model*, people are attracted to potential mates who display four qualities: (1) neoteny (i.e., youthful features such as full lips and large eyes), (2) sexual maturity (e.g., high cheek bones, curvy figure for women and broad shoulders for men), (3) expressivity (e.g., a large smile and confident posture), and (4) good grooming (e.g., cleanliness, nice hairstyle, and clothing). A speed-dating study also showed that weight is a major determinant of attraction; in short conversations with 25 different people, singles indicated more interest in getting to know those who were a healthy weight (Kurzban & Weeden, 2005).

Actual nonverbal communication also influences attraction. For example, the kinesic and vocal behaviors that people express in interaction can override the effects of initial attitudinal similarity or dissimilarity (Cappella & Palmer, 1990), and communication style rivals both physical attractiveness and similarity as a reason for people to be attracted to someone (Sunnafrank, 1992). Albada, Knapp, and Theune (2002) found further evidence for the important role that communication plays in the attraction process. In their study, people who exhibited negative communication styles during an interaction were rated about two points lower on a physical attractiveness scale than they had been before the interaction started.

Positive forms of communication also influence attraction. People tend to be attracted to those who use nonverbal cues that convey warmth, kindness, and sociability (Krueger & Caspi, 1993; Sprecher & Regan, 2002). Some research suggests that displays of agreeableness and warmth are more important for fostering attraction than are displays of dominance and confidence. In a study by Sadalla, Kenrick, and Vershure (1987), women observed men who were trained to be either dominant (by sitting in a relaxed position and talking in a loud, clear, and fast-paced voice) or nondominant (by sitting up straight and talking quietly). The women were more attracted to the men who were in the dominant condition. Two later studies extended this work by investigating both dominance and agreeableness (Graziano, Jensen-Campbell, Todd, & Finch, 1997; Jensen-Campbell, Graziano, & West, 1995). Although both dominance and agreeableness were predictive of attraction, agreeableness was even more predictive.

Finally, environmental cues such as ambient music and a comfortable temperature can increase attraction (Arriaga, Agnew, Capezza, & Lehmiller, 2008). In one study, women who were listening to rock music, which evoked positive emotion, rated men as more physically attractive than women who were either not listening to music or listening to alternative music, which evoked negative emotion (May & Hamilton, 1980). Most people know that low lighting enhances a romantic environment but are not aware that this effect could be partially due to pupil dilation: Low lighting leads to pupil dilation, and people perceive individuals with dilated pupils to be warmer and more attractive. Exciting environments may also foster attraction if, as the *excitation transfer hypothesis* suggests, people attribute the arousal (and sometimes the relief) they experience to their partner instead of to the situation (Zillman, 1978).

*Courtship.* Various scholars have developed models of courtship and quasi courtship (e.g., Cunningham & Barbee, 2008; Givens, 2005) that identify the nonverbal cues associated with stages of courtship as a progression from an "attention" stage to stages that involve sexual activity. The behavior that characterizes the early stages of these courtship models is generally timid and ambiguous, to help people save face if their advances are rejected. If, however, partners move successfully through these stages, their behaviors become bolder and more intimate.

Most models of the courtship process include an *attention stage*. Among the attention signals

that people display during social gatherings are smiling, nervous laughter, dressing and grooming oneself to try to stand out, and displaying possessions such as car keys or expensive electronic devices. When people spot someone specific whom they find attractive, their behavior shifts into a more ambivalent-tentative mode as they engage in behaviors such as sidelong glances, vacillating gaze (i.e., looking at and then away from the person), and shy or ambivalent smiles.

The next stage in the courtship process has been variously called *recognition, courtship readiness,* and *decide and approach.* At this stage, the primary goals are to acknowledge each other's interest, display signals showing availability, and eventually approach each other. Men may continue to appear vulnerable rather than bold during this stage, especially if the woman appears nervous. Signals related to availability and approachability include eyebrow raises; demure smiles; darting glances; head and hair tosses (especially for women); primping behaviors, such as fixing one's clothing or makeup; increased muscle tone (as people pull in their stomachs or stand straighter); and laughter (Moore, 1985). Although some studies suggest that smiling and gaze are especially critical for conveying interest and signaling availability in both heterosexual (Walsh & Hewitt, 1983) and lesbian (Rose & Zand, 2000) relationships, no single nonverbal cue may be as important as the total package of movement. Grammer, Honda, Juette, and Schmitt (1999) demonstrated that the speed, size, duration, and complexity of a woman's movements is correlated with how much she is interested in a man. Of course, people can misinterpret each other's nonverbal cues at this stage, as demonstrated aptly by Abbey's (1982) foundational work showing that men often overestimate the extent to which women are acting seductively rather than just being friendly.

Once two people approach each other, the next stage, which has been called *positioning, interaction,* or *talk and decide,* is to get to know each other better. Although talk also is a major factor at this stage, nonverbal behaviors may create and reinforce not only physical closeness but also psychological closeness through mutual gaze, direct body orientation, and inclusive postures that signal to others that a couple wishes to be alone. Nonverbal behaviors are also responsible for producing an interaction that is smooth, synchronized, animated, and pleasantly arousing, which in turn fosters attraction.

If couples continue to move through the courtship stages, they typically display more sexual interest in each other. The next stage focuses on touching and synchronizing behavior. Courtship rituals that involve music and dancing may help partners feel comfortable touching each other while also increasing the synchronization of movement. There are two phases related to sexual exploration and activity. The first of these focuses on signaling sexual interest through bolder, more provocative behaviors (e.g., exposing one's thigh when crossing legs), grooming behaviors (e.g., smoothing the partner's hair), and carrying and clutching activities (such as playing with someone's fingers or leading someone to the dance floor). More subtle nonverbal behaviors also occur at this stage. For example, men's voices may shift from high to low pitched and from fast to slow as the interaction becomes more sexually charged (see Farinelli, 2008, for a summary of vocal patterns related to affection and courtship). The second phase is the *resolution stage*, which occurs when couples have sex.

*Relationship Maintenance.* Research has shown that nonverbal communication is a key ingredient in relationship development, with couples exhibiting especially high levels of nonverbal affection, including touch, when they are in the process of moving their relationship from casual to committed (e.g., Guerrero & Andersen, 1991; Johnson & Edwards, 1991). Affectionate communication also helps people maintain satisfying relationships (Floyd, 2006; Punyanunt-Carter, 2004), as do expressions of positive emotion.

Indeed, after reviewing the literature, Kelly, Fincham, and Beach (2003) concluded that

> when one studies the interactions of happy couples, it is often not the verbal content that stands out. Instead, what is remarkable is the pleasurable emotions couples appear to be experiencing—the smiles, laughs, affection, and warmth that happy couples show. (p. 729)

Behaviors such as smiling, nodding in agreement, and displaying empathy through facial expressions are more predictive of marital satisfaction than is verbal communication (Gottman, Levenson, & Woodin, 2001), and expressions of positive emotion can help counterbalance some of the negativity that occurs in relationships (Fincham, Bradbury, Arias, Byrne, & Karney, 1997).

But it is not just the behaviors themselves that are reflective of relationships. The ways in which partners make sense of each other's nonverbal cues is also related to how happy they are with each other. Scholars (e.g., Fincham & Bradbury, 1992) have found a tendency for happily married (satisfied) couples to form what are called "relationship- or spouse-enhancing attributions" for a range of behaviors, including nonverbal cues. Attributions are the causes people see behind behavior, and they become "enhancing" when they support a positive view of another. So if a wife touched her husband on his arm, he could make sense of it in a way that reflected well on his wife and their relationship (i.e., "She did that because she is an affectionate woman"). Conversely, dissatisfied couples make attributions known as "distress-maintaining," where behaviors are judged to be caused by something that puts the partner or the relationship in a less favorable light (e.g., "She touched me because she is so disapproving").

Manusov and her colleagues (summarized in Manusov, 2007; see also Noller, 2006) have looked more precisely at how this works. They reached several conclusions: (a) that negative nonverbal cues are more likely to instigate attributions, (b) that relational satisfaction tends to be related to noticing more positive behavior, (c) that the attributions one partner makes are likely to affect that partner's subsequent behavior (e.g., smiling), and (d) that distress-maintaining and relationship-enhancing attributions can occur in both happy and unhappy relationships, though the former are more common in unhappy ones and the latter are more likely when couples are happy.

*Conflict Management.* In addition to the valence of behaviors and our attributions of those behaviors, effective conflict management is another key skill that helps people maintain satisfying relationships. Marital research has shown that conflicts often take the form of reciprocal escalating spirals of nonverbal hostility, with nonverbal expressions of affect emerging as a deciding factor in whether conflicts are managed or not (e.g., Gottman, Markman, & Notarius, 1977; Huston & Vangelisti, 1991). Gottman's (1994) *cascade model* describes a sequence consisting of four behaviors—(1) complaints and criticisms, (2) contempt, (3) defensiveness, and (4) stonewalling—that is especially destructive and can lead to divorce. Contempt is communicated by behaviors such as using a sarcastic or patronizing voice, appearing astonished or disgusted, looking down at someone, wrinkling one's nose, and rolling one's eyes. Defensive behaviors include sitting in closed positions, putting one's hands on one's hips, crossing one's arms across one's chest, backing away, whining, and shaking one's head while the partner is speaking. Finally, stonewalling consists of withdrawal or noninvolvement behaviors such as gaze aversion, lack of kinesic and vocal animation, head-down positions, and silence (Guerrero & Floyd, 2006). Partners often react to these types of behaviors by becoming emotionally flooded and increasingly aggressive or avoidant (Gottman, 1994).

In contrast, partners who manage conflict effectively display nonverbal cues that communicate warmth and help them focus on the issues at hand. Behaviors such as vocal interest, slower speech, longer speaking turns, smooth turn taking, and a relaxed posture are related to problem solving and validation during conflict interaction (Newton & Burgoon, 1990; Sillars, Coletti, Parry, & Rogers, 1982). Feeney, Noller, Sheehan, and Peterson (1999) also claim that "increased gaze, more facial expressiveness, more gestures, and more head nods" communicate that a person is trying to be cooperative during conflict (p. 353). Satisfied couples also communicate more warmth (in terms of positive affect and affection) to one another during conflict than do dissatisfied couples (Margolin, Burman, & John, 1989). Perceptions are critical as well. People tend to notice, react to, and overestimate the negativity they perceive in their partner's behavior but to underestimate the extent to which their partner is trying to communicate positive emotions (e.g., Gaelick, Bodenhausen, & Wyer, 1985; Manusov, Floyd, & Kerssen-Griep, 1997).

# Deception

This function concerns the ways in which people send messages designed to foster beliefs contrary to what the actor believes is the true state of affairs. Deception may take many forms, including falsehoods, white lies, equivocations, evasions, hyperbole, and omissions. The streams of research on deception, from communication to psychology, criminal justice, and information systems, run deep. Here, we summarize just a small fraction of what has been found. The reader is directed to several summaries in Aamodt and Custer (2006), Bond and DePaulo (2006), Burgoon and Levine (2009), DePaulo et al. (2003), Knapp (2008), Sporer and Schwandt (2007), and Vrij (2008). Because many view deception as impression management or self-presentation (Buller & Burgoon, 1994; DePaulo et al., 2003), a subset of the principles and findings we cover here is also applicable to impression management. What follows is a brief overview of the primary theories and lines of deception research most relevant to interpersonal communication.

## Deception Theories

Perhaps the most pervasive and cited "theory" is the *leakage hypothesis* articulated by Ekman and Friesen (1969). The leakage hypothesis proposes that the act of deception produces certain inward emotional and cognitive states that have associated outward telltale signs such as indications of arousal and stress. The nonverbal indicators of deception are thus involuntary and uncontrollable or uncontrolled signs of internal states. As part of the leakage principle is a leakage hierarchy that is based on the contention that deceivers attempt to censor and control facial expressions more than body and limb movements because they expect others to watch their face. Therefore, the least controllable or controlled channels and cues should be the best indicators of deceit. Subsequent work has challenged both the degree to which signs of deception are uncontrollable and whether the face is the "leakiest" channel, while still conceding that some indicators of deceit reflect involuntary reactions and unmonitored, uncensored behaviors (DePaulo et al., 2003; Zuckerman & Driver, 1985).

Expanding on this hypothesis, Zuckerman, DePaulo, and Rosenthal (1981) advanced a *four-factor theory*, positing that changes in deceivers' behavior are the result of four psychological processes: (1) *physiological arousal* (due to detection apprehension), (2) *emotional reactions* (arising from guilt or fear of detection), (3) *cognitive load* (the extra cognitive effort required to formulate deceptive messages), and (4) *behavioral control* (efforts to suppress telltale signs and to create a credible demeanor). Thus, the cues exhibited during deception should arise from these factors. In a similar vein, Hocking and Leathers (1980) theorized that people would attempt to control those cues stereotypically associated with deception.

In an attempt to move beyond examining leakage cues and to better understand the interpersonal dynamics involved in deceptive interaction, Buller and Burgoon (1996; Burgoon & Buller, 2008) developed *interpersonal deception theory* (IDT). IDT applies interpersonal communication

principles to deception. It makes an assumption, common to interpersonal communication, that communication is goal directed, which means that people have (albeit sometimes tacit and unconscious) strategies to construct plausible untruths, to evade detection, and to promote believability. In that respect, it shares the same assumption that underlies impression management. Interpersonal deception also requires that senders and receivers attend to the other previously cited communication functions. In the process of engaging in deceit, deceivers are usually motivated to protect their image and self-identity while also successfully influencing the other. To do so, they need to manage their communication performance so as to avoid negative relational messages that spoil their identity or relationship while sending positive relational messages that promote trust. They also need to manage their emotions so as to minimize clues to arousal, guilt, anxiety, or fear prompted by engaging in deceit. And they must maintain their conversational responsibilities so that the interaction proceeds smoothly.

Attending to this multiplicity of functions could make the task of deceiving more demanding on deceivers than on receivers and thus make it easier for receivers to detect deception, but in practice, it turns out that the net advantage usually goes to the deceiver; that is, deceit often escapes detection. Why this is so is explained in several of the propositions (empirically testable statements) of IDT. We mention just a few here. These various principles derive from a number of communication and psychology theories; IDT was intended to try and synthesize them into a "big-picture" view of deception and its detection.

1. *Interactive deception differs fundamentally from noninteractive deception.* The idea behind this proposition is that different conversational demands and characteristics come into play when sender and receiver engage in interpersonal interaction rather than, say, observing the interaction of others or delivering a monologue to a seen or unseen audience.

2. *Credibility is the central message feature to which both participants are attuned.* This proposition articulates a basic maxim of all communication, that participants expect one another to be truthful. Senders, therefore, attempt to craft their behavior and messages in ways that engender believability. Receivers in turn are attentive to any clues that "the truth, the whole truth, and nothing but the truth" is not being presented.

3. *Deception is manifested through a combination of strategic and nonstrategic behaviors.* General strategies might include adopting a submissive, agreeable demeanor; increasing uncertainty not only through verbal vagueness but also via mixed nonverbal messages about one's commitment to what is being said; conveying composure by being still and suppressing behaviors indicative of nervousness; increasing nonverbal involvement to suggest that they have nothing to hide; or, more generally, attempting to approximate their own normal demeanor. IDT recognizes that communicators may still display nonstrategic behavior such as indicators of arousal and nervousness, negative or dampened emotional expressions, inattentiveness, poor conversational management, and nonfluent communication performances. Thus, IDT embraces elements of the leakage hypothesis and the four-factor theory while emphasizing that deception is also a goal-driven communicative act that means actively managing what is being said and how it is being said (see also DePaulo, 1992; DePaulo et al., 2003, for a complementary self-presentational perspective that also emphasizes intentional, impression-enhancing behavior).

4. *Suspicion is manifested through a combination of strategic and nonstrategic behaviors.* Receivers also engage in strategic behavior. Like deceivers, when receivers' suspicions have been piqued, they engage in various strategies to ascertain whether deception is occurring and to uncover the truth. Similarly, arousal (in this case engendered by uncertainty), emotional reactions (engendered by negative reactions to being deceived as well as distress over how to proceed), and task complexity (prompted by the need to detect deception without alerting the deceiver) all may produce "leakage" by the receiver.

5. *Receivers recognize deceit and senders recognize suspicion when present.* Because deceit alters a sender's behavior and suspicion alters a receiver's behavior, those with whom they are interacting are posited to attune to such deviations. The result is that receivers regard rate deceptive communicators as less honest than truthful ones, even though they are reluctant to label them liars without further observation and verification. Likewise, senders may tune into sender skepticism as feedback to them, whether or not they go so far as to attribute suspicion to them.

6. *Relational familiarity alters behaviors, perceptions, and interpretations.* The interpersonal literature is replete with evidence that once people become acquainted, a host of new considerations emerge, such as prior familiarity with the person's behavior, anticipated future interactions, relational schemas and expectations, and a desire for continued pleasant interactions. These should produce interactions and attributions that are qualitatively different from interactions between strangers. Far less is known about how deception plays out between familiar others than strangers.

7. *Deceptive displays change over time.* To the extent that interpersonal interactions are dynamic events with iterative moves and countermoves and feedback loops between sender and receiver, deceptive interchanges should be changeable across the time course of an interaction and a relationship.

8. *Successful deception and its detection depend on communication skills, relational familiarity, behavioral familiarity, and training, among other variables.*

## Actual and Perceived Cues to Deception

Perhaps no area of deception research has attracted more attention than the quest for valid nonverbal indicators of deceit. Several meta-analyses, reviews, and experiments have attempted to sort out this issue. The consensus is that there is a mismatch between what people believe and what behaviors actually detect deceit reliably. Perhaps the most prominent stereotype worldwide is that the eyes are the best place to look for signs of deception, as deceivers are believed to avert their gaze (Bond & The Global Deception Research Team, 2006). Other cues people commonly cite when asked how they can tell whether someone is lying are signs of anxiety or stress, such as blushing, blinking, nervous gestures, fidgeting, postural shifts (squirming), more nonpurposive arm and hand movements, tension, blushing, inexpressive or negative facial expressions, hesitations (pauses), slower speech, speech errors, vocal uncertainty and unpleasantness, and abnormal behaviors. Comparatively, among the cues that have been confirmed as actually displayed by deceivers in face-to-face interactions, these are fairly reliable and have produced robust effects: dilated pupils, more blinking, reduced involvement, rigid and immobile postures, reduced illustrator gesturing and head movements, more slight hand or finger fidgeting, longer response latencies, shorter utterances, higher pitch, slower speaking tempo, more speech errors (nonfluencies), and a number of verbal indicators. Thus, the subjective impressions are partially right but also include both reliance on a number of behaviors that have no relationship to deception and failure to take account of many that are related strongly. An especially common tendency is to overrely on facial cues and underrely on the more informative vocal cues.

Also confounding receivers' detection ability is the complexity of deception displays—there is no Pinocchio's nose (i.e., no single telltale sign)—as different cues may be displayed under different conditions. Put differently, there is no single profile of deceptive behavior. Other complexities may derive from communicator characteristics such as gender, dominance, age, social skill, self-monitoring ability, personality, relational familiarity, amount of planning and rehearsal, and type of message content (emotional, factual, or attitudinal).

## Effects of Suspicion

Several interpersonal communication experiments have examined the effects of suspicion on sender and receiver behavioral displays (see, e.g., Buller, Strzyzewski, & Comstock, 1991; Burgoon, Buller, Ebesu, Rockwell, & White, 1996; McCornack & Levine, 1990; McCornack & Parks, 1986; Stiff, Kim, & Ramesh, 1992). Fortunately for deceivers, most people tend to hold a *truth bias*, an assumption that others' messages are honest and forthright. This is especially true among acquainted individuals. As a consequence, suspicion may not be that prevalent. Nevertheless, when it arises, it causes subtle changes in the suspecter's behavior, but these changes may depend on the level of suspicion. Suspecters who are moderately suspicious have been found to differ in their nonverbal behavior from those who are highly suspicious. Deceivers need not be overtly aware of these specific behavioral changes, but they do sense suspicion when it is present; that is, something in the suspecter's demeanor telegraphs the suspicions to them. More skilled individuals may use this feedback to their advantage, adjusting their demeanor to create a more honest-appearing presentation (see, e.g., Strömwall, Hartwig, & Granhag, 2006; White & Burgoon, 2001). However, senders under suspicion often suffer decrements in their own performance. This is true for truth tellers as well. Thus, being subjected to suspicion can cause a self-fulfilling prophecy, leading truth tellers to look dishonest and, thus, confirming the suspecter's suspicions.

*Detection Strategies and Detection Accuracy.* The combination of truth biases, other biases, and reliance on the wrong cues makes untrained observers relatively inaccurate in detecting discrepant and deceptive messages. In fact, people's deception and truth detection accuracies average only 47% and 57%, respectively (Aamodt & Custer, 2006; Bond & DePaulo, 2006), which means that people would typically be as well off flipping a coin, which produces a 50:50 accuracy rate. Although greater familiarity with deception— be it through exposure to previous samples of behavior (behavioral) or training (knowledge)— can improve detection success, too much experience with deception can lead to a lie bias and a concomitant reduction in deception success. This may explain why many professionals are no more accurate than lay people in detecting deception. However, some professionals do show exceptional ability, providing evidence that training and/or experience may boost detection accuracy (Bond, 2008; Ekman, O'Sullivan, & Frank, 1999). Although the research on the effectiveness of training has been mixed, training is likely to be more successful when subjects are motivated, the training is relevant to the type of detection task being undertaken, stimuli are judged in context, and training occurs over multiple rather than single training sessions (Blair, Levine, & Shaw, 2010; Frank & Feeley, 2003; George et al., in press; Hartwig, Granhag, Strömwall, & Kronkvist, 2006; Masip, Garrido, & Herrero, 2004).

## Summary

Nonverbal signals are essential ingredients in the interpersonal communication mix. Research substantiates that rather than being mere auxiliaries to the verbal stream, they carry significant social meanings in face-to-face interchanges. In analyzing the role of nonverbal signals in interpersonal communication, we have emphasized those behaviors that form a socially shared coding system and affect the overall process of communication. Codes that form the nonverbal communication system are kinesics, vocalics, haptics, proxemics, chronemics, physical appearance, olfactics, and artifacts. These coordinate with one another and with the verbal stream to achieve particular functions or purposes, several of which may be in force simultaneously. The many social functions that are accomplished include message production and processing, identification, impression formation, impression management, emotional communication, relational communication, conversation management, social influence, and deception. The research is impressive in documenting how much responsibility is shouldered by the nonverbal codes in accomplishing these fundamental communication objectives. For each of these functions, a rich amount of research and theory has emerged, only a fraction of which has been reviewed here. That newcomers to the nonverbal communication enterprise have included disciplines such as computer science and engineering, information systems, management, and evolutionary biology speaks to the significant role nonverbal communication plays in wide-ranging aspects of human relationships.

## References

Aamodt, M. G., & Custer, H. (2006). Who can best catch a liar? A meta-analysis of individual differences in detecting deception. *The Forensic Examiner, 15,* 6–11.

Abbey, A. (1982). Sex differences in attributions for friendly behavior: Do males misperceive females' friendliness? *Journal of Personality and Social Psychology, 42,* 830–838.

Aida, Y., & Falbo, T. (1991). Relationships between marital satisfaction, resources, and power strategies. *Sex Roles, 24,* 43–56.

Albada, K. F., Knapp, M. L., & Theune, K. E. (2002). Interaction appearance theory: Changing perceptions of physical attractiveness through social interaction. *Communication Theory, 12,* 8–40.

Ambady, N., Krabbenhoft, M. A., & Hogan, D. (2006). The 30-sec sale: Using thin-slice judgments to evaluate sales effectiveness. *Journal of Consumer Behavior, 16,* 4–13.

Ambady, N., & Rosenthal, R. (1993). Half a minute: Predicting teacher effectiveness from thin slices of nonverbal behavior and physical attractiveness. *Journal of Personality and Social Psychology, 64,* 431–441.

Andersen, P. A. (1991). When one cannot not communicate: A challenge to Motley's traditional communication postulates. *Communication Studies, 42,* 309–325.

Andersen, P. A., & Guerrero, L. K. (1998). Principles of communication and emotion in social interaction. In P. A. Andersen & L. K. Guerrero (Eds.), *Handbook of communication and emotion: Research, theory, applications, and contexts* (pp. 49–96). San Diego, CA: Academic Press.

Aronoff, J., Barclay, A. M., & Stevenson, L. A. (1988). The recognition of threatening facial stimuli. *Journal of Personality and Social Psychology, 54,* 647–655.

Aronoff, J., Woike, B. A., & Hyman, L. M. (1992). Which are the stimuli in facial displays of anger and happiness? Configurational bases of emotion recognition. *Journal of Personality and Social Psychology, 62,* 1050–1066.

Arriaga, X. B., Agnew, C. R., Capezza, N. M., & Lehmiller, J. J. (2008). The social and physical environment of relationship initiation: An interdependence analysis. In S. Sprecher, A. Wenzel, & J. Harvey (Eds.), *Handbook of relationship initiation* (pp. 197–215). New York: Psychology Press.

Banse, R., & Scherer, K. R. (1996). Acoustic profiles in vocal emotion expression. *Journal of Personality and Social Psychology, 70,* 614–636.

Barge, J. K., Schlueter, D. W., & Pritchard, A. (1989). The effects of nonverbal communication and gender on impression formation in opening statements. *Southern Communication Journal, 54,* 330–349.

Barrett, K. C. (1993). The development of nonverbal communication of emotion: A functionalist perspective. *Journal of Nonverbal Behavior, 17,* 145–169.

Barrett, K. C. (1998). A functionalist perspective to the development of emotions. In M. F. Mascolo & S. Griffin (Eds.), *What develops in emotional development?* (pp. 109–133). New York: Plenum Press.

Bavelas, J. B. (1990). Behaving and communicating: A reply to Motley. *Western Journal of Speech Communication, 54,* 593–602.

Bavelas, J. B., Black, A., Lemery, C. R., & Mullett, J. (1986). "I show how you feel": Motor mimicry as a communicative act. *Journal of Personality and Social Psychology, 50,* 322–329.

Baxter, L. A. (1992). Forms and functions of intimate play in personal relationships. *Human Communication Research, 18,* 336–363.

Bell, E., & Blaeuer, D. (2006). Performing gender and interpersonal communication research. In J. Wood & B. Dow (Eds.), *The gender and communication handbook* (pp. 9–23). Thousand Oaks, CA: Sage.

Ben-Ari, A., & Lavee, Y. (2007). Dyadic closeness in marriage: From the inside story to a conceptual model. *Journal of Social and Personal Relationships, 24,* 627–644.

Berger, C. R. (2009). Message production processes. In C. R. Berger, M. E. Roloff, & D. R. Roskos-Ewoldsen (Eds.), *Handbook of communication science* (2nd ed., pp. 111–128). Thousand Oaks, CA: Sage.

Bernieri, F. J. (2001). Toward a taxonomy of interpersonal sensitivity. In J. A. Hall & F. J. Bernieri (Eds.), *Interpersonal sensitivity: Theory and measurement* (pp. 3–20). Mahwah, NJ: Lawrence Erlbaum.

Bernieri, F. J., & Rosenthal, R. (1991). Interpersonal coordination: Behavior matching and interactional synchrony. In R. S. Feldman & B. Rimé (Eds.), *Fundamentals of nonverbal behavior* (pp. 401–432). Cambridge, UK: Cambridge University Press.

Birdwhistell, R. L. (1970). *Kinesics and context: Essays on body motion communication.* Philadelphia: University of Pennsylvania Press.

Blair, J. P., Levine, T. R., & Shaw, A. S. (2010). Content in context improves deception detection accuracy. *Human Communication Research, 36,* 423–442.

Bond, C. F., & DePaulo, B. M. (2006). Accuracy of deception judgments. *Personality and Social Psychology Review, 10,* 214–234.

Bond, C. F., & The Global Deception Research Team. (2006). A world of lies. *Journal of Cross-Cultural Psychology, 37,* 60–74.

Bond, G. D. (2008). Deception detection expertise. *Law and Human Behavior, 32,* 339–351.

Boulgouris, N., Plataniotis, K. N., & Micheli-Tzanakou, E. (2010). *Biometrics.* Hoboken, NJ: Wiley Interscience.

Brewer, M. B., & Hewstone, M. (Eds.). (2004). *Self and social identity.* Malden, MA: Blackwell.

Brody, L. R., & Hall, J. A. (2010). Gender, emotion, and socialization. In J. C. Chrisler & D. R. McCreary (Eds.), *Handbook of gender research in psychology* (pp. 429–454). New York: Springer.

Buck, R. (1984). *The communication of emotion.* New York: Guilford Press.

Buck, R., & VanLear, C. A. (2002). Verbal and nonverbal communication: Distinguishing symbolic, spontaneous, and pseudo-spontaneous communication. *Journal of Communication, 52,* 522–541.

Buller, D. B., & Burgoon, J. K. (1994). Deception. In J. A. Daly & J. M. Wiemann (Eds.), *Communicating strategically: Strategic interpersonal communication* (pp. 191–223). Hillsdale, NJ: Lawrence Erlbaum.

Buller, D. B., & Burgoon, J. K. (1996). Interpersonal deception theory. *Communication Theory, 6,* 203–242.

Buller, D. B., Strzyzewski, K. D., & Comstock, J. (1991). Interpersonal deception: I. Deceivers' reactions to receivers' suspicions and probing. *Communication Monographs, 58,* 1–24.

Burgoon, J. K. (1985). The relationship of verbal and nonverbal codes. In B. Dervin & M. J. Voight (Eds.), *Progress in communication sciences* (Vol. 6, pp. 263–298). Norwood, NJ: Ablex.

Burgoon, J. K. (1991). Relational message interpretations of touch, conversational distance, and posture. *Journal of Nonverbal Behavior, 15,* 233–259.

Burgoon, J. K. (1993). Interpersonal expectations, expectancy violations, and emotional communication. *Journal of Language and Social Psychology, 12,* 30–48.

Burgoon, J. K. (1994). Nonverbal signals. In M. L. Knapp & G. R. Miller (Eds.), *Handbook of interpersonal communication* (pp. 344–390). Thousand Oaks, CA: Sage.

Burgoon, J. K., & Bacue, A. (2003). Nonverbal communication skills. In B. R. Burleson & J. O. Greene (Eds.), *Handbook of communication and social interaction skills* (pp. 179–219). Mahwah, NJ: Lawrence Erlbaum.

Burgoon, J. K., & Buller, D. B. (2008). Interpersonal deception theory. In L. A. Baxter & D. O. Braithwaite (Eds.), *Engaging theories in interpersonal communication: Multiple perspectives* (pp. 227–239). Thousand Oaks, CA: Sage.

Burgoon, J. K., Buller, D. B., Ebesu, A., Rockwell, P., & White, C. (1996). Testing interpersonal deception theory: Effects of suspicion on nonverbal behavior and relational messages. *Communication Theory, 6,* 243–267.

Burgoon, J. K., & Dunbar, N. (2000). An interactionist perspective on dominance–submission: Interpersonal dominance as a dynamically, situationally contingent social skill. *Communication Monographs, 67,* 96–121.

Burgoon, J. K., Guerrero, L. K., & Floyd, K. (2010). *Nonverbal communication.* Boston: Allyn & Bacon.

Burgoon, J. K., & Hale, J. L. (1984). The fundamental topoi of relational communication. *Communication Monographs, 51,* 193–214.

Burgoon, J. K., & Hubbard, A. E. (2005). Expectancy violations theory and interaction adaptation theory. In W. B. Gudykunst (Ed.), *Theorizing about intercultural communication* (pp. 149–171). Thousand Oaks, CA: Sage.

Burgoon, J. K., Johnson, M. L., & Koch, P. T. (1998). The nature and measurement of interpersonal dominance. *Communication Monographs, 65,* 309–335.

Burgoon, J. K., & Le Poire, B. A. (1993). Effects of communication expectancies, actual communication, and expectancy disconfirmation on evaluations of communicators and their communication behavior. *Human Communication Research, 20,* 75–107.

Burgoon, J. K., & Le Poire, B. A. (1999). Nonverbal cues and interpersonal judgments: Participant and observer perceptions of intimacy, dominance, composure, and formality. *Communication Monographs, 66,* 105–124.

Burgoon, J. K., & Levine, T. R. (2009). Advances in deception detection. In S. W. Smith & S. R. Wilson (Eds.), *New directions in interpersonal communication research* (pp. 201–220). Thousand Oaks, CA: Sage.

Burgoon, J. K., Newton, D. A., Walther, J. B., & Baesler, E. J. (1989). Nonverbal expectancy violations and conversational involvement. *Journal of Nonverbal Behavior, 13,* 97–120.

Burgoon, J. K., Segrin, C., & Dunbar, N. E. (2002). Nonverbal communication and social influence. In J. P. Dillard & M. Pfau (Eds.), *The persuasion handbook: Developments in theory and practice* (pp. 445–473). Thousand Oaks, CA: Sage.

Burleson, B. R., & Denton, W. H. (1997). The relationship between communication skill and marital satisfaction: Some moderating effects. *Journal of Marriage and the Family, 59,* 884–902.

Burleson, B. R., & Planalp, S. (2000). Producing emotion(al) messages. *Communication Theory, 10,* 221–250.

Cappella, J. N. (1993). The facial feedback hypothesis in human interaction: Review and speculation. *Journal of Language and Social Psychology, 12,* 13–29.

Cappella, J. N., & Palmer, M. T. (1990). Attitude similarity, relational history, and attraction: The mediating effects of kinesic and vocal behaviors. *Communication Monographs, 57,* 161–183.

Carton, J. S., Kessler, E. A., & Pape, C. L. (1999). Nonverbal decoding skills and relationship well-being in adults. *Journal of Nonverbal Behavior, 23,* 91–100.

Cash, T. F., & Janda, I. H. (1984, December). The eye of the beholder. *Psychology Today, 46–52.*

Cash, T. F., & Kilcullen, R. N. (1985). The eye of the beholder: Susceptibility to sexism and beautyism in the evaluation of managerial applicants. *Journal of Applied Social Psychology, 15,* 591–605.

Coker, D. A., & Burgoon, J. K. (1987). The nature of conversational involvement and nonverbal encoding patterns. *Human Communication Research, 13,* 463–494.

Coulson, M. (2004). Attributing emotion to static body postures: Recognition accuracy, confusions and viewpoint dependency. *Journal of Nonverbal Behavior, 24,* 117–139.

Cunningham, M. R., & Barbee, A. P. (2008). Prelude to a kiss: Nonverbal flirting, opening gambits, and other communication dynamics in the initiation of romantic relationships. In S. Sprecher, A. Wenzel, & J. Harvey (Eds.), *Handbook of relationship initiation* (pp. 97–120). New York: Psychology Press.

Cunningham, M. R., Barbee, A. P., & Philhower, C. (2002). Dimensions of facial physical attractiveness: The intersection of biology and culture. In G. Rhodes & L. Zebrowitz (Eds.), *Advances in visual cognition: Vol. 1. Facial attractiveness* (pp. 193–238). Stanford, CT: JAI/Ablex.

Custrini, R. J., & Feldman, R. S. (1989). Children's social competence and nonverbal encoding and decoding of emotion. *Journal of Clinical Child Psychology, 18,* 336–342.

Darwin, C. (1998). *The expression of emotion in man and animals.* New York: Oxford University Press. (Original work published 1872)

DePaulo, B. M. (1992). Nonverbal behavior and self-presentation. *Psychological Bulletin, 111,* 203–243.

DePaulo, B. M., Lindsay, J. J., Malone, B. E., Muhlenbruck, L., Charlton, K., & Cooper, H. (2003). Cues to deception. *Psychological Bulletin, 129,* 74–118.

Dillard, J. P. (1998). The role of affect in communication, biology, and social relationships. In P. A. Andersen & L. K. Guerrero (Eds.), *Handbook of communication and emotion* (pp. xvii–xxxii). San Diego, CA: Academic Press.

Dovidio, J. F., Hebl, M., Richeson, J. A., & Shelton, J. N. (2006). Nonverbal communication, race, and intergroup interaction. In V. Manusov & M. L. Patterson (Eds.), *The Sage handbook of nonverbal communication* (pp. 481–500). Thousand Oaks, CA: Sage.

Dow, B., & Wood, J. T. (Eds.). (2006). *The Sage handbook of gender and communication.* Thousand Oaks, CA: Sage.

Dunbar, N. (2003, November). *An experimental test of dyadic power theory.* Paper presented at the annual meeting of the National Communication Association, Miami, FL.

Dunbar, N. E. (2004). Dyadic power theory: Constructing a communication-based theory of relational power. *Journal of Family Communication, 4,* 235–248.

Dunbar, N. E., & Burgoon, J. K. (2005). Perceptions of power and dominance in interpersonal encounters. *Journal of Social and Personal Relationships, 22,* 207–233.

Eagly, A. H., & Koenig, A. M. (2006). *Social role theory of sex differences and similarities: Implication for prosocial behavior.* In D. J. Canary & K. Dindia (Eds.), *Sex differences and similarities in communication* (2nd ed., pp. 156–172). Mahwah, NJ: Lawrence Erlbaum.

Eibl-Eibesfeldt, I. (1973). Expressive behaviour of the deaf and blind born. In M. von Cranach & I. Vine (Eds.), *Social communication and movement* (pp. 163–194). New York: Academic Press.

Ekman, P. (1973). Cross-cultural studies of facial expression. In P. Ekman (Ed.), *Darwin and facial expression: A century of research in review* (pp. 169–222). New York: Academic Press.

Ekman, P. (1993). Facial expression and emotion. *American Psychologist, 48,* 376–379.

Ekman, P., & Friesen, W. V. (1969). Nonverbal leakage and clues to deception. *Psychiatry, 32,* 88–105.

Ekman, P., O'Sullivan, M., & Frank, M. G. (1999). A few can catch a liar. *Psychological Science, 10,* 263–266.

Elfenbein, H. A., & Ambady, N. (2002). On the universality and cultural specificity of emotional recognition: A meta-analysis. *Psychological Bulletin, 128,* 205–235.

Elfenbein, H. A., & Ambady, N. (2003). When familiarity breeds accuracy: Cultural exposure and facial emotion recognition. *Journal of Personality and Social Psychology, 85,* 276–290.

Farinelli, L. (2008). The sounds of seduction. In L. K. Guerrero & M. L. Hecht (Eds.), *The nonverbal communication reader* (pp. 160–168). Long Grove, IL: Waveland Press.

Feeney, J. A., Noller, P., Sheehan, G., & Peterson, C. (1999). Conflict issues and conflict strategies as contexts for nonverbal behavior in close relationships. In P. Phillipot, R. S. Feldman, & E. J. Coats (Eds.), *The social context of nonverbal behavior* (pp. 348–371). Paris: Cambridge University Press.

Felmlee, D. H. (1994). Who's on top? Power in romantic relationships. *Sex Roles, 31,* 275–295.

Fincham, F. D., & Bradbury, T. N. (1992). Assessing attributions in marriage: The relationship attribution measure. *Journal of Personality and Social Psychology, 62,* 457–468.

Fincham, F. D., Bradbury, T. N., Arias, I., Byrne, C. A., & Karney, B. R. (1997). Marital violence, marital distress, and attributions. *Journal of Family Psychology, 11,* 367–372.

Floyd, K. (1999). All touches are not created equal: Effects of form and duration on perceptions of an embrace. *Journal of Nonverbal Behavior, 23,* 283–299.

Floyd, K. (2006). *Communicating affection: Interpersonal behavior and social context.* Cambridge, UK: Cambridge University Press.

Floyd, K., Hesse, C., & Haynes, M. T. (2007). Human affection exchange: XV. Metabolic and cardiovascular correlates of trait expressed affection. *Communication Quarterly, 55,* 79–94.

Floyd, K., Mikkelson, A. C., Tafoya, M. A., Farinelli, L., La Valley, A. G., Judd, J., et al. (2007). Human affection exchange: XIV. Relational affection predicts resting heart rate and free cortisol secretion during acute stress. *Behavioral Medicine, 32,* 151–156.

Floyd, K, & Morman, M. T. (1998). The measurement of affection communication. *Communication Quarterly, 46,* 144–162.

Floyd, K., Ramirez, A., & Burgoon, J. K. (2008). Expectancy violations theory. In L. K.Guerrero, J. A. DeVito, & M. L. Hecht (Eds.), *The nonverbal communication reader: Classic and contemporary readings* (3rd ed., pp. 503–510). Prospect Heights, IL: Waveland Press.

Floyd, K., & Riforgiate, S. (2008). Affectionate communication received from spouses predicts stress hormone levels in healthy adults. *Communication Monographs, 75,* 351–368.

Forbes, R. J., & Jackson, P. R. (1980). Non-verbal behavior and the outcome of selection interviews. *Journal of Occupational Psychology, 53,* 65–72.

Frank, M. G., & Feeley, T. H. (2003). To catch a liar: Challenges for research in lie detection training. *Journal of Applied Communication Research, 31,* 58–75.

Fridlund, A. J., & Duchaine, B. (1996). Facial expressions of emotion and the delusion of the hermetic self. In R. Harrè & W. G. Parrott (Eds.), *The emotions: Social, cultural, and biological dimensions* (pp. 259–284). Thousand Oaks, CA: Sage.

Fridlund, A. J., & Russell, J. A. (2006). The functions of facial expressions: What's in a face? In V. Manusov & M. L. Patterson (Eds.), *The Sage handbook of nonverbal communication* (pp. 299–319). Thousand Oaks, CA: Sage.

Frijda, N. H. (1993). Moods, emotion episodes, and emotions. In M. Lewis & J. M. Haviland (Eds.), *Handbook of emotions* (pp. 381–403). New York: Guilford Press.

Funder, D. C., & Colvin, C. R. (1991). Explorations in behavioral consistency: Properties of persons, situations, and behaviors. *Journal of Personality and Social Psychology, 60,* 773–794.

Gaelick, L., Bodenhausen, G. V., & Wyer, R. S., Jr. (1985). Emotional communication in close relationships. *Journal of Personality and Social Psychology, 49,* 1246–1265.

Galati, D., Scherer, K. R., & Ricci-Bitti, P. (1997). Voluntary facial expression of emotion: Comparing congenitally blind to normal sighted encoders. *Journal of Personality and Social Psychology, 73,* 1363–1379.

Gallaher, P. E. (1992). Individual differences in nonverbal behavior: Dimensions of style. *Journal of Personality and Social Psychology, 63,* 133–145.

Gallois, C., Ogay, T., & Giles, H. (2005). Communication accommodation theory: A look back and a look ahead. In W. B. Gudykunst (Ed.), *Theorizing about intercultural communication* (pp. 121–148). Thousand Oaks, CA: Sage.

George, J. F., Biros, D. P., Burgoon, J. K., Crews, J. M, Cao, J., Marett, K., et al. (in press). Defeating deception through e-training. *Management Information Systems Quarterly Executive.*

Gifford, R. (2006). Personality and nonverbal behavior: A complex conundrum. In V. Manusov & M. L. Patterson (Eds.), *The Sage handbook of nonverbal communication* (pp. 159–179). Thousand Oaks, CA: Sage.

Giles, H., Coupland, N., & Coupland, J. (1991). Accommodation theory: Communication, context, and consequence. In H. Giles, J. Coupland, & N. Coupland (Eds.), *Contexts of accommodation: Developments in applied sociolinguistics* (pp. 1–68). Cambridge, UK: Cambridge University Press.

Givens, D. B. (2005). *Love signals: A practical field guide to the body language of courtship.* New York: St. Martin's Press.

Gottman, J. M. (1994). *What predicts divorce? The relationship between marital processes and marital outcomes.* Hillsdale, NJ: Lawrence Erlbaum.

Gottman, J., Levenson, R., & Woodin, E. (2001). Facial expressions during marital conflict. *Journal of Family Communication, 1,* 37–57.

Gottman, J. M., Markman, H. J., & Notarius, C. I. (1977). The topography of marital conflict: A sequential analysis of verbal and nonverbal behaviors. *Journal of Marriage and the Family, 39,* 461–477.

Gottman, J. M., & Porterfield, A. L. (1981). Communicative competence in the nonverbal behavior of married couples. *Journal of Marriage and the Family, 43,* 817–824.

Grammer, K., Honda, M., Juette, A., & Schmitt, A. (1999). Fuzziness of nonverbal courtship communication unblurred by motion energy detection. *Journal of Personality and Social Psychology, 77,* 487–508.

Gray, H. M., & Ambady, N. (2006). Methods for the study of nonverbal communication. In V. Manusov & M. L. Patterson (Eds.), *The Sage handbook of nonverbal communication* (pp. 41–58). Thousand Oaks, CA: Sage.

Graziano, W. G., Jensen-Campbell, L. A., Todd, M., & Finch, J. (1997). Interpersonal attraction from an evolutionary psychology perspective: Women's reactions to dominant and prosocial men. In J. A. Simpson & D. Kenrick (Eds.), *Evolutionary social psychology* (pp. 141–167). Hillsdale, NJ: Lawrence Erlbaum.

Guerrero, L. K., & Andersen, P. A. (1991). The waxing and waning of relational intimacy: Touch as a function of relational stage, gender, and touch avoidance. *Journal of Social and Personal Relationships, 8,* 147–165.

Guerrero, L. K., & Floyd, K. (2006). *Nonverbal communication in close relationships.* Mahwah, NJ: Lawrence Erlbaum.

Guerrero, L. K., Jones, S. M., & Boburka, R. R. (2006). Sex differences in emotional communication. In D. J. Canary & K. Dindia (Eds.), *Sex differences and similarities in communication* (2nd ed., pp. 241–261). Mahwah, NJ: Lawrence Erlbaum.

Guerrero, L. K., & Reiter, R. L. (1998). Expressing emotion: Sex differences in social skills and communicative responses to anger, sadness, and jealousy. In D. J. Canary & K. Dindia (Eds.), *Sex differences and similarities in communication* (pp. 321–350). Mahwah, NJ: Lawrence Erlbaum.

Haggard, E. A., & Isaacs, F. S. (1966). Micromomentary facial expressions as indicators of ego mechanisms in psychotherapy. In L. A. Gottschalk & A. H. Auerback (Eds.), *Methods of research in psychotherapy* (pp. 154–165). New York: Appleton-Century-Crofts.

Halberstadt, A. G., & Saitta, M. B. (1987). Gender, nonverbal behavior, and perceived dominance: A test of the theory. *Journal of Personality and Social Psychology, 53,* 257–272.

Hall, E. T. (1977). *Beyond culture.* Garden City, NY: Anchor Books.

Hall, J. A. (1979). Gender, gender roles, and nonverbal communication skills. In R. Rosenthal (Ed.), *Nonverbal communication* (pp. 32–67). Cambridge, MA: Oelgeschlager, Genn & Hain.

Hall, J. A., Andrzejewski, S. A., & Yopchick, J. E. (2009). Psychosocial correlates of interpersonal sensitivity: A meta-analysis. *Journal of Nonverbal Behavior, 33,* 149–180.

Hall, J. A., Carter, J. D., & Horgan, T. G. (2000). Gender differences in nonverbal communication of emotion. In A. H. Fischer (Ed.), *Gender and emotions: Social psychological perspectives* (pp. 136–158). Baltimore: John Hopkins University Press.

Hall, J. A., Murphy, N. A., & Schmid Mast, M. (2006). Recall of nonverbal cues: Exploring a new definition of interpersonal sensitivity. *Journal of Nonverbal Behavior, 30,* 141–155.

Hartwig, M., Granhag, P. A., Strömwall, L. A., & Kronkvist, O. (2006). Strategic use of evidence during police interviews: When training to detect deception works. *Law and Human Behavior, 30,* 603–619.

Hatfield, E., Cacioppo, J. T., & Rapson, R. L. (1994). *Emotional contagion.* New York: Cambridge University Press.

Hatfield, E. E., & Sprecher, S. (1986). *Mirror, mirror: The importance of looks in everyday life.* Albany: State University of New York Press.

Heilman, M. E., & Saruwatari, L. R. (1979). When beauty is beastly: The effects of appearance and sex on evaluations of job applicants for managerial and non-managerial jobs. *Organizational Behavior and Human Performance, 23,* 360–372.

van Hemert, D. A., Poortinga, Y. H., & van de Vijver, F. J. R. (2007). Emotion and culture: A meta-analysis. *Cognition & Emotion, 21,* 913–943.

Henley, N. M. (2001). Body politics. In A. Branaman (Ed.), *Self and society: Blackwell readers in sociology* (pp. 288–297). Malden, MA: Blackwell.

Hertenstein, M. J., Keltner, D., App, B., Bulleit, B. A., & Jaskolka, A. R. (2006). Touch communicates distinct emotions. *Emotion, 6,* 528–533.

Hess, U., Blairy, S., & Kleck, R. E. (1997). The intensity of emotional facial expressions and decoding accuracy. *Journal of Nonverbal Behavior, 21,* 241–257.

Hocking, J. E., & Leathers, D. G. (1980). Nonverbal indicators of deception: A new theoretical perspective. *Communication Monographs, 47,* 119–131.

Huston, T. L., & Vangelisti, A. L. (1991). Socioemotional behavior and satisfaction in marital relationships: A longitudinal study. *Journal of Personality and Social Psychology, 61,* 721–733.

Izard, C. E. (1977). *Human emotions.* New York: Plenum Press.

Jensen-Campbell, L. A., Graziano, W. G., & West, S. (1995). Dominance, prosocial orientation, and female preferences: Do nice guys really finish last? *Journal of Personality and Social Psychology, 68,* 427–440.

Johnson, K. L., & Edwards, R. (1991). The effects of gender and type of romantic touch on perceptions of relational commitment. *Journal of Nonverbal Behavior, 15,* 43–55.

Jones, E. E., & Pittman, T. S. (1982). Toward a general theory of strategic self-presentation. In J. Suls (Ed.), *Psychological perspectives on the self* (Vol. 1, pp. 231–262). Hillsdale, NJ: Lawrence Erlbaum.

Juslin, P. N., & Laukka, P. (2003). Communication of emotions in vocal expression and musical performance: Different channels, same code? *Psychological Bulletin, 12,* 770–814.

Kaiser, S., & Wehrle, T. (2001). The role of facial expression in intra-individual and inter-individual emotion regulation. In D. Canamero (Ed.), *Proceedings of the AAAI Fall Symposium, Emotional and intelligent II: The tangled knot of social cognition* (pp. 61–66). Menlo Park, CA: AAAI Press.

Kelly, A. B., Fincham, F. D., & Beach, S. R. H. (2003). Communication skills in couples: A review and discussion of emerging perspectives. In J. O. Greene & B. R. Burleson (Eds.), *Handbook of communication and social skills* (pp. 723–751). Mahwah, NJ: Lawrence Erlbaum.

Kemper, T. D. (1984). Power, status, and emotions: A sociological contribution to a psychophysiological domain. In K. R. Scherer & P. Ekman (Eds.), *Approaches to emotion* (pp. 369–383). Hillsdale, NJ: Lawrence Erlbaum.

Kenny, D. A., Horner, C., Kashy, D. A., & Chu, L. (1992). Consensus at zero acquaintance: Replication, behavioral cues, and stability. *Journal of Personality and Social Psychology, 62,* 88–97.

Kitayama, S. (2002). Cultural and basic psychological processes—toward a system view of culture: Comment on Oyserman et al. (2002). *Psychological Bulletin, 128,* 189–196.

Kitayama, S., & Ishii, K. (2002). Words and voice: Spontaneous attention to emotional utterances in two languages. *Cognition & Emotion, 16,* 29–59.

Kitayama, S., Markus, H. T., & Matsumoto, A. (1995). Culture, self, and emotion: A cultural perspective on "self-conscious" emotions. In P. J. Tangney & K. W. Fischer (Eds.), *Self-conscious emotions: The psychology of shame, guilt, embarrassment, and pride* (pp. 439–465). New York: Guilford Press.

Knapp, M. L. (2008). *Lying and deception in human interaction.* Boston: Allyn & Bacon.

Knapp, M. L., & Hall, J. A. (2010). *Nonverbal communication in human interaction* (7th ed.). Belmont, CA: Wadsworth.

Krueger, R. F., & Caspi, A. (1993). Personality, arousal, and pleasure: A test of competing models of interpersonal attraction. *Personality and Individual Differences, 14,* 105–111.

Kurzban, R., & Weeden, J. (2005). HurryDate: Mate preferences in action. *Evolution & Human Behavior, 26,* 227–244.

Lee, J. W., & Guerrero, L. K. (2001). Types of touch in cross-sex relationships between coworkers: Perceptions of relational and emotional messages, inappropriateness, and sexual harassment. *Journal of Applied Communication Research, 29,* 197–220.

Le Poire, B. A., & Burgoon, J. K. (1996). Usefulness of differentiating arousal responses within communication theories: Orienting response of defensive arousal within theories of expectancy violation. *Communication Monographs, 63,* 208–230.

Levenson, R. W., Ekman, P., & Friesen, W. V. (1990). Voluntary facial action generates emotion-specific autonomic nervous system activity. *Psychophysiology, 27,* 363–384.

Levy, R. I. (1973). *Tahitians: Mind and experience in the Society Islands.* Chicago: Chicago University Press.

Manstead, A. S. R., & Fischer, A. H. (2002). Beyond the universality-specificity dichotomy. *Cognition & Emotion, 16,* 1–9.

Manusov, V. (1991). Perceiving nonverbal messages: Effects of immediacy and encoded intent on receiver judgments. *Western Journal of Speech Communication, 55,* 235–253.

Manusov, V. (2007). Attributions and interpersonal communication: Out of our heads and into behavior. In D. R. Rosko-Ewoldson & J. Monahan (Eds.), *Communication and social cognition: Theories and methods* (pp. 141–169). Mahwah, NJ: Lawrence Erlbaum.

Manusov, V., Floyd, K., & Kerssen-Griep, J. (1997). Yours, mine, and ours: Mutual attributions for nonverbal behaviors in couples' interactions. *Communication Research, 24,* 234–260.

Manusov, V., & Patterson, M. L. (Eds.). (2006). *The Sage handbook of nonverbal communication.* Thousand Oaks, CA: Sage.

Margolin, G., Burman, B., & John, R. (1989). Home observations of marital couples reenacting naturalistic marital conflicts. *Behavioral Assessment, 11,* 101–118.

Markus, H. R., & Kitayama, S. (1991). Culture and the self: Implications for cognition, emotion, and motivation. *Psychological Review, 98,* 224–253.

Marsh, A. A., Elfenbein, H. A., & Ambady, N. (2007). Separated by a common language: Nonverbal accents and cultural stereotypes about Americans and Australians. *Journal of Cross-Cultural Psychology, 38,* 284–301.

Masip, J., Garrido, E., & Herrero, C. (2004). The nonverbal approach to the detection of deception: Judgemental accuracy. *Psychology in Spain, 8,* 48–59.

Matsumoto, D. (2006). Culture and nonverbal behavior. In V. Manusov & M. L. Patterson (Eds.), *The SAGE handbook of nonverbal communication* (pp. 219–235). Thousand Oaks, CA: Sage.

May, J. L., & Hamilton, P. A. (1980). Effects of musically evoked affect on women's interpersonal attraction toward and perceptual judgments of physical attractiveness of men. *Motivation and Emotion, 4,* 217–228.

Mayer, J. D., & Salovey, P. (1997). What is emotional intelligence? In P. Salovey & D. Sluyter (Eds.), *Emotional development and emotional intelligence: Implications for educators* (pp. 3–31). New York: Basic Books.

McCornack, S. A., & Levine, T. T. (1990). When lovers become leery: The relationship between suspicion and accuracy in detecting deception. *Communication Monographs, 57,* 218–230.

McCornack, S. A., & Parks, M. R. (1986). Deception detection and relationship development: The other side of trust. In M. L. McLaughlin (Ed.), *Communication yearbook 9* (pp. 337–389). Newbury Park, CA: Sage.

McGovern, T., & Ideus, H. (1978). Impact of nonverbal behavior on the employment interview. *Journal of College Placement, 38,* 51–53.

Mead, M. (1975). Review of Darwin and facial expression: A century of research in review by P. Ekman. *Journal of Communication, 25,* 209–213.

Mehrabian, A., & Ferris, S. A. (1967). Inference of attitudes from nonverbal communication in two channels. *Journal of Counseling Psychology, 31,* 248–252.

Mehrabian, A., & Wiener, M. (1967). Decoding of inconsistent communications. *Journal of Personality and Social Psychology, 6,* 109–114.

Mesquita, B., & Karasawa, M. (2002). Different emotional lives. *Cognition & Emotion, 16,* 127–141.

Metts, S., & Grohskopf, E. (2003). Impression management: Goals, strategies, and skills. In J. O. Greene & B. R. Burleson (Eds.), *Handbook of communication and social interaction skills* (pp. 357–399). Mahwah, NJ: Lawrence Erlbaum.

Moore, M. M. (1985). Nonverbal courtship patterns in women: Context and consequences. *Ethology and Sociobiology, 6,* 237–247.

Morris, D. (1977). *Manwatching: A field guide to human behavior.* New York: Abrams.

Motley, M. T. (1990). On whether one can(not) communicate: An examination via traditional communication postulates. *Western Journal of Speech Communication, 54,* 1–20.

Motley, M. T., & Camden, C. T. (1988). Facial expression of emotion: A comparison of posed expressions versus spontaneous expressions in an interpersonal setting. *Western Journal of Speech Communication, 52,* 1–22.

Nelson, H. (2007). Encoding and decoding mutual grooming: Communication with a specialized form of touch. *Dissertation Abstracts International, B. The Physical Sciences and Engineering, 68*(4B), 2664.

Newton, D. A., & Burgoon, J. K. (1990). Nonverbal conflict behaviors: Functions, strategies, and tactics. In D. D. Cahn (Ed.), *Intimates in conflict: A communication perspective* (pp. 77–104). Hillsdale, NJ: Lawrence Erlbaum.

Noller, P. (2006). Nonverbal communication in close relationships. In V. Manusov & M. L. Patterson (Eds.), *The Sage handbook of nonverbal communication* (pp. 403–420). Thousand Oaks, CA: Sage.

Nowicki, S., & Duke, M. P. (1994). Individual differences in the nonverbal communication of affect: The diagnostic analysis of nonverbal accuracy scale. *Journal of Nonverbal Behavior, 18,* 9–35.

Olivola, C. Y., & Todorov, A. (2010). Elected in 100 milliseconds: Appearance based trait inferences and voting. *Journal of Nonverbal Behavior, 34,* 83–111.

Owren, M. J., & Bachorowski, J. (2003). Reconsidering the evolution of nonlinguistic communication: The case of laughter. *Journal of Nonverbal Behavior, 27,* 183–200.

Patterson, M. L. (1983). *Nonverbal behavior: A functional perspective.* New York: Springer-Verlag.

Planalp, S. (2008). Varieties of emotional cues in everyday life. In L. K. Guerrero & M. L. Hecht (Eds.), *The nonverbal communication reader: Classic and contemporary readings* (pp. 397–401). Long Grove, IL: Waveland Press.

Planalp, S., DeFrancisco, V. L., & Rutherford, D. (1996). Varieties of cues to emotion in naturally occurring situations. *Cognition & Emotion, 10,* 137–153.

Plutchik, R. (1984). Emotions: A general psychoevolutionary theory. In K. R. Scherer & P. Ekman (Eds.), *Approaches to emotion* (pp. 197–219). Hillsdale, NJ: Lawrence Erlbaum.

Poggi, I. (2002). Towards the alphabet and the lexicon of gesture, gaze, and touch. In P. Bouissac (Ed.), *Multimodality of human communication: Theories,* *problems and applications* (Virtual Symposium). Retrieved March 23, 2011, from www.semioticon .com/virtuals/virtual_index.html

Prager, K. J. (2000). Intimacy in personal relationships. In C. Hendrick & S. S. Hendrick (Eds.), *Close relationships: A sourcebook* (pp. 229–242). Thousand Oaks, CA: Sage.

Punyanunt-Carter, N. M. (2004). Reported affectionate communication and satisfaction in marital and dating relationships. *Psychological Reports, 95,* 1154–1160.

Register, L. M., & Henley, T. B. (1992). The phenomenology of intimacy. *Journal of Social and Personal Relationships, 9,* 467–481.

Reis, H. T., Wilson, I. M., Monestere, C., Bernstein, S., Clark, K., Seidl, E., et al. (1990). What is smiling is beautiful and good. *European Journal of Social Psychology, 20,* 259–267.

Remland, M. S., & Jones, T. S. (1989). The effects of nonverbal involvement and communication apprehension on state anxiety, interpersonal attraction, and speech duration. *Communication Quarterly, 37,* 170–183.

Ridgeway, C. L., Berger, J., & Smith, L. (1985). Nonverbal cues and status: An expectation states approach. *American Journal of Sociology, 90,* 955–978.

Riggio, R. E. (1992). Social interaction skills and nonverbal behavior. In R. S. Feldman (Ed.), *Applications of nonverbal behavior: Theories and research* (pp. 3–30). Hillsdale, NJ: Lawrence Erlbaum.

Rose, S., & Zand, D. (2000). Lesbian dating and courtship from young adulthood to midlife. *Journal of Gay and Lesbian Social Services, 11,* 77–104.

Roskos-Ewoldsen, D. R., & Roskos-Ewoldsen, B. (2009). Message processing. In C. R. Berger, M. E. Roloff, & D. R. Roskos-Ewoldsen (Eds.), *Handbook of communication science* (2nd ed., pp. 129–144). Thousand Oaks, CA: Sage.

Russell, J. A. (1980). A circumplex model of affect. *Journal of Personality and Social Psychology, 39,* 1161–1178.

Russell, J. A. (1994). Is there universal recognition of emotion from facial expressions? A review of the cross-cultural studies. *Psychological Bulletin, 115,* 102–141.

Sadalla, E. K., Kenrick, D. T., & Vershure, B. (1987). Dominance and heterosexual attraction. *Journal of Personality and Social Psychology, 52,* 730–738.

Sauter, D. A., Eisner, F., Ekman, P., & Scott, S. K. (2010). Cross-cultural recognition of basic emotions through nonverbal emotional vocalizations. *Proceedings of the National Academy of Sciences of the United States of America, 107*, 2408–2412.

Scherer, K. R. (1986). Vocal affect expression: A review and a model for future research. *Psychological Bulletin, 99*, 143–165.

Scherer, K. R., & Wallbott, H. G. (1994). Evidence for universality and cultural variation of differential emotion response patterning. *Journal of Personality and Social Psychology, 66*, 310–328.

Schmidt, K. L., Cohn, J. F., & Tian, Y. (2003). Signal characteristics of spontaneous facial expressions: Automatic movement in solitary and social smiles. *Biological Psychology, 65*, 49–66.

Segrin, C. (2000). Social skills deficits associated with depression. *Clinical Psychology Review, 20*, 379–403.

Sillars, A. L., Coletti, S. F., Parry, D., & Rogers, M. A. (1982). Coding verbal conflicts: Nonverbal and perceptual correlates of the "avoidance-distributive-integrative" distinction. *Human Communication Research, 9*, 83–95.

Smith, H. J., Archer, D., & Costanzo, M. (1991). "Just a hunch": Accuracy and awareness in person perception. *Journal of Nonverbal Behavior, 15*, 3–18.

Sporer, S. L., & Schwandt, B. (2007). Moderators of nonverbal indicators of deception: A meta-analytic synthesis. *Public Policy, and Law, 13*, 1–34.

Sprecher, S., & Felmlee, D. (1997). The balance of power in romantic heterosexual couples over time from "his" and "her" perspectives. *Sex Roles: A Journal of Research, 37*, 361–379.

Sprecher, S., & Regan, P. C. (2002). Liking some things (in some people) more than others: Partner preferences in romantic relationships and friendships. *Journal of Social and Personal Relationships, 19*, 436–481.

Staley, C. C., & Cohen, J. L. (1988). Communicator style and social style: Similarities and differences between the sexes. *Communication Quarterly, 36*, 192–202.

Stamp, G. H., & Knapp, M. L. (1990). The construct of intent in interpersonal communication. *Quarterly Journal of Speech, 76*, 282–299.

Stiff, J. B., Kim, H. J., & Ramesh, C. N. (1992). Truth biases and aroused suspicion in relational deception. *Communication Research, 19*, 326–345.

Street, R. L., & Cappella, J. N. (Eds.). (1985). *Sequence and pattern in communicative behaviour*. London: Edward Arnold.

Strömwall, L. A., Hartwig, M., & Granhag, P. A. (2006). To act truthfully: Nonverbal behaviour and strategies during a police interrogation. *Psychology, Crime & Law, 12*, 207–219.

Sunnafrank, M. (1992). On debunking the attitude similarity myth. *Communication Monographs, 59*, 164–179.

Swann, W. B. (1987). Identity negotiation: Where two roads meet. *Journal of Personality and Social Psychology, 53*, 1038–1051.

Tajfel, H., & Turner, J. C. (1986). The social identity theory of inter-group behavior. In S. Worchel & L. W. Austin (Eds.), *The social psychology of inter-group relations* (pp. 7–24). Chicago: Nelson-Hall.

Thayer, S. (Ed.). (1986). The psychology of touch [Special issue]. *Journal of Nonverbal Behavior, 10*, 7–80.

Tomkins, S. S. (1963). *Affect, imagery, consciousness: Vol. 2. The negative affects*. New York: Springer-Verlag.

Tomkins, S. S. (1984). Affect theory. In K. R. Scherer & P. Ekman (Eds.), *Approaches to emotion* (pp. 163–195). Hillsdale, NJ: Lawrence Erlbaum.

Tracy, J. C., & Matsumoto, D. (2008). The spontaneous expression of pride and shame: Evidence for biologically innate nonverbal displays. *Proceedings of the National Academy of Sciences, 105*, 11665–11660.

Tropp, L. R., & Wright, S. C. (2001). Ingroup identification as the inclusion of ingroup in the self. *Personality and Social Psychology Bulletin, 27*, 585–600.

Vrij, A. (2008). *Detecting lies and deceit: Pitfalls and opportunities*. New York: Wiley.

Wagner, H. L., & Smith, J. (1991). Facial expression in the presence of friends and strangers. *Journal of Nonverbal Behavior, 15*, 201–214.

Walsh, D. G., & Hewitt, J. (1983). Giving men the come on: Effect of eye-contact and smiling in a bar environment. *Perceptual and Motor Skills, 61*, 873–874.

Watzlawick, P., Beavin, J., & Jackson, D. D. (1967). *Pragmatics of human communication: A study of interactional patterns, pathologies, and paradoxes*. New York: W. W. Norton.

White, C. H., & Burgoon, J. K. (2001). Adaptation and communicative design: Patterns of interaction in truthful and deceptive conversations. *Human Communication Research, 27*, 9–37.

Wright, G. E., & Multon, K. D. (1995). Employers' perceptions of nonverbal communication in job interviews for persons with physical disabilities. *Journal of Vocational Behavior, 47*, 214–227.

Yee, N., & Bailenson, J. (2007). The Proteus effect: The effect of transformed self-representation on behavior. *Human Communication Research, 33,* 271–290.

Zebrowitz, L. A. (1997). *Reading faces: Window to the soul?* Boulder, CO: Westview Press.

Zillman, D. (1978). Attribution and misattribution of excitatory reactions. In J. H. Harvey, W. Ickes, & R. F. Kidd (Eds.), *New directions in attribution research* (Vol. 2, pp. 335–368). Hillsdale, NJ: Lawrence Erlbaum.

Zuckerman, M., DePaulo, B. M., & Rosenthal, R. (1981). Verbal and nonverbal communication of deception. In L. Berkowitz (Ed.), *Advances in experimental social psychology* (Vol. 14, pp. 2–59). New York: Academic Press.

Zuckerman, M., & Driver, R. E. (1985). Telling lies: Verbal and nonverbal correlates of deception. In W. A. Siegman & S. Feldstein (Eds.), *Multichannel integration of nonverbal behavior* (pp. 129–147). Hillsdale, NJ: Lawrence Erlbaum.

Zuckerman, M., Miyake, K., & Hodgins, H. S. (1991). Cross-channel effects of vocal and physical attractiveness and their implications for interpersonal perception. *Journal of Personality and Social Psychology, 60,* 545–554.

# PART IV

# Processes and Functions

# CHAPTER 9

# Emotion Experience and Expression

## Current Trends and Future Directions in Interpersonal Relationship Research

*Sandra Metts*

*Sally Planalp*

F ew aspects of the human condition are more important, ubiquitous, and complicated than emotions. Although humans share with other animals the basic drives to explore, seek pleasure, and avoid distress or threat, the complex social structures that have evolved and the languages that give them meaning separate the emotion systems of humans from all other animals. It is no surprise then that they have engaged the interest of scholars across theoretically and methodologically diverse disciplines, including physiology, neurology, psychology, sociology, philosophy, and the various areas of interest within communication, including rhetoric, mass communication, organizational communication, and interpersonal communication.

In the years since the previous version of this chapter (Metts & Planalp, 2002), interpersonal communication scholars have developed an increasingly rich and coherent profile of the role

of emotion in relationships. We no longer need to refer generically to the distal and proximal factors that influence emotional experience and expression as we did previously. Research now incorporates existing relationship theories and models such as the emotion-in-relationships model to guide investigations of emotion experience and, of particular importance, has developed instruments to measure emotion expression that reflect communication principles.

To provide a focus for this chapter, we will synthesize the current theory and research on the experience and expression of emotion in personal relationships such as those with friends, dating partners, and spouses. The distinguishing feature of these relationships is a unique relationship history and mutual interdependence, which together constitute a framework within which emotions are elicited, interpreted, and expressed. In close relationships, emotions are experienced in response to the actual or attributed messages of others and when expressed, intentionally or unintentionally, function as messages that fold back into the interaction. They accumulate in the background of these relationships and eventually shape the relational climate (e.g., relationship satisfaction, enduring affection, or lingering resentment), the unfolding of conflict episodes, and, in some cases, the management of relationship transgressions resulting in reconciliation or termination.

Before moving to the research on emotions in close relationships that has emerged since the previous publication of this chapter, we first summarize the conceptual and definitional issues that remain under discussion in the emotion literature by highlighting the key differences across three broad perspectives on emotion: (1) the basic- or discrete-emotion approach, (2) the appraisal theory perspectives, and (3) the dimensional approach. These issues are important to clarify because conceptual definitions direct methodological decisions. Clarity in both domains provides greater opportunity for research on emotion within and across disciplines to proceed systematically.

For example, the increasing interest in the role of emotion in persuasion and media effects has recently prompted media scholars to discuss the most useful conceptualization of emotion. As might be expected, the debate centers on the relative value of a clearly defined and limited set of basic emotions compared with a broadly conceived set of flexible and emergent affective states that reflect situational variability. For Nabi (2010), the more clearly focused and finite set of specified emotions, the "discrete-emotion" position, is the most useful approach "as what little might be lost in parsimony is more than offset by the precision gained in prediction" (p. 153). Bolls (2010), however, advocates the much broader "dimensional approach," bridging neurology, psychology, and phenomenology. He argues that the dimensional approach offers a methodological advantage for studying communication episodes because emotion expression (physiologically, linguistically, and behaviorally) can be "reliably organized according to the dimensions of valence and arousal" (p. 149).

Scholars who study close relationships also acknowledge the tension between the practical utility of narrow definitions of emotion and the explanatory utility of broader conceptualizations that can accommodate the complexity inherent in close relationships. The increasing use of a third approach to emotions, appraisal theory, in the relational communication area may reflect a compromise of sorts. Basic emotions can be examined, and dimensions of intensity and valence can be assessed while also including the influence of relationship-relevant appraisals, such as violations of expectations, the significance of goal obstruction, and the perceived intentionality of a partner's behavior.

We turn now to a more detailed discussion of conceptual and theoretical approaches to defining emotion and emotion experience. In addition, because the experience of emotion is only one piece of the puzzle when constructing a profile of the role of emotions in personal relationships, we also present the current views, positions, and research on emotion regulation and expression. We will then focus on emotions in close relationships during the stages of initiation, maintenance, and termination. Finally, we close this chapter with a discussion of new developments and directions in emotion research in close relationships, followed by what we see as unanswered questions that merit attention in future research.

## Approaches to Emotions and Emotional Experience

Much of the difficulty in defining emotions stems from their inherent complexity. They vary not only on dimensions such as valence, duration, and intensity but also on functions served through experience and expression, and on direction of focus (self or other directed). These features coalesce into complex formulations. They are an aspect of human nature that initially served basic survival needs but have since become embedded within the matrix of cultural norms, rules, and languages, blurring the lines between basic and social emotions (Matsumoto, 2007).

Emotion theorists have attempted to organize this complexity by focusing on related aspects within the emotion process. For example, in an integrative summary of the prominent emotion theories, Moors (2009) abstracts five components constituting what she terms the *emotion episode*, noting that each component has a certain "independence" but is itself a process that varies in duration. These include the somatic component (central and peripheral physiological response), the feeling component (the quality, or pleasantness/unpleasantness of emotional experience), the cognitive component (the meaning of the emotional event), the motivational component (state of action readiness), and the motor component (facial, vocal, and behavioral expressions). She then notes that differences in theoretical and methodological perspectives arise from differences in the number of these components included within a model or theory, whether they are temporally or causally related, and how the attributes within each component are defined. The cognitive component, for example, is sometimes broadly defined as general and automatic "mental awareness" or more narrowly as intentional, rule based, and nonautomatic. Likewise, the component of feeling is used in the narrow sense of phenomenal experience as well as in the broader conception as a composite of all other components (appraisals, action tendencies, and somatic and motor responses). These variations in conceptualizing emotions and components of the emotion experience are reflected in the theories we summarize below.

## Discrete-Emotion Models

Of the three perspectives we review here, the discrete-emotion model is perhaps the most coherent. The unifying assumption is that a limited number of innate "affect programs" constitute the basic or discrete emotions (e.g., Ekman, 1992, 1999, 2009; Ekman, Levenson, & Friesen, 1983; Izard, 2007, 2009; Izard, Ackerman, Schoff, & Fine, 2000). These emotions are believed to be qualitatively distinct neurological responses originating in the amygdala and the neocortex

regions of the brain (Izard, 2007) and are accompanied by physiological arousal patterns. The arousal systems are activated by an automatic (evolutionary based) appraisal of the environment (e.g., "Something important to our welfare is occurring") (Ekman, 2009). From the discrete-emotion perspective, these relevance appraisals are not cognitive in the sense of being intentional, conceptual, or propositional representations (Moors, 2009; Siemer & Reisenzein, 2007). They are more similar to alert signals or stimuli that are recognized cognitively (i.e., mental awareness) and thereby activate the relatively brief and prewired affective response or feeling as part of a neurobiological process that is then experienced as the emotion. Finally, the physiological arousal patterns that characterize the basic emotions are assumed to be manifested in universal facial expressions and in the corresponding action tendencies. For example, interest motivates orienting and exploring; anger motivates the removal of a goal obstruction.

Although there is general agreement among scholars about which emotions fall within the parameters of basic or discrete emotions, the categories are not identical (Ortony & Turner, 1990; Parrot, 2001). Frijda (1986) lists six emotions: desire, happiness, interest, surprise, wonder, and sorrow. Tomkins (1984) lists eight basic emotions: interest, surprise, enjoyment, distress, fear, shame, contempt, and anger. Ekman (2009) lists six basic emotions: anger, disgust/contempt, fear, sadness, surprise, and joy. Izard (2009) lists ten: joy, interest, surprise, sadness, anger, disgust, fear, shame, contempt, and guilt.

The inclusion or exclusion of particular emotions stems from the criteria embedded within each scholar's particular definitional criteria. For example, Ekman (2009) recognizes that other emotions, particularly guilt, shame, embarrassment, and envy, meet many of the criteria he lists for emotions, but he does not include them within the basic emotions because they do not have comparable forms in other primates (suggesting that they may have arisen later in our evolutionary history) and they have no efficient, clear, and universal signal. He also argues that jealousy is not an emotion but rather an emotional scene or plot because it involves the interface of emotions across three people—the rival (who may feel guilty, ashamed, afraid, angry, or contemptuous), the jealous person (who might feel angry, afraid, sad, or disgusted), and the person whose attention is being sought (who may feel any number of different emotions).

Izard (2009), however, does include shame and guilt as basic emotions because according to his differential emotions theory, basic emotions can be independent or dependent. The independent emotions are those arousal states that are present at birth in the infant's brain (i.e., joy, interest, sadness, anger, surprise, and disgust). The dependent discrete emotions (i.e., shame and guilt) are dependent in the sense that their coherence depends on the development of self-awareness and self-concept, both of which develop as language is acquired. For example, Izard argues that the activation of shame depends on the self-reflective appraisal of the situation; however, once activated, shame has the status of a discrete emotion because the neural, behavioral, and experiential components of shame are universal patterns that resulted from evolutionary circumstances. Finally, according to Izard, shame and guilt are dependent discrete emotions because they do not have a "consistent and specific expressive signature" (but cf. Lewis, Haviland-Jones, & Barrett, 2008) as they involve combinations of other emotions (e.g., fear and anger) that may influence expression depending on their salience in a given context (Izard et al., 2000).

The discrete-emotion perspective continues to be endorsed by emotion scholars, but the fundamental premise that basic emotions are coherent patterns of prewired, adaptive neurological and expressive responses is not consistently confirmed (Larsen, Berntson, Poehlmann, Ito, & Cacioppo, 2008). Regarding expression patterns, for example, Ekman (2009) provides evidence that facial expressions, when represented in pictures, evoked by films, and activated by verbal descriptions, are consistent across cultures with varying degrees of Western influence (e.g., Chile, Argentina, Brazil, Japan, Indonesia, and Papua New Guinea). Although concerns have been raised about the validity of the early findings based on emotion recognition in pictures of posed expressions (e.g., Russell, 1994), more recent research supports the assumption of universality by testing the premise that coherent expressions of the basic emotions evolved to serve a protective function for groups. Chiao et al. (2008) used pictures of faces with the same emotional intensity of fearful, happy, or angry expressions taken from Japanese and Caucasian posers (20 men and 20 women from each group). Respondents from each cultural group pressed a button to indicate the emotion shown and were also assessed for brain responses using functional magnetic resonance imaging (fMRI). Results indicated more rapid and successful recognition of expressions of fear when posed by members of one's own culture as well as greater activation in regions of the left and right amygdala than if the fear faces were posed by members of another culture.

However, the predicted coherent, preprogrammed patterns of characteristic facial expressions and bodily responses may be influenced in important ways by the intensity and valence of the emotional state. In a study of covert facial expressions using facial electromyography (EMG) of the brow, cheek, and perioral muscle regions, Cacioppo, Berntson, Larsen, Poehlmann, and Ito (2000) found that muscle regions moved toward distinctive profiles only when displays were for strong or intense emotions and were more consistently associated with broad, positive and negative affective states. A similar profile emerged for the dimension of activation in a study of body movements and emotion by Wallbott (1998). Professional actors were told to portray specific emotions (e.g., happiness, sadness, fear, cold anger, hot anger, disgust, contempt, shame, and guilt) during an evocative scene. These enactments were videotaped and analyzed for body movements and postures. Although some specific movements characterized a particular emotion (e.g., arms crossed in front of the chest for pride), many reflected aspects of activation rather than particular emotion display patterns.

The assumption that basic emotions are processed in particular areas of the brain also yields mixed results depending on the methods used to assess emotional experience (e.g., self-report vs. neural imaging) and the valence of emotional response. Anderson and Phelps (2002) used terms from the Positive and Negative Affect Schedules (e.g., attentive, inspired, excited, enthusiastic, and distressed, hostile, irritable/angry, fearful, ashamed, guilty, nervous, and jittery) to compare subjects with amygdala damage to a control group matched on age, sex, and education level. They found no differences between the groups on ratings of typicality or on magnitude and frequency of experience over a 30-day period for both the positive and the negative affective states. The authors concluded that "the human amygdala may be recruited during phenomenal affective states in the intact brain, but is not necessary for the production of these states" (p. 709).

By contrast, when more emotionally evocative visual stimuli are used (which do not require linguistic processing), amygdala damage does yield significant differences. In a study of amygdala patients, Adolfs, Russell, and Tranel (2004) used pictures of faces that gradually changed from faint to pronounced expressions of sadness and happiness, as well as neutral faces. When asked to rate the intensity of the expressions, subjects with bilateral amygdala damage showed a specific impairment in rating sad faces but performed normally in rating happy faces. Similar patterns emerged in a study by Berntson, Bechara, Damasio, Tranel, and Cacioppo (2007), in which participants who had lesions of the brain involving the amygdala and those with lesions of the brain that did not involve the amygdala rated pictures of emotion expression on dimensions of positivity, negativity, and arousal. Patients with amygdala lesions were able to recognize and categorize both the positive and the negative emotions displayed in the pictures, but they reported arousal only when viewing the positive-emotion displays.

Taken together, these studies using amygdala-impaired adults suggest that the amygdala plays an important role in the experience of the negative emotions, particularly sadness, but the positive emotions are less centralized in the amygdala. Meta-analyses of neurological studies also support the critical role played by the amygdala in emotion processing (Costafreda, Brammer, David, & Fu, 2008; Murphy, Nimmo-Smith, & Lawrence, 2003). As Costafreda et al. (2008) conclude from their meta-analysis of 385 studies using both impaired and healthy subjects, negative and positive emotions activate the amygdala, although more predictably with inductions of fear and disgust than with inductions of happiness. In a more systematic meta-analysis of Cobalt-55 PET (positron emission tomography) and fMRI studies of emotion in healthy subjects with no brain lesions, Phan, Wager, Taylor, and Liberzon (2002) created a schema of the brain divided into 20 regions and located results for individual emotions (positive, negative, happiness, fear, anger, sadness, disgust), different induction methods (visual, auditory, recall, imagery), and emotional tasks (with and without cognitive demand) within each region. The emotion profiles that emerged support the underlying premise of the discrete-emotion perspective. For example, fear was specific to the amygdala, sadness activated the subcallosal cingulate, and happiness activated the basal ganglia, the area of the brain associated with motivation and approach action tendencies.

Although the discrete-emotions approach is parsimonious and the research is extensive and systematic, the question of its utility for interpersonal scholars remains unanswered. In the dynamic and complicated world of interpersonal relationships, profiling the basic emotions of fear, happiness, disgust, anger, or sadness may have limited utility. While certainly present in relationship interactions, the basic emotions are also likely to merge with other affective states, producing more complex emotions such as envy, jealousy, hurt, and embarrassment. These emotions and their manifestations arise from appraisals of a partner's actions in particular situations.

## Appraisal Theories

The appraisal perspective on emotion experience is somewhat less coherent than the discrete-emotions approach, with several points of agreement as well as disagreement. Appraisal scholars agree that emotions are not innate, coherent, and automatic neurological and physiological arousal patterns. Rather, they are generated by some level of cognitive evaluation or interpretation of an event, broadly defined as a change in the environment that was not expected or the absence of change when one was anticipated (Roseman & Smith, 2001). Emotion experience and the manifestation (or suppression) of emotional states are initiated by evaluations of these events as "significant" in some way to a person's goals, motives, needs, and/or well-being (Ellsworth & Scherer, 2003; Roseman & Smith, 2001). Once this process begins, feelings of arousal are experienced, and action tendencies are activated and subject to regulation if appraisals change (McLaren & Solomon, 2008; Siemer, 2008; Smith & Kirby, 2004). Thus, anger is the likely result of an unexpected event being appraised as an obstruction to reaching a goal or satisfying a need, often attributed to an intentional act of another person (although objects such as a nonresponsive computer also prompt anger). Assessments of obstruction are likely to generate a coping response that includes eliminating the obstruction or correcting a person who is the source of the obstruction by demonstrating power or even using aggressive action (Scherer & Ellgring, 2007). In sum, although appraisal theorists acknowledge that a few intuitive appraisal patterns may have evolved as successful coping mechanisms that facilitated survival (Roseman & Smith, 2001), humans are capable of complex and flexible responses to emotion-eliciting situations, responses that may be effective or ineffective depending on the particular patterns of appraisal and the behaviors they motivate.

However, appraisal scholars differ on issues such as whether appraisals "cause" emotions or are "components" of the total emotional experience (Roseman & Evdokas, 2004). They also differ in the extent to which they view appraisals as fully conscious cognitive actions or, at least initially, as unconscious responses that prompt more conscious attention and/or recruit existing emotion schemas from memory (Roseman & Smith, 2001). Finally, appraisal scholars differ in the extent to

which they endorse the phasic model of appraisal sequences. For instance, the traditional two-step model of primary and secondary appraisal offered by Lazarus (1991, 2006) includes an immediate assessment of an event's relevance to our well-being followed by an assessment of how to cope. A third step, reappraisal, is also employed by some scholars (Lazarus, 2008). Reappraisal is a conscious reflection on the emotion experience as initially appraised and the effectiveness of alternative coping strategies. This phase in the appraisal sequence has received empirical attention in the long tradition of emotional support and comforting episodes (Burleson, 2003; Burleson & Goldsmith, 1998). Presumably, the results of reappraisal fold back into our affective memory for events and influence future appraisal processes when in similar situations.

Appraisal theories have several advantages over other approaches to emotion experience, particularly in explaining the variability that is evident in emotion experience. That is, the cultural and normative influences on appraisal dimensions acquired through childhood allow theorists to account for commonly shared emotion experiences within cultures. For example, in a study of adults who had lived in both the United States and Europe, Kotchemidova (2010) found that normative influences on situational appraisals facilitated the integration of individuals into new cultures. The strong presence of cheerfulness during interpersonal interactions in the United States was noted by respondents who eventually reconceptualized their emotional responses toward greater positivity than initially experienced.

However, the subjective interpretations of events (appraisal configurations) also allow theorists to explain the variability within cultures, such as why people experience different emotions or levels of intensity in similar situations but experience the same emotion in different situations. It provides an explanation for individual differences by locating the source of variability within appraisal patterns influenced by past experiences in emotion regulation (John & Gross, 2007) and personality factors that become salient in certain situations, such as aggressive tendencies in anger episodes (Kuppens, van Mechelen, & Rijmen, 2008) or attachment orientation in close relationships (Mikulincer & Shaver, 2005), particularly hurt (Shaver, Mikulincer, Lavy, & Cassidy, 2009).

Given the broad and inclusive nature of appraisal models, it is not surprising that a mechanism to distinguish them has emerged in the literature. Roseman and Smith (2001) distinguish two areas of focus within appraisal research: structural models and process models. Structural models focus on the types of appraisal dimensions (e.g., positive/negative, strong/weak), whereas process models focus on appraisal as part of the unfolding emotional state(s).

### Structural Appraisal Models

Structural models attempt to specify the types of evaluations that underlie emotion experiences, although they differ in the breadth of these appraisal categories. Some scholars focus on broad (molar) appraisal categories, or relational themes, that are likely to evoke certain types of emotions (Scherer, Dan, & Flykt, 2006). For example, sadness is felt when experiencing an irrevocable loss, fear when encountering immediate physical danger, happiness when making progress toward a desired goal, and anger when achieving a desired goal is obstructed (Lazarus, 1991; Scherer et al., 2006; Smith & Lazarus, 1993).

Other structural models more explicitly acknowledge the complexity of blended and social emotions by including elements within appraisal categories (molecular models). For example, Scherer (2001) proposes a typology of stimulus evaluation checks (SECs), which he argues represent the smallest set of criteria necessary to account for the differentiation among emotional states. These checks are subjective perceptions of and inferences about the specific characteristics of the event. Scherer groups individual SECs into four appraisal objectives: (1) relevance detection (novelty check, intrinsic pleasantness check, and goal relevance check), (2) implication assessment (causal attribution check, discrepancy from expectation check, goal/need conduciveness check, and

urgency check), (3) coping potential determination (control check, power check, and adjustment check if unable to control the situation), and (4) normative significance evaluation (internal standards check and external standards check). Scherer et al. (2006) subsequently confirmed these criteria in a study using ratings of content and affective reactions to pictures from the International Affective Picture System (IAPS) (e.g., pictures of snakes, a starving child, and a mother with her baby). Although Scherer (2001) proposes that simple and intuitive assessments of relevance typically precede assessments of implication, coping, and significance, it is possible for the SECs to be processed simultaneously (see also Lazarus, 2008). Indeed, this flexibility is at the core of the component process model.

### Process Appraisal Models

Process-oriented models of appraisal concentrate on the actual operation of emotional processes to specify the cognitive principles and operations underlying these appraisal modes. The most comprehensive approach is the component process model recently developed by Scherer (2001, 2009; Scherer & Ellgring, 2007) in light of the expanding neurological research. Rather than as sequential phases of appraisal, this model presents appraisal as a component of the emotion experience. As evident in the SEC model, recursive evaluation of events in terms of a number of criteria, such as novelty, intrinsic pleasantness, goal conduciveness, and normative significance of the event, as well as the coping potential contribute to feeling states or "efferent effects," which then stimulate response patterns in physiological reactions, motor expression, and action preparation (Ellsworth & Scherer, 2003).

Accordingly, appraisal is seen as a "continuously operating evaluation process" that activates the "organismic subsystems." These systems are "multiply and recursively interrelated" (Scherer, 2001). Table 9.1 details the functions, components, and subsystems of the emotion experience according to the component process model (Scherer, 2001).

**Table 9.1**  Component Process Model

| Emotion Function | Emotion Component | Organismic Subsystem |
|---|---|---|
| Evaluation of objects and events | Cognitive component | Information processing (CNS) |
| System regulation | Peripheral efference component | Support (CNS, NES, ANS) |
| Preparation and direction of action | Motivational component | Executive (CNS) |
| Communication of reaction and behavioral intention | Motor expression component | Action (SNS) |
| Monitoring of internal state and organism environment interaction | Subjective feeling component | Monitor (CNS) |

NOTE: ANS = autonomic nervous system; CNS = central nervous system; NES = neuro-endocrine system; SNS = somatic nervous system.

Support for the component process model as well as potential future directions are emerging within the research on brain activity in response to emotion-eliciting stimuli. For example, variations in appraisal patterns associated with certain personality traits appear to be manifested in amygdala activation. Trait anxiety in adolescents has been predictive of greater amygdala activation in response to fearful faces (Killgore & Yurgelun-Todd, 2005), whereas extraversion was predictive of greater amygdala activation in response to happy faces (Canli, Sivers, Whitfield, Gotlib, & Gabrieli, 2002).

## Dimensional Models of Emotion

Dimensional models are not so much concerned with the process of emotional experience as with the qualities, sensations, or feelings that characterize emotions. Although these theorists recognize that a few basic emotions have evolved to serve survival and reproductive needs, they share with appraisal theorists the perspective that basic emotions do not necessarily have a coherent response pattern or characteristic facial display. However, basic emotions are central to dimension models because they form the "core affects," which Russell and Barrett (1999) describe as the "most elementary consciously

accessible affective feelings" (p. 806) that people experience and which Ellsworth and Scherer (2003) describe as the "nexus" where dimensions are most clearly represented and from which other emotions can be distinguished. For example, on a dimension of valence, sadness and happiness are opposites, as are fear and anger; on a dimension of arousal, anger and rage are both negative affective states, but rage is a much more intense arousal. Although valence and arousal are the most common dimensions, some models also incorporate activation/deactivation, pleasant/unpleasant (Russell, 2003), avoidable/approachable (Blasi et al., 2008), and potency control/unpredictability (Fontaine, Scherer, Roesch, & Ellsworth, 2007).

Perhaps the most familiar dimensional models are the circumplex models of Plutchik (1980, 2001, 2002; Plutchik & Conte, 1997) and Russell (2003). In Plutchik's model, eight core emotions fall within the quadrants of high/low intensity and positive/negative valence: anger, fear, sadness, joy, disgust, surprise, expectancy, and acceptance. All other emotions are combinations or variations in arousal or intensity of these eight. Interestingly, although Plutchik does not explicitly refer to appraisal, several of the blended emotions he identifies imply some level of appraisal of the meaning of emotion-eliciting events. For example, *fiero* is experienced when someone triumphs over adversity, as occurs during athletic competition; *naches* is feeling pride in the accomplishments of close others, such as awards or honors given to a spouse or close friend; and *elevation* (which some would call gratitude) is the special type of joy experienced when someone receives unexpected kindness.

Russell's (2003) current circumplex model is similar in structure to Plutchik's (1980, 2001, 2002; Plutchik & Conte, 1997), but the dimensions that underlie (blend to create) the core affects are hedonic (pleasure/displeasure) and arousal (sleepy/activated). In addition, the theoretical framework includes acknowledgment of the role of appraisal. Russell does not consider appraisal to be the cause of a core affect but suggests that appraisals of "objects" (i.e., problems or opportunities) can facilitate changes in core affect (e.g., from anger to rage). When core affects blend to create new emotions or emotion episodes, information processing, including appraisal, is incorporated into that process.

As is true for all perspectives on emotional experience, the dimensional approach has received mixed support in empirical research. In a test of the assumption that opposite core affects cannot be experienced simultaneously, Larsen, McGraw, and Cacioppo (2001) asked college students to describe the emotion they experienced after watching the film *Life Is Beautiful* and the emotions they anticipated feeling when moving out of their dormitories or graduating from college. The students reported feeling both happy and sad in all three contexts. Larsen et al. suggest that although affective experiences may typically be bipolar, in some circumstances, the experience of emotion is better characterized as "bivariate."

Recent attempts to embed circumplex models within neuroscience have also yielded mixed results. Posner, Russell, and Peterson (2005) present compelling evidence that the dimensions of valence (pleasure/displeasure) and arousal or alertness are neurophysiological systems. They argue that "the prefrontal cortex integrates, organizes,

and structures the primitive sensations of pleasure and arousal with knowledge of the temporal contingencies that link prior experiences of stimuli within varying life contexts and expectations for the future" (p. 723). Support for this position is evident in a study by Blasi et al. (2008), in which respondents were required to make complex social decisions (i.e., approach or avoid) about either relatively unambiguous (i.e., angry, fearful, happy) or ambiguous (i.e., neutral) facial expressions. In addition to amygdala activation and differential patterns in the prefrontal cortex, results indicated that angry and fearful expressions were more frequently judged as avoidable and happy expressions most often as approachable, whereas neutral expressions took longer to evaluate and were equally judged as avoidable and approachable.

However, in a specific test of whether the eight affective states that constitute the circumplex model are perceived by respondents to reflect the dimensions of evaluation and activity, Remington, Fabrigar, and Visser (2000) found that although some of the affective states fell into their predicted regions, others did not. In fact, no affective states consistently fell in three regions of the circle: (1) positive evaluation/high arousal, (2) no evaluation/high arousal, and (3) no evaluation/low arousal. In another test of the circumplex model, Terracciano, McCrae, Hagemann, and Costa (2003) failed to find support for the model as a universal structure. Instead, the placement of emotions on the circular structure with axes of activation and valence emerged only for respondents who were affectively "sophisticated" (college students and adults with high scores on Openness to Feelings and measures of negative emotionality). For those adults and college students who scored low on Openness to Feelings and negative emotionality, a single dimension of positive and negative affect accounted for the dominant patterns of emotional experience.

Some working model of emotion underlies each piece of research on emotion, either implicitly or explicitly. Whether emotions are studied as a small number of discrete basic emotions or as more subtle and continuous emotional states guides the corresponding approach to emotional communication. In the research on emotional expression and communication, it is apparent that neither approach dominates the issues we address, and in some cases (as with the relationship between expression and experience), the choice remains controversial.

## Trends in Emotional Expression and Communication

Research on emotional expression and communication reveals several issues that continue to engage researchers within the field of communication and across disciplines since the last version of this chapter was published (Metts & Planalp, 2002). Since that time, no dramatically new topics have emerged, but several new foci of research are notable, usually building on long-standing and well-established foundational research (for a recent review, see Planalp, Metts, & Tracy, 2010). We turn now to an overview of that research.

## Communication Channels

One of the basic issues for the study of emotional communication concerns the modes, cues, or channels of communication for emotion. The usual suspects dominate: face, voice, to a lesser extent verbal expression (words, metaphors, and complex texts such as poetry), and to an even lesser extent body movement, posture, and touch (for reviews, see chapters in Lewis et al., 2008). A new arrival is olfaction, including topics such as body odor providing kinship information, pheromones signaling sexual attraction, and odors indicating moods (Haviland-Jones & Wilson, 2008).

Most of the work continues to focus on understanding separate modalities and cues, perhaps because cues are complicated enough when considered in isolation. One notable exception is Gottman's system for analyzing emotional expressions in marital interaction

(Coan & Gottman, 2007). The coding system is truly impressive in the huge range of cues that are observed in multiple modalities, including but by no means limited to (a) facial cues such as minute changes in facial musculature, eye rolls, and glowering; (b) acoustic cues such as sighing and changes in pitch; (c) body cues such as forward leans, bobbing heads, and finger pointing; (d) a large range of complex verbal statements such as caring statements, sarcasm, blaming, and ultimatums; and even (e) combinations such as a whiny protest, which combines verbal and vocal cues. Cues are ultimately synthesized into 16 emotions or emotion-laden behaviors (such as belligerence) that are used to describe affective processes in interaction. It is an ambitious undertaking, and it should be noted that it has been built on decades of research on a specific type of interaction (conflict) in a specific type of relationship (marriage) with a specific goal (to predict divorce). Because it is hard to imagine that this system would work in understanding children's play or hostage negotiations, for example, it illustrates the scope of the research challenge involved in understanding how communication cues and modalities work together as integrated expressions that are interpreted as gestalts in specific situations.

## The Relationship Between Experience of Emotion and Expression

Controversy continues over the extent to which expressions are linked to the emotional experiences to which they are assumed (more or less) to correspond (for more background, see Metts & Planalp, 2002, and the previous discussion of basic emotions). The case that facial expressions are an integral part of biologically coherent emotional packages (i.e., basic emotions) continues to be made on the grounds of universality, similarities in nonhuman primates, and strong links with other components of emotion, such as experience, appraisal, and physiological responses (Matsumoto, Keltner, Shiota, O'Sullivan, & Frank, 2008).

Traditional experimental and observational methodologies are now being supplemented and almost overshadowed by neuroimaging techniques in trying to isolate distinctive emotional packages that may include expressive components. The explosion of research in affective neuroscience is arguably the most important development in the study of emotion since the decade began. For example, in the 2008 edition of the *Handbook of Emotions*, two new chapters on neurological research (Craig, 2008; Wager et al., 2008) were added to the single chapter in the second edition (Ledoux & Phelps, 2003, 2008). It is clear that emotions have effects on neural circuitry that are quantifiable, visually observable through increasingly sophisticated brain scans, and of great heuristic value. As yet, no simple one-to-one relationship has been found between a particular experienced emotion and distinctive forms of neural activation, so it is not clear if neuroimaging will help establish inherent links between emotions and their expressions.

Especially promising is work on mirror neurons. First discovered in monkeys, mirror neurons are so called because they fire in the same brain regions for observers as for the person undertaking or even intending the action being observed. The findings have led to arguments that mirror neurons may be the evolutionary foundation of imitation, empathy, and even language (Rizzolatti & Craighero, 2004). Although they seem to provide an automatic link between expression and recognition (automatic empathy, if you will), and mirror neuron dysfunction has been linked to autism (Dapretto et al., 2005), a key question that remains is how motor neurons are controlled because it is clear that mimicry and empathy are not inevitable (Iacoboni & Dapretto, 2006).

Other voices make the case that control, flexibility, and adaption (Fischer, Manstead, & Zaalberg, 2003) are critical to understanding the full range of human emotional expression and recognition (more accurately called "communication"

when seen in this light). Russell, Bachorowski, and Fernández-Dols (2003) claim that emotional expressions are not simply observable manifestations of well-defined internal emotional states. The evidence most familiar to communication scholars would be display rules that are used to mask, simulate, accentuate, minimize, or otherwise alter expressions of emotion so that they fit a socially appropriate or expected enactment (Ekman & Friesen, 1975) and to serve social functions (Zaalberg, Manstead, & Fischer, 2004). Indeed, display rules and emotion regulation more generally are learned during childhood, beginning in infancy and continuing through adolescence, as part of the broader socialization process. Children realize early that the expression of emotion to particular others (e.g., peers compared with parents) is a message that not only serves an interactive function (e.g., sadness elicits support; fear elicits protection) but also invites potential attributions associated with the emotional experience (e.g., feeling sadness or fear may evoke unwanted attributions of weakness from peers) (Metts & Smith, 2009; Shipman, Zeman, Nesin, & Fitzgerald, 2003).

In sum, the argument that emotional expressions are much more flexible and serve complicated social functions is well documented in three ways: (1) expressions are adapted to receivers and contexts, (2) recognition is less like decoding and more like interpretation (e.g., complex understandings of and reactions to others' expressed emotions), and (3) what is sent may not be a tightly packaged and standardized basic emotion but rather more subtle emotional cues about nuanced emotional states (e.g., Russell et al., 2003).

The current state of the research seems to be that researchers are moving ahead on both ends of the continuum from "expressions as manifestations of basic emotions" to "emotional expressions as social communication." Nevertheless, there are indications that each side recognizes the validity of the other and that some yet to be understood, more complicated interaction between the two will ultimately emerge, perhaps following the model of getting beyond the false dichotomy between nature and nurture.

## The Effects of Expression on Expressors

This third continuing concern for research on emotional expression finds its roots in Freud's "talking cure" and has developed over the past few decades to specify how emotional expression affects the expressor on at least three levels: physiologically, psychologically, and socially. The research is too extensive to review thoroughly here, but in a recent reflection and synthesis, Smyth and Pennebaker (2008) concluded that effect sizes for expressive writing are quite small ($d = 0.08$). They conclude that expressive writing is helpful for interventions, but more needs to be known about how, for whom, and in what ways emotional expression works. Their questions do appear as themes in the research on how writing should be done (e.g., with optimism, from a certain point of view), with what special populations they might be helpful (e.g., with those having attention deficit disorder [ADD], posttraumatic stress disorder [PTSD], alexithymia, or human immunodeficiency virus [HIV]), and with what effects (e.g., on physical health, memory, or social relationships).

The most notable contribution from communication scholars is Floyd's (2006) program of research on human affection exchange, which focuses on the link between expression of affection and physiological indicators of disease processes, such as cholesterol (Floyd, Mikkelson, Hesse, & Pauley, 2007) and stress recovery (Floyd, Mikkelson, Tafoya, et al., 2007), and also includes special populations such as alexithymics (Hesse & Floyd, 2008) and social outcomes such as more satisfying father–son relationships (Morman & Floyd, 2002). Also related is work on the need (one might even say compulsion) to share emotions socially ("get it off one's chest"), both after powerful emotional experiences and in everyday

interaction. In his review of current research, Rimé (2009) found no evidence that social sharing aided emotional recovery from traumatic events, but it was perceived to be beneficial and cognitively helpful and elicited comfort from recipients.

## Social Regulation of Expression

The fourth persistent concern is how emotional expression is regulated interpersonally for individuals, the interaction at hand, and/or the relationship. Regardless of whether a felt emotion is suppressed or a fake emotion is displayed (or any number of other options) intentionally or unintentionally, regulation of expression is part and parcel of interpersonal interaction. Expressions may be regulated to signal cooperativeness and trustworthiness (Boone & Buck, 2003), manage face (Ting-Toomey, 2005), elicit support (Caughlin et al., 2009), signal hurt (Vangelisti, 2007), abuse others (Metts, Cupach, & Lippert, 2006), or perform any number of other social functions, prosocial or nefarious. Indeed, emotional regulation in social situations is identified as an important component of general emotional competence or intelligence (Saarni, 1999; Salovey, Detweiler-Bedell, Detweiler-Bedell, & Mayer, 2008). Recent edited books by Gross (2007) and Philippot and Feldman (2004) primarily review the literature on intrapersonal emotional regulation (but cf. Rimé, 2007; Shiota, Campos, Keltner, & Hertenstein, 2004). Work on emotional regulation in communication is dominated by the study of social support, but beyond that, it focuses on communication that tends to be emotion specific, for example, Bevan and Stetzenbach's (2007) exploration of jealousy expression in relationships and Domagalski and Steelman's (2007) examination of anger expression in the workplace.

We move now to a more detailed discussion of theoretical and empirical work on emotions in relationships.

# Emotion in Close Relationships

The form, function, and consequence of emotions in close relationships are necessarily framed by the nature of the relationship (e.g., dating, married, friends), relationship quality (e.g., satisfaction and commitment), and the degree of interdependence that is present between partners in that relationship. We begin with a discussion of emotions in relationship initiation, followed by a discussion of emotions in relationship maintenance, and then emotions in relationship termination.

## Initiation: Put on a Happy Face

If asked what initially attracted them to a potential romantic partner, many people would no doubt comment on appearance or physical attributes. Others, however, might mention the bright smile, welcoming demeanor, and other signs of approachability. As suggested in both appraisal theories and dimensional approaches, positive arousal (e.g., pleasantness, interest, and attention) is more likely to be experienced in situations perceived as not threatening and holding the potential for goal achievement. The interesting question is whether relationship initiation episodes are appraised as promising and not threatening, which promotes positive displays, or whether the positive displays present in these episodes influence the appraisal process and lead to positive emotional arousal and expression. The answer is that both explanations are reasonable accounts for the initiation process. For those who enter initiation episodes feeling happy, positive outcomes are likely to follow and confirm the preexisting emotion. Research indicates that feeling happy promotes activation, outgoingness, and the urge to approach other people (Miron, Parkinson, & Brehm, 2007). More specifically, according to Fredrickson and Branigan's (2005) broaden-and-build theory, positive emotions, compared to neutral states and negative emotions, broaden an individual's "momentary

thought–action repertoire." This enhanced perceptual openness, attention, and creativity in processing environmental and social stimuli provide a greater range of psychological resources that facilitates successful interaction during the initiation episode (Waugh & Fredrickson, 2006).

Of course, not everyone enters relationship initiation episodes in a state of happiness. Research indicates that because relationship initiation entails the evaluation of one's current attractiveness and potential value as a partner, the process is not intrinsically positive. College student respondents report feeling an array of negative affective states when engaging in relationship initiation episodes, such as feeling nervous, anxious, uneasy, cautious, uncomfortable, hesitant, afraid, and scared (Avtgis, West, & Anderson, 1998; Kunkel, Wilson, Olufowote, & Robson, 2003). What then accounts for the absence of these negative-affect displays and the presence of positive-affect displays? It is possible that potential daters follow display rules by simulating positive-emotion displays even when none are felt or even masking their apprehension and negative feelings with positive displays because normative scripts mandate positive displays (Ekman & Friesen, 1982; Metts & Mikucki, 2008). In addition, to the extent that formulating facial expressions of happiness generates the actual experience of happiness, as suggested by the facial-feedback hypothesis (Buck, 1980; Knapp & Hall, 2010; McIntosh, 1996), people who follow the social expectations for positive-emotion displays may ultimately benefit from the social and psychological advantages inherent in the positive-emotion experience. It is also possible that the prevailing positive atmosphere and the presence of positive-affect displays from others (e.g., at a party or in a bar) arouse comparable positive affect through emotional contagion (Barsade, 2002). As a result, secondary appraisal or reappraisal may serve to reformulate initial interpretations of threat and the corresponding withdrawal tendencies into interpretations of promise and potential success with corresponding approach tendencies.

In situations where people are seeking to establish a relationship (or are open to the possibility), normative expectations for displays of happiness, whether fully experienced or simulated, are highly successful mechanisms to facilitate that process (Metts & Mikucki, 2008). Of course, those relationships that emerge from the initial encounters experience a host of changes over time as they develop. The generally scripted nature of initial conversations gives way to relationship-specific and partner-specific expectations that must be negotiated if the relationship is to endure.

## Relationship Maintenance: Managing the Paradox of Interdependence

The behavioral and emotional interdependence that develops in close relationships is in some ways paradoxical. On the one hand, it provides the advantage of increased resources, opportunities for shared activities and novel experiences, enrichment through extended social networks, and the potential for personal growth or self-expansion (Aron, Aron, & Norman, 2001; Aron, Norman, Aron, McKenna, & Heyman, 2000). Even in difficult situations when a conflict of interest is present, partners learn to balance self-interest with the risk of exploitation to generate a pattern of mutual responsiveness (Murray & Holmes, 2009). Over time, as partners coordinate their needs, goals, and behaviors and discuss their perceptions of events and situations, congruent patterns of appraisal emerge. Eventually, emotional similarity leads to emotional convergence, which, in turn, facilitates an emotionally open communication climate, mutual trust, and relationship satisfaction (Anderson, Keltner, & John, 2003). On the other hand, interdependence is also the triggering mechanism for emotional arousal because partners' actions (or inactions) have implications for the well-being and goal achievement of the other (Clark & Brissette, 2003). For example, although interdependence enables need fulfillment, when judgments of equality and equity frame the attempt to gratify these needs, interactions elicit emotions, both positive and

negative. And while interdependence promotes goal achievement through increased resources, it also sometimes obstructs goal achievement, arousing negative emotions such as anger or hurt (Fitness & Warburton, 2009).

To more fully develop the emotional profiles that emerge within interdependent relationships, we first review the research on emotional convergence. We then turn to the extensive research on emotions associated with events that are appraised as entailing *threat, injustice/inequity,* and *goal obstruction.*

### Emotional Convergence

The development of emotional similarity in close relationships provides several advantages. For example, it facilitates easier coordination between partners in their thoughts and actions; contributes to a more accurate perception of each other's feelings, motivations, and intentions; and provides an implicit validation of situational appraisals and emotional responses. Over time, similarity in emotion experience contributes to an automatic, open, and comfortable expression of emotion and, eventually, emotional convergence. Emotional convergence should then predict relationship satisfaction and stability (Anderson et al., 2003).

This expectation is confirmed in existing research. Anderson and colleagues (2003) conducted three studies using friends and dormitory roommates. In the first study, they found that although friends did not develop similar personality traits over a six-month period of time, they did develop significant similarity in the emotions they experienced, and this similarity was a significant predictor of their satisfaction. In the second study of roommates, they found no correlation in emotional experience and expression profiles during the first two weeks of the semester, but at the end of the academic year, substantial correlations were evident. In addition, more emotionally similar roommates reported greater closeness, greater trust, and higher confidence that they would remain friends in the coming years. These patterns held across both male and female roommates.

In a third study, roommates (of seven months) were separated and paired with an unknown companion while they viewed film clips designed to induce emotions. Remarkably, roommates reported similar appraisals, similar emotional responses, and produced similar emotional expressions as coded by the independent coders.

The positive relational effects of emotional similarity in romantic couples have also been identified. Gonzaga, Campos, and Bradbury (2007) used both dating couples who engaged in laboratory interactions and newlywed couples who were assessed over a one-year period. Results across three studies indicated that although personality similarity was associated with relationship quality, emotion similarity mediated the association. Likewise, although personality convergence was associated with relational satisfaction, emotion convergence mediated the association.

Recognizing the positive effects of emotional expression and emotional convergence on relational closeness and satisfaction is not meant to suggest that unfettered communication of all emotional states is relationally healthy. As we elaborate below, some forms of negative-emotion expression are damaging to the relationship, particularly aggressive expressions of anger and jealousy. The most effective approach to emotional expression when problematic emotions are experienced is emotion regulation (Gross, 2007). That is, rather than suppressing strong negative emotions and inhibiting all signs of genuinely felt emotions, regulating the emotional experience through cognitive reappraisal before response tendencies are enacted and then controlling their manifestation is less psychologically draining and more socially adaptive (Kashdan, Volkmann, Breen, & Han, 2007; Kennedy-Moore & Watson, 2001; Richards, Butler, & Gross, 2003) and relationally constructive (Rivers, Brackett, Katulak, & Salovey, 2007).

### Appraisal Processes: Threat, Injustice/Inequity, and Goal Obstruction

As would be expected given the pervasive presence of emotion in close relationships and the interdisciplinary nature of its appeal, no single theory dominates the scholarly discourse on the origin, expression, and consequences of emotion in close relationships. However, a synthesis of the literature suggests that appraisal perspectives, whether explicitly articulated or implied within the rationale and methods, emerge as a prevailing backdrop for most empirical work on emotions in relationships.

The incorporation of appraisal principles is intuitively reasonable. Although basic or discrete emotions are certainly experienced within close relationships, their evocation and characteristic/spontaneous-response tendencies are deeply embedded within the constraints of relationship norms, expectations, and history. When experienced within this relationship environment, basic emotions often activate related or qualifying affective states, leading to complex affective composites that trigger more conscious appraisal. For example, regarding the experience of hurt, Planalp and Fitness (1999) note that humans may register betrayal affectively and immediately (i.e., feeling hurt), before much conscious cognitive processing occurs, with conscious reflection on the causes and implications of the betrayal event coming later. Moreover, emotional states, even the basic emotions, are more typically "communicated" rather than simply "expressed." Emotional states, their cause, and their relevance to the partner are often verbalized (effectively or ineffectively, constructively or destructively) and/or signaled in strategic actions such as silence or withdrawal. Indeed, appraisal theorists have recently begun to include "social appraisal" within the general appraisal model—an evaluative judgment centered on anticipation of appropriateness and the likely consequences of expressing emotion to another person (Evers, Fischer, Rodriguez Mosquera, & Manstead, 2005). When partners respond to these messages in some way, emotion communication episodes unfold.

Finally, dimensions of arousal such as intensity, valence, and pleasantness are at some level of consciousness responsive to relational cues within the environment, during both the initial appraisal of emotion recognition and the secondary appraisal guiding response or expression

(Russell, 2003). For example, entering a coffee shop and unexpectedly seeing one's partner talking to another person might elicit arousal that is simply experienced as interest or perhaps pleasure at the sight of one's partner. However, if the other person is recognized as a former romantic partner, inducing a sense of threat, and/or cues of intimate conversation are perceived, appraisal will formulate arousal patterns into the recognizable emotion of jealousy.

We organize the following discussion around three appraisal themes: threat, injustice/inequity, and goal obstruction. Although each theme can be distinguished conceptually, in actual practice, they frequently intersect into a complex matrix of emotional experience and expression.

### Threat Appraisals: Jealousy and Hurt

The typical response to threatening cues in one's environment is fear; however, in circumstances where environmental cues are relationally, rather than physically, relevant, appraisal processes sometimes lead to jealousy or hurt. Jealousy and hurt share in common some degree of fear and general negative affect associated with uncertainty, but jealousy is more likely to have some degree of anger as its core emotional component, whereas hurt is more likely to have some degree of sadness as its core emotional component.

*Jealousy.* Romantic jealousy is experienced when the perceived threat is focused on a romantic relationship that is assumed to be emotionally and sexually exclusive (Bringle & Boebinger, 1990). Research on romantic jealousy experience and expression suggests that the qualities constituting the experience of jealousy are systematically associated with its expression in various types of communicative actions and strategies. Of course, these patterns of association reflect the variations within scholars' conceptualization of the jealousy construct and assessment tools for the modes of expression.

One broad approach to jealousy experience reflects the appraisal circumstances of its evocation—is it evoked by actual knowledge of a partner's betrayal or by suspicions that are not confirmed? Barelds and Barelds-Dijkstra (2007) use this distinction in formulating two types of jealousy: reactive and anxious jealousy. Reactive jealousy results from knowledge that the partner has actually engaged in acts of perceived infidelity (flirting to sexual contact), while anxious jealousy is elicited by feelings of distrust and suspicions leading to rumination and images of the partner's infidelity. The authors also propose a third type of jealousy, possessive jealousy, which is a behavioral manifestation of jealousy feelings and includes efforts to control a partner's opportunity to interact with real or perceived rivals. The results of three studies using married and cohabiting couples indicated that reactive jealousy is positively associated with relational quality but anxious jealousy and possessive jealousy are negatively related. In terms of emotion experience and expression theories, this finding can be interpreted as the functional utility of reactive jealousy, compared with anxious jealousy, in that it is aroused by an actual event, involves recognizing and acknowledging one's jealousy, and facilitates open expression, negotiation, and greater potential for resolution rather than suppression of the jealous feelings.

A more common approach in interpersonal communication research is to conceptualize and, therefore, measure jealousy as a blend of more specific affective states/qualities and to use a typology of communicative responses, some of which are productive and some of which are not. For example, Guerrero, Trost, and Yoshimura (2005) explored patterns of association among component elements within the jealousy experience and communicative responses in two studies. In the first study, respondents' descriptions of actual jealousy episodes in their romantic relationships were coded for affective components comprising jealousy and strategies used to communicate jealousy to partners (i.e., active distancing, negative-affect expression, integrative communication, distributive communication, avoidance/denial, violent communication, surveillance, compensatory restoration, manipulation attempts, and rival contacts). In the second study, seriously dating, engaged, or married respondents indicated how they would typically feel and typically react when experiencing jealousy. The survey included 24 emotions that were factored into six clusters (passion, fear/envy, hostility, sadness, irritation, and guilt), and the same 11 communicative responses that were used in Study 1. Results indicated similar patterns in jealousy experience and communicative responses across both studies. In general, when strong negative emotions such as anger and hostility are salient in the experience of jealousy, partners are less likely to use integrative communication strategies and more likely to use distributive communication, active distancing, and manipulation.

Communication scholars have also extended the study of jealousy from romantic relationships to other categories of relationships. Bevan and Samter (2004), for example, examined intensity ratings for types of jealousy in cross-sex friendships and communicative responses as depicted in hypothetical scenarios. The types of jealousy included friend jealousy (relationship with another friend), family jealousy (relationship with family members), activity jealousy (involvement in activities outside the friendship, such as school, work, or hobbies), power jealousy (losing influence over a friend to another person), intimacy jealousy (feeling that more advice is sought from or disclosed to others), and romantic jealousy (a perceived third-party threat to the relationship). As might be expected, given the important role of emotional support and self-disclosure in friendship, intimacy jealousy was rated as most likely to be experienced and most likely to be negotiated directly through integrative communication (I would explain my feelings to my partner) and to a lesser degree through denial/avoidance (I would act like I didn't care).

Finally, an important complement to traditional jealousy research is the emerging focus on the person who is the target of another person's jealousy expressions regarding his or her increased relational and partner uncertainty (Bevan, 2006) or more specific emotional responses

(Yoshimura, 2004). Bevan and Hale (2006) used scenarios depicting jealousy expression strategies in several types of relationships, including with siblings, cross-sex friends, and dating partners. Consistent with previous research, they used three forms of jealousy expression: (1) distributive communication (direct and aggressive messages such as accusations or sarcasm), (2) integrative communication (direct, nonaggressive, and constructive messages), and (3) negative-affect expression (nonverbal behaviors such as crying or acting anxious, which are subject to interpretation by the jealousy target). Respondents rated the extent to which they would experience negative emotions, including sadness, anger, frustration, guilt, fear, insecurity, and surprise, in response to types of jealousy expressions. Results indicated that scenarios describing jealousy expression from siblings and dating partners elicited more intense negative-emotion ratings than scenarios describing jealousy expression from cross-sex friends. In addition, distributive communication was associated with more rumination than integrative communication or negative-affect expression.

Before moving from jealousy to perceptions of threat appraisals, which lead to the emotion of hurt, we believe it is important to briefly address the issue of sex differences in jealousy responses to infidelity. A common theme in romantic jealousy research is that men and women differ in their degree of felt jealousy depending on whether the infidelity is an emotional involvement or a sexual one. Presumably, men experience more jealousy in response to sexual infidelity and women experience more jealousy in response to emotional infidelity. Evolutionary psychology is often used as an explanatory framework to reason that a man is threatened by the possibility of investment in a child that is not his own and a woman is threatened by the potential loss of resources provided by her man (Buss, 1992, 2004; Cann, Mangum, & Wells, 2001; Shackelford et al., 2004). Although empirical support for sex differences is available, critiques of the methods used to assess jealousy experience suggest that this assumption be taken with caution. When Desteno, Bartlett, and Salovey (2002) tested the forced-choice method (i.e., respondents must select either sexual or emotional infidelity) against continuous-level measures (i.e., Likert scales), they found no sex differences in jealousy responses; both men and women rated sexual infidelity as the more distressing event. Desteno et al. concluded that "the intimate contact involved in this event presents the clearest signals that the rival has been elevated by the partner to a position equal to or greater than that of the jealous individual" (p. 1115). Raising a different methodological issue, Sagarin and Guadagno (2004) argue that the sex differences in reports of intense jealousy in romantic relationships may be attributable to the anchors used in Likert-type measures. They reason that women are simply more likely to report higher scores when the anchors are, for example, *not at all jealous* or *extremely jealous* on a Likert-type scale or the question is how bothered they would be by certain types of behaviors (e.g., flirting with or kissing someone else), with response options ranging from *strongly agree* to *strongly disagree*. After the upper anchor of the scale was altered to include contextual information (e.g., *as jealous as you could feel in a romantic relationship*), men and women did not differ in ratings of intensity of jealousy.

*Hurt.* Research on hurt in close relationships tends to parallel that on jealousy, with scholars addressing three related foci: (1) the affective components of the hurt, (2) the methods of communicating hurt feelings, and (3) the consequences of expressing hurt (Vangelisti, 2009).

Although hurt is generally considered to result from a person's belief that he or she is less valued than he or she desires, it is a particularly complex and diffuse emotion. Hurt often co-occurs with sadness and anger, configurations that emerge from relationship appraisal patterns that are not yet fully understood (Leary & Leder, 2009). Research efforts to understand the types of events or messages that elicit hurt and their affective correlates typically involve the analysis of actual hurtful experiences provided by respondents. In some cases, the analysis is explicitly guided by theory, and in others, the analysis is based on content categories derived from written descriptions.

A study by Zhang and Stafford (2008) provides an interesting illustration of how theory originally created to explain social identity (face management theory, by Goffman, 1967, and politeness theory, by Brown & Levinson, 1987) can be usefully imported to explain the causes and consequences of hurt. An analysis of episodes when respondents received what they perceived to be honest but hurtful messages from a romantic partner indicated that messages concerning the state of the relationship were rated by respondents as more threatening to negative face (i.e., a desire for autonomy) than those concerning personality, physical appearance, or behaviors. Also, the greater the perceived face threat, the greater the hurt and the greater the negative relational consequences reported. In a similar vein, Goldsmith and Donovan-Kicken (2009) use politeness theory as an integrative framework for synthesizing the empirical research on hurt. They conclude with the observation that "theories of face and politeness would call for attention to hurt that derives from disrupted social performances" (p. 68).

Employing a more emergent approach to conceptualizing hurt, Vangelisti, Young, Carpenter-Theune, and Alexander (2005) asked respondents to describe a particular interaction that hurt their feelings in a "script-like format," indicating the behaviors or messages that hurt them. Fourteen types of hurtful actions were identified by coders and subsequently reduced to eight broad categories: (1) relational denigration, (2) humiliation, (3) verbal/nonverbal aggression, (4) intrinsic flaw, (5) shock (unexpected), (6) ill-conceived humor, (7) mistaken intent, and (8) discouragement.

Using a similar approach, Feeney (2004) identified five general categories of hurtful actions: (1) active dissociation (denying or retracting feelings of love and commitment), (2) passive disassociation (ignoring or excluding a partner from plans and activities), (3) criticism, (4) sexual infidelity, and (5) deception (lying, breaking promises and confidences). In a subsequent two-part study designed to identify the affective components of hurt, Feeney (2005) coded respondent accounts of a hurtful event and then asked a second sample to sort the emotionally descriptive terms into emotion categories of anger, fear/anxiety, sadness, shame/inadequacy, and hurt/injury. Terms that were placed only in the hurt/injury category included *hurt, in pain, damaged, torn apart,* and *shattered.* The terms *betrayed, deceived,* and *used* were placed in anger as well as hurt, and *heartbroken, aching heart, let down, disappointed, deflated, misunderstood, numb,* and *unsupported* were also placed with sadness. The complexity of these overlapping profiles reflects the emergent, subjective, and situationally contingent nature of hurt.

A study of hurt experience and expression by McLaren and Solomon (2008) is noteworthy for its theoretical grounding in appraisal theory. A sample of college students were instructed to recall a minimally hurtful message or an extremely hurtful message from a friend or dating partner. Respondents also rated appraisal dimensions such as relationship quality, judgments of intentionality, intensity of hurt, frequency of hurt, as well as the relational consequences (distancing) of the hurtful message (i.e., more close or distant, relaxed or tense, more friendly or hostile, more intimate or remote, and more open or closed). Results indicated main effects on relational distancing for appraisals of intentionality, intensity of hurt, relational quality, and frequency of hurt. Interesting sex difference emerged as well. For males in dating relationships, intensity of hurt was not associated with relational distancing regardless of perceived intentionality or frequency friendships, but for females in dating relationships, intensity of hurt was positively associated with distancing when hurtful messages were perceived as frequent. In addition, for females in friendships, a positive association was found between intensity of hurt and relational distancing when hurtful messages were perceived as unintentional and infrequent, suggesting that the uncertainty associated with unpredictable

(unexpected) hurts may be especially uncomfortable. In a replication of this study using daily diaries over a 14-day period, McLaren and Solomon (2008) confirm the validity of these findings.

Investigations of communicative responses to hurt also vary in breadth and detail. May and Jones (2005) distinguish two types of hurt responses: (1) introjective (internalizing and magnifying the hurtful experience by self-criticism and self-punishment) and (2) retaliatory (lashing out angrily). Four hypothetical scenarios were created: deeply hurt by someone close either intentionally or not and being hurt in a public or private setting. Results indicated that both types of hurt responses were higher when the hurtful messages were intentional, and for introjective hurt, when the act was also committed in private. This suggests that when a close other intentionally sends a hurtful message in a private context, appraisal processes promote a strongly negative response that can be fully communicated without the constraints of having to manage face in the presence of other people. This is an important aspect of the emotional communication episode that is not typically included in emotion research.

### Inequity/Injustice Appraisals

One of the defining features of close relationships is that they provide partners the opportunity to fulfill needs for intimacy, belonging, enjoyment, companionship, support, and tangible resources (Prager & Buhrmester, 1998). Based on the fundamental premise of appraisal theory, we would expect that when a need fulfillment goal is met, an event is perceived as pleasant and gratifying; when it is not met, the event is perceived as unpleasant and not gratifying (Fitness & Fletcher, 1993). To the extent that one's own need fulfillment goals are satisfied significantly less often than are one's partner's, perceptions of relational injustice are likely to emerge and elicit negative emotions. Strong support for this assumption is provided by Mikula, Scherer, and Athenstaedt's (1998) study, which included data from 37 countries (2,921 student participants). They found consistent patterns of appraisal and reactions within descriptions of situations when joy, anger, fear, sadness, disgust, shame, and guilt were experienced. Specifically, strong main effects emerged for perceptions of injustice across all negative emotions, particularly anger, and unjust events were perceived to have negative effects on personal relationships.

Recent studies using the concepts of equality and equity illustrate the pervasive effects of these justice appraisals. Le and Agnew (2001) examined partners' perceived equality in need fulfillment and their experience of self-focused emotion and relationship-focused emotions. Although appraisal processes were not explicitly measured, Le and Agnew asked respondents to rate their positive affect (e.g., happy, enthusiastic, and trusting) and negative affect (e.g., gloomy, sad, mistrusting, and jealous) over a four-day period. As predicted, need fulfillment was a significant predictor of positive and negative affective states. Specifically, partners who perceived inequality in need fulfillment experienced more negative relationship-related emotions than did participants who perceived the relationship to be mutually dependent.

Guerrero, La Valley, and Farinelli (2008) further elaborate the role of perceived inequity in the emotion process by (a) measuring using more specific basic emotions (i.e., anger, guilt, and sadness) rather than general affective states, (b) incorporating the traditional equity model (i.e., underbenefitted inequity and overbenefitted inequity), and, of particular importance, (c) assessing communicative responses to the felt emotions. Married couples were asked to complete surveys measuring perceived equity status relative to partner, emotional experience, and likelihood of using particular expressive strategies for each emotion. The expressive strategies for anger included integrative assertion (discussing the problem), distributive aggression (criticizing the partner), passive aggression (the silent treatment), and nonassertive denial (keeping

angry feelings to myself). For guilt, strategies included apology/concession, explanations/justifications, appeasement, and denial/withdrawal, and for sadness, they included positivity/distraction, social support seeking, immobilization, and solitude.

Results indicated, as expected, that feeling underbenefited was associated with anger and sadness (for wives), while feeling overbenefited was associated with guilt. In addition, self-reported expression patterns were generally constructive when spouses perceived the relationship to be equitable (e.g., using assertive integration to express anger) but destructive when they felt underbenefited (e.g., using distributive aggression to express anger) or overbenefited (using nonassertive denial to express anger). Finally, Guerrero et al. (2008) raise the interesting possibility that "while UBI [Underbenefited Inequity] itself may be distressing, the experience and aggressive expression of anger may be more proximally related to low levels of marital satisfaction than UBI per se" (p. 720).

In a subsequent study, Guerrero, Farinelli, and McEwan (2009) extended these findings by including positive affect (love, appreciation, and affection) as well as negative affect and adding attachment-style dimensions: security/confidence, dismissiveness, preoccupation, and fear of intimacy. They surveyed romantic couples on how they expressed emotions using communicative strategies similar to those in Guerrero et al. (2008), with the addition of open expression for positive affect ("I show a lot of affection to my partner"). Results indicated that people's reports of how they believed they expressed emotions were predictive of their partner's relational satisfaction. Specifically, perceived expression of anger using assertive (rather than aggressive or passive–aggressive) strategies, expression of sadness using positive activity and social support–seeking (rather than immobilization or dependent behavior) strategies, and expressing positive emotions such as affection predicted partner satisfaction. In addition, satisfaction was higher when partners reported secure attachment style dimensions compared with dismissive or preoccupied dimensions.

## Goal Obstruction Appraisals and Relational Turbulence

One of the first theories of close relationships to explicitly build on the premises of emotion theory is Berscheid's emotion-in-relationships model (ERM; Berscheid, 1983; Berscheid & Ammazzalorso, 2004; Fehr & Harasymchuk, 2005). The fundamental premise is that interdependence links the actions and expectations of partners such that disruptions in routine action sequences (i.e., goal obstructions) elicit arousal. When the event is appraised as beneficial to self or to the relationship, positive arousal is experienced; when it is appraised as detrimental to self or the relationship, negative arousal is experienced. ERM has recently been recognized by communication scholars and used as a framework to study emotions in relationships.

Knobloch, Miller, and Carpenter (2007) applied ERM to dating relationships in various stages of increasing interdependence, from casual dating to serious dating. Surveys were used to measure perceived interference or facilitation from the partner relevant to the respondent's goals, relational intimacy, and a variety of emotions that represented the emotion families of anger (angry, mad, annoyed), sadness (sad, gloomy, depressed, sorrowful), fear (afraid, scared, frightened, fearful), and jealousy (jealous, insecure). As predicted from the interference model, interference and uncertainty were positively correlated with all four categories of negative emotions, while facilitation was negatively associated with them. Of particular importance for understanding how the experience of negative emotions may affect relational intimacy is the finding that relational uncertainty and interference mediated the association between negative emotions and relational intimacy. Of course, the full understanding of this process cannot be determined with cross-sectional data given that decreasing intimacy over time may lead to negative emotions, which, in turn, motivate goal-obstructive behavior.

This caveat aside, Knobloch (2008) presents additional confirmation of the tenets of ERM in an analysis of videotaped conversations of married couples who were instructed to talk about the positive aspects of their marriage for 10 minutes and then about a recent surprising event (positive or negative) that caused them to feel uncertain about or to question some aspect of the marriage for 10 minutes. Affiliative behaviors (e.g., smiling, pleasant tone of voice, touch, forward body lean, and eye contact) and disaffiliative behaviors (e.g., absence of affiliative cues and signals of uncoordinated conversation) during the conversations were coded. Perceived interference (e.g., "interferes with the plans I make," "makes it harder for me to schedule my activities") and facilitation (e.g., "helps me do the things I need to do each day," "helps me in my efforts to make plans") and emotions aroused by the conversations (anger, sadness, and happiness) were measured with self-report scales. Results indicated that perceived interference from partners, although generally rated as low, was still associated with uncoordinated conversations, disaffiliative messages, unfavorable cognitive appraisals, and negative emotional reactions to the conversations. Facilitation produced the opposite pattern.

One other example of uncertainty and partner interference is presented here, although it focuses on the emotion of hurt covered previously. Theiss, Knobloch, Checton, and Magsamen-Conrad (2009) describe hurtful experiences as involving extreme emotions, rumination, and polarized communication. Based on this perspective, they "conceptualize hurt as a manifestation of relational turbulence" (p. 589). They collected data from both partners once a week for six weeks. They measured uncertainty, interference, intensity of hurt, perceived intentionality, and damage to the relationship (e.g., decreased trust in the partner, weakened relational quality). In addition, they included three items for assessing communication of hurt to the partner: (1) "I didn't openly admit to my partner that he/she hurt me," (2) "I confronted my partner directly about the fact that he/she hurt me," and (3) "I explicitly told my partner that he/she hurt my feelings" (p. 600). Consistent with the previous studies referenced above, interference and relational uncertainty predicted intensity of hurt, appraisals of intentionality, and perceived damage to the relationship, all of which were associated with more direct communication about the hurtful event.

Whether any of the emotions discussed above that result from appraisals of relationship events lead directly to relationship termination is an open question. It is possible that the discovery of a partner's infidelity is an immediate and direct cause of termination, especially for men who discover their partner's sexual infidelity (Shackelford, Buss, & Bennett, 2002). However, other consequences from more benign but persistent occurrences of emotion-eliciting events, such as hurtful messages, may lead more indirectly to termination through a process of relational distancing (McLaren & Solomon, 2008; Vangelisti, 2006). Indeed, the sometimes positive responses to breakups, happiness and relief, may be the consequence of feeling free from the strain entailed in unsuccessfully managing the challenges of interdependence and the negative emotions experienced in those interactions. Whatever the origin and process of relational termination, the emotions evoked are complex and responsive to a number of contextual factors.

### Relationship Termination: Anger, Sadness, and, Sometimes, Relief

Although space does not permit an exhaustive summary of the research on termination across all relationship types (e.g., friendships, dating, and marriage), a synthesis of current romantic-termination research indicates that three contextual factors are relevant to emotional responses and their intensity. These include the role as the initiator or recipient (i.e., the rejector or the rejectee), the

time since the breakup, and the attachment style of the respondent. These factors are interrelated and often included within the same study because they function to moderate the effects of the breakup on a person's adjustment (i.e., increase the risk of poor outcomes in adjustment or protect from poor outcomes) (Sbarra & Law, 2009).

As might be expected for the role of initiator, romantic partners who report high levels of distress after a breakup also report that the other person initiated the breakup and that it was unexpected; they report feeling rejected and betrayed, although these feeling lessen over time (e.g., Field, Diego, Pelaez, Deeds, & Delgado, 2009). In a diary study of change over time, Sbarra and Emery (2005) found that participants who had recently experienced a breakup, compared with those still in a relationship, experienced more emotional volatility initially, and "feelings of Love [sic] decreased more slowly than feelings of sadness, which decreased slower still than feelings of anger" (p. 228). Interestingly, when diary accounts included contact with the former partner, feelings of both love and sadness increased on that day.

The development of attachment-style dimensions such as security, insecurity, and anxiety in early formative relationships has proven useful in understanding emotional responses and recovery from relationship terminations in adulthood. For example, Davis, Shaver, and Vernon (2003) found that high attachment-related anxiety was associated with a variety of dysfunctional coping responses to relationship loss, such as extreme distress, angry and vengeful behavior, and exaggerated attempts to gain back the partner. By contrast, low anxiety was associated with functional coping strategies such as seeking social support.

One particular type of attachment orientation, preoccupation (anxious/ambivalent attachment dimensions), has emerged as particularly influential in emotional responses to breakups. Barbara and Dion (2000), for example, found in an analysis of survey data that preoccupation scores were the most consistent predictor of breakup criteria, such as beliefs that a partner wanted out of the relationship and was a "villain" who controlled the breakup, and that participants experienced more negative emotions (e.g., hurt, resentment, anger, hate) than positive emotions (e.g., happiness, satisfaction, joy, relief). Sbarra (2006) collected daily-emotion ratings over four weeks from individuals whose romantic relationship had recently ended. Attachment preoccupation (as well as love and anger) was associated with less sadness recovery over that time period, while attachment security was associated with greater anger recovery.

While much work has been done on emotional communication in close relationships, both within and outside the field of communication, much remains to be done. In the next section, we turn to future possibilities.

# New Developments and Directions

Our review of recent developments in research on emotion and communication leads us to consider possible new directions for such research in the years to come. Some can be seen as extensions of existing trends, and some are fundamental issues that have yet to be addressed.

## Communicating Positive Emotions

One development in the study of emotion that is striking to scholars and laypeople alike is work on happiness and well-being (including but not limited to positive psychology). The literature is too broad to review here, but as evidence of its popular appeal, see the special issue of *Time* magazine on "The New Science of Happiness" (2005), and as evidence of its scholarly heuristic value, see the hundreds of recent popular and scholarly books in many disciplines (e.g., philosophy, economics, history, political science, and sociology). One key ingredient has long been known to be good social relationships (Myers & Diener, 1995), a finding that should motivate interpersonal communication scholars

to learn more. For example, in a study based on daily diary reports over a period of a month, Cohn, Fredrickson, Brown, Mikels, and Conway (2009) found that momentary, in situ experiences of happiness contributed to growth in ego resilience (e.g., emotion regulation skills, problem-solving skills), which then predicted life satisfaction.

Even the basic question of what kind of interpersonal interaction makes for happy people, productive interactions, and satisfying relationships remains unanswered and provides the much needed communication angle on positive emotions. Promising candidates based on existing research might be expressions of positive affect that may build upward spirals (Fredrickson & Joiner, 2002) and be emotionally contagious (Hatfield, Cacioppo, & Rapson, 1994), laughter (Reysen, 2006), and optimistic talk (Carver, Scheier, & Segerstrom, 2010). Within the realm of close relationships, expressions of gratitude are important not only for an individual's own subjective well-being (Emmons & McCullough, 2004) but also as a mechanism for increased relationship satisfaction. As Algoe, Gable, and Maisel (2010) concluded from a study of cohabiting couples, "Gratitude may help to turn 'ordinary' moments into opportunities for relationship growth, even in the context of already close, communal relations" (p. 232). Likewise, the critically important functions of affection communication within families, as exemplified by Morman and Floyd's work on father–son interactions (e.g., Morman & Floyd, 2002), merits continued attention.

Along the same lines, research on how communication can be used to overcome negative feelings and restore positive ones, especially in close relationships, is blossoming. Most notable is the explosion of work on forgiveness by communication scholars. Although long recognized by psychologists as an emotional resource that facilitates a general prosocial orientation (Karremans, Van Lange, & Holland, 2005), forgiveness as an emotional transformation emerging from the communication of partners (Waldron & Kelley, 2005) is an important new direction for scholarship. Communication scholars have substantiated the importance not only of the offending partner providing an account and an apology for the hurtful action, betrayal, or transgression (Bachman & Guerrero, 2006; Metts & Cupach, 2007; Morse & Metts, 2011) but also of the offended partner clearly communicating his or her forgiveness (Kelley & Waldron, 2005; Merolla, 2008; Waldron & Kelley, 2005). When ambiguous or "conditional," forgiveness induces guilt rather than gratitude in the offending partner and leads the offending partner to infer that anger, hurt, and/or resentment will continue to plague the relationship, and reconciliation is impaired. The interactive accomplishment of forgiveness in relationship maintenance is a promising area for communication scholars.

## Interpersonal Communication and New Technologies

New technologies seem to be affecting interpersonal communication in profound and truly novel ways. In particular, the quick and widespread adoption of social networking technologies (from Facebook to Instant Messaging, not to mention the taken-for-granted cell phone, e-mail, and phone cameras) is almost certainly changing the way emotion is communicated in interpersonal exchanges. From emoticons to flaming, to sexting, to cyber-bullying, even the neologisms reveal new emotional phenomena arising from technological change.

Many of the phenomena of interest in the context of new technologies have their grounding in face-to-face (F2F) interaction. There are many CMC (computer-mediated communication) versions of F2F emotional phenomena, such as jealousy in response to Internet infidelity, that are being studied comparatively (they are very similar, according to Groothof, Dijkstra, & Barelds, 2009) as well as in their own right (Docan-Morgan & Docan, 2007). Likewise, the generalized social preference for positive-emotion expression in F2F interaction is evident in MySpace comments, particularly those of

women (Thelwall, Wilkinson, & Uppal, 2010). In a recent review of the role of emotion in computer-mediated emotional communication, Derks, Fischer, and Bos (2008) concluded that CMC and F2F communication are "surprisingly similar," and if anything, emotion communication is more explicit and frequent in CMC than in F2F. Topics traditional to interpersonal communication and related to emotion are studied in the CMC context (e.g., identity, lying, influence, social support, power), as are traditional topics in emotional communication (e.g., cues, contagion, emotional intelligence). In addition, a recent review of CMC (Walther, 2010) hints at questions that move from the "whether" questions to the "how" questions. We no longer need to ask *whether* emotional involvement develops through CMC but *how* it does so, not *whether* emotional connections arise among online group members but *how* they do so.

## Basic Questions Still Not Answered

While it is important to attend to new developments related to emotional communication in other disciplines and in the world, it is equally important not to lose track of basic issues that have been there all along and have yet to be addressed adequately in the research. For interpersonal scholars, one of the most important issues still on the table is understanding the dynamics of emotional communication in actual, situated, context-rich episodes of interaction. Too often, emotional expression and interpretation have been treated as if they could be understood as single acts free of context (e.g., posed expressions), when all the evidence indicates that emotional communication is highly adaptive to interpersonal dynamics and situational constraints (see Russell et al., 2003, as discussed earlier). Emotional communication also has its own emergent properties during an unfolding interaction, as does all communication.

The best model available is Gottman's work, which provides a rich portrait of marital conflict in situ (e.g., Coan & Gottman, 2007, as discussed earlier). But on the whole, it is a still portrait rather than a film in which one episode is interpreted in light of what came before and affects what comes after. For example, Rimé (2009) speculates on the dynamic of social sharing: Initial sharing leads to interest, which leads to more social sharing, which may lead to emotional arousal in the listener, which may lead to empathy, efforts to help, and enhanced affection and closeness. He even adds that early verbal expressions of emotional experience move to more nonverbal expressions, suggesting that the types of cues used to share an experience also evolve in response to the listener's response.

Also in play in conversations is the process of social appraisal, articulated by Evers et al. (2005). Partners in conversation appraise not only what communication scholars would call the content of the interaction but also the social dimension (what the other is thinking, feeling, and doing and how they would likely respond to emotional expression). To that we might add the self, the relationship, and the situation. For example, one might respond emotionally to the content (an accusation), the other person (angry facial expression), one's own state ("I can't handle any conflict right now!"), the relationship ("I've got to work with her!"), or the situation ("This is causing a terrible scene"). Moreover, as Evers et al. argue, the person making the accusation may have anticipated the social implication in designing the message ("I'll accuse her so that it will make a scene and intimidate her"). These kinds of multilayered and probably highly subjective emotional expressions and interpretations might be studied effectively using the technique pioneered by Ickes for studying participants' perspectives on unstructured interaction (Ickes, 2003).

## Conclusion

Our review of the current research literature on emotion in interpersonal communication contains three themes. The first theme concerns unresolved basic issues and problems that have implications for research. Among those are how to define emotion and the nature of emotional experience. The section continues the debate or tension over whether emotion should be thought of as expressed or regulated. We suspect that neither issue will be resolved in favor of one camp or the other but that research will proceed in both camps with the hope of peaceful and productive cooperation. Scholars also continue to try to understand emotion communication in all its richness and subtlety as it unfolds in natural interactions. The issue here is not any particular controversy as much as it is about how to come to terms with the overwhelming complexity of the emotional interaction. The second theme concerns new developments that we have noted since reviewing the literature for the 2002 edition of this *Handbook*. One is the enormous surge of research on emotion by neuroscientists. It is not yet clear how that research will affect communication research, but it holds promise, as demonstrated in research on mirror neurons, for example. Another is research on emotion in CMC, which gathers momentum as new communication forms emerge and evolve and the opportunities for (and constraints in) communicating emotion evolve with them.

The third theme concerns bodies of research that continue to develop on the same trajectory they were on in 2002 but have now produced further contributions to our understanding of emotional communication. The most prominent is work on emotional issues and dynamics over the course of relationship change and across different types of relationships. Research has addressed both "what" and "how" questions: what emotions, both positive and negative, emerge and fall away in relationship development, maintenance, and deterioration and how those emotions are shared, negotiated, and managed through communication.

## References

Adolfs, R., Russell, J. A., & Tranel, D. (2004). Impaired judgments of sadness but not happiness following bilateral amygdala damage. *Journal of Cognitive Neuroscience, 16,* 453–462.

Algoe, S. B., Gable, S. L., & Maisel, N. C. (2010). It's the little things: Everyday gratitude as a booster shot for romantic relationships. *Personal Relationships, 17,* 217–233.

Anderson, A. K., & Phelps, E. A. (2002). Is the human amygdala critical for the subjective experience of emotion? Evidence of intact dispositional affect in patients with amygdale lesions. *Journal of Cognitive Neuroscience, 14,* 709–720.

Anderson, C., Keltner, D., & John, O. P. (2003). Emotional convergence between people over time. *Journal of Personality and Social Psychology, 84,* 1054–1068.

Aron, A., Aron, E. N., & Norman, C. (2001). The self expansion model of motivation and cognition in close relationships and beyond. In M. Clark & G. Fletcher (Eds.), *Blackwell handbook of social psychology: Vol. 2. Interpersonal processes* (pp. 478–501). Oxford, UK: Blackwell.

Aron, A., Norman, C., Aron, E., McKenna, C., & Heyman, R. (2000). Couples' shared participation in novel and arousing activities and experienced relationship quality. *Journal of Personality and Social Psychology, 78,* 273–284.

Avtgis, T. A., West, D. V., & Anderson, T. L. (1998). Relationship stages: An inductive analysis identifying cognitive, affective, and behavioral dimensions of Knapp's relational stages model. *Communication Research Reports, 15,* 280–287.

Bachman, G. F., & Guerrero, L. K. (2006). Forgiveness, apology, and communicative responses to hurtful events. *Communication Reports, 19,* 45–56.

Barbara, A. M., & Dion, K. L. (2000). Breaking up is hard to do, especially for strongly preoccupied lovers. *Journal of Personal and Interpersonal Loss, 5,* 315–342.

Barelds, D. P. H., & Barelds-Dijkstra, P. (2007). Relations between different types of jealousy and self and partner perceptions of relationship quality. *Clinical Psychology & Psychotherapy, 14,* 176–188.

Barsade, S. G. (2002). The ripple effect: Emotional contagion and its influence on group behavior. *Administrative Science Quarterly, 47,* 644–675.

Berntson, G. G., Bechara, A., Damasio, H., Tranel, D., & Cacioppo, J. T. (2007). Amygdala contribution to selective dimensions of emotion. *Social Cognitive and Affective Neuroscience, 2,* 123–129.

Berscheid, E. (1983). Emotion. In Kelley, H. H., Berscheid, E., Christensen, A., Harvey, J. H., Huston, T. L., Levinger, G., et al. (Eds.), *Close relationships* (pp. 110–168). New York: W. H. Freeman.

Berscheid, E., & Ammazzalorso, H. (2004). Emotional expression in close relationships. In M. B. Brewer & M. Hewstone (Eds.), *Perspectives on social psychology* (pp. 47–69). Oxford, UK: Blackwell.

Bevan, J. L. (2006). Testing and refining a consequence model of jealousy across relational contexts and jealousy expression messages. *Communication Reports, 19,* 31–44.

Bevan, J. L., & Hale, J. L. (2006). Negative jealousy-related emotion rumination as consequences of romantic partner, cross-sex friend, and sibling jealousy expression. *Communication Studies, 57,* 363–379.

Bevan, J. L., & Samter, W. (2004). Toward a broader conceptualization of jealousy in close relationships: Two exploratory studies. *Communication Studies, 55,* 14–28.

Bevan, J. L., & Stetzenbach, K. A. (2007). Jealousy expression and communication satisfaction in adult sibling relationships. *Communication Research Reports, 24,* 71–77.

Blasi, G., Hariri, A. R., Alce, G., Tuarisano, P., Sambataro, F., Das, S., et al. (2008). Preferential amygdala reactivity to the negative assessment of neutral faces. *Biological Psychiatry, 66,* 847–853.

Bolls, P. D. (2010). Understanding emotion from a superordinate dimensional perspective: A productive way forward for communication processes and effects studies. *Communication Monographs, 77,* 146–152.

Boone, R. T., & Buck, R. (2003). Emotional expressivity and trustworthiness. *Journal of Nonverbal Behavior, 27,* 163–182.

Bringle, R. G., & Boebinger, K. L. G. (1990). Jealousy and the "third" person in the love triangle. *Journal of Social and Personal Relationships, 7,* 119–133.

Brown, P., & Levinson, S. (1987). *Politeness: Some universals in language usage.* Cambridge, UK: Cambridge University Press.

Buck, R. (1980). Nonverbal behavior and the theory of emotion: The facial feedback hypothesis. *Journal of Personality and Social Psychology, 38,* 811–824.

Burleson, B. R. (2003). Emotional support skill. In J. O. Greene & B. R. Burleson (Eds.), *Handbook of communication and social interaction skills* (pp. 551–594). Mahwah, NJ: Lawrence Erlbaum.

Burleson, B. R., & Goldsmith, D. J. (1998). How the comforting process works: Alleviating emotional distress through conversationally induced reappraisals. In P. A. Andersen & L. K. Guerrero

(Eds.), *Handbook of communication and emotion: Research, theory, applications, and contexts* (pp. 245–280). San Diego, CA: Academic Press.

Buss, D. M. (1992). Sex differences in jealousy: Evolution, physiology, and psychology. *Psychological Reports, 3,* 251–255.

Buss, D. M. (2004). *The evolution of desire: Strategies of human mating.* New York: Basic Books.

Cacioppo, J. T., Berntson, G. G., Larsen, J. T., Poehlmann, K. M., & Ito, T. A. (2000). The psychophysiology of emotion. In M. Lewis & J. M. Haviland-Jones (Eds.), *Handbook of emotions* (2nd ed., pp. 173–191). New York: Guilford Press.

Canli, T., Sivers, H., Whitfield, S. L., Gotlib, I. H., & Gabrieli, J. D. E. (2002). Amygdala response to happy faces as a function of extraversion. *Science, 296,* 2191.

Cann, A., Mangum, J. L., & Wells, M. (2001). Distress in response to relationship infidelity: The roles of gender and attitudes about relationships. *Journal of Sex Research, 38,* 185–190.

Carver, C. S., Scheier, M. F., & Segerstrom, S. C. (2010). Optimism. *Clinical Psychology Review, 30,* 879–889.

Caughlin, J. P., Bute, J. J., Donovan-Kicken, E., Kosenko, K. A., Ramey, M. E., & Brashers, D. E. (2009). Do message features influence reactions to HIV disclosures? A multiple-goals perspective. *Health Communication, 24,* 270–283.

Chiao, J. Y., Iidaka, T., Gordon, H. L., Nogawa, J., Bar, M., Aminoff, E., et al. (2008). Cultural specificity in amygdala response to fear faces. *Journal of Cognitive Neuroscience, 20,* 2167–2174.

Clark, M. S., & Brissette, I. (2003). Two types of relationship closeness and their influence on people's emotional lives. In R. J. Davidson, K. R. Scherer, & H. H. Goldsmith (Eds.), *Handbook of the affective sciences* (pp. 824–835). Oxford, UK: Oxford University Press.

Coan, J. A., & Gottman, J. M. (2007). The specific affect coding system (SPAFF). In. J. A. Coan & J. J. B. Allen (Eds.), *Handbook of emotion elicitation and assessment* (pp. 267–285). New York: Oxford University Press.

Cohn, M. A., Fredrickson, B. L., Brown, S. L., Mikels, J. A., & Conway, A. M. (2009). Happiness unpacked: Positive emotions increase life satisfaction by building resilience. *Emotion, 9,* 361–368.

Costafreda, S. G., Brammer, M. J., David, A. S., & Fu, C. H. Y. (2008). Predictors of amygdala activation during the processing of emotional stimuli: A meta-analysis of 385 PET and fMRI studies. *Brain Research Reviews, 58,* 57–70.

Craig, A. D. (2008). Interoception and emotion. In M. Lewis, J. M. Haviland-Jones, & L. F. Barrett (Eds.), *Handbook of emotions* (3rd ed., pp. 272–288). New York: Guilford Press.

Dapretto, M., Davies, M. S., Pfeifer, J. H., Scott, A. A., Sigman, M., Bookheimer, S. Y., et al. (2005). Understanding emotions in others: Mirror neuron dysfunction in children with autism spectrum disorders. *Nature Neuroscience, 9,* 28–30.

Davis, D., Shaver, P. R., & Vernon, M. L. (2003). Physical, emotional, and behavioral reactions to breaking up: The roles of gender, age, emotional involvement, and attachment style. *Personality and Social Psychology Bulletin, 29,* 871–884.

Derks, D., Fischer, A. H., & Bos, A. E. R. (2008). The role of emotion in computer-mediated communication: A review. *Computers in Human Behavior, 24,* 766–785.

DeSteno, D., Bartlett, M. Y., & Salovey, P. (2002). Sex differences in jealousy: Evolutionary mechanism or artifact of measurement? *Journal of Personality and Social Psychology, 83,* 1103–1116.

Docan-Morgan, T., & Docan, C. A. (2007). Internet infidelity: Double standards and the differing views of women and men. *Communication Quarterly, 55,* 317–334.

Domagalski, T. A., & Steelman, L. A. (2007). The impact of gender and organizational status on workplace anger expression. *Management Communication Quarterly, 20,* 297–315.

Ekman, P. (1992). An argument for basic emotions. *Cognition & Emotion, 6,* 169–200.

Ekman, P. (1999). Basic emotions. In T. Dalgleish & M. J. Power (Eds.), *Handbook of cognition and emotion* (pp. 45–60). Chichester, UK: Wiley.

Ekman, P. (2009). *Emotions revealed: Recognizing faces and feelings to improve communication and emotional life* (2nd ed). New York: Holt.

Ekman, P., & Friesen, W. V. (1975). *Unmasking the face.* Englewood Cliffs, NJ: Prentice Hall.

Ekman, P., & Friesen, W. V. (1982). Measuring facial movement with the facial action coding system. In P. Ekman (Ed.), *Emotion in the human face* (pp. 178–211). Cambridge, UK: Cambridge University Press.

Ekman, P., Levenson, R. W., & Friesen, W. V. (1983). Autonomic nervous system activity distinguishes among emotions. *Science, 221,* 1208–1210.

Ellsworth, P. C., & Scherer, K. R. (2003). Appraisal processes in emotion. In Davidson, R. J., Scherer, K. R., & Goldsmith, H. H. (Eds.), *Handbook of affective sciences* (pp. 572–595). New York: Oxford University Press.

Emmons, R. A., & McCullough, M. E. (Eds.). (2004). *The psychology of gratitude.* New York: Oxford University Press.

Evers, C., Fischer, A. H., Rodriguez Mosquera, P. M., & Manstead, A. S. R. (2005). Anger and social appraisal: A "spicy" sex difference? *Emotion, 5,* 258–266.

Feeney, J. A. (2004). Hurt feelings in couple relationships: Toward integrative models of the negative effects of hurtful events. *Journal of Social and Personal Relationships, 21,* 487–508.

Feeney, J. A. (2005). Hurt feelings in couple relationships: Exploring the role of attachment and perceptions of personal injury. *Personal Relationships, 12,* 253–271.

Fehr, B., & Harasymchuk, C. (2005). The experience of emotion in close relationships: Toward an integration of the emotion-in-relationships and interpersonal scripts models. *Personal Relationships, 12,* 181–196.

Field, T., Diego, M., Pelaez, M., Deeds, O., & Delgado, J. (2009). Breakup distress in university students. *Adolescence, 44,* 705–728.

Fischer, A. H., Manstead, A. S. R., & Zaalberg, R. (2003). Social influences on the emotion process. *European Review of Social Psychology, 14,* 171–201.

Fitness, J., & Fletcher, G. J. O. (1993). Love, hate, anger and jealousy in close relationships: A prototype and cognitive appraisal analysis. *Journal of Personality and Social Psychology, 65,* 942–958.

Fitness, J., & Warburton, W. (2009). Thinking the unthinkable: Cognitive appraisals and hurt feelings. In A. L. Vangelisti (Ed.), *Feeling hurt in close relationships* (pp. 34–49). New York: Cambridge University Press.

Floyd, K. (2006). *Communicating affection: Interpersonal behavior and social context.* New York: Cambridge University Press.

Floyd, K., Mikkelson, A. C., Hesse, C., & Pauley, P. M. (2007). Affectionate writing reduces total cholesterol: Two randomized, controlled trials. *Human Communication Research, 33,* 19–142.

Floyd, K., Mikkelson, A. C., Tafoya, M. A., Farinelli, L., La Valley, A. G., Judd, J., et al. (2007). Human affection exchange: XIII. Affectionate communication accelerates neuroendocrine stress recovery. *Health Communication, 22,* 123–132.

Fontaine, J. R. J., Scherer, K. R., Roesch, E. B., & Ellsworth, P. C. (2007). The world of emotions is not two-dimensional. *Psychological Science, 18,* 1050–1057.

Fredrickson, B. L., & Branigan, C. (2005). Positive emotions broaden the scope of attention and thought-action repertoires. *Cognition & Emotion, 19,* 313–332.

Fredrickson, B. L., & Joiner, T. (2002). Positive emotions trigger upward spirals toward emotional well-being. *Psychological Science, 13,* 172–175.

Frijda, N. H. (1986). *The emotions.* Cambridge, UK: Cambridge University Press.

Goffman, E. (1967). *Interaction ritual: Essays in face-to-face interaction.* Garden City, NY: Doubleday.

Goldsmith, D. J., & Konovan-Kicken, E. (2009). Adding insult to injury: The contributions of politeness theory to understanding hurt feelings in close relationships. In A. L. Vangelisti (Ed.), *Feeling hurt in close relationships* (pp. 50–72). New York: Cambridge University Press.

Gonzaga, G. C., Campos, B., & Bradbury, T. (2007). Similarity, convergence, and relationship satisfaction in dating and married couples. *Journal of Personality and Social Psychology, 93,* 34–48.

Groothof, H. A. K., Dijkstra, P., & Barelds, D. P. H. (2009). Sex differences in jealousy: The case of Internet infidelity. *Journal of Social and Personal Relationship, 26,* 1119–1129.

Gross, J. J. (Ed.). (2007). *Handbook of emotion regulation.* New York: Guilford Press.

Guerrero, L. K., Farinelli, L., & McEwan, B. (2009). Attachment and relational satisfaction: The mediating effect of emotional communication. *Communication Monographs, 76,* 487–514.

Guerrero, L. K., La Valley, A. G., & Farinelli, L. (2008). The experience and expression of anger, guilt, and sadness in marriage: An equity theory explanation. *Journal of Social and Personal Relationships, 25,* 699–724.

Guerrero, L. K., Trost, M. R., & Yoshimura, S. M. (2005). Romantic jealousy: Emotions and communicative responses. *Personal Relationships, 12,* 233–252.

Hatfield, E., Cacioppo, J. T., & Rapson, R. L. (1994). *Emotional contagion.* New York: Cambridge University Press.

Haviland-Jones, J. M., & Wilson, P. J. (2008). A "nose" for emotion: Emotional information and challenges in odors and semiochemicals. In M. Lewis, J. M. Haviland-Jones, & L. F. Barrett (Eds.),

*Handbook of emotions* (3rd ed., pp. 235–248). New York: Guilford Press.

Hesse, C., & Floyd, K. (2008). Affectionate experience mediates the effects of alexithymia on mental health and interpersonal relationships. *Journal of Social and Personal Relationships, 25*, 793–810.

Iacoboni, M., & Dapretto, M. (2006).The mirror neuron system and the consequences of its dysfunction. *Nature Neuroscience, 7*, 942–951.

Ickes, W. (2003). *Everyday mind reading: Understanding what other people think and feel.* New York: Prometheus Press.

Izard, C. (2007). Basic emotions, natural kinds, emotion schemas, and a new paradigm. *Perspectives on Psychological Science, 2*, 260–280.

Izard, C. E. (2009). Emotion theory and research: Highlights, unanswered questions, and emerging issues. *Annual Review of Psychology, 60*, 1–25.

Izard, C. E., Ackerman, B. P., Schoff, K. M., & Fine, S. E. (2000). Self-organization of discrete emotions, emotion patterns, and emotion-cognition relations. In M. D. Lewis & I. Granic (Eds.), *Emotion, development, and self-organization: Dynamic systems approaches to emotional development* (pp. 15–36). New York: Cambridge University Press.

John, O. P., & Gross, J. J. (2007). Individual differences in emotion regulation. In J. J. Gross (Ed.), *Handbook of emotion regulation* (pp. 351–372). New York: Guilford Press.

Karremans, J. C., Van Lange, P. A. M., & Holland, R. W. (2005). Forgiveness and its associations with prosocial thinking, feeling, and doing beyond the relationship with the offender. *Personality and Social Psychology Bulletin, 31*, 1315–1326.

Kashdan, T. B., Volkmann, J. R., Breen, W. E., & Han, S. (2007). Social anxiety and romantic relationships: The costs and benefits of negative emotion expression are context-dependent. *Journal of Anxiety Disorders, 21*, 475–492.

Kelley, D. L., & Waldron, V. R. (2005). An investigation of forgiveness-seeking communication and relational outcomes. *Communication Quarterly, 53*, 339–358.

Kennedy-Moore, E., & Watson, J. C. (2001). How and when does emotional expression help? *Review of General Psychology, 5*, 187–212.

Killgore, W. D. S., & Yurgelun-Todd, D. A. (2005). Social anxiety predicts amygdala activation in adolescents viewing fearful faces. *NeuroReport, 16*, 1671–1675.

Knapp, M. L., & Hall, J. A. (2010). *Nonverbal communication in human interaction* (7th ed.). Boston: Wadsworth/Cengage Learning.

Knobloch, L. K. (2008). Extending the emotion-in-relationships model to conversation. *Communication Research, 35*, 822–848.

Knobloch, L. K., Miller, L. E., & Carpenter, K. E. (2007). Using the relational turbulence model to understand negative emotion within courtship. *Personal Relationships, 14*, 91–112.

Kotchemidova, C. (2010). Emotion, culture, and cognitive constructions of reality. *Communication Quarterly, 58*, 207–234.

Kunkel, A. D., Wilson, S. R., Olufowote, J., & Robson, S. (2003). Identity implications of influence goals: Initiating, intensifying, and ending romantic relationships. *Western Journal of Communication, 67*, 382–412.

Kuppens, P., Van Mechelen, I., & Rijmen, F. (2008). Toward disentangling sources of individual differences in appraisal and anger. *Journal of Personality, 76*, 969–1000.

Larsen, J. T., Berntson, G. G., Poehlmann, K. M., Ito, T. A., & Cacioppo, J. T. (2008). The psychophysiology of emotion. In M. Lewis & J. M. Haviland-Jones (Eds.), *Handbook of emotions* (3rd ed., pp. 180–195). New York: Guilford Press.

Larsen, J. T., McGraw, A. P., & Cacioppo, J. T. (2001). Can people feel happy and sad at the same time? *Journal of Personality and Social Psychology, 81*, 684–696.

Lazarus, R. S. (1991). *Emotion and adaptation.* New York: Oxford University Press.

Lazarus, R. S. (2006). Emotions and interpersonal relationships: Toward a person-centered conceptualization of emotions and coping. *Journal of Personality, 74*, 9–46.

Lazarus, R. S. (2008). Relational meaning and discrete emotions. In R. Scherer, A. Schorr, & T. Johnstone (Eds.), *Appraisal processes in emotion: Theory, methods, research* (pp. 37–67). New York: Oxford University Press.

Le, B., & Agnew, C. R. (2001). Need fulfillment and emotional experience in interdependent romantic relationships. *Journal of Social and Personal Relationships, 18*, 423–440.

Leary, M. R., & Leder, S. (2009). The nature of hurt feelings: Emotional experience and cognitive appraisals. In A. L. Vangelisti (Ed.), *Feeling hurt in close relationships* (pp. 15–33). New York: Cambridge University Press.

Ledoux, J. E., & Phelps, E. A. (2003). Emotional networks in the brain. In M. Lewis, J. M. Haviland-Jones, *Handbook of emotions* (2nd ed., pp. 157–172). New York: Guilford Press.

Ledoux, J. E., & Phelps, E. A. (2008). Emotional networks in the brain. In M. Lewis, J. M. Haviland-Jones, & L. F. Barrett (Eds.), *Handbook of emotions* (2nd ed., pp. 159–179). New York: Guilford Press.

Lewis, M., Haviland-Jones, J. M., & Barrett, L. F. (Eds.). (2008). *Handbook of emotions* (3rd ed.). New York: Guilford Press.

Matsumoto, D. (2007). Culture, context, and behavior. *Journal of Personality, 75,* 1285–1318.

Matsumoto, D., Keltner, D., Shiota, M., O'Sullivan, M., & Frank, M. (2008). Facial expressions of emotion. In M. Lewis, J. M. Haviland-Jones, & L. F. Barrett (Eds.), *Handbook of emotions* (3rd ed., pp. 211–234). New York: Guilford Press.

May, L. N., & Jones, W. H. (2005). Differential reaction to hurt. *Journal of Worry and Affective Experience, 1,* 54–59.

McIntosh, D. N. (1996). Facial feedback hypotheses: Evidence, implications, and directions. *Motivation and Emotion, 20,* 121–147.

McLaren, R. M., & Solomon, D. H. (2008). Appraisals and distancing responses to hurtful messages. *Communication Research, 35,* 339–357.

Merolla, A. J. (2008). Communicating forgiveness in friendships and dating relationships. *Communication Studies, 59,* 114–131.

Metts, S., & Cupach, W. R. (2007). Responses to relational transgressions: Hurt, anger, and sometimes forgiveness. In B. H. Spitzberg & W. R. Cupach (Eds.), *The dark side of interpersonal communication* (2nd ed., pp. 243–273). Mahwah, NJ: Lawrence Erlbaum.

Metts, S., Cupach, W. R., & Lippert, L. (2006). Forgiveness in the workplace. In J. M. Harden Fritz & B. L. Omdahl (Eds.), *Problematic relationships in the workplace* (pp. 249–278). New York: Peter Lang.

Metts, S., & Mikucki, S. L. (2008). The emotional landscape of romantic relationship initiation. In S. Sprecher, A. Wenzel, & J. Harvey (Eds.), *Handbook of relationship initiation* (pp. 353–374). New York: Taylor & Francis.

Metts, S., & Planalp, S. (2002). Emotional communication. In M. Knapp & J. A. Daly (Eds.), *Handbook of interpersonal communication* (3rd ed., pp. 339–373). Thousand Oaks, CA: Sage.

Metts, S., & Smith, A. (2009). Emotion regulation, developmental influences. In H. T. Reis & S. Sprecher (Eds.), *Encyclopedia of human relationships* (Vol. 1, pp. 504–507). Thousand Oaks, CA: Sage.

Mikula, G., Scherer, K. R., & Athenstaedt, U. (1998). The role of injustice in the elicitation of differential emotional reactions. *Personality and Social Psychology Bulletin, 24,* 769–783.

Mikulincer, M., & Shaver, P. R. (2005). Attachment theory and emotions in close relationships: Exploring the attachment-related dynamics of emotional reactions to relational event. *Personal Relationships, 12,* 149–168.

Miron, A. M., Parkinson, S. K., & Brehm, J. W. (2007). Does happiness function like a motivational state? *Cognition & Emotion, 21,* 248–267.

Moors, A. (2009). Theories of emotion causation: A review. *Cognition & Emotion, 23,* 625–662.

Morman, M. T., & Floyd, K. (2002). A "changing culture of fatherhood": Effects on affectionate communication, closeness, and satisfaction in men's relationships with their fathers and their sons. *Western Journal of Communication, 66,* 395–411.

Morse, C., & Metts, S. (2011). Situational and communicative predictors of forgiveness following a relational transgression. *Western Journal of Communication, 75,* 1–20.

Murphy, F. C., Nimmo-Smith, I., & Lawrence, A. D. (2003). Functional neuroanatomy of emotion: A meta-analysis. *Cognitive, Affective, and Behavioral Neuroscience, 3,* 207–233.

Murray, S. L., & Holmes, J. G. (2009). The architecture of interdependent minds: A motivation-management theory of mutual responsiveness. *Psychological Review, 116,* 908–928.

Myers, D. G., & Diener, E. (1995). Who is happy? *Psychological Science, 6,* 10–19.

Nabi, R. L. (2010). The case for emphasizing discrete emotions in communication research. *Communication Monographs, 77,* 153–159.

The new science of happiness. (2005, January 17). *Time,* pp. A1–A68.

Ortony, A., & Turner, T. J. (1990). What's basic about basic emotions? *Psychological Review, 97,* 315–331.

Parrott, W. G. (2001). The nature of emotion. In A. Tesser & N. Schwarz (Eds.), *Blackwell handbook of social psychology: Vol. 1. Intraindividual processes* (pp. 375–390). Oxford, UK: Basil Blackwell.

Phan, K. L., Wager, T. D., Taylor, S. F., & Liberzon, I. (2002). Functional neuroanatomy of emotion:

A meta-analysis of emotion activation studies in PET and fMRI. *Neuroimage, 16,* 331–348.

Philippot, P., & Feldman, R. S. (Eds.). (2004). *The regulation of emotion.* Mahwah, NJ: Lawrence Erlbaum.

Planalp, S., & Fitness, J. (1999). Thinking/feeling about social and personal relationships. *Journal of Social and Personal Relationships, 16,* 731–750.

Planalp, S., Metts, S., & Tracy, S. (2010). The social matrix of emotion expression and regulation. In C. R. Berger, M. E. Roloff, & D. Roskos-Ewoldsen (Eds.), *Handbook of communication science* (2nd ed., pp. 363–379). Thousand Oaks, CA: Sage.

Plutchik, R. (1980). *Emotion: Theory, research, and experience: Vol. 1. Theories of emotion.* New York: Academic Press.

Plutchik, R. (2001). The nature of emotions. *American Scientist, 89,* 344–350.

Plutchik, R. (2002). *Emotions and life: Perspectives from psychology, biology, and evolution.* Washington, DC: American Psychological Association.

Plutchik, R., & Conte, H. (1997). *Circumplex models of personality and emotions.* Washington, DC: American Psychological Association.

Posner, J., Russell, J. A., & Peterson, B. (2005). The circumplex model of affect: An integrative approach to affective neuroscience, cognitive development, and psychopathology. *Development and Psychopathology, 17,* 715–734.

Prager, K. J., & Buhrmester, D. (1998). Intimacy and need fulfillment in couple relationships. *Journal of Social and Personal Relationships, 15,* 435–469.

Remington, N. A., Fabrigar, L. R., & Visser, P. S. (2000). Reexamining the circumplex model of affect. *Journal of Personality and Social Psychology, 79,* 286–300.

Reysen, S. (2006). A new predictor of likeability: Laughter. *North American Journal of Psychology, 8,* 373–382.

Richards, J. M., Butler, E. A., & Gross, J. J. (2003). Emotion regulation in romantic relationships: The cognitive consequences of concealing feelings. *Journal of Social and Personal Relationships, 20,* 599–620.

Rimé, B. (2007). Interpersonal emotion regulation. In J. J. Gross (Ed.), *Handbook of emotion regulation* (pp. 466–485). New York: Guilford Press.

Rimé, B. (2009). Emotion elicits the social sharing of emotion: Theory and empirical review. *Emotion Review, 1,* 60–85.

Rivers, S. E., Brackett, M. A., Katulak, N. A., & Salovey, P. (2007). Regulating anger and sadness: An exploration of discrete emotions in emotion regulation. *Journal of Happiness Studies, 8,* 393–427.

Rizzolatti, G.1., & Craighero, L. (2004). The mirror-neuron system. *Annual Review of Neuroscience, 27,* 169–192.

Roseman, I. J., & Evdokas, A. (2004). Appraisals cause experienced emotions: Experimental evidence. *Cognition & Emotion, 18,* 1–28.

Roseman, I. J., & Smith, C. A. (2001). Appraisal theory: Overview, assumptions, varieties, controversies. In K. R. Scherer, R. Klaus, A. Schorr, & T. Johnstone (Eds.), *Appraisal processes in emotion: Theory, methods, research* (pp. 3–19). New York: Oxford University Press.

Russell, J. A. (1994). Is there universal recognition of emotion from facial expressions?: A review of the cross-cultural studies. *Psychological Bulletin, 115,* 102–141.

Russell, J. A. (2003). Core affect and the psychological construction of emotion. *Psychological Review, 110,* 145–172.

Russell, J. A., Bachorowski, J.-A., & Fernández-Dols, J.-M. (2003). Facial and vocal expressions of emotion. *Annual Review of Psychology, 54,* 329–349.

Russell, J. A., & Barrett, L. F. (1999). Core affect and the psychological construction of emotions. *Journal of Personality and Social Psychology, 76,* 805–819.

Saarni, C. (1999). *The development of emotional competence.* New York: Guilford Press.

Sagarin, B. J., & Guadagno, R. E. (2004). Sex differences in the contexts of extreme jealousy. *Personal Relationships, 11,* 319–328.

Salovey, P., Detweiler-Bedell, P. T., Detweiler-Bedell, J. B., & Mayer, J. D. (2008). Emotional intelligence. In M. Lewis, J. M. Haviland-Jones, & L. F. Barrett (Eds.), *Handbook of emotions* (3rd ed., pp. 533–547). New York: Guilford Press.

Sbarra, D. A. (2006). Predicting the onset of emotional recovery following nonmarital relationship dissolution: Survival analyses of sadness and anger. *Personality and Social Psychology Bulletin, 32,* 298–312.

Sbarra, D. A., & Emery, R. E. (2005). The emotional sequelae of nonmarital relationship dissolution: Analysis of change and intraindividual variability over time. *Personal Relationships, 12,* 213–232.

Sbarra, D. A., & Law, R. W. (2009). Dissolution of relationships, coping and aftermath. In H. T. Reis & S. Sprecher (Eds.), *Encyclopedia of human relationships* (Vol. 1, pp. 440–445). Thousand Oaks, CA: Sage.

Scherer, K. R. (2001). Appraisal considered as a process of multilevel sequential checking. In K. R. Scherer, A. Schorr, & T. Johnstone (Eds.), *Appraisal processes in emotion: Theory methods, research* (pp. 92–129). New York: Oxford University Press.

Scherer, K. R. (2009). The dynamic architecture of emotion: Evidence for the component process model. *Cognition & Emotion, 23,* 1307–1351.

Scherer, K. R., Dan, E. S., & Flykt, A. (2006). What determines a feeling's position in affective space? A case for appraisal. *Cognition & Emotion, 29,* 92–113.

Scherer, K. R., & Ellgring, H. (2007). Are facial expressions of emotion produced by categorical affect programs or dynamically driven by appraisal? *Emotion, 7,* 113–130.

Shackelford, T. K., Buss, D. M., & Bennett, K. (2002). Forgiveness or breakup: Sex differences in responses to a partner's infidelity. *Cognition and Emotion, 16,* 299–307.

Shackelford, T. K., Voracek, M., Schmitt, D. P., Buss, D. M., Weekes-Shackelford, V. A., & Michalski, R. L. (2004). Romantic jealousy in early adulthood and in later life. *Human Nature, 15,* 283–300.

Shaver, P. R., Mikulincer, M., Lavy, S., & Cassidy, J. (2009). Understanding and altering hurt feelings: An attachment-theoretical perspective on the generation and regulation of emotions. In A. L. Vangelisti (Ed.), *Feeling hurt in close relationships* (pp. 92–122). New York: Cambridge University Press.

Shiota, M. N., Campos, B., Keltner, D., & Hertenstein, M. (2004). Positive emotion and the regulation of interpersonal relationships. In P. Philippot & R. S. Feldman (Eds.), *The regulation of emotion* (pp. 129–158). Mahwah, NJ: Lawrence Erlbaum.

Shipman, K. L., Zeman, J., Nesin, A. E., & Fitzgerald, M. (2003). Children's strategies for displaying anger and sadness: What works with whom? *Merrill-Palmer Quarterly, 49,* 100–122.

Siemer, C. A., & Reisenzein, R. (2007). Emotions and appraisals: Can you have one without the other? *Emotion, 7,* 26–29.

Siemer, M. (2008). Beyond prototypes and classical definitions: Evidence for a theory-based representation of emotion concept. *Cognition & Emotion, 22,* 620–632.

Smith, C. A., & Kirby, L. D. (2004). Appraisal as a pervasive determinant of anger. *Emotion, 4,* 133–138.

Smith, C. A., & Lazarus, R. S. (1993). Appraisal components: Core relational themes and the emotions. *Cognition and Emotion, 7,* 233–269.

Smyth, J. M., & Pennebaker, J. W. (2008). Exploring the boundary conditions of expressive writing: In search of the right recipe. *British Journal of Health Psychology, 13,* 1–7.

Terracciano, A., McCrae, R. R., Hagemann, D., & Costa, P. T., Jr. (2003). Individual difference variables, affective differentiation, and the structures of affect. *Journal of Personality, 71,* 669–701.

Theiss, J., Knobloch, L. K., Checton, M. G., & Magsamen-Conrad, K. (2009). Relationship characteristics associated with the experience of hurt in romantic relationships: A test of the relational turbulence model. *Human Communication Research, 35,* 588–615.

Thelwall, M., Wilkinson, D., & Uppal, S. (2010). Data mining emotion in social network communication: Gender differences in MySpace. *Journal of the American Society for Information Science and Technology, 61,* 190–199.

Ting-Toomey, S. (2005). The matrix of face: An updated face-negotiated theory. In W. Gudykunst (Ed.), *Theorizing about intercultural communication* (pp. 71–92). Thousand Oaks, CA: Sage.

Tomkins, S. S. (1984). Affect theory. In K. R. Scherer & P. Ekman (Eds.), *Approaches to emotion* (pp. 163–196). Hilldale, NJ: Lawrence Erlbaum.

Vangelisti, A. (2006). Hurtful interaction and the dissolution of intimacy. In M. A. Fine & J. H. Harvey (Eds.), *Handbook of divorce and relationship dissolution* (pp. 133–152). Mahwah, NJ: Lawrence Erlbaum.

Vangelisti, A. (2007). Communicating hurt. In B. H. Spitzberg & W. R. Cupach (Eds.), *The dark side of interpersonal communication* (2nd ed., pp. 121–142). Mahwah, NJ: Lawrence Erlbaum.

Vangelisti, A. (Ed.). (2009). Feeling hurt in close relationships. New York: Cambridge University Press.

Vangelisti, A. L., Young, S. L., Carpenter-Theune, K. E., & Alexander, A. L. (2005). Why does it hurt? The perceived causes of hurt feelings. *Communication Research, 32,* 433–477.

Wager, T. D., Barrett, L. F., Bliss-Moreau, E., Lindquist, K. A., Duncan, S., Kober, H., et al. (2008). The neuroimaging of emotion. In M. Lewis, J. M. Haviland-Jones, & L. F. Barrett (Eds.), *Handbook of emotions* (3rd ed., pp. 249–271). New York: Guilford Press.

Waldron, V. R., & Kelley, D. L. (2005). Forgiving communication as a response to relational transgressions. *Journal of Social and Personal Relationships, 22,* 723–742.

Wallbott, H. G. (1998). Bodily expression of emotion. *European Journal of Social Psychology, 28,* 879–896.

Walther, J. B. (2010). Computer-mediated communication. In C. R. Berger, M. E. Roloff, & D. Roskos-Ewolsen (Eds.), *Handbook of communication science* (2nd ed., pp. 489–505). Thousand Oaks, CA: Sage.

Waugh, C. E., & Fredrickson, B. L. (2006). Nice to know you: Positive emotions, self-other overlap, and complex understanding in the formation of a new relationship. *Journal of Positive Psychology, 1,* 93–106.

Yoshimura, S. M. (2004). Emotional and behavioral responses to romantic jealousy expressions. *Communication Reports, 17,* 85–101.

Zaalberg, R., Manstead, A. S. R., & Fischer, A. H. (2004). Relations between emotions, display rules, social motives, and facial behaviour. *Cognition & Emotion, 18,* 183–207.

Zhang, S., & Stafford, L. (2008). Perceived face threat of honest but hurtful evaluative messages in romantic relationships. *Western Journal of Communication, 72,* 19–39.

# CHAPTER 10

# Supportive Communication

*Erina L. MacGeorge*

*Bo Feng*

*Brant R. Burleson*

In the decade since the previous edition of this *Handbook*, the authors of this chapter were fortunate to experience many successes and joys. Bo earned a PhD and found a faculty position, Erina earned tenure, each of us received awards and honors (especially Brant!), Brant married Erina, and we all delighted in the arrival of three healthy babies. However, like most readers, we also had our share of significant stresses, troubles, and sorrows: Among these were having to move across the country, suffering a miscarriage, and coping with the death of a parent. Most recently, Brant battled metastatic esophageal cancer, ultimately passing away before this chapter was completed, leaving us bereft not only of a coauthor but of a mentor, friend, and (for Erina) spouse. We know that many of our readers knew Brant and share in our profound sense of loss.

Through each of our difficulties, along with the lesser challenges of everyday life, we have been repeatedly reminded of how much we rely on interactions with others to sustain us in times of stress. As scholars, these experiences highlight for us the phenomenon of *supportive communication* and its impact on human well-being. In this chapter, we define supportive communication as *verbal and nonverbal behavior produced with the intention of providing assistance to others perceived as needing that aid*. At a multitude of points in our lives, all of us engage in this fundamental form of human interaction. The ubiquity of supportive communication, however, is only an incidental reason for its study. There are several more substantive warrants for scholarship in this arena (Burleson, Albrecht, & Sarason, 1994).

One warrant is pragmatic. Since the 1970s, a massive body of research findings has accumulated documenting the positive effects of supportive interactions and relationships on the health and well-being of individuals. For example, effective support reduces distress and improves coping (Jones, 2004), fosters psychological adjustment (Cramer, Henderson, & Scott, 1996; Kawachi & Berkman, 2001), improves resistance to and recovery from disease (Ikeda & Kawachi, 2010), and reduces mortality (Berkman et al., 2004). Clearly, we need to understand supportive communication processes if we are to facilitate these beneficial outcomes (Cohen & Janicki-Deverts, 2009; Gottlieb, 2000).

A second warrant for the study of supportive communication is theoretical. There is a wide range of interesting questions to be answered, such as "Why are some supportive messages more helpful than others, and under what conditions does this hold true?" and "Why do some people provide more skillful support than do others?" Beyond addressing these specific questions, the study of supportive communication provides a venue for exploring fundamental communication processes, including message production (see Burleson, 2007), message reception (see Burleson, 2010), and conversational interaction (Shaw & Kitzinger, 2007).

A third warrant is moral in character. Many writers have observed that supportive communication represents a form of altruistic or pro-social behavior (e.g., Eisenberg, 2002). Even supportive messages produced out of obligation (acting in conformity with norms) or in an effort to foster dependency have moral and ethical overtones (see Ray, 1993). Consequently, the study of supportive communication can inspire and enhance ethical sensibilities. It can also transform action, motivating us to increase the quality and quantity of supportive behavior in our communities.

Despite the power of these warrants, the formal study of supportive communication has a relatively short history. Arguably, the initial critical mass was not reached until the late 1980s or early 1990s, when a spate of articles, special issues of journals, and books focused attention on this subject (e.g., Albrecht & Adelman, 1987; Burleson, Albrecht, & Sarason, 1994; Sarason, Sarason, & Pierce, 1990). Since that time, research on supportive communication has grown considerably, so that this chapter could be focused exclusively on this literature. However, the study of supportive communication owes much to an older and broader tradition of interdisciplinary inquiry centered on the concept of *social support*. We believe that an appreciation for this broader domain of inquiry is necessary preparation for

understanding and contributing to the scholarship on supportive communication.

Accordingly, we pursue a threefold purpose in the current chapter. Initially, we provide a brief, broad-sweeping treatment of research on social support as conducted in the sociological and psychological traditions. Then, we review and critique theory and research focused on supportive communication. Although space does not permit us to provide an entirely comprehensive review, we address many of the major ideas, theories, and research findings, and touch briefly on methodological paradigms so that scholars new to the area will find this a useful introduction. Our conclusion focuses on an agenda for future research, emphasizing directions that researchers in the field can take in the decade ahead.

## Social Support: An Overview

The earliest work on "social support" appeared more than a century ago, when English and French demographers argued from statistical data that marriage is a health-promoting institution (Bertillion, 1879; Farr, 1885/1975). However, today's research on social support was given its primary stimulus by essays and books published in the mid-1970s (Caplan, 1974, 1976; Cassel, 1976; Cobb, 1976; Moss, 1973). Drawing on studies from multiple disciplines from the 1940s through the early 1970s, these scholars argued that stressful conditions place individuals at greater risk for psychological disorder, disease, and mortality but that social support provides protection.

In these early formulations, social support was conceptualized and defined in a variety of overlapping but somewhat distinctive ways. For example, Caplan (1976) emphasized the types of relationships that constitute a support network (everything from marriage and parenthood to acquaintanceships with service providers) and identified forms of supportive behavior, presaging later typologies of support. Cobb (1976) focused more closely on the experience of the support recipient, defining social support as information "leading the subject to believe that he is cared for and loved . . . esteemed and valued" (p. 300) (for a review of other early definitions, see Albrecht & Adelman, 1987.).

Stimulated by the formation of a definitional and theoretical framework, researchers from diverse disciplinary backgrounds began to examine the relationship between social support and well-being. Two major perspectives gradually emerged. The first, dominated by epidemiologists and sociologists, conceptualized and assessed social support as being (or resulting from) participation in a social network, often termed social integration. A second perspective, dominated by psychologists, defined and measured social support as the perceived availability of helpful persons or behaviors. Current work on social support continues to reflect both of these perspectives, so we will review each of them (for other reviews, see Cohen & Janicki-Deverts, 2009; Uchino, 2004).

## The Sociological Perspective

In an early and influential study, the epidemiologists Berkman and Syme (1979) examined the association between social support and morbidity in a nine-year follow-up of a representative sample of residents ($N = 6,928$) of Alameda County, California. Social support was measured as a composite of diverse indicators of social integration, including whether the individual was married, had contacts with extended family and close friends, attended church, and was involved in other social groups. Those who were more socially integrated at the study's beginning (in 1965) were found to have lower mortality nine years later, and this effect remained even when the researchers controlled for multiple potentially confounding factors. The more socially integrated were also less likely to have experienced various health-related problems, such as heart, digestive, and respiratory diseases.

Berkman and Syme's (1979) study illustrates two key characteristics of social support investigations in the sociological tradition. First, social support was operationalized as social integration. Measures of social integration typically tap role differentiation (participation in different kinds of social relationships), social participation (the frequency with which the individual engages in various social activities), perceived integration (the individual's feelings of community and belonging), or some combination of these three constructs—the so-called complex indicators—such as those employed by Berkman and Syme (for a review of social integration measures, see Brissette, Cohen, & Seeman, 2000).

A second characteristic of the Berkman and Syme (1979) study is its methodological strength in the domains of sampling, design, and statistical controls. Epidemiological and sociological studies typically use large and representative regional or national samples and control for multiple factors that might confound associations between social support and health. Moreover, many of these studies employ longitudinal, prospective designs to assess whether social support at one point in time predicts well-being at a future date (see review by Ikeda & Kawachi, 2010). These methodologically rigorous studies thus provide some of the best empirical evidence for the benefits of social support. Since Berkman and Syme's (1979) work, the association between social integration and longevity has been documented repeatedly in prospective research (see Berkman et al., 2004; Ikeda & Kawachi, 2010). In addition, a large body of work has documented the positive effects of social integration on multiple facets of physical and psychological health (for reviews, see Ikeda & Kawachi, 2010; Kawachi & Berkman, 2001; Uchino, 2004).

*Theoretical Issues.* Over the past three decades, researchers in the sociological tradition have addressed many significant theoretical issues. An early but important controversy concerned whether social support exercises its positive influence primarily in the context of stressful events (a "buffering" effect) or whether it has a beneficial effect regardless of stress levels (a "main" effect; see Cohen & Wills, 1985). The research evidence indicates that both types of effects occur, with social integration typically having a main rather than buffering effect on well-being, probably because most social integration measures fail to capture network qualities or behaviors that are specifically relevant to stressful events. Accordingly, most of the theorizing about the mechanisms through which social integration affects health has focused on factors that should be operative across the broad spectrum of life events (Brissette et al., 2000; Cohen, Gottlieb, & Underwood, 2000). Buffering effects are most likely to be observed when social support is operationalized as perceptions of support availability or adequacy in the presence of stressful conditions (see the discussion on perceived support later in this chapter).

At present, the most central theoretical issue for the sociological perspective concerns the nature of the causal mechanisms linking social integration with health outcomes (Cohen & Janicki-Deverts, 2009; Gruenewald & Seeman, 2010). Multiple cognitive, emotional, and behavioral mechanisms have been proposed, such as (a) *social influence*, in which integration with network members act to promote or constrain health-relevant behaviors; (b) *social resources*, in which network members provide access to health-protective "goods" such as information, money, and direct forms of assistance; and (c) *positive affect*, which could promote positive psychological and physiological states (for reviews, see Berkman, Glass, Brissette, & Seeman, 2000; Cohen, 1988; Cohen & Lemay, 2007). Increasingly, theorists have also argued for biological mechanisms explaining the effects of social integration (Gruenewald & Seeman, 2010; Uchino, 2006). This line of theorizing is supported by a growing body of epidemiological and laboratory studies demonstrating relationships between social integration and the biological processes that contribute to disease outcomes, including hypertension, immune response, and inflammatory response (for reviews, see Brissette et al., 2000; Kiecolt-Glaser, Gouin, & Hantsoo, 2010). Because social integration and health are both multidimensional

constructs, specifying the diverse mechanisms is challenging and remains a theoretical priority for research in the sociological tradition (Brissette et al., 2000).

## The Psychological Perspective

Whereas scholars in the sociological tradition have conceptualized social support in terms of integration within a social network, psychologists have developed approaches consistent with their discipline's traditional concern with the cognitive and emotional processes of individuals. Most of the research informed by the psychological perspective has been loosely connected by its focus on the *perceived availability of support*. Broadly, the perception that support is available (and, sometimes, that the available support is adequate; see Brock & Lawrence, 2010) is viewed as buffering the individual against stress and its health-damaging effects, as well as enhancing the individual's coping (Lakey & Cohen, 2000). However, the focus on perceived availability represents an evolution from an earlier focus on *enacted* and *received support*.

*Enacted Support.* Some of the earliest work in the psychological tradition (e.g., Barrera, 1981) was based on the plausible hypothesis that those who experience a stressful event but receive high levels of assistance from their social networks will be happier and healthier than those who experience such an event and receive less assistance. The intuitive notion underlying this "supportive actions" perspective (Lakey & Cohen, 2000) was that resources provided by helpers assisted recipients to cope more effectively with environmental demands, thereby reducing stress and protecting the target's health. Various classifications of support resources or functions were proposed (e.g., House, 1981), with most including variations on *emotional support* (affection, trust, esteem), *informational support* (advice, information, guidance), and *instrumental or tangible support* (money, labor, material assistance) (for a review of typologies, see Cutrona & Russell, 1990).

Despite the intuitive appeal of this approach, few researchers actually observed enacted support or assessed its effects. Beyond the difficulty of observing support provision in real-world settings, there was concern that behaviors enacted by helpers might not be perceived as supportive by their recipients. Studies found that the effects of enacted support were often qualified by a host of moderating variables, which made generalization quite difficult (see Goldsmith, 2004; Lakey, Orehek, Hain, & VanVleet, 2010; Rini & Dunkel-Schetter, 2010). These problems stimulated the study of received support.

*Received Support.* As an alternative to studying enacted support using observational data, self-report measures were designed to assess what is termed *received support*: perceptions of how much supportive behavior has been received from social network members in the recent past. For example, the popular Inventory of Socially Supportive Behaviors (Barrera, Sandler, & Ramsey, 1981) has respondents indicate how often during the previous four weeks they received each of 40 emotional, tangible, and informational support behaviors (for a review of measures of received support, see Wills & Shinar, 2000).

Initial research with measures of received support generated several conceptual and methodological issues to be addressed. Correlations between enacted support (measured from the perspective of the support provider) and received support (measured from the perspective of the support recipient) were modest at best (e.g., Antonucci & Israel, 1986). Furthermore, many early studies reported *positive* correlations between measures of received support and measures of stress and health problems (e.g., Sandler & Barrera, 1984). Although these correlations probably indicate that people marshal support resources when they are stressed (Barrera, 1986), psychologists sought a way of measuring social support that would more readily demonstrate its beneficial impact on health. Since comparative studies suggested that the competing construct of perceived availability of support explained more variance in physical and mental

health outcomes than did received support (for a meta-analysis, see Haber, Cohen, Lucas, & Baltes, 2007), most psychologists turned their attention to perceived availability of support.

*Perceived Availability of Support.* Concurrent with, and in response to, the empirical "failures" of received support measures, influential researchers argued that the critical element of social support is the perception that it is available if needed (Cohen & Wills, 1985; Kessler, 1992). This conceptual movement was presaged by early social support definitions that emphasized perceptions of care, value, or positive regard over behaviors that may produce such perceptions (see review by Sarason & Sarason, 2006). Instruments designed to measure perceived support typically have respondents indicate the availability to them of various types of support, should the need arise (for a review of measures, see Wills & Shinar, 2000).

The conceptual and methodological shift from enacted or received support to perceived support availability was part of a shift in theorizing about the mechanisms through which social support affects well-being. Enacted support and received support fit most naturally in a "coping assistance" model, in which supportive behaviors help stressed individuals deal more effectively with problems. The construct of perceived support availability is future oriented and de-emphasizes the role of supportive behavior. Correspondingly, appraisal theory was invoked to account for its effects. Appraisal theory explains stress as arising not from events themselves but from their interpretation or "appraisal," including evaluations of available coping resources (Lazarus & Folkman, 1984). Thus, to the extent that people perceive support as available to help with coping, they may experience less stress from negatively appraised events (Uchino, 2009a), regardless of whether they actually receive support from others.

This theoretical shift provokes questions about the etiology of perceived support availability. Although it is often assumed to be founded on the receipt of past supportive behaviors (Hobfoll, 2009), measures of perceived support availability frequently correlate only weakly with measures of recent received support (Haber et al., 2007). A very different possibility is that the perception of support availability is a stable personality characteristic originating from attachment experiences in infancy and childhood (Sarason, Sarason, & Shearin, 1986). Evidence supporting this view includes consistency over time in individuals' reports of support experiences and expectations (Sarason, Sarason, & Gurung, 1997) and correlations between perceived support availability and measures of attachment style and other personality traits (Asendorpf & Wilpers, 2000; Lakey & Lutz, 1996).

To date, studies of perceived support availability and health have been conducted with respect to a diversity of stressors and populations and have employed a vast array of research designs and measures. In fact, the literature is now so large that most reviews are either impressionistic or specific to particular stressors, populations, or outcomes. As one might expect from such a large and heterogeneous literature, there is considerable variation in the size and consistency of the observed effects, but altogether the findings strongly support the positive influence of perceived support availability on physical and mental health (for reviews, see Gruenewald & Seeman, 2010; Uchino, 2009a).

*Current Issues.* Many researchers working within the psychological perspective are currently focusing on identifying the causal mechanism, or mechanisms, through which perceived support availability influences well-being. Theorists have articulated with growing specificity different explanatory mechanisms, suggesting that mediators include appraisal processes, self-esteem, relational schemas, and self-conceptions, among others (for reviews, see Gruenewald & Seeman, 2010; Uchino, 2009a). An increasing number of studies are evaluating the operation of proposed mechanisms (see DiMatteo, 2004; Eisenberger, Taylor, Gable, Hilmert, & Lieberman, 2007; Uchino, 2009b).

Conceptualizations of social support as received versus perceived also continue to fuel

controversy and research. Although some theorists continue to maintain that only perceived availability has shown consistent, appropriate outcomes with assessments of well-being (Kessler, 1992; Sarason, Pierce, & Sarason, 1990), another popular perspective (e.g., Bolger, Zuckerman, & Kessler, 2000) suggests that received support may contribute to well-being but does so largely when it is "invisible" to the support recipient (i.e., the recipient is unaware of being helped) and therefore does not create embarrassment or obligation. In contradiction to both of these views, several recent studies have used measures of received support focused on types of supportive behavior especially relevant to given stressors; these studies have detected positive (and even strong) associations between received support and various well-being outcomes (e.g., Reynolds & Perrin, 2004; Rini, Dunkel-Schetter, Hobel, Glynn, & Sandman, 2006). These findings show that the study of enacted or received support should not be abandoned just because its effects are complex and challenging to document (Goldsmith, 2004; Hobfoll, 2009).

## Summary

Research in the sociological and psychological perspectives clearly indicates the relevance of social support—however defined—to physical and mental well-being. The theoretical questions that remain to be addressed in these traditions are both important and exciting. However, in this chapter, our primary focus is on an alternative to the sociological and psychological perspectives, one with a distinctive focus on social support as a *communication* process.

The sociological and psychological perspectives implicitly recognize that communication plays a role in the origin and impact of social support. The sociological perspective takes for granted that social networks are maintained through communication between network members, and many mechanisms through which social integration may affect well-being necessarily imply communication. In the psychological perspective, communication is an assumed but largely invisible vehicle through which perceptions of support availability are created, whether in childhood or in recent interactions. Sociological and psychological research on social support typically has not examined these functions of communication, making this another venue for theoretical development within these traditions.

But communication also deserves—and has earned—a far more central place in the study of social support. We believe that "social support should be studied as *communication* [italics added] because it is ultimately conveyed through messages directed by one individual to another in the context of a relationship that is created and sustained through interaction" (Burleson, Albrecht, Goldsmith, & Sarason, 1994, p. xviii).

# The Supportive Communication Perspective

At about the same time the sociological and psychological perspectives on social support were being articulated and refined (roughly 1975–1990), scholars in several academic disciplines were developing research programs examining what eventually would be called *supportive communication*. This emerging perspective was informed by a variety of empirical traditions, including research on psychotherapy by clinical psychologists (Elliott, 1985), research on "troubles talk" by ethnomethodologists (Jefferson, 1988), research on "comforting communication" and advice by communication researchers (Burleson, 1984), as well as work on "received support" in the psychological tradition (Barrera et al., 1981) (for a more extensive review of contributing research programs, see Burleson & MacGeorge, 2002). These diverse literatures remained largely segregated through the early 1990s, when scholars began to recognize the common focus on communicative efforts to help others in need and a distinctive communication or interactional perspective on social support

began to emerge. In the next section, we explicate the central commitments of this perspective.

## Distinctive Features of the Communication Perspective

The communication perspective on social support is distinct from the sociological and psychological perspectives in several respects. First and foremost among these is the *centrality of the role allotted to communication*. In this perspective, social support is not a hidden mechanism or a perceptual outcome; rather, it is fundamentally communicative in character. Thus, from a communication perspective, the study of "social support" *is the study of supportive communication*: verbal and nonverbal behaviors intended to provide or seek help. The object of study thus resembles what psychologists originally termed *enacted support* (see Goldsmith, 2004).

A second distinguishing feature of the communication perspective is the assumption of a relatively *direct connection between communication and well-being*. In both sociological and psychological perspectives, the connection between communication and well-being is indirect (e.g., communication fosters social integration, which in turn promotes well-being). In contrast, the communication perspective takes as its primary focus those communicative acts specifically intended to improve the well-being of another person who is currently experiencing a problematic situation. Thus, scholars in the communication perspective examine behaviors enacted in pursuit of goals such as reducing distress and promoting the resolution of problems.

A third defining attribute of the communication perspective is its focus on *helpers' intentional responses to targets' perceived needs*. Such needs may stem from a variety of acute or chronic stressful experiences, ranging from major losses and challenges (e.g., bereavement, loss of a job) to the myriad upsets and hassles that arise in everyday life. Emphasis is placed on understanding *intentional* helping in response to the perception of such events in others' lives, with research examining how and why "a 'provider' attempts to proffer support and a 'recipient' may be helped or benefited by the attempt" (Dunkel-Schetter & Skokan, 1990, p. 437). Several theorists provide detailed discussions of the character of supportive intentions (e.g., Burleson, 1994; Goldsmith, 2004).

A fourth distinctive characteristic of the communication perspective is that research within it typically *exhibits a normative focus*. Theory in the sociological and psychological traditions tends to incorporate the assumption that increased *quantity* of social integration, perceived support availability, or received support will lead to better outcomes (see Rini & Dunkel-Schetter, 2010; Vaux, 1990). In contrast, the communication perspective does *not* include a "more is better" orientation but instead appreciates that some forms of supportive communication are qualitatively better than others—at least in some situations, with respect to certain goals, and as evaluated by certain criteria (Burleson, 2003a; MacGeorge, Feng, & Thompson, 2008). This motivates research efforts to identify the features that distinguish more and less effective forms of support and to develop theory that explains why these features are efficacious.

A fifth distinguishing characteristic of the communication perspective is its emphasis on documenting the effects of supportive communication on various forms of well-being. Historically, communication scholars have focused most on *interaction and relationship outcomes* rather than the physical and psychological health outcomes that have been the primary focus in the sociological and psychological traditions. Of particular interest in the supportive communication tradition is the extent to which specific features of supportive messages and interactions have an immediate (or relatively immediate) impact on emotional distress, problem-solving capacity, and other proximal coping outcomes. Theory and research on this topic—representing the core of communication research on social support—is reviewed in subsequent sections on supportive interactions and their component messages.

Substantial attention has also been given to the effects of supportive communication on *relational outcomes* (Burleson, 2003a, 2003b; Burleson & Denton, 1997; Xu & Burleson, 2004). As Cobb (1976) pointed out long ago, supportive communication can signal care, commitment, interest, compassion, and even love. Consistent with this observation, several lines of research indicate that supportive communication can powerfully influence the quality of our interpersonal relationships, whether romantic, familial, or collegial (Burleson, 1990; Cunningham & Barbee, 2000; Hart, Newell, & Olsen, 2003; Reis, 2001). For example, among married and long-term romantic partners, relationship satisfaction and stability is associated with the receipt of sensitive support from one's partner (Brock & Lawrence, 2008; Cutrona, Shaffer, Wesner, & Gardner, 2007). Correspondingly, communication is represented as central to relationship satisfaction in several theoretical models of intimate relationships, including the relationship enhancement model (Cutrona, Russell, & Gardner, 2005), the vulnerability–stress–adaptation model (Bradbury, Cohan, & Karney, 2000), and attachment theory (Collins & Feeney, 2010). Since these, and other relational implications of supportive communication, are extensively reviewed in several other sources (Burleson, 2003a, 2003b), we will allow this brief review to suffice.

For many scholars and laypersons, the *health outcomes* of social support are the most compelling justification for its study (see Street, Makoul, Arora, & Epstein, 2009). In the prior edition of this chapter (Burleson & MacGeorge, 2002), Burleson and MacGeorge critiqued research on supportive communication for having given relatively little attention to this type of outcome and suggested the need to demonstrate that supportive communication indeed influenced health. Clearly, doing this is important for multiple reasons, including the development of stronger theoretical connections with the sociological and psychological perspectives on social support.

Although some evidence directly linking supportive communication and health was available when the last chapter was written (Thorsteinsson & James, 1999), the past decade has seen the development of a critical mass of studies, with work examining how supportive interactions influence various cognitive, affective, behavioral, and physiological processes associated with physical and psychological health (e.g., Brashers, Neidig, & Goldsmith, 2004; Floyd & Riforgiate, 2008; MacGeorge, Samter, & Gillihan, 2005). Given this progress, we devote the next section to the growing evidence that supportive *communication*—and not just social integration or perceived support availability—affects health.

## Supportive Communication and Health

There is now substantial evidence that supportive communication affects both psychological and physical health. We organize our discussion of this evidence around several mechanisms that connect different forms of supportive communication with various aspects of health. Identifying these mechanisms is central to building theoretical explanations and to the implementation of effective interventions (Gottlieb, 2000). We recognize (and will discuss in a later section) the fact that well-intended communication can have minimal or even negative effects. Here, however, we focus on the evidence that supportive communication promotes health by (a) providing health-relevant information, (b) motivating healthy behavior, (c) promoting self-esteem and self-care, and (d) reducing emotional distress.

### Providing Health-Relevant Information

Perhaps the most direct connection between supportive communication and health comes through the provision of information relevant to health, including information about medical treatments, nutrition, exercise, social services, and a host of other matters. When acted on, this informational support can help maintain or improve health by influencing health-related behavior (Kreps, 2003; Uchino, 2009a). Information provided in supportive interactions can also function to reduce distress by helping manage uncertainty about health-related matters (Brashers et al., 2004). For example, in the context of illness, supportive communication from nurses and doctors can reduce uncertainty and anxiety about medical prognosis and treatment, as well as enhancing patient perceptions of practitioner competence (e.g., Proctor, Morse, & Khonsari, 1996).

### Motivating Healthy Behavior

Many people find it challenging to stop unhealthy behaviors or undertake healthy ones (e.g., quitting smoking or exercising regularly). Supportive communication from caring others can encourage or persuade people to act in ways that help safeguard or restore their health (Helgeson, Novak, Lepore, & Eton, 2004; Pauley & Hesse, 2009; Roski, Schmid, & Lando, 1996). Motivational support, sometimes referred to as "direct social control" (Lewis & Rook, 1999), may operate in part by enhancing self-efficacy (Olds et al., 1997). For example, Saltzman and Holahan (2002) conducted a longitudinal study with 300 college students and found that supportive communication increased feelings of self-efficacy. These feelings in turn increased psychological adjustment and decreased depression over a five-week period.

### Promoting Self-Esteem and Self-Care

Psychological distress often arises from events that undermine one's feelings of self-worth, competence, and social acceptance. Esteem support, in which support providers express interest, concern, affection, and positive appraisal, can help maintain or restore recipients' self-esteem and self-worth (Cramer, 1994, 2003; Holmstrom & Burleson, in press). Typically, these expressions are not directly intended to improve the recipient's health. However, increases in self-esteem can improve psychological function (e.g., Colarossi & Eccles, 2003). Moreover, people who feel more positively about themselves tend to have more concern for their personal welfare, leading to more positive health practices and correspondingly better physical health (Johnson, Meyer, Winett, & Small, 2000; Yarcheski, Mahon, & Yarcheski, 2003).

## Reducing the Health Impact of Emotional Distress

One of the most common objectives pursued in supportive communication is emotional support—that is, helping recipients feel better about some upsetting problem or situation. There is substantial evidence that emotional support from a wide range of sources (e.g., acquaintances, friends, spouses; see Cutrona & Suhr, 1994; Hill, 1996; Samter, 1994) can help reduce emotional upset generated by events ranging from open-heart surgery (Kulik & Mahler, 1993) to recounting of distressing situations from the past (Jones & Burleson, 2003). Numerous mechanisms may underlie the salutary psychological impact of emotional support, including distraction, catharsis, problem solving, sensemaking, and cognitive reappraisal (Burleson & Goldsmith, 1998; Priem & Solomon, 2009). There is also evidence that ameliorating immediate distress with emotional support improves longer term psychological outcomes, including psychological adjustment (Cramer, 2000), greater optimism (McNicholas, 2002), and lower levels of loneliness and depression (Segrin, 2003). These distal outcomes are typically not directly intended by helpers but are consequences that emerge over time (Hobfoll, 2009).

There is also impressive evidence that supportive communication can affect physical health by buffering physiological reactions to stress. Experimental (e.g., Fritz, Nagurney, & Helgeson, 2003; Gerin, Pieper, Levy, & Pickering, 1992) and field studies (e.g., Gump, Polk, Kamarck, & Shiffman, 2001; Karlin, Brondolo, & Schwartz, 2003) show that supportive interactions can reduce physiological arousal in the face of stressful events, including reductions in cardiovascular reactivity (CVR) (Thorsteinsson & James, 1999; Uchino, Carlisle, Birmingham, & Vaughn, 2010) and cortisol production (e.g., Floyd & Riforgiate, 2008; Priem & Solomon, 2009). CVR is a reliable predictor of cardiovascular health, including susceptibility to strokes, heart attacks, and other diseases (Krantz & McCeney, 2002), and cortisol contributes to decreased immune system function (Kiecolt-Glaser, McGuire, Robles, & Glaser, 2002). Thus, by reducing CVR and/or cortisol levels when people experience stress, supportive communication can protect physical health and even save lives. Importantly, the beneficial influence of supportive interaction on physiological arousal is more consistent than the influence of perceived availability of support (see review by Uchino et al., 2010).

## Summary

Growing evidence indicates that supportive communication can contribute to the psychological and physical well-being of its recipients through several different mechanisms. Of course, many issues related to supportive communication and health need more intensive study. For example, there are likely to be mechanisms other than those identified here, and all of the mechanisms need to be better understood. Furthermore, despite the very significant value of existing research, much of the work on supportive communication and health has been conducted by researchers who are not trained as communication scholars. As a consequence, the role of communication, while clearly recognized, tends to be undertheorized. While there are certainly exceptions (e.g., Craig & Deichert, 2002; Fontana, Diegman, Villeneuve, & Lepore, 1999), most studies have done more to show that supportive communication has a positive impact on health (and that certain qualities of support providers moderate health outcomes, e.g., Holt-Lunstad, Uchino, Smith, & Hicks, 2007) than to identify specific characteristics of supportive messages that are responsible for the more or less positive effects of supportive interactions. We believe that a comprehensive understanding of how, why, and under what conditions supportive communication affects health outcomes will ultimately depend as much on detailed analyses of interactional and message features as on understanding the physiology of stress. Analyses of supportive interactions and messages are already available—and developing—and are at the heart of social support research by communication scholars. Therefore, we turn to a review of this work.

## Supportive Communication: Interactions and Messages

Burleson, Albrecht, Goldsmith, et al. (1994) asserted that researching social support as communication

> means studying the *messages* through which people both seek and express support; studying the *interactions* in which supportive messages are produced and interpreted; and studying the *relationships* that are created by and contextualize the supportive interactions in which people engage." (p. xviii; for a similar view, see Reis & Collins, 2000)

In the current section, we identify components of supportive communication that have an impact on well-being, explore why certain characteristics of interactions and messages have outcomes of interest, and consider why these characteristics are strengthened or weakened by specific conditions. We begin by reviewing research on the character of supportive interactions and then give detailed consideration to the properties of the messages that compose these interactions.

### Supportive Interactions

A decade ago, Heller and Rook (2001) observed that "a crucial gap in knowledge exists about the effective ingredients in supportive interactions"

(p. 120). As researchers have begun to fill this gap, two sets of issues have captured scholarly attention. The first of these concerns the structure of supportive interactions, especially the nature and sequence of the events composing these interactions. The second major issue pertains to the problematics of supportive interactions or the myriad challenges that providers and recipients face in their efforts to give or receive support.

*Interaction Structure.* Social psychologists and communication researchers have studied supportive interactions using a standard suite of social-scientific research methods (e.g., experiments, self-reports, observation of behavior elicited in the laboratory). Supportive interactions have also been studied using conversation analysis, which is an inductive, microanalytic approach grounded in ethnomethodology (e.g., work on "troubles talk"; Jefferson, 1988). Remarkably, these diverse approaches converge to suggest that supportive interactions have a typical structure composed of four phases or events, sequenced in a characteristic order.

Barbee and Cunningham (1995) provide an explicit characterization of these four phases. The first is *support activation* by the target, which can be intentional (e.g., the target asks for help) or unintentional (e.g., the helper notices that the target appears upset and indicates concern). The term *support seeking* is often used to describe support activation when it appears that the target is acting intentionally to elicit support from the helper. The second phase, *support provision*, involves the helper producing messages directed at assisting the target. The third phase, *target reactions*, encompasses the target's immediate behavioral responses to the helper's supportive messages. These reactions reflect the target's receipt and processing of the helper's support attempt and may be either spontaneous/automatic (i.e., minimally mediated by cognition) or systematic/controlled (i.e., reflective of deeper interpretation and planning; Fiske & Taylor, 2007). The fourth phase, *helper responses*, occurs when helpers reference and respond to the reactions of the target.

These helper behaviors serve to continue the supportive episode (e.g., commenting on the target's reactions, offering additional supportive comments) or close it (e.g., acknowledging changes in the target, redirecting the focus of the interaction).

Several aspects of the proposed interactional sequence merit comment. First, the sequence is not invariant; supportive interactions can also contain interruptions, topic changes, and other occurrences that complicate or disrupt the overall process (Jefferson & Lee, 1992). The occurrence of each event later in the sequence is made relevant and probable by antecedent events but is not guaranteed by them (e.g., a target may seek support but be ignored by a potential helper). Of course, the occurrence of events later in the sequence assumes that antecedent events have transpired or at least are perceived to have transpired (e.g., helper responses to target reactions would not occur in the absence of those reactions). Thus, this four-event sequence is a schema or script that channels actors' expectations, interpretations, and actions in support episodes.

Second, the events identified in this analysis are open structures, or slots, that can be filled appropriately by a variety of content. For example, support seeking or activation can occur through direct verbal acts (asking), indirect verbal acts (hinting or complaining), direct nonverbal acts (crying or pouting), or indirect nonverbal acts (e.g., sighing or sulking; Barbee & Cunningham, 1995). Each of the four support events also has a variable internal structure and may consist of anything from a brief bit of behavior to long, complex behavioral sequences.

Third, although the four-phase structure has received considerable empirical support, analyses of supportive interactions may also be broadened to include some additional phases, as well as deepened to observe relevant structures within phases. For example, Dirks and Metts (2010) describe a *decision phase* that is posited to occur prior to support activation, in which individuals experience a stressful event and decide whom to approach for support. To the extent that identifying additional

phases or subphases contributes to more insightful examination of supportive interactions, researchers should not be overly restricted by the currently dominant four-phase description.

Finally, relatively few studies have examined the full sequence of events in supportive interactions, usually focusing on a single event. The vast majority of studies have examined support provision, and a growing body of work focuses on support seeking or activation (for a review, see Feng & Burleson, 2006), but only limited research has directly examined target reactions to support efforts or helper responses to those reactions (e.g., Cheuk & Rosen, 1993).

*Interaction Structure and Its Outcomes.* Despite increasing attention given to supportive interaction structure, research examining the relationship between the structure and outcomes of supportive interactions remains in its infancy. To date, there are only a handful of studies examining contingencies in support provider and recipient behavior both across and within interaction phases. These studies do suggest that the dyadic interplay of behaviors can be consequential for support recipients. For example, several studies indicate that when support is more strongly desired or solicited, it is subsequently evaluated more positively by recipients (Dirks & Metts, 2010; Goldsmith, 2000; MacGeorge, Feng, Butler, & Budarz, 2004). Barbee and Cunningham (1995) summarized evidence indicating that helper use of approach behaviors (solve, solace) is more likely to follow target use of direct (compared with indirect) support activation behaviors (see also Horowitz et al., 2001). Saitzyk, Floyd, and Kroll (1997) found that helper expressions of confidence in and esteem for the target increased the likelihood of target disclosure of thoughts and feelings and that the giving of advice by helpers tended to promote targets expressing problem-solving ideas of their own. Feng (2009) recently reported that advice received more positive evaluations when given subsequent to emotional support and problem analysis than when these supportive behaviors occurred in a different sequence (e.g., when advice preceded emotional support and problem analysis). As researchers become more accustomed to the complexities of design and statistical analysis needed for research on contingent behaviors (see Saitzyk et al., 1997), studies connecting interactional structures and outcomes will make increasingly valuable contributions to theorizing about supportive communication.

*Problematics of Supportive Interactions.* Despite the paucity of precise findings linking interactional contingencies to support outcomes, there is ample evidence that supportive interactions are filled with perils, pitfalls, paradoxes, and predicaments for both helpers and targets. These problematics of supportive interactions stem from a wide variety of sources, such as self-presentational dilemmas and threats to face (Goldsmith, 2004), equity concerns (Brock & Lawrence, 2010), and the challenge of simultaneously pursuing multiple interaction goals, such as providing emotional support while seeking to achieve social control (see Sarason & Sarason, 2006). Various communicative strategies are available for managing many of these problematics (see Burleson & Goldsmith, 1998), but the high incidence of "support" that is either ineffective or insensitive (see Holmstrom, Burleson, & Jones, 2005) suggests that many people lack or do not employ the skills necessary to meet the challenges of providing support successfully (Goldsmith, 2004).

Sometimes supportive communication efforts are so inept or injurious that one must wonder if they were genuinely intended to help. Some instances of poor-quality supportive communication *do* stem from a lack of interest or motivation on the part of providers. For example, multiple studies indicate that when people view support seekers as responsible for their own problems, they generate interaction goals that are less supportive in character (Crocker & Canevello, 2008; MacGeorge, 2001) and correspondingly produce emotional support messages that are less sensitive (MacGeorge, Gillihan, Samter, & Clark, 2003). However, in many cases, it appears that

unhelpful, "failed" support efforts were sincerely intended to assist their recipients (Ford & Ellis, 1998; Vangelisti, 2009). Unfortunately, these inept efforts to seek and provide support are consequential. Research indicates that inept supportive interactions can have a variety of negative consequences, such as exacerbating stress and intensifying negative emotions, damaging psychological and physical health, and undermining relationship satisfaction and stability (e.g., Beehr, Bowling, & Bennett, 2010; Figueiredo, Fries, & Ingram, 2004). These research findings underscore the observation that support must be competently provided if it is to benefit recipients.

*Summary.* The available findings thus suggest that engaging in competent supportive communication—producing interactions that facilitate the elicitation and provision of helpful support—can be a demanding task requiring both ability and motivation (Burleson, 2003a). In the last major section of this chapter, we discuss the individual and situational factors that influence the skill with which support is provided in any given interaction. At present, we examine the theory and research on each phase of supportive interaction, with a focus on identifying key characteristics or properties of communication in each phase, demonstrating the connection between these properties and relevant outcomes, and describing the mechanisms that drive these connections. We begin by giving attention to support seeking, followed by consideration of support provision, the reception of supportive messages by their targets, and subsequent responses by the support provider.

## Support Seeking

Supportive interactions can be initiated by a support provider who notices an apparent need and offers support. In fact, it may be desirable that social networks respond to the needs of their members and offer help without being asked (Bolger et al., 2000). However, in many cases, support-giving behaviors do not materialize without indication of need by the stressed individual (Cutrona, Suhr, & MacFarlane, 1990). Support seeking, sometimes referred to as support activation (Barbee et al., 1993), elicitation (Cutrona et al., 1990), or mobilization (Cortina, 2004), can be defined as *intentional communicative activity with the aim of eliciting supportive actions from others.*

The body of research on support seeking is not as large as that focused on support provision. In addition, much of the research attention given to support seeking has focused on the likelihood of seeking support (e.g., whether or how frequently support is sought), the sources of support, or the types of support sought (Feng & Burleson, 2006), rather than the character and outcomes of communication involved in support seeking. We therefore briefly address these issues before examining what is known about communicative strategies for seeking support.

*Likelihood of Seeking Support.* An individual's likelihood of seeking support during times of stress or difficulty is influenced by a variety of factors. Various models of coping indicate that individuals' perceptions of stressful situations influence their selection of coping strategies, including support seeking (e.g., Li & Yang, 2009). In addition, the likelihood of support seeking is influenced by factors that include the seeker's self-efficacy (Shen, 2009), attachment style (Collins & Feeney, 2010), and gender (Day & Livingstone, 2003).

One growing area of theoretical development is concerned with the influence of culture on support seeking (Feng & Burleson, 2006; Kim, Sherman, & Taylor, 2008). Much of this work has focused on the differences between national groups or ethnicities characterized as individualistic or collectivistic (i.e., having the tendency to emphasize individual identities, rights, and achievements vs. group identity, obligations, and concerns; Gudykunst & Matsumoto, 1996; Hofstede, 1991; Triandis, 1994). Members of collectivist cultures (e.g., Chinese, Thais, Koreans, Asian Americans, Latinos) are less likely than members of individualist cultures

(e.g., U.S. Americans, Western Europeans) to seek social support as a means of coping (Mortenson, Burleson, Feng, & Liu, 2009; Taylor et al., 2004). One explanation for these cultural differences is that members of collectivist cultures may be comparatively hesitant to disturb the harmony of their in-groups by focusing the attention of group members on their distressed emotional states (Gao, 1996). Another explanation is that Asian philosophical and religious traditions (especially Buddhism and Taoism) promote the virtue of acceptance and endurance in the fate of adversity (Marsella, 1993), making active support seeking seem inappropriate or superfluous (Wong, Wong, & Scott, 2006).

*Sources of Support.* Support can come from a wide variety of sources, including everyone from close friends and relatives to acquaintances and professional helpers, such as therapists and members of the clergy. Even strangers may provide support, an occurrence that has become more common due to increased use of online support groups (Barak, Boniel-Nissim, & Suler, 2008). However, given that close relationships are generally seen as the locus of intimacy and care (McConatha, Lightner, & Deaner, 1994), it is not surprising to find that immediate family members, friends, and romantic partners are reported as the most frequent sources of support across cultures (e.g., Cortina, 2004). At the same time, research suggests that choices about whom to approach for support depend on the perceived ability and willingness of those sources to provide the support. For example, support seeking from a particular relational partner is affected by the quality of supportive interactions that have previously occurred (Brock & Lawrence, 2010). Research also indicates that gender and culture influence preferences for sources of support. Women tend to be preferred more than men (Burleson & Kunkel, 2006), and people from collectivist cultures are more likely than people from individualistic cultures to confine support seeking to close personal relationships, especially members of their immediate families (for a review, see Feng & Burleson, 2006).

*Types of Support Sought.* The type of support people seek generally depends on how they appraise their problems (Harlow & Cantor, 1995). Because many stressors are multifaceted, it is common to seek multiple forms of support (e.g., Boudioni et al., 2001). It is also possible for people to be unsure, unreflective, or inaccurate about the types of support they need, sometimes resulting in support seeking that is not well suited to the need (e.g., Prinstein, Borelli, Cheah, Simon, & Aikins, 2005). Some factors seem to predispose the seeking of particular types of support. For example, women are more likely than men to seek emotional support (Day & Livingstone, 2003), as are individuals who are more expressive (Reevy & Maslach, 2001).

*Strategies for Seeking Support.* Although research on the likelihood of seeking support, the sources of support, and the types of support sought provides important context, work on strategies for seeking support has the most direct relevance for scholars of supportive communication. These strategies are frequently classified as verbal or nonverbal (e.g., talking vs. crying) and direct or indirect (e.g., explicit requests for help vs. hinting that a problem exists; Barbee & Cunningham, 1995; Barbee, Rowatt, & Cunningham, 1998).

Some work has examined how the use of these strategies is influenced by various factors, such as gender and culture. There is evidence that women are more likely than men to use verbal messages to seek support, especially emotional support (Tamres, Janicki, & Helgeson, 2002), and that European Americans are more likely than Asians or Asian Americans to make use of explicit disclosure of a problem and overt expressions of negative feelings (Mortenson et al., 2009). Use of direct versus indirect strategies is also influenced by perceived risk from their use. Indirect strategies allow the support seeker to keep his or her problem hidden or only partially disclosed (Williams & Mickelson, 2008) and may thus reduce the degree of threat to the support seeker's face (Goldsmith, 1994). Consistent with these ideas, research indicates that when individuals are embarrassed,

ambivalent, or perceive stigma associated with seeking support directly, they use indirect activation strategies to protect self-esteem (Barbee, Rowatt, et al., 1998; Williams & Mickelson, 2008).

Do different support-seeking strategies produce different outcomes? As the typical "first act" in support interactions, support seeking is almost certain to affect whether support is received, the type of support provided, and the quality of that support, in turn affecting the outcomes of the interaction for the support recipient and the relationship between provider and recipient (e.g., Barbee & Cunningham, 1995; Goldsmith, 2000). However, research directly examining outcomes of support-seeking communication is sparse. There is evidence suggesting that direct strategies are more likely to elicit emotional support while indirect strategies are more likely to result in avoidant reactions from potential support providers (Williams & Mickelson, 2008). The use of direct support-seeking strategies is likely to entail disclosure of the problematic situation, which may, in turn, facilitate smooth and supportive interactions between the help seeker and the provider (Burleson & Goldsmith, 1998). In contrast, because indirect strategies may be vague about the character of the problem, support providers may be unsure of their ability to help and may therefore respond negatively or apathetically (Barbee, Derlega, Sherburne, & Grimshaw, 1998).

Clearly, there is much left to be examined with respect to support-seeking communication. One important direction is the development of more sophisticated theory about the properties of support-seeking messages that are likely to affect support providers' responses and recipients' outcomes. Distinctions such as direct versus indirect are relatively simple and have had heuristic value, but other features of support-seeking messages may do a better job of predicting relevant outcomes (Goldsmith, 1995). For example, it seems likely that support seekers need to communicate strategically if they are in any way responsible for their own problems and may need to highlight the efforts they have made to cope independently (see MacGeorge, 2001).

## Support Provision: Supportive Messages

The preponderance of research concerned with supportive communication has focused on the *provision* of support through supportive messages, where supportive messages are defined as *specific lines of communicative behavior enacted by one party with the intent of benefiting or helping another* (Burleson & MacGeorge, 2002). In particular, research has focused on (a) identifying the characteristics or properties of more and less effective supportive messages, (b) developing theoretical descriptions of these message features (e.g., person centeredness), (c) determining why these characteristics contribute to effectiveness, and (d) specifying the conditions that produce variability in message effectiveness. We begin by reviewing the historical development of research on "support types" and segue to examine more current work on the properties and outcomes of comforting, advice, and esteem support messages.

*Support "Types" and Matching Models.* One of the earliest contributions to the study of support provision was the common-sense observation that people provide different types of support to those in distress, because support is given in response to different types of problematic situations (for a review of typologies, see Cutrona & Russell, 1990). For example, Cutrona and Suhr's (1994) well-known typology includes the categories of emotional support (expressions of care, concern, and sympathy), esteem support (reassurance of worth, expressions of liking for or confidence in the other), network support (expressions of connection and belonging), informational support (information and advice), and tangible assistance (offers of money, physical intervention, material aid).

The observation that there are parallel support and problem types subsequently evolved into a group of theories about the relative effectiveness of different types of support. These theories are known as "matching models" and include Cohen and McKay's (1984) stressor-support

specificity model as well as Cutrona's (1990) even more influential optimal-matching model (OMM). The key idea underlying these models is that the type of support offered will be effective to the extent that it is *relevant* to the particular stressor being experienced by the target. This notion has strong intuitive appeal; after all, offering sympathy to a motorist who has run out of gas is "obviously" less effective than providing directions (or a ride) to a gas station.

Despite their appeal and frequent citation in the support literature, matching models have not fared well empirically. Leading proponents of the OMM found little support for the matching hypothesis in a detailed study of supportive messages exchanged by married couples and concluded that the model was a "significant over-simplification" (see also Cutrona et al., 2007; Cutrona & Suhr, 1994). More generally, studies have typically found that distressed people benefit from emotional support messages regardless of the character of the problem (e.g., Pasch, Bradbury, & Davila, 1997). Furthermore, the impact of informational support messages is highly variable but appears to depend on factors that go well beyond the "relevance" of providing information (e.g., placement in the sequence of supportive interaction; Feng, 2009; for a review, see MacGeorge et al., 2008).

For what reasons do matching models fail, and what does this indicate about the character of effective support? It is important to start by observing that both stressors and supportive messages are complex in ways not adequately addressed by the OMM. Losing one's job, for example, may result not only in financial problems but also in loss of self-esteem, depression, and the need to locate to a new position. No single type of support will be sufficient to address this situation. Furthermore, supportive messages and interactions are often, even typically, multifunctional—containing a variety of elements (MacGeorge, Graves, Feng, Gillihan, & Burleson, 2004), addressing a range of objectives (Dillard, 2008), and producing multifaceted effects (e.g., Feng & MacGeorge, 2010). Although it is analytically useful to distinguish among different types of stressors and forms of support, theorizing about supportive communication must reject the assumption of one-to-one correspondence between stressors and types of support and incorporate the recognition that messages can have impacts that are not "matched" to their types (e.g., emotional support may influence problem-solving motivation, and instrumental support may influence emotional states; Burleson & Goldsmith, 1998; Tardy, 1994).

Still more problematic for matching models is their foundation in two related assumptions. The first of these is that relevance is the primary determinant of the effectiveness of support efforts, and the second is that, assuming relevance exists, the quantity of support is the next most important factor (the "more is better" mentality; see Rini & Dunkel-Schetter, 2010). Relevance is surely a part of what influences helpfulness (as suggested by the example of the out-of-gas motorist), but messages can be equally relevant to a stressor (e.g., expressions of sympathy to someone suffering bereavement) while differing dramatically in other important ways (e.g., in the sensitivity with which sympathy is conveyed). Similarly, there are many reasons why more of a particular type of support may be ineffective or even harmful (Brock & Lawrence, 2010; Goldsmith, 2004).

In short, matching models have proven inadequate as theories of supportive communication effectiveness because they do not address the central issue of support quality. More useful theories require identifying specific elements of supportive messages and interactions that make supportive behavior "work" (or fail), explaining why those identified elements have the effects they do, and stipulating the conditions under which these elements have a stronger or weaker influence on outcomes. To date, this type of theorizing has been developed most extensively with respect to emotional support (Burleson, 2003a), complemented by growing attention to informational support (MacGeorge et al., 2008) and, most recently, to esteem support (Holmstrom & Burleson, 2011). Theory and research on these forms of supportive communication are presented in the sections that follow.

*Emotional Support or Comforting Messages.* Among communication scholars, emotional support messages are often referred to as "comforting" messages and are typically defined as messages having the goal of alleviating or lessening the emotional distress experienced by others (Burleson, 1984). An extensive research program by Burleson and his associates (for a review, see Burleson, 2003a) has identified the key features of more and less sensitive comforting messages and has shown that these features contribute to important message outcomes.

*Features of Effective Comforting Messages.* Applegate (1980) and Burleson (1982) proposed that comforting messages should be differentiated by the extent to which they reflect a person-centered orientation to discourse. Person centeredness refers to how much message behavior "reflects an awareness of and adaptation to the subjective, affective, and relational aspects of communicative contexts" (Burleson, 1987, p. 305). Thus, messages that are low in person centeredness deny the other's feelings and perspective (e.g., by criticizing the feelings, challenging their legitimacy, or telling the other how to act and feel). Messages displaying a moderate degree of person centeredness afford an implicit recognition of the other's feelings (e.g., distracting attention from the troubling situation, offering expressions of sympathy, or presenting explanations of the situation intended to reduce the other's distress). Highly person-centered comforting messages explicitly recognize and legitimate the other's feelings (e.g., helping to articulate the feelings, elaborating reasons why those feelings are present, and helping to place the feelings in a broader context). Similar analyses of sensitivity or sophistication in the provision of emotional support have been offered by several other scholars (Carkhuff & Berenson, 1977; Fruzzetti & Worrall, 2010; Greenberg, Rice, & Elliott, 1993; Rogers, 1957).

In multiple studies, Burleson and his colleagues (e.g., Burleson & Samter, 1985a; Kunkel & Burleson, 1999) have developed evidence that highly person-centered comforting messages are viewed as more sensitive and effective methods of managing another's distressed emotions than are less person-centered messages (see the review by Burleson, Samter, et al., 2005). Moreover, several experimental studies (Jones, 2004; Jones & Guerrero, 2001) show that highly person-centered comforting messages are not just perceived as more sensitive and effective; they actually do a better job of reducing emotional distress than less person-centered forms of comforting. Beyond their immediate impact on support recipients, the person-centered quality of comforting messages can influence the perceptions of helpers (Burleson, Delia, & Applegate, 1992; Samter & Burleson, 1990). For example, Samter, Burleson, & Murphy (1987) found that the person-centered quality of the messages used by a helper predicted observers' liking for and attraction to the helper (see Jones & Guerrero, 2001). Other research indicates that, over the long term, the person-centered quality of the comforting messages employed by parents and peers predict the developing child's social-cognitive and functional-communication skills, including comforting skills (Applegate, Burleson, & Delia, 1992; Burleson & Kunkel, 2002). In sum, the person-centered quality of comforting messages has been found to influence the cognitive, affective, and behavioral outcomes of support situations, both short- and long term.

*Mechanisms Explaining Comforting-Message Effectiveness.* Through what mechanisms do highly person-centered messages produce these beneficial outcomes? With regard to reducing emotional distress, Burleson and Goldsmith's (1998) *theory of conversationally induced reappraisals* asserts that highly person-centered messages do a better job than messages lower in person centeredness because they facilitate cognitive reappraisal of the upsetting event. Appraisal theories of emotion (Lazarus, 1991) maintain that people's appraisals (cognitive representations and judgments) of events generate their emotional reactions. Thus, to change a support recipient's emotional state, a support provider must foster cognitive *re*appraisal—a different perspective on the situation. Because highly person-centered messages are feeling focused and compassionate, they encourage a support recipient to reflect on, talk about, and understand his or her feelings, facilitating eventual acceptance and reorientation to existing challenges and opportunities. Experimental work (Jones & Wirtz, 2006) has recently provided direct support for this theoretical account of the causal mechanism through which highly person-centered messages facilitate positive emotional change.

The theory of conversationally induced reappraisals also helps explain liking for and attraction toward peers who use highly person-centered comforting, because reductions in distress and improvements in coping ability tend to generate positive feelings toward the support provider. However, children's development of sophisticated socio-cognitive and communication skills as a function of parents' highly person-centered communication is probably due more to the modeling of message strategies and attentiveness to the feelings and perspectives of others (for a fuller explication of this socialization process, see Burleson, Delia, & Applegate, 1995; Burleson & Kunkel, 1996).

*Moderators of Comforting-Message Effectiveness.* Studies have demonstrated that the effects of person centeredness on message evaluations are moderated by a host of recipient factors. These include (a) sex- and gender-related factors (Burleson et al., 2009), (b) ethnicity or culture (Burleson & Mortenson, 2003), (c) cognitive variables such as cognitive complexity (Burleson & Samter, 1985b), and (d) personality dimensions such as attachment style (Bodie et al., 2011), expressivity (Burleson, 2008a), religiosity (Wilkum & MacGeorge, 2010), and perceived availability of support (Servaty-Seib & Burleson, 2007). Features of the message source (support provider) and the problem situation have also been found to affect evaluations of comforting messages, including the sex of the source (Holmstrom et al., 2005), the closeness of the relationship between source and recipient (Bodie et al., 2011), the severity of the problem (Burleson, 2008b), and recipient responsibility for the problem (Jones & Burleson, 1997). A comprehensive review of the factors moderating the influence of message person centeredness is given in Bodie and Burleson (2008). Mechanisms that help explain moderating effects are reviewed in a subsequent section that examines the reception of comforting messages.

Despite this evidence of various moderators affecting the relationship between person centeredness and comforting effectiveness, it is critical to note the pattern of moderation: In all cases, the main effect of person centeredness substantially outweighs the effects of the moderators (Bodie & Burleson, 2008). For example, one of the most studied moderators is recipient sex. In this case, it has been consistently found that women evaluate highly person-centered messages somewhat more positively than men while men evaluate messages low in person centeredness somewhat more positively than women (e.g., MacGeorge, Graves, et al., 2004). However, both women and men still evaluate highly person-centered messages much more positively than messages low in person centeredness (for reviews, see Burleson & Hanasono, 2010; Burleson & Kunkel, 2006).

Although the person-centered quality of comforting messages appears to capture a key aspect of effective emotional support, there remain limitations in our understanding of comforting message effectiveness. Burleson (2010) recently critiqued his theory of conversationally induced reappraisal for failing to explain why messages that are not highly person-centered (especially moderately person-centered messages) can still produce positive emotional change (albeit less than that produced by highly person-centered messages). A dual-process theory of supportive message processing may help redress this limitation (Bodie & Burleson, 2008; Burleson, 2010). It is discussed in

a subsequent section on the reception of supportive messages. There are also features other than person centeredness that demonstrably affect comforting-message efficacy and therefore deserve more research attention. These include religious content (Wilkum & MacGeorge, 2010) and multiple aspects of nonverbal behavior (Jones & Guerrero, 2001; Jones & Wirtz, 2007).

*Advice.* As theory and research on comforting began to mature, supportive communication scholars began to pursue a parallel line of research on informational support, with particular focus on advice, defined as messages that make recommendations about what to do, think, or feel in response to a problematic situation (MacGeorge et al., 2008). Because informational support exhibits highly variable outcomes (compare Servaty-Seib & Burleson, 2007; Verhofstadt, Ickes, & Buysse, 2010), researchers were stimulated to identify and explain the specific features that differentiate between more and less effective advice.

*Features of More and Less Effective Advice Messages.* Early research on advice as a form of supportive communication focused on the style with which advice was given, especially the extent to which advice threatened or attended to the face needs of the recipient. More recently, attention has turned to examination of how advice outcomes are influenced by aspects of advice content and the sequencing of advice in supportive interactions.

*Facework.* Theories of face needs and facework (especially politeness theory; Brown & Levinson, 1987) suggest that advice is potentially threatening to "negative face" (i.e., recipients' desire to be autonomous and unimpeded) and to "positive face" (i.e., recipients' desire to be treated as competent and likeable). Correspondingly, "politeness" or "facework" features in advice messages should influence perceptions of face threat and therefore influence advice outcomes (Goldsmith, 1994).

Many studies have tested the effects of these features (Caplan & Samter, 1999; Goldsmith, 1994; Goldsmith & MacGeorge, 2000; MacGeorge,

Lichtman, & Pressey, 2002). These studies have been grounded in politeness theory (Brown & Levinson, 1987), which distinguishes between bald-on-record message strategies (in which the propositional content of a message is delivered bluntly) and several types of polite or mitigating strategies (in which language is used as facework to "redress" the threat posed by the propositional content). Several studies have demonstrated that advice including one or more forms of mitigating facework is preferred to advice that is bald-on-record (Feng & Burleson, 2008; Goldsmith, 1994; MacGeorge, Lichtman, et al., 2002). There is also evidence that politeness attending to positive face needs (i.e., "positive politeness") may be preferred to that which attends to negative face needs (i.e., "negative politeness"; Caplan & Samter, 1999; Goldsmith, 1994), though one large-scale study failed to detect any differences between forms of politeness as specified by politeness theory (Goldsmith & MacGeorge, 2000).

*Content Features.* Although facework strategies appear to be important to the way advice is evaluated by recipients, recent research has turned attention to the content of the advice message, especially content focused on the actions being advised. MacGeorge, Feng, and colleagues (Feng & MacGeorge, 2010; MacGeorge, Feng, et al., 2004) have shown that perceptions of an advised action's efficacy (whether it will work), feasibility (whether the advice recipient can do it), and limitations (the extent to which the action has risks or drawbacks) are important influences on advice evaluations and outcomes. Additional evidence that these are key features of advice content comes from a study showing that advice messages containing explicit argument about the advised action's efficacy, feasibility, and limitations are evaluated more positively and result in greater intention to implement the advice than messages that do not explicitly address these issues (Feng & Burleson, 2008).

*Interactional Sequence.* Several studies indicate that advice recipients are influenced not only by

message style and content but also by the interactional sequence in which advice is offered. Consistent with the observation that people who report being receptive to advice evaluate it more positively (MacGeorge, Feng, et al., 2004), unsolicited advice is more likely to be viewed as intrusive, unsupportive, and face threatening (Goldsmith, 2000; Goldsmith & Fitch, 1997). In addition, a recent message perception study shows that advice is evaluated more positively when it is preceded by emotional support and problem analysis (Feng, 2009). Continued research in this vein is important not only to theorizing about advice effectiveness but also to developing a more sophisticated understanding of supportive interactions.

*Theories of Advice Effectiveness.* As researchers have explored the effects of different features of advice messages, they have developed, tested, and elaborated several theories of advice outcomes. Theories of face and facework (Brown & Levinson, 1987; Metts & Cupach, 2008) have guided research demonstrating that mitigating facework strategies can improve advice outcomes. More recent examinations of content features in advice messages have been guided by the idea of stases or stock issues, a rhetorical concept originally developed to explain the necessary components of an effective policy speech (Ehninger & Brockriede, 1978). For example, the stock issue of "cure" refers to the necessity that speakers show how policies being proposed will adequately address the problem under consideration. Since advice, in essence, is a personalized "policy speech," the concept of cure suggests that advice recipients will be concerned with the efficacy and feasibility of the advised action (for a fuller discussion of stock issues as a basis for theorizing about advice, see MacGeorge, Feng, et al., 2004.

Recently, Feng and MacGeorge (2010) outlined an integrative theoretical framework they now title *advice response theory.* This theory incorporates the prior theoretical claims that specific content and stylistic elements are important influences on advice outcomes. However, it also proposes that advice message features (both content and style) will have greater or lesser influence on outcomes depending on the characteristics of the source and how the recipient processes the message. Accordingly, we will consider this theory after discussing the effects of source and recipient characteristics on advice outcomes.

*Source and Recipient Characteristics as Main Effects and Moderators.* Complementing research on advice message features are studies that have examined the characteristics of advice sources and recipients as influences on advice outcomes (for reviews, see Bonaccio & Dalal, 2006; MacGeorge et al., 2008). However, in contrast to the research literature on comforting messages, where source and recipient characteristics have generally been examined as moderators of the effect of person centeredness, the majority of studies of source and recipient characteristics have been conducted by social psychologists and consequently have not attended to message characteristics (Feng & MacGeorge, 2010).

Several studies of source characteristics on advice outcomes indicate that recipients are positively influenced by source expertise, trustworthiness, and expressed confidence in the advice, along with similarity to the recipient and closeness and liking in the relationship with the recipient (Bonaccio & Dalal, 2010; Feng & MacGeorge, 2006; Van Swol & Sniezek, 2005). A smaller number of studies have examined recipients' traits and situational perceptions as influences on responses to advice. For example, expressivity (MacGeorge, Graves, et al., 2004) and rational thinking style (Feng & Lee, 2010) have been found to be associated with more positive evaluations of advice, as has receptiveness to advice, defined as the desire to receive advice from a particular person in response to a specific situation (MacGeorge, Feng, et al., 2004).

To what extent do these source and recipient characteristics moderate the observed influences of advice message content and style? MacGeorge, Feng, et al. (2004) found that increased receptiveness resulted in usefulness (a precursor to the concept of efficacy) having a weaker influence and

absence of limitations having a stronger influence on advice outcomes. The study found no other significant interactions between these and several other variables. More recently, Feng and MacGeorge (2010) found that a set of source characteristics (liking, similarity, closeness, and expertise) moderated the influence of a set of message characteristics (efficacy, feasibility, absence of limitations, politeness, and confirmation, defined as the extent to which the advice supported an action the recipient already intended to take). As the influence of the set of message characteristics increased in magnitude, the influence of the set of source characteristics decreased, and vice versa. More research is needed to examine the interactions between different variables that affect advice evaluations.

*Advice Response Theory.* As described earlier, the advice response theory of Feng and MacGeorge (2010) proposes that message features (including both content and stylistic features such as politeness) are stronger influences on advice outcomes than source characteristics and that the influence of source characteristics is mediated through their effects on perceptions of message features. It further proposes, based on dual-process models of persuasion and supportive communication (Bodie & Burleson, 2008; Petty, Rucker, Bizer, & Cacioppo, 2004), that message features will have a stronger influence on advice outcomes when recipients "process" or think about advice messages more carefully (e.g., when a problem is very serious) and source characteristics become more influential when advice messages are thought about less carefully (e.g., when a problem is not serious). Initial research largely supports the theory (Feng & MacGeorge, 2010), but the influence of source characteristics did not decline as problem seriousness increased, perhaps because the average level of perceived problem seriousness was too high. As previously noted, this study also provided evidence of a moderating relationship between message features and source characteristics. Like its predecessor theories, advice response theory should help promote further research and theoretical development with regard to advice.

*Esteem Support.* Esteem support, sometimes referred to as identity or ego support, can be defined as a form of social support that is provided to enhance how recipients feel about themselves and their attributes, abilities, or accomplishments (Holmstrom & Burleson, 2011). Historically, esteem support has often been treated as an aspect of emotional support (Dakof & Taylor, 1990; Graetz, Shute, & Sawyer, 2000). Thus, until recently, there has been little direct attention to the properties or outcomes of esteem support (Carels & Baucom, 1999; Holmstrom & Burleson, 2011).

*Features of Effective Esteem Support Messages.* Drawing from attribution and appraisal theories (Lazarus, 1991; Weiner, 1986), the cognitive-emotional theory of esteem support messages (CETESM; Holmstrom & Burleson, 2011) states that the characteristics distinguishing more and less effective esteem support messages are distinct from those identified with respect to emotional support messages. Specifically, CETESM posits that esteem support messages can be scaled for the extent to which they are emotion focused or problem focused (i.e., concerned with the target's appraisals and attributions or focused on changing problematic behavior related to the esteem-threatening event) and assertive or inductive (designed to force or induce changes in the target's cognitions or behaviors). Consistent with their theorizing and some earlier research (Samter, 1989), Holmstrom and Burleson's (2011) study revealed that emotion-focused/inductive messages were generally perceived as better than problem-focused/assertive messages in terms of several outcomes, including self-esteem, self-worth, self-efficacy, and feelings of acceptance.

*Mechanisms Explaining Esteem Support Message Effectiveness.* The CETESM suggests that emotion-focused and inductive messages are the most effective forms of esteem support because of what they try to change and how they try to change it. It is believed that threats to self-esteem arise from negative attributions and appraisals about esteem-relevant events. Hence, emotion-focused esteem support is more effective than problem-focused esteem support because it directly addresses the cognitions that give rise to the target's negative self-conscious emotions (e.g., shame, guilt, embarrassment) as opposed to trying to manage behaviors related to the esteem-relevant event. Inductive esteem support is more effective than assertive esteem support because it does more to engage recipients in active sifting and sorting of information about the self and the esteem-threatening situation and, as such, the target is more likely to "own" the outcome of the inductive processes (Holmstrom & Burleson, 2011). This theory is an exciting new contribution that deserves further development and testing.

*Summary.* Research on the provision of support, and specifically on the effectiveness of the messages used to instantiate it, is at the heart of research on supportive communication. It is conducted primarily by scholars in the communication discipline and exhibits the quintessential features of the supportive communication perspective and, as such, provides a model for continuing research on the role of communication in the exchange of social support. Nonetheless, there is ample room for theoretical development. Some of the topics that need continued attention are addressed above. An additional important issue is discussed in the next section, which describes a very recent move to explain how message reception processes influence the effectiveness of supportive messages.

## Support Reception

Message reception is the process of interpreting the communicative behavior of others in an effort to understand the meaning and implications of that behavior (Burleson, 2007). Although this process necessarily occurs within any communicative interaction, it has only lately been given direct attention as an important influence on supportive interactions. In the theories of message effectiveness reviewed previously, cognitive processing of supportive behavior has been assumed, but the focus has been on evaluations and outcomes that are subsequent to message reception. Recently, however, Burleson and colleagues have focused theoretical attention on message reception in supportive interactions (Burleson, 2010).

Burleson and colleagues title their theory as "dual-process theory of supportive communication outcomes," noting its connections with dual-process theories of persuasive message reception (Fiske & Taylor, 2007; Petty et al., 2004). The theory asserts that various features of messages can influence the outcomes of supportive interactions (e.g., the person centeredness of comforting messages), as can features of sources, recipients, and virtually any other element or structure of supportive communication. However, the influence of these elements is postulated to vary as a function of the amount of scrutiny (or cognitive processing) message recipients give to different elements. Different outcomes are expected when certain elements are closely scrutinized as opposed to being given limited attention (these alternatives are the "dual processes"). Of particular importance is the idea that message content will have its strongest effect on outcomes when recipients scrutinize this content extensively, but when message content receives little scrutiny, other elements can trigger heuristics, associations, or sensations that influence outcomes. Message content generally receives more extensive processing when the recipient is more motivated and able to scrutinize that content (Petty et al., 2004; Todorov, Chaiken, & Henderson, 2002). Thus, various ability and motivation factors ultimately influence message outcomes.

Variation in the influence of person centeredness on comforting outcomes is explainable in terms of the dual-process model (for an extensive review, see Bodie & Burleson, 2008). Furthermore, several tests of the model have shown that evaluations of comforting messages are more strongly influenced by level of person centeredness under conditions where the recipients have greater ability or motivation to think carefully about message content, such as when the difficulties being faced by message recipients are more serious (Burleson, 2008b, Study 3; Rack, Burleson, Bodie, Holmstrom, & Servaty-Seib, 2008). However, additional research is still needed to support the validity of the theory and extend its explanatory power. The studies being conducted include more direct assessments of how closely messages are being processed (thought listing, reaction time, and self-report of engagement with the message, e.g., Bodie, Burleson, & Jones, 2009). They have also begun to address one of the major complexities associated with any dual-process model, which is that source, recipient, and other situational factors may influence message outcomes in a variety of ways (see Petty et al., 2004; Todorov et al., 2002), sometimes influencing the extent of processing (i.e., influencing ability or motivation), sometimes functioning as a cue that activates decisional heuristics or other low-elaboration processes, and sometimes functioning as a "biasing" influence on the direction of cognition if the level of message scrutiny is high. As Burleson and colleagues note, it is essential to specify and test the conditions under which situational elements operate in these diverse ways. Nonetheless, this developing theory already makes a unique contribution by stimulating systematic attention to the recipient's cognitive processing as an influence on message outcomes. We now move beyond provision and reception to consider the expressed reactions of support recipients and the responses of support providers.

## Support Recipient Reactions and Support Provider Responses

Over the course of a supportive interaction, support recipients typically must reply in an ongoing fashion to the communication behaviors of support providers. Thus, as they receive supportive messages and process them (to whatever degree), they must generate behaviors of their own, such as disclosing more aspects of the situation, soliciting advice, or turning the conversation to other topics. Throughout this give-and-take, support recipients experience cognitive and affective reactions to the efforts of the support provider, and some of these are reflected in their behaviors. Consequently, support providers will often be able to obtain some sense of how the recipient is reacting to their supportive efforts (e.g., Does the recipient stop crying, decide on a problem-solving action, or terminate the interaction?). In some cases, recipients will overtly communicate their evaluation of the supportive communication they have received, either during the interaction ("Mmm, that's an interesting suggestion.") or subsequent to it ("You really helped me."). The support provider then has the opportunity to respond to the reactions of the support recipient.

Although it is relatively easy to spin out this description of support recipient reactions and provider responses, there is very little research focused on these components of supportive interactions. The research reviewed in prior sections provides considerable insight into how recipients evaluate supportive communication but has not focused on how these evaluations are communicated to support providers. Nor has this research considered how support providers respond when support recipients react.

However, existing research indicates that these processes of reacting and responding to support are consequential and worthy of greater attention by scholars of supportive communication. Some of this work focuses on negative reactions and responses. For example, helpers whose assistance is rejected or "spurned" by confederates often experience negative affect and generate negative evaluations of the intended help recipient (e.g., viewing them as stubborn, proud, or lacking in understanding; Cheuk & Rosen, 1993), and the repeated experience of spurning contributes to helpers becoming disinterested in helping (e.g., K. S. Wong, Cheuk, & Rosen, 2007). Other work shows that support providers tend to become frustrated and less sympathetic if their assistance appears ineffective over time (see Joiner, 2000).

On the positive side, recent studies show that support providers respond positively to grateful reactions from support recipients. In a longitudinal study, trait gratitude predicted social support received over time (Wood, Maltby, Gillett, Linley, & Joseph, 2008). One interpretation of this result is that individuals with higher trait gratitude expressed more gratefulness for support to their support providers, which in turn motivated additional support. Consistent with this interpretation, a set of recent laboratory studies and a field experiment demonstrated that helpers who receive a thankful response are not only more willing to continue helping the original recipient but are also more likely to help others they encounter thereafter (Grant, 2010).

These studies suggest that reactions and responses are key components of supportive interactions, affecting relationships and subsequent support provision. However, research is needed to increase knowledge about the specific ways in which reactions and responses affect outcomes for recipients and providers and, especially, to determine how to be skillful in the management of these phases of interaction. For example, if a support recipient reacts negatively to support provision, what are the effective means for recipients or providers to improve the trajectory of the interaction? Are there ways for recipients to show gratitude that are more motivating to providers (and avoid damaging feelings of indebtedness for the recipient)?

As the prior sections have indicated, supportive interaction is a complex, highly contingent process involving (at a minimum) phases of support seeking, provision, reception, reaction, and response. Theory and research have progressed considerably in the past two decades, with notable increases since the previous version of this chapter. However, further work is necessary to develop more accurate—and practical—theory about how and why supportive messages and interactions affect coping processes, relationships, and health. As a complement to this process, it is important that theorists attend to individual difference factors that explain why some individuals exhibit greater skill in supportive interactions, as well as situational factors that tend to promote (or inhibit) the provision of effective support (Burleson, 2003a). This is the topic of the next section.

## Factors That Influence the Skillful Production of Supportive Messages

Studies have found that individuals' production of supportive messages is influenced by a variety of factors (for reviews, see Barbee, Rowatt, et al., 1998; Burleson, 2003a; Burleson & Kunkel, 2002). These include *demographic characteristics* (e.g., gender, culture), *personality traits* (e.g., attachment styles, trait empathy), *cognitive variables* (e.g., cognitive complexity, attribution processes), *affective states* (e.g., helper and target mood states and emotions), *relationship qualities* (e.g., type, length, or quality of relationship), *interactional contingencies* (e.g., support activation behavior, success of prior helping efforts), and *situational variables* (e.g., problem severity, responsibility for the problem). Although this diversity of factors has been organized in a variety of ways, often involving the distinction between trait and situational influences, it is theoretically useful to observe the distinction between factors affecting the *ability* to provide effective support and those that affect the *motivation* to do so (Burleson, 1985, 2003a).

In the category of trait variables that influence ability, interpersonal cognitive complexity and related perspective-taking traits are the most studied (Burleson, 1985; Burleson & Caplan, 1998), with numerous studies demonstrating that cognitive complexity explains substantial variability in the capacity to produce sophisticated comforting messages. Some attention has also been given to potential support providers' negative emotions as situation-based influences on their ability to comfort. For example, in some circumstances, a support provider may experience anxiety or embarrassment (Copenhaver, Lash, & Eisler, 2000). Emotions may generate cognitive interference, undermining the mental processes necessary for effective comforting (Burleson & Planalp, 2000).

A wide variety of trait and situational factors are likely to influence potential helpers' motivation or desire to provide support. Trait factors include emotional empathy (Tamborini, Salomonson, & Bahk, 1993), communication apprehension (Samter & Burleson, 1984), and self-efficacy at providing support (MacGeorge, Clark, & Gillihan, 2002). These traits are likely to be activated by perceptions of target need and affect the degree of effort individuals are willing to expend in pursuit of support-related goals (Burleson, 1985). A very wide range of situational factors also influence motivation, such as problem severity or recipient need (Hale, Tighe, & Mongeau, 1997) and the recipient's responsibility for the problem and effort to solve it (MacGeorge, 2001). The level of motivation aroused by factors such as these should influence an individual's willingness to expend effort in pursuit of support-related goals; such motivation should be manifest not only in the quality or sophistication of the messages produced but also in the persistence of supportive efforts, especially in the face of resistance. Some factors appear to influence both ability and motivation to provide quality support. In particular, there is evidence that support provider's gender affects both the ability (MacGeorge et al., 2003) and the motivation to provide support (Burleson, Holmstrom, & Gilstrap, 2005) via different mechanisms (for reviews, see Burleson & Kunkel, 2006; Eagly, 2009).

Recently, theorists have emphasized the multidimensionality of both ability and motivation. Drawing from current theories of message production, Burleson and Planalp (2000) describe message production as involving processes of interpretation (e.g., defining the situation, making attributions), goal generation (e.g., forming intentions pertaining to instrumental and relational objectives), planning and action assembly (building cognitive representations of communicative behaviors), enactment (executing the communicative action), and monitoring (observing and evaluating the outcomes of behavior). Thus, the production of a highly person-centered comforting message, for instance, depends on ability in interpretation, goal generation, planning, and so forth. In a similar move to specify the construct of motivation, Burleson, Holmstrom, et al. (2005) have argued for three distinct components of motivation: (1) goal motivation—the desire to achieve a particular social outcome, such as relieving the emotional distress of the target or helping the target solve a problem; (2) effectance motivation—the belief in one's ability to achieve an outcome, such as improving another's emotional state or fixing the person's problem; and (3) normative motivation—the desire to behave in role-appropriate ways, such as saying the "correct" things when comforting or advising others, according to salient social norms.

These theoretical extensions suggest that different variables should affect the ultimate quality of a comforting message by influencing specific aspects of ability or motivation. For example, interpersonal cognitive complexity is conceptualized as an index of interpretive capacity and should therefore influence support provision behaviors primarily by affecting a support provider's mental representations of the recipient's situation and, through these, the complexity of his or her interaction goals (Burleson & Caplan, 1998; Burleson & Rack, 2008). However, little research to date has investigated how specific trait or situational factors might affect particular aspects of ability or motivation (for one exception, see Burleson, Holmstrom, et al., 2005). Thus, theoretical development will depend on more systematic attention to the complex relationships between trait and situational factors, ability and motivation, and message outcomes. Since the vast majority of studies have focused on the provision of comforting, it is also important that future studies examine how traits, situational characteristics, abilities, and motivations influence (a) the provision of advice and other types of support (see MacGeorge, Feng, et al., 2004)

and (b) skill in other aspects of supportive interaction, such as support seeking.

## Conclusion

In this chapter, we have reviewed the scholarly literature on supportive communication and positioned this work in the context of the older, larger tradition of research on social support. We have emphasized the distinctiveness of studying social support as communication, the theoretical and empirical contributions of scholars working from this perspective, and the many questions that remain to be addressed. Nonetheless, as we (Erina and Bo) write this conclusion, we are acutely aware of the 30-plus years of perspective on supportive communication that was lost with Brant's untimely death. Accordingly, we have chosen to use this remaining space to highlight a few themes we believe he would have emphasized in his own research and mentoring of new scholars over the next decade.

First, Brant would have urged scholars of supportive communication to continue improving on what they have already done best: identifying the characteristics of supportive messages and interactions that lead to better (and worse) outcomes and developing theory that explains why those characteristics have their effects, including why such effects may be variable across individuals and situations. A large part of his intellectual energy in the past several years was focused on the development of the dual-process theory of supportive message reception, and he hoped that his co-theorists, Graham Bodie, Amanda Holmstrom, and others, would carry this work forward. Correspondingly, he supported the development and use of research methods that expanded, combined, and improved on the traditional research paradigms (see Burleson, 2003a; Burleson & MacGeorge, 2002) to address increasingly sophisticated questions about cause and effect, mediation, and moderation (e.g., Feng & MacGeorge, 2010; Jones & Wirtz, 2007).

Second, Brant wanted to see further development and testing of theory to explain how and why supportive communication affects psychological and physical health outcomes. As we searched the literature to revise this chapter, he was extremely excited about the evidence, much of it recent, that supportive interactions affect physiological processes (e.g., CVR, cortisol levels) in direct and powerful ways. For him (and us), this work was a personal vindication of his long-held contention that social support is a *fundamentally* communicative process and that the health effects of social support stem in significant measure from enacted behaviors and their reception (see also Goldsmith, 2004). But he was also concerned about the lack of precision about communicative processes in work focused on health outcomes and wanted communication scholars to engage with the effort to specify what features or qualities of interactions were most strongly connected to health outcomes.

Third, as much as Brant loved and was identified with the study of emotional support, he was increasingly interested, and encouraged others to be interested, in other types of support. These included not only advice and esteem support, previously discussed, but also the concept of motivational support, which he had planned to examine as a Fulbright scholar doing research on peer support and excessive drinking among college students in the United States and Finland. In addition, in one of his last official acts as a faculty member, he proudly signed off on Jennifer McCullough's (2010) completed dissertation, which focuses on the idea of celebratory support. Instead of looking at how to make distressed people feel better, McCullough's work focuses on how we can communicate to enhance others' happiness about the good things that happen to them. Brant found this idea truly delightful and believed that it was worthy of further empirical investigation.

Finally, Brant would have encouraged you, the reader, to take to heart the moral warrant for the study of supportive communication. He wanted to see more effort devoted to education and training in supportive communication and to the

development of effective social support interventions (Burleson, 2003a; Verderber, Verderber, & Berryman-Fink, 2009). He also wanted us to practice what we research and teach, imbuing our scholarship with personal, everyday commitment to supporting others as effectively as possible. His students, friends, and loved ones, including those writing this chapter, can attest to his powerful skills in providing support and the extent to which our lives are brighter and deeper because of the ways he chose to live what he studied. If you, too, will miss Brant and his work, please remember him not only in your choice of scholarly projects but in the way you comfort, advise, uplift, celebrate, and otherwise give to the people in your lives.

# References

Albrecht, T. L., & Adelman, M. B. (Eds.). (1987). *Communicating social support.* Newbury Park, CA: Sage.

Antonucci, T. C., & Israel, B. A. (1986). Verdicality of social support: A comparison of principal and network members' responses. *Journal of Consulting & Clinical Psychology, 54,* 432–437.

Applegate, J. L. (1980). Adaptive communication in educational contexts: A study of teachers' communicative strategies. *Communication Education, 29,* 158–170.

Applegate, J. L., Burleson, B. R., & Delia, J. G. (1992). Reflection-enhancing parenting as antecedent to children's social-cognitive and communicative development. In I. E. Sigel, A. V. McGillicuddy-Delisi, & J. J. Goodnow (Eds.), *Parental belief systems: The psychological consequences for children* (2nd ed., pp. 3–39). Hillsdale, NJ: Lawrence Erlbaum.

Asendorpf, J. B., & Wilpers, S. (2000). Attachment security and available support: Closely linked relationship qualities. *Journal of Social and Personal Relationships, 17,* 115–138.

Barak, A., Boniel-Nissim, M., & Suler, J. (2008). Fostering empowerment in online support groups. *Computers in Human Behavior, 24,* 1867–1883.

Barbee, A. P., & Cunningham, M. R. (1995). An experimental approach to social support communications:

Interactive coping in close relationships. In B. R. Burleson (Ed.), *Communication yearbook 18* (pp. 381–413). Thousand Oaks, CA: Sage.

Barbee, A. P., Cunningham, M. R., Winstead, B. A., Derlega, V. J., Gulley, M. R., Yankeelov, P. A., et al. (1993). Effects of gender role expectations on the social support process. *Journal of Social Issues, 49*(3), 175–190.

Barbee, A. P., Derlega, V. J., Sherburne, S. P., & Grimshaw, A. (1998). Helpful and unhelpful forms of social support for HIV-positive individuals. In V. J. Derlega & A. P. Barbee (Eds.), *HIV and social interaction* (pp. 83–105). Thousand Oaks, CA: Sage.

Barbee, A. P., Rowatt, T. L., & Cunningham, M. R. (1998). When a friend is in need: Feelings about seeking, giving, and receiving social support. In P. A. Andersen & L. K. Guerrero (Eds.), *Handbook of communication and emotion: Research, theory, applications, and contexts* (pp. 281–301). San Diego, CA: Academic Press.

Barrera, M. (1981). Social support in the adjustment of pregnant adolescents. In B. H. Gottlieb (Ed.), *Social networks and social support* (pp. 69–96). Beverly Hills, CA: Sage.

Barrera, M. (1986). Distinctions between social support concepts, measures, and models. *American Journal of Community Psychology, 14,* 413–445.

Barrera, M., Sandler, I. N., & Ramsey, T. B. (1981). Preliminary development of a scale of social support: Studies on college students. *American Journal of Community Psychology, 9,* 435–447.

Beehr, T. A., Bowling, N. A., & Bennett, M. M. (2010). Occupational stress and failures of social support: When helping hurts. *Journal of Occupational Health Psychology, 15,* 45–59.

Berkman, L., & Syme, S. L. (1979). Social networks, host resistance, and mortality: A nine-year follow-up study of Alameda County residents. *American Journal of Epidemiology, 109,* 186–204.

Berkman, L. F., Glass, T., Brissette, I., & Seeman, T. E. (2000). From social integration to health: Durkheim in the new millennium. *Social Science & Medicine, 51,* 843–857.

Berkman, L. F., Melchior, M., Chastang, J.-F., Niedhammer, I., Leclerc, A., & Goldberg, M. (2004). Social integration and mortality: A prospective study of French employees of Electricity of France–Gas of France. *American Journal of Epidemiology, 159,* 167–174.

Bertillion, M. J. (1879). Les celibataires, les veufs and les divorces au point de vue du marriage [Single persons, widowers and divorcees in view of marriage]. *Revue Scientifique, 16,* 776–783.

Bodie, G. D., & Burleson, B. R. (2008). Explaining variations in the effects of supportive messages: A dual-process framework. In C. Beck (Ed.), *Communication yearbook 32* (pp. 354–398). New York: Routledge.

Bodie, G. D., Burleson, B. R., Gill-Rosier, J., McCullough, J. D., Holmstrom, A. J., Rack, J. J., Hanasono, L., & Mincy, J. (2011). Explaining the impact of attachment style on evaluations of supportive messages: A dual-process framework. *Communication Research, 38,* 228–247.

Bodie, G. D., Burleson, B. R., & Jones, S. M. (in press). Explaining the relationships among supportive message quality, evaluations, and outcomes: A dual-process approach. *Communication Monographs.*

Bolger, N., Zuckerman, A., & Kessler, R. C. (2000). Invisible support and adjustment to stress. *Journal of Personality and Social Psychology, 79,* 953–961.

Bonaccio, S., & Dalal, R. S. (2006). Advice taking and decision-making: An integrative review of the literature. *Organizational Behavior and Human Decision Processes, 101,* 127–151.

Bonaccio, S., & Dalal, R. S. (2010). Evaluating advisors: A policy-capturing study under conditions of complete and missing information. *Journal of Behavioral Decision-Making, 23,* 227–249.

Boudioni, M., McPherson, K., Moynihan, C., Melia, J., Boulton, M., Leydon, G., et al. (2001). Do men with prostate or colorectal cancer seek different information and support from women with cancer? *British Journal of Cancer, 85,* 641–648.

Bradbury, T. N., Cohan, C. L., & Karney, B. R. (2000). Optimizing longitudinal research for understanding and preventing marital dysfunction. In T. N. Bradbury (Ed.), *The developmental course of marital dysfunction* (pp. 279–311). Cambridge, UK: Cambridge University Press.

Brashers, D., Neidig, J., & Goldsmith, D. (2004). Social support and the management of uncertainty for people living with HIV or AIDS. *Health Communication, 16,* 305–331.

Brissette, I., Cohen, S., & Seeman, T. E. (2000). Measuring social integration and social networks. In S. Cohen, L. G. Underwood, & B. H. Gottlieb

(Eds.), *Social support measurement and intervention* (pp. 29–54). New York: Oxford University Press.

Brock, R. L., & Lawrence, E. (2008). A longitudinal investigation of stress spillover in marriage: Does spousal support adequacy buffer the effects? *Journal of Family Psychology, 22,* 11–20.

Brock, R. L., & Lawrence, E. (2010). Support adequacy in marriage: Observing the platinum rule. In K. T. Sullivan & J. Davila (Eds.), *Support processes in intimate relationships* (pp. 3–25). New York: Oxford University Press.

Brown, P., & Levinson, S. C. (1987). *Politeness: Some universals in language usage.* Cambridge, UK: Cambridge University Press.

Burleson, B. R. (1982). The development of comforting communication skills in childhood and adolescence. *Child Development, 53,* 1578–1588.

Burleson, B. R. (1984). Comforting communication. In H. E. Sypher & J. L. Applegate (Eds.), *Communication by children and adults: Social cognitive and strategic processes* (pp. 63–104). Beverly Hills, CA: Sage.

Burleson, B. R. (1985). The production of comforting messages: Social-cognitive foundations. *Journal of Language and Social Psychology, 4,* 253–273.

Burleson, B. R. (1987). Cognitive complexity. In J. C. McCroskey & J. A. Daly (Eds.), *Personality and interpersonal communication* (pp. 305–349). Newbury Park, CA: Sage.

Burleson, B. R. (1990). Comforting as everyday social support: Relational consequences of supportive behaviors. In S. Duck (Ed.), *Personal relationships and social support* (pp. 66–82). London: Sage.

Burleson, B. R. (1994). Comforting messages: Features, functions, and outcomes. In J. A. Daly & J. M. Wiemann (Eds.), *Strategic interpersonal communication* (pp. 135–161). Hillsdale, NJ: Lawrence Erlbaum.

Burleson, B. R. (2003a). Emotional support skills. In J. O. Greene & B. R. Burleson (Eds.), *Handbook of communication and social interaction skills* (pp. 551–594). Mahwah, NJ: Lawrence Erlbaum.

Burleson, B. R. (2003b). The experience and effects of emotional support: What the study of cultural and gender differences can tell us about close relationships, emotion, and interpersonal communication. *Personal Relationships, 10,* 1–23.

Burleson, B. R. (2007). Constructivism: A general theory of communication skill. In B. B. Whaley & W. Samter (Eds.), *Explaining communication:*

*Contemporary theories and exemplars* (pp. 105–128). Mahwah, NJ: Lawrence Erlbaum.

Burleson, B. R. (2008a). *Does expressive orientation mediate sex differences in perceived support availability?* Unpublished manuscript, Purdue University, West Lafayette, IN.

Burleson, B. R. (2008b). What counts as effective emotional support? Explorations of individual and situational differences. In M. T. Motley (Ed.), *Studies in applied interpersonal communication* (pp. 207–227). Thousand Oaks, CA: Sage.

Burleson, B. R. (2010). Explaining recipient responses to supportive messages: Development and tests of a dual-process theory. In S. W. Smith & S. R. Wilson (Eds.), *New directions in interpersonal communication* (pp. 159–179). Thousand Oaks, CA: Sage.

Burleson, B. R., Albrecht, T. L., Goldsmith, D. J., & Sarason, I. G. (1994). The communication of social support. In B. R. Burleson, T. L. Albrecht, & I. G. Sarason (Eds.), *Communication of social support: Messages, interactions, relationships, and community* (pp. xi–xxx). Thousand Oaks, CA: Sage.

Burleson, B. R., Albrecht, T. L., & Sarason, I. G. (Eds.). (1994). *Communication of social support: Messages, interactions, relationships, and community.* Thousand Oaks, CA: Sage.

Burleson, B. R., & Caplan, S. E. (1998). Cognitive complexity. In J. C. McCroskey, J. A. Daly, M. M. Martin, & M. J. Beatty (Eds.), *Communication and personality: Trait perspectives* (pp. 230–286). Cresskill, NJ: Hampton Press.

Burleson, B. R., Delia, J. G., & Applegate, J. L. (1992). Effects of maternal communication and children's social-cognitive and communication skills on children's acceptance by the peer group. *Family Relations, 41,* 264–272.

Burleson, B. R., Delia, J. G., & Applegate, J. L. (1995). The socialization of person-centered communication: Parental contributions to the social-cognitive and communication skills of their children. In M. A. Fitzpatrick & A. L. Vangelisti (Eds.), *Explaining family interactions* (pp. 34–76). Thousand Oaks, CA: Sage.

Burleson, B. R., & Denton, W. H. (1997). The relationship between communication skills and marital satisfaction: Some moderating effects. *Journal of Marriage and the Family, 59,* 884–902.

Burleson, B. R., & Goldsmith, D. J. (1998). How the comforting process works: Alleviating emotional distress through conversationally induced reappraisals. In P. A. Andersen & L. K. Guerrero (Eds.), *Handbook of communication and emotion: Research, theory, applications, and contexts* (pp. 245–280). San Diego, CA: Academic Press.

Burleson, B. R., & Hanasono, L. K. (2010). Explaining cultural and sex differences in responses to supportive communication: A dual-process approach. In K. T. Sullivan & J. Davila (Eds.), *Support processes in intimate relationships* (pp. 291–317). New York: Oxford University Press.

Burleson, B. R., Hanasono, L. K., Bodie, G. D., Holmstrom, A. J., Rack, J. J., Rosier, J. G., et al. (2009). Explaining gender differences in responses to supportive messages: Two tests of a dual-process approach. *Sex Roles, 61,* 265–280.

Burleson, B. R., Holmstrom, A. J., & Gilstrap, C. M. (2005). "Guys can't say *that* to guys": Four experiments assessing the normative motivation account for deficiencies in the emotional support provided by men. *Communication Monographs, 72,* 468–501.

Burleson, B. R., & Kunkel, A. W. (1996). The socialization of emotional support skills in childhood. In G. R. Pierce, B. R. Sarason, & I. G. Sarason (Eds.), *Handbook of social support and the family* (pp. 105–140). New York: Plenum Press.

Burleson, B. R., & Kunkel, A. W. (2002). Parental and peer contributions to the emotional support skills of the child: From whom do children learn to express support? *Journal of Family Communication, 2,* 79–97.

Burleson, B. R., & Kunkel, A. W. (2006). Revisiting the different cultures thesis: An assessment of sex differences and similarities in supportive communication. In K. Dindia & D. J. Canary (Eds.), *Sex differences and similarities in communication* (2nd ed., pp. 137–159). Mahwah, NJ: Lawrence Erlbaum.

Burleson, B. R., & MacGeorge, E. L. (2002). Supportive communication. In M. L. Knapp & J. A. Daly (Eds.), *Handbook of interpersonal communication* (3rd ed., pp. 374–424). Thousand Oaks, CA: Sage.

Burleson, B. R., & Mortenson, S. R. (2003). Explaining cultural differences in evaluations of emotional support behaviors: Exploring the mediating influences of value systems and interaction goals. *Communication Research, 30,* 113–146.

Burleson, B. R., & Planalp, S. (2000). Producing emotion(al) messages. *Communication Theory, 10,* 221–250.

Burleson, B. R., & Rack, J. J. (2008). Constructivism theory. In L. A. Baxter & D. O. Braithwaite (Eds.), *Engaging theories in interpersonal communication* (pp. 51–64). Thousand Oaks, CA: Sage.

Burleson, B. R., & Samter, W. (1985a). Consistencies in theoretical and naive evaluations of comforting messages. *Communication Monographs, 52,* 103–123.

Burleson, B. R., & Samter, W. (1985b). Individual differences in the perception of comforting messages: An exploratory investigation. *Central States Speech Journal, 36,* 39–50.

Burleson, B. R., Samter, W., Jones, S. M., Kunkel, A. W., Holmstrom, A. J., Mortenson, S. T., et al. (2005). Which comforting messages *really* work best? A different perspective on Lemieux and Tighe's "receiver perspective." *Communication Research Reports, 22,* 87–100.

Caplan, G. (1974). *Support systems and community mental health.* New York: Behavioral Publications.

Caplan, G. (1976). The family as a support system. In G. Caplan & M. Killilea (Eds.), *Support systems and mutual help* (pp. 19–36). New York: Grune & Stratton.

Caplan, S. E., & Samter, W. (1999). The role of facework in younger and older adults' evaluations of social support messages. *Communication Quarterly, 47,* 245–264.

Carels, R. A., & Baucom, D. H. (1999). Support in marriage: Factors associated with on-line perceptions of support helpfulness. *Journal of Family Psychology, 13,* 131–144.

Carkhuff, R. R., & Berenson, B. G. (1977). *Beyond counseling and therapy* (2nd ed.). New York: Holt, Rinehart & Winston.

Cassel, J. (1976). The contribution of the social environment to host resistance. *American Journal of Epidemiology, 104,* 107–123.

Cheuk, W. H., & Rosen, S. (1993). How efficacious, caring Samaritans cope when their help is rejected unexpectedly. *Current Psychology, 12,* 99–112.

Cobb, S. (1976). Social support as a moderator of life stress. *Psychosomatic Medicine, 38,* 300–314.

Cohen, S. (1988). Psychosocial models of the role of social support in the etiology of physical disease. *Health Psychology, 7,* 269–297.

Cohen, S., Gottlieb, B. H., & Underwood, L. G. (2000). Social relationships and health. In S. Cohen, L. G. Underwood, & B. H. Gottlieb (Eds.), *Social support measurement and intervention* (pp. 3–25). New York: Oxford University Press.

Cohen, S., & Janicki-Deverts, D. (2009). Can we improve our physical health by altering our social networks? *Perspectives on Psychological Science, 4,* 375–378.

Cohen, S., & Lemay, E. P. (2007). Why would social networks be linked to affect and health practices? *Health Psychology, 25,* 410–417.

Cohen, S., & McKay, G. (1984). Social support, stress, and the buffering hypothesis: A theoretical analysis. In A. Baum, J. E. Singer, & S. E. Taylor (Eds.), *Handbook of psychology and health* (Vol. 4, pp. 253–263). Hillsdale, NJ: Lawrence Erlbaum.

Cohen, S., & Wills, T. A. (1985). Stress, social support, and the buffering hypothesis. *Psychological Bulletin, 98,* 310–357.

Colarossi, L. G., & Eccles, J. S. (2003). Differential effects of support providers on adolescents' mental health. *Social Work Research, 27,* 19–30.

Collins, N. L., & Feeney, B. C. (2010). An attachment theoretical perspective on social support dynamics in couples: Normative processes and individual differences. In K. T. Sullivan & J. Davila (Eds.), *Support processes in intimate relationships* (pp. 89–120). New York: Oxford University Press.

Copenhaver, M. M., Lash, S. J., & Eisler, R. M. (2000). Masculine gender-role stress, anger, and male intimate abusiveness: Implications for men's relationships. *Sex Roles, 42,* 405–416.

Cortina, L. M. (2004). Hispanic perspectives on sexual harassment and social support. *Personality and Social Psychology Bulletin, 30,* 570–584.

Craig, F. W., & Deichert, N. T. (2002). Can male-provided social support buffer the cardiovascular responsivity to stress in men? It depends on the nature of the support provided. *International Journal of Men's Health, 1,* 105–118.

Cramer, D. (1994). Self-esteem and Rogers' core conditions in close friends: A latent variable path analysis of panel data. *Counseling Psychology Quarterly, 7,* 327–337.

Cramer, D. (2000). Social desirability, adequacy of social support and mental health. *Journal of Community and Applied Social Psychology, 10,* 465–474.

Cramer, D. (2003). Facilitativeness, conflict, demand for approval, self-esteem, and satisfaction with romantic relationships. *Journal of Psychology, 137,* 85–98.

Cramer, D., Henderson, S., & Scott, R. (1996). Mental health and adequacy of social support: A four-wave panel study. *British Journal of Social Psychology, 35,* 285–295.

Crocker, J., & Canevello, A. (2008). Creating and undermining social support in communal relationships: The role of compassionate and self-image goals. *Journal of Personality and Social Psychology, 95,* 555–575.

Cunningham, M. R., & Barbee, A. P. (2000). Social support. In C. Hendrick & S. S. Hendrick (Eds.), *Close relationships: A sourcebook* (pp. 272–285). Thousand Oaks, CA: Sage.

Cutrona, C. E. (1990). Stress and social support: In search of optimal matching. *Journal of Social and Clinical Psychology, 9,* 3–14.

Cutrona, C. E., & Russell, D. W. (1990). Types of social support and specific stress: Toward a theory of optimal matching. In B. R. Sarason, I. G. Sarason, & G. R. Pierce (Eds.), *Social support: An interactional view* (pp. 319–366). New York: Wiley.

Cutrona, C. E., Russell, D. W., & Gardner, K. A. (2005). The relationship enhancement model of social support. In T. A. Revenson, K. Kayser, & G. Bodenmann (Eds.), *Couples coping with stress* (pp. 3–23). Washington, DC: American Psychological Association.

Cutrona, C. E., Shaffer, P. A., Wesner, K. A., & Gardner, K. A. (2007). Optimally matching support and perceived spousal sensitivity. *Journal of Family Psychology, 21,* 754–758.

Cutrona, C. E., & Suhr, J. A. (1994). Social support communication in the context of marriage: An analysis of couples' supportive interactions. In B. R. Burleson, T. L. Albrecht, & I. G. Sarason (Eds.), *Communication of social support: Messages, interactions, relationships, and community* (pp. 113–135). Thousand Oaks, CA: Sage.

Cutrona, C. E., Suhr, J. A., & MacFarlane, R. (1990). Interpersonal transactions and the psychological sense of support. In S. Duck (Ed.), *Personal relationships and social support* (pp. 30–45). London: Sage.

Dakof, G. A., & Taylor, S. E. (1990). Victims' perceptions of support attempts: What is helpful from whom? *Journal of Personality and Social Psychology, 58,* 80–89.

Day, A. L., & Livingstone, H. A. (2003). Gender differences in perceptions of stressors and utilization of social support among university students. *Canadian Journal of Behavioural Science, 35,* 73–83.

Dillard, J. P. (2008). Goals-plan-action theory of message production. In L. A. Baxter & D. O. Braithwaite

(Eds.), *Engaging theories in interpersonal communication: Multiple perspectives* (pp. 65–76). Thousand Oaks, CA: Sage.

DiMatteo, M. R. (2004). Social support and patient adherence to medical treatment: A meta-analysis. *Health Psychology, 23,* 207–218.

Dirks, S. E., & Metts, S. (2010). An investigation of the support process: Decision, enactment, and outcome. *Communication Studies, 61,* 391–411.

Dunkel-Schetter, C., & Skokan, L. A. (1990). Determinants of social support provision in personal relationships. *Journal of Social and Personal Relationships, 7,* 437–450.

Eagly, A. H. (2009). The his and hers of prosocial behavior: An examination of the social psychology of gender. *American Psychologist, 64,* 644–658.

Ehninger, D., & Brockriede, W. (1978). *Decision by debate* (2nd ed.). New York: Harper & Row.

Eisenberg, N. (2002). Empathy-related emotional responses, altruism, and their socialization. In R. J. Davidson & A. Harrington (Eds.), *Visions of compassion: Western scientists and Tibetan Buddhists examine human nature* (pp. 131–164). London: Oxford University Press.

Eisenberger, N. I., Taylor, S. E., Gable, S. L., Hilmert, C. J., & Lieberman, M. D. (2007). Neural pathways link social support to attenuated neuroendocrine stress responses. *Neuroimage, 35,* 1601–1612.

Elliott, R. (1985). Helpful and nonhelpful events in brief counseling interviews: An empirical taxonomy. *Journal of Counseling Psychology, 32,* 307–322.

Farr, W. (1975). Marriage and mortality. In N. Humphreys (Ed.), *Vital statistics: A memorial volume of selections from the reports and writings of William Farr* (pp. 469–476). Metuchen, NJ: Scarecrow Press. (Original work published 1885)

Feng, B. (2009). Testing an integrated model of advice-giving in supportive interactions. *Human Communication Research, 35,* 115–129.

Feng, B., & Burleson, B. R. (2006). Exploring the support-seeking process across cultures: Toward an integrated analysis of similarities and differences. In M. P. Orbe, B. J. Allen, & L. A. Flores (Eds.), *The same and different: Acknowledging the diversity within and between cultural groups* (pp. 243–266). Washington, DC: National Communication Association.

Feng, B., & Burleson, B. R. (2008). The effects of argument explicitness on responses to advice in supportive interactions. *Communication Research, 35,* 849–874.

Feng, B., & Lee, K. J. (2010). The influence of thinking styles on responses to supportive messages. *Communication Studies, 61,* 224–238.

Feng, B., & MacGeorge, E. L. (2006). Predicting receptiveness to advice: Characteristics of the problem, the advice-giver, and the recipient. *Southern Communication Journal, 71,* 67–85.

Feng, B., & MacGeorge, E. L. (2010). The influences of message and source factors on advice outcomes. *Communication Research, 37,* 576–598.

Figueiredo, M. I., Fries, E., & Ingram, K. M. (2004). The role of disclosure patterns and unsupportive social interactions in the well-being of breast cancer patients. *Psycho-Oncology, 13,* 96–105.

Fiske, S. T., & Taylor, S. E. (2007). *Social cognition: From brains to culture.* Boston: McGraw-Hill.

Floyd, K., & Riforgiate, S. (2008). Affectionate communication received from spouses predicts stress hormone levels in healthy adults. *Communication Monographs, 75,* 351–368.

Fontana, A. M., Diegman, T., Villeneuve, A., & Lepore, S. J. (1999). Nonevaluative social support reduces cardiovascular reactivity in young women during acutely stressful performance situations. *Journal of Behavioral Medicine, 22,* 75–91.

Ford, L. A., & Ellis, B. H. (1998). A preliminary analysis of memorable support and nonsupport messages received by nurses in acute care settings. *Health Communication, 10,* 37–63.

Fritz, H. L., Nagurney, A. J., & Helgeson, V. S. (2003). Social interactions and cardiovascular reactivity during problem disclosure among friends. *Personality and Social Psychology Bulletin, 29,* 713–725.

Fruzzetti, A. E., & Worrall, J. M. (2010). Accurate expression and validating responses: A transactional model for understanding individual and relationship distress. In K. T. Sullivan & J. Davila (Eds.), *Support processes in intimate relationships* (pp. 121–150). New York: Oxford University Press.

Gao, G. (1996). Self and OTHER: A Chinese perspective on interpersonal relationships. In W. B. Gudykunst, S. Ting-Toomey, & T. Nishida (Eds.), *Communication in personal relationships across cultures* (pp. 81–101). Thousand Oaks, CA: Sage.

Gerin, W., Pieper, C., Levy, R. I., & Pickering, T. G. (1992). Social support in social interaction: A moderator of cardiovascular reactivity. *Psychosomatic Medicine, 54,* 324–336.

Goldsmith, D. J. (1994). The role of facework in supportive communication. In B. R. Burleson, T. L. Albrecht, & I. G. Sarason (Eds.), *Communication of social support: Messages, interactions, relationships, and community* (pp. 29–49). Thousand Oaks, CA: Sage.

Goldsmith, D. J. (1995). The communicative microdynamics of support. In B. R. Burleson (Ed.), *Communication yearbook 18* (pp. 414–433). Thousand Oaks, CA: Sage.

Goldsmith, D. J. (2000). Soliciting advice: The role of sequential placement in mitigating face threat. *Communication Monographs, 67,* 1–19.

Goldsmith, D. J. (2004). *Communicating social support.* New York: Cambridge University Press.

Goldsmith, D. J., & Fitch, K. (1997). The normative context of advice as social support. *Human Communication Research, 23,* 454–476.

Goldsmith, D. J., & MacGeorge, E. L. (2000). The impact of politeness and relationship on perceived quality of advice about a problem. *Human Communication Research, 26,* 234–263.

Gottlieb, B. H. (2000). Selecting and planning support interventions. In S. Cohen, L. G. Underwood, & B. H. Gottlieb (Eds.), *Social support measurement and intervention* (pp. 195–220). New York: Oxford University Press.

Graetz, B. W., Shute, R. H., & Sawyer, M. G. (2000). An Australian study of adolescents with cystic fibrosis: Perceived supportive and nonsupportive behaviors from families and friends and psychological adjustment. *Journal of Adolescent Health, 26,* 64–69.

Grant, A. M. (2010). A little thanks goes a long way: Explaining why gratitude expressions motivate prosocial behavior. *Journal of Personality and Social Psychology, 98,* 946–955.

Greenberg, L. S., Rice, L. N., & Elliott, R. (1993). *Facilitating emotional change: The moment-by-moment process.* New York: Guilford Press.

Gruenewald, T. L., & Seeman, T. E. (2010). Social support and physical health: Links and mechanisms. In A. Steptoe (Ed.), *Handbook of behavioral medicine* (pp. 224–236). New York: Springer Science.

Gudykunst, W. B., & Matsumoto, Y. (1996). Cross-cultural variability of communication in personal relationships. In W. B. Gudykunst, S. Ting-Toomey, & T. Nishida (Eds.), *Communication in personal relationships across cultures* (pp. 19–56). Thousand Oaks, CA: Sage.

Gump, B. B., Polk, D. E., Kamarck, T. W., & Shiffman, S. M. (2001). Partner interactions are associated with reduced blood pressure in the natural environment: Ambulatory monitoring evidence from a healthy, multiethnic adult sample. *Psychosomatic Medicine, 63,* 423–433.

Haber, M. G., Cohen, J. L., Lucas, T., & Baltes, B. (2007). The relationship between self-reported received and perceived social support: A meta-analytic review. *American Journal of Community Psychology, 39,* 133–144.

Hale, J. L., Tighe, M. R., & Mongeau, P. A. (1997). Effects of event type and sex on comforting messages. *Communication Research Reports, 14,* 214–220.

Harlow, R. E., & Cantor, N. (1995). To whom do people turn when things go poorly: Task orientational and functional social contacts. *Journal of Personality and Social Psychology, 69,* 329–340.

Hart, C. H., Newell, L. D., & Olsen, S. F. (2003). Parenting skills and social-communicative competence in childhood. In J. O. Greene & B. R. Burleson (Eds.), *Handbook of communication and social interaction skills* (pp. 753–799). Mahwah, NJ: Lawrence Erlbaum.

Helgeson, V. S., Novak, S. A., Lepore, S. J., & Eton, D. T. (2004). Spouse social control efforts: Relations to health behavior and well-being among men with prostate cancer. *Journal of Social and Personal Relationships, 21,* 53–68.

Heller, K., & Rook, K. S. (2001). Distinguishing the theoretical functions of social ties: Implications for support interventions. In B. R. Sarason & S. Duck (Eds.), *Personal relationships: Implications for clinical and community psychology* (pp. 119–139). Chichester, UK: Wiley.

Hill, C. A. (1996). Interpersonal and dispositional influences on problem-related interactions. *Journal of Research in Personality, 30,* 1–22.

Hobfoll, S. E. (2009). Social support: The movie. *Journal of Social and Personal Relationships, 26,* 93–101.

Hofstede, G. (1991). *Cultures and organizations: Software of the mind.* London: McGraw-Hill.

Holmstrom, A. J., & Burleson, B. R. (2011). An initial test of a cognitive-emotional theory of esteem support messages. *Communication Research, 38,* 326–355.

Holmstrom, A. J., Burleson, B. R., & Jones, S. M. (2005). Some consequences for helpers who deliver "cold comfort": Why it's worse for women than men to be inept when providing emotional support. *Sex Roles, 53,* 153–172.

Holt-Lunstad, J. L., Uchino, B. N., Smith, T. W., & Hicks, A. (2007). On the importance of relationship quality: The impact of ambivalence in friendships on cardiovascular functioning. *Annals of Behavioral Medicine, 33,* 278–290.

Horowitz, L. M., Krasnoperova, E. N., Tater, D. G., Hansen, M. B., Person, E. A., Galvin, K. L., et al. (2001). The way to console may depend on the goal: Experimental studies of social support. *Journal of Experimental Social Psychology, 37,* 49–61.

House, J. S. (1981). *Work stress and social support.* Reading, MA: Addison-Wesley.

Ikeda, A., & Kawachi, I. (2010). Social networks and health. In A. Steptoe (Ed.), *Handbook of behavioral medicine: Methods and applications* (pp. 237–262). New York: Springer.

Jefferson, G. (1988). On the sequential organization of troubles-talk in ordinary conversation. *Social Problems, 35,* 418–441.

Jefferson, G., & Lee, J. R. E. (1992). The rejection of advice: Managing the problematic convergence of a "troubles-telling" and a "service encounter." In P. Drew & J. Heritage (Eds.), *Talk at work: Interaction in institutional settings* (pp. 521–548). Cambridge, UK: Cambridge University Press.

Johnson, S. L., Meyer, B., Winett, C., & Small, J. (2000). Social support and self-esteem predict changes in bipolar depression but not mania. *Journal of Affective Disorders, 58,* 79–86.

Joiner, T. E. (2000). Depression's vicious scree: Self-propagating and erosive processes in depression. *Clinical Psychology: Science and Practice, 7,* 203–218.

Jones, S. M. (2004). Putting the person into person-centered and immediate emotional support: Emotional change and perceived helper competence as outcomes of comforting in helping situations. *Communication Research, 31,* 338–360.

Jones, S. M., & Burleson, B. R. (1997). The impact of situational variables on helpers' perceptions of comforting messages: An attributional analysis. *Communication Research, 24,* 530–555.

Jones, S. M., & Burleson, B. R. (2003). Effects of helper and recipient sex on the experience and outcomes of comforting messages: An experimental investigation. *Sex Roles, 48,* 1–19.

Jones, S. M., & Guerrero, L. A. (2001). The effects of nonverbal immediacy and verbal person centeredness in the emotional support process. *Human Communication Research, 27,* 567–596.

Jones, S. M., & Wirtz, J. (2006). How *does* the comforting process work?: An empirical test of an appraisal-based model of comforting. *Human Communication Research, 32,* 217–243.

Jones, S. M., & Wirtz, J. (2007). "*Sad monkey see, monkey do*": Nonverbal matching in emotional support encounters. *Communication Studies, 58,* 71–86.

Karlin, W. A., Brondolo, E., & Schwartz, J. (2003). Workplace social support and ambulatory cardiovascular activity in New York City Traffic Agents. *Psychosomatic Medicine, 65,* 167–176.

Kawachi, L., & Berkman, L. F. (2001). Social ties and mental health. *Journal of Urban Health, 78,* 458–467.

Kessler, R. C. (1992). Perceived support and adjustment to stress. In H. O. F. Veiel & U. Baumann (Eds.), *The meaning and measurement of social support* (pp. 259–271). New York: Hemisphere.

Kiecolt-Glaser, J. K., Gouin, J.-P., & Hantsoo, L. (2010). Close relationships, inflammation, and health. *Neuroscience and Biobehavioral Reviews, 35,* 33–38.

Kiecolt-Glaser, J. K., McGuire, L., Robles, T. F., & Glaser, R. (2002). Emotions, morbidity, and mortality: New perspectives from psychoneuroimmunology. *Annual Review of Psychology, 53,* 83–107.

Kim, H. S., Sherman, D. K., & Taylor, S. E. (2008). Culture and social support. *American Psychologist, 63,* 518–526.

Krantz, D. S., & McCeney, M. K. (2002). Effects of psychological and social factors on organic disease: A critical assessment of research on coronary heart disease. *Annual Review of Psychology, 53,* 341–369.

Kreps, G. L. (2003). The impact of communication on cancer risk, incidence, morbidity, mortality, and quality of life. *Health Communication, 15,* 161–170.

Kulik, J. A., & Mahler, H. I. M. (1993). Emotional support as a moderator of adjustment and compliance after coronary artery bypass surgery: A longitudinal study. *Journal of Behavioral Medicine, 16,* 45–61.

Kunkel, A. W., & Burleson, B. R. (1999). Assessing explanations for sex differences in emotional support: A test of the different cultures and skill specialization accounts. *Human Communication Research, 25,* 307–340.

Lakey, B., & Cohen, S. (2000). Social support theory and measurement. In S. Cohen, L. G. Underwood, & B. H. Gottlieb (Eds.), *Social support measurement and intervention* (pp. 29–52). New York: Oxford University Press.

Lakey, B., & Lutz, C. J. (1996). Social support and preventive and therapeutic interventions. In G. R. Pierce,

B. R. Sarason, & I. G. Sarason (Eds.), *Handbook of social support and the family* (pp. 435–465). New York: Plenum Press.

Lakey, B., Orehek, E., Hain, K. L., & VanVleet, M. (2010). Enacted support's links to negative affect and perceived support are more consistent with theory when social influences are isolated from trait influences. *Personality and Social Psychology Bulletin, 36,* 132–142.

Lazarus, R. S. (1991). *Emotion and adaptation.* New York: Oxford University Press.

Lazarus, R. S., & Folkman, S. (1984). *Stress, appraisal, and coping.* New York: Springer.

Lewis, M. A., & Rook, K. S. (1999). Social control in personal relationships: Impact on health behaviors and psychological distress. *Health Psychology, 18,* 63–71.

Li, M., & Yang, Y. (2009). Determinants of problem solving, social support seeking, and avoidance: A path analytic model. *International Journal of Stress Management, 16,* 155–176.

MacGeorge, E. L. (2001). Support providers' interaction goals: The influence of attributions and emotions. *Communication Monographs, 68,* 72–97.

MacGeorge, E. L., Clark, R. A., & Gillihan, S. J. (2002). Sex differences in the provision of skillful emotional support: The mediating role of self-efficacy. *Communication Reports, 15,* 17–28.

MacGeorge, E. L., Feng, B., Butler, G. L., & Budarz, S. K. (2004). Understanding advice in supportive interactions: Beyond the facework and message evaluation paradigm. *Human Communication Research, 30,* 42–70.

MacGeorge, E. L., Feng, B., & Thompson, E. R. (2008). "Good" and "bad" advice: How to advise more effectively. In M. T. Motley (Ed.), *Studies in applied interpersonal communication* (pp. 145–164). Thousand Oaks, CA: Sage.

MacGeorge, E. L., Gillihan, S. J., Samter, W., & Clark, R. A. (2003). Skill deficit or differential motivation? Accounting for sex differences in the provision of emotional support. *Communication Research, 30,* 272–303.

MacGeorge, E. L., Graves, A. R., Feng, B., Gillihan, S. J., & Burleson, B. R. (2004). The myth of gender cultures: Similarities outweigh differences in men's and women's provision of and responses to supportive communication. *Sex Roles, 50,* 143–175.

MacGeorge, E. L., Lichtman, R., & Pressey, L. (2002). The evaluation of advice in supportive interactions:

Facework and contextual factors. *Human Communication Research, 28,* 451–463.

MacGeorge, E. L., Samter, W., & Gillihan, S. J. (2005). Academic stress, supportive communication, and health. *Communication Education, 54,* 365–372.

Marsella, A. J. (1993). Counseling and psychotherapy with Japanese Americans: Cross-cultural considerations. *American Journal of Orthopsychiatry, 63,* 200–208.

McConatha, J. T., Lightner, E., & Deaner, S. L. (1994). Culture, age, and gender as variables in the expression of emotions. *Journal of Social Behavior & Personality, 9,* 481–488.

McCullough, J. D. (2010). "Celebrate good times, come on!": Defining effective message features of celebratory support. Unpublished dissertation, Department of Communication, Purdue University, West Lafayette, IN.

McNicholas, S. L. (2002). Social support and positive health practices. *Western Journal of Nursing Research, 24,* 772–787.

Metts, S., & Cupach, W. R. (2008). Face theory. In L. A. Baxter & D. O. Braithwaite (Eds.), *Engaging theories in interpersonal communication: Multiple perspectives* (pp. 203–214). Thousand Oaks, CA: Sage.

Mortenson, S. T., Burleson, B. R., Feng, B., & Liu, M. (2009). Cultural similarities and differences in seeking social support as a means of coping: A comparison of Americans and Chinese and an evaluation of the mediating effects of self-construal. *Journal of International and Intercultural Communication, 2,* 208–239.

Moss, G. E. (1973). *Illness, immunity, and social interaction.* New York: Wiley.

Olds, D., Eckenrode, J., Henderson, C. R., Jr., Kitzman, H., Powers, J., Cole, R., et al. (1997). Long-term effects of home visitation on maternal life course and child abuse and neglect: 15-year follow-up of a randomized trial. *Journal of the American Medical Association, 278,* 637–643.

Pasch, L. A., Bradbury, T. N., & Davila, J. (1997). Gender, negative affectivity, and observed social support behavior in marital interaction. *Personal Relationships, 4,* 361–378.

Pauley, P. M., & Hesse, C. (2009). The effects of social support, depression, and stress on drinking behaviors in a college student sample. *Communication Studies, 60,* 493–508.

Petty, R. E., Rucker, D. D., Bizer, G. Y., & Cacioppo, J. T. (2004). The elaboration likelihood model of persuasion. In J. S. Seiter & R. H. Gass (Eds.), *Perspectives on persuasion, social influence, and compliance gaining* (pp. 65–89). Boston: Allyn & Bacon.

Priem, J. S., & Solomon, D. H. (2009). Comforting apprehensive communicators: The effects of reappraisal and distraction on cortisol levels among students in a public speaking class. *Communication Quarterly, 57,* 259–281.

Prinstein, M. J., Borelli, J. L., Cheah, C. S. L., Simon, V. A., & Aikins, J. W. (2005). Adolescent girls' interpersonal vulnerability to depressive symptoms: A longitudinal examination of reassurance-seeking and peer relationships. *Journal of Abnormal Psychology, 114,* 676–688.

Proctor, A., Morse, J. M., & Khonsari, E. S. (1996). Sounds of comfort in the trauma center: How nurses talk to patients in pain. *Social Science and Medicine, 42*(12), 1669–1680.

Rack, J. J., Burleson, B. R., Bodie, G. D., Holmstrom, A. J., & Servaty-Seib, H. L. (2008). Bereaved adults' evaluations of grief management messages: Effects of message person centeredness, recipient individual differences, and contextual factors. *Death Studies, 32,* 399–427.

Ray, E. B. (1993). When the links become chains: Considering dysfunctions of supportive communication in the workplace. *Communication Monographs, 60,* 106–111.

Reevy, G. M., & Maslach, C. (2001). Use of social support: Gender and personality differences. *Sex Roles, 44,* 437–459.

Reis, H. T. (2001). Relationship experiences and emotional well-being. In C. D. Ryff & B. H. Singer (Eds.), *Emotion, social relationships, and health* (pp. 57–86). New York: Oxford University Press.

Reis, H. T., & Collins, N. (2000). Measuring relationship properties and interactions relevant to social support. In S. Cohen, L. G. Underwood, & B. H. Gottlieb (Eds.), *Social support measurement and intervention* (pp. 136–192). New York: Oxford University Press.

Reynolds, J. S., & Perrin, N. A. (2004). Mismatches in social support and psychosocial adjustment to breast cancer. *Health Psychology, 23,* 425–430.

Rini, C., & Dunkel-Schetter, C. (2010). The effectiveness of social support attempts in intimate relationships. In K. T. Sullivan & J. Davila (Eds.), *Support processes in intimate relationships* (pp. 26–67). New York: Oxford University Press.

Rini, C., Dunkel-Schetter, C., Hobel, C. J., Glynn, L. M., & Sandman, C. A. (2006). Effective social support: Antecedents and consequences of partner support during pregnancy. *Personal Relationships, 13,* 207–229.

Rogers, C. R. (1957). The necessary and sufficient conditions of therapeutic personality change. *Journal of Consulting Psychology, 21,* 95–103.

Roski, J., Schmid, L. A., & Lando, H. A. (1996). Long-term associations of helpful and harmful spousal behaviors with smoking cessation. *Addictive Behaviors, 21,* 173–185.

Saitzyk, A. R., Floyd, F. J., & Kroll, A. B. (1997). Sequential analysis of autonomy-interdependence and affiliation-disaffiliation in couples' social support interactions. *Personal Relationships, 4,* 341–360.

Saltzman, K. M., & Holahan, C. J. (2002). Social support, self-efficacy, and depressive symptoms: An integrative model. *Journal of Social and Clinical Psychology, 21,* 309–322.

Samter, W. (1989). *Communication skills predictive of interpersonal acceptance among college students in a group living situation: A sociometric study.* Unpublished doctoral dissertation, Purdue University, West Lafayette, IN.

Samter, W. (1994). Unsupportive relationships: Deficiencies in the support-giving skills of the lonely person's friends. In B. R. Burleson, T. L. Albrecht, & I. G. Sarason (Eds.), *The communication of social support: Messages, interactions, relationships, and community* (pp. 195–214). Thousand Oaks, CA: Sage.

Samter, W., & Burleson, B. R. (1984). Cognitive and motivational influences on spontaneous comforting behavior. *Human Communication Research, 11,* 231–260.

Samter, W., & Burleson, B. R. (1990, June). *The role of affectively oriented communication skills in the friendships of young adults: A sociometric study.* Paper presented at the International Communication Association, Dublin, Ireland.

Samter, W., Burleson, B. R., & Murphy, L. B. (1987). Comforting conversations: Effects of strategy type on evaluations of messages and message producers. *Southern Speech Communication Journal, 52,* 263–284.

Sandler, I. N., & Barrera, M., Jr. (1984). Toward a multimethod approach to assessing the effects of social support. *American Journal of Community Psychology, 12,* 37–52.

Sarason, B. R., Pierce, G. R., & Sarason, I. G. (1990). Social support: The sense of acceptance and the role of relationships. In B. R. Sarason, I. G. Sarason, & G. R. Pierce (Eds.), *Social support: An interactional view* (pp. 95–128). New York: Wiley.

Sarason, B. R., & Sarason, I. G. (2006). Close relationships and social support: Implications for the measurement of social support. In A. L. Vangelisti & D. Perlman (Eds.), *The Cambridge handbook of personal relationships* (pp. 429–443). New York: Cambridge University Press.

Sarason, B. R., Sarason, I. G., & Gurung, R. A. R. (1997). Close personal relationships and health outcomes: A key to the role of social support. In S. Duck (Ed.), *Handbook of personal relationships* (2nd ed., pp. 547–573). Chichester, UK: Wiley.

Sarason, B. R., Sarason, I. G., & Pierce, G. R. (Eds.). (1990). *Social support: An interactional view.* New York: Wiley.

Sarason, I. G., Sarason, B. R., & Shearin, E. N. (1986). Social support as an individual difference variable: Its stability, origins, and relational aspects. *Journal of Personality and Social Psychology, 50,* 845–855.

Segrin, C. (2003). Age moderates the relationship between social support and psychosocial problems. *Human Communication Research, 29,* 317–342.

Servaty-Seib, H. L., & Burleson, B. R. (2007). Bereaved adolescents' evaluations of the helpfulness of support-intended statements: Associations with person centeredness and demographic, personality, and contextual factors. *Journal of Social and Personal Relationships, 24,* 207–223.

Shaw, R., & Kitzinger, C. (2007). Problem presentation and advice giving on a home birth helpline. *Feminism & Psychology, 17,* 203–213.

Shen, Y. E. (2009). Relationships between self-efficacy, social support, and stress coping strategies in Chinese primary and secondary school teachers. *Stress and Health, 25,* 129–138.

Street, R. L., Makoul, G., Arora, N. K., & Epstein, R. M. (2009). How does communication heal? Pathways linking clinician–patient communication to health outcomes. *Patient Education and Counseling, 74,* 295–301.

Tamborini, R., Salomonson, K., & Bahk, C. (1993). The relationship of empathy to comforting behavior following film exposure. *Communication Research, 20,* 723–738.

Tamres, L., Janicki, D., & Helgeson, V. S. (2002). Sex differences in coping behavior: A meta-analytic review. *Personality and Social Psychology Review, 6,* 2–30.

Tardy, C. H. (1994). Counteracting task-induced stress: Studies of instrumental and emotional support in problem-solving contexts. In B. R. Burleson, T. L. Albrecht, & I. G. Sarason (Eds.), *Communication of social support: Messages, interactions, relationships, and community* (pp. 71–87). Thousand Oaks, CA: Sage.

Taylor, S. E., Sherman, D. K., Kim, H. S., Jarcho, J., Takagi, K., & Dunagan, M. S. (2004). Culture and social support: Who seeks it and why? *Journal of Personality and Social Psychology, 87,* 354–362.

Thorsteinsson, E. B., & James, J. E. (1999). A meta-analysis of the effects of experimental manipulations of social support during laboratory stress. *Psychology and Health, 14,* 869–886.

Todorov, A., Chaiken, S., & Henderson, M. D. (2002). The heuristic-systematic model of social information processing. In J. P. Dillard & M. Pfau (Eds.), *The persuasion handbook: Developments in theory and practice* (pp. 195–211). Thousand Oaks, CA: Sage.

Triandis, H. C. (1994). *Culture and social behavior.* New York: McGraw-Hill.

Uchino, B. N. (2004). *Social support and physical health: Understanding the health consequences of relationships.* New Haven, CT: Yale University Press.

Uchino, B. N. (2006). Social support and health: A review of physiological processes potentially underlying links to disease outcomes. *Journal of Behavioral Medicine, 29,* 377–387.

Uchino, B. N. (2009a). Understanding the links between social support and physical health: A life-span perspective with emphasis on the separability of perceived and received support. *Perspectives on Psychological Science, 4,* 236–255.

Uchino, B. N. (2009b). What a lifespan approach might tell us about why distinct measures of social support have differential links to physical health. *Journal of Social and Personal Relationships, 26,* 53–62.

Uchino, B. N., Carlisle, M., Birmingham, W., & Vaughn, A. A. (2011). Social support and the reactivity hypothesis: Conceptual issues in examining the efficacy of received support during acute psychological stress. *Biological Psychology, 86,* 137–142.

Van Swol, L. M., & Sniezek, J. A. (2005). Factors affecting the acceptance of expert advice. *British Journal of Social Psychology, 44,* 443–461.

Vangelisti, A. L. (2009). Challenges in conceptualizing social support. *Journal of Social and Personal Relationships, 26,* 39–51.

Vaux, A. (1990). An ecological approach to understanding and facilitating social support. *Journal of Social and Personal Relationships, 7,* 507–518.

Verderber, K. S., Verderber, R. F., & Berryman-Fink, C. (2009). *Inter-act: Interpersonal communication concepts, skills, and contexts* (12th ed.). New York: Oxford University Press.

Verhofstadt, L. L., Ickes, W., & Buysse, A. (2010). "I know what you need right now": Empathic accuracy and support provision in marriage. In K. T. Sullivan & J. Davila (Eds.), *Support processes in intimate relationships* (pp. 71–88). New York: Oxford University Press.

Weiner, B. (1986). Attribution, emotion, and action. In R. M. Sorrentino & E. T. Higgins (Eds.), *Handbook of motivation and cognition: Foundations of social behavior* (pp. 281–314). New York: Guilford Press.

Wilkum, K., & MacGeorge, E. L. (2010). Does God matter?: Religious content and the evaluation of comforting messages in the context of bereavement. *Communication Research, 37,* 723–745.

Williams, S. L., & Mickelson, K. D. (2008). A paradox of support seeking and rejection among the stigmatized. *Personal Relationships, 15,* 493–509.

Wills, T. A., & Shinar, O. (2000). Measuring perceived and received social support. In S. Cohen, L. G. Underwood, & B. H. Gottlieb (Eds.), *Social support measurement and intervention* (pp. 86–135). New York: Oxford University Press.

Wong, K. S., Cheuk, W. H., & Rosen, S. (2007). Experience of being spurned: Coping style, stress preparation, and depersonalization in beginning kindergarten teachers. *Journal of Research in Childhood Education, 22,* 141–154.

Wong, P. T. P., Wong, L. C. J., & Scott, C. (2006). Beyond stress and coping: The positive psychology of transformation. In P. T. P. Wong & L. C. J. Wong (Eds.), *Handbook of multicultural perspectives on stress and coping* (pp. 1–26). New York: Springer.

Wood, A. M., Maltby, J., Gillett, R., Linley, P. A., & Joseph, S. (2008). The role of gratitude in the development of social support, stress, and depression: Two longitudinal studies. *Journal of Research in Personality, 42,* 854–871.

Xu, Y., & Burleson, B. R. (2004). The association of experienced spousal support with marital satisfaction: Evaluating the moderating effects of sex, ethnic culture, and type of support. *Journal of Family Communication, 4,* 123–145.

Yarcheski, T. J., Mahon, N. E., & Yarcheski, A. (2003). Social support, self-esteem, and positive health practices of early adolescents. *Psychological Reports, 92,* 99–103.

# CHAPTER 11

# Social Networks and the Life of Relationships

*Malcolm R. Parks*

Social networks link person to person to person, leading us to knowledge, love and friendship, danger, and adventure. My aim in this chapter is to encourage scholars of interpersonal communication to think more about social networks. Social network perspectives, I argue, cast new light on central interpersonal processes, point to new lines of research, and create bridges connecting interpersonal communication research with other areas and disciplines.

Interest in social networks has increased over the past decade as scholars in a variety of disciplines have discovered or, more properly, rediscovered how useful network thinking can be (Barabási, 2002; Christakis & Fowler, 2009; Lewis, 2009; Watts, 2003). The number of citations referencing social or communication networks in *Communication and Mass Media Complete* grew nearly 10-fold between 1999 and 2009. Unfortunately, only a few of these addressed issues of direct interest to interpersonal communication researchers.

Although the seeds of contemporary network perspectives were sown nearly a century ago in the work of Georg Simmel and others (Freeman, 1996; Simmel, 1922/1955), they have yet to fully take root in the study of interpersonal communication. My goal is not to lament the inattention to networks but rather to make the positive case by illustrating the relevance and explanatory value of viewing interpersonal interaction within the broader context of relationships among relationships. To do so, I begin by identifying the characteristics of networks that are of greatest relevance for interpersonal communication and by articulating several broad principles of network functioning. I will then illustrate the value of a network perspective by illustrating how it contributes to our understanding of how interpersonal relationships form, develop, and deteriorate over time. In the closing section, I will examine several implications of the work on networks and relationship change processes for the study of interpersonal communication more generally.

# Network Essentials for Interpersonal Communication Researchers' Network

## Building Blocks: Nodes and Links

Networks of all kinds consist of *nodes* and *links*. The way nodes and links are defined varies across disciplines and research questions. Interpersonal communication researchers are typically interested in networks in which the nodes are individuals and the links between them are defined in terms of either the content or frequency of their interaction or the overall strength of their relationship. But even here, there is substantial variety. Kim and McKay-Semmler (2009), for example, examined the association between racial attitudes and the degree of ethnic diversity among individuals' regular contacts, while Ye (2006) explored the role of traditional and online support networks in cultural adaptation. Other researchers have investigated topics as diverse as the relationship between workplace friendship networks and job satisfaction (Raile et al., 2008) and the role of networks of friends and family in facilitating weight loss among overweight individuals (Wing & Jeffery, 1999).

*Nodes.* Interpersonal networks are typically delineated in one of three conceptually distinct, but often empirically related, ways. One approach is to examine relationships among people who are found within a particular spatial area, such as a neighborhood or a housing development (Hampton & Wellman, 2003). A second approach is to examine relationships among people who belong to some recognized social entity, such as a company or a voluntary organization (e.g., Lau & Liden, 2008). The third and most common approach, however, is to examine the network contacts of a particular individual. The size or structure of these *egocentric networks* is then typically linked to some cognitive-affective, relational,

or health outcome for that individual. Because most of the research discussed in this chapter will fall into this category, it may be useful to identify the general ways in which egocentric networks are defined. Rather than trying to account for every social contact an individual may have, researchers typically focus on particular types of relationships, such as those with friends, family members, or members of particular groups. Researchers have, for example, tracked changes in the gender composition of adolescents' friendship networks to predict the emergence of romantic relationships (Connolly, Furman, & Konarski, 2000). In another study, researchers found that elderly women were less likely to experience dementia if they had regular contact with a greater number of friends, kin, and support providers (Crooks, Lubben, Petitti, Little, & Chiu, 2008).

*Links.* Approaches to conceptualizing the linkage between network members also vary with the goal of the research. Moreover, definitions of nodes and links are not always independent. Investigators might, for instance, ask respondents to identify their "friends" (nodes) and then assess how close the respondent feels to each friend (linkages). Or they may ask respondents to generate a list of people who provide social support (nodes) and then ask how frequently each network member provides a particular kind of support (linkages). Broadly speaking, however, links between network members are usually assessed in one of three ways: (1) the frequency of contact or interaction, (2) the strength of the relationship, or (3) the frequency with which certain types of information or behavior are exchanged between network members.

The first strategy yields an *interactive network* that includes all of those people with whom the participant has had some minimum level of interaction within a given period of time. Milardo (1989), for example, telephoned participants several times over a 21-day period to prompt them to list the people with whom they had interacted voluntarily for five minutes or more during the previous 24 hours.

The second strategy yields what has been called the *psychological network,* largely because it is based on subjective judgments of the importance or strength of the relationships among network members (Milardo, 1992). Studies in which respondents are asked to list close friends, family members, and others deemed to be important fall into this category (e.g., de Klepper, Sleebos, van de Bunt, & Agneessens, 2010; Laumann, 1973; Lewis, 1973b). Studies in which participants are asked to list those individuals who are particularly important to them or to whom they feel close also fall into this category (e.g., Johnson & Milardo, 1984; Kalmijn, 2003). So, too, do studies in which investigators have asked respondents to complete multidimensional measures of link strength or relational development (Parks, 2007).

A third strategy is based on the specific *message or behavioral content* flowing through the links among network members. Support networks are perhaps the most obvious example of networks that have been defined in this manner. Here, participants either identify those who provide social support, generally or of some specific type, or rate the extent to which network members identified in some other way provide such support (e.g., Suitor & Keeton, 1997; Ye, 2006). Researchers may assess the presence or absence of support providers generally (e.g., Crooks et al., 2008; Kouzis & Eaton, 1998), or they may be concerned with network contacts who provide a certain kind of support or support on a specific topic (Brashers, Neidig, & Goldsmith, 2004). Examples of the latter range from studies on the discussion of marital troubles with network members (Julien et al., 2000; Julien, Markman, Léveillé, Chartrand, & Bégin, 1994) to studies of how people negotiate informational and emotional support to cope with an illness or a traumatic event (e.g., Barnett & Hwang, 2006; Goldsmith, 2004). Similarly, networks may be defined in terms of the people with whom the participant discusses a specific topic or is engaged in a particular type of behavior. Respondents to the General Social Survey in the United States have been asked, for example, to report the number of people with whom they discuss "important matters" (Marsden, 1987; McPherson, Smith-Lovin, & Brashears, 2006). Investigators have examined networks defined by doing favors (Goeree, McConnell, Mitchell, Tromp, & Yariv, 2008) or sexual activity (Bearman, Moody, & Stovel, 2004).

Differences in the networks generated using alternative strategies will be greatest when the threshold for inclusion is set relatively high. Thus, for a given individual, the network of people with whom she or he has interacted for at least 10 minutes in the past 24 hours will probably not overlap greatly with a network generated by asking the individual to list the 10 people to whom she or he feels the closest (Milardo, 1989). Before leaving the question of how links are defined, however, it is worth noting three larger points. First, the networks generated using different strategies are not so much different networks as different sectors of the same network. Second, the two approaches are frequently combined (Burt, 1983; Parks, 2007). For example, Fischer (1977) asked men to name "the three men who are your closest friends and whom you see the most often" (p. 45). Finally, apart from the strategy used to identify them, most definitions allow links to be *reciprocated* or *unreciprocated.* I may say, "I've interacted with you in the past week," but you may or may not say that you've interacted with me when asked. You may name me as a source of social support, but I may not list you as one of my sources of support.

## Network Structures

The value of network analysis ultimately resides in the identification of larger patterns or structures created by the way network members are connected to one another. These structures both create and reflect a wide range of social phenomena. Networks with numerous gaps—"structural holes" (Burt, 1992) that make it difficult for network members to reach each other efficiently—will be less cohesive or resilient. Effective collective action becomes less likely. On the other hand, networks with more connections and shorter pathways linking members will be more cohesive and better able to mount coordinated efforts. Individuals occupying different structural positions will have markedly different opportunities to influence others, to receive new information, to provide support, and to access a wide range of other resources. They will be exposed to markedly different levels of risk. To note just one example, adolescents with few or weaker ties to friends and parents are more likely to be the targets of bullies (Spriggs, Iannotti, Nansel, & Haynie, 2007). The number, strength, and length of pathways linking network members therefore have a major bearing on the opportunities, risks, and constraints experienced by individual network members and the network as a whole.

Interpersonal communication research has traditionally focused on the attributes of messages or communicators and, to a lesser extent, on the attributes of the relationship between sender and receiver. Taking a network perspective, however, shifts our focus to the larger structure of connections among communicators. Rather than describing individuals in terms of their personalities or other attributes, individuals are described in terms of their relative location within a larger social network structure. Many different approaches have been advanced to describe networks (for overviews see Hanneman & Riddle, 2005; Knoke & Yang, 2008; Kolaczyk, 2009). I will focus on four broad families of measures: size, reach, centrality, and overall network structure.

*Measures of Network Size.* In most cases, network size refers straightforwardly either to the total number of links a given individual has or to the total number of individuals in the network as a whole. As we noted earlier, most researchers do not attempt to assess the total size of an individual's social network but instead are concerned with the size of some subset of interest. But even here size matters. During the 2004 U.S. elections, for example, Eveland and Hively (2009) found that those who regularly discussed political issues with a larger network of people were more likely

to discuss issues with people with opposing views and to participate in political activity.

It is often useful to distinguish between *in-degree* and *out-degree* contacts. The number of people with whom Mary discusses her marital problems (out-degree network size) may not be the same as the number of people who discuss their marital problems with Mary (in-degree network size). And that difference may have very real consequences for Mary's level of stress as well as how she is perceived by others. Although this issue has not been explored extensively, we do know that worries about burdening others and about reciprocity are concerns for people engaged in "troubles talk" (Goldsmith, 2004).

The distinction between in-degree and out-degree activity also highlights the role of reciprocity in networks. In some analyses, researchers will assume that links are reciprocal (i.e., the link from A to B is equivalent to the link from B to A). In other cases, the degree of reciprocity will be of substantive interest. Whether the people whom I list as close friends also consider me to be a close friend, for instance, will have implications for my ability to draw support from those relationships and perhaps even for my own sense of well-being.

*Measures of Reach Within Networks.* When we think of the size of an individual's network, we typically think of the number of persons to whom the individual is directly connected. But these "first-degree" links do not capture the full range of an individual's connections. If Cho has a direct, first-degree, connection to Min-suh, he will have an indirect, second-degree connection to Min-suh's friend Hee Sun as well as an indirect, third-degree connection to Hee Sun's husband Tim. One index of these indirect ties is the *two-step reach*, which represents the percentage of network members that a given individual can reach in just two steps. Individuals with a low two-step reach are able to reach fewer network members through "friends of friends." Because of this, they will have access to less diverse information and be less influential within the network as a whole.

There are a number of situations in which scholars of interpersonal communication might be interested in the length of the path connecting particular pairs of people in the network. Relationship researchers, for instance, have considered the social distance separating individuals from potential, but as yet unmet, romantic partners (Parks, 2007). Social support researchers might be concerned with whether an individual has links that lead to a source of assistance or to resources that are not available through immediate relationships. Those interested in intercultural or intergroup relations might examine the length of the paths separating individuals from different groups. To date, most investigations have focused on the direct and second-order linkages between members of differing groups (Pettigrew & Tropp, 2006; Vonofakou et al., 2008). Network analysts, however, have developed a variety of tools for more completely assessing the indirect connections between individuals or groups. Distance (sometimes called *geodesic distance*) represents the number of links separating two individuals along the shortest pathway connecting them. Measures of *reachability* reveal whether it is possible to connect any given pair of individuals directly or indirectly, while measures such as *point connectivity* assess the number of nodes that would need to be removed in order to make it no longer possible for two individuals to reach each other (Hanneman & Riddle, 2005). When connectivity between individuals or groups is high, the flow of information between them should be more durable and less vulnerable to disruptions caused by the loss of intermediaries.

*Measures of Centrality in Networks.* Some individuals occupy more central locations than others within the network. At the most specific or local level, differences in centrality can be viewed in terms of triadic relationships among network members by examining the ways in which one individual can be positioned between two other network members. Research on triadic relationships has a long history in balance theory

and in the study of small groups (Heider, 1958). More recently, Fernandez and Gould (1994) extended traditional conceptions of the individual's relationships with group members by considering a variety of ways by which individuals might connect, or "broker" groups. The individual (ego) may, for instance, function as a "coordinator" by facilitating interactions between unconnected members of a group to which the ego belongs, or he or she may serve as a "consultant" by linking members of a group to which he or she does not belong. Following previous analyses, Fernandez and Gould include roles such as "gatekeeper" (the ego regulates contact between his or her own group and another group) and "liaison" (the ego links two groups but is not a part of either) and also less frequently discussed roles such as "representative" (the ego conveys the interest of his or her group to outsiders). Their analysis recognizes subtle but important differences in the direction of information flow. Gatekeepers, for example, regulate the flow of information coming into the group, while representatives regulate the flow of information coming out of the group. Brokering has been applied to relations between professionals and institutions (e.g., Meyer, 2010), but interpersonal scholars have not yet exploited its potential for helping us understand family communication, conflict management, third-party roles in the formation and dissolution of dyadic relationships, and a variety of other areas. One notable exception is recent work illustrating how bilingual family members broker conversations between other family members who are having difficulty reaching consensus because of a language mismatch (Ng, 2007).

Other approaches to assessing centrality go beyond the analysis of triads to encompass the network as a whole. The four most widely used measures of centrality today can be traced in the work of Freeman (1978–1979) and Bonacich (1972, 1987). They are degree centrality, closeness centrality, betweenness centrality, and eigenvector centrality. To appreciate these measures, consider the network portrayed in Figure 11.1.

**Figure 11.1**   Example of a Social Network

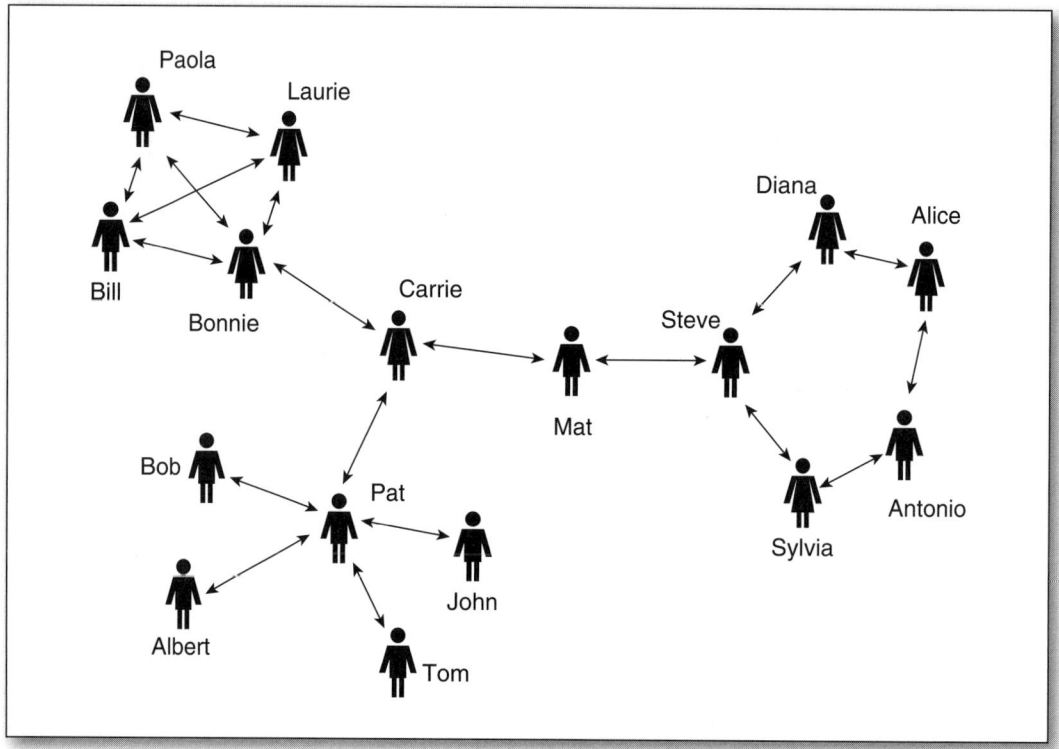

The most straightforward measure of centrality is *degree centrality.* It presents the number of people to whom a given individual is directly linked (e.g., the size of the ego's first-degree network). With direct ties to five other network members, Pat has the highest degree centrality in the network in Figure 11.1. Individuals with more ties are likely to exert more influence, though this will depend on several additional factors, including the directionality of the ties.

The *closeness centrality* of a given individual is usually assessed in terms of his or her distance from others in the network. Specific measures differ from one another largely because there are alternative ways of determining how close or far network members are from one another. Perhaps the most common is the *geodesic path distance,* which is the sum of the shortest paths from the individual to each other network member (Freeman, 1978–1979). In our model network

(Figure 11.1), the person with the highest closeness centrality is Carrie. Although Pat may have the most direct links, the paths linking Carrie to other network members are shorter in the aggregate. Messages from those with higher closeness centrality diffuse across the network more rapidly or efficiently than messages from less central persons (Sabidussi, 1966).

Measures of *betweenness centrality* reflect the extent to which a given individual lies between other pairs of network members. In Figure 11.1, for example, Mat lies between Steve and Carrie, who are only able to communicate through Mat. Betweenness can be determined by inspection in small networks, but researchers rely on quantitative measures of betweenness centrality in larger networks. There are several different algorithms for determining betweenness, but perhaps the most common was developed by Freeman (1978–1979). It estimates the betweenness for each person by calculating how frequently he or she falls on each of the paths linking all possible pairs of network members—that is, how often he or she stands "between" another pair of people in the network. Carrie has the highest betweenness centrality in our example.

The final measure of centrality to be discussed here is *eigenvector centrality*. This measure, as its name implies, is based on the principal eigenvector of the adjacency matrix (Bonacich, 1972). This measure registers the subtleties missed by measures such as degree centrality, which are concerned only with first-degree links. Although Pat has the most first-degree links, only one of his contacts (Carrie) is linked to anyone else. Mat is a powerful liaison connecting network segments, but he is somewhat more distant from others who are well connected. Eigenvector centrality assesses the extent to which a given individual is linked to others who are themselves more central in the network. It is Bonnie rather than Carrie, Mat, or Pat who has the highest eigenvector centrality because she is linked to people who are more directly linked to a greater number of people themselves. Put simply, having high eigenvector centrality means you know people who know people.

Different measures of centrality may covary in quite distinct ways with other variables of interest. For instance, in an investigation of the association between job satisfaction and various types of centrality in the workplace friendship network, Raile et al. (2008) found that closeness centrality was positively related to job satisfaction but that betweenness and degree centrality were not.

*Measures of Overall Network Structure.* The measures discussed thus far have focused on the relative locations of individuals rather than on the overall structure of the network generated by those individuals. Although some of the measures previously discussed can be generalized to the network (e.g., size), new measures come into play as we gain altitude to view the network as a whole.

The most common of these is *density*, which measures the degree to which the overall network is loosely or tightly knit. Density is usually measured as the proportion of actual to possible ties. In a network of size N, the total number of possible asymmetrical links is $N(N - 1)$, while the number of symmetrical or reciprocated (nondirectional) links is half of that. In our hypothetical network of 16 people in Figure 11.1, for example, there are 120 possible reciprocal relationships. Of these, 19 actually exist, resulting in a density coefficient of .158, or 15.8%. The overall density of a network is substantively important because it is both empirically and theoretically associated with social cohesion and innovativeness (Burt, 2004; Eagle, Macy, & Claxton, 2010; Fuchs, 2001).

Several other measures are available for assessing the more specific aspects of the overall network. Some, such as *network transitivity* and *average geodesic distance*, also reflect how generally close-knit or cohesive a network is. A network may be analyzed in terms of the possible three-person or triadic relationships within it. A triad is "transitive" if A is linked to B, B to C, and A to C. In our example, the triad linking Paola, Laurie, and Bill is transitive, but the triad linking Diana, Alice, and Antonio is not because Alice and Antonio are not directly linked. Although imbalanced or intransitive triads are common, balance theorists argue that interpersonal relationships will generally gravitate toward transitivity over time (Heider, 1958; Newcomb, 1953). Overall, transitivity is sometimes assessed as the proportion of total possible triads within the network that are transitive (excluding "vacuous" triads, in which none of the possible links actually exist). Another approach is to calculate the mean of the shortest paths linking all network members who can be connected directly or indirectly. The resulting measure of average geodesic distance will be small when the network is close-knit but will grow large as gaps in the network (structural holes) become more frequent. Information should diffuse less rapidly and less evenly in networks with greater average geodesic distances.

Connections among network members typically cluster together to form "local neighborhoods" whose density is greater than the density of the network as a whole (Hanneman & Riddle, 2005). Our network in Figure 11.1 consists of three clusters, with the "Paola–Laurie–Bonnie–Bill" cluster accounting for nearly a third of the total links in the network. Measures of *clustering* typically begin by calculating the density among the people to whom each network member is linked directly and then averaging that across all network members. Differences in the densities of network members' local neighborhoods are worth examining in their own right. Among other things, they may be related to the development and stability of particular relationships within the neighborhood. In many cases, researchers will be interested in the degree of linkage between clusters that have been defined according to some other attribute of interest. Examples would include studies examining the links between ethnic groups, between work or community groups, or even between those who do and do not engage in a particular behavior (e.g., smoking). Several measures of ties between groups have been developed, including Krackhardt and Stern's (1988) External–Internal Index, which, as its name implies, is based on the relative difference in ties to people inside and outside the group. Ties between groups not only are important for managing intergroup relations and prejudice but also figure prominently in the spread of behaviors between groups as well as in the overall resiliency of the larger organization or community in which the groups are set (Krackhardt & Stern, 1988; Pettigrew & Tropp, 2006).

## Four Themes in Network Perspectives on Interpersonal Communication

As we explore applications of network thinking to interpersonal communication, it is useful to consider four larger principles regarding communication in interpersonal networks. First, interpersonal networks are the living tissue of social structure and culture (Parks, 2007). They are the circulatory system carrying and shaping the behaviors and interactions that give these and every other higher order social concept meaning. However abstract, these concepts have to refer to something that is enacted and reenacted in the way people actually communicate. Tracking "who talks to whom about what" is not simply a tool for linking relationships to one another, but instead, it taps the ontological and experiential essence of norms, rituals, social structures, and cultures. Network analysis bridges the micro- and macrolevels of analysis (Granovetter, 1973). It provides a framework for understanding the larger social implications of interpersonal interactions for relating the broader historical or cultural trends to the lived experience of individuals.

Second, individuals actively "work the network" rather than simply being passive registers for forces imposed by larger network structures. This stands in marked contrast to traditional structuralist approaches that explain individual behavior in terms of larger social structures such as one's position in a network, one's role in a group, or membership in a social class or culture (e.g., Blau, 1977a, 1977b; Newman, Barabási, & Watts, 2006). The more active perspective adopted here is reflected in a number of recent studies of interpersonal networks (Christakis & Fowler, 2009; Parks, 2007). It also reflects a family of theories traditionally known as action theories—theories that emphasize our ability as individuals to selectively evaluate social situations, to form plans, and to act strategically (Emirbayer & Mische, 1998; Fararo, 1989). Throughout this chapter, we will see instances in which individuals view their interpersonal networks not as social webs in which they have become entangled but rather as pathways to be explored and exploited in their search for the satisfaction of their personal needs and desires.

Third, what happens in a relationship often does not stay in that relationship. Putting it in more technical terms, interpersonal behavior is frequently transitive across individuals within a social network, thus creating social-contagion effects. Observing an individual blame someone else for a failure, for example, has been shown to increase the likelihood that the observer will also blame others for his or her own, unrelated failures (Fast & Tiedens, 2010). Transitivity links otherwise separate social domains. Hence, the aggressive acts experienced by one spouse in the workplace have been shown to cross over to influence the level of psychological distress experienced by the other spouse (Haines, Marchand, & Harvey, 2006). Cases of broader emotional contagion in groups, schools, and entire communities have been documented so regularly over time that they must be considered a common feature of social behavior (Bartholomew, 2000; Bartholomew & Sirois, 1996; Boss, 1997). Traditional approaches to interpersonal communication have struggled to account for these "relationships among relationships" because they lack a conceptual framework for describing the spread of behavior across a social network. Network perspectives are beginning to provide new tools for documenting the extent of social transitivity. Christakis and Fowler (2009) have proposed a provocative "three-degrees rule of social influence"—that is, what we say and do extends to influence others up to three degrees from us in the social network (e.g., our friends' friends' friends).

Fourth, individuals are rarely aware of the influence of networks on their thoughts, feelings, and behavior. At first, this might appear to contradict the view that people actively manage their network, but in fact, it points to an important asymmetry in lay perspectives on networks. While we are often quite deliberate about our social actions, we usually do not consider how far they might extend beyond their immediate targets or how the social situation we inhabit in the moment might have been influenced by the actions of people not even present. Thus, our decision to befriend, say, a person from a different ethnic group, is usually experienced in terms of our own values and motives or the characteristics of the other person. But research demonstrates that the structure of the broader network in which we are embedded, specifically the ethnic heterogeneity of that network, will also influence our likelihood of selecting friends from other ethnic groups (Moody, 2001). Even if we wished

to know how we fit into larger networks, it is unlikely that we would have the information necessary to do so. We know who our friends are, but do we really know who their friends are? Do people know if their sexual partners are faithful or if they have additional partners? Research suggests that individuals often make dubious, if not downright incorrect, assumptions about their sexual partners' activities (e.g., Carey, Senn, Seward, & Vanable, 2010).

# Networks and the Life Cycle of Interpersonal Relationships

The paradigm for interpersonal communication research shifted dramatically approximately 35 years ago, when researchers began to conceptualize interpersonal communication as a developmental process in which interaction becomes more personalized and complex over time (Altman & Taylor, 1973; Berger & Calabrese, 1975; Miller & Steinberg, 1975). The developmental perspective and the theories it spawned continue to guide research and pedagogy (e.g., Knapp & Vangelisti, 2009). And it is within the developmental perspective that research on social networks has made its greatest contribution to the study of interpersonal communication. After a brief theoretic overview, I will explore that contribution across three broad phases of the relational life cycle: (1) initiation, (2) development, and (3) managing and dissolving of relationships.

## Social Contextual Theory

Social contextual theory (Parks, 2007) synthesizes and extends several lower order theoretical concepts to provide a more comprehensive explanation of the role of networks in the development and deterioration of interpersonal relationships. At its heart are two explanatory principles. The first, relational sensemaking, builds on familiar theories of interpersonal communication, while the second, network structuring, introduces issues largely overlooked in the study of interpersonal relationships.

*Relational Sensemaking.* The management of uncertainty is central to several theories of interpersonal communication (Afifi & Weiner, 2004; Babrow, 2007; Berger & Calabrese, 1975; Brashers, 2001; Knobloch & Solomon, 1999). Social contextual theory (SCT) generalizes the concept of uncertainty management to relational sensemaking and then extends it to the network level, thus revealing several ways in which people actively draw on their social networks to help them make sense of what is going on in a particular relationship.

Interactions among network members provide vast amounts of information about individuals within the network. Information about an individual obtained from network members can be more uncertainty reducing than information obtained directly from the individual in question (Parks & Adelman, 1983). Network members may be asked about the partner's past or expected future behavior. Relational participants may seek guidance and support from network members (Goldsmith, 1988). They compare their relationship with the relationships of other couples in their network (Titus, 1980) and may attempt to manage their own uncertainty about the relationship's image in the eyes of network members (Crowley, 2010; Leslie, Huston, & Johnson, 1986).

The role of network members in relational sensemaking is not limited to the exchange of information. Human sensemaking often revolves around aesthetic principles of symmetry and balance. Balance theories predict that attraction to a relational partner's network should go hand in hand with attraction to the partner (Heider, 1958; Newcomb, 1961). Cultural expectations reference principles of balance so that people in close relationships generally expect to meet their partner's other close associates. Imbalances and unmet expectations in network contact disrupt the sensemaking process, creating doubts about the viability of the relationship.

*Network Structuring.* Network factors are integral to the relational life cycle because they influence opportunities to meet, influence the amount and quality of interaction relational participants have, and regulate the availability of alternative relational partners (Parks, 2007). Unacquainted individuals' location relative to each other in the network (reachability, geodesic distance) influences whether they will ultimately meet. This aspect of network structuring may occur either passively, as shifts in network structure reduce the number of links separating prospective partners, or quite actively, as individuals manipulate their networks to increase access to prospective partners. Later on, network structuring facilitates relational development and maintenance as participants realign their networks to position their relationship more centrally, reduce contact with unsupportive members, and increase connections among members of their respective networks.

If their relationship begins to deteriorate, relational partners may seek to protect themselves by restricting access to information, severing contact with some network members, and seeking additional support from other network members who will take their side. This restructuring may be deliberate, but it can also occur as the consequence of any number of individual- and network-level actions, including changes of job, residence, or interests, or the actions of those further out in the network. Thus, trouble in the relationship may drive changes in the network, or changes in the network may create troubles in the relationship. One particularly sensitive aspect of network structure is the way in which it regulates perceptions of the availability and attractiveness of alternative partners. The mutual network formed by relational partners as their relationship develops acts as a barrier to the dissolution of their relationship (Levinger, 1979). But as the density and transitivity of this network decreases, alternative partners come into view, and this, in turn, may hasten the end of one relationship and the formation of a new one.

## Networks and the Initiation of Relationships

The central question about the initiation of inter-personal relationships is why two particular individuals meet and begin a relationship. Unfortunately, because they are focused on inter-actions after people meet, theories of interpersonal communication fail to account for why people meet people in the first place. Instead, we fall back on theories derived from other disciplines, which assume that relationships are usually initiated between people who live or work closer together (physical proximity) and between people who share basic socioeconomic characteristics and values (social homophily). A critique of these theories is beyond the scope of the present discussion, but two points should be made here. First, they fail to account for why we meet some people and not others who are within the same geographic radius or who are equally similar to us. Second, they overlook important contributors to the process of relationship initiation. SCT has identified two additional factors that help account for first meetings and the early development of interpersonal relationships: social proximity effects and third-party effects (Parks, 2007).

*Social Proximity and Relationship Initiation.* We usually think of the history of a relationship beginning when people meet for the first time. But it is possible to think about the "prehistory" if we adopt a social network perspective. That is, we may determine prospective partners' changing locations relative to one another within their broader network. Consider again, for example, the network portrayed in Figure 11.1. Paola and Antonio have not met and in fact are separated by the proverbial "six degrees of separation." But Figure 11.1 is just one frame in a film that continues to move forward. Imagine what might happen over time if Bonnie introduces her friend Paola to her favorite coworker Carrie and if Sylvia introduces Antonio to Steve. Each meeting makes the next more likely as Paola and Antonio are carried toward each other by

dynamic shifts in the structure of their network. Suppose that a few months later Carrie and Mat decide to have a party for some of their friends, who bring some of their friends. At this point, Paola and Antonio actually meet for the first time. Their relational prehistory ends and the history of their relationship begins. Importantly, the bulk of this prehistory occurs beyond the awareness of Paola and Antonio. One may think of this process as a sort of social plate tectonics, with individuals drifting on the "plates" created by shifting local network densities that determine how close or far apart they are in social rather than physical terms (Parks, 2007).

Several studies have confirmed the existence of social proximity effects. In a national sample of 3,432 adults, researchers found that 68% of married participants and 64% of cohabiting participant in the United States had been introduced to their partners by someone they knew and that 53% of unmarried participants involved in "short-term" relationships had been introduced to their sexual partners by someone they knew (Laumann, Gagnon, Michael, & Michaels, 1994). Similar findings emerged from a national sample of married and cohabiting couples in the Netherlands, where almost 50% reported having friends in common before they met and an additional 14% reported that members of their immediate families had known each other (Kalmijn & Flap, 2001). These findings are also consistent with our studies on the initiation of dating relationships and close friendships. In a sample of 858 adolescents and young adults, we found that 66% had met at least one member of their prospective partner's circle of close friends and relatives in advance of meeting the prospective partner for the first time (Parks, 2007). Almost 20% had met 4 or more of the prospective partner's 12 closest social contacts. Prior contact was significantly greater for the initiation of romantic relationships than it was for the initiation of same-sex friendships, suggesting that people do not "reach" as far into their social networks for romantic partners as they do for friendships.

*Third-Party Effects in Relationship Initiation.* The formal role of "matchmaker" has been recognized for generations, but the far more general and often more subtle impact of the informal help given by network members has gone largely unexplored. To better understand the nature of third-party help, we conducted an exploratory study of 437 young adults, in which we asked questions regarding the types of "help" they had given others or had received in starting a new romantic relationship during the previous year (Parks, 2007). The results offered striking confirmation of the belief that "we get by with a little help from our friends."

Network members commonly gave and received in the relationships we studied. Approximately 55% of the respondents reported helping at least one and usually more than one other couple "get a romantic relationship started" in the last year. And nearly two thirds (64%) of those who had started a new romantic relationship within the past year said that they had received assistance from one or more third parties. Respondents who had received third-party help dated significantly more extensively than those who did not. Far from being usual, third-party help appeared to be the norm in the formation of the romantic relationships we examined. Third-party assistance was particularly common among the members of organized living groups, such as fraternities and sororities, perhaps because of expectations within these groups or because belonging to such groups increases the size and densities of members' networks to the point where they can more effectively link to prospective partners.

The results also challenged several common stereotypes about relational help. Contrary to gender stereotypes, males and females were equally likely to both give and receive help. Moreover, helping is not a clandestine activity. In 70% to 80% of the cases, at least one of the recipients was aware of the helper's activities. And in many of these, one of the prospective partners had actually sought the assistance of network members. About 45% of the recipients had "worked the network" by directly asking for the network member's help, and even in the absence of a direct request, 64% of the helpers reported that the recipients had clearly hinted that their assistance was desired. Finally, it was apparent that third-party assistance went well beyond arranging for prospective romantic partners to meet for the first time. Network members also said or did things in an effort to make one recipient more attractive in the eyes of the other (e.g., noting positive qualities or downplaying negative qualities). In some instances, they went so far as to enlist other network members to say positive things about one prospective partner to the other. In addition, they often coached one person on how best to approach the other and relayed questions and answers between prospective partners.

## Networks and the Development of Relationships

The role of network members extends far beyond the initial stages of relational formation. Contemporary approaches to understanding the role of networks in the development of relationships can be traced to the pioneering work of Robert Lewis (1973a, 1973b). Lewis's studies of premarital dyads provided the foundation for other researchers who extended his work over the next decade (Johnson & Leslie, 1982; Milardo, 1982; Milardo, Johnson, & Huston, 1983; Parks & Adelman, 1983; Parks, Stan, & Eggert, 1983). Later studies extended the work in a variety of directions, which I will summarize in this section. The most extensive of these was a series of studies conducted over several years on same-sex friendships and opposite-sex dating relationships involving two different age groups (Parks, 2007).

*Networks in the Development of Same-Sex Friendships.* It is difficult to underestimate the richness or the personal and social importance of same-sex friendships (Rawlins, 2009; Rubin, Bukowski, & Laursen, 2009). They are culturally universal, yet they reflect the unique qualities of their participants, perhaps even more than do romantic or kin relationships. They are essential for our personal sense of well-being, yet they serve the broader social function of informally linking groups, institutions, and cultures.

To better understand how friendships evolve within the social context of the participants' surrounding social networks, we examined three aspects of friendship development: (1) how often the friends communicated with each other, (2) how close they felt to each other, and (3) how committed they were to maintaining their friendship. We expected, based on SCT, that these dimensions of friendship development would be strongly associated with four aspects of the participants' social networks. These included the extent to which the partners perceived that the members of their own and their friend's social network approved or supported their friendship. In addition, we measured the level of contact and density of the participants' joint social network—specifically, how many people partners had met in the other's network and how often they communicated with the ones they had met.

Data were gathered from 478 adolescents and young adults who completed surveys regarding one of their same-sex friendships. They responded to items assessing multiple aspects of their communication, closeness, and commitment to their friend. They also listed the 12 kin and nonkin to whom they felt the closest and obtained a similar list from their friend. They were then asked to report the degree to which they believed that each of these people supported or approved of their friendship as well as how often they communicated with each person in the partner's network. Confirmatory factor analysis was used to determine the associations among the relational and network factors as well as the overall goodness of fit of the entire model. Our interest here is with the highest layer of the final model, which contains the correlations among the factors. (Further information on this and other models discussed below may be found in Parks, 2007, especially in Appendix B.)

The correlations displayed in Figure 11.2 are all statistically significant ($p < .0001$) and point to a rich pattern of association among and between the measures of relationship development and the measures of network activity. Considering first the associations among the relationship measures, it appears that friends who communicate more often with each other are also closer and more committed to their relationship. Or, put the other way, friends who are close and highly committed also communicate more often. On the network side, perceptions of support for the relationship from one's own and the partner's network are associated with greater levels of contact and communication with the partner's close associates. Although our data did not allow a direct test, we believe that these are mutually causal relationships. That is, greater contact and communication with network members are both the cause and the effect of how supportive they are perceived to be. We should also recognize that perceptions of support are often quite selective and highly managed. Friends may downplay critical comments from network members and network members may soften or withhold criticism in the hope that the individual will soon discover the friend's faults. Or one may only introduce the friend to network members who are supportive, thus leading the friend to overestimate the level of support. The strong association between perceptions of support from one's own network and the friend's network could reflect a perceptual generalization on the part of the participants or could also reflect actual consistencies in perceptions among network members. For all these reasons, we might expect that perceptions of support from network members might be different from network members' actual opinions. However, this does not make them any less potent. Depression among adolescents, for example, appears to be much more strongly linked to their perception of peer approval than to their peers' actual levels of approval (Zimmer-Gembeck, Hunter, & Pronk, 2007).

**Figure 11.2**   Networks in the Development of Same-Sex Friendships

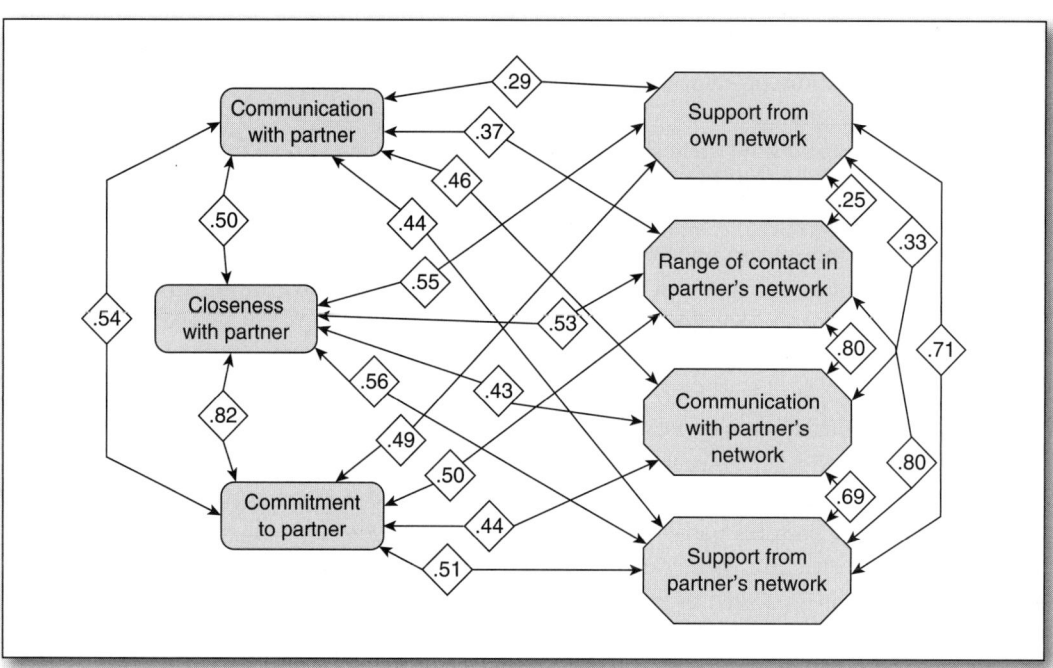

Our greatest interest, of course, is in the associations linking the relational and network factors. Consistent with SCT, we found that each of the measures of friendship (communication, closeness, and commitment) was positively and significantly correlated with each of the four network factors. Thus, the development of same-sex friendships is closely associated with the range of contact and the amount of communication individuals have with members of their friend's network and the extent to which they perceive that members of their own and their friend's network support their friendship. Again, we consider these associations to represent a mutual process in which friendship development and changes in the surrounding network drive each other. As friendships develop, the individuals meet more members of their partner's network and communicate with them more frequently, and network members become more supportive. Or viewed the other way, when networks converge and express support for a friendship, the friends will interact

more often and experience greater feelings of closeness and commitment.

Friendship is sometimes characterized as having quite distinct meanings and processes for men and women (e.g., Wood, 2007). However, we found relatively few differences between same-sex male and female friendships. With few exceptions, then, networks tend to function in the same way for both men and women in the development of same-sex friendships.

*Networks in the Development of Opposite-Sex Romantic Relationships.* As young people progress from early adolescence to young adulthood, their social networks become larger and diversify to include more members of the opposite sex. Romantic relationships typically begin to appear in middle or late adolescence (Connolly et al., 2000). Though often short-lived, these early romantic relationships leave a legacy. They offer opportunities to learn and test social and emotional skills, provide support, serve as points of reference for future relationships, and, sadly, are the site of significant risks for young people in terms of disappointment, abuse, and disease. Over the past 30 years, several groups of researchers have attempted to understand how these relationships developed within the context created by romantic partners' networks of friends and family. In some cases, researchers have tracked couples for periods of time ranging from months to years (Milardo et al., 1983; Parks & Adelman, 1983; Sprecher, Felmlee, Orbuch, & Willetts, 2002). Most studies, however, have been limited to cross-sectional data on very limited assessments of both relationships and networks. Although our approach has also been primarily cross-sectional, we have attempted to examine a much richer set of relational and network factors in more diverse samples.

We begin with a summary model (Figure 11.3) showing the linkages between communication, closeness, and commitment between romantic partners and measures of contact, communication, and support from members of their surrounding social networks. This model was derived from the confirmatory factor analyses of data obtained through surveys of 135 adolescents and 246 young adults involved in heterosexual romantic relationships at varying stages of development (Parks, 2007).

The frequency of interaction between romantic partners, their feelings of intimacy or closeness, and their level of commitment to their relationship were all closely linked in our overall sample. So, too, were the network measures. Perceptions of contact, communication, and support from the partner's network were positively correlated with each other and with the level of support for the relationship perceived from members of the participant's own network ($p < .0001$).

Correlations between relationship factors and network factors were uniformly significant ($p < .0001$) and positive. These findings suggest that romantic relationships flourish when they are supported by the partners' friends and families. Participants felt closer to their partners, were more committed to their relationship, and

**Figure 11.3**    Networks in the Development of Opposite-Sex Romantic Relationships

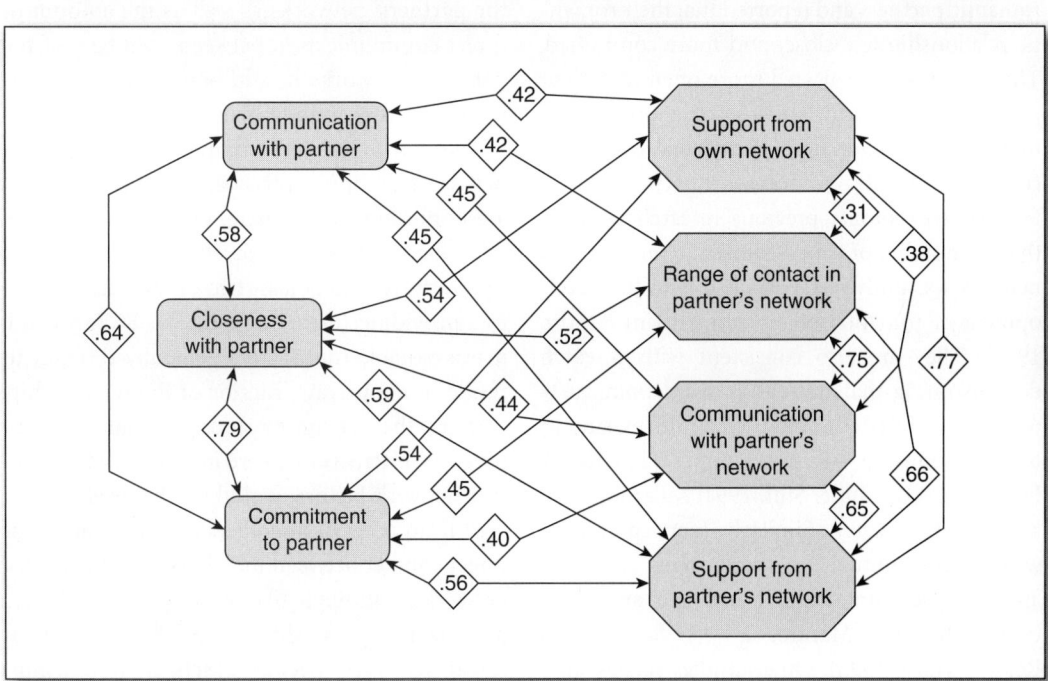

communicated more with each other when they perceived that their friends and family supported the relationship. In the same way, support from the partner's friends and family was associated with greater closeness, commitment, and communication. Support from one's own network and the partner's network functioned in similar ways in the overall model. Indeed, tests comparing the correlations of support from one's own versus one's partner's network revealed no significant differences. Some have contended that opposition from network members, specifically from parents, can create a "Romeo and Juliet effect," which intensifies the partners' romantic feelings (Driscoll, Davis, & Lipetz, 1972). However, our findings as well as the findings of nearly every other study suggest that romantic relationships prosper when network members are perceived to be supportive rather than oppositional (e.g., Lewis, 1973b; Sprecher, 1988; Sprecher & Felmlee, 2000).

The level of development in romantic relationships was also closely tied with the level of interaction with members of the partner's network. Those who met a greater number of people in the partner's network interacted more with their romantic partners and reported that their romantic relationship was closer and more committed. Those who communicated more often with their partner's friends and family also reported more frequent interaction and greater closeness and commitment with their romantic partners. These findings corroborate previous research showing that the number of people known in the partner's network was positively associated with the development of romantic relationships (Kim & Stiff, 1991). They are also consistent with research demonstrating that mutual or overlapping networks of unmarried romantic couples expand as their relationship advances (Agnew, Loving, & Drigotas, 2001; Kim & Stiff, 1991; Milardo, 1983; Milardo et al., 1983). Similarly, married couples with larger mutual or overlapping networks appear to be more satisfied, intimate, and committed (Julien & Markman, 1991; Stein, Bush, Ross, & Ward, 1992). Other studies suggest that having a common network may be more important in the early stages of relationships (Julien, Chartrand, & Begin, 1999; Kearns & Leonard, 2004; Sprecher & Felmlee, 2000). Thus, contact with the partner's network and the emergence of a mutual network may have their greatest effects early in relationships and after major relational transitions, such as marriage.

In the next study, we sought to examine a more detailed set of linkages between personal relationships and networks (Parks, 2007). This study involved 232 participants, about half of whom represented ethnic or racial groups other than European American. Most studies in this area have been limited to just a few rather general measures. (For reviews, see Milardo & Helms-Erikson, 2000; Sprecher et al., 2002.) In addition to measures of commitment and communication between the partners, we examined the depth (intimacy) of their interaction, how synchronized they felt their interactions were, the extent to which they reported using communication styles that were unique to the relationship (code personalization), and the degree of perceived predictability and understanding. On the network side, we examined the degree of overlap in the partners' networks as well as the amount of direct communication between members of the partners' networks in addition to the four network factors examined in our previous studies.

Though a complete summary of the results is beyond the scope of this chapter, several findings are important to note here. First, each of the six relational factors was correlated positively and significantly with at least two of the network factors providing further support for SCT. Second, it was notable that factors generally thought to reside in the private interior of the relationship, such as the synchrony and personalization of partners' interactions, were in fact linked to exterior network factors, including the level of support from network members and the amount of direct contact between members of the partners' networks. Although the causal sequence is still unknown, it is clear that network factors are associated with very specific aspects of relationships and not just with broad relational perceptions. Finally, the amount of communication between the romantic partners appears to be particularly sensitive to network factors. It was the only aspect of relationship development that was significantly associated with all six network factors and the only dimension linked to cross-network communication, network overlap, and the amount of communication with members of the partner's network. Romantic partners spent more time together when members of their individual networks had greater contact with each other, when they had a larger overlapping or mutual network, and when they communicated more often with members of their partner's network. Sometimes partners may need to spend time with network members in order to spend more time together, but the causal influence could just as reasonably flow the other way as well. As romantic partners begin spending more time together, network members begin paying more attention to the relationship and expect to meet and spend time with the previously unknown partner. Another plausible scenario begins even before the partners meet, when their social networks begin to slide together and each prospective partner begins communicating with a few members of the other's network. After being carried closer and closer in social space by these changes, the prospective partners meet for the first time, and a relationship begins. Shortly after that, they discover not only that they have a number of common acquaintances but that they also spend a lot of time with some of the same people. These discoveries motivate further interaction, and that in turn energizes all of the other dimensions of development.

*Links Between Networks and Relational Development Appear to Be Robust.* Uncertainty management and network structuring, the twin explanatory mechanisms of SCT, predict that partners' feelings toward each other and their interaction with members of each other's social networks should be intertwined across many relational types and settings. Additional research is obviously needed

to determine if these linkages extend to other types of relationships and across a wider range of age groups. However, the work to date suggests that links between networks and relational development are rather robust. We have already noted that measures of relational development and network involvement covaried in very similar ways in male and female friendships. But we can also compare the model for same-sex friendships (Figure 11.2) with the model for opposite-sex romantic relationships (Figure 11.3). When that was done, significant differences were found in only 3 of the 21 correlations in the final models, and only 1 of those involved a correlation between a network factor and a relationship factor. Greater support from one's own network was associated with more frequent communication with one's partner in both relationships, but the correlation was significantly stronger in romantic relationships than in friendships. Communication with the partner was also more strongly associated with commitment in romantic relationships and in same-sex friendships. On the other hand, perceived support from the partner's network was more strongly associated with the amount of communication the participant had with the partner's network in friendships than in romantic relationships. Even in these cases, however, the differences were relatively small.

More differences emerged when we compared adolescents still in high school with young adults who were in college. The greatest difference occurred in the structure of the network variables. Among high school students, the number of people participants had met in their partner's network and how often they communicated with them were so highly correlated that they loaded on a common factor. These measures were also correlated among university students, but not as strongly and could thus be treated as separate factors. I believe that this difference reflects a more general difference in the environments experienced by high school and university students. Our adolescent participants attended a medium-sized high school with a relatively homogeneous student body drawn from a confined geographic area. Because of this, and the fact that high school students have comparatively less control over their schedules, we would expect that they would be more likely to spend time around the people they met. University students, on the other hand, inhabit a more fluid social environment, where meeting someone does not necessarily lead to spending time interacting with them. This looser, more fluid context may have also accounted for the fact that the ties between relationship and network factors were generally stronger in the university samples than in the high school samples. Further investigation is obviously needed to account for the differences between these age groups. For both groups, however, relational development—closeness, commitment, and communication—was closely associated with the partners' surrounding social networks of friends and family. What friends and family thought of the relationship and how the new relationship fit with existing relationships were closely associated with the development of relationships in both age groups.

### Managing Relationships Among Relationships

Each of our relationships is part of a larger network whose ecology involves multiple participants linked in multiple ways and pursuing multiple goals. Unfortunately, this richer relational ecology receives little attention in even the best interpersonal texts (Canary, Cody, & Manusov, 2008; Floyd, 2009; Knapp & Vangelisti, 2009; McCornack, 2010). Nor has the problem received concerted attention in the research literature. Nevertheless, it is possible to piece several bodies of work together to form an initial picture of how people "manage relationships among relationships." Three concepts warrant particular attention: (1) social boundaries, (2) information management at the network level, and (3) the management of problematic relationships within a network.

*Social Boundaries.* The concept of individual and relational boundaries provides a foundation for

considering how people manage relationships in networks. Boundaries are critical not only because they maintain the integrity of individuals and relationships but also because they frame decisions regarding the flow and ownership of information. Boundaries may be described in terms of who gets to set them, who owns a given piece of information, whether ownership is exclusive or shared, and what levels of permeability or access are considered legitimate (Petronio, 2002). Most scholars have assumed that interpersonal boundaries are established and regulated with rule systems more or less analogous to the rules countries work out to manage their borders. Thus, stepfamilies, for example, may seek to establish explicit rules governing the disclosure of information both within the family and with those in the network (Afifi, 2003). But the boundaries between individuals and relationships are considerably more fluid than those between nations. Explicit negotiation of boundaries is rarely sufficient, and instead, people must rely on vacillating, often ambiguous, sometimes contradictory rules that they have inferred from interaction or that they have extracted from humor or gossip within the network (Baxter, Dun, & Sahlstein, 2001).

Two additional factors complicate the regulation of interpersonal boundaries. First, at any one time, an individual typically occupies multiple social positions and participates in multiple relationships, sometimes making it difficult to know which boundary expectations take precedence (Petronio, Ellemers, Giles, & Gallois, 1998). Second, relational participants have to be concerned not only with their boundaries as individuals and as a pair but also with one or more *network boundaries* that shape the paths information is likely to travel once it leaves the dyad and is diffused among the network members. Individuals have little control over how far information travels once it is disclosed. Indeed, without knowing how central the recipient of a disclosure is within the broader network, it is impossible to estimate how quickly and how far one's disclosure might be spread. Those who disclose may pledge recipients to secrecy, but such promises are often not kept, and the information spreads far beyond its intended limits (Petronio & Bantz, 1991). The fact that people regularly post vast amounts of personal and relational information to Internet sites only makes the challenges of understanding and managing network boundaries all the greater (Tufekci, 2008).

Boundaries—personal, relational, and network—are sites of conflicting relational goals and conditions. The concept of contradictory forces in social life can be traced to the work of Georg Simmel in the late 19th and early 20th centuries (Simmel, 1950). Contemporary research, however, draws most often from the boundary management theories of Petronio (2002; Petronio & Reierson, 2009) and the work on relational dialectics by Baxter (1988, 1993). These perspectives envision life at the social boundaries in terms of tensions between revealing and concealing, between accepting and changing, and between autonomy and connection.

*Information Management Strategies.* We still have much to learn about the strategies people use to manage these complex, inherently contradictory aspects of life in networks. Drawing together research from a variety of areas, I have proposed (Parks, 2007) that our strategic options fall generally into six categories: (1) granting access and making disclosures, (2) withdrawing and withholding, (3) selective access and disclosure, (4) ambiguity and equivocation, (5) relational tests, and (6) participating in boundary rituals. The first two represent rather direct but opposing choices, while the remaining four make room for more subtle, even artful, choices.

There are, of course, many reasons why people reveal information that they would normally keep to themselves or within a particular relationship—to apply for credit, to get a passport, to obtain medical care or spiritual guidance, to establish friendships, or to maintain family relationships (Petronio & Reierson, 2009). We disclose otherwise private information not only to obtain support from others but also to offer support to others (Goldsmith, 2004). This does not mean that disclosures that are intended to help are always perceived as helpful. Pregnant couples, for example, often experience stress when network members go too far in sharing their own experiences or in offering "friendly advice" (Petronio & Jones, 2006). Sometimes disclosures to network members are not intended to benefit the immediate recipient but rather to insert information into a pathway that one expects to lead to the ultimate target ("If I tell mom about the dent in the car, I know she'll tell dad, and then I won't have to break the bad news to him."). In this way, disclosure to one network member functions as a way to avoid disclosure to another. In many cases, however, withdrawal and withholding are the options of first choice. By withdrawing or concealing, individuals reinforce their sense of autonomy, and relational partners may enhance the sense that their relationship is special. More generally, information may be withheld to maintain control, to steer clear of conflicts among network members, to avoid burdening network members, and to protect the positive image of the self or relationship in the eyes of others. Given the larger dialectic tensions they seek to address, decisions to disclose or withhold information to network members are often fraught with trade-offs. Mothers and adolescent daughters who extensively discuss the problems each faces report having a more positive relationship, but the adolescents are also more anxious and more prone to depression (Waller & Rose, 2010).

These trade-offs often lead individuals to favor selective disclosure over full disclosure or concealment. One may be selective with respect to *topics*, *targets*, or *timing*. Thus, an individual may disclose some topics or aspects of a topic but not others, to some targets or recipients but not others, and at some times but not others. These options may be applied to the other dynamic tensions at the boundary as well. One may, for instance, actively seek novelty or change in some aspects of one's network while preserving stability in others. Sometimes people artfully construct strategies that appear to respond simultaneously to contradictory interests or demands. We can easily imagine a person whose desires for connection lead to the development of many close relationships with network members but whose desire for autonomy leads him or her to keep those relationships relatively separate from one another, thus minimizing pressures for accountability and conformity to the group.

A fourth approach to managing boundary tensions involves ambiguity and equivocation (Bavelas, Black, Chovil, & Mullett, 1990; Eisenberg, 2007). Both allow people to provide satisfactory responses to network members who have opposing expectations or to respond to network members in ways that are honest but not perhaps altogether complete. Consider cases in which an individual or institution needs to issue an apology. Bavelas (2003), for example, examined the language that four Canadian church organizations used in official apologies for historic mistreatment of indigenous peoples. Although the churches faced tremendous external pressure to fully acknowledge past wrongs, they also recognized that a full apology that took responsibility for specific injustices could create legal liabilities as well as internal conflict. To manage this dilemma, most of the actual "apologies" were phrased equivocally in ways that noted that injustices had occurred but did not actively express responsibility. Ambiguity and equivocation are particularly useful when the information to be conveyed to network members is potentially stressful or even devastating, as in the case of physicians who have to give bad news to patients and their families. Through the skillful use of implicit, and hence somewhat ambiguous, language, physicians are able to deliver bad news honestly but in a less damaging way (Del Vento, Bavelas, Healing, MacLean, & Kirk, 2009).

Researchers have long recognized that relational partners often rely on indirect strategies to assess their relationship. Some of the most common of these are "secret tests" involving network members (Baxter & Wilmot, 1984). For example, one partner may directly seek information from the other partner's friends. Loyalty may be tested by placing one's partner in the presence of an attractive alternative partner, or the definition of the relationship may also be tested by creating a situation in which a particular definition would be expected (e.g., testing a new romantic partner's vision for the relationship with a visit to a family holiday gathering). Although secret tests were originally viewed as indirect strategies for managing uncertainty, later research has suggested that relational partners may use these tests to incite the other to either commit more fully to the relationship or break it off (Chory-Assad & Booth-Butterfield, 2001). All of the research to date has examined the use of secret tests as a way for partners to test or alter the status of their own relationship. Many of the tests identified thus far, however, could just as easily be used to test relationships among network members. For example, "joking" is a test in which the individual teases the partner about the status of the relationship to elicit the partner's response. One can do the same regarding the possible relationships among network members (e.g., "Hey, did you dress up tonight just because you knew Brad was going to be here?").

Relational rituals offer a final set of options for managing information and dialectic tensions within networks. Rituals establish sequences of interaction in which roles are known and harmonized and in which conflicting obligations and expectations are reconciled. Families that invest more time and energy on maintaining their rituals tend to have stronger attachment and greater intimacy (Crespo, Davide, Costa, & Fletcher, 2008). Rituals are no less useful in the management of relations among network members more generally. The scripted roles and sequences of wedding ceremonies, for example, give the bride or groom whose parents are divorced opportunities to include and honor all parties while containing them to specific tasks and minimizing potential conflict (Parks, 2007). Another example comes from lesbian families, where participating in rituals such as regular church attendance helps them to be seen as legitimate within their broader family and community network (Suter, Daas, &

Bergen, 2008). Here, too, the structured nature of ritual both supports family identity and effectively encapsulates potential threats.

*Managing Enemies and Disliked Friends of Friends.* Traditional principles of balance and transitivity predict that we should like those who are liked by the people we like (Heider, 1958; Newcomb, 1953). Your friends should be my friends. Yet when we asked high school and university students if any of their close friends was close to someone that they disliked, 82% said yes. In fact, nearly 30% of their close friends were close to at least one person that the participant disliked (Parks, 2007). Strongly disliked people, people who are seen as attempting to block or thwart one's efforts—in a word, *enemies*—also appear to be common. In one U.S. study, 70% of the young adults surveyed reported having or having had a personal enemy, usually a coworker or former romantic partner (Holt, 1989). And there is evidence that even higher percentages of people in some other cultures think of themselves as having a personal enemy (Adams, 2005). Most people therefore occupy networks containing both liked and disliked persons, and it is common for people we like to like others whom we do not like. To make matters worse, we are often unable to avoid these people.

How do we cope with disliked, but unavoidable, people in our networks? In what to our knowledge is the only study to address this question directly, we developed a typology of 33 strategies for coping with disliked friends of friends. We then asked 137 adolescents and young adults to rate how often they used each strategy (Parks, 2007). Contrary to balance theory predictions, we found that people generally did very little to alter the relational imbalance. Only 5 of the 33 strategies were used very often. The most common strategy was simply to try to tolerate the disliked other by being polite. The next most common was to avoid thinking about the disliked other.

There were a number of individual and situational variations in strategies for dealing with disliked friends of friends. Predictably, males reported being somewhat more confrontational (e.g., arguing with the friend, confronting the disliked person). Respondents whose dislike was greater for their friend's friend also reported using more direct and confrontational strategies. On the other hand, respondents reported being more accepting and less confrontational if they believed that their friend was particularly close to the disliked other and if they were able to spend less time in the presence of the disliked other. Much more work needs to be done on this topic, but our results suggest that passively tolerating disliked others is a common feature of life in social networks.

## Networks and the Deterioration of Relationships

The vast majority of our social relationships never become very close, and most of those that do are relatively short-lived. Young adults in one study, for example, stayed in touch with only about half of those named as contacts just six months earlier (Feld, 1997). In another study, only 8% of those identified as close business associates were named again three years later (Burt, 2000). Only 27% of those named as intimate ties in the local community were named again 10 years later (Wellman, Wong, Tindall, & Nazer, 1997). Estimates of divorce rate vary by method and by age group, but it is likely that 35% to 45% of first marriages in the United States will end in divorce (Hurley, 2005).

Yet even when they deteriorate, relationships may continue in some lesser form or be transformed from one kind of relationship to another. Those whose direct interaction ends may maintain indirect contact through intermediaries in the networks. Network perspectives have the advantage of encompassing the complicated ways in which relationships deteriorate, transform, and realign over time. To illustrate, I will examine the deterioration process in relation to three network factors: (1) distance or reach to specific types of people in the network, (2) several specific aspects of network structure derived from measures of centrality and density, and (3) link content, particularly attraction and support, among network members.

*Relational Deterioration and Network Distance or Reach.* Previously, I outlined several measures of proximity between individuals within a network. I also illustrated how these measures could help us understand the earliest stages of relationship formation. At least two aspects of network distance/reach are relevant for our understanding of how relationships deteriorate. The first is the *distance from alternative partners.* Earlier, I portrayed development as a process in which the partners' developed an increasingly interconnected and mutual network. As Levinger (1979) observed, these changes in network structure effectively reduce access to alternative partners and thereby create barriers to the dissolution of the relationship. Alternative partners should become more distant and less reachable when individuals have forged a mutual network with their relational partners, when they regularly interact with the partner's network (cross-network contact), and when the members of their network interact regularly with the members of their partner's network (cross-network density). This does mean, however, that their networks fully insulate relational participants from alternative partners. In her study of divorced couples who had remarried, for example, Ambert (1989) reported that 11% of the new relationships had started as affairs while the original couple was still living together. Even setting aside the specter of an affair originating within the couple's network, it is likely that the networks of many romantic couples are only moderately dense and overlapping. If so, alternative partners may only be a few links away.

An indirect relationship through the network may continue to exist even after partners stop interacting with each other directly. The *distance from the former partner* should have important implications for support and adjustment following the termination of relationships. After divorce, for example, continued contact with the former partner may present a source of support for parenting or create intrusion and risk. A person may continue to have an influence on the former partner when the distance from the former partner is short enough so that information on his or her activities is readily available. Because of this, relationships may not truly be over when they're "over." Interpersonal communication researchers have yet to explore how such indirect linkages and monitoring might affect former relational partners. First-person accounts, however, make it clear that former partners take advantage of the Internet to track and monitor each other's behavior (e.g., Pollitt, 2004). The consequences of this range from cases of "cyberstalking" (Parsons-Pollard & Moriarty, 2009) to cases in which ex-partners productively use e-mail to avoid face-to-face confrontations (Zaslow, 2005).

*Relational Deterioration and Changes in Network Size and Structure.* As relationships begin to deteriorate, we would expect to see reductions both in the size of the partner's shared network and in the amount of contact between members of their respective networks (cross-network density). There is substantial evidence demonstrating that sharing a common network enhances the stability of premarital relationships (Agnew et al., 2001; Parks & Adelman, 1983). Research on marital relationships also supports the association between network overlap and marital satisfaction and stability (Cotton, Cunningham, & Antill, 1993; Kearns & Leonard, 2004). People are also less likely to end work relationships or to leave their jobs when their networks are more highly linked and when they are connected with a larger number of people in the organization (Burt, 2000; Feeley, 2000).

It follows from these findings that relationships should deteriorate when participants' networks begin to diverge. One reason for this is that relational sensemaking is disrupted and uncertainty increases. Diminishing contact with the partner's network reduces access to information about the partner and eliminates an important frame of reference for interpreting the partner's actions. The concept of network structuring also helps explain why relationships should come apart when networks come apart. When the network is highly overlapping, participants will worry that ending the relationship will cost them not only a partner but many friends and perhaps a broader social status as well (Kalmijn, 2003; Milardo, 1987). This barrier to dissolution no longer functions as effectively once the shared network begins to pull apart. Alternative partners and activities become more available and attractive as the shared network comes apart.

The deterioration of the relationship itself leads to still further reductions, often quite dramatic ones, in the level of network overlap and the amount of contact partners have with the members of each other's network. Following divorce, for example, the network of shared friends shrinks significantly, sometimes by as much as 40% for women, according to some estimates (Duffy, 1993; Hughes, Good, & Candell, 1993). Even when predivorce relationships are maintained, the level of contact with friends and other relatives by marriage is usually far lower than it was prior to the divorce (Albeck & Kaydar, 2002; Ambert, 1988). Moreover, contact and support from friends in one's own network may fall following a divorce (Huddleston & Hawkings, 1993; Spanier & Thompson, 1984).

Changes in the relationship not only affect partners' contact with each other's networks but also contact between the networks (cross-network density). In one of our studies, cross-network density was strongly associated with both the number of people the romantic partners had met in each other's network and how often they communicated with them (Parks, 2007). These factors, in turn, were linked with many aspects of the relationship, including how often the partners interacted, how well they felt they understood each other, how intimate they were, and how committed they were to maintaining the relationship. Conversely, reductions in the amount of communication between the partners' networks should trigger a wide range of indirect but negative effects inside the relationship. Effects

can also flow the other way as troubles inside the relationship work their way out to reduce cross-network density. Married couples whose relationship is beginning to flounder, for example, often avoid socializing together (Vaughan, 1986). As social events that brought network members into contact become less frequent, network members now have less opportunity to interact with each other. One spouse may also actively discourage network members from socializing with those in the other spouse's network. We should, however, keep in mind that loosening of network connections can have positive as well as negative consequences. It may bring relief from enmeshed, dysfunctional relationships and thus create new, more adaptive options for network members and relational participants alike.

*Relational Deterioration and Changes in the Content of Communication With Network Members.* The content that flows through links among network members also changes as relationships deteriorate. Chief among these are changes in attraction and support. Although our studies (Parks, 2007) reveal that dislike for the partner's network usually had negative effects on the relationship, Sprecher and Felmlee (2000) found that attraction to the partner's friends and family was unrelated to the likelihood of terminating a romantic relationship over a five-year period. Both of these studies, however, relied on averaged or global judgments about network members as a group. What counts, however, is probably not whether one likes everyone in the partner's network or whether the average level of attraction to the partner's network is high. The vital questions may be whether there is at least one person to like, whether one likes those the partner sees as important to like, and whether one can minimize interaction with those one strongly dislikes. If not, the relationship should either not develop very far or, if already established, should deteriorate rapidly.

These effects flow both ways. Troubles inside the relationship may lead to negative feelings toward members of the partner's network. This can happen in a number of ways. When the relationship is in trouble, information shared with members of one's own network is usually biased toward blaming the other partner (Gray & Silver, 1990). Network members then alter their behavior toward the blamed partner, and in turn, their increasingly negative response may cause the partner to dislike the network members in question. Unfortunately, these may be the very people whom it is most crucial to like. As the relationship deteriorates further, individuals may assume that negative accounts have become widely known in the partner's network, and this may cause the average or overall level of attraction to network members to drop. Much of this is conjecture, but we do know that couples who break up typically report decreased liking for their former partner's family and friends. Sprecher and Felmlee (2000) found that both men and women liked their former partner's family and friends less after the breakup.

Support from friends and family can play a critical role in the decision to end a relationship. Researchers have generally found that the less the support dating couples perceive from the partner's family and friends for their relationship, the more likely they are to end their relationship within the following year (e.g., Felmlee & Greenberg, 1999; Lewis, 1973a; Parks & Adelman, 1983). Similar findings have emerged from studies of marriage and divorce—those who perceive less support for their relationship are less satisfied, less committed, more likely to consider ending their relationship, and more likely to actually end it (Bryant & Conger, 1999; Cleek & Pearson, 1985; Greeff, 2000).

Relationships with in-laws are particularly crucial in marriage. The potential complexity of these linkages was revealed in a four-year study of couples who had been married for many years (Bryant, Conger, & Meehan, 2001). For both husbands and wives, conflict with their mother-in-law was associated with lower satisfaction, commitment, and relational stability a year later. The same pattern emerged for relationships with the father-in-law, although not

as consistently for the husbands as for the wives. The causal pattern was also somewhat different for husbands and wives. For wives, conflict with in-laws spoiled the marriage, but there was no evidence that the quality of the marriage at one point in time was related to the level of conflict with in-laws at a later point. For husbands, conflict with in-laws and relational deterioration appeared to drive each other: Greater conflict with in-laws reduced marital quality, and reduced marital quality resulted in more conflict with the in-laws.

This last finding reminds us that the association between relational deterioration and support from network members is often a two-way street. Lack of support from network members can have deleterious effects on the quality of the marriage or dating relationship. By the same token, as the relationship deteriorates, network members may reevaluate their previous positions and shift to supporting the end rather than the continuance of the relationship. Recently divorced people typically report that network members approved of the divorce (Huddleston & Hawkings, 1993; Spanier & Thompson, 1984; Sprecher & Felmlee, 2000).

## Networks and Relationships: Summary and Implications

The development and deterioration of interpersonal relationships depends only in part on the characteristics of the participants and their interaction with one another. As the foregoing discussion illustrates, the fate of relationships also depends on the participants' location within a larger social network and on their interactions with network members. Relationships, in other words, can only be understood within the context of other relationships—within a network.

Because network terminology is so varied, I began by describing those aspects of networks that are most relevant for scholars of interpersonal communication. Social networks consist of links between "nodes," typically individual communicators. Network structure is defined by the pattern of linkages between individuals. Some are linked; some are not. Links are usually conceptualized in terms of the amount of interaction, the strength or importance of the relationship between individuals, or the presence of some specific type of message content (e.g., support messages). The pattern of linkages among people, regardless of how the linkage is defined, will create a network structure whose characteristics have implications for the flow of information and support, for innovation, for group cohesion, and for interpersonal conflict. Wide interdisciplinary interest has resulted in quite diverse approaches to describing network structure, but four aspects would appear to have particular relevance for researchers interested in interpersonal communication: network size, reach, and central and overall structure. As we revisit each in this closing section, I will first summarize its role in helping us understand the life cycle of personal relationships and then explore how it might be applied to other interpersonal processes.

## Interpersonal Communication and the Size of Networks

The first way to describe a network is in terms of its size. How many close friends does a given person have? How many people does the individual in question receive support from? How many people does the individual provide support to? Depending on the question being examined, it may be helpful to distinguish between in-degree and out-degree links or reciprocated and unreciprocated links. The size of an individual's social network will have implications for access to information, for the ability to enlist others in taking collective action, and for a variety of affective, cognitive, and physiological states, including loneliness, happiness, stress, and overall health (e.g., Christakis & Fowler, 2009).

Network size enters into the development and deterioration of personal relationships at three points. First, other things being equal, the size of

an individual's network determines the range of potential relational partners. People with larger personal networks, especially if those networks have diverse ties, will be socially proximal to a greater number of people and thus encounter a larger pool of potential partners. They will also have more people to draw on for third-party assistance early in a relationship. Second, once a relationship is initiated, the proportion of people in the partner's network with whom one has contact will be closely associated with the relationship's development. Research has consistently demonstrated that for both romantic relationships and same-sex friendships, the proportion of people one interacts with in the partner's network will be positively associated with the amount of interaction, intimacy, and commitment one has for the partner. Although proportion is undoubtedly important, many intriguing questions remain regarding how many people one needs to meet, how people manage oppositional network members, and how they obtain support from members of their own and their partner's network. Indeed, the entire question of how individuals marshal support for their relationships from other members of the network is only beginning to be explored (Crowley, 2010). Finally, the size of particular network components, such as the support network, will influence the stability of relationships. Support networks not only provide resources that help maintain relationships but, as we noted earlier, also function to insulate partners from alternatives to their relationship. One of the critical turning points in the decline of a relationship occurs when partners stop nurturing a network that supports the relationship and begin building a network that supports them as individuals independent of the relationship.

Network size is also implicated in a variety of other processes of interest to interpersonal communication researchers. Most obviously, the size of one's personal network is a measure, albeit a crude one, of one's social influence. Those who have greater numbers of contacts with others in the network are often viewed as opinion leaders (Buller, Dignan, Buller, & Gadt, 2001; Cohen, Havlin, & ben-Avraham, 2003). The size of one's personal network is also undoubtedly related to one's health and well-being, though clearly not in a simple way. Recent research on loneliness suggests, for example, that loneliness is not affected by the total size of one's social network or even by the size of one's kin network but is negatively associated with the size of one's friendship network (Cacioppo, Fowler, & Christakis, 2009). This research also suggests that therapeutic interventions aimed at helping lonely people will be maximally effective when they are aimed at individuals at the periphery of social networks. The benefits of a large network are further complicated by expectations of reciprocity. Having a large number of people from whom one can draw support is protective; however, having a large number of people who also expect support in return may outstrip one's emotional and material resources. Furthermore, a large network may be rich in one type of support but impoverished in another. Tardy and Hale (1998), for example, identified two quite different types of social support that mothers obtained from a playgroup for their toddlers. One was affirmation or "bonding" support. The other involved the exchange of practical advice that allowed mothers to "crack the code" of the various institutions providing health and other child care services. One can easily imagine a group in which mothers form a very cohesive, "bonded" group but whose members lack the skill and experience needed to work effectively with external institutions. Thus, what appears to be a large network may in fact be deficient with regard to a particular need or requirement.

Finally, it is worth considering network size in relationship to the "dark side" of interpersonal communication (Spitzberg & Cupach, 2007). Although there is a great deal of work on the positive effects of social support, little attention has been given to the possible negative affects of a network dominated by complaint and rumination. Supporters lift, but being caught in a network of those who rehash negative experiences can lead to depression, particularly in adolescent females (Starr & Davila, 2009; Stone, Uhrlass, & Gibb, 2010). Ruminating in female friendships has been shown to increase rather than mitigate hormonal stress responses to life stressors (Byrd-Craven, Geary, Rose, & Ponzi, 2008).

## Interpersonal Communication and Reach in Networks

The concept of "reach" generally refers to the distance separating any two individuals within a broader network. As I noted previously, it contributes to our understanding of how relationships both begin and end. SCT (Parks, 2007) is unique in its conceptualization of the "prehistory" of relationships as one of decreasing network distance between future partners. At the other end of the relational life cycle, deterioration and its aftermath can be described in part as increasing network distance between former partners and decreasing network distance to alternative partners.

Network reach and distance are also relevant for several other aspects of interpersonal communication. Two particularly promising areas for further research involve efforts to improve intergroup relations and to enhance the effectiveness and efficiency of health campaigns. With regard to the first, there is now substantial evidence to suggest that contact between groups often, though not automatically, results in reduced tensions (Harwood, 2010; Pettigrew & Tropp, 2006). Although much of the work to date has focused on direct contacts, indirect contacts between groups can also reduce tension. For one thing, people from different groups are more likely to interact in a positive manner if they discover that they already have friends in common. Beyond this, however, simply discovering that one has indirect links to members of a disliked group may itself reduce perceptions of dissimilarity (Aron, Mashek, & Aron, 2004; Wright, Aron, McLaughlin-Volpe, & Ropp, 1997). Interventions that increase knowledge of indirect ties with members of disliked groups may offer a practical way to reduce intergroup prejudice.

Understanding the reach of indirect ties also creates opportunities for social action. A common problem for public health agencies is how to engage those who have not yet been diagnosed or who are not already receiving treatment. This is true for a variety of conditions, but I will focus on the case of HIV (human immunodeficiency virus) because infection rates are higher in hard-to-reach minority communities than in the general population and because nearly half of all new infections are believed to have come from sexual contact with people who are not aware that they have HIV (Marks, Crepaz, & Janssen, 2006). Attempts to reach those with undiagnosed HIV through media campaigns and community-based campaigns have generally met with little success. Recently, however, researchers have turned to "peer-recruiting" strategies in which HIV-positive individuals were enlisted to recruit peers from their social, sexual, or drug-using networks. This strategy proved to be more than five times more effective at linking previously undiagnosed individuals with health care providers than a more traditional strategy (Kimbrough et al., 2009). In our terms, these researchers used direct ties to extend their reach to indirect, second-order ties.

## Interpersonal Communication and Centrality in Networks

How central one is in a local or broader network has implications for an array of interpersonal processes. Several different measures of centrality have been described in this chapter, but broadly speaking, people who are more central know more people who know more people. Previously, I described several ways in which one's relational opportunities and outcomes may depend on centrality. Individuals who are more central in a network will have more opportunities to initiate relationships than those who are in peripheral positions. The principle of social proximity implies that the probability of as yet unacquainted individuals meeting increases as the number of indirect links separating them is reduced—that is, as they "drift" toward a more central region of an emerging mutual network. Furthermore, our research on third-party helping implies that those closer to the center of networks are in a better position, first, to introduce previously unacquainted individuals to one another and, second, to provide additional assistance, including social support, to nascent relationships. As friendships and romantic relationships grow closer, each partner becomes more central in the other's social network, and their relationship becomes more central in their emerging joint network. Greater centrality in turn opens channels of information and support that allow the partners to manage uncertainty and enhance the stability of the relationship. Increased centrality in a joint or shared network also increases the stability of the relationship by reducing access to alternative partners. The research on relationship termination suggests, conversely, that when this centrality is threatened, either by troubles inside the relationship or by rifts in the network created by external forces, the relationship between the partners will begin to deteriorate.

Measures of centrality may illuminate other interpersonal processes as well. At the microlevel, researchers may find new ways to understand the dynamics of families and work groups by examining the various ways in which an individual may "broker" relationships between other group members (Fernandez & Gould, 1994). Ng's (2007) work on how bilingual family members broker family decision making illustrates the potential for research on brokering relationships to help us understand how groups bridge differences in language, culture, and goals. Beyond this, measures of centrality offer important tools for understanding flows of information and influence in social networks. They offer a counterbalance to traditional approaches that have relied, perhaps too heavily, on measures of motivation or personality to account for why some individuals are more influential or better informed than others. This is theoretically important, but it is also rich in practical implications for those who are attempting to understand how to disseminate messages efficiently and effectively within social systems.

## Interpersonal Communication and Overall Network Structure

Several more general aspects of network structure will be of interest to interpersonal communication scholars. These include the overall density or connectedness of the network of interest, the level of transitivity within the network as a whole, and the presence of clusters or "local neighborhoods" within the overall network. Relationship development and deterioration, as I have argued throughout, are best understood when we augment our traditional concerns with individuals and dyads with an appreciation of the changing local densities within the participants' larger social networks. Changes in the level of connection among members of those larger networks mediate opportunities to meet, access to alternative partners, uncertainty and support, and the overall stability of any given dyadic relationship.

The role of local network densities and structures in the life cycle of interpersonal relationships can easily be extended to a variety of other interpersonal processes. The effects of changing local densities on access to alternative partners, for example, are closely related to questions about change and innovation more generally. Questions about how people manage uncertainty and obtain support for a particular relationship in the network are merely specific instances of broader questions about how people make sense of their social environment. What we have learned about the bridging of networks in the development of friendships and romantic relationships can easily be extended to ideas about how to bridge ethnic and cultural differences.

The study of interpersonal communication continues to suffer from a strong disciplinary, and perhaps cultural, bias toward explaining behavior in terms of individual differences and isolated interactions. By shifting our attention to the relationships between network members and to the structures in which individuals and interactions are embedded, social network perspectives have the potential to expand dramatically both the power of our theories and the value of our contribution to the solution of a wide variety of social problems.

## References

Adams, G. (2005). The cultural grounding of personal relationship: Enemyship in North American and West African worlds. *Journal of Personality and Social Psychology, 88,* 948–968.

Afifi, T. D. (2003). "Feeling caught" in stepfamilies: Managing boundary turbulence through appropriate communication privacy rules. *Journal of Social and Personal Relationships, 20,* 729–755.

Afifi, W. A., & Weiner, J. L. (2004). Toward a theory of motivated information management. *Communication Theory, 14,* 167–190.

Agnew, C. R., Loving, T. J., & Drigotas, S. M. (2001). Substituting the forest for the trees: Social networks and the prediction of romantic relationship state and fate. *Journal of Personality and Social Psychology, 81,* 1042–1057.

Albeck, S., & Kaydar, D. (2002). Divorced mothers: Their network of friends pre- and post-divorce. *Journal of Divorce & Remarriage, 36*(3–4), 111–138.

Altman, I., & Taylor, D. (1973). *Social penetration: The development of interpersonal relationships.* New York: Holt, Rinehart, & Winston.

Ambert, A. (1988). Relationships with former in-laws: A research note. *Journal of Marriage and Family, 50,* 679–686.

Ambert, A. (1989). *Ex-spouses and new spouses: A study of relationships.* Greenwich, CT: JAI Press.

Aron, A., Mashek, D. J., & Aron, E. N. (2004). Closeness as including other in the self. In D. J. Mashek & A. Aron (Eds.), *Handbook of closeness and intimacy* (pp. 27–41). Mahwah, NJ: Lawrence Erlbaum.

Babrow, A. S. (2007). Problematic integration theory. In B. B. Whaley & W. Samter (Eds.), *Explaining communication: Contemporary theories and exemplars* (pp. 181–200). Mahwah, NJ: Lawrence Erlbaum.

Barabási, A.-L. (2002). *Linked: How everything is connected to everything else and what it means for business, science, and everyday life.* New York: Penguin Books.

Barnett, G. A., & Hwang, J. M. (2006). The use of the Internet for health information and social support: A content analysis of online breast cancer discussion groups. In M. Murero & R. E. Rice (Eds.), *The Internet and health care: Theory, research, and practice.* (pp. 233–253). Mahwah, NJ: Lawrence Erlbaum.

Bartholomew, R. E. (2000). Re: "Epidemic hysteria: A review of the published literature." *American Journal of Epidemiology, 151,* 2006–2207.

Bartholomew, R. E., & Sirois, F. (1996). Epidemic hysteria in schools: An international and historical overview. *Educational Studies, 22*(3), 285–311.

Bavelas, J. B. (2003). *A field test of equivocation theory: Apologies by Canadian churches to indigenous people.* Paper presented at the annual conference of the International Communication Association, San Diego, CA.

Bavelas, J. B., Black, A., Chovil, N., & Mullett, J. (1990). *Equivocal communication.* Newbury Park, CA: Sage.

Baxter, L. A. (1988). A dialectical perspective on communication strategies in relationship development. In S. Duck (Ed.), *Handbook of personal relationships* (pp. 257–273). New York: Wiley.

Baxter, L. A. (1993). The social side of personal relationships: A dialectical perspective. In S. Duck (Ed.), *Social context and relationships* (pp. 139–165). Newbury Park, CA: Sage.

Baxter, L. A., Dun, T., & Sahlstein, E. (2001). Rules for relating communicated among social network members. *Journal of Social and Personal Relationships, 18*(2), 173–199.

Baxter, L. A., & Wilmot, W. W. (1984). "Secret tests": Social strategies for acquiring information about the state of the relationship. *Human Communication Research, 11,* 171–202.

Bearman, P. S., Moody, J., & Stovel, K. (2004). Chains of affection: The structure of adolescent romantic and sexual networks. *American Journal of Sociology, 110,* 44–91.

Berger, C. R., & Calabrese, R. J. (1975). Some explorations in initial interaction and beyond: Toward a developmental theory of interpersonal communication. *Human Communication Research, 1,* 99–112.

Blau, P. M. (1977a). A macrosociological theory of social structure. *American Journal of Sociology, 83,* 26–54.

Blau, P. M. (1977b). *Inequality and heterogeneity: A primitive theory of social structure.* New York: Free Press.

Bonacich, P. (1972). Factoring and weighting approaches to status scores and clique identification. *Journal of Mathematical Sociology, 2,* 113–120.

Bonacich, P. (1987). Power and centrality: A family of measures. *American Journal of Sociology, 92,* 1170–1182.

Boss, L. P. (1997). Epidemic hysteria: A review of the published literature. *Epidemiological Reviews, 19,* 233–243.

Brashers, D. E. (2001). Communication and uncertainty management. *Journal of Communication, 51,* 477–497.

Brashers, D. E., Neidig, J. L., & Goldsmith, D. J. (2004). Social support and the management of uncertainty for people living with HIV or AIDS. *Health Communication, 16*(3), 305–331.

Bryant, C., & Conger, R. (1999). Marital success and domains of social support in long-term relationships: Does the influence of network members never end? *Journal of Marriage and Family, 61,* 437–450.

Bryant, C., Conger, R., & Meehan, J. M. (2001). The influence of in-laws on change in marital success. *Journal of Marriage and Family, 63,* 614–626.

Buller, D., Dignan, M., Buller, M. K., & Gadt, M. (2001). A pilot study to improve dietary behaviors at the worksite with peer leaders. *AWHP's Worksite Health, Spring,* 38–41.

Burt, R. S. (1983). Distinguishing relational contents. In R. S. Burt & M. J. Minor (Eds.), *Applied network analysis: A methodological introduction* (pp. 35–74). Beverly Hills, CA: Sage.

Burt, R. S. (1992). *Structural holes: The social structure of competition.* Cambridge, MA: Harvard University Press.

Burt, R. S. (2000). Decay functions. *Social Networks, 22,* 1–28.

Burt, R. S. (2004). Structural holes and good ideas. *American Journal of Sociology, 110,* 349–399.

Byrd-Craven, J., Geary, D. C., Rose, A. J., & Ponzi, D. (2008). Co-ruminating increases stress hormone levels in women. *Hormones and Behavior, 53*(3), 489–492.

Cacioppo, J. T., Fowler, J. H., & Christakis, N. A. (2009). Alone in the crowd: The structure and spread of loneliness in a large social network. *Journal of Personality and Social Psychology, 97*(6), 977–991.

Canary, D. J., Cody, M. J., & Manusov, V. L. (2008). *Interpersonal communication: A goals based approach* (4th ed.). Boston: Bedford/St. Martin's.

Carey, M. P., Senn, T. E., Seward, D. X., & Vanable, P. A. (2010). Urban African-American men speak out on sexual partner concurrency: Findings from a qualitative study. *AIDS and Behavior, 14*(1), 38–47.

Chory-Assad, R. M., & Booth-Butterfield, M. (2001). Secret test use and self-esteem in deteriorating relationships. *Communication Research Reports, 18*(2), 147–157.

Christakis, N., & Fowler, J. H. (2009). *Connected: The surprising power of our social networks and how they shape our lives.* New York: Little, Brown.

Cleek, M., & Pearson, T. A. (1985). Perceived causes of divorce: An analysis of interrelationships. *Journal of Marriage and Family, 47,* 179–191.

Cohen, R., Havlin, S., & ben-Avraham, D. (2003). Efficient immunization strategies for computer networks and populations. *Physical Review Letters, 91*(24), 247901-1–247904-4.

Connolly, J. A., Furman, W., & Konarski, R. (2000). The role of peers in the emergence of heterosexual romantic relationships in adolescence. *Child Development, 71,* 1395–1408.

Cotton, S., Cunningham, J., & Antill, J. (1993). Network structure, network support and the marital satisfaction of husbands and wives. *Australian Journal of Psychology, 45,* 176–181.

Crespo, C., Davide, I. N., Costa, M. E., & Fletcher, G. J. O. (2008). Family rituals in married couples: Links with attachment, relationship quality, and closeness. *Personal Relationships, 15*(2), 191–203.

Crooks, V. C., Lubben, J., Petitti, D. B., Little, D., & Chiu, V. (2008). Social network, cognitive function, and dementia incidence among elderly women. *American Journal of Public Health, 98*(7), 1221–1227.

Crowley, J. (2010). *Marshaling network support for romantic relationships: Towards the development of a typology.* San Francisco: National Communication Association.

Del Vento, A., Bavelas, J. B., Healing, S., MacLean, G., & Kirk, P. (2009). An experimental investigation of the dilemma of delivering bad news. *Patient Education and Counseling, 77,* 443–449.

Driscoll, R., Davis, K. E., & Lipetz, M. E. (1972). Parental interference and romantic love: The Romeo and Juliet effect. *Journal of Personality and Social Psychology, 24,* 1–10.

Duffy, M. (1993). Social networks and social support of recently divorced women. *Public Health Nursing, 10*(1), 19–24.

Eagle, N., Macy, M., & Claxton, R. (2010). Network diversity and economic development. *Science, 328,* 1029–1031.

Eisenberg, E. M. (2007). *Strategic ambiguities: Essays on communication, organization, and identity.* Thousand Oaks, CA: Sage.

Emirbayer, M., & Mische, A. (1998). What is agency? *American Journal of Sociology, 103,* 962–1023.

Eveland, W. P., Jr., & Hively, M. H. (2009). Political discussion frequency, network size, and heterogeneity of discussion as predictors of political knowledge and participation. *Journal of Communication, 59*(2), 205–224.

Fararo, T. J. (1989). *The meaning of general theoretical sociology: Tradition and formalization.* Cambridge, UK: Cambridge University Press.

Fast, N. J., & Tiedens, L. Z. (2010). Blame contagion: The automatic transmission of self-serving attributions. *Journal of Experimental Social Psychology, 46*(1), 97–106.

Feeley, T. H. (2000). Testing a communication network model of employee turnover based on centrality. *Journal of Applied Communication Research, 28,* 262–278.

Feld, S. L. (1997). Structural embeddedness and the stability of interpersonal relations. *Social Networks, 19,* 91–95.

Felmlee, D., & Greenberg, S. (1999). A dynamic systems model of dyadic interaction. *Journal of Mathematical Sociology, 23,* 155–180.

Fernandez, R. M., & Gould, R. V. (1994). A dilemma of state power: Brokerage and influence in the national health policy domain. *American Journal of Sociology, 99,* 1455–1491.

Fischer, C. S. (1977). *Networks and places: Social relations in the urban setting.* New York: Free Press.

Floyd, K. (2009). *Interpersonal communication: The whole story.* New York: McGraw-Hill.

Freeman, L. (1978–1979). Centrality in social networks: Conceptual clarification. *Social Networks, 1,* 215–239.

Freeman, L. (1996). Some antecedents of social network analysis. *Connections, 19,* 39–42.

Fuchs, S. (2001). *Against essentialism: A theory of culture and society.* Cambridge, MA: Harvard University Press.

Goeree, J. K., McConnell, M. A., Mitchell, T., Tromp, T., & Yariv, L. (2008). *The 1/d law of giving.* Retrieved

May 20, 2010, from www.hss.caltech.edu/~lyariv/
Papers/Westridge.pdf

Goldsmith, D. J. (1988). *To talk or not to talk: The flow
of information between romantic dyads and members of their communication networks.* Unpublished
master's thesis, University of Washington, Seattle.

Goldsmith, D. J. (2004). *Communicating social support.*
New York: Cambridge University Press.

Granovetter, M. S. (1973). The strength of weak ties.
*American Journal of Sociology, 78,* 1361–1380.

Gray, J. D., & Silver, R. C. (1990). Opposite sides of the
same coin: Former spouses' divergent perspectives in coping with their divorce. *Journal of
Personality and Social Psychology, 59,* 1180–1191.

Greeff, A. P. (2000). Characteristics of families that
function well. *Journal of Family Issues, 21,* 948–962.

Haines, V. Y., III, Marchand, A., & Harvey, S. (2006).
Crossover of workplace aggression experiences in
dual-earner couples. *Journal of Occupational
Health Psychology, 11*(4), 305–314.

Hampton, K., & Wellman, B. (2003). Neighboring in
Netville: How the Internet supports community
and social capital in a wired suburb. *City &
Community, 2*(4), 277–311.

Hanneman, R. A., & Riddle, M. (2005). *Introduction to
social network methods.* Riverside, CA: University
of California. Retrieved March 31, 2011, from
http://faculty.ucr.edu/~hanneman/

Harwood, J. (2010). The contact space: A novel framework for intergroup contact research. *Journal of
Language and Social Psychology, 29*(2), 147–177.

Heider, F. (1958). *The psychology of interpersonal relations.* New York: Wiley.

Holt, R. R. (1989). College students' definitions and
images of enemies. *Journal of Social Issues, 45,* 33–50.

Huddleston, R. J., & Hawkings, L. (1993). The reation
of friends and family to divorce. *Journal of Divorce
& Remarriage, 19*(1–2), 195–207.

Hughes, R., Good, E., & Candell, K. (1993). A longitudinal study of the effects of social support on
the psychological adjustment of the divorced
mothers. *Journal of Divorce & Remarriage, 19*(1–2),
37–56.

Hurley, D. (2005, April 19). Divorce rate: It's not as high
as you think. *New York Times.* Retrieved March 31,
2011, from www.nytimes.com/2005/04/19/health/
19divo.html

Johnson, M. P., & Leslie, L. A. (1982). Couple involvement and network structure: A test of the dyadic
withdrawal hypothesis. *Social Psychology Quarterly,
45,* 34–43.

Johnson, M. P., & Milardo, R. M. (1984). Network
interference in pair relationships: A social psychological recasting of Slater's theory of social
regression. *Journal of Marriage and Family, 46,*
893–899.

Julien, D., Chartrand, E., & Begin, J. (1999). Social networks, structural interdependence, and conjugal
adjustment in heterosexual, gay, and lesbian couples. *Journal of Marriage and Family, 61,* 516–530.

Julien, D., & Markman, H. J. (1991). Social support
and social networks as determinants of individual
and marital outcomes. *Journal of Social and Personal
Relationships, 8,* 549–568.

Julien, D., Markman, H. J., Léveillé, S., Chartrand, É., &
Bégin, J. (1994). Networks' support and interference with regard to marriage: Disclosure of marital problems to confidants. *Journal of Family
Psychology, 8,* 16–31.

Julien, D., Tremblay, N., Bélanger, I., Dubé, M., Bégin, J.,
& Bouthillier, D. (2000). Interaction structure of
husbands' and wives' disclosure of marital conflict to their respective best friend. *Journal of
Family Psychology, 14*(2), 286–303.

Kalmijn, M. (2003). Shared friendship networks and
the life course: An analysis of survey data on married and cohabiting couples. *Social Networks, 25,*
231–249.

Kalmijn, M., & Flap, H. (2001). Assortative meeting
and mating: Unintended consequences of organized settings for partner choices. *Social Forces,
79,* 1289–1312.

Kearns, J. N., & Leonard, K. E. (2004). Social networks,
structural interdependence, and marital quality
over the transition to marriage: A prospective
analysis. *Journal of Family Psychology, 18,* 383–395.

Kim, H. J., & Stiff, J. B. (1991). Social networks and the
development of close relationships. *Human
Communication Research, 18,* 70–91.

Kim, Y. Y., & McKay-Semmler, K. (2009). *Interethnic
communication among college students: An examination of behavioral and contextual factors.*
Chicago: International Communication Association.

Kimbrough, L. W., Fisher, H. E., Jones, K. T., Johnson, W.,
Thadiparthi, S., & Dooley, S. (2009). Accessing
social networks with high rates of undiagnosed
HIV infection: The social networks demonstration project. *American Journal of Public Health,
99*(6), 1093–1099.

de Klepper, M., Sleebos, E., van de Bunt, G., &
Agneessens, F. (2010). Similarity in friendship
networks: Selection or influence? The effect of

constraining contexts and non-visible individual attributes. *Social Networks, 32*(1), 82–90.

Knapp, M. L., & Vangelisti, A. L. (2009). *Interpersonal communication and human relationships* (6th ed.). Boston: Allyn & Bacon.

Knobloch, L. K., & Solomon, D. H. (1999). Measuring the sources and content of relational uncertainty. *Communication Studies, 50*, 261–278.

Knoke, D., & Yang, S. (2008). *Social network analysis* (2nd ed.). Thousand Oaks, CA: Sage.

Kolaczyk, E. D. (2009). *Statistical analysis of network data: Methods and models.* New York: Springer.

Kouzis, A. C., & Eaton, W. W. (1998). Absence of social networks, social support and health services utilization. *Psychological Medicine, 28*, 1301–1310.

Krackhardt, D., & Stern, R. (1988). Informal networks and organizational crises: An experimental simulation. *Social Psychology Quarterly, 51*(2), 123–140.

Lau, D. C., & Liden, R. C. (2008). Antecedents of coworker trust: Leaders' blessings. *Journal of Applied Psychology, 93*(5), 1130–1138.

Laumann, E. O. (1973). *Bonds of pluralism: The form and substance of urban social networks.* New York: Wiley.

Laumann, E. O., Gagnon, J. H., Michael, R. T., & Michaels, S. (1994). *The social organization of sexuality: Sexual practices in the United States.* Chicago: University of Chicago Press.

Leslie, L. A., Huston, T. L., & Johnson, M. P. (1986). Parental reactions to dating relationships: Do they make a difference? *Journal of Marriage and Family, 48*, 57–66.

Levinger, G. (1979). A social exchange view of the dissolution of pair relationships. In R. L. Burgess & T. L. Huston (Eds.), *Social exchange in developing relationships* (pp. 169–193). New York: Academic Press.

Lewis, R. A. (1973a). A longitudinal test of a developmental framework for premarital dyadic formation. *Journal of Marriage and Family, 35*(1), 16–25.

Lewis, R. A. (1973b). Social reaction and the formation of dyads: An interactionist approach to mate selection. *Sociometry, 36*(3), 409–418.

Lewis, T. G. (2009). *Network science: Theory and applications.* Oxford, UK: Wiley-Blackwell.

Marks, G., Crepaz, N., & Janssen, R. S. (2006). Estimating sexual transmission of HIV from persons aware and unaware they are infected with the virus in the United States. *AIDS, 20*(10), 1147–1450.

Marsden, P. V. (1987). Core discussion networks of Americans. *American Sociological Review, 52*, 122–131.

McCornack, S. (2010). *Reflect & relate: An introduction to interpersonal communication* (2nd ed.). Boston: Bedford/St. Marten's.

McPherson, M., Smith-Lovin, L., & Brashears, M. E. (2006). Social isolation in America: Changes in core discussion networks over two decades. *American Sociological Review, 71*, 353–375.

Meyer, M. (2010). The rise of the knowledge broker. *Science Communication, 32*(1), 118–127.

Milardo, R. M. (1982). Friendship networks in developing relationships: Converging and diverging social environments. *Social Psychology Quarterly, 45*, 162–172.

Milardo, R. M. (1983). Social networks and pair relationships: A review of substantive and measurement issues. *Sociology and Social Research, 68*, 1–18.

Milardo, R. M. (1987). Changes in social networks of women and men following divorce. *Journal of Family Issues, 8*, 78–96.

Milardo, R. M. (1989). Theoretical and methodological issues in the identification of the social networks of spouses. *Journal of Marriage and Family, 51*, 165–174.

Milardo, R. M. (1992). Comparative methods for delineating social networks. *Journal of Social and Personal Relationships, 9*, 447–461.

Milardo, R. M., & Helms-Erikson, H. (2000). Network overlap and third-party influence in close relationships. In C. Hendrick & S. Hendrick (Eds.), *Close relationships: A sourcebook* (pp. 33–45). Thousand Oaks, CA: Sage.

Milardo, R. M., Johnson, M. P., & Huston, T. L. (1983). Developing close relationships: Changing patterns of interaction between pair members and social networks. *Journal of Personality and Social Psychology, 44*, 964–976.

Miller, G. R., & Steinberg, M. (1975). *Between people: A new analysis of interpersonal communication.* Chicago: Science Research.

Moody, J. (2001). Race, school integration, and friendship segregation in America. *American Journal of Sociology, 107*, 679–716.

Newcomb, T. M. (1953). An approach to the study of communicative acts. *Psychological Review, 60*, 391–404.

Newcomb, T. M. (1961). *The acquaintance process.* New York: Holt, Rinehart, & Winston.

Newman, M., Barabási, A.-L., & Watts, D. J. (Eds.). (2006). *The structure and dynamics of networks.* Princeton, NJ: Princeton University Press.

Ng, S. H. (2007). From language acculturation to communication acculturation: Addressee orientations and communication brokering in conversations. *Journal of Language and Social Psychology, 26*(1), 75–90.

Parks, M. R. (2007). *Personal relationships and personal networks.* Mahwah, NJ: Lawrence Erlbaum.

Parks, M. R., & Adelman, M. B. (1983). Communication networks and the development of romantic relationships: An expansion of uncertainty reduction theory. *Human Communication Research, 10,* 55–79.

Parks, M. R., Stan, C. M., & Eggert, L. L. (1983). Romantic involvement and social network involvement. *Social Psychology Quarterly, 46*(2), 116–131.

Parsons-Pollard, N., & Moriarty, L. J. (2009). Cyberstalking: Utilizing what we do know. *Victims & Offenders, 4*(4), 435–441.

Petronio, S. (2002). *Boundaries of private disclosures.* New York: SUNY Press.

Petronio, S., & Bantz, C. (1991). Controlling the ramifications of disclosure: "Don't tell anybody but . . . ." *Journal of Language and Social Psychology, 10,* 263–269.

Petronio, S., Ellemers, N., Giles, H., & Gallois, C. (1998). (Mis)communicating across boundaries. *Communication Research, 25,* 571–595.

Petronio, S., & Jones, S. M. (2006). When "friendly advice" becomes a privacy dilemma for pregnant couples: Applying communication privacy management theory. In L. H. Turner & R. West (Eds.), *The family communication sourcebook* (pp. 201–218). Thousand Oaks, CA: Sage.

Petronio, S., & Reierson, J. (2009). Regulating the privacy of confidentiality: Grasping the complexities through communication privacy management theory. In T. D. Afifi & W. A. Afifi (Eds.), *Uncertainty, information management, and disclosure decisions: Theories and applications* (pp. 365–383). New York: Routledge.

Pettigrew, T. F., & Tropp, L. R. (2006). A meta-analytic test of intergroup contact theory. *Journal of Personality and Social Psychology, 90*(5), 751–783.

Pollitt, K. (2004, January 19). Webstalker: When it's time to stop checking on your ex. *The New Yorker, 409,* 38–42.

Raile, A. N. W., Kim, R. K., Jounghwa, C., Serota, K. B., Hee Sun, P., & Dong Wook, L. (2008). Connections at work: How friendship networks relate to job satisfaction. *Communication Research Reports, 25*(2), 168–178.

Rawlins, W. K. (2009). *The compass of friendship: Narratives, identities, and dialogues.* Thousand Oaks, CA: Sage.

Rubin, K. H., Bukowski, W. M., & Laursen, B. (2009). *Handbook of peer interactions, relationships, and groups.* New York: Guilford Press.

Sabidussi, G. (1966). The centrality index of a graph. *Psychometrika, 31,* 581–603.

Simmel, G. (1950). *The sociology of Georg Simmel* (K. H. Wolff, Trans.). Glencoe, IL: Free Press.

Simmel, G. (1955). *Conflict & the web of group affiliations* (K. H. Wolff & R. Bendix, Trans.). Glencoe, IL: Free Press. (Original work published 1922)

Spanier, G. B., & Thompson, L. (1984). *Parting: The aftermath of separation and divorce.* Beverly Hills, CA: Sage.

Spitzberg, B. H., & Cupach, W. R. (Eds.). (2007). *The dark side of interpersonal communication.* Mahwah, NJ: Lawrence Erlbaum.

Sprecher, S. (1988). Investment model, equity, and social support determinants of relationship commitment. *Social Psychology Quarterly, 51,* 318–328.

Sprecher, S., & Felmlee, D. (2000). Romantic partners' perceptions of social network attributes with the passage of time and relationship transitions. *Personal Relationships, 7,* 325–340.

Sprecher, S., Felmlee, D., Orbuch, T. L., & Willetts, M. C. (2002). Social networks and change in personal relationships. In H. T. Reis, M. A. Fitzpatrick, & A. L. Vangelisti (Eds.), *Stability and change in relationships* (pp. 257–284). Cambridge, UK: Cambridge University Press.

Spriggs, A. L., Iannotti, R. J., Nansel, T. R., & Haynie, D. L. (2007). Adolescent bullying involvement and perceived family, peer and school relations: Commonalities and differences across race/ethnicity. *Journal of Adolescent Health, 41*(3), 283–293.

Starr, L. R., & Davila, J. (2009). Clarifying co-rumination: Associations with internalizing symptoms and romantic involvement among adolescent girls. *Journal of Adolescence, 32*(1), 19–37.

Stein, C. H., Bush, E. G., Ross, R. R., & Ward, M. (1992). Mine, yours and ours: A configural analysis of the networks of married couples in relation to marital satisfaction and individual well-being. *Journal of Social and Personal Relationships, 9,* 365–383.

Stone, L. B., Uhrlass, D. J., & Gibb, B. E. (2010). Co-rumination and lifetime history of depressive disorders in children. *Journal of Clinical Child and Adolescent Psychology, 39*(4), 597–602.

Suitor, J., & Keeton, S. (1997). Once a friend, always a friend? Effects of homophily on women's support networks across a decade. *Social Networks, 19,* 51–62.

Suter, E. A., Daas, K. L., & Bergen, K. M. (2008). Negotiating lesbian family identity via symbols and rituals. *Journal of Family Issues, 29*(1), 26–47.

Tardy, R. W., & Hale, C. L. (1998). Bonding and cracking: The role of informal, interpersonal networks in health care decision making. *Health Communication, 10*(2), 151–173.

Titus, S. L. (1980). A function of friendship: Social comparisons as a frame of reference for marriage. *Human Relations, 33,* 409–431.

Tufekci, Z. (2008). Can you see me now? Audience and disclosure regulation in online social network sites. *Bulletin of Science, Technology & Society, 28,* 20–36.

Vaughan, D. (1986). *Uncoupling: Turning points in intimate relationships.* New York: Oxford University Press.

Vonofakou, C., Hewstone, M., Voci, A., Paolini, S., Turner, R. N., Tausch, N. T., et al. (2008). The impact of direct and extended cross-group friendships on improving intergroup relations. In U. Wagner, L. R. Tropp, G. Finchilescu, & C. Tredoux (Eds.), *Improving intergroup relations: Building on the legacy of Thomas F. Pettigrew* (pp. 107–123). Malden, MA: Blackwell.

Waller, E. M., & Rose, A. J. (2010). Adjustment trade-offs of co-rumination in mother-adolescent relationships. *Journal of Adolescence, 33,* 487–497.

Watts, D. J. (2003). *Six degrees: The science of a connected age.* New York: W. W. Norton.

Wellman, B., Wong, R. Y., Tindall, D., & Nazer, N. (1997). A decade of network change: Turnover, persistence and stability in personal communities. *Social Networks, 19,* 27–50.

Wing, R. R., & Jeffery, R. W. (1999). Benefits of recruiting participants with friends and increasing social support for weight loss and maintenance. *Journal of Consulting and Clinical Psychology, 67*(1), 132–138.

Wood, J. T. (2007). *Gendered lives: Communication, gender and culture* (7th ed.). Belmont, CA: Thomson Wadsworth.

Wright, S. C., Aron, A., McLaughlin-Volpe, T., & Ropp, S. A. (1997). The extended contact effect: Knowledge of cross-group friendships and prejudice. *Journal of Personality and Social Psychology, 73,* 73–90.

Ye, J. (2006). Traditional and online support networks in the cross-cultural adaptation of Chinese international students in the United States. *Journal of Computer-Mediated Communication, 11*(3), 863–876.

Zaslow, J. (2005). Emailing the ex: Technology can help ease dealings between divorced couples. *Wall Street Journal, Eastern Edition, 246*(95), D1–D1.

Zimmer-Gembeck, M. J., Hunter, T. A., & Pronk, R. (2007). A model of behaviors, peer relations and depression: Perceived social acceptance as a mediator and the divergence of perceptions. *Journal of Social and Clinical Psychology, 26*(3), 273–302.

# CHAPTER 12

# Interpersonal Influence

*James Price Dillard*

*Leanne K. Knobloch*

**A**t the moment of birth, children express their desire to be held and fed through the only means available to them. As they age, they discover the many ways in which language can be used to acquire playthings and ice cream as well as guide their younger siblings away from harm and, occasionally, toward adventure. With adolescence comes the need to learn the communicative skills that establish and coordinate more complex peer relationships. From there, many individuals move into careers such as politics or counseling, both of which have interpersonal influence as their core function. The later stages of life may be characterized by requests for preferred medication in preferred quantities. Even after death, some individuals make an effort to shape the actions of friends and relatives via the executor of their will.

The implications of these examples are both numerous and clear. For one, interpersonal influence is a cradle-to-grave undertaking. It occurs over the entirety of one's life span. Moreover, it is part of virtually every type of social relationship from the superficial to the deeply intimate. And it is consequential. Skillful mentors guide confused adolescents toward happy and productive lives. Senior citizens lose their life savings to scurrilous scams that promise financial security. In short, interpersonal influence is a phenomenon that pervades every aspect of humanity and does so in ways that matter. These facts more than justify the research attention that the topic has received. For present purposes, we define interpersonal influence as *symbolic efforts designed (a) to preserve or change the behavior of another individual or (b) to maintain or modify aspects of another individual that are proximal to behavior, such as cognitions, emotions, and identities.*

## A Brief History of Interpersonal Influence

The previous version of this chapter (i.e., Dillard, Anderson, & Knobloch, 2002), provided a detailed examination of the history of interpersonal influence, which we will not repeat here (see Wilson, 2002, for another account). However, a few broad comments on the chronology of this research tradition will help to contextualize the pages that follow and to explain the structure of the chapter.

To begin, there are two streams of research that we review: (1) message production and (2) message effects. As the phrase suggests, the message production literature focuses on how and why individuals generate messages. Obviously, the topic is broader than interpersonal influence. But it is fair to say that interpersonal influence has been one of the arenas in which message production has been examined most consistently. If we locate the beginning of influence message production research in the mid-1970s (Dillard et al., 2002), there were two clearly discernable approaches to the problem. Cognitive theories emphasized the mental processes that individuals move through in the course of formulating a string of words and behaviors (e.g., Dillard, 1990a; Hample & Dallinger, 1990; Kellermann & Shea, 1996; Meyer, 1990; Wilson, 1995), whereas discourse models gave greater emphasis to the form of the utterances and to their location in the social surround (Fitch & Sanders, 1994; Ifert & Roloff, 1994; Kim, 1994; O'Keefe, 1990). Recent years have seen a synthesis of perspectives that is epitomized in Wilson's revised analysis of face and facework (e.g., Cai & Wilson, 2000), which we use to structure our review of the message production literature.

Research on message effects presents the other side of the influence coin. Although many points in time could mark the commencement of research on the effects of interpersonal influence (Pratkanis, 2007), one that is both convenient

and defensible is Freedman and Fraser's (1966) paper on the foot-in-the-door technique. That was the first in a corpus of studies that focused on how seemingly minor variations in the language of requests could produce significant and sometimes large variations in behavioral compliance. We organize our examination of the message effects literature around the communicative structure of the various techniques.

## Message Production

### Goals That Motivate Interpersonal Influence

There is surely some truth to the notion that human interaction is infinitely complex. As such, it might seem that people seek to persuade others for an enormous variety of reasons. Yet research on the goals of interpersonal influence suggests that perceptions of immense diversity are unwarranted. Studies reported by Cody, Canary, and Smith (1994), Dillard (1989), and Rule, Bisanz, and Kohn (1985) embraced a data-driven approach to the identification of influence goals that (a) asked individuals why they sought to influence others and then (b) grouped the resulting data via statistical or interpretative means. The most frequently identified reasons for influencing others are listed in Table 12.1, along with a description and an example of each (cf. Kellermann, 1992).

**Table 12.1**   Influence Goals

| Type | Description | Examples |
|------|-------------|----------|
| Gain assistance | Obtain material or nonmaterial resources | Can I borrow your class notes? |
| Give advice | Provide counsel (typically about health and relationships) | I think that you should quit smoking. |
| Share activity | Promote joint endeavors between source and target | Let's do something tonight. |

| Type | Description | Examples |
|------|-------------|----------|
| Change orientation | Alter target's stance toward a sociopolitical issue | Here's why you are wrong about gun control. |
| Change relationship | Alter the nature of the source–target relationship of other people | We should agree not to date. |
| Obtain permission | Secure the endorsement of the (more powerful) target | Hey, Dad. Can I use the car? |
| Enforce rights and obligations | Compel target to fulfill commitment or role requirement | You promised that you would take out the trash. So, how about it? |

## Influence Goals as Contexts

Context is an essential element in many theories of human communication. But it is sometimes evoked as a category that embraces all of the causal mechanisms, situational parameters, and boundary conditions that the theory itself leaves unspecified. One dissatisfying result is that any knowledge claims emerging from the theory must be qualified by the phrase "depending on the context." The ambiguity inherent in such open-ended views has motivated some investigators to adopt research strategies that rely heavily on lay conceptualizations of context. Studies of courtroom discourse (Tracy, 2009), crisis negotiations (Agne, 2007), and maternity leave requests (Meisenbach, Remke, Buzzanell, & Liu, 2008) are three examples that define context via people's perceptions of specific situations. This tack circumvents the problems that emerge from catch-all definitions of context, but at the cost of limiting the knowledge claims to the boundaries of the context.

A middle ground treats influence goals themselves as context. Variations on this theme can be found in several programs of research focused on interpersonal influence. For one, Cody and his associates (Cody et al., 1994, 1986; Cody & McLaughlin, 1980) contend that influence goals are associated with particular configurations of situational dimensions. A complementary approach treats social reality as embedded in *social densities* (Dillard & Solomon, 2000), where social densities are complex constellations of obstacles and opportunities that constitute social life. Because individuals are cognizant of the ways in which social densities curtail certain options while encouraging others, goals arise within social densities. A third perspective, advanced by Kellermann (2004), analyzes goals with regard to their potential to create negative affect and restrict the freedom of the message target.

Additional insight into goal-defined contexts comes from juxtaposing specific influence goals with actors' tacit knowledge of the conditions that define compliance seeking. Identity implications theory (Wilson, Aleman, & Leatham, 1998; Wilson, Kunkel, Robson, Olufowote, & Soliz, 2009) follows Searle (1969) in defining goals in terms of six *constitutive rules* or logical preconditions that regulate an influence attempt: (1) Is there a need for the action? (2) Is there a need for the directive? (3) Is the hearer able to perform the action? (4) Is the hearer willing or obligated to perform the desired action? (5) Is the request legitimate? and (6) Does the speaker sincerely want the hearer to perform the action? Identity implications theory treats this set of questions "as a template that can be overlaid onto specific influence goals to predict possible threats to face" (Wilson et al., 1998, p. 69). Consistent with a goal-as-context framework, the answers to those six questions vary substantially as a function of goal type. Indeed, Wilson's work demonstrates the effectiveness of pairing goals with constitutive rules to understand the positive and negative face threats salient to both persuaders and targets

(Cai & Wilson, 2000; Wilson et al., 1998, 2009; Wilson & Kunkel, 2000) even across cultures (Kim et al., 2009). Following Wilson et al.'s (1998, 2009) analysis, the following subsections treat goals as definitions of influence situations. We consider seven goals derived from empirical investigations of social influence (see Table 12.1; Kellermann, 2004, for a more extensive list).

## Asking a Favor

### Definition

The *ask-favor* goal encompasses episodes in which an individual seeks physical, financial, informational, or material aid from a target (Cody et al., 1994; Dillard, 1989). Favor asking occurs relatively often within interaction (Cody et al., 1994), and although favors can be asked of anyone (Dillard, 1989; cf. Goldschmidt, 1998), they are typically requested within intimate relationships (Dillard, 1989; Goldschmidt, 1998). In successful attempts to gain assistance, resources flow toward the source and away from the target (Cody et al., 1994; Dillard, 1989).

### Constitutive Rules

The defining features of favor-asking episodes include assumptions that (a) the source needs help, (b) providing aid is an imposition on the target, and (c) the target may be willing and able to help but is not obligated to help (Goldschmidt, 1996, 1998; Wilson et al., 1998; Wilson & Kunkel, 2000). A variety of potential threats to the source's face and the target's face arise in conjunction with these constitutive rules (Cai & Wilson, 2000; Kim et al., 2009; Wilson et al., 1998; Wilson & Kunkel, 2000). Threats to the target's negative face are especially acute because, by definition, asking a favor imposes on the target's autonomy. Of course, the source may also suffer threats to his or her own negative face. Asking for help is an implicit admission that the source cannot resolve the problem alone, so he or she risks looking lazy or needy. Moreover, if

the target provides assistance, a debt has been incurred (e.g., Roloff, Janiszewski, McGrath, Burns, & Manrai, 1988). Because the target may call on the source to satisfy this debt in the future, the source suffers a loss of autonomy. Notably, the salience of these face threats vary according to the nature of the relationship between the source and the target.

### Situational Features and Constraints

Whereas the constitutive rules governing favor-asking episodes give rise to particular face threats likely to be salient during interaction (Cai & Wilson, 2000; Wilson et al., 1998; Wilson & Kunkel, 2000), the constitutive rules and face threats, in turn, translate into specific contextual parameters of favor-asking episodes. Seeking assistance typically coincides with secondary concerns for identity, interaction, and relationship management (Schrader & Dillard, 1998). When asking favors of friends, people perceive relatively low levels of apprehension, short-term consequences for the relationship, low levels of target resistance, and high levels of homophily and intimacy (Cody et al., 1986). These situation perceptions change in predictable ways when asking favors of acquaintances: Individuals perceive relatively low levels of target dominance, short-term consequences for the relationship, and low levels of intimacy (Cody et al., 1986).

### Research

Goldschmidt (1998) identified a three-stage sequence of favor-asking episodes. The *prefavor* serves both to define the upcoming episode and to alert the target to the source's need. In some instantiations, the prefavor seeks permission to pose the request.

"I need a favor."

"May I ask you a favor?"

The *favor* itself is specified in the second stage with varying degrees of elaboration and supporting rationale.

"Could you give me a ride to the post office?"

"I need to get to the post office before it closes, but my car won't start. I have to get my job application in the mail so that it arrives by the deadline."

Elaboration of the favor clarifies the parameters of the request and signals the level of assistance needed. The supporting rationale explains why the source is imposing on the target and, in doing so, mitigates the threat to the target's negative face. Behavior in these episodes tends to be submissive (Cody et al., 1994; Dillard, 1989), to incorporate self-focused reasons for needing help (Wilson & Kunkel, 2000), and to express approval for the target (Cai & Wilson, 2000; Wilson et al., 1998). Requests for favors vary in explicitness, in part as a function of the status of the target and the intimacy of the relationship (Cody et al., 1994).

The third and final stage in asking a favor is the *hearer's response* (Goldschmidt, 1998). The response may be governed by attributions of the source's culpability for the problem, the target's emotional reactions to the request, and the target's inclination to comply or refuse. Of course, a variety of options are available beyond pure compliance or pure refusal. Targets may signal resistance or offer a conditional response.

"I don't think I know how to get to the post office."

"Sure, I can take you if we can go right away."

Any response other than clear compliance allows the interaction to continue. Sources might reiterate or embellish their request, seek information regarding the conditions needed for compliance, or attempt to satisfy those conditions.

## Conclusions and Directions for Future Work

To date, work focused on gain-assistance attempts has illuminated the defining features of these episodes (e.g., Goldschmidt, 1996, 1998). Comparably less is known, however, about the effects that correspond with those messages. In particular, work on message effects should attend to the relational implications of gain-assistance requests. Because ongoing relationships are governed by social exchange, asking a favor necessarily generates a social indebtedness that has to be rectified at a subsequent opportunity (e.g., Han, Li, & Hwang, 2005; Roloff et al., 1988). Hence, work that sheds light on the relational aspects of the gain-assistance goal, in addition to its instrumental ramifications, would be particularly valuable.

# Giving Advice

## Definition

In advice-giving episodes, the source recommends a course of action to the target, who in turn must choose whether to follow the guidance (Wilson et al., 1998). Unlike most of the other influence goals reviewed in this chapter, advice-giving episodes are designed to benefit the target rather than the source (Cody et al., 1994; Dillard, 1989). Examples of advice-giving attempts include (a) advising a sibling to spend less time on extracurricular activities and more time on schoolwork, (b) encouraging a friend to quit smoking, (c) recommending that a grandparent follow his or her medical regime, and (d) persuading a spouse to take up a hobby (Fogarty & Youngs, 2000; Wilson et al., 1998).

## Constitutive Rules

Advice-giving attempts are governed by constitutive rules that define the nature of the episodes (Kim et al., 2009; Wilson et al., 1998; Wilson & Kunkel, 2000). Advice-giving situations arise when the source (a) believes that the target is choosing a course of action that is not ideal, (b) is motivated to offer advice that benefits the target rather than himself or herself, and (c) crafts a message to promote the target's well-being (Wilson et al., 1998). Although advice-giving attempts arise from the source's sincere recognition of a need for action, such episodes also reveal the source's perceptions of the target. Consequently, face threats are salient for both advisors and advisees (Goldsmith &

Fitch, 1997; Kim et al., 2009; Wilson et al., 1998). The target's negative face is threatened to the extent that the advice constrains his or her behavior; moreover, the target's positive face is jeopardized by the implication that he or she is incompetent, inefficient, or lazy. The source also incurs potential threats to his or her positive face: By offering advice, the source may seem nosy, overbearing, or bossy. These face threats contribute to three dilemmas of advice-giving episodes: (1) recipients may view the advice as helpful or intrusive, (2) advice givers must balance the need for honesty with the need for supportiveness, and (3) recipients should show gratitude for the advice but retain the autonomy to make their own decision about its implementation (Goldsmith & Fitch, 1997).

## Situational Features and Constraints

The secondary motivations of giving advice involve relationship maintenance (Schrader & Dillard, 1998). Whereas the secondary goal of relational resource is prominent within advice-giving episodes involving both friends and parents (Schrader & Dillard, 1998), the contextual parameters depend on the nature of the relationship between interactants. For example, dispensing advice to friends involves low apprehension, low target dominance, low personal benefit, and moderate homophily (Cody et al., 1986). Conversely, offering advice to parents involves low apprehension, high intimacy, high target dominance, high target resistance, and low benefits to the source (Cody et al., 1986). Thus, work focused on the contextual parameters of advice-giving episodes suggests that people must balance their desires to help the target versus preserve the relationship.

## Research

*Message Production and Perception.* Work stemming from the discourse-analytic tradition illustrates what talk in advice-giving episodes looks like. For example, researchers have analyzed

advice giving within the context of radio call-in shows (Hutchby, 1995), social support telephone lines (Pudlinski, 1998, 2002), online forums (Morrow, 2006), conversations between patients and health care providers (Kinnell & Maynard, 1996; Kiuru, Poskiparta, Kettunen, Saltevo, & Liimatainen, 2004), and interactions between students and teachers (Vehvilainen, 2009). This research has yielded detailed descriptions of advice-giving sequences (e.g., Kinnell & Maynard, 1996; Pudlinski, 1998; Vehvilainen, 2009) among partners with a limited history.

Other research sheds light on the form and function of advice-giving attempts within more intimate relationships (Goldsmith, 2000; Goldsmith & Fitch, 1997). For example, Goldsmith (2000) employed retrospective accounts to identify six ways to initiate advice-giving episodes: (1) advisee asks for advice, (2) advisee asks for information, (3) advisee identifies a problem, (4) advisee announces a plan of action, (5) advisor identifies advisee's problem, or (6) advisor gives unprompted advice. Notably, these methods of initiation range from fully solicited advice (i.e., the target requests it) to completely unsolicited advice (i.e., the source volunteers it). Degree of solicitation, in turn, corresponds with face wants: People's perceptions of both negative and positive face needs increase as perceived solicitation increases (Goldsmith, 2000). Face management issues, in turn, constrain message production (Goldsmith & Fitch, 1997).

Still other scholarship has evaluated people's perceptions of message effectiveness. Individuals tend to perceive advice more favorably when the message incorporates facework and politeness strategies (Feng & Burleson, 2008; Goldsmith & MacGeorge, 2000; MacGeorge, Lichtam, & Pressey, 2002), when the advisor is explicit about the efficacy and feasibility of the recommended behavior (Feng & Burleson, 2008), when the drawbacks of implementing the advice are minimal (Feng & Burleson, 2008; MacGeorge, Feng, Butler, & Budarz, 2004), and when the target is receptive to the advice (MacGeorge et al., 2004; Thompson & O'Hair, 2008). Recipients are more receptive to advice when their relationship with the advisor is close and when the advisor has expertise in the nature of the problem (Feng & MacGeorge, 2006), but they tend to resist advice when it is undesired, inappropriate, or replete with limitations (Feng & Burleson, 2008; Feng & MacGeorge, 2006; Thompson & O'Hair, 2008).

All three lines of research are incorporated into Feng's (2009) integrated model of advice giving in supportive interactions. Her data documented the effectiveness of a three-step advice-giving sequence. In the first step, an individual responds to the target's distress by providing *emotional support* to help the target cope with feelings of anger, sadness, anxiety, and fear (e.g., "It's understandable that you're upset about failing that exam. But remember, your grade doesn't depend on just one exam."). In the second step, *problem inquiry and analysis*, individuals seek information about the nature of the problem and determine whether advice is the appropriate response (e.g., "Do you know why you didn't do well? Do you think you can earn a better grade on the next one?"). A third step involves *offering advice* (e.g., "You could try studying with people in your class next time. Studying with classmates may help you learn the material better."). Feng (2009) found that participants rated advice embedded in the three-step sequence to be more effective than advice that did not follow the pattern.

## Conclusions and Directions for Future Work

As is evident from our review, work stemming from the discourse-analytic and interpersonal communication traditions privilege different aspects of advice-giving episodes. These lines of inquiry have asked different questions, employed distinct methods, and offered unique findings. Clearly, the literatures have the capacity to inform one other: The discourse-analytic work provides information about the nature of advice-giving episodes, and the interpersonal communication research sheds light on the forces shaping message production and processing. We echo

Goldsmith and Fitch's (1997) call, issued more than a decade ago, for scholars to integrate their work to achieve a more comprehensive understanding of advice giving.

## Changing or Maintaining Sociopolitical Orientation

### Definition

These episodes occur when the source attempts to alter or solidify the target's attitudes and/or behaviors concerning a civic issue (Schrader & Dillard, 1998; Southwell & Yzer, 2007, 2009). Actors attempt to change or maintain another person's sociopolitical orientation to enhance the welfare of a group, community, or society (as the actors perceive that welfare) rather than to enhance the welfare of the interactants themselves (Dillard, 1989). The source must be prepared for potential resistance to his or her position given the potentially heterogeneous attitudes of targets and the "truly public" nature of political talk (Schudson, 1997). Accordingly, attempts to change or maintain a target's orientation arise when individuals perceive a need for action and are willing to risk considerable face threat.

### Constitutive Rules

An examination of Searle's (1969) constitutive rules sheds light on the relevant contextual parameters. The source must believe that (a) an influence attempt is necessary, (b) the target may be willing and able to be persuaded, and (c) the source has a legitimate right to advocate a particular position. These constitutive rules suggest a number of face threats. By voicing an influence message, the source threatens the target's positive face by implying that the target's opinion is less desirable. Similarly, the source's positive face is jeopardized because he or she opposes the target's viewpoint. Of course, the target's negative face is threatened if the source's suggestions constrain his or her autonomy in social decision making.

## Situational Features and Constraints

Individuals attempting to change or maintain a target's orientation are motivated by secondary concerns such as preserving one's identity, maintaining the relationship between interactants, and skillfully negotiating the interaction (Schrader & Dillard, 1998). Moreover, people tend to view these attempts as high in both group benefit and publicness (Dillard, 1989). A clear implication is the difficulty of achieving compliance: In fact, Cody et al. (1994) reported that trying to change someone's sociopolitical orientation was among the least successful of the influence episodes they examined.

## Research

Scholars have examined change- or maintain-orientation episodes in diverse settings, including talking about public affairs in casual conversation (Wyatt, Katz, & Kim, 2000; Wyatt, Kim, & Katz, 2000), discussing politics with social network members (Cho et al., 2009; Pan, Shen, Paek, & Sun, 2006), and conversing about organ donation with family members (Morgan, Harrison, Long, Afifi, & Stephenson, 2008). These episodes appear to occur quite frequently. For example, Greenberg (1975) found that more than 25% of naturally occurring conversations concerned issues of public affairs; of those, nearly 66% contained overtly identifiable influence attempts. Similarly, Infante and Rancer (1993) concluded from their retrospective recall data that politics was the topic of conversation that people most frequently argued about. Influence attempts about sociopolitical issues can be very persuasive: In a study that compared the relative effectiveness of various communication channels, Kinsey and Chaffee (1996) found that interpersonal talk about political issues, rather than attention to mass media, was the strongest predictor of presidential approval ratings.

Qualities of individuals play a role in attempts to change or maintain a person's sociopolitical orientation. People high in trait argumentativeness, for example, attempt to influence others regarding political issues more frequently (Infante & Rancer, 1993). Individuals who attach personal importance to politics are especially likely to seek information about political events and vote in elections; conversely, those who value politics because of normative expectations are particularly vulnerable to persuasion attempts (Koestner, Losier, Vallerand, & Carducci, 1996). Even a person's mood influences the processing of political information: Findings support a "rally around the flag" effect such that people experiencing negative affect perceive political leaders more favorably (Way & Masters, 1996). As a set, these findings underscore the importance of individual characteristics.

Other research, compiled in a 2009 special issue of *Communication Theory*, suggests factors that predict when interpersonal communication may shape the outcomes of mass media campaigns. Scholars have theorized that interpersonal interaction may facilitate inoculation (Compton & Pfau, 2009), that figurative language in a campaign may spur conversation (Hoeken, Swanepoel, Saal, & Jansen, 2009), that interpersonal communication may ebb and flow during a political election cycle (Hardy & Scheufele, 2009), that the density of people's social networks may shape how mass-mediated ideas become adopted by individuals (Morgan, 2009), and that interpersonal conversation may mediate the effects of media exposure on people's political participation (Cho et al., 2009). Taken together, this research suggests that interpersonal conversations exert an important influence on the effects of mass-mediated messages.

## Conclusions and Directions for Future Work

Change- or maintain-orientation episodes are exceedingly valuable within a democratic society (Wyatt, Katz, et al., 2000; but see Schudson, 1997). Face-to-face deliberation of social issues helps people gain information, form opinions, and become involved in the public realm. Despite the significance of interpersonal influence attempts surrounding sociopolitical matters, however, little is known about the content of these conversations. In fact, Southwell and Yzrer (2009) called for scholars to more closely examine "what people actually say" (p. 5). Work is needed to delineate the message features that characterize these episodes.

# Obtaining Permission

## Definition

In an obtain-permission episode, the source seeks authorization from the target to perform some behavior (Canary, Cody, & Marston, 1986; Cody et al., 1994; Rule et al., 1985). By definition, obtain-permission attempts are characterized by a power imbalance such that the target possesses the ability to control the source's behavior. Examples include (a) children asking a babysitter for permission to play past their normal bedtime, (b) students asking a professor to enroll them in a class that is already full, (c) employees asking a supervisor if they may leave work early, and (d) doctors asking patients for permission to conduct a physical exam (Canary et al., 1986; Cody et al., 1994; Robinson & Stivers, 2001; Rule et al., 1985).

## Constitutive Rules

The constitutive rules governing obtain-permission attempts reveal the defining features of these episodes. Obtain-permission episodes are characterized by the source's perceptions that (a) the target's permission is needed for the source to perform a desired action, (b) the target would not grant permission unless the source enacts a request, (c) the target may be willing and able to grant permission, and (d) the source has a legitimate right to seek permission from the target. These constitutive rules set the stage for a variety

of face threats to arise. Most notably, the source's negative face is jeopardized because he or she lacks the freedom to perform the behavior in the absence of permission. In addition, the source's positive face is threatened if the target disapproves of the requested behavior (e.g., permission to eat an extra dessert, to attend an all-night party, to take a vacation during a busy time at the office). The target's positive face is threatened if denial of the request incurs the source's annoyance, anger, or resentment (e.g., a "temper tantrum"). In turn, the target's negative face is threatened if the source exerts so much pressure to comply that the target feels forced to acquiesce.

## Situational Features and Constraints

Work by Cody and his colleagues has illuminated the situational features and constraints of people's requests for permission in particular role relationships. Within the context of parent–child interaction, for example, obtain-permission attempts are characterized by short-term consequences, high intimacy, high target dominance, and low apprehension (Cody et al., 1994). In contrast, within the context of professor–student interaction, obtain-permission requests coincide with high target dominance, low intimacy, and relatively high target resistance (Cody et al., 1994). The common denominator between the two instantiations of obtain-permission episodes is target dominance: By definition, obtain-permission episodes occur in relationships with an unequal distribution of power (Canary et al., 1986; Cody et al., 1994; Rule et al., 1985).

Other research has examined situational factors that predict people's perceptions of secondary goals. Meyer (2002) found that people ascribed more importance to addressing the target's negative face when they were seeking permission to enact a behavior with high personal benefit. In contrast, individuals were less concerned with addressing the target's positive and negative face when asking permission from a high-status target. In intimate relationships, individuals were less concerned with addressing the target's positive and negative face when they expected considerable resistance from the target.

## Research

Relative to the other six influence goals examined in this chapter, the obtain-permission goal has been vastly understudied with respect to message behavior. The two studies we located examined permission seeking as a precursor to engaging in socially undesirable behavior. Sundstrom and Sundstrom (1977) found that when a stranger asks permission to engage in a personal space invasion (i.e., to sit on an already occupied public bench), men are less likely to leave the scene but women are more likely to leave the scene. Campbell, Svenson, and Jarvis (1993) discovered that people frequently deny others permission to smoke in both public venues (i.e., restaurants, schools) and private venues (i.e., cars, homes). Together, these studies demonstrate that individuals may enact obtain-permission requests before engaging in socially undesirable behavior to mitigate negative reactions from those around them.

## Conclusions and Directions for Future Work

The scarcity of work focused on the obtain-permission goal points to a considerable need for additional research. Most obviously, work should examine how and why targets decide to comply with requests for permission. Second, scholars should investigate how people negotiate these episodes within dyads marked by shifts in power over time. Fluctuating levels of dominance characterize many kinds of relationships: Children mature into adults, students graduate, employees earn promotions. Thus, research could shed light on the ongoing management of power by examining how people's communication in obtain-permission episodes varies according to power dynamics.

## Enforcing Obligations

### Definition

Because social relationships are built on a complex web of rights and obligations, people are motivated to act when they perceive that another person has abrogated his or her societal responsibilities, contractual obligations, or role requirements (e.g., Cai & Wilson, 2000; Cody et al., 1994; Kim et al., 2009; Wilson et al., 1998). In episodes of enforcing obligations, the aggrieved party issues a complaint that (a) expresses dissatisfaction with the actions of the target and (b) requests that the target fulfill his or her obligation (Cody et al., 1986; Newell & Stutman, 1989/90, 1991; Wilson et al., 1998). Successful enforce-obligation attempts, like successful gain-assistance attempts, are characterized by a redistribution of resources from the target to the source (Cody et al., 1994). Examples of enforce-obligation attempts include requests for landlords to repair leaky plumbing, roommates to wash their dishes, and friends to pay overdue loans (e.g., Cody et al., 1994; Wilson et al., 1998).

### Constitutive Rules

The constitutive rules governing enforce-obligation episodes dictate three logical preconditions to people's influence attempts: (1) the source believes that the target has made a previous commitment to performing some action, (2) the target has not yet performed the action, and therefore (3) the source has a right to persuade the target to fulfill the overdue obligation (Cai & Wilson, 2000; Kim et al., 2009; Wilson et al., 1998). These constitutive rules generate a specific constellation of face threats (Cai & Wilson, 2000; Wilson et al., 1998). For example, a request to enforce an obligation may threaten the target's negative face by suggesting that he or she is required to comply. It also may threaten the target's positive face by implying that he or she is incompetent, unreliable, disorganized, irresponsible, or lazy. Indeed, disapproval of the target's behavior is implicit in enforce-obligation episodes (Kellermann, 2004). An enforce-obligation episode may jeopardize the source's autonomy, and thereby threaten his or her negative face, if the target expects him or her to offer a concession in exchange for compliance (Wilson et al., 1998).

## Situational Features and Constraints

Not only do people attach considerable importance to enforcing obligations relative to other goal types (Cai & Wilson, 2000; Schrader & Dillard, 1998), but they also manage secondary concerns for identity and interaction (Schrader & Dillard, 1998). Individuals perceive enforce-obligation episodes to entail high rights to persuade, low target resistance, and low target dominance (Cody et al., 1986). They also report low concern for the target's perspective but strong consequences for the relationship (Wilson et al., 1998).

## Research

Research focused on the message behavior people enact in enforce-obligation episodes offers a sizeable base of descriptive information. Above all, this work implies that people are straightforward and assertive when pursuing the enforce-obligation goal. Individuals endorse the strategies of direct requests, negative manipulation of feelings, exchange tactics, and rationality (Canary et al., 1986; Cody et al., 1986), but they rarely select indirect tactics or strategies that benefit the target (Cody et al., 1986). Moreover, people are willing to exert pressure on the target to comply, but they are unwilling to express their approval of the target to gain compliance (Cai & Wilson, 2000). Individuals, particularly those who have an independent sense of self (Kim et al., 2009), rarely withdraw from an enforce-obligation episode if the target does not acquiesce after the first request (Cody et al., 1986). Relative to other goal contexts, then,

individuals pursue the enforce-obligation goal in a direct and resolute manner.

In contrast to work illuminating how people's communication behavior in enforce-obligation attempts compares with communication behavior in other goal episodes, lines of research focused on complaining, social confrontation, and consumer complaints have situated enforce-obligation requests within particular settings. Following the organization of the literature, we structure our review around these three venues for enforcing obligations.

*Interpersonal Complaining.* Kowalski's (1996, 2003; Kowalski & Erickson, 1997; Kowalski, Walker, Wilkinson, Queen, & Sharpe, 2003) research on complaining behavior emphasizes the connection between cognition and message production. She suggests that people experience dissatisfaction when events do not measure up to their ideals. Motivation to reduce negative affect spurs them to evaluate the utility of complaining, which, in turn, determines the likelihood that they will complain. An important point is that not all complaints are attempts to change the behavior of another person. Whereas authentic complaints emerge from genuine dissatisfaction with the behavior of another person (Kowalski, 1996, p. 190), inauthentic complaints stem from any of the other motivations for complaining (e.g., self-presentation). Only authentic complaints fit within our conception of interpersonal influence.

Discourse analytic work has documented a three-turn complaint sequence marked by (1) a question from the source ("What are you doing?"), (2) a response from the target ("I'm making dumplings."), and (3) a complaint from the source ("But they're supposed to be half that size."). The question-and-answer presequence helps the source gather information and establish grounds for the complaint (Monzoni, 2008). Complaints issued with laughter and irony can help the source signal the kind of response he or she desires (Edwards, 2005). And, of course, targets can respond in a variety of ways: They can express regret, apologize, take or deny responsibility, offer an appeal, demonstrate concern for the source, offer to repair, or promise to end the behavior (e.g., Bergman & Kasper, 1993; Eslami-Rasekh, 2004).

Theorizing focused on the chilling effect suggests the conditions under which partners decide to express or withhold complaints (Roloff & Cloven, 1990). The chilling effect framework argues that individuals are less likely to express complaints to a partner who appears willing to end the relationship (e.g., perceived dependence power) or to engage in symbolic or physical aggression (e.g., perceived punitive power). Empirical data underscore the utility of the perspective for understanding people's decisions to voice complaints within courtships (Cloven & Roloff, 1993; Solomon & Samp, 1998), marriages (Solomon, Knobloch, & Fitzpatrick, 2004), and family relationships (Afifi & Olson, 2005; Afifi, Olson, & Armstrong, 2005).

*Social Confrontation.* Newell and Stutman (1989/90, 1991) contend that social confrontation emerges from cocreated interaction, is identifiable only in retrospect (even by the participants), and is embodied in multiple speech acts rather than a single utterance. A complaint marks the onset of a social confrontation episode, whereby one actor signals that the other has violated a rule for appropriate conduct. The response of the accused is a second fundamental feature of social confrontation episodes (Newell & Stutman, 1989/90). The transgressor could reject the complaint by ignoring it, engaging in countercomplaining, or challenging the legitimacy of the speaker's assertion. Alternatively, the transgressor could accept the claim and indicate acceptance by offering sympathy, remedy, or excuses. He or she could also treat the complaint as irrelevant, typically by denying responsibility or agency. Interactions are only social confrontation episodes if the accused accepts the role definition offered by the speaker.

Movement toward resolution is a third essential element of social confrontation episodes. Such movement is not synonymous with compliance by the accused but rather is manifested in

talk that acknowledges the existence of a problem. To close the episode, the interactants must show some effort to deal with the problem or acknowledge their inability to do so (Newell & Stutman, 1991). Newell and Stutman argue that all three elements must be present to classify an episode as social confrontation.

*Consumer Complaints.* Given the number of commercial transactions that occur every day, customers will inevitably view some percentage as unsatisfactory. Dissatisfying consumer experiences motivate a variety of behaviors, including (a) ignoring the problem; (b) boycotting the product class, brand, or seller; (c) complaining to social network members; (d) seeking redress; and (e) registering a complaint with a legal, media, or consumer protection organization (Stephens & Gwinner, 1998; Strauss & Hill, 2001). Although diverse, these forms of consumer complaints represent goal-directed activity (e.g., Singh & Wilkes, 1996): *Voice behaviors* entail complaints to the company responsible for the problem, *private behaviors* involve exiting from a relationship with that company, and *third-party behaviors* encompass complaints to other consumers or agencies (Dart & Freeman, 1994; Hansen, Swan, & Powers, 1997). Consumers may enact behaviors from multiple categories when seeking redress (e.g., Nyer & Gopinath, 2005; Singh & Wilkes, 1996).

Customers who do not register a formal complaint deny organizations the opportunity to rectify the problem, promote repeat business, and enhance brand loyalty. For this reason, substantial research has documented consumer qualities (e.g., Blodgett & Anderson, 2000; Bodey & Grace, 2007) and situational antecedents (e.g., Susskind, 2000) governing the likelihood that people will voice a formal complaint. Scholars have developed sophisticated conceptual frameworks that (a) link consumers' decisions to their cognitive appraisals (Singh & Wilkes, 1996; Stephens & Gwinner, 1998) and (b) identify the remedial tactics that consumers evaluate positively (Bolkan & Daly, 2009). Evidence that consumer complaint behavior varies cross-culturally (e.g., Liu & McClure, 2001), particularly according to market practices (e.g., Blodgett, Hill, & Bakir, 2006), is especially notable given the growth of international commerce.

## Conclusions and Directions for Future Work

Research has examined multiple facets of communication behavior within enforce-obligation episodes. These bodies of work emerge from distinct traditions and seek to answer specialized questions about enforce-obligation attempts: (a) investigations of message production relative to other goal contexts identify people's preferences for negotiating enforce-obligation episodes, (b) research on complaining illustrates features of discourse and individuals' motivations, (c) work on social confrontation delineates the sequential nature of enforce-obligation episodes, and (d) findings drawn from consumer complaint studies indicate how people seek redress. Although the four lines of research shed light on components of enforce-obligation episodes, work is needed to integrate them.

# Sharing Activity

## Definition

Share-activity episodes involve persuading a target to engage in a mutual activity (Canary et al., 1986; Rule & Bisanz, 1987). This goal includes requests to participate in both recreational activities (e.g., eating out, playing sports, attending movies) and instrumental activities (e.g., cleaning, doing laundry, grocery shopping) with the target (Canary & Dainton, 2006; Dindia, 2003). Not surprisingly, share-activity episodes are typically embedded in the parameters of close relationships. Indeed, share-activity requests commonly function as relationship maintenance behaviors within friendships (Dainton, Zelley, & Langan, 2003), family relationships (Vogl-Bauer, Kalbfleisch, & Beatty, 1999), heterosexual romantic

relationships (Dainton & Aylor, 2002; Yum & Canary, 2009), and homosexual romantic relationships (Haas, 2003).

## Constitutive Rules

Share-activity attempts arise when one person desires to participate in collaborative action with a partner. Other social parameters include the following: (a) a request is necessary to instantiate the mutual activity, (b) the target may be willing and able to spend time with the source, (c) the source has a legitimate right to make such a request of the target, and (d) the source is willing to engage in collaborative action if the target agrees to do so. These defining features suggest several face threats that may be relevant to share-activity episodes. The source may incur threats to his or her positive face from uncertainty about whether (a) the target is amenable to spending time together and/or (b) he or she has a justifiable right to make such a request of the target (e.g., Knobloch, 2006). Similarly, the target's positive face may be threatened if he or she (a) is unwilling to engage in the shared activity or (b) is willing but unable to comply with the particular request. Finally, the target's negative face may be jeopardized if he or she feels pressure to comply.

## Situational Features and Constraints

Although share-activity requests, like all influence attempts, have the potential to threaten face, they are fundamentally collaborative because they offer potential benefits to both the source and the target (e.g., Flora & Segrin, 1998). Perhaps for this reason, share-activity requests also are notably routine. People attempt to accomplish this goal quite frequently in interpersonal relationships (Rule & Bisanz, 1987; Rule et al., 1985); they report high levels of ease, comfort, and confidence in making their requests (Canary et al., 1986); and they indicate that they are generally successful in gaining compliance (Cody et al., 1994). Share-activity requests typically coincide with the secondary goal of relational preservation (Schrader & Dillard, 1998), particularly when liking is high and when the request benefits the source (Meyer, 2002). To a lesser extent, identity and interaction concerns are also salient (Schrader & Dillard, 1998).

Share-activity episodes are important because relationships deteriorate in the absence of relational maintenance behaviors (Canary & Dainton, 2006; Dainton & Aylor, 2002; Stafford & Canary, 2006). As Canary and Stafford (1994) point out, "Without maintenance efforts, desired characteristics of a relationship decay like any system that has been neglected" (p. 7). Thus, whereas successful share-activity requests generally function to preserve relationships (Canary & Dainton, 2006), unsuccessful attempts may lead to conflict or negative outcomes within relationships (Flora & Segrin, 1998; Reissman, Aron, & Bergen, 1993).

## Research

Date requests have been the backdrop for most research on the communication strategies people employ during share-activity episodes. One example is a program of research conducted by Berger and his associates (Berger, 1988; Berger & Bell, 1988; Berger & diBattista, 1992), which focused on the connection between planning and interpersonal influence. Their work shows that people's date request strategies include seeking similarities, showing interest, engaging in small talk, and asking the target out on a date. Other work sheds light on the linguistic features of date requests (Knobloch, 2006; Knobloch & Schmelzer, 2008; Solomon, 1997). Research asking people to role-play leaving a voice mail message for a romantic partner reveals variation in linguistic features such as fluency, affiliativeness, and politeness (Knobloch, 2006; Knobloch & Schmelzer, 2008):

> "Hey, it's me. I just wanted to see if you were available to hang out any time today or maybe go get some dinner. So, give me a call back and let me know. All right, talk to you later. Bye."

> "Uh, hey, what's up? It's me. I'm just, uh, seeing what you were up to right now. I was thinking about maybe just, uh, kind of relaxing tonight, seeing a movie or something. So, just give me a call back when you get this, and, uh, let me know what you're up to. Alright, later."

Explicitness also appears to be a key linguistic parameter. Solomon (1997), in her study of date requests embedded within telephone conversations, identified nine categories ordered by decreasing explicitness: (1) mood derivable requests ("Go out with me."), (2) explicit performative requests ("I am asking you if you want to have dinner."), (3) hedged performative requests ("I'd like to ask you to go out with me."), (4) obligation statements ("You have to go out with me."), (5) want statements ("I'd like you to eat with me."), (6) a suggestory formula ("Let's have dinner tonight."), (7) conditional assessment ("Could you go out on Friday?"), (8) strong hints ("Will you be on campus later?"), and (9) mild hints ("I haven't seen you for awhile.").

Although an explicitness dimension is relevant to share-activity attempts (Berger & Bell, 1988; Berger & diBattista, 1992; Knobloch, 2006; Solomon, 1997), the nature of the effect is less clear. On the one hand, participants in a study conducted by Canary et al. (1986) reported that they were more likely to use direct-request strategies in response to a hypothetical share-activity scenario than in response to hypothetical scenarios of other influence episodes. Conversely, Dillard (1989) found that people's retrospective accounts of a share-activity episode were rated by independent observers to contain low directness; this finding also is relative to other types of influence episodes.

One way to reconcile these findings involves attending to the nature of the source's relationship with the target. Intimacy and relational uncertainty, in particular, are two relationship characteristics that predict the explicitness of date requests. For example, Solomon's (1997) data supported her theorizing that people employ (a) explicit date requests at low levels of intimacy to diminish the opportunity for miscommunication that exists in the absence of shared relational history, (b) implicit date requests at moderate levels of intimacy because uncertainty about nonreciprocated affection makes face threats especially salient, and (c) explicit date requests at high levels of intimacy because mutually defined commitment to the relationship allows them to privilege efficiency over face management concerns. Knobloch (2006) documented evidence that individuals who are uncertain about the status of their courtship craft date request messages that are more implicit. Taken together, these findings imply that the nature of the relationship may govern the explicitness of share-activity requests.

## Conclusions and Directions for Future Work

Although the relatively brief, casual, and idiosyncratic nature of share-activity attempts complicate investigations of this goal, such work is clearly important given the connection to relationship maintenance. Up to this point, scholars have focused almost exclusively on date requests within courtship. Thus, we encourage a next generation of research to examine the relationship characteristics, strategies, and linguistic features of share-activity requests in other contexts.

# Relationship (Re)definition

## Definition

All influence goals have implications for the relationship between the source and the target, but the relationship (re)definition goal is unique because it specifies the relationship itself as the domain of change. It involves a person's attempt to alter the nature of a relationship, typically by seeking to increase or decrease intimacy (Kunkel, Wilson, Olufowote, & Robson, 2003; Wilson et al., 2009). The class of relationship (re)definition goals includes a number of specific aims,

such as initiating a friendship via face-to-face or computer-mediated interaction (e.g., Ramirez & Burgoon, 2004; Sprecher, Wenzel, & Harvey, 2008), asking a romantic partner to date exclusively (e.g., Wilson et al., 2009), and terminating a relationship (e.g., Kellas & Manusov, 2003). As is evident from these examples, the relational change goal highlights the dyad as a central focus of the interaction.

Relationship (re)definition episodes are conceptually similar to share-activity episodes because issues of interpersonal relating are primary motivations for both goals. The two differ, however, in both the nature and the duration of the desired compliance. Whereas the share-activity goal represents people's short-term desire to preserve the current definition of the relationship, the relationship (re)definition goal involves people's attempts to modify the status of the relationship in the long term. Thus, relational change attempts have considerable ramifications for the future of the relationship (e.g., Baxter & Bullis, 1986; Honeycutt, Cantrill, & Greene, 1989).

## Constitutive Rules

An examination of the constitutive rules governing relationship (re)definition episodes provides insight into the contextual parameters of this goal (Kunkel et al., 2003, Table 1). By definition, relationship (re)definition episodes occur when a person seeks to modify the level of intimacy that exists in his or her relationship with a target. The source believes that (a) a directive is necessary because the target would not alter his or her perceptions of the relationship in the absence of such a request, (b) the target may be willing and able to change his or her definition of the association, and (c) the source has a legitimate right to ask for the modification. By making such a request, the source indicates that he or she is willing to modify his or her perceptions of the relationship if the target agrees.

Relationship (re)definition attempts also evoke face threats (Kunkel et al., 2003; Wilson et al., 2009). The target's negative face is at risk if he or she feels pressure to comply with the request, and the target's positive face is at risk if the request makes him or her feel inadequate. With respect to the source's negative face, a relational change request is threatening if it damages a current desired relationship or precludes a future desired relationship with a different partner. In terms of the source's positive face, a relational change request is perilous if the source appears unattractive, forward, needy, or insensitive. Above all, the source's positive face is threatened to the extent that the target is not willing or able to comply.

Although people may desire to effect change at any point in a relationship's history, scholars tend to divide relationship (re)definition attempts into categories focused on people's requests to initiate relationships, escalate relationships, and de-escalate relationships (e.g., Kunkel et al., 2003; Wilson et al., 2009). Following the nature of the literature, then, we organize our discussion around these developmental junctures. For each juncture, we define the contextual parameters of relational change and then discuss relevant research.

## Initiating Relationships

*Situational Features and Constraints.* Initiating a relationship is a high-stakes situation because it involves potential personal gain, long-term relational consequences, possible embarrassment, face threats, and uncertainty about the target's response. Indeed, the target exerts substantial control over the outcome of a relationship initiation attempt: He or she can comply, refuse, reject the source, or respond ambiguously (Besson, Roloff, & Paulson, 1998). Substantial face threats correspond with attempts to initiate a relationship (Baxter, 1987), particularly the risks of appearing unattractive, being pushy, and pressuring the partner (Kunkel et al., 2003; Wilson et al., 2009). Not surprisingly, the secondary goals of personal resource and arousal management are especially relevant to relationship initiation (Schrader & Dillard, 1998), and

apprehension and anxiety coincide with these episodes (Cody et al., 1994).

*Research.* Although research on how people communicate to initiate relationships is far too extensive to be summarized in this chapter, a recent handbook edited by Sprecher et al. (2008) offers a comprehensive synthesis of the topic. Chapters in that volume describe communication processes such as verbal and nonverbal initiation strategies (Cunningham & Barbee, 2008), uncertainty management (Knobloch & Miller, 2008), information seeking (Afifi & Lucas, 2008), and self-disclosure (Derlega, Winstead, & Greene, 2008). Popular strategies for initiating relationships include complimenting and praising, emphasizing similarity, disclosing information, creating a positive image both in person and online, employing clever opening gambits, using humor, and relying on assistance from third parties (Baxter & Philpott, 1982; Clark, Shaver, & Abrahams, 1999; Cunningham & Barbee, 2008).

Work from the interpersonal influence tradition offers insight into the factors that predict people's choice of strategies. Linguistic features of initiate-relationship episodes include (a) positive politeness strategies of giving compliments and showing interest in the target and (b) negative politeness strategies of hedging and inviting the target's input (Wilson et al., 2009). Individuals who perceive more severe face threats tend to employ more positive and negative politeness strategies (Wilson et al., 2009). Moreover, people initiating relationships are less likely to persist in the face of initial resistance by the target (Kunkel et al., 2003; Wilson et al., 2009).

## Escalating Relationships

*Situational Features and Constraints.* The relational-change goal takes the form of escalating intimacy when an individual attempts to create more closeness within an already initiated relationship (Kunkel et al., 2003; Wilson et al., 2009). Cody et al. (1994, p. 57) defined relationship escalation events as those in which an actor "plans to engage in an activity or persuade a dating partner to advance to a more intimate or personal level." Relationship escalation attempts are nonroutine, complex episodes that require special attention to be implemented effectively (Schrader & Dillard, 1998). Moreover, relationship escalation attempts include situational parameters such as high intimacy, high homophily, low resistance, mutual benefits for partners, low apprehension, and high rights for the source to persuade the target (Cody et al., 1994). Secondary goals relevant to relationship escalation attempts include relational resource, identity, and interaction concerns (Honeycutt, Cantrill, Kelly, & Lambkin, 1998). Face threats include the risks of pressuring the target, damaging the current relationship, precluding a more desirable future relationship, appearing unattractive, and looking needy (Kunkel et al., 2003).

*Research.* A variety of strategies are available to people attempting relationship escalation, including ingratiating and explaining (Honeycutt et al., 1998), disclosing intimate information and displaying physical affection (Honeycutt et al., 1989), showing interest in the target and minimizing the imposition of the request (Wilson et al., 2009), and facilitating increased contact and rewards, offering social support, and verbally expressing affection (Tolhuizen, 1989). People use multiple strategies in combination to attempt relationship escalation (e.g., Honeycutt et al., 1989, 1998), and their requests tend to be direct and forthright (Cody et al., 1986; Kunkel et al., 2003). Notably, however, people are unlikely to persist in their attempt to escalate the relationship if the target offers initial resistance (Kunkel et al., 2003).

## De-Escalating Relationships

*Situational Features and Constraints.* Relationship de-escalation episodes comprise people's attempts to decrease intimacy or terminate the relationship altogether (Kunkel et al., 2003; Sahlstein & Dun, 2008; Wilson et al., 2009), which implicitly suggests disapproval of the target

(Kellermann, 2004). Compared with other goal types, people report that the relationship de-escalation goal is relatively important for them to accomplish; conversely, individuals who are attempting relationship de-escalation do not endorse the secondary goal of protecting relational resources (Schrader & Dillard, 1998). Secondary goals that constrain message production include avoiding embarrassing the target, being clear to prevent confusion, presenting a considerate image, and managing arousal (Canary et al., 1986). Prominent face threats include fears of pressuring the target to comply, making the target feel inadequate, appearing insensitive, and regretting the decision in the future (Kunkel et al., 2003; Wilson et al., 2009). Targets, for their part, may respond to these relationship de-escalation attempts with anger, hostility, and negative emotion or agreement, relief, and goodwill (Wilmot, Carabaugh, & Baxter, 1985).

*Research.* We refer readers to Fine and Harvey (2006) for a review of the voluminous literature on relationship dissolution. For our purposes, suffice it to say that relationship de-escalation attempts can be arrayed on a continuum of directness (Baxter, 1984; Wilmot et al., 1985). Global strategies for enacting relationship de-escalation include (a) direct relationship talk (explicit conversation with the partner), (b) distance cueing (implicit signals that the individual is no longer motivated to maintain the relationship), and (c) cost escalation (decreasing the partner's rewards and increasing the partner's costs to show that the relationship is no longer worth the partner's investment; Baxter, 1987; Baxter & Philpott, 1982).

Other scholarship has focused on the politeness strategies that people endorse for accomplishing relationship termination. Commonly identified politeness strategies include hedging, giving compliments, and expressing caring (Wilson et al., 2009). As perceptions of face threat increase, people's reports of using positive politeness strategies (e.g., apologizing or asking for input from the source) tend to decrease

(Wilson et al., 2009). Individuals indicate that they would persist despite initial resistance from the target (Kunkel et al., 2003; Wilson et al., 2009). Given the intricacies of the global strategies and conversation tactics that people use in combination to terminate relationships, these episodes are probably best understood as a sequence of events that unfold in relationships over time (Honeycutt, Cantrill, & Allen, 1992; Kellas & Manusov, 2003).

## Conclusions and Directions for Future Work

Although extant work offers a descriptive base for the conditions that define attempts to initiate, escalate, and de-escalate relationships, two directions for future inquiry are evident. First, whereas scholars of close relationships have paid particular attention to how the characteristics of the dyad provide a backdrop for relationship (re)definition episodes, work stemming from the interpersonal influence tradition has tended to ignore the nature of the relationship between people. We see value in efforts to synthesize the two paradigms. Second, investigators should attend to the linguistic features of relationship (re)definition episodes in conversation. Relative to the other influence goals, much remains unknown about how people attempt to change relationships within the back-and-forth interplay of discourse.

## Message Effects

Although messages might have many types of effects (Dillard et al., 2002), given space limitations, this section focuses on only one: compliance. The phrase *compliance technique* has been used to convey that research in this area emphasizes scripted methods for enhancing compliance, not spontaneous, top-of-the-head utterances. Implicitly, the technique literature assumes a linear model of communication in which the source and the target are clearly differentiated

and influence flows in one direction. The source seeks to control the interaction for the purpose of producing behavior change in the target, often with the aim of garnering tangible resources.

Some influence attempts are quite brief, consisting of no more than a request and a response. Others unfold in stages, with each segment of the interaction establishing the grounds for what follows. Accordingly, we partition the research literature on compliance techniques based on the degree of interaction between the message source and the target. Single-interact compliance techniques are those in which the source makes a single utterance and the target either complies or refuses. In other words, the source and the target produce one communicative act each, which together constitute a single interact.

Triple-interact techniques are those in which, prior to making the request for compliance, the source uses some type of set-up that requires engagement on the part of the target. A set of four acts—Request #1, Response #1, Request #2, Response #2—yields three pairs of acts, or a triple interact. Compliance procedures that fall in this category are also known as sequential request techniques because they include two ordered requests. Multi-interact techniques are defined as interaction sequences in which more than two ordered requests are planned as the means of achieving compliance.

### Single-Interact Techniques

*That's-not-all (TNA).* The TNA sales technique presents a prospective buyer with a product, a price, and a request to purchase. But before the target can respond, the salesperson sweetens the deal either by reducing the price or adding something else of value. The first effort to scientifically assess the effectiveness of the TNA employed the guise of a psychology club bake sale (Burger, 1986). In the control condition, potential customers were informed that they could purchase a cupcake and two cookies for a total of US$ 0.75.

Participants were told by the experimenter that the cupcake alone was US$ 0.75. But immediately after that cost information was provided, a second experimenter stopped the exchange by holding up his hand, conferred with the first experimenter, and then announced that actually the cupcake plus two cookies could be purchased for US$0.75. The TNA proved superior (73% compliance vs. 40%), a finding that was replicated in five subsequent experiments. Burger went on to argue that the effect might be accounted for either by a felt need for reciprocity or by perceptual contrast. Subsequent work on TNA indicated that its effectiveness is probably limited to conditions in which the message recipient is processing superficially (Pollock, Smith, Knowles, & Bruce, 1998). This finding implies that TNA is unlikely to be effective in big-ticket transactions, where individuals are motivated to carefully evaluate the message, unless systematic processing can be reduced by some other means. But this is one of the few compliance techniques that appears to be well suited to commercial interactions.

*The Lure.* Although Joule, Gouilloux, and Weber (1989) call this technique the lure, another phrase that is equally apt is bait-and-switch. As both descriptors suggest, the technique is one in which the target is offered and agrees to an attractive deal. Once the decision is made, he or she is told that circumstances have changed: "We are out of that shoe in your size." Next, the target is provided with an opportunity to execute a substitute course of action but, importantly, one that lacks the advantages of the original offer: "We do stock some very similar shoes that would fit you, but they are not on sale." In the only scientific test of the technique known to us, Joule et al. report mixed evidence of the technique's effectiveness.

*Disrupt-Then-Reframe (DTR).* The DTR depends on momentarily confusing the message target (Knowles, Butler, & Linn, 2001). The underlying logic of the approach assumes that individuals possess cognitive scripts for request interactions,

where scripts are defined as expectations regarding sequences of behavior. The oft-used illustration is that of restaurant behavior in which customers first order, then eat, and then pay. Obviously, people may possess multiple versions of this script that vary the order of some behaviors (such as when payment occurs), but the larger point is the important one: Individuals learn to expect that certain things will happen in a certain order. When they comprehend the interaction as a request sequence, the natural culmination is compliance. When message targets are thinking in typical fashion, they may have reason to question whether or not they should comply. But the confusion induced by mild perturbation distracts them from evaluating the request. The result is enhanced compliance.

In one application of the DTR (Knowles et al., 2001), control participants were asked, "Would you be interested in donating some money to the Richardson Center [for developmentally delayed adults]?" The persuasive reframing followed immediately: "You could make a difference!" In the DTR condition, a syntactically illegal construction was produced by reversing the words *money* and *some*—that is, "Would you be interested in donating money some to the Richardson Center?" The result was 65% compliance in the DTR group compared with 30% in the control group. Compliance in a third condition, which reversed the words *Center* and *Richardson* in addition to *money* and *some*, produced only 25% compliance. From the latter result, the researchers concluded that anything more than a mild disruption reduces the effectiveness of the technique.

Although research on the DTR is still in its infancy, Carpenter and Boster (2009) located six articles that contained 14 separate tests of the compliance technique. A meta-analysis of those data indicated a substantial effect of DTR on compliance: $r = .28$. When Carpenter and Boster partitioned the data by type of organization, the effect was even more dramatic. DTR used in the service of nonprofit organizations produced compliance at four times the rate of the control group. But even when the technique was used to increase sales for profit-oriented organizations, compliance was roughly two and half times greater than in the control group.

The results of the Carpenter and Boster (2009) meta-analysis are consistent with the idea that the DTR inhibits critical evaluation of the behavioral sequence. But other accounts are possible as well. For instance, Fennis, Das, and Pruyn (2004) offer a counterarguing explanation. Kardes, Fennis, Hirt, Tormala, and Bullington (2007) suggest that the ambiguity is aversive and that the DTR is successful to the extent that the reframing portion of the sequence provides a sense of closure.

*Legitimizing Paltry Contributions (LPC).* It seems self-evident that likelihood of compliance should be inversely related to the size of the request. If true, this presents a decision point for the compliance-seeking agent: Can resource acquisition be maximized by gathering many small donations or a few larger ones? Cialdini and Schroeder (1976; see also Weyant, 1984) suggest that the apparent dilemma can be avoided by legitimizing small contributions. By adding the phrase "Even a penny will help" to their standard door-to-door solicitation, they were able to increase the frequency of contributions without affecting the size of donations. Other studies have produced similar results with some slight variation in wording (e.g., "even a few minutes will help") (Takada & Levine, 2007).

In a meta-analysis, the LPC literature estimated the technique's effectiveness at $r = .18$, which is equivalent to an odds ratio of 2.41 (Andrews, Carpenter, Shaw, & Boster, 2008). That research also provided some indication that LPC's impact is limited to face-to-face encounters. However, given the paucity of data on this point, it must be accepted with caution. A different investigation suggested that the LPC effect might be moderated by individual differences in the ability of the message target to take the perspective of others (Takada & Levine, 2007).

There are, at present, no compelling explanatory accounts of the LPC technique. But analysis

of the phenomenon implies that there may be two components of decision making about charitable giving. One is the question of whether or not to give, while the other focuses on how much to give. It appears that minimizing the latter concern removes a barrier to the former. A more complete account is needed.

## Triple-Interact Techniques

*Pique.* Santos, Leve, and Pratkanis (1994) hypothesized that phrasing a request with unusual specificity might be sufficient to pique the target's interest, increase mindful processing, and enhance compliance. To test this idea, experimenters acting as panhandlers asked passersby for 17 or 37 cents (as well as control requests that included "a quarter" and "any change"). Targets who heard one of the pique requests were 60% more likely to comply than were targets in the control conditions. However, a follow-up study showed that the effect was limited to individuals who asked what the money would be used for (Burger, Hornisher, Martin, Newman, & Pringle, 2007). While leaving open the question of why the technique stimulates compliance, this finding suggests that the pique is best conceived as a triple-interact, not a single-interact, technique.

*Pregiving.* Throughout the history of humankind, every society has embraced a norm of reciprocity (Gouldner, 1960). This norm directs individuals to return in kind the actions, objects, and, to a lesser extent, affections that are provided to them by others: tit for tat, an eye for an eye. Application of the reciprocity principle is apparent in the marketing efforts of charitable organizations that send small, unsolicited gifts such as calendars and address labels along with their appeal for funds. These are examples of a strategy dubbed *pregiving* (Bell, Cholerton, Davison, Fraczek, & Lauter, 1996; Bell, Cholerton, Fraczek, Rohlfs, & Smith, 1994). One necessary condition for the effective implementation of pregiving is that the message recipient actually accept the initial offering. Without the indebtedness created by acceptance, recipients would have no need to reciprocate. But if the gift is too large, audience members may balk at accepting it, presumably because they would become indebted past the point of comfort (Bell et al., 1994).

A second variable that moderates the effectiveness of the technique is whether or not the target believes that the influencing agent will learn of his or her compliance (Whately, Webster, Smith, & Rhodes, 1999). That individuals apparently feel compelled to discharge the debt even when the pregiver will not know of their action points toward an internalized norm of reciprocity. But compliance is further enhanced when the target expects that the source will learn of his or her compliance. This latter finding implies the operation of social concerns that extend beyond an internalized norm.

Boster, Rodriguez, Cruz, and Marshall (1995) suggest a third moderator variable. Their experiment, which varied the intimacy of the source–recipient relationship, showed that pregiving produced more compliance than a direct request only when the influencing agent and recipient were strangers. In fact, one of the defining features of friendship is that reciprocity takes place in an extended time frame (Hatfield, Utne, & Traupmann, 1979). If a source uses pregiving and also indicates a desire for immediate reciprocity, he or she signals that the relationship is *not* one of friendship. Conversely, there is evidence that pregiving produces liking (Whately et al., 1999) and that liking, not obligation, explains the effectiveness of pregiving (Goei, Lindsey, Boster, Skalski, & Bowman, 2003). Other research, focused on date requests, suggests a role for gratitude as well as liking (Hendrickson & Goei, 2009).

*Unit Relationship Techniques.* Whereas pregiving may be a means of establishing a relationship, compliance rates may be enhanced by reminding message targets of their existing relationship with a message source even when (a) the two interactants are previously unknown to each another

and (b) the basis for the relationship is wholly arbitrary. Here, we overview what is really a class of techniques that presumably function to create the perception of what Heider (1958) called a unit relationship. In his words, "Separate entities [e.g., individuals] comprise a unit when they are seen as belonging together" (p. 176). The perception of a unit relationship is the basis for positive sentiment or some broad form of liking.

One illustration of a unit relationship technique comes from Aune and Basil (1994), who report a fivefold increase in compliance among college students when the target request was preceded by this interact: "Hi! Are you a student here at ____ ? Oh, that's great, so am I." In line with Roloff's (1987) thinking on relational obligations, the authors speculate that calling explicit attention to the relationship was sufficient to stimulate a sense of obligation in the message target. Other research points to liking for the source as the operative mediator (Burger, Soroka, Gonzago, Murphy, & Somervell, 2001), but the effects are difficult to disentangle because individuals both like and are obligated to those with whom they have a unit relationship (but see Goei et al., 2003). Evidently, the perception of a unit relationship can be created by a brief dialogue prior to the target request (e.g., "How are you feeling today?" "How many exams are you taking?") (Dolinski, Nawrat, & Rudak, 2001) or by learning that one shares a first name or a birthday (Burger, Messian, Patel, del Prado, & Anderson, 2004).

*The Door-in-the-Face (DITF).* The DITF technique begins with a request large enough that it will be rejected by most individuals. That initial appeal is then followed by a smaller, but still substantial, request (Cialdini et al., 1975; Millar, 2001). The available evidence is clear that the DITF enhances compliance. Ceteris paribus, it increases compliance 10% to 15% over a single message control condition. Five well-identified scope conditions govern the potency of the effect (Dillard, Hunter, & Burgoon, 1984; Fern, Monroe, & Avila, 1986; O'Keefe & Hale, 1998, 2001).

Specifically, the two requests must be delivered close together in time, in a face-to-face interaction, by the same requester, and on behalf of the same prosocial beneficiary. O'Keefe and Hale (2001) report that when all of these factors are favorable, the DITF roughly doubles the likelihood of compliance relative to the single-request control group (odds ratio = 1.86). When any of these elements are absent, the efficacy of the technique is diminished and may even be reversed.

Early efforts to explain the DITF posited a reciprocal concessions corollary to the general principle of reciprocity: "You should make concessions to those who make concessions to you" (Cialdini et al., 1975, p. 206). That view has been criticized by some as vague and incompatible with the research findings (e.g., O'Keefe, 1999; Tusing & Dillard, 2000). However, it retains many adherents, and it is difficult to definitively refute (Hale & Laliker, 1999; Lecat, Hilton, & Crano, 2009; Turner, Tamborini, Limon, & Zuckerman-Hyman, 2007). One alternative account of the effect is the *perceptual contrast* explanation, which holds that large requests cause the target to perceive the smaller request as less costly, thereby making compliance more likely (Cantrill & Seibold, 1986). The *self-presentation* perspective contends that rejecting the first request causes targets to be concerned that they will be evaluated negatively by the requester. Complying with the second request allows targets to alleviate this concern (Bell, Abrahams, Clark, & Schlatter, 1996; Pendleton & Batson, 1979). The *availability hypothesis* predicts that a concession on the part of the requester is recorded as favorable information in working memory, subsequently informing the receiver to comply with the second request (Tybout, Sternthal, & Calder, 1983). However, reciprocal concessions aside, the data have not been kind to any of these alternatives. None is seen as a plausible account of the DITF effect (Cantrill & Seibold, 1986; Dillard et al., 1984; Fern et al., 1986; O'Keefe & Hale, 1998).

To fill the resulting theoretical void, O'Keefe and Figge (1997) offered a guilt-based explanation of the DITF. They suggested that guilt arises from the juxtaposition of the moral or social standard (made salient by the first request) and the target's awareness that he or she has failed to behave in accordance with that standard by virtue of refusing the first request. Direct measures of guilt were not supportive of the notion that felt guilt mediates compliance (O'Keefe & Figge, 1999; Turner et al., 2007). But Millar (2002), who experimentally increased and decreased guilt, provided the best evidence of the mediating role of guilt in the DITF. Still, given the inconsistent findings across studies, the viability of the guilt account is not firmly established.

*The Foot-in-the-Door (FITD).* The FITD technique begins with a small request to which almost anyone would be likely to acquiesce (e.g., "Would you mind displaying a small sign in the window of your home that reads 'Be a safe driver'?"). This is followed by a second request that is not so innocuous. In the initial investigation of the FITD, the second request asked participants if they would be willing to have an imposing billboard erected in their front yard for a period of one week (Freedman & Fraser, 1966). Those who had previously committed to the first request complied at a rate twice that of those who had not been exposed to the initial request. Although subsequent work showed the effect in that study to be unusually large, the meta-analyses of the FITD literature leave little doubt as to the efficacy of the technique (Burger, 1999; Dillard et al., 1984; Fern et al., 1986).

The most commonly invoked explanation for the FITD is self-perception theory (Bem, 1972) or some variant thereof (Dillard, 1990b; but see Gorassini & Olson, 1995; Guadagno, Asher, Demaine, & Cialdini, 2001). The essential premise of the theory is that individuals infer their attitudes from their actions. Although self-perception theory is silent concerning what might prompt compliance with the initial FITD request, it straightforwardly suggests that the target infers the existence of a favorable attitude from compliance, which, in turn, serves as a guide to action on presentation of the second request. From that general premise, it is possible to deduce several factors that should increase the potency of the technique: (a) actually performing the initial request (rather than simply agreeing to do so), (b) labeling the target as helpful or supportive of the cause, (c) requiring more than a minimal amount of effort to enact the initial request, and (d) making the second request topically similar to the first. In fact, Burger (1999) presents meta-analytic evidence supportive of each of these hypotheses.

However, direct evidence of a change in self-perception has proven elusive (Rittle, 1981; Scott, 1977). Whereas Dillard (1990b) provided evidence consistent with a self-inference process in a between-subjects design, Gorassini and Olson (1995) did not find support for self-concept as a mediator in their within-subjects investigation. The matter is further complicated by the supposition that the FITD is only truly effective among a subset of potential targets (Gamian-Wilk & Lachowicz-Tabaczek, 2007). For example, Cialdini, Trost, and Newsom (1995) report that only persons high in preference for consistency show the FITD effect (see also Guadagno et al., 2001). Similarly, Burger and Guadagno (2003) observed the FITD effect only among persons with high self-concept clarity. And only persons high in self-concept clarity showed enhanced perceptions of their own helpfulness (Burger & Guadagno, 2003). As a group, these studies seem supportive of the self-perception account of the FITD, at least insofar as it applies to a trait-differentiated group of individuals. But interpretation of the data is often troubled by the fact that there was no significant overall FITD effect, thereby leaving one to wonder how primary studies or meta-analyses that did not partition subjects on these individual differences were able to observe an FITD effect.

*The Low Ball.* The low ball is a technique whose development is generally attributed to automobile dealerships (Carlson, 1973). In the first step of the sequence, the salesperson offers a car at an unexpectedly low price. After securing a commitment to purchase from the buyer, the salesperson leaves to clear the transaction with the management. When he or she returns, the buyer is told that the management has rejected the deal because the dealership would lose money at that price. Thus, the dealer can only offer the sale at a new, higher price. In addition to its apparent effectiveness for selling cars, Cialdini, Cacioppo, Bassett, and Miller (1978) provide systematic evidence of the technique's potency in other contexts. However, the low ball may be limited to circumstances in which the same person makes both the first and the second request (Burger & Petty, 1981). Some research shows the low ball producing higher rates of compliance than the FITD (Brownstein & Katzev, 1985; Hornik, Zaig, & Shadmon, 1991; Joule, 1987) but lower rates than the DITF (Wang, Brownstein, & Katzev, 1989; cf. Brownstein & Katzev, 1985). The paucity of comparative data suggests that such conclusions should be drawn cautiously.

*The Foot-in-the-Mouth (FITM).* Howard's (1990) FITM technique holds that asking individuals how they feel prior to making a request results in heightened effectiveness relative to a single-request control condition (also see Fointiat, 2000). He reasons that when individuals publicly commit themselves to feeling good—as the majority of individuals do when asked this common question—they experience an internal pressure to behave consistently with that statement. This pressure results in enhanced compliance. Although there may be merit to his argument, Howard's data show declining compliance rates when targets are grouped on the favorability of their response (e.g., "I feel good" vs. "I'm fine" vs. "I'm making it"). This pattern suggests that mood state may be responsible for variations in compliance and that these statements are simply accurate self-reports of those moods. If true, this would either undermine the commitment account or point toward the need for a multiple-process understanding of the FITM. Similar to the DITF, Howard suggests that the effectiveness of the technique is limited to prosocial requesters.

## Multi-Interact Techniques

*The High-Probability Procedure.* One technique, called the high-probability (high-p) procedure (Mace et al., 1988), bears some superficial resemblance to the FITD. But rather than a single initial request, the high-p procedure calls for the source to pose a series of questions, each one of which is likely to produce compliance. These high-p requests are followed by the target appeal, which is, relatively speaking, a low-probability request. Although no one has yet undertaken a quantitative synthesis of this literature, several investigations indicate that the procedure does reliably increase compliance (e.g., Davis, Brady, Williams, Hamilton, 1992; Harchik & Putzier, 1990; Kennedy, Itkonen, & Lindquist, 1995; Mace et al., 1988; Sanchez-Fort, Brady, & Davis, 1996; but see Hughes, 2009; Wilder, Zonneveld, Harris, Marcus, & Reagan, 2007).

Research on the high-p technique is notably different from FITD inquiry in four respects. First, whereas the FITD has been examined in the general population, high-p research has targeted special populations such as toddlers (McComas, Wacker, & Cooper, 1998), second-grade children (Ardoin, Martens, & Wolfe, 1999), emotionally disordered children (Davis & Reichle, 1996), developmentally disabled children (Ducharme & Worling, 1994), mentally retarded adolescents (Mace, Mauro, Boyajian, & Eckert, 1997), and hostage takers (Hughes, 2009). The difference in target populations is a manifestation of the distinct aims of the researchers. Second, whereas FITD is essentially a one-episode interaction designed to benefit the requester, high-p researchers study the use of longer term behavior-shaping methods to prevent self-injurious behavior or promote socially appropriate action. Low-probability behaviors that clinical researchers wish to render high probability include sharing

(e.g., "Hand [peer] a soda") and cooperation (e.g., "Help build the city with [peer]") (Davis & Reichle, 1996, p. 474). This goal highlights a third way in which high-probability research is distinct from FITD. In contrast to the large-sample, between-subjects FITD work, high-p research typically uses within-subject designs on a very small number of subjects, sometimes as few as one (e.g., McComas et al., 1998).

A final difference concerns conceptual explanations for the two techniques. Whereas self-perception is typically called on to explain the FITD effect, the researchers account for the high-p procedure in terms of reinforcement principles. Nevin's (1996) behavioral momentum metaphor equates rate of responding with velocity and resistance to extinction with mass. Although the metaphor is not without its critics (Houlihan & Brandon, 1996), it has provided the basis for much research into conditions that moderate the effect. In particular, the effectiveness of the high-p procedure for increasing the frequency of low-probability behaviors is enhanced by (a) shorter intervals between the first series of requests (Mace et al., 1988), (b) the use of "do" requests (vs. "don't" requests) (Ducharme & Worling, 1994), (c) the use of a variant sequence rather than an invariant sequence (Davis & Reichle, 1996), (d) a greater number of high-probability requests (Eckert, Boyajian, & Mace, 1995, cited in Mace, 1996), and (e) the use of "higher quality reinforcers" (e.g., food is more effective than praise) (Mace et al., 1997; Zuluaga & Normand, 2008).

*Dump-and-Chase (DAC).* Whereas the techniques described thus far all implicitly entail two interactants moving through a single sequence of moves, the DAC is unique in its appreciation of the fact that conversations are cocreated (Boster et al., 2009): They might head off in unexpected directions or involve an unspecified number of interacts. Therefore, rather than assume a single sequence, the DAC posits multiple possible paths toward (non)compliance. The simplest sequence involves a request followed by compliance. But, as obstacles researchers have pointed out, sometimes message targets offer reasons for their noncompliance rather than refusing outright (Roloff & Janiszewski, 1989). Conversations continue to the extent that the compliance seeker is able to defuse the reasons for noncompliance. This constitutes a second, more elaborate path toward compliance.

The third and most complex sequence occurs when the target simply declines to comply with the initial request. This sets the stage for the compliance agent to pursue information about the reasons for refusal and then to attempt to overcome those obstacles, perhaps repeatedly. Hence, the persistent agent presents a communicative pattern of *dumping* the proffered reasons for resistance and *chasing* the target in the direction of compliance. To date, only two studies have evaluated the effectiveness of the DAC (Boster et al., 2009). Both demonstrate the promise of the technique and provide some initial evidence of its efficacy relative to the FITD and DITF.

## Conclusions

For purely pragmatic reasons, we have partitioned our review of the influence literature into message production and message effects. This provided a clear structure for our efforts, and it reflects a division that captures how the research is actually carried out. But the true relationships between the two is something more akin to that of yin and yang. Like these ancient concepts in Chinese philosophy, production and effects are not really distinct from one another. Rather, they are two complementary aspects of the single process known as interpersonal influence or, more broadly, communication. That is not to say that the production-versus-effects distinction has not proven useful. In fact, it has served the research community well as a means of breaking down a complex problem into smaller, more manageable parts. But we should not lose sight of the few efforts to study the process as a whole (e.g., Fitch & Sanders, 1994; Hample & Dallinger, 1992; Keck &

Samp, 2007) or the larger truth: That deeper understanding of interpersonal influence will require multiprocess accounts of interactive behavior.

## References

Afifi, T. D., & Olson, L. (2005). The chilling effect in families and the pressure to conceal secrets. *Communication Monographs, 72,* 192–216.

Afifi, T. D., Olson, L. N., & Armstrong, C. (2005). The chilling effect and family secrets: Examining the role of self protection, other protection, and communication efficacy. *Human Communication Research, 31,* 564–598.

Afifi, W. A., & Lucas, A. A. (2008). Information seeking in the initial stages of relationship development. In S. Sprecher, A. Wenzel, & J. Harvey (Eds.), *Handbook of relationship initiation* (pp. 135–151). New York: Psychology Press.

Agne, R. R. (2007). Reframing practices in moral conflict: Interaction problems in the negotiation standoff at Waco. *Discourse & Society, 18,* 549–578.

Andrews K. R., Carpenter, C. J., Shaw, A. S., & Boster, F. J. (2008). The legitimization of paltry favors effect: A review and meta-analysis. *Communication Reports, 21,* 59–69.

Ardoin, S. P., Martens, B. K., & Wolfe, L. A. (1999). Using high-probability instruction sequences with fading to increase student compliance during transitions. *Journal of Applied Behavior Analysis, 32,* 339–351.

Aune, R. K., & Basil, M. D. (1994). A relational obligations approach to the foot-in-the-mouth effect. *Journal of Applied Social Psychology, 24,* 546–556.

Baxter, L. A. (1984). Trajectories of relationship disengagement. *Journal of Social and Personal Relationships, 1,* 29–48.

Baxter, L. A. (1987). Cognition and communication in the relationship process. In R. Barnett, P. McGhee, & D. Clarke (Eds.), *Accounting for relationships* (pp. 192–212). London: Methuen.

Baxter, L. A., & Bullis, C. (1986). Turning points in developing romantic relationships. *Human Communication Research, 12,* 469–493.

Baxter, L. A., & Philpott, J. (1982). Attribution-based strategies for initiating and terminating friendships. *Communication Quarterly, 30,* 217–224.

Bell, R. A., Abrahams, M. F., Clark, C L., & Schlatter, C. (1996). The door-in-the-face compliance strategy: An individual difference analysis of two models in an AIDS fundraising context. *Communication Quarterly, 44,* 107–124.

Bell, R. A., Cholerton, M., Davison,V., Fraczek, K. E., & Lauter, H. (1996). Making health communication self-funding: Effectiveness of pregiving in an AIDS fundraising/education campaign. *Health Communication, 8,* 331352.

Bell, R. A., Cholerton, M., Fraczek, K. E., Rohlfs, G. S., & Smith, B. A. (1994). Encouraging donations to charity: A field study of competing and complementary factors in tactic sequencing. *Western Journal of Communication, 58,* 98–115.

Bem, D. J. (1972). Constructing cross-situational consistencies in behavior: Some thoughts on Alker's critique of Mischel. *Journal of Personality, 40,* 17–26.

Berger, C. R. (1988). Planning, affect, and social action generation. In L. Donohew, H. E. Sypher, & E. T. Higgins (Eds.), *Communication, social cognition, and affect* (pp. 93–116). Hillsdale, NJ: Lawrence Erlbaum.

Berger, C. R., & Bell, R. A. (1988). Plans and the initiation of social relationships. *Human Communication Research, 15,* 217–235.

Berger, C. R., & diBattista, P. (1992). Information seeking and plan elaboration: What do you need to know to know what to do? *Communication Monographs, 59,* 368–387.

Bergman, M. L., & Kasper, G. (1993). Perception and performance in native and nonnative apology. In G. Kasper & S. Blum-Kulka (Eds.), *Interlanguage pragmatics* (pp. 83–107). New York: Oxford University Press.

Besson, A. L., Roloff, M. E., & Paulson, G. D. (1998). Preserving face in refusal situations. *Communication Research, 25,* 183–199.

Blodgett, J. G., & Anderson, R. D. (2000). A Bayesian network model of the consumer complaint process. *Journal of Service Research, 2,* 321–338.

Blodgett, J., Hill, D., & Bakir, A. (2006). Cross-cultural complaining behavior? An alternative explanation. *Journal of Consumer Satisfaction, Dissatisfaction and Complaining Behavior, 19,* 103–117.

Bodey, K., & Grace, D. (2007). Contrasting "complainers" with "noncomplainers" on attitude toward complaining, propensity to complain, and key personality characteristics: A nomological look. *Psychology & Marketing, 24,* 579–595.

Bolkan, S., & Daly, J. A. (2009). Organizational responses to consumer complaints: An examination of effective remediation tactics. *Journal of Applied Communication Research, 37,* 21–39.

Boster, F. J., Rodriguez, J. I., Cruz, M. G., & Marshall, L. (1995). The relative effectiveness of a pre-giving message on friends and strangers. *Communication Research, 22,* 475–484.

Boster, F. J., Shaw, A. S., Hughes, M., Kotowski, M. R., Strom, R. E., & Deatrick, L. M. (2009). Dump-and-Chase: The effectiveness of persistence as a sequential request compliance-gaining strategy. *Communication Studies, 60,* 219–234.

Brownstein, R., & Katzev, R. (1985). The relative effectiveness of three compliance techniques in eliciting donations to a cultural organization. *Journal of Applied Social Psychology, 15,* 564–574.

Burger, J. M. (1986). Increasing compliance by improving the deal: The that's-not-all technique. *Journal of Personality and Social Psychology, 51,* 277–283.

Burger, J. M. (1999). The foot-in-the-door compliance procedure: A multiple process analysis. *Personality and Social Psychology Review, 3,* 303–325.

Burger, J. M. (2003). Self-concept clarity and the foot-in-the-door procedure. *Basic and Applied Social Psychology, 25,* 79–86.

Burger, J. M., Hornisher, J., Martin, V. E., Newman, G., & Pringle, S. (2007). The pique technique: Mindlessness or shifting heuristics. *Journal of Applied Social Psychology, 37,* 2086–2096.

Burger, J. M., Messian, N., Patel, S., del Prado, A., & Anderson, C. (2004). What a coincidence! The effects of incidental similarity on compliance. *Personality and Social Psychology Bulletin, 30,* 35–43.

Burger, J. M., & Petty, R. E. (1981). The low-ball compliance technique: Task or person commitment? *Journal of Personality and Social Psychology, 40,* 492–500.

Burger, J. M., Soroka, S., Gonzago, K., Murphy, E., & Somervell, E. (2001). The effect of fleeting attraction on compliance to requests. *Personality and Social Psychology Bulletin, 27,* 1578–1586.

Cai, D. A., & Wilson, S. R. (2000). Identity implications of influence goals: A cross-cultural comparison of interaction goals and facework. *Communication Studies, 51,* 307–328.

Campbell, R. L., Svenson, L. W., & Jarvis, G. K. (1993). Age, gender, and location as factors in permission to smoke among university students. *Psychological Reports, 72,* 1231–1234.

Canary, D. J., Cody, M. J., & Marston, P. J. (1986). Goal types, compliance-gaining and locus of control. *Journal of Language and Social Psychology, 5,* 249–269.

Canary, D. J., & Dainton, M. (2006). Maintaining relationships. In A. L. Vangelisti & D. Perlman (Eds.), *The Cambridge handbook of personal relationships* (pp. 727–743). New York: Cambridge University Press.

Canary, D. J., & Stafford, L. (1994). Maintaining relationships through strategic and routine interaction. In D. J. Canary & L. Stafford (Eds.), *Communication and relational maintenance* (pp. 6–23). New York: Academic.

Cantrill, J. G., & Seibold, D. R. (1986). The perceptual contrast explanation of sequential request strategy effectiveness. *Human Communication Research, 13,* 253–267.

Carlson, M. D. (1973). *How to get your car repaired without getting gypped.* New York: Harrow Books.

Carpenter, C. J., & Boster, F. J. (2009). A meta-analysis of the effectiveness of the Disrupt-Then-Reframe compliance gaining technique. *Communication Reports, 22,* 55–62.

Cho, J., Shah, D. V., McLeod, J. M., McLeod, D. M., Scholl, R. M., & Gotlieb, M. R. (2009). Campaigns, reflections, and deliberation: Advancing an O-S-R-O-R model of communication effects. *Communication Theory, 19,* 66–88.

Cialdini, R. B., Cacioppo, J. T., Bassett, R., & Miller, J. A. (1978). Low-ball procedure for producing compliance: Commitment then cost. *Journal of Personality and Social Psychology, 36,* 463–476.

Cialdini, R. B., & Schroeder, D. A. (1976). Increasing compliance by legitimizing paltry contributions: When even a penny helps. *Journal of Personality and Social Psychology, 34,* 599–604.

Cialdini, R. B., Trost, M. R., & Newsom, J. T. (1995). Preference for consistency: The development of a valid measure and the discovery of surprising behavioral implications. *Journal of Personality and Social Psychology, 69,* 318–328.

Cialdini, R. B., Vincent, J. E., Lewis, S. K., Catalan, J., Wheeler, D., & Darby, B. L. (1975). Reciprocal concessions procedure for inducing compliance: The door-in-the-face technique. *Journal of Personality and Social Psychology, 34,* 206–215.

Clark, C. L., Shaver, P. R., & Abrahams, M. F. (1999). Strategic behaviors in romantic relationship initiation. *Personality and Social Psychology Bulletin, 2,* 707–720.

Cloven, D. H., & Roloff, M. E. (1993). The chilling effect of aggressive potential on the expression of complaints in intimate relationships. *Communication Monographs, 60,* 199–219.

Cody, M. J., Canary, D. J., & Smith, S. W. (1994). Compliance-gaining goals: An inductive analysis of actor's goal types, strategies, and successes. In J. A. Daly & J. M. Wiemann (Eds.), *Strategic interpersonal communication* (pp. 33–90). Hillsdale, NJ: Lawrence Erlbaum.

Cody, M. J., Greene, J. O., Marston, P. J., O'Hair, H. D., Baaske, K. T., & Schneider, M. J. (1986). Situation perceptions and message strategy selection. In M. L. McLaughlin (Ed.), *Communication Yearbook, 9* (pp. 390–420). Beverly Hills, CA: Sage.

Cody, M. J., & McLaughlin, M. L. (1980). Perceptions of compliance gaining situations: A dimensional analysis. *Communication Monographs, 47,* 132–148.

Compton, J., & Pfau, M. (2009). Spreading inoculation: Inoculation, resistance to influence, and word-of-mouth communication. *Communication Theory, 19,* 9–28.

Cunningham, M. R., & Barbee, A. P. (2008). Prelude to a kiss: Nonverbal flirting, opening gambits, and other communication dynamics in the initiation of romantic relationships. In S. Sprecher, A. Wenzel, & J. Harvey (Eds.), *Handbook of relationship initiation* (pp. 97–120). New York: Psychology Press.

Dainton, M., & Aylor, B. (2002). Routine and strategic maintenance efforts: Behavioral patterns, variations associated with relational length, and the prediction of relational characteristics. *Communication Monographs, 69,* 52–66.

Dainton, M., Zelley, E., & Langan, E. (2003). Maintaining friendships throughout the lifespan. In D. J. Canary & M. Dainton (Eds.), *Maintaining relationships through communication: Relational, contextual, and cultural variations* (pp. 79–102). Mahwah, NJ: Lawrence Erlbaum.

Dart, J., & Freeman, K. (1994). Dissatisfaction response styles among clients of professional accounting firms. *Journal of Business Research, 29,* 75–81.

Davis, C. A., Brady, M., Williams, R., & Hamilton, R. (1992). Effects of high-probability requests on the acquisition and generalization of responding to requests in young children with behavior disorders. *Journal of Applied Behavior Analysis, 25,* 905–916.

Davis, C. A., & Reichle, J. (1996). Variant and invariant high-probability requests: Increasing appropriate behaviors in children with emotional-behavioral disorders. *Journal of Applied Behavior Analysis, 29,* 471–482.

Derlega, V. J., Winstead, B. A., & Greene, K. (2008). Self-disclosure and starting a close relationship. In S. Sprecher, A. Wenzel, & J. Harvey (Eds.), *Handbook of relationship initiation* (pp. 153–174). New York: Psychology Press.

Dillard, J. P. (1989). Types of influence goals in personal relationships. *Journal of Social and Personal Relationships, 6,* 293–308.

Dillard, J. P. (1990a). A goal-driven model of interpersonal influence. In J. P. Dillard (Ed.), *Seeking compliance* (pp. 41–56). Scottsdale, AZ: Gorsuch Scarisbrick.

Dillard, J. P. (1990b). Self-inference and the foot-in-the-door technique: Quantity of behavior and attitudinal mediation. *Human Communication Research, 16,* 422–447.

Dillard, J. P., Anderson, J. W., & Knobloch, L. K. (2002). Interpersonal influence. In M. Knapp & J. Daly (Eds.), *The handbook of interpersonal communication* (pp. 423–474). Thousand Oaks, CA: Sage.

Dillard, J. P., Hunter, J. E., & Burgoon, M. (1984). Sequential request persuasive strategies: Meta-analysis of foot-in-the-door and door-in-the-face. *Human Communication Research, 10,* 461–488.

Dillard, J. P., & Solomon, D. H. (2000). Conceptualizing context in message-production research. *Communication Theory, 10,* 167–175.

Dindia, K. (2003). Definitions and perspectives on relational maintenance communication. In D. J. Canary & M. Dainton (Eds.), *Maintaining relationships through communication: Relational, contextual, and cultural variations* (pp. 1–28). Mahwah, NJ: Lawrence Erlbaum.

Dolinski, D., Nawrat, N., & Rudak, I. (2001). Dialogue involvement as a social influence technique. *Personality and Social Psychology Bulletin, 27,* 1395–1406.

Ducharme, J. M., & Worling, D. E. (1994). Behavioral momentum and stimulus fading in the acquisition and maintenance of child compliance in the home. *Journal of Applied Behavior Analysis, 27,* 639–647.

Edwards, D. (2005). Moaning, whinging, and laughing: The subjective side of complaints. *Discourse Studies, 7,* 5–29.

Eslami-Rasekh, Z. (2004). Face-keeping strategies in reaction to complaints: English and Persian. *Journal of Asian Pacific Communication, 14,* 181–197.

Feng, B. (2009). Testing an integrated model of advice giving in supportive interactions. *Human Communication Research, 35,* 115–129.

Feng, B., & Burleson, B. R. (2008). The effects of argument explicitness on responses to advice in supportive interactions. *Communication Research, 35,* 849–874.

Feng, B., & MacGeorge, E. L. (2006). Predicting receptiveness to advice: Characteristics of the problem, the advice-giver, and the recipient. *Southern Journal of Communication, 71,* 67–85.

Fennis, B. M., Das, E. H. H. J., & Pruyn, A. Th. A. (2004). If you can't dazzle them with brilliance, baffle them with nonsense: Extending the impact of the disrupt-then-reframe technique of social influence. *Journal of Consumer Psychology, 14,* 280–290.

Fern, E. F., Monroe, K. B., & Avila, R. A. (1986). Effectiveness of multiple request strategies: A synthesis of research results. *Journal of Marketing Research, 23,* 144–152.

Fine, M. A., & Harvey, J. H. (Eds.). (2006). *Handbook of divorce and relationship dissolution.* Mahwah, NJ: Lawrence Erlbaum.

Fitch, K. L., & Sanders, R. E. (1994). Culture, communication, and preferences for directness in expression of directives. *Communication Theory, 4,* 219–245.

Flora, J., & Segrin, C. (1998). Joint leisure time in friend and romantic relationships: The role of activity type, social skills and positivity. *Journal of Social and Personal Relationships, 15,* 711–718.

Fogarty, J., & Youngs, G. A., Jr. (2000). Psychological reactance as a factor in patient noncompliance with medication taking: A field experiment. *Journal of Applied Social Psychology, 30,* 2365–2391.

Fointiat, V. (2000). "Foot-in-the-mouth" versus "door-in-the-face" requests. *Journal of Social Psychology, 140,* 264–266.

Freedman, J. L., & Fraser, S. L. (1966). Compliance without pressure: The foot-in-the-door technique. *Journal of Personality and Social Psychology, 4,* 195–202.

Gamian-Wilk, M., & Lachowiscz-Tabaczek, K. (2007). Implicit theories and compliance with the foot-in-the-door technique. *Polish Psychological Bulletin, 38,* 50–63.

Goei, R., Lindsey, L. L. M., Boster, F. J., Skalski, P. D., & Bowman, J. M. (2003). The mediating role of liking and obligation on the relationship between favors and compliance. *Communication Research, 30,* 178–197.

Goldschmidt, M. (1996). From the addressee's perspective: Imposition in favor-asking. In S. M. Gass & J. Neu (Eds.), *Speech acts across cultures: Challenges to communication in a second language* (pp. 241–256). New York: Mouton de Gruyter.

Goldschmidt, M. M. (1998). Do me a favor: A descriptive analysis of favor asking sequences in American English. *Journal of Pragmatics, 29,* 129–153.

Goldsmith, D. J. (2000). Soliciting advice: The role of sequential placement in mitigating face threat. *Communication Monographs, 67,* 1–19.

Goldsmith, D. J., & Fitch, K. (1997). The normative context of advice as social support. *Human Communication Research, 23,* 454–476.

Goldsmith, D. J., & MacGeorge, E. L. (2000). The impact of politeness and relationship on perceived quality of advice about a problem. *Human Communication Research, 26,* 234–263.

Gorassini, D. R., & Olson, J. M. (1995). Does self-perception change explain the foot-in-the-door effect? *Journal of Personality and Social Psychology, 69,* 91–105.

Gouldner, A. W. (1960). The norm of reciprocity: A preliminary statement. *American Sociological Review, 25,* 161–178.

Greenberg, S. R. (1975). Conversations as units of analysis in the study of personal influence. *Journalism Quarterly, 52,* 128–131.

Guadagno, R. E., Asher, T., Demaine, L. J., & Cialdini, R. B. (2001). When saying yes leads to saying no: Preference for consistency and the reverse foot-in-the-door effect. *Personality and Social Psychology Bulletin, 27,* 859–867.

Haas, S. M. (2003). Relationship maintenance in same-sex couples. In D. J. Canary & M. Dainton (Eds.), *Maintaining relationships through communication: Relational, contextual, and cultural variations* (pp. 209–230). Mahwah, NJ: Lawrence Erlbaum.

Hale, J. L., & Laliker, M. (1999). Explaining the door-in-the-face: Is it really time to abandon reciprocal concessions? *Communication Studies, 50,* 203–210.

Hample, D., & Dallinger, J. M. (1990). Arguers as editors. *Argumentation, 4,* 153–169.

Hample, D., & Dallinger, J. M. (1992). The use of multiple goals in cognitive editing of arguments. *Argumentation and Advocacy, 28,* 109–122.

Han, K. H., Li, M. C., & Hwang, K. K. (2005). Cognitive responses to favor requests from different social targets in a Confucian society. *Journal of Social and Personal Relationships, 22,* 283–294.

Hansen, S. W., Swan, J. E., & Powers, T. L. (1997). Vendor relationships as predictors of organizational buyer complaint response styles. *Journal of Business Research, 40,* 65–77.

Harchik, A., & Putzier, V. (1990). The use of high-probability requests to compliance with instructions to take medication. *Journal of the Association for Persons with Severe Handicaps, 15,* 40–43.

Hardy, B. W., & Scheufele, D. A. (2009). Presidential campaign dynamics and the ebb and flow of talk as a moderator: Media exposure, knowledge, and political discussion. *Communication Theory, 19,* 89–101.

Hatfield, E., Utne, M. K., & Traupmann, J. (1979). Equity theory and intimate relationships. In R. L. Burgess & T. L. Huston (Eds.), *Social exchange in developing relationships* (pp. 99–133). New York: Academic Press.

Heider, F. (1958). *The psychology of interpersonal relations.* New York: Wiley.

Hendrickson, B., & Goei, R. (2009). Reciprocity and dating: Explaining the effects of favor and status on compliance with a date request. *Communication Research, 36,* 585–608.

Hoeken, H., Swanepoel, P., Saal, E., & Jansen, C. (2009). Using message form to stimulate conversations: The case of tropes. *Communication Theory, 19,* 49–65.

Honeycutt, J. M., Cantrill, J. G., & Allen, T. (1992). Memory structures for relational decay: A cognitive test of sequencing of deescalating actions and stages. *Human Communication Research, 18,* 528–562.

Honeycutt, J. M., Cantrill, J. G., & Greene, R. W. (1989). Memory structures for relational escalation: A cognitive test of the sequencing of relational actions and stages. *Human Communication Research, 16,* 62–90.

Honeycutt, J. M., Cantrill, J. G., Kelly, P., & Lambkin, D. (1998). How do I love thee? Let me consider my options: Cognitions, verbal strategies, and the escalation of intimacy. *Human Communication Research, 25,* 39–63.

Hornik, J., Zaig, T., & Shadmon, D. (1991). Reducing refusals in telephone surveys on sensitive topics. *Journal of Advertising Research, 31,* 49–56.

Houlihan, D., & Brandon, P. K. (1996). Compliant in a moment: A commentary on Nevin. *Journal of Applied Behavior Analysis, 29,* 549–555.

Howard, D. J. (1990). The influence of verbal responses to common greetings on compliance behavior: The foot-in-the-mouth effect. *Journal of Applied Social Psychology, 20,* 1185–1196.

Hughes, J. (2009). A pilot study of naturally-occurring high-probability request sequences in hostage negotiations. *Journal of Applied Behavior Analysis, 42,* 491–497.

Hutchby, I. (1995). Aspects of recipient design in expert advice giving on call-in radio. *Discourse Processes, 19,* 219–238.

Ifert, D. E., & Roloff, M. E. (1994). Anticipated obstacles to compliance: Predicting their presence and expression. *Communication Studies, 45,* 120–130.

Infante, D. A., & Rancer, A. S. (1993). Relations between argumentative motivation, and advocacy and refutation on controversial issues. *Communication Quarterly, 41,* 415–426.

Joule, R. V. (1987). Tobacco deprivation: The foot-in-the-door technique versus the low-ball technique. *European Journal of Social Psychology, 17,* 361–365.

Joule, R. V., Gouilloux, G., & Weber, F. (1989). The lure: A new compliance procedure. *Journal of Social Psychology, 129,* 741–749.

Kardes, F. R., Fennis, B. M., Hirt, E. R., Tormala, Z. L., & Bullington, B. (2007). The role of the need for cognitive closure in the effectiveness of the disrupt-then-reframe influence technique. *Journal of Consumer Research, 34,* 377–385.

Keck, K. L., & Samp, J. A. (2007). The dynamic nature of goals and message production as revealed in sequential analysis of conflict interactions. *Human Communication Research, 33,* 27–47.

Kellas, J. K., & Manusov, V. (2003). What's in a story? The relationship between narrative completeness and adjustment to relationship dissolution. *Journal of Social and Personal Relationships, 20,* 285–307.

Kellermann, K. (2004). A goal-directed approach to gaining compliance: Relating differences among goals to differences in behaviors. *Communication Research, 31,* 397–445.

Kellermann, K., & Shea, B. C. (1996). Threats, suggestions, hints, and promises: Gaining compliance efficiently and politely. *Communication Quarterly, 44,* 145–165.

Kennedy, C., Itkonen, T., & Lindquist, K. (1995). Comparing interspersed requests and social comments as antecedents for increasing student compliance. *Journal of Applied Behavior Analysis, 28,* 97–98.

Kim, M. S. (1994). Cross-cultural comparisons of perceived importance of conversational constraints. *Human Communication Research, 21,* 128–151.

Kim, M. S., Wilson, S. R., Anastasiou, L., Aleman, C., Oetzel, J., & Lee, H. R. (2009). The relationship between self-construals and perceived face threats in influence goals. *Journal of International and Intercultural Communication, 2,* 318–343.

Kinnell, A. M., & Maynard, D. W. (1996). The delivery and receipt of safer sex advice in pre-test counseling sessions for HIV and AIDS. *Journal of Contemporary Ethnography, 24,* 405–437.

Kinsey, D. F., & Chaffee, S. H. (1996). Communication behavior and presidential approval: The decline of George Bush. *Political Communication, 13,* 281–291.

Kiuru, P., Poskiparta, M., Kettunen, T., Saltevo, J., & Liimatainen, L. (2004). Advice-giving styles by Finnish nurses in dietary counseling concerning Type 2 diabetes care. *Journal of Health Communication, 9,* 337–354.

Knobloch, L. K. (2006). Relational uncertainty and message production within courtship: Features of date request messages. *Human Communication Research, 32,* 244–273.

Knobloch, L. K., & Miller, L. E. (2008). Uncertainty and relationship initiation. In S. Sprecher, A. Wenzel, & J. Harvey (Eds.), *Handbook of relationship initiation* (pp. 121–134). New York: Psychology Press.

Knobloch, L. K., & Schmelzer, B. (2008). Using the emotion-in-relationships model to predict features of interpersonal influence attempts. *Communication Monographs, 75,* 219–247.

Knowles, E., Butler, S., & Linn, J. (2001). Increasing compliance by reducing resistance. In J. P. Forgas & K. D. Williams (Eds.), *Social influence: Direct and indirect processes* (pp. 41–60). Philadelphia: Taylor & Francis.

Koestner, R., Losier, G. F., Vallerand, R. J., & Carducci, D. (1996). Identified and introjected forms of political internalization: Extending self-determination theory. *Journal of Personality and Social Psychology, 70,* 1025–1036.

Kowalski, R. M. (1996). Complaints and complaining: Functions, antecedents, and consequences. *Psychological Bulletin, 119,* 179–196.

Kowalski, R. M. (2003). *Complaining, teasing, and other annoying behaviors.* New Haven, CT: Yale University Press.

Kowalski, R. M., & Erickson, J. R. (1997). Complaining: What's all the fuss about? In R. M. Kowalski (Ed.), *Aversive interpersonal behaviors* (pp. 92–110). New York: Plenum Press.

Kowalski, R. M., Walker, S., Wilkinson, R., Queen, A., & Sharpe, B. (2003). Lying, cheating, complaining, and other aversive interpersonal behaviors: A narrative examination of the darker side of relationships. *Journal of Social and Personal Relationships, 20,* 471–490.

Kunkel, A. D., Wilson, S. R., Olufowote, J., & Robson, S. (2003). Identity implications of influence goals: Initiating, intensifying, and ending romantic relationships. *Western Journal of Communication, 67,* 382–412.

Lecat, B., Hilton, D. J., & Crano, W. D. (2009). Group status and reciprocity norms: Can the door-in-the-face effect be obtained in an outgroup context? *Group Dynamics: Theory, Research, and Practice, 13,* 178–189.

Liu, R. R., & McClure, P. (2001). Recognizing cross-cultural differences in consumer complaint behavior and intentions: An empirical examination. *Journal of Consumer Marketing, 18,* 54–75.

Mace, F. C. (1996). In pursuit of general behavioral relations. *Journal of Applied Behavior Analysis, 29,* 557–563.

Mace, F. C., Hock, M. L., Lalli, J. S., West, B. J., Belfiore, P., Pinter, E., et al. (1988). Behavioral momentum in the treatment of non-compliance. *Journal of Applied Behavior Analysis, 21,* 123–141.

Mace, F. C., Mauro, B. C., Boyajian, A. E., & Eckert, T. L. (1997). Effects of reinforcer quality on behavioral momentum: Coordinated applied and basic research. *Journal of Applied Behavior Analysis, 30,* 1–20.

MacGeorge, E. L., Feng, B., Butler, G. L., & Budarz, S. K. (2004). Understanding advice in supportive interactions: Beyond the facework and message evaluation paradigm. *Human Communication Research, 30,* 42–70.

MacGeorge, E. L., Lichtman, R. M., & Pressey, L. C. (2002). The evaluation of advice in supportive interactions: Facework and contextual factors. *Human Communication Research, 28,* 451–463.

McComas, J. J., Wacker, D. P., & Cooper, L. J. (1998). Increasing compliance with medical procedures: Application of the high-probability request procedure to a toddler. *Journal of Applied Behavior Analysis, 31,* 287–290.

Meisenbach, R. J., Remke, R. V., Buzzanell, P. M., & Liu, M. (2008). "They allowed": Pentadic mapping of women's maternity leave discourse as organizational rhetoric. *Communication Monographs, 75,* 1–24.

Meyer, J. R. (1990). Cognitive processes underlying the retrieval of compliance-gaining strategies: An implicit rules model. In J. P. Dillard (Ed.), *Seeking compliance: The production of interpersonal influence messages* (pp. 123–142). Scottsdale, AZ: Gorsuch Scarisbrick.

Meyer, J. R. (2002). Contextual influences on the pursuit of secondary goals in request messages. *Communication Monographs, 69,* 189–203.

Millar, M. G. (2001). Promoting health behaviours with door-in-the-face: The influence of the beneficiary of the request. *Psychology, Health, & Medicine, 6,* 115–119.

Millar, M. G. (2002). Effects of guilt induction and guilt reduction on door in the face. *Communication Research, 29,* 666–680.

Monzoni, C. M. (2008). Introducing direct complaints through questions: The interactional achievement of "pre-sequences"? *Discourse Studies, 10,* 73–87.

Morgan, S. E. (2009). The intersection of conversation, cognitions, and campaigns: The social representation of organ donation. *Communication Theory, 19,* 29–48.

Morgan, S. E., Harrison, T. R., Long, S. D., Afifi, W. A., & Stephenson, M. T. (2008). In their own words: A multicultural qualitative study of the reasons why people will (not) donate organs. *Health Communication, 23,* 23–33.

Morrow, P. R. (2006). Talking about problems and giving advice in an Internet discussion forum: Some discourse features. *Discourse Studies, 8,* 531–548.

Nevin, J. A. (1996). The momentum of compliance. *Journal of Applied Behavior Analysis, 29,* 535–547.

Newell, S. E., & Stutman, R. K. (1989/90). Negotiating confrontation: The problematic nature of initiation and response. *Research on Language and Social Interaction, 23,* 139–162.

Newell, S. E., & Stutman, R. K. (1991). The episodic nature of social confrontation. In J. A. Anderson (Ed.), *Communication yearbook 14* (pp. 359–413). Thousand Oaks, CA: Sage.

Nyer, P. U., & Gopinath, M. (2005). Effects of complaining versus negative word of mouth on subsequent changes in satisfaction: The role of public commitment. *Psychology & Marketing, 22,* 937–953.

O' Keefe, B. J. (1990). The logic of regulative communication: Understanding the rationality of message designs. In J. P. Dillard (Ed.), *Seeking compliance: The production of interpersonal influence messages* (pp. 87–104). Scottsdale, AZ: Gorsuch-Scarisbrick.

O'Keefe, D. J. (1999). Three reasons for doubting the adequacy of the reciprocal concessions explanation of door-in-the-face effects. *Communication Studies, 50,* 211–220.

O'Keefe, D. J., & Figge, M. (1997). A guilt-based explanation of the door-in-the-face influence strategy. *Human Communication Research, 24,* 64–81.

O'Keefe, D. J., & Figge, M. (1999). Guilt and expected guilt in the door-in-the-face technique. *Communication Monographs, 66,* 312–324.

O'Keefe, D. J., & Hale, S. L. (1998). The door-in-the-face influence strategy. In M. E. Roloff (Ed.), *Communication yearbook 21* (pp. 1–33). Thousand Oaks, CA: Sage.

O'Keefe, D. J., & Hale, S. L. (2001). An odds-ratio-based meta-analysis of research on the door-in-the-face influence strategy. *Communication Reports, 14,* 31–38.

Pan, Z., Shen, L., Paek, H. J., & Sun, Y. (2006). Mobilizing political talk in a presidential campaign: An examination of campaign effects in a deliberative framework. *Communication Research, 33,* 315–345.

Pendleton, M. G., & Batson, C. D. (1979). Self-presentation and the door-in-the-face technique for reducing compliance. *Personality and Social Psychology Bulletin, 5,* 77–81.

Pollock, C. L., Smith, S. D., Knowles, E. S., & Bruce, H. J. (1998). Mindfulness limits compliance with the that's-not-all technique. *Personality and Social Psychology Bulletin, 24,* 1153–1157.

Pratkanis, A. R. (2007). *The science of social influence: Advances and future progress.* London, UK: Psychology Press.

Pudlinski, C. (1998). Giving advice on a consumer-run warm line: Implicit and dilemmatic practices. *Communication Studies, 49,* 322–341.

Pudlinski, C. (2002). Accepting and rejecting advice as competent peers: Caller dilemmas on a warm line. *Discourse Studies, 4,* 481–500.

Ramirez, A., Jr., & Burgoon, J. K. (2004). The effect of interactivity on initial interactions: The influence of information valence and modality and information richness on computer-mediated interaction. *Communication Monographs, 71,* 422–447.

Reissman, C., Aron, A., & Bergen, M. R. (1993). Shared activities and marital satisfaction: Causal direction and self-expansion versus boredom. *Journal of Social and Personal Relationships, 10,* 243–254.

Rittle, R. H. (1981). Changes in helping behavior: Self-versus situational perceptions as mediators of the foot-in-the-door effect. *Personality and Social Psychology Bulletin, 7,* 431–437.

Robinson, J. D., & Stivers, T. (2001). Achieving activity transitions in physician-patient encounters. *Human Communication Research, 27,* 253–298.

Roloff, M. E. (1987). Interpersonal communication: The social exchange approach. Beverly Hills, CA: Sage.

Roloff, M. E., & Cloven, D. H. (1990). The chilling effect in interpersonal relationships: The reluctance to speak one's mind. In D. D. Cahn (Ed.), *Intimates in conflict: A communication perspective* (pp. 49–76). Hillsdale, NJ: Lawrence Erlbaum.

Roloff, M. E., & Janiszewski, C. A. (1989). Overcoming obstacles to interpersonal compliance: A principle of message construction. *Human Communication Research, 16,* 33–61.

Roloff, M. E., Janiszewski, C. A., McGrath, M. A., Burns, C. S., & Manrai, L. A. (1988). Acquiring resources from intimates: When obligation substitutes for persuasion. *Human Communication Research, 14,* 364–396.

Rule, B. G., & Bisanz, G. L. (1987). Goals and strategies of persuasion: A cognitive schema for understanding social events. In M. P. Zanna, J. M. Olson, & C. P. Herman (Eds.), *Social influence: The Ontario symposium* (Vol. 5, pp. 185–206). Hillsdale, NJ: Lawrence Erlbaum.

Rule, B. G., Bisanz, G. L., & Kohn, M. (1985). Anatomy of a persuasion schema: Targets, goals, and strategies. *Journal of Personality and Social Psychology, 48,* 1127–1140.

Sahlstein, E., & Dun, T. (2008). "I wanted time to myself and he wanted to be together all the time": Constructing breakups as managing autonomy-connection. *Qualitative Research Reports in Communication, 9,* 37–45.

Sanchez-Fort, M., Brady, M., & Davis, C. (1996). Using behavioral momentum to increase the use of signed vocabulary words of young children with moderate to severe disabilities. *Education and Training in Mental Retardation and Developmental Disabilities, 30,* 151–165.

Santos, M. D., Leve, C., & Pratkanis, A. R. (1994). Hey, buddy, can you spare seventeen cents? Mindful persuasion and the pique technique. *Journal of Applied Social Psychology, 24,* 755–764.

Schrader, D. C., & Dillard, J. P. (1998). Goal structures and interpersonal influence. *Communication Studies, 49,* 276–293.

Schudson, M. (1997). Why conversation is not the soul of democracy. *Critical Studies in Mass Communication, 14,* 297–309.

Scott, C. A. (1977). Modifying socially conscious behavior: The foot-in-the-door technique. *Journal of Consumer Research, 4,* 156–164.

Searle, J. R. (1969). *Speech acts: An essay in the philosophy of language.* Cambridge, UK: Cambridge University Press.

Singh, J., & Wilkes, R. E. (1996). When consumers complain: A path analysis of the key antecedents of consumer complaint response estimates. *Journal of the Academy of Marketing Science, 24,* 350–365.

Solomon, D. H. (1997). A developmental model of intimacy and date request explicitness. *Communication Monographs, 64,* 99–118.

Solomon, D. H., Knobloch, L. K., & Fitzpatrick, M. A. (2004). Relational power, marital schema, and decisions to withhold complaints: An investigation of the chilling effect on confrontation in marriage. *Communication Studies, 55,* 146–167.

Solomon, D. H., & Samp, J. A. (1998). Power and problem appraisal: Perceptual foundations of the chilling effect in dating relationships. *Journal of Social and Personal Relationships, 15,* 191–209.

Southwell, B. G., & Yzer, M. C. (2007). The roles of interpersonal communication in mass media campaigns. In C. Beck (Ed.), *Communication Yearbook 31* (pp. 420–462). New York: Lawrence Erlbaum.

Southwell, B. G., & Yzer, M. C. (2009). When (and why) interpersonal talk matters for campaigns. *Communication Theory, 19,* 1–8.

Sprecher, S., Wenzel, A., & Harvey, J. (Eds.). (2008). *Handbook of relationship initiation.* New York: Psychology Press.

Stafford, L., & Canary, D. J. (2006). Equity and interdependence as predictors of relational maintenance strategies. *Journal of Family Communication, 6,* 227–254.

Stephens, N., & Gwinner, K. P. (1998). Why don't some people complain? A cognitive-emotive process model of consumer complaint behavior. *Journal of the Academy of Marketing Science, 26,* 172–189.

Strauss, J., & Hill, D. J. (2001). Consumer complaints by e-mail: An exploratory investigation of corporate responses and customer reactions. *Journal of Interactive Marketing, 15,* 63–73.

Sundstrom, E., & Sundstrom, M. G. (1977). Personal space invasions: What happens when the invader asks permission? *Environmental Psychology and Nonverbal Behavior, 2,* 76–82.

Susskind, A. M. (2000). Efficacy and outcome expectations related to customer complaints about service experiences. *Communication Research, 27,* 353–378.

Takada, J., & Levine, T. R. (2007). The effects of the Even-a-Few-Minutes-Would-Help strategy, perspective taking, and empathic concern on the successful recruiting of volunteers on campus. *Communication Research Reports, 24,* 177–184.

Thompson, S., & O'Hair, H. D. (2008). Advice-giving and the management of uncertainty for cancer survivors. *Health Communication, 23,* 340–348.

Tolhuizen, J. H. (1989). Communication strategies for intensifying dating relationships: Identification, use and structure. *Journal of Social and Personal Relationships, 6,* 413–434.

Tracy, K. (2009). How questioning constructs judge identities: Oral argument about same-sex marriage. *Discourse Studies, 11,* 199–221.

Turner, M. M., Tamborini, R., Limon, M. S., & Zuckerman-Hyman, C. (2007). The moderators and mediators of door-in-the-face requests: Is it a negotiation or a helping experience? *Communication Monographs, 74,* 333–356.

Tusing, K. J., & Dillard, J. P. (2000). The psychological reality of the door-in-the-face: It's helping, not bargaining. *Journal of Language and Social Psychology, 19,* 5–25.

Tybout, A., Sternthal, B., & Calder, B. J. (1983). Information availability as a determinant of multiple request effectiveness. *Journal of Marketing Research, 20,* 280–290.

Vehvilainen, S. (2009). Student-initiated advice in academic supervision. *Research on Language and Social Interaction, 42,* 163–190.

Vogl-Bauer, S., Kalbfleisch, P. J., & Beatty, M. J. (1999). Perceived equity, satisfaction, and relational maintenance strategies in parent-adolescent dyads. *Journal of Youth and Adolescence, 28,* 27–49.

Wang, T., Brownstein, R., & Katzev, R. (1989). Promoting charitable behavior with compliance techniques. *Applied Psychology: An International Review, 38,* 165–183.

Way, B. M., & Masters, R. D. (1996). Emotion and cognition in political information-processing. *Journal of Communication, 46,* 48–65.

Weyant, J. M. (1984). Applying social psychology to induce charitable donations. *Journal of Applied Social Psychology, 14,* 441–447.

Whately, M. A., Webster, J. M., Smith, R. H., & Rhodes, A. (1999). The effect of a favor on public and private compliance: How internalized is the norm of reciprocity? *Basic and Applied Social Psychology, 21,* 251–259.

Wilder, D. A., Zonneveld, K., Harris, C., Marcus, & Reagan, R. (2007). Further analysis of antecedent interventions on preschoolers' compliance. *Journal of Applied Behavior Analysis, 40,* 535–539.

Wilmot, W. W., Carabaugh, D. A., & Baxter, L. A. (1985). Communicative strategies used to terminate romantic relationships. *Western Journal of Speech Communication, 49,* 204–216.

Wilson, S. R. (1995). Elaborating the cognitive rules model of interaction goals: The problem of accounting for individual differences in goal formation. In B. R. Burleson (Ed.), *Communication yearbook 18* (pp. 3–25). Thousand Oaks, CA: Sage.

Wilson, S. R. (2002). *Seeking and resisting compliance: Why people say what they do when trying to influence others.* Thousand Oaks, CA: Sage.

Wilson, S. R., Aleman, C. G., & Leatham, G. B. (1998). Identity implications of influence goals: A revised analysis of face-threatening acts and application to seeking compliance with same-sex friends. *Human Communication Research, 25,* 64–96.

Wilson, S. R., & Kunkel, A. W. (2000). Identity implications of influence goals: Similarities in perceived face threats and facework across sex and close relationships. *Journal of Language and Social Psychology, 19,* 195–221.

Wilson, S. R., Kunkel, A. D., Robson, S. J., Olufowote, J. O., & Soliz, J. (2009). Identity implications of relationship (re)definition goals: An analysis of face threats and facework as young adults initiate, intensify, and disengage from romantic relationships. *Journal of Language and Social Psychology, 28,* 32–61.

Wyatt, R. O., Katz, E., & Kim, J. (2000). Bridging the spheres: Political and personal conversation in public and private spheres. *Journal of Communication, 51,* 71–92.

Wyatt, R. O., Kim, J., & Katz, E. (2000). How feeling free to talk affects ordinary political conversation, purposeful argumentation, and civic participation. *Journalism & Mass Communication Quarterly, 77,* 99–114.

Yum, Y. O., & Canary, D. J. (2009). Cultural differences in equity theory predictions of relational maintenance strategies. *Human Communication Research, 35,* 384–406.

Zuluaga, C. A., & Normand, M. P. (2008). An evaluation of the high-probability instruction sequence with and without programmed reinforcement for compliance with high-probability instructions. *Journal of Applied Behavior Analysis, 41,* 453–457.

# CHAPTER 13

# Interpersonal Conflict: Recent Trends

*Michael E. Roloff*

*Benjamin W. Chiles*

The third edition of the *Handbook of Interpersonal Communication* was the first to include a chapter exclusively dedicated to reviewing the interpersonal conflict literature (Roloff & Soule, 2002). In addition to discussing recently published research, it provided a historical overview of the field. Since that time, literature reviews have been published that are focused on specific processes associated with interpersonal conflict, such as skills (Canary, 2003), emotions (Guerrero & La Valley, 2006), resolvability (Miller, Roloff, & Malis, 2008), and social cognition (Roloff & Miller, 2006b).

Reviews have also focused on the relational contexts in which interpersonal conflict occurs (Caughlin & Vangelisti, 2006; Koerner & Fitzpatrick, 2006; Roloff & Miller, 2006a) and the theories used to study interpersonal conflict (Sillars, 2010). The aforementioned scholarship provides a useful foundation for understanding research in the area as well as in specific subareas within it. Our review will build on previous ones by updating the broader literature and by highlighting emerging themes and trends, such as the

influence of conflict on both personal and relational well-being. The review will be organized into three sections. (1) The first will focus on conflict and will examine new conceptualizations of conflict, the factors that predict conflict, and some of the effects of conflict. (2) The second will focus on conflict management. This section will first examine some of the new approaches to understanding conflict management, the factors that predict the occurrence of different conflict management behaviors, and some of the effects of the different types of conflict management. (3) Finally, we will summarize what we perceive to be important trends in the recent literature and propose some new directions for future research.

## Interpersonal Conflict

### Definition

Many scholars have sought to understand and define interpersonal conflict. As a result, many definitions exist. Although each of these varying perspectives highlights something important about interpersonal conflict, they can also create confusion as well as difficulty in establishing uniform methods of operationalization. Consequently, it becomes difficult to generalize across studies. To rectify these problems, Barki and Harwick (2004) synthesized a wide variety of definitions into one that characterized conflict as "a dynamic process that occurs between interdependent parties as they experience negative emotional reactions to perceived disagreements and interference with the attainment of their goals" (p. 234). Based on this definition, the authors created a framework for understanding conflict that identified three properties: disagreement, negative emotion, and interference. They also identified two targets of interpersonal conflict: task and relationships. Combining properties and targets provides two insights. The authors argue that when conflict is confined to disagreement over tasks, it can stimulate open deliberation that is functional for decision making, but when task disagreements give rise to negative emotions, and interference or conflict is about relational issues, conflict produces negative outcomes. Moreover, they believe that not all situations that technically fall within the parameters of their definition will be experienced by ordinary people as interpersonal conflict. Indeed, they speculate that situations in which there is only disagreement about tasks may not be experienced as conflict, whereas the strongest feelings of being in conflict arise from the joint occurrence of disagreement, negative emotion, and interference.

Although much of their speculation remains untested, Barki and Harwick (2004) provide a useful definition of interpersonal conflict. It stresses the various processes that can occur in a conflict, including those that are cognitive (perceived disagreement), affective (negative emotion), and behavioral (interference), and it recognizes that conflict may be focused on task or relational issues. However, it does not inform as to what causes conflict. We look at that next.

## Predictors of Conflict

Relative to other forms of communication, conflict is a rare occurrence (e.g., Alberts, Yoshmiura, Rabby, & Loshiavo, 2005). For the most part, individuals get along. However, because conflict can produce negative consequences, researchers are interested in what causes it to appear. Two approaches have been taken to understanding the origins of conflict: (1) those that focus on relational factors and (2) those that examine individual differences.

*Relational Approaches.* Barki and Harwick's (2004) definition of interpersonal conflict requires that some degree of interdependency must exist for individuals to be in conflict. That implies that they are in a relationship of some sort. Appropriately, several recent perspectives have focused on conflict arising from relational dynamics. One such perspective is the relational turbulence model.

The relational turbulence model posits that individuals experience periods of turbulence during relational transitions as they adopt new relational definitions and behavioral patterns (Solomon & Knobloch, 2001, 2004). During transitions, relational uncertainty increases, and because of increasing interdependency, partner interference also increases. If so, conflict due to interference should be especially evident during transitional times. However, once a couple successfully makes the transition, turbulence should decrease. With regard to courtship, such transitions are evident when a couple is moving from casual dating to serious involvement. During this transition, the relationship has become more intimate but has not yet stabilized at a higher level, and this creates turbulence. Research verifies that individuals in such transitional states view their partner's irritating behavior as more severe (Solomon & Knobloch, 2001), experience more negative emotions (Knobloch, Miller, & Carpenter, 2007), try to avoid discussing difficult topics (Knobloch & Carpenter-Theune, 2004), and report more relational turbulence (Knobloch, 2007) than do those whose relationship is at a stable point of intimacy. Importantly, interference from the partner partly mediates the nonlinear relationship between intimacy and turbulence (Knobloch, 2007), suggesting that this property of interpersonal conflict may be especially important during relational transitions. Similarly, Roloff and Johnson (2002) argued that during the different stages of a relationship, certain issues may emerge that stimulate repeated arguing, and such disagreements may continue until couples adjust to the new stage.

Relational turbulence is stimulated by relational transitions. Other models examine ongoing and sometimes desirable relational processes that could stimulate conflict. For example, Kumashiro, Rusbult, and Finkel (2008) created a personal–relational equilibrium model that posits that individuals try to keep a balance between personal and relational needs. Although individuals can engage in actions that meet both sets of needs, sometimes one set may be given less priority than the other. When either is out of balance, individuals engage in behavior that will restore equilibrium. This implies that when individuals perceive that they have sacrificed their personal needs to further the relationship, they may cut back on relational activity under some conditions that could stimulate conflict. This possibility is illustrated by Impett, Gable, and Peplau (2005), who studied daily relational sacrifice. They posited that when people self-sacrifice for approach motivations (e.g., love for a partner, wanting to make the partner happy), their self-sacrifice increases both personal and relational well-being, whereas doing so for avoidance motivations (e.g., fear of partner, dependency, guilt) has a negative impact. Importantly, they found that sacrificing for avoidance motives on a given day was positively associated with interpersonal conflict the following day. Interestingly, when people experience conflict on a given day, the following day they were more likely to engage in sacrifice for approach motives, which may

indicate that they are trying to repair relational damage due to conflict.

It is also possible that conflict is a natural by-product of relational escalation. Cunningham, Shamblen, Barbee, and Ault (2005) argued that as relationships develop, partners may develop social allergens for some of each other's behaviors. The relevant behaviors, or social allergens, are actions that create an undesirable emotional reaction that is of greater intensity in a person's relational partner than in others with whom he or she does not have a relationship. The development of social allergens is thought to result from increased awareness of a partner's annoying behavior as the initially high levels of passion decline, increased awareness of a partner's decreasing concern for positive impression management, increased emotionality resulting from repeated exposure to an irritant, and the growing tendency to see the annoying behaviors as intentional. Cunningham et al. (2005) found that social allergens develop over time, and the more often they are repeated, the stronger the partner's negative emotional reactions and the greater the relational harm.

Although the aforementioned perspectives identify relational dynamics as causes of conflict, other researchers have focused on individual differences in sensitivity to actions that give rise to conflict. We examine those next.

*Individual-Difference Approaches.* Barki and Harwick (2004) argued that interpersonal conflict is grounded in individual perceptions and that individuals may differ in their perceptions of a conflict, including whether it exists.

Some researchers have investigated whether men and women differ with regard to the kinds of partner behaviors they find annoying. For example, Ter Laak, Olthof, and Aleva (2003) noted that both evolutionary psychology (Buss, 1989) and self-construal theory (Cross & Madson, 1997) posit that men and women should differ with regard to how negatively they view a partner's behavior. They asked men and women to judge how annoying they find 13 partner behaviors.

Consistent with self-construal theory, women reported that a partner's relationship-threatening behavior (e.g., acting condescending, neglectful, self-centered) was more annoying, whereas men reported being more annoyed by their partner's autonomy-threatening behavior (e.g., acting moody, jealous). As predicted by evolutionary psychology, women found their partners' sexually aggressive behavior to be especially annoying relative to men, and men found their partner's sexually withholding behavior to be especially annoying relative to women.

Other researchers have investigated the degree to which perceptions of conflict are related to attachment styles. Bowlby (1971) argued that interactions with intimates early in life create expectations for adult relationships. Anxiety is one dimension that differentiates attachment styles, with anxious individuals worrying about being rejected by their partners. Fraley and Shaver (2000) argued that anxiety reflects an appraisal/monitoring system whereby individuals scrutinize their relationships so as to ensure that there is sufficient relational closeness. However, this system is biased in that it is focused more on rejection than on support, which increases perceptions of conflict. Indeed, highly anxious individuals report more daily conflict with their dating partners and were more likely to report that it escalated than do individuals who were not anxiously attached (Campbell, Simpson, Boldry, & Kashy, 2005).

In addition to attachment style, a person's commitment to an interpersonal relationship can influence sensitivity to conflict. Individuals who are highly committed to the continuation of their relationship should be motivated to maintain it, including downplaying relational threats arising from their partner's traits and actions. Consistent with this view, Arriaga, Slaughterbeck, Capezza, and Hmurvoic (2007) discovered that individuals who were highly committed to their relationship were less affected after becoming aware of their partner's negative traits than were those who were less committed. In addition, less committed partners

experienced greater relational uncertainty after becoming aware of their partner's negative traits than did those who were more committed. Similarly, Menzies-Toman and Lydon (2005) found that relational commitment increased the likelihood of individuals making benign appraisals of their partner's transgressions (i.e., seeing them as less severe than other people judge them to be). Importantly, for understanding conflict, making benign appraisals was negatively related to voicing concerns to the partner about the transgression but positively related to remaining silently loyal.

The notion that conflict is relatively rare was apparent in earlier literature reviews (e.g., Roloff & Soule, 2002). However, recent research more fully informs as to when conflict emerges, and conceptual frameworks have been developed that explain why. And although it is somewhat infrequent, interpersonal conflict has significant effects for the individuals involved. Recent research has made strides in examining this area as well.

## Interpersonal Conflict Effects

Scholars have long investigated the consequences of engaging in conflict (Roloff & Soule, 2002). In most cases, the effects were confined to the relationship and included outcomes such as reduction in relational satisfaction and increased likelihood of relationship termination. Recent scholarship has studied three types of effects: (1) the first type is focused on the efficacy of conflict for resolving problems, (2) the second is the effect of conflict on personal well-being, and (3) the last one is the effect of conflict on the relationship.

*Efficacy.* Scholars have long noted that conflict may be a necessary condition for promoting change. In one sense, conflict is thought to make individuals aware of their problematic behavior and to prompt improvement. Without confrontation, they might not realize that there is a need to change. In a second sense, conflict is thought to improve problem solving as individuals share information. When individuals disagree, they learn about alternative viewpoints, which may improve their understanding and performance. We will look at the ability of conflict to promote change and to improve problem solving.

Overall, Fletcher, and Simpson (2006) note that individuals have ideal standards that they use to evaluate their partner's behaviors. These standards include warmth/trustworthiness, attractiveness/vitality, and status/resources. When the partner is perceived to be deficient on these standards, individuals often try to regulate their partner's behavior so that they improve. In doing so, they make the partner aware that he or she does not measure up and needs to change. The researchers found that most regulation attempts fail. When partners become aware that they are perceived to be inadequate, they resist changing, and relational satisfaction falls. Rather than producing change, confronting partners about their inadequacies seems to produce resistance.

There is also minimal evidence that conflict improves problem solving. Most of the research was conducted on teams and in learning contexts but still has implications for interpersonal conflict. One approach involves focusing on different types of conflict. As noted by Barki and Harwick (2004), interpersonal conflict can be focused on task or relational issues. Task conflict occurs when decision makers perceive that they have different ideas, opinions, and preferences, while relational conflict arises when they perceive personal incompatibility, such as tension, animosity, and annoyance (Jehn, 1997). Task conflict is hypothesized to increase the quality of decision making, especially when making nonroutine decisions, as individuals share solutions and gain insights into their needs. On the other hand, relational conflict is expected to harm decision making as individuals harden or polarize their positions. Contrary to expectations, a meta-analysis of research conducted in group contexts shows that both types of conflict are negatively related to team performance, which includes decision quality (De Dreu & Weingart, 2003). Although some subsequent research suggests that task conflict may be beneficial, the effects only occur under rare and

stringent conditions, and even when improving performance, conflict has other negative consequences (De Dreu, 2008).

Education researchers have investigated whether conflict can be functional for learning. When two individuals work on a joint task, they may find that they disagree as to its nature. This disagreement is characterized as socio-cognitive conflict and has both a cognitive and a social component (Buchs, Butera, Mugny, & Darnon, 2004). As individuals become aware of multiple and discrepant views, they experience uncertainty about the nature of the task and its solution, as well as uncertainty about whose solution is best. In these situations, individuals use one of two techniques for coping with the conflict. Individuals may engage in epistemic conflict regulation, during which they evaluate the validity of the various views of the task. Alternatively, individuals may engage in relational conflict regulation, during which they try to establish their competency by showing that their solution is best. When individuals are motivated to increase their mastery of a knowledge domain, epistemic conflict regulation emerges, but when their goal is to improve their performance, relational conflict regulation dominates (Darnon, Muller, Schrager, Pannuzzo, & Butera, 2006).

Epistemic conflict regulation is thought to increase learning as individuals sort through options, while relational conflict regulation retards learning as individuals try to promote their own positions. When individuals believe that they have complementary information about a task relative to when they have identical information, they engage in more epistemic conflict regulation than relational conflict regulation, which improves their immediate and delayed performance (Darnon, Buchs, & Butera, 2002). However, when compared with situations in which two individuals do not have different views of a task (i.e., they are not in conflict), the performance of individuals engaged in relational conflict regulation is much worse, but the performance of those experiencing epistemic conflict regulation does not differ (Darnon et al., 2002).

In effect, relative to no conflict, relational conflict regulation reduces learning, but epistemic conflict regulation does not improve it.

It is possible that the ineffectiveness of conflict for improving decision making and learning may result from inherent reactions to disagreement. De Dreu and Van Knippenberg (2005) found that when in conflict, individuals quickly take ownership of the positions and arguments they espouse and link them to their self-concepts. This linkage increases the likelihood of competitive communication, unfavorable impressions of each other, and attitudinal polarization. Although holding individuals accountable for their actions and self-esteem moderates the aforementioned tendencies, they only reduce in magnitude rather than reversing the direction of the patterns. If so, destructive tendencies such as relational conflict or relational conflict regulation emerge during any disagreement and can potentially reduce the efficacy of conflict for solving problems.

Research conducted on the efficacy of conflict provides a rather discouraging picture. Confronting partners about their deficiencies seems counterproductive, and trying to focus on the tangible rather than the relational issues also seems to reduce problem solving or, at best, results in learning that is no better than not being in a conflict.

*Personal Well-Being Effects.* Although daily conflict is relatively rare, it is among the most frequently reported sources of stress (e.g., Almeida, Wethington, & Kessler, 2002). Appropriately, researchers are increasingly studying how conflict-induced stress influences individual well-being. As such, a stress process perspective has been developed that guides this research (Choi & Marks, 2008). This perspective posits that the stress arising from ongoing interpersonal conflict creates a number of physiological responses that compromise the effectiveness of the immune system, promotes unhealthy stress reactions (e.g., increased cigarette smoking and alcohol consumption), and reduces the likelihood that relational partners will convince each other to take care of their health, all of which undermine physical well-being. There is both experimental and correlational evidence supporting this view (e.g., Bookwala, 2005; Kiecolt-Glaser et al., 2005; Kivimaki, Vahtera, Elovainio, Lillrank, & Kevin, 2002; Robles & Kiecolt-Glaser, 2003).

Recently, researchers have extended the stress process model to psychological well-being. In a longitudinal study, Choi and Marks (2008) looked at the degree to which marital conflict is associated with both functional impairment (e.g., inability to accomplish daily tasks due to a mental or physical condition) and depression in middle-aged individuals or the elderly. The results indicate that marital conflict was positively associated with functional impairment over the first 5 years of the study and with depression over the 10-year span of the study. In addition, the link between marital conflict and depression was partly mediated by functional impairment. There was no evidence supporting the notion that the relationship between marital conflict and functional impairment was mediated by depression. Thus, continuing conflict seems to increase both physical and mental problems over the long term.

Some researchers have investigated whether all the features of ongoing conflict are stressful and if the stress can be mitigated by coping. Gunlicks-Stoessel and Powers (2009) examined the degree to which a person's typical coping style is related to the degree of physiological stress experienced during and immediately after a conflict. They found that males who typically deal with stress by seeking social support showed higher levels of stress throughout the encounter than did those who do not seek social support. Moreover, both males and females with partners who typically need social support experienced greater stress than did those whose partners do not need social support. Other forms of coping such as distraction and disengagement were not related to stress. The researchers speculated that individuals who rely on their partners for social support become especially upset during conflict because their partners are not supportive, and their own stress may transfer to the partners.

Malis and Roloff (2006b) examined the stress reactions (e.g., hyperarousal, intrusive thinking, avoidance) and physical problems (e.g., eating and sleeping problems, interference with daily activities) that were reported after a recent episode of a serial argument. Serial arguments are repeated argumentative episodes over a given issue. Results indicated that neither the number of times an argument had occurred or how long it had been occurring was significantly related to the dependent variables, but the perceived resolvability of the argument was negatively related to stress, hyperarousal, and eating problems. Also, coping with conflict by adopting a resigned stance was positively correlated with stress-related reaction, while selectively ignoring the argument was negatively correlated.

Although there is no evidence that a single conflict can impair health, ongoing conflict seems to reduce personal well-being. It may also impede relational functioning.

*Relational Well-Being Effects.* Roloff and Soule (2002) noted that interpersonal conflict is related to lower levels of relational functioning but that the degree is moderated by a number of factors. Recent research has continued to investigate moderators so as to better understand why conflict has a more negative influence on some relationships than on others.

One obvious moderating variable is the importance of the topic about which relational partners are in conflict. If a topic is of minimal importance, it would seem as though individuals might be better able to resolve it and avoid relational harm than if it is of critical importance. However, research does not support its role as a moderator. Miller and Roloff (2006) asked individuals to describe a conflict that they had successfully resolved, one that was ongoing and resolvable, or one that was ongoing and irresolvable. The three types of conflicts did not differ with regard to the importance of the issue. Furthermore, Cramer (2002) found that conflict processes involved in minor and major issues were positively correlated and that conflict was negatively related to relational satisfaction regardless of the importance of the issue.

A person's attachment style appears to be a more useful moderator than the topic. Mikulincer and Shaver (2003) developed an attachment activation model that assumes that relational actions, including interpersonal conflict, can activate attachment. Individuals who are securely attached react to conflict by trying to connect with the partner through relational maintenance behavior. However, individuals who are anxiously attached perceive conflict as relationally threatening, which stimulates negative behavior toward the partner as well as causes distress and lower levels of relational satisfaction. Campbell et al. (2005) analyzed diary accounts of conflict and discovered that anxiously attached individuals reported more frequent and serious conflicts that created more distress and relational harm than did those who were securely attached. Moreover, the researchers reported that observers of taped conflict interactions perceived that anxiously attached individuals overacted and escalated the conflict. Not surprisingly, both anxiously attached individuals and their partners reported feeling more distressed after the conflict than did those who were securely attached. Research also indicates that anxiety attachment, especially among females, is positively related to making negative attributions about a partner's problematic behavior, which is positively related to the self-reported use of negative conflict behaviors and postconflict distress (Pearce & Halford, 2008). Finally, Saavedra, Chapman, and Rogge (2010) found that anxious attachment was negatively related to relational satisfaction but the relationship was much stronger when hostile conflict was frequent rather than infrequent. Moreover, the researchers found that over time, anxious individuals who reported frequent hostile conflict were most likely to experience reduced levels of relational satisfaction.

Other researchers investigated whether implicit theories of interpersonal relationships moderate the relationship between conflict and relational functioning. Knee (1998) noted that some individuals espouse the belief that relationships grow gradually over time, and require maintenance, and that by dealing with problems, partners can make the relationship stronger. Such a "growth" perspective should help individuals deal with interpersonal conflict, and hence, their relational feelings should be less affected by it. Knee, Patrick, Vietor, and Neighbors (2004) examined diary entries about conflict and discovered that conflict, especially unresolved conflict, is negatively related to subsequent relational commitment but that this association is smaller among individuals who endorsed growth beliefs. When analyzing an actual conflict discussion, the researchers found that relational commitment after the confrontation was positively related to whether the conflict was resolved but this relationship was only significant among individuals who did not endorse growth beliefs. Hence, the degree to which the conflict was resolved seems to matter less to individuals who hold growth beliefs.

Current research has identified a variety of moderators, and importantly, researchers are working from theoretical perspectives that identify variables that account for the relationships. However, research continues to indicate that ongoing conflict reduces relational quality rather than increases it.

## Summary

A number of trends are evident in the study of interpersonal conflict. First, research more fully informs as to the specific factors that stimulate conflict as well as those that moderate its effects. Importantly, these factors are embedded within theoretical perspectives rather than reflecting a variable-analytic approach. Second, the effects of conflict have expanded to include its efficacy as well as how it influences personal and relational well-being. Although moderators have been found, interpersonal conflict does not seem to increase problem solving and seems to reduce both personal and relational well-being. Many readers may respond to the latter conclusion by noting that conflict per se may be less important than how individuals manage it. We turn to that next.

# Conflict Management

## Definition

Although *conflict management* is a term that is more commonly used by scholars studying conflict in organizations rather than in informal relationships, it is a useful concept for understanding interpersonal conflict research. Conflict management can be broadly conceived of as the actions that occur prior to, during, and after a conflict is perceived. The relevant behaviors can range from attempts to avoid the conflict to those that involve active engagement. Although some researchers focus on a given type of action (e.g., disclosure, insults), many researchers study clusters of actions that are organized with regard to their functionality. Hence, actions are categorized as constructive, functional, positive, supportive, or integrative, as opposed to destructive, maladaptive, negative, unsupportive, or distributive. When assessing conflict management, researchers typically focus on the likelihood of actions or the frequency with which they are observed or are reported. Thus, data related to conflict management are assessed from diary accounts, responses to hypothetical scenarios, and interactions observed in a laboratory. In addition, researchers sometimes focus on individual actions (e.g., insults, acknowledgments, solution generation), while others investigate sequences of actions (e.g., demand–withdraw, mutual hostility, escalation). Although the diversity of assessments makes organizing the results difficult, some general patterns can be identified.

## Predictors of Conflict Management

Three recent approaches have been used to predict conflict management: goal-based approaches, appraisal approaches, and intimacy approaches.

*Goal-Based Approaches.* Increasingly, researchers have adopted a goal-based approach to understanding conflict management. An implicit assumption of this approach is that individuals initiate conflict with the primary objective of creating change in their partner, and once confronted, partners formulate their own goals, including accepting or resisting the change. These goals are associated with their attempts to manage the conflict.

Heyman, Hunt-Maroano, Malik, and Smith Slep (2009) asked heterosexual cohabitating and married couples about the areas in which they wanted their partners to change. Although both genders wanted to see their partners improve, women wanted greater change in more areas than did men. When observed discussing each partner's most desired change, differences in positivity (e.g., disclosures, acceptances) and negativity (e.g., hostility, withdrawal) were observed. Regardless of gender, individuals were less positive when discussing their own issue than their partner's. However, women responded more positively during encounters over their partner's issues than did men. Women were somewhat more likely to act negatively during discussion of their own versus their partner's issues, but men's negative responses did not differ in this respect. Finally, women were more negative than men regardless of whose issue was being discussed. The findings are somewhat complex but indicate that at a minimum, individuals enact fewer positive behaviors when discussing the areas in which they want their partners to change relative to those in which their partner wants them to change, and perhaps because they want greater change in more areas, women tend to be more negative when discussing their own issues.

Baucom, McFarland, and Christensen (2010) examined how the area of change under discussion is related to demand–withdraw sequences in both homosexual and heterosexual couples. Regardless of sexual orientation, they found that individuals were more demanding (e.g., blaming, pressuring) when discussing their own relative to

their partner's issues and were more withdrawing (e.g., topic avoidance) when discussing their partner's relative to their own issues. However, women were more demanding than were men, and men withdrew more than women, regardless of their sexual orientation. Finally, demanding increased during the interaction, whereas the frequency of withdrawing did not change. Perhaps because they were encountering resistance, individuals who wanted change increased pressure as the discussion continued. Thus, regardless of sexual orientation, individuals are more confrontational when discussing their own issues and more withdrawing when discussing their partner's, but perhaps because women want more change in their relationships, they generally are more demanding.

Although the desire for change is a driving force in conflict, other goals may also influence conflict management. Keck and Samp (2007) asked relational partners to discuss an area of relational change and while watching a tape of the interaction indicate their goals at one-minute intervals. The goals were then related to enacted strategies separately for individuals who initiated the change and those who resisted. During an encounter, initiators and resistors expressed both singular and multiple goals. The initiators often combined their instrumental goals (e.g., convincing the partner) with relational (e.g., maintaining the relationship), self-identity (e.g., restoring or maintaining one's own sense of self), and other-identity (e.g., supporting the partner) goals or pursued a single relational goal. On the other hand, the resistors often pursued a single relational goal or a combination of identity and relational goals. For the initiators, the combination of self and instrumental goals increased the likelihood of acting distributively (e.g., trying to control the conversation). For the resistors, holding instrumental goals or a combination of instrumental and self-identity goals increased the likelihood of distributive actions, whereas having other-identity goals or a combination of identity and relationship goals increased the use of integrative behaviors (e.g., disclosures, offering solutions). Also, the results indicated that the strategies enacted by one individual influence the partner's subsequent goals. When the initiators acted distributively, the resistors increased the importance of their instrumental goals while decreasing the importance of other goals, but when the initiators were integrative, the resistors were less instrumentally motivated and other goals became important. On the other hand, distributive behavior by the resistors increased the initiators' commitment to self-identity goals while reducing the importance of relational goals, but the resistors' integrative actions increased the importance they attached to relational goals and decreased their commitment to the combination of self-identity and instrumental goals. Although the results are complicated, this study provides useful information in that it looks at the relationship between goals and actions as dynamic and changing over the course of a given interaction.

Goal perspectives have also been used to study repeated argumentative episodes over a given topic. Bevan, Finan, and Kaminsky (2008) noted that when engaged in serial arguing, individuals often form both positive and negative interaction goals that may influence their motivation to continue to try to achieve their objectives in future episodes. They found that trying to achieve mutual understanding/resolution or expressing positive relational feelings stimulated integrative actions and rumination about the conflict that increased motivation to achieve the objectives. In effect, holding positive goals prompts positive actions and thoughts that maintain goal commitment. However, when trying to achieve negative objectives, such as hurting the partner or changing the partner, both distributive and integrative actions stimulated rumination about the conflict that resulted in less motivation to achieve the goals. Thus, when seeking negative goals, both positive and negative actions stimulate rumination that, in this case, reduces goal commitment. Although not part of the study, the latter findings might indicate that negative goals stimulate actions and thoughts that cause individuals to abandon their goals.

Such goal abandonment could result from the emotions that are expressed during conflict. Sanford (2007) noted that conflict may cause hard emotions such as anger or soft emotions such as sadness and guilt. These emotions may influence appraisals of how difficult it will be to resolve a conflict as well as how important it is to try. In a study involving marital conflict, soft emotions increased appraisals that a conflict would be difficult to resolve and that it is important to resolve. On the other hand, hard emotions were positively related to anticipated difficulty for both husbands and wives, but among husbands, hard emotions were negatively related to believing that the conflict was important to resolve. Hence, soft emotions may keep partners engaged even if the conflict is difficult to resolve, whereas hard emotions may cause men to disengage.

*Appraisal Approaches.* This approach assumes that individuals try to make sense of their past interactions via appraisals, which in turn influence their behaviors in present and future interactions. Appraisals include expectations of how a partner will behave during a conflict. Sanford (2006) looked at expectancies that a partner will be understanding or will engage in negative behavior, as well as attributions about the causes of a spouse's behavior related to an individual's behavior across four conflict interactions. Expecting the partner to engage in negative behaviors increased the likelihood that wives would act negatively and decreased the likelihood that they would engage in positive behaviors. The most consistent predictor was the degree to which the spouse was expected to be understanding, which for husbands and wives reduced the likelihood of negative behavior while increasing the likelihood of positive actions. Importantly, an individual's expectancies for the partner showed a stronger relationship to his or her behavior than did the partner's actual behavior.

DiPaola, Roloff, and Peters (2010) also found that expectations are related to how conflict is experienced. When individuals reported on a conflict they initiated, the degree to which they anticipated that it would be intense was positively related to the degree to which the conflict was upsetting, personal attacks were exchanged, and emotional reactions arising from the conflict interfered with their life afterward. The aforementioned relationships were much smaller when another person initiated the conflict. In effect, the unanticipated beginning of the conflict may have attenuated the influence of expectations.

*Social Support Approaches.* These approaches assume that the support that relational partners provide each other influences the way they manage conflict. Individuals in close relationships value the respect and support they receive from one another, and when it is provided, they grow more intimate. However, when not receiving support, individuals feel invalidated and uncared for. Consequently, when problems arise, they are prone to enact negative conflict behaviors. In a longitudinal study involving newlyweds, Sullivan, Pasch, Johnson, and Bradbury (2010) found that the quality of support that couples provided each other predicted their negative but not positive conflict management. Spouses who initially provided each other inadequate support were more likely to engage in negative actions during conflict than those who were supportive. Importantly, negative conflict management was not significantly related to the subsequent quality of support, and the relationship between initial support and subsequent marital satisfaction was mediated by negative actions during a conflict. This model assumes that negative conflict management is simply a reflection of inadequate social support skills that are evident at the beginning of a relationship.

Recent research more fully informs as to the factors that stimulate certain forms of conflict management. In some cases, the type of conflict management depends on interaction goals and appraisals of the situation, but one approach suggests that conflict management really reflects partners' social support skills.

## Conflict Management Effects

As with research on interpersonal conflict, scholars have also investigated how various approaches to managing conflict are effective and influence personal and relational well-being.

*Efficacy.* Research indicates that the degree to which conflict is resolved is significantly related to other processes such as relational satisfaction (e.g., Cramer, 2002). Until recently, however, there has been limited research investigating the efficacy of approaches to conflict management.

One such strain of research has investigated how demand–withdraw patterns are related to resolution. When individuals demand that their partners change and the partner withdraws, it seem unlikely that the conflict will be resolved. Consistent with this view, Papp, Kouros, and Cummings (2009) found that demand–withdraw patterns enacted in marital conflicts were negatively related to conflict resolution. However, research indicates that demand–withdraw patterns may not be related to all features of conflict resolution. McGinn, McFarland, and Christensen (2009) examined accounts of actual conflicts and coded their outcomes. In 40% of the cases, both partners mutually resolved the conflict; in 37%, only one partner felt that the issue was resolved; and in the remaining 23% of the cases, both felt that the conflict was unresolved. Among the conflicts that were resolved, 63% did not include an agreed-on change in behavior. Demand–withdraw patterns were not significantly related to resolution, but when conflicts were resolved, demand–withdraw patterns were negatively related to agreed-on patterns of change. Hence, some couples who enact demand–withdraw patterns may be able to resolve the conflict, but they are less likely to agree on specific change than are those who do not enact this pattern.

Mitnick, Heyman, Malik, and Smith Slep (2009) investigated whether "nondemanding" requests for change can avoid partner resistance and withdrawal. They coded marital conflicts for the degree to which requests for change used the pronoun *we* rather than *you* (e.g., "We need to be stricter with the children" vs. "You should be stricter with the children"), asked the partner to increase rather than decrease behavior (e.g., do more of something rather than less), and made specific rather than vague requests. For both husbands and wives, phrasing requests with "you" increased the spouse's resistance; however, "we" statements reduced resistance but only when used by wives. Wives who requested that their husbands decrease a behavior encountered resistance, whereas husbands who requested that their wives increase a behavior encountered resistance. The specificity of the request was unrelated to resistance for both spouses. Although these results are useful, they provide more information about request forms that create (e.g., "you" statements) rather than reduce resistance.

The aforementioned research suggests that being demanding lacks efficacy because it prompts partner withdrawal and resistance. However, Overall, Fletcher, Simpson, and Sibley (2009) recently reported a study that partly calls that finding into question. They noted that conflict strategies vary with regard to whether they are direct and positive. Direct strategies may be positive (e.g., reasoning) or negative (coercive), just as indirect strategies can be positive (e.g., acting charming, supporting the partner's view) or negative (manipulation, acting hurt or weak). They examined the degree to which romantic couples enacted behaviors that varied on the two dimensions when trying to get a partner to change and related the behaviors to immediate success at convincing the partner to change as well as the degree to which the partner changed over the next year. At the end of the interaction, both partners perceived direct strategies (regardless of whether they were positive or negative) to be ineffective, as were negative strategies (regardless of whether they were indirect or direct). Only positive indirect strategies were judged by both partners to be relatively effective at achieving commitment to change. However, over the course of a year, only positive-direct and negative-direct strategies resulted in the targeted partner's reporting

changes in his or her behavior, and among women requesting change, the use of positive-direct strategies was positively associated with changes in their partner's behavior. Moreover, the effectiveness was not mediated by increased discussion of the issue during the next year. Hence, the initial encounter appeared to be sufficient to set off the change. One important caveat to this study is that direct messages were not significantly related to problem seriousness over the year. Thus, although directness increased partner changes, there was no evidence that it reduced the seriousness of the problem.

*Personal Well-Being Effects.* As noted earlier, ongoing interpersonal conflict, and especially hostile conflict, can be stressful. Researchers have also investigated whether all conflict management strategies are stressful.

Malis and Roloff (2006a) looked at the degree to which demand–withdraw patterns are related to postepisodic stress arising from a recent episode of serial arguing. The results indicated that self-demand/partner withdraw was positively related to hyperarousal, intrusive thoughts, thought avoidance, and task interference arising from physical problems. The partner demand/self-withdraw pattern was positively related to postepisodic stress, thought avoidance, and task interference with tasks. Thus, both negative patterns were associated with subsequent stress-related problems.

Roloff and Reznick (2008) compared the stress impact of mutual hostility (e.g., yelling, insults) with constructive communication (e.g., suggesting compromises and solutions) enacted during a recent episode of serial arguing. Across nine indicators of stress-related problems (e.g., stress, hyperarousal, sleeping problems), mutual hostility was positively related to nine. Constructive communication was negatively related to seven, but the relationship was only statistically significant for two. Three interactions were found between constructive communication and mutual hostility, and in each case, the negative relationship between constructive communication and stress-related problems was weaker when mutual hostility was present. These results indicate that negative communication has a much stronger relationship with stress than does constructive communication, and when the two forms of conflict co-occur, constructive communication has a trivial relationship with stress.

In a recent study, Reznick, Roloff, and Miller (2010) investigated the relationship between integrative, distributive, and avoidant conflict actions enacted during a recent episode of serial arguing and postepisodic health problems. A path analysis indicated that all three conflict actions were positively related to postepisodic hyperarousal, which was positively related to health problems. This finding was then replicated with a second sample. This study indicates that all three types of conflict management are positively related to stress and stress-related health problems. However, one study indicates that some actions may help reduce stress for some individuals. Robles, Shaffer, Malarkey, and Keicolt-Glaser (2006) studied changes in physiological measures of stress during a marital conflict. Changes in husbands' stress levels were not related to positive or negative actions, but the stress level of wives decreased when mutual negative actions were frequent and their husbands acted in a supportive manner (e.g., agreed, accepted responsibility, approved). Hence, problem solving may not mitigate stress, but for women, a supportive partner does.

Based on the aforementioned research, one might argue that one should avoid expressing one's feelings during conflict and instead be superficially cooperative or engaged. However, such a move may be problematic. Harper and Welsh (2007) found that individuals who self-silence (i.e., avoid expressing their thoughts and feelings) concede more to their partners during the conflict but their partners feel frustrated and uncomfortable when communicating with them. Moreover, individuals who suppress their emotions during a stressful conversation increase their own and their partner's stress and reduce mutual rapport and attraction (Butler et al., 2003). In addition, suppressing emotions during a conflict may actually increase recollection of them afterward (Richards, Butler, & Gross, 2003). Finally, marital couples in which both spouses hold in their anger have higher mortality rates than do those in which one or both spouses express their anger (Harburg, Kaciroti, Gleiberman, Julius, & Schork, 2008).

Thus, negative actions aimed at resolving a conflict seem to be stressful, with constructive/supportive attempts having rather limited effects on stress.

*Relational Effects.* Traditionally, research has found that negative actions occurring during conflict are related to reductions in relational quality, with constructive communication showing smaller and less consistent relationships with relational quality. Recent research continues to show this pattern.

Stanley, Markman, and Whitton (2002) conducted a survey of marital couples and looked at how their self-reported conflict management is related to their potential for divorce (thinking or talking about divorcing). For both spouses, negative conflict behaviors (e.g., criticizing, invalidations, and escalation) were positively related to divorce potential, although for wives, remaining positive about the relationship (e.g., being satisfied, viewing the relationship as fun) was more strongly related to their divorce potential than was negativity. Also, couples in which the parties reported that both withdrew from interaction reported more negativity than did those reporting that neither withdrew, which could mean that negativity decreases the likelihood of resolution as partners disengage.

Hanzal and Segrin (2009) examined the degree to which some couples are more vulnerable to relational problems arising from conflict management than are others. They examined how negative affectivity (i.e., the tendency to respond to a situation with negative emotions) is related to conflict management and marital satisfaction. Regardless of gender, negative affectivity was positively related to conflict engagement (e.g., exploding, getting out of control), compliance (e.g., giving in), and withdrawal (e.g., refusing to talk) but negatively related to positive problem solving (e.g., focusing on the problem). Negative affectivity was also negatively related to both spouses' satisfaction. A mediation analysis indicated that some forms of conflict management mediated the relationship between negative affectivity and satisfaction, although only partially. For husbands, their own positive problem solving, engagement, and withdrawal and their wife's positive problem solving and engagement were significant mediators, whereas for wives, their own positive problem solving and their husband's conflict engagement and withdrawal were mediators. This study indicates that some couples may be especially vulnerable to marital dissatisfaction resulting from their conflict management but also indicates that both positive and negative actions play a role in disenchantment.

Markman, Rhoades, Whitton, Stanley, and Ragan (2010) investigated how self-reported and observed conflict management were related to marital distress over the first years of marriage. They found that self-reported and observed premarital negative communication (e.g., negative affect, escalation, withdraw) were negatively related to marital adjustment over the first five years. Regardless of subsequent marital distress, all couples engaged in lower levels of negative conflict over the first five years. However, individuals whose marriages were distressed after five years reported higher levels of premarital negative conflict actions, and both their reported and observed negative actions increased over the first years of marriage relative to those whose marriages were not distressed. Although some significant patterns were found for changes in positive communication (e.g., positive affect, problem solving, supporting communication), they were inconsistent, and the authors concluded that negative conflict management has a much stronger influence than positive management.

Sanford (2003) examined how topic difficulty, negative communication, and marital satisfaction might be related. Married couples communicated about unresolved problems in their relationship during four interactions. Both the difficulty of the problems and conflict actions were coded. The results indicated that couples did not vary their actions (e.g., how negatively or positively they expressed their views or responded to their partner's statements) with the difficulty of the problem being discussed. However, those couples who discussed one difficult problem had lower overall levels of marital satisfaction and were more negative when discussing relational problems regardless of how difficult they were to discuss. A subsequent analysis indicated that discussing difficult problems decreases marital satisfaction and that increases the likelihood of negative conflict management. Hence, rather than assuming that negative actions cause marital dissatisfaction, it is possible that over time, negative actions and marital satisfaction are in a mutually dependent relationship.

McNulty and Russell (2010) recently reported a study that indicates that direct-negative problem solving may help rather than hinder relational quality. They conducted two longitudinal studies of newlyweds and related the behaviors they engaged in during a reenacted conflict to relational processes. Their research indicates that when discussing a relatively minor relational problem, direct-negative problem-solving behavior (e.g., blaming, commanding, and rejecting the partner) decreases marital conflict largely because such behaviors make the problem more serious. However, direct-negative behaviors increase marital satisfaction by reducing the seriousness of major problems. Interestingly, the seemingly positive impact of direct-negative problem solving for dealing with serious problems does not extend to indirect-negative behaviors such as negative mind-reading statements or sarcasm. This study seems to indicate that when facing serious problems, condemning a partner's actions or character may actually stimulate change and improve the relationship, although such behavior is counterproductive when occurring in discussions of minor problems. Thus, this research suggests that direct-negative behavior effectively solves problems that have the effect of increasing relational quality.

Although the aforementioned research investigated how actions occurring within a conflict exchange are related to relational quality, other researchers have focused on whether avoiding conflict influences relational quality. Conflict avoidance has generally been viewed as harmful to relationships, especially when individuals perceive that their partners are avoiding discussing certain topics (Sargent, 2002). Caughlin and Afifi (2004) looked at the relationship between reasons for avoiding discussing topics and relational satisfaction in romantic and parent–child relationships. The degree to which romantic partners reported that they avoided discussing certain topics to prevent conflict was not significantly correlated with their own satisfaction and neither was an individual's perception that his or her partner avoided issues to prevent conflict. Among parents and children, avoiding topics to prevent conflict was negatively correlated with their relational satisfaction, but perceiving that their partner avoided topics for conflict prevention was not significantly correlated with satisfaction. Although some motives for avoiding discussing a topic were negatively related to relational satisfaction (e.g., the partner is unresponsive, there is a lack of closeness), conflict avoidance was not a strong predictor.

However, conflict avoidance may be more problematic for some individuals than for others. Afifi, McManus, Steuber, and Coho (2009) looked at the degree to which couples tried to avoid conflict during an interaction, including changing the topic and being evasive. Gender differences were discovered. Only among women did perception of partner avoidance reduce their satisfaction levels. Moreover, only among women was there a bidirectional effect between satisfaction and avoidance. Although men and women who were initially dissatisfied engaged in conflict avoidance, only women who perceived that their partner avoided conflict became less satisfied. In addition, the more women avoided conflict because they anticipated that their partner might become angry, the more they avoided it during the conversation, and

the more dissatisfied they became. The same pattern was not statistically significant among men. Thus, this study suggests that the negative effects of avoidance only occur for women.

## Summary

Research on conflict management indicates that it is driven by interaction goals and appraisals but may also reflect inadequate social skills. When individuals seek to achieve negative goals or have negative expectations for the partner, negative conflict management results. Importantly, such goals and appraisals are not fixed and can change during disputes. Generally, negative conflict behaviors are ineffective, although under some conditions, direct behaviors may be effective in the long term. Negative behavior may also increase stress and reduce relational quality in the short term. The consequences of constructive communication are generally weak.

## Conclusion

Synthesizing results from the literature is a difficult and inexact process. Generalizing results that use diverse methods, measures, samples, and analyses requires caution and might be better left to meta-analysis. However, we can offer the following observations about the results of recent research, with the caveat that we are only noting what we perceive to be important trends rather than statistically identifying definitive patterns. These trends fall into three rough categories: themes, findings, and methodological approaches. Finally, based on this analysis, we would like to propose a few general directions for future research.

When reviewing recent research on interpersonal conflict and its management, we noted the presence of two general themes. First, researchers continue to be interested in what causes conflict and conflict management and have increasingly focused on moderators. Second, researchers continue to study the effects of interpersonal conflict. Importantly though, research has expanded from an exclusive focus on relational effects to studying the efficacy of interpersonal conflict as well as its influence on personal well-being.

With regard to findings, there are a number of different factors that predict when conflict will arise as well as how it will be managed. Conflict tends to be more common at certain times in a relationship, and some people are more sensitive to it than are others. Moreover, how people manage conflict is related to their goals, appraisals of the situation, and social skills. Second, frequent arguments and negative forms of conflict management are ineffective at resolving conflict, and they reduce personal and relational well-being at least in the short term and for some individuals. However, recent research suggests that some direct forms of negative conflict management might be effective and might improve relational functioning in the long term. The third main finding, on the other hand, is that there is little evidence that frequent conflict or constructive communication is effective or has strong effects on either personal or relational well-being.

Several important methodological developments also have taken place in recent research. First, research is increasingly theory driven, and numerous perspectives have been developed as a result. Very few variable-analytic studies have appeared. At the same time, there has been no move to create an overarching perspective that integrates the various "mini theories." Consequently, much of the work remains scattered and disconnected. Second, researchers have increasingly used more sophisticated designs, varied samples, and complex statistical analyses. In particular, although cross-sectional designs are still reported, there is a growing use of longitudinal designs that include both partners in a dispute. These moves have greatly increased the overall quality of results. However, they also have made it increasingly difficult to interpret the results. In some cases, the explanation of the statistical procedures is longer than the presentation of the results and is written in such a fashion as to be impenetrable to some readers. Presumably, as the improved methods and analyses become more

common, the need for such dense presentation will decrease, and it will become more reader-friendly. Third, interpersonal conflict research remains strongly multidisciplinary and is increasingly becoming interdisciplinary. In particular, the use of physiological assessments of stress reflects a welcome extension of conflict effects beyond the relational into physical health. At the same time, measures are used that are foreign to many in the social sciences, and although their nuances are understood by the researchers who use them, they may not be readily accessible to all readers.

When considering future research directions in the field of interpersonal conflict, we would like to share three suggestions. First, we are hopeful that researchers will simultaneously investigate the three levels of effects we discussed in our review: efficacy, personal well-being, and relational well-being. In most cases, reported studies continue to focus on one effect (e.g., relational effects), but a few have expanded the focus to include several effects (e.g., Choi & Marks, 2008; McNulty & Russell, 2010). Considering multiple effects allows us to better understand their interrelationship. For example, some forms of conflict management may be very effective at resolving a conflict and perhaps improving a relationship but at the same time may be very stressful during and immediately after a conflict episode. Alternatively, some processes may be ineffective at resolving a conflict and also stimulate stress, both of which eventually undercut commitment to a relationship. Although we currently lack a theory that would delineate and predict possible configurations, it seems fruitful to create one. Second, we found some research that suggests that dysfunctional conflict behavior such as direct negativity may be functional in some circumstances. This counterintuitive finding raises the possibility that functional behavior may be dysfunctional in other respects. For example, integrative actions might enhance relational satisfaction, but they are also stressful to enact. If so, it is important to determine how the negative consequences of a positive strategy can be mitigated. Finally, our review indicates that the oft-touted benefits of interpersonal conflict and constructive communication remain elusive, yet research does not yet inform as to why their positive effects are sparse. Clearly, some individuals act positively during conflict, but apparently, their behavior is not consistently successful. What is it about interpersonal conflict that reduces the effectiveness of disclosure, empathic listening, solution generation, and other integrative techniques that logically should resolve a conflict with minimal stress and relational harm? That remains an open question.

Overall, we believe that recent research on interpersonal conflict continues to advance knowledge in important ways partly because of increased links to theory and the use of more sophisticated methods and analyses.

# References

Afifi, T. D., McManus, T., Steuber, K., & Coho, A. (2009). Verbal avoidance and dissatisfaction in intimate conflict situations. *Human Communication Research, 35,* 357–383.

Alberts, J. K., Yoshimura, C. G., Rabby, M., & Loshiavo, R. (2005). Mapping the topography of couples' daily conversation. *Journal of Social and Personal Relationships, 22,* 299–322.

Almeida, D. W., Wethington, E., & Kessler, R. C. (2002). The daily inventory of stressful events: An interview-based approach for measuring daily stressors. *Assessment, 9,* 41–55.

Arriaga, X. B., Slaugherbeck, E. S., Capezza, M. M., & Hmurovic, J. L. (2007). From bad to worse: Relationship commitment and vulnerability to partner imperfections. *Personal Relationships, 14,* 389–409.

Barki, H., & Hartwick, J. (2004). Conceptualizing the construct of interpersonal conflict. *International Journal of Conflict Management, 15,* 216–244.

Baucom, B. R., McFarland, P. T., & Christensen, A. (2010). Gender, topic, and time in observed demand–withdraw interaction in cross- and same-sex couples. *Journal of Personality and Social Psychology, 24,* 233–242.

Bevan, J. L., Finan, A., & Kaminsky, A. (2008). Modeling serial arguments in close relationships: The serial

argument process model. *Human Communication Research, 34,* 600–624.

Bookwala, J. (2005). The role of marital quality in physical health during the mature years. *Journal of Aging and Health, 17,* 85–104.

Bowlby, J. (1971). *Attachment and loss: Vol. 1. Attachment.* New York: Pelican Books.

Buchs, C., Butera, F., Mugny, G., & Darnon, C. (2004). Conflict elaboration and cognitive outcomes. *Theory Into Practice, 43,* 23–30.

Buss, D. M. (1989). Conflict between the sexes: Strategic inference and the evocation of anger and upset. *Journal of Personality and Social Psychology, 56,* 735–747.

Butler, E. A., Egloff, B., Wilhelm, F. H., Smith, N. C., Erickson, E. A., & Gross, J. J. (2003). The social consequences of expressive suppression. *Emotion, 3,* 48–67.

Campbell, L., Simpson, J. A., Boldry, J., & Kashy, D. A. (2005). Perceptions of conflict and support in romantic relationships: The role of attachment anxiety. *Journal of Personality and Social Psychology, 88,* 510–531.

Canary, D. J. (2003). Managing interpersonal conflict: A model of events related to strategic choices. In J. O. Green & B. R. Burleson (Eds.), *Handbook of communication and social interaction skills* (pp. 515–550). Thousand Oaks, CA: Sage.

Caughlin, J. P., & Afifi, T. D. (2004). When is topic avoidance unsatisfying? Examining moderators of the association between avoidance and dissatisfaction. *Human Communication Research, 30,* 479–513.

Caughlin, J. P., & Vangelisti, A. L. (2006). Conflict in dating and marital relationships. In J. G. Oetzel & S. Ting-Toomey (Eds.), *The Sage handbook of conflict communication: Integrating theory, research, and practice* (pp. 129–158). Thousand Oaks, CA: Sage.

Choi, H., & Marks, N. F. (2008). Marital conflict, depressive symptoms, and functional impairment. *Journal of Marriage and Family, 70,* 377–390.

Cramer, D. (2002). Relationship satisfaction and conflict over minor and major issues in romantic relationships. *Journal of Psychology, 136,* 75–81.

Cross, S. E., & Madson, L. (1997). Models of self: Self-construals and gender. *Psychological Bulletin, 122,* 5–37.

Cunningham, M. R., Shamblen, S. R., Barbee, A. P., & Ault, L. K. (2005). Social allergies in romantic relationships: Behavioral repetition, emotional sensitization, and dissatisfaction in dating couples. *Personal Relationships, 12,* 273–295.

Darnon, C., Buchs, C., & Butera, F. (2002). Epistemic and relational conflict in sharing information during cooperative learning. *Swiss Journal of Psychology, 61,* 139–151.

Darnon, C., Muller, D., Schrager, S. M., Pannuzzo, N., & Butera, F. (2006). Mastery and performance goals predict epistemic and relational conflict regulation. *Journal of Educational Psychology, 98,* 766–776.

De Dreu, C. K. W. (2008). The virtue and vice of workplace conflict: Food for (pessimistic) thought. *Journal of Organizational Behavior, 29,* 5–18.

De Dreu, C. K. W., & Van Knippenberg, D. (2005). The possessive self as a barrier to constructive conflict management: Effects of mere ownership, process accountability, and self-concept clarity on competitive cognitions and behavior. *Journal of Personality and Social Psychology, 89,* 345–357.

De Dreu, C. K. W., & Weingart, L. R. (2003). Task versus relationship conflict, team member satisfaction, and team effectiveness: A meta-analysis. *Journal of Applied Psychology, 88,* 741–749.

DiPaola, B. M., Roloff, M. E., & Peters, K. M. (2010). College students' expectations of conflict intensity: A self-fulfilling prophecy. *Communication Quarterly, 58,* 59–76.

Fraley, R. C., & Shaver, P. R. (2000). Adult romantic attachment: Theoretical developments, emerging controversies, and unanswered questions. *Review of General Psychology, 4,* 132–154.

Guerrero, L. K., & La Valley, A. G. (2006). Conflict, emotion, and communication. In J. G. Oetzel & S. Ting-Toomey (Eds.), *The Sage handbook of conflict communication: Integrating theory, research, and practice* (pp. 69–96). Thousand Oaks, CA: Sage.

Gunlicks-Stoessl, M. L., & Powers, S. I. (2009). Romantic partners' coping strategies and patterns of cortisol reactivity and recovery in response to relationship conflict. *Journal of Social and Clinical Psychology, 28,* 630–649.

Hanzal, A., & Segrin, C. (2009). The role of conflict resolution styles in mediating the relationship between enduring vulnerabilities and marital quality. *Journal of Family Communication, 9,* 150–169.

Harburg, E., Kaciroti, N., Gleiberman, L., Julius, M., & Schork, M. A. (2008). Marital pair anger-coping types may act as an entity to affect mortality: Preliminary findings from a prospect study (Tecumseh, Michigan, 1971–1988). *Journal of Family Communication, 8,* 44–61.

Harper, M. S., & Welsh, D. P. (2007). Keeping quiet: Self-silencing and its association with relational and individual functioning among adolescent romantic couples. *Journal of Social and Personal Relationships, 24,* 99–116.

Heyman, R. E., Hunt-Maroano, A. N., Malik, J., & Smith Slep, A. M. (2009). Desired change in couples: Gender differences and effects on communication. *Journal of Family Communication, 23,* 474–484.

Impett, E. A., Gable, S. L., & Peplau, L. A. (2005). Giving up and giving in: The costs and benefits of daily sacrifice in intimate relationships. *Journal of Personality and Social Psychology, 89,* 327–344.

Jehn, K. (1997). A qualitative analysis of conflict types and dimensions in organizational groups. *Administrative Science Quarterly, 42,* 530–557.

Keck, K. L., & Samp, J. A. (2007). The dynamic nature of goals and message production as revealed in a sequential analysis of conflict interactions. *Human Communication Research, 33,* 27–47.

Kiecolt-Glaser, J. K., Loving, T. J., Stowell, J. R., Malarkey, W. B., Lemeshow, S., Dickinson, S. L., et al. (2005). Hostile marital interactions proinflamatory cytokine production and wound healing. *Archives of General Psychiatry, 62,* 1377–1384.

Kivimaki, M., Vahtera, J., Elovainio, M., Lillrank, B., & Kevin, M. V. (2002). Death or illness of a family member, violence, interpersonal conflict, and financial difficulties as predictors of sickness absence: Longitudinal cohort study on psychological and behavioral links. *Psychosomatic Medicine, 64,* 817–825.

Knee, C. R. (1998). Implicit theories or relationships: Assessment and prediction or romantic relationships initiation, coping and longevity. *Journal of Personality and Social Psychology, 74,* 360–370.

Knee, C. R., Patrick, H., Vietor, N. A., & Neighbors, C. (2004). Implicit theories of relationships: Moderators of the link between conflict and commitment. *Personality and Social Psychology Bulletin, 30,* 617–628.

Knobloch, L. K. (2007). Perceptions of turmoil within courtship: Associations with intimacy, relational uncertainty, and interference from partners. *Journal of Social and Personal Relationships, 24,* 363–384.

Knobloch, L. K., & Carpenter-Theune, K. E. (2004). Topic avoidance in developing romantic relationships:

Association with intimacy and relational uncertainty. *Communication Research, 31,* 173–205.

Knobloch, L. K., Miller, L. E., Bond, B. J., & Mannone, S. E. (2007). Relational uncertainty and message processing in marriage. *Communication Monographs, 74,* 154–180.

Knobloch, L. K., Miller, L. E., & Carpenter, K. E. (2007). Using the relational turbulence model to understand negative emotion within courtship. *Personal Relationships, 14,* 91–112.

Koerner, A. F., & Fitzpatrick, M. A. (2006). Family conflict communication. In J. G. Oetzel & S. Ting-Toomey (Eds.), *The SAGE handbook of conflict communication: Integrating theory, research, and practice* (pp. 159–184). Thousand Oaks, CA: Sage.

Kumashiro, M., Rusbult, C. E., & Finkel, E. J. (2008). Navigating personal and relational concerns: The quest for equilibrium. *Journal of Personality and Social Psychology, 95,* 94–110.

Malis, R. S., & Roloff, M. E. (2006a). Demand–withdraw patterns in serial arguments: Implications for well-being. *Human Communication Research, 32,* 198–216.

Malis, R. S., & Roloff, M. E. (2006b). Features of serial arguing and coping strategies: Links with stress and well-being. In R. M. Dailey & B. A. Le Poire (Eds.), *Applied communication matters: Family, health and community relations* (pp. 39–66). New York: Peter Lang.

Markman, H. J., Rhoades, G. K., Whitton, S. W., Stanley, S. M., & Ragan, E. P. (2010). The premarital communication roots of marital distress and divorce: The first five years of marriage. *Journal of Family Psychology, 24,* 289–298.

McGinn, M. M., McFarland, P. T., & Christensen, A. (2009). Antecedents and consequences of demand/withdraw. *Journal of Family Psychology, 23,* 749–757.

McNulty, J. K., & Russell, V. M. (2010). When "negative" behaviors are positive: A contextual analysis of the long-term effects of problem-solving behaviors on changes in relationship satisfaction. *Journal of Personality and Social Psychology, 98,* 587–604.

Menzies-Toman, D. A., & Lydon, J. E. (2005). Commitment-motivated benign appraisals of partner transgressions: Do they facilitate accommodation? *Journal of Social and Personal Relationships, 22,* 111–128.

Mikulincer, M., & Shaver, P. R. (2003). The attachment behavioral system in adulthood: Activation, psychodynamics, and interpersonal processes. In M. P. Zanna (Ed.), *Advances in experimental social psychology* (Vol. 35, pp. 53–152). New York: Academic Press.

Miller, C. W., & Roloff, M. E. (2006). The perceived characteristics of irresolvable, resolvable and resolved intimate conflicts. *International Journal of Conflict Management, 17,* 291–315.

Miller, C. W., Roloff, M. E., & Malis, R. S. (2008). Understanding interpersonal conflicts that are difficult to resolve: A review of literature and presentation of an integrated model. In C. A. Beck (Ed.), *Communication yearbook 31* (pp. 118–173). New York: Lawrence Erlbaum.

Mitnick, D. M., Heyman, R. E., Malik, J., & Smith Slep, A. M. (2009). The differential association between change request qualities and resistance, problem resolution, and relationships satisfaction. *Journal of Family Psychology, 23,* 464–473.

Overall, N. C., Fletcher, G. O., & Simpson, J. A. (2006). Regulation processes in intimate relationships: The role of ideal standards. *Journal of Personality and Social Psychology, 91,* 662–685.

Overall, N. C., Fletcher, G. J. O., Simpson, J. A., & Sibley, C. G. (2009). Regulating partners in intimate relationships: The costs and benefits of different communication strategies. *Journal of Personality and Social Psychology, 96,* 620–639.

Papp, L. M., Kouros, C. D., & Cummings, E. M. (2009). Demand–withdraw patterns in marital conflict in the home. *Personal Relationships, 16,* 285–300.

Pearce, Z. J., & Halford, W. K. (2008). Do attributions mediate the association between attachment and negative couple communication? *Personal Relationships, 15,* 155–170.

Reznick, R. M., Roloff, M. E., & Miller, C. W. (2010). Communication during interpersonal arguing: Implications for stress symptoms. *Argumentation and Advocacy, 46,* 193–213.

Richards, J. M., Butler, E. A., & Gross, J. J. (2003). Emotional regulation in romantic relationships: The cognitive consequences of concealing feelings. *Journal of Social and Personal Relationships, 20,* 599–620.

Robles, T. F., & Kiecolt-Glaser, J. K. (2003). The physiology of marriage: Pathways to health. *Physiology & Behavior, 79,* 409–416.

Robles, T. F., Shaffer, V. A., Malarkey, W. B., & Kiecolt-Glaser, J. K. (2006). Positive behaviors during marital conflict: Influences on stress hormones.

*Journal of Social and Personal Relationships, 23,* 305–325.

Roloff, M. E., & Johnson, L. J. (2002). Serial arguing over the relational life course: Antecedents and consequences. In A. L. Vangelisti, H. T. Reis, & M. A. Fitzpatrick (Eds.), *Stability and change in relationships* (pp. 107–128). Cambridge, UK: Cambridge University Press.

Roloff, M. E., & Miller, C. W. (2006a). Mulling about family conflict and communication: What we know and what we need to know. In L. H. Turner & R. West (Eds.), *Family communication: A reference of theory and research.* Thousand Oaks, CA: Sage.

Roloff, M. E., & Miller, C. W. (2006b). Social cognition approaches to understanding interpersonal conflict and communication. In J. G. Oetzel & S. Ting-Toomey (Eds.), *The Sage handbook of conflict communication: Integrating theory, research, and practice* (pp. 97–128). Thousand Oaks, CA: Sage.

Roloff, M. E., & Reznik, R. M. (2008). Communication during serial arguments: Connections with individuals' mental and physical well-being. In M. T. Motley (Ed.), *Studies in applied interpersonal communication* (pp. 97–120). Thousand Oaks, CA: Sage.

Roloff, M. E., & Soule, K. P. (2002). Interpersonal conflict: A review. In M. L. Knapp & J. A. Daly (Eds.), *Handbook of interpersonal communication* (3rd ed., pp. 475–528). Thousand Oaks, CA: Sage.

Saavedra, M. C., Chapman, K. E., & Rogge, R. D. (2010). Clarifying links between attachment and relationship quality: Hostile conflict and mindfulness as moderators. *Journal of Family Psychology, 24,* 380–390.

Sanford, K. (2003). Problem-solving conversations in marriage: Does it matter what topics couples discuss? *Personal Relationships, 10,* 97–112.

Sanford, K. (2006). Communication during marital conflict: When couples alter their appraisal, they change their behavior. *Journal of Family Psychology, 20,* 256–265.

Sanford, K. (2007). Hard and soft emotion during conflict: Investigating married couples and other relationships. *Personal Relationships, 14,* 65–90.

Sargent, J. (2002). Topic avoidance: Is this the way to a more satisfying relationship? *Communication Research Reports, 19,* 175–182.

Sillars, A. L. (2010). Interpersonal conflict. In C. R. Berger, M. E. Roloff, & D. R. Roskos-Ewoldsen (Eds.), *The handbook of communication sciences* (2nd ed., pp. 273–290). Thousand Oaks, CA: Sage.

Solomon, D. H., & Knobloch, L. K. (2001). Relationship uncertainty, partner interference, and intimacy within dating relationships. *Journal of Social and Personal Relationships, 18,* 804–820.

Solomon, D. H., & Knobloch, L. K. (2004). A model of relational turbulence: The role of intimacy, relational uncertainty, and interference from partners in appraisal of irritations. *Journal of Social and Personal Relationships, 21,* 795–816.

Stanley, S. M., Markman, H. J., & Whitton, S. W. (2002). Communication, conflict, and commitment: Insights on the foundations of relationship success from a national survey. *Family Process, 41,* 659–675.

Sullivan, K. T., Pasch, L. A., Johnson, M. D., & Bradbury, T. N. (2010). Social support, problem solving, and the longitudinal course of newlywed marriage. *Journal of Personality and Social Psychology, 98,* 631–644.

Ter Laak, J. J. F., Olthoff, T., & Alkeva, E. (2003). Sources of annoyance in close relationships: Sex-related differences in annoyance with partner behaviors. *Journal of Psychology, 137,* 545–559.

# CHAPTER 14

# Theories of Computer-Mediated Communication and Interpersonal Relations

*Joseph B. Walther*

omputer-mediated communication (CMC) systems, in a variety of forms, have become integral to the initiation, development, and maintenance of interpersonal relationships. They are involved in the subtle shaping of communication in almost every relational context. We may observe or participate in the conversations of huge numbers of social actors, from the Twitter messages of experts we have never met to one's family's blog and from messaging a barely acquainted Facebook friend to coordinating with one's spouse through texting about who will pick up the kids that day or saying via e-mail that one is sorry about the fight they had that morning. Individuals exploit the features of these media to make their best impression and attract attention or to ward off undesired contacts (Tong & Walther, 2011a). We continually form and re-form our impressions and evaluations of others online, from deciding whose recommendations to trust in discussion boards (Van Der Heide, 2008) to evaluating the friend who portrays himself online in a not quite accurate way (DeAndrea & Walther, in press). Although many people perceive that social media messages are trivial and banal, so is the stuff by which relationships are maintained (Duck, Rutt, Hurst, & Strejc, 1991; Tong & Walther, 2011b).

The ubiquity of CMC is not sufficient impetus for it to be a focus of study in interpersonal communication research. How CMC changes our messages—how they are constructed, whether for specific relational purposes or with lesser or greater effect—remain important questions that continue to drive inquiry in interpersonal CMC research. How does the Internet affect the likelihood of having relationships? With whom? And how do we manage these relationships? How do disclosures and affectations influence others and ourselves, and how do online interpersonal processes affect the instrumental and group dynamics that technology enables? How do we exploit existing technologies for relational purposes, and how do we evade the potential dampening effects that technologies otherwise may impose on relational communication? How do technology developers incorporate features into communication systems specifically designed to support and enhance relational functions?

There are many methodologies employed in studying CMC and social interaction. Large-scale, sophisticated surveys enumerate what people are doing online and why they say they are doing them (e.g., Katz & Rice, 2002; the Pew Internet & American Life Project at http://pewinternet.org/). There are accounts of the metaphors that define the online experience for Internet date seekers (e.g., Heino, Ellison, & Gibbs, 2010) and interpretive investigators' insights from interacting with groups of young people about what is going on and what it means online (boyd, 2007). Conference proceedings from design experiments report cognitive and affective responses to variations in the representation of others' online behaviors or different interface characteristics with which to behave online (e.g., the ACM Digital Library at http://portal.acm.org/dl.cfm). A number of recent and forthcoming volumes address different aspects of interpersonal interaction online, including works by Amichai-Hamburger (2005), Baym (2010), Joinson, McKenna, Postmes, and Reips (2007), Konijn, Utz, Tanis, and Barnes (2008), Papacharissi (2010), Whitty and Carr (2006), and Wright and Webb (2011), among others. Any of these approaches provide glimpses into the changing landscape of interpersonal communication and CMC. No one chapter can paint this landscape or summarize it well. Worse yet, such an amalgamation of facts would suffer from a lack of coherence, reflecting a field with more work being done than consensus on what work should be done. Moreover, to describe what people are doing interpersonally with CMC today would be to invite obsolescence very quickly, given the pace of change in communication and technology. Readers who expect such an accounting in this essay will be disappointed.

Alternatively, despite the field's youth, there are now a greater number of theoretical positions directly related to CMC than any single overview of the field has previously described. Some theories have matured and are due for evaluation,

both in light of a number of empirical tests of their validity, and intensions and extensions of their explanatory power. New technological developments may have enlarged or diminished their relative scope. Newer theories have also arisen, some barely tested, the ultimate utility of which remains to be seen. This is not to suggest that the only theories the field needs are those focusing specifically on CMC. As Yzer and Southwell (2008) suggested, the most useful explanations of CMC may be those that rest strongly on robust theories developed in traditional contexts. For the present purposes, the chapter focuses on CMC-specific theoretical formulations. As Scott (2009) observed, "We can't keep up with new innovations, so we need theory and models that can" (p. 754).

This chapter provides, first, a description and evaluation of 13 major and minor theories of CMC. Although readers may find many of these approaches reviewed in other sources, particular efforts have been made to review the theories' development and status since the publication of the previous edition of this *Handbook* (see Walther & Parks, 2002). These theories are classified according to their conceptualization of the way users respond to the characteristics of CMC systems, particularly in the adaptation to cue systems that differ from face-to-face communication. These theories include the now standard classification of cues-filtered-out theories, which assert that systematic reductions in the nonverbal cues conveyed by different communication systems lead to impersonal orientations among users. There are differences among the foci of impersonal orientations, some of which are asocial and others quite specific and social in nature. The second group of theories depicts how characteristics of communicators, their interactions with others, and contextual factors affect the perceived capacities of different communication systems. These perceptions, in turn, affect the expressiveness and normative uses of these same technologies as if the capacities themselves had changed. The next set of theories reflects the ways in which communicators adapt to or exploit the cue limitations of CMC systems to achieve or surpass face-to-face levels of affinity. Finally, new theoretical ideas are mentioned that address the utility of different media over the progression of usage sequences or relational stages or compare media effects of different kinds based on the relative effortfulness of different channels. The discussion includes numerous examples from research that help exemplify critical findings related to these frameworks.

The chapter ends with a few notes of concern about trends in contemporary CMC research. These trends represent understandable developments given the nature of the field, yet they also present potential problems in the further development of knowledge in certain domains. These concerns involve the role of face-to-face comparisons in technology-focused research, the potential impact of new technologies on earlier CMC theories, and the implications of multimodality in relationships (i.e., how to learn about the usage of a variety of communication systems within any single relationship).

## Cues-Filtered-Out Theories

As numerous reviews have reflected, Culnan and Markus (1987) coined the term *cues-filtered-out* to describe a group of theories sharing the premise that CMC has no nonverbal cues and therefore occludes the accomplishment of social functions that typically involve those cues.

### Social Presence Theory

Social presence theory was imported from teleconferencing research as one of the first analytic frameworks applied to CMC. Short, Williams, and Christie's (1976) theory argued that various communication media differed in their capacity to transmit classes of nonverbal communication in addition to verbal content. The fewer the number of cue systems a system supported, the less warmth and involvement users experienced with one another. Hiltz, Johnson, and Agle (1978)

and Rice and Case (1983) first applied this model to CMC, using it to predict that CMC rendered less socio-emotional content than other, multimodal forms of communication. Numerous experiments supported these contentions. Nevertheless, a number of theoretical and methodological critiques by other researchers challenged the social presence explanation of CMC dynamics (e.g., Lea & Spears, 1992; Walther, 1992). These critiques challenged several assumptions of the social presence model and identified artifacts in the research protocols that supported its application to CMC.

Despite the demise of social presence in some quarters of CMC research, extensive research and definition efforts have continued with respect to the role of presence with regard to settings such as virtual reality and computer-based gaming. Biocca, Harms, and Burgoon (2003) suggested definitional issues that a robust theory of social presence might require and the prospective benefits of a renewed social presence theory for comparing effects among various media. K. M. Lee (2004) highlighted the various conceptions of presence in related literatures, including telepresence, copresence, and social presence, as each construct describes somewhat different states of awareness of the self and others during electronic communication (see also Lombard & Ditton, 1997). Nevertheless, the various constructs and related measures are often used interchangeably or in duplication. Nowak and Biocca's (2003) experiment on the optimal level of anthropomorphism for avatars, for example, compared the research participants' responses to lifelike, cartoonish, or abstract avatars on measures of presence, copresence, and social presence. Each of the presence variables reflected the same result: Abstract rather than lifelike avatars stimulated the greatest presence responses.

Although researchers have in large part rejected the notion that CMC is inherently inferior to traditional communication media on outcomes such as social presence, there appears to be a resurgence of presence-related evaluations that

that were common in first-generation CMC (i.e., text-based e-mail, chat, and discussions) being applied to next-generation CMC, which features photos, graphics, avatars, or videos. Many individuals apparently assume that we no longer need to concern ourselves with earlier forms of minimal-cue CMC (or research about them) now that we have systems with greater bandwidth and presence. Education technologists, in particular, have been eager to recommend avatar-based interactions in Second Life as a cure for what remains, in the view of many, an impoverished level of social presence in plain-text educational conferencing (see Baker, Wentz, & Woods, 2009; Barnes, 2009; Childress & Braswell, 2006; Gunawardena, 2004), without much evidence of avatars' interpersonal impact beyond what may be expected due to novelty or to the hyperpersonal intercultural potential of asynchronous learning networks (e.g., Oren, Mioduser, & Nachmias, 2002). In a world where we know our communication partners by photo if not by face, plain-text CMC with no additional multimedia is, in some corners, being retro-conceptualized as never having been quite good enough, especially in comparison with the more presence-bearing media that seem (for now) to be here to stay. It appears that, although the formal theory of social presence has become disregarded in many quarters of CMC research, the concept of social presence as an inherent consequence of multiple cues remains alive and well (e.g., Bente, Rüggenberg, Krämer, & Eschenburg, 2008).

It remains to be seen whether social presence or some other construct and framework will emerge to account for why individuals use various new media for various relational activities. Observers of the new multimodal world of relationships have yet to identify coherent explanations about the relational functions and goals to which older new media and newer new media are being strategically applied. Meanwhile, plain-text messaging through e-mail, mobile phones, and the 140-character Twitter tweet suggest that text-based CMC is not at all gone. The subject of multiple media, interpersonal

functions, and sequences is discussed once more at the end of this chapter.

## Lack of Social Context Cues

Like social presence theory, the lack of social context cues hypothesis (Siegel, Dubrovsky, Kiesler, & Mcguire, 1986; Sproull & Kiesler, 1986) once guided numerous studies on the interpersonal and group impacts of CMC, although it has been more or less set aside in response to contradictions that became apparent in native Internet environments (see Sproull & Faraj, 1997), as well as to formal theoretical and empirical challenges. The framework originally specified that CMC occluded the cues to individuality and normative behavior that face-to-face interaction transacts nonverbally. As a result, according to the model, CMC users became deindividuated and normless; CMC prevented users from attuning to others' individual characteristics, such as charisma, dominance, or affection, resulting in a cognitive reorientation of its users. The lack of nonverbal cues led them to become self-focused and resistant to influence, disinhibited, belligerent, and affectively negative.

As with social presence theory, a number of critical issues related to the research paradigms accompanying the lack of social context cues approach, and to the various theoretical issues it raised, have led to the model's retreat. Negative social responses to CMC have been accounted for theoretically through more complex frameworks that can explain both negative affective outcomes as well as positive ones, in formulations incorporating CMC's impersonal, interpersonal, and hyperpersonal effects (see Walther, 1996). Researchers articulated alternative assumptions and employed different research designs, leading to the development of second-generation theories of CMC. These latter positions predict different social and interpersonal effects of CMC media depending on other contextual factors (Walther, 2010).

That said, research still surfaces that shares the basic premises of the lack of social context cues hypothesis, and such studies, ironically, often include methodological strategies that were criticized with regard to the original research on the lack of social context cues and social presence models. One such approach has appeared in several experiments on compliance gaining and social influence in CMC (e.g., Guadagno & Cialdini, 2002): The absence of nonverbal cues in CMC is said to prevent communicators from detecting demographic, personality, and interpersonal characteristics of others. The implication in this case is that CMC confers no peripheral cues to persuasion (see Petty & Cacioppo, 1986). As a result, it is suggested, CMC users process messages based on argument strength—that is, through central routes to persuasion alone—and they experience less overall attitude change than do off-line communicators. Methodologically, such research has employed very short interaction sessions among strangers in CMC and face-to-face (e.g., Di Blasio & Milani, 2008), an approach that has been demonstrated elsewhere to impose a time-by-medium interaction effect, artifactually dampening impression formation in CMC (for a review, see Walther, 1992, 1996).

Other persuasion research following a lack of social context cues approach apparently employed short, scripted real-time chat sessions as the operationalization of e-mail yet made claims about e-mail's persuasion-related potential on that platform (Guadagno & Cialdini, 2007). Whereas gender-by-medium differences in persuadability are obtained in such research, it is difficult to know how to generalize these findings. Using synchronous CMC chat to describe asynchronous e-mail is a questionable, although certainly not a novel, approach. This conflation should be of concern, although differences due to synchronous versus asynchronous CMC remain understudied in CMC research.

In a similar vein, Epley and Kruger (2005) argued that e-mail's lack of nonverbal cues prevents users from deciphering others' individual characteristics following the presentation of a false pre-interaction expectancy about a pending conversational partner. The authors conducted several experiments in which they primed interviewers to expect a high or low level of intelligence or extraversion from an interviewee. Some dyads communicated using a voice-based system, while so-called e-mail communicators used a real-time CMC chat system. In the voice conditions, although conversations were restricted to simple, predetermined questions and spontaneous answers, they constituted actual interactions between two real (randomly assigned) persons. In contrast, there was no real interaction between CMC interviewers and their ostensible interviewees, since the responses interviewers received to their questions were sent by a researcher who had transcribed what a voice-based interviewee had said to a different, voice-based interviewer. This research strategy was intended to prevent the introduction of random variations in CMC users' language in order to provide a true test of the difference between CMC and speech. Epley and Kruger found that expectancies persisted in the post-CMC evaluations of partners, although they dissipated in voice.

A replication of this work by Walther, DeAndrea, and Tong (2010) challenged the former study's methods, particularly the use of transcribed speech as the operationalization of CMC interviewee responses. This concern focused on the lack of real interactions in the prior study and the employment of language that had been generated accompanying voice, in speech, as if it was structurally and functionally identical to the language that is generated in spontaneous CMC, where communicators know that there are no vocal cues to convey identity and social meanings. Walther, DeAndrea, and Tong argued that CMC users adapt to the medium by altering their language in a way that compensates for the absence of nonverbal cues. Their study therefore involved bona fide interviewees in both voice and CMC who could generate naturalistic responses to interviewers in both media. CMC users' postdiscussion impressions were rated as more intelligent than those of voice-based partners, in contrast to Epley and Kruger's (2005) findings and consistent with the hyperpersonal model of CMC (Walther, 1996). Impressions changed in conjunction with the number of utterances exchanged, consistent with the social information processing theory of CMC (Walther, 1992).

Indeed, the history of contradictions between cues-filtered-out findings and the more prosocial effects of CMC can be explained in part by the methodological constraints on CMC interaction, which reflect competing theoretical orientations about communication and CMC (Fulk & Gould, 2009; Walther, 2010).

## Media Richness

Media richness theory (Daft & Lengel, 1986), also known as information richness theory (Daft & Lengel, 1984), originally modeled the relative efficiency of different communication media for reducing equivocality in organizational decision making. It has also been applied to interpersonal situations either formally or informally. The term *rich media* is often used casually in the literature to signify multimodal or greater-bandwidth media, that is, communication media that support multiple verbal and nonverbal cue systems.

Media richness theory seems to be one of the most popular models of CMC (for a review, see D'Urso & Rains, 2008). This may be because some of its core constructs are so intuitively appealing, especially the media richness construct. This construct, in turn, is defined theoretically by four subdimensions: (1) the number of cue systems supported by a medium, (2) the immediacy of feedback provided by a medium (from unidirectional to asynchronously bidirectional to simultaneous bidirectional interaction), (3) the potential for natural language (compared with the more formal genre of memoranda, business letters, or data printouts), and (4) message personalization (i.e., the degree to which a message can be made to address a specific individual). So in the original formulation, face-to-face communication is the richest mode because it includes multiple-cue systems, simultaneous sender-and-receiver

exchanges (providing great immediacy of feedback), natural language, and message personalization. Telephones, letters, and memoranda each offer progressively declining levels of richness. The second core construct of the model is the equivocality of a messaging situation. Equivocality is defined as the degree to which a decision-making situation and information related to it are subject to multiple interpretations.

The theory argues that there is a match between the equivocality of a message situation and the richness of the medium with which to address it: To be most efficient, greater equivocality requires more media richness, and lesser equivocality requires leaner media. Although the theory was originally formulated so that the result of optimal match (or of mismatch) affects efficiency, it is often described in the literature as being related to communication effectiveness.

It is somewhat surprising that the theory remains as frequently employed as it does given that, even within the domain of organizational communication, it has a poor history of empirical support. The first empirical investigation of the theory (Daft, Lengel, & Trevino, 1987) addressed it indirectly by asking managers to indicate in a questionnaire what media they would use to address a list of various communication situations. These situations had been rated by other research participants in terms of their equivocality. The degree to which the test managers' media selections (in terms of richness) matched the situations' equivocality led to a media sensitivity score for each manager. Through inspection of the same managers' personnel evaluations, researchers found a correlation between media sensitivity and managerial performance. These results were interpreted as supporting the theory.

One can see that the investigation described above does not actually test the theoretical relationships specified by the theory; rather, it evaluates peripheral processes and implications that may be related to the model less directly. That is, rather than examining direct relationships between the actual use of differently rich media, equivocal message situations, and efficiency (e.g., the time and effort required), Daft et al. (1987) examined organizationally related implications of managers' projections of media selection. Such findings have been contested by other researchers in a variety of ways. For example, Markus (1994) questions whether the projective, self-report approach to asking managers what media they would choose for various communication tasks generalizes to managers' actual media use. In her own study, Markus found that managers express media selection preferences very consistent with the matches prescribed by Daft and Lengel (1986) when completing questionnaires. By shadowing several managers, however, Markus found that their media selection behavior frequently departed from their questionnaire responses. It appears that managers hold normative beliefs about media choice that align with the media richness model but the normal constraints and spontaneous-communication needs that they face lead them to select media in ways that defy media richness sensibilities, and according to Markus, they do not suffer any decrement in performance as a result.

A second significant threat to the model came in the form of an experiment by Dennis and Kinney (1998) that sought to test directly the core theoretical dynamics of media richness theory as well as its extension toward interpersonal perceptions of online collaborators. This study involved small groups that addressed a simple or equivocal task, using videoconferencing (greater in richness) or text-based messaging (lower in richness). They found that media richness produced differences in the time it took different groups to complete their tasks. Media richness did not, however, interact with task equivocality to affect decision quality or interpersonal perceptions. More recent work examined media richness variations with differences in high-context versus low-context cultural backgrounds of users (Setlock, Quinones, & Fussell, 2007). Researchers predicted that there would be more benefit from using videoconferencing than from a reduced-bandwidth medium among those from a high-context culture (see Hall, 1976). Culture, however,

did not interact with media richness differences on conversational efficiency, task performance, or satisfaction.

Walther and Parks (2002) criticized the model as being unable to generate hypotheses that apply to many forms of CMC. Their concern focused on the four subdimensions of richness. When applying these criteria to traditional media, it is easy to see that all four dimensions tend to vary in conjunction with one another as one compares media. As one moves away from face-to-face to memoranda, for example, there are fewer code systems, less immediacy of feedback, less natural language, and little message personalization. However, e-mail does not fit into this scheme so neatly. Although e-mail is generally text based and therefore low in multiple codes, it may be exchanged relatively rapidly (if all addressees are online at the same time), it may use natural language (or formal language), and its capacity for message personalization is great. Likewise, one may use Facebook to broadcast information about oneself to a large audience, but Facebook also features public displays of relatively private one-to-one messages between friends that are sometimes very personally, even idiosyncratically, encoded. As these examples should make clear, media richness theory offers no clear method for ascribing a unitary richness value when the underlying criteria that constitute richness may reflect very different values, and researchers cannot apply the model to media that offer so much variation among richness characteristics. This issue may be an underlying factor that has contributed to the troubling level of empirical support for the model in CMC research.

Notwithstanding the troubling level of empirical support, media richness theory continues to be applied to new media and new interpersonal settings (without much success). For instance, Cummings, Lee, and Kraut (2006) used media richness theory to predict that friends from high school use telephone and face-to-face contact more frequently than CMC to maintain their friendships when they transition to college. Their results showed, however, that CMC was the most frequently used medium among such friends. Rather than abandon the media richness framework, the authors conjectured that the relatively greater expense of making long-distance phone calls interfered with their predictions.

In a different vein, Hancock, Thom-Santelli, and Ritchie (2004) used media richness theory in a study comparing individuals' media preferences for deceiving another person. They argued that lying can be considered an equivocal message, and therefore, individuals should select rich media such as face-to-face or telephone for deception more often than they would choose text-based chat or e-mail. Results of a diary study did not support the hypothesis. Telephone was the most frequently used medium for deception, followed by face-to-face and instant messaging (which did not differ from each other), and e-mail was the least frequently used medium for deception. Hancock et al. (2004) concluded with a features-based explanation of their findings: Individuals resist the use of media that are recordable (such as CMC) so that their lies cannot be caught later or provide evidence with which to hold them to account. The recordability characteristic of new media, they argued, questions the applicability of media richness's assumption that communication channels differ along a single dimension. Interestingly, more recent research identifying an abundance of deception in date-finding websites has yet to be reconciled with this study's conclusion that liars avoid recordable and accountable media.

## The Social Identity Model of Deindividuation Effects

The social identity model of deindividuation effects, or SIDE model, has had an interesting evolution in the literature. Although its developers have argued that it is decidedly not about interpersonal communication, at least in terms of the mechanisms that generate its predictions (e.g., Postmes & Baym, 2005), it has been applied to many settings that appear to be interpersonal in

nature. At one point, SIDE was one of the most dominant theories of CMC. Changes to the theory in response to empirical challenges and changes in communication technology—attributes that bear on the theory's central assumptions—appear to have accompanied a marginal decline in its popularity and scope. In certain contexts, however, it remains a most parsimonious and robust explanatory framework for CMC dynamics.

The SIDE model is included here as a cues-filtered-out theory because it, like others, considers the absence of nonverbal cues in CMC as an impersonalizing deterrent to the expression and detection of individuality and the development of interpersonal relations online. The SIDE model differs from other cues-filtered-out approaches, however, in that rather than leave users with no basis for impressions or relations at all, it predicts that CMC shifts users toward a different form of social relations based on social self-categorization. The SIDE model (Lea & Spears, 1992; Reicher, Spears, & Postmes, 1995) specifies two factors that drive online behavior. The first factor is the visual anonymity that occurs when CMC users send messages to one another through text (in real-time chat or in asynchronous conferencing and e-mail). When communicators cannot see each other, the model puts forth, communicators do not attune themselves to one another on the basis of their interindividual differences. Drawing on principles of social identification and self-categorization theories (Tajfel, 1978; Tajfel & Turner, 1979), the model originally argued that visual anonymity led to deindividuation, or a loss of awareness with regard to one's own (and others') individuality. When in such a state of deindividuation, the second major factor in the theory comes into play: whether CMC users orient themselves to some salient social category or group (i.e., a social identification). If a CMC user experiences a social identification, the user will relate to other CMC users on the basis of in-group (or out-group) dynamics. These classifications then drive users' perceptions of similarity and attraction toward online partners in gross terms, that is, as a unified perception based on of whether others online seem to belong to the same group that is salient to the user, rather than as a sum or average of one's perceptions of each other partner in a conversation.

The model also specified, theoretically, that when a deindividuated CMC user orients to an individualistic identification rather than a social identification, then systematic effects on similarity and attraction should not occur. The model views interpersonal (rather than group) attraction toward other members as an aggregation of randomly distributed values based on a person's attraction to each idiosyncratic individual. That is, when perceiving others individually, one may like one person a lot, dislike another person a lot, and like others to different degrees, which, on balance, should average to some neutral level. Attraction to a group to which one belongs, in contrast, should be systematically positive. This difference in the form of attraction marks a key distinction between a group-based and an interpersonally based approach to the social dynamics of CMC (Lea, Spears, & de Groot, 2001; for a review, see Walther & Carr, 2010).

The most basic research strategy that provided evidence for SIDE involved experiments manipulating the two factors, visual anonymity and type of identification. In a prototypical experiment, one half of the small groups of CMC users in an experiment would communicate with one another using a text-based chat system only, whereas the other half would use the chat system and be shown photos that were supposed to represent the members. The former condition provides visual anonymity, presumably instigating deindividuation, whereas the latter condition involves visual identification and individuation. The second factor, group identification, is manipulated by prompting participants explicitly to look for the unique and distinctive characteristics of the group in which they were involved rather than to try to detect what made the individuals with whom they were conversing unique and different from one another. Such research has produced predicted interaction effects of visual

anonymity/identifiability by group/interpersonal identity, with conditions involving both visual anonymity and group identity providing the greatest scores on attraction (e.g., Lea & Spears, 1992).

The SIDE model's advocates originally argued that the nature of group memberships with which CMC users identified comprised fairly general social categories (e.g., English vs. Dutch nationalities, psychology vs. business majors, men vs. women, etc.). Although attempts to arouse these kinds of identifications have been employed in SIDE experiments, they have not produced effects as clearly as when identification was targeted only with the local group, that is, the unique and specific small group involved in the interaction. These results have led to revisions of the SIDE model, and recent versions focus on visually anonymous CMC leading to in-group identification with the group of participants rather than via larger social categories.

Although the SIDE model is distinctively not about an interpersonal basis for online relations, it has been argued to offer an explanatory framework for what others consider to be interpersonal phenomena. Lea and Spears (1995) argued that SIDE can explain the development of romantic relationships online. Rejecting notions that intimate attraction is necessarily and exclusively premised on physical appearance or the exchange of nonverbal cues (a rejection with which several other CMC theories in this chapter, described below, concur), they argued that intimacy may result from the perceptions of similarity that arise from a couple's shared membership in a variety of social categories (see also Sanders, 1997). From this perceptive, although partners who communicate romantically online may believe that they love each other interpersonally, this would be an illusion. Their projection of interpersonal intimacy would be an outgrowth and projection of the similarity/attraction they share on the basis of their social (rather than interpersonal) identifications. Other essays have made quite strident pronouncements about the superiority of a groups-based, rather than an interpersonally-based, approach to understanding a variety of online social responses. They have gone so far as to suggest that interpersonally based explanations for systematic social effects in online behavior are empirically conflicting and conceptually misleading and that they have impeded theoretical understanding about CMC effects (Postmes & Baym, 2005).

Despite these pronouncements about its overarching superiority as an organizing model for the entire field, the SIDE model seems now to be taking a more appropriately limited place in CMC research. This change appears to be due to uncertainties about the components of the model itself, empirical "competitions" in which social and interpersonal components both appear, and new media forms that alternately extend or restrict the scope of SIDE's domain.

The deindividuation aspect of the model itself has been redefined (see E.-J. Lee, 2004). Although visual anonymity is still a key predictor of SIDE's effects, empirical studies have led to questions about the deindividuation that anonymity was said to produce, in terms of its actual potency and its theoretical necessity in the model. Research has found that in some cases SIDE-like responses to an anonymous online crowd are greater when a CMC user is more, rather than less, self-aware (Douglas & McGarty, 2001). This and other studies have led SIDE theorists to argue that it is not deindividuation but rather depersonalization—the inability to tell who is who online—that is (and always has been) the construct on which SIDE phenomena depend. It is admirable that the theory is open to such modification, although it represents a significant departure from the important elements of social identity theory on which it originally drew and from assertions that were argued strongly in earlier articulations of the model.

Responding in part to SIDE advocates' claims that their model could explain seemingly interpersonal effects, researchers made efforts to demonstrate more carefully whether group or interpersonal factors were operating in their CMC studies. Greater attention has been paid to whether the operationalizations and measurements

involved in research can discern group-based constructs from interpersonally based constructs (Wang, 2007). Moreover, experiments have directly compared SIDE-based versus interpersonally-based factors in the same study for their effects on the responses of CMC groups. Rogers and Lea (2004), for example, studied a number of virtual groups composed of students in England and the Netherlands who worked over an extended period of time via asynchronous conferencing and real-time chat. Steps were employed to maximize the salience of each virtual group's unique identity (i.e., researchers addressed groups by their collective name only, rather than individually by member). Repeated measures indicated that group attraction did not maintain evenly or increase over time. To the contrary, interpersonal affiliation among members reflected marginal increases over the duration of the groups' experience. More recently, Wang, Walther, and Hancock's (2009) experiment with visually anonymous online groups involved a SIDE-based assignment of four members to two distinct subgroups. The researchers further prompted one member of each four-person group to enact interpersonally friendly (or unfriendly) behaviors toward the rest of the members. In general, other members evaluated the deviants in each group on the basis of the individuals' interpersonal behaviors and not on the basis of those individuals' in-group or out-group status with respect to other subgroup members. These results suggest that SIDE is less robust than previously suggested when CMC users confront bona fide behavioral differences among members while remaining visually anonymous. A recent essay offers a more tempered view of when SIDE and other intergroup dynamics are likely to arise in CMC and when they give way to interpersonal dynamics (Walther & Carr, 2010).

Recent revisions to the SIDE model have also retracted its previous assertions that visually anonymous CMC users cannot, theoretically, relate to one another as individuals (Postmes, Baray, Haslam, Morton, & Swaab, 2006; Postmes, Spears, Lee, & Novak, 2005). Now individuals are seen, over time and under conditions of visual anonymity, to form relationships with each other first and then to identify with and form attachments to the small, interacting group. Group identification arises inductively in this new perspective. These formulations represent a major departure from SIDE's previous assumptions. They also leave unaddressed the mechanisms by which interacting individuals online become sufficiently attracted to one another to provide the interpersonal motivation, attraction, and reward that may be required to facilitate the durations of interaction required for individuals to develop an emergent group identity.

New media forms also raise interesting issues with regard to SIDE's scope. Many new technologies seem quite amenable to SIDE analysis of their effects on users, while others seem distinctly out of its reach. Communication systems such as social network sites, which confront CMC users with photos of prospective interactants, resemble the control group conditions in the prototypical SIDE experiment, that is, the visually identified conditions for which SIDE predicts no systematic effects. Alternatively, some new Web-based communication systems are very compatible with SIDE dynamics (see Walther, 2009): CMC systems display anonymous comments with no visual identification of other commenters, no interaction with other commenters, and the relatively clear implication that participants belong to the same social group. A recent study drew on SIDE theory successfully to predict readers' responses to the comments apparently left by other YouTube viewers in reaction to antimarijuana public service announcements. Researchers appended experimentally created comment sets (featuring all-positive or all-negative comments) to institutionally produced antimarijuana videos on YouTube pages. The more the participants identified with the ostensible commenters, the more the valence of those comments affected viewers' attitudes about the public service announcement videos and about marijuana (Walther, DeAndrea, Kim, & Anthony, 2010). The propagation of visually and authorially anonymous

reviews or talk-back sites on the Web merits further analysis from a SIDE perspective.

## Signaling Theory

Donath (1999) was the first to suggest a theoretical basis underlying the skepticism CMC users often hold about the legitimacy of others' online self-presentation and how CMC facilitates such deception. Prior to Donath's position, references abounded (and are still heard) regarding the anonymity of the Internet facilitating deception, although anonymity is a complex concept with various potential meanings pertaining to online interaction (see Rains & Scott, 2007). Anonymity's lack of utility in the case of deception is captured in the fact that individuals may lie about themselves (online or off) using their real names or pseudonyms. A better explanation for why people mistrust others' self-presentations is needed, and Donath's (1999) approach provides a reasonable one to explain why people trust many forms of information that are communicated off-line but tend to mistrust the kind of information individuals provide about themselves that is most prevalent in CMC discussions.

According to Donath, the fields of economics and biology have contributed to the development of signaling theory, which Donath then applied to the evaluation of self-presentational claims in text-based discussion fora. Signaling theory, Donath reviews (2007), shows "why certain signals are reliable and others are not. For a signal to be reliable, the costs of deceptively producing the signal must outweigh the benefits." Within signaling theory there are two types of signals. *Assessment signals* are artifacts that have an inherent and natural relationship with some characteristic with which they are associated. An animal that has very large horns, for example, must be strong; strength is required to support large, heavy horns. It would be impossible to support very heavy horns without being strong, that is, to deceive about one's strength using such horns; one could not falsely bear heavy horns if one did not actually possess the strength to do so. Conventional signals, on the other hand, bear socially determined symbolic relationships with their referents. Verbal claims about the possession of some attribute such as strength may be conventionally understood in terms of the intention of the claim, but ultimately, conventional signals are not as trustworthy as assessment signals. Conventional signals cost little to manufacture or construct, and they are therefore less trustworthy.

Text-based online discussions, Donath (1999) proposed, are dominated by conventional signals since such discussions are composed only of verbal statements. Because self-descriptive claims can easily be faked through verbal discourse, she argues, there is (rightfully) considerable wariness about whether online discussants can be trusted entirely to be who they say they are.

> Rare in the animal world, conventional signals are very common in human communication. The self-descriptions in online profiles are mostly conventional signals—it is just as easy to type 24 or 62 as it is to enter one's actual age, or to put M rather than F as one's gender. (Donath, 2007)

In the context of text-based CMC, Donath's (1999, 2007) application of signaling theory appears to have limited predictive utility and to raise certain validity questions. The perspective suggests no limiting factor to the general proposition that users should be suspicious of verbal claims and self-descriptions in CMC. Although the framework helps us understand online skepticism, it does not provide much in terms of variations in observers' assessments of others' online veracity, although questions of credibility in CMC have received ample attention from several other perspectives (e.g., Metzger, Flanagin, Eyal, Lemus, & McCann, 2003; Sundar, 2008). Second, the perspective does not consider whether there are indeed characteristics that are transmitted sufficiently reliably through text and language alone. It is hard to imagine, for instance, that an individual could convey being articulate

or being humorous online unless the individual actually possessed those characteristics. In such cases, verbal behavior should constitute assessment signals rather than conventional signals. These and other qualities that language might reliably convey are not considered in the application of signaling theory to CMC.

To her credit, Donath (2007) has expanded the application of signaling to explain the benefits and potentials of social network sites in helping observers assess the veracity of others' online claims. Like Walther and Parks' (2002) warranting theory (described below), she contends that the ability to contact other individuals in a target's social network reduces the likelihood that the target will engage in deception. From a signaling theory perspective, an observer's ability to discern a target's deception may result in social sanctions or punishment for the target. These negative repercussions are seen as costly in the parlance of economic theory, and knowing that these costs could accrue provides a disincentive for social network site users to prevaricate in their profiles. Thus, social network sites, unlike text-based discussion systems that are divorced from an individual's off-line social network, should reduce deception and increase the trust that CMC users place in others. These suggestions are yet to be tested, although the findings reported by Toma, Hancock, and Ellison (2008) and Warkentin, Woodworth, Hancock, and Cormier (2010) are consistent with this notion. DeAndrea and Walther (in press) found, however, that individuals are quite well aware of their friends' distorted self-presentations on Facebook profiles.

## Experiential and Perceptual Theories of CMC

### Electronic Propinquity Theory

The theory of electronic propinquity (Korzenny, 1978) received brief mention in the previous edition of the *Handbook*'s chapter on CMC (Walther & Parks, 2002). Those comments noted that relatively little attention had been paid to the theory since its first appearance in 1978 and its original follow-up in 1981 (Korzenny & Bauer, 1981; cf. Monge, 1980). Possibly because the most advanced technology mentioned in its introduction was interactive closed-circuit television, the theory has almost escaped the attention of the CMC research literature. Its formal structure and the nature of its constructs, however, leave it quite amenable to forms of CMC that can be characterized in terms of their bandwidth and interactivity. The theory has received a modicum of renewed attention since 2002, including empirical research that may contribute to a renewal of interest in its potential.

The central construct in electronic propinquity theory is the psychological closeness experienced by communicators. Whereas physical closeness or proximity is generally associated with interpersonal involvement in face-to-face communication, Korzenny (1978) argued that communicators connected through electronic media could also experience a sense of closeness, or electronic propinquity.

The theory specified the main and interaction effects on electronic propinquity from a number of specific factors. The first factor is bandwidth, or the capacity of a channel to convey multiple-cue systems (like the first factor in media richness, described above, which followed propinquity theory historically); the greater the bandwidth, the more the propinquity. Mutual directionality (like immediacy of feedback) increases propinquity, as do users' greater communication skills, the lower (rather than higher) level of complexity of a task, fewer communication rules, and fewer choices among alternative media. These factors also interact with each other, as specified in a series of derived theorems: The greater the bandwidth, the less the effect of task difficulty; the greater users' skills, the less the effect of more communication rules; and the fewer the choices among media, the less the effect of bandwidth.

Although the theory predated the Internet, these theoretical properties provide a sufficiently open-ended definitional framework in which specific media may be considered even though they did not exist when the theory was created. Therefore CMC, with or without auditory and/or visual cues, can fit neatly into electronic propinquity's calculus. Owing in part to a failed test using traditional media in an experiment by Korzenny and Bauer (1981), until recently, no such application to CMC had been examined empirically.

A recent replication of electronic propinquity theory's original test has indicated greater validity for the theory and has successfully applied it to CMC. Walther and Bazarova (2008) identified a confound in Korzenny and Bauer's (1981) original experiment that they attempted to isolate in a new empirical study. The confound had to do with the theory's proposition that the fewer the number of media choices one has, the greater the propinquity one experiences with the remaining medium, a dynamic that may have been present in Korzenny and Bauer's study but was unplanned and unchecked. Walther and Bazarova investigated this factor directly. They created experimental groups that alternatively had two media among their members (e.g., audioconferencing among all members but additional videoconferencing among a subset of members) or had only one medium connecting everyone. Media included face-to-face discussion, videoconferencing, audio conferencing, and text-based chat.

Results supported the proposition about the effect of media choice and bandwidth. Those who had no choices (i.e., only one medium) experienced greater propinquity using that medium than did those who used the same medium among two media present, when it was the lower bandwidth medium of the two. For example, text-based chat produced greater propinquity and satisfaction ratings when chat was the only channel a group was able to use, compared with ratings of chat in groups where a member used both chat and audio conferencing. These patterns persisted along all the media combinations evaluated in the study: "There were no differences between ratings obtained as a result of chat, voice, video, or FtF communication among groups who used only one medium"

(Walther & Bazarova, 2008, p. 640), although the use of two media consistently led to less propinquity for the lower bandwidth medium. The experiment offered further support for the theory. It demonstrated complex interactions among choice, bandwidth, communicator skill, and task difficulty, which generally supported electronic propinquity's predictions.

In addition to the renewed potential for the application of propinquity theory to emerging media, Walther and Bazarova (2008) suggested that these results may help account for discrepancies in the existing literature on the social effects of CMC. Numerous studies that have examined natural CMC uses in field settings often indicate that it is less preferred by users for relationships and group maintenance than other, higher bandwidth media and face-to-face interactions. In contrast, numerous experimental studies show relatively high levels of satisfaction and positive relational communication using CMC alone under various circumstances. Electronic propinquity theory's unique focus on the effects of media choice helps resolve this discrepancy. It alerts us to the notion that when communicators are aware or have a history of alternative media options for a specific relationship, CMC should be expected to be the least satisfying. Where communicators are constrained to one channel alone, as experiments often require, electronic propinquity theory explains how users quite readily apply communication skills to make the remaining available medium effective and satisfying. Whether there are many real-world settings where users are constrained in this way to a single medium is a different question, but electronic propinquity theory helps unlock what had been an unexplained paradox in the research literature with regard to these conflicting empirical findings.

## Social Influence Theory

The social influence approach to media richness (Fulk, Schmitz, & Steinfield, 1990; Fulk, Steinfield, Schmitz, & Power, 1987), like channel expansion theory (described below; Carlson & Zmud, 1999), focuses on the factors that change users' perceptions about the capacities of CMC and their consequent uses of the medium. It may be important to note that this approach shifts the definition of media richness to a perceptually based phenomenon describing how expressively a medium may be used. This departs from media richness theory's approach, which defines media richness based on the a priori properties of media.

Social influence theory rejects those aspects of media richness (and social presence) theory that argue that certain properties of media exclusively determine their expressive capabilities and their utility in interpersonal (and other) domains. Instead, Fulk et al. (1987) argue, the nature of media and their potentials are socially constructed, and the richness and utility of a medium are affected by interaction with other individuals in one's social network. Following from this network-analytic perspective, the theory predicts that one's strong ties have more influence on one's perception of CMC richness than do one's weak ties. In organizational settings, these distinctions include one's close coworkers versus workers in other organizational units. The authors of the model suggest that social interaction with network ties may include overt discussions about communication media and their uses. It may also include communications with one's ties via a given CMC medium, and the qualities of those exchanges also shape perceptions about that medium's potential and normative uses.

Social influence has received robust support in previous empirical studies. Research testing the model shows stronger correspondence between individuals' perceptions of e-mail's richness and those of their strongly tied coworkers than those of weakly tied coworkers. Research has established the cognitive and perceptual basis of these effects: One's attitudes about e-mail's utility correspond primarily with one's perceptions about one's coworkers' perceptions and secondarily with those coworkers' actual attitudes. These differences between direct perceptions and metaperceptions help demonstrate that the social influence process is not a magic bullet but a communication process that leads to individuals' reconstructions of others' messages (Fulk, Schmitz, & Ryu, 1995).

The social influence model has not received very much research attention recently. Its developers have shifted their focus after having set a precedent for complex research strategies exploring social influence that would not be simple to replicate. Nevertheless, how users construct perceptions about the potential and preferred uses of newer communication technologies may be a topic of renewed attention. Social network websites, for example, make most visible one's strong and weak ties. They make evident what the normative expressive and usage practices of one's friends are. These phenomena correspond quite clearly to the theoretical factors implicated in social influence theory, and future research on how different groups of users evolve different standards and norms for messaging via these systems can benefit from a social influence approach.

## Channel Expansion Theory

Channel expansion theory (Carlson & Zmud, 1994, 1999) also takes issue with the fixed properties ascribed to various media in media richness theory. Whereas social influence theory focuses on how dynamic interaction in a social network of communicators predicts and explains how users come to perceive CMC's richness, the primary focus of channel expansion theory is on internal, experiential factors. The theory's original, central argument is that as individuals gain more experience with a particular communication medium, the medium becomes richer for them (Carlson & Zmud, 1994). That is, theoretically, it becomes more capable for the conduct of equivocal and interpersonally oriented communication tasks. With experience, the authors argued, users learn how to encode and decode affective messages using a particular channel.

The channel expansion theory was expanded to include increasing familiarity with an interaction partner as a second major factor affecting the richness or expressiveness of a medium that is used to communicate with that partner, with experience related to the conversational topic

and organizational experience as additional, potential factors (Carlson & Zmud, 1999). Social influence by other communicators was posited to affect richness perceptions as well. The model was tested by its developers in a cross-sectional survey and in a longitudinal panel study, in both cases focusing only on e-mail. The first study produced a moderate correlation between experience using e-mail and e-mail richness perceptions (see also Foulger, 1990) as well as a correlation between familiarity with the conversational partner and e-mail richness (Carlson & Zmud, 1999). The panel study likewise found an increase in perceived e-mail richness commensurate with e-mail experience over time. Social influence was not significant.

The theory lay dormant until D'Urso and Rains (2008) replicated and expanded investigation of the model. These researchers included traditional media (face-to-face and telephone) as well as text-based chat, along with e-mail, in a survey of organizational users. Results were fairly consistent with Carlson and Zmud's (1999) findings with respect to new media. For chat and e-mail, experience with the media, and no other variables, affected media richness ratings. For traditional media, only social influence and experience with one's conversation partner, and not experience with the medium, affected richness perceptions.

Channel expansion theory offers an antidote to the inconsistencies of media richness research in a sense. The learning-based explanation that channel expansion theory offers is reasonable and intuitive. At the same time, other approaches deal with several of the theory's elements in more sophisticated (as well as in more complicated) ways. For instance, CMC users' ability to encode and decode personal and social cues is central to the social information processing theory of CMC (see below); the influence of others' richness perceptions is demonstrated more particularly in social influence theory; and electronic propinquity theory offers a different account for why the same medium may offer more psychological closeness and satisfaction in some circumstances and less in others by specifying a constellation of situational, media, and user characteristics.

# Theories of Interpersonal Adaptation and Exploitation of Media

## Social Information Processing

The social information processing (SIP) theory of CMC (Walther, 1992) has become a widely used framework for explaining and predicting differences between text-based CMC and off-line communication, and recent work has made efforts to expand its scope to include newer, multimedia forms of online communication. The theory seeks to explain how, with time, CMC users are able to accrue impressions of and relations with others online, and these relations achieve the level of development that is expected through off-line communication.

The theory articulates several assumptions and propositions concerning what propels these effects. It explicitly recognizes that CMC is devoid of the nonverbal communication cues that accompany face-to-face communication. It differs, however, from theories of CMC that argue that the lack of nonverbal cues impedes impressions and relations or reorients users' attention to impersonal states or to group-based forms of relating. The SIP theory articulates the assumption that communicators are motivated to develop interpersonal impressions and affinity regardless of medium. It further proposes that when nonverbal cues are unavailable, communicators adapt their interpersonal (as well as instrumental) communication to whatever cues remain available through the channel that they are using. Thus, in text-based CMC, the theory expects individuals to adapt the encoding and decoding of social information (i.e., socioemotional or relational messages) into language and the timing of messages. Although many readers of the theory have interpreted this argument to refer to emoticons (typed-out smiles, frowns, and other

faces; e.g., Derks, Bos, & von Grumbkow, 2007), the theory implicates language content and style characteristics as more primary conduits of interpersonal information.

A second major contention of SIP is that CMC operates at a rate different from face-to-face communication in terms of users' ability to achieve levels of impression and relational definition equivalent to face-to-face interaction. Because verbal communication with no nonverbal cues conveys a fraction of the information of multimodal communication, communication functions should require a longer time to take place. CMC users need time to compensate for the slower rate in order to accumulate sufficient information with which to construct cognitive models of partners and to emit and receive messages with which to negotiate relational status and definition.

With respect to the first major theoretical contention, recent research has demonstrated that communicators adapt social meanings into CMC language that they would otherwise express nonverbally. Walther, Loh, and Granka (2005) had dyads discuss a controversial issue: face-to-face or via real-time computer chat. In each dyad, prior to their dyadic discussion, the researchers privately prompted one of the members to increase or decrease his or her friendliness toward the other individual by whatever means that person chose to do so. The naive partner rated the ad hoc confederate after the interaction was over, providing ratings of the confederate's immediacy and affection dimensions of relational communication. Coders then analyzed recordings of the face-to-face confederates for the kinesic, vocalic, and verbal behaviors that corresponded to variations in immediacy and affection ratings. A number of vocalic cues provided the greatest influence on relational communication, followed by a group of specific kinesic behaviors; the confederates' verbal behaviors had no significant influence on perceptions of their immediacy and affection. In contrast, in the CMC transcripts, several specific verbal behaviors bore significant association with differences in relational communication. No less variance was accounted for by the verbal cues in CMC than the nonverbal cues accounted for in face-to-face interaction. This research provides confirmation about the hypothetical process mechanisms of the SIP theory, beyond confirmation of a relationship between distal antecedents and consequents.

The theory is somewhat equivocal about the second major element, the temporal dimension. The primary theoretical explanation for the additional time CMC requires for impression development and relational management is that electronic streams of verbal communication without nonverbal accompaniments contain less information than multimodal face-to-face exchanges. Even in so-called real-time CMC, chat communication cues are not fully duplexed in terms of seeing a partner's reactions at the same time that they generate an utterance. From this perspective, even a constant and uninterrupted exchange of real-time CMC should provide a relatively smaller accumulation of interpersonal information than would face-to-face communication over the same time interval. However, discussions of the theory also reflect that more time may be needed for relational effects to accrue in CMC because CMC is generally used in a more sporadic manner than face-to-face communication. Online communication often involves asynchronous media, that is, systems that allow one communicator to create a message at one time and recipients to obtain it later at a point in time they choose. The SIP perspective can account for both approaches to temporal distortion theoretically, and both approaches have been used in empirical research: Recent studies have added support for SIP by using strictly asynchronous communication (Peter, Valkenburg, & Schouten, 2005; Ramirez, Zhang, McGrew, & Lin, 2007) or real-time chat episodes repeated over several consecutive days (Hian, Chuan, Trevor, & Detenber, 2004; Wilson, Straus, & McEvily, 2006). However, greater theoretical precision would enhance understanding of the theory's scope and application.

The SIP theory has been expanded by researchers other than its original developer to incorporate media other than text-based CMC, although these formulations are tentative. Tanis and Postmes (2003) established that the presentation of partners' photos or the exchange of pre-interaction biographies of CMC users works equivalently well in instilling interpersonal expectations in CMC settings. Previously, SIP research had been more oriented to verbal exchanges, such as CMC users' biographical disclosures, attitudinal statements, and style. Therefore, it is noteworthy that photographic information appears to function similarly as biographical text.

Westerman, Van Der Heide, Klein, and Walther (2008) offered a more sophisticated approach to the potential effects of photos and other multimedia information online within SIP framework. These researchers reconsidered SIP's root proposition that lesser bandwidth media transmit less information per exchange than do greater bandwidth media, affecting the rate of impression formation and relational development. They examined various forms and channels of personal information from this perspective. As a result, they argued that some mediated forms of information are faster (i.e., they transmit more social information in a respective time interval, e.g., photos or videos) and others are slower. This simple assertion is consistent with SIP; yet an expanded view of faster and slower media allows for greater scope and a wider range of predictions about new, multimodal media than the theory was originally conceived to explain.

Despite these potential adjustments with which to integrate visual information in the SIP framework, recent studies have demonstrated considerably limited additional effects on attraction and uncertainty reduction when additional modalities accompany text-based CMC. In one study, Antheunis, Valkenburg, and Peter (2007) compared face-to-face dyadic communication with an instant messaging system, and a hybrid instant messenger that displayed visual information about a dyadic partner alongside textual CMC. After a get-to-know-you session, no significant differences in interpersonal attraction arose between these conditions. Visual cues actually increased the frequency of disclosures and personal questions, in contrast to previous findings that disclosure and personal questions were proportionately more frequent in CMC than in face-to-face interactions (Tidwell & Walther, 2002).

Finally, a recent examination of uncertainty reduction processes via social network sites focused explicitly on the potential obsolescence of SIP theory in light of new media characteristics providing information aside from the interactive exchanges on which SIP traditionally focuses. Another study by Antheunis, Valkenburg, and Peter (2010) argued that social network sites provide an abundance of asynchronous and unintrusive biographical, multimodal (pictorial), and sociometric information about other people. Therefore, they predicted that these alternative forms of social information should be expected to be the primary sources of uncertainty reduction about others, without need of recourse to interactive communication via text. Results of the study showed that despite the appeal of these newer forms of information display, interactive communication contributed the most to uncertainty reduction about another individual.

## Hyperpersonal CMC

The hyperpersonal model of CMC (Walther, 1996) proposes a set of concurrent theoretically based processes to explain how CMC may facilitate impressions and relationships online that exceed the desirability and intimacy that occur in parallel off-line interactions. The model follows four common components of the communication process to address how CMC may affect cognitive and communication processes relating to message construction and reception: (1) effects due to receiver processes, (2) effects among message senders, (3) attributes of the channel, and (4) feedback effects. The model has received a great deal of attention in the literature. At the same time, extensions and revisions to the model have been proposed on the basis of both conceptual and empirical contributions. Certain aspects of the model remain underresearched—such as the holistic integrity of its subcomponents as well as the reciprocal effects of feedback—although some progress has been made with respect to these issues.

*Receivers.* When receiving messages from others in CMC, an individual may tend to exaggerate perceptions of the message sender. In the absence of the physical and other cues that face-to-face encounters provide, rather than fail to form an impression, receivers fill in the blanks with regard to missing information. This often takes the form of idealization if the initial clues about another person are favorable. The original articulation of the model drew explicitly on SIDE theory (Lea & Spears, 1992) in formulating receiver dynamics. The SIDE model also describes how CMC users make overattributions of similarity when communicating under conditions of visual anonymity if contextual cues suggest that a conversational partner shares some salient social identity with the receiver. It further proposes that communicators experience heightened attraction in these circumstances. The SIDE model argues that the specific form of attraction is focused on one's attachment to the group identity rather than to the individual person.

Recent rearticulations of the hyperpersonal model, however, have attempted to broaden the concepts related to receiver dynamics (see Walther, 2006). The hyperpersonal approach now suggests that an initial impression may be activated not only by group identifications but through individual stereotypes, such as personality characteristics, or due to the vague resemblance of an online partner to a previously known individual (see Jacobson, 1999). Analysis of online impressions using social relations analysis (Kenny, 1994), which assesses how uniform or differentiated one's impressions of other group members are, offers a promising approach to the question of group- or interpersonally based impressions in CMC (see Markey & Wells, 2002).

*Senders.* Text-based CMC facilitates selective self-presentation. Online, one may transmit only cues that an individual desires others to have. It need not be apparent to others what one's physical characteristics are (unless one discloses them verbally), nor do individuals generally transmit unconscious undesirable interaction behaviors such as interruptions, mismanaged eye contact, or nonverbal disfluencies of the kind that detract from desired impressions face-to-face. Instead, CMC senders may construct messages that portray themselves in preferential ways, emphasizing desirable characteristics and communicating in a manner that invites preferential reactions. Self-disclosure quite naturally plays a role in this process, by which individuals not only disclose what content they wish to be known but also, through disclosure, breed intimacy. Research has found that disclosure and personal questions constitute greater proportions of utterances in online discussions among strangers than they do in comparable face-to-face discussion (Joinson, 2001; Tidwell & Walther, 2002). This may be a simple adaptation to the lack of nonverbal expressive behavior, which would normally provide uncertainty-reducing information. Yet CMC users' disclosures are more intimate than those of face-to-face counterparts, suggesting a strategic aspect to this difference as well.

Apart from explicit disclosures, much of what senders selectively self-present is conveyed through the content of the exchanges in terms of how communicators express their evaluations of various subjects, their agreement with partners, word choice, and any number of ordinary expressions of affinity. A recent study (Walther, Van Der Heide, Tong, Carr, & Atkin, 2010) asked one member of an online dyad, who was about to discuss the topic of hamburgers with an online partner, to behave online in a way that prompted the other person to like or to dislike the individual. The significant differences in liking for the actor following the CMC conversation were associated with the actor's level of agreements versus disagreements and concurrence versus divergence in statements about the other partner's favorite hamburger. Online (and perhaps elsewhere), we manipulate our desirability to others

not so much by overt statements of interpersonal affect but through the way we complement or contest others' views of things in the world. In other research, systematic differences among individuals' construction of stories about themselves online led to changes in their self-perceptions. Gonzales and Hancock (2008) asked participants to write about their experiences in a manner that would lead others to perceive them as either extraverted or introverted. Half of the participants in the experiment posted these responses in a blog, presumably accessible to other CMC users, whereas the other half of the participants recorded their answers in a private document for ostensible analysis at a later time, anonymously. The blog writers generated significantly different self-perceived extraversion/introversion scores following the experience, in accordance with the characteristic they had been assigned. Gonzales and Hancock concluded that selective self-presentation online provides a potent influence not only on others but also on the transformation of an individual's self, a phenomenon they called "identity shift."

*Channel.* The third dimension of the hyperpersonal model involves characteristics of the channel and how CMC as a medium contributes to the deliberate construction of favorable online messages. One part of the channel factor focuses on the mechanics of the CMC interface, suggesting that users exploit the ability to take time to contemplate and construct messages mindfully. In many CMC applications (especially asynchronous systems), users may take some time to create optimally desirable messages without interfering with conversational flow, very much unlike the effects of face-to-face response latencies. The hyperpersonal model further suggests that CMC users capitalize on the ability to edit, delete, and rewrite messages to make them reflect intended effects before sending them. The introduction of the model further suggested that CMC users may redirect cognitive resources into enhancing one's messages, without the need to pay attention to the physical behaviors of one's conversational partner or oneself, or to the ambient elements where one is physically located when communicating (in contrast to these demands on attention in face-to-face conversations). CMC users can focus their attention on message construction to a greater extent than they would in face-to-face conversations.

Recent research supported a number of these suggestions (Walther, 2007). A study led college student participants to believe that they were joining an asynchronous discussion with a prestigious professor, who was described in much detail; with a relatively undesirable high school student in another state, also described in detail; or with another college student, about whom no details were provided except for the student's name. Participants' message composition was recorded in real time and later coded and rated, and a different group of participants provided ratings of how desirable each type of target would be as an interaction partner. Results of the study revealed that the more desirable the partner was, the more editing (deletions, backspaces, and insertions) the participants exercised in composing their messages to that partner. The degree of editing corresponded to the degree of relational affection ascribed to the messages by raters. Participants self-reported their level of mindfulness during message production, which had been expected to differ based on the attractiveness of the ostensible message target. It did not, and neither did the time they spent composing their messages differ as a result of the different types of targets. However, those who were more mindful spent more of their time editing the messages they had written, whereas those who were lower in mindfulness spent more time choosing what to write. These results add a level of verification to the model's contention that CMC users exploit the unique mechanical features of the medium to enhance relational qualities of their messages.

Another facet of the channel component of the hyperpersonal model has been more difficult to interpret, and research results have challenged the model's original assertions about asynchronous versus synchronous CMC. The model originally posited that asynchronous CMC allowed users to avoid the problems of entrainment associated with face-to-face meetings. Entrainment, in the small group communication literature (Kelly & McGrath, 1985), refers to the ability to synchronize attention and interaction with collaborators. It is proposed to be difficult to accomplish when participants have competing demands on their time and attention. Time pressures work against entrainment in face-to-face meetings, leading communicators to neglect group maintenance behaviors in favor of impersonal, task-related discussions. Since CMC users working asynchronously can interact with others at times that are convenient and available to them, the model suggested that CMC should not suffer from a lack of maintenance behavior. CMC users would be more likely to engage in off-task, interpersonal discussions than in face-to-face meetings since, without meeting in real time, there is no time pressure constraining such exchanges.

This aspect of the model was challenged very quickly. Roberts, Smith, and Pollock's (1996) ethnographic observations and interviews reflected that individuals who enter real-time, multiplayer online games and chat systems (as opposed to asynchronous discussions) very rapidly exhibit sociable exchanges. Likewise, Peña and Hancock (2006) demonstrated that the conversations in a real-time multiparty sword-fighting game reflected more socio-emotional utterances than game-related statements even during online duels. The sociability benefits originally ascribed to asynchronous CMC in the introduction of the model are fairly clearly an aspect of many synchronous systems as well, at least those in which socializing is a goal that users bring to the system. A recent review of communication that takes place in certain online, real-time, role-playing games describes a great proportion and a wide variety of interpersonal communication behaviors among associates and fellow "clan" members (Klimmt & Hartmann, 2008). Although these findings suggest greater scope for the development of hyperpersonal dynamics, the entrainment explanation has not been tested since the model was developed, and the conceptual and empirical status of this aspect of the channel component of the model is unclear.

*Feedback.* The hyperpersonal model of CMC suggested that the enhancements provided by idealization, selective self-presentation, and channel effects reciprocally influenced matters, forming a feedback system by which the CMC intensified and magnified the dynamics that each component of the model contributes. That is, when a receiver gets a selectively self-presented message and idealizes its source, that individual may respond in a way that reciprocates and reinforces the partially modified personae, reproducing, enhancing, and potentially exaggerating them. The manner in which the dynamics of these reciprocated expectations may modify participants' character was suggested to reflect the process of behavioral confirmation.

Behavioral confirmation (Snyder, Tanke, & Berscheid, 1977) describes how one interaction partner's impression about a target partner leads the first partner to behave and how that behavior alters the responses of the target partner in return. The original behavioral confirmation study involved male participants who were shown photos priming them to believe that their upcoming female telephone interaction partners were physically attractive or unattractive (even though the actual partners were not really those depicted in the photos but were randomly selected female participants). Not only did this expectation affect the males' involvement, it affected the females' personality-related responses as well, as revealed in outside raters' evaluations of the females' personalities based on audio recordings of their conversations. The hyperpersonal model appropriated this construct, suggesting that one's idealized impressions of an online partner may lead a CMC user to reciprocate based on that impression, transmitting messages that, in turn, may shape the partner's responses, shifting the target's personality in the direction of the communicators' mutually

constructed and enacted impression. In this way, feedback may intensify the hyperpersonal effects of idealization, selective self-presentation, and channel exploitation.

The feedback component of the hyperpersonal model has received little formal research attention until recently. One study (Walther, Liang, et al., 2011) examined whether feedback to a CMC communicator enhanced the identity shift phenomenon described by Gonzales and Hancock (2008; see above). As Gonzales and Hancock had done, this experiment called on half the participants to answer several questions as if they were extraverted and the other half, as if introverted. Participants posted their responses to a blog or pasted them into a Web-based form. Departing from Gonzales and Hancock, in each condition, participants either did or did not receive feedback confirming their (extraverted or introverted) personality performances. When participants subsequently completed self-report measures of their extraversion/introversion, those who received feedback expressed more extreme scores in the direction of the initial prompting. This study also helps establish a link between two components of the hyperpersonal model—selective self-presentation and feedback—showing that the activation of these components jointly produces stronger effects than in isolation.

Several CMC studies have generated findings consistent with a *behavioral disconfirmation* effect (see Ickes, Patterson, Rajecki, & Tanford, 1982; Burgoon & Le Poire, 1993). Behavioral disconfirmation takes place when one individual anticipates an unpleasant interaction with a target person and, to avert the unpleasantness, overaccommodates in order to improve the person's demeanor. One was the Walther (2007) study described above, in which participants anticipated online communication with a high school–age loner, a college student, or a professor. Despite pretest indications that the high schoolers were the least desired communication partners, male participants who believed that they were communicating with a male high schooler expressed greater editing and affection than with a male peer or professor. No voice-based or face-to-face comparisons were done in that study.

As discussed earlier, two recent studies explored the effects of preinteraction expectancies on subsequent impressions following CMC or voice-based communication (Epley & Kruger, 2005; Walther, DeAndrea, & Tong, 2010). Manipulations in both studies instilled preinteraction expectancies among interviewers regarding their partners' high or low intelligence. Manipulations in both studies involved the bogus presentation of one of two sets of a partner's ostensible photograph, grade point average, major, and self-reported greatest high school achievement. In Epley and Kruger's (2005) research, half the interviewers used a phonelike system to speak to a real interviewee, and half the interviewers used CMC to obtain responses that were transcribed from a person other than the actual interviewee. The results superficially appear to reflect greater behavioral confirmation in CMC than on the phone: Interviewers' post-test assessments of interviewees' intelligence were different in CMC but not in voice conditions. The methodology in that study, however, was such that the CMC interviewer could not actually have influenced his or her partner's behavior. Walther, DeAndrea, and Tong's (2010) replication involved actual interviewees in both voice and CMC conditions. The post-CMC ratings indicated relatively greater intelligence assessments than did those following the voice-based interviews, reflecting behavioral disconfirmation in CMC relative to voice. Further research is exploring the reasons for these voice versus CMC differences in confirmation and disconfirmation.

*Extensions.* In addition to research that has added, supported, or challenged the hyperpersonal model's claims, a variety of extensions to the model have been made, and it has been applied to new social technologies as well.

Research exploring the dynamics of online date-finding systems has applied aspects of the hyperpersonal model in several ways. Many of these systems require users to create profiles that feature photos and self-descriptions. Ellison, Heino, and Gibbs's (2006) interviews with online daters revealed that users make overattributions from minimal cues that prospective dates exhibit. These include gross inferences based on spelling errors and projections about individuals' character on the basis of what time of day or night he or she initiates a date request. Gibbs, Ellison, and Heino (2006) also drew on selective self-presentation principles in their documentation of the dilemmas faced by daters when honest self-presentations produce fewer dates than do self-aggrandizing or deceptive self-presentations (see also Whitty, 2008).

Research on deceptive self-presentation in online dating profiles has made particular use of the hyperpersonal model. Innovatively acquired data demonstrate that most online daters misrepresent their age, weight, and/or height online (Toma et al., 2008; see also Hall, Park, Song, & Cody, 2010). In several cases, these findings have been attributed to CMC's facility for selective self-presentation and editing under asynchronous communication conditions (Toma et al., 2008). This hyperpersonal perspective has most recently been applied to the manner in which dating system users select or retouch the photographs they post to their electronic profiles (Hancock & Toma, 2009).

Additional work has added new explanatory extensions to the model. Jiang, Bazarova, and Hancock (2011) developed a framework for understanding the exceptional impact of self-disclosure on intimacy in CMC compared with face-to-face communication. Although individuals disclose proportionately more, and more intimately, in CMC than in face-to-face communication (Tidwell & Walther, 2002), questions remained over whether receivers (over) interpret disclosures in a way that increases intimacy in CMC more intensively than in off-line interactions. Jiang et al. (2011) hypothesized that the degree to which receiving disclosure from a conversational partner affects intimacy is shaped by the attributions a receiver makes for the partner's motivation to disclose. A 2 × 2 experiment included CMC chat versus face-to-face interactions between a naive participant and a confederate who offered several personal disclosures in one condition and no disclosures in a control condition. Posttest measures revealed that the CMC participants receiving disclosures experienced greater intimacy than did face-to-face participants. Among those who were exposed to a greater degree of disclosure, the CMC participants more frequently perceived that the discloser's behavior was motivated by some aspect of their relationship rather than by the medium or the discloser's disposition, compared with the face-to-face participants. The type of attribution fully mediated the relationship between the disclosure-by-medium interaction and intimacy. In addition to documenting a hyperpersonal effect of disclosure on intimacy, this study provided a new attributional mechanism to explain the effect, which is also affected by the medium.

A self-attribution dynamic may also be operating online that leads to exaggerated intimacy as a result of online self-disclosure, a hypothesis that has not appeared in the literature previously. Although it is commonly understood that when another person discloses to us, we experience intimacy with that person, Collins and Miller's (1994) meta-analysis of the relationship between disclosure and liking demonstrates an alternative connection as well: When we disclose to another person, our own disclosure increases our feelings of intimacy toward the recipient. Thus, when users naturally adapt to the absence of nonverbal cues in CMC by disclosing proportionately more than they do in face-to-face interaction (Joinson, 2001; Tidwell & Walther, 2002), it may be due to their own expression of relatively greater disclosure (in addition to or instead of the reception of others' disclosures) that they attribute greater intimacy to disclosive CMC conversations. Although this contention warrants empirical verification, it suggests an interesting contribution to the hyperpersonal cycle.

Another form of self-perception affecting intimacy can be hypothesized on the basis of findings that it takes several times longer to have a conversation online than exchanging the same

amount of verbal content in a face-to-face meeting (see Tidwell & Walther, 2002). If CMC chatters have an online conversation that feels as though it should only have taken an hour but turns out to have taken four hours, and if the communication rate differential is not apparent to CMC interactants (as it is apparently unapparent to online game players; Rau, Peng, & Yang, 2006), this temporal distortion may also lead to exaggerated inferences about the desirability of the online partner. When time seems to pass more quickly than it actually does, people attribute enjoyment to the events that occurred during that time (Sackett, Nelson, Meyvis, Converse, & Sackett, 2009).

Other researchers have also examined the role of disclosures in the development of relatively more intimate relations online and their effects. Valkenburg and Peter (2009) identify three relationships among four specific processes that explain how CMC may be related to improvements in adolescents' well-being. For reasons that have appeared in the literature (see above; for a review Kim & Dindia, 2011; see also Schouten, Valkenburg, & Peter, 2007), the first important relationship in the model is the effect of CMC in promoting online self-disclosure. Drawing on extensive literature, Valkenburg and Peter (2009) proceed to connect self-disclosure with the development of higher quality relationships among people. Finally, the authors point out the connection between high-quality relationships and development of psychological well-being. The first two linkages in particular implicate CMC as a catalyst in the relationally-based development of adolescent adjustment.

In contrast to Valkenburg and Peter's depiction of the beneficial effects of CMC to well-being, another application of the hyperpersonal model is seen in Caplan's (2003) approach to the study of *problematic Internet use.* Caplan focuses on the usage and consequences of CMC by individuals who have social skill deficits in their face-to-face communication abilities and who experience disruptive communication-related anxieties. To such people, Caplan has shown that

Internet interaction is especially appealing, particularly real-time discussion systems. Because CMC provides individuals greater control over their messages and their self-presentation, it reduces anxiety (see also Amichai-Hamburger, 2007). Under these conditions, individuals may develop what Caplan (2005) refers to as a *preference for online social interaction*, "characterized by beliefs that one is safer, more efficacious, more confident, and more comfortable with online interpersonal interactions and relationships than with traditional (face-to-face) social activities" (p. 723). This use of CMC is paradoxical and problematic, according to Caplan's research, because such individuals experience a decline in their off-line social skills in conjunction with their more socially rewarding online interactions.

## Warranting

A new theoretical construct, known as the warranting construct, was introduced in the previous edition of the *Handbook of Interpersonal Communication* (Walther & Parks, 2002). Warranting pertains to the perceived legitimacy and validity of information about another person that one may receive or observe online. Individuals often come to learn quite a lot about each other through discussions in topical online discussion groups or through online role-playing games (see Parks & Floyd, 1996; Parks & Roberts, 1998), as well as from personal homepages and other forms of online interaction and self-presentation, including online dating sites (see Ellison et al., 2006). However, as Donath (1999) explained, it is widely suspected that the information one obtains through interaction in such venues leaves open the possibility for distorted self-presentations and outright deception with respect to participants' off-line characteristics. As a relationship develops online, there may come a point at which it becomes very important to interactants to have information that they believe reliably describes a partner's off-line characteristics. This may become

especially acute if they decide to initiate an off-line meeting, as many online friends and prospective romantic partners decide to do (Parks & Roberts, 1998).

The introduction of the warranting construct argued that an individual is less likely to distort his or her self-presentation when the receiver has access to other members of the sender's social circle, since others can corroborate the individual's real-life characteristics and hold that person accountable for misrepresentation. To increase a partner's confidence in one's self-descriptions, an individual may make efforts to put an online partner in touch with members of the individual's off-line network.

The greater value of the warranting construct is found in its definition of what kind of information provides more confidence to receivers about the potentially true nature of an individual's off-line self. From this perspective, receivers are expected to be more confident about their impressions based on information that is more likely to warrant, or connect, the online persona to the off-line body and person (see Stone, 1995). Information is more likely to be seen as truthful to a receiver to the extent that the receiver perceives it to be "immune to manipulation by the person to whom it refers," according to Walther and Parks (2002, p. 552). They argued that CMC users may take deliberate steps to provide online partners with information having relatively great warranting value by using links to individuals in one's social network or hyperlinks to websites or archives containing information about the user over which the user himself or herself has no control.

Recent research has provided several empirical tests of the warranting construct. Although warranting was originally conceptualized in the context of relationships originating in text-based online discussions, recent research has applied and extended the construct to contemporary multimedia websites in interesting ways. The first reference to warranting came in a study of impression management in online dating sites. Ellison et al. (2006) reported that online date seekers warrant their claims about their proclivities or participation in certain activities by including photographs on their user profiles that depict them engaged in the activity they are claiming. Showing oneself rock climbing, for instance, would be difficult to manipulate or manufacture if it was not an individual's actual activity (see Donath, 1999, and below). Other research from an online dating context (Toma et al., 2008) found that individuals who used online date-finding services distorted their online self-presentation to a lesser extent the more their off-line acquaintances knew they were using these services. Similarly, Warkentin et al. (2010) investigated whether individuals' displays of information that could be used to hold them to account for self-presentations affected the frequency and degree of deception they displayed with respect to their claims about demographic characteristics and personal tastes and preferences. Although chat systems featured more deception than was present in social network profiles and e-mail, the presence of cues to off-line identity in any of these platforms reduced the level of deception in that medium, according to Warkentin et al.

Walther, Van Der Heide, Hamel, and Shulman (2009) tested warranting experimentally by juxtaposing flattering versus unflattering statements about an individual on mock-up Facebook profiles. The comments were made to appear to have been posted by the profile owner or by the owner's Facebook friends. Facebook provides a format in which an individual can indicate qualities about himself or herself via "about me" descriptions, favorite quotations, current activities, and so on and where one's acquaintances can also post comments reflecting the activities and characteristics of the profile host via postings on the host's "wall" (and other commenting systems). When individuals' suggestions about their own physical attractiveness (either positive and self-promoting or negative and self-denigrating) were contradicted by the cues contained in wall postings from friends, observers' ratings of the profile owner significantly reflected the friends' comments more than the profile owner's self-claims. A replication focusing on profile owners and friends' assessments of an individual's extraversion provided more ambiguous results. In related research, an experiment that varied only the coefficients representing the number of friends a Facebook profile owner appeared to have found a curvilinear relationship between the number of one's friends and the observers' ratings of the profile owner's popularity and social attractiveness (Tong, Van Der Heide, Langwell, & Walther, 2008). Although the sociometric friend coefficient did not contradict any particular self-generated claim of the profile owner, its effect nevertheless reinforces the influential nature of online information about a user that is beyond the immediate reach of the user to manipulate. A similar study by Utz (2010) examined observers' ratings of a profile owner's popularity and social attractiveness via the Dutch Hyves social network site. Profile mock-ups reflected variations in self-claims for extraversion, the photographically depicted extraversion of nine of one's friends, and the number of friends a profile owner had. An interaction effect between the number of friends and the apparent extraversion of friends significantly affected the social attractiveness ratings of the profile owner.

The warranting principle remains a relatively new construct at this time, although its empirical application in contemporary multimedia systems suggests that it is likely to see additional rather than decreased use. Concerns about the legitimacy of others' online self-presentations has been a pernicious issue related to CMC since before the widespread diffusion of the Internet (see Van Gelder, 1985), and sensationalistic accounts of identity deception and manipulation still attract headlines (Labi, 2007). Likewise, as systems for meeting new friends and lovers shift from the casual discussion site to purposive online dating sites, concerns about others' online authenticity continues (Lawson & Leck, 2006). Theoretical structures that help explain how

CMC users assess the veridicality of others' online self-presentations may increase in value.

## Efficiency Framework

A new framework was developed to resolve previously contradictory findings about satisfaction with, and the effectiveness of, CMC collaboration. Its investigation has incorporated very novel CMC technologies and has implicated presence as a mediating factor.

The framework's developers, Nowak, Watt, and Walther (2005, 2009), noted that many studies of CMC generated relatively low ratings on interpersonal satisfaction and related notions (typically in field experiments or surveys) compared with ratings of face-to-face communication or video communication. Although researchers are frequently aware of the known linkage between interpersonal cohesiveness and productivity or quality, many of the same studies in which CMC earned lower sociability ratings found no deleterious effects of CMC on task accomplishment. For example, Galagher and Kraut (1994) found that text-based CMC groups were less satisfied with their communication than video-mediated groups but that there were no significant differences in the quality of the outputs that these conditions produced. Research assessing CMC often relies on measurements of its subjective appeal and does not consider its instrumental utility for communicative tasks independently.

Nowak et al. (2009) argue that users are likely to conflate their impressions of CMC's presence and satisfaction with their estimates of its utility. Enjoyment or frustration responses override an individual's objective assessment of effectiveness, and individuals may be expected to dislike CMC when there are easier alternatives (see Korzenny's, 1978, electronic propinquity theory, described above). People are cognitive and behavioral misers, as Nowak et al. (2009) note, and prefer to do a task using less effort than using more effort. Compared with face-to-face communication, CMC is more effortful. Face-to-face communication is intuitive and provides rapid exchange of

information through multiple modalities. Drawing on SIP theory, CMC may be just as capable as face-to-face interaction in achieving task and social outcomes, but it requires more time and effort, which are inherently less desirable in most cases than doing things in an easier way. There is a natural efficiency to face-to-face communication that is often satisfying.

Satisfaction and utility may be unrelated, however, or even inversely related, depending on the task. When people collaborate on writing something together, for instance, talk is only useful to a point. In contrast, if collaborators plan, organize, and execute a writing task via the written (and stored and editable) medium of CMC, it may provide a greater efficiency in the long run, since things have been made recorded, retrievable, and reusable in a way that speech is not. This process is not less effortful than talk. Greater effort, however, in addition to being frustrating, may lead to better outcomes. In this way, the efficiency framework attempts to explain how, within and across studies, CMC may be rated as socially unsatisfactory but, nevertheless, may offer instrumental benefits. To evaluate CMC on an affective basis alone, which is common, may be misleading from a utilitarian perspective.

Empirical research on the efficiency framework has been extremely limited. One study involved small groups collaborating on the preparation of presentations for five weeks, using face-to-face meetings, text-based real-time chats at specific times, asynchronous text-based conferencing, real-time videoconferencing, or an asynchronous video communication system that allowed members to record, leave, and play multimodal messages to and from one another (Nowak et al., 2009). Consistent with previous research and the efficiency framework's predictions, self-administered questionnaires showed higher scores on presence and conversational involvement for face-to-face communication above all other conditions. A greater number of cue systems also led to greater subjective project quality and satisfaction, as did synchronous (compared with asynchronous) media. With respect to the objective quality of their projects, however, external coders' ratings identified the asynchronous video condition as having facilitated the best actual work, with no other differences between conditions. Real-time versus asynchronous comparisons did not affect the quality of the work.

Although this perspective seems especially suited for the study of mediated collaborations, its central lessons may apply to a variety of interpersonal as well as instrumental settings as media characteristics evolve: Those media that are the easiest to use may not, in fact, offer the greatest instrumental benefit. As interface options increase and become more natural, more research will be needed that separates affective reactions from those pertaining to interaction goals. In strictly recreational social settings, these two aspects—social and purposive outcomes—may be isomorphic. As new electronic media such as avatar-based systems and desktop video are employed for an increasing number of activities, including the common instrumentalities that make up so much of the maintenance of ongoing relationships, whether easier is better or not, will deserve continued reexamination.

## ICT Succession

Perhaps the most recent new framework about CMC is Stephens's (2007) prescriptive formulation involving the strategic sequencing of messages across multiple communication channels. This approach recognizes different forms of information and communication technologies (ICTs), including traditional media, face-to-face channels, and newer forms of CMC. It primarily concerns how combinations of ICTs predict communication effectiveness in organizational communication, although it includes predictions related to the use of the media for "tasks that are personal and social in nature" (p. 499).

In terms of its structure, the ICT succession model presents several propositions inferred by the author from principles and findings in a wide variety of literatures, rather than deriving them from a set of related higher order constructs. The major theoretical terms of the model can be identified as (a) successive (vs. single) message transmissions and (b) complementary (vs. singular) channel usage. The central proposition of the model is that the repetition of a message through two different types of communication channels causes the greatest communication effectiveness and efficiency (for certain types of tasks). For example, a message sent once face-to-face might be followed up by e-mail, or vice versa, which should be more effective than repeating messages using a single medium (or no repetitions at all).

Among these terms and relationships, singular versus successive messaging is easily defined: A communicator may send a message once or send it more than once. The definition of complementary modalities is less clear. The model reflects a variety of different approaches to identify groupings of channels based on criteria found in other CMC theories as well as in perceptual studies of media uses and gratifications (Flanagin & Metzger, 2001), rather than on the basis of some underlying functional property. It clusters channels into the following groups: face-to-face, mass media, oral media, or textual media. Although a proposition refers to "maximizing modalities through complementary successive ICT use" (Stephens, 2007, p. 496), the theory does not indicate what kind of combinations among different ICT groups would be optimally complementary. It may be that the use of two nominally different ICTs constitutes sufficient complementarity, although later propositions address the superiority of mass media as an initial medium and elsewhere the benefit of text-based media for subsequent messages.

The ICT succession model received mixed empirical support in a recent experiment (Stephens & Rains, 2011). Research confederates either e-mailed a persuasive message to participants encouraging them to use the career services center at their universities or read the message face-to-face to the participant. A few minutes later, based on the experimental condition, one of several events transpired: (a) a confederate then communicated a second message, with different content, that also advocated using the career services center, using either the same channel (e-mail or face-to-face) as the first message or the other of the two channels, or (b) a confederate provided a message about a different topic using one or other of the media combinations. This experimental design allowed the researchers to examine the influence of media succession on outcomes independently of the effect of the simple addition of more persuasive arguments. Results revealed significantly greater intention to use the career services center when messages were conveyed using complementary successive messages than when other message/media combinations were used, although attitudes (rather than intentions), information effectiveness perceptions, and recall did not differ among the conditions as predicted. Complementary media effects overrode the simple effects of being exposed to multiple messages.

In one sense, the ICT succession theory offers a modest digital-age update and elaboration to conventional suggestions. As Koehler, Anatol, and Applbaum wrote in their 1976 organizational communication textbook, "We suggest that a combination of oral and written (printed) media are more effective in achieving employee understanding than either oral or written messages alone" (p. 204). The initial empirical research compared two media that are rather conventional by current standards, and despite the Stephens and Rains (2011) article's title alluding to interpersonal interaction, no interpersonal processes per se seem to have been involved. Nevertheless, other aspects of the researchers' discussion of the model offer a glimpse at research to come that may expand the scope of the predictions beyond conventional wisdom or first-generation Internet applications. When the authors point out that "ICTs such as mobile phones, e-mail, text messaging, and instant messaging have made it increasingly possible to communicate repeated messages over time" (p. 102), they open the door to the discovery of media selection strategies that may go well

beyond choices based on differences in the number of code systems supported by different media. How communication partners may choose among many more options than simply just written versus oral ones may be an interesting focus of inquiry and illuminate much about communicators' literacies, opportunities, effort economies, and communication strategies. These issues will bear repeated attention across both organizational and relational contexts such as the development of friendships, courtship, maintenance, conflict, and perhaps relational dissolution. The issue of multimodality is addressed more fully below, after some other concluding observations.

## Challenges to CMC Research

This review ends with some notes of concern about current trends in CMC research. These concerns focus on three issues: (1) the increasing neglect of off-line comparisons in CMC studies, potentially undermining broad theoretical understanding and leading to potentially inflated views of CMC's effects; (2) how and whether new technologies affect the utility of theories that were developed in the context of somewhat older technological contexts; and (3) how we study interpersonal communication when many relationships are radically multimodal.

There appears to be an increasing tendency for CMC research to focus on different features and different users of CMC and not to make comparisons with face-to-face communication or communication using other traditional media. This trend is supported by different disciplinary orientations about what questions should concern us and by the development of research tools that make CMC much easier to analyze than its off-line counterpart. For a number of years, many researchers have extolled the end of the face-to-face "gold standard" for CMC research (for a review, see Nardi & Whittaker, 2002), meaning that online behavior itself is a legitimate and significant focus of study and that descriptions of it, or comparisons of different interfaces or users, are sufficiently interesting without having to compare observations of online to off-line behavior. Technology design research, for example, may largely be uninformed by what happens off-line, since its focus is on the discovery of technology users' needs and preferences and the evaluation of technology features that optimally address those criteria.

Additionally, there has been significant growth in the development of low-cost computer programs that provide powerful analyses of digitally represented behavior. In particular, language analysis programs that can be applied to large corpuses of digital texts have made online behavior more amenable to analysis and made textual analysis far less onerous than it previously was. The ease, cost, availability, and power of these applications make them very appealing. At the same time, their availability may privilege analysis of the kind of digital primary data to which the programs are especially well suited and facilitate disregard for the analysis of analog face-to-face interaction recordings, which require significant resources to transcribe and/or prepare for digital analysis.

These factors, as well as others, may be promoting the analysis of online interpersonal behavior more frequently and of off-line behavior less so. Although to many of us the dynamics of organic online behavior are often quite interesting, the lack of comparison with off-line behaviors has the potential to lead to artificial conclusions. We may infer support using native digital sources for theoretically universal effects when the effects are limited. We may likewise conclude that certain behaviors are primarily or exclusively the result of various qualities of media, but without comparison with off-line behavior that may exhibit similar patterns, such conclusions may be fallacious and misleading.

Second, questions arise whether new technologies should lead us to retire theories that were developed in light of other, older technologies. Good ways to ask these questions examine the boundary conditions and scope of extant theories. We should always assess how the topography of new technologies' features meet or violate the assumptions of a theory. As discussed above, theories that were premised on the lack of

visual information about one's partners may not hold as much utility for multimedia interfaces. At the same time, advances in technology-enabled social arrangements allow us to see if theories can stretch their original assumptive boundaries. Human and Lane (2008), for instance, have appropriated elements of electronic propinquity theory and the hyperpersonal model to try to account for the idealization that emerges through the online communication that takes place between the occasional face-to-face meetings of geographically separated off-line relational partners. Exploring the degree to which the processes implicated in older models may be reconfigured for newer media presents intriguing possibilities (as is demonstrably the case with electronic propinquity theory). To the extent that the older media's boundary conditions continue to appear within other, newer systems, the vitality of the theories remains even if the scope of their application declines. When multimedia news stories or videos appear in a Web 2.0 application but are accompanied by user-generated comments appearing as anonymous, plain-text messages, for example, theories premised on unimodal media and focused on anonymity remain quite potent with respect to the effects of the comments.

Finally, just as the previous *Handbook* suggested that relationships may develop through multiple modalities (Walther & Parks, 2002), many researchers have come to suggest that interpersonal communication research must explicitly recognize that contemporary relationships are not conducted through one medium or another but often through a great variety of channels. Multimodality has become the primary channel characteristic of interpersonal relationships:

> We conduct our relationships face-to-face, over the phone, and online through modes as diverse as e-mail, instant messaging, social network friending, personal messages, comments, shared participation in discussion forums and online games, and the sharing of digital photos, music, and videos. (Baym, 2009, p. 721)

Research has yet to conceptualize what this means for the study of relationships, except by reference to media ecologies (e.g., Barnes, 2009), the implications of which are not yet clear beyond phenomenological levels. Even advocates of a multimodal perspective at times do no more than survey individuals about the use of all their Internet and mobile applications and enter their total new technology use as one undifferentiated predictor variable comparing new technology, old media, and face-to-face interaction on relational outcomes of some kind. In contrast, other researchers have advanced good questions based on established theories applied to new media to describe and explain the disappointing effects of moving a new relationship from online to off-line and back (e.g., Ramirez & Wang, 2008; Ramirez & Zhang, 2007).

We will need new theoretical concepts with which to describe the functional attributes of groups of technologies. Qualities such as the opportunistic availability of different media (e.g., texting or mobile-enabled microblogging) may be such a concept. Economy of effort may be a useful property with which to describe social media that allow one to contribute to the maintenance of numerous relationships with a single message. Knowing which applications provide asymmetrical interpersonal information-seeking (I can Google you without you knowing it) or symmetrical requirements (You have to grant me access to your Facebook profile before you can see mine) may be a useful frame, depending on the theoretical questions these phenomena arouse. It is also likely that different media are used in functional, strategic sequences (beyond repetition) that may illuminate relational patterns. Our chapter in the previous *Handbook* quoted Mitchell (1995): "Hacker lore has it that burgeoning cyberspace romances progress through broadening bandwidth and multiplying modalities—from exchange of e-mail to phone and photo, then taking the big step of going (face-to-face), then climbing into bed" (p. 19). Lore aside, technology sequences and their relational significance deserve an update: If a man takes an interest in a woman he sees in a class, he

may want to scan the Web for information about her. If that search suggests potential reward, he may talk to her to establish a minimal basis of familiarity so that he can request access to her social network profile and be able to see how many friends she has, what they look like, what their comments have to say about her, and how she interacts with them in turn. If results are encouraging, a face-to-face conversation may come next, followed by a reinforcing e-mail or social network posting. Do increases in channel access signify relational escalation? Do we meet new partners' Flickr family photo collection before we meet the parents, and why? Rather than resign ourselves to undifferentiated, massive multimodality, future research may begin to contemplate the strategic and interpersonal signification possibilities it presents as its users exploit the vast relational potentials of CMC.

# References

Amichai-Hamburger, Y. (Ed.). (2005). *The social net: Understanding human behavior in cyberspace.* Oxford, UK: Oxford University Press.

Amichai-Hamburger, Y. (2007). Personality, individual differences and Internet use. In A. Joinson, K. McKenna, T. Postmes, & U.-D. Reips (Eds.), *The Oxford handbook of Internet psychology* (pp. 187–204). Oxford, UK: Oxford University Press.

Antheunis, M. L., Valkenburg, P. M., & Peter, J. (2007). Computer-mediated communication and interpersonal attraction: An experimental test of two explanatory hypotheses. *CyberPsychology & Behavior, 10,* 831–835.

Antheunis, M. L., Valkenburg, P. M., & Peter, J. (2010). Getting acquainted through social network sites: Testing a model of online uncertainty reduction and social attraction. *Computers in Human Behavior, 26,* 100–109.

Baker, S. C., Wentz, R. K., & Woods, M. M. (2009). Using virtual worlds in education: Second life as an educational tool. *Teaching of Psychology, 36,* 59–64.

Barnes, S. B. (2009). Relationship networking: Society and education. *Journal of Computer-Mediated Communication, 14,* 735–742.

Baym, N. K. (2009). A call for grounding in the face of blurred boundaries. *Journal of Computer-Mediated Communication, 14,* 720–723.

Baym, N. K. (2010). *Personal connections in the digital age.* Cambridge, UK: Polity Press.

Bente, G., Rüggenberg, S., Krämer, N. C., & Eschenburg, F. (2008). Avatar-mediated networking: Increasing social presence and interpersonal trust in net-based collaborations. *Human Communication Research, 34,* 287–318.

Biocca, F., Harms, C., & Burgoon, J. K. (2003). Toward a more robust theory and measure of social presence: Review and suggested criteria. *Presence: Teleoperators and Virtual Environments, 12,* 456–480.

boyd, d. (2007). Why youth ♥ social network sites: The role of networked publics in teenage social life. In D. Buckingham (Ed.) *Youth, identity, and digital media* (pp. 119–142). Cambridge: MIT Press.

Burgoon, J. K., & Le Poire, B. A. (1993). Effects of communication expectancies, actual communication, and expectancy disconfirmation on evaluations of communicators and their communication behavior. *Human Communication Research, 20,* 67–96.

Caplan, S. E. (2003). Preference for online social interaction: A theory of problematic Internet use and psychosocial well-being. *Communication Research, 30,* 625–648.

Caplan, S. E. (2005). A social skill account of problematic Internet use. *Journal of Communication, 55,* 721–736.

Carlson, J. R., & Zmud, R. W. (1994). Channel expansion theory: A dynamic view of media and information richness perceptions. In D. P. Moore (Ed.), *Academy of Management: Best papers proceedings 1994* (pp. 280–284). Madison, WI: Omnipress.

Carlson, J. R., & Zmud, R. W. (1999). Channel expansion theory and the experiential nature of media richness perceptions. *Academy of Management Journal, 42,* 153–170.

Childress, M. D., & Braswell, R. (2006). Using massively multiplayer online role-playing games for online learning. *Distance Education, 27,* 187–196.

Collins, N. L., & Miller, L. C. (1994). Self-disclosure and liking: A meta-analytic review. *Psychological Bulletin, 116,* 457–475.

Culnan, M. J., & Markus, M. L. (1987). Information technologies. In F. M. Jablin, L. L. Putnam, K. H. Roberts, & L. W. Porter (Eds.), *Handbook of organizational communication: An interdisciplinary perspective* (pp. 420–443). Newbury Park, CA: Sage.

Cummings, J. M., Lee, J. B., & Kraut, R. E. (2006). Communication technology and friendship during the transition from high school to college. In R. E. Kraut, M. Brynin, & S. Kiesler (Eds.), *Computers, phones, and the Internet: Domesticating information technology* (pp. 265–278). New York: Oxford University Press.

Daft, R. L., & Lengel, R. H. (1984). Information richness: A new approach to managerial behavior and organization design. In B. M. Staw & L. L. Cummings (Eds.), *Research in organizational behavior* (Vol. 6, pp. 191–233). Greenwich, CT: JAI Press.

Daft, R. L., & Lengel, R. H. (1986). Organizational information requirements, media richness and structural design. *Management Science, 32,* 554–571.

Daft, R. L., Lengel, R. H., & Trevino, L. K. (1987). Message equivocality, media selection, and manager performance: Implications for information systems. *MIS Quarterly, 11,* 355–368.

DeAndrea, D. C., & Walther, J. B. (in press). Attributions for inconsistencies between online and offline self-presentations. *Communication Research.*

Dennis, A. R., & Kinney, S. T. (1998). Testing media richness theory in the new media: The effects of cues, feedback, and task equivocality. *Information Systems Research, 9,* 256–274.

Derks, D., Bos, A. E. R., & von Grumbkow, J. (2007). Emoticons and social interaction on the Internet: The importance of social context. *Computers in Human Behavior, 23,* 842–849.

Di Blasio, P., & Milani, L. (2008). Computer-mediated communication and persuasion: Peripheral vs. central routes to opinion shift. *Computers in Human Behavior, 24,* 798–815.

Donath, J. (1999). Identity and deception in the virtual community. In M. A. Smith & P. Kollock (Eds.), *Communities in cyberspace* (pp. 29–59). New York: Routledge.

Donath, J. (2007). Signals in social supernets. *Journal of Computer-Mediated Communication, 13*(1), Article 12. Retrieved January 20, 2008, from http://jcmc.indiana.edu/vol13/issue1/donath.html

Douglas, K. M., & McGarty, C. (2001). Identifiability and self-presentation: Computer-mediated communication and intergroup interaction. *British Journal of Social Psychology, 40,* 399–416.

Duck, S., Rutt, D. J., Hurst, M. H., & Strejc, H. (1991). Some evident truths about conversations in everyday relationships: All communications are not created equal. *Human Communication Research, 18,* 228–267.

D'Urso, S. C., & Rains, S. A. (2008). Examining the scope of channel expansion: A test of channel expansion theory with new and traditional communication media. *Management Communication Quarterly, 21,* 486–507.

Ellison, N. B., Heino, R. D., & Gibbs, J. L. (2006). Managing impressions online: Self-presentation processes in the online dating environment. *Journal of Computer-Mediated Communication, 11*(2), Article 2. Retrieved January 30, 2007, from http://jcmc.indiana.edu/vol11/issue2/ellison.html

Epley, N., & Kruger, J. (2005). What you type isn't what they read: The perseverance of stereotypes and expectancies over e-mail. *Journal of Experimental Social Psychology, 41,* 414–422.

Flanagin, A. J., & Metzger, M. J. (2001). Internet use in the contemporary media environment. *Human Communication Research, 27,* 153–181.

Foulger, D. A. (1990). *Medium as process: The structure, use, and practice of computer conferencing on IBM's IBMPC computer conferencing facility.* Unpublished doctoral dissertation, Temple University, Pennsylvania.

Fulk, J., & Gould, J. J. (2009). Features and contexts in technology research: A modest proposal for research and reporting. *Journal of Computer-Mediated Communication, 14,* 764–770.

Fulk, J., Schmitz, J., & Ryu, D. (1995). Cognitive elements in the social construction of communication technology. *Management Communication Quarterly, 8,* 259–288.

Fulk, J., Schmitz, J., & Steinfield, C. (1990). A social influence model of technology use. In J. Fulk & C. Steinfeld (Eds.), *Organizations and communication technology* (pp. 71–94). Newbury Park, CA: Sage.

Fulk, J., Steinfield, C., Schmitz, J., & Power, J. G. (1987). A social information processing model of media use in organizations. *Communication Research, 14*(5), 529–552.

Galagher, J., & Kraut, R. E. (1994). Computer-mediated communication for intellectual teamwork: An experiment in group writing. *Information Systems Research, 5,* 110–138.

Gibbs, J. L., Ellison, N. B., & Heino, R. D. (2006). Self-presentation in online personals: The role of anticipated future interaction, self-disclosure, and perceived success in Internet dating. *Communication Research, 33,* 1–26.

Gonzales, A. L., & Hancock, J. T. (2008). Identity shift in computer-mediated environments. *Media Psychology, 11,* 167–185.

Guadagno, R. E., & Cialdini, R. B. (2002). Online persuasion: An examination of gender differences in computer-mediated interpersonal influence. *Group Dynamics: Theory Research and Practice, 6,* 38–51.

Guadagno, R. E., & Cialdini, R. B. (2007). Persuade him by email, but see her in person: Online persuasion revisited. *Computers in Human Behavior, 23,* 999–1015.

Gunawardena, C. N. (2004). Designing the social environment for online learning: The role of social presence. In D. Murphy, R. Carr, J. Taylor, & T. Wong (Eds.), *Distance education and technology: Issues and practice* (pp. 255–270). Hong Kong: Open University of Hong Kong Press.

Hall, E. T. (1976). *Beyond culture.* New York: Doubleday.

Hall, J. A., Park, N., Song, H., & Cody, M. J. (2010). Strategic misrepresentation in online dating: The effects of gender, self-monitoring, and personality traits. *Journal of Social and Personal Relations, 27,* 117–135.

Hancock, J. T., Thom-Santelli, J., & Ritchie, T. (2004). Deception and design: The impact of communication technologies on lying behavior. In E. Dykstra-Erickson & M. Tscheligi (Eds.), *Proceedings of the ACM Conference on Human Factors in Computing Systems* (CHI 2004, Vol. 6, pp. 130–136). New York: ACM.

Hancock, J. T., & Toma, C. L. (2009). Putting your best face forward: The accuracy of online dating photographs. *Journal of Communication, 59,* 367–386.

Heino, R. D., Ellison, N. B., & Gibbs, J. L. (2010). Relationshopping: Investigating the market metaphor in online dating. *Journal of Social and Personal Relationships, 27,* 427–447.

Hian, L. B., Chuan, S. L., Trevor, T. M. K., & Detenber, B. H. (2004). Getting to know you: Exploring the development of relational intimacy in computer-mediated communication. *Journal of Computer-Mediated Communication, 9*(3). Retrieved January 3, 2007, from http://jcmc.indiana.edu/vol9/issue3/detenber.html

Hiltz, S. R., Johnson, K., & Agle, G. (1978). *Replicating Bales' problem solving experiments on a computerized conference: A pilot study* (Research Report No. 8). Newark, NJ: New Jersey Institute of Technology, Computerized Conferencing and Communications Center.

Human, R., & Lane, D. (2008, November). *Virtually friends in cyberspace: Explaining the migration from FtF to CMC relationships with electronic functional propinquity theory.* Paper presented at the annual meeting of the National Communication Association, San Diego, CA.

Ickes, W., Patterson, M. L., Rajecki, D. W., & Tanford, S. (1982). Behavioral and cognitive consequences of reciprocal versus compensatory responses to pre-interaction expectancies. *Social Cognition, 1,* 160–190.

Jacobson, D. (1999). Impression formation in cyberspace: Online expectations and offline experiences in text-based virtual communities. *Journal of Computer-Mediated Communication, 5*(1). Retrieved March 31, 2011, from http://jcmc.indiana.edu/vol5/issue1/jacobson.html

Jiang, C. L., Bazarova, N. N., & Hancock, J. T. (2011). The disclosure-intimacy link in computer-mediated communication: An attributional extension of the hyperpersonal model. *Human Communication Research, 37,* 58–77.

Joinson, A. N. (2001). Self-disclosure in computer-mediated communication: The role of self-awareness and visual anonymity. *European Journal of Social Psychology, 31,* 177–192.

Joinson, A., McKenna, K., Postmes, T., & Reips, U.-D. (Eds.). (2007). *The Oxford handbook of Internet psychology.* Oxford, UK: Oxford University Press.

Katz, J. E., & Rice, R. E. (2002). *Social consequences of Internet use: Access, involvement, and interaction.* Cambridge: MIT Press.

Kelly, J. R., & McGrath, J. E. (1985). Effects of time limits and task types on task performance and interaction of four-person groups. *Journal of Personality and Social Psychology, 49,* 395–407.

Kenny, D. A. (1994). *Interpersonal perception: A social relations analysis.* New York: Guilford Press.

Kim, J., & Dindia, K. (2011). Online self-disclosure: A review of research. In K. B. Wright & L. M. Webb (Eds.), *Computer-mediated communication in personal relationships* (pp. 156–181). New York: Peter Lang.

Klimmt, C., & Hartmann, T. (2008). Mediated interpersonal communication in multiplayer video-games: Implications for entertainment and relationship management. In E. A. Konijn, S. Utz, M. Tanis, & S. B. Barnes (Eds.), *Mediated interpersonal communication* (pp. 309–330). New York: Routledge.

Koehler, J. W., Anatol, K. W. E., & Applbaum, R. L. (1976). *Organizational communication: Behavioral perspectives.* New York: Holt, Rinehart, & Winston.

Konijn, E. A., Utz, S., Tanis, M., & Barnes, S. B. (Eds.). (2008). *Mediated interpersonal communication.* New York: Routledge.

Korzenny, F. (1978). A theory of electronic propinquity: Mediated communication in organizations. *Communication Research, 5,* 3–24.

Korzenny, F., & Bauer, C. (1981). Testing the theory of electronic propinquity. *Communication Research, 8,* 479–498.

Labi, N. (2007, September). An IM infatuation turned to romance. Then the truth came out. *WIRED, 15*(9), 149–153.

Lawson, H. M., & Leck, K. (2006). Dynamics of Internet dating. *Social Science Computer Review, 24,* 189–208.

Lea, M., & Spears, R. (1992). Paralanguage and social perception in computer-mediated communication. *Journal of Organizational Computing, 2,* 321–341.

Lea, M., & Spears, R. (1995). Love at first byte? Building personal relationships over computer networks. In J. T. Wood & S. Duck (Eds.), *Understudied relationships: Off the beaten track* (pp. 197–233). Thousand Oaks, CA: Sage.

Lea, M., Spears, R., & de Groot, D. (2001). Knowing me, knowing you: Anonymity effects on social identity processes within groups. *Personality and Social Psychology Bulletin, 27,* 526–537.

Lee, E.-J. (2004). Effects of visual representation on social influence in computer-mediated communication. *Human Communication Research, 30,* 234–259.

Lee, K. M. (2004). Presence, explicated. *Communication Theory, 14,* 27–50.

Lombard, M., & Ditton, T. (1997). At the heart of it all: The concept of presence. *Journal of Computer-Mediated Communication, 3*(2). Retrieved March 9, 1999, from http://jcmc.indiana.edu/vol3/issue2/lombard.html

Markey, P. M., & Wells, S. M. (2002). Interpersonal perception in Internet chat rooms. *Journal of Research in Personality, 36,* 134–146.

Markus, M. L. (1994). Electronic mail as the medium of managerial choice. *Organization Science, 5,* 502–527.

Metzger, M. J., Flanagin, A. J., Eyal, K., Lemus, D. R., & McCann, R. M. (2003). Credibility for the 21st century: Integrating perspectives on source, message, and media credibility in the contemporary media environment. In P. J. Kalbfleisch (Ed.),

*Communication yearbook 27* (pp. 293–335). New York: Routledge.

Mitchell, W. J. (1995). *City of bits: Space, place, and the infobahn.* Cambridge: MIT Press.

Monge, P. R. (1980). Multivariate multiple regression. In P. R. Monge & J. N. Cappella (Eds.), *Multivariate techniques in human communication research* pp. 13–56. New York: Academic Press.

Nardi, B., & Whittaker, S. (2002). The place of face to face communication in distributed work. In P. J. Hinds & S. Kiesler (Eds.), *Distributed work: New research on working across distance using technology* (pp. 83–110). Cambridge: MIT Press.

Nowak, K., Watt, J. H., & Walther, J. (2005). The influence of synchrony and sensory modality on the person perception process in computer mediated groups. *Journal of Computer-Mediated Communication, 10* (3). Retrieved February 1, 2006, from http://jcmc.indiana.edu/vol10/issue3/nowak.html

Nowak, K., Watt, J. H., & Walther, J. B. (2009). Computer mediated teamwork and the efficiency framework: Exploring the influence of synchrony and cues on media satisfaction and outcome success. *Computers in Human Behavior, 25,* 1108–1119.

Nowak, K. L., & Biocca, F. (2003). The effect of the agency and anthropomorphism on users' sense of telepresence, copresence, and social presence in virtual environments. *Presence: Teleoperators and Virtual Environments, 12,* 481–494.

Oren, A., Mioduser, D., & Nachmias, R. (2002). The development of social climate in virtual learning discussion groups. *International Review of Research in Open and Distance Learning, 3*(1), 1–19.

Papacharissi, Z. (Ed.). (2010). *A networked self: Identity, community and culture on social network sites.* New York: Routledge.

Parks, M. R., & Floyd, K. (1996). Making friends in cyberspace. *Journal of Communication, 40,* 80–97.

Parks, M. R., & Roberts, L. (1998). Making MOOsic: The development of personal relationships on line and a comparison to their off-line counterparts. *Journal of Social and Personal Relationships, 15,* 517–537.

Peña, J., & Hancock, J. T. (2006). An analysis of socio-emotional and task-oriented communication in an online multiplayer video game. *Communication Research, 33,* 92–109.

Peter, J., Valkenburg, P. M., & Schouten, A. P. (2005). Developing a model of adolescent friendship formation on the Internet. *Cyberpsychology & Behavior, 8,* 423–430.

Petty, R. E., & Cacioppo, J. T. (1986). The elaboration likelihood model of persuasion. *Advances in Experimental Social Psychology, 19,* 123–205.

Postmes, T., Baray, G., Haslam, S. A., Morton, T., & Swaab, R. (2006). The dynamics of personal and social identity formation. In T. Postmes & J. Jetten (Eds.), *Individuality and the group: Advances in social identity* (pp. 215–236). London: Sage.

Postmes, T., & Baym, N. (2005). Intergroup dimensions of Internet. In J. Harwood & H. Giles (Eds.), *Intergroup communication: Multiple perspectives* (pp. 213–238). New York: Peter Lang.

Postmes, T., Spears, R., Lee, A. T., & Novak, R. J. (2005). Individuality and social influence in groups: Inductive and deductive routes to group identity. *Journal of Personality and Social Psychology, 89,* 747–763.

Rains, S. A., & Scott, C. R. (2007). To identify or not to identify: A theoretical model of receiver responses to anonymous communication. *Communication Theory, 17,* 61–91.

Ramirez, A., Jr., & Wang, Z. (2008). When online meets offline: An expectancy violation theory perspective on modality switching. *Journal of Communication, 58,* 20–39.

Ramirez, A., Jr., & Zhang, S. (2007). When online meets offline: The effect of modality switching on relational communication. *Communication Monographs, 74,* 287–310.

Ramirez, A., Jr., Zhang, S., McGrew, K., & Lin, S.-F. (2007). Relational communication in computer-mediated interaction: A comparison of participant-observer perspectives. *Communication Monographs, 74,* 492–516.

Rau, P.-L. P., Peng, S.-Y., & Yang, C.-C. (2006). Time distortion for expert and novice online game players. *CyberPsychology & Behavior, 9,* 396–403.

Reicher, S. D., Spears, R., & Postmes, T. (1995). A social identity model of deindividuation phenomena. *European Review of Social Psychology, 6,* 161–198.

Rice, R. E., & Case, D. (1983). Electronic message systems in the University: A description of use and utility. *Journal of Communication, 33*(1), 131–152.

Roberts, L. D., Smith, L. M., & Pollock, C. (1996, September). *A model of social interaction via computer-mediated communication in real-time text-based virtual environments.* Paper presented at the meeting of the Australian Psychological Society, Sydney, New South Wales, Australia.

Rogers, P., & Lea, M. (2004). Cohesion in online groups. In K. Morgan, C. A. Brebbia, J. Sanchez, & A. Voiskounsky (Eds), *Human perspectives in the Internet society: Culture, psychology and gender* (pp.115–124). Southampton, UK: WIT Press.

Sackett, A. M., Nelson, L. D., Meyvis, T., Converse, B. A., & Sackett, A. L. (2009). You're having fun when time flies: The hedonic consequences of subjective time progression. *Psychological Science, 21,* 111–117.

Sanders, R. E. (1997). Find your partner and do-si-do: The formation of personal relationships between social beings. *Journal of Social and Personal Relationships, 14,* 387–415.

Schouten, A. P., Valkenburg, P. M., & Peter, J. (2007). Precursors and underlying processes of adolescents' online self-disclosure: Developing and testing an "Internet-attribute-perception" model. *Media Psychology, 10,* 292–315.

Scott, C. R. (2009). A whole-hearted effort to get it half right: Predicting the future of communication technology scholarship. *Journal of Computer-Mediated Communication, 14,* 753–757.

Setlock, L. D., Quinones, P.-A., & Fussell, S. R. (2007). Does culture interact with media richness? The effects of audio vs. video conferencing on Chinese and American dyads. In *Proceedings of the 40th annual Hawaii International Conference on System Sciences.* Retrieved September 1, 2009, from http://csdl2.computer.org/comp/proceedings/hicss/2007/2755/00/27550013.pdf

Short, J., Williams, E., & Christie, B. (1976). *The social psychology of telecommunications.* London: Wiley.

Siegel, J., Dubrovsky, V., Kiesler, S., & Mcguire, T. W. (1986). Group processes in computer-mediated communication. *Organizational Behavior and Human Decision Processes, 37,* 157–187.

Snyder, M., Tanke, E. D., & Berscheid, E. (1977). Social perception and interpersonal behavior: On the self-fulfilling nature of social stereotypes. *Journal of Experimental Social Psychology, 35,* 656–666.

Sproull, L., & Faraj, S. (1997). Atheism, sex, and databases: The Net as a social technology. In S. Kiesler (Ed.), *Cultures of the Internet* (pp. 35–51). Mahwah, NJ: Lawrence Erlbaum.

Sproull, L., & Kiesler, S. (1986). Reducing social context cues: Electronic mail in organizational communication. *Management Science, 32,* 1492–1512.

Stephens, K. K. (2007). The successive use of information and communication technologies at work. *Communication Theory, 17,* 486–507.

Stephens, K. K., & Rains, S. A. (2011). Information and communication technology sequences and message repetition in interpersonal interaction. *Communication Research, 38,* 101–122.

Stone, A. R. (1995). *The war of desire and technology at the close of the mechanical age.* Cambridge: MIT Press.

Sundar, S. S. (2008). The MAIN model: A heuristic approach to understanding technology effects on credibility. In M. J. Metzger & A. J. Flanagin (Eds.), *Digital media, youth, and credibility* (pp. 73–100). Cambridge: MIT Press.

Tajfel, H. (1978). *Differentiation between social groups: Studies in the social psychology of intergroup relations.* London: Academic Press.

Tajfel, H., & Turner, J. C. (1979). An integrative theory of intergroup conflict. In W. Austin & S. Worchel (Eds.), *The social psychology of intergroup relations* (pp. 33–47). Monterey, CA: Brooks/Cole.

Tanis, M., & Postmes, T. (2003). Social cues and impression formation in CMC. *Journal of Communication, 53,* 676–693.

Tidwell, L. C., & Walther, J. B. (2002). Computer-mediated communication effects on disclosure, impressions, and interpersonal evaluations: Getting to know one another a bit at a time. *Human Communication Research, 28,* 317–348.

Toma, C. L., Hancock, J. T., & Ellison, N. B. (2008). Separating fact from fiction: An examination of deceptive self-presentation in online dating profiles. *Personality and Social Psychology Bulletin, 34,* 1023–1036.

Tong, S. T., Van Der Heide, B., Langwell, L., & Walther, J. B. (2008). Too much of a good thing? The relationship between number of friends and interpersonal impressions on Facebook. *Journal of Computer-Mediated Communication, 13,* 531–549.

Tong, S. T., & Walther, J. B. (2011b). Relational maintenance and computer-mediated communication. In K. B. Wright & L. M. Webb (Eds.), *Computer-mediated communication in personal relationships* (pp. 98–119). New York: Peter Lang.

Tong, S. T., & Walther, J. B. (2011a). Just say "No thanks": Romantic rejection in computer-mediated communication. *Journal of Social and Personal Relationships 28,* 488–506.

Utz, S. (2010). Show me your friends and I will tell you what type of person you are: How one's profile, number of friends, and type of friends influence impression formation on social network sites.

*Journal of Computer-Mediated Communication, 15*, 314–335.

Valkenburg, P. M., & Peter, J. (2009). Social consequences of the Internet for adolescents: A decade of research. *Current Directions in Psychological Science, 15*, 1–5.

Van Der Heide, B. (2008, May). *Persuasion on the 'net: A synthetic propositional framework.* Paper presented at the annual meeting of the International Communication Association, Montreal, Quebec, Canada.

Van Gelder, L. (1996). The strange case of the electronic lover. In C. Dunlop & R. Kling (Eds.), *Computerization and controversy: Value conflicts and social choices* (pp. 533–547). Boston: Academic Press.

Walther, J. B. (1992). Interpersonal effects in computer-mediated interaction: A relational perspective. *Communication Research, 19*, 52–90.

Walther, J. B. (1996). Computer-mediated communication: Impersonal, interpersonal, and hyperpersonal interaction. *Communication Research, 23*, 3–43.

Walther, J. B. (2006). Nonverbal dynamics in computer-mediated communication, or :( and the net :('s with you, :) and you :) alone. In V. Manusov & M. L. Patterson (Eds.), *Handbook of nonverbal communication* (pp. 461–479). Thousand Oaks, CA: Sage.

Walther, J. B. (2007). Selective self-presentation in computer-mediated communication: Hyperpersonal dimensions of technology, language, and cognition. *Computers in Human Behavior, 23*, 2538–2557.

Walther, J. B. (2009). Theories, boundaries, and all of the above. *Journal of Computer-Mediated Communication, 14*, 748–752.

Walther, J. B. (2010). Computer-mediated communication. In C. R. Berger, M. E. Roloff, & D. R. Roskos-Ewoldsen (Eds.), *Handbook of communication science* (2nd ed., pp. 489–505). Thousand Oaks: Sage.

Walther, J. B., & Bazarova, N. (2008). Validation and application of electronic propinquity theory to computer-mediated communication in groups. *Communication Research, 35*, 622–645.

Walther, J. B., & Carr, C. T. (2010). Internet interaction and intergroup dynamics: Problems and solutions in computer-mediated communication. In H. Giles, S. Reid, & J. Harwood (Eds.), *The dynamics of intergroup communication* (pp. 209–220). New York: Peter Lang.

Walther, J. B., DeAndrea, D., Kim, J., & Anthony, J. (2010). The influence of online comments on perceptions of anti-marijuana public service announcements on YouTube. *Human Communication Research, 36*, 469–492.

Walther, J. B., DeAndrea, D. C., & Tong, S. T. (2010). Computer-mediated communication versus vocal communication in the amelioration of pre-interaction stereotypes: An examination of theories, assumptions, and methods in mediated communication research. *Media Psychology, 13*, 364–386.

Walther, J. B., Liang, Y., DeAndrea, D. C., Tong, S. T., Carr, C. T., Spottswood, E. L., et al. (2011). The effect of feedback on identity shift in computer-mediated communication. *Media Psychology, 14*, 1–26.

Walther, J. B., Loh, T., & Granka, L. (2005). Let me count the ways: The interchange of verbal and nonverbal cues in computer-mediated and face-to-face affinity. *Journal of Language and Social Psychology, 24*, 36–65.

Walther, J. B., & Parks, M. R. (2002). Cues filtered out, cues filtered in: Computer-mediated communication and relationships. In M. L. Knapp & J. A. Daly (Eds.), *Handbook of interpersonal communication* (3rd ed., pp. 529–563). Thousand Oaks, CA: Sage.

Walther, J. B., Van Der Heide, B., Hamel, L., & Shulman, H. (2009). Self-generated versus other-generated statements and impressions in computer-mediated communication: A test of warranting theory using Facebook. *Communication Research, 36*, 229–253.

Walther, J. B., Van Der Heide, B., Tong, S. T., Carr, C. T., & Atkin, C. K. (2010). The effects of interpersonal goals on inadvertent intrapersonal influence in computer-mediated communication. *Human Communication Research, 36*, 323–347.

Wang, Z. (2007, November). *Interpersonal and group level measures in attraction and group identification: A factor analysis approach.* Paper presented at the annual meeting of the National Communication Association, Chicago.

Wang, Z., Walther, J. B., & Hancock, J. T. (2009). Social identification and interpersonal communication in computer-mediated communication: What you do versus who you are in virtual groups. *Human Communication Research, 35*, 59–85.

Warkentin, D., Woodworth, M., Hancock, J. T., & Cormier, N. (2010). Warrants and deception in computer-mediated communication. In K. Inkpen & C. Gutwin (Eds.), *Proceedings of the 2010 ACM Conference on Computer Supported Cooperative Work* (pp. 9–12). New York: ACM.

Westerman, D. K., Van Der Heide, B., Klein, K. A., & Walther, J. B. (2008). How do people really seek information about others? Information seeking across Internet and traditional communication sources. *Journal of Computer-Mediated Communication, 13,* 751–767.

Whitty, M. (2008). Revealing the "real" me, searching for the "actual" you: Presentations of self on an Internet dating site. *Computers in Human Behavior, 24,* 1707–1723.

Whitty, M., & Carr, A. (2006). *Cyberspace romance: The psychology of online relationships.* New York: Palgrave MacMillan.

Wilson, J. M., Straus, S. G., & McEvily, W. J. (2006). All in due time: The development of trust in computer-mediated and face-to-face groups. *Organizational Behavior and Human Decision Processes, 99,* 16–33.

Wright, K. B., & Webb, L. M. (Eds.). (2011). *Computer-mediated communication in personal relationships.* New York: Peter Lang.

Yzer, M. C., & Southwell, B. G. (2008). New communication technologies, old questions. *American Behavioral Scientist, 25,* 8–20.

# CHAPTER 15

# Interpersonal Skills

*Brian H. Spitzberg*

*William R. Cupach*

Interpersonal skills are the sine qua non of social life. And yet, few things in life are so taken for granted as interpersonal and social skills. Like eating and walking, talking and interacting are part of the mundane landscape of everyday behavior. Ordinarily, we take notice of our own, or someone else's, interpersonal skills when they are exceptionally bad, exceptionally good, or simply not at all what we expected. The rest of the time, interpersonal skills tend to represent the ground for whatever is the focus of attention.

Despite the extent to which interpersonal skills occupy the status of "scenery" to everyday experience, there are few characteristics as vital to quality of life. Social and interpersonal skills are the means through which all human relationships are initiated, negotiated, maintained, transformed, and dissolved. They are the means through which conflicts are resolved, face is negotiated, and predicaments are managed. In short, interpersonal skills are the fulcrum on which the levers of social life are maneuvered. This chapter reviews the research and theory relevant to interpersonal skills and the role such skills play in interpersonal communication. It initially suffices to treat "interpersonal skills" and "social skills" as synonymous and as primitive terms referring to behaviors that facilitate competence in interaction. More precise definitions and distinctions will be explicated later in this chapter.

## The Rationale of Interpersonal Skills

### A Synoptic History of Interpersonal Skills

By most accounts, social scientific interest in interpersonal skills is relatively recent in origin. When the discipline of communication is traced to its historical origins, public speaking and persuasion are found to be the focal point of most literature. This again suggests the extent to which interpersonal skills serve as a mere backdrop to what are considered more important activities.

Nevertheless, intellectual interest in interpersonal skills can be found even among the pantheon of the most noted and influential communication scholars and philosophers. One of the earliest historical references to communication being treated as a skill is implicit in the characterization of the sophistic rhetorics of ancient Sicily (Kennedy, 1963). When property and status were made contingent on a person's ability to persuade judges in a forensic context, teachers arose to instruct people in the arts and skills of communication. Aristotle (1926), the most influential early philosopher of rhetoric, wrote relatively little about the interpersonal context per se but identified several important distinctions that would later be replicated in more contemporary discussions of interpersonal skills. For example, he noted that ultimately "the object of rhetoric is judgment," such that a communicator needs to "know how to put the judge into a certain frame of mind" (p. 169). The art and "skill" of rhetoric, therefore, was concerned with creating preferred impressions in the minds of the interlocutor or the audience. This key notion presages the contemporary interest in impression management. Cicero (1959) briefly discussed "tact" in conversation, which was considered necessary to avoid talking excessively about oneself, ignoring the status of conversants, or simply being "in any way awkward or tedious" (p. 211). Quintillian (1903) discusses several similar topics, including appropriateness of style, decorum, aptitude, adaptation ("One kind of style cannot suit every cause, or every auditor, or every character, or every occasion" X, 1, 4, p. 310), and specifically employs the phrase *skilled in speaking* in defining the competent rhetor.

Medieval literature is relatively silent regarding interpersonal skills (Menache, 1990). Wine (1981), however, suggests that the dominant model of social competence during this era was predicated on a "defect" conception of behavior. People who were socially incompetent were literally defective. Defect was diagnosed by the manifestation of deviant behavior, which in turn was attributable to physical, mental, or demonological causes. While the understanding of specific causes has changed considerably through the ages since, the basic notion of social competence being tied to personal defect is still very much in evidence in modern conceptions of competence.

Western intellectual interest in interpersonal skills heightened considerably during the Renaissance. After the plague, accumulated wealth was concentrated among a much smaller surviving population, which still operated by feudal and hereditary status structures. Among the societal trends that developed was an acute elaboration of the code of conduct in the context of royalty and "the court." The "art of conversation" became a popular subject of writing and education (Burke, 1993). Writers like Machiavelli emphasized the tactics through which a person achieves and maintains status, whereas others such as Stephano Guazzo emphasized aptitudes such as decorum. Decorum described a style of conversation that adapts vocal quality and verbal content to the context (Mohrmann, 1972). European writers such as de Sculdéry, Bussy-Rabutin, de Sévigné, and Boursault created models of communication in the salon, in which "conversation was the best indicator of the worth of an individual or of an entire group, enabling members of society to both measure and construct their personal status" (Goldsmith, 1988, p. 12). The rhetoric of the banquet became an art unto itself (Jeanneret, 1991).

Ehninger (1975) describes this era of rhetoric as one of ingratiation, the strategic attempt to create positive impressions of self by pleasing others. It is no accident that the development of elaborate codes of conduct, such as mannerisms, forms of address, and formal table manners served to erect social barriers potentially stronger than economic ones. A person might be able to come into wealth, but "manner" is something learned through the long enculturation process of being "born" into royalty and wealth. Meanwhile, as Wine (1981) suggests, outside the gilded courts and palaces during this era, explorations in biology and medicine altered the demonological defect model into a more "medical" defect model. The basic assumption of this model is that deviant behavior was the product of underlying structural defects of the body, which were often revealed through surface manifestations such as lesions, skull shape, or illness.

The 18th century brought forth the elocutionary movement, which was concerned with the "just and graceful management of the voice, countenance, and gesture in speaking" (Sheridan, 1762, p. II, 1). Textbooks identified precise behavioral representations of emotional displays, gestural flourishes, and the meticulous mapping of body movements designed to communicate specific messages and moods (e.g., Austin, 1966; Bulwer, 1974). While still focusing almost entirely on the public oratorical context, such approaches clearly presaged a "skills" philosophy of communication. Excellent communication consists of (a) a specific set of behaviors that (b) can be learned and refined.

By the transition into the 20th century, America was experiencing its own renaissance. The Industrial Revolution, combined with the natural resources of the then settled United States, established another concentration of wealth among a relative minority of the society's populace. Once again, interest in interpersonal skills was revealed in an expanding literature oriented to educating people in the social graces. Manners and etiquette books taught proper behavior, and often, the more proper the behavior, the more elaborate, formal, and privileged the context (Ewbank, 1987). The aristocracy found ways of not only restricting the entry of the lower classes but also of stigmatizing the nouveau riche (Bushman, 1992; Kasson, 1990).

Throughout the 20th century, other trends began to take hold that would significantly influence academic interest in interpersonal skills. In perhaps the earliest social scientific analog, Thorndike (1920) speculated on the nature of social intelligence, a concept that has become closely yoked to interpersonal and social skills (Marlowe, 1985). The social scientific interest in intelligence led to a series of studies attempting to develop a measurable and developmental model of social competence that was an analog to a general factor ($g$) of mental intelligence (see Bradway, 1937, 1938; Doll, 1953; Otness, 1941). If a social intelligence quotient could be

identified and validly operationalized, then there would be a way of diagnosing mental illness and identifying appropriate interventions. Of course, most of the ideological biases that surround theories and measures of mental intelligence apply equally (see Gould, 1981; Howe, 1997), if not more so, to social intelligence. For example, it no longer seems reasonable to view *social idiot* (Bassett, Longwell, & Bulow, 1939) as an objective clinical diagnostic term.

As social competence lost momentum as an exact analog to mental intelligence, clinical interest in interpersonal and communication skills found voice in other theories of mental health. Ruesch (1951) reviewed the role of communication in psychiatric trends and identified "successful communication" as "the only criterion" of mental health: "It is obvious that people are mentally healthy only when their means of communication permit them to manage their surroundings successfully" (p. 87). This perspective sowed the seeds of the Palo Alto group's conception of disturbed communication processes as underlying most mental illness and relational disorder. This mantle was taken up as well by other programs of research that presumed a social skills basis of mental health (Phillips & Zigler, 1961; Zigler & Levin, 1981, Zigler & Phillips, 1960, 1961). It also prefigured the movement in counseling theories toward a communication skills model of helping (e.g., Carkhuff, & Truax, 1966; Truax, 1967).

If psychologists were viewing social skills as the foundation of mental health, others were viewing social skills as the basis for family and relational health. Terman (1938) conducted some of the earliest social scientific research on marital satisfaction and provided perhaps the first in a long line of studies revealing "communication" as a primary source of healthy marital functioning. As the study of marriage became virtually a discipline of its own, interpersonal skills and processes increasingly became recognized as central to marital success (e.g., Boland & Follingstad, 1987; Feeney, Noller, & Ward, 1997; Gottman, 1994).

This selective synopsis of scholarly interest in interpersonal skills throughout recorded history suggests that such conceptions are always subject to the prevailing ideological paradigms and societal praxis of a given era. Although interpersonal skills may not always be prominent in the writings of a given era, their importance to the everyday life of any era is indisputable. A brief review of the literature on the importance of interpersonal skills evidences this claim.

## Importance of Interpersonal Skills

The rationale for interpersonal skills is developed through the premises of an axiomatic syllogism: Interpersonal skills are vital to the development of human relationships. Human relationships are vital to personal well-being. Therefore, interpersonal skills are vital to well-being. These axioms are developed below.

*Interpersonal skills are vital to the development of human relationships.* Interpersonal communication is the means through which relationships are initiated, negotiated, maintained, and ended (Burleson, Metts, & Kirch, 2000; Miczo, Segrin, & Allspach, 2001). It follows, then, that skill in interpersonal communication is essential to managing relationships. For example, research consistently reveals communication as one of the most important factors in determining the satisfaction and dissatisfaction of marriages (e.g., Gottman, 1994) and close relationships (Burleson et al., 2000; Kelly, Fincham, & Beach, 2003). The skill of managing relational conflict and negative affect in particular appears to be immensely important to the developmental success of relationships (e.g., Gottman 1994; Kline, Pleasant, Whitton, & Markman, 2006; Spitzberg, Canary, & Cupach, 1994). In the previous edition of this chapter, more than 80 communication skills constructs were identified that demonstrated a correlation to relationship satisfaction (Spitzberg & Cupach, 2002). The sheer complexity of this landscape has led some to search for a simpler schema for skills intervention (e.g., Gottman & Rushe, 1995). Indeed, it seems unlikely that there need to be 80 distinct skills, and instead, there is likely to be a higher order structure to such

communication skills. Regardless of the complexity, studies and reviews of varied communication intervention and training programs generally reveal significant subsequent improvements in marital satisfaction and duration (e.g., Hawkins, Blanchard, Baldwin, & Fawcett, 2008; Shadish & Baldwin, 2003; Wood, Crane, Schaalje, & Law, 2005).

Human relationships and interpersonal skills are vital to personal well-being. Attachment theory has long placed considerable emphasis on the importance of bonding (e.g., Ainsworth, Blehar, Waters, & Wall, 1978; Bowlby, 1969, 1973, 1980). Most theories of human motivation have also posited interpersonal (Maslow, 1968), love (Freedman, Leary, Ossorio, & Coffey, 1951; Leary & Coffey, 1955), approach (Horney, 1945), belonging (Baumeister & Leary, 1995; Schutz, 1966), connection (Baxter & Montgomery, 1996), or analogous intimacy (McAdams, 1988) drives. Feeling "competent" appears to be an important ingredient of daily well-being (Sheldon, Ryan, & Reis, 1996). It follows that to the extent relationships are neither established nor sustained, or are managed incompetently, well-being will suffer.

*Risk Behavior.* People deficient in their interpersonal skills over time may experience a pattern of disturbed relationships that distort normal feedback processes, diminish self-esteem, and create pathways to deviant and risky behavior. Although research is not very direct or extensive, there is evidence that deficits of social skills are related to various risk-oriented behavior patterns. These risky behavior patterns include smoking, alcohol, and drug abuse (Anda et al., 1999; Herrmann & McWhirter, 1997; Wilsnack, Wilsnack, Kristjanson, & Harris, 1998), risky sexual activity (e.g., Noar, Carlyle, & Cole, 2006), delinquency and criminal activity (e.g., Bullis, Walker, & Stieber, 1998; Dreznick, 2003; Emmers-Sommer et al., 2004; Leschied, Chiodo, Nowicki, & Rodger, 2008; Swanson et al., 1998), and intimate partner violence (Babcock, Waltz, Jacobson, & Gottman, 1993; Roberts & Noller, 1998; Sabourin, Infante, & Rudd, 1993).

*Health.* The precise mechanisms by which the social body affects the physical body are still very much the source of speculation. What is no longer considered particularly speculative is the proposition that the two are integrally related. Several lines of research have demonstrated some of these links (e.g., Eaker, Sullivan, Kelly-Hayes, D'Agostino, & Benjamin, 2007; Everson-Rose & Lewis, 2005; Myrtek, 2007; Robles & Kiecolt-Glaser, 2003; Whitson & El-Sheikh, 2003; Yarcheski, Mahon, Yarcheski, & Cannella, 2004). Specific traumatic childhood relational experiences affect the risk of adult health. Felitti et al. (1998) and Anda et al. (1999) had more than 9,000 HMO (health maintenance organization) patients report on several childhood experiences, including psychological (e.g., parent insulted the child), physical (e.g., parent pushed [or hit] the child), and sexual (e.g., parent sexually touched the child) abuse; interparental violence (e.g., mother was hit); as well as some less interactional factors (i.e., parental substance abuse, mental illness, familial criminal behavior). Generally, odds ratios indicated that the more these events were reported, the more likely the adults were to smoke, to be severely obese, to have experienced two or more weeks of depression in the past year, to have attempted suicide, to report alcoholism, to inject drugs, to have had a sexually transmitted disease, to display ischemic heart disease, to be diagnosed with cancer, to experience a stroke, or to report bronchitis or emphysema. Interpersonal types of trauma in childhood appear to have potentially devastating impacts on health as adults.

Research indicates the significant health benefits afforded by marital relationships. Compared with married persons, single, widowed, and separated/divorced couples tend to display greater odds ratios of having been a psychiatric outpatient or inpatient, having been imprisoned, having committed suicide, or having died from any cause (Argyle, 1981). Similar results have been reported for accidents and assaults (Cheung, 1998). Importantly, however, Ren (1997) found that it was not just the existence of relational status but also the quality of the relationship that

revealed significant health effects (cf. Dalgard & Lund Håheim, 1998; see also McCabe, Cummins, & Romeo, 1996; Reis & Franks, 1994). Thus, couples who were unhappy in the relationship, occasionally uncooperative, or sometimes violent during disagreements tended to report poorer health. Indeed, research indicates that relatively specific interaction skills such as affect regulation, affective expressiveness, and avoiding defensiveness and withdrawal may be associated with both marital stability and health (Gottman & Levenson, 1992). The health benefits of marriage may be moderated and complex but nevertheless appear resilient and real (cf. Barrett, 2000; DePaulo, 2011; Eaker et al., 2007; Johnson, Backlund, Sorlie, & Loveless, 2000; Manzoli, Villari, Pironec, & Boccia, 2007; Westermeyer, 1998).

If primary relationships such as marriage and childhood relations with parents demonstrate material effects on health, the more extended web of familial, social, organizational, and community relationships may also provide important benefits. Several large-scale epidemiological studies bear this out (Bosworth & Schaie, 1997; Dalgard & Lund Håheim, 1998; Ford, Ahluwalia, & Galuska, 2000; Glass, de Leon, Marottoli, & Berkman, 1999; House, Landis, & Umberson, 1988; Schrodt, Witt, & Messersmith, 2008; Su & Ferraro, 1997).

The mechanisms by which relationships benefit health are not well understood. Apart from the tangible sources of support they may provide, relational partners may provide beneficial models and act as tangible facilitators of healthier behavior practices (Broman, 1993; Ford et al., 2000; Lewis & Rook, 1999) and recovery (de Leon et al., 1999; Regehr & Marziali, 1999). Socially skilled persons may be better able to mobilize support and facilitate healthier practices in self and others (Lewis & Rook, 1999). Research is also beginning to isolate specific stress-linked (e.g., Floyd et al., 2007; Powers, Pietromonaco, Gunlicks, & Sayer, 2006; Thorsteinsson & James, 1999) hormonal and physiological effects of communication and supportive relationships (Davis & Swan, 1999; Floyd & Riforgiate, 2008). Analogous studies are isolating the physiological influences of negative interaction patterns in marriages (e.g., Gottman & Levenson, 1999a, 1999b; Miller, Dopp, Myers, Stevens, & Fahey, 1999; Thomsen & Gilbert, 1998). These latter findings serve as an important reminder that it is rarely just the existence of relationships but their interactional quality that determines the nature of the health benefit (Burg & Seeman, 1994; McCabe et al., 1996; Miller, Kemeny, Taylor, Cole, & Visscher, 1997; Rook, 1984, 1991, 1998).

*Achievement.* People with better communication skills may employ those skills to negotiate their education and subsequent career objectives (Morreale & Pearson, 2008). Research suggests that social skills and competence are positively related to indicators of educational achievement (Burleson & Samter, 1992; Kahn, Nauta, Gailbreath, Tipps, & Chartrand, 2002; Rosenfeld, Grant, & McCroskey, 1995; Rubin, Graham, & Mignerey, 1990), although the relationships may be ambivalent (e.g., Landsheer, Maassen, Bisschop, & Adema, 1998; Strahan, 2003). Once out of school, better communicators probably interview better (Peterson, 1997; Salgado & Moscoso, 2002) and are more likely to master their relational connections to achieve status and career success (Alexander, Penley, & Jernigan, 1992; Bahniuk, Kogler Hill, & Darus, 1996; Dobos, Bahniuk, & Kogler Hill, 1991; Kolb, 1996; Lleras, 2008; Payne, 2005; Penley, Alexander, Jernigan, & Henwood, 1991). The finding that homelessness is associated with the risk of a breakdown in social ties (Muñoz, Vázquez, Bermejo, & Vázquez, 1999) and lack of social skills (Bearsley-Smith, Bond, Littlefield, & Thomas, 2008) is suggestive that unemployment and employability may also be related to interpersonal skills (Conference Board, 2006; Ramsay, Gallois, & Callan, 1997; Salgado & Moscoso, 2002; Waldron & Lavitt, 2000; Waldron, Lavitt, & McConnaughy, 2001; Young, Arthur, & Finch, 2000). It is not surprising, therefore, that communication competencies are viewed as among the most central and vital qualifications and needs of the workforce (Curtis, Winsor, & Stephens, 1989;

Daly, 1994; DiSalvo, 1980; Glaser & Eblen, 1986; Hawkins & Fillion, 1999; O'Neil, Allred, & Baker, 1997).

*Psychological Well-Being.* In 1981, Michael Argyle, one of the pioneers of social skills models, reviewed the relatively meager evidence to claim a link between social skills deficits and the development and maintenance of childhood disturbance, schizophrenia, depression, neurosis, and alcoholism. In the years since, research has excavated these and other links and is continuing to uncover ever greater complexity in these links.

Interpersonal skills are the means through which everyday social interactions are negotiated. If interpersonal skills are deficient, then social relations are likely to be less effective and more negatively reinforcing. Such outcomes extended over a long period of time are likely to significantly lower a person's self-esteem (Franks & Morolla, 1976; Richmond, McCroskey, & McCroskey, 1989), diminish a person's popularity and social status with peers (Burleson, 1986; Burleson, Delia, & Applegate, 1992; Newcomb, Bukowski, & Pattee, 1993), constrain adjustment to social stresses (Krumrei, Coit, Martin, Fogo, & Mahoney, 2007), and potentially, lead to mental illness (Procidano, 1992). Furthermore, if a family of origin sustains distorted and deviant forms of interaction, the children of that family are likely to develop similarly distorted social skills, which also present risk factors for adult adjustment (Schrodt et al., 2008). Not surprisingly, research consistently identifies correlations between various forms of mental disturbance and deficient social skills (e.g., Gresham, Cook, Crews, & Kern, 2004; Magee Quinn, Kavale, Mathur, Rutherford, & Forenss, 1999). Even if social and interpersonal skills do not cause mental disturbance, there is strong evidence that improvements in social skills facilitate adjustment among those already diagnosed with mental disorders such as schizophrenia (Kurtz & Mueser, 2008). Thus, there are many interpersonal communication paths to mental health and illness.

Evidence is beginning to indicate very strong influences of family-of-origin communication dynamics and later adolescent and adult health. Parents who are depressed or schizophrenic, or who display deviant and negative patterns of communication with their children tend to increase significantly the risk of those children developing social incompetence, schizophrenia, and other mental disorders (Wichstrøm, Anderson, Holte, & Wynne, 1996). Many studies have found that measures of social "competence prove to be the most powerful predictors of course and outcome for adult schizophrenics" (Weintraub & Neale, 1984, p. 279). Such patterns of findings have led some to theorize that social skills are the primary means through which mental adjustment and health are achieved and maintained (Brokaw & McLemore, 1991). Longitudinal studies have also revealed that the amount and quality of social relationships are protective of mental health. In one study, minimal angry behavior, satisfactory peer social adjustment, and having a mentor relationship at Time 1 predicted over a quarter of the variance in overall mental health over 30 years later (Westermeyer, 1998).

If interpersonal skills are vital to the initiation and maintenance of relationships, then it seems an axiomatic extension that such skills should be related to syndromes such as social anxiety, loneliness, and depression. While there is no shortage of research drawing such links (e.g., Gable & Shean, 2000; Garland & Fitzgerald, 1998; Shaver, Furman, & Buhrmester, 1985; Spitzberg & Canary, 1985), other research is far more circumspect and ambivalent (e.g., Flora & Segrin, 1998; Segrin, 1999; Shean & Heefner, 1995; Vandeputte et al., 1999). Generally, the more carefully research specifies interpersonal skills, the more qualified the findings become. Thus, it appears that there are causal connections between certain social skills deficits and depression, but they tend to be small in magnitude (e.g., Segrin, 1992; for a review, see Segrin, 1998, 1999). Social skills may also play a fairly specific role in mediating interactant vulnerability to psychosocial problems

(e.g., Segrin & Flora, 2000). In contrast, when the construct of psychological well-being is viewed generally, the available evidence indicates that interpersonal skills are likely very facilitative of psychological quality of life. For example, Reis, Sheldon, Gable, Roscoe, and Ryan (2000) found that daily well-being is best predicted by "meaningful talk and feeling understood and appreciated by interaction partners" (p. 419).

In summary, the vast majority of available research, across several disciplines, methodologies, and theoretical perspectives, evidences support for the conclusion that interpersonal skills facilitate well-being. Interpersonal skills are probably a necessary but not sufficient factor in this relationship. Being "interpersonal," any given person's skills are contingent in part on the skills of those with whom he or she interacts. Thus, ceteris paribus, the more interpersonally skilled people are, the better their quality of life.

## The Prevalence of (In)Competence

Given the conclusion that interpersonal skills are vital to the collective state of social and personal health, the natural question arises as to the extent to which people in general *are* competent in their everyday lives. There is surprisingly little research directly addressing this question. As a baseline of comparison, Bassett, Whittington, and Staton-Spicer (1978) found that approximately a third of the U.S. adult population was "functionally incompetent" in the basic skills of math, reading, and problem solving (see also Ilott, 2001). Compared with this, research across a variety of approaches to operationalizing competence suggests that about 7% to 25% of the adult population is interpersonally incompetent (Bryant & Trower, 1974; Bryant, Trower, Yardley, Urbieta, & Letemendia, 1976; Curran, Miller, Zwick, Monti, & Stout, 1980; Hecht & Wittchen, 1988; Schoon, Parsons, Rush, & Law, 2010; Vangelisti & Daly, 1989; Verhulst & Althaus, 1988). In an Australian study, about 7% of people were socially isolated, and 9% experienced some social isolation (Hawthorne, 2008). In a Swedish study, between 14% and 17% of people met the criteria for social phobia (Furmark et al., 1999). When further broken down into specific communication competencies, the prevalence of incompetence can be substantially higher. A study of college students presented with a set of 19 communication tasks revealed that

> 22% of the students tested had problems asking a question; 33% could not give accurate directions; 35% could not adequately express and defend a point of view; . . . and 49% could not describe the point of view of a person who disagreed with them. (Rubin, 1981, p. 30)

The Conference Board (2006) survey of employers found that high percentages of graduates with only a high school degree were "deficient" in a variety of skills considered very important for entering the job market, including written communication (81%), critical thinking/problem solving (70%), oral communications (53%), reading comprehension (38%), teamwork/collaboration (35%), information technology application (22%), and English language (21%). Even substantial percentages of two-year college and technical school graduates were considered deficient in written communications (47%), writing in English (46%), critical thinking/problem solving (23%), and oral communications (21%). Four-year college graduates were considered deficient mostly in written communications (28%), writing in English (26%), and leadership skills (24%). It is worth emphasizing that according to the College Board Survey of high school students ($N =$ 828,516), 89% of students rate themselves above average in "ability to get along with others," 63% to 64% rate themselves above average in "written expression" and "spoken expression," and 70% rate themselves above average in "leadership" abilities (Kruger, 1999).

An alternative way of thinking about population levels of competence is illustrated by asking what percentage of everyday interactions "go poorly" rather than well. Zelenski and Larsen (2000) found that although most encounters involved happiness and relaxation, 45% of interactions involved boredom, frustration, or anxiety, and 16% involved fear, anger, or disgust. Spitzberg and Cupach (2007) review various estimates of dark-side experiences, including anger, breaches of propriety, bullying, communicative apprehension, disaffinity, discouraging conversations, hassles, hurt feelings, profanity, social rejection, sexual aggression, sexual harassment, shyness, social stress, threats, or troublesome relationships. The relative ubiquity with which most people encounter one or more of these forms of relationship or interaction suggests that interpersonal communication is a minefield of challenges to competence. Social skills are known to influence the experience of everyday interaction quality (Nezlek, 2001), so these problematic types of encounters are also likely a function of at least situational constraints on communication competence. Thus, the available evidence indicates that there is a substantial need for better interpersonal skills among a significant proportion of the populace. Presumably, the rest of the population also has room for meaningful improvement as well. While there is evidence that good communication experiences outnumber bad communication experiences in everyday life (e.g., Drury, Catan, Dennison, & Brody, 1998; Duck, Rutt, Hurst, & Strejc, 1991), the less frequent negative communication encounters may disproportionately influence well-being (Rook, 1984).

## The Nature of Interpersonal Skills

Digesting the available scholarship regarding interpersonal skills is challenging and sometimes frustrating. The relevant literature is vast, and several overlapping terms are employed, including symbolic competence, linguistic competence, pragmatic competence, social skill, interpersonal skill, social competence, interpersonal competence, and communicative competence. According to Hargie (1997), "quite often researchers and theorists in this area have been working in differing contexts, with little cross-fertilisation between those involved in clinical, professional and developmental settings" (p. 10). As a consequence, numerous conceptualizations have been offered, and terminology is inconsistent across authors. Different authors use different terms to refer to roughly the same phenomena, and authors using the same term often define it in very different ways. Thus, what one author calls skill, another might label competence, and vice versa. Some argue that skill subsumes competence, while others maintain that competence subsumes skill (Hargie). So it is not surprising that several authors have noted the lack of consensus in skills/competence terminology (e.g., Kramsch & Whiteside, 2008; Morreale, 2008; Rickheit, Strohner, & Vorwerg, 2008; Spitzberg, 2009b; Spitzberg & Chagnon, 2009; Spitzberg & Cupach, 1989; Wilson & Sabee, 2003). Rather than review the plethora of overlapping and unique conceptualizations of skills, we offer a set of definitions and distinctions that derive from our own model of interpersonal competence (Spitzberg, 2000, 2009a; Spitzberg & Cupach, 1984). In the present discussion, social skills are considered synonymous with interpersonal skills.

## Situating Interpersonal Skills: A Model of Interpersonal Competence

Interpersonal skills are usefully situated within a broader conceptualization of interpersonal competence. An individual's interpersonal skills, along with the accompanying knowledge and motivation, enable the occurrence of certain outcomes that are judged interpersonally competent in a particular interactional context. Interpersonal skills can be defined as repeatable goal-directed behaviors, behavioral patterns, and behavior sequences that are appropriate to the interactional context (Spitzberg, 2003). Thus, the domain of skills is circumscribed to observable performance (Bellack & Hersen, 1978; Curran, 1979), although not all behaviors would be considered skills. According to Hargie (1997), "skilled behavior is therefore more complex than instinctive or reflexive movements" (p. 8). Since skilled behavior is performed in the service of desired outcomes, it is repeatable and intentional rather than accidental or coincidental.

Interpersonal skills are performed at several levels of abstraction. Similar to goals, skills are organized hierarchically, with simpler, more microscopic behaviors (e.g., smiling, nodding the head) combining to form more abstract behaviors (e.g., showing interest). Skills are therefore structurally and temporally coordinated in complex ways.

While interpersonal skills per se can be viewed "as behavioral pathways or avenues to an individual's goals" (Kelly, 1982, p. 3), they are tied to, and distinguishable from, the underlying cognitive and affective processes that enable and generate them. This is akin to Trower's (1980, 1982, 1984) distinction between social *skills* and social *skill*. Skills "are the actual normative component behaviors or actions," whereas *skill* "refers to the process of generating skilled behavior" (Trower, 1982, p. 418). These generative mechanisms include knowledge and motivation.

Two distinct types of knowledge appear in the literature: content and procedural. *Content knowledge* (i.e., knowing what) includes possessing information about relational partners, conversational topics (Roloff & Kellermann, 1984), social contexts (Forgas, 1983b), and the rules of language (Chomsky, 1965), conversation (McLaughlin, 1984), and face concerns (Kunkel, Wilson, Olufowote, & Robson, 2003). Competent communicators generally possess more elaborate and discriminating representations of interaction episodes (Forgas, 1983b; Hazleton, Cupach, & Canary, 1987).

*Procedural knowledge* (i.e., knowing how) includes processes such as formulating and prioritizing goals (e.g., Bochner & Kelly, 1974;

Kunkel et al., 2003; Wilson, Kunkel, Robson, Olufowote, & Soliz, 2009), solving problems (e.g., Shure, 1981; Spivack, Platt, & Shure, 1976), explaining and predicting others' behavior (Hazleton & Cupach, 1986), and selecting, coordinating, and implementing relevant skills. Greene's (1984, 1997; Greene & Graves, 2007) action assembly theory, for example, explains how performance deficits can be attributable to the *functional properties of the cognitive system*. According to action assembly theory, the *procedural record*, a long-term memory structure acquired through social experience, contains symbolic representations of key elements of social interaction. Specifically, procedural records consist of nodes and associative pathways that represent contingencies among actions, outcomes, and salient features of social situations. According to Greene (1984), "the task facing the communicator, then, is the integration of these various procedural records and activated knowledge from the conceptual store to form a coherent output representation of action to be taken" (p. 293). Unskilled performance can occur when a person fails to retrieve from memory the appropriate elements of procedural records or when cognitive effort is diverted from the "assembly of components of the output representation where it is needed" (Greene & Geddes, 1993, p. 40). In this way, performance deficits can be explained by glitches in cognitive processing.

*Motivation* is the affective force that energizes performance and guides a person's approach–avoidance orientation to a social situation. It includes both the aversive and the avoidant dimensions of communication, such as anxiety, apprehension, and shyness (Kashdan, 2007; Sibley, 2007), as well as the more approach-oriented dimensions, such as the identification and pursuit of goals through social interaction (Nezlek, Schütz, & Sellin, 2007). Possession of both knowledge and motivation enhances the likelihood of skilled performance but does not ensure it. By analogy, a stage actor may be thoroughly familiar with the script, very knowledgeable about acting techniques, and highly motivated to do well, yet give a weak performance.

Interpersonal skills, along with knowledge and motivation, facilitate interpersonal competence. We define *interpersonal competence* as the evaluative impression of the quality of interaction (Spitzberg, 2000, 2009a; Spitzberg & Cupach, 1984). Thus, competence is inferred, in large part, based on the observation of skills. In this sense, the judgment that one has given a "skilled performance" is tantamount to perceiving one's behavior as interpersonally competent. When the possession of knowledge and motivation leads to the performance of appropriate skills, the likelihood of the individual being seen as competent is enhanced. The performance of appropriate skills, however, *cannot guarantee* that an actor will be seen as interpersonally competent. The characteristics of the observer, whether the actor is observing his or her own behavior, or another person is observing the actor (Dunning, Heath, & Suls, 2004), and the criteria employed by the observer also influence judgments of competence.

## Criteria of Interpersonal Skills

As suggested by the synoptic review above, interpersonal skills have been conceptualized in many different ways. One era seeks sincerity, whereas another seeks politeness. One era seeks conciseness, whereas another seeks elaborateness. These historical shifts reflect in part a shifting of the criteria by which the quality of behavior is evaluated (Spitzberg, 1994b). Skills are always evaluated in terms of some criterion or set of criteria (Spitzberg, 2000). A person may be skilled at loud, high-pitched whistling noises by expelling air through the nose, but this skill is unlikely to be viewed as an interpersonal skill because its relation to higher criteria of competence and quality is unclear. Therefore, an examination of the criteria of competence in interpersonal interaction is in order. At least six criteria of quality interaction have been articulated in connection with interpersonal relations: fidelity, satisfaction, efficiency, effectiveness, appropriateness, and ethics.

*Fidelity Criteria.* A layperson's definition of competent communication is likely to refer to clear communication, or communication in which a person's meanings are clearly understood (McCroskey, 1982; Powers & Lowry, 1984). Communication is widely presumed to be a means of making one's intentions and meanings apparent to an audience (Grimshaw, 1980), and therefore, a conduit metaphor of communication is implied (Axley, 1984; Reddy, 1979). Accuracy reflects the extent to which the meaning or information in one person's mind (i.e., location) is replicated in another person's mind (i.e., location). The extent to which meaning is incomplete, biased, or distorted represents error in the signal transfer and, thus, interference, inability, intentional misrepresentation, or some combination of these influences.

Many approaches toward competent communication, and indeed entire perspectives toward communication, have stressed one or another version of these fidelity and veracity criteria (e.g., Cahn, 1990; Coupland, Wiemann, & Giles, 1991; Davis, 1999; Mieth, 1997; Mortensen, 1997; Powers & Lowry, 1984; Wood, 1998). The underlying assumptions of these approaches provide an indirect rationale for many of the constructs closely associated with competence, such as empathy, perspective taking, interpersonal sensitivity, and cognitive complexity (Zebrowitz, 2001). That is, constructs thought to facilitate adaptation of messages to the receiver, and facilitate perception and interpretation of the partner, are likely to enhance fidelity, veracity, and co-orientation as well.

To be clear, the criteria associated with accuracy and understanding require some elucidation. Clarity, or fidelity, is generally used to describe message characteristics, somewhat independently of receiver perceptions. A message is clear to the extent that it represents the information it is intended to represent or information available in a referent. As an example, in Rubin's (1985) measure of competence, one of the items prompts the student subject to give directions to a location on that person's campus. The directions are, in essence, coded to determine the extent to which they would actually get a person to that location. So there is an explicit assumption that there is an objective foundation of information relevant to the message, and competence is determined by the message's representation of that information in a relatively error-free manner. Clarity also tends to imply aspects of Grice's maxims of not only representing the information but doing so in a concise, efficient manner (Cappella, 1995; Grice, 1989). That is, clear communication avoids unnecessary information. The assumption is that all communication involves certain promissory and consensual features, and therefore, competence consists of using communication in a way that does justice and minimal damage to these features (Mieth, 1997).

Co-orientation, or understanding, is concerned with the extent to which a Coactor comprehends the intended meaning(s) of an Actor's message. Understanding has been operationalized in numerous ways, including perceived understanding (i.e., Actor's perception of Coactor's and Actor's correspondence in meanings) and actual understanding (i.e., Coactor's actual correspondence of meaning with Actor). Some applications of such criteria, for example, indicate high rates of unsuccessful communication of specific elements of patient care instructions across work shifts in hospital contexts (Chang, Arora, Lev-Ari, D'Arcy, & Keysar, 2010; Hinami, Farnan, Meltzer, & Arora, 2009). Other studies find relatively high rates of agreement between patients and doctors in consultations (Žebiene et al., 2008). These types of understanding can further be taken to "meta" levels, such as Actor's perception of Coactor's perception of Actor's meanings (see Allen & Thompson, 1984; Ickes, 1997; Kenny, 1994; Laing, Phillipson, & Lee, 1966).

Accuracy and co-orientation also need to be distinguished from agreement (Mortensen, 1997). Agreement is the extent to which Actor and Coactor possess similar attitudes or beliefs, independent of the source of those correspondences. Two people may simply hold similar beliefs even though they may never have communicated, or they may have simply discovered (vs. achieved) their agreement through communication. To the extent that agreement is achieved through communication, it becomes more of an effectiveness criterion than a meaning-based criterion, given that some form of persuasion is implied. All possible combinations exist theoretically among agreement–disagreement, accurate–inaccurate, and understood–misunderstood (see Table 15.1).

Despite the intuitive cachet of fidelity, veracity, and co-orientation criteria, there are several problems with predicating interpersonal competence on their accomplishment (Spitzberg, 1993, 1994a, 1994b). First, the conduit metaphor reifies meaning as an objective, discrete, and static entity that has some implicit or explicit one-to-one correspondence with reality or an operational representation of that reality. Thus, to be clear in communicating a belief about the death penalty, it must be assumed that there is a belief and that this belief has distinct characteristics that can be identified and objectively mapped by verbal and nonverbal behavior (cf. Wittgenstein, 1958, 1963). Understanding thereby presupposes that this mapping can be "back-translated" in the mind of the receiver. Such conduit metaphors vastly oversimplify the nature of cognitive processing, symbolic subtlety, and complexity. Furthermore, such approaches tend to presuppose awareness of intentions as well as the ability of people to articulate their intentions. These are clearly problematic suppositions (e.g., Levinson, 1995; Nisbett & Ross, 1980).

Second, the clarity criterion runs afoul of useful and common forms of communication such as idiomatic messages (e.g., Bell & Healey, 1992; Bruess & Pearson, 1993; Hopper, Knapp, & Scott, 1981), humor (e.g., Graham, Papa, & Brooks,

**Table 15.1** Possible Combinations of Clarity, Agreement, and Understanding as Criteria of Competence

| |
|---|
| Clear/Agreement/Understanding (e.g., Actor accurately encodes personal attitude and belief about the death penalty; Coactor shares this belief and comprehends the meanings intended by Actor) |
| Clear/Disagreement/Understanding (e.g., Actor accurately encodes personal attitude and belief about the death penalty; Coactor holds an oppositely valenced attitude based on beliefs divergent from those of Actor but nonetheless comprehends the meanings intended by Actor) |
| Clear/Agreement/Misunderstanding (e.g., Actor accurately encodes personal attitude and belief about the death penalty; Coactor shares this belief but misapprehends Actor's intended meanings) |
| Clear/Disagreement/Misunderstanding (e.g., Actor accurately encodes personal attitude and belief about the death penalty; Coactor holds an oppositely valenced attitude based on beliefs divergent from those of Actor and misapprehends Actor's intended meanings) |
| Unclear/Agreement/Understanding (e.g., Actor inaccurately encodes personal attitude and belief about the death penalty; Coactor shares the same "underlying" belief as Actor and comprehends meanings intended by Actor despite the unclear encoding) |
| Unclear/Disagreement/Understanding (e.g., Actor inaccurately encodes personal attitude and belief about the death penalty; Coactor holds an oppositely valenced attitude based on beliefs divergent from those of Actor and comprehends the meanings intended by Actor despite the unclear encoding) |
| Unclear/Agreement/Misunderstanding (e.g., Actor inaccurately encodes personal attitude and belief about the death penalty; Coactor shares the same "underlying" belief as Actor but misapprehends the meanings intended by Actor despite the unclear encoding) |

1992), teasing (Alberts, Kellar-Guenther, & Corman, 1996; Kowalski, 2000), equivocation, ambivalence and ambiguity (e.g., Chovil, 1994; Eisenberg, 1984), paradox (Wilder & Collins, 1994), and the ineffable (Branham, 1980). Even forms of communication such as poetry, metaphor, and socio-emotional interaction (e.g., small talk) seem ill represented by a clarity criterion.

Third, the understanding criterion shows mixed empirical support. Although many studies reveal mutual understanding to be positively associated with relational satisfaction (see Allen & Thompson, 1984; Boland & Follingstad, 1987), some studies suggest that mutual understanding is either unrelated or negatively related to relational adjustment (e.g., Garland, 1981; Tucker & Anders, 1999). Certainly, understanding seems to play a complex role in the management of relationships (Sanford, 1998; Sillars, 1998; Sillars, Weisberg, Burggraf, & Zietlow, 1990; Simpson, Ickes, & Blackstone, 1995; Tucker & Anders, 1999), as it may reveal all the finer grained points of difference between any two individuals, which then may engender both a sense of psychological distance and interactional conflict.

Fourth, such criteria seem to ideologically marginalize deception as an intrinsically incompetent form of communication. Yet deception is a relatively common form of interpersonal communication (DePaulo, Kashy, Kirkendol, Wyer, & Epstein, 1996; Ryan & Shim, 2006; Serota, Levine, & Boster, 2010), which is often intended to benefit the person being deceived (Camden, Motley, & Wilson, 1984; Lippard, 1988), and may even fulfill a variety of positive relational functions (Hunt & Manning, 1991; Tooke & Camire, 1991). For example, much of politeness behavior, which is widely considered a universal pragmatic (Brown & Levinson, 1987), relies on deception as its modus operandi. Politeness is a key aspect of appropriate, and therefore competent, interaction, even though it trades on the social capital of equivocation and deception for its competence. Conversely, savage, mean-spirited, even evil communication can be frighteningly clear and well understood, even though intuitively most interactants would be hesitant to consider such behavior competent.

*Satisfaction Criteria.* Most people prefer communication that "feels good." Satisfaction is the extent to which a communication encounter produces or is associated with a psychological sense of positively valenced feeling(s). Hecht (1978) defined communication satisfaction as the affective reaction to the extent of fulfillment of positively valenced interactional expectations. A communicator develops expectations regarding a given type of interpersonal encounter. Most of these expectations will have valences attached to them. To the extent that an encounter fulfills the positively valenced expectations, it will be satisfying. Furthermore, satisfaction sometimes arises from doing the best under the circumstances or through violation of negatively valenced expectations (Spitzberg & Brunner, 1991). Thus, a college student may go to an information interview hopeful of getting a job offer but satisfied with simply making a good impression. Married couples may dislike conflict but may be satisfied when a conflict was not nearly as bad as expected. Satisfaction has been employed in several investigations as a criterion of competent interaction (see Spitzberg & Cupach, 1984, for a review).

Satisfaction is also an intuitive criterion of interpersonal skill. It too, however, is a flawed criterion. First, satisfaction is a solipsist criterion. A person who enjoys being mean spirited, evil, and savage in his or her communication can be defined as competent under a satisfaction criterion. Conversely, if satisfaction is reserved for the receiver of communication, then perfectly clear and normatively appropriate behavior may not satisfy any given Coactor. Some people are harder to satisfy than others, and some people may never be satisfied. For example, lonely and depressed interactants, compared with nonlonely or nondepressed interactants, tend to view all others as less competent (Segrin, 1998). Such a solipsist criterion, therefore, relegates interpersonal skills to the whim and subjectivity of the individual's affective mood in response to the encounter at hand.

Second, it is unclear what role satisfaction plays in novel interactions that have no expectations or in interactions that have little or no affective valence. Unexpected and unfamiliar encounters, on the one hand, and routine or administrative communication encounters, on the other, illustrate interactions in which satisfaction may simply be relatively irrelevant. Yet interpersonal skills are presumably involved in such encounters.

Third, the most important interactions may occasionally be encounters that have little or no potential to be satisfying. Relational breakups, conflicts, criticisms, rejections, and episodic personal sacrifices may be critical incidents or turning points and, in the long run, perhaps even life altering. But they are seldom viewed as intrinsically satisfying. Related, short-term dissatisfactions may produce longer term forms of satisfactions, thereby distancing the connection between episodic satisfaction and more enduring relational competence. For example, when people have approach motives for making personal sacrifices in their relationships, they tend to experience higher well-being, but when they have avoidance motives for such sacrifices, they fare poorly (Impett, Gable, & Peplau, 2005). Thus, dissatisfying encounters may still produce competent outcomes.

*Efficiency Criteria.* Efficiency refers to the extent to which skills are used to achieve some outcome with a minimum of effort, time, complexity, and investment of resources. In general, according to Berger (2000), "when individuals succeed in their endeavors, the ease and speed with which they do so may be used as bases for judging their skill" (p. 160). Interpersonal skills are efficient if they accomplish their intended function in a parsimonious manner. If presented with an interpersonal objective (e.g., ask a person out on a date), an interactant may be able to envision several different behavioral approaches to achieve that objective. As a criterion of interpersonal skill, efficiency would require that these approaches be arrayed in terms of their relative time, effort, difficulty, and likelihood of success. Efficiency has been employed as a criterion of competence in several studies (e.g., Kellermann, Reynolds, & Chen, 1991; Kellermann & Shea, 1996).

Given that communication is functional, efficiency has an intuitive appeal. Given two paths to fulfilling a certain function, it seems reasonable to assume that it is more competent to select the path that requires less effort relative to its chance of success. There are, however, several problems with efficiency. First, because efficiency is inherently comparative (i.e., relative to alternatives forgone), it is empirically problematic. Because communication is irreversible, there is no reasonable empirical way to determine what the relative success *would have been* had other paths been taken instead of the one that was.

Second, efficiency permits highly objectionable behavior to be considered competent. For example, it may be far more efficient to tell people to "take a hike" or "to get out of my face" when interaction is unwanted. But it is hardly what most people would consider competent. Politeness phenomena, therefore, often involve more elaborate performance codes. It may be argued that such objectionable behaviors are not efficient if they do not achieve their function, but if the function is to communicate rejection, this argument fails. If the function, in contrast, is to communicate rejection in an appropriate manner, then efficiency becomes confounded or redundant with other criteria of competence.

Third, efficiency seems relatively orthogonal to some types of interaction. For example, small talk, play, teasing, storytelling, humor, and social support seem rather difficult to evaluate in terms of their efficiency, given that part of the function of such episodes is to invest in the function of bonding with another. The investment of resources such as time and effort is itself part of the measure of the value of the encounter. Therefore, efficiency seems ideologically wedded to not only a conduit metaphor but also an almost mechanical or physicalist model of communication.

Fourth, efficiency seems too much an extension of the mechanical or computer analog of human behavior. These analogs have been common (Vroon, 1987) but risk considerable reductionism (Marshall, 1977) and seem too dependent on concepts of error and time, prioritizing minimization and planning over creativity and spontaneity. Perhaps communication is ultimately a process analogous to machines and computers, but such engineering metaphors suggest a rationality and design that may not characterize the more unanticipated features of the human communication condition.

*Effectiveness Criteria.* Effectiveness represents the extent to which an interactant accomplishes preferred outcomes through communication (Spitzberg & Cupach, 1984). In many senses, therefore, effectiveness is inclusive of satisfaction and superordinate to efficiency. When people achieve preferred outcomes, they are more likely to be satisfied. Furthermore, the attainment of a preferred outcome is likely to be more important to most people than the efficiency with which it is accomplished, at least as long as inefficiencies do not outweigh the value of the outcome itself. The term *preferred* fits better than the term *desirable* because of the pragmatics of avoidance–avoidance types of conflicts. There may be instances in which communicators are faced with "no-win" contexts. In such cases, selection of the "least-punishing" communication tactic(s) will be more effective, even though the outcomes may be undesirable (Spitzberg, 2000).

Effectiveness represents one of the oldest and most established criteria of competence. Classical rhetoric was primarily concerned with issues surrounding persuasion, in which effectiveness is the point of communication. All functional approaches to communication implicitly or explicitly rely on notions of effectiveness because they assume that communication varies in its efficacy in accomplishing certain functions. For example, fidelity concerns presuppose the importance of the goal of achieving mutual understanding and are therefore subordinate to the broader goal of effectiveness. Attributional approaches to communication also imply effectiveness criteria. Causal questions such as "Why did she or he say or do that?" often are only resolved by addressing the issue of what outcome the communicator was attempting to accomplish. Finally, any approaches to communication that are based on plans (e.g., Berger, 1997) or communicator goals (e.g., Kunkel et al., 2003; Nezlek et al., 2007; Wilson et al., 2009) implicitly or explicitly incorporate an effectiveness criterion of competence. A communicator's competence is determined by the extent to which preferred goals, plans, or intentions are fulfilled.

Like the other criteria, effectiveness has substantial intuitive appeal. It nevertheless runs afoul of a few problems. First and foremost, effectiveness as a sole criterion of competence presents any number of ethical and normative difficulties. Preferred outcomes can be accomplished through the use of force, coercion, threat, manipulation, deception, exploitation, and the entire communicative arsenal of the darker sides of interaction (e.g., Cupach & Spitzberg, 1994; Spitzberg & Cupach, 1998). While these forms of communication may have their functional and even preferred aspects, normatively they are widely considered incompetent and unethical. It seems that there is less concern over a theory of competence based on effectiveness (e.g., Parks, 1995) than there is a philosophy of communication implicit in such a theory. What does it say about the human condition if a theory of competence predicated exclusively on effectiveness envisions the darker side of communication as competent and skilled (Spitzberg & Cupach, 2007)?

The second difficulty with the effectiveness criterion revolves around issues of intentions and empiricism. Preferred outcomes can occur for reasons that have little or nothing to do with a communicator's performance (McCroskey, 1982; cf. Spitzberg, 1983). Thus, a communicator may receive preferred outcomes due to luck, circumstance, or coincidence. Communicators should not be considered competent or skilled merely because desirable things happen to them. Unless a communicator applied communicative behavior to the intention of producing such preferred outcomes, competence should not be attributed. Intentions, however, are formidably difficult to operationalize. For example, communicators tend to be biased in their retroactive attribution of intention to self for positively valenced outcomes (Dunning et al., 2004; Kruger, 1999), and online or real-time intentions are often relatively inaccessible. Thus, effectiveness may become a proxy for self-esteem or satisfaction rather than represent actual performance-based accomplishment.

Finally, like satisfaction, effectiveness is a solipsist criterion of competence. Only a given individual can know whether or not the outcomes that occurred were the preferred outcomes. The individual actor therefore is the sole *arbiter elegantiae* of any given communicative performance. There is no necessary normative point of reference in this criterion of competence, and as such, it permits competence to be disconnected from the larger societal context in which communication occurs.

*Appropriateness Criteria.* Appropriateness is the extent to which a communicative performance is judged legitimate within a given context (Spitzberg & Cupach, 1984). Appropriateness may be the most common theoretical criterion of competent communication (e.g., Larson, Backlund, Redmond, & Barbour, 1978). Given that competent communication is viewed as inherently contextual in nature, it follows that the standards of appropriateness for any given context must be taken into account in the evaluation of competence. It is therefore generally assumed that contexts "possess" such standards of appropriateness. Although appropriateness often is defined in terms of behavior "conforming" to the "rules" of a context, the notion of being legitimate seems better suited (Spitzberg, 2000). To conform is to abide by *existing* standards of appropriateness. This standard would therefore imply a highly conservative standard of competence in which norms of acceptable behavior would be strongly anchored in the preservation of the status quo. Creativity, innovation, evolution, and revolution of communicative behavior would implicitly be discouraged as modes of competence in such a perspective. Instead, the most competent communicators may be those who are able to renegotiate the applicable rules of conduct in a given context (Pearce & Cronen, 1980). Thus, competence is viewed as appropriate to the extent it is viewed as legitimate within the *extant* rules of a context, including those rules that may have been newly negotiated as applicable.

If effectiveness is problematic in part because of its solipsism, appropriateness is problematic because it is too based on the judgments of other(s). In any given situation, a communicator may have to choose between satisfying self-objectives and those of others in the context. In such situations, there is little a priori basis for privileging the judgments of others (cf. Linell, 1998). Mob rule, the distortions of peer influence, and the sometimes coercive nature of group pressures (e.g., Fishbein, 1996; Stafford & Dainton, 1994) all warn against the automatic evaluation of competence in strict terms of the other. Appropriateness "glorifies the collective while diminishing the importance of the individual" (Burgoon, 1995, p. 469). Even though legitimacy in terms of extant rules may permit creativity, appropriateness as a criterion still seems spring-loaded to preserve the status quo. If this is so, then appropriateness as a sole criterion is biased by a conformist and traditionalist ideology.

Finally, appropriateness, as an other-oriented criterion, becomes problematic because there often is no identifiable or singular "other." Communication is often performed to multiple audiences, and these different audiences may apply very different standards of appropriateness even within a given context. Therefore, there is no obvious calculus for determining who the appropriate judge of appropriateness is, or how to reconcile conflicting evaluations of appropriateness, in a given context.

*Ethical Criteria.* To a large extent, the criteria up to this point have largely focused on functional, or ends-oriented, approaches to identifying skilled communication. In contrast, there are more means-oriented approaches (Penman, 1992). Various approaches have taken a moralistic stance to delimiting ideal communication. Often influenced by Buber's philosophy of dialogue as well as the critical theories of Habermas and feminism, these approaches can be broadly described as dialogical. Dialogical approaches tend to define communication as competent to the extent that it fulfills various values of equal access, confirmation of other(s), and veracity. Dialogue requires (a) an "exchange of rational arguments among (more or less) equal persons," (b) "joint action that ties people together and creates the temporary world they experience," (c) interaction that is "appealing to all participants," and (d) "the expression of individual and constantly changing perspectives and individual or shared inspirations, enchantments, and desires" (Riikonen, 1999, p. 141).

Several variations of the dialogic approach appear in the scholarly literature (e.g., Ayim, 1997; Habermas, 1970, 1981, 1987; Johannesen, 1971; Kristiansen & Bloch-Poulson, 2000; Linell, 1998; McNamee & Gergen, 1999; Pearce & Littlejohn, 1997; Pearce & Pearce, 2000). Core common principles in these approaches represent concepts of equality, otherness, and freedom. Such notions seem to envision both a theoretical and a metatheoretical framework. In such a framework, "good communication theory and practice would be those that enrich our experience and increase our options and opportunities for actions. Bad communication, conversely, restricts or negates our experiences and options" (Penman, 1992, p. 241). Communication as dialogue envisions interpersonal skills as means that should abide by a moral coda. This moral coda, in turn, envisions a world in which ideal speech situations could empower all and provide respect and voice to each person regardless of station or stereotype. Thus, unlike the criteria of competence, which indicate what good communication accomplishes (i.e., the ends), these moral criteria focus instead on what good

communication *is* (i.e., the means). On the other hand, critical approaches espouse moral criteria that envision the world that would result from the enactment of such dialogical communication and, thus, build a vision of the ends into the means themselves. Furthermore, many critical approaches are essentially operationalizing a particular set of appropriateness criteria for communication competence.

These ethical approaches are unabashedly ideological, and this may be both their strength and the reason for their relative lack of attention in the interpersonal skills literature. These approaches may purport a "political ideology" (Burgoon, 1995, p. 477) in which "the prototypical competent communicator is described as open, warm, caring, and so on" (Burgoon, 1995, p. 469; see also Katriel & Philipsen, 1981). In doing so, they may reflect a "feminization" of interpersonal skills (Parks, 1995, p. 488) that merely replaces old ideological dilemmas with new ones. For example, to the extent that collectivist concerns are privileged over individualistic concerns, the individual voice may be diminished. To the extent that interpersonal skills are constrained through feminization, then communicators are likewise constrained in their abilities to construct new and divergent identities that may or may not accord with existing notions of feminine voice. Thus, the ideological objective of moral behavior may clash with the postmodern objective of celebrating self-determination (Burgoon, 1995; Parks, 1995; Spitzberg, 1993, 1994a, 1994b, 2000).

*Criteria Summary.* The mere production of a behavior is rarely considered a sufficient basis for claiming that a person is "skilled." Skills are generally viewed as performances that are put to socially valued purposes. Once such evaluative and normative considerations are applied, issues of the underlying criteria of such considerations become paramount: By what standards should skilled or competent communication behavior be evaluated? This deceptively complex question leads to answers that unravel the more carefully they are examined.

This discussion of criteria of competence in communication suggests that any single criterion is flawed. It is because of the limitations of singular standards of evaluation that most theorists have incorporated multiple or hybrid criteria. The most common hybrid is to claim that competent communication is both appropriate *and* effective (e.g., Spitzberg, 2009a, 2009b; Spitzberg & Chagnon, 2009; Spitzberg & Cupach, 1984). Communication that accomplishes preferred objectives in a manner judged legitimate by others is likely to be satisfying and ethical as well. In any given context, a communicator obviously may give preference to one criterion over another and thereby sacrifice a degree of optimal competence to the pragmatics of a given encounter. Such sacrifices are suggestive of the central role of context in discussions of competent and skilled interaction.

## Contextual Dimensions of Interpersonal Skills

The contextual nature of interpersonal skills is axiomatic. That is, what is presumed to be skilled in one context is not necessarily presumed to be skilled in another. This axiom is reasonable but also overly vague. It is not very useful to claim that interpersonal skills are contextual unless the concept of context can be systematically unpacked.

Context can be defined as a subjective interpretation of the frame within which interaction occurs (Goffman, 1974). The boundaries of this frame are minimally interpreted through the matrix or intersection of five dimensions: culture, time, relationship, place, and function (Spitzberg, 2000). These dimensions combine in various ways to both construct, and be constructed by, interaction.

### Cultural Context

Culture represents the intergenerational patterns of belief, value, and behavior that are relatively consensual and transferable within the group. Although several pancultural dimensions have been identified (e.g., Hofstede, 1984; Spitzberg, 1989; Triandis, 1995), it is generally accepted that each culture will have its own instantiations of these dimensions as they apply to competent interaction. That is, all cultures may employ the same criteria of competence and dimensions for comprehending communication, but the specific behaviors that fulfill these criteria or "load" on those dimensions differ considerably across cultures. For example, research has consistently demonstrated that in reference to certain behaviors, different ethnic and national groups differ significantly in their evaluations of competence (Hecht, Collier, & Ribeau, 1993; Nicotera, 1997; Wyatt, 1999). Furthermore, various models of interpersonal competence have presupposed the contextual relevance of culture by identifying skills of cultural openness and adaptability as key competencies (e.g., Spitzberg & Changon, 2009).

### Chronological Context

Time refers to several features of context that are relevant to competent interaction. First, time refers to stability of skills. Skill in interaction has variously been viewed as either a set of epiphenomenal states or a set of dispositional traits (e.g., Cupach & Spitzberg, 1983; Spitzberg, 1990, 1991, 1994c; Spitzberg & Brunner, 1991; Spitzberg & Cupach, 1989). Whether skills are viewed as strictly situational or more dispositional depends on whether they are assumed to generalize across space and time. Thus, time as a dimension of context concerns the stability of skills over time. Second, time refers to the timing of skilled performance. In this sense, time is concerned with issues such as the synchronicity of behaviors (VanLear, 1991), the management of speaking turns and talk time (e.g., Boltz, 2005; Nevile, 2007), the appropriateness of interactional beginnings and closings (Kellermann et al., 1991; Markman, 2009), and other aspects of behavior sequencing in the interactional time stream

(Higginbotham & Wilkins, 1999). Research consistently demonstrates the importance of timing in terms of interaction management skills (e.g., Dillard & Spitzberg, 1984; Kramsch & Whiteside, 2008; Wilson & Wilson, 2005).

## Relational Context

Relationship refers to the subjective and structural pattern of interdependence and closeness between interactants (Kelley et al., 1983). Research has shown that the type of relationship is a natural cognitive category for organizing social information (Baldwin, 1992; Sedikides, Olsen, & Reis, 1993) and significantly influences expectations and evaluations of appropriate interpersonal motivation (e.g., Graham, Barbato, & Perse, 1993) and behavior (e.g., Baxter & Simon, 1993; Hecht, 1984; Knapp, Ellis, & Williams, 1980). Various perspectives have attempted to identify the relatively unique skills and competencies involved in initiating and maintaining close relationships (e.g., Burleson & Samter, 1994; Carpenter, 1993; Davis & Oathout, 1987; Rubin, Booth, Rose-Krasnor, & Mills, 1995). In addition, much of the marital satisfaction literature can be interpreted as investigating implicit models of relational competence in a particular relationship context (e.g., Gottman & Porterfield, 1981; Spitzberg & Cupach, 2002), and contemporary dialectical models of relationships also implicitly suggest competencies unique to particular relational forms and needs (e.g., Baxter & Montgomery, 1996). As with culture, there may be common underlying dimensions involved in the comprehension of relationship types (e.g., Burgoon & Hale, 1984), but specific competencies vary significantly across these dimensions depending on the particular relationship type being evaluated.

## Situational Context

Place refers to the physical situation in which interaction occurs. Research on social situations shows that place is a significant influence on expectations and evaluations of appropriateness of behavior (e.g., Argyle, Furnham, & Graham, 1981; Forgas, 1978, 1982, 1983a; Pavitt, 1989; Smith-Lovin, 1979). As with culture and relationship, there may be common underlying dimensions along which place is comprehended (e.g., Forgas, 1979; Heise, 1979; Wish, D'Andrade, & Goodnow, 1980; Wish & Kaplan, 1977), but the competence of any given behavior will vary significantly along these from one place to the next.

## Functional Context

Function refers to the motives (e.g., intentions, objectives, goals, purposes) or pragmatic influences of behavior in the interactional system in which they are enacted. Articulated in speech act theory (e.g., Austin, 1962; Searle, 1969) and systems conceptions (e.g., Bochner & Eisenberg, 1987) of interaction, the assumption is that communication behavior *does* rather than just *is.* Communication has effects, and these effects represent how communication functions in an encounter. Communication occurs in the service of certain effects on interactants, and these effects, or outcomes, are indicators of interactional effectiveness and practical achievement. Communication in the service of conflict is likely to be quite distinct from communication in the service of a job interview. Various approaches to communication have attempted to identify the competencies associated with primary functions (e.g., Burleson & Denton, 1997; Burleson, Kunkel, Samter, & Werking, 1996) or motives (e.g., Rubin, Perse, & Barbato, 1988) of interaction. Research has demonstrated that what is considered competent varies according to which functions are being pursued or fulfilled (e.g., Ryan & Shim, 2006; Tazelaar, Van Lange, & Ouwerkerk, 2004; Tyler & Feldman, 2004).

*Summary.* One of the least contextual claims about competent interaction is that it is contextual. What this precisely means, however, is rarely a subject of direct inquiry or conceptualization.

Context reveals at least five socially relevant facets: culture, time, relationship, place, and function. The matrix of these intersecting facets produces relatively consensual expectations and guidelines for conducting interaction, and yet these aspects are also relatively negotiable by the interactants. Competence is likely to result from a complex interplay of the extent to which interactants fulfill the expectancies associated with their context and their ability to negotiate the very relevance and nature of those expectations (Burgoon, Stern, & Dillman, 1995; Spitzberg & Brunner, 1991). Thus, any approach to conceptualizing and operationalizing interpersonal skills must account for the role of context in the competence of those skills.

## Toward a Taxonomy of Interpersonal Skills

In their review of the literature, Spitzberg and Cupach (1989; see also Spitzberg & Chagnon, 2009) identified more than a hundred conceptual constructs, and more than another hundred factor-analytically based constructs, associated with interpersonal competence (see Table 15. 2). While it is possible that this is an accurate reflection of the complexity of the terrain of interpersonal skills, there is a strong intuitive and empirical sense in which there are higher order structures by which this panoply of skills could be organized (Spitzberg, 1989; Spitzberg & Chagnon, 2009). There obviously has been no shortage of efforts to identify a more parsimonious yet reasonably comprehensive taxonomy of skills and functions (e.g., Heggestad & Morrison, 2008). Several problems, however, continue to plague such efforts.

### Obstacles to a Taxonomy of Interpersonal Skills

First, skills vary considerably by their level of abstraction. Eye contact is a fairly specific behavior. It has been further operationalized in terms of micromomentaries, gaze, aversions, mutual eye contact, and related constructs. Eye contact is significantly related to impressions of competence and social skill (e.g., Dillard & Spitzberg, 1984). Yet relatively few interpersonal skill taxonomies identify "eye contact" as a major interpersonal skill. In contrast, assertiveness and empathy are ubiquitous in the interpersonal skills literature (e.g., Spitzberg & Cupach, 1984, 1989), but the specific behavioral components that constitute these skills are far from consensual (for assertiveness, see, e.g., Gervasio & Crawford, 1989; Kolotkin, Wielkiewicz, Judd, & Weiser, 1983; Linehan & Walker, 1983; Pitcher & Meikle, 1980; Wildman & Clementz, 1986; for empathy, see, e.g., Bryant, 1987; Chlopan, McCain, Carbonell, & Hagen, 1985; Cliffordson, 2002; Davis, 1983; Leibetseder, Laireiter, & Köller, 2007; Spreng, McKinnon, Mar, & Levine, 2009). Both assertiveness and empathy are likely to depend in part on eye contact. So which is the "skill," eye contact or assertion? Both are skills, but they exist at different levels of abstraction. Skills vary from the microscopic (e.g., eye contact, asking questions, etc.), to the mezzoscopic (e.g., expressiveness, composure, etc.), to the macroscopic (e.g., distributive, integrative, avoidant, etc.) levels of abstraction.

A second problem with organizing skills is the complexity of determining what concept should guide organization. Most efforts attempt to organize skills according to one or more of three approaches: contextual, functional, or topographical. *Contextual approaches* attempt to identify the types of skills involved in particular interaction contexts, for example, in heterosexual (e.g., Davis & Oathout, 1992; VanWesenbeeck, van Zessen, Ingham, Jaramazovi, & Stevens, 1999), organizational (e.g., DeWine, 1987; Wellmon, 1988), marital (e.g., Carroll, Badger, & Yang, 2006), and health care (e.g., Cegala, McNeilis, McGee, & Jonas, 1995; Gruppen et al., 1997; Scherz, Edwards, & Kawail, 1995) types of contexts. *Functional approaches* attempt to identify the types of skills involved in competently accomplishing certain interaction functions, such as conflict (e.g., Spitzberg et al., 1994), support (e.g., Barry, Bunde, Brock, & Lawrence, 2009;

**Table 15.2** Factor-Analytic Skills and Competencies Attributed to the Macroconcepts of "Social Skills," "Interpersonal Competence," and "Interpersonal Skills"

**Altercentrism**

| |
|---|
| Acceptance |
| Affiliation |
| Aggressiveness/aggression(–)[a] |
| Altercentrism |
| Attention |
| Attentiveness |
| Boorish (–) |
| Confirmation |
| Cooperativeness |
| Cultural empathy |
| Decoding |
| Disapproval/criticism of others (–) |
| Disdainful of others (–) |
| Distance (–) |
| Enhancement |
| Emotional sensitivity |
| Emotional support |
| Empathy |
| Enmeshment |
| Evaluation and acceptance of feedback |
| Friendliness/outgoing |
| Helping |
| Hostile depression (–) |
| Hostile domination (–) |

| |
|---|
| Interpersonal diplomacy |
| Intimacy/warmth |
| Listening |
| Negative assertion (–) |
| Other orientation/directedness |
| Perceptiveness |
| Personality traits (empathy, tolerance) |
| Prosocial competence/skills |
| Reflecting |
| Responsiveness |
| Self-centeredness (–) |
| Social interaction (display respect, appropriate behavior) |
| Social offensiveness (–) |
| Social sensitivity |
| Understanding |

**Composure**

| |
|---|
| Ability to deal with psychological stress |
| Anxiety (comfort, composure, confidence, nervous movements) (–) |
| Assertiveness |
| Autonomy |
| Avoidance/social withdrawal (–) |
| Commitment |
| Coping with feelings |
| Dominance (–) |
| Emotional control |
| Impersonal endeavors/perils |
| Initiation |
| Instrumental skills |
| Intentionality |

*(Continued)*

## Table 15.2 (Continued)

| |
|---|
| Interpersonal skills (establish relationship, initiate talking) |
| Managerial ability (motivation, creativity) |
| Need for achievement |
| Persuasiveness |
| Pleading |
| Self-efficacy |
| Self-orientation |
| Social control |
| Social manipulation |
| Social instrumental skills |
| Social relaxation/ease |
| Social superiority |
| **Coordination** |
| Ability to effectively communicate (deal with misunderstandings, different styles) |
| Conversational skills |
| Decoding and encoding |
| Interaction management/skills |
| Message orientation |
| Verbal skills |
| **Expressiveness** |
| Ability to be understood |
| Activity in the conversation |
| Affective skills |
| Animation |
| Articulation |
| Body nonverbal behavior |
| Clarity |
| Confrontation/anger expression |
| Openness/confiding |
| Emotional control |
| Emotional expressivity |
| Emotionality |
| Encoding |
| Expressiveness/expressivity |
| Facial expressiveness and vocalic behavior |

| |
|---|
| Nonverbal behavior |
| Personal appearance/physical attractiveness |
| Self-disclosure/expression |
| Social expressivity |
| Vocalic skills |
| Wit |
| **Contextual competencies** |
| Conflict management/handling differences |
| Heterosocial contact |
| Relations with authority figures |
| Social activity/experience |
| **Macrolevel competencies** |
| Ability to establish interpersonal relationships |
| Adaptability |
| Awareness |
| Creativity |
| Similarity |
| Social ability/skill |
| **Outcomes** |
| Appropriateness |
| Communicative competence |
| Communication satisfaction |
| Effectiveness |
| Rewarding impression |
| Task completion |

SOURCES: Expanded from Spitzberg (1994b) and Spitzberg and Cupach (1989). Studies added since the Spitzberg and Cupach (1989) and Spitzberg (1994b) source include Bubaš (2000), Burleson et al. (1996), Cui (1989), Farrell, Rabinowitz, Wallander, and Curran (1985), and Hammer, Gudykunst, and Wiseman (1978).

NOTES: Labels were excluded or adapted for any of the following reasons: (a) labels had minimal interactional or communicative referent (e.g., "self-concept" or "self-perception"); (b) the label referent was unclear (e.g., "completion" or "corruption"); and (c) cognate labels have been combined (e.g., "social anxiety," "anxiety," and "apprehension" become "anxiety"; "confirmation" and "social confirmation" become "confirmation").

a. Skills or competencies with negative loadings or predicted relationships to competence are annotated with a "(–)" symbol.

Riggio, Watring, & Throckmorton, 1993; Riggio & Zimmerman, 1991), medical consultation (e.g., Gremigni, Sommaruga, & Peltenburt, 2008; Lie et al., 2009; Piccolo, Mazzi, Scardoni, Gobbi, & Zimmermann, 2008), and so forth. Other functional approaches have attempted to locate more inclusive functions, such as instrumental and expressive functions (e.g., Ickes, 1981, 1985; Lamke, Sollie, Durbin, & Fitzpatrick, 1994; Newcomb et al., 1993). *Topographical approaches* attempt to identify clusters of behaviors that seem to bear structural resemblance in form or function, such as self-disclosure and openness (e.g., Derlega & Grzelak, 1979; Miller, Berg, & Archer, 1983), empathy (e.g., Ickes, 1997), and assertiveness (e.g., Rakos, 1991).

To identify these as approaches to interpersonal skills is a generous attribution to the literature. In practice, most scholarly approaches to interpersonal skills have been piecemeal, poorly conceptualized, and surprisingly lacking in rationale. They often reflect what Spitzberg and Cupach (1989) referred to as the "list" technique, in which a list of independently reasonable skills candidates is assembled. Given the daunting complexities of identifying a rationale for an appropriate underlying organizing set of structural or functional features, such bootstrap approaches are not surprising. This difficulty in identifying underlying features reflects the third, and closely related, problem in organizing interpersonal skills: multifunctionality.

Systems theory has identified two vexing principles: equifinality and multifinality (Spitzberg, 2009a). Equifinality refers to the idea that many means can lead to a given outcome (von Bertalanffy, 1968). For example, one person may flirt using relatively blatant tactics, whereas another person may flirt using rather subtle and manipulative tactics. Both tactics may succeed in achieving the outcome of gaining someone's attraction (Egland, Spitzberg, & Zormeier, 1996). Multifinality indicates that any given means can lead to multiple possible outcomes (Ramaprasad, 1983). Thus, both obvious and subtle forms of flirtation may lead to outright rejection, feigned interest, genuine interest with caution, or outright attraction. If skills are multifunctional in these senses (McFall, 1982), then there can be no fixed underlying functional taxonomy of skills. That is, no single skill can be tethered to a single function. This has implications for topographical approaches as well. For example, characterizing certain skills as constituting "expressiveness" implicitly suggests that they serve the function of regulating affect display and disclosure. Yet expressive skills can function in instrumental, persuasive, manipulative, and status-based ways as well.

The multifunctionality of skills is closely related to a final problem in organizing such skills: Skills have a "dark side" to them (Spitzberg, 1993, 1994a). Counseling psychologists have discovered that "dysfunctional behavior is typically enacted in a highly skilled manner" (Brokaw & McLemore, 1991, p. 73). Most scholars view self-disclosure as an important interpersonal skill (e.g., Derlega, Metts, Petronio, & Margulis, 1993). Yet someone very skilled in self-disclosure may employ it in manipulative and exploitative ways. Deception is a skill as well, and it can be used in very competent, prosocial ways (e.g., Ryan & Shim, 2006; Serota et al., 2010). Yet self-disclosure is frequently touted as a vital interpersonal skill, and deception is rarely espoused as a vital interpersonal skill. Employing aggression so as to escalate a conflict might be a very useful skill, and one that is clearly overlooked by most approaches to conflict management skills. There are times when conflicts need to be escalated rather than reduced, and this escalation may involve moving against another person. Taxonomies of interpersonal skills, in other words, tend to be ideologically normative and therefore incomplete. They identify only those skills that have a normatively positive valence or "bright-side" connotation.

These problems make a taxonomy of interpersonal skills particularly difficult to construct. The alternative of listing more than 100 skill components, however, seems equally flawed. While there is no obvious resolution in sight, it is possible to construct a heuristic model to bridge some of these problems and set the stage for future refinement of these taxonomic issues.

## A Working Taxonomy of Interpersonal Skills

Figure 15. 1 illustrates an approach to an interpersonal skills taxonomy. It is not presented here as a final or comprehensive taxonomy. It is instead intended to establish a framework through which such a practical taxonomy could be empirically refined. The taxonomy attempts to incorporate facets of several previous approaches (Baxter & Montgomery, 1996; Bochner, 1984; Bubaš, 2000; Burgoon & Dunbar, 2000; Burleson et al. 1992; Greene, 1997; Horney, 1945; Patterson, 1994; Rubin et al., 1988; Spitzberg, 1994c), including five decades of research on the fundamental dimensions of interpersonal behavior (e.g., see Dillard, Solomon, & Palmer, 1999; Spitzberg, 1989; Spitzberg & Brunner, 1991). At the highest level of abstraction, the taxonomy identifies three macro-interaction functions. Skills can be employed to move with or toward another person, as with integrative, cooperative, and bonding moves (Horney, 1945; Newcomb et al., 1993; Santelli, Bernstein, Zborowski, & Bernstein, 1990). Skills can also be employed to move away from another person, as with avoidance, ambivalence, and equivocation. Finally, skills can be employed to move against another, as with aggression, coercion, and control. These macrofunctions represent a generic map of the ways in which behavior can function to affect a relationship to another person. These functions need not be viewed as mutually exclusive. They represent interpersonal rather than personal functions because they are defined in terms of the effects of Actor's behavior on a Coactor. Finally, the approach includes the overwhelming evidence of the importance of the affiliation and status dimensions of circumplex research (e.g., Hatcher & Rogers, 2009; Locke, 2000; Moskowitz & Zuroff,

2005), but adds the recognition that interpersonal behavior can be moving away from someone in addition to moving with or against that person.

Although skills are multifunctional, multifinal, and equifinal, this taxonomy permits certain skills to have stronger links with certain functions than with others. For example, skills associated with empathy and giving support tend to affect one's negotiation of intimacy and openness with another more than negotiating autonomy in relation to that person. Offering support *could* be employed so as to affect autonomy and may always have certain peripheral effects on autonomy, but it is functionally weighted more prominently in its effects on intimacy.

Similarly, microscopic skills have differential weightings in their linkage to mezzoscopic skills, which in turn have a differential impact on macroscopic skills. Any given microscopic skill can be employed in the service of any and all of the mezzo- and macroscopic skills and by extension, therefore, to any of the mezzo- and macroscopic functions. It is expected, however, that research will reveal that some microscopic skills will be linked more to certain mezzo- and macroscopic skills than to others. Such anticipated weightings are illustrated in the figure through the use of solid (primary link) versus dashed (peripheral linkage) lines.

Such a taxonomy is, in some ways, just as complex as a listing of 100 separate skills. But it helps unpack some of the potential conceptual and operational oversights of many discussions of social skills. First, it is flexible. It can accommodate additional terms and components in any column, so long as those components are distinguishable from those already noted. There may be a place in this taxonomy for other forms and functions, such as face management, self-expansion, trust, altruism, and so forth.

Second, it helps identify why so many measures reveal such distinct factor structures. Such measures often haphazardly mix items from several levels of abstraction and thereby suggest

**Figure 15.1** A Heuristic Taxonomy of Interpersonal Skills and Functions

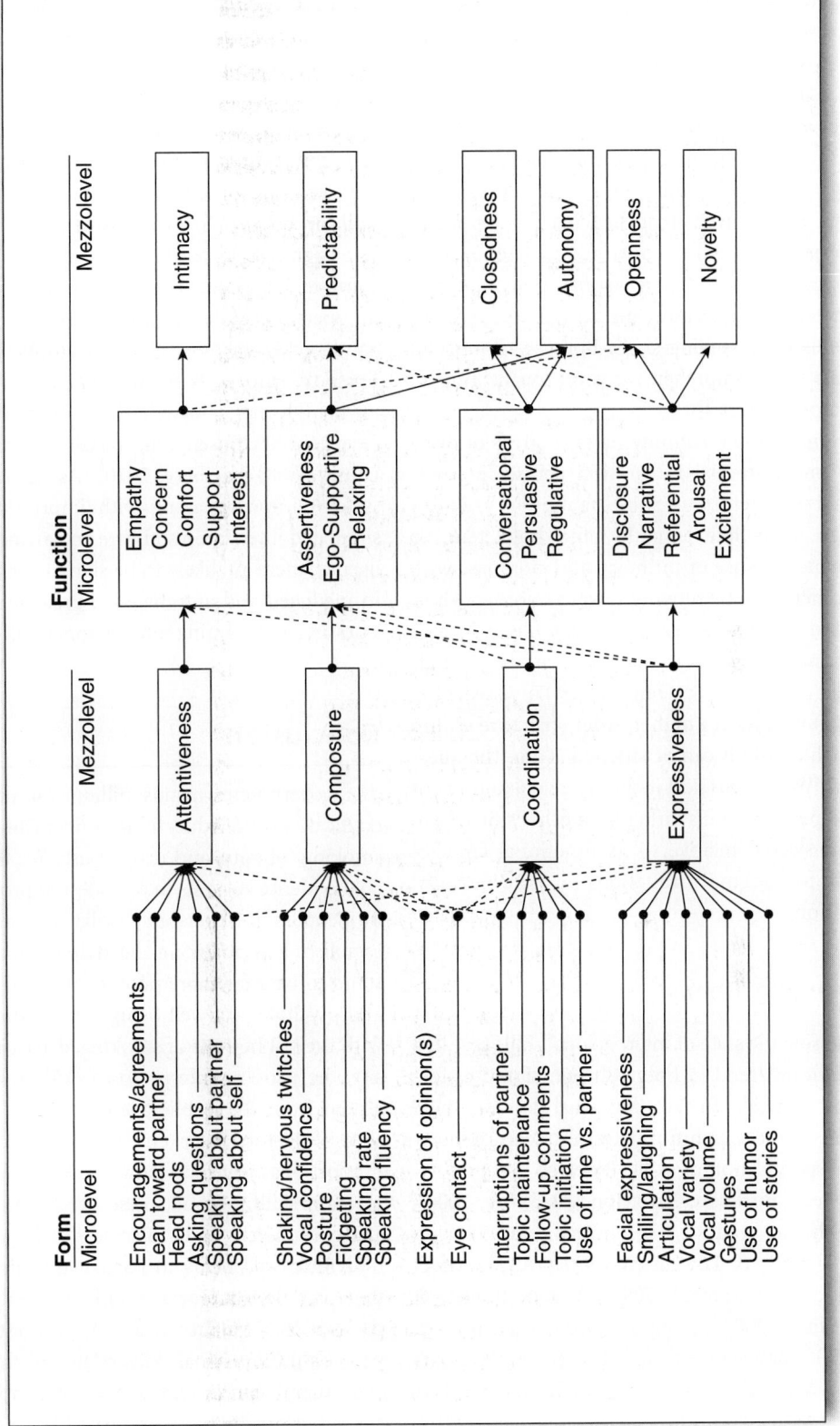

NOTE: Solid lines/arrows represent conjectured main loadings or paths; dashed lines/arrows represent secondary loadings or paths.

empirically indeterminate factor interpretations (Spitzberg, 1994b). Recognition of these varying levels of abstraction should also lead to more conceptually rigorous and valid measures of interpersonal skills.

Third, this taxonomy reveals that topography (e.g., form) and function are interrelated but both are involved in identifying the nature of interpersonal skills. Form reduces to a more micro feature of interpersonal skills, whereas function concerns more mezzo and macro orientations to classifying skills. Both are important levels in a comprehensive conceptualization of interpersonal skills.

Finally, the taxonomy suggests areas of overlap and potential integration across interpersonal skill literatures. Showing support probably often looks like empathy, and both tend to enhance a sense of intimacy and closeness with another, thereby moving toward another. Thus, lists of skills that are sometimes noted in current measures of social and interpersonal skills (e.g., Burleson & Denton, 1997; Carpenter, 1993) now have a higher order structure within which the skills can be situated. Thus, the question "Why is *this* skill included in a taxonomy of interpersonal skills rather than other skills?" can be answered relative to its functional connection to the macrofunctions of interpersonal relations.

### Emerging Trends

Assessing the state of interpersonal skills reveals a significant trend in both conceptual and assessment domains. In the conceptual domain, there seems to be a significant trend toward contextual specification of skills. Research on comforting (e.g., Burleson, 2010; Jones & Wirtz, 2006), health care contexts (e.g., Iramaneerat, Myford, Yudkowsky, & Lowenstein, 2009; Klakovich & Cruz, 2006; Makoul, 2001; Zanten, Boulet, & McKinley, 2007), group contexts (e.g., Stewart, 2006), management and leadership contexts (e.g., Madlock, 2008; Payne, 2005; Riggio & Lee, 2007; Wisecarver, Carpenter, & Kilcullen, 2007),

mediated contexts (e.g., Perrin & Ehrensberger-Dow, 2008; Spitzberg, 2006), intercultural contexts (see Deardorff, 2009; Spitzberg & Chagnon, 2009), and a host of other contexts illustrates that parallel to ongoing research on the general structure and nature of interpersonal skills, there is increasing specialization and contextualization of skill conceptions. In the assessment domain, there is a significant trend toward development of computer- and video-assisted forms of assessing interpersonal skills (e.g., Bakx, Sijtsma, Van der Sanden, & Taconis, 2002; Campbell, Lison, Borsook, Hoover, & Arnold, 1995; Hasler, 2009; Payne, Horner, Boswell, Schroeder, & Stine-Cheyne, 2009; Rosengren, Hartzler, Baer, Wells, & Dunn, 2008; Spitzberg, 2010). As virtual reality systems improve, along with improvements in simulated interaction software and artificial intelligence, there are likely to be significant advances in mediated and automated approaches to both assessing and training interpersonal skills.

## Conclusion

The government spends billions of dollars to eradicate crime, educational underachievement, smoking, obesity, and drug abuse. Yet the available evidence suggests that modest improvements in people's interpersonal skills and ability to establish and maintain satisfying relationships stand to be a far more potent source of physical and psychological well-being. Yet in comparison with the hot buttons of smoking, drugs, and obesity, the issue of interpersonal skills is virtually absent from the public agenda. Several conclusions therefore bear emphasizing. First, large proportions of the population lack basic communication skills. Second, these deficits are associated with severe costs to society at large and to individual well-being in particular. Third, while there is little basis for a specific odds ratio comparison, the evidence is at least suggestive that people's interpersonal skills related to the initiation, maintenance, and quality of relationships are substantially *more* important to social and personal well-being than quitting smoking, losing weight, rehabilitating criminals, improving educational expenditures, and reducing drug abuse in society! Yet, despite the extensive evidence, the agenda of interpersonal skills is rarely, if ever, even mentioned in this discourse, much less given the same weight as these other societal agendas.

Perhaps one of the primary reasons why the agenda of interpersonal skills has not received greater priority in social and political discourse is that the concept itself has lacked clarity. This lack of clarity, in turn, has been exacerbated by the sheer multiplicity of approaches and constructs associated with interpersonal skills. Certainly, interpersonal skills have seemed prismatic: The more one peers into the concept, the more facets and shades are discerned. This chapter has attempted to specify many of these facets but with the intent of providing a relatively comprehensive and integrated approach. While the approach discussed within falls far short of a theory of interpersonal skills, we do believe that it provides the conceptual parameters within which such a theory will eventually be formulated. Thus, what this architecture lacks in theoretical detail we hope will be made up for with its theoretical heurism and integrative comprehensiveness.

# References

Ainsworth, M. D. S., Blehar, M. C., Waters, E., & Wall, S. (1978). *Patterns of attachment: A psychological study of the strange situation.* Hillsdale, NJ: Lawrence Erlbaum.

Alberts, J. K., Kellar-Guenther, Y., & Corman, S. R. (1996). That's not funny: Understanding recipients' responses to teasing. *Western Journal of Communication, 60,* 337–357.

Alexander, E. R., III., Penley, L. E., & Jernigan, I. E. (1992). The relationship of basic decoding skills to managerial effectiveness. *Management Communication Quarterly, 6,* 58–73.

Allen, A., & Thompson, T. (1984). Agreement, understanding, realization, and feeling understood as predictors of communicative satisfaction in marital dyads. *Journal of Marriage and the Family, 46,* 915–921.

Anda, R. F., Croft, J. B., Felitti, V. J., Nordenberg, D., Giles, W. H., Williamson, D. F., et al. (1999). Adverse childhood experiences and smoking during adolescence and adulthood. *Journal of the American Medical Association, 282,* 1652–1658.

Argyle, M. (1981). Social competence and mental health. In M. Argyle (Ed.), *Social skills and mental health* (pp. 159–187). New York: Methuen.

Argyle, M., Furnham, A., & Graham, J. A. (1981). *Social situations.* London: Cambridge University Press.

Aristotle. (1926). *The "art" of rhetoric* (J. H. Freese, Trans.). New York: Putnam's.

Austin, G. (1966). *Chironomia or, a treatise on rhetorical delivery.* Carbondale: Southern Illinois University Press.

Austin, J. L. (1962). *How to do things with words.* Cambridge, MA: Harvard University Press.

Axley, S. R. (1984). Managerial and organizational communication in terms of the conduit metaphor. *Academy of Management Review, 9,* 428–237.

Ayim, M. N. (1997). *The moral parameters of good talk: A feminist analysis.* Waterloo, Ontario, Canada: Wilfrid Laurier University Press.

Babcock, J. C., Waltz, J., Jacobson, N. S., & Gottman, J. M. (1993). Power and violence: The relation between communication patterns, power discrepancies, and domestic violence. *Journal of Consulting and Clinical Psychology, 61,* 40–50.

Bahniuk, M. H., Kogler Hill, S. E., & Darus, H. J. (1996). The relationship of power-gaining communication strategies to career success. *Western Journal of Communication, 60,* 358–378.

Bakx, A. W. E. A., Sijtsma, K., van der Sanden, J. M. M., & Taconis, R. (2002). Development and evaluation of s astudent-centered multimedia self-assessment instrument for social-communicative competence. *Instructional Science, 30,* 335–359.

Baldwin, M. W. (1992). Relational schemas and the processing of social information. *Psychological Bulletin, 112,* 461–484.

Barrett, A. E. (2000). Marital trajectories and mental health. *Journal of Health and Social Behavior, 41,* 451–464.

Barry, R. A., Bunde, M., Brock, R. L., & Lawrence, E. (2009). Validity and utility of a multidimensional model of received support in intimate relationships. *Journal of Family Psychology, 23,* 48–57.

Bassett, D. M., Longwell, S. G., & Bulow, H. V. (1939). Social and occupational competence of idiots.

*American Association on Mental Deficiency, 44,* 97–102.

Bassett, R. E., Whittington, N., & Staton-Spicer, A. (1978). The basics in speaking and listening for high school graduates: What should be assessed? *Communication Education, 27,* 293–303.

Baumeister, R. F., & Leary, M. R. (1995). The need to belong: Desire for interpersonal attachments as a fundamental human motivation. *Psychological Bulletin, 117,* 497–529.

Baxter, L. A., & Montgomery, B. M. (1996). *Relating: Dialogues and dialectics.* New York: Guilford Press.

Baxter, L. A., & Simon, E. P. (1993). Relationship maintenance strategies and dialectical contradictions in personal relationships. *Journal of Social and Personal Relationships, 10,* 225–242.

Bearsley-Smith, C. A., Bond, L. M., Littlefield, L., & Thomas, L. R. (2008). The psychosocial profile of adolescent risk of homelessness. *European Child & Adolescent Psychiatry, 17,* 226–234.

Bell, R. A., & Healey, J. G. (1992). Idiomatic communication and interpersonal solidarity in friends' relational cultures. *Human Communication Research, 18,* 307–335.

Bellack, A. S., & Hersen, M. (1978). Chronic psychiatric patients: Social skills training. In M. Hersen & A. S. Bellack (Eds.), *Behavior therapy in the psychiatric setting* (pp. 169–195). Baltimore: Williams & Wilkins.

Berger, C. R. (1997). *Planning strategic interaction.* Mahwah, NJ: Lawrence Erlbaum.

Berger, C. R. (2000). Goal detection and efficiency: Neglected aspects of message production. *Communication Theory, 10,* 156–166.

von Bertalanffy, L. (1968). *General system theory: Foundations, development, applications* (Rev. ed.). New York: George Braziller.

Bochner, A. P. (1984). The functions of human communication in interpersonal bonding. In C. C. Arnold & J. W. Bowers (Eds.), *Handbook of rhetorical and communication theory* (pp. 544–621). Boston: Allyn & Bacon.

Bochner, A. P., & Eisenberg, E. M. (1987). Family process: System perspectives. In C. R. Berger & S. H. Chaffee (Eds.), *Handbook of communication science* (pp. 540–563). Newbury Park, CA: Sage.

Bochner, A. P., & Kelly, C. W. (1974). Interpersonal competence: Rationale, philosophy, and implementation of a conceptual framework. *Speech Teacher, 23,* 270–301.

Boland, J. P., & Follingstad, D. R. (1987). The relationship between communication and marital satisfaction: A review. *Journal of Sex and Marital Therapy, 13,* 286–313.

Boltz, M. G. (2005). Temporal dimensions of conversational interaction: The role of response latencies and pauses in social impression formation. *Journal of Language & Social Psychology, 24,* 103–138.

Bosworth, H. B., & Schaie, K. W. (1997). The relationship of social environment, social networks, and health outcomes in the Seattle longitudinal study: Two analytical approaches. *Journal of Gerontology: Psychological Sciences, 52B,* P197–P205.

Bowlby, J. (1969). *Attachment and loss: Vol. 1. Attachment.* New York: Basic Books.

Bowlby, J. (1973). *Attachment and loss: Vol. 2. Separation: Anxiety and anger.* New York: Basic Books.

Bowlby, J. (1980). *Attachment and loss: Vol. 3. Loss: Sadness and depression.* New York: Basic Books.

Bradway, K. P. (1937). Social competence of exceptional children: II. The mentally subnormal. *Journal of Exceptional Children, 4,* 38–42.

Bradway, K. P. (1938). Social competence of grade school children. *Journal of Experimental Education, 6,* 326–331.

Branham, R. J. (1980). Ineffability, creativity, and communication competence. *Communication Quarterly, 28,* 11–21.

Brokaw, D. W., & McLemore, C. (1991). Interpersonal models of personality and psychopathology. In D. G. Gilbert & J. J. Connolly (Eds.), *Personality, social skills, and psychopathology: An individual differences approach* (pp. 49–83). New York: Plenum Press.

Broman, C. L. (1993). Social relationships and health-related behavior. *Journal of Behavioral Medicine, 16,* 335–350.

Brown, P., & Levinson, S. C. (1987). *Politeness: Some universals in language usage.* Cambridge, UK: Cambridge University Press.

Bruess, C. J., & Pearson, J. C. (1993). "Sweet pea" and "pussy cat": An examination of idiom use and marital satisfaction over the life cycle. *Journal of Social and Personal Relationships, 10,* 609–615.

Bryant, B., & Trower, P. E. (1974). Social difficulty in a student sample. *British Journal of Educational Psychology, 44,* 13–21.

Bryant, B., Trower, P., Yardley, K., Urbieta, H., & Letemendia, F. J. (1976). A survey of social inadequacy among psychiatric outpatients. *Psychological Medicine, 6,* 101–112.

Bryant, B. K. (1987). Critique of comparable questionnaire methods in use to assess empathy in children and adults. In N. Eisenberg & J. Strayer (Eds.), *Empathy and its development* (pp. 361–373). Cambridge, UK: Cambridge University Press.

Bubaš, G. (2000, March). *The structure of agency and communion dimensions in interpersonal communication interaction.* Paper presented at the European Communication Association Experts' Conference, Manchester, UK.

Bullis, M., Walker, H. M., & Stieber, S. (1998). The influence of peer and educational variables on arrest status among at-risk males. *Journal of Emotional and Behavioral Disorders, 6,* 141–152.

Bulwer, J. (1974). *Chirologia: Or the natural language of the hand* and *Chironomia: or the art of manual rhetoric.* Carbondale: Southern Illinois University Press.

Burg, M. M., & Seeman, T. F. (1994). Families and health: The negative side of social ties. *Annals of Behavioral Medicine, 16,* 109–115.

Burgoon, J. K., & Dunbar, N. E. (2000). An interactionist perspective on dominance-submission: Interpersonal dominance as a dynamic, situationally contingent social skill. *Communication Monographs, 67,* 96–121.

Burgoon, J. K., & Hale, J. L. (1984). The fundamental topoi of relational communication. *Communication Monographs, 51,* 193–214.

Burgoon, J. K., Stern, L. A., & Dillman, L. (1995). *Interpersonal adaptation: Dyadic interaction patterns.* Cambridge, UK: Cambridge University Press.

Burgoon, M. (1995). A kinder, gentler discipline: Feeling good about being mediocre. In B. R. Burleson (Ed.), *Communication yearbook 18* (pp. 464–479). Thousand Oaks, CA: Sage.

Burke, P. (1993). *The art of conversation.* Ithaca, NY: Cornell University Press.

Burleson, B. R. (1986). Communication skills and childhood peer relationships: An overview. In M. Burgoon (Ed.), *Communication yearbook* (Vol. 9, pp. 143–180). Beverly Hills, CA: Sage.

Burleson, B. R. (2010). Explaining recipient responses to supportive messages: Development and tests of a dual-process theory. In S. W. Smith & S. R. Wilson (Eds.), *New directions in interpersonal communication research* (pp. 159–179). Thousand Oaks, CA: Sage.

Burleson, B. R., Delia, J. G., & Applegate, J. L. (1992). Effects of maternal communication and children's social-cognitive and communication skills on children's acceptance by the peer group. *Family Relations, 41,* 264–272.

Burleson, B. R., & Denton, W. H. (1997). The relationship between communication skill and marital satisfaction: Some moderating effects. *Journal of Marriage and the Family, 59,* 884–902.

Burleson, B. R., Kunkel, A. W., Samter, W., & Werking, K. J. (1996). Men's and women's evaluations of communication skills in personal relationships: When sex differences make a difference—and when they don't. *Journal of Social and Personal Relationships, 13,* 201–224.

Burleson, B. R., Metts, M. W., & Kirch, M. W. (2000). Communication in close relationships. In C. Hendrick & S. S. Hendrick (Eds.), *Close relationships: A sourcebook* (pp. 244–258). Thousand Oaks, CA: Sage.

Burleson, B. R., & Samter, W. (1992). Are there gender differences in the relationship between academic performance and social behavior? *Human Communication Research, 19,* 155–175.

Burleson, B. R., & Samter, W. (1994). A social skills approach to relationship maintenance: How individual differences in communication skills affect the achievement of relationship functions. In D. J. Canary & L. Stafford (Eds.), *Communication and relational maintenance* (pp. 61–90). San Diego, CA: Academic.

Bushman, R. L. (1992). *The refinement of America: Persons, houses, cities.* New York: Alfred A. Knopf.

Cahn, D. D. (1990). Perceived understanding and interpersonal relationships. *Journal of Social and Personal Relationships, 7,* 231–244.

Camden, C., Motley, M. T., & Wilson, A. (1984). White lies in interpersonal communication: A taxonomy and preliminary investigation of social motivations. *Western Journal of Speech Communication, 48,* 309–325.

Campbell, J. O., Lison, C. A., Borsook, T. K., Hoover, J. A., & Arnold, P. H. (1995). Using computer and video technologies to develop interpersonal skills. *Computers in Human Behavior, 11,* 223–239.

Canary, D. J., & MacGregor, I. M. (2008). Differences that make a difference in assessing student communication competence. *Communication Education, 57,* 41–63.

Cappella, J. N. (1995). An evolutionary psychology of Gricean cooperation. *Journal of Language and Social Psychology, 14,* 167–181.

Carkhuff, R. R., & Truax, C. B. (1966). Toward explaining success or failure in interpersonal experience. *Personnel and Guidance Journal, 44,* 723–728.

Carpenter, B. N. (1993). Relational competence. In D. Perlman & W. H. Jones (Eds.), *Advances in personal relationships: A research annual* (Vol. 4, pp. 1–28). Philadelphia: Jessica Kingsley.

Carroll, J. S., Badger, S., & Yang, C. (2006). The ability to negotiate or the ability to love? Evaluating the developmental domains of marital competence. *Journal of Family Issues, 27,* 1001–1032.

Cegala, D. J., McNeilis, K. S., McGee, D. S., & Jonas, A. P. (1995). A study of doctors' and patients' perceptions of information processing and communication competence during the medical interview. *Health Communication, 7,* 179–203.

Chang, V. Y., Arora, V. M., Lev-Ari, S., D'Arcy, M., & Keysar, B. (2010). Interns overestimate the effectiveness of their hand-off communication. *Pediatrics, 125,* 491–496.

Cheung, Y-B. (1998). Accidents, assaults, and marital status. *Social Science and Medicine, 47,* 1325–1329.

Chlopan, B. E., McCain, M. L., Carbonell, J. L., & Hagen, R. L. (1985). Empathy: Review of available measures. *Journal of Personality and Social Psychology, 48,* 635–653.

Chomsky, N. (1965). *Aspects of the theory of syntax.* Cambridge: MIT Press.

Chovil, N. (1994). Equivocation as an interactional event. In W. R. Cupach & B. H. Spitzberg (Eds.), *The dark side of interpersonal communication* (pp. 105–124). Hillsdale, NJ: Lawrence Erlbaum.

Cicero. (1959). *De Oratore I, II* [The orator] (E. W. Sutton, Trans.). Cambridge, MA: Harvard University Press. (Original work published 1942)

Cliffordson, C. (2002). The hierarchical structure of empathy: Dimensional organization and relations to social functioning. *Scandinavian Journal of Psychology, 43,* 49–59.

Conference Board. (2006). *Are they really ready to work? Employers' perspectives on the basic knowledge and applied skills of new entrants to the 21st century U.S. workforce.* New York: Author.

Coupland, N., Wiemann, J. M., & Giles, H. (1991). Talk as "problem" and communication as "miscommunication": An integrative analysis. In N. Coupland, H. Giles, & J. M. Wiemann (Eds.), *"Miscommunication" and problematic talk* (pp. 1–17). Newbury Park, CA: Sage.

Cui, G. (1989). *Measuring intercultural effectiveness: An integrative approach.* Paper presented at the International Communication Conference, San Francisco.

Cupach, W. R., & Spitzberg, B. H. (1983). Trait versus state: A comparison of dispositional and situational measures of interpersonal communication competence. *Western Journal of Speech Communication, 47,* 364–379.

Cupach, W. R., & Spitzberg, B. H. (Eds.). (1994). *The dark side of interpersonal communication.* Hillsdale, NJ: Lawrence Erlbaum.

Curran, J. P. (1979). Social skills: Methodological issues and future directions. In A. S. Bellack & M. Hersen (Eds.), *Research and practice in social skills training* (pp. 319–354). New York: Plenum Press.

Curran, J. P., Miller, I. W., III, Zwick, W. R., Monti, P. M., & Stout, R. L. (1980). The socially inadequate patient: Incidence rate, demographic and clinical features, and hospital and posthospital functioning. *Journal of Consulting and Clinical Psychology, 48,* 375–382.

Curtis, D. B., Winsor, J. L., & Stephens, R. D. (1989). National preferences in business and communication education. *Communication Education, 38,* 6–14.

Dalgard, O. S., & Lund Håheim, L. L. (1998). Psychosocial risk factors and mortality: A prospective study with special focus on social support, social participation, and locus of control. *Journal of Epidemiology and Community Health, 52,* 476–481.

Daly, J. A. (1994). Assessing speaking and listening: Preliminary considerations for a national assessment. In A. Greenwood (Ed.), *The national assessment of college student learning: Identification of the skills to be taught, learned, and assessed* (Report of the Proceedings of the Second Study Design Workshop, November 1992, pp. 113–180). Washington, DC: U.S. Department of Education.

Davis, M. C., & Swan, P. D. (1999). Association of negative and positive social ties with fibrinogen levels in young women. *Health Psychology, 18,* 131–139.

Davis, M. H. (1983). Measuring individual differences in empathy: Evidence for a multidimensional approach. *Journal of Personality and Social Psychology, 44,* 113–126.

Davis, M. H., & Oathout, H. A. (1987). Maintenance of satisfaction in romantic relationships: Empathy and relational competence. *Journal of Personality and Social Psychology, 53,* 397–410.

Davis, M. H., & Oathout, H. A. (1992). The effect of dispositional empathy on romantic relationship behaviors: Heterosexual anxiety as a moderating influence. *Personality and Social Psychology Bulletin, 18,* 76–83.

Davis, O. (1999). Confusional consequences of illogical interaction. *Psychiatry, 62,* 250–264.

Deardorff, D. K. (2009). Synthesizing conceptualizations of intercultural competence: A summary of emerging themes. In D. K. Deardorff (Ed.), *The Sage handbook of intercultural competence* (pp. 264–270). Los Angeles, CA: Sage.

DePaulo, B. (2011). Living single: Lightening up those dark, dopey myths. In W. R. Cupach & B. H. Spitzberg (Eds.), *The dark side of close relationships—II* (pp. 409–439) New York: Routledge.

DePaulo, B. M., Kashy, D. A., Kirkendol, S. E., Wyer, M. M., & Epstein, J. A. (1996). Lying in everyday life. *Journal of Personality and Social Psychology, 70,* 979–995.

Derlega, V. J., & Grzelak, J. (1979). Appropriateness of self-disclosure. In G. J. Chelune (Ed.), *Self-disclosure: Origins, patterns, and implications of openness in interpersonal relationships* (pp. 151–176). San Francisco: Jossey-Bass.

Derlega, V. J., Metts, S., Petronio, S., & Margulis, S. T. (1993). *Self-disclosure.* Newbury Park, CA: Sage.

DeWine, S. (1987). Evaluation of organizational communication competence: The development of the communication training impact questionnaire. *Journal of Applied Communication Research, 15,* 113–127.

Dillard, J. P., Solomon, D. H., & Palmer, M. T. (1999). Structuring the concept of relational communication. *Communication Monographs, 66,* 49–65.

Dillard, J. P., & Spitzberg, B. H. (1984). Global impressions of social skills: Behavioral predictors. In R. N. Bostrom (Ed.), *Communication yearbook 8* (pp. 446–463). Beverly Hills, CA: Sage.

DiSalvo, V. S. (1980). A summary of current research identifying communication skills in various organizational contexts. *Communication Education, 29,* 283–290.

Dobos, J., Bahniuk, M. H., & Kogler Hill, S. E. (1991). Power-gaining communication strategies and career success. *Southern Communication Journal, 57,* 35–48.

Doll, E. A. (1953). *The measurement of social competence.* Darien, CT: Educational Publishers, Educational Test Bureau.

Dreznick, M. T. (2003). Heterosocial competence of rapists and child molesters: A meta-analysis. *Journal of Sex Research, 40,* 170–178.

Drury, J., Catan, L., Dennison, C., & Brody, R. (1998). Exploring teenagers' accounts of bad communication: A new basis for intervention. *Journal of Adolescence, 21,* 177–196.

Duck, S., Rutt, D. J., Hurst, M. H., & Strejc, H. (1991). Some evident truths about conversations in everyday relationships: All communications are not created equal. *Human Communication Research, 18,* 228–267.

Dunning, D., Heath, C., & Suls, J. M. (2004). Flawed self-assessment: Implications for health, education, and the workplace. *Psychological Science in the Public Interest, 5,* 69–106.

Eaker, E. D., Sullivan, L. M., Kelly-Hayes, M., D'Agostino, R. B., & Benjamin, E. J. (2007). Marital status, marital strain, and risk of coronary heart disease or total mortality: The Framingham offspring study. *Psychosomatic Medicine, 69,* 509–513.

Egland, K. L., Spitzberg, B. H., & Zormeier, M. M. (1996). Flirtation and conversational competence in cross-sex platonic and romantic relationships. *Communication Reports, 9,* 105–118.

Ehninger, D. (1975). A synoptic view of systems of Western rhetoric. *Quarterly Journal of Speech, 61,* 448–453.

Eisenberg, E. M. (1984). Ambiguity as strategy in organizational communication. *Communication Monographs, 51,* 227–242.

Emmers-Sommer, T. M., Allen, M., Bourhis, J., Sahlstein, E., Laskowski, K., Falato, W. L., et al. (2004). A meta-analysis of the relationship between social skills and sexual offenders. *Communication Reports, 17,* 1–10.

Everson-Rose, S. A., & Lewis, T. T. (2005). Psychosocial factors and cardiovascular diseases. *Annual Review of Public Health, 26,* 469–500.

Ewbank, H. L. (1987). The rhetoric of conversation in America: 1776–1828. *Southern Speech Communication Journal, 53,* 49–64.

Farrell, A. D., Rabinowitz, J. A., Wallander, J. L., & Curran, J. P. (1985). An evaluation of two formats for the intermediate-level assessment of social skills. *Behavioral Assessment, 7,* 155–171.

Feeney, J. A., Noller, P., & Ward, C. (1997). Marital satisfaction and spousal interaction. In R. J. Sternberg & M. Hojjat (Eds.), *Satisfaction in close relationships* (pp. 160–189). New York: Guilford Press.

Felitti, V. J., Anda, R. F., Nordenberg, D., Williamson, D. F., Spitz, A. M., Edwards, V., et al. (1998). Relationship of childhood abuse and household dysfunction to many of the leading causes of death in adults: The adverse childhood experiences (ACE) study. *American Journal of Preventative Medicine, 14,* 245–257.

Fishbein, H. D. (1996). *Peer prejudice and discrimination: Evolutionary, cultural, and developmental dynamics.* Boulder, CO: Westview Press.

Flora, J., & Segrin, C. (1998). Joint leisure time in friend and romantic relationships: The role of activity type, social skills, and positivity. *Journal of Social and Personal Relationships, 15,* 711–718.

Floyd, K., Mikkelson, A. C., Tafoya, M. A., Farinelli, L., La Valley, A. G., Judd, J., et al. (2007). Human affection exchange: XIV. Relational affection predicts resting heart rate and free cortisol secretion during acute stress. *Behavioral Medicine, 32,* 151–156.

Floyd, K., & Riforgiate, S. (2008). Affectionate communication received from spouses predicts stress hormone levels in healthy adults. *Communication Monographs, 75,* 351–368.

Ford, E. S., Ahluwalia, I. B., & Galuska, D. A. (2000). Social relationships and cardiovascular disease risk factors: Findings from the third national health and nutrition examination survey. *Preventative Medicine, 30,* 83–92.

Forgas, J. P. (1978). The effects of behavioural and cultural expectation cues on the perception of social episodes. *European Journal of Social Psychology, 8,* 203–213.

Forgas, J. P. (1979). *Social episodes: The study of interaction routines.* New York: Academic Press.

Forgas, J. P. (1982). Episode cognition: Internal representations of interaction routines. *Advances in Experimental Social Psychology, 15,* 59–101.

Forgas, J. P. (1983a). The effects of prototypicality and cultural salience on perceptions of people. *Journal of Research in Personality, 17,* 153–173.

Forgas, J. P. (1983b). Social skills and the perception of interaction episodes. *British Journal of Clinical Psychology, 22,* 195–207.

Franks, D. D., & Marolla, J. (1976). Efficacious action and social approval as interacting dimensions of self-esteem: A tentative formulation through construct validation. *Sociometry, 39,* 324–341.

Freedman, M. B., Leary, T. F., Ossorio, A. G., & Coffey, H. S. (1951). The interpersonal dimension of personality. *Journal of Personality, 20,* 143–161.

Furmark, T., Tillfors, M., Everz, P.-O., Marteinsdottir, I., Gefvert, O., & Fredrikson, M. (1999). Social phobia in the general population: Prevalence and sociodemographic profile. *Social Psychiatry and Psychiatric Epidemiology, 34,* 416–424.

Gable, S. L., & Shean, G. D. (2000). Perceived social competence and depression. *Journal of Social and Personal Relationships, 17,* 139–150.

Garland, D. R. (1981). Training married couples in listening skills: Effects on behavior, perceptual accuracy and marital adjustment. *Family Relations, 30,* 297–306.

Garland, M., & Fitzgerald, M. (1998). Social skills correlates of depressed mood in normal young adolescents. *Irish Journal of Psychological Studies, 15,* 19–21.

Gervasio, A. H., & Crawford, M. (1989). Social evaluations of assertiveness: A critique and speech act reformulation. *Psychology of Women Quarterly, 13,* 1–25.

Glaser, S. R., & Eblen, A. (1986). Organizational communication effectiveness: The view of corporate administrators. *Journal of Applied Communication Research, 14,* 119–132.

Glass, T. A., de Leon, C. M., Marottoli, R. A., & Berkman, L. F. (1999). Population based study of social and productive activities as predictors of survival among elderly Americans. *British Medical Journal, 319,* 478–483.

Goffman, E. (1974). *Frame analysis: An essay on the organization of experience.* Cambridge, MA: Harvard University Press.

Goldsmith, E. C. (1988). *Exclusive conversations: The art of interaction in seventeenth-century France.* Philadelphia: University of Pennsylvania.

Gottman, J. M. (1994). *What predicts divorce? The relationship between marital processes and marital outcomes.* Hillsdale, NJ: Lawrence Erlbaum.

Gottman, J. M., & Levenson, R. W. (1992). Marital processes predictive of later dissolution: Behavior, physiology, and health. *Journal of Personality and Social Psychology, 63,* 221–233.

Gottman, J. M., & Levenson, R. W. (1999a). Rebound from marital conflict and divorce prediction. *Family Process, 38,* 287–292.

Gottman, J. M., & Levenson, R. W. (1999b). What predicts change in marital interaction over time? A study of alternative models. *Family Process, 38,* 143–158.

Gottman, J. M., & Porterfield, A. L. (1981). Communicative competence in the nonverbal behavior of married couples. *Journal of Marriage and the Family, 43,* 817–824.

Gottman, J. M., & Rushe, R. (1995). Communication and social skills approaches to treating ailing marriages: A recommendation for a new marital therapy called "minimal marital therapy." In W. O'Donohue & L. Krasner (Eds.), *Handbook of psychological skills training: Techniques and applications* (pp. 287–305). Boston: Allyn & Bacon.

Gould, S. J. (1981). *The mismeasure of man.* New York: W. W. Norton.

Graham, E. E., Barbato, C. A., & Perse, E. M. (1993). The interpersonal communication motives model. *Communication Quarterly, 41,* 172–186.

Graham, E. E., Papa, M. J., & Brooks, G. P. (1992). Functions of humor in conversation: Conceptualization and measurement. *Western Journal of Communication, 56,* 161–183.

Greene, J. O. (1984). A cognitive approach to human communication: An action assembly theory. *Communication Monographs, 51,* 289–306.

Greene, J. O. (1997). A second generation action assembly theory. In J. O. Greene (Ed.), *Message production: Advances in communication theory* (pp. 151–170). Mahwah, NJ: Lawrence Erlbaum.

Greene, J. O., & Geddes, D. (1993). An action assembly perspective on social skill. *Communication Theory, 3,* 26–49.

Greene, J. O., & Graves, A. R. (2007). Cognitive models of message production. In D. R. Roskos-Ewoldsen & J. L. Monahan (Eds.), *Communication and social cognition: Theories and methods* (pp. 17–45). Mahwah, NJ: Lawrence Erlbaum.

Gremigni, P., Sommaruga, M., & Peltenburg, M. (2008). Validation of the Health Care Communication Questionnaire (HCCQ) to measure outpatients' experience of communication with hospital staff. *Patient Education and Counseling, 71,* 57–64.

Gresham, F. M., Cook, C. R., Crews, S. D., & Kern, L. (2004). Social skills training for children and youth with emotional and behavioral disorders: Validity considerations and future directions. *Behavioral Disorders, 30,* 32–46.

Grice, H. P. (1989). *Studies in the way of words.* Cambridge, MA: Harvard University Press.

Grimshaw, A. D. (1980). Mishearings, misunderstandings, and other nonsuccesses in talk: A plea for redress of speaker-oriented bias. *Sociological Inquiry, 50,* 31–74.

Gruppen, L. D., Garcia, J., Grum, C. M., Fitzgerald, J. T., White, C. A., Dicken, L., et al. (1997). Medical students' self-assessment accuracy in communication skills. *Academic Medicine, 72*(Suppl. 1), S57–S59.

Habermas, J. (1970). Toward a theory of communicative competence. In H. P. Dreitzel (Ed.), *Recent sociology* (No. 2, pp. 115–148). New York: Macmillan.

Habermas, J. (1981). *The theory of communicative action: Vol. 1. Reason and the rationalization of society.* Boston: Beacon Press.

Habermas, J. (1987). *The theory of communicative action: Vol. 2. The critique of functionalist reason.* Cambridge, UK: Polity Press.

Hammer, M. R., Gudykunst, W. B., & Wiseman, R. L. (1978). Dimensions of intercultural effectiveness: An exploratory study. *International Journal of Intercultural Relations, 2,* 382–393.

Hargie, O. D. W. (1997). Communication as skilled performance. In O. D. W. Hargie (Ed.), *The handbook of communication skills* (2nd ed., pp. 7–28). London: Routledge.

Hasler, B. S. (2009). *Virtual assessment center: A media comparison study on the diagnostic of face-to-face and online role-play for social competence assessment.* Doctoral thesis, University of Zurich, Zurich, Switzerland.

Hatcher, R. L., & Rogers, D. T. (2009). Development and validation of a measure of interpersonal strengths: The Inventory of Interpersonal Strengths. *Psychological Assessment, 21,* 554–569.

Hawkins, A. J., Blanchard, V. L., Baldwin, S. A., & Fawcett, E. B. (2008). Does marriage and relationship education work? A meta-analytic study. *Journal of Consulting and Clinical Psychology, 76,* 723–734.

Hawkins, K. W., & Fillion, B. P. (1999). Perceived communication skill needs for work groups. *Communication Research Reports, 16,* 167–174.

Hawthorne, G. (2008). Perceived social isolation in a community sample: Its prevalence and correlates with aspects of peoples' lives. *Social Psychiatry, 43,* 140–150.

Hazleton, V., Jr., & Cupach, W. R. (1986). An exploration of ontological knowledge: Communication competence as a function of the ability to describe, predict, and explain. *Western Journal of Speech Communication, 50,* 119–132.

Hazleton, V., Jr., Cupach, W. R., & Canary, D. J. (1987). Situation perception: Interactions between competence and messages. *Journal of Language and Social Psychology, 6,* 57–63.

Hecht, H., & Wittchen, H.-U. (1988). The frequency of social dysfunction in a general population sample and in patients with mental disorders: A comparison using the social interview schedule (SIS). *Social Psychiatry and Psychiatric Epidemiology, 23,* 17–29.

Hecht, M. L. (1978). The conceptualization and measurement of interpersonal communication satisfaction. *Human Communication Research, 4,* 253–264.

Hecht, M. L. (1984). Satisfying communication and relationship labels: Intimacy and length of relationship as perceptual frames of naturalistic conversations. *Western Journal of Speech Communication, 48,* 201–216.

Hecht, M. L., Collier, M. J., & Ribeau, S. A. (1993). *African American communication: Ethnic identity and cultural interpretations.* Newbury Park, CA: Sage.

Heggestad, E. D., & Morrison, M. J. (2008). An inductive exploration of the social effectiveness construct space. *Journal of Personality, 76,* 839–874.

Heise, D. R. (1979). *Understanding events: Affect and the construction of social action.* New York: Cambridge University Press.

Herrmann, D. S., & McWhirter, J. J. (1997). Refusal and resistance skills for children and adolescents: A selected review. *Journal of Counseling and Development, 75,* 177–187.

Higginbotham, D. J., & Wilkins, D. P. (1999). Slipping through the timestream: Social issues of time and timing in augmented interactions. In D. Kovarsky, J. F. Duchan, & M. Maxwell (Eds.), *Constructing (in)competence: Disabling evaluations in clinical and social interaction* (pp. 49–82). Mahwah, NJ: Lawrence Erlbaum.

Hinami, K., Farnan, J. M., Meltzer, D. O., & Arora, V. M. (2009). Understanding communication during hospitalist service changes: A mixed methods study. *Journal of Hospital Medicine, 4,* 535–540.

Hofstede, G. (1984). *Culture's consequences: International differences in work-related values* (abridged ed.). Newbury Park, CA: Sage.

Hopper, R., Knapp, M. L., & Scott, L. (1981). Couples' personal idioms: Exploring intimate talk. *Journal of Communication, 31,* 23–33.

Horney, K. (1945). *Our inner conflicts: A constructive theory of neurosis.* New York: W. W. Norton.

House, J. S., Landis, K. R., & Umberson, D. (1988). Social relationships and health. *Science, 241,* 540–545.

Howe, M. J. A. (1997). *IQ in question: The truth about intelligence.* Thousand Oaks, CA: Sage.

Hunt, J., & Manning, P. K. (1991). The social context of police lying. *Symbolic Interaction, 14,* 51–70.

Ickes, W. (1981). Sex-role influences in dyadic interaction: A theoretical model. In C. Mayo & N. M. Henley (Eds.), *Gender and nonverbal behavior* (pp. 95–128). New York: Springer-Verlag.

Ickes, W. (1985). Sex-role influences on compatibility in relationships. In W. Ickes (Ed.), *Compatible and incompatible relationships* (pp. 187–208). New York: Springer-Verlag.

Ickes, W. (Ed.). (1997). *Empathic accuracy.* New York: Guilford Press.

Ilott, I. (2001). Incompetence: An unspoken consensus. In J. Raven & J. Stephenson (Eds.), *Competence in the learning society* (pp. 57–66). New York: Peter Lang.

Impett, E. A., Gable, S. L., & Peplau, L. A. (2005). Giving up and giving in: The costs and benefits of daily sacrifice in intimate relationships. *Journal of Personality and Social Psychology, 89,* 327–344.

Iramaneerat, C., Myford, C. M., Yudkowsky, R., & Lowenstein, T. (2009). Evaluating the effectiveness of rating instruments for a communication skills assessment of medical residents. *Advances in Health Sciences Education, 14,* 575–594.

Jeanneret, M. (1991). *A feast of words: Banquets and table talk in the renaissance.* Chicago: University of Chicago Press.

Johannesen, R. L. (1971). The emerging concept of communication as dialogue. *Quarterly Journal of Speech, 57,* 373–382.

Johnson, N. J., Backlund, E., Sorlie, P. D., & Loveless, C. A. (2000). Marital status and mortality: The national longitudinal mortality study. *Annals of Epidemiology, 10,* 224–238.

Jones, S. M., & Wirtz, J. G. (2006). How does the comforting process work? An empirical test of an appraisal-based model of comforting. *Human Communication Research, 32,* 217–243.

Kahn, J. H., Nauta, M. M., Gailbreath, R. D., Tips, J., & Chartrand, J. M. (2002). The utility of career and personality assessment in predicting academic progress. *Journal of Career Assessment, 10,* 3–23.

Kashdan, T. B. (2007). Social anxiety spectrum and diminished positive experiences: Theoretical synthesis and meta-analysis. *Clinical Psychology Review, 27,* 348–365.

Kasson, J. F. (1990). *Rudeness and civility: Manners in nineteenth-century urban America.* New York: Hill & Wang.

Katriel, T., & Philipsen, G. (1981). "What we need is communication": "Communication" as a cultural category in some American speech. *Communication Monographs, 48,* 301–317.

Kellermann, K., Reynolds, R., & Chen, J. B.-S. (1991). Strategies for conversational retreat: When parting is not sweet sorrow. *Communication Monographs, 58,* 362–383.

Kellermann, K., & Shea, B. C. (1996). Threats, suggestions, hints, and promises: Gaining compliance efficiently and politely. *Communication Quarterly, 44,* 145–165.

Kelley, H. H., Berscheid, E., Christensen, A., Harvey, J. H., Huston, T. L., Levinger, G., et al. (Eds.). (1983). *Close relationships.* New York: Freeman.

Kelly, A. B., Fincham, F. D., & Beach, S. R. H. (2003). Communication skills in couples: A review and discussion of emerging perspectives. In J. O. Greene & B. R. Burleson (Eds.), *Handbook of communication and social interaction skills* (pp. 723–752). Mahwah, NJ: Lawrence Erlbaum.

Kelly, J. (1982). *Social skills training: A practical guide for interventions.* New York: Springer.

Kennedy, G. (1963). *The art of persuasion in Greece.* Princeton, NJ: Princeton University Press.

Kenny, D. A. (1994). *Interpersonal perception: A social relations analysis.* New York: Guilford Press.

Klakovich, M. D., & Dela Cruz, F. A. (2006). Validating the interpersonal communication assessment scale. *Journal of Professional Nursing, 22,* 60–67.

Kline, G. H., Pleasant, N. D., Witton, S. W., & Markman, H. J. (2006). Understanding couple conflict. In A. L. Vangelisti & D. Perlman (Eds.), *The Cambridge handbook of personal relationships* (pp. 445–462). New York: Cambridge University Press.

Knapp, M. L., Ellis, D. G., & Williams, B. A. (1980). Perceptions of communication behavior associated with relationship terms. *Communication Monographs, 47,* 262–278.

Kolb, J. A. (1996). A comparison of leadership behaviors and competencies in high- and average-performance teams. *Communication Reports, 9,* 173–183.

Kolotkin, R. A., Wielkiewicz, R. M., Judd, B., & Weiser, S. (1983). Behavioral components of assertion: Comparison of univariate and multivariate assessment strategies. *Behavioral Assessment, 6,* 61–78.

Kowalski, R. M. (2000). "I was only kidding!": Victims' and perpetrators' perceptions of teasing. *Personality and Social Psychology Bulletin, 26,* 231–241.

Kramsch, C., & Whiteside, A. (2008). Language ecology in multilingual settings. Towards a theory of symbolic competence. *Applied Linguistics, 29,* 645–671.

Kristiansen, M., & Bloch-Poulsen, J. (2000). The challenge of the unspoken in organizations: Caring container as a dialogic answer? *Southern Communication Journal, 65,* 176–190.

Kruger, J. (1999). Lake Wobegon be gone! The "below-average effect" and the egocentric nature of comparative ability judgments. *Journal of Personality and Social Psychology, 77,* 221–232.

Krumrei, E., Coit, C., Martin, S., Fogo, W., & Mahoney, A. (2007). Post-divorce adjustment and social relationships: A meta-analytic review. *Journal of Divorce & Remarriage, 46,* 145–166.

Kunkel, A. D., Wilson, S. R., Olufowote, J., & Robson, S. (2003). Identity implications of influence goals: Initiating, intensifying, and ending romantic relationships. *Western Journal of Communication, 67,* 382–412.

Kurtz, M. M., & Mueser, K. T. (2008). A meta-analysis of controlled research on social skills training for schizophrenia. *Journal of Consulting and Clinical Psychology, 76,* 491–504.

Laing, R. D., Phillipson, H., & Lee, A. R. (1966). *Interpersonal perception: A theory and a method of research.* New York: Springer.

Lamke, L. K., Sollie, D. L., Durbin, R. G., & Fitzpatrick, J. A. (1994). Masculinity, femininity, and relationship satisfaction: The mediating role of interpersonal competence. *Journal of Social and Personal Relationships, 11,* 535–554.

Landsheer, H. A., Maassen, G. H., Bisschop, P., & Adema, L. (1998). Can higher grades result in fewer friends? A reexamination of the relation between academic and social competence. *Adolescence, 33,* 185–191.

Larson, C. E., Backlund, P., Redmond, M., & Barbour, A. (1978). *Assessing functional communication.* Falls Church, VA: Speech Communication Association.

Leary, T., & Coffey, H. S. (1955). Interpersonal diagnosis: Some problems of methodology and validation. *Journal of Abnormal and Social Psychology, 50,* 110–124.

Leibetseder, M., Laireiter, A-R., & Köller, T. (2007). Structural analysis of the E-scale. *Personality and Individual Differences, 42,* 547–561.

de Leon, C. F. M., Glass, T. A., Beckett, L. A., Seeman, T. E., Evans, D. A., & Berkman, L. F. (1999). Social networks and disability transitions across eight intervals of yearly data in the New Haven EPESE. *Journal of Gerontology: Social Sciences, 54B,* S162–S172.

Leschied, A., Chiodo, D., Nowicki, E., & Rodger, S. (2008). Childhood predictors of adult criminality: A meta-analysis drawn from the prospective longitudinal literature. *Canadian Journal of Criminology and Criminal Justice, 50,* 435–467.

Levinson, S. C. (1995). Interactional biases in human thinking. In E. N. Goody (Ed.), *Social intelligence and interaction: Expressions and implication of the social bias in human intelligence* (pp. 221–260). Cambridge, UK: Cambridge University Press.

Lewis, M. A., & Rook, K. S. (1999). Social control in personal relationships: Impact on health behaviors and psychological distress. *Health Psychology, 18,* 63–71.

Lie, D., Bereknyei, S., Braddock, C. H., III, Encinas, J., Ahearn, S., & Boker, J. R. (2009). Assessing medical students' skills in working with interpreters during patient encounters: A validation study of the Interpreter Scale. *Academic Medicine, 84,* 643–650.

Linehan, M. M., & Walker, R. O. (1983). The components of assertion: Factor analysis of a multimethod assessment battery. *British Journal of Clinical Psychology, 22,* 277–281.

Linell, P. (1998). *Approaching dialogue: Talk, interaction and contexts in dialogical perspectives.* Amsterdam: John Benjamins.

Lippard, P. V. (1988). "Ask me no questions, I'll tell you no lies": Situational exigencies for interpersonal deception. *Western Journal of Speech Communication, 52,* 91–103.

Lleras, C. (2008). Do skills and behaviors in high school matter? The contribution of noncognitive factors in explaining differences in educational attainment and earnings. *Social Science Research, 37,* 888–902.

Locke, K. D. (2000). Circumplex scales of interpersonal values: Reliability, validity, and applicability to interpersonal problems and personality disorders. *Journal of Personality Assessment, 75,* 249–267.

Madlock, P. E. (2008). The link between leadership style and communication competence, and employee satisfaction. *Journal of Business Communication, 45,* 61–78.

Magee Quinn, M., Kavale, K. A., Mathur, S. R., Rutherford, R. B., Jr., & Forness, S. R. (1999). A meta-analysis of social skill interventions for students with emotional or behavioral disorders. *Journal of Emotional and Behavioral Disorders, 7,* 54–64.

Makoul, G. (2001). The SEGUE framework for teaching and assessing interpersonal skills. *Patient Education and Counseling, 45,* 23–34.

Manzoli, L., Villari, P., Pironec, G. M., & Boccia, A. (2007). Marital status and mortality in the elderly: A systematic review and meta-analysis. *Social Science & Medicine, 64,* 77–94.

Markman, K. M. (2009). "So what shall we talk about." *Journal of Business Communication, 46,* 150–170.

Marlowe, H. A., Jr. (1985). Competence: A social intelligence perspective. In H. A. Marlowe Jr. & R. B. Weinberg (Eds.), *Competence development: Theory and practice in special populations* (pp. 50–82). Springfield, IL: Charles C. Thomas.

Marshall, J. C. (1977). Minds, machines and metaphors. *Social Studies of Science, 7,* 475–488.

Maslow, A. H. (1968). *Toward a psychology of being* (2nd ed.). New York: D. Van Nostrand.

McAdams, D. P. (1988). *Power, intimacy, and the life story: Personalogical inquiries into identity.* New York: Guilford Press.

McCabe, M. P., Cummins, R. A., & Romeo, Y. (1996). Relationship status, relationship quality, and health. *Journal of Family Studies, 2,* 109–120.

McCroskey, J. C. (1982). Communication competence and performance: A research and pedagogical perspective. *Communication Education, 31,* 1–8.

McFall, R. M. (1982). A review and reformulation of the concept of social skills. *Behavioral Assessment, 4,* 1–33.

McLaughlin, M. L. (1984). *Conversation: How talk is organized.* Beverly Hills, CA: Sage.

McNamee, S., & Gergen, K. J. (1999). *Relational responsibility: Resources for sustainable dialogue.* Thousand Oaks, CA: Sage.

Menache, S. (1990). *Vox Dei: Communication in the middle ages.* New York: Oxford University Press.

Miczo, N., Segrin, C., & Allspach, L. E. (2001). Relationship between nonverbal sensitivity, encoding, and relational satisfaction. *Communication Reports, 14,* 39–48.

Mieth, D. (1997). The basic norm of truthfulness: Its ethical justification and universality. In C. Christians & M. Traber (Eds.), *Communication ethics and universal values* (pp. 87–104). Thousand Oaks, CA: Sage.

Miller, G. E., Dopp, J. M., Myers, H. F., Stevens, S. Y., & Fahey, J. L. (1999). Psychosocial predictors of natural killer cell mobilization during marital conflict. *Health Psychology, 18,* 262–271.

Miller, G. E., Kemeny, M. E., Taylor, S. E., Cole, S. W., & Visscher, B. R. (1997). Social relationships and immune processes in HIV seropositive gay and bisexual men. *Annals of Behavioral Medicine, 19,* 139–151.

Miller, L. C., Berg, J. H., & Archer, R. L. (1983). Openers: Individuals who elicit intimate self-disclosure. *Journal of Personality and Social Psychology, 44,* 1234–1244.

Mohrmann, G. F. (1972). The civile conversation: Communication in the Renaissance. *Speech Monographs, 39,* 193–204.

Morreale, S. P. (2008). Competent and incompetent communication. In W. F. Eadie (Ed.), *21st century communication* (pp. 444–453). Thousand Oaks, CA: Sage.

Morreale, S. P., & Pearson, J. C. (2008). Why communication education is important: The centrality of the discipline in the 21st century. *Communication Education, 57,* 224–240.

Mortensen, C. D. (1997). *Miscommunication.* Thousand Oaks, CA: Sage.

Moskowitz, D. S., & Zuroff, D. C. (2005). Assessing interpersonal perceptions using the interpersonal grid. *Psychological Assessment, 17,* 218–230.

Muñoz, M., Vázquez, C., Bermejo, M., & Vázquez, J. J. (1999). Stressful life events among homeless people: Quantity, types, timing, and perceived causality. *Journal of Community Psychology, 27,* 73–87.

Myrtek, M. (2007). Type A behavior and hostility as independent risk factors for coronary heart disease. In J. Jordan, B. Bardé, & A. M. Szeiher (Eds.), *Contributions toward evidence-based psychocardiology: A systematic review of the literature*

(pp. 159–183). Washington, DC: American Psychological Association.

Nevile, M. (2007). Talking without overlap in the airline cockpit: Precision timing at work. *Text & Talk, 27,* 225–249.

Newcomb, A. F., Bukowski, W. M., & Pattee, L. (1993). Children's peer relations: A meta-analytic review of popular, rejected, neglected, controversial, and average sociometric status. *Psychological Bulletin, 113,* 99–128.

Nezlek, J. B. (2001). Causal relationships between perceived social skills and day-to-day social interaction: Extending the sociometer hypothesis. *Journal of Social and Personal Relationships, 18,* 386–403.

Nezlek, J. B., Schütz, A., & Sellin, I. (2007). Self-presentational success in daily social interaction. *Self and Identity, 6,* 361–379.

Nicotera, A. M. (1997). *The mate relationships: Cross-cultural applications of a rules theory.* Albany: State University of New York Press.

Nisbett, R., & Ross, L. (1980). *Human inference: Strategies and shortcomings of social judgment.* Englewood Cliffs, NJ: Prentice Hall.

Noar, S. M., Carlyle, K., & Cole, C. (2006). Why communication is crucial: Meta-analysis of the relationship between safer sexual communication and condom use. *Journal of Health Communication, 11,* 365–390.

O'Neil, H. F., Jr., Allred, K., & Baker, E. L. (1997). Review of workforce readiness theoretical frameworks. In H. F. O'Neil Jr. (Ed.), *Workforce readiness: Competencies and assessment* (pp. 3–25). Mahwah, NJ: Lawrence Erlbaum.

Otness, H. R. (1941). Educating for social competence. *Training School Bulletin, 38,* 21–32.

Parks, M. R. (1995). Ideology in interpersonal communication: Beyond the couches, talk shows, and bunkers. In B. R. Burleson (Ed.), *Communication yearbook 18* (pp. 480–497). Thousand Oaks, CA: Sage.

Patterson, M. L. (1994). Strategic functions of nonverbal exchange. In J. A. Daly & J. M. Wiemann (Eds.), *Strategic interpersonal communication* (pp. 273–293). Hillsdale, NJ: Lawrence Erlbaum.

Pavitt, C. (1989). Accounting for the process of communicative competence evaluation: A comparison of predictive models. *Communication Research, 16,* 405–433.

Payne, H. J. (2005). Reconceptualizing social skills in organizations: Exploring the relationship between communication competence, job performance, and supervisory roles. *Journal of Leadership and Organizational Studies, 11,* 63–71.

Payne, S. C., Horner, M. T., Boswell, W. R., Schroeder, A. N., & Stine-Cheyne, K. J. (2009). Comparison of online and traditional performance appraisal systems. *Journal of Managerial Psychology, 24,* 526–544.

Pearce, W. B., & Cronen, V. E. (1980). *Communication, action, and meaning.* New York: Praeger.

Pearce, W. B., & Littlejohn, S. W. (1997). *Moral conflict: When social worlds collide.* Thousand Oaks, CA: Sage.

Pearce, W. B., & Pearce, K. A. (2000). Combining passions and abilities: Toward dialogic virtuosity. *Southern Communication Journal, 65,* 161–175.

Penley, L. E., Alexander, E. R., Jernigan, I. E., & Henwood, C. I. (1991). Communication abilities of managers: The relationship to performance. *Journal of Management, 17,* 57–76.

Penman, R. (1992). Good theory and good practice: An argument in progress. *Communication Theory, 2,* 234–250.

Perrin, D., & Ehrensberger-Dow, M. (2008). Media competence. In G. Rickheit & H. Strohner (Eds.), *Handbook of communication competence* (pp. 277–312). New York: Mouton de Gruyter.

Peterson, M. S. (1997). Personnel interviewers' perceptions of the importance and adequacy of applicants' communication skills. *Communication Education, 46,* 287–291.

Phillips, L., & Zigler, E. (1961). Social competence: The action-thought parameter and vicariousness in normal and pathological behaviors. *Journal of Abnormal and Social Psychology, 63,* 137–146.

Piccolo, L. D., Mazzi, M. A., Scardoni, S., Silvia, G. M., & Zimmerman, C. (2008). A theory-based proposal to evaluate patient-centred communication in medical consultations: The Verona Patient-Centred Communication Evaluation scale (VR-COPE). *Health Education, 108,* 355–372.

Pitcher, S. W., & Meikle, S. (1980). The topography of assertive behavior in positive and negative situations. *Behavior Therapy, 11,* 532–547.

Powers, S. I., Pietromonaco, P. R., Gunlicks, M., & Sayer, A. (2006). Dating couples' attachment styles and patterns of cortisol reactivity and recovery in response to a relationship conflict. *Journal of Personality and Social Psychology, 90,* 613–628.

Powers, W. G., & Lowry, D. N. (1984). Basic communication fidelity: A fundamental approach. In R. N. Bostrom (Ed.), *Competence in communication: A multidisciplinary approach* (pp. 57–73). Beverly Hills, CA: Sage.

Procidano, M. E. (1992). The nature of perceived social support: Findings of meta-analytic studies. In C. D. Spielberger & J. N. Butcher (Eds.), *Advances in personality assessment* (Vol. 9, pp. 1–26). Hillsdale, NJ: Lawrence Erlbaum.

Quintillian. (1903). *Quintillian's institutes of oratory, or education of an orator* (J. S. Bell, Trans.). London: George Bell & Sons.

Rakos, R. F. (1991). *Assertive behavior: Theory, research, and training.* London: Routledge.

Ramaprasad, A. (1983). On the definition of feedback. *Behavioral Science, 28,* 4–13.

Ramsay, S., Gallois, C., & Callan, V. J. (1997). Social rules and attributions in the personnel selection interview. *Journal of Occupational and Organizational Psychology, 70,* 189–203.

Reddy, M. J. (1979). The conduit metaphor: A case of frame conflict in our language about language. In A. Ortony (Ed.), *Metaphor and thought* (pp. 284–324). Cambridge, UK: Cambridge University Press.

Regehr, C., & Marziali, E. (1999). Response to sexual assault: A relational perspective. *Journal of Nervous and Mental Disease, 187,* 618–623.

Reis, H. T., & Franks, P. (1994). The role of intimacy and social support in health outcomes: Two processes or one? *Personal Relationships, 1,* 185–197.

Reis, H. T., Sheldon, K. M., Gable, S. L., Roscoe, J., & Ryan, R. M. (2000). Daily well-being: The role of autonomy, competence, and relatedness. *Personality and Social Psychology Bulletin, 26,* 419–435.

Ren, X. S. (1997). Marital status and quality of relationships: The impact on health perception. *Social Scientific Medicine, 44,* 241–249.

Richmond, V. P., McCroskey, J. C., & McCroskey, L. L. (1989). An investigation of self-perceived communication competence and personality orientations. *Communication Research Reports, 6,* 30–38.

Rickheit, G., Strohner, H., & Vorwerg, C. (2008). The concept of communicative competence. In G. Rickheit & H. Strohner (Eds.), *Handbook of communication competence* (pp. 15–62). New York: Mouton de Gruyter.

Riggio, R. E., & Lee, J. (2007). Emotional and interpersonal competencies and leader development. *Human Resource Management Review, 17,* 418–426.

Riggio, R. E., Watring, K. P., & Throckmorton, B. (1993). Social skills, social support, and psychosocial adjustment. *Personality and Individual Differences, 15,* 275–280.

Riggio, R. E., & Zimmerman, J. (1991). Social skills and interpersonal relationships: Influences on social support and support seeking. In W. H. Jones & D. Perlman (Eds.), *Advances in personal relationships* (Vol. 2, 133–155). London: Jessica Kingsley.

Riikonen, E. (1999). Inspiring dialogues and relational responsibility. In S. McNamee & K. J. Gergen (Eds.), *Relational responsibility: Resources for sustainable dialogue* (pp. 139–150). Thousand Oaks, CA: Sage.

Roberts, N., & Noller, P. (1998). The associations between adult attachment and couple violence: The role of communication patterns and relationship satisfaction. In J. A. Simpson & W. S. Rholes (Eds.), *Attachment theory and close relationships* (pp. 317–350). New York: Guilford Press.

Robles, T. F., & Kiecolt-Glaser, J. K. (2003). The physiology of marriage: Pathways to health. *Physiology and Behavior, 79,* 409–416.

Roloff, M. E., & Kellermann, K. (1984). Judgments of interpersonal competence: How you know, what you know, and who you know. In R. N. Bostrom (Ed.), *Competence in communication: A multidisciplinary approach* (pp. 175–218). Beverly Hills, CA: Sage.

Rook, K. S. (1984). The negative side of social interaction: Impact on psychological well-being. *Journal of Personality and Social Psychology, 46,* 1097–1108.

Rook, K. S. (1991). Detrimental aspects of social relationships: Taking stock of an emerging literature. In H. O. F. Veiel & U. Baumann (Eds.), *The meaning and measurement of social support* (pp. 157–169). New York: Hemisphere.

Rook, K. S. (1998). Investigating the positive and negative sides of personal relationships: Through a lens darkly? In B. H. Spitzberg & W. R. Cupach (Eds.), *The dark side of close relationships* (pp. 369–393). Mahwah, NJ: Lawrence Erlbaum.

Rosenfeld, L. B., Grant, C. H., III, & McCroskey, J. C. (1995). Communication apprehension and self-perceived communication competence of academically gifted students. *Communication Education, 44,* 79–86.

Rosengren, D. B., Hartzler, B., Baer, J. S., Wells, E. A., & Dunn, C. W. (2008). The video assessment of simulated encounters-revised (VASE-R): Reliability and validity of a revised measure of motivational interviewing skills. *Drug and Alcohol Dependence, 97,* 130–138.

Rubin, K. H., Booth, C., Rose-Krasnor, L., & Mills, R. S. L. (1995). Social relationships and social skills: A conceptual and empirical analysis. In S. Shulman (Ed.), *Close relationships and socioemotional development* (pp. 63–94). Norwood, NJ: Ablex.

Rubin, R. B. (1981). *The development and refinement of a communication competency assessment instrument.* Paper presented at the Speech Communication Association Conference, Anaheim, CA.

Rubin, R. B. (1985). The validity of the communication competency assessment instrument. *Communication Monographs, 52,* 173–185.

Rubin, R. B., Graham, E. E., & Mignerey, J. T. (1990). A longitudinal study of college students' communication competence. *Communication Education, 39,* 1–14.

Rubin, R. B., Perse, E. M., & Barbato, C. A. (1988). Conceptualization and measurement of interpersonal communication motives. *Human Communication Research, 14,* 602–628.

Ruesch, J. (1951). Communication and mental illness: A psychiatric approach. In J. Ruesch & G. Bateson (Eds.), *Communication: The social matrix of psychiatry* (pp. 50–93). New York: W. W. Norton.

Ryan, A. M., & Shim, S. S. (2006). Social achievement goals: The nature and consequences of different orientations toward social competence. *Personality and Social Psychology Bulletin, 32,* 1246–1263.

Sabourin, T. C., Infante, D. A., & Rudd, J. E. (1993). Verbal aggression in marriages: A comparison of violent, distressed but nonviolent, and nondistressed couples. *Human Communication Research, 20,* 245–267.

Salgado, J. F., & Moscoso, S. (2002). Comprehensive meta-analysis of the construct validity of the employment interview. *European Journal of Work and Organizational Psychology, 11,* 299–324.

Sanford, K. (1998). Memories of feeling misunderstood, and a schema of partner empathic responding: New scales for marital research. *Journal of Social and Personal Relationships, 15,* 490–501.

Santelli, J., Bernstein, D. M., Zborowski, L., & Bernstein, J. M. (1990). Pursuing and distancing, and related traits: A cross-cultural assessment. *Journal of Personality Assessment, 55,* 663–672.

Scherz, J. W., Edwards, H. T., & Kallail, K. J. (1995). Communicative effectiveness of doctor-patient interactions. *Health Communication, 7*, 163–177.

Schoon, I., Parsons, S., Rush, R., & Law, J. (2010). Childhood language skills and adult literacy: A 29-year follow-up study. *Pediatrics, 125*, e459–e466.

Schrodt, P., Witt, P. L., & Messersmith, A. S. (2008). A meta-analytical review of family communication patterns and their associations with information processing, behavioral, and psychosocial outcomes. *Communication Monographs, 75*, 248–269.

Schutz, W. C. (1966). *The interpersonal underworld.* Palo Alto, CA: Science & Behavior Books.

Searle, J. R. (1969). *Speech acts: An essay in the philosophy of language.* Cambridge, UK: Cambridge University Press.

Sedikides, C., Olsen, N., & Reis, H. T. (1993). Relationships as natural categories. *Journal of Personality and Social Psychology, 64*, 71–82.

Segrin, C. (1992). Specifying the nature of social skill deficits associated with depression. *Human Communication Research, 19*, 89–123.

Segrin, C. (1998). The impact of assessment procedures on the relationship between paper and pencil and behavioral indicators of social skill. *Journal of Nonverbal Behavior, 22*, 229–251.

Segrin, C. (1999). Social skills, stressful life events, and the development of psychosocial problems. *Journal of Social and Clinical Psychology, 18*, 14–34.

Segrin, C., & Flora, J. (2000). Poor social skills are a vulnerability factor in the development of psychosocial problems. *Human Communication Research, 26*, 489–514.

Serota, K. B., Levine, T. R., & Boster, F. J. (2010). The prevalence of lying in America: Three studies of self-reported lies. *Human Communication Research, 36*, 2–25.

Shadish, W. R., & Baldwin, S. A. (2003). Meta-analysis of MFT interventions. *Journal of Marital & Family Therapy, 29*, 547–570.

Shaver, P., Furman, W., & Buhrmester, D. (1985). Transition to college: Network changes, social skills, and loneliness. In S. Duck & D. Perlman (Eds.), *Understanding personal relationships: An interdisciplinary approach* (pp. 193–220). Beverly Hills, CA: Sage.

Shean, G. D., & Heefner, A. S. (1995). Depression, interpersonal style, and communication skills. *Journal of Nervous and Mental Disease, 183*, 485–487.

Sheldon, K. M., Ryan, R., & Reis, H. T. (1996). What makes for a good day? Competence and autonomy in the day in the person. *Personality and Social Psychology, 22*, 1270–1279.

Sheridan, T. (1762). *A course of lectures in elocution: Together with two dissertations on language; and some other tracts relative to those subjects.* London: W. Strahan.

Shure, M. B. (1981). Social competence as a problem-solving skill. In J. D. Wine & M. D. Smye (Eds.), *Social competence* (pp. 158–188). New York: Guilford Press.

Sibley, C. G. (2007). The association between working models of attachment and personality: Toward an integrative framework operationalizing global relational models. *Journal of Research in Personality, 41*, 90–109.

Sillars, A. L. (1998). (Mis)understanding. In B. H. Spitzberg & W. R. Cupach (Eds.), *The dark side of close relationships* (pp. 73–102). Mahwah, NJ: Lawrence Erlbaum.

Sillars, A. L., Weisberg, J., Burggraf, C. S., & Zietlow, P. H. (1990). Communication and understanding revisited: Married couples' understanding and recall of conversations. *Communication Research, 17*, 500–522.

Simpson, J. A., Ickes, W., & Blackstone, T. (1995). When the head protects the heart: Empathic accuracy in dating relationships. *Journal of Personality and Social Psychology, 69*, 629–641.

Smith-Lovin, L. (1979). Behavior settings and impressions formed from social scenarios. *Social Psychology Quarterly, 42*, 31–43.

Spitzberg, B. H. (1983). Communication competence as knowledge, skill, and impression. *Communication Education, 32*, 323–328.

Spitzberg, B. H. (1989). Issues in the development of a theory of interpersonal competence in the intercultural context. *International Journal of Intercultural Relations, 13*, 241–268.

Spitzberg, B. H. (1990). The construct validity of trait-based measures of interpersonal competence. *Communication Research Reports, 7*, 107–116.

Spitzberg, B. H. (1991). An examination of trait measures of interpersonal competence. *Communication Research, 3*, 22–29.

Spitzberg, B. H. (1993). The dialectics of (in)competence. *Journal of Social and Personal Relationships, 10*, 137–158.

Spitzberg, B. H. (1994a). The dark side of (in)competence. In W. R. Cupach & B. H. Spitzberg (Eds.), *The dark side of interpersonal communication* (pp. 25–49). Hillsdale, NJ: Lawrence Erlbaum.

Spitzberg, B. H. (1994b). Ideological issues in competence assessment. In S. Morreale, M. Brooks, R. Berko, & C. Cooke (Eds.), *Assessing college student competency in speech communication* (1994 SCA Summer Conference Proceedings, pp. 129–148). Annandale, VA: Speech Communication Association.

Spitzberg, B. H. (1994c). Instructional assessment of interpersonal competence: The Conversational Skills Rating Scale. In S. Morreale, M. Brooks, R. Berko, & C. Cooke (Eds.), *Assessing college student competency in speech communication* (1994 SCA Summer Conference Proceedings, pp. 325–352). Annandale, VA: Speech Communication Association.

Spitzberg, B. H. (2000). What is good communication? *Journal of the Association for Communication Administration, 29,* 103–119.

Spitzberg, B. H. (2003). Methods of skill assessment. In J. O. Greene & B. R. Burleson (Eds.), *Handbook of communication and social interaction skills* (pp. 93–134). Mahwah, NJ: Lawrence Erlbaum.

Spitzberg, B. H. (2006). Toward a theory of computer-mediated communication competence. *Journal of Computer-Mediated Communication, 11*(2), Article 12. Retrieved April 5, 2011, from http://jcmc.indiana.edu/vol11/issue2/spitzberg.html

Spitzberg, B. H. (2009a). Axioms for a theory of intercultural communication competence [Invited article, Japanese Association of Communication and English Teachers]. *Annual Review of English Learning and Teaching, No. 14,* 69–81.

Spitzberg, B. H. (2009b). Interpersonal communication competence and social skills. In W. Donsbach (Ed.), *International encyclopedia of communication* (pp. 2486–2492). Oxford, UK: Blackwell.

Spitzberg, B. H. (2010, November). *Making an IMPACCT©: The Interactive Media Package for Assessment of Communication and Critical Thinking.* Paper presented at the National Communication Association Conference, San Francisco.

Spitzberg, B. H., & Brunner, C. C. (1991). Toward a theoretical integration of context and communication competence inference research. *Western Journal of Speech Communication, 55,* 28–46.

Spitzberg, B. H., & Canary, D. J. (1985). Loneliness and relationally competent communication. *Journal of Social and Personal Relationships, 2,* 387–402.

Spitzberg, B. H., Canary, D. J., & Cupach, W. R. (1994). A competence-based approach to the study of interpersonal conflict. In D. D. Cahn (Ed.), *Conflict in personal relationships* (pp. 183–202). Hillsdale, NJ: Lawrence Erlbaum.

Spitzberg, B. H., & Chagnon, G. (2009). Conceptualizing intercultural communication competence. In D. K. Deardorff (Ed.), *The SAGE handbook of intercultural competence* (pp. 2–52). Thousand Oaks, CA: Sage.

Spitzberg, B. H., & Cupach, W. R. (1984). *Interpersonal communication competence.* Beverly Hills, CA: Sage.

Spitzberg, B. H., & Cupach, W. R. (1989). *Handbook of interpersonal competence research.* New York: Springer-Verlag.

Spitzberg, B. H., & Cupach, W. R. (Eds.). (1998). *The dark side of close relationships.* Mahwah, NJ: Lawrence Erlbaum.

Spitzberg, B. H., & Cupach, W. R. (2002). Interpersonal skills. In M. L. Knapp & J. Daly (Eds.), *Handbook of interpersonal communication* (3rd ed., pp. 564–611). Newbury Park, CA: Sage.

Spitzberg, B. H., & Cupach, W. R. (2007). Disentangling the dark side of interpersonal communication. In B. H. Spitzberg & W. R. Cupach (Eds.), *The dark side of interpersonal communication* (2nd ed., pp. 3–28). Mahwah, NJ: Lawrence Erlbaum.

Spivack, G., Platt, J. J., & Shure, M. B. (1976). *The problem-solving approach to adjustment.* San Francisco: Jossey-Bass.

Spreng, R. N., McKinnon, M. C., Mar, R. A., & Levine, B. (2009). The Toronto Empathy Questionnaire: Scale development and initial validation of a factor-analytic solution to multiple empathy measures. *Journal of Personality Assessment, 91,* 62–71.

Stafford, L., & Dainton, M. (1994). The dark side of "normal" family interaction. In W. R. Cupach & B. H. Spitzberg (Eds.), *The dark side of interpersonal communication* (pp. 259–280). Hillsdale, NJ: Lawrence Erlbaum.

Stewart, J-A. (2006). High-performing (and threshold) competencies for group facilitators. *Journal of Change Management, 6,* 417–439.

Strahan, E. Y. (2003). The effects of social anxiety and social skills on academic performance. *Personality and Individual Differences, 34,* 347–366.

Su, Y.-P., & Ferraro, K. F. (1997). Social relations and health assessments among older people: Do the effects of integration and social contributions vary cross-culturally? *Journal of Gerontology: Social Sciences, 52B,* S27–S36.

Swanson, J., Swartz, M., Estroff, S., Borum, R., Wagner, R., & Hiday, V. (1998). Psychiatric impairment, social contact, and violent behavior: Evidence from a study of outpatient-committed persons with severe mental disorder. *Social Psychiatry and Psychiatric Epidemiology, 33* (Suppl), S86–S94.

Tazelaar, M. J. A., Van Lange, P. A. M., & Ouwerkerk, J. W. (2004). How to cope with "noise" in social dilemmas: The benefits of communication. *Journal of Personality and Social Psychology, 87,* 845–859.

Terman, L. M. (1938). *Psychological factors in marital happiness.* New York: McGraw-Hill.

Thomsen, D. G., & Gilbert, D. G. (1998). Factors characterizing marital conflict states and traits: Physiological, affective, behavioral and neurotic variable contributions to marital conflict and satisfaction. *Personality and Individual Differences, 25,* 833–855.

Thorndike, R. L. (1920). Intelligence and its uses. *Harper's Monthly, 140,* 227–235.

Thorsteinsson, E. B., & James, J. E. (1999). A meta-analysis of the effects of experimental manipulations of social support during laboratory stress. *Psychology and Health, 14,* 869–886.

Tooke, W., & Camire, L. (1991). Patterns of deception in intersexual and intrasexual mating strategies. *Ethology and Sociobiology, 12,* 345–364.

Triandis, H. C. (1995). *Individualism and collectivism.* Boulder, CO: Westview Press.

Trower, P. (1980). Situational analysis of the components and processes of socially skilled and unskilled patients. *Journal of Consulting and Clinical Psychology, 48,* 327–339.

Trower, P. (1982). Toward a generative model of social skills: A critique and synthesis. In J. P. Curran & P. M. Monti (Eds.), *Social skills training* (pp. 399–427). New York: Guilford Press.

Trower, P. (1984). A radical critique and reformulation: From organism to agent. In P. Trower (Ed.), *Radical approaches to social skills training* (pp. 48–88). London: Croom Helm.

Truax, C. B. (1967). A scale for the rating of accurate empathy. In C. R. Rogers (Ed.), *The therapeutic relationship and its impact* (pp. 555–568). Madison: University of Wisconsin Press.

Tucker, J. S., & Anders, S. L. (1999). Attachment style, interpersonal perception accuracy, and relationship satisfaction in dating couples. *Personality and Social Psychology Bulletin, 25,* 403–412.

Tyler, J. M., & Feldman, R. S. (2004). Cognitive demand and self-presentation efforts: The influence of situational importance and interaction goal. *Self and Identity, 3,* 364–377.

Vandeputte, D. D., Kemper, S., Hummert, M. L., Kemtes, K. A., Shaner, J., & Segrin, C. (1999). Social skills of older people: Conversations in same- and mixed-age dyads. *Discourse Processes, 27,* 55–76.

Vangelisti, A. L., & Daly, J. A. (1989). Correlates of speaking skills in the United States: A national assessment. *Communication Education, 38,* 132–143.

VanLear, C. A. (1991). Testing a cyclical model of communicative openness in relationship development: Two longitudinal studies. *Communication Monographs, 58,* 337–361.

VanWesenbeeck, I., van Zessen, G., Ingham, R., Jaramazovi, E., & Stevens, D. (1999). Factors and processes in heterosexual competence and risk: An integrated review of the evidence. *Psychology and Health, 14,* 25–50.

Verhulst, F. C., & Althaus, M. (1988). Persistence and change in behavioral/emotional problems reported by parents of children aged 4–14: An epidemiological study. *Acta Psychiatrica Scandinavica, 77*(Suppl. 339), 1–28.

Vroon, P. A. (1987). Man-machine analogs and theoretical mainstreams in psychology. In W. J. Baker, M. E. Hyland, H. Van Rappard, & A. W. Staats (Eds.), *Current issues in theoretical psychology* (pp. 393–414). North-Holland: Elsevier Science.

Waldron, V. R., & Lavitt, M. R. (2000). "Welfare-to-work": Assessing communication competencies and client outcomes in a job training program. *Southern Communication Journal, 66,* 1–15.

Waldron, V. R., Lavitt, M., & McConnaughy, M. (2001). "Welfare-to-work": An analysis of communication competencies taught in a job training program serving an urban poverty area. *Communication Education, 50,* 15–33.

Weintraub, S., & Neale, J. M. (1984). Social behavior of children at risk for schizophrenia. In N. F. Watt, E. J. Anthony, L. C. Wynne, & J. E. Rolf (Eds.),

*Children at risk for schizophrenia: A longitudinal perspective* (pp. 279–285). Cambridge, UK: Cambridge University Press.

Wellmon, T. A. (1988). Conceptualizing organizational communication competence: A rules-based perspective. *Management Communication Quarterly, 1,* 515–534.

Westermeyer, J. F. (1998). Predictors and characteristics of mental health among men at midlife: A 32-year longitudinal study. *American Journal of Orthopsychiatry, 68,* 265–273.

Whitson, S., & El-Sheikh, M. (2003). Marital conflict and health: Processes and protective factors. *Aggression and Violent Behavior, 8,* 283–312.

Wichstrøm, L., Anderson, M. C., Holte, A., & Wynne, L. C. (1996). Disqualifying family communication and childhood social competence as predictors of offspring's mental health and hospitalization. *Journal of Nervous and Mental Disease, 184,* 581–588.

Wilder, C., & Collins, S. (1994). Patterns of interactional paradoxes. In W. R. Cupach & B. H. Spitzberg (Eds.), *The dark side of interpersonal communication* (pp. 83–104). Hillsdale, NJ: Lawrence Erlbaum.

Wildman, B. G., & Clementz, B. (1986). Assertive, empathic assertive, and conversational behavior. *Behavior Modification, 10,* 315–331.

Wilsnack, R. W., Wilsnack, S. C., Kristjanson, A. F., & Harris, T. R. (1998). Ten-year prediction of women's drinking behavior in a nationally representative sample. *Women's Health: Research on Gender, Behavior, and Policy, 4,* 199–230.

Wilson, M., & Wilson, T. P. (2005). An oscillator model of the timing of turn-taking. *Psychonomic Bulletin & Review, 12,* 957–968.

Wilson, S. R., Kunkel, A. D., Robson, S. J., Olufowote, J. O., & Soliz, J. (2009). Identity implications of relationship (re)definition goals: An analysis of face threats and facework as young adults initiate, intensify, and disengage from romantic relationships. *Journal of Language and Social Psychology, 28,* 32–61.

Wilson, S. R., & Sabee, C. M. (2003). Explicating communicative competence as a theoretical term. In J. O. Greene & B. R. Burleson (Eds.), *Handbook of communication and social interaction skills* (pp. 3–50). Mahwah, NJ: Lawrence Erlbaum.

Wine, J. D. (1981). From defect to competence models. In J. D. Wine & M. D. Smye (Eds.), *Social competence* (pp. 3–35). New York: Guilford Press.

Wisecarver, M. M., Carpenter, T. D., & Kilcullen, R. N. (2007). Capturing interpersonal performance in a latent performance model. *Military Psychology, 19,* 83–101.

Wish, M., D'Andrade, R. G., & Goodnow, J. E., II. (1980). Dimensions of interpersonal communication: Correspondences between structures for speech acts and bipolar scales. *Journal of Personality and Social Psychology, 39,* 848–860.

Wish, M., & Kaplan, S. J. (1977). Toward an implicit theory of interpersonal communication. *Sociometry, 40,* 234–246.

Wittgenstein, L. (1958). *The blue and brown books.* New York: Harper & Row.

Wittgenstein, L. (1963). *Philosophical investigations.* Oxford, UK: Basil Blackwell.

Wood, J. T. (1998). *But I thought you meant . . .: Misunderstandings in human communication.* Mountain View, CA: Mayfield.

Wood, N. D., Crane, D. R., Schaalje, G. B., & Law, D. D. (2005). What works for whom: A meta-analytic review of marital and couples therapy in reference to marital distress. *American Journal of Family Therapy, 33,* 273–287.

Wyatt, T. (1999). An Afro-centered view of communicative competence. In D. Kovarsky, J. F. Duchan, & M. Maxwell (Eds.), *Constructing (in)competence: Disabling evaluations in clinical and social interaction* (pp. 197–223). Mahwah, NJ: Lawrence Erlbaum.

Yarcheski, A., Mahon, N. E., Yarcheski, T. J., & Cannella, B. L. (2004). A meta-analysis of predictors of positive health practices. *Journal of Nursing Scholarship, 36,* 102–108.

Young, B. S., Arthur, W., Jr., & Finch, J. (2000). Predictors of managerial performance: More than cognitive ability. *Journal of Business and Psychology, 15,* 53–72.

Zanten, M. van, Boulet, J. R., & McKinley, D. (2007). Using standardized patients to assess the interpersonal skills of physicians: Six years' experience with a high-stakes certification examination. *Health Communication, 22,* 195–205.

Žebiene, E., Švab, I., Šapoka, V., Kairys, J., Dotsenko, M., Radić, S., et al. (2008). Agreement in patient-physician communication in primary care: A study from Central and Eastern Europe. *Patient Education and Counseling, 73,* 246–250.

Zebrowitz, L. A. (2001). Groping for the elephant of interpersonal sensitivity. In J. A. Hall & F. J. Bernieri

(Eds.), *Interpersonal sensitivity theory and measurement* (pp. 333–350). Mahwah, NJ: Lawrence Erlbaum.

Zelenski, J. M., & Larsen, R. J. (2000). The distribution of basic emotions in everyday life: A state and trait perspective from experience sampling data. *Journal of Research in Personality, 34,* 178–197.

Zigler, E., & Levine, J. (1981). Premorbid competence in schizophrenia: What is being measured? *Journal of Consulting and Clinical Psychology, 49,* 96–105.

Zigler, E., & Phillips, L. (1960). Social effectiveness and symptomatic behaviors. *Journal of Abnormal and Social Psychology, 61,* 231–238.

Zigler, E., & Phillips, L. (1961). Social competence and outcome in psychiatric disorder. *Journal of Abnormal and Social Psychology, 63,* 264–271.

# PART V

# Contexts

# CHAPTER 16

# Interpersonal Communication in the Workplace

*Karen K. Myers*

*David R. Seibold*

*Hee Sun Park*

Communication serves many functions in the workplace, including information sharing, coordination, influence, motivation, decision making, and identification (Myers & Sadaghiani, 2010). Especially important, interpersonal interactions in work groups serve to create and maintain work *relationships* among team and organizational members (Sias, 2009). In turn, most significant work tasks, as well as many personal and organizational goals, are accomplished through communication-based interpersonal relationships in the workplace (Sias, Krone, & Jablin, 2002). Members rely on relationships with others in the organization to facilitate knowledge sharing and skill development, to aid in problem solving, to satisfy informational needs and to reduce uncertainty, to settle on—and settle into—their roles in the team, and to feel recognized for contributions to the work group and organization (Myers, 2009).

Recent reviews highlight the importance of interpersonal communication and relationships in the workplace. For example, Krone, Kramer, and Sias (2010) emphasize four areas of theoretical development in organizational communication that have clear ties with interpersonal communication: (1) supervisor–subordinate communication, (2) organizational assimilation/socialization, (3) emotion management, and (4) power and control. Seibold, Meyers, and Shoham (2010) survey research on organizational influence (social influence processing, diffusion of innovations, and network theory) in which interpersonal relationships and communication are salient. In their review of organizational and applied communication research, Seibold, Lemus, Ballard, and Myers (2009) acknowledge recent scholarship that is germane for understanding interpersonal communication in the workplace—for example, work on matters of difference in race and gender (Allen, 2005; Ashcraft, 2005); problematic workplace relationships (Tracy, Lutgen-Sandvik, & Alberts, 2006); emotion management (Waldron, 2000); organizational irrationality (Ashcraft & Trethewey, 2004); supervisory communication (Wagoner & Waldron, 1999), leadership (Fairhurst, 2007; Fairhurst & Sarr, 1996; Parker, 2001) and managerial reflexivity (Barge, 2004); customer service interactions (Ford, 2001, 2003); employee participation (Seibold & Shea, 2001); and certain organizational policies (Kirby & Krone, 2002).

Arguably, the most focused and yet most comprehensive reviews of interpersonal communication in the workplace have been those that appeared in three successive editions of this *Handbook*. Using a developmental, life span perspective, Jablin (1985) reviewed research on task/work relationships in terms of (a) anticipation of interpersonal communication at work (vocational/occupational development through communication from family, schools, media, peers, and part-time jobs and organizational choice from interactions in selection interviews and concerning job/organizational expectations); (b) interpersonal communication during assimilation and role making (via superior–subordinate communication, formal–informal interactions with coworkers, and assimilation outcomes related to communication climate and communication networks); and (c) interpersonal communication and disengagement from work (job transfer, voluntary exit, and retirement). In a full updating of the earlier chapter, Jablin and Krone (1994) used the same stage model of socialization and covered the same topics as Jablin (1985). Importantly, in their treatment of the outcomes of assimilation, Jablin and Krone (1994) added a review of findings related to cultural knowledge and shared meanings and to refinement of communication capacities and competencies. Finally, Sias et al. (2002) provided a sweeping focus on

workplace relationships from an ecological systems perspective and in a manner that enabled them to innovatively emphasize the dynamic and developmental nature of these relationships. The authors examined three relationship dimensions (status, intimacy, choice) across four system levels (microsystem, mesosystem, macrosystem, and exosystem) and studied equivalent-status relationships and different-status relationships at each level. They concluded that there were three biases in research up to that time (microsystem bias, intralevel bias, and unidirectional influence bias). We turn next to our focus in this chapter—the conceptual framework we use to organize the review—and the ways in which we hope this chapter will be read as a complement to the aforementioned chapters in the first three editions.

## Workplace Interaction and Interpersonal Processes of Assimilation

Jablin (1987) described the process of organizational members learning about the culture and how to get along in organizations as organizational assimilation. He argued that assimilation is the central determinant of how well individuals are able to function with others in the organizational environment. Some have referred to this process as membership negotiation (McPhee & Zaug, 2000; Myers, 2009; Scott & Myers, 2010). *Membership negotiation* is an appropriate term to use when considering contemporary workplace relationships because, in many ways, newcomers and old-timers alike must continuously assimilate into their changing organizational environments to retain productivity and to develop and maintain strong workplace relationships—the point of this chapter. Indeed, Korte (2010) found that integrating into an organization is largely a social process.

Our central propositions are that assimilation into the workplace is largely *interactive*, that the subprocesses inherent in members' assimilation in turn inhere in *interpersonal communication*, and that assimilation subprocesses are communicatively constituted in interpersonal *relationships* that simultaneously function to foster connections among members and facilitate work. Again the interpersonal interactions associated with assimilation are not limited to newcomers but continue throughout members' tenure in the organization (Jablin, 2001) and with others in the environment. We organize this review of interpersonal communication in the workplace around *seven processes of organizational assimilation* reported by Myers and Oetzel (2003) and later validated and refined by Gailliard, Myers, and Seibold (2010): (1) becoming familiar and working with supervisors, (2) becoming acquainted with coworkers, (3) acculturating, (4) being recognized, (5) becoming involved, (6) negotiating roles, and (7) developing job competency. Within each, we examine studies of the role of communication in workplace relationships.

We use the framework on member assimilation provided by Myers and colleagues (Gailliard et al., 2010; Myers & Oetzel, 2003) to organize this review for several reasons. First, the framework is theory based and empirically supported by the responses of nearly 900 employees from hundreds of organizations across the United States. Second, it focuses on *processes* central to organizational membership, processes in which interpersonal communication is vital and processes that generate other interpersonal communication in the workplace. Previous reviews have been organized by phase of development (Jablin, 1985, 2001; Jablin & Krone, 1994), by level of analysis (Jablin & Krone, 1987), topically (Krone et al., 2010; Seibold et al., 2010; Seibold, Lemus, et al., 2009), and in terms of ecological systems (Sias et al., 2002). They have not fully foregrounded the workplace (sub)processes in which interpersonal communication is central. Third, the process-oriented character of the assimilation framework we employ also represents a theoretical and empirical advance on the stage models that undergirded previous approaches to organizational socialization, including those underlying chapters parallel to ours in the first

two editions of this *Handbook*. Specifically, Jablin (1985) and Jablin and Krone (1994) reviewed communication in the work/organizational setting from a developmental, life span perspective that involved the stages of anticipation, assimilation, and disengagement. The present chapter offers an opportunity to reinterpret that perspective and, by extension, some of the early research that has become key to understanding interpersonal communication in the workplace. For example, reviews of research by Jablin (1985) and by Jablin and Krone (1994) concerning communication between supervisors and subordinates, and then between coworkers, provide a strong foundation for the first two processes of assimilation that we cover—becoming familiar and working with supervisors and becoming acquainted with coworkers. They also surveyed early research pertaining to other processes we emphasize: (a) becoming acculturated, (b) becoming involved, (c) feeling recognized, (d) negotiating one's role, and (e) developing job competency. Thus, we highlight and reinterpret those "foundational/early research" studies (published before 2000) in terms of each of the seven processes in the following sections. We do so in the hope that readers will have a fuller appreciation of both the history of scholarship and the core findings concerning each of the seven processes. We also hope readers will see how that core has been elaborated through the "advances/recent research" studies (published since 2000) that we then review in our discussion of each of the seven processes.

## Becoming Familiar and Working With Supervisors

Myers and Oetzel (2003) found that one of the most crucial objectives of new members is *becoming familiar with their supervisor*. By learning about a supervisor's preferences, workers can make judgments about how to engage and work with the supervisor: Does the supervisor expect progress updates, or would she prefer final reports? How should the member complete tasks? Does the supervisor expect employees to take the initiative or wait for direction? Should one try to figure out unfamiliar assignments alone or ask for clarification? By extension, all members must become accustomed to working with their supervisor.

Supervisors represent the organization to subordinates. They are the voice of the organization, framing organizational policies and decisions and often justifying them to workers (Barge, 2004). When employees have strong relational identification with their supervisors, they often generalize that identification to the organization (Sluss & Ashforth, 2007). This can have long-term effects on individuals' membership, including how committed they are to achieving organizational goals and even how likely they are to quit. In reviewing research related to becoming familiar and working with supervisors, we first treat traditional research on supervisor–subordinate communication.

### Foundations/Early Research

Superior–subordinate communication is vital to organizational assimilation and central to interpersonal workplace communication in general. Supervisors and organizational members interact in numerous ways, with the potential to forge the most significant relationships in organizations. Organizational members seek strong relationships with supervisors in the hope that supervisors will keep them informed about top-down changes, listen to their input, and give them favorable assignments and evaluations. Subordinates communicate with supervisors to obtain information about organizational policies and decisions, learn about situations and decisions that will affect them and their jobs, receive task direction, and assist in problem solving. For their part, supervisors depend on subordinates to put forth their best effort in completing assigned tasks and meeting designated deadlines, and depending on the relationship that emerges, supervisors are the source of worker empowerment. Katz and Kahn (1966) characterized supervisors' interactions with subordinates as including informing employees about the organization's and work group's

goals, directing their activities based on organizational polices and practices, providing job and/or task descriptions, and offering feedback to support good performance and improve it if lacking.

Redding (1972) noted the *openness/closedness* of supervisor–subordinate communication, whether interaction partners were willing to share and listen or whether they demonstrated defensiveness within the interactions. Workers who have more open communication with their supervisors are more likely to feel welcomed, and they are likely to believe that they can discuss concerns and even develop stronger relationships over time. Eisenberg and Witten (1987) later proposed that openness may not always be effective. They suggest that *strategic communication*— communicating with a level of ambiguity—can enable listeners to fill in missing detail or draw their own conclusions related to vague information, resulting in more satisfying communication for both supervisor and subordinates.

*Distortion*—miscommunication that occurs when employees communicate with individuals in more powerful positions—most frequently occurs when workers must communicate negative information to their supervisors. Workers frequently make negative issues seem less so, while positive information may be exaggerated to make themselves or situations appear better than they are. Downs and Conrad (1982) found that the workers rated most effective by their supervisors were more willing to openly communicate negative news to supervisors. *Upward influence* relates to the effect of the organizational hierarchy on a supervisor's relationship with his or her subordinates, as well as the influence individuals have on their supervisor or managers higher in the organization. In the first area, research on the *Pelz Effect*—subordinates' satisfaction is influenced by their supervisor's ability to have upward influence in the organization on behalf of their workers (Pelz, 1952)—revealed that workers' feelings of cooperation in work groups and of organizational control are positively influenced by their leader's upward influence (Anderson, Tolson, Fields, & Thacker, 1990).

Studies of the messages that workers use to *influence* their supervisors have identified nine *strategies:* (1) informal nonspecific behaviors to win favor, (2) formal exchanges with specific behaviors to win favors, (3) following rules, (4) logical presentation of worker input, (5) threats, (6) covert manipulation, (7) forging coalitions, (8) persistence, and (9) going above one's direct supervisor's head to make appeals (Kipnis, Schmidt, & Wilkinson, 1980; Schilit & Locke, 1982). Krone (1984) argued that the strategies can be generalized to three primary tactics: (1) open persuasion, (2) manipulative persuasion (hiding either the means of influence or the worker's actual desired outcome), and (3) manipulation (deception related to both the means of influence and the desired outcome). The tactics used are influenced by situational factors such as the tasks and goals involved, norms, and the likelihood of receiving resistance; relational factors such as closeness, power, and trust in the relationship; organizational characteristics such as type of organization and size, structure, and levels in the organization; personal characteristics such as gender, age, experience, self-confidence, and locus of control; perceived power of the target; and type of decision influence (Kipnis et al., 1980; Schilit & Locke, 1982).

Supervisors' communication *styles* and related *effectiveness* also have received considerable attention over the past several decades. The research concludes that effective leaders use definable communication styles such as openness, sensitivity to others, good listening skills, and persuasiveness. For example, Buller and Buller (1987) found that supervisors use affiliation or control/dominance styles in their communicative relationship and that workers whose supervisors use affiliation styles are more likely to report satisfaction in their work. Fairhurst's (1993) study of leader and member communication styles in speech communities found that speakers convey meanings or assert power differentials by employing various verbal strategies. Although Fairhurst identified 12 communication patterns in leader–member interactions, these generally fit into three categories: (1) aligning, or drawing closer together through value alliance and supportiveness; (2) accommodating, or demonstrating politeness and a desire to get along by making adjustments to the other; and (3) polarizing behaviors, or demonstrating power differentials, distancing, and competitiveness.

Scholars also found that supervisors use different styles of communication with different workers. In investigations of *vertical dyad linkages*, in which leaders forge better relationships with some workers than with others (Dansereau, Graen, & Haga, 1975), workers who have earned the favor of the supervisor are in the supervisor's *in-group*. In-group members earn their status by demonstrating trustworthiness, competence, and initiative and receive preferential treatment from supervisors. Communication between supervisors and in-group members is characterized as open, supportive, trusting, and respectful. In contrast, supervisors are less trusting and less open with *out-group* members (Fairhurst, Rogers, & Sarr, 1987).

Given its potential to influence worker productivity and organizational goals, supervisor *feedback* received extensive attention from communication researchers. As Jablin (1979) summarily concluded, "Feedback from superiors to subordinates appears related to subordinate performance and satisfaction . . . a subordinate's performance to a large extent controls the nature of his/her superior's feedback" (p. 1214). Subsequent investigations have examined how and why members seek feedback (Miller & Jablin, 1991; Morrison, 1993), feedback effects on worker motivation (Cusella, 1987; Morris, Gaveras, Baker, & Coursey, 1990), and the effects of attribution by the person giving and receiving the feedback (Kipnis, Schmidt, Price, & Stitt, 1981).

Other areas of early investigation that received considerable attention include *personal characteristics* that affect supervisor–subordinate communication, such as communication apprehension (McCroskey, Richmond, & Davis, 1986), communication competence (Johnson, 1992; Monge, Bachman, Dillard, & Eisenberg, 1982), and gender

(Baker, 1991; Graham, Unruh, & Jennings, 1991). Communication-based studies also examined *conflict management strategies* of workers and supervisors and conflict negotiation processes (Knapp, Putnam, & Davis, 1988; Putnam, 1988). Scholars also focused on sexual harassment, examining everyday talk that fosters a climate conducive to harassment (Clair, 1993b; Strine, 1992; Taylor & Conrad, 1992) and the effects of sex roles in the workplace that may contribute to harassment and perceptions of harassment (Bingham & Burleson, 1989; Clair, 1993a; Gutek & Morasch, 1982).

### Advances/Recent Research

Several lines of communication research have emerged in the past decade that are relevant to becoming familiar and working with supervisors: leader–member exchange relationships and their effect on burnout and expressions of dissent, the role of strong superior–subordinate relationships in motivating workers, supervisors' use of humor to build relationships, and supervisor-provided social support.

Although many contemporary organizations rely on self-managed work groups (Seibold, Kang, Gailliard, & Jahn, 2009), hierarchical leadership structures are normative in most workplaces. Supervisors are in positions to empower employees, fostering their growth and development; offer flexibility (Hornung, Rousseau, & Glaser, 2008); evaluate and reward and give preferred assignments (Miller, Johnson, Hart, & Peterson, 1999); or make daily life miserable and sideline an employee's career (Lutgen-Sandvik, Tracy, & Alberts, 2007). It is no surprise that, on entry, workers search for means to win favor and then to remain on the supervisor's good side (Teven, McCroskey, & Richmond, 2006).

Researchers continue to examine the vertical dyad linkage between supervisors and followers, reconceptualized as *leader–member exchange theory* (LMX). LMX specifies that leaders/managers develop different types of relationships with different members (Graen & Uhl-Bien, 1995). Becker, Halbesleben, and O'Hair (2005) found that

organizational members in out-group relationships are more likely to engage in defensive communication with their supervisor and more likely to experience *burnout* than their in-group counterparts. Accordingly, workers who enjoy in-group relationships with their supervisors are more likely to gain the attention of supervisors and to receive favorable treatment (Bhal, Bhaskar, & Ratnam, 2009; Graen & Scandura, 1987). In fact, in-group relationships could explain many special treatments found in recent studies. Kassing's (2000) work on employee *dissent* reveals that subordinates who reported that they had a high-quality relationship with their supervisors used more articulated dissent (open dissent expressed to the supervisor in the hope of improving the situation). Subordinates with low-quality relationships with their supervisors used more latent dissent (complaining to coworkers to express dissatisfaction). In-group members also may benefit through *idiosyncratic deals*, special negotiations between a worker and a supervisor to meet the worker's individual needs (Hornung et al., 2008; Lai, Rousseau, & Chang, 2009). These deals are intended to acknowledge the value of an employee, but they can aid the worker and the organization by strengthening the worker's commitment.

The importance of LMX and relationship quality with supervisors is evident in various nations as well. For example, LMX is positively related to affective commitment among expatriates in multinational corporation subsidiaries in China (Liu & Ipe, 2010). Among bank workers in India, LMX was positively related to receiving information and discussing job-related problems with superiors. Additionally, data from Korean engineering workers showed that in-group subordinates were more likely to ask their supervisors for direct feedback (Lee, Park, Lee, & Lee, 2007) and supervisors were more likely to seek both negative and positive feedback directly from their in-group subordinates (Lee, Lee, Lee, & Park, 2005).

Supervisors also appear to benefit from strong supervisor–subordinate relationships insofar as they increase workers' attachment to the organization and its mission, improve workers' task performance, and lower turnover. For example, Richmond and McCroskey (2000) found that supervisor–worker *nonverbal immediacy* positively influences relationships, leading to many desired outcomes such as job satisfaction, motivated followers, trusting relationships between workers and supervisors, and supervisor credibility. Other positive outcomes can result from strong supervisor–worker relationships. Martin, Rich, and Gayle (2004) suggested that the communication styles of supervisors and their subordinates may encourage *organizational citizenship behaviors* (behaviors that go above and beyond what is required of the job). Chory and Hubbell (2008) found that workers who trust their supervisor are less likely to engage in deception and obstructionism, harbor hostility, and behave aggressively.

One means of building relationships with workers may be as simple as laughter. Martin et al. (2004) found that managers and subordinates consciously used *humor* as part of their communication style. However, subordinates consistently use more positive humor (humor used to lighten the mood or make a situation more enjoyable) than do supervisors. Men are more likely than women to use expressive humor (humor used to let others know them) and negative humor (humor used to criticize). Martin et al. report dominance and sex (male) as predictors of negative humor use for both supervisors and subordinates. They conclude that supervisors use humor to enhance relational satisfaction between themselves and their subordinates, which also enhances the organizational climate. Both are likely to result in employees' willingness to engage in extracitizenship behaviors. Campbell, Martin, and Wanzer (2001) found that managers who use humor in interacting with workers foster employees' satisfaction with the supervisors, and those supervisors are also more likely to be judged as responsive to worker needs.

Research also continues to examine supervisors' communication of support to workers. Snyder (2009) argues that supervisors are the strongest organizational influence capable of reducing worker burnout. Supervisors are in the best position to offer workers instrumental support, including changing job duties or assigning additional workers to tasks (Apker & Ray, 2003). In addition, Barge and Schlueter's (2004) investigation of memorable messages found that most of the memorable messages given to newcomers were from managers or trainers with the purpose of facilitating the member's assimilation into the organization. Most of the messages were positive in nature, and more than 90% were given in face-to-face interactions.

## Becoming Acquainted With Coworkers

Beyond suggesting that developing and maintaining a relationship with one's supervisor is foundational to communication-based assimilation into an organization—and through roles in the organization thereafter—Myers and colleagues (Gailliard et al., 2010; Myers & Oetzel, 2003) found *familiarity with others* in the workplace to be important. They described this process as getting to know *coworkers* and then establishing friendly or at least productive relationships with them. This process involves feeling comfortable with coworkers and learning how to interact with them. When members feel familiar with coworkers, they often derive emotional support and generally feel a sense of community. Participants in Myers and Oetzel's (2003) study reported that when they felt familiar with others, they had a willingness to engage in task-related interactions such as problem solving, decision making, and debate with coworkers.

### Foundations/Early Research

Researchers have long known that coworkers are important in socializing newcomers (Jablin, 1982; Riordan & Griffeth, 1995). Coworkers informally guide newer members to the norms and attitudes of the work group and organization (Feldman, 1981; Van Maanen, 1975). New members often seek out information from supervisors, but at times, coworkers can be the preferred source (Feldman & Brett, 1983). Seeking information from coworkers is less risky because it may be less harmful to admit what we do not know to coworkers than it is to admit to supervisors (Morrison, 1993; Tidwell & Sias, 2005). Miller and Jablin (1991) argued that organizational members engage in *information seeking* to answer three questions: (1) What must I do to succeed? (2) Am I succeeding? (3) Am I being accepted? They proposed seven strategies that members use to obtain information: (1) overt, directly asking a question; (2) indirect, involving noninterrogative questions; (3) third party, seeking information from a substitute source; (4) testing limits, creating a situation to which information targets must respond about whether the member has broken a norm; (5) disguising conversations, concealing information seeking within another conversation; (6) observation, unobtrusively watching to gain information; and (7) surveillance, using retrospective sensemaking to draw conclusions based on observations, both past and present.

Many studies pertaining to the importance of becoming familiar with coworkers focus on work groups. Fellow group members provide newcomers with information beyond that provided in formal training and that guides workers in getting along in the workplace (Comer, 1991). Hackman (1976) found that group coworkers familiarize new members to the organizational and group reward system by identifying who allocates rewards and identifying the behaviors that are rewarded. *Social information processing* studies support that claim to the extent that they show the large part coworkers play in shaping newcomers' attitudes about their jobs and the organization (Caldwell & O'Reilly, 1982; Salancik & Pfeffer, 1978). Their attitudes are shaped by both ambient messages (which may be unintentional and are not directed to any one person) and discretionary intentional messages (typically, communication to particular members) (Hackman, 1976). Members not only learn how to perform tasks, but they acquire the group's attitude about their work. This adaptation may

be important in fitting in because acceptance into work groups is not guaranteed. Moreland and Levine (1982) proposed a model of group socialization specifying that group members evaluate new members before accepting them as one of their own. Group members who do not receive favorable assessments likely do not benefit as much from coworker socialization, nor do they receive long-term guidance and support.

Much of the early research examined the effects of communication and the resulting norms on the work group and its members. Research revealed that group functioning and members' perceptions about group coherence are greatly affected by the task (Hirokawa, 1990). Hackman and Vidmar (1970) concluded that group members in groups charged with problem solving often find others supportive in working through problem-solving tasks; group members involved in production tasks typically characterize interaction as filled with tension and conflict. Studies of task-focused groups have examined the effects of communication between members that destroys trust. When group members' trust has been eroded, member interactions become "tense, inflexible and personal" (Leathers, 1970, p. 186), communication can be distorted (Zand, 1972), verbal fluency drops (Prentice, 1975), and, ultimately, the group's effectiveness is diminished (Klimoski & Karol, 1976).

Although many individuals may seek to avoid *conflict* in the workplace, early research demonstrated that integrative conflict can contribute to group decision quality, group process, and relationship development (Wall, Galanes, & Love, 1987). Investigators began to view conflict management as a type of *negotiation* (Mannix, Thompson, & Bazerman, 1989; Thompson, Mannix, & Bazerman, 1988). By definition, conflict involves two or more people who disagree with one another. Accordingly, choosing a conflict management style and its effectiveness can depend on not only individual preferences but also the other persons in conflict. Examining both individual-level and group-level effects of conflict management styles on satisfaction with work group, Park and Park (2008) showed that individuals' preferred use of cooperative styles of conflict management has a positive effect on satisfaction with group processes. This positive effect is stronger in groups whose members have a similarly high level of preferences for cooperative styles than in groups whose members have different preferences for cooperative styles.

Orientation behavior also received attention early on. *Orientation behavior* is interaction intended to resolve conflicts, provide helpful suggestions, and ease tension, all to ensure that the group meets its goals. Kline (1972) found that members' orienting behaviors are associated with the likelihood that the group will reach a consensus. *Feedback to group performance* also received considerable attention. Chief among the findings was that feedback's impact is affected by numerous factors, including individual group members' differences, such as their goals; group task structure; members' means and ability to process feedback; as well as the nature of the feedback, such as overall content, usefulness of the information, and aggregation level (see Nadler, 1979).

Workplace friendships differ from nonwork friendships because they carry the expectation that in addition to performing well socially, friends will be productive. Furthermore, workplace relationships may be complicated by multiplex interdependency, and they can be overtly or covertly competitive in nature (Myers, 2009). Those differences and caveats notwithstanding, coworkers play a vital role in members' integration into the organization by providing *social support* and *friendship*. They offer social support by giving feedback that may affect coworkers' self-concept; assist in making sense of organizational events, structures, and policies; and reduce uncertainty through the shared group experience and collective sensemaking (Jablin & Sussman, 1983; Ray, 1987). In addition, the workplace is an important source of friendships. These *relationship blends* (Bridge & Baxter, 1992) can make work more enjoyable, and they may also embed workers in their organizations, making them less likely to quit.

Putnam and Stohl (1990) proposed that individuals are simultaneously members of multiple groups and also members in organizations in which many are embedded. According to their *bona fide group perspective*, group members are affected by their various memberships, and they bring to the workplace diverse interests and experiences. They also are affected by pressures from their memberships in other groups, which can affect their performance, commitment, and relationships with coworkers.

## Advances/Recent Research

Recent communication-related studies pertaining to becoming acquainted and working with others have examined coworkers' evaluation of fellow members, the benefits of workplace friendships, the function of humor among coworkers, and dissolving work-based friendships.

Studies offer evidence for the importance of coworkers in members' assimilation and for long-term satisfaction in the work environment. When newcomers enter a work group, incumbent members evaluate the newcomer's ability to contribute both interpersonally and productively to the group's overall performance and social atmosphere (Dillard, Solomon, & Samp, 1996; Moreland & Levine, 2001). At the same time, newcomers assess the existing members of the group for many of the same reasons to determine whether they have made a good choice in joining. They ask themselves, "How will I benefit from being a part of this collective?" and "Will I be capable of contributing both functionally and socially?" When newcomers determine that being a part of the organization or work group is not advantageous, they may choose to quit, try to change the collective more to their liking, or limit their interaction with other members. When existing members make a negative assessment of newcomers and their potential to contribute to and fit into the organization or group, the newcomers might be marginalized or barely tolerated, or long-time members may provide newcomers negative feedback in the hope that they conform.

When newcomers and old-timers make mostly positive assessments of each other, constructive interaction and relationships can result. Developing productive relationships with open communication enables coworkers to draw on diverse perspectives and skills and collaborate on tasks, all conducive to productivity.

At times, managers not only condone but encourage the development of friendly relationships between coworkers, perhaps because friendships appear to foster productivity (Berman, West, & Richter, 2002). Ross (1997) reported that work groups composed of friends have higher levels of productivity than work groups that include only acquaintances. Friendships between organizational members foster open exchange of information and supportiveness. In fact, employees who have closer relationships tend to have more job satisfaction (Rath, 2006; Winstead, Derlega, Montgomery, & Pilkington, 1995) and more involvement in their jobs (Marshall & Stohl, 1993). They also are more likely to identify strongly with the organization (Bullis & Bach, 1989) and less likely to quit (Friedman & Holtom, 2002). The reason may be that social support from coworkers is an effective means of coping with job stressors. Friends enable workers to better understand organizational issues from different perspectives and to feel more in control of work-related stressors (Apker & Ray, 2003).

Feeley, Hwang, and Barnett (2008) found that workers with more friends in the workplace were less likely to have quit after three months. The data revealed that having a number of friends on whom workers could rely is more important in reducing *turnover* than having a small number of close friends. Freeley et al. concluded that their results point to the importance of socially integrating workers on entry. They also advocate the use of the same, or nearly the same, level of workers to introduce and acquaint workers with coworkers.

Because workplace friendship can involve both task and social dimensions, however, balance or imbalance in task activities as well as social activities can have implications for coworker relationships (Kingsley Westerman & Park, 2010). In a study that tested equity theory, Kingsley Westerman, Park, and Lee (2007) showed that when a coworker friend does not complete his or her fair share of work contributing to productivity or nonwork social activities, individuals' liking of their coworker friend decreases and they have to consider the unpleasant task of confronting the coworker friend and asking him or her to change the behavior. Although the importance of maintaining equitable relationships with coworker friends is universal, people in different national cultures may react differently to unfairness in workplace friendship. Kingsley Westerman et al. showed that when in an inequitable relationship with coworker friends, Koreans were more likely to take action to restore relational fairness than Americans, possibly because Koreans may be more concerned with maintaining harmonious relationships with their coworkers.

Recently, workplace *humor* has received the attention of several researchers (Lynch, 2009; Martin, 2004; Tracy, Myers, & Scott, 2006). These studies are discussed later in this chapter, but they demonstrate that humor among coworkers has many positive benefits in the workplace. Through shared jokes, members build a common understanding about situations and experiences, and they develop mutual identity. Humor also enables coworkers to establish and maintain control by joking about or teasing members who do not conform. It also can be a means of resistance when workers wish to express discontent without direct confrontation. "Humor begets bonding; in return bonding begets more ingroup humor" (Lynch, 2009, p. 446).

Workplace relationships can have negative consequences for coworkers and work groups (Seibold, Kang, et al., 2009), especially when those relationships deteriorate (Hess, Omdahl, & Fritz, 2006). Interpersonal communication scholars, of course, have long been interested in *relational disengagement*. For example, Baxter (1985) found that individuals dissolve relationships using methods that are either direct or other focused. Sias and colleagues (Sias, 2005;

Sias, Fix, Heath, Perry, & Silva, 2004; Sias & Perry, 2004) have investigated dissolving relationships in organizational settings. As they note, workplace relationships may be more difficult to end because organizational tasks may necessitate continued interaction. Sias et al. (2004) investigated the reasons for organizational members choosing to end organizational relationships. Interviews with organizational members revealed several reasons: (a) *betrayal*, one party believes the other has been disloyal or betrayed the trust of the other; (b) *problem personality*, the personality of one party is intolerable to the other; (c) *distracting life events*, when a coworker's personal life continually intrudes on the workplace, causing coworkers to choose to distance themselves; (d) *conflicting expectations*, one party's expectations for the relationship conflicts with the expectations of the other; and (e) *promotion*, when one person is promoted to a position of authority over the other, making an interpersonal relationship difficult to maintain.

Sias and Perry (2004) extended the Sias et al. (2004) research by investigating whether the reasons for ending workplace relationships could be linked to particular strategies for ending those relationships. Based on the Sias et al. findings, Sias and Perry (2004) derived three strategies workers use to dissolve relationships with coworkers: (1) *escalating-costs* tactics involve making interaction uncomfortable for the other person by using a condescending tone, responding with an obvious tone of dislike, or something similar; (2) *depersonalization* tactics involve avoiding conversations and using a distant tone in actions; and (3) *state-of-the-relationship* tactics, a more direct approach, are used when partners openly discuss ending the relationship. Sias and Perry found that in conflicting expectations and promotions, workers are most likely to use escalating costs or depersonalization. Workers who experience betrayals and problem personalities are more likely to choose depersonalization. With distracting life events, workers often use escalating costs.

## Acculturating

*Acculturation* involves learning about and accepting the culture. Interviewees in Myers and Oetzel's (2003) study described acculturation as learning the norms of the organization and "how things get done" within their respective organizations. The organization's culture dictates what it is like to work in the organization, how employees feel about their work, and how they relate to supervisors, coworkers, and other stakeholders (Burns, 1955; Feldman, 1977). According to Bauer, Morrison, and Callister (1998), developing a common organizational framework is a part of socialization and acculturating. Acculturating helps members understand how we view and value customers, the community, our competitors, and ourselves (Bauer et al., 1998).

### Foundations/Early Research

Early communication scholarship on organizational acculturation examined, among many topics, antecedents such as individuals' experiences and socialization's potential role in acculturating members, the socially constructed attitudes about jobs that permeate work groups and organizations, the effect of task on member interaction, and how insiders socialize newcomers to organizational norms (Jablin, 1985; Jablin & Krone, 1994).

Acculturation-related interactions are not limited to adults who are entering organizations. Children and adolescents are exposed to elements of organizational culture as part of their *vocational anticipatory socialization* (Jablin, 1987). Parents play an important role in preparing their children for workplace culture. Nachmann (1960) proposed that parents' communication, behaviors, and attitudes may affect their children's occupational and organizational choices and, therefore, the organizational cultures they will experience. For example, when children have grown up in an environment that encourages and values analytical debate, as adults they might choose an occupation and an organization that enables them to engage in similar discussions with colleagues. Alternatively, children whose parents were driven by a passion for material possessions or appearances may instill those values in their sons and daughters. As adults, those children may choose to enter occupations with related cultures that mirror those material values (Goldstein & Oldham, 1979). Relatedly, educational institutions introduce young people to workplace culture. Schoolchildren must learn to successfully function in an organization. As part of that acculturation, they learn about hierarchies, following directions, getting along with others, adhering to rules, completing tasks, and timeliness (Bowles & Gintis, 1976). Adolescents may later think that they would like the culture of a given occupation or sector because they have seen depictions of them in the media, although Turow (1974) observed that these depictions often are largely misrepresentations.

Occupational cultures may be quite different from what young people realize. Early research demonstrated that *screening interviews* are important information sources for job candidates about the culture of organizations (Teigen, 1983). According to Teigen (1983), as many as 38% of communicative exchanges are related to climate/cultural issues. Applicants who recruiters wished to attract were given more and more positive information about the organization's culture than applicants who were seen as less desirable.

As discussed earlier, *social information processing* research suggests that attitudes about jobs are socially constructed (Salancik & Pfeffer, 1978; Seibold et al., 2010). The cultural environment appears to have a strong influence on the attitude workers will develop about their work and the organization. O'Reilly and Caldwell (1979) found that coworkers' job satisfaction is influenced by day-to-day discourse about topics such as how workers are treated by supervisors, whether organizational policies are fair, and whether compensation is deemed adequate for the work. Thus, part of acculturating is learning about "how we feel about our work."

Tasks and technology affect the organizational culture, but their especially strong influence on work group culture has long been documented (Hackman & Vidmar, 1970). Some tasks require members to work together, coordinating their tasks with a great deal of face-to-face interaction, while other tasks in other jobs are performed fairly autonomously or from remote locations, using technology to submit work or reports to the organization. These factors affect the nature of interpersonal communication among members. However, tasks also play a role in the spatial nature of the work. Some jobs are performed outside in remote locations by small work groups, while other jobs are performed in one location in close contact with many people from the organization. In addition, some jobs or industries are gendered (e.g., nursing, elementary school teaching, waste management), shaping the culture and interpersonal interaction in the organization and work group. These differences are evident in the culture, and becoming assimilated involves adjusting to a job's particular culture and interaction patterns (Jablin & Sussman, 1983). Indeed, members' interactions about both work tasks and technologies have been found to shape the culture of temporality in work groups (Ballard & Seibold, 2004), which in turn affects the communication dynamics in those units, including willingness to engage in interpersonal communication (or to avoid it), coordination and conflict, and perceptions of communication load (Ballard & Seibold, 2006).

Learning about the norms of the work group and organization is a fundamental part of organizational acculturation. Coworkers play an important part in communicating these informal rules of behavior to new members. Very early research by Seashore (1954) found that socializing newcomers to these roles so that they can perform as one of the group, and the act of communicating these norms to newcomers, works to strengthen group cohesiveness. However, recent research indicates that if newcomers are not accepted by coworkers, they may not receive as many of these guiding messages (Myers & McPhee, 2006).

## Advances/Recent Research

Recent studies of workplace interactions that affect organizational members' acculturation include organizational culture expectations formed through pre-entry (anticipatory) socialization, organizational identification and concertive control and their effect on organizational culture, the effects and functions of dissent and gossip, workplace civility practices, and the personal and relational uncertainty surrounding corporate mergers that effectively marry two organizational cultures.

Although it is assumed that members acculturate to a particular organization after they join, research indicates that members gain exposure to the atmosphere and expectations of the work environment long *before* they enter. Medved, Brogan, McClanahan, Morris, and Shepherd (2006) investigated the socializing influence of parents' messages about balancing career and family. They found that parents frequently advise their children to select occupations that will enable them to enjoy their future families and allow them to balance work with family obligations. Hymlö (2006) found that movies targeted toward adolescent girls communicate that anyone can (and should) become rock stars, actresses, and top models. These movies and other media targeted at the adolescent girl lead girls to aspire to enter careers that will enhance their beauty and make them rich. These studies demonstrate that a variety of communication sources may influence adolescents' choices of the organizational culture they may enter someday, in part by instilling the values that young people use to evaluate various career paths. Several other studies demonstrate how acculturation to a particular organization may begin in childhood through what Gibson and Papa (2000) term *organizational osmosis*, in which individuals are acculturated through communication-based secondary

exposure, thus enabling them to learn about and potentially accept the organization's culture before they join it.

For example, most firefighters in Myers's (2005) study of municipal firefighters became acquainted with the Cactus City Fire Department through family communication. A large number of Cactus City firefighters had other family members in the department, and the firefighters often learned about the job and lifestyle of firefighting as children, visiting their parent or other family member at the station and hearing about the occupation and the department during mealtime conversations. Similarly, in the Gibson and Papa (2000) study of manufacturing workers, young people in the town learned about the harsh working conditions found in the community's largest employer, Industry International, through interaction with family members, neighbors, and others in the community. The workers boasted and bragged about their ability to withstand the physical demands of the job—subjecting themselves to backbreaking effort in a workplace that did not allow workers to take vacations or call in sick. Even though the culture was brutal by most standards, many young men of the town joined Industry International knowing what to expect, which made their assimilation easier.

Gibson and Papa's (2000) work underscores that many cultures thrive because workers have strong identification with their organization. Cheney (1983) and Tompkins and Cheney (1985) described *organizational identification* as value congruence between the member and the organization such that a member will make decisions on the basis of what is best for the organization. In organizations in which strong identification is part of the workplace culture, members feel extreme pressure to assist in meeting organizational goals. Members' behaviors and interactions are influenced, even dictated, by means of *concertive control*, or control exerted by coworkers, causing them to conform to behaviors that fit in with the organization's dominant ideology (Tompkins & Cheney, 1985). Concertive control is a powerful means of unobtrusive control because it extends the power of surveillance and monitoring from management to rank-and-file workers. When concertive control is widespread in organizations, members are monitored not only by supervisors but also by all members of their work group.

Kassing (2000) predicted that organizational cultures that promote more open discussion and debate (freedom of speech) also promote higher levels of organizational identification with employees. He found that employees in organizational cultures that promote freedom of speech use more *articulated dissent* (proactive dissent with the objective of rectifying the problem) and less latent dissent (complaining about the problem in an unproductive way).

Gossip can influence the organization's culture and affect workplace relationships. Hafen (2004) defines *gossip* as "healing talk that connects us intimately to one another in communication based on community; skill-building talk, as we compare our behaviors to others; and dis/empowering talk that evokes feelings of dominance for gossiper and subordination for gossipee" (p. 226). Due to its covert nature, gossip gives less powerful individuals a source of power. It is a means of resisting others' power and even inflicting pain on coworkers and management. Hafen argued that gossip serves at least three purposes. First, it can discretely inform newcomers about other members of the organization, which can be an invaluable part of socialization (Laing, 1993). Second, gossip can be an indirect guide about values and behavioral norms in the organization—if people are gossiping about the behavior, it might be best to avoid that behavior in the future. Third, learning about the gossip climate and uses of gossip in the organization can inform members about what is appropriate gossip behavior and what is not.

The culture of an organization can also have a strong influence on how members treat one another in face-to-face exchanges. Sypher (2004) argues that *workplace civility* must be reclaimed in organizations:

> I cannot think of an issue more in need of intellectual clarity and debate than the way in which we should treat one another at work, especially in the face of difference and certainly in the face of the day-to-day interactions that capture the majority of our waking lives. (p. 258)

Among the causes for incivility, Sypher cites a feeling of disconnection from others as a result of suburban lifestyles, longer workweeks, more demands at home, and sleep deprivation. The results of incivility, she continues, include insomnia, problems in workers' home lives, and physical aggression in the workplace.

Organizational members experience uncertainty throughout their membership but particularly acutely in two situations: (1) at organizational entry and (2) when two cultures marry as a result of an organizational merger. A merger can force all members—even longtime members—to acculturate all over again. According to *uncertainty reduction theory* (URT) (Berger & Calabrese, 1975), individuals seek information when they experience uncertainty, and that uncertainty is reduced with increased communication. The theory also specifies that reduced uncertainty has a positive effect on individuals. In one study, researchers found that continual communication throughout the merger and acquisition process reduced members' uncertainty better than a one-time interaction (Napier, Simmons, & Stratton, 1989). In another investigation, Kramer, Dougherty, and Pierce (2004) examined the uncertainty experienced by airline pilots who faced a corporate merger. They surveyed pilots three times during the merger process and found that in the pilots' view, the importance of information from official sources (e.g., corporate announcements, meetings, supervisor) increased over time, but the value of information from the union decreased. Overall, information obtained from the media was important throughout the merger. Information from official sources did decrease uncertainty for the pilots at all three data points. The survey also found that pilots' attitudes toward the merger grew more negative as the merger progressed. Finally, Kramer and colleagues found that uncertainty was not a mediator between communication and several outcomes (attitude toward the merger, job stress, job security, job satisfaction, and commitment). The researchers concluded that more information does not necessarily reduce uncertainty but more communication during a merger can directly affect several important membership outcomes.

## Being Recognized

Being *recognized* as valuable by superiors and coworkers is a significant part of feeling accepted into the organization. Also important is a feeling of self-efficacy, that one is able to contribute to the organization. Participants in Myers and Oetzel's (2003) study talked about receiving positive feedback from a supervisor or coworker. In one poignant example, a hotel worker recalled a day when the general manager panicked. He had several hotel employees in his office for a meeting, but he was unable to communicate with them because he only spoke English and they spoke only Spanish. She informed the manager that she could speak Spanish and, although it was not part of her job, volunteered to be a translator in the meeting. After the meeting, the hotel manager was quite appreciative, and he thanked her for rescuing him from a difficult situation. She recalled that the incident was so meaningful because she felt recognized by the hotel manager as someone who could contribute her skills to the organization's operations. Even though she was relatively new, from that time on, she knew that the general manager knew who she was and viewed her as a valuable employee.

### Foundations/Early Research

Despite its importance, there is a dearth of research concerning the role of recognition in organizational membership. An early study by Bullis and Bach (1989) also supports the value of member recognition. In their investigation of graduate student assimilation into a graduate program, students were asked about the types of *turning points* (experiences that had an effect, either positively or negatively) on their organizational identification. Bullis and Bach found that receiving *informal recognition*, such as acknowledgement by a professor for a job well done, had the most positive effect on their identification with the program.

Research on *supervisor feedback* has clear implications for understanding recognition. When workers receive positive feedback (recognition) from their supervisors, their future performance and job satisfaction often increase (Jablin, 1979). Cusella (1987) and O'Reilly and Anderson (1980) further conclude that when the supervisor is high in credibility (i.e., he or she has expertise and worker trust), his or her positive feedback can positively affect workers' satisfaction and motivation. A limited amount of research examines the effect of *feedback and recognition given by coworkers.* Moreland and Levine's (1982, 2001) model of work group socialization specifies that members are evaluated by coworkers to determine their contributions to the group, functionally and socially. Members recognized as valuable contributors are more likely to receive their coworkers' commitment to them and to be accepted as part of the group.

LMX research can also help in understanding recognition in the workplace. Graen and Scandura (1987) argue that because *some workers are recognized* as competent, trustworthy, and motivated, they become part of their supervisor's in-group. The preferential treatment they receive and the closer relationship that they develop as being a part of the in-group are likely to motivate them to continue their positive behaviors. Thus, recognition as a valuable team member by the supervisor is likely to continue. Recognition related to in-group members also extends to coworkers. Graen and Scandura found that in-group members are also judged by coworkers. When coworkers believe that an in-group member has earned the right to be in the leader's in-group—that is, the member is responsible, motivated, and excels in his or her work—coworkers recognize the member's right to be in the leader's in-group. They, too, have a positive valence for the worker. However, when coworkers do not judge the in-group member worthy of being in the in-group, he or she is unlikely to receive such recognition.

## Advances/Recent Research

Recent studies of several topics illuminate recognition in the workplace, a critical process in members' assimilation into organizations. These investigations focus on recognizing leadership potential in leaderless work groups and the challenges traditionally underrepresented members face in being recognized as leaders.

Recognition has been investigated by examining who becomes *recognized as the leader* in leaderless groups. Fisher's (1986) model of emergent leadership specifies that leaders emerge (i.e., are recognized as leaders) in three phases. First, some individuals are immediately discounted because they are too quiet, too uninformed, too dogmatic, or uninterested in leading. Second, one or a few potential candidates emerge as a result of support from fellow members. Finally, due to a variety of interpersonal factors (e.g., they are seen as too opinionated, too offensive), candidates drop out of consideration, and the leader is recognized. Limon and La France (2005) examined the effects of *argumentativeness* and *communication apprehension* on leadership emergence. They found a positive

association with argumentativeness and a negative association with communication apprehension in predicting who is likely to emerge as a leader. They also found that a combination of argumentativeness and low communication apprehension was an even better predictor than either one individually.

Traditionally *underrepresented workers*, such as women and persons of color, have long felt challenged to be recognized for their value to their organizations. Bligh and Kohles (2008) found that even women in the U.S. Senate felt constrained by their fellow senate members and their constituents to adhere to traditional rules of feminine discourse. They did not feel able to respond as directly and/or as aggressively as their male counterparts. Anderson and Buzzanell (2007) investigated females' leadership in Mac User Groups dominated by male "geeks." The researchers found that in this high-technology, traditionally male group context, women constructed identities that competed with traditional geekgendered identities to assert themselves as leaders. Parker (2002) notes that in American culture, in which leaders have traditionally been white males, African American female executives often must fight for recognition within the upper echelons of organizations. Being both African American and female can cause others, even other African Americans, to trivialize their contributions and to assume that an African American woman has advanced to the higher level position because of some form of social promotion (Allen, 2005; Parker, 2001). The women in Parker's (2001) study either directly confronted the problem or ignored the bias, considering it the other person's problem. Their responses varied from direct confrontation to assert power to slowly gaining others' confidence in their abilities and assuming that others will recognize their contributions over time (Parker, 2002). Although men and women report experiences in which they were undervalued or not recognized by coworkers or supervisors, Gersick, Bartunek, and Dutton (2000) found that women feel the lingering effects of those incidents even years after the incident.

*Workers with disabilities* often have difficulty receiving recognition as competent, capable contributors (Cohen & Avanzino, 2010). Able-bodied workers may believe that their disabled coworkers unnecessarily receive special privileges or advantages for their disability (Coopman, 2003). In what Fox, Giles, Orbe, and Bourhis (2000) labeled *interability communication*, able-bodied individuals may be unable to focus their attention in conversations on anything but the disability. Braithwaite and Harter (2000) propose that disabled individuals learn a wide variety of communication strategies to compensate for the various ways in which people perceive them. For example, some able-bodied coworkers are overly generous in their communication, or they display an overly positive attitude that helps them feel more comfortable in a disabled person's presence. As a result, many people with disabilities attempt to hide or deny their disabilities until it becomes impossible to do so. Cohen and Avanzino (2010) contend that denying the disability and being overly accommodative can impede, respectively, disabled and able-bodied workers' ability to develop open relationships with each other. These practices interfere with disabled workers' ability to develop identities as meaningful contributors and to be recognized for them.

## Becoming Involved

Research by Myers and colleagues (Gailliard et al., 2010; Myers & Oetzel, 2003) indicates that when members are *involved* with the organization, they seek ways to contribute in the workplace, often by volunteering to perform extra work or to take on added responsibility for the sake of the organization and its members. Workers who are involved seek out ways to improve programs, processes, and products and,

if they are capable, perform the additional effort necessary to make those improvements.

### Foundations/Early Research

Individuals learn to be involved in organizations, beginning with children's attendance at school (Jablin, 1985). Beyond academic requirements, school children learn that participation leads to contact with others and development of friendships, presumably in a context that is enjoyable or offers benefits. When friends join clubs or participate in sports or other activities, children may choose to enhance their involvement too. Years later, in the workplace, coworkers may have an influence on their involvement. The effects *of social information processing* may cause coworkers to adopt similar attitudes toward involvement (Caldwell & O'Reilly, 1982). Expectations of involvement in the form of prosocial behaviors is often communicated in employee training (George & Bettenhausen, 1990). Workers may choose to become involved in extra committees or extra roles because they see the activities or the goals as challenging or fun. They also may be motivated by the recognition they will receive. Conversely, they may become involved because so many others are "stepping up." According to social comparison theory (Festinger, 1954), people evaluate their behaviors by comparing themselves with the behaviors of similar others. When comparing, people pay attention to descriptive norms regarding others' behaviors, which can be a way to motivate people to contribute more or less (Cress & Kimmerle, 2007).

Involvement also relates to desiring to participate in organizational processes to meet organizational objectives. When employees *identify with their organization*, they feel invested in the well-being of the organization and, thus, are more likely to be involved participants in positive citizen behaviors. Meyer (2004) defined *citizenship* as "being a compliant, loyal follower . . . a dynamic, involved, problem-solving leader of a group. . . . being a 'good group member' or being a 'team player' or perhaps a dependable follower of orders" (p. 183).

Employee participation and involvement has other functional benefits for the organization. For example, members' involvement in organizational *communication networks* may cause them to become linked to areas of the organization outside their functional area. They can be the link that fills structural holes, communicatively linking others in the organization. Exposure to other areas of the organization gives them a broader view of the organization and the issues that affect it. Research demonstrates that worker participation (involvement) can lead to enhanced work life for members (Castrogiovanni & Macy, 1990; Lawler, 1982). For example, when members participate in discussions about concerns and decision making, they have less uncertainty, greater clarity about expectations, and greater performance–reward expectancy (Bullock, 1983).

### Advances/Recent Research

Although the early research on involvement reviewed above offered insights into workers' motivations to become involved and the outcomes of involvement for both worker and organization, involvement has been understudied by scholars. Recent research has investigated the relationship between involvement and burnout and citizenship behaviors, as well as a desire for meaningful work and empowerment.

Freudenberger (1974) first defined *burnout* as "wearing out" as a result of excessive work pressure. When workers do not feel involved in their work, they also are more prone to burnout. Under burnout, they experience (a) emotional exhaustion—feeling emotionally drained, (b) reduced personal accomplishment—feeling as though they are incapable of completing their work, and (c) depersonalization—feeling alone in the workplace (Maslach, 1993).

Relatedly, Avtgis, Thomas-Maddox, Taylor, and Patterson (2007) argue that employees want *more meaning and more personal gratification* from

their work than did previous generations. Research on the latest generation of workers, often called the *Millennials* or *Generation Y* (born between 1979 and 1994), found that millennials expect to be drawn into meaningful work, even as entry-level workers (Myers & Sadaghiani, 2010). Whereas workers from previous generations expected to pay their dues as young, inexperienced workers, contemporary workers want to feel involved in and passionate about their work from entry. This may offer positive and negative effects for organizations. On the one hand, members may be more dedicated and passionate about their work. On the other, if workers do not feel identified with the organization and their role in it or if they do not feel that they are able to be involved in a meaningful way, they are more likely to quit and seek fulfillment elsewhere. The implications for interpersonal and intergenerational communication are potentially significant. First, even acknowledging longstanding findings that subordinates prefer supervisory communication that is accepting and encouraging rather than neutral or negative, millennials' need for communication from supervisors and coworkers that is positive in valence and affirming in content feels burdensome to many senior and seasoned organizational members. Second, when millennials are marginalized by more senior coworkers and supervisors, they may experience two well-established dynamics: (1) the lack of informal organizational communication with them will negatively relate to their satisfaction and (2) low levels of communicative support from their supervisors could lead to turnover. Third, given Millennials' desire for open communication, and plenty of it, many are loathe to accept an organizational policy where information is communicated on a "need-to-know basis." Regardless of their low-level positions, millennial workers feel a need to be kept in the loop of information. Given supervisors' traditional preference for communication with other supervisors and managers more than with their subordinates, as well as supervisors' tendency to emphasize task instructions in their downward communication with subordinates more than socio-emotional content, supervisors report shock at millenials' expectation that supervisors share privileged information with them (Myers & Sadaghiani, 2010).

Feelings of *empowerment* are especially important for members' involvement, especially in the case of volunteers. Empowered workers feel a sense of self-efficacy or competence in being able to make decisions such as what, how, and when tasks will be completed (Chiles & Zorn, 1995). Workers who feel empowered often feel that they can affect achievement of organizational goals. When members do not feel empowered, they are less likely to feel inspired or motivated to do their work. In organizations that depend on volunteers, it is especially important that those members feel empowered (Foy, 1994). Theories of volunteerism stress that volunteers are motivated by the positive feeling that they derive from serving the organization and its clients (Omoto, Snyder, & Berghuis, 1993) and by the positive feelings of self-esteem (enhancing one's personal identity) that volunteering fosters (Piliavin & Callero, 1991). Recently, Ashcraft and Kedrowicz (2002) investigated how the volunteer–organization relationship was communicatively constructed in a domestic violence shelter and prevention organization called Haven. Many volunteers viewed their work at Haven as separate from their personal and professional lives. Because they already had a professional job, they did not mind that professional staff at Haven did not empower them to make decisions such as who they could allow to enter the shelter. Others felt like secondary members when the staff delegated the menial tasks to them, which caused some to question why they were volunteering. Ashcraft and Kedrowicz revealed a paradox in the self-proclaimed feminist organization. Although the staff strived for and touted a hierarchy-free organization, with every member (including volunteers) empowered to speak his or her mind, the lack of hierarchy had a disempowering effect on volunteers. Instead of a more traditional relationship in which staff gives volunteers social,

appraisal, and instrumental support, the staff saw the volunteers as equally empowered and thus requiring none of these types of support from them. These egalitarian practices squelched volunteers' feeling of empowerment and their desire to remain involved.

Becker and O'Hair (2007) investigated *citizenship behaviors* and their relationship to workers' treatment of coworkers. They described organizational citizenship behaviors as behaviors that are prosocial, cooperative, and demonstrate a feeling of responsibility to the organization, work group, or others. They anticipated that citizenship behaviors would be negatively related to *Machiavellianism*—a willingness to manipulate others for self-serving needs. Becker and O'Hair found that citizenship behaviors toward the organization have a stronger negative association with Machiavellianism than the negative association of organizational citizenship behaviors toward individuals or groups.

## Negotiating Roles

In the workplace, a *role* describes the duties one is tasked to perform and the manner in which the individual performs them (Katz & Kahn, 1966). Myers and Oetzel (2003) described *role negotiation* as a process in which newcomers compromise between their own expectations and the expectations of the organization. The negotiation process involves finding a stance between management's requirements for how the role should be performed and newcomers' perceptions concerning enactment of tasks and application of their abilities. Contributing to role negotiation is management's training (socializing) of members so that they adopt the role, usually with the intention that the new member will perform it in a custodial way much like his or her predecessor (described as *role taking* by Katz & Kahn, 1966). Role negotiation also involves *individualization,* or revising elements of the role to fit the individual's preferences or needs (Schein, 1968). Hess (1993) described this as *personalization* because it involves small (e.g., keeping the office door open rather than closed) and potentially larger (e.g., modifying job duties) changes. Role negotiation (described as *role making* by Katz & Kahn, 1966) suggests some give and take by the member, personalizing the role while also accommodating supervisor expectations, work group norms, and standards of the organization.

One of Myers and Oetzel's (2003) participants was an experienced hotel manager who had accepted a job with a company for whom he had never worked. The manager described a situation that caused him to negotiate his role:

> "Just before I joined the company, they had undergone a massive refinancing. There was a strong drive to control costs throughout the company. But, I decided I would rather spend a little more and be told I was spending too much than save the company a nickel and have the place get run down." While the company saw his position as "cost cutter," he chose instead to be "guardian of the property." (p. 444)

The manager reported that he received a promotion a few months later. He took this as an indication that he had successfully negotiated his role and benefited the organization at the same time.

### Foundations/Early Research

Jablin (1985) describes the importance of supervisor–subordinate interaction in role negotiation. Specifically, the supervisor is in a position to *role model* appropriate behaviors and attitudes (Weiss, 1977); members take cues from their supervisor about the importance of adhering to rules and organizational systems, the attitudes and relationships members have with upper management, and also the level of commitment expected in the work group and organization. Because supervisors are in a position to oversee, evaluate, reward, and punish members, their feedback (both positive and negative) can directly influence members' role-negotiating behaviors. Having a trusting (in-group) relationship

with a supervisor may facilitate role negotiation. In some cases, workers convince supervisors about the feasibility of the desired change by using influencing strategies such as open persuasion, manipulative persuasion, or manipulation (Krone, 1991, 1992).

Interactions with coworkers also can be a part of members' role negotiation. Coworkers are role models for normative workplace behaviors, and they frequently are information sources. For example, members may seek trusted colleagues' assistance in making sense of organizational events (Feldman, 1981). They may seek information from coworkers in their social and informational networks about organizational politics and what policies can be ignored or tested. Members may unify to challenge organizational policies and procedures, thereby collectively negotiating their roles. Just as likely, coworkers can resist and protest against other members' attempts to negotiate their roles. Their motivations for doing so may stem from concerns about how the changes will affect them in performing their own roles, concerns for customers or other stakeholders, or concerns based on perceptions of workplace equity (Kirby & Krone, 2002).

Role negotiation has been the focus of much of the research on *work–life balance*. These studies examine how workers negotiate flexibility in various dimensions of their work, such as (a) the schedule on which they will perform work (e.g., shifting hours to accommodate individual needs, working four 10-hour days instead of five days, working part-time) (Cowan & Hoffman, 2007; Kirby & Krone, 2002), (b) the location where the work will be performed (e.g., working some or all hours in a remote location) (Broadfoot, 2001; Edley, 2004; Hymlö, 2006), (c) autonomy in performing tasks (Brewer, 2000), (d) compensation (e.g., paid a salary versus commission, bonus for reaching goals) (Weisberg & Buckler, 1994), and (e) evaluation (e.g., how and how often workers are evaluated) (Broadfoot, 2001). Helmle, Seibold, and Afifi (in press) discuss the relevance of relational dialectics theory and findings from selected areas of interpersonal communication research (e.g., stress contagion effects, marital schemata and equity, and relationship conflict patterns) for understanding how married couples who own and run their own businesses (i.e., coprenuers) manage work–family life integration.

One type of role negotiation in the workplace is of special concern for women—negotiating maternity leave. Although maternity leaves are usually a part of formal organizational policies, many of the details are negotiated between employees and their supervisors. Miller, Jablin, Casey, Lamphear-Van Horn, and Ethington (1996) offered a model of the factors influencing the negotiation process of maternity leaves. Several antecedents can affect a supervisor's attitude about maternity leaves and his or her willingness to offer flexibility to particular employees, including (a) the supervisor's bias against leave takers, (b) the quality of the relationship between the worker and the supervisor, (c) the criticality of the worker's role (a critical role may be difficult to fill during the leave but her value is a powerful negotiating tool), and (d) the worker's career ambitions. According to Miller et al., the actual negotiations are affected by information seeking and negotiating tactics: What has been negotiated in the past? How have others responded to coworkers who negotiate flexibility? How skilled are the participants in giving, taking, and collaborating? The outcomes in the model are job satisfaction, satisfaction with the negotiation process, and the quality of the leader–member relationship. However, it seems likely that relationships with coworkers may also be affected as a result of this role negotiation.

## Advances/Recent Research

Recent role negotiation research has examined contextual issues affecting negotiations, the process used, negotiations within work groups, role negotiation by traditionally underrepresented members (workers with disabilities and female African Americans in leadership roles), and how humor and emotional displays facilitate (or impede) favorable role identity negotiations.

Meiners (2004) investigated a structural issue that affects role negotiation—the relationship between newcomers' *role development* and *time pressure*. He argues that newcomers are under pressure to quickly become contributing members of the organization. Meiners hypothesized and found that these time pressures cause workers to use fewer competitive tactics because these strategies can lengthen the negotiating process. Instead, they are likely to use integrative tactics. Integrative negotiations are characterized by both parties' willingness to compromise. Meiners reported a relationship between time pressure and the use of three integrative negotiation tactics in negotiating roles: (1) *directness*, openness or candor in revealing preferences and priorities; (2) *elaboration*, the extent to which information is unpacked and alternatives are explored; and (3) *mutual concessions*, a willingness to share control of the interaction and compromise. Many laud integrative negotiation for facilitating long-term relationships because it allows the parties to better understand the issues at stake and each other's priorities, thus better ensuring a mutually satisfying outcome (Folger & Poole, 1984). In this case, integrative methods of negotiating a role with supervisors should result in polite interaction and, perhaps, more favorable outcomes for both.

Most research on organizational roles examines the relationships that are negotiated between supervisors and their subordinates. Increasingly, organizations are organized around work groups that do not have traditional supervisor–worker reporting relationships (O'Toole & Lawler, 2006). Reporting relationships may be cross-functional or ad hoc, or members may work in autonomous or semiautonomous teams. Apker, Propp, and Ford (2005) studied these nontraditional reporting procedures in health care organizations, arguing that

> in many healthcare contexts employees are responsible to several colleagues rather than to one particular supervisor . . . Thus, interactions between team members may

be more significant in defining employees' role behaviors than their communication with a formally appointed leader. (p. 95)

Drawing on role dialectics (Baxter & Montgomery, 2000), they suggest that in these situations, roles are continually in flux, negotiated and renegotiated with individuals and frequently dependent on the situation. Apker et al. (2005) concluded that nurses must be aware of their team members' expectations of them. This awareness enables them either to communicatively accommodate their team members' expectations or to assert their status as a partner (rather than as a subordinate) in the team.

Newcomers directly or indirectly negotiate some aspects of their jobs. For example, workers may have distinctive ways of prioritizing and reporting completion of tasks to their supervisors. However, Cohen and Avanzino (2010) argue that *workers with disabilities* must participate in many more negotiations than people without disabilities. They must negotiate accommodation that enables them to work productively, often mindful of their supervisors' and coworkers' perceptions of these adaptations. Workers with disabilities that are progressive may find themselves in especially difficult relational circumstances. Degenerative physical abilities may necessitate reoccurring negotiations with their supervisors (Cohen & Avanzino, 2010). Unfortunately, supervisors who were mostly accommodative early on may become irritated by the repeated negotiations. Workers with disabilities then become challenged not only by their physical limitations but also by their eroding relationship with their supervisors.

Parker's (2002) investigation of African American female executives illuminates communication dynamics associated with another aspect of role negotiation. Parker focuses on how African American female executives overcome *cultural constraints* that may impede their leadership. She argues that the dominant culture has stringent expectations about how leaders should communicate, behave, and look. African American female executives contradict that dominant-culture

image not only in the view of white males but also at times for other African Americans. Parker found that upper- and senior-level white male colleagues interactively attempt to challenge African American women's authority or abilities. By not inviting them to informal meetings or social gatherings, they also exclude the women from interaction that could expand their strategic network. They subordinated the women by speaking to them in demeaning ways or not offering them opportunities. In other cases, the women's ideas were ignored or even co-opted. In interaction with other African Americans, the women were often met with direct conflict as a result of another's unmet expectations or with personal attacks made directly or indirectly in an attempt to challenge the women's position or authority. The women in the study discussed ways in which they negotiate their professional identities in response to these challenges. Some women turned to using unassertive means to allow white males to get used to the idea of working with a colleague who was an African American woman, but when the situation required it, they spoke up to directly assert their role and identity. Other women chose to take the matter head on from the start. They developed a reputation of being tough and verbally challenged the men who did not treat them as an equal-level colleague. Other strategies involved the use of humor to gain and hold attention, forcing their way into cliques, creating their own strategic networks, and avoiding the individuals who were attacking them or acknowledging personal attacks. Through these means, the women found their voice in dominant-culture organizations and negotiated their role within those cultures. In studies of the ways role negotiations occur communicatively, researchers found that *humor* is a valuable tool for enabling employees to negotiate their workplace roles. For example, Lynch (2009) acknowledges the power of humor to enhance relationships and argues that humor also can assist in boosting productivity, communicating resistance, and exerting control. Lynch found that humor helped professional chefs makes sense of their professional roles, thereby claiming and negotiating their professional identities as leaders in their domain of the organization. Tracy, Myers, et al. (2006) found that humor enabled participants from three occupations—firefighters, 911 call takers, and prison guards—to collectively make sense of their work and negotiate their roles. The researchers explain that workers in each of these professions must respond on a daily basis to the needs of prisoners, the mentally ill, drunks, and drug addicts. The workers' professional identities could easily be demeaned by serving what are often considered the lower elements of society. Through humor, the 911 call takers, firefighters, and prison guards were able to cognitively negotiate their roles by distancing themselves, claiming superiority, and drawing distinctions between themselves and the people they are hired to serve. In a third study that examined the use of humor by female middle managers, Martin (2004) proposed that individuals in middle management are often caught in the middle—having to answer to persons both up and down the hierarchy. Gender expectations further restrict women's abilities to be tough and confrontational in these roles. Martin found that the women in her study used humor to negotiate the challenges and paradoxes associated with being a female in the middle in gendered organizations. They used humor for a variety of purposes, including resisting upper management, softening managerial directives, negotiating conflicting options, and maintaining managerial control. Martin argues that humor helps women negotiate their constrained positional roles in the middle of the organization and their own femininity.

Other studies have examined the communication of emotions in the workplace according to normative professional display rules. Normative emotional displays involve the display of emotions that other organizational members and members of the public expect from the role. Morgan and Krone (2001) explored whether medical professionals negotiate their role performances through *emotional improvisation*, to resist those professional and organizational display rules. The researchers defined emotional improvisation as behaviors of medical personnel (e.g., physicians, nurses, and technicians who conduct heart catheterizations in a cardiac care center) that go against the organizational or professional norm of demonstrating detached concern. They found that emotional improvisations were not used often by medical professionals. When the researchers observed these improvisations, only a few were deemed successful by the interviewed participants. Morgan and Krone concluded that the established professional norms of emotional display served the medical personnel by assisting them in controlling the emotions of patients and patients' families. Because the norms of display assisted the medical personnel in communicatively performing their roles with patients and coworkers, most of them were followed.

## Developing Job Competency

Feldman (1981) argued, and Myers and colleagues supported (Gailliard et al., 2010; Myers & Oetzel, 2003), that members must have at least minimal levels of *job competency* to be contributing members of the work group and the organization. On the surface, developing task competency may not appear to be a communicative issue. However, the communication processes involved in training members to develop task competency, coordinate tasks with coworkers, and serve customers, along with the interaction that enables newcomers to hone their skills through information seeking and feedback, are significant aspects of organizational integration. Without task competency, newcomers are unlikely to successfully integrate. Moreland and Levine (1982, 2001) highlight the importance of task competency in their model of group socialization. The model specifies that members actively evaluate one another's "rewardingness" to the group. That is, members ask themselves (both consciously and subconsciously), "What are the rewards for having this member as part of our group?" Members who have job competency are more likely to be accepted by others in the workplace. However, members also assess their own task performance abilities. If they do not believe themselves to be able to accomplish the work, they are likely to feel a lack of accomplishment and are more prone to stress, burnout, and turnover.

## Foundations/Early Research

The primary purpose of *organizational training* is to develop newcomers' job competency. Van Maanen (1978) and Van Maanen and Schein (1979) proposed that organizations socialize members by means of six different tactics. Each tactic has two poles, but socialization is rarely at one extreme or the other. We will not review all six tactics, but two are particularly relevant because of the implications for interpersonal interaction. The first of these tactics involves *collective versus individual socialization*. Collective socialization means that newcomers are grouped to receive training, whereas individual socialization involves a one-on-one approach. An advantage of collective socialization is that new members are grouped, thus offering them the opportunity to become familiar with one another and potentially causing them to feel as though they are "in this together." Members of the group are more likely to rely on one another for social support, and they may facilitate one another's learning by reiterating lessons, clarifying understanding, or participating in group sensemaking (Jehn & Shah, 1997; Zorn & Gregory, 2005). Individual socialization is advantageous insofar as it enables the recruit to learn more details about his or her specific job and allows the newcomer to develop a more personal relationship with the individual who provides the training.

The second relevant socialization tactic is *serial versus disjunctive*. Serial socialization involves assigning a more experienced member to train and mentor the newcomer. The newcomer knows that she can ask questions and seek advice from the mentor because of the assigned relationship. Mentors can reduce uncertainty

and ease the transition into an organization (Cable & Parsons, 2001). Louis, Posner, and Powell (1983) surveyed recent college graduates who had recently entered organizations. Although fewer than half of the recruits were provided mentors as part of their socialization, mentors' assistance was significantly related to their job satisfaction. Cable and Parsons (2001) found that mentors also were associated with the protégé's perceptions of their fit in the organization. Landau and Scandura (2007) argue that having a positive mentoring relationship increases members' self-efficacy, encourages their continued learning, and enhances the development of job skills. In disjunctive socialization, newcomers are more or less left on their own after the initial training. They must judge for themselves to whom they should go with questions or to seek advice. They may find a mentor, but that relationship is one that is established informally. Ashforth and Saks (1996) offer a fuller description of the tactics and likely outcomes.

## Advances/Recent Research

Recent investigations establish the importance of interpersonal communication in the process of developing job competency. These studies examine the amount and appropriateness of communication, communication skills training for underprivileged job seekers, the factors influencing information seeking, task-related guidance and professional development from colleagues and friends, and the necessity of good interpersonal communication skills in customer service.

Supervisors are a primary source of job task information (Axley, 1996). Employees rely on their immediate supervisors to provide them with task guidance, including feedback that helps them improve their skills (Cusella, 1987). However, some supervisors may be better at providing information and task-related guidance than others. One factor may be *communication apprehension* (CA). CA often results in an individual's poorer performance in employment interviews (Ayres, Keereetaweep, Chen, & Edwards, 1998), limited job choice options (Harville, 1992), and more frequent turnover (Richmond & Roach, 1992). Recently, Bartoo and Sias (2004) speculated that the negative effects of CA also may have a deleterious effect on their relationship with subordinates. They proposed that CA may cause supervisors to limit their interactions with others and, thus, restrict the amount of information and feedback they provide to their subordinates. Bartoo and Sias found that supervisors with CA were less likely to provide their workers with information than supervisors who did not suffer from CA. Workers whose supervisor has CA may therefore experience *communication underload*, including the uncertainty and stress caused by lack of information. These workers may want feedback that would help them improve their job skills, but they may not receive it because of their supervisor's discomfort in communicating.

However, merely more communication may not contribute to task competency. Less is more in some occupations, and communication must conform to industry or occupational standards. A recent investigation of air traffic control and pilot interactions by Howard (2008) is illustrative. He found that more information communicated between air traffic controllers and pilots (more than was standard operating procedure) was problematic. Howard explained that cognitive and temporal resources are scarce and in high demand on the flight deck and in the control room. Communicative turns that included more information than necessary unduly increased cognitive demands. Howard also found out that when standardized linguistic protocol was violated, subsequent violations often occurred—including relational communication between parties who were acquainted.

Communication skills also can demonstrate *an ability to perform job tasks* prior to organizational entry and may be necessary for securing employment. Waldron and Lavitt (2000) examined the effects of communication training with clients in a "welfare-to-work" program. The training included topics designed to assist the clients in developing a *professional demeanor*, often expected by potential employers (Klein, 1999). Waldron and Lavitt (2000) described this demeanor as "the capacity to produce conversational behavior that is both effective (e.g., persuading an employer to make a positive hiring decision) and perceived as socially appropriate (e.g., assuming an appropriately 'professional' demeanor)" (p. 3). The participants who received the communication training showed significant improvements on interpersonal competence, interview plan specificity and complexity, self-assessments of interview plan confidence, and employer assessments of "plan convincingness." In practice interviews, the clients also improved in composure (e.g., confidence), altercentrism (e.g., attention to partner), expressiveness (e.g., nonverbal animation), and interaction management (e.g., turn taking).

Once hired, members who are uncertain about how to perform their job commonly engage in *information seeking*. As previously noted, Miller and Jablin (1991) proposed that organizational members may engage in several means of seeking information to determine what they must do to succeed, whether they are succeeding, and whether they are being accepted by others. Roderick and Knox (2002) examined the information-seeking practices of organizational members to determine whether age and organizational role influenced information-seeking strategies. They found that age was related to the information-seeking strategy chosen. Younger workers were less likely to use overt information-seeking methods (asking for information directly) than either middle-aged or older workers. Younger workers also were more likely to use testing strategies than middle-aged or older workers. Testing is intentionally breaking a rule to determine at what point the rule breaking is noticed and pointed out to the violator. Younger workers also used more indirect and observing strategies than older respondents. Indirect and observing strategies are indirect means of asking for or obtaining information that may not disclose the inquirer's ignorance or uncertainty.

Roderick and Knox conclude that less direct means of gathering information are used by younger workers to avoid disclosing their lack of knowledge or their discomfort with uncertainty. Middle-aged or older workers are less likely to be concerned about these issues. They also found that professionals, managers, and technical workers are more likely to seek information directly, while workers in customer service, sales, marketing, and lower level jobs are more likely to seek information through a less direct means.

As mentioned above, mentors can play an important role in training and guiding newcomers. However, less experienced members can receive some of the same benefits through other workplace relationships. For example, Gersick et al. (2000) recently studied professors' professional relationships with their colleagues. The most influential relationships the faculty had experienced were the relationships in which a more senior member helped a junior member by reading papers and providing reviews and by identifying which activities were worth getting involved in and which should be declined. Overall, the senior faculty members were instrumental in guiding junior faculty in performing job tasks and prioritizing those tasks to help them learn their role. According to the participants, these relationships were instrumental in helping them launch their careers.

*Friendships* can also facilitate the development of job competency. Zorn and Gregory (2005) examined medical students' socialization to medical school and the medical profession. Among several findings, the collective nature of their socialization fostered knowledge acquisition. Medical students often studied together, quizzing one another and helping one another to grasp concepts. When one student was unclear about a topic, the others helped by offering alternative means to understand the concept. An additional benefit was that teaching the topic to their classmate solidified their own knowledge.

Finally, *interpersonal communication skills* are not only instrumental in developing many job competencies but may also be critical job skills in

their own right. For example, effective interpersonal skills enable customer service workers to provide customers with more personalized service, aiding in the development of provider–customer relationships (Ford, 2001). Customers who have relationships with service providers are consistently more satisfied with the service they receive than those who do not (Gutek, Bhappu, Liao-Troth, & Cherry, 1999). According to Stern, Thompson, and Arnould (1998) and Gremler and Gwinner (2000), customers desire service providers who they perceive understand and care about them and reinforce their values. Customer service representatives who engage in personalized service practices to establish personal connections with customers may ultimately have more satisfied and loyal customers. This is especially true in professional services because customers have high expectations of relationships with professional service providers (Ford, 2001). Ford (2003) surveyed customers to assess their expectations of and experiences with physicians, dentists, auto mechanics, and hairdressers. Results indicated that expectations for personalized service communication were high. Ford also found that customer satisfaction and loyalty were predicted by communicative expectations and service provider performance or solely by the provider's communicative performance. These results were true in all four organizational contexts.

## Conclusion

In this chapter, we discuss interpersonal communication in the workplace that occurs between coworkers, between supervisors and subordinates, and between workers and customers, and is associated with skill competency and relational development and maintenance. Just as Jablin (1985) and Jablin and Krone (1994) relied on an organizational socialization framework to organize their reviews in previous editions of this *Handbook,* we have employed a member assimilation perspective to frame our examination of foundational studies and recent advances concerning interpersonal communication in the workplace. The processes of organizational assimilation proposed by Myers and Oetzel (2003), and later supported by Gailliard et al. (2010), reveal interaction subprocesses in assimilation and more general interpersonal communication processes in the workplace that have been found in early research (prior to 2000) and in more recent studies: (a) becoming familiar and working with supervisors, (b) becoming acquainted with coworkers, (c) acculturating, (d) being recognized, (e) becoming involved, (f) negotiating roles, and (g) developing job competency. Although these communicative processes enable newcomers to assimilate into organizations, they are integral aspects of workplace interaction throughout a member's tenure.

There are many questions that remain about these processes of organizational assimilation, answers to which would also greatly increase our understanding of interpersonal communication in the workplace. For example, first, since developing a strong, supportive relationship with a supervisor is important throughout members' organizational tenure, future research should examine how the relationship between supervisors and workers evolves over time. Do subordinates shift from being in-group members to out-group members and vice versa? If so, are there predictable factors and patterns? Second, the effect of interpersonal interaction with coworkers on organizational integration and long-term membership tenure is ripe for further investigation. For example, how do changing uses of media and technology by adolescents affect their expectations for interaction within the organization? How does more continual connection with individuals outside the organization via social media during the workday affect coworkers' interaction? Third, with regard to acculturating, how do newcomers determine what rules can be broken and which policies can be ignored? How are cultures talked into existence by members? In increasingly diverse workplaces, how do factors such as age and race affect interactions and the culture of the organization?

Fourth, concerning involvement and following the work of Avtgis et al. (2007), how do generational differences affect the desire to become involved? Fifth, future research on role negotiation should examine the effect of shorter organizational tenures on role negotiation. Will negotiations be more aggressive, or will such negotiations be less important? How will changing work–life balance issues affect the necessity to negotiate? How will a more diverse workforce influence workers' motivations and desired outcomes? Will generational differences caused by a broader age range of workers cause workers to engage in more negotiations?

Interpersonal interaction in organizations among people from different national cultures is another important area that this chapter has only touched on. Workplaces are globalized not only by workers from different national cultures interacting face-to-face but also through communication technologies with people around the world. For example, when a Korean company opens a U.S.-based factory and hires American employees, how do Korean supervisors and American workers manage assimilation and acculturation (e.g., how do workers and supervisors negotiate acceptable rules)? Do American workers assimilate to Korean organizational culture, or do Korean supervisors assimilate to U.S. workplace cultures? How do these differences affect supervisor–subordinate interaction and relationships? When customer service representatives serve customers who reside in other cultures, are the representatives able to toggle between their home country's normative workplace interaction and the norms expected by the customers they serve? How does the customers' perception of the foreign representative's communication competency (often related to cultural norms) affect their satisfaction with the exchange? Future research needs to examine the extent to which theories and research findings documented in Western cultures generalize in other cultures and whether the research findings discussed in this chapter are applicable to interpersonal communication among individuals from different national cultures.

In conclusion, we hope we have intrigued readers about the intersection of interpersonal communication and the workplace and the many potential directions for new research. The past few decades have introduced numerous changes in organizations, from increased diversity related to gender, ability, class, and experience to dispersed workers working from homes, across the country, and in different time zones across the globe. These factors can make interaction among members more complicated and sometimes more difficult. In addition, increased worker mobility and the recent economic turmoil have changed the relationship members have with their organization, potentially affecting workers' trust, motivation, and loyalty. These changes have affected many of the advances we reviewed in research on interpersonal communication in the workplace, and they open many possibilities for future research and discovery.

# References

Allen, B. J. (2005). Social constructionism. In S. May & D. K. Mumby (Eds.), *Engaging organizational communication: Theory and research* (pp. 35–54). Thousand Oaks, CA: Sage.

Anderson, L. R., Tolson, J., Fields, M. W., & Thacker, J. W. (1990). Extension of the Pelz Effect: The impact of leaders' upward influence on group members' control within the organization. *Basic and Applied Social Psychology, 11,* 19–32.

Anderson, W. K., & Buzzanell, P. M. (2007). "Outcast among outcasts": Identity, gender, and leadership in a Mac users group. *Women and Language, 30,* 32–44.

Apker, J., Propp, K. M., & Ford, W. S. Z. (2005). Negotiating status and identity tensions in health-care team interactions: An exploration of nurse role dialectics. *Journal of Applied Communication Research, 33,* 93–115.

Apker, J., & Ray, E. B. (2003). Stress and social support in health care organizations. In T. Thompson, A. Dorsey, K. Miller, & R. A. Parrott (Eds.), *Handbook of health communication* (pp. 347–368). Mahwah, NJ: Lawrence Erlbaum.

Ashcraft, K. L. (2005). Feminist organizational communication studies: Engaging gender in public and private. In S. May & D. K. Mumby (Eds.), *Engaging organizational communication: Theory and research* (pp. 141–170). Thousand Oaks, CA: Sage.

Ashcraft, K. L., & Kedrowicz, A. (2002). Self-direction or social support? Nonprofit empowerment and the tacit employment contract of organizational communication studies. *Communication Monographs, 69,* 88–110.

Ashcraft, K. L., & Trethewey, A. (2004). Developing tension: An agenda for applied research on the organization of irrationality. *Journal of Applied Communication Research, 32,* 171–181.

Ashforth, B. E., & Saks, A. M. (1996). Socialization tactics: Longitudinal effects on newcomer adjustment. *Academy of Management Journal, 39,* 149–178.

Avtgis, T., Thomas-Maddox, C., Taylor, E., & Patterson, B. (2007). The influence of employee burnout syndrome on the expression of organizational dissent. *Communication Research Reports, 24,* 97–102.

Axley, S. R. (1996). *Communication at work: Management and the communication-intensive organization.* Westport, CT: Quorum Books.

Ayres, J., Keereetaweep, T., Chen, P., & Edwards, P. A. (1998). Communication apprehension and employment interviews. *Communication Education, 47,* 1–17.

Baker, M. A. (1991). Gender and verbal communication in professional settings. *Management Communication Quarterly, 5,* 36–63.

Ballard, D. I., & Seibold, D. R. (2004). Communication-related organizational structures and work group temporal experiences: The effects of coordination method, technology type, and feedback cycle on members' construals and enactments of time. *Communication Monographs, 71,* 1–27.

Ballard, D. I., & Seibold, D. R. (2006). The experience of time at work: Relationship to communication load, job satisfaction, and interdepartmental communication. *Communication Studies, 57,* 317–340.

Barge, J. K. (2004). Reflexivity and managerial practice. *Communication Monographs, 71,* 70–96.

Barge, J. K., & Schlueter, D. W. (2004). Memorable messages and newcomer socialization. *Western Journal of Communication, 68,* 233–256.

Bartoo, H., & Sias, P. M. (2004). When enough is too much: Communication apprehension and employee information experiences. *Communication Quarterly, 52*, 15–26.

Bauer, T., Morrison, E. W., & Callister, R. R. (1998). Organizational socialization: A review and direction for future research. In G. R. Ferris & K. M. Rowland (Eds.), *Research in personnel and human resource management* (Vol. 16, pp. 149–214). Greenwich, CT: JAI Press.

Baxter, L. A. (1985). Accomplishing relationship deterioration. In S. Duck & D. Perlman (Eds.), *Understanding personal relationships* (pp. 243–265). London: Sage.

Baxter, L. A., & Montgomery, B. M. (2000). Rethinking communication in personal relationships from a dialectical perspective. In K. Dindia & S. Duck (Eds.), *Communication and personal relationships* (pp. 31–53). New York: Wiley.

Becker, J. A. H., Halbesleben, J. R. B., & O'Hair, H. (2005). Defensive communication and burnout in the workplace: The mediating role of leader–member exchange. *Communication Research Reports, 22*, 145–152.

Becker, J. A. H., & O'Hair, H. D. (2007). Machiavellians' motives in organizational citizenship behavior. *Journal of Applied Communication Research, 35*, 246–267.

Berger, C. R., & Calabrese, R. J. (1975). Some explorations in initial interaction and beyond: Toward a developmental theory of interpersonal communication. *Human Communication Research, 1*, 99–112.

Berman, E. M., West, J. P., & Richter, M. N., Jr. (2002). Workplace relations: Friendship patterns and consequences (according to managers). *Public Administration Review, 62*, 217–230.

Bhal, K. T., Bhaskar, A. U., & Ratnam, C. S. V. (2009). Employee reactions to M & A: Role of LMX and leader communication. *Leadership & Organization Development Journal, 30*, 604–624.

Bingham, S. G., & Burleson, B. R. (1989). Multiple effects of messages with multiple goals: Some perceived outcomes of response to sexual harassment. *Human Communication Research, 16*, 184–216.

Bligh, M. C., & Kohles, J. C. (2008). Negotiating gender role expectations: Rhetorical leadership and women in the US Senate. *Leadership, 4*, 381–402.

Bowles, S., & Gintis, H. (1976). *Schooling in capitalist America: Educational reforms and the contradictions of economic life.* New York: Basic Books.

Braithwaite, D. O., & Harter, L. M. (2000). Communication and the management of dialectical tensions in the personal relationships of people with disabilities. In D. O. Braithwaite & T. L. Thompson (Eds.), *Handbook of communication and people with disabilities: Research and application* (pp. 17–33). Mahwah, NJ: Lawrence Erlbaum.

Brewer, A. M. (2000). Work design for flexible work scheduling: Barriers and gender implications. *Gender, Work, and Organization, 7*, 33–44.

Bridge, K., & Baxter, L. A. (1992). Blended relationships: Friends as work associates. *Western Journal of Communication, 56*, 200–225.

Broadfoot, K. J. (2001). When the cat's away, do the mice play? *Management Communication Quarterly, 15*, 110–114.

Buller, M. K., & Buller, D. B. (1987). Physicians' communication style and patient satisfaction. *Journal of Health and Social Behavior, 28*, 375–388.

Bullis, C., & Bach, B. W. (1989). Socialization turning points: An examination of change in organizational identification. *Western Journal of Speech Communication, 53*, 273–293.

Bullock, J. R. (1983). Participation and pay. *Group & Organization Studies, 8*, 127–136.

Burns, T. (1955). The reference of conduct in small groups: Cliques and cabals in occupational milieux. *Human Relations, 8*, 467–486.

Cable, D. M., & Parsons, C. K. (2001). Socialization tactics and person-organization fit. *Personnel Psychology, 54*, 1–23.

Caldwell, D. F., & O'Reilly, C. A. (1982). Task perceptions and job satisfaction: A question of causality. *Journal of Applied Psychology, 67*, 361–369.

Campbell, K. L., Martin, M. M., & Wanzer, M. (2001). Employee perceptions of manager humor orientation, assertiveness, responsiveness, approach/avoidance strategies, and satisfaction. *Communication Research Reports, 18*, 67–74.

Castrogiovanni, G. J., & Macy, B. A. (1990). Organizational information processing capabilities and degree of employee participation: A longitudinal field experiment. *Group & Organizational Studies, 15*, 313–336.

Cheney, G. (1983). The rhetoric of identification and the study of organizational communication. *Quarterly Journal of Speech, 69*, 143–158.

Chiles, A. M., & Zorn, T. E. (1995). Empowerment in organizations: Employees' perceptions of the influences on empowerment. *Journal of Applied Communication Research, 23,* 1–25.

Chory, R. M., & Hubbell, A. P. (2008). Organizational justice and managerial trust as predictors of antisocial employee responses. *Communication Quarterly, 56,* 357–375.

Clair, R. P. (1993a). The use of framing devices to sequester organizational narratives: Hegemony and harassment. *Communication Monographs, 60,* 113–136.

Clair, R. P. (1993b). The bureaucratization, commodification, and privatization of sexual harassment through institutional discourses: A study of the Big 10 universities. *Management Communication Quarterly, 7,* 123–157.

Cohen, M., & Avanzino, S. (2010). We are people first: Framing organizational assimilation experiences of the physically disabled using co-cultural theory. *Communication Studies, 61,* 272–303.

Comer, D. R. (1991). Organizational newcomers' acquisition of information from peers. *Management Communication Quarterly, 5,* 64–89.

Coopman, S. (2003). Communicating disability: Metaphors of oppression, metaphors of empowerment. *Communication Yearbook, 27,* 337–394.

Cowan, R., & Hoffman, M. F. (2007). The flexible organization: How contemporary employees construct the work/life border. *Qualitative Research Reports in Communication, 8,* 37–44.

Cress, U., & Kimmerle, J. (2007). Guidelines and feedback in information exchange: The impact of behavioral anchors and descriptive norms in a social dilemma. *Group Dynamics: Theory, Research, and Practice, 11,* 42–53.

Cusella, L. P. (1987). Feedback, motivation, and performance. In F. M. Jablin, L. L. Putnam, K. H. Roberts, & L. W. Porter (Eds.), *Handbook of organizational communication: An interdisciplinary perspective* (pp. 624–678). Newbury Park, CA: Sage.

Dansereau, F., Graen, G., & Haga, W. J. (1975). A vertical dyad linkage approach to leadership within formal organizations. *Organizational Behavior and Human Performance, 13,* 46–78.

Dillard, J. P., Solomon, D. H., & Samp, J. A. (1996). Framing social reality: The relevance of relational judgments. *Communication Research, 23,* 703–723.

Downs, C. W., & Conrad, C. (1982). Effective subordinancy. *Journal of Business Communication, 19,* 27–37.

Edley, P. (2004). Entrepreneurial mothers' balance of work and family. In P. M. Buzzanell, H. Sterk, &

L. Turner (Eds.), *Gender in applied communication contexts* (pp. 255–273). Thousand Oaks, CA: Sage.

Eisenberg, E. M., & Witten, M. G. (1987). Reconsidering openness in organizational communication. *Academy of Management Review, 12,* 418–426.

Fairhurst, G. T. (1993). The leader-member exchange patterns of women leaders in industry: A discourse analysis. *Communication Monographs, 60,* 321–351.

Fairhurst, G. T. (2007). *Discursive leadership: In conversation with leadership psychology.* Thousand Oaks, CA: Sage.

Fairhurst, G. T., Rogers, L. E., & Sarr, R. A. (1987). Manager-subordinate control patterns and judgments about the relationship. In M. McLaughlin (Ed.), *Communication yearbook 10* (pp. 395–415). Newbury Park, CA: Sage.

Fairhurst, G. T., & Sarr, R. A. (1996). *The art of framing: Managing the language of leadership.* San Francisco: Jossey-Bass.

Feeley, T. H., Hwang, J., & Barnett, G. A. (2008). Predicting employee turnover from friendship networks. *Journal of Applied Communication Research, 36,* 56–73.

Feldman, D. C. (1977). The role of initiation activities in socialization. *Human Relations, 30,* 977–990.

Feldman, D. C. (1981). The multiple socialization of organizational members. *Academy of Management Review, 6,* 309–319.

Feldman, D. C., & Brett, J. M. (1983). Coping with new jobs: A comparative study of new hires and job changers. *Academy of Management Journal, 26,* 258–272.

Festinger, L. (1954). A theory of social comparison processes. *Human Relations, 7,* 117–140.

Fisher, A. B. (1986). Leadership: When does the difference make a difference? In R. Y. Hirokawa & M. S. Poole (Eds.), *Communication and group decision-making* (pp. 197–215). Beverly Hills, CA: Sage.

Folger J. P., & Poole, M. S. (1984). *Working through conflict: A communication perspective.* Glenview, IL: Scott Foresman.

Ford, W. S. Z. (2001). Customer expectations for interactions with service providers: Relationship versus encounter orientation and personalized service communication. *Journal of Applied Communication Research, 29,* 1–29.

Ford, W. S. Z. (2003). Communication practices of professional service providers: Predicting customer satisfaction and loyalty. *Journal of Applied Communication Research, 31,* 189–211.

Fox, S., Giles, H., Orbe, M., & Bourhis, R. Y. (2000). Inter-ability communication: Theoretical perspectives. In D. O. Braithwaite & T. L. Thompson (Eds.), *Handbook of communication and people with disabilities: Research and application* (pp. 193–222). Mahwah, NJ: Lawrence Erlbaum.

Foy, N. (1994). *Empowering people at work.* Brookfield, VT: Gower.

Freudenberger, H. J. (1974). Staff burn-out. *Journal of Social Issues, 30,* 159–165.

Friedman, R. A., & Holtom, B. (2002). The effects of network groups on minority employee turnover intentions. *Human Resource Management, 41,* 405–421.

Gailliard, B., Myers, K. K., & Seibold, D. R. (2010). Organizational assimilation: A multidimensional reconceptualization and measure. *Management Communication Quarterly, 24,* 552–578.

George, J. M., & Bettenhausen, K. (1990). Understanding prosocial behavior, sales performance, and turnover: A group-level analysis in a service context. *Journal of Applied Psychology, 75,* 698–709.

Gersick, C. J. G., Bartunek, J. M., & Dutton, J. E. (2000). Learning from academia: The importance of relationships in professional life. *The Academy of Management Journal, 43,* 26–44.

Gibson, M., & Papa, M. (2000). The mud, the blood, and the beer guys: Organizational osmosis in blue-collar work groups. *Journal of Applied Communication Research, 28,* 68–88.

Goldstein, B., & Oldham, J. (1979). *Children and work: A study of socialization.* New Brunswick, NJ: Transaction.

Graen, G. B., & Scandura, T. A. (1987). Toward a psychology of dyadic organizing. In B. Staw & L. Cummings (Eds.), *Research in organizational behavior* (Vol. 9, pp. 175–208). Greenwich, CT: JAI Press.

Graen, G. B., & Uhl-Bien, M. (1995). Relationship-based approach to leadership: Development of a leader-member exchange (LMX) theory of leadership over 25 years—Applying a multi-level multi-domain perspective. *Leadership Quarterly, 6,* 219–247.

Graham, G. H., Unruh, J., & Jennings, P. (1991). The impact of nonverbal communication in organizations: A survey of perceptions. *Journal of Business Communication, 28,* 45–62.

Gremler, D. D., & Gwinner, K. P. (2000). Customer-employee rapport in service relationships. *Journal of Service Research, 3,* 82–104.

Gutek, B. A., Bhappu, A. D., Liao-Troth, M. A., & Cherry, B. (1999). Distinguishing between service relationships and encounters. *Journal of Applied Psychology, 84,* 218–233.

Gutek, B. A., & Morasch, B. (1982). Sex ratios, sex role spillover, and sexual harassment of women at work. *Journal of Social Issues, 38,* 55–74.

Hackman, J. R. (1976). Group influences on individuals. In M. D. Dunnette (Ed.), *Handbook of industrial and organizational psychology* (pp. 1455–1525). Chicago: Rand McNally.

Hackman, J. R., & Vidmar, N. (1970). Effects of size and task type of group performance and member reactions. *Sociometry, 33,* 37–54.

Hafen, S. (2004). Organizational gossip: A revolving door of regulation and resistance. *Southern Communication Journal, 69,* 223–240.

Harville, D. L. (1992). Person/job fit model of communication apprehension in organizations. *Management Communication Quarterly, 27,* 55–61.

Helmle, J. R., Seibold, D. R., & Afifi, T. D. (in press). Work and family in copreneurial family businesses: Extending and integrating communication research. In C. Salmon (Ed.), *Communication yearbook 35.* Thousand Oaks, CA: Sage.

Hess, J. A. (1993). Assimilating newcomers into an organization: A cultural perspective. *Journal of Applied Communication Research, 21,* 189–210.

Hess, J. A., Omdahl, B. L., & Fritz, J. M. H. (2006). Turning points in relationships with disliked coworkers. In J. M. H. Fritz & B. L. Omdahl (Eds.), *Problematic relationships in the workplace* (pp. 205–232). New York: Peter Lang.

Hirokawa, R. Y. (1990). The role of communication in group decision-making efficacy: A task contingency perspective. *Small Group Research, 21,* 190–204.

Hornung, S., Rousseau, D. M., & Glaser, J. (2008). Creating flexible work arrangements through idiosyncratic deals. *Journal of Applied Psychology, 93*(3), 655–664.

Howard, J. W., III. (2008). "Tower, am I cleared to land?": Problematic communication in aviation discourse. *Human Communication Research, 34*(3), 370–391.

Hymlö, A. (2006). Girls on film: An examination of gendered vocational socialization messages found in motion pictures targeting teenage girls. *Western Journal of Communication, 70,* 167–185.

Jablin, F. M. (1979). Superior-subordinate communication: The state of the art. *Psychological Bulletin, 86,* 1201–1222.

Jablin, F. M. (1982). Organizational communication: An assimilation approach. In M. E. Roloff & C. R. Berger (Eds.), *Social cognition and communication* (pp. 255–286). Beverly Hills, CA: Sage.

Jablin, F. M. (1985). Task/work relationships: A life-span perspective. In M. L. Knapp & G. R. Miller (Eds.), *Handbook of interpersonal communication* (pp. 615–654). Beverly Hills, CA: Sage.

Jablin, F. M. (1987). Organizational entry, assimilation, and exit. In F. Jablin, L. Putnam, K. Roberts, & L. Porter (Eds.), *Handbook of organizational communication* (pp. 679–740). Newbury Park, CA: Sage.

Jablin, F. M. (2001). Organizational entry, assimilation, and exit. In F. Jablin & L. Putnam (Eds.), *The new handbook of organizational communication* (pp. 732–818). Thousand Oaks, CA: Sage.

Jablin, F. M., & Krone, K. J. (1987). Organizational assimilation. In C. R. Berger & S. H. Chaffee (Eds.), *Handbook of communication science* (pp. 711–746). Newbury Park, CA: Sage.

Jablin, F. M., & Krone, K. J. (1994). Task/work relationships: A life-span perspective. In M. L. Knapp & G. R. Miller (Eds.), *Handbook of interpersonal communication* (2nd ed., pp. 621–675). Thousand Oaks, CA: Sage.

Jablin, F. M., & Sussman, L. (1983). Organizational group communication: A review of the literature and model of the process. In H. H. Greenbaum, R. L. Falcione, & S. A. Hellweg (Eds.), *Organizational communication: Abstracts, analysis, and overview* (Vol. 8, pp. 11–50). Beverly Hills, CA: Sage.

Jehn, K. A., & Shah, P. P. (1997). Interpersonal relationships and task performance: An examination of mediating processes in friendship and acquaintance groups. *Journal of Personal and Social Psychology, 72,* 775–790.

Johnson, G. M. (1992). Subordinate perceptions of superior's communication competence and task attraction related to superior's use of compliance-gaining tactics. *Western Journal of Communication, 56,* 54–67.

Kassing, J. W. (2000). Investigating the relationship between superior-subordinate relationship quality and employee dissent. *Communication Research Reports, 17,* 58–69.

Katz, D., & Kahn, R. L. (1966). *The social psychology of organizations.* New York: Wiley.

Kingsley Westerman, C. Y., & Park, H. S. (2010). Managing blended friendships: Using empirical data to prepare students and employees for relational outcomes. *Journal of Career Development, 36,* 246–261.

Kingsley Westerman, C. Y., Park, H. S., & Lee, H. E. (2007). A test of equity theory in multidimensional friendships: A comparison of the United States and Korea. *Journal of Communication, 57,* 575–597.

Kipnis, D., Schmidt, S. M., Price, K., & Stitt, C. (1981). Why do I like thee: Is it your performance or my orders? *Journal of Applied Psychology, 65,* 324–328.

Kipnis, D., Schmidt, S. M., & Wilkinson, I. (1980). Intraorganizational influence tactics: Explorations in getting one's way. *Journal of Applied Psychology, 65,* 440–452.

Kirby, E., & Krone, K. (2002). "The policy exists but you can't really use it": Communication and the structuration of work-family policies. *Journal of Applied Communication Research, 30,* 50–77.

Klein, K. (1999, May 12). Small business/entrepreneur of the year awards. *Los Angeles Times,* p. C7.

Klimoski, R. J., & Karol, B. L. (1976). The impact of trust on creative problem solving groups. *Journal of Applied Psychology, 61,* 630–633.

Kline, J. A. (1972). Orientation and group consensus. *Central States Speech Journal, 23,* 44–47.

Knapp, M. L., Putnam, L. L., & Davis, L. L. (1988). Measuring interpersonal conflict in organizations: Where do we go from here? *Management Communication Quarterly, 1,* 414–429.

Korte, R. (2010). First, get to know them: A relational view of organizational socialization. *Human Resource Development Quarterly, 7,* 233–252.

Kramer, M. W., Dougherty, D. S., & Pierce, T. A. (2004). Managing uncertainty during a corporate acquisition: A longitudinal study of communication during an airline acquisition. *Human Communication Research, 30,* 71–101.

Krone, K. J. (1984). *A framework for studying upward influence messages in decision making contexts.* Paper presented at the annual meeting of the International Communication Association, San Francisco.

Krone, K. J. (1991). The effects of leader-member exchange on subordinates' upward influence attempts. *Communication Research Reports, 8,* 9–18.

Krone, K. J. (1992). A comparison of organization, structural, and relationship effects on subordinates' upward influence choices. *Communication Quarterly, 40,* 1–15.

Krone, K. J., Kramer, M. W., & Sias, P. M. (2010). Theoretical developments in organizational communication research. In C. R. Berger, M. E. Roloff, & D. Roskos-Ewolsen (Eds.), *Handbook of communication science* (2nd ed., pp. 165–182). Thousand Oaks, CA: Sage.

Lai, L., Rousseau, D. M., & Chang, K. T. T. (2009). Idiosyncratic deals: Coworkers as interested third parties. *Journal of Applied Psychology, 94,* 547–556.

Laing, M. (1993). Gossip: Does it play a role in the socialization of nurses? *Image: Journal of Nursing Scholarship, 25,* 37–43.

Landau, M. J., & Scandura, T. A. (2007). Mentoring as a forum for personal learning in organizations. In B. R. Ragins & K. E. Kram (Eds.), *The handbook of mentoring at work: Theory, research, and practice* (pp. 95–122). Thousand Oaks, CA: Sage.

Lawler, E. E. (1982). Increasing worker involvement to enhance organizational effectiveness. In P. S. Goodman & Associates (Eds.), *Change in organizations: New perspectives on theory, research, and practice* (pp. 280–315). San Francisco: Jossey-Bass.

Leathers, D. G. (1970). The process effects of trust-destroying behavior in small groups. *Speech Monographs, 37,* 180–187.

Lee, H. E., Park, H. S., Lee, T. S., & Lee, D. W. (2007). Relationships between LMX and subordinates' feedback seeking behaviors. *Social Behavior and Personality, 35,* 359–374.

Lee, T. S., Lee, D. W., Lee, H. E., & Park, H. S. (2005). Superior-subordinate relationship in Korean civil engineering companies. *Journal of Management in Engineering, 21,* 159–163.

Limon, M., & La France, B. H. (2005). Communication traits and leadership emergence: Examining the impact of argumentativeness, communication apprehension, and verbal aggressiveness in work groups. *Southern Communication Journal, 70,* 123–133.

Liu, Y., & Ipe, M. (2010). The impact of organizational and leader-member support on expatriate commitment. *International Journal of Human Resource Management, 21,* 1035–1048.

Louis, M. R., Posner, B. Z., & Powell, G. N. (1983). The availability and helpfulness of socialization practices. *Personnel Psychology, 36,* 857–866.

Lutgen-Sandvik, P., Tracy, S. J., & Alberts, J. K. (2007). Burned by bullying in the American workplace: Prevalence, perception, degree, and impact. *Journal of Management Studies, 44,* 835–860.

Lynch, O. H. (2009). Kitchen antics: The importance of humor and maintaining professionalism at

work. *Journal of Applied Communication Research, 37,* 444–464.

Mannix, E. A., Thompson, L. L., & Bazerman, M. H. (1989). Negotiation in small groups. *Journal of Applied Psychology, 74,* 508–517.

Marshall, A. A., & Stohl, C. (1993). Participating as participation: A network approach. *Communication Monographs, 60,* 137–157.

Martin, D. M. (2004). Humor in middle management: Women negotiating the paradoxes of organizational life. *Journal of Applied Communication Research, 32,* 147–170.

Martin, D. M., Rich, C. O., & Gayle, B. (2004). Humor works: Communication style and humor functions in manager/subordinate relationships. *Southern Communication Journal, 69,* 206–222.

Maslach, C. (1993). Burnout: A multidimensional perspective. In W. B. Schaufeli, C. Maslach, & T. Marek (Eds.), *Professional burnout: Recent developments in theory and research* (pp. 19–32). Washington: Taylor & Francis.

McCroskey, J. C., Richmond, V. P., & Davis, L. M. (1986). Apprehension about communicating with supervisors: A test of a theoretical relationship between types of communication apprehension. *Western Journal of Speech Communication, 50,* 171–182.

McPhee, R. D., & Zaug, P. (2000). The communicative constitution of organizations: A framework for explanation. *Electronic Journal of Communication/ La Revue Electronique de Communication, 10*(1–2). Retrieved April 15, 2011, from www.cios.org/getfile/ MCPHEE_V10N1200

Medved, C. E., Brogan, S. M., McClanahan, A. M., Morris, J. F., & Shepherd, G. J. (2006). Family and work socializing communication: Messages, gender, and ideological implications. *Journal of Family Communication, 6,* 161–180.

Meiners, E. B. (2004). Time pressure: An unexamined issue in organizational newcomers' role development. *Communication Research Reports, 21,* 243–251.

Meyer, J. C. (2004). Organizational discourse and citizenship: A special issue introduction. *Southern Communication Journal, 69,* 183–187.

Miller, V. D., & Jablin, F. M. (1991). Information seeking during organizational entry: Influences, tactics, and a model of the process. *Academy of Management Review, 16,* 92–120.

Miller, V. D., Jablin, F. M., Casey, M. K., Lamphear-Van Horn, M., & Ethington, C. (1996). The maternity leave as a role negotiation process. *Journal of Managerial Issues, 8,* 286–309.

Miller, V. D., Johnson, J. R., Hart, Z., & Peterson, D. L. (1999). A test of antecedents and outcomes of employee role negotiation ability. *Journal of Applied Communication Research, 27,* 24–48.

Monge, P. R., Bachman, S. G., Dillard, J. P., & Eisenberg, E. M. (1982). Communicator competence in the workplace: Model testing and scale development. In M. Burgoon (Ed.), *Communication yearbook 5* (pp. 505–527). New Brunswick, NJ: Transaction.

Moreland, R. L., & Levine, J. M. (1982). Group socialization: Temporal changes in individual-group relations. In L. Berkowitz (Ed.), *Advances in experimental social psychology* (Vol. 15, pp. 137–192). New York: Academic Press.

Moreland, R. L., & Levine, J. M. (2001). Socialization in organizations and work groups. In M. E. Turner (Ed.), *Groups at work: Theories and research* (pp. 69–112). Mahwah, NJ: Lawrence Erlbaum.

Morgan, J. M., & Krone, K. J. (2001). Bending the rules of "professional" display: Emotional improvisation in caregiver performances. *Journal of Applied Communication Research, 29,* 317–340.

Morris, G. H., Gaveras, S. C., Baker, W. L., & Coursey, M. L. (1990). Aligning actions at work: How managers confront problems of employee performance. *Management Communication Quarterly, 3,* 303–333.

Morrison, E. W. (1993). Newcomer information seeking: Exploring types, modes, sources, and outcomes. *Academy of Management Journal, 36,* 557–589.

Myers, K. (2005). A burning desire: Assimilation into a fire department. *Management Communication Quarterly, 18,* 344–384

Myers, K. K. (2009). Workplace relationships. In S. Smith & S. R. Wilson (Eds.), *New directions in interpersonal communication* (pp. 135–156*)*. Thousand Oaks, CA: Sage.

Myers, K. K., & McPhee, R. D. (2006). Influences on member assimilation in workgroups in high reliability organizations: A multilevel analysis. *Human Communication Research, 32,* 440–468.

Myers, K. K., & Oetzel, J. G. (2003). Exploring the dimensions of organizational assimilation: Creating and validating a measure. *Communication Quarterly, 51,* 438–457.

Myers, K. K., & Sadaghiani, K. (2010). Millennials in the workplace: A communication perspective on Millennials' organizational relationships and performance. *Journal of Business and Psychology, 25,* 225–238.

Nachmann, B. (1960). Childhood experiences and vocational choice in law, dentistry and social work. *Journal of Counseling Psychology, 7,* 243–250.

Nadler, D. A. (1979). The effects of feedback on task group behavior: A review of experimental research. *Organizational Behavior and Human Performance, 23,* 309–338.

Napier, N. K., Simmons, G., & Stratton, K. (1989). Communication during a merger: The experience of two banks. *Human Resource Planning, 12,* 105–122.

Omoto, A., Snyder, M., & Berghuis, J. P. (1993). The psychology of volunteerism: A conceptual analysis and a program of action research. In J. B. Pryor & G. Reeder (Eds.), *The social psychology of HIV infection* (pp. 333–356). Hillsdale, NJ: Lawrence Erlbaum.

O'Reilly, C. A., & Anderson, J. C. (1980). Trust and the communication of performance appraisal information: The effect of feedback and performance and job satisfaction. *Human Communication Research, 6,* 290–298.

O'Reilly, C. A., & Caldwell, D. F. (1979). Informational influence as a determinant of task characteristics and job satisfaction. *Journal of Applied Psychology, 64,* 157–165.

O'Toole, J., & Lawler, E. E., III. (2006). *The new American workplace.* New York: Palgrave.

Park, H. S., & Park, M. (2008). Multilevel effects of conflict management preferences on satisfaction with group processes. *International Journal of Conflict Management, 19,* 57–71.

Parker, P. S. (2001). African American women executives within dominant culture organizations: (Re) conceptualizing notions of instrumentality and collaboration. *Management Communication Quarterly, 15,* 42–82.

Parker, P. S. (2002). Negotiating identity in raced and gendered workplace interactions: The use of strategic communication by African American women senior executives within dominant culture organizations. *Communication Quarterly, 50,* 251–268.

Pelz, D. (1952). Influence: A key to effective leadership in the first line supervisor. *Personnel, 29,* 209–217.

Piliavin, J. A., & Callero, P. (1991). *Giving blood: The development of an altruistic identity.* Baltimore: Johns Hopkins University Press.

Prentice, D. S. (1975). The effect of trust-destroying communication on verbal fluency in the small group. *Speech Monographs, 42,* 262–270.

Putnam, L. L. (1988). Communication and interpersonal conflict in organizations. *Management Communication Quarterly, 1,* 293–301.

Putnam, L. L., & Stohl, C. (1990). Bona fide groups: A reconceptualization of groups in context. *Communication Studies, 41,* 248–265.

Rath, T. (2006). *Vital friends: The people you can't afford to live without.* New York: Gallup Press.

Ray, E. B. (1987). Supportive relationships and occupational stress in the workplace. In T. Albrecht & M. Adelman (Eds.), *Communicating social support* (pp. 172–191). Newbury Park, CA: Sage.

Redding, W. C. (1972). *Communication within the organization: An interpretive review of theory and research.* New York: Industrial Communication Council.

Richmond, V. P., & McCroskey, J. C. (2000). The impact of supervisor and subordinate immediacy on relational and organizational outcomes. *Communication Monographs, 67,* 85–95.

Richmond, V. P., & Roach, D. K. (1992). Willingness to communicate and employee success in U.S. organizations. *Journal of Applied Communication Research, 31,* 95–115.

Riordan, C. M., & Griffeth, R. W. (1995). The opportunity for friendship in the workplace: An underexplored construct. *Journal of Business and Psychology, 10,* 141–154.

Roderick, R., & Knox, R. L. (2002). Information seeking among organizational members. *Communication Research Reports, 19,* 372–379.

Ross, J. A. (1997). Does friendship improve job performance? *Harvard Business Review, 75,* 8–9.

Salancik, G. R., & Pfeffer, J. (1978). A social information processing approach to job attitudes and task design. *Administrative Science Quarterly, 23,* 224–253.

Schein, E. H. (1968). Organizational socialization and the profession of management. *Industrial Management Review, 9,* 1–16.

Schilit, W. K., & Locke, E. A. (1982). A study of upward influence in organization. *Administrative Science Quarterly, 27,* 304–316.

Scott, C. W., & Myers, K. K. (2010). Toward an integrative theoretical perspective of membership negotiations: Socialization, assimilation, and the duality of structure. *Communication Theory, 20,* 79–105.

Seashore, S. (1954). *Group cohesiveness in the industrial work group.* Ann Arbor: University of Michigan Institute for Social Research.

Seibold, D. R., Kang, P., Gailliard, B. M., & Jahn, J. (2009). Communication that damages teamwork: The dark side of teams. In P. Lutgen-Sandvik & B. Davenport Sypher (Eds.), *Destructive organizational communication: Processes, consequences, and constructive ways of organizing* (pp. 267–289). New York: Routledge.

Seibold, D. R., Lemus, D. R., Ballard, D. I., & Myers, K. K. (2009). Organizational communication and applied communication research: Parallels, intersections, integration, and engagement. In L. R. Frey & K. N. Cissna (Eds.), *The Routledge handbook of applied communication research* (pp. 331–354). New York: Routledge.

Seibold, D. R., Meyers, R. A., & Shoham, M. D. (2010). Social influence in groups and organizations. In C. R. Berger, M. E. Roloff, & D. Roskos-Ewolsen (Eds.), *Handbook of communication science* (2nd ed., pp. 237–253). Thousand Oaks, CA: Sage.

Seibold, D. R., & Shea, C. (2001). Participation and decision making. In F. M. Jablin & L. L. Putnam (Eds.), *Handbook of organizational communication: Advances in theory, research, and methods* (pp. 664–703). Thousand Oaks, CA: Sage.

Sias, P. M. (2005). Narratives of workplace friendship deterioration. *Journal of Social and Personal Relationships, 21,* 321–340.

Sias, P. M. (2009). *Organizing relationships: Traditional and emerging perspectives on workplace relationships.* Thousand Oaks, CA: Sage.

Sias, P. M., Fix, B., Heath, R. G., Perry, T., & Silva, D. (2004). Narratives of workplace friendship deterioration. *Journal of Social and Personal Relationships, 21,* 321–340.

Sias, P. M., Krone, K. J., & Jablin, F. M. (2002). An ecological perspective on workplace relationships. In M. L. Knapp & J. A. Daly (Eds.), *Handbook of interpersonal communication* (3rd ed., pp. 615–642). Thousand Oaks, CA: Sage.

Sias, P. M., & Perry, T. (2004). Disengaging from workplace relationships: A research note. *Human Communication Research, 30,* 589–602.

Sluss, D. M., & Ashforth, B. E. (2007). Relational identity and identification: Defining ourselves through work relationships. *Academy of Management Review, 32,* 9–32.

Snyder, J. (2009). The role of coworker and supervisor social support in alleviating the experience of burnout for caregivers in the human-services industry. *Southern Communication Journal, 74,* 373–389.

Stern, B. B., Thompson, C. J., & Arnould, E. J. (1998). Narrative analysis of a marketing relationship: The customer's perspective. *Psychology & Marketing, 15,* 195–214.

Strine, M. (1992). Understanding "how things work": Sexual harassment and academic culture. *Journal of Applied Communication Research, 20,* 391–400.

Sypher, B. (2004). Reclaiming civil discourse in the workplace. *Southern Communication Journal, 69,* 257–269.

Taylor, B., & Conrad, C. (1992). Narratives of sexual harassment: Organizational dimensions. *Journal of Applied Communication Research, 20,* 401–418.

Teigen, C. W. (1983). *Communication of organizational climate during job screening interviews: A field study of interviewee perceptions, "actual" communication behavior and interview outcomes.* Unpublished doctoral dissertation, Department of Speech Communication, University of Texas, Austin.

Teven, J. J., McCroskey, J. C., & Richmond, V. P. (2006). Communication correlates of perceived Machiavellianism of supervisors: Communication orientations and outcomes. *Communication Quarterly, 54*(2), 127–142.

Thompson, L. L., Mannix, E. A., & Bazerman, M. H. (1988). Group negotiation: Effects of decision rules, agendas and aspiration. *Journal of Personality and Social Psychology, 54,* 86–95.

Tidwell, M., & Sias, P. (2005). Personality and information seeking: Understanding how traits influence information-seeking behaviors. *Journal of Business Communication, 42,* 51–77.

Tompkins, P. K., & Cheney, G. (1985). Communication and unobtrusive control in contemporary organizations. In R. D. McPhee & P. K. Tompkins (Eds.), *Organizational communication: Traditional themes and new directions* (pp. 179–210). Beverly Hills, CA: Sage.

Tracy, S. J., Lutgen-Sandvik, P., & Alberts, J. K. (2006). Nightmares, demons, and slaves: Exploring the painful metaphors of workplace bullying. *Management Communication Quarterly, 20,* 148–185.

Tracy, S. J., Myers, K. K., & Scott, C. (2006). Cracking jokes and crafting selves: A multi-site analysis of humor, sensemaking, and identity management among human service workers. *Communication Monographs, 73,* 283–308.

Turow, J. (1974). Advising and ordering in daytime, primetime. *Journal of Communication, 24,* 138–141.

Van Maanen, J. (1975). Breaking in: Socialization to work. In R. Dubin (Ed.), *Handbook of work, organization, and society* (pp. 67–120). Chicago: Rand McNally.

Van Maanen, J. (1978). People processing: Strategies of organizational socialization. *Organizational Dynamics, 7,* 19–36.

Van Maanen, J., & Schein, E. (1979). Toward a theory of organizational socialization. *Research in Organizational Behavior, 1,* 209–264.

Wagoner, R., & Waldron, V. R. (1999). How supervisors convey routine bad news: Facework at UPS. *Southern Communication Journal, 64,* 193–210.

Waldron, V. R. (2000). Relational experiences and emotion at work. In S. Fineman (Ed.), *Emotion in organizations* (2nd ed., pp. 64–82). Thousand Oaks, CA: Sage.

Waldron, V. R., & Lavitt, M. R. (2000). "Welfare-to-work": Assessing communication competencies and client outcomes in a job training program. *Southern Communication Journal, 66,* 1–15.

Wall, V. D., Galanes, G. J., & Love, S. B. (1987). Small, task-oriented groups: Conflict management, satisfaction, and decision quality. *Small Group Behavior, 18,* 31–55.

Weisberg, A. C., & Buckler, C. A. (1994). *Everything a working mother needs to know about pregnancy rights, maternity leave, and making her career work for her.* New York: Doubleday.

Weiss, H. M. (1977). Subordinate imitation of supervisor behavior: The role of modeling in organizational socialization. *Organizational Behavior and Human Performance, 19,* 89–105.

Winstead, B. A., Derlega, V. J., Montgomery, M. J., & Pilkington, C. (1995). The quality of friendships at work and job satisfaction. *Journal of Social and Personal Relationships, 12,* 199–215.

Zand, D. E. (1972). Trust and managerial problem solving. *Administrative Science Quarterly, 17,* 229–239.

Zorn, T. E., & Gregory, K. W. (2005). Learning the ropes together: Assimilation and friendship development among first-year male medical students. *Health Communication, 17,* 211–232.

# CHAPTER 17

# Intercultural Perspectives on Interpersonal Communication

*John G. Oetzel*

*Stella Ting-Toomey*

## Intercultural Interpersonal Relationships

Intercultural interpersonal relationships (e.g., friendships, dating, and marriage) are becoming more prevalent and accepted compared with past decades. For example, Reiter, Krause, and Stirlen (2005) surveyed the dating behavior of 468 university students from various ethnic groups in the United States and found that 66% of the participants who were in a relationship reported being involved in an intercultural romantic relationship (defined as dating someone from a different ethnic group/race, national culture, or religious background). Jacobson and Johnson (2006) revealed that 85% of a sample of 934 African Americans approve of interracial marriage. Although more young adults in the United States are dating and cohabiting with someone of a different cultural background, Joyner and Kao (2005) found that interracial romantic relationships are still considerably less likely than same-race romantic relationships to lead to marriage. Furthermore, there are differences among other ethnic groups in the pattern of interracial dating and marital relationships: Hispanics had the highest rate of interracial relationships: 45% of 18- to 19-year-olds and 33% of 24- to 25-year-olds were in interracial dating relationships in the early 2000s compared with African Americans (20% and 14%, respectively) and white Americans (16% and 12%, respectively) (Joyner & Kao, 2005). While society is becoming more accepting of intercultural marriage in general, the idea of intermixing of some racial groups on the marital bonding level still meets with societal resistance (Joyner & Kao, 2005).

Despite the growing acceptance of certain types of intercultural relationships, intercultural relationships are more difficult than intracultural relationships because of both communication difficulties within the relationship and societal constraints and continuing prejudice and discrimination against certain individuals from all cultural groups (Chen, 2003; Diggs & Clark, 2002; Thompson & Collier, 2006). The struggle of intercultural relationships is essentially a struggle of managing multiple identities through mindless versus mindful intercultural communication practice (Collier, 2005; Ting-Toomey, 2005a). Identity is "a person's conception of self within a particular social, geographical, cultural, and political context" (Yep, 1998, p. 79) and consists of personal, relational, and social (or cultural) membership components. Personal identities are unique qualities of ourselves such as personality traits, personal self-image, and individuated self-concept. Relational identities refer to relational role expectations such as sibling relationships, friendships, and dating relationships, and a sense of relational couplehood. Social identities are aspects we share with other individuals who belong to the same perceived social or cultural membership group (Gallois, Ogay, & Giles, 2005; Hecht, Warren, Jung, & Krieger, 2005; Imahori & Cupach, 2005). Throughout this chapter, we consider intercultural relationships as occurring between individuals who differ on one or more social or cultural identities. Most intercultural relationships involve negotiating multiple cultural identity membership differences (e.g., different religion, ethnicity, and nationality at the same time).

The purpose of this chapter is to review the extant literature to identify the key findings about cultural perspectives on interpersonal relationships. Specifically, we seek to examine the various ways in which the study of identity management/negotiation in intercultural interpersonal relationships is accomplished. Reviewing this research is important because of the challenges intercultural relationships present. Identifying key themes in the literature can help researchers and practitioners work with intercultural partners to establish healthy and satisfying relationships. To this end, the opening section presents an overview of three approaches to the study of intercultural communication. To understand how culture frames interpersonal

communication and relationships, we need to understand different conceptualizations of key interpersonal and cultural terms. The second section then reviews the research literature of three types of intercultural relationships—friendship, dating, and marital/cohabiting/family. We focus on these three relationship types due to the fact that most of the existing intercultural/interracial communication-based research studies focused on these three relationship arenas. The final section establishes future directions for the study of intercultural interpersonal relationships.

## Three Approaches for Studying Intercultural Interpersonal Relationships

The study of how identities are negotiated and managed across and between cultures has been undertaken by a variety of scholars using different theoretical perspectives and methods. The subdiscipline of intercultural communication primarily uses three major approaches to study intercultural interpersonal relationships: social scientific, interpretive, and critical. Within each of these approaches, there are subtle differences in specific approaches, but these larger strands provide a general framework for understanding how culture and communication relate in intercultural relationships. This section presents an overview of these three approaches by including three key subsections: (1) definitions of key terms (culture, identity, communication, competence, and relationship), (2) a description of research goals and methods to study intercultural relationships, and (3) an exemplar theoretical framework for examining intercultural relationships (see Table 17.1 for an overview of the approaches).

## Social-Scientific Approach

The social-scientific approach was the predominant approach to the study of intercultural communication in the 1980s, but today it is simply one of three major approaches. Within the

**Table 17.1**    Key Concepts in the Three Approaches to Studying Intercultural Interpersonal Relationships

|  | *Social Scientific* | *Interpretive* | *Critical* |
|---|---|---|---|
| Culture | Shared system of meanings/patterns; apriori group membership | Shared system of meanings; speech community | Site of power struggle; site of contested meaning |
| Identity | Discrete choice; evolving and negotiated | Distinct system of communal practices | Nonnegotiated social category and group right; multiple and contextualized |
| Communication | Process of creating meaning through exchange of messages | Speech codes; communal function | Discourse |
| Communication competence | Knowledge, motivation, and skills to interact effectively and appropriately | Appropriate and effective communication; feeling as well as behavior | Rational/unconstrained communication versus distorted communication |
| Relationship | Develops through stages: initial interaction, formation, progression, and maintenance | Develops through stages constructed by speech codes | Recognition of power in relationships (e.g., alliances) |
| Research goals | Identify patterns of cultural influences on communication; comparison of multiple cultures; etic | Deep description of individual cultural community; emic | Unmask power and domination in the system to achieve social justice |
| Research methods | Quantitative: survey and experimental design | Qualitative: ethnography, interviews, case studies; interpretive analysis: grounded theory and ethnography of speaking | Qualitative: interviews, case study, ethnography; critical analysis: discourse analysis and textual analysis |

social-scientific approach, scholars study culture and communication in interpersonal relationships from a cross-cultural and intercultural perspective. Much of the foundational social-scientific work on intercultural communication research is based on comparisons of two or more cultures (often national or ethnic groups). These comparisons help identify how the aspects of culture and communication patterns vary in different cultural groups. These communication patterns presumably provide information about what to expect when interacting with members from different cultures. This type of research is classified as cross-cultural. For example, in a cross-cultural self-disclosure research study, researchers are interested in comparing the similarities and differences on self-disclosure patterns between Mexican friendship pairs and Korean friendship pairs. In contrast, intercultural communication is the exchange of messages between people from different cultural groups (Gudykunst, 2003a). Gudykunst (2003a) argued that "understanding cross-cultural communication is a prerequisite to understanding intercultural communication" (p. vii). For example, in an intercultural self-disclosure study, researchers are interested in studying how cultural membership factors (e.g., Mexican cultural value and identity issues vs. Korean cultural value and identity issues) affect the intercultural self-disclosure twist-and-turn processes. However, other scholars suggested that the study of intercultural interaction is distinctively different from cross-cultural communication research because individuals communicating in an intergroup/intercultural context can mutually adjust or adapt to each other, and there are also exponentially more social/cultural identity–based factors to consider (e.g., cultural/ethnic identity salience factors, language interaction issues, intercultural competence/incompetence factors, etc.) with people from a different culture than with people from the same culture (Adler & Graham, 1989; Barnett & Lee, 2003). Social scientists who study cross-cultural communication and those who study intercultural communication share research perspectives and methods. The purpose of the social-scientific perspective is to identify patterns of communication and connect these patterns to the underlying cultural values. This subsection explores this purpose in more depth.

*Key Terms.* While there are hundreds of definitions of cultures, researchers from a social-scientific perspective typically emphasize that culture is shared among members. Specifically, they share patterns of behavior and ways to make sense of the world. For example, Ting-Toomey and Takai (2006) defined culture as

> a learned system of meanings that fosters a particular sense of shared identity-hood and community-hood among its group members. It is a complex frame of reference that consists of a pattern of traditions, beliefs, values, norms, symbols, and meanings that are shared to varying degrees by interacting members of an identity group. (p. 691)

From the social science point of view, culture provides an overarching system-level perspective about a group of people that can best be understood by comparing one culture with another. Culture is not meant to pigeonhole or stereotype people; it simply describes general patterns that influence, to a certain degree, the members of the culture. However, social scientists tend to look on single aspects of culture (e.g., nationality or ethnicity or religion) in any given study and not multiple aspects of culture simultaneously. This is a potential limitation of the social-scientific perspective.

Culture is often conceived as an a priori membership in a group and as a variable (Hall, 1992; Martin & Nakayama, 1999). To this end, social-scientific researchers study culture by identifying and operationalizing the variables associated with patterns of culture. The most popular social-scientific perspective on culture was offered by Hofstede (1991, 2001). Hofstede surveyed more than 100,000 employees of IBM in more than 50 nations around the world. He identified broad patterns that he found distinguished the cultures; the patterns are labeled dimensions of cultural variability because they describe how cultures vary on a set of common conceptions on the membership systems level and included the following dimensions: individualism–collectivism (broad value tendencies of people in a culture to emphasize the individual identity vs. group identity and individual rights vs. group obligations, Triandis, 1995), power distance (the extent to which "the less powerful members of institutions and organizations within a country expect and accept that power is distributed unequally," Hofstede, 1991, p. 28), uncertainty avoidance (the extent to which "the members of a culture feel threatened by uncertain or unknown situations," Hofstede, 1991, p. 113), masculinity–femininity (the extent to which a society emphasizes achievement or nurture, Hofstede, 1991), and short-term versus long-term orientation (orientation toward short-term gains and immediate tangible outcomes vs. traditions, social obligations, and long-term relationship building, Hofstede, 2001).

A key component of culture is identity. While there is agreement across the approaches that identity includes both social and personal components, there is difference in the ways that identity is conceptualized. Kim (2007) identified five different themes of how identity is conceptualized and studied. Three of these themes are consistent with the social-scientific perspective: (1) identity is a discrete category and a choice; (2) identity is adaptive and evolving; and (3) identity is flexible and negotiated. The first theme emphasizes that individuals choose their identity (e.g., bicultural identity). For example, Berry's (2008) model of acculturation strategies centers on two key questions: (1) Is your home culture of value and to be retained? and (2) Is the host culture and positive relations with the larger society of value and to be sought? The result is four choices of identity: integration (yes, yes), assimilation (no, yes), separation (yes, no), and marginalization (no, no). The second theme centers on identity as dynamic and evolving over time. Kim's (2005, 2009) theory of cross-cultural adaptation emphasizes this point. Briefly, Kim explains that individuals' cultural identity undergoes a gradual transformation as a result of the desire for individuals to establish a relatively stable and functional relationship with the environment and the interactions that these individuals have within a host culture. The third theme emphasizes the need to negotiate and reconcile individuals' cultural identity vis-à-vis other people. For example, Imahori and Cupach's (2005) identity management theory and Ting-Toomey's (2005a) identity negotiation theory both emphasize the importance of negotiating cultural identity in the development of competent interpersonal relationships. In sum, these three themes have variations, but all emphasize concrete social categories that are important to describe and use (and move beyond the static conceptualization of "national culture," "ethnic background," or static "race" category) to explain positive and negative intercultural relationships. Furthermore, cultural identities are variables that can be measured and used to explain communication in these relationships.

Culture and identity are distinct from communication. Communication is a process that includes positive and negative factors; communication does not have any value judgments and simply is what results when people exchange verbal and nonverbal messages. For example, "communication is a process whereby people collectively create and transmit meaning through the exchange of verbal and nonverbal messages in a particular context" (Oetzel, 2009, p. 11). The process of message exchange includes various types of communication processes relevant to intercultural relationships, such as stereotypes, social power, social support, self-disclosure, and commitment/attachment (Chen, 2003).

Given that communication includes both negative and positive components, social-scientific researchers seek to define and describe intercultural communication competence. Intercultural communication competence is "the knowledge, motivation, and skills to interact effectively and appropriately with members of different cultures" (Wiseman, 2003, p. 192). Effectiveness refers to achieving interpersonal communication goals, while appropriateness emphasizes the ability to maintain relationships by performing culture-sensitive role behaviors. Intercultural communication competence is of vital importance to establish and maintain intercultural relationships. Intercultural relationships are constituted through communication; incompetent communication usually derails or damages relationships, while competent communication usually nurtures relationships. Several theoretical approaches to intercultural communication place a primary emphasis on competence, including anxiety uncertainty management theory (Gudykunst, 2005) and conversational constraints theory (Kim, 2005). While competence is often implicit in theories of intercultural communication, these particular theories make it a primary focus as a communication process and outcome.

Satisfying relationships result from individuals using competent communication to negotiate cultural identities and cultural differences to build a positive relational culture. A relational culture refers to "processes, structures, and practices that create, express, and sustain personal relationships and identities of partners" (Wood, 1997, p. 150). In essence, relational partners develop their own culture, which is a mix of both their larger cultural backgrounds and their idiosyncratic behaviors and personalities. From this perspective, a relationship develops in phases such as initial interaction, relationship formation, relational sustenance and progression, and relational maintenance (Chen, 2003).

*Research Goals and Methods.* The social-scientific perspective seeks to describe/understand and predict the effect of culture (or cultural variables) on communication variables and the subsequent effect of communication on various outcomes, such as intercultural relationships. Ideally, this perspective seeks to identify the causal effects of culture, but because of limitations in the methods of studying culture, many studies are only able to identify associations with culture. A strong emphasis has been placed on constructing and/or using theoretical frameworks to understand the relationships among culture, identity, communication, and relationship development. In this manner, social-scientific researchers use etic (as opposed to emic—see "Interpretive Approach") approaches for studying cross-cultural and intercultural communication. Etic approaches involve the use of a structure (such as a theory or a model) created by the researcher and using preestablished criteria/ frameworks for studying communication (Gudykunst, 2003b). The researcher also positions herself or himself from a point outside the system of study. The purpose is to describe and explain the system from the etic structure employed by the researcher.

Overall, the main purpose of research is to explain and improve the quality of the intercultural process and outcomes from such encounters. Intercultural communication competence has often been defined as communicating appropriately and effectively in a diverse range of intercultural situations (for a detailed review, see Spitzberg & Changnon, 2009). It can also encompass both the desired internal dimension (e.g., cultural frame shifting, flexibility, and cultural empathy) and the desired external outcome dimension (e.g., appropriate and effective communication in a situated intercultural context) (Deardorf, 2006). Thus, research questions of interest tend to be within two broad areas: (1) How do cultural factors contribute to competent or incompetent communication in intercultural relationships? and (2) What are the results of competent or incompetent communication for the development of intercultural relationships? These questions are addressed in a variety of issues and processes related to intercultural relationship development, including (but not limited to) anxiety management in interpersonal relationships (Gudykunst, 2005), communication accommodation (Gallois et al., 2005), conflict management (Oetzel & Ting-Toomey, 2003; Ting-Toomey, 2005b), and cultural adaptation (Kim, 2005).

There are two predominant methods used by most social-scientific researchers who study interpersonal relationships: (1) survey questionnaire and (2) experimental design. The survey questionnaire is by far the most frequently used research method (e.g., Oetzel et al., 2001; Rao, Singhal, Ren, & Zhang, 2001). For example, Oetzel et al. (2001) surveyed 768 college students in four national cultures: China, Japan, Germany, and the United States. They used these data to compare and contrast the conflict management behavior of university students in interpersonal conflicts. Experimental designs are the "gold standard" of social-scientific research because of the control of variables, which enables causal relationships to be examined. Culture is not a variable that lends itself well to experimental manipulation, and thus, experimental designs are relatively rare. Rather than controlling culture, researchers typically manipulate the composition of groups or dyads to be intra- or intercultural. These experiments collect a combination of self-report information (e.g., cultural and individual variables) as well as videotaped interaction. For example, Cai, Wilson, and Drake (2000) examined 80 U.S. and international students in a negotiated task. The authors coded the interactions for information sharing, offers, and distributive tasks and asked participants to complete a self-report questionnaire on individualism–collectivism. They then correlated individualism–collectivism to participant behavior and negotiated outcomes.

*Theoretical Exemplar.* Imahori and Cupach's (2005) cultural identity theory attempts to "explain how cultural identities are negotiated through development of an interpersonal relationship" (p. 196). Imahori and Cupach argued that the successful negotiation of cultural identities in interpersonal relationships also involves the negotiation of relational identities. This negotiation is engaged through competence facework. The theory includes two propositions focused on face problematics and identity management phases.

The first proposition describes four challenges that people in relationships experience related to cultural identity management. The first challenge (Proposition 1a) occurs when people from different cultural backgrounds only view their interaction partner as a member of a cultural group and ignore other aspects of their identity (labeled identity freezing). The second challenge (Proposition 1b) is the opposite of the first challenge and occurs when people's cultural identities are ignored, thus not supporting people's desire to have positive cultural identities (labeled nonsupport problematic). The third challenge (Proposition 1c) is managing the dialectic between supporting your own cultural identity versus that of the other person (labeled self–other face dialectic). Imahori and Cupach (2005) argued that this challenge is more difficult to manage the more distinct the cultural identities are. The final challenge (Proposition 1d) is the dialectical choice between supporting the partner's negative or positive face. Negative face is the desire for freedom and autonomy, while positive face is the desire for interpersonal acceptance and approval.

The second proposition examines the unique features of identity management at three highly

interdependent and cyclical phases of intercultural interpersonal relationships: trial, enmeshment, and renegotiation. The trial phase focuses on the initial interactions and development of a relationship. During the trial phase, identity management involves balancing the self–other and negative–positive dialectics while avoiding the identity freezing and nonsupport problematics (Proposition 2a). Furthermore, Imahori and Cupach (2005) noted that identity management during the trial period involves some degree of face threat for relational partners to discover the balance point of the dialectics (Proposition 2b). The enmeshment phase involves the development of a personal relationship resulting from enough commonalities between the partners. During the enmeshment phase, increased interaction results in the co-development of symbols and rules that create an integrated interpretive framework for understanding each other and the relationship (Proposition 2c). As a result of this integration, identity management during the enmeshment phases de-emphasizes cultural identities and emphasizes relational identities (Proposition 2d). The renegotiation phase involves redefining the relationship as new face challenges are presented. During renegotiation, relational partners manage identities and face problematics by increasing symbolic and rule convergence, as evidenced by a salient relational identity (Proposition 2e). Furthermore, intercultural partners are able to deal directly with cultural differences that were largely ignored during the trial phases as these differences are seen as "integral and positive aspects of their relationship (Proposition 2f)" (Imahori & Cupach, 2005, p. 205).

Identity management theory is illustrative of the conceptualizations of the key terms and research methods presented in this section. This theory identifies cultural identities as a key factor that results in communication difficulties in intercultural relationships. Managing these communication difficulties occurs through competent and interpersonally sensitive facework, which results in personalized relationship development (assuming sufficient commonalities). The purpose of the theory is to describe and predict relationships among the key constructs, thereby fitting the criteria established for the social-scientific perspective. Furthermore, Imahori and Cupach (2005) reviewed the research supporting the propositions of the theory, which was predominantly conducted through survey questionnaires.

## Interpretive Approach

The interpretive perspective provides detailed descriptions of culture and cultural communication. The goal of interpretive research is to identify a unified culture and the ways of knowing and understanding that culture. From this perspective, understanding the subtle nuances and meanings of behaviors is vital to understand culture. This perspective centers on meaning and on describing the way people construct meaning within a culture. The interpretive researcher wants to understand the practices of another community from a native or insider perspective. That is, the meanings that are important are the ones that the members themselves attune to and respond to in particular situational contexts. There are different interpretive approaches used to study intercultural communication, such as ethnography of communication (EOC; Hymes, 1972) and phenomenology (Orbe & Spellers, 2005). In brief, EOC applies ethnographic methods to understand the communication patterns of a cultural community. Phenomenology examines how individuals experience their world from a descriptive and first-person point of view. This section explores the larger framework (rather than individual perspectives) of interpretive research as it relates to intercultural relationships.

*Key Terms.* Although there are many definitions of culture within the interpretive perspective, the one aspect at the core of these definitions is culture as a system of sensemaking that is shared by a community. One definition of culture that is often used within the interpretive perspective is Geertz's (1973): Culture "denotes an historically transmitted pattern of meanings embodied in symbols, a system of inherited conceptions expressed in symbolic forms by means of which men [sic] communicate, perpetuate, and develop their knowledge about and attitudes toward life" (p. 89). Geertz explained that these systems of symbols are webs of significance that we as humans have created to make sense of our lives. This sensemaking focus lies at the heart of a variety of definitions of culture that have taken their lead from Geertz's work. For example, Philipsen (1992) stated that culture is a "socially constructed and historically transmitted pattern of symbols, meanings, premises, and rules" (p. 7).

From the interpretive perspective, a culture then is not a geopolitical, religious, or ethnic community; rather, it is a shared code for communicating. Some interpretive scholars (e.g., Hymes, 1972; Philipsen, 1992) use the concept of speech community in conjunction with culture. A speech community refers to a group of people who share a code (linguistic features) and the norms for producing and interpreting communication (Hymes, 1972). Members of a speech community may use labels connected to religious, ethnic, or national groups, but the culture is not these groups themselves. Two people from England may not be from the same culture or speech community, whereas two people from China and Australia may be part of the same culture because they had the same sensemaking system passed on to them. Furthermore, people can belong to multiple speech communities/cultures. Difficulties can occur in intercultural relationships when the partners come from different speech communities. For example, when strangers who come from different speech communities meet, they make sense of their world through their own interaction patterns and community relationships. Developing friendships can be difficult if those sensemaking processes cause us to label the other person in a negative way when they are actually behaving in a manner that is appropriate in their own community.

The sensemaking process of culture is recognized as something that is passed on to others over time and helps offer those individuals a sense of communal identity. Cultural identity in the interpretive perspective is a distinct system of communal practices (Kim, 2007). Specifically, Kim argued that "cultural identity is conceived as a communally shared system of communicative practices that is unique to the community and enduring over time" (p. 246). Cultural identity includes the shared practices, rituals, and patterns that constitute a community and connote a common tradition and future.

As noted in the description of culture, communication in the interpretive perspective consists of a speech code for making sense of the world (Philipsen, 1992). Communication performs a communal function; that is, it is the means for linking individuals into communities of shared identity (Philipsen, 1989). Thus, communication and culture are inextricably linked, and interpretive researchers often do not try to separate them. The meanings of communication are unique to the particular speech communities. For example, Carbaugh (1989) identified 50 terms for talk (i.e., communication) in six different cultural communities. This study was a cross-cultural comparison of four levels of communication—act, event, style, and function—and the salient messages within the cultural categories of speech (messages about communication, social relations, and personhood). Carbaugh explicated unique and native ways of communicating messages at the three levels that are understood by the community. For example, *dugri* speech in Israel represents a relatively direct mode of communication, while sweet speech in Fiji represents an indirect mode. The key point is that while there may be a framework to compare these definitions of communication, their meanings are unique to the cultural community. These patterns of communication are ways to develop interpersonal relationships. For example, *dugri* speech, or "straight talk," demonstrates respect for the other—that is, concern enough to share one's thoughts. Similarly, sweet speech also displays respect by maintaining the harmonic fabric of the interpersonal relationship and preserving communal peace.

In the interpretive perspective, communication competence has a similar conceptualization to that of the social-scientific perspective. That is, competent communication involves appropriate and effective outcomes. One distinction is that to truly participate in a culture one must know what to feel (Carbaugh, 1990). Thus, competence is also the ability to feel as members do rather than simply the ability to act in appropriate and effective ways. That is, one not only is able to take the perspective of the other person but also has similar experiential emotions to others when the same stimulus arises. Furthermore, the specific means of performing competent communication are unique to a cultural community. For example, Philipsen (1989) identified, through a review of the literature, patterns of competent communication in several distinct communities. In "Teamsterville" (a working-class suburb of Chicago), community members needed to perform a communication style that showed that they were members of the community because performing in a "place" is such an important component. In "Nacirema" (*American* spelled backward), members have to express their unique and true self in their relationships with others. In "Appalacia," members use acts such as "huddling" and "passing the time" to demonstrate that they experienced their lives with each other. Similarly, Covarrubias and Windchief (2009) illustrated how silence helped perform three key functions for American Indian students attending a mainstream U.S. university: (1) maintaining traditional cultural practices, (2) distinguishing cultural practices from those of non-Indians, and (3) safekeeping cultural elements. These functions help one develop and maintain interpersonal relationships (i.e., the particular communication practice reinforces cultural identity). They also function only for members who are part of the cultural membership group or accepted as allies of the cultural group.

Relationships are also created and made sense of through unique speech codes. Compared with the social-scientific perspective, in which interpersonal relationships develop from initial phases to enmeshed phases, the interpretive perspective emphasizes the constructed meanings of these developmental relationships. The latter perspective also stresses the importance of investigating the repeated speech codes that are used in a distinctive speech community and the normative rules for maintaining various forms of interpersonal relationships in each interactional community. For example, Philipsen's (1992) study of "Teamsterville" illustrates appropriate types of relationships and speaking for men. It emphasizes factors such as the importance of hierarchical relationships among men, the importance of speaking as an insider, ascribed identity, and physical response to insults and threats. Additionally, Griefat and Katriel (1989) examined *musayara* as a code for describing relationships with others in one's culture. *Musayara* "refers to 'going with' or 'accompanying' one's partner in conversation" (p. 121). It focuses on "tactful and smooth talks" in maintaining harmony in both social and personal relationships.

*Research Goals and Methods.* The interpretive perspective seeks to understand and describe a cultural community. In contrast to the social-scientific perspective, the description and understanding are not for comparative purposes per se but simply to understand how meaning is constructed. Thus, the purpose is to describe the meanings that community members construct and how they make sense of the world. Interpretive researchers compare/contrast speech communities with others; however, they do not attempt to judge meanings and behaviors but rather to present them as they are. Interpretive researchers use emic approaches for studying interpersonal communication. Emic approaches involve the study of only one culture or cultural community using structures that are discovered by the researcher (Gudykunst, 2003b). The researchers also place themselves in a position within the system of study and use criteria constructed by the members of the community. Understanding of communities and the systems

of meanings they create arises from a very careful exploration of the members' discourse in context and must resonate with the underlying meanings displayed by the members of the community in question. The experts in this sense are the members of a community rather than the researcher.

General research areas for the interpretive research orientation as it relates to culture and communication are varied. Among several themes are the following: (a) identifying cultural norms of communication, (b) investigating the native terms and the meanings these communication terms convey, (c) examining identity construction as it relates to cultural communities, and (d) investigating intercultural couples' negotiation of cultural differences. One example of research inquiry specifically related to intercultural relationships (i.e., the latter point) is Leeds-Hurwitz's (2002) study of 112 intercultural weddings. Her research examined intercultural weddings—interracial, interethnic, interfaith, international, and interclass—to identify how the couples cope with cultural differences. She examined how the couples displayed different cultural identities simultaneously in their wedding ceremonies. Her purpose was to describe how these couples engaged in successful identity negotiation and not to predict the factors that led to the successful negotiation (the latter being a social-scientific focus).

The methods of interpretive research involve different types of qualitative data collection approaches, such as ethnography, case studies, and in-depth interviews. Regardless of the approach to collecting data, the analysis of the data centers on interpretive frameworks such as grounded theory, ethnography of speaking, and phenomenology. For example, ethnography of speaking (Hymes, 1972) has been used by researchers using ethnographic data collection and interview protocols. Probably the most famous example of an interpretive approach to understanding a speech community is Philipsen's (1992) study of "Teamsterville." Initially, Philipsen spent 21 months working as a social worker. Then, he spent an additional 9 months exclusively conducting fieldwork. He used participant observation, interviewing, and native reactions to "out-of-role" behavior. The data were analyzed with the ethnography of speaking framework. Similarly, Covarrubias and Windchief's (2009) study of American Indian college students' use of silence illustrates the use of ethnography of speaking. The authors used 34 one- to three-hour interviews to collect data. They used these data in conjunction with the participant observation method to explore how these students use silence to construct meanings and interpersonal relationships (from acquaintance to friendship) with other American Indians and non-Indians in a mainstream U.S. university.

*Theoretical Exemplar.* The most popular interpretive perspective on cultural communication is speech codes theory. It attempts to interpret or explain observed communication conduct by referencing situated speech codes. A speech code is "a system of socially-constructed symbols and meaning, premises, and rules, pertaining to communication conduct" (Philipsen, Coutu, & Covarrubias, 2005, p. 57). Speech codes theory has six specific propositions. The first proposition is that each cultural community has a distinct speech code. Culture is a community of people who share similar ways of speaking (i.e., speech codes). For example, Arab Israelis use *musayara* to guide a complex system of meanings around social relations (Griefat & Katriel, 1989). What makes the Arab Israelis a cultural community is not that they share ancestry or physical geography but rather that they share speech codes.

Second, any given cultural community has multiple speech codes. These codes are often used to juxtapose one community with another. For example, Philipsen's (1992) study of "Teamsterville" illustrates that community members need to know another person's ethnicity/nationality in order to understand whether they fit into a community. The third proposition is that speech codes reference specific psychological, sociological, and rhetorical content. Speech codes describe the way community members see the world, how

individuals relate to one another, and how to engage in strategic behavior (including verbal and nonverbal messages). These actions are the basic content of speech codes.

Fourth, speech codes constitute the meanings of communicative acts. This proposition centers on the interpretive process of speech codes. That is, speech codes inform the members of a speech community how to interpret their own and others' actions. The fifth proposition is that the rules and underlying premises of a speech code are found within the act of speaking itself. The act of speaking includes the rules, symbols, and meanings of communicative conduct. Finally, the artful use of a shared speech code predicts and explains the intelligibility and morality of communication conduct. Thus, community members use speech codes to make sense of the world and to provide a code of ethics for themselves.

Speech code theory provides a strong example of the interpretive perspective of culture. It does not explicitly examine intercultural relationships. Much of the research related to speech code theory examines how codes and culture are related on a general level. However, speech code theory does provide a framework for understanding how people from different cultures may have difficulties understanding one another and developing satisfying interpersonal relationships. In this manner, it can explain that intercultural relationships are challenging because the partners have a different sensemaking system and rules for communication conduct.

## Critical Approach

The third approach that scholars take toward intercultural communication is the critical perspective. These scholars emphasize power differences between different cultures and study the domination of groups by others. They examine ways in which certain communication patterns privilege certain individuals over others and try to point out this privilege. Given the interest in critical studies to unmask all forms of domination as they occur in everyday social relations, critical researchers invest in the notion of their knowledge having the potential to reform the investigated social/cultural conditions (Moon, 1996). A further goal of critical scholars is to identify how culture is used to privilege and reinforce the power of certain groups at the expense of other groups. This focus on power/privilege and the potential for reform are the distinguishing features of critical scholarship in comparison with most social-scientific and interpretive research. There are a variety of approaches within the critical framework that have differing philosophies and theoretical perspectives, such as postcolonialism, Western Marxism, critical rhetorical studies, cultural studies, and postmodernism (e.g., Halualani, 2000; Hasian, 2001; Martin & Nakayama, 1999). Although some scholars (e.g., Burrell & Morgan, 1988) distinguish critical scholarship from postmodern approaches, the general principles and conceptualizations are consistent. Furthermore, many intercultural communication scholars organize these approaches into a single framework (e.g., see textbooks such as Martin & Nakayama, 2009; Oetzel, 2009). Thus, this section presents the key terms, research goals and methods, and a theoretical exemplar as a single framework recognizing that critical inquiry (like interpretive and social-scientific approaches) is not homogeneous.

*Key Terms.* From the critical perspective, culture is the site of a power struggle that involves competing interests and a multitude of meanings (Hall, 1986). This contrasts with the interpretive and social-scientific perspective of shared meanings among cultural members. In fact, critical theorists challenge hegemonic concepts of culture to explore voices that have not been represented by the dominant culture (Moon, 1996). Furthermore, culture involves the social context and structures where power struggles and clash of meanings exist. Thus, culture also reflects the structural and material disparities that shape our everyday engagement with members of different cultural groups (Collier, 2009; Kelly, 2006). In sum, critical scholars are not interested in the shared meanings and values among members of a particular culture per se. Rather, their interest centers on ways the power is wielded and used to marginalize and silence people who are not part of the mainstream culture.

Cultural identity also centers on issues of privilege and contextualization. For example, Kim (2007) argued that most critical scholarship centers on cultural identity as a nonnegotiable social category and group right (Kim, 2007). Research on cultural identity emphasizes the (lack of) power in which members of traditionally underrepresented groups find themselves given the structural oppression in the system. They emphasize the importance of resisting mainstream perspectives of identity (e.g., Flores, 2001; Hegde, 1998). Furthermore, critical scholars emphasize the framing of context on cultural identities. The plurality of identity is an important distinction as it represents the fact that individuals have multiple cultural identities that change and reflect the influence of context (Collier, 2005). In intercultural relationships, this point emphasizes that relational partners have many cultural identities, and these vary in different situations.

Communication, from the critical perspective, tends to center on discourse. Discourses are written and verbal texts that reflect a way of thinking about a subject. Discourse is a way of framing communication from the critical perspective and is linked to theoretical and analytical approaches to the study of phenomena. For example, Collier (2009) studied the discourse of female Palestinian and Israeli teens who were participants in a peace-building project. The discourse was captured through interviews with the participants, and the author then identified the themes of the discourse. In general, critical discourse about culture focuses on factors such as history, power relations, ideology, the communicative experiences of cultural processes, the discursive production of cultures, and the communication contexts of race, gender, sexuality, class, caste, and nationality (Collier, 2009; Hall, 1986). Thus, in intercultural relationships, discourses are themes or ways of thinking about the relationship.

Critical scholars make salient discourses that privilege certain groups (e.g., Israeli teens vs. Palestinian teens) and lead to imbalanced relationships (e.g., Collier, 2005). For example, the conversational partner from the group with less privilege often has to adapt to the more privileged person to maintain the relationship rather than the other way around.

Communication competence has particular meaning within the context of power relations among different cultural groups. Habermas's (1987) distinction between distorted communication and rational or unconstrained communication characterizes incompetent and competent communication. Those with the dominant worldview (i.e., the people who have the most power) distort communication to get those who have less power to accept the dominant worldview as their own (Habermas). This is incompetent communication as it serves to reproduce inequities. Unconstrained or rational communication involves speaking authentically and accurately with regard to social relationships. It also involves the willingness of those in power to cooperate with those who resist domination. In this manner, competent communication results in more equality in relationships. Identifying the meaning of authenticity, resistance, equality, "rational" versus "distorted" communication, and so on is a challenge for critical scholars (interpretive scholars also can be interested in these meanings) as they investigate competent communication as "equalizing the negotiation table" and is usually done by closely considering the structural, historical, and contextual factors that frame the phenomena of study.

In studying developmental interpersonal relationships, critical perspective holds some similarities to the social-scientific and interpretive perspectives. They progress from initial to enmeshed phases. The key distinction is the central role that power plays in various types of interpersonal relationship. Critical scholars call attention to this power in all types of social and personal relationships. In addition, they examine particular types of relationships that are not accepted by the

mainstream culture (e.g., gay marriage) or specifically involve aspects of power imbalance process. For example, Halualani (1995) examined how perspectives of romance reinforce patriarchal power relationships, male dominance, and female subordination in an Asian mail-order bride catalog. Thus, she called attention to the unequal power dynamics of interpersonal relationships that begin through mail order. Furthermore, Collier (2009) studied intercultural alliances. Using the term *alliance* to describe the relationships that intercultural partners have calls particular attention to the role that power has in a particular context. That is, individuals need to form an alliance to balance the unequal power structure in order to address issues of interpersonal concern (in her case Palestinian and Israeli relations).

*Research Goals and Methods.* The general focus within the critical research orientation is the deconstruction of oppressive ideologies and the social transformation of cultural representations together with the disempowering cultural conditions of communication. In other words, critical scholars want to identify the communication/discourse that is reinforcing the structural domination of one group by another and suggest ways in which the situation could be improved (i.e., by enhancing equality). Researcher biases are emphasized and made explicit in critical scholarship in contrast to social-scientific scholarship, where the goal is to minimize bias and promote objectivity. Furthermore, critical scholars emphasize the role of context in shaping intercultural relationships; the relationship does not exist in the vacuum of the involved partners but rather occurs within the larger societal contexts as well as the social networks of the partners. To accomplish these research goals, critical scholars take the role of experts who critically examine intercultural communication in relationships. Similar to the social-scientific perspective, they use their own theories and concepts to frame the object of study.

Research is largely focused on three areas of critical scholarship in interpersonal relationships. First, critical scholars might examine media and other texts that reinforce unequal relationships among people from different cultural groups (or genders). Halualani's (1995) critique of the hegemonic discourse in the Asian mail-order bride catalog is an example of this approach. Second, critical scholars might examine how people from different cultures form relationships (e.g., friendships and alliances) that work on addressing inequalities and challenges in their own relationships or challenges in society. Diggs and Clark (2002) conducted an auto-ethnography to examine the challenges that they faced in forming and maintaining an intercultural friendship. Additionally, Collier's (2009) study of Palestinian–Israeli alliances is an example of the study of intercultural relationships that help in addressing societal challenges. Third, critical scholars might examine the structural and ideological constraints that inhibit the effective development of intercultural relationships (including the negotiation of intercultural identities). Thompson and Collier's (2006) study of interracial couples in the United States examined the contextual factors that shape identity negotiation between the partners.

The methods of data collection for critical scholars are largely consistent with those of interpretive scholars. Critical scholars use ethnography, open-ended interviews, and case studies to collect data. Furthermore, critical scholars engage in scholarly critique of existing texts such as movies, magazines, and other forms of media. The actual analytical approach of critical scholars is different from that of interpretive scholars because of the difference in research goals. Critical scholars are not interested in description of the data but rather the critique of the data. As a result, approaches include discourse analysis, textual analysis, and phenomenology. Collier's (2009) study of Palestinian–Israeli alliances involved discourse analysis to identify key themes. Halualani's (1995) study of the mail-order bride catalog is an example of textual analysis. Using a phenomenological approach, Orbe (1994) examined the communication processes of 35 African American men, partly situated in the context of interracial relationships with white men.

Orbe's (1998) continued research on co-cultural communication focuses on how power relations shape co-cultural communication processes and vice versa, based on the framework articulated within his theoretical co-culture model. This focus on power demonstrates how interpretive frameworks such as phenomenology and muted group approach can be used for critical theory purposes.

*Theoretical Exemplar.* Collier's (2005) theory of cultural identifications has been applied to intercultural relationships (Thompson & Collier, 2006). The theory identifies three key aspects of the politics of identity: (1) differing levels of agency affecting intercultural relationships, (2) privilege and subjugating ascriptions, and (3) cultural identities' intersection with historical and societal context. First, agency focuses on the freedom to choose a range of actions and to enact identity(ies) (Collier, 2005). Collier noted that members of different cultural groups have different levels of agency. For example, Collier argued that members of traditionally underrepresented groups take greater risks and experience more severe consequences for choosing to speak up and express their preferences and identities. Furthermore, those from the dominant group may perceive that their partners have the same level of agency as them. This perception creates difficulties in the relationship because the severe consequences of expressing identity are not recognized.

Second, privilege (from social class or ethnicity) often results in subjugated ascriptions. Subjugated ascriptions are identities given to others that put them in an inferior position. Collier (2005) noted that privilege (e.g., whiteness) is often invisible to members of the dominant group and therefore difficult to challenge. Thompson and Collier (2006) identified one way that interracial couples use to maintain their relationship, which is to disassociate from the label "interracial." Collier argued that this is evidence that the privilege of whiteness ideology is evident in intercultural relationships because it forces couples to move away from their cultural identities and accept a neutral identity category.

Third, Collier (2005) explained that cultural identities cannot be separated from the societal and historical context. Collier pointed out that specific events of the past shaped current society, and generations pass on their perspectives about identity. She illustrated several examples of participants in South Africa and Palestine/Israel to demonstrate how certain identities are salient in specific situations. Furthermore, multiple identities are enacted depending on historical and societal contexts. Related to intercultural relationships, Thompson and Collier (2006) found that interracial couples often protected their relationship and the other partner from racism/discrimination (given the social context of the United States).

Collier's (2005) theoretical lens on cultural identifications illustrates how the critical approach is applied to intercultural relationships. The theory emphasizes the necessity to negotiate cultural identity in interpersonal relationships and also the importance that power and context have in shaping identity negotiation. The three approaches to the study of intercultural relationships all contribute valuable insights to the rewards and challenges of forming and maintaining diverse types of interpersonal relationship in multiple embedded contexts.

## Communication Patterns in Intercultural Friendship and Romantic Relationships

The three approaches to studying intercultural–interpersonal relationships provide insight to the manner in which scholars study relationships and also what they might be able to uncover. However, the review of the extant literature does not demonstrate an equivalent investigation of intercultural relationships from these three approaches. In fact, the review of the literature demonstrates that the vast majority of research has been conducted from the social-scientific perspective. To develop the grounding of the research literature on intercultural personal relationships, it is necessary to synthesize the key themes in the research. The following subsections identify what has been covered and the essential areas that require further research and attention. This section has two major subsections: (1) intercultural friendships and (2) intercultural romantic relationships.

## Intercultural Friendships

The *Brown vs. Board of Education* U.S. Supreme Court decision (1954) outlawed segregated public schools and increased the opportunity to form interracial friendships in the United States. Furthermore, global migration and increased virtual communication have increased the opportunities for various types of intercultural friendships. While there are opportunities to make intercultural friends, there are challenges as well. This section examines some of the key communication challenges and differences in forming intercultural friendships: culture shock, self-disclosure, and perception biases.

*Culture Shock.* People encounter culture shock whenever they uproot themselves from a familiar setting and move to an unfamiliar one. Millions of U.S. Americans cross cultural boundaries every year to work, to study, to engage in government service, and to volunteer their time in global humanitarian work. Likewise, millions of international students, cultural exchange teachers, artists, scientists, and business people come to the United States to learn, to teach, to perform, to experiment, and to conduct business. The term *culture shock* basically refers to a stressful transitional period when individuals move from a familiar environment into an unfamiliar territory (Ting-Toomey & Chung, 2005). In this unfamiliar environment, the individual's identity appears to be stripped of all protection. Previously familiar cues and scripts are suddenly inoperable in the new cultural setting.

From how to say a proper "hello" to how to say a proper "goodbye," from how to develop a meaningful friendship to how to ask someone out for a "date," every cultural contact moment creates potential awkwardness. Unfamiliarity creates perceived identity threat, and perceived identity threat triggers emotional defense and vulnerability. In fact, Ward, Bochner, and Furnham (2001) discussed the ABCs of culture shock in terms of the affective, behavioral, and cognitive disorientation dimensions. Affectively, sojourners in the initial culture shock stage often experience anxiety, bewilderment, and perplexity as well as an intense desire to be elsewhere. Behaviorally, they are at the confusion stage in terms of the norms and rules that guide communication appropriateness and effectiveness. They are often at a loss in terms of how to initiate and maintain smooth conversations with their hosts or newfound friends. Cognitively, they lack cultural-interpretive competence to explain many of the "bizarre" behaviors that are occurring in their unfamiliar cultural settings.

Ward et al. (2001) also discussed two concepts that are critical to a sojourner's adjustment process: (1) sociocultural adjustment and (2) psychological adjustment. *Sociocultural adjustment* refers to the ability to fit in and execute appropriate and effective interactions in a new cultural environment. It can include factors such as the quality or quantity of interpersonal relationships established in the host culture and the length of residence in the host country. International students, for example, reported greater satisfaction with their host culture when host nationals took the initiative to befriend them. It has also been revealed that international students' friendship networks typically consist of the following patterns: (a) a primary, monocultural friendship network that consists of close friendships with other compatriots from similar cultural backgrounds (e.g., German international students developing friendship ties with other European students); (b) a bicultural network that consists of social bonds between sojourners and host nationals, whereby professional aspirations and goals are pursued; and (c) a multicultural network that consists of acquaintances from diverse cultural groups for recreational activities (Ward

et al.). Research further indicates that greater sociocultural adjustment and social support in the new cultural environment are associated with lower levels of depression and hopelessness in international students. Overall, culture-specific knowledge, language fluency, more extensive contact with host nationals, and a longer period of residence in the host culture are associated with lower levels of sociocultural difficulty in the new culture (Ward, 2004).

*Psychological adjustment* refers to the feelings of intrapersonal well-being and personal satisfaction during cross-cultural transitions (Ward et al., 2001). Chronic strain, low self-esteem, and low mastery have a direct effect on adjustment depression. As cultural distance widens and stress level increases, newcomers need to expand more energy and effort to overcome the culture shock barriers. Supportive, close friendships, in this context, will help serve as a buffer to the everyday roller-coaster of challenges faced by the sojourners.

*Self-Disclosure and Intercultural/Interracial Friendship Development.* According to research on intercultural friendship development, international students generally experience major roadblocks and challenges in developing interpersonal ties with U.S. American students (Gareis, 2000; Kudo & Simkin, 2003; Lee, 2006). While the majority of college international students ($N = 671,616$ for the academic year of 2008–2009) studying in the United States are culled from India, China, South Korea, Canada, and Japan (Institute of International Education: Open Door Report, 2009, from http://opendoors.iienetwork.org), the majority of U.S. American students ($N = 262,416$ for the academic year 2008–2009) studying abroad tended to choose the United Kingdom, Italy, Spain, France, and China as their study destinations. While international students tended to stay several years to obtain their bachelor, master, or doctoral degrees at various U.S. universities (the top three are University of Southern California, New York University, and Columbia University), U.S. American students typically spend a shorter duration (from an eight-week program to an academic year) on their cultural experience abroad. This may partly explain why international students tended to encounter more stressors and challenges during their lengthier sojourns, especially due to contrastive cultural value and communication style differences.

The intercultural and interpersonal research literature suggests one of the ways to counteract stressful life events is to maintain meaningful close friendship ties. One of the key factors in sustaining and developing close friendship ties is self-disclosure. In examining the self-disclosure patterns of East Asian international students (with a small sample size of 74) from four different countries (China, Japan, South Korea, and Taiwan), Chen (2006) found that the East Asian students self-disclosed slightly more in intracultural friendships than in intercultural friendships. In addition, attitudes and opinions, tastes and interests, studies or work, and personality were perceived as "superficial topics" of self-disclosure, while money and financial matters, and body and appearances were considered as "intimate topics." However, there was no clear distinction concerning the amount of self-disclosure and the positive/negative content of self-disclosure in these two friendship types.

In a follow-up study, Chen and Nakazawa (2009) investigated the self-disclosure patterns of U.S. American students in intercultural and interracial friendship types. Altogether, 252 U.S. American college students participated in the study, with 63 reporting on an intercultural friendship between a U.S. citizen and a non-U.S. citizen and 189 reporting on an interracial friendship. Based on self-report survey data, the research findings indicated that the level of relational intimacy played a strong role in both intercultural and interracial friendship's self-disclosure patterns: As relational intimacy level increased, friends had greater intent to disclose, they disclosed in greater amount and depth, and they also engaged in more honest/accurate self-disclosure. Furthermore, individualism was found to correlate

positively with self-disclosure intention, depth, and honesty/accuracy, while collectivism was discovered to correlate positively with self-disclosure intention and honesty/accuracy only but not with depth. In both intercultural and interracial friendship situations, respondents reported equivalent levels of reciprocal self-disclosure in all six areas. Likewise, in comparing self-disclosure patterns in Japanese and U.S. American students, Kito (2005) found that both groups were drawn to their newfound friends because of perceived similarity. Both young adult groups also cited trust, respect, understanding, and sincerity as common characteristics of friendship. The Japanese respondents also cited togetherness, trust, and warmth as the top friendship priorities, while the U.S. Americans cited understanding, respect, and sincerity as top friendship indicators. It seems that while Asian collectivists stress more on an interpersonal "relationship atmosphere" of harmony and warmth, American individualists emphasize more the intrinsic friendship qualities of "being oneself" and "self-transparency of honesty."

*Perception Biases.* Interestingly, in a recent interracial friendship self-disclosure study, the researchers (Shelton, Trail, West, & Bergsieker, 2010) studied the relationship between self-disclosure and perceived partner responsiveness in African American and European American college students. They asked the participants to select a black and a white potential friend whom they did not know very well at the beginning of the study but wanted to befriend over time. Every 2 weeks, across a total of 10 weeks, the participants completed a questionnaire about the nature of self-disclosure and interactions in the intra-racial friendship context and in the interracial friendship context. Results indicated that among African American respondents, distinctive differences were found in self-disclosure, perceived friend disclosure, and perceived partner responsiveness in the two friendship types. The African American students reported more own self-disclosure, perceived partner's self-disclosure, and perceived partner's responsiveness with their fellow African American friends than with their European American friends. It appears that African American students at a

> predominantly white university particularly appreciate having a potential in-group friend with whom to socialize and become friends. That is, because black students are scarce at such universities, black student encountering a potential black friend may be more likely to self-disclose extensively and feel connected to this person on the basis of their shared ethnic group membership. (Shelton et al., 2010, p. 84)

In comparison, results did not reveal any significant self-disclosure pattern difference among European American respondents with their fellow European American friends and their African American friends. This might be due to possible social desirability effect, that is, the white students might want to avoid expressing any self-disclosure pattern distinction in regard to the two friendship groups. However, the same white students did report lower levels of intimacy (i.e., less closeness and liking) with black friends than with white friends. Thus, an alternative interpretation of the result could be that European American students might actually believe that they treated both black and white friends comparably and also perceived similar self-disclosure patterns. However, there continues to exist some psychological gap or intergroup emotional distance among the interracial friendship pairs (Shelton et al., 2010). Interestingly, for both African American and European American groups, perceived partner's responsiveness (i.e., perceived acceptance, validation, and caring) served as an important mediating factor that boosts their perceptions of self- and partner disclosure and intimacy level in both interracial and interracial friendship contexts. Believing that partners are concerned and receptive to one's self-disclosure process is essential to reduce anxiety and uncertainty in intergroup–interracial contact encounters (Gudykunst, 2005).

Indeed, in another study, White et al. (2009) investigated the role of friendship quality and interracial contact in high school–age adolescents and university-age adolescents (with Anglo-Australian, Arab, and Asian students) in Sydney, Australia. The research findings revealed that while high school adolescents reported higher levels of blatant prejudice and subtle prejudice, college students reported a higher level of subtle prejudice and a lower level of blatant prejudice. Moreover, a higher level of prejudice was directed at the Arab students than at the Asians for both samples. It appears that the targets of prejudiced attitude also change according to the historical and cultural contexts in contemporary society. Furthermore, high school–age adolescents who reported a strong friendship quality with their close Anglo-Australian friends also reported very similar levels of blatant prejudice toward fellow Asian and Arab students. Last, high school adolescents who reported having no Asian friends reported a higher level subtle prejudice, whereas high school adolescents who reported having Asian friends and frequent contacts with them also reported significantly lower levels of both blatant and subtle prejudice. Meanwhile, university-age adolescents with "no Asian" friends actually reported higher Asian-directed, blatant prejudice than those with Asian friends. Of course, the study and the essentialization of the broad categorical use of labels such as "Asian students" and "Arab students" could be one of the key problems and challenges for future researchers studying intercultural and interpersonal relationship formation processes. A mindful differentiation and layered perspective in examining the multiple identity facets within particular groups of "Asians" or "Arabs" may help yield more theoretically meaningful findings in future research studies. Pragmatically, the researchers in the interracial contact study suggested the importance of developing cooperative contact strategies in the classroom and promoting positive social interdependence among diverse cultural and racial students to debunk rigid stereotypes and reduce intergroup racial prejudice.

In fact, Welner (2006) advocated the importance of designing race-conscious classroom assignments to promote better interracial/intergroup friendship developments. He found that through positive intergroup racial contacts, K–12 students held improved, positive racial attitudes, had greater civic engagement, and cultivated a "critical mass" that enabled them to promote racial and cultural tolerance in their school environment. Such efforts would help counteract some of the research findings that revealed that minority group students (e.g., African American and Asian American students) continued to have low to moderate interracial contact with other racial group members due to perceived social and psychological distance (Kohatsu et al., 2000).

In summary, research on intercultural friendships has tended to examine the challenges and difficulties that arise when different cultural frames influence communication. Culture shock research examines the challenges that occur during initial encounters. Research on self-disclosure identifies different patterns of revealing information that make developing friendships challenging. Additionally, research on perception biases also demonstrates challenges in forming friendships with people from different cultural backgrounds. Overall, this research has been conducted from the social-scientific approach, with some critical scholarship in the area of perception biases.

## Intercultural/Interracial Romantic Relationships

Research on intercultural romantic relationships examines challenges and benefits. In discussing interracial intimate relationship development, Foeman and Nance (1999) concluded that interracial couples move through the following stages of "racial" awareness and awakening in their intimate relationship process: racial awareness, coping, identity emergence, and relationship maintenance. The first stage, racial awareness, refers to the gradual awakening stage, when the partners in an interracial relationship become conscious of each other's views and societal views on intimate racial relationships. The second stage, coping, refers to the struggles the couple have to face in gaining approval from their families and friends and the strategies they come up with in dealing with such external pressures. In the third stage, identity emergence, both partners gain a new sense of security and bravely announce their intimate relationship to their families and in-groups. The fourth stage, relationship maintenance, refers to the continuous hard work the couple have to face in dealing with new challenges, such as having children, moving to new neighborhoods, and entering new social circles.

Despite the many pressure points in intercultural/interracial relationships, many intimate couples often mention the following rewards from their relationship (Karis & Killian, 2009; Romano, 2001; Ting-Toomey, 2009b): (a) experiencing personal enrichment and growth due to the day-to-day opportunity to continuously clarify their own beliefs, values, and prejudices; (b) developing multiple cultural frames of reference due to the opportunity of integrating multiple value systems such as "doing" *and* "being," "controlling" *and* "yielding"; (c) experiencing greater diversities and emotional vitality in their lifestyles because of participating in different customs, ceremonies, languages, celebrations, foods, and cultural network circles; (d) developing a stronger and deeper relationship with each other because they have weathered intercultural prejudice and racist opposition and arrived at a forgiving, healing place; and (e) raising open-minded, resourceful children who see the world from a multicultural lens and have the ability to be "at home" wherever they find themselves. These stages of challenge and benefit provide the overall picture of intercultural romantic relationships. In this subsection, we explore the key trends in the research literature about these relationships in four parts: (1) factors associated with intercultural dating, (2) love and emotional intimacy, (3) conflict, and (4) relational transgressions and terminations.

*Factors Associated With Intercultural Dating.* With the increase of cultural and ethnic diversification in the United States, the likelihood of being attracted to members of other cultures and races will also increase. Age, generation, ethnic identity, and racial/intergroup attitude appear to be four important predictors of interethnic dating and marriages. For example, Firmin and Firebaugh (2008) found that age and generation appeared to be two key predictors for intimate relationship formation, with younger people and succeeding generations more open to interracial dating than older and preceding ones. The later the generation in the United States, the more likely the individuals are to date out-group members. Additionally, the less prejudice they perceive in intergroup relations, the more likely they are open to date members from that group. For example, third-generation Asian Americans are five times more likely to marry outside their ethnic groups than first-generation Asian Americans (Kitano, Fujino, & Sato, 1998).

Chung and Ting-Toomey (1999), in examining interethnic dating attraction in Asian Americans, found that the strength of individuals' ethnic identities was related to intergroup attraction and dating. Individuals with assimilated, bicultural, or marginal identities have a greater tendency to date out of their own groups than those who view their ethnic identities and traditions as very important aspects of their self-concept. There were also times during which individuals were attracted to culturally dissimilar others because they perceived their partners as typical or atypical of their own culture. This means that people do activate their stereotyping process in the initial intercultural attraction stages—be they positive or negative stereotypes. In addition, there is also a "Romeo and Juliet" effect at work in an intercultural intimate relationship: The more the respective families are against this intimate relationship, the more the couples want to rebel against their parents and "do their own thing," and therefore, they find each other more attractive (Ting-Toomey & Chung, 2005).

Martin, Bradford, Drzewiecka, and Chitgopekar (2003) surveyed 316 European American young adults regarding their openness to and experience with interracial dating. The results indicated that respondents who were raised in more diverse neighborhoods and have diverse acquaintances were significantly more likely to date outside their race. The reasons given for encouraging interracial dating included compatibility, physical and sexual attraction, and curiosity. The reasons offered for discouraging interracial dating included lack of desire, lack of proximity, and personal, familial, or societal pressure. Levin, Taylor, and Caudle (2007), in examining interracial dating patterns in more than 2,000 college students (from diverse racial/ethnic backgrounds) in a longitudinal study, discovered that students who exhibited lower levels of in-group favoritism bias, intergroup anxiety, and in-group identification were more likely to date members of other racial and ethnic groups during college. In addition, students who dated outside their group more during college showed less in-group favoritism bias and intergroup anxiety at the end of college. In particular, Asian American students who dated outside their group more during college also felt more pressure not to socialize with or date members of other groups at the end of college. Latinos whose families had been in the United States for more generations were also more likely to date intercultural/interracial partners. They also reported experiencing less bias directed against them as intergroup dating partners than other minority groups because of both historical factors and physical characteristics. Interestingly, intergroup dating in college was less prevalent among those who had a greater proportion of precollege in-group friendships. The influence of such close friendships and the in-group attitudes (e.g., intergroup anxiety and prejudice) may outweigh opportunities to branch outward and seek interracial/intergroup dating opportunities.

Kreager (2008), analyzing the data from the National Longitudinal Study of Adolescent Health with a sample of 13,000 students from

Grades 7 to 12, found that a positive relationship existed between adolescent interracial dating and peer trouble at school. Such peer troubles are often very subtle (such as awkward glances, under-the-breath comments, head shaking, expressions of disbelief or verbal intimidation) as compared with blatant violent reactions. In particular, African American students in interracial romances perceived the greatest peer trouble, while Asians and Latinos showed little differences from their intra-racial dating peers. These patterns likely stem from heightened perceptions of norm violation and prejudice associated with black–nonblack romances. Two other ideas emerged from this study. First, black male adolescents were more likely to have interracial dating relationships than black female dating relationships. Second, Asian female adolescents were more likely involved in interracial dating relationships than Asian male adolescents.

*Love and Emotional Intimacy.* Kline, Horton, and Zhang (2008) examined cultural differences in communicating love among 143 young adults from the United States and the East Asian countries of China, Japan, and South Korea. Through open-ended and closed-ended questionnaire format, the U.S. American and East Asian international students answered some of the questions along the dimensions of attitudes/beliefs, activities, and expressions of love concerning friendship and love concerning marriage. The narrative thought units were coded by three coders using a set of common procedures. The East Asian respondents were more likely to believe that marriage is about trust, caring, and respect and that it takes hard work; U.S. American respondents were more likely to believe that love in marriage is essential and unconditional. East Asian students also tended to express love and affection in close friendships during particular "talking" activities, such as while having dinner together and when drinking together, whereas U.S. American students tended to express love and affection in close friendships during sports and exercise, when going to the movies or concerts,

while shopping, and while having dinner and drinking together. In expressing love and affection in marriage, both sample groups considered the same activities important—talking, having dinner together, doing things together, and physical intimacy—as vehicles for love expressions. Both groups also subscribed to the importance of belief similarity, faithfulness, and commitment in marital relationships, more so than in close friendships.

Taking a close look at emotional intimacy in European Canadian and Chinese Canadian dating partners (sample size = 62 dating couples: 31 European Canadian and 31 Chinese Canadian couples), Marshall (2010) designed two studies exploring individualism–collectivism and gender-role ideology in self-disclosure and responsiveness. She found that both groups conceptualized intimacy via self-disclosure and partner responsiveness. In Study 1, using the actor–partner interdependence model analysis, Chinese Canadian immigrants and their partners scored lower in the intimacy/expressing emotional support dimension than their European Canadian counterparts. More important, Chinese Canadians' lower intimacy rating was mediated by their more traditional gender-role ideology but not by their collectivism. The lower intimacy score also mediated their lower relationship satisfaction score and higher risk of relationship termination. In Study 2, Marshall (2010) further discovered that the Chinese Canadian males' traditionalism and associated lower self-disclosure contributed to their partners' lower intimacy. In contrast to the results for self-disclosure, there were no mean cultural differences in responsiveness. In both studies, the role of intimacy appeared to be the key link to relational satisfaction or relationship termination in both Chinese Canadian and European Canadian samples. The author attributed the effect of acculturation (an average of eight years of Canadian residence in the Chinese Canadian sample) and some aspects of deep-rooted Confucian values to the influence of gender-role traditionalism in the Chinese Canadian male sample.

*Conflicts.* Research on conflict in intercultural relationships has tended to take two approaches. First, there is research that has centered on the individualism–collectivism value dimension as an explanatory framework. Second, research (particularly from an interpretive and social-scientific approach) has examined conflict styles in various ethnic groups.

The individualism–collectivism framework has been tested in many interpersonal contexts, such as acquaintanceship, friendship, and family relationships. People in individualistic cultures (compared with collectivistic cultures) tend to communicate directly, whereas people from collectivistic culture (compared with individualistic cultures) tend to be indirect when they communicate in interpersonal communication situations (Gudykunst et al., 1996). In the context of conflict communication styles, while culture-based value differences such as individualism/collectivism, small/large power distance, and personality traits have been viewed as the primary explanatory factors for orientation, situational features such as relational intimacy and distance, in-group/out-group assessment, and mindset filters and biases have also been considered as critical mediating factors that moderate cultural members' facework orientations and conflict communication styles (Ting-Toomey, 2009a; Ting-Toomey, Oetzel, & Yee-Jung, 2001). Overall and in comparison terms, individualists tend to focus on pursuing self-interest conflict goals and using competing and dominating conflict strategies to pursue their goals, while collectivists tend to be more attuned to mutual-interest conflict goals and preferred to use compromising, accommodating, and conflict-avoidant strategies in stressful conflict situations. For example, in comparing Japanese and U.S. American conflict behaviors in close-friendship and relative-stranger situations, Oetzel, Ting-Toomey, Yokochi, Masumoto, and Takai (2000) found that Japanese college students rated the use of avoidance facework strategy higher and integrative, problem-solving strategy lower than their U.S. American counterparts.

In examining the use of conflict facework strategies with same-sex siblings and parents, Oetzel et al. (2003) found that members from individualistic, small–power distance cultures tended to emphasize self-face conflict issues and reported the use of defensive conflict tactics, whereas members from collectivistic, large–power distance cultures tended to emphasize other-face and mutual-face conflict issues and reported the use of conflict denials or sidestepping pretension strategies more than their counterparts. More specifically, the German respondents also reported a higher degree of self-face concern and tended to use more defensive facework strategies in dealing with family conflicts than their U.S. American cohorts. Additionally, the Japanese respondents tended to be more emotionally expressive in dealing with family conflicts than their Mexican counterparts. The unexpected differences between the two collectivistic cultures could be due to the different types of culture-based collectivism at work in the Japanese and the Mexican cultures. Since the Japanese participants (coming from an emotionally understated, collectivistic culture) often tended to pretend that conflicts do not exist for the most part, especially in workplace settings, when a family conflict erupted, they may actually express their gut emotions openly and let their pent-up emotions be known to their in-group family members. In comparison, since Mexican culture tends to be an emotionally expressive, relational culture, the Mexican respondents may actually prefer to reign in their emotions during family conflicts for the sake of family harmony and the well-being of individuals in the family system (for a recent analytical critique on the individualism–collectivism value system, see Ting-Toomey, 2010). Last, participants with independent self-construals tended to emphasize self-face concern and defensive conflict tactics in dealing with family conflicts, while participants with interdependent self-construals tended to be sensitive to self-face, other-face, and mutual-face family conflict concerns and also preferred the use of both integrative problem-solving and conflict avoidance tactics.

In terms of different ethnic conflict styles within the multicultural U.S. population, distinctive and similar conflict style patterns do exist in different ethnic groups in the United States. According to Orbe and Everett (2006), the following factors greatly shape the use of particular conflict styles in co-culture group members (i.e., interactions among underrepresented and dominant group members) in the diverse U.S. society: cultural/ethnic and racial identity salience issues, social inequality, in-group/out-group tensions, perceptual differences, rigid stereotyping, media influence, and the lack of contact with or exposure to co-cultural membership differences (e.g., ethnic minority group members, gays and lesbians, people with disabilities, etc.). For example, African American conflict styles are influenced simultaneously by both individualistic and collectivistic value tendencies and also by both small– and large–power distance value patterns. At the same time that traditional African values are collectivistic (e.g., community, interdependence, being one with nature, and church/religious participation) and large power distance based (e.g., respecting grandparents and pastors), African Americans are also in constant struggle against the power dominance of the whites in the white-privileged U.S. society (Asante & Asante, 1990). The white-privileged social position refers to the general favored state of whites holding power over other minority group members in key decision-making roles in major policy-making institutions (Orbe & Spellers, 2005). There is also a general tendency for European Americans or whites to view racism episodes as individual acts rather than as part of a truncated, power imbalance institutional package. Thus, assertive conflict styles and emotionally expressive conflict styles may be one method for African Americans to uphold self and in-group membership solidarity and dignity.

In terms of Asian American conflict orientations, it has been found that the philosophy of Confucianism strongly influences proper facework rituals and conflict interaction performance. Confucianism remains the fundamental philosophy that underlies many Asian cultures (e.g., China, Taiwan, Singapore, Korea, and Japan). Confucius was a Chinese philosopher of practical ethics who lived from 551 to 479 BCE. His practical code of conduct emphasizes a hierarchical societal structure (i.e., large power distance) and appropriate family role performance. Some core Confucian values include a dynamic long-term orientation, perseverance, ordering relationships by status, having a sense of shame, and emphasizing collective face-saving (Gao & Ting-Toomey, 1998). An interdependent sense of shame includes the constant awareness of other people's expectations of one's own or in-group performance and particular sensitivity for mutual face-saving, face losing, and face giving (i.e., a give-and-take face enhancement process) behaviors. Asian Americans who adhere to traditional Asian values (e.g., recent Asian immigrants) tend to use avoidant or obliging conflict styles to deal with the conflict at hand. They sometimes also use "silence" as a powerful high-context conflict mode. They may also resort to familiar third-party help—especially from trusted family members or networks—to mediate the conflict situation (Sue & Sue, 2003). Asian Americans who identify strongly with the larger U.S. culture also tend to use an integrative conflict style to find substantive solutions to address the conflict problem more than Asian Americans who identify weakly with the larger U.S. culture (Ting-Toomey et al., 2000). Given the diversity of the Asian American population, we should also pay close attention to the country of origin, the immigration experience, acculturation patterns, the generational level, language mastery, family socialization norms, and ethnic identity salience factors, which contribute to the enormous differences between and within these multiple groups.

In the context of traditional Latino/Latina Americans' conflict practices, tactfulness and consideration of others' feelings are deemed to be important face-sensitive conflict norms. Tactfulness and considerateness are conveyed through the use of other-oriented facework behaviors, such as the use of an obliging or "smoothing over" conflict style or an avoidance style (Garcia, 1996). They also tend to seek out trusted third-party help more than the European American group (Ting-Toomey et al., 2000). More specifically, in a tradition-based Mexican American group, for example, the term *respeto* connotes honor, respect, and "face," which individuals accord to listeners in accordance with their roles and hierarchical status. Thus, diplomatic and circumspective face-sensitive behaviors, especially in dealing with unequal-status family conflicts, are critical in promoting competent conflict communication. In addition, since Mexican American facework is closely related to family loyalty, honor, name, respect, and extended family approval issues, family members are expected to uphold their family dignity at all times and not bring shame to their extended family unit. However, in dealing with close friendship conflict, while the Mexican American interviewees believed that conveyance of empathy for the other person's feelings is critical, they also endorsed an emotionally expressive, confrontational conflict style in dealing with friendship problems (Collier, 1991). Overall, collectivism and large–power distance values are the underlying value patterns that undergird Latino/Latina American conflict expectations. Research also revealed that Latino/Latina Americans who identify strongly with their traditional ethnic values tend to use more emotionally expressive conflict styles than Latino/Latina Americans who do not strongly identify with their traditional ethnic values (Ting-Toomey et al., 2000). Thus, under the broad category of "collectivism," while the Latino/Latina group tends to endorse an emotionally expressive norm in some conflict situations, the Asian group tends to emphasize emotional restraint in some conflict contexts. With the tremendous diversities under the "Latino/Latina American" label, we will do well to increase the complexity of our understanding of the values and distinctive conflict patterns of each group (e.g., the Puerto Rican group, Cuban group, Mexican group, El Salvadorian group, etc.) and the relational and situational features

that shape the norms and expectations of a particular conflict style.

Collectivism and larger–power distance values also permeate traditional Native American tribes. Overall, Native Americans tend to prefer the use of verbal self-restraint and verbal self-discipline in uncertainty conflict situations (Basso, 1990). Some of the value patterns of Native Americans that have been identified by researchers are (a) mutual sharing—honor and respect are gained by sharing and giving; (b) in-group cooperation—the family and tribe take precedence over the individual; (c) noninterference—they are taught to observe and not to react impulsively and, especially, not to meddle in other people's affairs; (d) time orientation—they tend to be more present oriented than future oriented, and life is to be lived fully in the present; (e) extended family orientations—they have a strong respect for elders and their wisdom and generational knowledge; and (f) harmony with nature—they tend to prefer to flow with nature rather than control or master their natural environment (Sue & Sue, 2003).

Given these value patterns, we can infer that in terms of conflict styles, Native Americans tend to be more understated and emotionally restrained in dealing with conflicts in their everyday lives. Out of consideration for the other person's face or in-group face, they tend to use a more subtle, high-context conflict style in trying to resolve their conflict peacefully. They are also likely to go to a third-party elder to solicit her or his wisdom in resolving the conflict issue, thus helping each other maintain face. They also tend to use more deliberate silence in conveying their displeasure. However, given the fact that there are more than 500 American Indian groups, any ethnic-based generalizations should only serve as a starting point to go more in-depth to understand the complexity of each interethnic conflict scene. (This admonition applies to other large groups as well—Asians, Arabs, Europeans, African Americans, etc.) For example, American Indians who live on or near reservations are more likely to subscribe to traditional values, while other American Indians may adhere to predominant, mainstream values or maintain a set of bicultural values (Ting-Toomey & Oetzel, 2001).

*Relational Transgressions and Terminations.* Using individualism–collectivism as an explanatory frame, Zhang, Ting-Toomey, and Lee (2010) explored how U.S. American college students (i.e., data collections from a southwestern university in the United States) and Chinese college students (i.e., data collected from a western university in China) differ when they respond to their dating partners' Internet relational transgressions. They also assessed how different self-construal personality types influence relational response strategies. Overall, they found that the U.S. respondents tend to prefer exit and anger voice responses more than the Chinese respondents in reacting to an emotional infidelity episode. Comparatively, the Chinese respondents tend to prefer loyalty, passive neglect, and third-party help responses. It seems that for the Chinese respondents, loyalty is a passive–active strategy: A patient, self-disciplined reaction moderates upfront confrontation and would not aggravate the conflict situation further. Furthermore, while seeking help from family and close friends might seem to be passive in the U.S. Americans' mindset, it is an active strategy for the Chinese participants because it shows that the individual is caring and committed to the intimate relationship and that he or she is actually doing something to salvage the relationship by seeking third-party advice. Both culture groups, however, also preferred the use of a high degree of integrative, problem-solving voice response, which contradicted the previous U.S.–Japan interpersonal research study.

Furthermore, the researchers (Zhang et al., 2010) also uncovered that participants with different levels of self-construal differed when they responded to their dating partners' relational transgression action. Self-construal is one's conception of self and consists of interdependent and independent aspects. Interdependent self-construal emphasizes connection to others, while independent self-construal emphasizes autonomy and distinction from others. The participants with high independent self-construal tend to prefer exit and anger voice responses, whereas those with high relational self-construal tend to prefer the use of integrative voice and third-party help-seeking responses.

Past research has also examined self-construal in various contexts. Hara and Kim (2004) found that independent self-construal is negatively associated with the indirect verbal message and that interdependent self-construal is positively associated with an indirect verbal style. In Kapoor, Hughes, Baldwin, and Blue's (2003) study, the researchers found that most Asian Indians subscribe to interdependent self-construal and prefer silence and indirect communication compared with U. S. Americans. These research findings are consistent with Gudykunst et al.'s (1996) earlier finding that people with independent self-construal prefer to use direct messages, while people with interdependent self-construal prefer to use indirect messages due to their social sensitivity and interpersonal-harmony orientation. Ting-Toomey et al. (2001) also found that biconstrual individuals (those who are high on both independent and interdependent traits) tend to have the most diverse conflict repertoire to deal with a conflict situation in comparison with independent, interdependent, and ambivalent (low on both independent and interdependent traits) personality types. However, the degree of intimacy between the conflict partners, the nature of the conflict, and the conflict context greatly influence individuals' expectancies concerning the appropriate and effective conflict competence outcome in different intercultural/interracial conflict situations.

Moving beyond interracial/interethnic communication styles and response to transgressions, Bratter and King (2008), using the National Survey of Family Growth 2002 data (males = 1,606, females = 4,070), examined the divorce rates for interracial couples in comparison with same-race couples. Comparisons across marriage cohorts revealed that overall, interracial couples have higher rates of divorce, particularly those marrying during the late 1980s. Compared with same-race, white–white marriages, they found that black male/white female marriages and Asian male/white female marriages were more prone to divorce. Also, white male/nonwhite female marriages and Hispanic/non-Hispanic marriages had a lower risk for divorce. The influence of gender/sex, specifically the elevated divorce rate in white female interracial marriages, highlights the distinctive nature of interracial marriage. The researchers explained this distinctive phenomenon via the notion that interracial black male/white female couples continue to experience negative reactions and stigmas from strangers and diminished support from family and friends. In addition, white female mothers also may have the added pressure of being perceived as "unqualified to raise and nurture non-White offspring because of their lack of experience in navigating American culture as a minority" (Bratter & King, 2008, p. 170). Such an unwelcoming and distancing environment from both racial in-groups may add additional strain and social isolation to the interracial marriage.

However, in a recent study, Zhang and Van Hook (2009), using the Six Panels of Survey of Income and Program Participants ($N = 23,139$ married couples), found that after controlling for couple characteristics, the risk of divorce or separation among interracial couples was similar to the risk in the more divorce-prone origin group. Although marital dissolution was found to be strongly associated with race or ethnicity (especially concerning black male/white female marriages, followed by Hispanic–white marriages), the results failed to provide clear evidence that interracial marriage per se is associated with an elevated risk of marital dissolution. Based on qualitative interview data, Yancey (2007) reported that whites who married blacks experienced more firsthand racism than whites who married other, nonblack minorities. Specifically, white females reported encountering more racial incidents with their black husbands (e.g., inferior restaurant service, racial profiling, and racism against their children) and more hostilities from families and friends than other interracial pairings.

In summary, the research on intercultural romantic relationships has examined several key factors. First, the research identifies the factors that lead to intercultural dating. Second, once couples start dating, research examines differences in the expression of love and intimacy that can create challenges for maintaining the relationship. Third, in addition to intimacy expression, differences in conflict patterns have been identified, and these differences can exacerbate conflict in these relationships. Finally, the research explores relational transgressions and communication styles as potential factors for relationship termination. The social-scientific approach predominates the research on intercultural relationships, but there is more interpretive scholarship than in the intercultural friendship area.

## Directions for Future Intercultural Interpersonal Relationship Research

Overall, there continues to be a dearth of theoretically driven and communication-anchored research studies in the intercultural/interracial personal relationship development realm. In reviewing the research studies on intercultural/interracial friendship, the dating relationship, and the marital relationship, here are some common threads: (a) cross-cultural relationship studies have focused their research investigations moderately on self-disclosure patterns and perceived partner responsiveness across different cultures; (b) interracial relationship studies tended to examine self-disclosure patterns in interracial pairings; (c) cross-cultural relationship studies also emphasized the theme of cross-cultural comparisons of love and emotional expressions of intimacy across different cultures; (d) interracial relationship studies tended to emphasize intergroup racial anxiety and attitudes in interracial dating dyads; (e) cross-cultural relationship studies tended to draw from the theoretical base of the individualism–collectivism value dimension as their theoretical framework; (f) interracial friendship and dating studies tended to draw from social identity theory and its variants; (g) cross-cultural studies tended to compare a U.S. American sample with some Asian samples as their data sets; (h) interracial relationships studies tended to either go for the existing sociological, demographic data set or emphasize strongly the interracial interpersonal relationship formation process between blacks and whites; (i) cross-cultural research studies tended to emphasize predictor or mediating factors in linking cultural group membership, on the one hand, and relational communication responses, on the other, and thus underaddressed critical cross-cultural or intercultural relationship competence outcome issues; and (j) interracial interpersonal studies tended to emphasize the discovery of predictor factors that prompt interracial dating, in particular the factors of age, generation, and sex in interracial dating and marital relationships. Methodologically, we know more about (a) U.S. college adolescents' friendship patterns and dating relationship patterns than about any other age groups or generation groups; (b) research designs that were drawn from the social-scientific approach than from the interpretive approach or the critical approach; (c) heterosexual dating and marital relationships than gay relationships across cultures or racial lines; (d) interpersonal relationship intimacy development in the United States than in any other global cultural regions; and (e) the static race category in the formation and development of close relationships than a dynamic view of shifting cultural/ethnic identity allegiance issues and their relationship to intimate communication patterns.

As scholars and researchers in the area of cross-cultural and intercultural interpersonal relationship development, we need to pay more close attention to the theories and research perspectives in the domains of both intercultural and interpersonal communication. For example, theories in intercultural and intergroup communication (e.g., integrative communication theory by Kim, 2005; identity negotiation theory by Ting-Toomey, 2005a; communication accommodation theory by Gallois et al., 2005) can inform interpersonal scholars

concerning the importance of sociocultural membership identity issues in conjunction with emerging interpersonal relationship development constructs (e.g., online intercultural/interracial dating, Facebook friendship maintenance, and text message abbreviated communication).

On the other hand, interpersonal communication theories (e.g., expectancy violation theory by Burgoon & Ebesu Hubbard, 2005; relational dialectics theory by Baxter and Montgomery, 1996; and communication privacy management theory by Petronio, 2002) can help explain particular relational and situational features that are salient to the escalation, oscillation, and de-escalation of intercultural/interracial friendships and romantic relationships. A mindful, cross-fertilization approach may help both domains develop richer intercultural interpersonal theories or personal relationship development models across a wide variety of situated cultural and ethnic settings. In addition, both intercultural and interpersonal scholars have barely scratched the surface of how, for example, bicultural identity individuals (i.e., via the immigrant socialization experience), multicultural global nomads (i.e., via a lifetime of fluid boundary crossing), or multiethnic/mixed-race hybrid individuals (i.e., via dual or triple parental ethnic socialization heritages) engage in competent (or incompetent) identity negotiation and relationship development formation with other kindred spirits or monocultural individuals.

In today's dynamic and mobile society, ethnic and racial category is no longer a single-checkmark category. More and more individuals in the global world have mosaic oppositional or compatible cultural identities (Benet-Martiniz, Leu, Lee, & Morris, 2002; Bonam & Shih, 2009; Chen, Benet-Martinez, & Bond, 2008; Cheng & Lee, 2009). The more intercultural and interpersonal researchers tend to examine the dynamic interplay of multiple sociocultural identity and personal identity issues (in conjunction with situational dynamic issues) within hybrid individuals, the more likely we are to catch on to the cultural frame-switching cognition and emotion that drive such individuals to form and shape their close relationships. The more we pay close attention to the culture-sensitive relational and situational features that prompt the meaning construction processes of individuals who hold divergent or convergent sociocultural membership identities (and situated personal identity issues), the more likely we are to increase the heuristic value of our theory-building processes in the intercultural interpersonal communication domain.

In particular, while there has been incremental growth in the mainstream interpersonal literature in incorporating some cultural or racial variations in their interpersonal research design, collectively, as scholars in interpersonal communication, we can do more of the following. From the social-scientific paradigm, we can ask more of the following research questions: How do different cultural/ethnic identity types (e.g., ethnic oriented, assimilated, bicultural, marginal identity) influence the various interpersonal communication strategies or responses in diverse cultural and ethnic groups? How would biracial/hybrid individuals choose to disclose or not disclose their identity salience issues? How do they regulate identity boundary and privacy issues, and how does perceived self-disclosure responsiveness affect such self-disclosure? How do individuals with different identity types negotiate identity issues and manage their conflicts in an experimental lab setting? What constitutes intercultural intimate relationship satisfaction? How does intercultural relationship satisfaction or intercultural relationship adaptation vary among different age groups, generation groups, and personality types?

From the interpretive research paradigm, we can ask more of the following research questions: What is the meaning of intercultural relationship satisfaction for diverse cultural and ethnic groups? What are the relationship expectations and obligations between close friends and between committed intercultural partners? What are the roles of family and social network in shaping the development of a meaningful, intimate relationship? What are the critical turning points or phases that an intercultural or interethnic romantic relationship has to pass through in

order to arrive at the crystallization stage? What are some of the essential indigenous emic concepts that are not being captured in the mainstream interpersonal U.S.-based literature? How do concepts such as destiny, relationship patience, authenticity, and interpersonal forgiveness play out in different ethnic and cultural groups? What are the distinctive differences and similarities among particular groups (e.g., Cuban, Puerto Rican, and Mexican) under the broad umbrella, for example, of "Latinos" in interpreting some of the core interpersonal symbols, metaphors, premises, contexts, and meanings?

From the critical research paradigm, we can ask more of the following research questions: How can we better access the theme of power in intimate intercultural/interracial relationships? How can we help abused partners in an asymmetrical intimate relationship to get out of the dysfunctional cycle and, at the same time, be sensitive to the traditional cultural worldviews and assumptions? How can we promote better multiracial alliance building in the school environment so that young children can embrace intercultural/interracial friendships with ease and security? How can we educate immigrant parents to respect the rights of their young adolescents to date and choose their intercultural or interracial partners without subjecting them to more pressure? How can we design the educational curriculum so that multicultural/multiethnic youngsters also develop an appreciation of the sacrifices, immigration stories, and hard work of their parents or grandparents? How can we develop a strong base for non-Hispanic white students and all minority students to develop more intercultural interpersonal empathy for their fellow classmates who sound different and look different from them—whether on a visible or an invisible level?

In addition to addressing these types of questions, intercultural scholars should also consider more complex models that emphasize the fluid nature of cultural identity(ies) and relationship negotiation. One such model that holds great promise for advancing scholarship on intercultural interpersonal relationship development is the social ecological framework (Oetzel 2009; Oetzel, Ting-Toomey, & Rinderle, 2006). Social ecology was developed by scholars in many different fields of study (e.g., the family system or health care system) to better address the influences of cultural and social contexts or environments on human behavior. The social ecological framework can be visually displayed by thinking about a series of concentric circles to represent different levels of intercultural relations. In the inner circle is the individual and includes factors such as identities, emotions, and social cognitions. The next circle includes the interpersonal relationships (such as family relations, friendships, romantic relationships, and/or social networks) we create with others. The third circle represents the organizations and institutions (such as work and religions) that frame our various relationships. The outer circle illustrates the cultural structure and societal structure that we live in. In this way, individuals are in relationships within embedded contexts that are within particular cultural layers. Additionally, the social ecological framework emphasizes that not only do the inner circles influence the outer circles but the outer circles also influence the inner ones in a bidirectional manner.

The advantage of the social ecological framework is fourfold. First, it emphasizes that the individual and interpersonal communication are influenced by the cumulative effect of multiple physical, social, and cultural contextual factors. Second, it emphasizes that the individual and interpersonal communication are also affected by individual and interpersonal attributes. Third, the social ecological perspective is interdisciplinary and incorporates different analytical methods for understanding how an intercultural interpersonal relationship develops. In this manner, the framework allows for multiple theoretical approaches (i.e., social scientific, interpretive, and critical). Finally, the framework emphasizes that interpersonal relationship formation and cultural orientation are dynamic, fluid, interdependent, and situationally grounded. Thus, the framework provides an overarching tapestry map for understanding the benefits, challenges, and evolving processes of intercultural acquaintanceship,

friendship, and/or other intimate relationship formation, escalation, and de-escalation. It also emphasizes that the intercultural personalized relationship development process is framed by multiple embedded factors such as cultural worldviews and values, societal hierarchical structures, institutional policies and workplaces, social network reactions, and other relational and situational factors. Concurrently, individual partners also co-create the meanings, expectations, rules, and norms of their relational culture via their own unique personal attributes, life scripts, and sociocultural membership identities within the confines and the creative options of weaving their own interpersonal threads, patterns, and colors.

This chapter covered the three primary approaches (i.e., social scientific, interpretive, and critical) in the study of intercultural interpersonal relationships. In addition, key terms, theoretical exemplars, and research goals under each approach have been reviewed. The chapter then turned to address some of the selective research topics of intercultural/interracial friendship and romantic relationship development. Last, directions for future research under the three research paradigms have been addressed. Both international and interethnic research collaboration efforts are urgently needed to understand the rich fabric of interpersonal relationship formation from diverse cultural, ethnic, racial, linguistic, religious, gender, and gender orientation perspectives. The indigenous narrative approach, cross-cultural comparative social-scientific approach, and critical empowering approach are all needed for us to truly understand the multiple voices, authentic stories, and communication dynamics of what constitute satisfying and dissatisfying intercultural interpersonal relationships in embedded macro-, meso-, and microcontextual systems.

# References

Adler, N. J., & Graham, J. L. (1989). Cross-cultural interaction: The international comparison fallacy. *Journal of International Business Studies, 20,* 515–537.

Asante, M., & Asante, K. (Eds.). (1990). *African culture: The rhythms of unity.* Trenton, NJ: African World Press.

Barnett, G. A., & Lee, M. (2003). Issues in intercultural communication research. In W. B. Gudykunst (Ed.), *Cross-cultural and intercultural communication* (pp. 259–273). Thousand Oaks, CA: Sage.

Basso, K. (1990). "To give up on words": Silence in Western Apache culture. In D. Carbaugh (Ed.), *Cultural communication and intercultural communication* (pp. 303–320). Hillsdale, NJ: Lawrence Erlbaum.

Baxter, L., & Montgomery, B. (1996). *Relating: Dialogues and dialectics.* New York: Guilford Press.

Benet-Martinez, V., Leu, J., Lee, F., & Morris, M. (2002). Negotiating biculturalism: Cultural frame switching in biculturals with oppositional versus compatible cultural identities. *Journal of Cross-Cultural Psychology, 33,* 492–516.

Berry, J. W. (2008). Globalisation and acculturation. *International Journal of Intercultural Relations, 32,* 328–336.

Bonam, C., & Shih, M. (2009). Exploring multiracial individuals' comfort with intimate interracial relationships. *Journal of Social Issues, 65,* 97–103.

Bratter, J., & King, R. (2008). "But will it last?": Marital instability among interracial and same-race couples. *Family Relations, 57,* 160–171.

Burgoon, J., & Ebesu Hubbard, A. (2005). Cross-cultural and intercultural applications of expectancy violations theory and interaction adaptation theory. In W. B. Gudykunst (Ed.), *Theorizing about intercultural communication* (pp. 149–171). Thousand Oaks, CA: Sage.

Burrell, G., & Morgan, G. (1988). *Sociological paradigms and organizational analysis.* Portsmouth, NH: Heinemann.

Cai, D. A., Wilson, S. R., & Drake, L. E. (2000). Culture in the context of intercultural negotiation: Individualism-collectivism and paths to integrative agreements. *Human Communication Research, 26,* 591–617.

Carbaugh, D. (1989). Fifty terms for talk: A cross-cultural study. In S. Ting-Toomey & F. Korzenny (Eds.), *Language, communication and culture: Current directions* (pp. 93–120). Newbury Park, CA: Sage.

Carbaugh, D. (1990). Toward a perspective on cultural communication and intercultural contact. *Semiotica, 80,* 15–35.

Chen, L. (2003). Communication in intercultural relationships. In W. B. Gudykunst (Ed.), *Handbook of international and intercultural communication* (2nd ed., pp. 241–257). Thousand Oaks, CA: Sage.

Chen, S. X., Benet-Martiniz, V., & Bond, M. (2008). Bicultural identity, bilingualism, and psychological adjustment in multicultural societies: Immigration-based and globalization-based acculturation. *Journal of Personality, 76*(4), 803–837.

Chen, Y.-W. (2006). Intercultural friendship from the perspectives of East Asian international students. *China Media Research, 2,* 43–58.

Chen, Y.-W., & Nakazawa, M. (2009). Influences of culture on self-disclosure as relationally situated in intercultural and interracial friendships from a social penetration perspective. *Journal of Intercultural Communication Research, 38*(2), 77–98.

Cheng, C.-Y., & Lee, F. (2009). Multiracial identity integration: Perceptions of conflict and distance among multiracial individuals. *Journal of Social Issues, 65,* 51–68.

Chung, L., & Ting-Toomey, S. (1999). Ethnic identity and relational expectations among Asian Americans. *Communication Research Reports, 16,* 157–166.

Collier, M. J. (1991). Conflict competence within African, Mexican, and Anglo American friendships. In S. Ting-Toomey & F. Korzenny (Eds.), *Cross-cultural interpersonal communication* (pp. 132–154). Newbury Park, CA: Sage.

Collier, M. J. (2005). Theorizing cultural identifications: Critical updates and continuing evolution. In W. B. Gudykunst (Ed.), *Theorizing about intercultural communication* (pp. 235–256). Thousand Oaks, CA: Sage.

Collier, M. J. (2009). Contextual negotiation of cultural identifications and relationships: Interview discourse with Palestinian, Israeli, and Palestinian/Israeli young women in a U.S. peace-building program. *Journal of International and Intercultural Communication, 2,* 344–368.

Collier, M. J., & Thomas, M. (1988). Cultural identity: An interpretive perspective. In Y. Y. Kim & W. B. Gudykunst (Eds.), *Theories in intercultural communication* (pp. 99–120). Newbury Park, CA: Sage.

Covarrubias, P. O., & Windchief, S. R. (2009). Silences in stewardship: Some American Indian college students examples. *Howard Journal of Communications, 20,* 333–352.

Deardorf, D. K. (2006). Identification and assessment of intercultural competence as a student outcome of internalization student outcome of internationalization at institutions of higher education in the United States. *Journal of Studies in Intercultural Education, 10,* 241–266.

Diggs, R. D., & Clark, K. D. (2002). It's a struggle, but worth it: Identifying and managing identities in an interracial friendship. *Communication Quarterly, 50,* 368–390.

Firmin, N., & Firebaugh, S. (2008). Historical analysis of college campus interracial dating. *College Student Journal, 42,* 782–788.

Flores, L. (2001). Challenging the myth of assimilation: A Chicana feminist response. In M. J. Collier (Ed.), *Constituting cultural difference through discourse* (pp. 26–46). Thousand Oaks, CA: Sage.

Foeman, A. K., & Nance, T. (1999). From miscegenation to multiculturalism: Perceptions and stages of interracial relationship development. *Journal of Black Studies, 29,* 540–557.

Gallois, C., Ogay, T., & Giles, H. (2005). Communication accommodation theory. In W. B. Gudykunst (Ed.), *Theorizing about intercultural communication* (pp. 121–148). Thousand Oaks, CA: Sage.

Gao, G., & Ting-Toomey, S. (1998). *Communicating effectively with the Chinese.* Thousand Oaks, CA: Sage.

Garcia, W. R. (1996). Respeto: A Mexican base for interpersonal relationships. In W. Gudykunst, S. Ting-Toomey, & T. Nishida (Eds.), *Communication in personal relationships across cultures* (pp. 137–155). Thousand Oaks, CA: Sage.

Gareis, E. (2000). Intercultural friendship: Five case studies of German students in the USA. *Journal of Intercultural Studies, 21,* 67–91.

Geertz, C. (1973). *The interpretation of cultures.* New York: Basic Books.

Griefat, Y., & Katriel, T. (1989). Life demands musayara: Communication and culture among Arabs in Israel. In S. Ting-Toomey & F. Korzenny (Eds.), *Language, communication and culture: Current directions* (pp. 121–138). Newbury Park, CA: Sage.

Gudykunst, W. B. (2003a). Forward. In W. B. Gudykunst (Ed.), *Cross-cultural and intercultural communication* (pp. vii–ix). Thousand Oaks, CA: Sage.

Gudykunst, W. B. (2003b). Issues in cross-cultural research. In W. B. Gudykunst (Ed.), *Cross-cultural and intercultural communication* (pp. 149–161). Thousand Oaks, CA: Sage.

Gudykunst, W. B. (2005). An anxiety/uncertainty management (AUM) theory of stranger's intercultural adjustment. In W. B. Gudykunst (Ed.), *Theorizing about intercultural communication* (pp. 419–457). Thousand Oaks, CA: Sage.

Gudykunst, W., Matsumoto, Y., Ting-Toomey, S., Nishida, T., Kim, K. S., & Heyman, S. (1996). The influence of cultural individualism-collectivism, self construals, and individual values on communication styles across cultures. *Human Communication Research, 22,* 510–543.

Habermas, J. (1987). *The theory of communicative action: Lifeworld and system* (Vol. 2; T. McCarthy, Trans.). Boston: Beacon Press.

Hall, B. J. (1992). Theories of culture and communication. *Communication Theory, 2,* 50–70.

Hall, S. (1986). The problem of ideology: Marxism without guarantees. In D. Morley & K. H. Chen (Eds.), *Stuart Hall: Critical dialogues in cultural studies* (pp. 25–46). London: Routledge.

Halualani, R. T. (1995). The intersecting hegemonic discourses of an Asian mail-order bride catalog: Pilipina "Oriental Butterfly" dolls for sale. *Women's Studies in Communication, 18,* 45–64.

Halualani, R. T. (2000). Rethinking "ethnicity" as structural-cultural project(s): Notes on the interface between cultural studies and intercultural communication. *International Journal of Intercultural Relations, 24,* 579–602.

Hara, K., & Kim, M.-S. (2004). The effect of self-construals on conversational indirectness. *International Journal of Intercultural Relations, 28,* 1–18.

Hasian, M. (2001). When rhetorical theory and practice encounter postcolonialism: Rethinking the meaning of Farrakhan and the Million Man March address. In M. J. Collier (Ed.), *Constituting cultural difference through discourse* (pp. 77–106). Thousand Oaks, CA: Sage.

Hecht, M., Warren, J., Jung, E., & Krieger, J. (2005). A communication theory of identity: Development, theoretical perspective, and future directions. In W. B. Gudykunst (Ed.), *Theorizing about intercultural communication* (pp. 257–277). Thousand Oaks, CA: Sage.

Hegde, R. (1998). Swinging the trapeze: The negotiation of identity among Asian Indian immigrant women in the United States. In D. V. Tanno & A. Gonzalez (Eds.), *Communication and identity across cultures* (pp. 34–55). Thousand Oaks, CA: Sage.

Hofstede, G. (1991). *Culture and organizations: Software of the mind.* London: McGraw-Hill.

Hofstede, G. (2001). *Culture's consequences: Comparing values, behaviors, institutions, and organizations across nations* (2nd ed.). Thousand Oaks, CA: Sage.

Hymes, D. (1972). Models of the interaction of language and social life. In J. J. Gumperz & D. Hymes (Eds.), *Directions in sociolinguistics: The ethnography of communication* (pp. 35–71). New York: Holt, Rinehart & Winston.

Imahori, T. T., & Cupach, W. R. (2005). Identity management theory: Facework in intercultural relationships. In W. B. Gudykunst (Ed.), *Theorizing about intercultural communication* (pp. 195–210). Thousand Oaks, CA: Sage.

Institute of International Education. (2009). *Open doors 2009 report.* Retrieved May 1, 2010, from http://opendoors.iienetwork.org

Jacobson, C. K., & Johnson, B. R. (2006). Interracial friendship and African American attitudes about interracial marriage. *Journal of Black Studies, 36,* 570–584.

Joyner, K., & Kao, G. (2005). Interracial relationships and the transition to adulthood. *American Sociological Review, 70,* 563–582.

Kapoor, S., Hughes, P. C., Baldwin, J. R., & Blue, J. (2003). The relationship of individualism-collectivism and self-construals to communication styles in India and the United States. *International Journal of Intercultural Relations, 27,* 683–700.

Karis, T., & Killian, K. (Eds.). (2009). *Intimate couples: Exploring diversity in intimate relationships.* New York: Routledge.

Kelly, W. (2006). Applying a critical metatheoretical approach to intercultural relations: The case of U.S.–Japanese communication. *China Media Research, 2,* 9–21.

Kim, M. S. (2005). Culture-based conversational constraints theory: Individual- and culture-level analyses. In W. B. Gudykunst (Ed.), *Theorizing about intercultural communication* (pp. 71–92). Thousand Oaks, CA: Sage.

Kim, Y. Y. (2005). Adapting to a new culture: An integrative communication theory. In W. B. Gudykunst (Ed.), *Theorizing about intercultural communication* (pp. 375–400). Thousand Oaks, CA: Sage.

Kim, Y. Y. (2007). Ideology, identity, and intercultural communication: An analysis of differing academic conceptions of cultural identity. *Journal of Intercultural Communication Research, 36,* 237–254.

Kim, Y. Y. (2009). The identity factor in intercultural competence. In D. K. Deardorff (Ed.), *The Sage handbook of intercultural competence* (pp. 53–65). Thousand Oaks, CA: Sage.

Kitano, H., Fujino, D., & Sato, J. (1998). Interracial marriages. In L. Lee & N. Zane (Eds.), *Handbook of Asian American psychology* (pp. 223–260). Thousand Oaks, CA: Sage.

Kito, M. (2005). Self-disclosure in romantic relationships and friendships among American and Japanese college students. *Journal of Social Psychology, 145,* 127–140.

Kline, S., Horton, B., & Zhang, S. (2008). Communicating love: Comparisons between American and East Asian university students. *International Journal of Intercultural Relations, 32,* 200–214.

Kohatsu, E., Dulay, M., Lam, C., Concepcion, W., Perez, P., & Lopez, C. (2000). Using racial identity theory to explore racial mistrust and interracial contact among Asian Americans. *Journal of Counseling & Development, 78,* 334–342.

Kreager, D. (2008). Guarded borders: Adolescent interracial romance and peer trouble at school. *Social Forces, 87,* 887–910.

Kudo, K., & Simkin, K. A. (2003). Intercultural friendship formation: The case of Japanese students at an Australian university. *Journal of Intercultural Studies, 24,* 91–114.

Lee, P.-W. (2006). Bridging cultures: Understanding the construction of relational identity in intercultural friendship. *Journal of Intercultural Communication Research, 35,* 3–22.

Leeds-Hurwitz, W. (2002). *Wedding as text: Communicating cultural identity through ritual.* Mahwah, NJ: Lawrence Erlbaum.

Levin, S., Taylor, P., & Caudle, E. (2007). Interethnic and interracial dating in college: A longitudinal study. *Journal of Social and Personal Relationships, 24,* 223–341.

Marshall, T. (2010). Cultural differences in intimacy: The influence of gender-role ideology and individualism–collectivism. *Journal of Social and Personal Relationships, 25,* 143–168.

Martin, J., Bradford, L., Drzewiecka, J., & Chitgopekar, A. (2003). Intercultural dating patterns among young white U.S. Americans: Have they changed in the past 20 years. *Howard Journal of Communication, 14,* 53–73.

Martin, J. N., & Nakayama, T. K. (1999). Thinking dialectically about culture and communication. *Communication Theory, 9,* 1–25.

Martin, J. N., & Nakayama, T. K. (2009). *Intercultural communication in contexts* (5th ed.). New York: McGraw-Hill.

Moon, D. (1996). Concepts of "culture": Implications for intercultural communication research. *Communication Quarterly, 44,* 70–84.

Oetzel, J. G. (2009). *Layers of intercultural communication.* New York: Pearson Education.

Oetzel, J. G., & Ting-Toomey, S. (2003). Face concerns and facework during conflict: A test of the face-negotiation theory. *Communication Research, 30,* 599–624.

Oetzel, J. G., Ting-Toomey, S., Chew-Sanchez, M., Harris, R., Wilcox, R., & Stumpf, S. (2003). Face and facework in conflicts with parents and siblings: A cross-cultural comparison of Germans, Japanese, Mexicans, and U.S. Americans. *Journal of Family Communication, 3,* 67–93.

Oetzel, J. G., Ting-Toomey, S., Masumoto, T., Yokochi, Y., Pan, X., Takai, J., et al. (2001). Face and facework in conflict: A cross-cultural comparison of China, Germany, Japan, and the United States. *Communication Monographs, 68,* 235–258.

Oetzel, J. G., Ting-Toomey, S., & Rinderle, S. (2006). Conflict communication in contexts: A social ecological perspective. In J. G. Oetzel & S. Ting-Toomey (Eds.), *The Sage handbook of conflict communication* (pp. 727–739). Thousand Oaks, CA: Sage.

Oetzel, J. G., Ting-Toomey, S., Yokochi, Y., Masumoto, T., & Takai, J. (2000). A typology of facework behaviors in conflicts with best friends and relative strangers. *Communication Quarterly, 48,* 397–419.

Orbe, M. P. (1994). "Remember, it's always whites' ball". Descriptions of African American male communication. *Communication Quarterly, 42,* 287–300.

Orbe, M. P. (1998). From the standpoint(s) of traditionally muted groups: Explicating a co-cultural communication theoretical model. *Communication Theory, 8*(1), 1–26.

Orbe, M. P., & Everett, M. (2006). Interracial and inter-ethnic conflict and communication in the United States. In J. Oetzel & S. Ting-Toomey (Eds.), *The Sage handbook of conflict communication* (pp. 575–594). Thousand Oaks, CA: Sage.

Orbe, M. P., & Spellers, R. E. (2005). From the margins to the center: Utilizing co-cultural theory in diverse contexts. In W. Gudykunst (Ed.), *Theorizing about intercultural communication* (pp. 173–191). Thousand Oaks, CA: Sage.

Petronio, S. (2002). *Boundaries of privacy: Dialectics of disclosure.* Albany: State University of New York Press.

Philipsen, G. (1989). Speech and communal function in four cultures. In S. Ting-Toomey & F. Korzenny (Eds.), *Language, communication and culture: Current directions* (pp. 79–92). Newbury Park, CA: Sage.

Philipsen, G. (1992). *Speaking culturally: Explorations in social communication.* Albany: State University of New York Press.

Philipsen, G., Coutu, L. M., & Covarrubias, P. (2005). Speech codes theory: Restatement, revisions, and response to criticism. In W. Gudykunst (Ed.), *Theorizing about intercultural communication* (pp. 55–68). Thousand Oaks, CA: Sage.

Rao, N., Singhal, A., Ren, L., & Zhang, J. (2001). Is the Chinese self-construal in transition? *Asian Journal of Communication, 11,* 68–95.

Reiter, M. D., Krause, J. M., & Stirlen, A. (2005). Intercouple dating on a college campus. *College Student Journal, 39,* 449–456.

Romano, D. (2001). *Intercultural marriage: Promise and pitfalls* (2nd ed.). Yarmouth, ME: Intercultural Press.

Shelton, J. N., Trail, T., West, T., & Bergsieker, H. B. (2010). From strangers to friends: The interpersonal process model of intimacy in developing interracial friendships. *Journal of Social and Personal Relationships, 27,* 71–90.

Spitzberg, B., & Changnon, G. (2009). Conceptualizing intercultural competence. In D. K. Deardorff (Ed.), *The Sage handbook of intercultural competence* (pp. 2–52). Thousand Oaks, CA: Sage.

Sue, D. W., & Sue, D. (2003). *Counseling the culturally different: Theory and practice* (4th ed.). New York: Wiley.

Thompson, J., & Collier, M. J. (2006). Toward contingent understandings of intersecting identifications among selected U.S. interracial couples: Integrating interpretive and critical views. *Communication Quarterly, 54,* 487–506.

Ting-Toomey, S. (2005a). Identity negotiation theory: Crossing cultural boundaries. In W. B. Gudykunst (Ed.), *Theorizing about intercultural communication* (pp. 211–234). Thousand Oaks, CA: Sage.

Ting-Toomey, S. (2005b). The matrix of updated face negotiation theory. In W. B. Gudykunst (Ed.), *Theorizing about intercultural communication* (pp. 71–92). Thousand Oaks, CA: Sage.

Ting-Toomey, S. (2009a). Intercultural conflict competence as a facet of intercultural competence development: Multiple conceptual approaches. In D. K. Deardorff (Ed.), *The Sage handbook of intercultural competence* (pp. 100–120). Thousand Oaks, CA: Sage.

Ting-Toomey, S. (2009b). A mindful approach to managing conflicts in intercultural-intimate couples. In T. A. Karis & K. Killian (Eds.), *Intercultural couples: Exploring diversity in intimate relationships* (pp. 31–49). New York: Routledge.

Ting-Toomey, S. (2010). Applying dimensional values in understanding intercultural communication. *Communication Monographs, 77,* 169–180.

Ting-Toomey, S., & Chung, L. C. (2005). *Understanding intercultural communication.* Los Angeles: Roxbury.

Ting-Toomey, S., & Oetzel, J. G. (2001). *Managing intercultural conflict effectively.* Thousand Oaks, CA: Sage.

Ting-Toomey, S., Oetzel, J., & Yee-Jung, K. (2001). Self-construal types and conflict management styles. *Communication Reports, 14,* 87–104.

Ting-Toomey, S., & Takai, J. (2006). Explaining intercultural conflict: Promising approaches and future directions. In J. G. Oetzel & S. Ting-Toomey (Eds.), *The Sage handbook of conflict communication* (pp. 691–723). Thousand Oaks, CA: Sage.

Ting-Toomey, S., Yee-Jung, K., Shapiro, R., Garcia, W., Wright, T., & Oetzel, J. G. (2000). Cultural/ethnic identity salience and conflict styles in four U.S. ethnic groups. *International Journal of Intercultural Relations, 24,* 47–81.

Triandis, H. C. (1995). *Individualism and collectivism.* Boulder, CO: Westview Press.

Ward, C. (2004). Psychological theories of culture contact and their implications for intercultural training and interventions. In D. Landis, J. Bennett, & M. Bennett (Eds.), *Handbook of intercultural training* (3rd ed., pp. 185–216). Thousand Oaks, CA: Sage.

Ward, C., Bochner, S., & Furnham, A. (2001). *The psychology of culture shock* (2nd ed.). London: Routledge.

Welner, K. G. (2006). K–12 race-conscious student assignment policies: Law, social science, and diversity. *Review of Educational Research, 76,* 349–382.

White, F., Wooton, B., Man, J., Diaz, H., Rasiah, J., Swift, E., et al. (2009). Adolescent racial prejudice development: The role of friendship quality and interracial contact. *International Journal of Intercultural Relations, 33,* 524–534.

Wiseman, R. L. (2003). Intercultural communication competence. In W. B. Gudykunst (Ed.), *Cross-cultural and intercultural communication* (pp. 191–208). Thousand Oaks, CA: Sage.

Wood, J. (1997). *Gendered lives: Communication, gender, and culture* (2nd ed.). Belmont, CA: Wadsworth.

Yancey, G. (2007). Experiencing racism: Differences in the experiences of Whites married to Blacks and non-Black racial minorities. *Journal of Comparative Family Studies, 38,* 197–213.

Yep, G. A. (1998). My three cultures: Navigating the multicultural identity landscape. In J. M. Martin, T. K. Nakayama, & L. A. Flores (Eds.), *Readings in cultural contexts* (pp. 79–85). Mountain View, CA: Mayfield.

Zhang, R., Ting-Toomey, S., & Lee, P. (2010, June). *Culture and self-construal as predictors of relational responses to emotional infidelity: China and the United States.* Paper presented at the annual meeting of the International Communication Association, Singapore.

Zhang, Y., & Van Hook, J. (2009). Marital dissolution among interracial couples. *Journal of Marriage and Family, 71,* 95–107.

# CHAPTER 18

# Interpersonal Processes in Romantic Relationships

*Anita L. Vangelisti*

I nterpersonal communication is central to romantic relationships. The way two people interact when they first meet can either ignite or extinguish hopes of future romance (Davis, 1973). Couples' communication is associated with what partners think about each other (Sillars, Roberts, Leonard, & Dun, 2000), how they generally behave toward each other (Fitzpatrick, 1988), and how they feel about their relationship (Noller, 1984). Patterns of interaction can even determine whether a relationship continues or ends (Gottman, 1994). In short, communication not only reflects romantic relationships, it also defines them (Duck, 1994; Knapp, 1984).

The purpose of this chapter is to provide a selective review of the literature on interpersonal communication in romantic relationships. The chapter is divided into three parts. In the first section, theory and research associated with the initiation of romantic relationships are examined. In the second section, literature describing some of the interpersonal processes that typify ongoing romantic relationships is reviewed. Both individual characteristics (e.g., cognition and affect) and interpersonal patterns (e.g., couple types, behavioral sequences) are described. Finally, in the third section, studies focusing on relational dissolution and divorce are discussed.

It is important to acknowledge that the review of research and theory offered in this chapter is by no means comprehensive. A chapter of this length could not possibly do justice to a comprehensive review—the literature simply is too vast and too diverse. The effort here was to include many of the research findings that capture the spirit of what scholars know about interpersonal interaction in romantic relationships. Given this, difficult selections were made. In some cases, interesting studies were omitted. In others, topics that are relevant to romantic relationships were excluded. It is my hope that the reader will indulge these choices and use the ideas presented in this chapter as stimuli for further study.

# Initiating Romantic Relationships

The number of factors that can influence whether two people come together and form a long-term romantic relationship is daunting. Some researchers say that individuals' selection of one mate over another happens largely by chance (Lykken & Tellegen, 1993). Others argue that attraction and relationship initiation are the result of biochemical reactions in the body (Fisher, 1992). Yet others suggest that mate selection involves a series of strategies employed by individuals who are attempting to maximize their reproductive value (Buss, 1994).

Fortunately, the broad range of explanations offered for how and why people come together to form romantic relationships has not prevented researchers and theorists from systematically studying the phenomenon. Scholars have examined processes that affect the development of romantic relationships, and they have also studied the variables that encourage people to initiate relationships. For instance, research suggests that the initiation of romantic relationships is constrained by both physical and social contexts. People are more likely to start romantic relationships with individuals who are physically proximate than they are with those at a distance (Segal, 1974). Although the advent of social networking sites, Internet chat rooms, and online dating sites allows for the initiation of more long-distance relationships, people who start their relationships online usually progress to meeting face-to-face if they are interested in long-term romantic relationships (Parks & Roberts, 1998).

Because so many relationships are initiated through face-to-face interactions, the pool of potential partners available to people typically is limited by individuals' social network (Parks & Eggert, 1991). People tend to interact with others who are similar to themselves in terms of variables such as age, socioeconomic status, and education. As a consequence, the group from which individuals are likely to select a romantic partner is relatively homogeneous.

While the environmental constraints on relational initiation are stronger than many would like to admit, it is important to note that, within a relatively homogeneous pool of potential partners, individuals still make selections. The choices people make concerning relationship initiation may be influenced by any number of variables ranging from their perceptions of the other person's social competence to how lonely they feel when they first meet a potential partner.

## Theoretical Approaches to Relationship Initiation

Although scholars debate over which variables exert a stronger influence on relationship initiation, most agree that the information that individuals obtain about a potential partner is an important commodity for those who are interested in initiating romantic relationships. Indeed, the notion that people seek and exchange information when they initially interact is woven through many theories of relationship initiation. For instance, one of the most well-known theories of relationship development, Altman and Taylor's (1973) social penetration theory, conceives of information as a means for developing intimacy as well as a way to evaluate the rewards and costs that may be associated with a relationship. Altman and Taylor suggested that increases in relational breadth and depth are the result of individuals sharing information about themselves with one another. When people first meet, they exchange information that is relatively impersonal and limit the number of different topics they discuss. As they come to know and trust each other, partners share a greater number of topics (breadth) and disclose more intimate information to each other about those topics (depth). In fact, research has revealed that partners who disclose more to each other report greater emotional involvement in their relationships (Rubin, Hill, Peplau, & Dunkel-Schetter, 1980) as well as greater relational satisfaction (Hendrick, 1981). Although, as Altman and Taylor suggested, disclosure is a vital component of relational development, it is important to note that the rate at which partners exchange intimate information varies over the course of their relationship. For instance, as partners come to know each other, their need to disclose information typically decreases (Derlega, Metts, Petronio, & Margulis, 1993). They begin to establish a balance between the disclosure of intimate information and privacy (Petronio, 1991), and for various reasons, they may even declare some topics off limits for discussion (Baxter & Wilmot, 1985; Roloff & Ifert, 1998).

Drawing from social exchange theories (Burgess & Huston, 1979; Thibaut & Kelley, 1959), Altman and Taylor argued that people move further into a relationship only as long as the perceived rewards associated with the relationship exceed the costs. If, for example, partners perceive that their interactions are more pleasing than not, they are likely to continue their association with each other. In addition to assessing how rewarding their interactions are, individuals consider what other alternative relationships might be available to them as well as how those alternatives compare with their current relationship. Rusbult's (1983) investment model suggests that partners' perception of their alternatives, their satisfaction, and the investments they make in their relationship operate together to influence how committed they are to continuing the relationship.

Rather than propose that partners' assessments of rewards and costs are the key factors in determining whether or not relationships will develop, Berger and Calabrese (1975) argued that "when strangers meet, their primary concern is one of uncertainty reduction or increasing predictability about the behavior of both themselves and others in the interaction" (p. 100). Uncertainty reduction theory suggests that to reduce uncertainty during initial interactions, partners engage in information-seeking behaviors. When potential partners initially encounter each other, they discuss relatively innocuous items—the weather, where they are from, what they do for a living (Berger, Gardner, Clatterbuck, & Schulman, 1976). Normally, they do not talk about highly charged personal matters such as their fears, anxieties, or fantasies (Knobloch & Carpenter-Theune, 2004). According to Berger and Calabrese (1975), as the amount of verbal communication between partners increases, their uncertainty tends to decrease. It is only after people come to know each other that they begin to exchange more intimate information because their uncertainty has faded.

Of course, people experience uncertainty about their partner's thoughts, values, and feelings after they have initiated and established their relationship as well (Parks & Adelman, 1983). In fact, researchers who have examined uncertainty in established relationships have argued that it can stem from a number of sources (Afifi & Reichert, 1996). To adapt the concept of uncertainty to the context of close relationships, Knobloch and Solomon (1999, 2002) coined the term *relational uncertainty* and defined it in terms of the confidence that people have in their perceptions of involvement within their interpersonal associations. Knobloch and Solomon suggested that relational uncertainty comes from three interrelated but distinct sources: (1) self-uncertainty (which occurs when people perceive that they are unable to predict or explain their own relationship-relevant attitudes or behaviors), (2) partner uncertainty (which reflects individuals' perceived inability to predict the other person's attitudes or behaviors), and (3) relationship uncertainty (which involves people's questions about the status of their relationship with their partner). Although the role of uncertainty in ongoing relationships is complex, researchers have found that relational uncertainty generally is inversely associated with marital quality (e.g., Knobloch, 2008).

Both social penetration theory and uncertainty reduction theory suggest that partners' willingness to exchange different sorts of information is central to relational development. Although the information that people exchange when they initially meet provides an important perspective on what happens when relationships first are initiated, it obviously represents only a part of the picture. While they seek and provide information, people also enact behaviors to make themselves attractive and likable to others. Indeed, Bell and Daly (1984) argued that individuals intentionally engage in behaviors to generate affinity in others. Using a four-step conceptual model, these researchers identified the strategies people typically use to actively initiate relationships. The various strategies clustered into seven general categories: (1) focusing on commonalities (e.g., highlighting similarities, demonstrating equality), (2) showing self-involvement (e.g., finding ways of regularly "running into" the other), (3) involving the other (e.g., participating in activities the other person enjoys, including the other in activities), (4) demonstrating caring and concern (e.g., listening, being altruistic), (5) displaying politeness (e.g., letting the other have control over plans, acting interested), (6) encouraging mutual trust (e.g., being honest, being reliable), and (7) demonstrating control and visibility (e.g., being dynamic, looking good).

In addition to enacting behaviors to make themselves more attractive, individuals bring other, more stable qualities to initial interactions that affect how, and whether, those interactions progress. Two of the most frequently studied qualities associated with the initiation of romantic relationships are physical attraction and similarity.

## Physical Attraction

Even though most people have been told not to "judge a book by its cover," physical attractiveness is one of the primary cues that individuals employ in deciding whether to initiate a relationship with another person (see, e.g., Walster, Aronson, Abrahams, & Rottman, 1966). People make decisions about approaching potential partners based, in large part, on how physically attractive they perceive those partners to be. After they have approached and talked to a potential partner, the way they evaluate the interaction also is affected by physical attractiveness. Indeed, Reis, Nezlek, and Wheeler (1980) found that physical attractiveness was associated with the degree to which interactions with others were perceived as pleasant.

Researchers and theorists suggest that part of the reason for the primacy of physical attractiveness in the initiation of romantic relationships is that people believe that physical attractiveness is associated with positive qualities (see Eagly, Ashmore, Makhijani, & Longo, 1991, for a meta-analysis). In one of the first of many studies to suggest that "what is beautiful is good," Dion, Berscheid, and Walster (1972) found that both men and women judged physically attractive people as more likely than those who were physically unattractive to have a number of positive characteristics, including kindness, sexual warmth and responsiveness, poise, sociability, and sensitivity. Participants also thought that those who were more physically attractive had better characters and would be more exciting dates than those who were unattractive. When asked about the future of physically attractive and unattractive individuals, people noted that those who were attractive would be more likely to have a happy marriage, to have social and professional success, to be competent in marriage, and to have more fulfilling lives. Many scholars have noted that the bias individuals have for beauty is the result of stereotypes associated with attractiveness: that is, in selecting a physically attractive partner, people believe that they get a partner with a number of other desirable characteristics as well. Other researchers have suggested that the bias reflects individuals' goals: that people want to have close social ties to attractive partners and they project their desires onto potential partners (Lemay, Clark, & Greenberg, 2010).

Although physical attractiveness plays a major role in the choices people make concerning their selection of potential partners, the role that it plays is qualified by a number of variables. For instance, while people generally prefer to date those who are highly attractive, they often pair up with partners who approximate their own attractiveness (Walster et al., 1966). This *matching phenomenon* has been confirmed by work showing an inverse association between individuals' physical attractiveness and their ratings of others' attractiveness as well as a tendency for those who are relatively unattractive to anticipate rejection from potential partners (Montoya, 2008). Research also has demonstrated that people's preferences for an attractive partner do not necessarily predict their choices. For example, individuals who reported that physical attractiveness was important to them prior to attending a speed dating event were not more likely, after the event, to say that they wanted to date the person they rated as most physically attractive (Eastwick & Finkel, 2008). Furthermore, it is important to note that the role of physical attractiveness in relationships changes as relationships develop. People's perceptions of their partner's physical attractiveness can change over time (Albada, Knapp, & Theune, 2002), and their ratings of a partner's physical attractiveness have been associated with relational qualities such as commitment, passion, intimacy, satisfaction, and marital adjustment (Barelds & Dijkstra, 2009; McNulty, Neff, & Karney, 2008).

Perhaps the most well-studied variable associated with the role of physical attractiveness in mate selection is gender. Researchers have repeatedly found a gender difference with regard to the importance that men and women initially assign to physical attractiveness. More specifically, men report stronger preferences for physically attractive mates than do women; women, in contrast, report stronger preferences than do men for partners who have good earning potential or other valued resources (Buss, 1989; Sprecher, Sullivan, & Hatfield, 1994).

One of the most popular explanations provided for this gender difference is rooted in evolutionary psychology (Buss, 1994; Simpson & Kenrick, 1996). Scholars argue that, for example, men place greater importance on the physical attractiveness of their mates because they are seeking mates who are fertile and able to produce healthy offspring. Women, in contrast, place more importance on the earning potential of their partners because they are seeking mates who will be "good providers" for their children. This explanation is difficult to refute, in part because the gender difference in question has

been replicated across a number of cultures (Buss, 1989). Even so, there are alternative explanations. For instance, it is possible that the difference is due to the distinct ways in which men and women are socialized to talk and think about their choices in romantic partners. In support of this explanation, Sprecher (1989) found that differences in the importance that men and women assign to the physical attractiveness of potential partners were larger when self-report data were examined than when behavioral data were tested. When Sprecher asked men and women to report their preferences in potential mates, men were more likely to say that physical attractiveness affected their choice than were women, and women were more likely than were men to report that their preference was based on the other's earning potential and expressiveness. However, when she examined the participants' behavior, she found that both men's and women's choice of a partner was most influenced by the partner's physical attractiveness.

## Similarity

In addition to focusing on the role of physical attractiveness in relationship initiation, scholars have studied the association between similarity and attraction. For instance, the literature on mate selection has yielded substantial evidence that people tend to choose spouses who are relatively similar to them in terms of race, religion, ethnicity, education, and age (see Surra, Gray, Boettcher, Cottle, & West, 2006). Furthermore, studies examining the dynamics of ongoing relationships indicate that partners who have similar preferences with regard to role performance and leisure activities are more compatible that those who do not (e.g., Houts, Robins, & Huston, 1996).

While researchers have explored attraction and partners' similarity with regard to a number of different variables, the association between attitudinal similarity and attraction has received the most attention. Most scholars suggest that the impetus for this line of research was a longitudinal investigation conducted by Newcomb (1961) examining friendships that were formed between college housemates. Newcomb assessed housemates' value similarity before they were acquainted and then later looked at the association between that variable and attraction. He found that value similarity was positively linked to the attraction that developed between housemates over the course of a semester.

To further establish the association between attraction and attitude similarity, Byrne (1971) conceived what is now known as the "bogus stranger" experimental paradigm. This procedure involved researchers first measuring people's attitudes about a number of topics. Then, attitude similarity was manipulated by presenting participants with what was supposed to be another set of attitudes toward the same topics. People typically were told that this second set of attitudes belonged to a stranger, who was portrayed as another participant. Finally, the participants were asked to report the extent to which they were attracted to the bogus stranger. Byrne and his associates found that people reported greater attraction to strangers who were attitudinally similar to them than to those who were dissimilar (e.g., Byrne & Griffitt, 1966; Byrne & Nelson, 1965).

In spite of the evidence amassed by Byrne and his colleagues (e.g., Byrne, 1971; Byrne & Griffitt, 1966; Byrne & Nelson, 1965), a number of resaerchers have questioned the association between attitude similarity and attraction. For instance, Rosenbaum (1986) provided evidence that the link between these two variables was not due to people being attracted to similar others but that, instead, it was based on their feelings of repulsion for those who are dissimilar. Condon and Crano (1988) found that the association between attitude similarity and attraction was influenced by people's assumption that others would evaluate them positively. Perhaps the most celebrated study on this issue in the field of communication is one conducted by Sunnafrank and Miller (1981). Following a modification of the bogus stranger manipulation, these researchers asked dyads to engage in a conversation with each other. They selected conversational partners based on their similarity or dissimilarity on two controversial topics and told the participants that

they would meet and work together on a project involving those topics. Individuals who were in a no-interaction condition responded to Byrne's measure of attraction. Those in an initial-interaction condition talked to each other for five minutes and then responded to the same questionnaire. Sunnafrank and Miller found that the association between attitude similarity and attraction was eliminated when people were given the opportunity to interact (see also Sunnafrank, 1983, 1986). In line with these findings, a meta-analysis of the literature on similarity and attraction indicated that actual similarity was important in studies that involved no interaction or only a short interaction. Perceived similarity, by contrast, predicted attraction in studies that involved no interaction, a short interaction, and existing relationships (Montoya, Horton, & Kirchner, 2008).

Clearly, discussion concerning the nature of the link between attitude similarity and attraction is ongoing. Two decades ago, this discussion was characterized by relatively extreme views. Some scholars argued that the attitude similarity/attraction effect was "dead" (Bochner, 1991); others said that similarity was of "fundamental importance" to human relationships (Duck & Barnes, 1992). As noted by Cappella and Palmer (1992), the intensity of researchers' comments was "testimony to the centrality of attitude similarity in the study of relationship formation" (p. 180). Today, researchers are more interested in examining different types of similarity and the outcomes associated with similarity than they are in arguing about its importance. For example, Gonzaga, Campos, and Bradbury (2007) found that the association between personality similarity and relationship satisfaction was mediated by partners' shared emotional experiences. Rusbult, Kumashiro, Kubacka, and Finkel (2009) examined similarity to support the *Michelangelo phenomenon*—an interpersonal model suggesting that partners in close relationships promote each other's ideal selves. They found that one partner's similarity to the other's ideal self affirmed the other's ideals and that, as a consequence, each partner moved closer to his or her own ideal self.

# Interpersonal Processes in Romantic Relationships

Research and theory on similarity and physical attraction clearly illustrate the centrality of interpersonal communication to the initiation of romantic relationships. When people initiate relationships, they have to communicate—whether to gather information about potential partners, to give information about themselves to partners, or to present themselves as attractive and likable. Obviously these, and other, interpersonal behaviors do not cease once romantic relationships are established. The specific behaviors enacted by individual partners may change over time, and certainly the way in which people think about and respond to certain behaviors will change. As their relationships develop, partners also will begin to engage in patterns of interaction that they did not enact when they first met.

Studies on the interpersonal processes that take place in the context of romantic relationships have focused both on the behavior of individual partners as well as on the patterns of behavior enacted by romantic dyads. Individuals' communication patterns and the patterns of communication enacted by dyads are influenced by the cognitive and affective characteristics that individuals bring to their initial interactions. Furthermore, because romantic relationships are dynamic and reflexive, the cognitive and affective characteristics that emerge from partners' interactions influence, and are influenced by, their relationship.

## Individual Characteristics of Relational Partners

### Cognition

The ways people think about potential partners and relationships clearly influence whether and how they initiate relationships with others. Those who see relationships as risky and dangerous are likely to approach potential partners differently than those who view relationships as

stable and rewarding. Similarly, once individuals are involved with a romantic partner, their thoughts about their partner and about their relationship are likely to affect their relational outcomes. Research suggests that cognition in and about romantic relationships is associated with the way people feel about their relationship, the way they behave toward their partner, and even the way their partner behaves toward them (e.g., Fletcher, Overall, & Friesen, 2006).

While the literature on cognition in close relationships is quite diverse in terms of focus, three aspects of partners' cognition have received a great deal of attention from researchers and theorists. These include (1) descriptive knowledge structures (e.g., relational schemas), (2) evaluative knowledge structures (e.g., beliefs and standards), and (3) explanatory knowledge structures (e.g., attributions and accounts).

*Descriptive Knowledge Structures.* People have mental representations that reflect their predictions about the qualities that describe individuals and relationships. These descriptive knowledge structures influence the way people interpret information about their partner as well as the way they behave in the context of their relationship. A number of terms have been used to study the "coherent frameworks of relational knowledge" (Planalp, 1985) that individuals bring to their close relationships, including schemas, scripts, working models, and mental models.

Although scholars differ with regard to their opinions concerning the specific components and functions of descriptive relational knowledge structures, most agree that, among other things, they include understandings about the *self*, the *other*, and the *relationship between self and other*. These representations differ from those traditionally discussed by psychologists (e.g., Markus, 1977) in that they are necessarily social. While it is possible to have distinct views of the self, the other, or the relationship (e.g., "I like chocolate," "He has grey hair," "We've been married for 17 years"), relational knowledge structures define what a person is like in relationship to others (e.g., "I'm a good listener," "He is a caring person," "We still like each other") (Andersen, Reznik, & Chen, 1997). Knowledge structures about the self, the other, and the relationship, thus, are interdependent: Each influences and is influenced by the other. Furthermore, each of these cognitive structures affects the way people experience and behave within their romantic relationships.

For instance, research on the way relational partners view themselves shows that self-representations affect partners' experiences within romantic relationships. Individuals tend to be drawn toward others who see them as they see themselves (Deutsch & Solomon, 1959). Swann, Hixon, and De La Ronde (1992) found that people with negative self-concepts were more committed to spouses who evaluated them negatively than to partners who evaluated them positively. Perhaps because they do not view themselves as strong or independent, people with low self-esteem also seem to be more swayed by their love experiences than do those with high self-esteem. Individuals with low self-esteem note that they have more intense experiences of love, report that their love experiences are less rational, and view their partners more positively than do people with high self-esteem (Dion & Dion, 1988). Individuals who doubt themselves also underestimate the strength of their partner's love for them (Murray, Holmes, Griffin, Bellavia, & Rose, 2001). They respond to being hurt by behaving badly toward their partner, and their partner, in turn, rates them as overly dependent, selfish, and needy (Murray, Bellavia, Rose, & Griffin, 2003). It may not be surprising, then, that when they feel inferior to their partner, those with low self-esteem engage in behaviors that function to increase their partner's dependence on them (Murray et al., 2009).

Studies on cognitive representations of potential partners similarly illustrate that activating particular expectations about a partner can influence social interaction. In a classic study, Snyder, Tanke, and Berscheid (1977) found that men who were told that a woman they were about to interact with for the first time was physically attractive rated the woman more favorably than did men who were told that their interactional partner was unattractive. Furthermore, when outside observers rated the women's conversational behavior, the researchers found that, indeed, the women behaved in more socially skillful ways. Snyder et al. concluded that the men's impressions of women's physical attractiveness created a self-fulfilling prophecy. When the men expected the women to behave in more positive ways, the women did so.

In a similar vein, Andersen and Baum (1994) found that activating descriptive knowledge structures associated with a significant other can influence the way people evaluate strangers. These researchers asked people to describe a significant other whom they either liked or disliked. They also asked the participants to interact with a stranger who was portrayed as having the traits that the participants used to describe their significant other. The researchers found that individuals "transferred" the schema of their significant other to the stranger—that is, the participants evaluated the stranger based, in part, on the traits associated with their significant other.

Although studies focusing on representations of the self or the other provide interesting information about the way descriptive knowledge structures can influence people's relationships, they constitute a relatively small sector of the literature. Research on descriptive knowledge structures in relationships has been dominated by work emphasizing the way partners represent their relationships with others. These investigations may be best exemplified by research and theory on adult attachment.

The literature on adult attachment is founded on the work of Bowlby (e.g., 1969), who argued that individuals develop "internal working models" of relationships from the interactions they had as infants with caregivers. According to Bowlby, these models comprise two distinct parts. One is a representation of the self or a self-schema that portrays the self as either worthy or unworthy of love and caring. The other is a representation of the caregiver that characterizes him or her as responsive and sensitive to the infant or as unresponsive and insensitive. Bowlby argues that the attachment relationship infants form with their adult caregivers influences individuals' behavior well past infancy into adulthood.

Of course, in adulthood, attachments change. As people mature, they become less attached to their adult caregiver and, in many cases, become attached to a romantic partner. Hazan and Shaver (1987) argued that the attachments people develop as infants are later embodied in their romantic relationships. Based on the three categories of attachment identified by Ainsworth, Blehar, Waters, and Wall (1978) to characterize infants' attachments to their caregivers, Hazan and Shaver posited three types of adult attachment. The first of these is *secure*. Individuals with a secure attachment style find it easy to get close to others, are comfortable depending on others, and tend not to be concerned about being abandoned or having someone become too emotionally close to them. The second type is *avoidant*. People who are avoidant tend to get nervous when others get too close to them and are uncomfortable trusting or depending on others. The third, and final, type of adult attachment described by Hazan and Shaver is *anxious-ambivalent*. Those who are anxious-ambivalent find that others are reluctant to get as intimate with them as they would like. They worry that their romantic partners do not really care about them, and they often want to become extremely close to their partners.

Bartholomew and Horowitz (1991) provide a slightly different conceptualization of adult attachment. Like Bowlby, they suggest that internal working models are made up of representations of the self and the other. Because, as Bartholomew and Horowitz argue, both the self and the other can be evaluated in a positive or a negative fashion, combining these two dimensions yields four categories: (1) one in which people have a positive view of the self and of others (*secure*), (2) one in which they have a positive view of the self and a negative view of others (*dismissing*), (3) one with a negative view of the self and a positive view of others (*preoccupied*), and (4) the final one with a negative view of the self and a negative view of others (*fearful*). Other researchers (Collins & Read, 1990) argue that two or three dimensions (e.g., comfort with closeness, anxiety about being abandoned or unloved, comfort with depending on others) can capture the essence of people's attachment styles.

Regardless of whether attachment is conceived of as a style or as dimensions along which individuals vary, a plethora of findings suggest that people who are secure tend to be involved in relationships that are more committed and satisfying than do those who are insecure (e.g., either anxious-ambivalent or avoidant). Those who are secure tend to be more trusting, have higher self-esteem, and have more positive beliefs about others. They experience more positive emotions and fewer negative emotions in the context of their relationships, and they appear to be more comfortable expressing their feelings to relational partners. In short, people who are secure tend to be better off—both as individuals and as relational partners—than are those who are insecure. (For reviews, see Cassidy & Shaver, 2008; Feeney & Noller, 1996.)

The consistent associations between attachment and positive individual and relational outcomes raise important questions about whether these knowledge structures are subject to change. Is attachment stable or unstable? If an individual is insecurely attached as a child, is he or she doomed to a life of failed relationships?

Bowlby originally conceived of attachment as relatively stable. Indeed, much of the literature on social cognition emphasizes the stability of knowledge structures. People often seek out and attend to information that is consistent with their expectations (Rosenthal, 1993; Stangor & McMillan, 1992), they resist data that contradict their beliefs (Ross, Lepper, & Hubbard, 1975), and they bias their memories of events or circumstances to fit with their current perceptions and expectations (Ross, 1989). Recent work on attachment similarly suggests that secure attachment is associated with greater accessibility of a "secure-base script," deeper processing of script-relevant information, and faster script-relevant judgments (Mikulincer, Shaver, Sapire-Lavid, & Avihou-Kanza, 2009). In line with the notion that there is a fair amount of stability in descriptive knowledge representations, studies on adult attachment have demonstrated that approximately 70% of people evaluate their own attachment style consistently over time periods ranging from one week to four years (Baldwin & Fehr, 1995; Kirkpatrick & Hazan, 1994).

Although researchers and theorists have emphasized the stability of individuals' knowledge structures, most also acknowledge that these structures are dynamic and responsive to changes in the social environment. For instance, Davila, Karney, and Bradbury (1999) found that, on average, individuals' attachment representations changed in a predictable way over the early years of marriage. More specifically, spouses tended to become more secure, perhaps reflecting increased comfort with their relationship. These researchers also found significant changes in spouses' attachment based on both individual differences (e.g., psychological vulnerabilities) and interpersonal variables (e.g., relational satisfaction). Little, McNulty, and Russell (2010) similarly found that although attachment anxiety and attachment avoidance were negatively associated with marital satisfaction, both were influenced by couples' sexual behavior. Attachment avoidance was unrelated to daily ratings of satisfaction for partners who reported more frequent sex, and attachment anxiety was unrelated to daily satisfaction when partners reported more satisfying sex. As Davila and her colleagues (1999) noted, it appears that people's "past experiences, their current states of mind about relationships, and their experiences with partners all affect how secure they feel in relationships" (p. 798).

*Evaluative Knowledge Structures.* In addition to including "internal working models" that provide partners with a basis for predicting the qualities individuals and relationships *will* have, most theorists suggest that relational knowledge structures include beliefs or standards about the qualities that individuals and relationships *should* have (Baucom, Epstein, Sayers, & Sher, 1989). Partners' evaluative knowledge structures have been studied under a number of different labels, including implicit theories of relationships, relational standards, prototype interaction pattern models, unrealistic beliefs, and ideal standards. Although each of the concepts associated with these labels carries a slightly different meaning, they all reflect criteria that provide people with a way to evaluate their relationships with others.

Evaluative knowledge structures such as relationship beliefs or standards are central to a number of well-known theories, including social exchange (Huston & Burgess, 1979) equity (Walster, Walster, & Berscheid, 1978), interdependence (Kelley & Thibaut, 1978; Thibaut & Kelly, 1959), and investment (Rusbult, 1983) theories. Scholars who employ these, and other, theories suggest that comparisons between individuals' beliefs or standards and their perceptions of their current relationship serve as a basis for the way people feel about their romantic partner (Lederer & Jackson, 1968). When individuals' relational standards or beliefs are met or upheld, partners are relatively satisfied with their relationship; when people's standards or beliefs are not fulfilled, they are likely to become dissatisfied or distressed.

Empirical research generally has confirmed the association between relational quality and the degree to which people report that their standards or beliefs are fulfilled. For instance, studies examining commonly held relational standards have demonstrated that when individuals' standards were met, partners tended to be relatively satisfied with their relationship; in contrast, when those standards were unfulfilled, partners tended to be less satisfied (Vangelisti & Daly, 1997). The same association emerged when the standards individuals held for their relational partners were examined: There was a positive association between the fulfillment of people's standards for their partners and their relational satisfaction (Fletcher, Simpson, Thomas, & Giles, 1999). Research also suggests that individuals are happier when they match their partner's ideal standards (Campbell, Simpson, Kashy, & Fletcher, 2001).

Of course, some beliefs or standards are more difficult to meet than others. A number of researchers have examined beliefs about relationships that are "unrealistic." Because unrealistic relational beliefs involve extreme standards that are difficult, if not impossible, to meet (e.g., "happy couples never fight"), partners who hold such beliefs are more likely to be disappointed in their relationships (Baucom & Epstein, 1990). Indeed, Bradbury and Fincham (1987) found a negative link between unrealistic romantic beliefs and marital satisfaction. Kurdek (1992) further reported that unrealistic beliefs were negatively associated with satisfaction in both heterosexual and homosexual couples.

People with unrealistic or extreme beliefs about relationships not only tend to be less relationally satisfied, they also tend to be less optimistic about their partner changing than those with more realistic expectations (Epstein & Eidelson, 1981). Furthermore, those who are dissatisfied tend to expect more negative behaviors and fewer positive behaviors from their partners during conflict episodes than do those who are satisfied (Vanzetti, Notarius, & NeeSmith, 1992). The negative views held by individuals who have unrealistic relationship beliefs and the disappointment they feel about their relationship may create a very undesirable relational context for partners: People who have unrealistic beliefs are more likely to be dissatisfied with their relationship; individuals who are dissatisfied, in turn, anticipate negative behaviors from their partner. Given the negative views these individuals have concerning their partner and their relationship, they are likely to become entrenched in their disappointment, regardless of whether their partner tries to change.

Another quality of beliefs and standards that affects relational satisfaction is their flexibility. Neff and Karney (2003) looked at changes in partners' standards and perceptions of each other early in marriage. They found that marital satisfaction was more stable when partners' standards

were flexible. That is, couples who were consistently satisfied tended to modify their standards so that they matched the current strengths of their relationship.

While it is apparent that unfulfilled relational beliefs and standards are linked to the quality of romantic relationships, the nature of the association appears to differ somewhat for women and men. For example, when Vangelisti and Daly (1997) asked people to rate the importance of various relational standards, they found that women and men rated the standards similarly. Women, however, believed that their standards were fulfilled less often than did men. Fitzpatrick and Sollie (1999) further examined what they called unrealistic gendered beliefs—beliefs that focused on irreconcilable differences in men's and women's relational needs. These researchers found that women's unrealistic beliefs were associated with more alternatives, lower matches to ideal comparison levels, and lower commitment. By contrast, men's unrealistic gendered beliefs were not associated with either investment or commitment. The authors argued that the links between women's unrealistic beliefs and various aspects of relational investment may reflect the notion that women are supposed to be "relational experts." That is, because women see unfulfilled beliefs as having important implications for their romantic relationships, the association between women's unmet beliefs and their relational investment may be stronger than it is for men.

*Explanatory Knowledge Structures.* Knowledge structures such as beliefs and standards serve as a framework for interpreting and evaluating relationships. While these structures have been the focus of a great deal of theoretical and empirical work, the processes and structures that they influence are interesting subjects of study as well. Research on attribution and accounts provides a glimpse of the explanatory processes and structures that affect, and are affected by, romantic relationships.

For instance, the attributions people provide for their partner's behavior often reveal something about the way they regard their relationship.

Studies suggest that individuals are particularly likely to seek out such explanations when something happens that is negative, unexpected, or out of the ordinary (Pyszczynski & Greenberg, 1981). People like their experiences to "make sense" (Heider, 1958). When romantic partners feel or behave in ways that are out of character, those who notice the discrepancy typically search for a way to explain it. Because their explanations may comment on the thoughts, feelings, or behavior of the other (e.g., "because she's tired," "because he's stingy," "because she's a neat person"), they reflect a certain relational context—one that may be satisfying, dissatisfying, affectionate, or hostile.

A large body of research on marital and romantic partners' attributions supports the notion that people's explanations for their partner's behavior are linked to their relational satisfaction (Bradbury & Fincham, 1990). Studies have repeatedly revealed that those who are dissatisfied with their relationship tend to opt for explanations that magnify the potential impact of their partner's negative behavior and discount the influence of the partner's positive behavior. Satisfied people, in contrast, select attributions that highlight their partner's positive behavior and minimize his or her negative behavior. In short, dissatisfied individuals tend to make relatively negative, "distress-maintaining" attributions for their partner's behavior, while those who are satisfied make more positive, "relationship-enhancing" attributions (Holtzworth-Munroe & Jacobson, 1985).

While the association between partners' attributions and the quality of their relationship is well established, the nature of that association has not always been clear. Researchers and theorists have long argued that the causal direction of the link between maladaptive attributions and relational distress is bidirectional—that is, not only are attributions influenced by relational satisfaction, but relational satisfaction also is affected by attributions (e.g., Fincham & Bradbury, 1989). Evidence from longitudinal studies now has confirmed that the attributions made by partners are associated with the deterioration of marital

relationships (Karney & Bradbury, 2000). Studies also show that negative, distress-maintaining attributions are associated with elevated rates of negative behaviors during problem-solving discussions (Bradbury, Beach, Fincham, & Nelson, 1996).

In line with the literature on attributions, research on accounts suggests that the explanations people provide for events associated with their romantic relationships are linked to relational quality. For example, Surra and her colleagues (Surra, Arizzi, & Asmussen, 1988; Surra, Batcheler, & Hughes, 1995) have studied people's accounts of "turning points" in courtship—times when relational partners perceive that the chance that they will marry either increases or decreases (see also Baxter & Bullis, 1986; Lloyd & Cate, 1985). Using an interview procedure developed by Huston, Surra, Fitzgerald, and Cate (1981), these researchers asked respondents to explain what happened at each perceived turning point. Their findings indicated that individuals' explanations for relational turning points were associated with relational satisfaction four years after marriage. Partners' satisfaction was positively linked to their comments about spending time together and disclosure and negatively associated with references to alternative dating partners and attributions concerning one or both partners' social network.

Research on accounts (see Harvey, Orbuch, & Weber, 1992) also has focused on the story-like explanations people construct to deal with stressful life events such as incest (Harvey, Orbuch, Chwalisz, & Garwood, 1991) or relationship dissolution (Sorenson, Russell, Harkness, & Harvey, 1993). These investigations have demonstrated that those who formulate accounts to explain the trauma they experience and who then confide their accounts to close-relationship partners are better off, both physically and psychologically, than those who do not. Whether accounts are elicited by events associated with individuals' romantic relationship or by other events, it appears that people benefit from sharing their explanations with those they are close to. The ability to talk about stressful events with a romantic partner may not only reflect the quality of the romantic relationship, it also may affect individuals' well-being (see Pennebaker, 1990).

In spite of the potential link between people's ability to express their explanations for traumatic events to others and their personal well-being, there are a number of reasons why individuals may decide not to disclose the explanations they generate to their romantic partner. They may feel that the information is irrelevant to their partner, that it is too personal to discuss, or that it will be judged negatively. Most of the literature on accounts and attributions has focused on explanations that individuals may opt not to disclose to others. Because these internal, cognitive explanations affect people's personal relationships, they are a very important area for research. But distinguishing individuals' unspoken attributions and accounts from those they communicate also should yield interesting data about how individuals perceive their romantic relationships. What types of explanations are people unwilling to discuss, and why? How are unspoken attributions modified when they emerge in conversations between romantic partners? What can spoken attributions and accounts tell us about partners' relationships that unspoken ones cannot?

Although scholars have noted that distinctions between expressed and unexpressed explanations are important (Antaki, 1987; Hilton, 1990), few have contrasted the two. This is part of the reason why we know relatively little about how the attributions and accounts people generate for themselves to meet their own needs differ from those they generate for the public eye. Baumeister and Newman (1994) underline the importance of this distinction when they discuss possible differences in the narratives people construct to interpret their experiences and those they devise to communicate with others. These researchers suggest that stories based on *interpretive* motives meet people's needs to make sense of their lives, whereas those constructed for *interpersonal* purposes focus on achieving a particular effect on another person. Because interpretive

motives emphasize the needs of the individual rather than the impact of the individual on others, they should exert a less potent influence on the explanations people generate when they talk to relational partners than should interpersonal motives.

### Affect

Even a cursory review of the literature on cognition in romantic relationships reveals that partners' affect is closely tied to what and how they think. Internal working models of relationships are organized, in part, around individuals' affective orientation toward themselves and others. The beliefs and standards that people hold for their relationships evoke certain emotions when they are unmet. The attributions and accounts that people generate are influenced by the way individuals feel toward their relational partner. Clearly, affect and the expression of affect are central components of romantic relationships.

The literature on romantic partners' expressions of affect generally suggests that individuals in distressed relationships display more negative affect, less positive affect, and more reciprocity of negative affect than do those who are not distressed (Notarius & Johnson, 1982). In addition, although partners who are happy tend to engage in more positive behaviors than those who are unhappy (Weiss & Heyman, 1990), negative behaviors often are deemed the more sensitive barometer of marital satisfaction (Huston & Vangelisti, 1991). Studies demonstrate that partners' negative behaviors are more strongly linked to marital satisfaction than are their positive behaviors, particularly when couples are dissatisfied with their relationship (Jacobson, Waldron, & Moore, 1980).

Longitudinal research further suggests that the association between the expression of negative affect and relational satisfaction holds up over time. Indeed, premarital assessments of negative affect and the intensity of couples' conflict predict satisfaction in the marriage later

(Kelly, Huston, & Cate, 1985). Even when initial levels of satisfaction are controlled, the expression of negative affect predicts declines in relational satisfaction over time (Levenson & Gottman, 1985).

Although studies have consistently established an association between negative affective behaviors and relational satisfaction, it is important to note that the link between these two variables may not be as straightforward as it first appears. Researchers and theorists who have focused their attention on romantic partners' expression of affect argue that the decline in relational satisfaction associated with negative behaviors is qualified by several issues.

First, while there is evidence that negative behavior often outweighs positive behavior in terms of its impact on relational quality, researchers who have studied the effect of positive behavior on relationships argue that positive behavior can be just as influential. These scholars suggest that the impact of positive behavior on relationships is more difficult to detect than that of negative behavior because it is relatively subtle and complex. Some argue that the influence of positive behaviors may emerge at certain times in relationships. For example, Cutrona (1996) noted that positive supportive behaviors may contribute to relational quality when partners are under a great deal of stress. She suggested that under stressful circumstances, the expression of positive affect can prevent emotional withdrawal and isolation, and as a consequence, it can help alleviate damage to the relationship.

Other theorists have focused on the unique functions of positive affect for individuals and their relationships. For instance, Fredrickson's (2001) *broaden-and-build* model suggests that the experience and expression of positive emotions function to broaden thought–action repertoires and build resources that people can use to enhance or maintain their well-being. Taking a slightly different tack from Frederickson, Gable, Reis, Impett, and Asher (2004) argue that *capitalization*—the process of sharing positive events—helps people enjoy the positive events they experience and build personal and social resources. In line with this argument, Reis et al. (2010) found that sharing positive events with an enthusiastic listener increased the perceived value of the events. They also found that enthusiastic responses to shared positive events were associated with trust and a prosocial concern for others.

A second issue that affects the link between partners' negative behaviors and their satisfaction is gender. A number of studies suggest that there are important gender differences in the expression of affect and the influence of affective expressions on relational satisfaction. Research has shown that, on average, wives express more negativity as well as more positivity in their relationships than do husbands (Noller, 1984; Notarius & Johnson, 1982). Women tend to be more critical when they interact with their partners than do men (Hahlweg, Revenstorf, & Schindler, 1984). Furthermore, wives who are distressed are more likely than distressed husbands to behave negatively toward their spouse (Notarius, Benson, Sloane, Vanzetti, & Hornyak, 1989). Distressed wives also have a greater tendency than those who are not distressed to reciprocate negative behavior from their partner (Notarius & Pellegrini, 1987).

In addition to expressing more negativity toward their husbands, it appears that distressed wives have difficulty countering their husbands' negative behavior with positive behavior. Notarius and his colleagues (1989) found that distressed wives were less likely than distressed husbands to respond positively to negative messages. These wives, as a consequence, are less likely than others (distressed husbands, nondistressed husbands, and nondistressed wives) to break the cycle of negativity that characterizes the interactions of many dissatisfied couples.

Studies that have examined the behaviors of both partners suggest that there may be good reason for the greater negativity of distressed wives: Distressed wives are particularly likely to have unresponsive husbands. Because men experience greater physiological arousal during conflict than do women, Gottman and Levenson (1988) argued that men have a greater tendency than women to withdraw during conflict episodes. Inasmuch as this is the case, Gottman and Krokoff (1989) suggested that the increased negativity of wives may be due, in part, to a tendency among distressed husbands to suppress their negative behaviors during conflict. In other words, the ways in which distressed husbands and wives respond to the negative feelings they experience during a conflict may actually "feed" on each other. Wives who are distressed may be particularly likely to express their negative feelings because their husbands are unresponsive. Distressed husbands may withdraw and act unresponsive as a consequence of their wives' increased negativity.

It is important to note that although wives (particularly those who are distressed) express more negativity in their relationships than do husbands, the negativity of wives does not necessarily affect couples' satisfaction as might be expected. Social learning theorists would predict that the greater negativity of wives would be experienced by husbands as punishing or costly and, as a consequence, would create declines in husbands' satisfaction. However, this does not appear to be the case. In fact, husbands' negativity seems to have more of an impact on spouses' satisfaction than does wives' negativity. Gottman and Krokoff (1989), for example, found that husbands' negativity, rather than wives' negativity, predicted declines in partners' relational satisfaction. Furthermore, wives appear to be more sensitive to their partner's negativity than do husbands. Huston and Vangelisti (1991) found that husbands' negativity predicted declines in wives' satisfaction, but wives' negativity did not similarly affect husbands' satisfaction.

A third issue that complicates the association between negative behaviors and satisfaction involves the way negative behaviors are coded and defined. When negative behaviors are coded in concert with other behaviors or examined based on their form or function, the inverse association between negative behaviors and satisfaction becomes more nuanced. Some researchers have found that the impact of positive behaviors is only evident when positive behaviors are examined in context with negative behaviors. Huston and Chorost (1994) studied whether partners' expressions of affection moderated the longitudinal association between negative behavior and relational quality. They found that the link between negativity and the quality of couples' relationships was buffered by partners' expressions of affection for each other. Gottman and Levenson (1992) argued that the ratio of positive to negative behaviors has a stronger influence on couples' satisfaction than does the absolute frequency of either positive or negative behaviors. These researchers tested their argument by classifying couples into two groups: regulated and unregulated. Regulated couples were those in which both partners displayed more positivity than negativity when they spoke to each other. Unregulated couples, by contrast, were those in which both partners showed more negativity than positivity during interaction. Over a period of four years, Gottman and Levenson found that regulated couples were more satisfied, less likely to have considered divorce, less likely to have separated, and less likely to have divorced.

Rather than examine the ratio of positive to negative behaviors, Overall, Fletcher, Simpson, and Sibley (2009) looked at communication strategies varying in valence and directness. They found that direct negative strategies initially were perceived by partners as unsuccessful but that these strategies predicted increases in desired change over time. McNulty and Russell (2010) also looked at direct versus indirect negative behaviors. They found that direct negative behaviors interacted with the severity of couples' problems to affect relational satisfaction. More specifically, couples' tendency to engage in these behaviors predicted declines in their satisfaction when they faced relatively minor problems but more stable satisfaction when they faced severe problems. Indirect negative behaviors, by comparison, were linked to consistently lower levels of satisfaction, regardless of problem severity. The researchers suggested that direct negative behaviors can help partners resolve problems over time because they provide a relatively clear understanding of the issues at hand. In a similar vein, Graham, Huang, Clark, and Helgeson (2008) argued that expressing negative emotions can promote relational development and intimacy by providing information about partners' needs. The results of their study indicated that willingness to express negative emotions was associated with positive outcomes such as the provision of social support, building new close relationships, and greater intimacy in people's closest relationships.

## Interaction Patterns of Couples

Although research has demonstrated fairly consistent links between the positive and negative affect expressed by partners and their relational satisfaction, couples may differ in terms of the way they enact and interpret affective behaviors. Some couples may maintain very satisfying relationships while engaging in a relatively high number of negative behaviors because they enact an even greater number of positive behaviors. Other couples who enact relatively few negative behaviors may be somewhat dissatisfied because the number of positive behaviors they engage in is so low. The patterns of interaction that couples engage in are important predictors of relational satisfaction and stability (Gottman & Levenson, 1992; Heavey, Christensen, & Malamuth, 1995).

Scholars have studied the interaction patterns of couples in several different ways. Some researchers have employed the amount of time couples spend together as a general indicator of their behavior and have examined the links between that time and relational quality. Others have used partners' behaviors and attitudes as a basis for grouping couples into categories or "types." Scholars also have analyzed specific behavioral sequences and have tested the associations between those sequences and partners' relational happiness.

### Time Together

Most researchers would agree that evaluating the amount of time partners spend together is a rather crude way to measure couples' interaction patterns. It does not provide any information about partners' beliefs, values, or specific behaviors. Assessing couples' time together, however, does offer a potentially interesting (albeit indirect) indication of partners' attitudes and their behavioral intentions. Couples who have maintained their relationship over a period of 50 years likely regard their partner and their relationship differently than do those who have been together for 2 or 3 years. Similarly, those who spend a great deal of time with each other on a daily basis probably have different attitudes toward each other than do those who spend very little time together.

Researchers have studied the amount of time couples spend together in both global and specific ways. Globally, they have examined the duration of a couple's relationship in terms of its association with marital satisfaction. Specifically, they have focused on the amount of time couples spend engaged in various activities together on a day-to-day basis.

*Global Assessments.* The duration of couples' relationship is regarded by many as a measure of relational stability. Partners who have been together for long periods of time are said to have more stable relationships than those who have been together for short periods or those who have ended their relationship. Although stability—conceived of as the duration of a couple's relationship—is an important variable, examining stability apart from variations in partners' satisfaction yields limited information about the quality of the relationship. Relationships can be stable and happy or they can be stable and unhappy. They can be stable with regard to duration but quite volatile in terms of partners' feelings toward each other (Bradbury, Fincham, & Beach, 2000). Perhaps for these reasons, researchers often have examined the length of couples' relationship in terms of its association with partners' satisfaction.

Over time, marital satisfaction declines for many couples. The greatest decrease in satisfaction appears to take place during the first few years of marriage (Glenn, 1998). Theorists have long argued that this initial decline in satisfaction occurs as newlyweds' infatuation with each other wanes (Waller, 1938). Partners who might have been particularly careful to engage in positive, affectionate behaviors prior to marriage may begin to settle into more stable behavioral patterns after marriage (MacDermid, Huston, & McHale, 1990). Indeed, Huston, Robins, Atkinson, and McHale (1987) found that the frequency with which spouses engaged in affectionate behaviors decreased significantly shortly after marriage. The frequency of partners' negative behaviors, by contrast, remained relatively stable. These findings suggest that the decline in marital satisfaction that occurs during the first few years of marriage may be due more to a decrease in positive behaviors than an increase in negative ones.

Although research suggests that satisfaction declines continuously over the first few years of marriage, many textbooks that discuss this issue note that spouses' satisfaction tends to increase in the later years of marriage (typically after the children leave home). This curvilinear pattern is regarded by many scholars with some skepticism. Researchers' questions about the U-shaped satisfaction curve stem from two issues: The first involves the explanation typically given for the drop and subsequent rise in the level of partners' happiness, and the second involves the nature of the data used to identify the pattern.

First, the explanation often provided for the initial decline in satisfaction is the arrival of children. Although there is evidence suggesting that couples who do not have children tend to be happier than those who do (Glenn & McLanahan, 1982), the presence of children, per se, does not seem to cause marital dissatisfaction. Studies that compare couples who have children during the initial years of marriage with those who do not

show that both groups experience declines in marital satisfaction (McHale & Huston, 1985). Some research also has demonstrated that the presence of children delays the divorces of many couples who are unhappy with their marriage (White, Booth, & Edwards, 1986). The results of studies such as these suggest that changes often attributed to the transition to parenthood instead may be associated with the duration of couples' relationship as well as systematic differences between couples who opt to have children and those who do not (Huston & Kramer Holmes, 2004; Huston & Vangelisti, 1995).

The second reason why many scholars regard the U-shaped satisfaction curve with caution is that much of the research supporting the curvilinear pattern is based on either cross-sectional or retrospective data. The findings associated with cross-sectional data are subject to scrutiny because, as noted by Glenn (1990), they may reflect the effects of a number of factors, including "(a) duration of marriage, (b) the removal of many marriages from each marriage cohort through divorce as the cohort grows older, and (c) differences among different marriage cohorts" (p. 823). Furthermore, Vaillant and Vaillant (1993) argue that the trajectory of partners' satisfaction differs depending on whether it is evaluated using retrospective reports or measurements of satisfaction at several points in time. In a longitudinal study, these researchers found that the curvilinear pattern appeared in partners' retrospective reports but not in periodic measurements of their satisfaction. When looking back on their relationship, spouses may perceive that they experienced a decline and a subsequent increase in their satisfaction. Those perceptions, however, do not necessarily match up with the feelings they reported at various points in time over the course of their relationship. It may be that partners who stay together for long periods recognize that they have experienced ups and downs in their relationship, and they may take pride in having overcome the difficulties. Indeed, Buehlman, Gottman, and Katz (1992) found that the most satisfied couples in their study told stories of having overcome difficulties together.

*Specific Assessments.* In addition to examining the duration of couples' relationship, some scholars have looked at the amount of time partners spend together on a day-to-day basis. In general, the literature suggests that satisfied couples report spending more time together than do couples who are dissatisfied with their relationship (Kirchler, 1989). During courtship, partners who are more involved in their relationship tend to engage in more activities together (Surra, 1985). Studies further have revealed a positive association between marital happiness and the frequency of partners' interaction (Johnson, Amoloza, & Booth, 1992) as well as the amount of time partners spend talking to each other (Dickson-Markman & Markman, 1988).

It also is interesting to note that marital satisfaction has been positively linked to the number of pleasurable activities partners engage in together (Marini, 1976). Although this pattern undoubtedly varies from culture to culture (Wong & Goodwin, 2009), it appears that people who are happy in their relationship not only spend more time together, but they also engage in activities that make their time together particularly rewarding.

### Couple Types

Although the amount of time couples are willing to spend together provides some indication of the degree to which they are involved in their relationship, it offers only a very general picture of the interaction patterns that typify different couples. Fitzpatrick (1977) developed a typology for characterizing married couples that reflects variations in the patterns of behaviors and beliefs reported by partners. Her model is based on the work of Kantor and Lehr (1975) and focuses on the associations between partners' ongoing patterns of interaction and marital satisfaction. Using the Relational Dimension Instrument (RDI), Fitzpatrick identified four different types of couples.

Couples who are *traditional* have relatively conventional ideological values about marriage.

They tend to be very interdependent, reporting that they share time, space, and leisure activities together. These partners are not extremely assertive, but they do not avoid conflict. In *independent* couples, both partners have relatively nonconventional values about relational and family life. Because independents do not make assumptions about the roles men and women should assume in relationships, they have difficulty negotiating a daily time schedule. These partners maintain separate physical spaces but demonstrate a great deal of interdependence in their marriage and tend to engage in, rather than avoid, conflict. *Separate* couples are ambivalent about their values concerning marriage and family life. They report having a conventional orientation toward marriage but a nonconventional orientation toward individual freedom. These partners usually have less companionship and sharing than do the other couple types. They report being assertive, but they tend to avoid conflict. Finally, *mixed* couples are those in which each partner has a different definition of the relationship (e.g., the wife is an independent, and the husband is a traditional).

Gottman (1993) later put forth a typology of couples that, as he noted, is similar in many ways to that of Fitzpatrick's (1977). Gottman suggested that stable partnerships can include *validator* couples (those who display moderate negative affect, moderate positive affect, and a great deal of neutral interaction), *volatile* couples (those who express a great deal of negative affect, even more positive affect, and relatively little neutral interaction), and *avoider* couples (those who demonstrate little negative affect, little positive affect, and a great deal of neutral interaction).

While typologies such as these cannot capture the full range of variation in couples' behaviors and attitudes, they do offer at least three advantages over models that categorize couples as either satisfied or dissatisfied (Koerner & Fitzpatrick, in press). First, instead of placing partners at one of two extremes on a continuum of marital satisfaction, they include couples who are moderately satisfied or who disagree about the degree to which they are satisfied. Second, these typological approaches typically allow for increased variability because partners' scores on measures of marital quality often are skewed in a positive direction (Terman, 1938). Third, because the typologies include an assessment of characteristics other than partners' satisfaction, they can provide researchers with an indication of the criteria couples use to evaluate their relationship as satisfactory or unsatisfactory.

## Behavioral Sequences

Rather than use assessments of partners' behavior as one of several means for grouping couples into categories, a number of researchers have examined couples' behaviors in their own right. Similar to research that has focused on the individual behaviors of each partner, studies that have emphasized the behavioral patterns of couples generally suggest that couples who are dissatisfied engage in more negative behaviors and fewer positive behaviors than do those who are satisfied. For instance, distressed couples display more negative and fewer positive nonverbal cues than do nondistressed couples (Noller, 1982). Those who are unhappy with their relationship tend to engage in fewer supportive behaviors than do those who are happy (Pasch & Bradbury, 1998). Couples who are distressed also report more frequent conflict, more time spent in conflict, and more conflict avoidance (Schaap, Buunk, & Kerkstra, 1988). Furthermore, during conflict episodes, distressed couples engage in more criticizing, complaining, disagreeing, and sarcasm than do couples who are not distressed (Ting-Toomey, 1983). The conflict of distressed couples' also tends to be marked by expressions of contempt, criticism, defensiveness, and avoidance or "stonewalling" (Gottman, 1994). (For a review of the literature on couples' conflict, see Sillars & Canary, in press.)

In addition to a general tendency to communicate increased negativity and decreased positivity, dissatisfied couples tend to exhibit two patterns of behavior that distinguish them from satisfied couples. These two behavioral sequences not only set dissatisfied couples apart from couples who are satisfied, but they also predict declines in partners' satisfaction over time.

*Negative Affect Reciprocity.* The first of these patterns involves the reciprocity of negative affect. Research has demonstrated that while both satisfied and dissatisfied partners reciprocate each other's positive behaviors, dissatisfied partners also reciprocate negative behaviors (Weiss & Heyman, 1990). Partners who are dissatisfied, in other words, respond to their spouses' negative behavior with more negative behavior. Research by Gaelick, Bodenhausen, and Wyer (1985) offers one interesting explanation for why some couples may engage in more negative affect reciprocity than positive affect reciprocity. These researchers found that individuals tended to reciprocate the emotion that they thought their partner was conveying. The participants in this study also perceived that their partners reciprocated their own affect. At first glance, these findings might suggest that partners would be equally likely to reciprocate negative and positive affect. However, Gaelick et al. found that the spouses had some difficulty decoding their partners' expressions of love. Because the partners were able to decode expressions of hostility more accurately, hostility was reciprocated more frequently than love. Inasmuch as dissatisfied couples are more likely to express negative than positive affect, this effect probably is intensified for couples who are unhappy with their marriage.

In some couples, the reciprocity of negative affect takes a form that appears to make it a particularly potent predictor of relational distress. Levenson and Gottman (1985) found that a decline in marital satisfaction over time was associated with more reciprocity of the husband's negative affect by the wife and less reciprocity of the wife's negative affect by the husband. This mismatch, or lack of symmetry, in the reciprocity of spouses' affect creates a situation where the affect of one partner (in this case, that of the husband) appears to exert more control over the course of the interaction than does the affect of the other (in this case, that of the wife). Of course, one partner's affect only has this sort of influence if it is reciprocated. Given this, a number of researchers argue that partners' ability to avoid reciprocating negative affect, and thus to extricate themselves from negative sequences of communication, is an important skill (Escudero, Rogers, & Gutierrez, 1997).

*Demand–Withdraw.* The gender difference in negative affect reciprocity identified by Levenson and Gottman (1985) is closely related to the second communication pattern that distinguishes dissatisfied couples from satisfied ones. Typically labeled the demand–withdraw pattern, this sequence of behaviors occurs during conflict when one partner communicates in "demanding" ways (e.g., attempts to discuss a problem or concern) while the other withdraws (e.g., attempts to avoid the conversation). Research consistently has demonstrated a link between the demand–withdraw pattern and both marital dissatisfaction and divorce (Heavey et al., 1995; Noller, Feeney, Bonnell, & Callan, 1994).

A number of studies examining the demand–withdraw pattern have found that wives more frequently engage in demanding behavior than their husbands, whereas husbands tend to withdraw more often than their wives (Christensen & Shenk, 1991; but see Papp, Kouros, & Cummings, 2009). Several theorists have offered a social-structural explanation for this particular finding (e.g., Christensen & Heavey, 1990; Heavey, Layne, & Christensen, 1993; Klinetob & Smith, 1996). These scholars argue that because wives typically have less power in their marriage than do husbands, wives tend more often to be less satisfied with the state of affairs in the relationship. As a consequence, wives may be more likely than their husbands to desire changes in the marriage. Their desire for change may encourage wives to complain or demand. By contrast, because husbands have more relational power, they tend to desire relatively few changes in the relationship.

Husbands may have little reason to engage in demanding behaviors and quite a few reasons to withdraw. For husbands, withdrawing may be a way to maintain the status quo and avoid their wives' demands for change.

Researchers who have tested the social-structural explanation for the demand–withdraw pattern have found that when partners discussed an issue about which husbands desired more change than wives, the tendency for wives to demand more frequently than husbands disappeared (Christensen & Heavey, 1990; Heavey et al., 1993). Furthermore, one study suggested that husband demand/wife withdraw occurred more often than wife demand/husband withdraw when partners discussed an issue about which husbands desired more change than wives (Klinetob & Smith, 1996).

Although the social-structural explanation has received some support, there also is evidence that the causal forces behind the demand–withdraw pattern may be more complex than originally thought. For instance, Caughlin and Vangelisti (1999) found that individuals' desire for change in their partner was positively associated with both husband demand/wife withdraw and wife demand/husband withdraw. Partners' desire for change, in other words, may be related to their engaging in both demanding and withdrawing behaviors. In addition, Caughlin (2002) found that the demand–withdraw pattern predicts increases in wives' satisfaction over time. Caughlin suggests that the influence of the demand–withdraw pattern on marital satisfaction may depend on how long couples have been married as well as the way partners enact demand–withdraw sequences.

# Relational Dissolution and Divorce

Although the popular media and political pundits argue that people often enter romantic relationships with the idea that they can end them with little difficulty, research suggests that relational dissolution is a very stressful, unpleasant process for most couples (Kitson & Morgan, 1990). Those who are divorced or separated tend to experience lower happiness and more symptoms of psychological distress than do those who are married (Mastekaasa, 1997). After a romantic breakup, people report less clarity about the way they view themselves (Slotter, Gardner, & Finkel, 2010). They have a greater tendency to be depressed and report lower levels of satisfaction with their life (Glenn & Weaver, 1988). People who are divorced are more likely to have health problems (Murphy, Glaser, & Grundy, 1997) and tend to be at a greater risk of mortality than those who are married (Hemstrom, 1996).

The picture put forth in the literature of individuals who have experienced relational dissolution is fairly bleak. Yet it is important to remember that this picture is one derived from between-group differences—typically differences between those who have experienced the termination of a long-term relationship and those who are involved in an ongoing relationship. Variations also exist within the group of individuals who have dissolved their marital or romantic relationships.

Indeed, a number of scholars have identified certain traits that are associated with divorce. Partners bring individual characteristics with them into marriage (e.g., depression, neuroticism) that decrease the stability of their relationship and increase the chance that they will divorce (Davila, Bradbury, Cohan, & Tochluk, 1997). Using data from monozygotic and dizygotic twins, some scholars even argue that people have genetic predispositions toward certain behaviors or qualities that increase their risk of divorce (Lykken, 2002). The overarching assumption behind much of this research is that individuals who are poorly adjusted are "selected out" of marriage. People who divorce are perceived as relatively unfit to select partners, maintain long-term romantic relationships, or deal with the disruptions that occur in their relationships.

An alternative perspective is one that regards divorce and relational dissolution as a stressor or a crisis that individuals adjust to with varying levels of success. Although some adopting this latter perspective have characterized the termination of relationships as a singular event, most now recognize that it is an event embedded in a system of other events and circumstances. Relational dissolution, in other words, can be seen as a chronic strain (Amato, 2000). It sets the stage for changes in partners' relationship, their social network, their economic well-being, and sometimes their parental status. These changes, in turn, create stressful conditions that individuals must adjust to over time.

Clearly, some individuals are better able to adjust to relational dissolution and divorce than others. Research suggests that people's ability to cope with the termination of their relationships is affected by structural, social, and psychological resources. For instance, concrete, structural resources such as income and employment can influence people's well-being. If partners' socioeconomic status is significantly diminished following a divorce, they are likely to have more difficulty adjusting to the separation than if their socioeconomic status remained relatively stable (McLanahan & Booth, 1989). Similarly, social resources such as network support can affect individuals' ability to adjust. Partners who have supportive social networks tend to experience less difficulty than those who do not (Gerstel, 1988).

Individuals' personal or psychological resources are particularly important contributors to postdivorce well-being. Part of the reason for this is that relational dissolution often depletes both structural and social resources. People (particularly women) can lose substantial income, and social networks often are disrupted. As a consequence, individuals' ability to identify and recover their losses following the termination of their relationship can be critical. Those who are unable to do so may experience distress not only because of their limited psychological resources but also because those limited psychological resources put them at a disadvantage when it comes to accessing structural and social resources. Given this, it is not surprising that studies show that partners who experience reduced clarity about the way they view themselves after a breakup are more distressed (Slotter et al., 2010) or that those who feel guilty or preoccupied about their divorce generally have more problems adjusting to their postdivorce state (Masheter, 1991).

Harvey and Fine (2006) underline the importance of partners' psychological resources when they suggest that a critical factor in people's recovery from traumatic events such as relational dissolution is their ability to formulate accounts. Accounts provide individuals with a way of making sense of what happened in their relationship and give them a basis for talking about the termination of their relationship to others (Sorenson et al., 1993). The explanations people generate for why their relationship ended can offer them a way to save face with regard to an event that some might see as a major failure: Rather than portray themselves as unable to maintain a satisfactory relationship, individuals may depict themselves as making a decision that will improve the quality of their life. Indeed, research suggests that people's descriptions of relational termination often are biased in a self-serving manner. For example, Hill, Rubin, and Peplau (1976) found that people who had experienced the breakup of a dating relationship tended to report that they wanted to end the relationship more than their partner did. In studying divorced couples, Gray and Silver (1990) found that former spouses had relatively positive perceptions of themselves and negative perceptions of their partner. Similarly, when Hopper and Drummond (1991) compared a conversation between two partners who were ending their relationship with later conversations between the partners and others in their social network, they found that the individuals reconstructed their breakup conversation to portray themselves in a positive light.

In addition to helping people save face, accounts can reflect the way partners feel about their relationship ending. For instance, women who attempt to end physically abusive relationships may explain the dissolution as caused by unstable, external factors (e.g., the stress their partner has experienced on the job) or by stable, internal characteristics of their partner (e.g., his immaturity, his inability to control his temper). The accounts these women formulate to frame the termination of their relationship may not only reflect how they feel about their partner, they also may provide them with a reason to avoid going back to an abusive relationship (Herbert, Silver, & Ellard, 1991).

Although existing research offers a fair amount of information about the factors that may influence partners' adjustment following relational dissolution or divorce, it does not provide a great deal of information about the dissolution process itself. Certainly, gathering data on the interpersonal processes that occur as relationships dissolve is no easy task. Partners who are in the midst of ending their relationships are unlikely to volunteer to bare their souls to researchers. In some cases, these individuals may not even be aware that their relationship is in the process of coming apart. Nevertheless, scholars have formulated models that may be used to begin to explore the communication processes that are involved in relational dissolution.

## Stage Models

Researchers and theorists have posited a number of different models to illustrate the various stages that partners go through as they dissolve their romantic relationships. Two models frequently cited by communication scholars include one proposed by Duck (1982) and one put forth by Knapp (1978). Duck's model suggests that partners move through four phases when their relationships come apart. The first is labeled the *intrapsychic* phase. During this period, individuals evaluate their partner's behavior and consider the extent to which that behavior provides a justification for ending the relationship. They also assess the positive aspects of alternative relationships and the costs of relationship dissolution. The *dyadic* phase is next. In this phase, partners begin to discuss the problems they perceive. They talk about the costs associated with terminating the relationship as well as whether the relationship should be repaired. In the *social* phase, partners begin to think about how they will present the dissolution of their relationship to their network of friends and family members. In doing so, individuals construct stories or accounts that help them (and others) make sense of the relationship. Finally, the *grave-dressing* phase is a period when partners focus on ending the relationship. They reformulate the account of their breakup and start to disseminate that account to their social network. They also engage in behaviors that help them "get over" the relationship and their relational partner.

Knapp's (1978) model is similar to the one posited by Duck (1982), but it places slightly more emphasis on what takes place between partners and slightly less emphasis on the interface between partners and their social network. Knapp argues that the process of dissolution begins with what he calls the *differentiating* stage. When partners start to disengage from each other, they begin to talk more about their differences. Joint possessions and joint activities become individualized. In some cases, communication during this stage is characterized by conflict, but partners also may express the distinctions between them in ways that do not include overt disagreement. The next phase described by Knapp is the *circumscribing* stage. During this period, communication between partners becomes more restricted and controlled. Partners opt to talk about "safe" topics and begin to avoid issues that they perceive as sensitive. They usually communicate less frequently; less information is exchanged, and the information that is exchanged is less intimate. In the *stagnating* stage, partners' communication nearly comes to a halt. Even relatively superficial topics sometimes are avoided. Partners often believe that communication is useless. They

usually share the same physical environment, but emotionally, they are quite distant. Next, in the *avoiding* stage, partners do their best to avoid social contact. When they do communicate, they make it clear that they are not interested in each other or in the relationship. Interaction often is very direct (e.g., "I don't have time for you") because partners have little, if any, concern about the impact of what they say on each other. When individuals reach the *terminating* stage, their relationship finally ends. Partners may engage in a conversation in which they agree that they will no longer see each other, or they may avoid such an interaction and allow the relationship to fade away. If they do talk about the end of the relationship, their interaction is likely to be characterized by messages that emphasize the distance between them—whether psychological, physical, or both. (See Koenig Kellas, Bean, Cunningham, & Cheng, 2008, for a study of postdissolution relationships.)

Both Knapp and Duck note that the models they describe should be interpreted with caution. By describing the stages or phases that may be experienced by partners, these theorists are not implying that people will move toward dissolution in a direct, linear fashion. In fact, both of these scholars argue that partners may move forward through the various stages of dissolution or backward from what appears to be a more advanced stage to one that is less advanced. They also note that some individuals may skip some stages altogether. The models, in short, offer a template that can be used by researchers and laypeople alike to explore and explain some of the experiences individuals have when their relationships come apart.

## Directions for Future Study

The studies reviewed in this chapter offer only a glimpse of what has become a substantial scholarly literature (Perlman & Duck, 2006). In spite of the size and diversity of this literature, it is possible to identify a number of trends that have begun to influence what researchers study as well as how they study it.

## Identifying Patterns of Behavior

Research on behavioral sequences such as the demand–withdraw pattern (Christensen & Heavey, 1990) and the reciprocity of negative affect (Levenson & Gottman, 1985) has yielded important information about the influence of behavior on partners' relationships. Rather than isolating and identifying communication behaviors out of context, these and other similar studies have pinpointed the behavioral patterns that affect the quality of partners' relationship over time (e.g., Heavey et al., 1995). Given the relatively sophisticated analytic strategies that have emerged in recent years (e.g., Kenny, Kashy, & Cook, 2006) as well as the increasing tendency of researchers to focus on couples as opposed to individual partners, it is likely that scholars will continue to identify the behavioral sequences enacted by couples and explore the ways in which various patterns of behavior affect relational qualities.

## Changing the Outcome Variable

Researchers and laypeople alike want to know what makes for a happy marriage. Perhaps for this reason, relational satisfaction has been the outcome variable of choice for most scholars studying interpersonal communication in romantic relationships. The underlying assumption made by many has been that if partners are happy, their relationship is likely to remain intact, whereas if they are unhappy, their relationship may come apart. In spite of the premium placed on relational happiness, scholars have begun to acknowledge that satisfaction—typically operationalized as partners' feelings about their relationship at a given point in time—is not the only way to conceptualize relational success. For instance, Glenn (1990) argued that a "marriage that is intact and

satisfactory to both spouses is successful, while one that has ended in divorce or separation or is unsatisfactory to one or both spouses is a failure" (p. 821). Successful relationships, in short, may be conceived as those that are both intact and satisfying. Because satisfaction is integral to successful relationships, it certainly will continue to be a focus of interest for researchers. But variables other than satisfaction that are associated with intact relationships also have begun to move to the forefront. Researchers, for example, are examining outcome variables such as commitment (Rusbult, Coolsen, Kirchner, & Clarke, 2006), sacrifice (Van Lange et al., 1997), trust (Rempel, Holmes, & Zanna, 1985), and forgiveness (McCullough, Worthington, & Rachal, 1997). They also have begun to reassess the structure of relational satisfaction, noting that positive and negative evaluations of relationships can be measured as separate, albeit related, variables (Fincham & Beach, 2006).

## Reexamining the Structure of Variables

Relational satisfaction is not the only variable that has come under scrutiny in recent years. The structure of other variables has been reassessed as well. For instance, most researchers now conceive of positive and negative affect as two separate dimensions rather than as a single, bipolar dimension (e.g., Cacioppo & Berntson, 1994). Similarly, instead of looking at partners' behavior on a unidimensional continuum ranging from positive to negative, scholars have begun to examine positive and negative behavior separately (e.g., Caughlin & Huston, 2006). Distinguishing positive and negative affect as well as positive and negative behavior is not simply a matter of developing more sophisticated measures. It also represents an important theoretical issue. When the positivity and negativity that characterizes couples are assessed using unidimensional measures, couples who are rated as highly positive cannot also be evaluated as highly negative. Likewise, those who are assessed as low in positivity cannot also be rated as low in negativity. Similar concerns have been raised about other variables such as commitment (Adams & Jones, 1997; Johnson, 1991) and love (Hendrick & Hendrick, 1986; Marston, Hecht, & Robers, 1987; Sternberg, 1986). Researchers examining these variables have argued, for example, that there are different forms of commitment and different types of love. Inasmuch as this is the case, using unidimensional measures to assess variables such as commitment or love may oversimplify constructs that are actually relatively complex and may even offer a distorted view of couples' relationships.

## Including Physiological Measures

Researchers have long known that close relationships can influence people's physical well-being (Berkman, 1995). Supportive relationships have been linked to individuals' health (Robles & Kiecolt-Glaser, 2003) as well as their longevity (Rohrbaugh, Mehl, Shoham, Reilly, & Ewy, 2008). To identify the mechanisms by which relationships affect people's physical health, a number of researchers have begun to include physiological measures in their studies. These studies have yielded a range of interesting findings. For instance, close attachment relationships have been associated with decreased threat-related brain activity (Coan, Schaefer, & Davidson, 2006). In a similar vein, people who reported receiving affectionate communication from their spouses tended to have lower levels of cortisol (a stress hormone) (Floyd & Riforgiate, 2008). By contrast, when individuals were hurt by something their partner said, their cortisol levels tended to be higher (Priem, McLaren, & Solomon, 2010), and partners' negativity during problem-solving interactions has been associated with decreased immune function (Kiecolt-Glaser et al., 1997) and delayed healing of wounds (Kiecolt-Glaser et al., 2005).

Although there are clear associations between partners' communication behavior and a number of physiological measures, the precise mechanisms by which these associations occur still are unclear. For instance, Saxbe and Repetti (2010) found that individuals' cortisol level was positively associated with their partner's cortisol level over several days but that marital satisfaction weakened this effect for wives. While these findings suggest that partners' cortisol levels are linked, they also raise any number of questions about whether there are relatively direct causal associations between communication and physiological variables, whether the associations are moderated or mediated by other variables such as relational quality, or both.

## Exploring the Role of Technology

In addition to assessing physiological variables, researchers are beginning to examine the influence of technology on partners' relationships. The explosion of technological advances has made this a difficult issue to ignore: Computers, cell phones, and the Internet are integral to many people's lives and, as a consequence, touch their relationships. Much of the research that has been conducted in this area has focused on people's use of computer-mediated communication and the Internet. For example, researchers have examined the influence of the restricted communication channels associated with computer-mediated communication on intimacy as well as the personality characteristics of those who spend a great deal of time on the Internet (see Chapter 14, by Walther, this volume). Given that a growing number of romantic relationships are initiated in online settings, the nature of those relationships and the various ways by which partners negotiate those relationships is intriguing. Examining romantic relationships that are developed or maintained online may provide researchers with an interesting point of comparison for variables that have heretofore been studied in face-to-face settings. For instance, while studies have established the importance of social networks for the development of romantic relationships (Parks, 2006), the Internet provides people with a context in which they can initiate relationships with little influence from network members. As Sprecher, Felmlee, Orbuch, and Willets (2002) note, couples may experience greater difficulty maintaining such relationships over time without network support. In addition to its obvious influence on relationships that are initiated online, the Internet may shape face-to-face romantic relationships indirectly by affecting partners' communication with their social network. People who, in the past, have had little contact with family members may develop closer family relationships via the Internet. Those closer family ties, in turn, may influence their relationship with their partner. Individuals also may develop friendships or sexual relationships online that affect their existing romantic relationship. When this occurs, couples may have to negotiate rules about what they can and cannot do online and develop strategies to deal with violations of those rules (Whitty, 2009).

## Concluding Comments

The research reviewed in this chapter underlines the notion that interpersonal communication is a defining feature of romantic relationships. People have to communicate when they initiate relationships. The way they approach potential partners, the type of questions they ask, and the information they disclose all influence whether and how their relationships develop. Communication also is central to partners' ongoing associations with each other. The cognitive and affective processes that partners bring to their relationships are reflected in their communication behavior. Furthermore, the interactions that individuals and couples engage in provide important information about the quality of their relationships. Even when relationships come apart, the way partners communicate shapes the dissolution process.

Researchers and theorists who study romantic relationships are moving forward along several paths that are likely to highlight the centrality of communication to relational partners and relationships. They are examining patterns rather than isolated instances of behavior. They are expanding the scope of what they study, refining relevant variables, and exploring the impact of physiology and technological advances on romantic partners and romantic relationships. Surely, these are steps in the right direction.

## References

Adams, J. M., & Jones, W. H. (1997). The conceptualization of marital commitment. *Journal of Personality and Social Psychology, 72,* 1177–1196.

Afifi, W. A., & Reichert, T. (1996). Understanding the role of uncertainty in jealousy experience and expression. *Communication Reports, 9,* 93–103.

Ainsworth, M. D. S., Blehar, M. C., Waters, E., & Wall, S. (1978). *Patterns of attachment: Assessed in the strange situation and at home.* Hillsdale, NJ: Lawrence Erlbaum.

Albada, K. F., Knapp, M. L., & Theune, K. E. (2002). Interaction appearance theory: Changing perceptions of physical attractiveness through social interaction. *Communication Theory, 12,* 8–40.

Altman, I., & Taylor, D. A. (1973). *Social penetration: The development of interpersonal relationships.* New York: Holt, Rinehart, & Winston.

Amato, P. R. (2000). The consequences of divorce for adults and children. *Journal of Marriage and the Family, 62,* 1269–1287.

Andersen, S. M., & Baum, A. (1994). Transference in interpersonal relations: Inferences and affect based on significant other representations. *Journal of Personality, 62,* 459–498.

Andersen, S. M., Reznik, I., & Chen, S. (1997). The self in relation to others: Motivational and cognitive underpinnings. In J. G. Snodgrass & R. L. Thompson (Eds.), *The self across psychology: Self-recognition, self-awareness, and the self-concept* (pp. 233–275). New York: Academy of Science.

Antaki, C. (1987). Performable and unperformable: A guide to accounts of relationships. In R. Burnet, P. McGhee, & D. Clarke (Eds.), *Accounting for* relationships: *Explanation, representation, and knowledge* (pp. 97–113). New York: Methuen.

Baldwin, M. W., & Fehr, B. (1995). On the instability of attachment style ratings. *Personal Relationships, 2,* 247–261.

Barelds, D. P., & Dijkstra, P. (2009). Positive illusions about a partner's physical attractiveness and relationship quality. *Personal Relationships, 16,* 263–283.

Bartholomew, K., & Horowitz, L. M. (1991). Attachment styles among young adults: A test of a four-category model. *Journal of Personality and Social Psychology, 61,* 226–244.

Baucom, D. H., & Epstein, N. (1990). *Cognitive-behavioral marital therapy.* New York: Brunner/Mazel.

Baucom, D. H., Epstein, N., Sayers, S., & Sher, T. G. (1989). The role of cognitions in marital relationships: Definitional, methodological, and conceptual issues. *Journal of Consulting and Clinical Psychology, 57,* 31–38.

Baumeister, R. F., & Newman, L. S. (1994). How stories make sense of personal experiences: Motives that shape autobiographical narratives. *Personality and Social Psychology Bulletin, 20,* 676–690.

Baxter, L. A., & Bullis, C. (1986). Turning points in developing romantic relationships. *Human Communication Research, 12,* 469–493.

Baxter, L. A., & Wilmot, W. W. (1985). Taboo topics in close relationships. *Journal of Social and Personal Relationships, 2,* 253–269.

Bell, R. A., & Daly, J. A. (1984). The affinity-seeking function of communication. *Communication Monographs, 51,* 91–115.

Berger, C. R., & Calabrese, R. J. (1975). Some explorations in initial interaction and beyond: Toward a developmental theory of interpersonal communication. *Human Communication Research, 1,* 99–112.

Berger, C. R., Gardner, R. R., Clatterbuck, G. W., & Schulman, L. S. (1976). Perceptions of information sequencing in relationship development. *Human Communication Research, 3,* 34–39.

Berkman, L. F. (1995). The role of social relations in health promotion. *Psychosomatic Medicine, 57,* 245–254.

Bochner, A. P. (1991). On the paradigm that would not die. In J. A. Anderson (Ed.), *Communication yearbook 14* (pp. 484–491). Newbury Park, CA: Sage.

Bowlby, J. (1969). *Attachment and loss: Vol. 1. Attachment.* New York: Basic Books.

Bradbury, T. N., Beach, S. R. H., Fincham, F. D., & Nelson, G. (1996). Attributions and behavior in functional and dysfunctional marriages. *Journal of Consulting and Clinical Psychology, 64,* 569–576.

Bradbury, T. N., & Fincham, F. D. (1987). Affect and cognition in close relationships: Toward an integrative model. *Cognition & Emotion, 1,* 59–67.

Bradbury, T. N., & Fincham, F. D. (1990). Attributions in marriage: Review and critique. *Psychological Bulletin, 107,* 3–33.

Bradbury, T. N., Fincham, F. D., & Beach, S. R. H. (2000). Research on the nature and determinants of marital satisfaction: A decade in review. *Journal of Marriage and the Family, 62,* 964–980.

Buehlman, K. T., Gottman, H. M., & Katz, L. F. (1992). How a couple views their past predicts their future: Predicting divorce from an oral history interview. *Journal of Family Psychology, 5,* 295–318.

Burgess, R. L., & Huston, T. L. (Eds.). (1979). *Social exchange in developing relationships.* New York: Academic Press.

Buss, D. M. (1989). Sex differences in human mate preferences: Evolutionary hypotheses tested in 37 cultures. *Behavioral & Brain Sciences, 12,* 1–49.

Buss, D. M. (1994). *The evolution of desire: Strategies of human mating.* New York: Basic Books.

Byrne, D. (1971). *The attraction paradigm.* New York: Academic Press.

Byrne, D., & Griffitt, W. (1966). Similarity versus liking: A clarification. *Psychometric Science, 6,* 295–296.

Byrne, D., & Nelson, D. (1965). Attraction as a linear function of proportion of positive reinforcements. *Journal of Personality and Social Psychology, 1,* 659–663.

Cacioppo, J. T., & Berntson, G. C. (1994). Relationship between attitudes and evaluative space: A critical review, with emphasis on the separability of positive and negative substrates. *Psychological Bulletin, 115,* 401–423.

Campbell, L., Simpson, J. A., Kashy, D. A., & Fletcher, G. J. O. (2001). Ideal standards, the self, and flexibility of ideals in close relationships. *Personality and Social Psychology Bulletin, 27,* 447–462.

Cappella, J. N., & Palmer, M. T. (1992). The effect of partners' conversation on the association between attitude similarity and attraction. *Communication Monographs, 59,* 180–189.

Cassidy, J., & Shaver, P. R. (2008). *Handbook of attachment: Theory, research, and clinical applications* (2nd ed.). New York: Guilford Press.

Caughlin, J. P. (2002). The demand/withdraw pattern of communication as a predictor of marital satisfaction over time: Unresolved issues and future directions. *Human Communication Research, 28,* 49–85.

Caughlin, J. P., & Huston, T. L. (2006). The affective structure of marriage. In A. L. Vangelisti & D. Perlman (Eds.), *The Cambridge handbook of personal relationships* (pp. 131–155). New York: Cambridge University Press.

Caughlin, J. P., & Vangelisti, A. L. (1999). Desire for change in one's partner as a predictor of the demand/withdraw pattern of marital communication. *Communication Monographs, 66,* 66–89.

Christensen, A., & Heavey, C. L. (1990). Gender and social structure in the demand/withdraw pattern of marital conflict. *Journal of Personality and Social Psychology, 59,* 73–81.

Christensen, A., & Shenk, J. L. (1991). Communication, conflict, and psychological distance in nondistressed, clinic, and divorcing couples. *Journal of Consulting and Clinical Psychology, 59,* 458–463.

Coan, J. A., Schaefer, H. S., & Davidson, R. J. (2006). A capability model of individual differences in frontal EEG asymmetry. *Biological Psychology, 72,* 198–207.

Collins, N. L., & Read, S. J. (1990). Adult attachment, working models, and relationship quality in dating couples. *Journal of Personality and Social Psychology, 58,* 644–663.

Condon, J. W., & Crano, W. D. (1988). Inferred evaluation and the relation between attitude similarity and interpersonal attraction. *Journal of Personality and Social Psychology, 54,* 789–797.

Cutrona, C. (1996). *Social support in couples.* Thousand Oaks, CA: Sage.

Davila, J., Bradbury, T, N., Cohan, C. L., & Tochluk, S. (1997). Marital functioning and depressive symptoms: Evidence for a stress generation model. *Journal of Personality and Social Psychology, 73,* 849–861.

Davila, J., Karney, B. R., & Bradbury, T. N. (1999). Attachment change processes in the early years of marriage. *Journal of Personality and Social Psychology, 76,* 783–802.

Davis, M. (1973). *Intimate relations.* New York: Free Press.

Derlega, V., Metts, S., Petronio, S., & Margulis, S. T. (1993). *Self disclosure.* Newbury Park, CA: Sage.

Deutsch, M., & Solomon, L. (1959). Reactions to evaluations by others as influenced by self evaluations. *Sociometry, 22,* 93–112.

Dickson-Markman, F., & Markman, H. J. (1988). The effect of others on marriage: Do they help or hurt? In P. Noller & M. A. Fitzpatrick (Eds.), *Perspectives on marital interaction* (pp. 294–322). Clevedon, UK: Multilingual Matters.

Dion, K. K., Berscheid, E., & Walster, E. (1972). What is beautiful is good. *Journal of Personality and Social Psychology, 24,* 285–290.

Dion, K. L., & Dion, K. K. (1988). Romantic love: Individual and cultural perspectives. In R. J. Sternberg & M. L. Barnes (Eds.), *The psychology of love* (pp. 100–118). New Haven, CT: Yale University Press.

Duck, S. W. (1982). A topography of relationship disengagement and dissolution. In S. Duck (Ed.), *Personal relationships: Vol. 4. Dissolving personal relationships* (pp. 1–30). New York: Academic Press.

Duck, S. W. (1994). *Meaningful relationships: Talking, sense, and relating.* Thousand Oaks, CA: Sage.

Duck, S., & Barnes, M. K. (1992). Disagreeing about agreement: Reconciling differences about similarity. *Communication Monographs, 59,* 199–208.

Eagly, A. H., Ashmore, R. D., Makhijani, M. G., & Longo, L. C. (1991). What is beautiful is good, but. . . . : A metaanalytic review of research on the physical attractiveness stereotype. *Psychological Bulletin, 110,* 109–128.

Eastwick, P. W., & Finkel, E. J. (2008). Sex differences in mate preferences revisited: Do people know what they initially desire in a romantic partner? *Journal of Personality and Social Psychology, 94,* 245–264.

Epstein, N., & Eidelson, R. J. (1981). Unrealistic beliefs of clinical couples: Their relationship to expectations, goals, and satisfaction. *American Journal of Family Therapy, 9,* 13–22.

Escudero, V., Rogers, L., & Gutierrez, E. (1997). Patterns of relational control and nonverbal affect in clinic and nonclinic samples. *Journal of Social and Personal Relationships, 14,* 5–29.

Feeney, J., & Noller, P. (1996). *Adult attachment.* Thousand Oaks, CA: Sage.

Fincham, F. D., & Beach, S. R. H. (2006). Relationship satisfaction. In A. L. Vangelisti & D. Perlman (Eds.), *The Cambridge handbook of personal relationships* (pp. 579–594). New York: Cambridge University Press.

Fincham, F. D., & Bradbury, T. N. (1989). The impact of attributions in marriage: An individual difference analysis. *Journal of Social and Personal Relationships, 6,* 69–85.

Fisher, H. E. (1992). *The anatomy of love: The natural history of monogamy, adultery, and divorce.* New York: W. W. Norton.

Fitzpatrick, M. A. (1977). A typological approach to communication in relationships. In B. Rubin (Ed.), *Communication yearbook 1* (pp. 263–275). Rutgers, NJ: Transaction Books.

Fitzpatrick, M. A. (1988). *Between husbands and wives.* Newbury Park, CA: Sage.

Fitzpatrick, J., & Sollie, D. L. (1999). Unrealistic gendered and relationship-specific beliefs: Contributions to investments and commitment in dating relationships. *Journal of Social and Personal Relationships, 16,* 852–867.

Fletcher, G. J. O., Overall, N. C., & Friesen, M. D. (2006). Social cognition in intimate relationships. In A. L. Vangelisti & D. Perlman (Eds.), *The Cambridge handbook of personal relationships* (pp. 353–368). New York: Cambridge University Press.

Fletcher, G. J. O., Simpson, J. A., Thomas, G., & Giles, L. (1999). Ideals in intimate relationships. *Journal of Personality and Social Psychology, 76,* 72–89.

Floyd, K., & Riforgiate, S. (2008). Affectionate communication received from spouses predicts stress hormone levels in healthy adults. *Communication Monographs, 7,* 351–368.

Fredrickson, B. (2001). The role of positive emotions in positive psychology: The broaden-and-build theory of positive emotions. *American Psychologist, 56,* 218–226.

Gable, S. L., Reis, H. T., Impett, E., & Asher, E. R. (2004). What do you do when things go right? The intrapersonal and interpersonal benefits of sharing positive events. *Journal of Personality and Social Psychology, 87,* 228–245.

Gaelick, L., Bodenhausen, G., & Wyer, R. S. (1985). Emotional communication in close relationships. *Journal of Personality and Social Psychology, 49,* 1246–1265.

Gerstel, N. (1988). Divorce and kin ties: The importance of gender. *Journal of Marriage and the Family, 50,* 209–219.

Glenn, N. D. (1990). Quantitative research on marital quality in the 1980s: A critical review. *Journal of Marriage and the Family, 52,* 818–831.

Glenn, N. D. (1998). The course of marital success and failure in five American 10-year marriage cohorts. *Journal of Marriage and the Family, 60,* 569–576.

Glenn, N. D., & McLanahan, S. (1982). Children and marital happiness: A further specification of the relationship. *Journal of Marriage and the Family, 44,* 63–72.

Glenn, N. D., & Weaver, C. N. (1988). The changing relationship of marital status to reported happiness. *Journal of Marriage and the Family, 50,* 317–324.

Gonzaga, G. C., Campos, B., & Bradbury, T. (2007). Similarity, convergence, and relationship satisfaction in dating and married couples. *Journal of Personality and Social Psychology, 93,* 34–48.

Gottman, J. M. (1993). The roles of conflict engagement, escalation, and avoidance in marital interaction: A longitudinal view of five types of couples. *Journal of Consulting and Clinical Psychology, 61,* 6–15.

Gottman, J. M. (1994). *What predicts divorce? The relationship between marital processes and marital outcomes.* Hillsdale, NJ: Lawrence Erlbaum.

Gottman, J. M., & Krokoff, L. J. (1989). Marital interaction and satisfaction: A longitudinal view. *Journal of Consulting and Clinical Psychology, 57,* 47–52.

Gottman, J. M., & Levenson, R. W. (1988). The social psychophysiology of marriage. In P. Noller & M. A. Fitzpatrick (Eds.), *Perspectives on marital interaction* (pp. 182–200). Philadelphia: Multilingual Matters.

Gottman, J. M., & Levenson, R. W. (1992). Marital processes predictive of later dissolution: Behavior, physiology, and health. *Journal of Personality and Social Psychology, 63,* 221–233.

Graham, S. M., Huang, J. Y., Clark, M. S., & Helgeson, V. S. (2008). The positives of negative emotions: Willingness to express negative emotions promotes relationships. *Personality and Social Psychology Bulletin, 34,* 394–406.

Gray, J. D., & Silver, R. C. (1990). Opposite sides of the same coin: Former spouses' divergent perspectives in coping with their divorce. *Journal of Personality and Social Psychology, 59,* 1180–1191.

Hahlweg, K., Revenstorf, D., & Schindler, L. (1984). Effects of behavioral marital therapy on couples' communication and problem-solving skills. *Journal of Consulting and Clinical Psychology, 52,* 553–566.

Harvey, J. H., & Fine, M. A. (2006). Social construction of accounts in the process of relationship termination. In M. A. Fine & J. H. Harvey (Eds.), *Handbook of divorce and relationship dissolution* (pp. 189–200). Mahwah, NJ: Lawrence Erlbaum.

Harvey, J. H., Orbuch, T. L., Chwalisz, K., & Garwood, G. (1991). Coping with sexual assault: The roles of account-making and confiding. *Journal of Traumatic Stress, 4,* 515–531.

Harvey, J. H., Orbuch, T. L., & Weber, A. L. (1992). (Eds.). *Attributions, accounts, and close relationships.* New York: Springer-Verlag.

Hazan, C., & Shaver, P. (1987). Romantic love conceptualized as an attachment process. *Journal of Personality and Social Psychology, 52,* 511–524.

Heavey, C. L., Christensen, A., & Malamuth, N. M. (1995). The longitudinal impact of demand and withdrawal during marital conflict. *Journal of Consulting and Clinical Psychology, 63,* 797–801.

Heavey, C. L., Layne, C., & Christensen, A. (1993). Gender and conflict structure in marital interaction: A replication and extension. *Journal of Consulting and Clinical Psychology, 61,* 16–27.

Heider, F. (1958). *The psychology of interpersonal relations.* New York: Wiley.

Hemstrom, O. (1996). Is marriage dissolution linked to differences in mortality risks for men and women? *Journal of Marriage and the Family, 58,* 366–378.

Hendrick, C., & Hendrick, S. S. (1986). A theory and method of love. *Journal of Personality and Social Psychology, 50,* 392–402.

Hendrick, S. S. (1981). Self-disclosure and marital satisfaction. *Journal of Personality and Social Psychology, 40,* 1150–1159.

Herbert, T. B., Silver, R. C., & Ellard, J. H. (1991). Coping with an abusive relationship: I. How and why do women stay? *Journal of Marriage and the Family, 53,* 311–325.

Hill, C. T., Rubin, Z., & Peplau, L. A. (1976). Breakups before marriage: The end of 103 affairs. *Journal of Social Issues, 32,* 147–168.

Hilton, D. J. (1990). Conversational processes and causal explanation. *Psychological Bulletin, 107,* 65–81.

Holtzworth-Munroe, A., & Jacobson, N. S. (1985). Causal attributions of married couples: When do they search for causes? What do they conclude when they do? *Journal of Personality and Social Psychology, 48,* 1398–1412.

Hopper, R., & Drummond, K. (1991). Emergent goals at a relational turning point: The case of Gordon and Denise. *Journal of Language and Social Psychology, 9,* 39–65.

Houts, R. M., Robins, E., & Huston, T. L. (1996). Compatibility and the development of premarital relationships. *Journal of Marriage and the Family, 58,* 7–20.

Huston, T. L., & Burgess, R. L. (1979). Social exchange in developing relationships: An overview. In R. L. Burgess & T. L. Huston (Eds.), *Social exchange in developing relationships* (pp. 3–28). New York: Academic Press.

Huston, T. L., & Chorost, A. F. (1994). Behavioral buffers on the effect of negativity on marital satisfaction: A longitudinal study. *Personal Relationships, 1,* 223–239.

Huston, T. L., & Kramer Holmes, E. (2004). Becoming parents. In A. L. Vangelisti (Ed.), *Handbook of family communication* (pp. 105–133). Mahwah, NJ: Lawrence Erlbaum.

Huston, T. L., Robins, E., Atkinson, J., & McHale, S. M. (1987). Surveying the landscape of marital behavior: A behavioral self-report approach to studying marriage. *Applied Social Psychology Annual, 7,* 45–72.

Huston, T. L., Surra, C. A., Fitzgerald, N. M., & Cate, R. M. (1981). From courtship to marriage: Mate selection as an interpersonal process. In S. W. Duck & R. Gilmore (Eds.), *Personal relationships 2: Developing personal relationships* (pp. 53–88). New York: Academic Press.

Huston, T. L., & Vangelisti, A. L. (1991). Socioemotional behavior and satisfaction in marital relationships. *Journal of Personality and Social Psychology, 61,* 721–733.

Huston, T. L., & Vangelisti, A. L. (1995). How parenthood affects marriage. In M. A. Fitzpatrick & A. L. Vangelisti (Eds.), *Explaining family interactions* (147–176). Thousand Oaks, CA: Sage.

Jacobson, N. S., Waldron, H., & Moore, D. (1980). Toward a behavioral profile of marital distress. *Journal of Consulting and Clinical Psychology, 48,* 696–703.

Johnson, D. R., Amoloza, T. O., & Booth, A. (1992). Stability and developmental change in marital quality: A three wave panel analysis. *Journal of Marriage and the Family, 54,* 582–594.

Johnson, M. P. (1991). Commitment to personal relationships. In W. H. Jones & D. Perlman (Eds.), *Advances in personal relationships* (Vol. 3, pp. 117–143). London: Jessica Kingsley Press.

Kantor, D., & Lehr, W. (1975). *Inside the family: Toward a theory of family process.* San Francisco: Jossey-Bass.

Karney, B. R., & Bradbury, T. N. (2000). Attributions in marriage: State or trait? A growth curve analysis. *Journal of Personality and Social Psychology, 78,* 295–309.

Kelley, H. H., & Thibaut, J. W. (1978). *Interpersonal relations: A theory of interdependence.* New York: Wiley.

Kelly, C., Huston, T. L., & Cate, R. M. (1985). Premarital relationship correlates of the erosion of satisfaction in marriage. *Journal of Social and Personal Relationships, 2,* 167–178.

Kenny, D. A., Kashy, D. A., & Cook, W. (2006). *Dyadic data analysis.* New York: Guilford Press.

Kiecolt-Glaser, J. K., Glaswer, R., Cacioppo, J. T., MacCallum, R. C., Snydersmith, M., Kim, C., et al. (1997). Marital conflict in older adults: Endocrinological and immunological correlates. *Psychosomatic Medicine, 59,* 339–349.

Kiecolt-Glaser, J. K., Loving, T. J., Stowell, J. R., Malarkey, W. B., Lemeshow, S., Dickinson, S., et al. (2005). Hostile marital interactions, proinflammatory cytokine production, and wound healing. *Archives of General Psychiatry, 62,* 1377–1384.

Kirchler, E. (1989). Everyday life experiences at home: An interaction diary approach to assess marital relationships. *Journal of Family Psychology, 2,* 311–336.

Kirkpatrick, L., & Hazan, C. (1994). Attachment styles and close relationships: A four-year prospective study. *Personal Relationships, 1,* 123–142.

Kitson, G. C., & Morgan, L. A. (1990). The multiple consequences of divorce: A decade in review. *Journal of Marriage and the Family, 52,* 913–924.

Klinetob, N. A., & Smith, D. A. (1996). Demand-withdraw communication in marital interaction: Tests of interspousal contingency and gender role hypotheses. *Journal of Marriage and the Family, 58,* 945–958.

Knapp, M. L. (1978). *Social intercourse: From greeting to goodbye.* Boston: Allyn & Bacon.

Knapp, M. L. (1984). *Interpersonal communication and human relationships.* Boston: Allyn & Bacon.

Knobloch, L. K. (2008). The content of relational uncertainty within marriage. *Journal of Social and Personal Relationships, 25,* 467–495.

Knobloch, L. K., & Carpenter-Theune, K. E. (2004). Topic avoidance in developing romantic relationships: Associations with intimacy and relational uncertainty. *Communication Research, 31,* 173–205.

Knobloch, L. K., & Solomon, D. H. (1999). Measuring the sources and content of relational uncertainty. *Communication Studies, 50,* 261–278.

Knobloch, L. K., & Solomon, D. H. (2002). Information seeking beyond initial interaction: Negotiating relational uncertainty within close relationships. *Human Communication Research, 28,* 243–257.

Koenig Kellas, J., Bean, D., Cunningham, C., & Cheng, K. Y. (2008). The ex-files: Trajectories, turning points, and adjustment in the development of post-dissolutional relationships. *Journal of Social and Personal Relationships, 25,* 23–50.

Koerner, A. F., & Fitzpatrick, M. A. (in press). Communication in intact families. In A. L. Vangelisti (Ed.), *The Routledge handbook of family communication* (2nd ed.). New York: Routledge.

Kurdek, L. (1992). Assumptions versus standards: The validity of two relationship conditions in heterosexual and homosexual couples. *Journal of Family Psychology, 6,* 164–170.

Lederer, W., & Jackson, D. O. (1968). *The mirages of marriage.* New York: W. W. Norton.

Lemay, E. P., Jr., Clark, M. S., & Greenberg, A. (2010). What it beautiful is good because what is beautiful is desired: Physical attractiveness stereotyping as projection of interpersonal goals. *Personality and Social Psychology Bulletin, 36,* 339–353.

Levenson, R. W., & Gottman, J. M. (1985). Physiological and affective predictors of change in relationship satisfaction. *Journal of Personality and Social Psychology, 49,* 85–94.

Little, K. C., McNulty, J. K., & Russell, V. M. (2010). Sex buffers intimates against the negative implications of attachment insecurity. *Personality and Social Psychology Bulletin, 36,* 484–498.

Lloyd, S. A., & Cate, R. M. (1985). Attributions associated with significant turning points in premarital relationship development and dissolution. *Journal of Social and Personal Relationships, 2,* 419–436.

Lykken, D. T. (2002). How relationships begin and end. In A. L. Vangelisti, H. T. Reis, & M. A. Fitzpatrick (Eds.), *Stability and change in relationships* (pp. 83–102). New York: Cambridge University Press.

Lykken, D. T., & Tellegen, A. (1993). Is human mating adventitious or the result of lawful choice? A twin study of mate selection. *Journal of Personality and Social Psychology, 65,* 56–68.

MacDermid, S. M., Huston, T. L., & McHale, S. M. (1990). Changes in marriage associated with the transition to parenthood: Individual differences as a function of sex-role attitudes and changes in division of labor. *Journal of Marriage and the Family, 52,* 475–486.

Marini, M. (1976). Dimensions of marriage happiness: A research note. *Journal of Marriage and the Family, 38,* 443–447.

Markus, H. (1977). Self-schemata and processing information about the self. *Journal of Personality and Social Psychology, 35,* 63–78.

Marston, P. J., Hecht, M. L., & Robers, T. (1987). "True love ways": The subjective experience and communication or romantic love. *Journal of Social and Personal Relationships, 4,* 387–407.

Masheter, C. (1991). Postdivorce relationships between ex-spouses: The roles of attachment and interpersonal conflict. *Journal of Marriage and the Family, 53,* 103–110.

Mastekaasa, A. (1997). Marital dissolution as a stressor: Some evidence on psychological, physical, and behavioral changes during the preseparation period. *Journal of Divorce & Remarriage, 26,* 155–183.

McCullough, M. E., Worthington, E. L., Jr., & Rachal, K. C. (1997). Interpersonal forgiving in close relationships. *Journal of Personality and Social Psychology, 73,* 321–336.

McHale, S. M., & Huston, T. L. (1985). The effect of the transition to parenthood on the marriage relationship: A longitudinal study. *Journal of Family Issues, 6,* 409–433.

McLanahan, S. S., & Booth, K. (1989). Mother-only families: Problems, prospects, and politics. *Journal of Marriage and the Family, 51,* 557–580.

McNulty, J. K., Neff, L. A., & Karney, B. R. (2008). Beyond initial attraction: Physical attractiveness in newlywed marriage. *Journal of Family Psychology, 22,* 135–143.

McNulty, J. K., & Russell, V. M. (2010). When "negative" behaviors are positive: A contextual analysis of the long-term effects of problem-solving behaviors on changes in relationship satisfaction. *Journal of Personality and Social Psychology, 98,* 587–604.

Mikulincer, M., Shaver, P. R., Sapir-Lavid, Y., & Avihou-Kanza, N. (2009). What's inside the minds of securely and insecurely attached people? The secure-base script and its associations with attachment-style dimensions. *Journal of Personality and Social Psychology, 97,* 615–633.

Montoya, R. M. (2008). I'm hot, so I'd say you're not: The influence of objective physical attractiveness on mate selection. *Personality and Social Psychology Bulletin, 34,* 1315–1331.

Montoya, R. M., Horton, R. S., & Kirchner, J. (2008). Is actual similarity necessary for attraction? A meta-analysis of actual and perceived similarity. *Journal of Social and Personal Relationships, 25,* 889–922.

Murphy, M., Glaswer, K., & Grundy, E. (1997). Marital status and long-term illness in Great Britain. *Journal of Marriage and the Family, 59,* 156–164.

Murray, S. L., Aloni, M., Holmes, J. G., Derrick, J. L., Stinson, D. A., & Leder, S. (2009). Fostering partner dependence as trust insurance: The implicit contingencies of the exchange script in close relationships. *Journal of Personality and Social Psychology, 96,* 324–348.

Murray, S. L., Bellavia, G. M., Rose, P., & Griffin, D. W. (2003). Once hurt, twice hurtful: How perceived regard regulates daily marital interactions. *Journal of Personality and Social Psychology, 84,* 126–147.

Murray, S. L., Holmes, J. G., Griffin, D. W., Bellavia, G., & Rose, P. (2001). The mismeasure of love: How self-doubt contaminates relationship beliefs. *Personality and Social Psychology Bulletin, 27,* 423–436.

Neff, L. A., & Karney, B. R. (2003). The dynamic structure of relationship perceptions: Differential importance as a strategy of relationship maintenance. *Personality and Social Psychology Bulletin, 29,* 1433–1446.

Newcomb, T. M. (1961). *The acquaintance process.* New York: Holt, Rinehart, & Winston.

Noller, P. (1982). Channel consistency and inconsistency in the communications of married couples. *Journal of Personality and Social Psychology, 43,* 732–741.

Noller, P. (1984). *Nonverbal communication and marital interaction.* Oxford, UK: Pergamon Press.

Noller, P., Feeney, J. A., Bonnell, D., & Callan, V. (1994). A longitudinal study of conflict in early marriage. *Journal of Social and Personal Relationships, 11,* 233–252.

Notarius, C. I., Benson, P. R., Sloane, D., Vanzetti, N., & Hornyak, L. M. (1989). Exploring the interface between perception and behavior: An analysis of marital interaction in distressed and nondistressed couples. *Behavioral Assessment, 11,* 39–64.

Notarius, C. I., & Johnson, J. S. (1982). Emotional expression in husbands and wives. *Journal of Marriage and the Family, 45*, 483–489.

Notarius, C. I., & Pellegrini, D. S. (1987). Differences between husbands and wives: Implications for understanding marital discord. In K. Hahlweg & M. J. Goldstein (Eds.), *Understanding major mental disorder: The contribution of family interaction research* (pp. 231–249). New York: Family Process Press.

Overall, N. C., Fletcher, G. J. O., Simpson, J. A., & Sibley, C. G. (2009). Regulating partners in intimate relationships: The costs and benefits of different communication strategies. *Journal of Social and Personal Relationships, 96*, 620–639.

Papp, L. M., Kouros, C. D., & Cummings, E. M. (2009). Demand–withdraw patterns in marital conflict in the home. *Personal Relationships, 16*, 285–300.

Parks, M. R. (2006). *Personal relationships and personal networks.* Mahwah, NJ: Lawrence Erlbaum.

Parks, M. R., & Adelman, M. B. (1983). Communication networks and the development of romantic relationships: An expansion of uncertainty reduction theory. *Human Communication Research, 10*, 55–79.

Parks, M. R., & Eggert, L. L. (1991). The role of social context in the dynamics of personal relationships. In W. Jones & D. Perlman (Eds.), *Advances in personal relationships* (Vol. 2, pp. 1–34). London: Jessica Kingsley Press.

Parks, M. R., & Roberts, L. D. (1998). "Making Moosic": The development of personal relationships on line and a comparison to their off-line counterparts. *Journal of Social and Personal Relationships, 15*, 517–537.

Pasch, L. A., & Bradbury, T. N. (1998). Social support, conflict, and the development of marital dysfunction. *Journal of Consulting and Clinical Psychology, 66*, 219–230.

Pennebaker, J. (1990). *Opening up.* New York: Morrow Press.

Perlman, D., & Duck, S. (2006). The seven seas of the study of personal relationships: From "the thousand islands" to interconnected waterways. In A. L. Vangelisti & D. Perlman (Eds.), *The Cambridge handbook of personal relationships* (pp. 11–34). New York: Cambridge University Press.

Petronio, S. (1991). Communication boundary management: A theoretical model of managing disclosure of private information between marital couples. *Communication Theory, 1*, 311–335.

Planalp, S. (1985). Relational schemata: A test of alternative forms of relational knowledge as guides to communication. *Human Communication Research, 12*, 3–29.

Priem, J. S., McLaren, R. M., & Solomon, D. H. (2010). Relational messages, perceptions of hurt, and biological stress reactions to disconfirming interaction. *Communication Research, 37*, 48–72.

Pyszczynski, T. A., & Greenberg, J. (1981). Role of disconfirmed expectancies on the instigation of attributional processing. *Journal of Personality and Social Psychology, 40*, 31–38.

Reis, H. T., Nezlek, J., & Wheeler, L. (1980). Physical attractiveness in social interaction. *Journal of Personality and Social Psychology, 38*, 604–617.

Reis, H. T., Smith, S. M., Tsai, F., Charmichael, C. L., Caprariello, P. A., Rodrigues, A., et al. (2010). Are you happy for me? How sharing positive events with others provides personal and interpersonal benefits. *Journal of Personality and Social Psychology, 99*, 311–329.

Rempel, J. K., Holmes, J. G., & Zanna, M. P. (1985). Trust in close relationships. *Journal of Personality and Social Psychology, 49*, 95–112.

Robles, T. F., & Kiecolt-Glaser, J. K. (2003). The physiology of marriage: Pathways to health. *Physiology and Behavior, 79*, 409–416.

Rohrbaugh, M. J., Mehl, M. R., Shoham, V., Reilly, E. S., & Ewy, G. A. (2008). Prognostic significance of spouse *we* talk in couples coping with heart failure. *Journal of Consulting and Clinical Psychology, 76*, 781–789.

Roloff, M. E., & Ifert, D. (1998). Antecedents and consequences of explicit agreements to declare a topic taboo in dating relationships. *Personal Relationships, 5*, 191–205.

Rosenbaum, M. E. (1986). The repulsion hypothesis: On the nondevelopment of relationships. *Journal of Personality and Social Psychology, 51*, 1156–1166.

Rosenthal, R. (1993). Interpersonal expectations: Some antecedents and some consequences. In P. D. Blanck (Ed.), *Interpersonal expectations: Theory, research, and applications* (pp. 3–24). New York: Cambridge University Press.

Ross, L., Lepper, M. R., & Hubbard, M. (1975). Perseverance in self-perception and social perception: Biased attribution processes in the debriefing paradigm. *Journal of Personality and Social Psychology, 32,* 880–892.

Ross, M. (1989). Relation of implicit theories to the construction of personal histories. *Psychological Review, 96,* 341–357.

Rubin, Z., Hill, C. T., Peplau, L. A., & Dunkel-Schetter, C. (1980). Self disclosure in dating couples: Sex roles and the ethic of openness. *Journal of Marriage and the Family, 42,* 305–317.

Rusbult, C. E. (1983). A longitudinal test of the investment model: The development (and deterioration) of satisfaction and commitment in heterosexual involvements. *Journal of Personality and Social Psychology, 45,* 101–117.

Rusbult, C. E., Coolsen, M. K., Kirchner, J. L., & Clarke, J. A. (2006). Commitment. In A. L. Vangelisti & D. Perlman (Eds.), *The Cambridge handbook of personal relationships* (pp. 615–635). New York: Cambridge University Press.

Rusbult, C. E., Kumashiro, M., Kubacka, K. E., & Finkel, E. J. (2009). "The part of me that you bring out": Ideal similarity and the Michelangelo phenomenon. *Journal of Personality and Social Psychology, 96,* 61–82.

Saxbe, D., & Repetti, R. L. (2010). For better or worse? Coregulation of couples' cortisol levels and mood states. *Journal of Personality and Social Psychology, 98,* 92–103.

Schaap, C., Buunk, B., & Kerkstra, A. (1988). Marital conflict resolution. In P. Noller & M. A. Fitzpatrick (Eds.), *Perspectives on marital interaction* (pp. 245–270). Philadelphia: Multilingual Matters.

Segal, M. W. (1974). Alphabet and attraction: An unobtrusive measure of the effect of propinquity in a field setting. *Journal of Personality and Social Psychology, 30,* 654–657.

Sillars, A., & Canary, D. J. (in press). Family conflict communication and linkages to relational quality. In A. L. Vangelisti (Ed.), *The Routledge handbook of family communication* (2nd ed.). New York: Routledge.

Sillars, A., Roberts, L. J., Leonard, K. E., & Dun, T. (2000). Cognition during marital conflict: The relationship of thought and talk. *Journal of Social and Personal Relationships, 17,* 479–502.

Simpson, J. A., & Kenrick, D. T. (Eds.). (1996). *Evolutionary social psychology.* Mahwah, NJ: Lawrence Erlbaum.

Slotter, E. B., Gardner, W. L., & Finkel, E. J. (2010). Who am I without you? The influence of romantic breakup on the self-concept. *Personality and Social Psychology Bulletin, 36,* 147–160.

Snyder, M., Tanke, E. D., & Berscheid, E. (1977). Social perception and interpersonal behavior: On the self-fulfilling nature of social stereotypes. *Journal of Personality and Social Psychology, 35,* 656–666.

Sorenson, K. A., Russell, S. M., Harkness, D. J., & Harvey, J. H. (1993). Account-making, confiding, and coping with the ending of a close relationship. *Journal of Social Behavior and Personality, 8,* 73–86.

Sprecher, S. (1989). The importance to males and females of physical attractiveness, earning potential and expressiveness in initial attraction. *Sex Roles, 21,* 591–607.

Sprecher, S., Felmlee, D., Orbuch. T. L., & Willetts, M. C. (2002). Social networks and change in personal relationships. In A. L. Vangelisti, H. T. Reis, & M. A. Fitzpatrick (Eds.), *Stability and change in relationships* (pp. 257–284). New York: Cambridge University Press.

Sprecher, S., Sullivan, Q., & Hatfield, E. (1994). Mate selection preferences: Gender differences examined in a national sample. *Journal of Personality and Social Psychology, 66,* 1074–1080.

Stangor, C., & McMillan, D. (1992). Memory for expectancy-congruent and expectancy-incongruent information: A review of the social and social developmental literatures. *Psychological Bulletin, 111,* 42–61.

Sternberg, R. J. (1986). A triangular theory of love. *Psychological Review, 93,* 119–135.

Sunnafrank, M. (1983). Attitude similarity and interpersonal attraction in communication processes: In pursuit of an ephemeral influence. *Communication Monographs, 50,* 273–284.

Sunnafrank, M. (1986). Communicative influences on perceived similarity and attraction: An expansion of the interpersonal goals perspective. *Western Journal of Speech Communication, 50,* 158–170.

Sunnafrank, M., & Miller, G. R. (1981). The role of initial conversations in determining attraction to similar and dissimilar strangers. *Human Communication Research, 8,* 16–25.

Surra, C. A. (1985). Courtship types: Variations in interdependence between partners and social networks. *Journal of Personality and Social Psychology, 49,* 357–375.

Surra, C. A., Arizzi, P., & Asmussen, L. A. (1988). The association between reasons for commitment and the development and outcome of marital relationships. *Journal of Social and Personal Relationships, 5,* 47–63.

Surra, C. A., Batchelder, M. L., & Hughes, D. K. (1995). Accounts and the demystification of courtship. In M. A. Fitzpatrick & A. L. Vangelisti (Eds.), *Explaining family interactions* (pp. 112–145). Thousand Oaks, CA: Sage.

Surra, C. A., Gray, C. R., Boettcher, T. M. J., Cottle, N. R., & West, A. R. (2006). From courtship to universal properties: Research on dating and mate selection, 1950 to 2003. In A. L. Vangelisti & D. Perlman (Eds.), *The Cambridge handbook of personal relationships* (pp. 113–130). New York: Cambridge University Press.

Swann, W. B., Jr., Hixon, J. G., & De La Ronde, C. (1992). Embracing the bitter "truth": Negative self concepts and marital commitment. *Psychological Science, 3,* 118–121.

Terman, L. M. (1938). *Psychological factors in marital happiness.* New York: McGraw-Hill.

Thibaut, J. W., & Kelley, H. H. (1959). *The social psychology of groups.* New York: Wiley.

Ting-Toomey, S. (1983). An analysis of verbal communication patterns in high and low marital adjustment groups. *Human Communication Research, 9,* 306–319.

Vaillant, C. O., & Vaillant, G. E. (1993). Is the U curve of marital satisfaction an illusion? A 40 year study of marriage. *Journal of Marriage and the Family, 55,* 230–239.

Vangelisti, A. L., & Daly, J. A. (1997). Gender differences in standards for romantic relationships. *Personal Relationships, 4,* 203–219.

Van Lange, P. A. M., Rusbult, C. E., Drigotas, S. M., Arriaga, X. B., Witcher, B. S., & Cox, C. L. (1997). Willingness to sacrifice in close relationships. *Journal of Personality and Social Psychology, 72,* 1373–1395.

Vanzetti, N. A., Notarius, C. I., & NeeSmith, D. (1992). Specific and generalized expectancies in marital interaction. *Journal of Family Psychology, 6,* 171–183.

Waller, W. (1938). *The family: A dynamic interpretation.* New York: Cordon Press.

Walster, E., Aronson, V., Abrahams, D., & Rottman, L. (1966). Importance of physical attractiveness in dating behavior. *Journal of Personality and Social Psychology, 4,* 508–516.

Walster, E., Walster, G. W., & Berscheid, E. (1978). *Equity: Theory and research.* Boston: Allyn & Bacon.

Weiss, R. L., & Heyman, R. E. (1990). Observation of marital interaction. In F. D. Fincham & T. N. Bradbury (Eds.), *The psychology of marriage: Basic issues and applications* (pp. 87–117). New York: Guilford Press.

White, L. K., Booth, A., & Edwards, J. N. (1986). Children and marital happiness: Why the negative correlation? *Journal of Family Issues, 7,* 131–147.

Whitty, M. (2009). Technology and hurt in close relationships. In A. L. Vangelisti (Ed.), *Feeling hurt in close relationships* (pp. 400–416). New York: Cambridge University Press.

Wong, S., & Goodwin, R. (2009). Experiencing marital satisfaction across three cultures: A qualitative study. *Journal of Social and Personal Relationships, 26,* 1011–1028.

# CHAPTER 19

# Interpersonal Communication and Health Care

*Teresa L. Thompson*

*Jeffrey D. Robinson*

*Dale E. Brashers*

F or many, the study of communication in the context of health care has an importance that goes beyond that of other areas of communication inquiry. Most likely, this is because the outcomes of communication in health care settings are viewed as so significant and so relevant to daily life. When the consequences affect the quality of life or even the absence of life, the importance of communication processes is elevated.

Health communication is also one of the newer areas of study to be represented in the *Handbook of Interpersonal Communication*. The first edition of this volume did not include a chapter on health communication. Research on communication in health care has developed so much in the past 20 years, however, that it has become one of the most rapidly growing and interesting topics in the field. The past couple of decades have found many scholars whose backgrounds are in interpersonal, mass, or organizational communication turning their interests and research to the health care context. Most of this research focuses on communication in established provider–patient dyads, but some focuses on initial interactions.

---

*We were shocked and saddened by the untimely death of our friend, colleague, and coauthor, Dale Brashers. He was a remarkable scholar who made important contributions to our understanding of health communication in the context of persons living with HIV or AIDS. He was also a wonderful human being, and we will miss him greatly.*

Our review begins by discussing the links among communication and various health care processes and moves from there to a more specific discussion of health communication outcomes. A key variable in health communication is uncertainty, so we will talk in some detail about that. This is followed by a short discussion of disclosure processes that are particularly relevant to health communication, and then by more in-depth discussion of discourse issues and, after that, nonverbal communication in health care. A survey of some research on control concerns is followed by analyses of research relating to communication skills/competence and, subsequently, end-of-life discussions. Family communication in health care, communication about medical errors, and medical communication technology are then discussed. We conclude by focusing briefly on some of the theoretical perspectives that are most relevant to interpersonal communication in health care.

## Outcomes

One of the many reasons why interpersonal communication in health care contexts is important is because of the outcomes or effects of that communication. There is a long history of research on this topic, which documents many significant bottom-line consequences. In the second edition of the *Handbook of Interpersonal Communication,* Thompson (1994) included a table summarizing Beckman, Kaplan, and Frankel's (1989) list of health care outcomes, which were potentially important topics of study. These were divided into various types of outcomes that were ordered temporally from the time of a health care interaction to a later point in time. *Process outcomes* are elements that occur during the interaction, such as coparticipation, patient assertiveness or self-advocacy, and provider empathic behaviors. These elements can be thought of as "what happens" in the interaction. *Short-term outcomes* are those that occur immediately after the interaction (and are presumed to be the result of the

interaction), such as patient satisfaction, acquisition of health information, or intention to accept and comply with recommended treatments. *Intermediate outcomes* are more distal and include actual adherence to treatments, reduction in negative psychological effects (e.g., depression or anxiety), and increased self-confidence or self-efficacy. *Long-term outcomes* are the ultimate results or anticipated goals of the interaction. These factors could include symptom reduction, improved quality of life, cure, and/or survival rates. And notice that, even though we have given examples in terms of patient outcomes, a parallel set could be constructed for physicians, including process outcomes such as information seeking, immediate outcomes such as provider satisfaction, intermediate outcomes such as patient retention, and long-term outcomes such as reduction in malpractice suits.

We decided to return to this outcome-focused system again in this edition of the *Handbook* because we believe that it provides an important heuristic for theorizing about health communication. We also believe that perhaps the most important goal of health communication research is to provide a basis for improving health and well-being. One of the major contributions of this research should be highlighting the processes that link various features or patterns of communication with various health-related outcomes. The current research literature clearly indicates that there are connections between communication and health outcomes, but the reasons for these connections and the processes that shape them are not well understood. Health communication researchers should continue to develop theories about the *processes* of communication, delineating the roles of emotion, cognition, motivation, and so on. The results of these studies will help explain *how* and *why* communication is related to health (Goldsmith & Brashers, 2009). Theories that account for outcomes across various contexts may provide the best ways for us to think about how to reach the ultimate goal of improving mental and physical health outcomes. Although this approach is decidedly linear and does not account for the many other factors that will influence health and illness, the connections between these elements provide a starting point for understanding how improved communication can make a difference. Two examples of these possible connections in physician–patient communication are given below (and notice that we could do the same sort of exercise for outcomes of other interpersonal health communication domains, such as social support or self-disclosure):

1.  Low patient participation → Poor comprehension of treatment recommendations → Poor adherence → Decreased survival or poor quality of life

2.  Provider empathic behavior → Patient satisfaction → Less decisional regret → Continued relationships or fewer malpractice suits

Current research provides snapshots of some links in provider–patient communication, and we will review selected research on those associations in this chapter. The key outcomes on which we will focus in this chapter are satisfaction, adherence/compliance/cooperation, health status, malpractice litigation, and quality of life.

The outcome that is studied most frequently in the interpersonal health communication literature is patient satisfaction. It is likely that this variable is studied so often because it is an easier variable to examine than are many other outcomes and also because it is something to which people will immediately react. Most people, when they go to a health care provider, walk out of the interaction with a feeling of satisfaction or a lack thereof. It is something about which people complain and something that affects other outcomes (Duggan & Thompson, 2011). It is frequently difficult for people to accurately judge the quality of the health care that they receive, but it is not difficult to assess whether one is satisfied with the communication accompanying that care. Indeed, research has long shown that most patients are satisfied with health care per se, but they typically are not satisfied with

interpersonal communication during the health care interaction (Duggan & Thompson, 2011). Although few would argue that satisfaction is the most significant product of health communication, it does ultimately affect other, more important outcomes.

The topic of patients' satisfaction has occupied researchers for almost 40 years (e.g., Lebow, 1974). One type of patient satisfaction is that which results from particular visits. Visit satisfaction has been operationalized both as a single, global, perceptual judgment and as a composite of patients' perceptions of physicians' communication/behavior. The importance of visit satisfaction is seductive because numerous researchers have found it to be a valid indicator of both the subjective and the objective quality of physicians' medical care (DiMatteo & Hays, 1980; Roter et al., 1997; Roter, Hall, & Katz, 1987; Weaver, Ow, Walker, & Degenhardt, 1993). Consequently, visit satisfaction has become a determinant of health care organizations' and medical schools' communication-training objectives (Duffy et al., 2004) and is being used to adjust merit increases to physicians' salaries (Grumbach, Osmond, Vranizan, Jaffe, & Bindman, 1998). There are, however, enduring conceptual and measurement problems associated with satisfaction, such as scores being overwhelmingly high (i.e., a ceiling effect), with extremely little variation when broad measures are used (Bertakis & Callahan, 1992; Bertakis, Roter, & Putnam, 1991; Carr-Hill, 1992). Even those patients who are less satisfied are still usually not dissatisfied, according to these measures.

Various aspects of communication have been examined in relation to communication satisfaction. The earliest work on interpersonal health communication was conducted by a pediatrician, Barbara Korsch, and her colleagues (Korsch, Gozzi, & Francis, 1968). This work indicated that mothers typically were dissatisfied with the lack of (a) warmth, (b) consideration for parental concerns, and (c) diagnostic clarity on the part of pediatricians. Doctors' reliance on medical jargon also led to dissatisfaction in mothers. More recent research indicates that little has changed in the

40 years since that early work, in that those communicative behaviors consistently relate to parental and patient satisfaction and increased doctor–patient collaboration (Galil et al., 2006). Although more mothers are satisfied now than was the case in earlier research, those mothers who are dissatisfied are still reacting to the same types of behaviors as did dissatisfied mothers in the past. Korsch et al.'s (1968) finding regarding physicians' "warmth" foreshadowed the importance of the affective/relational dimension of physicians' communication. Patients distinguish between content (sometimes referred to as task/instrumental) and affective/relational dimensions of communication (Street & Wiemann, 1987). A recent meta-analysis of physician–patient communication in cancer care found that affective behavior (e.g., physicians' displays of approval, empathy, concern, worry, reassurance, and optimism) is significantly associated with patients' postvisit satisfaction; furthermore, this study found that affective behavior is significantly more strongly associated with satisfaction than instrumental behavior (e.g., physicians' question asking and counseling/direction giving and both physicians' and patients' information giving).

Of course, perceived competence and credibility on the part of the health care provider also negatively affect satisfaction (Paulsel, McCroskey, & Richmond, 2006). More important than perceived competence and credibility as determinants of satisfaction, however, are higher levels of information giving, positive affect from the care provider, more question asking on the part of the patient, less physician dominance, more nonverbal immediacy, and more psychosocial discussion within the dyad (Ong, Visser, Lammes, & de Haes, 2000; Pieterse, van Dulmen, Beemer, Bensing, & Ausems, 2007). Other communication processes that are associated with lower patient satisfaction include unclear communication about treatment benefits, side effects, and symptom control and patients' feelings of restriction due to physician behaviors (Butow, 2001). Note that these findings are based on more specific measures of satisfaction than the broader

measures mentioned above, which led to ceiling effects. Satisfaction itself has subsequent effects, in that it is positively associated with better health, more positive affect, more favorable patient ratings, and more mutual liking (Hall, Horgan, Stein, & Roter, 2002); however, health also affects satisfaction (Hall, Milburn, Roter, & Daltroy, 1998). It is not surprising that healthier patients are also more satisfied. The relationship is a nonrecursive one.

Beyond the effects of satisfaction that Hall et al. (2002) noted, satisfaction influences patient cooperation with treatment regimens. More satisfied patients are more likely to cooperate with their care providers (Duggan & Thompson, 2011). More important, however, other aspects of communication directly affect treatment compliance. This also means that satisfaction determines health outcomes and quality of life through the moderating impact of treatment adherence. This is based on the assumption that complying with the care provider's treatment suggestions leads to improved health and higher quality of life, which may not always be the case. Such a relationship is dependent on the appropriateness of the treatment recommendations themselves and whether they actually work to alleviate the patient's problem.

Research by Beach, Keruly, and Moore (2006) does show that patients who perceive that their doctors know them as individuals, not just as patients, more consistently cooperate with treatment recommendations and experience more positive health outcomes. Provider communication that is seen by patients as more collaborative also is associated with increased adherence (Schoenthaler et al., 2009). Fox et al. (2009) found that cooperation is improved when physicians demonstrate more warmth, openness, and interest; related research also associates cooperation with more shared decision making with patients (Lakatos, 2009; Schoenthaler et al., 2009) and less provider discord with and control over patients (Lakatos, 2009).

The impact of provider communication on patient adherence recently was summarized in

Zolnierek and DiMatteo's (2009) meta-analysis of 106 studies published from 1948 to 2008. Their results indicate a significant positive correlation between effective physician communication and patient adherence, with the data demonstrating "a 19% higher risk of nonadherence among patients whose physicians communicate poorly" (p. 826). This meta-analysis also confirmed the positive relationship between satisfaction and adherence. Commenting on this study, Roter and Hall (2009) noted that the effect is even stronger when physician behaviors are coded than when patient reports of physician behaviors are used. The latter is more frequently done in research, as it is easier to ask patients to respond to questionnaires than it is to get permission to tape interactions and to then transcribe and code communicative behaviors.

As noted above, communication both directly and indirectly affects health through the moderating influences of satisfaction and cooperation. The direct effects of communication on health are more difficult to examine because of the multitude of variables that also affect health. Although oft-cited research such as that conducted by Kaplan, Greenfield, and Ware (1989a, 1989b) reported that certain aspects of physician–patient communication are associated with "better health" as measured physiologically (blood pressure or blood sugar), behaviorally (functional status), or more subjectively (overall health status), it is likely that many other factors also affect these outcomes. Patient–provider communication that is structured to focus on patients' views positively influences patient quality of life and treatment satisfaction (Priebe et al., 2007), and more positive patient perception of physician communication is related to less decline in health status (Franks et al., 2005). Provider communicative competence also is related to outcomes such as improved glucose control in diabetic patients (Parchman, Flannagan, Ferrer, & Matamoras, 2009).

Although health communication scholars typically find the impact of communication on actual health outcomes of ultimate concern, physicians frequently are more interested in the effect of communication variables on malpractice litigation. This is true only, of course, of those physicians who become aware of this line of research, as most care providers often blame malpractice litigation on patient variables rather than on interactional variables. The research indicates, however, that it is not patients' individual differences that account for much of the variance in suing care providers for malpractice. Nor is it actual medical error that is the key determinant of such litigation. Instead, it is communicative variables that most commonly determine which doctors are sued and which are not (Vukmir, 2004). Vukmir's (2004) analysis of malpractice research from 1976 to 2003 reported that the likelihood of litigation was not related to severity of medical outcomes or any patient profile or sociodemographic variables. It was instead associated with patient–provider interaction and communication variables. We find, again, that satisfaction with communication plays a moderating role on the relationship between communication and litigation (Roter, 2006).

We know, for instance, that families who file medical malpractice claims following prenatal injuries report a lack of satisfaction with physician–patient communication. They also perceive that the physician who treated their family member would not listen or talk openly, attempted to mislead them, or did not warn them about long-term neuro-developmental problems (Hickson, Clayton, Githens, & Sloan, 1992). Mothers whose children have died are more likely to initiate malpractice suits if, in addition, their complaints did not meet with adequate response, they felt they were rushed or ignored, or they did not receive explanation for why certain tests were conducted (Hickson et al., 1994). Similarly, Beckman's (1995) analysis of 45 malpractice suits noted that patients and families who felt abandoned, discounted, or uninformed by their physicians were the most likely to initiate litigation. Those surgeons who are more dominant and communicate less concern paralinguistically are more likely to be sued as well (Ambady et al., 2002). Physician dominance was also identified as a key variable in research reported by Wissow (2004). While it is possible that some physicians who are effective communicators are still sued, the data indicate a substantially lower likelihood of legal action if the patient is satisfied with the provider's communicative attempts.

Malpractice lawyers are aware of these relationships and consistently advise physicians about the relevance of their communicative behaviors to litigation (Nichols, 2003). Hickson and Entman (2008) have also noted that more collaboration among members of the health care team is negatively related to malpractice litigation. And even specialists such as pathologists and radiologists, who did not traditionally have much direct contact with patients and showed little concern with communication variables, have now begun reporting a relationship between diagnostic certainty in communication and malpractice suits (Berlin, 2007; Skoumal, Florell, Bydalck, & Hunter, 1996). This notion of diagnostic certainty leads directly to our next topic—uncertainty in health communication.

## Uncertainty

How people respond to illness-related uncertainty has become a major focus of health communication research over the past two decades. Theories have been constructed to explain how health and illness might create uncertainty and how people might respond to uncertain situations. These various perspectives include uncertainty in illness theory (Mishel, 1988, 1990), problematic integration theory (Babrow, 1992), the theory of motivated information management (Afifi & Morse, 2009; Afifi & Weiner, 2006), and the theory of communication and uncertainty management (Brashers, 2001, 2007). Related theories of information seeking similarly shed light on the processes of uncertainty/information management, including the risk perception attitude framework (Rimal & Turner, 2009). Theories across these domains highlight the complexity of uncertainty management processes and their connection to interpersonal communication.

One area of complexity is the meaning of uncertainty itself, which has important implications for understanding how it is managed (Babrow & Matthias, 2009). Uncertainty has been described for patients (Brashers, Goldsmith, & Hsieh, 2002; Martin, Stone, Scott, & Brashers, 2010) and for their social network members (Donovan-Kicken & Bute, 2008; Stone & Jones, 2009). Babrow, Kasch, and Ford (1998) explicated the concept of uncertainty and provided an insightful analysis into the many ways in which it has been used across research domains. They noted that uncertainty can result from complex situations (e.g., multicausal or contingent pathways to outcomes), properties of information (e.g., clarity, completeness, volume, or consistency), probabilistic thinking (e.g., belief in a single probability or a range of probabilities), the structure of information (e.g., how or whether information is integrated with other information), and lay epistemology (e.g., individual beliefs about the nature of knowledge). Different forms of uncertainty might yield different ways of managing it. As Babrow and Matthias (2009) argued, uncertainty that results from too little information might lead to information seeking, whereas uncertainty that results from information overload might evoke an avoidance or selective-attention strategy.

Interpersonal health communication research has focused on uncertainty management processes in relationships among individuals and their friends, family members, and health care providers. For example, social support has been shown to be one interpersonal communication process that potentially can aid in uncertainty management (Ford, Babrow, & Stohl, 1996; Goldsmith, 2004). People seek and provide social support to enhance information seeking and avoiding, develop skills for coping, reinforce perceptions of relational stability, and encourage perspective shifts, although attempts at support may exacerbate uncertainty at times (Brashers, Neidig, & Goldsmith, 2004). Goldsmith (2009), for example, investigated dyadic coping in couples managing illness (myocardial infarction or cancer) as uncertainty management. She found that the couples dealt with uncertainty about the illness, about their identities, and about the relationship and that communication was both a source of uncertainty as well as a resource for managing it. Partners communicated directly and indirectly to manage uncertainty—raising some topics for discussion while avoiding communication about potentially stressful topics when needed. They revealed that they were sometimes uncertain about when and how to disclose their feelings or to seek social support. They also felt the need to communicate their preferences for uncertainty management—for example, revealing that they are overwhelmed so as to prevent or stop an onslaught of information from well-meaning friends and family.

Provider–patient relationships similarly can both aid in uncertainty management and be the source of uncertainty. Mishel (1988) described "credible authority" (i.e., the trust and confidence one has in health care providers) as an important predictor of uncertainty. Providers can be a valuable source of information and advice and can facilitate decision making; yet providers sometimes do experience and express uncertainty (Brashers, Hsieh, Neidig, & Reynolds, 2006; Gordon, Joos, & Byrne, 2000). Provider uncertainty can influence provider–patient communication, patient uncertainty (Clayton, Dudley, & Musters, 2008), and perhaps patient satisfaction and anxiety (Blanch, Hall, Roter, & Frankel, 2009). In addition, other patterns of behavior might create uncertainty for patients. For example, if health care providers reinforce the stigma attached to an illness, it can diminish the trust that people have in them and in the health care system (Rintamaki, Scott, Kosenko, & Jensen, 2007).

Uncertainty management by patients can be manifested in many ways during the medical encounter, including asking questions (Eggly et al., 2006) or sharing information (Nakash, Dargouth, Oddo, Gao, & Alegría, 2009). In addition, as part of their uncertainty management, patients today more frequently bring information they acquire elsewhere to the health care

encounter, such as from Internet sources (Lewis, Gray, Freres, & Hornik, 2009) or from direct-to-consumer advertising (DeLorme & Huh, 2009). People engaged in uncertainty management also may try to avoid distressing information that might result from health care interactions, including threatening diagnoses (Dawson, Savitsky, & Dunning, 2006).

These two areas of research (social support and provider–patient communication) reveal that uncertainty management can be, and perhaps often is, collaborative or negotiated between individuals. Individuals may have different and potentially conflicting goals, so careful coordination may be critical (Brashers et al., 2002). On the other hand, one party may have a skill set that the other does not (Bevan & Pecchioni, 2008), which may enhance the coping ability of the collective. And it may be that providers' perceptions of the medical competence of their patients may limit their willingness to engage in more participative decision making (Matthias, 2010).

Uncertainty management in interpersonal contexts other than illness (e.g., prevention contexts) also has garnered attention. Questions include what might motivate information seeking among individuals, such as those who are engaged in, planning, or seeking sexual behavior. We might think of conversations preceding sexual encounters as an uncertainty management activity, in which information about the partner's sexual health and sexual history might be the target of information seeking (Afifi & Weiner, 2006). Whether or not people conceal or reveal their sexual history may be a function of the goals they have for the interaction (Caughlin & Vangelisti, 2009), including managing uncertainty.

Another area of growing interest in communication and in the health sciences is screening for disease risk. Because of the probabilistic nature of genetics, screening for disease risk is a compelling area of study for researchers interested in uncertainty. Genetic susceptibility can be difficult for families to discuss (Galvin & Grill, 2009). Moreover, screening can be uncertain, with unexpected results for those being tested

(Frost, Venne, Cunningham, & Gerritsen-McKane, 2004; Skirton & Bylund, 2010). Still, these interactions can provide compelling evidence for the interactional nature of uncertainty management. Dillard and Carson (2005) examined the discourse of screening for cystic fibrosis (also see Dillard, Carson, Bernard, Laxova, & Farrell, 2004). They found that uncertainty management was coordinated between parents and genetic counselors and that parents sometimes would seek information (e.g., ask questions of the clinician) while at other times they preferred to avoid information (e.g., one mother said that she did not want information about cystic fibrosis until she knew whether her baby would be diagnosed with it).

Uncertainty management research within the interpersonal health communication domain has grown considerably over the past decade. Several areas seem particularly interesting and important for further expansion. For example, cultural variations in responses to uncertainty may be a fruitful avenue for these theorists to explore (e.g., Goldsmith, 2001). This could help promote more effective interactions when patients and health care providers are from different cultures and/or use different languages—circumstances in which uncertainty might be substantial and methods for managing it might diverge (e.g., Hsieh, 2006, 2007). It also is important to understand more explicitly the relationships between uncertainty and physical or mental health outcomes (e.g., see Knobloch & Knobloch-Fedders, 2010). As Mishel's (1988) theory of illness uncertainty predicts, unresolved uncertainty is associated with poorer adaptation (e.g., the fear of recurrence of cancer is associated with poorer mental health; see Bellizzi, Latini, Cowan, Duchane, & Carroll 2008). But we know little about how different communicative responses to uncertainty might alleviate or accelerate those effects. As we noted earlier, it is critical for advancing the science of health communication that researchers go beyond the immediate outcomes of interaction to examine how communication processes link to distal health outcomes. This enhanced understanding could lead to improved outcomes through communication-based uncertainty management interventions (Goldsmith & Brashers, 2008; e.g., Mishel et al., 2009). Disclosure or the lack thereof may relate to these uncertainty management interventions.

## Disclosure

The topic of disclosure is a common and important one in the field of interpersonal communication in general, and no less so in health communication. Within the health context, some relevant disclosure issues include patient disclosure to care providers, patient disclosure of health conditions to others, and provider disclosure to patients. The disclosure research is vast, so we will focus our discussion on some representative studies.

The first of these, patient disclosure to care providers, is obviously essential for accurate diagnosis and treatment. A health care provider cannot diagnose accurately without full information (Parrott, 1995). The positive health outcomes associated with effective provider–patient communication are accentuated by higher levels of self-disclosure by patients to providers (Weijts, 1994). Apart from disclosure as it pertains to diagnosis, patients must also give their health care providers private information that may not appear directly relevant to the immediate health problem, such as sexual orientation, sexual history, HIV+ status, other health problems, family history, and so on (Agne, Thompson, & Cusella, 2000).

Some of the issues noted above are stigmatizing, making disclosure much more difficult (Cline, 2011). This is even truer when disclosure is targeted toward friends and family than when one is disclosing to a health care provider. Caughlin et al. (2009) examined multiple message strategies for such disclosure, concluding that different approaches do indeed yield different reactions from others (also see Caughlin et al., 2008).

In addition to looking at disclosure from the patient's point of view, research has examined the predicaments faced by care providers as patients disclose to them (Petronio & Sargent, 2011). Petronio and Sargent (2011) examined these ethical dilemmas through the lens of communication privacy management theory (Petronio, 2002), a perspective with numerous applications to interpersonal issues arising with regard to health care. Also pertaining to provider disclosure, it is important to note that delivery of bad news is a salient topic in the study of interpersonal communication in health care (Maynard, 2003), as are provider disclosure of medical mistakes and end-of-life communication (both discussed below). And truth telling to patients is always an important concern (Thomasma, 1994). Providers in the United States are more willing than they used to be to be honest with patients, although this does not necessarily mean that they are always willing to tell patients everything they know, expect, or believe (Hsieh, 2010). Providers in some cultures disclose far less to their patients (Beisecker & Thompson, 1995). Some Native American cultures perceive that talking about impending terminality will actually bring about death. In some Asian cultures, norms against truth telling still remain. The notion of "full disclosure" is also a problematic one; how fully can one ever disclose, in that how much detail is indeed "full"? Although full disclosure is what the communicators negotiate it to be, it is likely never possible for a care provider to share all possible information with a patient.

Another aspect of disclosure from care providers that is consistently relevant in health care is informed consent (Gillotti, 2003), although the degree to which patients are actually "informed" during this process is variable (Wanzer et al., 2010). Raising questions about the message strategies used when obtaining informed consent, Olufowote (2010) argued that "radiologists—drawing upon interpretive schemes of patients as fearful, ignorant, and easily controlled—discursively and skillfully manipulate IC [informed consent] language and information in engineering patients' decisions" (p. 22). Informed

consent is not at all a straightforward process. Few patients actually understand the material about which they are allegedly "informed," and providers can "inform" in ways that also guide patients in the direction advocated by them (Wanzer et al., 2010). These analyses lead us to a more detailed discussion of the discourse of medical interaction.

## Patient Participation

One longstanding critique of research on physician–patient communication is that it is largely atheoretical (Hall, Roter, & Katz, 1988; Roter, Hall, & Katz, 1988), especially relative to mainstream research on interpersonal communication. However, there are established theories that appear to be good candidates for explaining the relationship between certain physician–patient behaviors and health outcomes, and thus for guiding future research. For one example closer to the heart of interpersonal communication, take self-determination theory (SDT). SDT posits that humans have at least three basic psychological needs, those for autonomy, relatedness, and competence (Ryan & Deci, 2000). SDT argues that these needs are energizing states that, if satisfied, are conducive to well-being and health. If they are not satisfied, they contribute to illness and pathology. SDT is concerned specifically with how these needs are either enabled or constrained by aspects of the social environment, including interactions in health care settings. Of special interest are the needs for autonomy and relatedness. The need for autonomy is concerned with human motivation. SDT predicts that intrinsically motivated health behaviors (i.e., those that have been internalized)—including health communication behaviors, such as question asking (Williams, Frankel, Campbell, & Deci, 2000)—are more strongly associated with positive health outcomes than behaviors that are both extrinsically motivated and noninternalized. SDT suggests that health care providers need to be autonomy-supportive rather than autonomy-controlling. The need for relatedness is concerned with humans' levels of security with, attachment to, and perceived caring of others. SDT predicts that patients' perceptions of their relatedness to (vs. disconnectedness with) their health care providers are associated with patients' positive health outcomes, such as satisfaction with health care providers and adherence to their medical recommendations (the latter being associated with the former). The dimensions of both of these needs—that is, autonomy-supportive versus autonomy-controlling, and relatedness versus disconnectedness—figure in almost all major typologies of the physician–patient relationship, with autonomy-controlling and disconnectedness representing paternalistic care and autonomy-supportive and relatedness representing patient-centered or relationship-centered care (Bensing, 2000; Williams et al., 2000). SDT was not originally developed with reference to physician–patient interaction, and clearly more testing/tailoring is needed. For example, there is evidence that some patients (e.g., older, less well-educated, male patients with severe medical conditions) may prefer something like an autonomy-controlling relationship (Benbassit, 1998).

SDT dovetails with a central form of relationship-centered care known as patient participation (Street & Gordon, 2006; Street & Millay, 2001). There are two broad aspects of patient participation, the first being patients' active participation, or communication that involves patients proactively (i.e., autonomously) initiating topics and independently directing the conversation. For instance, patients can (a) seek, confirm, and clarify information through questions; (b) express worry, anxiety, fear, anger, frustration, or other negative affect; and (c) assert rights, beliefs, interests, needs, desires, and so on. The second, and related, aspect of patient participation is physicians' facilitation, which includes verbal moves that encourage patients to ask questions, discuss their opinions, express their feelings, and otherwise participate in decision making. Physicians'

facilitation simultaneously involves building partnerships/relationships with patients and supporting their autonomy.

Patients are notoriously nonparticipative (i.e., nonautonomous). Robinson (2001) noted that, in physician–patient interaction, physicians usually initiate sequences (primarily questions) and topics and patients respond. Physician-initiated questions are typically restrictive, structured to obtain short, factual answers, and physicians frequently initiate questions during (i.e., in overlap with) patients' attempts to elaborate their answers. Physicians rarely give reasons for asking particular questions or shifting topics, and patients' responses are frequently neutral and nonevaluative.

As predicted by SDT, patient participation benefits health care outcomes. Compared with primary care patients, cancer patients are significantly more participatory (Street, Gordon, Ward, Krupat, & Kravitz, 2005). Patients' participation is associated positively with the amount of information that cancer specialists provide patients (Gordon, Street, Sharf, & Souchek, 2006) and with patients' cancer coping (Ong et al., 1999), psychological adjustment (Butow, Dunn, Tattersall, & Jones, 1995), satisfaction with specialists (Siminoff, Ravdin, Colabianchi, & Saunders Sturm, 2000), comprehension and recall of cancer information (Brown, Butow, Dunn, & Tattersall, 2001), and perceptions of control and responsibility over treatment decisions (Street & Voigt, 1997). Patients' participation is associated negatively with patients' anxiety (Brown et al., 2001) and regret about their cancer treatment decisions (Siminoff et al., 2000). Cancer specialists' verbal moves that facilitate patients' participation are positively associated with patients' participation (Street & Millay, 2001), satisfaction with specialists (Ong et al., 2000), satisfaction with cancer treatment decisions (Siminoff et al., 2000), and sense of being understood by the specialists (Takayama & Yamazaki, 2004). Cancer specialists' verbal moves that facilitate patients' participation are associated negatively with patients' regret about their cancer treatment decisions (Siminoff et al., 2000).

## Coding and Discourse Analysis

Understanding provider–client interaction is critical to explain health care outcomes. The predominant method for studying such interactions is the use of preexisting (vs. inductively generated) coding schemata to divide interaction into component speech acts and place them into mutually exclusive categories, which allows for the generation of frequency counts that can be statistically associated with other variables (for a review, see Heritage & Maynard, 2006). Some of the most productive contemporary examples of such coding schemata are Debra Roter's *Roter Interaction Analysis System* (RIAS; Roter & Larson, 2002), Donald Cegala's *PACE* system (Cegala, Street, & Clinch, 2007), and Richard Street's system for coding patient participation (Street & Millay, 2001). A complete review of the relationship between coded communication variables—such as physician information giving (medical, lifestyle, psychosocial), physician question asking, physician counseling, and patient question asking—and health outcomes is beyond the scope of this chapter (for more information, see Duggan & Thompson, 2011). Suffice it to say that physician–patient communication behaviors have been associated with reduction in patients' pain, anxiety, psychological distress, role limitations, and blood pressure; increases in patients' functional status; and the resolution of patients' symptoms (Stewart, 1995).

There are at least four limitations of traditional coding schemata as they examine the behaviors noted above. First, many coding schemata tend to conflate grammatical form and social action by operationalizing code categories according to the former. For example, common code categories are "physician (or patient) question" and "physician (or patient) information giving" (i.e., a type of declarative). However, a long tradition of discourse- and conversation-analytic research has demonstrated that people produce and understand communication primarily in terms of the social action(s) it accomplishes (Schegloff, 1995). For instance, most coding schemata categorize the physician utterances *You have cancer* and *You don't have cancer* as the same "thing" (i.e., the same code of "physician gives medical information"), but clearly they represent two different classes of action—the giving of bad and good medical news, respectively (Maynard, 2003).

For the first of two concrete examples, examine Extracts 1 and 2 (line 1 in each case). Both of these physician questions are issued at the beginning of acute, primary care visits to solicit patients' medical concerns. Most coding schemata would represent these questions as accomplishing "the same" action; that is, they would simply be coded as a "question" or a "prompt for information." Extract 1 (line 1) provides an example of what Heritage and Robinson (2006) termed a *general inquiry* question, such as the following: *What can I do for you today? How can I help? What are you here for? What brings you in? Tell me what's going on. What's the problem?*

```
Extract 1:   RIB PAIN [P3:25:05]

01 a-> DOC: What can I do for you today.

02          (0.5)

03 b-> PAT: We:ll- (0.4) I fee:l  like (.) there's something

04 b->      wro:ng do:wn underneath here in my rib area. . . .
```

Extract 2 (line 1) provides an example of a different type of question, what Heritage and Robinson (2006) termed a *request for confirmation*:

```
Extract 2: THROAT PAIN [P3:49:09]

01 a-> DOC: Sounds like you're uncomfortable.

02          (.)

03 b1> PAT: Yeah.

04 b2> PAT: My e:ar,=an' my- s- one side=of my throat hurt(s).
```

As Heritage and Robinson (2006) demonstrated, general inquiry questions, such as the one in Extract 1 (i.e., *What can I do for you today?*) encourage patients, *as a first order of business*, to present their chief complaint in their own terms. Furthermore, as designed, these questions tacitly claim that the physician lacks information about the patient's concerns, which *encourages* expanded problem presentation. In contrast, requests for confirmation, such as the one in Extract 2 (i.e., *Sounds like you're uncomfortable*) encourage patients, *as a first order of business*, to produce tokens of either confirmation or disconfirmation, which the patient does: "Yeah" (line 3). Only then do patients present their chief concerns: "My e:ar,=an' my- s- one side=of my throat hurt(s)" (line 4). Requests for confirmation tacitly claim that the physician possesses at least some information about the patient's concerns (e.g., information previously solicited and documented by nurses), which *discourages* expanded problem presentation.

Controlling for patients' age, sex, race, education, and problem type and for practice setting (e.g., urban vs. rural), Heritage and Robinson (2006) found that, compared with requests for confirmation, general inquiry questions resulted in patients producing significantly longer problem presentations (27 vs. 12 seconds) that included significantly more discrete symptoms. Robinson and Heritage (2006) found that, compared with requests for confirmation, when physicians solicited patients' problem presentations with general inquiry questions, patients reported

(immediately after the visit) significantly greater positive evaluations of physicians' listening behavior and positive affective/relational communication (potentially explainable in terms of empowering and/or facilitating patients' self-disclosure). In sum, patients do not orient to the questions or prompts for information in Extracts 1 and 2 as one and the same thing; each has strikingly different consequences for both the process and the outcomes of interaction.

For a second example of how subtle formatting changes of a question can matter for the action it accomplishes, the inclusion of certain *polarity items* in *Yes/No* interrogatives can establish an additional preference for either a *Yes* answer or a *No* answer (for a review, see Heritage, 2010). The polarity items *any* and *at all* (e.g., *Any chest pain? Do you smoke at all?*) are negative-polarity items and embody an additional preference—that is, beyond other sources of preference, including grammar (Sacks, 1987) and socio-medical issues (Heritage, 2010)—for a *No*-type answer. Alternatively, the positive-polarity items *some* and *still* (e.g., *Do you have some chest pain? Are you still taking your medicine?*) embody an additional preference for a *Yes*-type answer. After patients presented an initial medical concern, Heritage, Robinson, Elliot, Beckett, and Wilkes (2007) examined physicians' use of both the negative-polarity question *Are there any other issues you would like to address during the visit today?* and the positive-polarity question *Are there some other issues you would like to address during the visit today?* Compared with control cases, in which the physicians did not ask either question, Heritage et al. demonstrated that the positive-polarity question is significantly more likely to elicit previously unstated patient concerns; this was not the case for the negative-polarity question.

In sum, individual code categories (e.g., "asks questions" or "gives medical information") are blunt instruments and are dulled even further when, as is frequently the case during analysis, the categories are collapsed to meet the requirements of statistical analysis (e.g., when "asks open-ended questions" and "asks closed-ended questions" are collapsed into "asks questions"). However, during continuing medical education training, recommendations to, for example, "provide patients with more medical information" are frequently and arduously resisted by physicians who want to know "exactly what to say" and "exactly where to say it." This is not to deny the vast, and vastly important, findings that have been, and continue to be, produced via traditional coding schemata (for a review, see Heritage & Maynard, 2006). Furthermore, it needs to be recognized that the previously reviewed studies that were informed by the qualitative approach of conversation analysis ultimately coded communication behavior. Over time, there has been a social scientifically pragmatic and symbiotic relationship between discursive methods and traditional coding methods—the former qualitatively bringing validity to the latter, and the latter quantitatively empowering the former.

A second limitation of traditional coding methods is that because code category infrastructures are largely dominated by form (e.g., grammar) at the expense of function (i.e., action), they frequently exclude actions that are meaningful for participants and sometimes misrepresent the actions they are designed to capture (Patton, 1989; Stiles & Putnam, 1995). The discovery of action has been the *forte* of inductive studies of social interaction, such as those guided by discourse and conversation analysis and ethnography (for a review, see Heritage & Maynard, 2006). One exemplary discovery of action is what Heritage and Stivers (1999) termed physicians' "online commentary," or communication that is produced while examining patients and that "describes or evaluates what the physician is seeing, feeling or hearing" (p. 1501). Online commentary affords patients at least some access to physicians' diagnostic reasoning. As such, online commentary has the capacity to foreshadow the existence of medical problems (or lack thereof) and thus, ultimately, whether or not the physician will provide treatment. For an example, see Extract 3 (drawn from Heritage & Stivers, 1999), in which a patient with upper-respiratory concerns is examined:

```
Extract 3:

01      DOC:  An:' we're gonna have you look s:traight ahea:d,=h

02            (0.5)

03      DOC:  J's gonna check yer thyroid right no:w,

04            (9.5) ((physician examines patient))

05 -->  DOC:  .hh That feels normal?

06            (0.8)

07 -->  DOC:  I don't feel any: lymph node: swelling, .hh in yer

08            neck area,

09      DOC:  .hh Now what I'd like ya tuh do I wantchu tuh

10            breathe: with yer mouth open. . . .
```

After instructing the patient to "look s:traight ahea:d" (line 1), explaining the imminent examination procedure—"J's gonna check yer thyroid" (line 3), and examining the patient (line 4), the physician produces online commentary: "That feels normal? . . . I don't feel any: lymph node: swelling, .hh in yer neck area" (lines 5–8). Insofar as lymph node swelling is commonly recognized as a sign of infection (or at least a medical problem), the physician's online commentary contributes to foreshadowing at least "no treatable problem" and at most "no problem at all."

Online commentary can be generally categorized as that which foreshadows "no problem," including utterances such as *That feels normal* (see Extract 3, line 5, above), versus that which foreshadows a "problem," including utterances such as *There's inflammation there* and *That ear looks terrible* (Mangione-Smith, Stivers, Elliott, McDonald, & Heritage, 2003). Heritage and Stivers (1999) argued that online commentary has at least three functions. First, it is used to reassure patients about their health status (especially in the case of the "no problem" online commentary). Second, the "problem" online commentary is used to legitimize patients' decision to seek medical treatment. Third, the "no problem" online commentary is used to tacitly build a case, prior to the physician's official diagnosis that the patient's medical problem is not in need of medical treatment (e.g., antibiotics). Regarding this last function, Heritage, Elliott, Stivers, Richardson, and Mangione-Smith (2010) found that compared with physicians' provision of the "problem" online commentary, the provision of exclusively "no problem" commentary significantly reduced the likelihood of patients subsequently resisting or challenging physicians' treatment recommendations, which is important because such resistance can lead to physicians' inappropriate prescription of antibiotics. Heritage et al. operationalized, and coded for, the "no problem" and "problem" online commentaries, exposing once again the reciprocal relationship between qualitative methods and traditional coding methods, each having advantages and disadvantages.

The nature of online commentary exposes a third limitation of any coding method used for statistical purposes, regardless of how qualitatively informed the code category system is. The mathematical reliability of any coding schema used for statistical purposes depends on the assumption of independence of measures. Coding schemata are necessarily constructed as groupings of mutually exclusive categories that represent single meanings and actions. However, talk (and body deployment) is polysemic; communication behavior simultaneously contains multiple dimensions of meaning. Different types of online commentary have the capacity to serve two or more of the functions noted above (i.e., reassuring, legitimizing, and case building).

A fourth limitation is not of the method of coding, per se, but the fact that many (if not most) physician–patient communication studies that employ coding use the correlation coefficient to make claims about the effect of social actions (i.e., process variables) on outcome variables (e.g., adherence to medical recommendations). Stiles (1989) forcefully argued that the correlation coefficient is inappropriate for these purposes. Stiles's argument does not deal with the fact that inferring causation from correlation is invalid—although he recognizes this as further confounding the correlation tradition—but rather with the assumption that "finding a correlation is necessary if a causal relationship exists, so that null results are taken to deny a process component's importance" (p. 213).

According to Stiles (1989), the correlation coefficient incorrectly assumes that "patient requirements for the processes in question are constant across patients, or at least randomly distributed with respect to the processes" and that doctors' responsiveness to patients' requirements is randomly distributed (p. 213). Regarding the former, not all patients, during any particular visit for any particular medical problem, require the same amount of information giving, explanation giving, question asking, and so on. Furthermore, individual patient requirements may themselves differ in relation to their effect on particular outcome variables (e.g., some patients respond to a surplus of information neutrally, some negatively, and some positively). Thus, Stiles argued that patients frequently differ in terms of their desires, demands, and preferences regarding process variables and that these differences can attenuate, or even reverse, process–outcome correlations regardless of whether or not the process variables actually affect the outcomes.

Problems relating to patient requirements are compounded by those of physician responsiveness. Because communication is both interactive and responsive, it makes sense that physicians will respond in nonrandom ways to differing patient requirements. As Stiles (1989) noted,

> To the degree that physicians are appropriately responsive to patient requirements, process–outcome correlations will be attenuated. In the extreme, if physicians were perfectly responsive, the expected correlation would be zero, insofar as no outcome variance would be accounted for by inadequate levels of the process component. (p. 214)

Stiles (1989) concluded that traditional coding methods need to be much more strongly informed by inductive, qualitative research on the process of medical interaction itself. Additionally, it is always important to keep in mind the interrelationships between verbal and nonverbal communication.

## Nonverbal Communication

Because most medical concerns have at least some social and/or psychological dimensions (Balint, 1957; Engel, 1977; Waitzkin, 1991), physician–patient communication involves a large affective-relational dimension (e.g., warmth, reassurance, trustworthiness). Patients can discriminate between affective-relational and medical-technical dimensions of visit communication (Bensing & Dronkers, 1992) and base their evaluations of physicians' competence on both

dimensions (Cegala, McNeilis, McGee, & Jonas, 1995), which are correlated (Street & Buller, 1987). Importantly, though, *patients prioritize the affective-relational (vs. medical-technical) dimension* (Ben-Sira, 1982; Mechanic & Meyer, 2000). Although physicians' management of the affective-relational dimension of communication is accomplished both verbally and nonverbally (Roter, 1989), nonverbal communication is integral to the expression of affect and attitude generally (Ekman & Friesen, 1969), and specifically to the management of empathy and rapport (for a review, see Harrigan & Rosenthal, 1986). As a result, nonverbal communication significantly influences patients' biological, social, and psychological health outcomes.

### Physician Nonverbal Behaviors

*Physicians' Gaze Orientation.* Gaze orientation is the primary nonverbal behavior that persons use to communicate their immediately current engagement in (or disengagement from) collaborative social action, which includes the majority of talk in interaction. Gaze orientation not only communicates individuals' current attention to, availability for, and participation in others' actions (or lack thereof; Kendon, 1990), but gaze also indicates the intended recipients of individuals' actions (Sacks, Schegloff, & Jefferson, 1974).

Most likely due to methodological confounds, findings regarding the relationship between gaze orientation and visit outcomes are contradictory. One the one hand, Larsen and Smith (1981) found physicians' *direct facial orientation toward patients* to be negatively associated with patients' postvisit satisfaction. Relatedly, Harrigan, Oxman, and Rosenthal (1985) found physicians' increased and decreased *mutual gaze with patients* to be negatively and positively associated with external raters' evaluations of physicians' rapport with patients, respectively. On the other hand, Smith, Polis, and Hadac (1981) demonstrated that physicians' time spent *reading patients' medical records*, which was also physicians' time spent *gazing away from patients*, was negatively associated with patients' postvisit satisfaction and understanding. One explanation for these contradictory findings lies in the analysis of *where physicians are gazing while patients are talking*. For example, Harrigan et al. (1985) also showed that, compared with low-rapport physicians, high-rapport physicians gazed at patients' medical records more often when not gazing at the patients *but were more likely to continue to gaze at patients when the patients were talking*. Harrigan et al. concluded that the explanatory variable might be physicians' "reasonable degree of chart use," one that is yet to be operationalized or investigated. Concerning physicians' outcomes, Giron, Manjon-Arce, Puerto-Barber, Sanchez-Garcia, and Gomez-Beneyto (1998) found physicians' *eye contact while patients spoke* to be positively associated with physicians' psycho-diagnostic abilities. Bensing (1991) noted that physicians' *gaze toward patients* is positively associated with external physician raters' evaluations of the quality of the participant physicians' psychosocial care. In some cases, we may have (a) physicians looking away too much because they don't want to intimidate the patients, (b) looking away too much because they consider themselves of higher status and therefore do not need to look at patients as much as the patients look at them, or (c) looking away too much because they are matching the behavior of a patient who doesn't look at them.

A number of studies have also found associations between physicians' gaze orientation and communication processes. For example, the amount of time that physicians gaze at patients has been positively associated with the amount of psychosocial (vs. somatic) information given by patients (Bensing, Kerrsens, & van der Pasch, 1995; van Dulmen, Verhaak, & Bilo, 1997; Verhaak, 1988). Along similar lines, Duggan and Parrott (2001) demonstrated that physicians' *lack of direct facial orientation toward patients* was negatively associated with patients' self-disclosure (e.g., about life beyond symptoms).

*Physicians' Body Orientation.* Although gaze orientation communicates persons' *immediately current* engagement, the front of a person's body communicates a *frame of dominant orientation,* or a frame of space wherein the person's *long-term and dominant* social actions are most likely to be focused (Kendon, 1990; Schegloff, 1998). The orientation of persons' bodies communicates a locale of their availability or nonavailability for collaborative action, which includes most talk in interaction. When two persons bring each other into (or remove the other from) their frame of dominant orientation, they establish (or dismantle) a *participation framework* (Goodwin, 1981).

Larsen and Smith (1981) showed the amount of time physicians spend with their bodies oriented *toward patients* to be positively associated with patients' postvisit satisfaction and understanding. Street and Buller (1987) found physicians' *indirect* body orientation (i.e., away from patients) to be positively associated with patients' perceptions of physicians' dominance. Harrigan et al. (1985) reported that physicians' body orientation *away from patients* is negatively associated with external raters' evaluations of physicians' rapport with patients. According to Giron et al. (1998), physicians' *open face-to-face posture while patients spoke* was positively associated with physicians' psycho-diagnostic abilities.

*Physicians' Proximity to Patients.* Weinberger, Greene, and Mamlin (1981) demonstrated that physicians' proximity to patients was positively associated with patients' postvisit satisfaction. Smith et al. (1981) found physicians' time spent *within three feet* of patients to be positively associated with patients' postvisit understanding. Larsen and Smith (1981) showed physicians' *forward lean toward* patients and *backward lean away from* patients to be positively and negatively associated with patients' postvisit satisfaction and understanding, respectively. Along similar lines, Harrigan et al. (1985) and Harrigan and Rosenthal (1983) demonstrated that physicians' forward and backward lean are positively and negatively associated with external raters' evaluations of physicians' rapport with patients, respectively.

*Physicians' Head Nodding.* When people gaze at speakers, especially when the speakers are producing multi-unit turns (e.g., when patients produce illness narratives or when physicians explain treatments), the gazers nod their head frequently, which, at a minimum, communicates attention (Schegloff, 1982). According to Hall, Irish, Roter, Ehrlich, and Miller (1994), compared with male physicians, female physicians nodded more overall, and they nodded more to female patients. Harrigan and Rosenthal (1983) discovered that external raters' evaluations of physicians' nodding were positively associated with raters' perceptions of physician rapport. In a later study, however, Harrigan et al. (1985) found no association between nodding and rapport. Nodding is, however, more commonly studied in association with other variables than as an isolated cue, and the findings when nodding is viewed as part of a larger communicative function are more robust. For example, Weinberger et al. (1981) showed that physicians' nonverbal encouragement—operationalized in terms of nodding and gesture—was positively associated with patients' postvisit satisfaction. Duggan and Parrott (2001) showed likewise that physicians' facial reinforcement—operationalized in terms of nodding and facial animation—was positively associated with patients' self disclosure (about more psychosocial, vs. biomedical, issues).

*Physician Smiling.* Although some studies have found no associations regarding physicians' smiling (e.g., Harrigan et al., 1985), Duggan and Parrott (2001) demonstrated that physicians' smiling was positively associated with patients' self-disclosure (about more psychosocial, vs. biomedical, issues). According to Hall et al. (1994), compared with male physicians, female physicians smile more overall, and they smile more at male patients. In a different vein, Rosenblum et al. (1994) showed that medical students' smiling during actual patient interviews (evaluated for grades by clinician supervisors) was positively associated with the students'

final grades, which included evaluations of students' medical-technical skills.

*Touch.* Although some studies have found no associations regarding physicians' touch (e.g., Weinberger et al., 1981), Larsen and Smith (1981) demonstrated that *physicians' touch of patients* was negatively associated with patients' postvisit satisfaction and *patients' touch of physicians* was negatively associated with patients' postvisit understanding. According to Street and Buller (1987)—who distinguished between physicians' *social touch,* used to convey reassurance, friendliness, approval, concern, and/or affection, and physicians' *task touch,* used during physical examination—physicians produced significantly more social touch than patients, and physicians' task touch was positively associated with patients' postvisit evaluations of physicians as being dominant. Harrigan (1985) showed that patients performed more *hand-to-body self-touching* (which is a nonverbal expression of anxiety, among other things) than physicians and that patients self-touched more when answering questions than when being asked questions. Shreve, Harrigan, Kues, and Kagas (1988) revealed that, compared with when patients presented their initial medical agenda (i.e., their officially stated reason for visiting), patients engaged in more hand-to-body self-touching when they presented subsequent agendas that were psychosocially consequential, such as an unwanted pregnancy or unemployment.

*Patients' Physical Appearance.* Many of the established stereotypes associated with physical appearance appear to apply in physician–patient interaction. Nordholm (1980) demonstrated that health professionals rated *attractive* patients, as they appeared in pictures, as more friendly, likely to improve, intelligent, responsible, pleasant, trusting, insightful, approachable, cooperative, and motivated; attractive patients were also rated as less likely to complain and be aggressive. Alternatively, Hadjistavropoulos, Ross, and Von Baeyer (1990) found that medical residents rated *unattractive* (vs. attractive) female patients, as they appeared in pictures, as being less healthy; as experiencing more pain, distress, and negative affect; as needing more help; as getting more physician concern; and as being more likely to continue to have problems without treatment. According to Hooper, Comstock, Goodwin, and Goodwin (1982), patients' physical attractiveness was positively associated with both physicians' use of a patient-centered interviewing style (e.g., open-ended questions) and physicians' *nonverbal attention*, which was operationalized in terms of gaze and body orientation toward patients. Dealing with age as a matter of appearance, Matheson (1997) showed that, irrespective of patients' levels of reported pain and experimental condition of expressed pain (i.e., genuine, masked, posed, or baseline), independent raters, who were able to successfully distinguish the patients' chronological age, rated elderly patients as being in more pain than younger patients.

*Physicians' Tone of Voice.* A number of studies have examined physicians' tone of voice by examining "filtered speech," in which an electronic filter is used to remove high frequencies and mask speech content. Almost 40 years ago, Milmoe, Rosenthal, Blane, Chafetz, and Wolf (1967) found, somewhat counterintuitively, that external raters' evaluations of physicians' filtered speech as sounding "angry" were positively associated with patients seeking treatment for alcohol abuse. Twenty years later, Roter et al. (1987) again demonstrated that ratings of physicians' tonal anger were positively associated with patients' postvisit satisfaction with the affective-relational dimensions of physicians' communication. It is possible that although physicians' tonal negative affect may come across as "punishing," it may simultaneously communicate personal concern, which may motivate patients to adhere to physicians' directives. According to Hall et al. (1994), external raters evaluated male (vs. female) physicians as sounding more friendly, bored, and calm. Roter et al. (1987) also found external

raters' evaluations of physicians as sounding "less bored" to be positively associated with patients' postvisit evaluations of the medical-technical dimensions of physicians' communication. Finally, Harrigan, Gramata, Lucic, and Margolis (1989) showed that physicians' amplitude and speech rate were positively associated with external raters' evaluations of physicians' dominance.

*Physicians' Skill at Encoding and Decoding Emotion.* Based on Rosenthal's early work (Rosenthal, Hall, DiMatteo, and Rogers, 1979), DiMatteo and her colleagues (DiMatteo, Hays, & Prince, 1986; DiMatteo, Taranta, Friedman, & Prince, 1980) analyzed physicians' general capacities to "correctly" express (with their face, body, etc.) basic emotions (e.g., happiness, sadness, anger, and surprise) as well as to "correctly" interpret emotion expressed by others. They referred to these skills as nonverbal encoding and decoding, respectively. DiMatteo et al. (1980, 1986) showed that physicians' encoding and decoding skills were both positively associated with patients' postvisit evaluations of the affective-relational dimensions of physicians' communication (e.g., caring) but not with the medical-technical dimensions (e.g., giving medical explanations). Friedman, DiMatteo, and Taranta (1980) demonstrated that physicians' encoding skills were positively associated with external raters' evaluations of their "likeability." Physicians' encoding skills also have been positively associated with the density of physicians' workloads, which can be a measure of physicians' popularity (DiMatteo et al., 1986). Robbins, Kirmayer, Cathebras, Yaffe, and Dworkind (1994) found physicians' skills at nonverbal decoding to be positively associated with their documentation of psychosocial diagnoses in patients' medical records. Physicians' vocal-encoding errors—that is, encoding negative emotion when instructed to encode positive emotion—have been negatively associated with patients' postvisit evaluations of the socio-emotional dimensions of physicians' communication (DiMatteo et al., 1980; Friedman et al., 1980). Finally, there is evidence that medical students have worse nonverbal decoding skills than undergraduate nonscience (e.g., the liberal arts) majors and that medical students interested in specialized areas of care (e.g., surgery) have worse decoding skills than those interested in primary care (Giannini, Giannini, & Bowman, 2000).

*The Inseparability of Discrete Nonverbal Behaviors.* The social meaning of individual nonverbal behaviors can be altered when they are employed simultaneously. For example, Harrigan and Rosenthal (1983) revealed that external raters' evaluations of physicians' rapport were associated with the interrelationships between physicians' torso position (i.e., forward or backward lean), head nodding, and leg position (i.e., crossed or uncrossed). Later, based on these findings, Harrigan and Rosenthal (1986) asserted,

> Nonverbal units of behavior are difficult, if not impossible, to study in total isolation from one another. While the head is nodding, the trunk may be angled forward or back, the limbs may be still or moving, the face expressionless or animated, and the gaze steady, averted, or darting. Each unit of nonverbal behavior is interrelated in that each is capable of influencing the evaluation of another behavior. (p. 45)

Studies often have not tested for interaction effects between individual nonverbal behaviors. In fact, such interactions are obscured when individual nonverbal behaviors are collapsed into larger order variables, such as immediacy, which has been operationalized in terms of decreased physical proximity and increased touch, forward lean, gaze, and body orientation (Larsen & Smith, 1981). This is not to suggest that the aggregation of individual nonverbal behaviors is completely unprincipled. For instance, researchers often evaluate their coherence with statistical techniques, such as factor analysis. Aggregation is less principled, however, when it is motivated by professional demands involving acceptable levels of interrater reliability or significance, statistical demands involving cell size, and so on. Aggregation does, though, obscure the effects of individual nonverbal behaviors, as well as the fact that individual nonverbal behaviors do interact.

One of the most well-documented interrelationships is between gaze and body orientation (Mehrabian, 1967). Although different segments of the body (e.g., the head, torso, and legs) can be oriented in different directions (Kendon, 1990), there remains a socially understood body segment hierarchy in terms of persons' levels of attention and engagement. Specifically, even though gaze orientation communicates persons' current foci of attention, compared with upper body segments (e.g., the head), lower body segments (e.g., the legs) more strongly communicate a person's frame of dominant orientation (Kendon, 1990). Along these lines, in a nonmedical context, Mehrabian (1967) found the amount of time senders maintained head orientation toward receivers to be positively associated with external raters' evaluations of senders' positive attitudes toward receivers, but only when senders' bodies were also oriented toward receivers. In a medical context, Ruusuvuori (2001) examined patients' responses to physicians' opening questions (e.g., "What can I do for you today?") and showed that when the physicians removed their gaze from the patients (e.g., to read medical records or a computer screen) prior to the patients having completed their responses, the patients tended to produce disfluencies in order to (re)solicit the physicians' gaze. According to Ruusuvuori, the patients produced fewer disfluencies when the physicians' bodies were oriented toward (vs. away from) them. Ruusuvuori's findings suggest that in terms of physicians' levels of engagement with patients (i.e., attention to patients' responses), patients understand the absence or removal of physicians' gaze differently depending on the orientation of physicians' bodies.

## The Inseparability of Nonverbal and Verbal Behavior

Almost 20 years ago, Streeck and Knapp (1992) asserted that "the classification of communicative behavior as either 'verbal' or 'nonverbal' is misleading and obsolete" (p. 3). Although this position is not new, and has continued to be a mantra of research reform (see Chapter 8, by Burgoon, Guerrero, & Manusov, this volume), its implications often go ignored. There are at least two different ways of conceptualizing the relationship between verbal and nonverbal behavior that focus on their co-occurrence in social meaning. The first conceptualization is that verbal and nonverbal behavior constitute two distinct channels of communication that are attended to and processed separately by receivers (e.g., Ekman & Friesen, 1969). Researchers adopt this position tacitly whenever they examine phenomena whose functions entail both verbal and nonverbal communication (e.g., dominance) and yet analyze such phenomena exclusively in terms of one channel, or modality, of meaning.

The second, alternative conceptualization (which this chapter adopts) is that the meaning of communicative events is shaped by, and thus *depends* on, the "context" in which it is situated and that verbal and nonverbal behavior *are each forms of context* (Goodwin, 1995). From this perspective, the relationship between verbal and nonverbal behavior is neither additive nor multiplicative, in the sense that each constitutes a separate yet combinable factor of meaning. Rather, the relationship between a range of communicative modalities (e.g., verbal, nonverbal, artifactual) is holistic and metamorphic (for more on this, see McNeill, Cassell, & McCullough, 1994).

This second conceptualization shifts analytic attention away from the function of individual nonverbal behaviors to how they achieve their social meanings in and through interaction—to

the multimodal array of communication practices that participants rely on to accomplish certain meanings (Sanders, 1987). This conceptualization is in line with Burgoon's (1994) message perspective and Stamp and Knapp's (1990) interaction perspective on the nature of nonverbal communication. Robinson and Stivers (2001) supported the validity of a multimodal perspective in physician–patient interaction specifically. From this multimodal perspective, the first conceptualization (above) is statistically *reified* (rather than supported) by physician–patient studies showing that when controlling for verbal variables, nonverbal variables retain independent significance (e.g., Bensing, 1991).

Historically, in studies of physician–patient communication, nonverbal behavior has been unitized in terms of its duration/frequency (e.g., in seconds) across randomly selected segments or entire visits. In opposition to this, Robinson (2006) argued that physicians' production of nonverbal cues and patients' understandings of such cues cannot be separated from verbal interaction because they are organized by rules associated with designing particular turns of talk. For example, the exact same type of head nod can mean something different when produced at the beginning, middle, or end of a turn of talk, constructing particular social actions (e.g., nonverbal behaviors are produced and understood differently when physicians are delivering good vs. bad diagnostic news) and the sequencing of actions. As just one example of sequencing, there is evidence that physicians' and patients' nonverbal behaviors are nonrandom, patterned, and/or synchronized. For instance, Street and Buller (1987) found that physicians and patients "matched" their gaze orientation, body orientation, and illustrative gestures. Koss and Rosenthal (1997) showed that external raters' evaluations of physician–patient nonverbal synchrony were positively associated with raters' evaluations of physician–patient rapport. Several reviews (Kiesler & Auerbach, 2003; Lepper, Martin, & DiMatteo, 1995) have suggested that the presence or absence of physicians' and patients' nonverbal synchrony (or exchange) plays a role in a variety of participants' affective-relational attributions, such as affiliation and dominance, respectively.

The above correlational research is supported by focused studies of interaction. For example, in line with the observation that gaze communicates a person's current focus of attention, Heath (1988) showed that a physician's gaze shift to a female patient's chest can lead directly to the patient gazing at her own chest. Similarly, Heath (1986) showed that physicians' gaze shifts to objects of discussion, such as X-rays, can lead directly to patients gazing at the same objects.

Heath's (1986) finding shows subtle nonverbal control. Other issues of control are also apparent in health care.

# Control

The notion of interactional/relational control is relevant to all interpersonal communication, but it is relevant in a unique way to communication in the health care context. Unlike many interpersonal contexts, most health care interactions are inherently structured according to control patterns. Typically, the health care provider is "in control" of the interaction, and patients or family members have to struggle to make themselves heard and to share in that control. The relationship traditionally has been a paternalistic one. Although many providers now advocate shared control, the actions of most of them do not actually result in such sharing (Gwyn & Elwyn, 1999). Providers more commonly subtly control the interactions.

Several investigators have studied interactional control in health care through the application of relational coding systems, although the results have not been completely consistent. O'Hair (1989) reported that both physicians and patients attempted relational control maneuvers but patients were not always successful. McNeilis and Thompson (1998) also found much provider dominance. Von Friederichs-Fitzwater,

Callahan, Flynn, and Williams (1991), however, reported frequent examples of neutralized symmetry, in which patients respond to physicians' one-up statements with one-across statements rather than accepting physician dominance with a one-down response. Cecil (1998) found physicians showing more control submission (responding to patients' one-up statements with a one-down reply) and patients demonstrating greater control dominance (by initiating one-up statements) than had been the case in earlier research. Cecil's results also showed more patient compliance with less physician control assertiveness and less patient control submission.

More recently, research that illuminates issues of control has focused on patient-centered or relationship-centered care. These perspectives contend that health care should not be solely directed or controlled by the provider (the traditional biomedical, paternalistic model). It should instead be based on shared power/control. The concept of relationship-centered care is consistent with relational communication literature that looks at medical interactions as contexts of mutual influence and acknowledges that relationship development, multiple goals, and multiple identities influence the communication process and outcomes (Duggan & Thompson, 2011). Research focusing on this perspective looks at interruption sequences and whether interactants return to the topic under discussion once they have been interrupted. They typically do not. Providers also typically redirect communication even if they do not explicitly interrupt patients (Marvel, Epstein, Flowers, & Beckman, 1999). Shared control has positive outcomes, however, in that we know that asking about patients' needs, perspectives, and expectations; attending to the psychosocial context; and encouraging patient involvement in decisions predict lower expenditures for diagnostic tests, hospitalization, and ambulatory care (Epstein et al., 2005). De Haes and Bensing (2009) also suggested a shared approach to communication goals, focusing on building relationships, collaborative information gathering and provision, collective decision making, joint construction of treatment, and responding to emotions.

Beyond interactional issues, then, shared or collaborative decision making is an important control concern. The notion of a "shared mind" (Epstein & Peters, 2009) helps describe the desired state of consistent understanding of the patient's state of health on the part of both patient and provider, as well as accurate understanding of each other's perspectives and agreement on treatment options. The ideal goal of shared decision making is this statement of a shared mind. Requirements for this include communication that reflects patient involvement in consultation and the decision-making process and physician responsiveness when the patient asks questions, states preferences, expresses concerns, conveys understandings, and offers opinions (Politi & Street, 2011; Street & Millay, 2001). Shared decision making also "requires communication that is about exploring and clarifying and tolerating uncertainty about the known and unknown aspects of the decision" (Politi & Street, 2011, p. 402). Additionally, Politi and Street (2011) discuss the relevance of provider understanding of the patient's values, beliefs, and desires for collaborative decision making. They also note the role of uncertainty in the decision-making process, even though explicit consideration of uncertainty rarely occurs (Braddock, Edwards, Hasenberg, Laidley, & Levinson, 1999; Politi, Han, & Col, 2007). Physician discomfort with uncertainty is associated with more paternalistic approaches to care provision (Légaré, O'Connor, Graham, Wells, & Tremblay, 2006). By contrast, those physicians who acknowledge uncertainty more openly tend to have patients who are more satisfied (Gordon et al., 2000). These interactions also are characterized by more rapport, open information sharing, positive talk, and partnership-building statements (Gordon et al., 2000), thus showing the

interrelationships between collaboration and openness about uncertainty.

## Skills

Patient-centered consulting skills are crucial for the delivery of effective primary care (Mead & Bower, 2002). Research on communication skills, however, focuses on issues that are broader than just patient-centeredness. Some research in this area emphasizes the skills that are necessary for effective interaction and care and the outcomes of those skills; other work focuses on training to develop those skills.

Focusing on the medical interview, Barrier, Li, and Jensen (2003) identified three skill sets that, they argued, are essential for effective interviewing: (1) information gathering, (2) relationship building, and (3) patient education. Other work has differentiated between skills-based and "mindful 'being in relation'"–based approaches to provider–patient interaction, arguing that while they are conceptually distinct, both perspectives are useful (Zoppi & Epstein, 2002). Complications arise because of the vast differences among experts on communication skills regarding teachable moments appropriate for the improvement of the following skills: (a) rapport building, (b) agenda setting, (c) information management, (d) active listening for the patient's perspective, (e) responding to emotion, and (f) skill in reaching a common ground (Buyck & Lang, 2002). The variations in assessments among the experts, all of whom teach communication skills to medical students, were not only statistically significant, they were staggering. Similarly, Arnold et al. (2009) noted significant disparity in the terminology used by experts to talk about skills. These differences undoubtedly make evaluation of skills and subsequent training rather difficult.

Work on skill development and training generally does indicate that skills can be improved to some extent through workshops and other training programs. Sheldon (2005) reviewed 21 training programs and concluded that 19 of them led to improvement in communication skills, although improvement was not long lasting across all variables. Longer programs with consolidation workshops were the most effective. A systematic meta-analysis of research on training programs conducted by Smith et al. (2007) provides evidence that student ability to establish rapport with and gather information from patients improved after training and that workshops including small-group discussions and structured feedback were particularly efficacious. Modeling of the behavior of attending physicians is rarely effectively used for communication skills training (Burack, Irby, Carline, Root, & Larson, 1999), but it can be effective when done well (Janicik, Kalet, Schwartz, Zabar, & Lipkin, 2007). Chant, Jenkinson, Randle, Russell, and Webb (2002) reported that few of the training programs they reviewed were adequately evaluated and that methodological deficiencies were evident in most of those that did include evaluation components. Standardized patients have been effectively used, however, to assess provider interaction skills (van Zanten, Boulet, & McKinley, 2007).

The most thorough discussion of training is provided in the second edition of Kurtz, Silverman, and Draper's (2005) *Teaching and Learning Communication Skills in Medicine.* This volume, directed at those who train practitioners, is a how-to manual on the topic. It must be noted, however, as the authors emphasize, that the book does not focus on which skills should be taught but on how to teach those skills. Thus, the discrepancies noted above in expert assessment of necessary skills again become problematic. The content of training, however, is thoroughly assessed on theoretical, operational, and practical levels by Cegala and Lenzmeier-Broz (2002), and their article is a helpful resource for both scholars and trainers. Note also that it is likely that continued support for a physician once he or she returns to the office or hospital may well lead to higher success of training efforts.

As is evident from the above discussion, little research has focused on the communication skills of the patient in the medical encounter. For exceptions to this, see the work of Cegala, Coleman, and Turner (1998), Cegala, McClure, Marinelli, and Post (2000), Cegala, McGee, and McNeilis (1996), Eaton and Tinsley (1999), McGee (1997), and McGee and Cegala (1998). This work is most thoroughly summarized by Cegala (2003). McGee (1997) reported that patients who are trained in communication skills engage in significantly more information seeking and comprehension checking and recall more treatment information, and McGee and Cegala (1998) noted that trained patients sought more information through the use of both direct and indirect questions and acquired more helpful information. Cegala et al. (2000) developed and tested a patient-training program, finding that trained patients demonstrated more effective and efficient information seeking, provided physicians with more detailed information about their medical condition, and used more summarizing statements to verify information. Dyads containing a trained patient also showed more patient-centered communication than did other dyads (see also Cegala, 2003).

It is evident that training patients in effective communication also positively affects provider communication (Duggan & Thompson, 2011). Other effective patient training programs have been reported by Breslin, Mullan, and Montori (2008) and Belkora, Edlow, and Aviv (2008); both of these focus on uncertainty reduction as key variables.

As we talk about communication skills and training, it is particularly relevant to turn our attention to the health communication interactions that are especially problematic—namely, end-of-life discussions.

## End-of-Life Discussions

The importance of end-of-life discussions cannot be overemphasized, but they are rarely given an adequate examination or even enacted. This is an interesting conundrum—one of the most important things about which patients and care providers *should* talk is also the one that is most frequently avoided. This is true in many, but not all, cultures. There are some cultures in which death is seen as a natural state and discussion about it is seen as normative. There are other cultures, including the dominant U.S. culture, that are death-avoidant. We attempt to do everything we can to evade death; this includes avoiding discussion of it and fearing the aging process (Callahan, 2009; Glaser & Strauss, 1965; Ragan & Goldsmith, 2008). Talking about death makes it real and prevents us from evading it. There are some Native American cultures that take this even further, believing that the act of mentioning death may bring it on.

Regardless of the culture in which one has been raised, end-of-life discussion is going to be necessary at times. When death happens suddenly, the dying/deceased person and the survivors need not converse about death in great detail. It is still evident in such circumstances that euphemisms are used. We talk about people "passing away" or "moving on" rather than using terms such as *death* or *dead*. And most individuals feel uncomfortable talking with the loved one of an individual who has died; we claim that we "don't know what to say," which implies the fallacious notion that there *is* something that one can say that can make grief go away. We know that this is not true, although it is true that some of the things that we say make the bereaved feel worse.

It is when an individual is facing death that communication becomes particularly difficult, however. Although many cultures have evolved in recent decades toward more disclosure of impending terminality and a grim prognosis than used to be the case, such communication is still challenging. Friends and family members pretend that they do not know that the person is dying, because talking about it makes them too uncomfortable. The literature is replete with examples of terminally ill individuals being avoided by care providers, family, and friends and communication about terminality being

even more strongly avoided. Individuals who are terminal and want to talk about their feelings and/or fears or who want to talk about their plans for end-of-life frequently find it difficult to get others to hold such conversations with them. Sometimes family members and friends "protect" loved ones from such communication, regardless of whether this is desired by the terminally ill person. There is a pretense of normalcy and many layers of denial (Goldsmith, Wittenberg-Lyles, Ragan, & Nussbaum, 2011). These conversations have inherent within them the dialectic tension between hope and realistic expectations (Goldsmith et al., 2011). As Boyle, Miller, and Forbes-Thompson (2005) put it, "Even though good communication among clinicians, patients, and family members is identified as the most important factor in end-of-life care in ICUs, it is the least accomplished" (p. 302). Dialectical tensions in end-of-life communication have also been outlined in Miller and Knapp (1986).

Even research in this area is not embraced, perhaps because researchers themselves are uncomfortable with the topic and perhaps because it is difficult to "study" such challenging encounters. Those researchers who do undertake research in this area typically find that the bereaved welcome the opportunity to talk about the passing of their loved one. End-of-life discussions prior to death, however, are less accessible for study. This is true whether these discussions take place between the terminally ill individual and friends/family members or with care providers. Although we commonly think of end-of-life discussion as being most relevant in old age, death can actually strike at any age (Chatelle, 2008). Palliative care becomes relevant when there is any chronic health problem; hospice care is a concern only during what is expected to be the last six months of life (Goldsmith et al., 2011).

Family members typically become more involved in the health care process and health care decisions as an individual faces serious illness and impending terminality (Ragan, Wittenberg-Lyles, Goldsmith, & Sanchez-Reilly, 2008). This leads the family to share in the anxiety and depression that may be experienced by the patient (Ragan et al., 2008). The presence of the family, however, can also serve to raise relevant questions, provide more information, and ultimately increase adherence and subsequent health outcomes (Pecchioni & Keeley, 2011). Lack of family communication about impending terminality, however, may move the family into a state of crisis (Goldsmith et al., 2011; Lau, Downing, Wesperance, Shaw, & Kuziemsky, 2006; Wittenberg-Lyles, Goldsmith, Ragan, & Sanchez-Reilly, 2010), making decision making much more difficult (Holst, Lundren, Olsen, & Ishøy, 2009; Matsuyama, Reddy, & Smith, 2006). This also causes families to overestimate the likelihood of recovery (Goldsmith et al., in press).

This overestimation of the likelihood of recovery coupled with the lack of communication about end-of-life issues that typically occurs in most families makes the move from aggressive treatment to palliative and hospice care much more challenging (Goldsmith et al., 2011; Norton, Tilden, Tolle, Nelson, & Eggman, 2003). Compounding this difficulty is the lack of health literacy in most families (Cameron, Baker, & Wolf, 2011; Goldsmith et al., 2011), making it even more problematic for them to estimate the odds of their loved one's recovery. Family meetings are seen as central to end-of-life issues, but these meetings do not always include the patient (Hickman, 2002).

Despite the lack of communication about impending terminality consistently documented in the literature, the research also shows a strong desire on the part of both patients and family members for truthful disclosure from their primary care providers (Back et al., 2009). Most of us do not desire futile end-of-life treatment and want to be able to communicate our wishes about this (Goldsmith et al., 2011). Concomitantly, however, most of us know little about medical treatment options at the end of life and have not had these discussions with our providers or loved ones (Scharader, Nelson, & Eidsness, 2009). Our providers have not received adequate training about the initiation of such discussions, and

there is great variance among them (Larochelle, Rodriguez, Arnold, & Baranato, 2009). Care providers typically realize that they are not good at such tasks (Wittenberg-Lyles et al., 2010). Those who feel more competent about initiating end-of-life discussions do indeed do so more frequently (Jackson et al., 2008). Other physicians prefer to extend futile and inappropriate treatment for dying patients rather than talk to them about their impending death (Back, Arnold, Tulsky, Baile, & Fryer-Edwards, 2003). The training that is provided to most care givers is formulaic and scripted (Wittenberg-Lyles, Goldsmith, Sanchez-Reilly, & Ragan, 2008) and focuses only on increasing providers' confidence during such communication (Gueguen, Bylund, Brown, Levin, & Kissane, 2009).

Most care providers do not feel comfortable during the family meetings that are necessary at the end of life (Fineberg, 2005), as these meetings require a rather specific set of skills (Hudson, Quinn, O'Hanlon, & Aranda, 2008). Conversations related to end-of-life issues should focus on topics such as withdrawal of artificial nutrition or breathing equipment, nursing home placement, and hospice care (Goldsmith et al., 2011). Family meetings should focus on these topics, as well as making it clear that concerns need now to turn from cure to comfort. These meetings frequently require education of and mediation among family members (Wittenberg-Lyles et al., 2010). Wittenberg-Lyles et al.'s (2010) insightful discussion of family meetings makes it clear that many of the end-of-life practices advocated by care providers are instead strategically ambiguous and not in the best interests of the patient or the family. Complete avoidance of such family meetings makes misunderstandings even more likely (Holst et al., 2009) and leads to higher levels of guilt and dissatisfaction in family members (Goold, Williams, & Arnold, 2000; Hickman, 2002; Thompson, Menec, Chochinov, & McClement, 2008). Song's (2004) systematic review of the relevant literature identified no negative affective reactions to end-of-life discussion but reported a variety of positive outcomes.

The reluctance of care providers to initiate end-of-life discussions is not surprising considering the lack of control that they experience during such interactions compared with the level of control to which they are accustomed (Friedrichsen, Lipkin, & Hall, 2006). Care providers also lack knowledge about palliative care (Fadul et al., 2007; Ferrell, 2005; Johnson, Girgis, Paul, & Currow, 2008). The lack of health literacy in patients and families combined with providers' lack of knowledge of the power, mechanics, and role of palliative care most commonly leads to avoidance of end-of-life discussion and ineffective interaction when such discussions do take place. Not only do physicians avoid end-of-life discussions, but they frequently do not even read patients' advance directives (Westphal & McKee, 2009). Nurses are more likely to familiarize themselves with these directives. Physicians do indicate that they comply with family and patient wishes when they are familiar with them, but the lack of reading of advanced directives means that the burden of further communication about desires is put on the patient or family at a time that is already very difficult for them. One wonders about the purpose of advance directives if they are rarely read.

It is no surprise, then, that patients and families are typically dissatisfied with end-of-life communication (Dys, Shugarman, Lorenz, Mularski, & Lind, 2008). Hancock et al.'s (2007) meta-analysis of research on provider and patient perceptions of end-of-life communication indicated vast discrepancies between the interactants' perceptions, with patients perceiving that they had received much less information than the providers believed had been communicated. Patients also understood much less than the providers reported they had. Providers underestimated patient desires for full disclosure of the diagnosis and overestimated patients' fear of such disclosure. The fact that most patients express a desire to avoid futile treatment and be allowed to die comfortably but few are actually allowed to do so also helps explain the high levels of dissatisfaction

with end-of-life communication and care (Lamont, 2005; Weiner & Cole, 2004).

## Families

Implicit in several of the topics that we have already discussed in this chapter is the relevance of both communication among family members and communication between care providers and family members to the health care delivery process. Beyond those concerns that have been addressed elsewhere in this chapter and this volume, a key notion that must be considered is the importance of the family to health outcomes and health care (Pecchioni & Keeley, 2011). Although much health communication research focuses on formal provider–patient relationships, the majority of health care provided to individuals over the life span actually comes from family members. Additionally, the ways in which families talk about health-related issues have numerous important effects on attitudes and behaviors (Parrott, 2009), affecting both physical and mental health (Pecchioni, Thompson, & Anderson, 2006). We learn what is healthy and unhealthy from family members, while simultaneously learning what topics should and should not be discussed (Ormondroyd et al., 2008). Not discussing topics such as sexuality and sexual health can have serious consequences. Other key learning processes associated with family communication include teen risk behaviors, nutrition decisions, and lifestyle choices that affect health (Pecchioni et al., 2006). Family communication also plays a key role in social support, sensemaking, and coping (see Chapter 10, by MacGeorge, Feng, & Burleson, this volume).

The interdependence of family members means that their health behaviors and outcomes are also interrelated. When a health crisis affects one family member, others are also affected, as are family rules and levels of homeostasis (Pecchioni & Keeley, 2011). Scholars have also described the phenomenon of "compathy"—the contagion of physical distress among family members (Morse & Mitchum, 1997). As Pecchioni and Keeley (2011) describe it, "The more realistic picture of health communication interactions is that most are three-way conversations between the patient, health provider, and family member(s)" (p. 373), rather than the traditional, dyadic conceptualization of provider–patient interaction. Although such a perspective reminds researchers of the need to include family members in their work on health communication, other writing urges us to remember the role of the care provider in the family communication process (Majerovitz, Mollot, & Rudder, 2009).

Additionally, negative family communication patterns are likely to have health outcomes (Olson, 1993; Olson, Sprenkle, & Russell, 1979). How families react to crises also has serious health consequences (Pecchioni & Keeley, in press). Family communication is replete with dialectical tensions that are negotiated through communication (Baxter & Braithwaite, 2006, 2008; Baxter, Braithwaite, Golish, & Olson, 2002) and that influence health-related behaviors. "Communication about health issues is rarely a one-time discussion; often health dialogues are a stream of discussions until a clear meaning is achieved" (Pecchioni & Keeley, 2011, p. 368).

In addition to these dialectical tensions, nurturing and control are central concerns related to family health communication (Le Poire, 2006). Le Poire (2006) discusses their interrelationships in her work on inconsistent nurturing as control. Examining the paradoxical nature of many family behaviors, Le Poire's theory illuminates health problems such as drug and alcohol abuse, eating disorders, and depression (Duggan, Le Poire, Prescott, & Baham, 2009). Similarly, Floyd's work on the communication of affection indicates the interrelationships between numerous physical and mental health consequences and affectionate communication among family members (Floyd, 2001, 2006a, 2006b; Floyd, Hesse, & Haynes, 2007; Floyd,

Mikkelson, et al., 2007; see also Chapter 4, by Floyd & Affifi, this volume).

Decisions about organ donation, an important health outcome, are made through communication with family members (Smith, Lindsey, Kopfman, Yoo, & Morrison, 2008; Thompson, Robinson, & Kenny, 2003). Family communication has an influence on how genetically transmitted health disorders affect others, as well. Those families that do not talk about such issues have much more difficulty coping with them (Bauer, 2011). Also, any family member who is providing care for another who is ill is likely to experience high levels of stress (Roscoe, Corsentino, Watkins, McCall, & Sanchez-Ramos, 2009). These are, then, just a few examples of the interrelationships between family communication and health/health care delivery. Another issue with which both patients and families must cope, however, is medical errors.

## Disclosure of Medical Errors

One of the areas of interpersonal communication in health care that has received increasing attention in recent years is disclosure of medical errors/mistakes. Disclosure, of course, is an important and long-studied communicative process. It is only in recent years, however, that communication researchers and health care providers have turned their attention to writing and research on disclosure of medical errors per se. The salience of this topic should be obvious, as few question the well-documented seriousness of medical errors (Matlow, Stevens, Harrison, & Laxer, 2006) and the large number of patients affected by them. As recently as 2001, however, researchers and practitioners were "discussing" the wisdom of full disclosure of medical errors (see Hébert, Levin, & Robertson, 2001). The conclusion of these discussions was generally in support of full disclosure.

The data do indicate that full disclosure of errors discourages rather than encourages litigation and reduces the average settlement values (Pelt & Faldmo, 2008), and provides positive consequences for the well-being of physicians as well as their relationships with patients (Calvert & Hollander-Rodriguez, 2008). Nonetheless, the litigious nature of U.S. society likely leads people in positions of responsibility to feel great consternation at having to admit mistakes. Although there are cultural differences in expectations regarding disclosure of medical errors, the general expectation as demonstrated in the research is in favor of disclosure (Berlinger & Wu, 2005). Disclosure is advocated even when the mistakes affect large numbers of patients—a context in which disclosure is particularly difficult (Chafe, Levinson, & Sullivan, 2009). Publishing reports of medical errors in publicly available journals has also been advocated to allow other researchers to learn from these errors (Murphy, Stee, McEvoy, & Oshiro, 2007).

One important review of this line of research was offered by Mazor, Simon, and Gurwitz (2004), which confirmed that both patients and the public are in favor of disclosure. Physicians report support for it but do not always actually disclose medical errors. Mazor et al. found that little research has examined the disclosure process itself, its consequences, and the relationship between disclosure practices and its consequences.

A second review was published by Kaldjian, Jones, and Rosenthal (2006), who examined 881 articles listed in MEDLINE from 1975 to 2004. They identified 35 factors believed to facilitate disclosure of medical errors, including accountability, honesty, and restitution, and 41 factors believed to impede it, including professional repercussions, legal liability, and blame. The three most common goals of disclosure identified in the research were improvement of patient safety, enhancement of learning, and informing patients. Facilitating factors were more commonly discussed when the goal of disclosure was informing patients. If facilitating factors can be improved, and impeding factors removed, disclosure of medical errors

should be more likely. Increased disclosure, it is argued, should help decrease future errors. Building on this work, Kaldjian, Jones, Rosenthal, Tripp-Reimer, and Hillis (2006) developed an empirical taxonomy of facilitating and impeding factors.

Increased understanding of medical errors and the disclosure process has also been provided by Carmack's (2010) narrative analysis of physicians' stories of mistakes. Carmack's work shows how such stories enable physicians to *bear witness* to errors. The stories show the complexity of the processes that lead to medical errors and the role that communication plays in leading to mistakes. Rowe (2004) also provides a narrative analysis of medical mistakes and doctors' responses to them.

Based on the obvious need for disclosure and the accompanying data indicating the lack of skill health care providers demonstrate in disclosing, Hannawa (2009) offered a model of physician disclosure. She argues that the process begins with a cost–benefit analysis, followed by an assessment of informational and relational disclosure competence if the decision to disclose has been reached. Competence mediates the impact of disclosure on physician defensiveness and both long- and short-term outcomes. Organizational climate also plays a mediating role.

Finally, it should be noted that it is not only physicians who make medical errors. Using a qualitative method, Noland and Rickles (2009) analyzed the socialization of pharmacy students with regard to error avoidance and communication. Although the students reported receiving training on these issues, the study found inconsistent and incomplete socialization to the interrelationships between communication and medication mistakes. Similarly, Crigger (2004) discussed disclosure of nursing errors, recommending a three-step process: disclosure, apology, and making amends.

Just as disclosure of medical errors is a relatively new area of study within health communication, so, too, is the study of new communication technologies. We turn now to this last topic before we conclude the chapter.

## Health Applications of Communication Technologies

Communication technologies have influenced how people seek, handle, and use health information, through applications such as telemedicine, e-mail, electronic and personal health records, Internet health websites, and online support groups. These technologies affect interpersonal communication by providing new ways of sharing information about health and illness, providing and receiving social support, and communicating and negotiating with health care providers.

Telemedicine is defined broadly as the use of communication technologies in the provision of health care (Turner, 2003). It can range from distance instruction applications in medical education to mediated contexts for provider–patient interactions. Probably the most commonly used description of telemedicine is as a system that connects participants in the health care encounter who are in different locations. One such system is closed circuit television, in which both parties in the interaction are visible to each other through the use of a camera and a monitor in each location; this is often achieved today through Internet connections. This version of telemedicine has been used extensively in specialties in which visualization and/or verbalization are key to diagnosis, including dermatology, radiology, and psychiatry (Bashshur & Shannon, 2009). These consultations often are synchronous (except perhaps for radiological applications such as X-rays or scans) and may be facilitated by having a health care professional in the room with the patient. These telemedicine consultations provide access to providers for those who live in remote, rural, or otherwise underserved areas (Matusitz & Breen, 2007).

Telemedicine systems also have been developed with asynchronous applications. In a study

of dermatology consultations for acne, for example, patients engaged in follow-up visits by downloading pictures of their faces with a written update on their condition to a secured website (Watson, Bergman, Williams, & Kvedar, 2010). Those data subsequently were analyzed by a dermatologist, and recommendations or treatment modifications were communicated to the patient. Results of the study showed that the reduction in inflammatory lesion (i.e., acne) count, as judged by coders, was similar for onsite versus online consultations and that the time spent on diagnosis and communicating recommendations by the dermatologists across conditions was not statistically different. The time savings for the patients using online follow-up, however, were significant because they did not have to travel to the dermatologist's office. In addition to routine follow-up situations, telemedicine systems can allow health care providers to monitor patients' data and intervene in medically urgent (e.g., potentially life threatening) situations (Izquierdo et al., 2007).

E-mail use between health care providers and patients also has been a growing focus of health communication research. E-mail use is complicated because of concerns such as professional liability, provider reimbursement, and confidentiality (Masters, 2008). The complexity of these issues led the American Medical Association to develop guidelines for e-mail use by physicians (e.g., obtaining informed consent before using e-mail to communicate with a patient, never using e-mail for emergent situations, establishing an appropriate turnaround time for responses).

There is evidence that patients want to use e-mail to communicate with their physicians, especially when an office visit is deemed unnecessary (e.g., Singh, Fox, Peterson, Shethia, & Street, 2009). There is also evidence that physicians are adopting e-mail use and finding it beneficial in their practice (Patt, Houston, Jenckes, Sands, & Ford, 2003). The reasons that physicians give for using e-mail to talk with patients include saving time and delivering better care (Houston, Sands, Nash, & Ford, 2003). In one study, the most common types of e-mail messages from patients to physicians were information updates, requests for prescription renewals, health questions, questions about test results, and requests for referrals or appointments (White, Moyer, Stern, & Katz, 2004). E-mail messages can even contain socio-emotional content. Roter, Larson, Sands, Ford, and Houston (2008) found that the majority of e-mail message content was informational but that messages from both patients and providers also contained a substantial amount of emotionally supportive and partnership-building content.

Electronic medical records (EMR) and personal health records (PHR) are among the newest information management innovations in health care delivery. EMR allow health care organizations to compile and share information about a patient across different providers, which is intended to facilitate better health care interactions through faster and more accurate record keeping (Anderson & Kay, 2009). PHR provide patients with a mechanism to collect, store, and share their own health data. For example, MyCareTeam is a PHR system designed for patients with diabetes that allows "the opportunity to log in and find education, provides a portal for logging blood glucose (BG) readings, and creates a space where patients can discuss their condition with a HCP and exchange information related to diabetes management" (Levine, Turner, Robinson, Angelus, & Hu, 2009, p. 462). MyHealtheVet is a similar system maintained by the Veteran's Administration Hospitals (see www .myhealth.va.gov/), which provides access to a database of the patient's health profile, an electronic prescription refill service, an information-forwarding service for second opinions, access to lab results, mechanisms for uploading home monitoring data, and so on (Finn & Bria, 2009). These PHR systems help people integrate "personal, professional, and health-related information" and use "integrated information to make health-related decisions" (Pratt, Unruh, Civan, & Skeels, 2006, p. 53).

Information that people gather from the Internet is another area of interest for interpersonal communication researchers. That information has the potential to become a part of the dialogue in provider–patient interactions (e.g., patients may come with a candidate diagnosis or treatments in mind). Health information increasingly is acquired on the Internet, and people take that information to their doctors to discuss possible diagnoses and treatment plans (Lewis et al., 2009). Research also shows that doctors use the Internet to seek medical information, especially doctors who are younger, male, or specialists (Masters, 2008).

People also use the Internet to seek and provide social support through groups that are managed as discussion lists, chat rooms, or bulletin boards (e.g., Ancker et al., 2009). Online support groups provide an opportunity to share information in relative privacy and anonymity. This may be particularly beneficial when the illness is *rare*, which decreases opportunities for meeting others with the illness; *stigmatized*, which causes individuals to not want to reveal themselves in face-to-face settings; or *debilitating*, which decreases the likelihood that individuals with the illness can travel to face-to-face meetings (Davison, Pennebaker, & Dickerson, 2000). Support groups that meet online can develop their own unique cultures, which can be enforced through group norms or the influence of a moderator (Peterson, 2009). They can provide a variety of types of support, such as informational, emotional, and esteem (Mo & Coulson, 2008). They can be populated with peers, family members, or friends of those with the illness. Online support group interventions have been tested across a variety of illnesses. Rains and Young (2009) conducted a meta-analysis of these interventions and found that they "increased social support, decreased depression, increased quality of life, and increased self-efficacy to manage one's health condition" (p. 309). These effects were moderated by the size of the group, the types of communication channels available, and the length of the intervention, such that (a) larger groups were associated with better quality of life but lower perceptions of social support and

(b) groups in which both synchronous and asynchronous channels were available and those that met for longer periods of time were associated with increased perceptions of social support.

## Conclusion

As we move toward the end of this discussion of interpersonal communication in health care, we should briefly mention some of the theoretical perspectives that are commonly used in this area of study. Few of them are exclusively relevant to the health care setting, but many of them do have some particularly interesting applications to this unique context. We have referred earlier in our discussion to communication and uncertainty management theory (Brashers, 2001, 2007) and problematic integration theory (Babrow, 1992), as well as the theory of motivated information management (Afifi & Morse, 2009; Afifi & Weiner, 2006), the risk perception attitude framework (Rimal & Turner, 2009), and Mishel's (1988, 1990) uncertainty in illness theory. All of these examine the role of uncertainty and information seeking/processing as they pertain to health care. Numerous persuasion theories are used in this area of study, including Witte's (1992) extended parallel process model, the theories of reasoned action (Fishbein & Ajzen, 1975) and planned behavior (Ajzen, 1991), psychological reactance (Brehm & Brehm, 1981), prospect theory (Kahneman & Tversky, 1979), situational theory of problem solving (Kim & Grunig, in press), protection motivation theory (Rogers, 1983), the theory of normative social behavior (Rimal & Real, 2005), and inoculation theory (McGuire, 1961). We mentioned earlier Petronio's (2002) communication privacy management theory and Ryan and Deci's (2000) SDT; narrative theory has becoming increasingly pervasive and important in health communication (Harter, Japp, & Beck, 2005). Grounded theory is commonly used (Glaser & Strauss, 1967), and we have seen applications of politeness theory (Lambert, 1996; Spiers, 1998), accommodation theory (Street, 1991;

Watson & Gallois, 1998), and social exchange theory (Roter & Hall, 1991).

As the application of these theories suggests, interpersonal communication in health care settings is a rich and fascinating area of study. What we see operating here are interpersonal communicative processes in a unique and important setting. The process of communication is similar to that found in many other settings, but the subtleties and the consequences are distinctive and inimitable.

## References

Afifi, W. A., & Morse, C. R. (2009). Expanding the role of emotion in the theory of motivated information management. In T. D. Afifi & W. A. Afifi (Eds.), *Uncertainty, information management, and disclosure decisions* (pp. 87–105). New York: Routledge.

Afifi, W. A., & Weiner, J. L. (2006). Seeking information about sexual health: Applying the theory of motivated information management. *Human Communication Research, 32,* 35–57.

Agne, R., Thompson, T. L., & Cusella, L. P. (2000). Stigma in the line of face: Self-disclosure of patients' HIV status to health care providers. *Journal of Applied Communication Research, 28,* 235–261.

Ajzen, I. (1991). The theory of planned behavior. *Organizational Behavior and Human Decision Processes, 50,* 179–211.

Ambady, N., LaPlante, D., Nguyen, T., Rosenthal, R., Chaumeton, N., & Levinson, W. (2002). Surgeons' tone of voice: A clue to malpractice history. *Surgery, 132,* 5–9.

Ancker, J. S., Carpenter, K. M., Greene, P., Hoffman, R., Kukafka, R., Marlow, L. A., et al. (2009). Peer-to-peer communication, cancer prevention, and the Internet. *Journal of Health Communication, 14,* 38–46.

Anderson, P., & Kay, L. (2009). The therapeutic alliance: Adapting to the unthinkable with better information. *Health Communication, 25,* 775–778.

Arnold, W., Losh, D. P., Mauksch, L. B., Maresca, T. M., Storck, M. G., Wenrich, M. D., et al. (2009). Lexicon creation to promote faculty development in medical communication. *Patient Education and Counseling, 74,* 179–183.

Babrow, A. S. (1992). Communication and problematic integration: Understanding and diverging probability and value, ambiguity, ambivalence, and impossibility. *Communication Theory, 2,* 95–130.

Babrow, A. S., Kasch, C. R., & Ford, L. A. (1998). The many meanings of *uncertainty* in illness: Toward a systematic accounting. *Health Communication, 10,* 1–23.

Babrow, A. S., & Matthias, M. S. (2009). Generally unseen challenges in uncertainty management: An application of problematic integration theory. In T. D. Afifi & W. A. Afifi (Eds.), *Uncertainty, information management, and disclosure decisions* (pp. 9–25). New York: Routledge.

Back, A., Arnold, R. M., Tulsky, J. A., Baile, W. F., & Fryer-Edwards, K. (2003). Teaching communication skills to medical oncology fellows. *Journal of Clinical Oncology, 21,* 2433–2436.

Back, A., Young, J., McCown, E., Engelberg, R., Vig, E., & Reinke, L. (2009). Abandonment at the end of life from patient, caregiver, nurse, and physician perspectives. *Archives of Internal Medicine, 169,* 474–479.

Balint, M. (1957). *The doctor, his patient, and the illness.* New York: International Universities Press.

Barrier, P. A., Li, J. T.-C., & Jensen, N. M. (2003). Two words to improve physician-patient communication: What else? *Mayo Clinic Proceedings, 78,* 211–214.

Bashshur, R. L., & Shannon, G. W. (2009). *History of telemedicine: Evolution, context, and transformation.* New Rochelle, NY: Mary Ann Liebert.

Bauer, E. P. (2011). Mental illness, stigma, and disclosure. In M. Miller-Day (Ed.), *Family communication, connections, and health transitions: Going through this together* (193–228). New York: Peter Lang.

Baxter, L. A., & Braithwaite, D. O. (2006). Introduction: Metatheory and theory in family communication research. In D. O Braithwaite & L. A. Baxter (Eds.), *Engaging theories in family communication: Multiple perspectives* (pp. 1–15). Thousand Oaks, CA: Sage.

Baxter, L., & Braithwaite, D. O. (2008). Relational dialectics theory: Crafting meaning from competing discourses. In L. A. Baxter & D. O. Braithwaite (Eds.), *Engaging theories in interpersonal communication: Multiple perspectives* (pp. 349–361). Thousand Oaks, CA: Sage.

Baxter, L. A., Braithwaite, D. O., Golish, T. D., & Olson, L. N. (2002). Contradictions of interaction for wives of elderly husbands with adult dementia. *Journal of Applied Communication Research, 30,* 1–26.

Beach, M. C., Keruly, J., & Moore, R. D. (2006). Is the quality of the patient-provider relationship associated with better adherence and improved health outcomes for patients with HIV? *Journal of General Internal Medicine, 21,* 661–665.

Beckman, H. (1995). Communication and malpractice: Why patients sue their physicians. *Cleveland Clinic Journal of Medicine, 62(2),* 85–89.

Beckman, H., Kaplan, S. H., & Frankel, R. (1989). Outcome-based research on doctor-patient communication: A review. In M. Stewart & D. Roter (Eds.), *Communicating with medical patients* (pp. 223–227). Newbury Park, CA: Sage.

Beisecker, A., & Thompson, T. L. (1995). Physician-elderly patient interaction. In J. F. Nussbaum & J. Coupland (Eds.), *Handbook of communication and aging research* (pp. 397–416). Hillsdale, NJ: Lawrence Erlbaum.

Belkora, J., Edlow, B., & Aviv, C. (2008). Training community resource center and clinic personnel to prompt patients in listing questions for doctors: Follow-up interviews about barriers and facilitators to the implementation of consultation planning. *Implementation Science, 3,* 6.

Bellizzi, K. M., Latini, D. M., Cowan, J. E., Duchane, J., & Carroll, P. R. (2008). Fear of recurrence, symptom burden, and health-related quality of life in men with prostate cancer. *Urology, 72,* 1269–1273.

Benbassit, J. (1998). Patients' preferences for participation in clinical decision making: A review of published surveys. *Behavioral Medicine, 24,* 81–88.

Bensing, J. (1991). Doctor-patient communication and the quality of care. *Social Science & Medicine, 32,* 1301–1310.

Bensing, J. (2000). Bridging the gap: The separate worlds of evidence-based medicine and patient-centered medicine. *Patient Education and Counseling, 39,* 17–25.

Bensing, J., & Dronkers, J. (1992). Instrumental and affective aspects of physician behavior. *Medical Care, 30,* 283–298.

Bensing, J. M., Kerssens, J. J., & van der Pasch, M. (1995). Patient-directed gaze as a tool for discovering and handling psychosocial problems in general practice. *Journal of Nonverbal Behavior, 19,* 223–242.

Ben-Sira, Z. (1982). Stress potential and esotericity of health problems: The significance of the physician's affective behavior. *Medical Care, 20,* 414–424.

Berlin, L. (2007). Communicating results of all diagnostic radiological examinations directly to patients: Has the time come? *American Journal of Radiology, 189,* 1275–1282.

Berlinger, N., & Wu, A. W. (2005). Subtracting insult from injury: Addressing cultural expectations in the disclosure of medical error. *Journal of Medical Ethics, 31,* 106–108.

Bertakis, K. D., & Callahan, E. J. (1992). A comparison of initial and established patient encounters using the Davis observation code. *Family Medicine, 24,* 307–311.

Bertakis, K. D., Roter, D., & Putnam, S. M. (1991). The relationship of physician medical interview style to patient satisfaction. *Journal of Family Practice, 32,* 175–181.

Bevan, J. L., & Pecchioni, L. L. (2008). Understanding the impact of family caregiver cancer literacy on patient health outcomes. *Patient Education and Counseling, 71,* 356–364.

Blanch, D. C., Hall, J. A., Roter, D. L., & Frankel, R. M. (2009). Is it good to express uncertainty to a patient? Correlates and consequences for medical students in a standardized patient visit. *Patient Education and Counseling, 76,* 300–306.

Boyle, D. K., Miller, P. A., & Forbes-Thompson, S. A. (2005). Communication and end-of-life care in the intensive care unit: Patient, family, and clinician outcomes. *Critical Care Nursing Quarterly, 28,* 302–316.

Braddock, C. H., Edwards, K. A., Hasenberg, N. M., Laidley, T. L., & Levinson, W. (1999). Informed decision making in outpatient practice: Time to get back to basics. *JAMA, 282,* 2313–2320.

Brashers, D. E. (2001). Communication and uncertainty management. *Journal of Communication, 51,* 477–497.

Brashers, D. E. (2007). A theory of communication and uncertainty management. In B. Whaley & W. Samter (Eds.), *Explaining communication theory* (pp. 201–218). Mahwah, NJ: Lawrence Erlbaum.

Brashers, D. E., Goldsmith, D. J., & Hsieh, E. (2002). Information seeking and avoiding in health contexts. *Human Communication Research, 28,* 258–271.

Brashers, D. E., Hsieh, E., Neidig, J. L., & Reynolds, N. R. (2006). Managing uncertainty about illness: Health care providers as credible authorities. In R. M. Dailey & B. A. Le Poire (Eds.), *Applied interpersonal communication matters* (pp. 219–240). New York: Peter Lang.

Brashers, D. E., Neidig, J. L., & Goldsmith, D. J. (2004). Social support and the management of uncertainty for people living with HIV. *Health Communication, 16,* 305–331.

Brehm, S. S., & Brehm, J. W. (1981). *Psychological reactance: A theory of freedom and control.* New York: Academic Press.

Breslin, M., Mullan, R., & Montori, V. (2008). The design of a decision aid about diabetes medications for use during the consultation with patients with type 2 diabetes. *Patient Education and Counseling, 73,* 465–472.

Brown, R. F., Butow, P. N., Dunn, S. M., & Tattersall, M. H. N. (2001). Promoting patient participation and shortening cancer consultations: A randomised trial. *British Journal of Cancer, 85,* 1273–1279.

Burack, J. H., Irby, D. M., Carline, J. D., Root, R. K., & Larson, E. B. (1999). Teaching compassion and respect: Attending physicians' responses to problematic behaviors. *Journal of General Internal Medicine, 14,* 49–55.

Burgoon, J. K. (1994). Nonverbal signals. In M. L. Knapp & G. R. Miller (Eds.), *Handbook of interpersonal communication* (2nd ed., pp. 229–285). Thousand Oaks, CA: Sage.

Butow, P. (2001). The importance of communication skills to effective cancer care and support. *NSW Public Health Bulletin, 12*(10), 272–274.

Butow, P. N., Dunn, S. M., Tattersall, M. H. N., & Jones, Q. J. (1995). Computer-based interaction analysis of the cancer consultation. *British Journal of Cancer, 71,* 1115–1121.

Buyck, D., & Lang, F. (2002). Teaching medical communication skills: A call for greater uniformity. *Family Medicine, 34,* 337–343.

Callahan, D. (2009). Death, mourning, and medical progress. *Perspectives in Biological Medicine, 52,* 103–115.

Calvert, J. F., & Hollander-Rodriguez, J. (2008). What are the repercussions of disclosing a medical error? *Journal of Family Practice, 57,* 124–125.

Cameron, K., Baker, D., & Wolf, M. (2011). Integrating health literacy in health communication. In T. L. Thompson, R. Parrot, & J. F. Nussbaum (Eds.), *Routledge handbook of health communication* (2nd ed., pp. 306–319). New York: Routledge.

Carmack, H. J. (2010). Bearing witness to the ethics of practice: Storying physicians' medical mistake narratives. *Health Communication, 25,* 449–458.

Carr-Hill, R. A. (1992). The measurement of patient satisfaction. *Journal of Public Health Medicine, 14,* 236–249.

Caughlin, J. P., Brashers, D. E., Ramey, M. E., Kosenko, K. A., Donovan-Kicken, E., & Bute, J. J. (2008). The message design logics of responses to HIV disclosures. *Human Communication Research, 34,* 655–685.

Caughlin, J. P., Bute, J. J., Donovan-Kicken, E., Kosenko, K. A., Ramey, M. E., & Brashers, D. E. (2009). Do message features influence reactions to HIV disclosures? A multiple-goals perspective. *Health Communication, 24,* 270–283.

Caughlin, J. P., & Vangelisti, A. L. (2009). Why people conceal or reveal secrets: A multiple goals theory perspective. In T. D. Afifi & W. A. Afifi (Eds.), *Uncertainty, information management, and disclosure decisions* (pp. 279–299). New York: Routledge.

Cecil, D. W. (1998). Relational control patterns in physician-patient clinical encounters: Continuing the conversation. *Health Communication, 10,* 125–149.

Cegala, D. J. (2003). Patient communication skills training: A review with implications for cancer patients. *Patient Education and Counseling, 50,* 91–94.

Cegala, D. J., Coleman, M. T., & Turner, J. W. (1998). The development and partial assessment of the medical communication competence scale. *Health Communication, 10,* 261–288.

Cegala, D. J., & Lenzmeier-Broz, S. (2002). Physician communication skills training: A review of theoretical backgrounds, objectives and skills. *Medical Education, 36,* 1004–1016.

Cegala, D. J., McClure, L., Marinelli, T. M., & Post, D. M. (2000). The effects of communication skills training on patients' participation during medical interviews. *Patient Education and Counseling, 41,* 209–222.

Cegala, D. J., McGee, D. S., & McNeilis, K. S. (1996). Components of patients' and doctors' perceptions of communication competence during a primary care medical interview. *Health Communication, 8,* 1–27.

Cegala, D. J., McNeilis, K. S., McGee, D. S., & Jonas, A. P. (1995). A study of doctors' and patients' perceptions of information processing and communication competence during the medical interview. *Health Communication, 7,* 179–203.

Cegala, D. J., Street, R. L., Jr., & Clinch, C. R. (2007). The impact of patient participation on physicians' information provision during a primary care medical interview. *Health Communication, 21,* 177–185.

Chafe, R., Levinson, W., & Sullivan, T. (2009). Disclosing errors that affect multiple patients. *Canadian Medical Association Journal, 180,* 1125–1127.

Chant, S., Jenkinson, T., Randle, J., Russell, G., & Webb, C. (2002). Communication skills training in health care: A review of the literature. *Nurse Education Today, 29,* 189–202.

Chatelle, M. (2008). *Journeys of heartache and grace: Conversations and life lessons from young people with serious illnesses.* Austin, TX: LangMarc.

Clayton, M. F., Dudley, W. N., & Musters, A. (2008). Communication with breast cancer survivors. *Health Communication, 23,* 207–221.

Cline, R. J. W. (2011). Everyday interpersonal communication and health. In T. L. Thompson, R. Parrott, & J. F. Nussbaum (Eds.), *Routledge handbook of health communication* (2nd ed., pp. 377–396). New York: Routledge.

Crigger, N. J. (2004). Always having to say you're sorry: An ethical response to making mistakes in professional practice. *Nursing Ethics, 11,* 568–576.

Davison, K. P., Pennebaker, J. W., & Dickerson, S. S. (2000). Who talks? The social psychology of illness support groups. *American Psychologist, 55,* 205–217.

Dawson, E., Savitsky, K., & Dunning, D. (2006). "Don't tell me, I don't want to know": Understanding people's reluctance to obtain medical diagnostic information. *Journal of Applied Social Psychology, 36,* 751–768.

DeLorme, D. E., & Huh, J. (2009). Seniors' uncertainty management of direct-to-consumer advertising usefulness. *Health Communication, 24,* 494–503.

Dillard, J. P., & Carson, C. L. (2005). Uncertainty management following a positive newborn screening for cystic fibrosis. *Journal of Health Communication, 10,* 57–76.

Dillard, J. P., Carson, C. L., Bernard, C. J., Laxova, A., & Farrell, P. M. (2004). An analysis of communication following newborn screening for cystic fibrosis. *Health Communication, 16,* 195–205.

DiMatteo, M. R., & Hays, R. (1980). The significance of patients' perceptions of physician conduct: A study of patient satisfaction in a family practice center. *Journal of Community Health, 6,* 18–34.

DiMatteo, M. R., Hays, R. D., & Prince, L. M. (1986). Relationship of physicians' nonverbal communication skill to patient satisfaction, appointment noncompliance, and physician workload. *Health Psychology, 5,* 581–594.

DiMatteo, M. R., Taranta, A., Friedman, H. S., & Prince, L. M. (1980). Predicting patient satisfaction from physicians' nonverbal communication skills. *Medical Care, 18*, 376–387.

Donovan-Kicken, E., & Bute, J. J. (2008). Uncertainty of social network members in the case of communication-debilitating illness or injury. *Qualitative Health Research, 18*, 5–18.

Duffy, F. D., Gordon, G. H., Whelan, G., Cole-Kelly, K., Frankel, R., Buffone, N., et al. (2004). Assessing competence in communication and interpersonal skills: The Kalamazoo II report. *Academic Medicine, 79*, 495–50.

Duggan, A., Le Poire, B. A., Prescott, M. E., & Baham, C. S. (2009). Understanding the helper: The role of codependency in health care and health care outcomes. In D. E. Brashers & D. J. Goldsmith (Eds.), *Communicating to manage health and illness* (pp. 271–300). New York: Routledge.

Duggan, A. P., & Parrott, R. L. (2001). Physicians' nonverbal rapport building and patients' talk about the subjective component of illness. *Human Communication Research, 27*, 299–311.

Duggan, A. P., & Thompson, T. L. (2011). Provider–patient interaction and related outcomes. In T. L. Thompson, R. Parrott, & J. F. Nussbaum (Eds.), *Routledge handbook of health communication* (2nd ed., pp. 414–427). New York: Routledge.

van Dulmen, A. M., Verhaak, P. F. M., & Bilo, H. J. G. (1997). Shifts in doctor-patient communication during a series of outpatient consultations in non-insulin-dependent diabetes mellitus. *Patient Education and Counselling, 30*, 227–237.

Dys, S. M., Shugarman, L. R., Lorenz, K. A., Mularski, R. A., & Lind, J. (2008). A systematic review of satisfaction with care at the end of life. *Journal of the American Geriatric Society, 56*, 124–129.

Eaton, L. G., & Tinsley, B. H. (1999). Maternal personality and health communication in the pediatric context. *Health Communication, 11*, 75–96.

Eggly, S., Penner, L. A., Greene, M., Harper, F. W., Ruckdeschel, J. C., & Albrecht, T. A. (2006). Information seeking during "bad news" oncology interactions: Question asking by patients and their companions. *Social Science & Medicine, 63*, 2974–2985.

Ekman, P., & Friesen, W. V. (1969). The repertoire of nonverbal behavior: Categories, origins, usage, and coding. *Semiotica, 1*, 49–98.

Engel, G. L. (1977). The need for a new medical model: A challenge for biomedicine. *Science, 196*, 129–196.

Epstein, R. M., Franks, P., Sheilds, C. G., Meldrum, S. C., Miller, K. N., Campbell, T. L., et al. (2005). Patient-centered communication and diagnostic testing. *Annals of Family Medicine, 3*, 415–421.

Epstein, R. M., & Peters, E. (2009). Beyond information: Exploring patients' preferences. *JAMA, 302*, 195–197.

Fadul, N., Elsayem, A., Palmer, L., Zhang, T., Braitheh, F., & Bruera, E. (2007). Predictors of access to palliative care services among patients who died at a comprehensive cancer center. *Journal of Palliative Medicine, 10*, 1146–1152.

Ferrell, B. (2005). Late referrals to palliative care. *Journal of Clinical Oncology, 23*, 2588–2589.

Fineberg, I. C. (2005). Preparing professionals for family conferences in palliative care: Evaluation results of an interdisciplinary approach. *Journal of Palliative Medicine, 8*, 857–866.

Finn, N. B., & Bria, W. F. (2009). *Digital communication in medical practice*. London: Springer-Verlag.

Fishbein, M., & Ajzen, I. (1975). *Belief, attitude, intention, and behavior*. Reading, MA: Addison-Wesley.

Floyd, K. (2001). Human affection exchange: I. Reproductive probability as a predictor of men's affection with their sons. *Journal of Men's Studies, 10*, 39–50.

Floyd, K. (2006a). *Communicating affection: Interpersonal behavior and social context*. Cambridge, UK: Cambridge University Press.

Floyd, K. (2006b). Human affection exchange XII: Affectionate communication is associated with diurnal variation in salivary free cortisol. *Western Journal of Communication, 70*, 47–63.

Floyd, K., Hesse, C., & Haynes, M. T. (2007). Human affection exchange: XV: Metabolic and cardiovascular correlates of trait expressed affection. *Communication Quarterly, 55*, 19–94.

Floyd, K., Mikkelson, A. C., Tafoya, M. A., Farinelli, L., La Valley, A. G., Judd, J. H., et al. (2007). Human affection exchange: XIII: Affectionate communication accelerates neuroendocrine stress recovery. *Health Communication, 22*, 123–132.

Ford, L. A., Babrow, A. S., & Stohl, C. (1996). Social support messages and the management of uncertainty in the experience of breast cancer: An application of problematic integration theory. *Communication Monographs, 63*, 189–207.

Fox, S. A., Heritage, J., Stockdale, S. E., Asch, S. M., Duan, N., & Reise, S. P. (2009). Cancer screening adherence: Does physician–patient communication matter? *Patient Education and Counseling, 75,* 178–184.

Franks, P., Fiscella, K., Shields, C. G., Meldrum, S. C., Duberstein, P., Jerant, A. F., et al. (2005). Are patients' ratings of their physicians related to health outcomes? *Annals of Family Medicine, 3,* 229–234.

von Friederichs-Fitzwater, M. M., Callahan, E. J., Flynn, N., & Williams, J. (1991). Relational control in physician–patient interactions. *Health Communication, 3,* 17–36.

Friedman, H. S., DiMatteo, M. R., & Taranta, A. (1980). A study of the relationship between individual differences in nonverbal expressiveness and factors of personality and social interaction. *Journal of Research in Personality, 14,* 351–364.

Friedrichsen, M., Lipkin, M., & Hall, A. (2006). Concerns about losing control when breaking bad news to terminally ill patients with cancer: Physicians' perspective. *Journal of Palliative Medicine, 9,* 673–682.

Frost, C. J., Venne, V., Cunningham, D., & Gerritsen-McKane, R. (2004). Decision making with uncertain information: Learning from women in a high risk breast cancer clinic. *Journal of Genetic Counseling, 13,* 221–236.

Galil, A., Bachner, Y. G., Merrick, J., Flusser, H., Lubetzky, H., Heiman, N., & Carmel, S. (2006). Physician-parent communication as predictor of parent satisfaction with child development services. *Research in Developmental Disabilities, 27,* 233–242.

Galvin, K. M., & Grill, L. H. (2009). Opening up the conversation on genetics and genomics in families: The space for communication scholars. In C. Beck (Ed.), *Communication yearbook 33* (pp. 306–332). New York: Routledge.

Giannini, A. J., Giannini, J. D., & Bowman, R. K. (2000). Measurement of nonverbal receptive abilities in medical students. *Perceptual and Motor Skills, 90,* 1145–1150.

Gillotti, C. (2003). Medical disclosure and decision-making: Excavating the complexities of physician–patient information exchange. In T. L. Thompson, A. Dorsey, K. Miller, & R. Parrott (Eds.). *Handbook of health communication* (pp. 163–182). Mahwah, NJ: Lawrence Erlbaum.

Giron, M., Manjon-Arce, P., Puerto-Barber, J., Sanchez-Garcia, E., & Gomez-Beneyto, M. (1998). Clinical interview skills and identification of emotional disorders in primary care. *American Journal of Psychiatry, 155,* 530–535.

Glaser, B. G., & Strauss, A. L. (1965). *Awareness of dying.* San Francisco: Aldine.

Glaser, B. G., & Strauss, A. L. (1967). *The discovery of grounded theory: Strategies of qualitative research.* Hawthorne, NY: Aldine de Gruyter.

Goldsmith, D. J. (2001). A normative approach to the study of uncertainty and communication. *Journal of Communication, 51,* 514–533.

Goldsmith, D. J. (2004). *Communicating social support.* New York: Cambridge University Press.

Goldsmith, D. J. (2009). Uncertainty and communication in couples coping with serious illness. In T. D. Afifi & W. A. Afifi (Eds.), *Uncertainty, information management, and disclosure decisions* (pp. 203–225). New York: Routledge.

Goldsmith, D. J., & Brashers, D. E. (2008). Communication matters: Developing and testing social support interventions. *Communication Monographs, 75,* 320–330.

Goldsmith, D. J., & Brashers, D. E. (2009). Introduction: Communicating to manage health and illness. In D. E. Brashers & D. J. Goldsmith (Eds.), *Communicating to manage health and illness* (pp. 1–14). New York: Routledge.

Goldsmith, J., Wittenberg-Lyles, E., Ragan, S., & Nussbaum, J. F. (2011). Life span and end-of-life health communication. In T. L. Thompson, R. Parrot, & J. F. Nussbaum (Eds.), *Routledge handbook of health communication* (2nd ed., pp. 441–454). New York: Routledge.

Goodwin, C. (1981). *Conversational organization: Interaction between speakers and hearers.* New York: Academic Press.

Goodwin, C. (1995). Seeing in depth. *Social Studies of Science, 25,* 237–274.

Goold, S. D., Williams, B., & Arnold, R. M. (2000). Conflicts regarding decisions to limit treatment. *Journal of the American Medical Association, 283,* 909–914.

Gordon, G. H., Joos, S. K., & Byrne, J. (2000). Physician expressions of uncertainty during patient encounters. *Patient Education and Counseling, 40,* 50–65.

Gordon, H. S., Street, R. L., Sharf, B. F., & Souchek, J. (2006). Racial differences in doctors' information-giving and patients' participation. *Cancer, 107,* 1313–1320.

Grumbach, K., Osmond, D., Vranizan, K., Jaffe, D., & Bindman, A. B. (1998). Primary care physicians' experience of financial incentives in managed-care systems. *New England Journal of Medicine, 339,* 1516–1521.

Gueguen, J. A., Bylund, C. L., Brown, R. F., Levin, T. T., & Kissane, D. W. (2009). Conducting family meetings in palliative care: Themes, techniques, and preliminary evaluation of a communication skills module. *Palliative and Supportive Care, 7,* 171–179.

Gwyn, R., & Elwyn, G. (1999). When is a shared decision not (quite) a shared decision? Negotiating preferences in a general practice encounter. *Social Science & Medicine, 49,* 437–447.

Hadjistavropoulos, H. D., Ross, M. A., & von Baeyer, C. L. (1990). Are physicians' ratings of pain affected by patients' physical attractiveness? *Social Science & Medicine, 31,* 69–72.

de Haes, H., & Bensing, J. (2009). Endpoints in medical communication research, proposing a framework of functions and outcomes. *Patient Education and Counseling, 74,* 287–294.

Hall, J. A., Horgan, T. G., Stein, T. S., & Roter, D. L. (2002). Liking in the physician–patient relationship. *Patient Education and Counseling, 48,* 69–77.

Hall, J. A., Irish, J. T., Roter, D. L., Ehrlich, C. M., & Miller, L. H. (1994). Gender in medical encounters: An analysis of physician and patient communication in a primary care setting. *Health Psychology, 13,* 384–392.

Hall, J. A., Milburn, M. A., Roter, D. L., & Daltroy, L. H. (1998). Why are sicker patients less satisfied with their medical care? Tests of two explanatory models. *Health Psychology, 17,* 70–75.

Hall, J. A., Roter, D. L., & Katz, N. R. (1988). Meta-analysis of correlates of provider behavior in medical encounters. *Medical Care, 26,* 657–675.

Hancock, K., Clayton, J. M., Parker, S. M., Walder, S, Butow, P. N., & Carrick, S. (2007). Discrepant perceptions of end of life communication: A systematic review. *Journal of Pain and Symptom Management, 34,* 190–200.

Hannawa, A. (2009). Negotiating medical virtues: Toward the development of a physician mistake disclosure (PMD) model. *Health Communication, 24,* 391–399.

Harrigan, J. A. (1985). Self-touching as an indicator of underlying affect and language processes. *Social Science & Medicine, 20,* 1161–1168.

Harrigan, J. A., Gramata, J. F., Lucic, K. S., & Margolis, C. (1989). It's how you say it: Physicians' vocal behavior. *Social Science & Medicine, 28,* 87–92.

Harrigan, J. A., Oxman, T. E., & Rosenthal, R. (1985). Rapport expressed through nonverbal behavior. *Journal of Nonverbal Behavior, 9,* 95–110.

Harrigan, J. A., & Rosenthal, R. (1983). Physicians' head and body positions as determinants of perceived rapport. *Journal of Applied Social Psychology, 13,* 496–509.

Harrigan, J. A., & Rosenthal, R. (1986). Nonverbal aspects of empathy and rapport in physician–patient interaction. In P. D. Blanck, R. Buck, & R. Rosenthal (Eds.), *Nonverbal communication in the clinical context* (pp. 36–73). University Park: Pennsylvania State University Press.

Harter, L., Japp, P., & Beck, C. (2005). *Narratives in health and illness.* Mahwah, NJ: Lawrence Erlbaum.

Heath, C. (1986). *Body movement and speech in medical interaction.* Cambridge, UK: Cambridge University Press.

Heath, C. (1988). Embarrassment and interactional organization. In P. Drew & A. Wootton (Eds.), *Erving Goffman: Exploring the interaction order* (pp. 136–160). Boston: Northeastern University Press.

Hébert, P. C., Levin, A. V., & Robertson, G., (2001). Bioethics for clinicians: 23: Disclosure of medical error. *Canadian Medical Association Journal, 164,* 509–513.

Heritage, J. (2010). Questioning in medicine. In A. Freed & S. Ehrlich (Eds.), *"Why do you ask?": The function of questions in institutional discourse* (pp. 42–68). New York: Oxford University Press.

Heritage, J., Elliott, M., Stivers, T., Richardson, A., & Mangione-Smith, R. (2010). Reducing inappropriate antibiotics prescribing: The role of online commentary on physical examination findings. *Patient Education and Counseling, 81,* 119–125.

Heritage, J., & Maynard, D. (2006). Problems and prospects in the study of doctor-patient interaction: 30 years of research in primary care. *Annual Review of Sociology, 32,* 351–374.

Heritage, J., & Robinson, J. D. (2006). The structure of patients' presenting concerns: Physicians' opening questions. *Health Communication, 19,* 89–102.

Heritage, J., Robinson, J. D., Elliot, M. N., Beckett, M., & Wilkes, M. (2007). Reducing patients' unmet concerns in primary care: A trial of two question designs. *Journal of General Internal Medicine, 22*, 1429–1433.

Heritage, J. C., & Stivers, T. (1999). Online commentary in acute medical visits: A method of shaping patient expectations. *Social Science & Medicine, 49*, 1501–1517.

Hickman, S. (2002). Improving communication near the end of life. *American Behavioral Scientist, 46*, 252–267.

Hickson, G. B., Clayton, E. W., Entman, S. S., Miller, C. S., Githens, P. B., Whetten-Goldstein, K., & Sloan, F. A. (1994). Obstetricians' prior malpractice experience and patients' satisfaction with care. *Journal of the American Medical Association, 272*, 1583–1587.

Hickson, G. B., Clayton, E. W., Githens, P. B., & Sloan, F. A. (1992). Factors that prompted families to file medical malpractice claims following perinatal injuries. *Journal of the American Medical Association, 267*, 1359–1363.

Hickson, G. B., & Entman, S. S. (2008). Physician behavior and litigation risk: Evidence and opportunity. *Clinical Obstetrics and Gynecology, 51*, 688–699.

Holst, L., Lundren, M., Olsen, L., & Ishøy, T. (2009). Dire deadlines: Coping with dysfunctional family dynamics in an end-of-life care setting. *International Journal of Palliative Nursing, 15*, 34–41.

Hooper, E. M., Comstock, L. M., Goodwin, J. M., & Goodwin, J. S. (1982). Patient characteristics that influence physician behavior. *Medical Care, 20*, 630–638.

Houston, T. K., Sands, D. Z., Nash, B. R., & Ford, D. E. (2003). Experiences of physicians who frequently use email with patients. *Health Communication, 15*, 515–525.

Hsieh, E. (2006). Understanding medical interpreters: Reconceptualizing bilingual health communication. *Health Communication, 20*, 177–186.

Hsieh, E. (2007). Interpreters as co-diagnosticians: Overlapping roles and services between providers and interpreters. *Social Science & Medicine, 64*, 924–927.

Hsieh, E. (2010). Provider–interpreter collaboration in bilingual health care: Competitions of control over interpreter-mediated interactions. *Social Science & Medicine, 78*, 154–159.

Hudson, P., Quinn, K., O'Hanlon, B., & Aranda, S. (2008). Family meetings in palliative care: Multidisciplinary clinical practice guidelines. *BMC Palliative Care, 7*, 12.

Izquierdo, R., Meyer, S., Starren, J., Goland, R., Teresi, J., Shea, S., et al. (2007). Detection and remediation of medically urgent situations using telemedicine case management for older patients with diabetes mellitus. *Therapeutic and Clinical Risk Management, 3*, 485–489.

Jackson, V., Mack, J., Matsuyama, R., Lakoma, M. D., Sullivan, A. M., Arnold, R. M., et al. (2008). A qualitative study of oncologists' approaches to end-of-life care. *Journal of Palliative Medicine, 11*, 893–906.

Janicik, R., Kalet, A. L., Schwartz, M. D., Zabar, S., & Lipkin, M. (2007). Using bedside rounds to teach communication skills in the internal medicine clerkship. *Medical Education Online, 12*, 1–8.

Johnson, C., Girgis, A., Paul, C., & Currow, D. C. (2008). Cancer specialists' palliative care referral practices and perceptions: Results of a national survey. *Palliative Medicine, 22*, 51–57.

Kahneman, D., & Tversky, A. (1979). Prospect theory: An analysis of decision under risk. *Econometrica, 47*, 263–291.

Kaldjian, L. C., Jones, E. W., & Rosenthal, G. E. (2006). Facilitating and impeding factors for physicians' error disclosure: A structured literature review. *Joint Commission Journal on Quality and Patient Safety, 32*, 188–198.

Kaldjian, L. C., Jones, E. W., Rosenthal, G. E., Tripp-Reimer, T., & Hillis, S. L. (2006). An empirically derived taxonomy of factors affecting physicians' willingness to disclose medical errors. *Journal of General Internal Medicine, 21*, 942–948.

Kaplan, S. H., Greenfield, S., & Ware, J. E. (1989a). Assessing the effects of physician–patient interactions on the outcomes of chronic disease. *Medical Care, 27*, S110–S127.

Kaplan, S. H., Greenfield, S., & Ware, J. E. (1989b). Impact of the doctor–patient relationship on the outcomes of chronic disease. In M. Stewart & D. Roter (Eds.), *Communicating with medical patients* (pp. 228–245). Newbury Park, CA: Sage.

Kendon, A. (1990). *Conducting interaction: Patterns of behavior in focused encounters.* Cambridge, UK: Cambridge University Press.

Kiesler, D. J., & Auerbach, S. M. (2003). Integrating measurement of control and affiliation in studies of physician–patient interaction: The interpersonal circumplex. *Social Science & Medicine, 57*, 1707–1722.

Kim, J.-N., & Grunig, J. E. (in press). *Situational theory of problem solving: Communicative, cognitive, and perceptive bases.* New York: Routledge.

Knobloch, L. K., & Knobloch-Fedders, L. M. (2010). The role of relational uncertainty in depressive symptoms and relationship quality: An actor–partner interdependence model. *Journal of Social and Personal Relationships, 27,* 137–159.

Korsch, B. M., Gozzi, E. K., & Francis, V. (1968). Gaps in doctor–patient communication. *Pediatrics, 42,* 855–871.

Koss, T., & Rosenthal, R. (1997). Interactional synchrony, positivity, and patient satisfaction in the physician–patient relationship. *Medical Care, 35,* 1158–1163.

Kurtz, S., Silverman, J., & Draper, J. (2005). *Teaching and learning communication skills in medicine* (2nd ed.). Oxford, UK: Radcliffe.

Lakatos, P. L. (2009). Prevalence, predictors, and clinical consequences of medical adherence in IBD: How to improve it? *World Journal of Gastroenterology, 15,* 4234–4239.

Lambert, B. L. (1996). Face and politeness in pharmacist–physician interaction. *Social Science & Medicine, 43,* 1189–1198.

Lamont, E. B. (2005). A demographic and prognostic approach to defining the end of life. *Journal of Palliative Medicine, 8,* S12–S21.

Larochelle, M. R., Rodriguez, K., Arnold, R. M., & Baranato, A. E. (2009). Hospital staff attributions of the causes of physician variation in end-of-life treatment intensity. *Palliative Medicine, 23,* 460–470.

Larsen, K. M., & Smith, C. K. (1981). Assessment of nonverbal communication in the patient–physician interview. *Journal of Family Practice, 12,* 481–488.

Lau, F., Downing, M., Wesperance, M., Shaw, J., & Kuziemsky, C. (2006). Use of Palliative Performance Scale in end-of-life prognostication. *Journal of Palliative Medicine, 9,* 1066–1075.

Lebow, J. L. (1974). Consumer assessments of the quality of medical care. *Medical Care, 12,* 328.

Légaré, F., O'Connor, A. M., Graham, I. D., Wells, G. A., & Tremblay, S. (2006). Impact of the Ottawa Decision Support Framework on the agreement and the difference between patients' and physicians' decisional conflict. *Medical Decision Making, 26,* 373–390.

Le Poire, B. A. (2006). *Family communication: Nurturing and control in a changing world.* Thousand Oaks, CA: Sage.

Lepper, H. S., Martin, L. R., & DiMatteo, M. R. (1995). A model of nonverbal exchange in physician–patient expectations for patient involvement. *Journal of Nonverbal Behavior, 19,* 207–222.

Levine, B. A., Turner, J. W., Robinson, J. D., Angelus, P., & Hu, T. M. (2009). Communication plays a critical role in web-based monitoring. *Journal of Diabetes Science and Technology, 3,* 461–467.

Lewis, N., Gray, S. W., Freres, D. R., & Hornik, R. C. (2009). Examining cross source engagement with cancer-related information and its impact on doctor–patient relations. *Health Communication, 24,* 723–734.

Majerovitz, S. D., Mollot, R. J., & Rudder, C. (2009). We're on the same side: Improving communication between nursing home and family. *Health Communication, 24,* 12–20.

Mangione-Smith, R., Stivers, T., Elliott, M., McDonald, L., & Heritage, J. (2003). Online commentary during the physical examination: A communication tool for avoiding inappropriate antibiotic prescribing. *Social Science & Medicine, 56,* 313–320.

Martin, S. C., Stone, A. M., Scott, A. M., & Brashers, D. E. (2010). Medical, personal, and social forms of uncertainty across the transplantation trajectory. *Qualitative Health Research, 20,* 182–196.

Marvel, M. K., Epstein, R. M., Flowers, K., & Beckman, H. B. (1999). Soliciting the patient's agenda: Have we improved? *Journal of the American Medical Association, 281,* 283–287.

Masters, K. (2008). For what purpose and reasons do doctors use the Internet: A systematic review. *International Journal of Medical Informatics, 77,* 4–16.

Matheson, D. H. (1997). The painful truth: Interpretation of facial expressions of pain in older adults. *Journal of Nonverbal Behavior, 21,* 223–238.

Matlow, A., Stevens, P., Harrison, C., & Laxer, R. M. (2006). Disclosure of medical errors. *Pediatric Clinics of North America, 53,* 1091–1104.

Matsuyama, R., Reddy, S., & Smith, T. (2006). Why do patients choose chemotherapy near the end of life? A review of the perspective of those facing death from cancer. *Journal of Clinical Oncology, 24,* 3490–3496.

Matthias, M. S. (2010). The impact of uncertainty on decision making in prenatal consultations: Obstetricians' and midwives' perspectives. *Health Communication, 25,* 199–211.

Matusitz, J., & Breen, G. M. (2007). Telemedicine: Its effects on health communication. *Health Communication, 21,* 73–83.

Maynard, D. W. (2003). *Bad news, good news: Conversational order in everyday talk and clinical settings.* Chicago: University of Chicago Press.

Mazor, K. M., Simon, S. R., & Gurwitz, J. H. (2004). Communicating with patients about medical errors: A review of the literature. *Archives of Internal Medicine, 164,* 1690–1697.

McGee, D. S. (1997). In search of patient communication competence: A test of an intervention to improve communication in the primary-care medical interview. *Dissertation Abstracts International, 57*(7-A), 2739.

McGee, D. S., & Cegala, D. J. (1998). Patient communication skills training for improved communication competence in the primary care medical consultation. *Journal of Applied Communication Research, 26,* 412–430.

McGuire, W. (1961). Resistance to persuasion conferred by active and passive prior refutation of the same and alternative counterarguments. *Journal of Abnormal and Social Psychology, 63,* 326–332.

McNeilis, K., & Thompson, T. L. (1998). The impact of relational control on compliance in dentist–patient interactions. In G. Kreps & D. O'Hair (Eds.), *Relational communication and health outcomes* (pp. 57–72). Cresskill, NJ: Greenwood.

McNeill, D., Cassell, J., & McCullough, K. (1994). Communicative effects of speech-mismatched gestures. *Research on Language and Social Interaction, 27,* 223–237.

Mead, N., & Bower, P. (2002). Patient-centred consultations and outcomes in primary care: A review of the literature. *Patient Education and Counseling, 48,* 51–61.

Mechanic, D., & Meyer, S. (2000). Concepts of trust among patients with serious illness. *Social Science & Medicine, 51,* 657–668.

Mehrabian, A. (1967). Orientation behaviors and nonverbal attitude communication. *Journal of Communication, 17,* 324–332.

Miller, V. D., & Knapp, M. L. (1986). Communication paradoxes and the maintenance of living relationship with the dying. *Journal of Family Issues, 7,* 255–275.

Milmoe, S., Rosenthal, R., Blane, H. T., Chafetz, M. E., & Wolf, I. (1967). The doctor's voice: Postdictor of successful referral of alcoholic patients. *Journal of Abnormal Psychology, 72,* 78–84.

Mishel, M. H. (1988). Uncertainty in illness. *Image: Journal of Nursing Scholarship, 20,* 225–232.

Mishel, M. H. (1990). Reconceptualization of uncertainty in illness theory. *Journal of Nursing Scholarship, 22,* 256–262.

Mishel, M. H., Germino, B. B., Lin, L., Pruthi, R. S., Wallen, E. M., Crandell, J., et al. (2009). Managing uncertainty about treatment decision making in early stage prostate cancer: A randomized clinical trial. *Patient Education and Counseling, 77,* 349–359.

Mo, P. K., & Coulson, N. S. (2008). Exploring the communication of social support within virtual communities: A content analysis of messages posted to an online HIV/AIDS support group. *Cyberpsychology & Behavior, 11,* 371–374.

Morse, J. M., & Mitchum, C. (1997). Compathy: The contagion of physical distress. *Journal of Advanced Nursing, 26,* 64–7.

Murphy, J. G., Stee, L., McEvoy, M. T., & Oshiro, J. (2007). Journal reporting of medical errors. *Chest, 131,* 890–896.

Nakash, O., Dargouth, S., Oddo, V., Gao, S., & Alegría, M. (2009). Patient initiation of information: Exploring its role during the mental health intake visit. *Patient Education and Counseling, 75,* 220–226.

Nichols, J. D. (2003). Lawyer's advice on physician conduct with malpractice cases. *Clinical Orthopaedics and Related Research, 407,* 14–18.

Noland, C. A., & Rickles, N. M. (2009). Reflection and analysis of how pharmacy students learn to communicate about medication errors. *Health Communication, 24,* 351–360.

Nordholm, L. (1980). Beautiful patients are good patients: Evidence for the physical attractiveness stereotype in first impressions of patients. *Social Science & Medicine, 14,* 81–83.

Norton, S. A., Tilden, V. P., Tolle, S. W., Nelson, C. A., & Eggman, S. T. (2003). Life support withdrawal: Communication and conflict. *American Journal of Critical Care, 12,* 548–555.

O'Hair, D. (1989). Dimensions of relational communication and control during physician–patient interactions. *Health Communication, 2,* 97–115.

Olson, D. H. (1993). Circumplex model of marital and family systems: Assessing family functioning.

In F. Walsh (Ed.), *The family on the threshold of the 21st century: Trends and implications* (pp. 259–280). Mahwah, NJ: Lawrence Erlbaum.

Olson, D. H., Sprenkle, D. H., & Russell, C. S. (1979). Circumplex model of marital and family systems: I. Cohesion and adaptability dimensions, family types, and clinical applications. *Family Processes, 18,* 3–28.

Olufowote, J. (2010). Informed consent to treatment's sociohistorical discourse of traditionalism: A structurational analysis of radiology residents' accounts. *Health Communication, 25,* 22–31.

Ong, L. M. L., Visser, M. R. M., Lammes, F. B., & de Haes, J. C. J. M. (2000). Doctor–patient communication and cancer patients' quality of life and satisfaction. *Patient Education and Counseling, 41,* 145–156.

Ong, L. M. L., Visser, M. R. M., Van Zuuren, F. J., Rietbroek, R. C., Lammes, F. B., & De Haes, J. C. J. M. (1999). Cancer patients' coping styles and doctor–patient communication. *Psycho-Oncology, 8,* 155–166.

Ormondroyd, E., Moynihan, C., Ardern-Jones, A., Eeles, R., Foster, C., Davolls, S., et al. (2008). Communicating genetics research results to families: Problems arising when the patient participant is deceased. *Psycho-Oncology, 17,* 804–811.

Parchman, M. L., Flannagan, D., Ferrer, R. L., & Matamoras, M. (2009). Communication competence, self-care behaviors, and glucose control in patients with Type 2 diabetes. *Patient Education and Counseling, 77,* 55–59.

Parrott, R. (1995). Topic-centered and person-centered "sensitive subjects": Managing barriers to disclosure about health. In L. K. Fuller & L. M. Shilling (Eds.), *Communicating about communicable diseases* (pp. 177–190). Amherst, MA: Human Resource Development Press.

Parrott, R. (2009). *Talking about health: Why communication matters.* Oxford, UK: Wiley-Blackwell.

Patt, M. R., Houston, T. K., Jenckes, M. W., Sands, D. Z., & Ford, D. E. (2003). Doctors who are using email with their patients: A qualitative exploration. *Journal of Medical Internet Research, 5,* e9.

Patton, M. J. (1989). Problems with and alternatives to the use of coding schemes in research on counseling. *The Counseling Psychologist, 17,* 490–506.

Paulsel, M. L., McCroskey, J. C., & Richmond, V. P. (2006). Perceptions of health care professionals' credibility as a predictor of patients' satisfaction with their medical care and physician. *Communication Research Reports, 23,* 69–76.

Pecchioni, L., & Keeley, M. V. (2011). Insights about health from family communication theories. In T. L. Thompson, R. Parrott, & J. F. Nussbaum (Eds.), *Routledge handbook of health communication* (2nd ed., pp. 363–376). New York: Routledge.

Pecchioni, L. L., Thompson, T. L., & Anderson, D. J. (2006). Interrelations between family and health communication. In L. H. Turner & R. West (Eds.), *The family communication sourcebook* (pp. 447–468). Thousand Oaks, CA: Sage.

Pelt, J. L., & Faldmo, L. P. (2008). Physician error and disclosure. *Clinical Obstetrics and Gynecology, 51,* 700–708.

Peterson, J. L. (2009). "You have to be positive": Social support processes of an online support group for men living with HIV. *Communication Studies, 60,* 526–541.

Petronio, S. (2002). *Boundaries of privacy: Dialectics of disclosure.* New York: SUNY Press.

Petronio, S., & Sargent, J. (2011). Disclosure predicaments arising during the course of patient care: Nurses' privacy management. *Health Communication, 26,* 255–266.

Pieterse, A. H., van Dulmen, A. M., Beemer, F. A., Bensing, J. M., & Ausems, M. G. (2007). Cancer genetic counseling: Communication and counselees' post-visit satisfaction, cognitions, anxiety, and needs fulfillment. *Journal of Genetic Counseling, 16,* 85–96.

Politi, M. C., Han, P. K. J., & Col, N. C. (2007). Communicating the uncertainty of harms and benefits of medical interventions (Eisenberg Center 2006 White Paper Series). *Medical Decision Making, 7,* 681–695.

Politi, M., & Street, R. L. (2011). The importance of communication in collaborative decision making: Facilitating shared mind and the management of uncertainty. In T. Thompson, R. Parrott, & J. F. Nussbaum (Eds.), *Routledge handbook of health communication* (2nd ed., pp. 399–413). New York: Routledge.

Pratt, W., Unruh, K., Civan, A., & Skeels, M. (2006). Personal health information management. *Communications of the ACM, 49,* 51–55.

Priebe, S., McCabe, R., Bullenkamp, J., Hansson, L., Lauber, C., Martinez-Leal, R., et al. (2007). Structured patient–clinician communication and 1-year outcome in community mental healthcare: Cluster randomised controlled trial. *British Journal of Psychiatry, 191,* 420–426.

Ragan, S., & Goldsmith, J. (2008). End-of-life communication: The drama of pretense in the talk of dying patients and their M.D.'s. In K. Wright & S. Moore (Eds.), *Applied health communication* (pp. 207–228). Cresskill, NJ: Hampton Press.

Ragan, S., Wittenberg-Lyles, E. M., Goldsmith, J., & Sanchez-Reilly, S. (2008). *Communication as comfort: Multiple voices in palliative care.* New York: Routledge.

Rains, S. A., & Young, V. A. (2009). A meta-analysis of research on formal computer-mediated support groups: Examining group characteristics and health outcomes. *Human Communication Research, 35,* 309–336.

Rimal, R. N., & Real, K. (2005). How behaviors are influenced by perceived norms: A test of the theory of normative social behavior. *Communication Research, 32,* 389–414.

Rimal, R., & Turner, M. M. (2009). Use of the risk perception attitude (RPA) framework for understanding health information seeking. In T. D. Afifi & W. A. Afifi (Eds.), *Uncertainty, information management, and disclosure decisions* (pp. 145–163). New York: Routledge.

Rintamaki, L. S., Scott, A. M., Kosenko, K. A., & Jensen, R. E. (2007). Male patient perceptions of HIV stigma in health care contexts. *AIDS Patient Care and STDs, 21,* 956–960.

Robbins, J. M., Kirmayer, L. J., Cathebras, P., Yaffe, M. J., & Dworkind, M. (1994). Physician characteristics and the recognition of depression and anxiety in primary care. *Medical Care, 32,* 795–812.

Robinson, J. D. (2001). Asymmetry in action: Sequential resources in the negotiation of a prescription request. *Text, 21,* 19–54.

Robinson, J. D. (2006). Nonverbal communication and physician–patient interaction: Review and new directions. In V. Manusov & M. L. Patterson (Eds.), *The Sage handbook of nonverbal communication* (pp. 437–459). Thousand Oaks, CA: Sage.

Robinson, J. D., & Heritage, J. (2006). Physicians' opening questions and patients' satisfaction. *Patient Education and Counseling, 60,* 279–285.

Robinson, J. D., & Stivers, T. (2001). Achieving activity transitions in primary-care consultations: From history taking to physical examination. *Human Communication Research, 27,* 253–298.

Rogers, R. W. (1983). Cognitive and physiological processes in fear appeals and attitude change: A revised theory of protection motivation. In J. T. Cacioppo & R. E. Petty (Eds.), *Social psychology: A source book* (pp. 153–176). New York: Guildford Press.

Roscoe, L. A., Corsentino, E., Watkins, S., McCall, M., & Sanchez-Ramos, J. (2009). Well-being of family caregivers of persons with late-stage Huntington's disease: Lessons in stress and coping. *Health Communication, 24,* 239–248.

Rosenblum, N. D., Wetzel, M., Platt, O., Daniels, S., Crawford, J., & Rosenthal, R. (1994). Predicting medical student success in a clinical clerkship by rating students' nonverbal behavior. *Archives of Pediatric Adolescent Medicine, 148,* 213–219.

Rosenthal, R., Hall, J. A., DiMatteo, M. R., & Rogers, P. L. (1979). *Sensitivity to nonverbal communication: The PONS Test.* Baltimore: Johns Hopkins University Press.

Roter, D. (1989). Which facets of communication have strong effects on outcome: A meta-analysis. In M. Stewart & D. Roter (Eds.), *Communicating with medical patients* (pp. 183–196). Newbury Park, CA: Sage.

Roter, D. (2006). The physician–patient relationship and its implications for malpractice litigation. *Journal of Healthcare Law & Policy, 9,* 304–314.

Roter, D., & Larson, S. (2002). The Roter interaction analysis system (RIAS): Utility and flexibility for analysis of medical interactions. *Patient Education and Counseling, 46,* 233–234.

Roter, D. L., & Hall, J. A. (1991). Health education theory: An application to the process of patient-provider communication. *Health Education Research, 6,* 185–194.

Roter, D. L., & Hall, J. A. (2009). Communication and adherence: Moving from prediction to understanding. *Medical Care, 47,* 823–825.

Roter, D. L., Hall, J. A., & Katz, N. R. (1987). Relations between physicians' behaviors and analogue patients' satisfaction, recall, and impressions. *Medical Care, 25,* 437–451.

Roter, D. L., Hall, J. A., & Katz, N. R. (1988). Patient–doctor communication: A descriptive summary of the literature. *Patient Education and Counseling, 12,* 99–119.

Roter, D. L., Larson, S., Sands, D. Z., Ford, D. E., & Houston, T. (2008). Can email messages between patients and physicians be patient-centered? *Health Communication, 23,* 80–86.

Roter, D. L., Stewart, M., Putnam, S. M., Lipkin, M., Stiles, W., & Inui, T. S. (1997). Communication patterns of primary care physicians. *JAMA, 227,* 350–356.

Rowe, M. (2004). Doctors' responses to medical errors. *Critical Reviews in Oncology/Hematology, 52,* 147–163.

Ruusuvuori, J. (2001). Looking means listening: Coordinating displays of engagement in doctor–patient interaction. *Social Science & Medicine, 52,* 1093–1108.

Ryan, R. M., & Deci, E. L. (2000). Self-determination theory and the facilitation of intrinsic motivation, social development, and well being. *American Psychologist, 55,* 68–78.

Sacks, H. (1987). On the preference for agreement and contiguity in sequences in conversation. In G. Button & J. R. Lee (Eds.), *Talk and social organization* (pp. 54–69). Clevedon, UK: Multilingual Matters.

Sacks, H., Schegloff, E. A., & Jefferson, G. (1974). A simplest systematics for the organization of turn-taking for conversation. *Language, 50,* 696–735.

Sanders, R. E. (1987). The interconnection of utterances and nonverbal displays. *Research on Language and Social Interaction, 20,* 141–170.

Scharader, S., Nelson, M., & Eidsness, L. (2009). Dying to know: A community survey about dying and end-of-life care. *Omega, 60,* 33–50.

Schegloff, E. A. (1982). Discourse as an interactional achievement: Some uses of "uh-huh" and other things that come between sentences. In D. Tannen (Ed.), *Analyzing discourse: Text and talk* (pp. 71–93). Washington, DC: Georgetown University Press.

Schegloff, E. A. (1995). Discourse as an interactional achievement III: The omnirelevance of action. *Research on Language and Social Interaction, 28,* 185–211.

Schegloff, E. A. (1998). Body torque. *Social Research, 65,* 535–596.

Schoenthaler, A., Chaplin, W. F., Allegrante, J. P., Fernandez, S., Diaz-Gloster, M., Tobin, J. N., et al. (2009). Provider communication effects medication adherence in hypotensive African Americans. *Patient Education and Counseling, 75,* 185–191.

Sheldon, L. K. (2005). Communication in oncology care: The effectiveness of skills training workshops for health care providers. *Clinical Journal of Oncology Nursing, 9,* 305–312.

Shreve, E. G., Harrigan, J. A., Kues, J. R., & Kagas, D. K. (1988). Nonverbal expressions of anxiety in physician–patient interactions. *Psychiatry, 51,* 378–397.

Siminoff, L. A., Ravdin, P., Colabianchi, N., & Saunders Sturm, C. M. (2000). Doctor–patient communication patterns in breast cancer adjuvant therapy decisions. *Health Expectations, 3,* 26–36.

Singh, H., Fox, S. A., Peterson, N. J., Shethia, A., & Street, R. L. (2009). Older patients' enthusiasm to use email to communicate with their physicians: Cross sectional survey. *Journal of Medical Internet Research, 11,* e18.

Skirton, H., & Bylund, C. L. (2010). Management of uncertainty. In C. L. Gaff & C. L. Bylund (Eds.), *Family communication about genetics: Theory and practice* (pp. 136–151). New York: Oxford University Press.

Skoumal, S. M., Florell, S. R., Bydalek, M. K., & Hunter, W. J. (1996). Malpractice protection: Communication of diagnostic uncertainty. *Diagnostic Cytopathology, 14,* 385–389.

Smith, C. K., Polis, E., & Hadac, R. R. (1981). Characteristics of the initial medical interview associated with patient satisfaction and understanding. *Journal of Family Practice, 12,* 283–288.

Smith, S., Hanson, J. L, Tewksbury, L. R., Christy, C., Talib, N. J., Harris, M. A., et al. (2007). Teaching patient communication skills to medical students: A review of randomized controlled trials. *Evaluation and the Health Professions, 30,* 3–21.

Smith, S., Lindsey, L. L., Kopfman, J., Yoo, J., & Morrison, K. (2008). Predictors of engaging in family discussion about organ donation and getting organ donor cards witnessed. *Health Communication, 23,* 142–152.

Song, M. K. (2004). Effects of end-of-life discussions on patients' affective outcomes. *Nursing Outlook, 52,* 118–125.

Spiers, J. A. (1998). The use of face work and politeness theory. *Qualitative Health Research, 8,* 25–47.

Stamp, G. H., & Knapp, M. L. (1990). The construct of intent in interpersonal communication. *Quarterly Journal of Speech, 76,* 282–299.

Stewart, M. A. (1995). Effective physician–patient communication and health outcomes: A review.

*Canadian Medical Association Journal, 152,* 1423–1433.

Stiles, W. B. (1989). Evaluating medical interview process components: Null correlations with outcomes may be misleading. *Medical Care, 27,* 212–220.

Stiles, W. B., & Putnam, S. M. (1995). Coding categories for investigating medical interviews: A meta-classification. In M. Lipkin Jr., S. M. Putnam, & A. Lazare (Eds.), *The medical interview: Clinical care, education and research* (pp. 489–494). New York: Springer-Verlag.

Stone, A. M., & Jones, C. L. (2009). Sources of uncertainty: Experiences of Alzheimer's disease. *Issues in Mental Health Nursing, 30,* 677–686.

Streeck, J., & Knapp, M. (1992). The interaction of visual and verbal features in human communication. In F. Poyatos (Ed.), *Advances in nonverbal communication* (pp. 3–24). Amsterdam: Benjamins.

Street, R. L. (1991). Physicians' communication and parents' evaluations of pediatric consultations. *Medical Care, 29,* 1146–1152.

Street, R. L., & Buller, D. B. (1987). Nonverbal response patterns in physician–patient interactions: A functional analysis. *Journal of Nonverbal Behavior, 11,* 234–253.

Street, R. L., & Gordon, H. S. (2006). The clinical context and patient participation in post-diagnostic consultations. *Patient Education and Counseling, 64,* 217–224.

Street, R. L., Gordon, H. S., Ward, M. W., Krupat, E., & Kravitz, R. L. (2005). Patient participation in medical consultations: Why some patients are more involved than others. *Medical Care, 43,* 960–969.

Street, R. L., & Millay, B. (2001). Analyzing patient participation in medical encounters. *Health Communication, 13,* 61–73.

Street, R. L., & Voigt, B. (1997). Patient participation in deciding breast cancer treatment and subsequent quality of life. *Medical Decision Making, 17,* 298–306.

Street, R. L., & Wiemann, J. (1987). Patients' satisfaction with physicians' interpersonal involvement, expressiveness, and dominance. *Communication Yearbook, 10,* 591–612.

Takayama, T., & Yamazaki, Y. (2004). How breast cancer outpatients perceive mutual participation in patient-physician interactions. *Patient Education and Counseling, 52,* 279–289.

Thomasma, D. C. (1994). Telling the truth to patients: A clinical ethics exploration. *Cambridge Quarterly Healthcare Ethics, 3,* 375–382.

Thompson, G. N., Menec, V. H., Chochinov, H. M., & McClement, S. E. (2008). Family satisfaction with care of a dying loved one in nursing homes: What makes the difference? *Journal of Gerontological Nursing, 34,* 37–44.

Thompson, T. L. (1994). Interpersonal communication and health care. In M. L. Knapp & G. R. Miller (Eds.), *Handbook of interpersonal communication,* (2nd ed., pp. 696–725). Thousand Oaks, CA: Sage.

Thompson, T. L., Robinson, J. D., & Kenny, R. W. (2003). Family conversations about organ donation. *Progress in Transplantation,* 49–55.

Turner, J. W. (2003). Telemedicine: Expanding healthcare into virtual environments. In T. L. Thompson, A. M. Dorsey, K. I. Miller, & R. Parrott (Eds.), *Handbook of health communication* (pp. 515–535). Mahwah, NJ: Lawrence Erlbaum.

Verhaak, P. F. M. (1988). Detection of psychological complaints by general practitioners. *Medical Care, 26,* 1009–1020.

Vukmir, R. B. (2004). Medical malpractice: Managing the risk. *Medicine and Law, 25,* 495–513.

Waitzkin, H. (1991). *The politics of medical encounters: How patients and doctors deal with social problems.* New Haven, CT: Yale University Press.

Wanzer, M. B., Wojtaszczyk, A. M., Schimert, J., Missert, L., Baker, S., Baker, R., et al. (2010). Enhancing the "informed" in informed consent: A pilot test of a multimedia presentation. *Health Communication, 25,* 365–374.

Watson, A. J., Bergman, H., Williams, C. M., & Kvedar, J. C. (2010). A randomized trial to evaluate the efficacy of online follow-up visits in the management of acne. *Archives of Dermatology, 146,* 406–411.

Watson, B., & Gallois, C. (1998). Nurturing communication by health professionals toward patients: A communication accommodation theory approach. *Health Communication, 10,* 343–355.

Weaver, M. J., Ow, C. L., Walker, D. J., & Degenhardt, E. F. (1993). A questionnaire for patients' evaluations of their physicians' humanistic behaviors. *Journal of General Internal Medicine, 8,* 135–139.

Weijts, W. (1994). Responsible health communication: Taking control of our lives. *American Behavioral Scientist, 38,* 257–270.

Weinberger, M., Greene, J. Y., & Mamlin, J. J. (1981). The impact of clinical encounter events on patient and physician satisfaction. *Social Science & Medicine, 15E,* 239–244.

Weiner, J. S., & Cole, S. A. (2004). Three principles to improve clinician communication for advanced care planning: Overcoming emotional, cognitive, and skill barriers. *Journal of Palliative Medicine, 7,* 817–829.

Westphal, D. M., & McKee, S. A. (2009). End-of-life decision making in the intensive care unit: Physician and nurse perspectives. *American Journal of Medical Quality, 24,* 222–228.

White, C. B., Moyer, C. A., Stern, D. T., & Katz, S. J. (2004). A content analysis of e-mail communication between patients and their providers: Patients get the message. *Journal of the American Medical Informatics Association, 11,* 260–267.

Williams, G. C., Frankel, R. M., Campbell, T. L., & Deci, E. L. (2000). Research on relationship-centered care and healthcare outcomes from the Rochester biopsychosocial program: A self-determination theory integration. *Families, Systems & Health, 18,* 79–90.

Wissow, L. S. (2004). Patient communication and malpractice: Where are we now? *Patient Education and Counseling, 52,* 3–5.

Witte, K. (1992). Putting the fear back into fear appeals: The extended parallel process model. *Communication Monographs, 59,* 329–349.

Wittenberg-Lyles, E. M., Goldsmith, J., Ragan, S., & Sanchez-Reilly, S. (2010). Medical students' views and ideas about palliative care communication training. *American Journal of Hospice & Palliative Medicine, 27,* 38–49.

Wittenberg-Lyles, E. M., Goldsmith, J., Sanchez-Reilly, S., & Ragan, S. L. (2008). Communicating a terminal prognosis in a palliative care setting: Deficiencies in current communication training protocols. *Social Science & Medicine, 66,* 2356–2365.

van Zanten, M., Boulet, J. R., & McKinley, W. (2007). Using standardized patients to assess the interpersonal skills of physicians: Six years experience with a high stakes certification examination. *Health Communication, 22,* 195–205.

Zolnierek, K. B. H., & DiMatteo, M. R. (2009). Physician communication and patient adherence to treatment: A meta-analysis. *Medical Care, 47,* 826–834.

Zoppi, K., & Epstein, R. M. (2002). Is communication a skill? Communication behaviors and being-in-relation. *Family Medicine, 43,* 319–324.

# CHAPTER 20

# Interpersonal Communication in Family Relationships

*John P. Caughlin*

*Ascan F. Koerner*

*Paul Schrodt*

*Mary Anne Fitzpatrick*

Family communication has been an enduring interest for interpersonal communication scholars. Indeed, every *Handbook of Interpersonal Communication* has included a chapter on family communication. Although interest in the topic has remained constant, the research literature on family communication has grown so much since the first handbook chapter (Fitzpatrick & Badzinski, 1985) that it now only faintly resembles the literature that was described less than a generation ago. Prior to the time of the first edition, only a handful of communication scholars were researching family communication specifically, with the vast majority of research on the topic being conducted by scholars outside the communication discipline, especially in family sociology and family therapy

(Rogers, 2006). Now, although interest in family interaction remains great outside the discipline, there are literally hundreds of communication scholars interested in family communication. In fact, a recent check of the National Communication Association membership roll revealed precisely 500 members of the Family Communication Division.

The growth in the family communication literature is also reflected in the diversity of research programs and theories addressing family communication. Fitzpatrick and Badzinski (1985) identified six theories that formed the grounding for almost all the research on family communication. By 2004, Stamp found that 16 different theories commonly guided family communication research, and this number does not even include other theories that have risen in prominence since then, such as communication privacy management theory (Petronio, 2002; Petronio & Caughlin, 2006). The increased breadth in research is also reflected in large-scaled projects focusing on family communication. Whereas it was possible in 1985 to provide a reasonable summary of the major streams of research in a single chapter, now research on family communication warrants a major handbook (Vangelisti, 2004) and other similar tomes (e.g., Turner & West, 2006).

The increased efforts spent on understanding family communication are justified because family communication "shapes how we interact in virtually every context of our lives" (Vangelisti, 1993, p. 42). Most people first learn how to communicate in families (Bruner, 1990), and the quality of family relationships is extremely important to individuals' well-being and sense of life satisfaction (Campbell, Converse, & Rodgers, 1976).

The current chapter provides an introduction to the growing literature on this important topic. It is by necessity highly selective. The chapter begins with discussions of some fundamental issues, including definitions of families, the changes in families that have occurred in recent decades, and the centrality of communication to families. The remainder of the chapter is divided into two main parts, the first adumbrating some research that highlights communication processes that operate in many different types of families and the second summarizing research that focuses on communication within specific types of families.

## Definitions of Family

Families affect humans in a number of ways, with important biological, psychological, social, political, and legal ramifications. Thus, it is no surprise that "family" is a highly complex and multifaceted social concept with multiple, competing, or even incompatible definitions that frequently are hotly contested by various stakeholders. Debates over the definition of family have become even more contentious over the past few decades as major changes in society have led scholars to question what were once presumed to be inherent properties of "the family." Indeed, the changes in families have been so salient that many scholars now avoid referring to "the family" as a singular institution, instead referring to families in the plural so as not to imply one particular type (Fitzpatrick, 2006). Given the changes in families and the debates over how to define the concept of family, no definition of family can be truly objective or scientifically neutral. Thus, our goal here is not to define family in the absolute sense but to briefly review how family has been defined in the area of family communication and to discuss the relative strengths and weaknesses of the various definitions. The main criterion for our evaluation is a definition's ability to focus attention on communication and its outcomes. Following Wamboldt and Reiss (1989), three classes of definitions of the family can be identified in the extant research on families: (1) family structure, (2) task orientation, and (3) transactional process.

### Family Structure

Most early definitions of family were based on family structure (Fitzpatrick, 2006). Structure here refers to who is in or out of the family and how family members are related to one another. Structural definitions most commonly refer to either the family of origin or the family of procreation. The *family of origin* is a group of individuals who have established biological, social, or legal legitimacy by virtue of shared genetics, marriage, or adoption. The family of origin is identified in reference to a child, usually because it is born into and/or raised by the family. In contrast, the *family of procreation* is identified in reference to an adult who is in a committed romantic relationship or a parent and refers to a smaller group living in the same household, also often called the nuclear family. Family structure definitions presuppose clear criteria for membership in the family and often identify hierarchies within the family based on sex and age. In addition, specific functions are associated with specific family roles, such as discipline with fathers, nurturance with mothers, and creating a sense of history with grandparents.

From a communication perspective, structural definitions are problematic because they seem to imply that family structure determines communication behaviors, an assertion not necessarily supported by empirical data (see the section on communication in various family types). In addition, social changes such as the high divorce rate, artificial reproduction technologies, and changing gender norms are making definitions of the family based solely on structural characteristics rather exclusive. For example, in 2008, only about 70% of all U.S. children lived in two-parent households, and fewer than 60% lived in households together with their married, biological parents (Federal Interagency Forum on Child and Family Statistics, 2009). Families have simply become too diverse to be described by any simple structural definition (Galvin, 2006).

Despite these obvious problems with structural definitions, much family research still uses "the household" or "the nuclear family" to operationalize the family. This trend is partly due to convenience; it is fairly easy to determine who lives with whom. In addition, studying only families with similar memberships avoids statistical confounds that can be created by the absence or presence of different family members or different constellations of family members.

## Psychosocial Task Definitions

The second class of definitions is based on whether certain tasks associated with family are performed (Wamboldt & Reiss, 1989). In these definitions, a family is a psychosocial group consisting of two or more members who work toward tasks such as mutual needs fulfillment, nurturance, and development. Task definitions are usually concerned with describing the functions of the family. A good example of a psychosocial task definition defines the family as the social unit that accepts responsibility for the socialization and nurturance of children (Lerner & Spanier, 1978). In this definition, a family consists of children and the adults who take responsibility for caring for them, regardless of whether there are one or more adults, whether the adults are married to one another, and whether the adults are the biological parents of the children. Thus, in psychosocial task definitions, structure is ignored but function emphasized.

Inclusiveness, especially of nontraditional families, is an obvious strength of psychosocial task definitions. Additionally, the emphasis on function clearly leads to a focus on what families do, such as how they communicate with one another. An obvious weakness of psychosocial task definitions are the fuzzy boundaries around the concept, especially given that contributing to the functions of a family does not require lengthy relationships. For example, a family friend visiting for the weekend might provide nurturing to a child, a camp counselor might impart education, and a music teacher instill self-confidence, yet few would feel compelled to consider these persons to be family.

## Transactional Process Definitions

A final class of definitions of the family gives central importance to transactional processes. A family is defined as a group of intimates who generate a sense of home and group identity, complete with strong ties of loyalty and emotion, and an experience of history and a future (Wamboldt & Reiss, 1989). Similar to psychosocial task definitions, the emphasis is on function, but relationships are described as intimate, that is, they are characterized by interdependence, commitment, a perception of closeness, and temporal stability. Thus, like psychosocial task definitions, function is emphasized, but unlike psychosocial task definitions, structure is not ignored. Rather, structure exists in the form of enduring, intimate relationships, but functions are properties of the group rather than individual family roles. Thus, discipline and nurturance, for example, result from the way families communicate with one another rather than only from the behaviors of a parent. In addition, transactional definitions are concerned with the sense of family identity that is created through communication. This attribute of a family is captured by the concept that Reiss (1981) has called "family paradigms," or the worldviews that families hold affecting how they process information from the surrounding environment. Identity for one family may be tied to its concept of surviving in a complex or hostile world, another family's identity may revolve around religion, and yet another's may focus on having fun.

From a communication perspective, the strengths of transactional definitions include emphasis on communication processes, flexibility regarding family structures, and emphasis on interdependence in family relationships. These strengths probably explain why most definitions in family communication textbooks are versions of transactional definitions, with communication framed as constituting the family structures (Floyd, Mikkelson, & Judd, 2006). One weakness of transactional definitions, however, is the relative fuzziness of the conceptual boundaries, which creates complications for researchers, such as statistical challenges. The fuzziness arises from families' ability to determine membership for themselves and from the lack of unequivocal criteria for family. For example, at what point does a relationship become intimate enough and have enough sense of a shared history and future that it counts as a form of kin?

## Summary

The three different types of family definitions emphasize different aspects of family. Family structure definitions include as family members those who have established biological or socio-legal legitimacy. A variety of societal changes make family structure definitions less viable than they once seemed. Psychosocial task definitions define the family as a group that works toward mutual needs fulfillment as well as the nurturance and development of the members. Although psychosocial task definitions help us focus on the goals of family life, the various stages and types of families have markedly different goals, making the definition less useful than it might be. Transactional process approaches define the family as a group of intimates who generate a sense of home and group identity, have strong ties of loyalty and emotion, and experience a history and a future. Admittedly, this definition is complex and contains many abstract concepts that themselves need to be defined. Yet the transactional definition has two advantages over the other two approaches. First, the transactional definition of the family places a very strong emphasis on communication as the major vehicle in establishing levels of interdependence and commitment, forming ties of loyalty and identity, and transmitting a sense of family identity, history, and future. Second, this definition can encompass the many forms of modern family life because this approach allows families to define themselves rather than basing the definition of the family on socio-legal or genetic criteria.

## What Do the Changes in the Family Mean?

It is not controversial to claim that the institution of family has changed over the past few generations. The implications of these changes, however, are widely debated. Both in popular culture and in scholarly literature, there are periodic exhortations to do something about the ostensibly deteriorating family. Inevitably, some scholars respond with arguments that the various changes are not necessarily negative. In the early 1990s, for example, worries about the state of the family were reflected in political campaigns promising to reinstitute family values, and some family scholars argued that "the sky is falling" (Cowan, 1993, p. 548) because of the downfall in the American family (Popenoe, 1993). Others responded that the changes in families are not inherently problematic and the concerns about such changes reflect biases toward overly rigid structural norms for families (Stacey, 1993).

More recently, the same kind of debate has resurfaced using slightly different terms. Waite and Gallagher (2000) argued that traditional heterosexual marriage has unique benefits for both men and women, making them happier and healthier. Waite and Gallagher's analysis received extensive attention in popular outlets, contributing to a sense that bolstering the institution of traditional marriage is extremely important. Yet many scholars questioned whether the benefits of marriage are unique. DePaulo and Morris (2005) suggested that the key is not marriage, per se, but having fulfilling and enduring relationships, which, they argue, many single people (especially women) are able to develop. Others argued that traditional marriage is a patriarchal institution that makes sense financially for women but typically undermines their overall well-being (England, 2001).

It is likely that such discussions over the fate of marriages and families will continue, and we cannot hope to resolve them here. Nevertheless, one obvious impediment to a constructive debate on such issues is the extent to which they are informed by overly positive perceptions about what families were like in the past. Historians have shown us that nostalgia for a lost family tradition that never existed has prejudiced our understanding of the contemporary family (Coontz, 2000a). Our understanding of family difficulties in the past, such as incest or violence, is severely hampered by a lack of accurate historical perspective and the strong tendency in the past to deny or suppress real problems in families (Gordon, 1988). Although providing a thorough historical perspective on families is beyond the

scope of this chapter, it is exceedingly clear that many people have misconceptions about families from the past. For example, one common concern is the supposedly unprecedented exposure that children have to information about sex, but from the colonial period in the United States to the 18th century, children were regularly exposed to such information. In colonial families, for example, children often shared a bed with sexually active parents (Gadlin, 1977), and it was common in the 1700s for the word "fornication" to be used in school spelling exercises (Coontz, 2000b). Table 20.1 summarizes a number of myths about families that have not been supported by careful historical analyses (Coontz, 2000a, 2000b; Cooper, 1999; Hareven, 1980). Families have always had problems, and it is important when assessing the meaning of changes in families to compare the modern state of families with what families were actually like in the past—not a romanticized version of families that never existed.

# Centrality of Communication for Families

As communication scholars, we often take the centrality of communication for families for granted, as a virtual truism. Even outside the field of communication, few would argue with the premise that communication is the means by which family relationships are established and maintained, attachment and intimacy are created, children are socialized, gender roles and expectations are formed, decisions are made, problems and conflicts are resolved, social support is provided, and the physical and mental well-being of others are affected. In fact, most of the early research that established the central role of communication for families emerged from scholars outside the discipline of communication, and arguably, the bulk of current research concerned with family communication is still conducted by researchers who are not identified as communication scholars.

**Table 20.1** Seven Myths Not Supported by Historical Research on the American Family

| | Myths | Facts |
|---|---|---|
| 1. | Large extended family households were common in preindustrial America. | Although extended family households did exist, they represented a small proportion of households. |
| 2. | Migration associated with industrialization contributed to the decline of close family ties. | Because family members often followed each other to new locations, such migration actually helped keep extended family ties close in many instances. |
| 3. | Diversity in the forms of families is a new challenge in America. | There have been diverse family forms throughout all periods of American history. |
| 4. | Substance abuse is a greater challenge to American families now than ever before. | Alcohol and drug use was higher at the end of the 19th century than at the beginning of the 21st century. |
| 5. | The value placed on motherhood has declined in modern times. | Motherhood was not glorified as a career until the 19th century. |
| 6. | Stability and uniformity in family life cycle transitions declined markedly in the 20th century compared with previous centuries. | In many ways, American families achieved unprecedented stability and uniformity in life cycle transitions in the 20th century; for example, shorter life spans in earlier centuries contributed to comparatively short marriages. |
| 7. | In recent years, families have allowed children greater access to information about sex than ever before. | Open discussions about sex in front of children were common from the colonial period through the 18th century. |

Family communication, however, is relevant not only as a process useful in predicting important outcomes, such as those described above. It is also relevant because it effectively mediates or moderates the effects of other constructs on important outcomes of family members. Thus, family communication is an important outcome in its own right because understanding how families communicate is necessary for appreciating how other, more distal factors affect families and individual family members. There is an overall negative effect of divorce on children, for example, but the effect of divorce depends on the nature of communication between divorcing or divorced parents (e.g., Amato & Afifi, 2006).

Family communication not only helps constitute the relationships within families, it also shapes the impact of all other factors that can influence families.

Given the central and varied functions of communication in families, it is not surprising that there is considerable plurality in our conceptualizations of family communication (Stamp, 2004). Although certain scholars have attempted to delineate a particular set of assumptions that underlie "a communication approach" (Whitchurch & Dickson, 1999, p. 693), the reality is that family communication scholars' research has become so diverse that no single set of assumptions describes it all. There are certain common foci, such as an interest in meaning within families, that distinguish most communication scholars from many (if not most) scholars who study family interaction in other disciplines, yet the specific questions about these common foci and the research paradigms used to address these foci vary widely within the field. In our view, this diversity in perspectives is unproblematic; indeed, families and family communication are so complex that no single perspective is likely to ever lead to a full understanding of either. For example, one very gross division within the family communication literature involves whether research is focused primarily on particular processes (e.g., conflict, support, typologies) that cut across various family forms or whether research foregrounds the influence of family forms (e.g., blended families, single-parent families) on communication and family outcomes. Because there is value in both of these broad approaches, we discuss each below.

## Research That Foregrounds Processes Across Families

Researchers interested in families often examine certain aspects or dimensions of communication without focusing on the type of family. Given the complexity of family communication, the number of potential constructs or dimensions is probably limitless. Consider just one construct that is important to family interaction—power. Even with this single general construct, there are many different legitimate ways to conceptualize and operationalize it; for instance, some researchers focus on evidence of power dynamics in observable patterns of interaction (e.g., Rogers & Farace, 1975; Watzlawick, Beavin, & Jackson, 1967), some place more emphasis on the social structures that shape interaction to benefit relatively more powerful family members (e.g., Eldridge & Christensen, 2002; Klein & Johnson, 1997), and others examine family members' perceptions

about who most influences family decisions (Caughlin & Ramey, 2005; Dornbusch et al., 1985). Rather than representing a problem, the multiple conceptualizations of power simply indicate that it is a multifaceted construct that shapes, and is shaped by, family communication in a number of ways. There are, therefore, many reasonable specific dimensions of power that can be assessed.

The same is true for other prominent dimensions of family communication, such as affective expression (Caughlin & Huston, 2006) and responsive communication (Reis, Clark, & Holmes, 2004). There are obviously many specific dimensions of affect and responsiveness. Moreover, research on such aspects of family communication illustrates the utility of focusing on general processes that cut across different types of family relationships. Such a focus allows us to understand processes that are widely applicable across different family relationships. For example, the connection between marital dissatisfaction and the expression of negative affect is perhaps the most replicated finding pertaining to family interaction (e.g., Caughlin, Huston, & Houts, 2000; Gottman, 1994; Karney & Bradbury, 1995). Such findings are similar to those showing that the affective quality of parental communication (e.g., negative expressions, warmth) is extremely important in parent–child interactions and in child development (e.g., Abe & Izard, 1999; Zhou et al., 2002).

Although it is clear that broad constructs such as affective expressions are important across different types of family relationships and across different types of families, it is sometimes difficult to recognize the extent of generalizability because the literatures focusing on different types of family relationships sometimes develop different vocabularies for similar communication constructs. In the marital interaction literature, for example, frequent complaints about what the other family member does typically would be labeled a form of negativity (e.g., Gottman, 1994), whereas a parent complaining about a child's behavior commonly would be labeled rejection (e.g., Shelton & Harold, 2008).

Within the broad range of studies that focus on processes within families, there are at least two major classes of research. The first examines communication processes such as family conflict and supportive communication, among many others. The second uses typological approaches to understanding communication in families. Illustrative examples of each of these approaches are summarized below.

## Communication Processes

### Family Conflict

Family conflict is simply interpersonal conflict experienced in family relationships. It can be defined as existing at the level of both psychology and behavior. At the psychological level, family conflict exists whenever a family member desires or pursues an outcome and perceives another family member as interfering with or preventing the family member from obtaining the outcome (Fincham, Bradbury, & Grych, 1990). At the behavioral level, family conflict exists whenever a family member engages in observable behavior intended to either interfere with or prevent the outcome or to reduce or remove the perceived interference (e.g., Cahn, 1992; Straus, 1990). These behaviors vary in how explicit or direct they are (Donohue & Kolt, 1992); the degree to which they are aggressive, hostile, and violent (Straus, 1990); whether they are unilateral or reciprocal; and the extent to which they are dyadic or involve multiple family members.

Family conflict is different from other types of interpersonal conflict in several important aspects. Compared with other interpersonal relationships, family relationships often are perceived to be less voluntary and more obligating, and they depend less on satisfaction for their stability (Vangelisti, 1993). This means that family conflict, particularly at the behavioral level, often is less avoided and more extreme. In addition, the meaning of conflict behaviors is

understood in the context of an enduring relationship that is full of personal history rather than in the context of the specific conflict episode. Also, because conflict takes place between family members who are embedded within family systems, the conflict is likely to also affect other interpersonal relationships within the family, whose dynamics might influence the behavior of the conflicting members. Finally, family conflict takes place within a societal context that defines a specific set of expectations, rules, and values for family relationships that are distinct from those of other relationships.

*Conflict Frequency and Intensity.* There is ample research demonstrating that conflict is frequent in families (e.g., Shantz & Hartup, 1992; Shantz & Hobart, 1989; Sillars, Canary, & Tafoya, 2004), in all likelihood because of the great intimacy and interdependence that characterize family relationships. Greater intimacy is associated with more conflict because it leads to greater directness in communication, an increased sense that one has the right to make requests of the other, and increased expectations that the other will comply with one's request. Similarly, greater interdependence is associated with more conflict because it means that family members are more likely to be able to interfere with desired outcomes and to be perceived as interfering (Deutsch, 1973).

As for conflict intensity, there can be little doubt that conflict can be particularly intense in family relationships (Straus, 1990). Few persons would perpetrate or allow verbal aggression or even physical violence in conflicts at work or with friends; however, family relationships are rife with verbally abusive and violent conflict. In representative samples of U.S. families, Straus and Gelles (1990) found instances of severe violence (such as kicking, punching, and attacks with objects) in 8% of all marital relationships, 11% of parent–child relationships, and 36% of sibling relationships. Straus found less severe violence (e.g., shoving, pushing, and slapping) in 16% of marriages, almost 100% of parent–child relationships with young children, 34%

of parent–adolescent relationships, and 64% of sibling relationships.

*Types of Family Conflict.* Family conflict is associated with a wide range of behaviors, which makes it difficult to theorize about conflict without first classifying conflicts or conflict behaviors into different types. One way to create types of family conflict is to focus on the outcomes of conflict behaviors, such as relational satisfaction, stability, or child adjustment, and to label them accordingly as either functional (i.e., constructive) or dysfunctional (i.e., destructive). Such a distinction makes sense as long as it can be assumed that specific types of conflict behaviors consistently lead to either positive or negative outcomes, which can be a problematic assumption. Not only is the meaning of most conflict behaviors ambiguous, but also the standards by which conflict behavior is judged are not always easy to determine and often lead to varying evaluations. What a particular conflict behavior means is shaped by many factors, including the particular relational history and climate of those engaged in the conflict (Caughlin & Vangelisti, 2006). Thus, whether a conflict behavior is constructive or destructive depends on whether conflict is judged using a long- or short-term perspective; whether these outcomes are psychological, behavioral, or relational; and finally, from whose perspective the outcomes are judged. Because at the root of many family conflicts are incompatible goals, it is almost inevitable that any outcome has to be evaluated differently depending on whose perspective is used when making the judgment. Thus, conflict behavior that achieves a desired outcome for one family member (and from that person's perspective is desirable) might be dysfunctional for another family member or even dysfunctional in some ways for the family member who apparently won the conflict. Some adolescents who win battles for greater autonomy from their parents, for example, later express surprise at the extent to which those disagreements undermined their relationship with their parents (Ramey, 2010).

A second way of classifying conflict behaviors is to focus on the behaviors themselves rather than their outcomes. Such typologies group types of conflict behaviors together based on some shared attribute, usually an underlying dimension, such as intensity. For example, Donohue and Kolt (1992) distinguished between *latent conflict, problem to solve, dispute,* and *fight.* Straus (1990) distinguished between *reasoning* (rational discussion and problem solving), *verbal aggression* (symbolically hurting the other), and *violence* (inflicting physical pain and/or injury). Finally, Sillars et al. (2004) categorized conflict behaviors using two underlying dimensions: *direct* versus *indirect* and *cooperation* versus *competition.*

A third way that researchers have classified conflict is based on who is involved, such as marital conflict, parent–child conflict, and sibling conflict. Such a classification makes sense, because there can be important attributes of the relationship that influence conflict behaviors and outcomes, such as the power differential between parents and children. In addition, there are a number of fairly normative goal incompatibilities between family members that make certain kinds of family conflict both common and predictable. For example, conflict between parents and preadolescent children most typically involves parents' attempts to regulate their children's behavior and children initially resisting and ultimately complying with their parents' demands (Laursen, 1993). Parent–child conflict is a normative part of the socialization process as children move from other-regulation to self-regulation, and such instances constitute much of family communication. As children move into adolescence, most of the conflicts remain centered on parents' attempts to control the child's behaviors, such as cleaning one's room and doing homework (Smetana, Daddis, & Chuang, 2003), although some parent–adolescent dyads begin to have conflicts in which adolescents attempt to change parents' behaviors, such as health risk behaviors (Caughlin & Ramey, 2005). The most salient change in parent–child conflict that occurs as children reach adolescence involves children becoming likely to strongly resist parents' demands on their behaviors (Collins & Laursen, 2004; Noller, 1995; Smetana & Asquith, 1994). One reason for this change is adolescents appear to develop a sense that they have a legitimate right to govern their own behaviors sooner than parents do (Smetana & Asquith, 1994).

*Functions of Family Conflict.* Family conflict can serve important functions for the family as a whole and for individual family members. As systems of interdependent individuals whose goals, interests, and needs are not always in alignment, families can benefit from responding to such incompatibilities in ways that maintain the system overall. Thus, one important function of family conflict is to allow families to recognize the needs of individual family members and to coordinate their behaviors such that they can facilitate goal achievement for their members while simultaneously maintaining the family system (Koerner & Fitzpatrick, 2006).

This is not to suggest that goal achievement is a necessary result of family conflict. Indeed, most single-conflict episodes yield very little progress in integrating family members' goals. Vuchinich's (1999; Vuchinich & Angelelli, 1995) line of research on communication and conflict in whole family units suggests that very little is resolved in most episodes of conflict. Vuchinich videotaped families while they had dinner and analyzed the observable conflicts. Vuchinich (1999) reported four common ways that families stop engaging in overt conflict: submission, compromise, withdrawal, and standoff. Vuchinich found that the majority of family conflicts ended in standoffs: Family members simply stopped discussing the issue, with no apparent resolution. This suggests that most families, even functional ones, consider family conflict to be a normal part of ongoing family life. It also suggests that most conflict episodes probably have no discernable impact on helping family members collectively achieve their goals but progress toward that end may occur over repeated discussions.

Another important function of family conflict is to facilitate the socialization and development of children. For example, one of the main ways that adolescents achieve a level of autonomy that is congruent with functional adulthood is through conflict with parents (Collins & Laursen, 2004; Smetana, 1996). Specifically, family communication serves five developmental functions for adolescents, all of which are achieved, at least in part, through family conflict (Noller, 1995). The functions are (1) renegotiation of roles, rules, and relationships; (2) identity exploration; (3) enhancing adolescents' self-esteem; (4) modeling and teaching problem-solving behaviors; and (5) enabling adolescents' decision making.

*Outcomes of Family Conflict.* Despite the functions that conflict can serve, most research examining conflict in families suggests that excessive conflict tends to have negative consequences. Chief among them is that conflict affects the quality of family relationships and family members' well-being (Cummings, Iannotti, & Zahn-Waxler, 1985; Gordis, Margolin, & John, 2001; Tucker, McHale, & Crouter, 2003). In addition, family conflict can contribute to poor socialization of children. Negative conflict behaviors that children learn in families of origin affect their family relationships (Reese-Weber & Bertle-Haring, 1998; Rinaldi & Howe, 2003), relationships with friends and peers (Jenkins, 2000), and subsequent interpersonal relationships as adults (Koerner & Fitzpatrick, 1997, 2002). Additionally, physical violence and child abuse, which are more likely to occur during family conflict than during any other time of family communication, appear to result in particularly acute negative effects on the mental and physical health of children (Salzinger et al., 2002).

One interesting apparent contradiction in the literature on conflict in families concerns the extent to which the negative effects of conflict are viewed as a function of the amount of conflict or the competence with which conflict is handled. In the marital conflict literature, scholars commonly argue that "the number and type of conflict areas . . . are less important than how couples handle these conflicts" (Clements, Cordova, Markman, & Laurenceau, 1997, p. 342). This is in stark contrast to the literature on parent–adolescent conflict, which has focused much more on the negative outcomes associated with the amount or intensity of conflict than the manner in which those conflicts are addressed (e.g., Cole & McPherson, 1993; Crouter, Bumpus, Maguire, & McHale, 1999; Turner, Larimer, & Sarason, 2000). At first glance, these literatures might seem to suggest that the amount of conflict is more important in parent–adolescent relationships, whereas the ways conflicts are addressed are more important in marriage. The apparent differences, however, actually appear to be a function of biases in researchers' attention. Despite frequent claims that the amount or type of conflicts in marriage are not important, there is actually very good evidence that some couples are faced with more difficult and relationship-threatening conflict than are others (Sanford, 2003), and the amount of conflict in marriage is an important predictor of dissatisfaction and divorce (Caughlin & Vangelisti, 2006; Noller & Feeney, 1998; Orbuch, Veroff, Hassan, & Horrocks, 2002). Whereas more research has focused on the amount of conflict in parent–adolescent relationships, handling conflict poorly, such as by engaging in a pattern in which the parent frequently nags and complains while the adolescent withdraws, predicts negative outcomes such as low self-esteem and risky behaviors among adolescents (Caughlin & Malis, 2004). In short, it appears that in both marriages and parent–adolescent dyads, both the amount of conflict and the manner in which conflicts are handled matter.

## Supportive Communication

Social support is a complex and multifaceted construct (Goldsmith, 2004; Sarason & Sarason, 2009; Vangelisti, 2009). Rather than attempting to summarize all research on social support, we focus on aspects of social support that are particularly important for understanding support

processes in marriages and families (for more on social support, see Chapter 10, "Supportive Communication," this volume). Supportive communication is extremely important for the well-being of marriages and families. Xu and Burleson (2004), for example, argued that "considerable research suggests that social support is one of the most important provisions of the marital relationship and an important determinant of marital satisfaction" (p. 123). Numerous studies using varied measures bolster the claim that social support is one key to marital well-being. For instance, Dehle, Larson, and Landers (2001) asked married individuals to keep diaries for a week and found that daily reports of spouses' support were associated with satisfaction. Also, Pasch and her associates (Pasch & Bradbury, 1998; Pasch, Bradbury, & Davila, 1997) developed a laboratory task designed to elicit social support. One spouse was asked to "talk about something you would like to change about yourself" (Pasch et al., 1997, p. 366), while the other was told to respond however he or she wanted. The ways the wives sought and provided social support predicted marital outcomes two years after these conversations.

The vast majority of research examining the importance of social support in families has focused on the marital relationship. Even social support studies that do not specifically label themselves as pertaining to marriage often use marital relationships as the context for understanding support; for instance, Goldsmith, Lindholm, and Bute's (2006) study of how "couples" cope with serious cardiac events was based almost exclusively on married individuals.

Despite the emphasis on marriage in support research, supportive communication is also important in other family relationships. When college students were asked what they thought constituted good family communication, for example, there was nearly unanimous agreement that providing emotional and/or tangible support is a hallmark of high-quality family communication (Caughlin, 2003). Moreover, many of the challenges and issues that lead family members to need support are ones that affect the entire family. When one family member is diagnosed with cancer, for example, the experience typically affects multiple family members in numerous ways (e.g., Miller & Caughlin, 2011). Often, other family members experience as much uncertainty and distress as the patients themselves do (Goldsmith, 2009; Hagedoorn, Sanderman, Bolks, Tuinstra, & Coyne, 2008), leading some scholars to argue that cancer is not just an individual's disease but also a family issue (Veach, Nicholas, & Barton, 2002).

Despite the fact that challenges within families frequently affect multiple family members, most research on support processes treats social support as if there were a clearly defined individual in need of support, with others (including family members) acting as potential providers of support. The most common way that scholars recognize the challenges of nonpatients is with the concept of caregiving burden (Tang et al., 2008), which recognizes that providing support can be extremely stressful but maintains the division between recipients and providers of support. Given the interdependence of family members' experiences with stressors, such a division does not always make sense when thinking about support processes in families (Goldsmith, 2009). Although most research on supportive communication makes such a division, the research on dyadic coping and on communal coping are important exceptions.

*Dyadic and Communal Coping.* Dyadic coping (Badr, Carmack, Kashy, Cristofanilli, & Revenson, 2010; Bodenmann, 2005) and communal coping (Lyons, Mickelson, Sullivan, & Coyne, 1998) are conceptually distinct, but related, constructs that refer to the idea that some stressors are experienced and managed jointly. Dyadic and communal coping are not support processes in and of themselves, but they highlight the fact that support processes sometimes are coordinated, leading multiple individuals to orient toward managing a stressor together.

The construct of dyadic coping is defined in terms of pairs of individuals, but communal coping can occur in dyads, small groups, or even communities. Lawrence and Schiller Schigelone (2002), for example, examined communal coping in retirement communities. Communal coping is defined in terms of (a) a communal orientation toward a stressor (e.g., when a family defines a problem as "our" problem), (b) communicative efforts to address the issue, and (c) joint attempts to mitigate the adverse effects of the stressor (Lyons et al., 1998). Although most communal coping research has not examined families, per se, the construct is plainly relevant to families; for instance, communal coping has been observed in some postdivorce families (Afifi, Hutchinson, & Krouse, 2006).

Joint coping efforts often have benefits. For example, in a prospective study that followed couples over the first six months of treatment for metastatic breast cancer, patients' distress was inversely related to the extent to which they and their partner engaged in positive dyadic coping, such as mutual calming, expressions of solidarity, and joint problem solving (Badr et al., 2010). Yet communal coping efforts are not always helpful or functional; if joint coping is enacted with ambivalence or in a superficial manner, it can be counterproductive (Bodenmann, 2005). Also, even when family members are all oriented toward the same stressor, they may communicate in ways that undermine support for others; for example, in families dealing with the loss of a parent due to cancer, some family members who had provided direct care to the parent may resent others who were less involved and can even think that those other family members are unworthy of comforting (Stone et al., 2010). Even ostensibly positive collaborative coping efforts can be detrimental to some family members. Although positive dyadic coping was related to lower distress for patients in the Badr et al. (2010) study, it was related to increased distress for the partners. Similarly, parents and children establishing a collaborative orientation toward stressors can come at a cost: Afifi and McManus (2006) found that communal coping in postdivorce families can be detrimental to children's well-being.

## Typological Approaches

Whereas the research discussed above that focuses on family communication processes is powerful in delineating associations between specific behaviors and outcomes, it tends to ignore the context of these associations and, more important, the moderating influences that context has on such associations. One of the basic insights into communication, however, is that all communication is contextual. Intentions, interpretations, the meanings assigned to behaviors, and the consequences of communication behaviors all depend on the context in which they are performed (Watzlawick et al., 1967). Thus, while a kiss typically is an expression of affection that increases intimacy and satisfaction, it can also signify betrayal and deliver one to one's enemies (as in the case of Jesus and Judas).

One way to address this inherent complexity of human communication is the use of a typological approach (Van Lear, Koerner, & Allen, 2006). In creating family typologies, researchers essentially identify stable relationship contexts that have consistent effects on how communication behaviors function in these relationships. Although this assumption is not always made explicit, it is essential to communication typologies. The factors that determine which type a family belongs to can be structural (e.g., types based on family constellations), cognitive (e.g., types based on family communication schemata), behavioral (e.g., types based on parenting), or outcome based (e.g., types based on child adjustment).

### Marriage Types

The marital relationship is of tremendous importance for family relationships. For most families, it is the foundational relationship for procreation, it provides a model for children on how to relate and communicate, and it creates a context for other intrafamilial relationships. Thus, marital types are often reflected in family types (Fitzpatrick & Ritchie, 1994). Marital typologies often are based on differences in key behaviors. In some instances, the key behaviors underlying a typology are fairly concrete, such as in Gottman's (1993, 1994) marital typology, which is based primarily on differences in conflict behaviors and distinguishes between three functional (i.e., validating, volatile, and avoidant) and two dysfunctional (i.e., hostile and hostile-detached) types. In other instances, key behaviors underlying typologies are fairly abstract, such as in Rosenfeld, Bowen, and Richman's (1995) typology of dual-career marriages (collapsing, work directed, and traditional role), which is based on spouses' participation in family and work-related activities.

Yet other marital typologies are based on multiple key communication constructs. For example, Caughlin and Huston (2006) argued that positive affect and antagonism do not represent end points along a single continuum but rather exist independently. These researchers used these two key behaviors to define four marriage types: (1) *tempestuous* marriages are high on both affection and antagonism, (2) *warm* marriages are high on affection and low on antagonism, (3) *hostile* marriages are low on affection and high on antagonism, and (4) *bland* marriages are low on both dimensions. Unlike the other three types, hostile marriages are not very stable and usually end in divorce (Caughlin & Huston).

Other marriage typologies are based on behavioral and cognitive differences, that is, differences in the beliefs and values of spouses. Probably the best example is Fitzpatrick's (1988) marital typology, which is based on spouses' reports of their beliefs and behaviors regarding ideology, interdependence, and conflict avoidance and categorizes marriages into three types: (1) *traditionals* (conventional ideology, high interdependence, low conflict avoidance), (2) *independents* (unconventional ideology, high interdependence, low conflict avoidance), and (3) *separates* (conventional ideology, low interdependence, high conflict avoidance). In about two thirds of marriages, both spouses have the same marital type; the remaining marriages fall into a mixed type (most frequently a traditional wife and a separate husband).

A significant strength of Fitzpatrick's (1988) typology is that it is based on both theory (the underlying dimensions were based on prevailing marital theories) and empirical validation (the three types represent naturally occurring clusters in the conceptual space of eight possible types defined by the three dimensions). Additionally, it allows for different marriages to achieve similar outcomes in different ways, which produces rich descriptions of each marriage type. For example, independent and separate spouses have close relationships outside their marriages that provide emotional support, whereas traditional spouses depend almost exclusively on their spouses for emotional support. Thus, spouses in all three marriage types are able to obtain emotional support, albeit from different sources. Probably the greatest weakness of the typology is that about a third of all couples fall into the mixed category. Although there are six different types of mixed couples that should be expected to vary greatly in their communication, in research, they are usually treated as equivalent. This is not just a simple oversight but almost certainly wrong as these very different constellations constitute very different relational contexts.

### Parenting Types

Parenting is important because it is the behavior associated with the crucial function of raising, educating, and socializing children. Given its centrality to families, it is no surprise that parenting has been the focus of researchers interested in child development since the beginning of research on families. What is surprising is the astonishing consistency of researchers' use of concepts to define parenting as well as the consistency of their findings (Darling & Steinberg, 1993).

Essentially, parenting has been defined along two dimensions, which might be called affiliation (including warmth, acceptance, and involvement) and dominance (including strictness, monitoring, and control). Early uses include Symonds (1939), who used the labels *acceptance/rejection* and *dominance/submission,* and Schaefer (1959), who labeled the dimensions *love/hostility* and *autonomy/control.* A more recent example is Maccoby and Martin (1983), who used the labels *responsiveness* and *demandingness.*

There are several iterations of the typology that resulted from crossing these two dimensions, the most well established of which is Baumrind's (1967, 1971). Baumrind initially developed her typology based on observations of parents' interactions with their preschool-age children, yielding three parenting types. *Authoritative* parenting emphasizes both affiliation and control, which creates warm and supportive parent–child relationships as well as age-appropriate control and monitoring. This parenting style is generally associated with a warm and accepting family communication climate and well-adjusted children. *Authoritarian* parenting emphasizes control but neglects the emotional needs of children. This type of parenting is focused on rules and obedience. This parenting style is associated with a cold and unsupportive family communication climate as well as poorly adjusted children. Finally, *permissive* parenting focuses on meeting children's emotional needs but fails to meet their needs for structure and control. In other words, it is high on affiliation and low on control. This parenting style is associated with emotional and somewhat volatile relationships, a somewhat chaotic family communication climate, and less than optimal child adjustment.

Later, Baumrind also identified parents who were not very involved in the parenting of their children and labeled this the *uninvolved* or *neglecting* parenting style. Parents with this style are not particularly interested in their children and less inclined to meet any of their needs. That is, they are low on affiliation and control. This parenting style is associated with a cold and avoidant family communication climate and less than optimal child adjustment.

## Family Types

Much like typologies of marriages and of parenting, family typologies are most often based on communication behaviors and patterns of family members of varying degrees of abstraction. Typically, the observed behaviors or outcomes associated with the behaviors are used to establish the functioning of families. Examples are Kantor and Lehr's (1976) typology of closed, open, and random families, where open families are considered the most functional, and Reiss's (1981) typology of consensus-sensitive, interpersonal-distance-sensitive, and environment-sensitive families, where environment-sensitive families are best for the mental health of children.

Olson's (1993) typology based on his circumplex model of marital and family communication is also primarily concerned with explaining family functioning. It is unique in that the types are defined by families' psychosocial properties of cohesion and flexibility rather than by observable behaviors. Specifically, in this model, 16 family types are defined by their location along two orthogonal dimensions of cohesion (high to low: enmeshed, connected, separated, and disengaged) and flexibility (high to low: chaotic, flexible, structured, and rigid). Families moderate on both dimensions are considered *balanced* and most functional, families extreme on both dimensions are considered *unbalanced* and least functional, and families extreme on one dimension and moderate on the other are considered to be intermediate in functioning. Family communication behavior, in this model, is viewed as a third, facilitating dimension that enables families to change with regard to cohesion and flexibility (Olson).

Finally, there are also family typologies that are less concerned with outcomes but rather focus on the origins of family communication behaviors. One example is the typology of family communication patterns first described by McLeod and

Chaffee (1972) and further developed by Fitzpatrick and her associates (Fitzpatrick & Ritchie, 1994; Koerner & Fitzpatrick, 2002, 2004, 2006). According to these researchers, family communication patterns are the result of families' use of different strategies to establish shared social realities. One strategy is to focus on the environment itself and the concepts that represent it. That is, families can try to discover the objective reality of the environment. The other strategy is to focus on how others understand the environment. That is, families can align their interpretation of the environment with the interpretation of others, usually high-status family members.

According to the theory, families that focus on concepts when creating social reality are conversation oriented. When families focus on others' perceptions when creating social reality, they are conformity oriented (Fitzpatrick & Ritchie, 1994). Conversation orientation refers to open and frequent communication among family members with the purpose of codiscovering the meaning of symbols and objects. It is associated with warm and supportive relationships and mutual respect for one another. Conformity orientation, in contrast, refers to more restricted communication between parents and children, with the persons in authority, usually the parents, defining social reality for all family members. It is associated with strict parenting and less concern for the children's thoughts and feelings.

These two orientations define four family types. *Consensual* families are high on both conversation orientation and conformity orientation. Their communication is characterized by the pressure to agree and to preserve parental authority, on the one hand, and an interest in open communication and in exploring new ideas, on the other. Parents resolve this tension by listening to their children and explaining their values and beliefs with the expectation that the children will adopt the parents' belief system. Children in these families are usually well adapted and satisfied.

*Pluralistic* families emphasize conversation orientation over conformity orientation. Their communication is open and unconstrained and involves all family members and a wide range of topics. Parents in these families rarely attempt to control their children and are accepting of children's different opinions. Children of these families tend to be independent and autonomous and to communicate persuasively. They are generally satisfied with their family relationships.

*Protective* families emphasize conformity over conversation orientation. Their communication is more restricted, concerned with children's obedience and rarely concerned with conceptual matters. Parents in these families state their beliefs and values and expect their children to subscribe to them unquestioningly. Children in protective families tend to see little value in conversation and to distrust their own decision-making ability.

*Laissez-faire* families deemphasize both conformity and conversation orientation. Their communication is infrequent and usually uninvolving. Members of laissez-faire families often are emotionally divorced from one another, and parents are not very involved with their children. Children of these families tend to discount family relationships and make their own decisions. They do not receive much support from their parents and are especially susceptible to peer influence.

Family communication pattern types have been associated with a number of family processes, such as confirmation and affection (Schrodt, Ledbetter, & Ohrt, 2007), conflict (Koerner & Fitzpatrick, 1997), family rituals (Baxter & Clark, 1996), and understanding (Sillars, Koerner, & Fitzpatrick, 2005), as well as with outcomes, such as adult children's conflict behaviors (Koerner & Fitzpatrick, 2002), children's mental and physical health (Schrodt & Ledbetter, 2007), and children's resiliency (Fitzpatrick & Koerner, 2005). In addition to being theoretically developed and empirically well tested, family communication pattern types theory also converges with a larger body of research on human communication in general and family communication in particular, making it probably the most broad-ranging family

communication theory currently available. The two dimensions of conversation orientation and conformity orientation are closely related to the dimensions of affiliation and power, which have been recognized as central to interpersonal relationships (Haslam, 1994). In addition, conversation orientation and conformity orientation also are closely related to responsiveness and demandingness (Isaacs & Koerner, 2008), which underlie most typologies of parenting.

## Research That Foregrounds Different Family Forms

Contrary to research that foregrounds interpersonal communication processes within families, research that foregrounds different family forms examines how family structure shapes communication among family members. Here, the locus of inquiry shifts from interpersonal constructs that occur across different kinds of relationships to communication in particular family forms. In this section, we review empirical research on communication in four different family forms: divorced and single-parent families, stepfamilies, gay and lesbian families, and adoptive families.

Although communication scholars have identified a number of issues unique to each family form, it is important to note that all four family forms challenge traditional ideas of what constitutes a "normal" family, namely, the intact, two-parent biological family. An increasing number of children in the United States are being raised in nontraditional family forms (Fields, 2001; Koerner & Fitzpatrick, 2004). From the ongoing debate over the effects of divorce on children's well-being (Amato, 2000), to the deficit-comparison approach that characterized early stepfamily research (Ganong & Coleman, 2004), to the various ways in which gay and lesbian couples and families challenge heteronormativity (Biblarz & Stacey, 2010; Patterson, 2000), scholars continue to document the communication patterns of family relationships that challenge stereotypical understandings of what it means to belong to a "family."

## Divorced and Single-Parent Families

Although the divorce rate in the United States has leveled off over the past two decades (Bramlett & Mosher, 2001), nearly half of all marriages in the United States end in permanent separation or divorce (Tejada-Vera & Sutton, 2009). According to Amato (2000), slightly more than half of all divorces involve children under the age of 18, and thus, researchers have devoted substantial efforts toward understanding the impact of divorce on both adults' and children's adjustment. At the center of this body of work is an ongoing debate over the effects of divorce on children (Amato, 2000), a debate that is difficult to resolve due to the challenges associated with assessing the consequences of marital instability on children's lives. Some authors have posited that divorce is a major life disruption that incurs a host of psychological and social difficulties for children (e.g., Popenoe, 1996), whereas others have argued that both children and adults are quite resilient to divorce and that some children may benefit from being removed from a highly conflicted family environment (e.g., Amato & Afifi, 2006; Bray & Hetherington, 1993). In his most recent update of an earlier meta-analysis (i.e., Amato & Keith, 1991), Amato (2001) found that children with divorced parents in the 1990s continued to score significantly lower in measures of psychological well-being and social relations than children with continuously married parents. Nevertheless, there is a growing consensus among family researchers that interpersonal difficulties between parents, rather than divorce per se, is the primary detrimental influence on both parents' and children's adjustment (Afifi & Schrodt, 2003a; Amato & Afifi, 2006; Schrodt & Afifi, 2007). Consequently, in this section, we review interpersonal factors that influence the extent to

which divorce is associated with poor outcomes for family members.

### Conflict and Triangulation

Although conflict can serve important functions in families (Noller, 1995), children's exposure to destructive conflict can place them in an uncomfortable position as mediators (Afifi, 2003; Hetherington, 1999). Children's feelings of self-blame and perceived threat, which often occur as a function of witnessing marital conflict and experiencing loyalty binds (Grych, Seid, & Fincham, 1992), mediate the influence of marital conflict on children's anxiety and depression (Grych, Fincham, Jouriles, & McDonald, 2000; Stocker, Richmond, Low, Alexander, & Elias, 2003).

Consequently, communication scholars have compared empirical models of interparental conflict patterns and children's outcomes across divorced and nondivorced families. Afifi and Schrodt (2003a), for instance, tested adolescents' and young adults' feelings of being caught between their parents as a mediator between divorce and children's satisfaction with their parents. They found that divorce was largely associated with dissatisfaction through children's feeling of being caught, which, in turn, was a function of parents' demand–withdraw patterns and poor communication competence. Similarly, Amato and Afifi (2006) discovered that having parents in high-conflict marriages was associated with feeling caught in the middle, and feeling caught was associated with poor well-being. In fact, Amato and Afifi reported that young adults with divorced parents were no more likely than young adults who grew up with happily married parents to report feeling caught in the middle. Amato and Afifi concluded that children with parents in high-conflict marriages (who do not divorce) may be particularly likely to experience psychological distress because they are unable to escape from their parents' marital problems.

Consistent with this reasoning, Schrodt and Afifi (2007) found that relational closeness with parents moderates the degree to which parents' symbolic aggression, demand–withdraw patterns, and negative disclosures affect young adults' feelings of being caught, mental health, and family satisfaction. Also, Schrodt and Ledbetter (2007) reported that although young adults from divorced families were more likely to report feeling caught between their parents, after controlling for parents' demand–withdraw patterns and family conversation and conformity orientations, only young adults from nondivorced families experienced a decline in mental health as a function of feeling caught. In sum, witnessing marital conflict is likely to exacerbate children's feelings of being caught in both divorced and nondivorced families, though such feelings may actually be more detrimental to children from intact families because they are unable to escape from their parents' conflict patterns (Amato & Afifi, 2006; Schrodt & Ledbetter, 2007).

## Coparental Communication Between Ex-Spouses

The divorce process commonly involves former spouses dissolving their romantic relationship while maintaining their coparental partnership. Although some marriages dissolve amicably, most ex-spouses are faced with the challenging task of developing a separate togetherness while uncoupling without unfamilying (Graham, 2003; Masheter, 1997a, 1997b). Indeed, most ex-spouses maintain some form of direct contact for years after their divorce, although such contacts may diminish over time (Maccoby & Mnookin, 1992). Masheter (1997a, 1997b) and Graham (2003) contend that attachment to the ex-spouse is quite common, particularly when there are children involved. Some former spouses become friends (Masheter, 1997a), advise each other (Ahrons, 1994), and serve as confidants for each other regarding new romantic relationships (Ahrons & Rogers, 1987). Others maintain "business-like" partnerships suitable for coparenting children in both postdivorce single-parent families and stepfamilies (Braithwaite, McBride,

& Schrodt, 2003; Schrodt, Baxter, McBride, Braithwaite, & Fine, 2006).

Contact with an ex-spouse can be problematic. Masheter (1997b) found that preoccupation with the ex-spouse is inversely associated with well-being and postdivorce adjustment. Divorced individuals who are highly preoccupied with their former partners are likely to experience either hostility or maladaptive affection toward their ex-spouse (Masheter, 1997b). Although an affectionate relationship with an ex-spouse might seem positive, too much closeness and self-disclosure might signal an unhealthy preoccupation with the former spouse (Graham, 2003).

Perhaps the most extensive investigation of communication and coparenting to date is Maccoby and Mnookin's (1992) longitudinal study of more than 1,100 Californian postdivorce families. They identified three basic patterns of coparenting: (1) *disengaged* coparents managed their interpersonal conflict by avoidance and made little effort to coordinate their coparenting activities, (2) *conflicted* coparents maintained regular contact but were actively involved in disputes that spilled over into the parenting domain; and (3) *cooperative* coparents were able to suppress or insulate their conflicts from their children. Although there are a host of factors that undermine supportive and cooperative coparental relationships in postdivorce families, some of the most common include interparental hostility, legal difficulties over custody and visitation, incompatible values, and a general distrust of a former partner's parenting abilities (Maccoby & Mnookin, 1992; Schrodt et al., 2006).

## Parent–Child Disclosures and Divorce

Afifi and her colleagues (Afifi, Afifi, & Coho, 2009; Afifi & McManus, 2010; Afifi, McManus, Hutchinson, & Baker, 2007; Afifi & Schrodt, 2003b; Schrodt & Afifi, 2007) have advanced a program of research investigating parents' disclosures to their adolescent and young adult children in divorced and intact families and the impact that such disclosures have on parent–child relationships and children's well-being. Using uncertainty reduction and uncertainty management theories (Brashers, 2001), Afifi and Schrodt (2003b) found that the association between uncertainty about one's family relationships and avoidance of discussing the state of one's family was positive and linear for adolescents and young adults in postdivorce families. For the offspring from first-marriage families, however, this association was curvilinear in nature. In addition, Afifi et al. (2007) examined the factors that prompt inappropriate parental disclosures and the impact that such disclosures have on adolescents' well-being. They found that custodial parents' lack of control over their divorce-related stressors was the only factor associated with their inappropriate disclosures.

Afifi et al. (2009) found support for the hypothesis that the valence of parental disclosures—not the frequency of such disclosures—negatively affects adolescents' well-being, especially adolescents from divorced families. Also, adolescents typically perceive that their custodial parents disclose more negative information about the other parent than the parents perceive that they disclose (Afifi & McManus, 2010). Negative disclosures about the other parent might be associated with closer, more cohesive relationships between custodial parents and adolescents yet are associated with poor individual outcomes for the adolescents (Afifi & McManus, 2010; Schrodt & Afifi, 2007).

## Postdivorce and Unmarried Single-Parent Families

As of 2004, approximately 37% of all births in the United States were to unmarried parents, with even higher proportions occurring among ethnic and racial minorities (Martin et al., 2006). Many divorces also result in single parenting. Most studies of single-parent families consist of single-mother families with nonresidential fathers. Amato and Sobolewski (2004) found that a significant number of nonresident fathers still maintain ties with their children after divorce.

Within three years of the birth of a child outside marriage, however, the majority of fathers live away from their child (Carlson, McLanahan, & Brooks-Gunn, 2008). Given that children typically are more likely to thrive when fathers maintain an active presence in their lives (Amato & Gilbreth, 1999), researchers have devoted considerable effort toward identifying the factors that maintain children's relationships with their nonresidential fathers.

Positive coparenting is a strong predictor of nonresident fathers' future involvement with children born outside of marriage (Carlson et al., 2008; Sobolewski & King, 2005). The importance of coparenting implies that both mothers and fathers play a role in determining the father's involvement; indeed, some custodial mothers restrict access between fathers and their children because of resentment and hostility toward the fathers, who then avoid contact (Seltzer & Brandreth, 1994). Although mothers' control of fathers' access to their children might be detrimental in many cases, it is also important to recognize that mothers may have sound reasons for doing so. Former husbands who were abusive during marriage frequently engage in coparenting as a means of extending control over their ex-spouse, exposing both the mother and the children to continued risk of violence (Hardesty & Ganong, 2006). Regardless of the specific reasons, many custodial mothers and nonresidential fathers communicate infrequently about their adolescent children, and most coparents eventually minimize interaction across households (Maccoby & Mnookin, 1992).

In addition to examining coparenting relationships between former partners, researchers have also compared differences in parenting and child outcomes between single-mother and single-father households (Biblarz & Stacey, 2010). Single mothers are more likely to supervise their children, stay involved with them, communicate with them, and cultivate close relationships with them than are single fathers (Eitle, 2006; Hawkins, Amato, & King, 2006). Single mothers are also more likely to participate in their children's school and religious events and to know the names of their children's friends and their parents than are single fathers (Hawkins et al., 2006), but single mothers report more difficulty remaining firm and patient while controlling their children's behaviors (Hilton, Desrochers, & Devall, 2001). Perhaps as a function of increased parental involvement, adolescents in single-mother households are less likely to engage in substance abuse, misconduct, and delinquent behavior than are those from single-father households (Breivik & Olweus, 2006; Eitle, 2006).

One of the most notable conclusions drawn from research on single-parent families is that two parents (in a low-conflict relationship) generally provide more material and emotional resources to children than one parent (e.g., Amato, 2005; McLanahan & Sandefur, 1994). For parents, divorce is associated with more difficulties in raising children (Fisher, Fagor, & Leve, 1998), less authoritative parenting (Simons & Associates, 1996), less trust in the former partner's parenting abilities (Maccoby & Mnookin, 1992; Schrodt et al., 2006), and greater parental role strain among both noncustodial and custodial parents (Rogers & White, 1998).

There is evidence that many of the poor outcomes associated with single-parent families are a function of communication processes. For example, Breivik, Olweus, and Endresen (2009) compared antisocial behaviors and substance use among more than 4,000 adolescents living in postdivorce single-mother and single-father households in Norway. Children in both single-mother and single-father families reported more antisocial behavior and substance abuse than children in nondivorced, two-biological-parent families, but communication behaviors such as conflict and parental monitoring mediated the effects of single parenthood (Breivik et al., 2009). Given the challenges that divorced parents face, it is not surprising that most remarry (Coleman, Ganong, & Fine, 2000), and with remarriage comes the added challenges associated with communicating in a stepfamily.

## Stepfamilies

Defined as families in which "at least one of the adults has a child (or children) from a previous relationship" (Ganong & Coleman, 2004, p. 2), stepfamilies involve an array of personal relationships that vary considerably in form, structure, and complexity (Schrodt & Braithwaite, 2010). At a given time, at least 9% of married households and 11.5% of cohabiting couple households contain stepchildren (U.S. Bureau of the Census, 2003). The number of people who spend at least part of their lifetime in a stepfamily is much higher. Consequently, research on stepfamilies has intensified considerably since 1990 (Coleman et al., 2000), with three key areas of primary interest to interpersonal communication scholars: stepfamily development, dialectical tensions and relational change, and the stepparent role.

### Stepfamily Development

One of the fundamental questions in stepfamily scholarship is whether stepfamilies are qualitatively distinct from first-marriage, intact families. Historically, many family scholars investigated stepfamily relationships using a "deficit-comparison" approach (Coleman et al., 2000; Ganong & Coleman, 2004). This approach relies on a model of the conventional, "nuclear" family with which the stepfamily is compared and found to be problematic (Ganong & Coleman, 2004).

In response to the deficit comparison, communication scholars have examined interpersonal behaviors that contribute to different stepfamily developmental pathways and stepfamily types. Using retrospective interviews, for instance, Baxter, Braithwaite, and Nicholson (1999) identified 15 different types of turning points that stepfamily members experience, including changes in household configuration, conflicts, and spending quality time together. These scholars then provided a depiction of changes in "feeling like a family" that included five different trajectories of the first four years of stepfamily development. The *accelerated* trajectory reflected a pattern of quick and sustained movement toward higher levels of feeling like a family. The *declining* trajectory began with a high level of feeling like a family but quickly declined over time. The *prolonged* trajectory reflected stepfamilies in which movement toward feeling like a family progressed gradually, whereas the *stagnating* trajectory began and ended with relatively low levels of feeling like a family. Finally, the *high-amplitude turbulent* trajectory reflected stepfamilies that experienced rapid increases and decreases in levels of feeling like a family (Baxter et al., 1999).

In a somewhat different vein, Golish (2003) used family systems theory and extant research on coping and resilience to examine the communication strengths that differentiated strong stepfamilies from those that struggled. The communicative tactics used by stepfamilies to manage the challenges encountered differed according to the strength of the stepfamily. Communication in strong stepfamilies was characterized by frequent everyday talk, openness, communicating clear rules and boundaries, engaging in family problem solving, spending time together as a family, and promoting a positive image of the noncustodial parent.

Finally, Schrodt (2006b) developed a typology of stepfamilies based on various aspects of the family relationships. The first type, *bonded* stepfamilies, were characterized by low levels of dissension and avoidance and relatively high levels of stepfamily involvement, flexibility, and expressiveness. Second, *functional* stepfamilies were characterized by moderately high levels of stepfamily involvement, flexibility, and expressiveness, as well as moderately low levels of dissension and avoidance. Whereas *ambivalent* stepfamilies were characterized by slightly above-average levels of dissension and avoidance and slightly below-average levels of involvement, flexibility, and expressiveness, both *evasive* and *conflictual* stepfamilies were characterized by high levels of dissension and avoidance and relatively low levels of involvement and flexibility, with the primary difference between the final two types being levels of stepfamily expressiveness. People from bonded and functional stepfamilies reported higher competence and fewer mental health symptoms than did individuals from the other stepfamily types (Schrodt, 2006b).

## Dialectical Tensions and Relational Change

A considerable amount of research on communication in stepfamilies has been guided by relational dialectics theory (Baxter, 2011; Baxter & Braithwaite, 2010; Baxter & Montgomery, 1996). For example, Braithwaite, Baxter, and Harper (1998) explored the role of rituals in stepfamilies and discovered that the most productive ritual enactments were oriented to the management of the dialectical tensions between the "old" and the "new" experienced by family members. It is also common for stepchildren to want emotional closeness and a relationship with their stepparent yet, at the same time, desire emotional distance due to feelings of loyalty to the nonresidential parent (Baxter, Braithwaite, Bryant, & Wagner, 2004). Stepchildren may also desire both open and closed communication with the stepparent, and they sometimes express competing desires for parental authority to reside solely with their residential parent and for the stepparent to exert authority (Baxter et al., 2004). Finally, some stepchildren's talk suggests both a desire to be centered in the attention of their parents as well as a desire to avoid being caught in the middle of their parents' disputes (Braithwaite, Toller, Daas, Durham, & Jones, 2008).

These tensions are often interrelated. The competing discourses about being centered between the parents without being caught, for example, are related to the tension of openness–closedness. Stepchildren often want enough information from their parents to be able to know what is going on, and yet they simultaneously desire enough closeness from their parents to avoid hearing information that makes them uncomfortable (Braithwaite et al., 2008).

In addition to the competing dialectical tensions involving residential parents and stepparents, there are unique tensions in relationships between stepchildren and nonresidential parents (Braithwaite & Baxter, 2006). One involves a contradiction of parenting and nonparenting. Stepchildren commonly want nonresidential parents to be involved in parenting, yet they also resist parenting due to feelings of ambivalence with the nonresidential parent. Although not unique to relationships with nonresidential parents, the expression of contradictions about openness is shaped by this relational context. Whereas stepchildren typically express a desire to be open with the nonresidential parent, they often express hesitation to have such openness given the nonresidential parent's lack of familiarity with the child's everyday life.

### The Stepparent Role

Perhaps the most important and challenging task during the development of a stepfamily involves negotiating the role of the stepparent (Fine, Coleman, & Ganong, 1998; Ganong, Coleman, Fine, & Martin, 1999; Golish, 2003; Schrodt, Soliz, & Braithwaite, 2008). The stepparent role is what primarily distinguishes stepfamilies from other family types (Afifi & Schrodt, 2003b; Ganong et al., 1999; Schrodt, 2006a, 2006b), and family relationships with stepparents are a key to stepfamily functioning (Schrodt et al., 2008). One basic question about stepparenting concerns whether the stepparent should have an active or inactive role in the stepchildren's lives (Fine et al., 1998). Some scholars contend that the stepparent should do no more than try to build a friendship with the stepchild(ren), whereas others have found that the long-term benefits of having the stepparent act as a parent outweigh the short-term benefits of having the stepparent simply act as a friend (e.g., Hetherington, 1999).

Fine et al. (1998) reported different perceptions of the stepparent role, with children being much more likely than parents or stepparents to indicate that they preferred the stepparent act like a friend rather than as a parental figure.

Adults were generally more likely to discuss the stepparent role with each other than they were to discuss this role with their stepchildren, which in turn, produced inconsistencies in perceptions of parenting behaviors (e.g., warmth and control) that ultimately undermined stepfamily members' interpersonal adjustment (Fine et al., 1998).

Schrodt (2006a) argued that trying to fit the stepparent role into preexisting categories such as "parent" or "friend" is not as useful as focusing on processes, such as the establishing of positive regard between stepparents and stepchildren, whether and how stepchildren grant stepparents authority, and discussions of feelings between stepparents and stepchildren. Likewise, Ganong et al. (1999) explored the strategies that stepparents use to develop and maintain affinity with their stepchildren, and found three relatively distinct patterns of affinity-seeking and affinity-maintaining strategies among stepparents: *early-affinity-seeking* stepparents, *continuous-affinity-seeking* stepparents, and *nonseeking* stepparents. Not surprisingly, stepparents who continued their efforts at relationship building well beyond the formation of the stepfamily (i.e., continuous-affinity-seeking stepparents) were more likely than other stepparents to develop close stepparent–stepchild relationships.

Communication scholars also have examined patterns of engagement and topic avoidance in stepfamilies. Golish and Caughlin (2002), for instance, compared the types of topics avoided in parent–child versus stepparent–child relationships. In general, adolescents and young adults engaged in topic avoidance the most with their stepparents (regardless of stepparent sex), followed by their fathers and then their mothers. Consistent with such findings, Schrodt et al. (2007) compared patterns of everyday talk across parent–child, stepparent–child, and nonresidential parent–child relationships and found that children engaged in everyday talk (e.g., small talk, catching up) more frequently with residential parents than with residential stepparents or nonresidential parents. There were, however, only two notable differences between everyday talk with residential stepparents and nonresidential parents: Stepchildren engaged in more love talk with nonresidential parents than with stepparents but engaged in more small talk with stepparents than with nonresidential parents. Moreover, Schrodt et al. (2008) provided evidence of dyadic reciprocity in everyday talk and relational satisfaction for stepparents and stepchildren, such that stepparents who engaged in more everyday talk with their stepchildren were more likely to have stepchildren who reported being satisfied in their relationship with their stepparent. Taken together, the various findings pertaining to communication patterns in stepfamilies demonstrate the centrality of interpersonal communication to family members' negotiations of the stepparent role as well as the centrality of the stepparent role to stepfamily functioning.

## Gay and Lesbian Families

In addition to postdivorce families and stepfamilies, family scholars have also given increased attention to gay and lesbian families, as such families challenge stereotypical understandings of what constitutes "family" (Peplau & Beals, 2004). As Patterson (2000) noted, "The family lives of lesbian and gay people have been a subject of controversy during the past decade" (p. 1052). Not only do gay and lesbian family members face larger societal stigmas associated with having nonheterosexual identities, but many also face the prospect of living in communities that do not formally recognize same-sex marriages and often do so without the loving support of their families of origin. Although a detailed comparison of same-sex and cross-sex couples lies well beyond the space afforded here (see reviews by Patterson, 2000; Peplau & Spalding, 2000), researchers have demonstrated that (a) lesbians and gay men report as much satisfaction with their relationships as do heterosexual couples (Cardell, Finn, & Maracek, 1981; Kurdek & Schmidt, 1986); (b) the correlates of relationship quality for lesbian and gay couples include equal power distribution,

perceiving many attractions in and few alternatives to the relationship (Beals, Impett, & Peplau, 2002), engaging in shared decision making, and placing a high value on the relationship (Kurdek, 1994, 1995); (c) lesbian and gay couples, both those with and without children, tend to have an egalitarian division of household labor (Chan, Brooks, Raboy, & Patterson, 1998; Kurdek, 1993); and (d) common areas of conflict for lesbian and gay couples include finances, affection/sex, being overly critical, and division of household tasks (Kurdek, 1994, 1995).

In more recent research, Suter and her colleagues (Suter, Bergen, Daas, & Durham, 2006; Suter & Daas, 2007) adopted relational dialectics theory to examine the internal and external contradictions that lesbian couples manage as they co-construct their public and private identities through rituals. Specifically, Suter et al. (2006) found that lesbian couples experienced tensions of inclusion–seclusion and revelation–concealment at three ritual sites: anniversaries, commitment ceremonies, and holidays. During each of these rituals, the lesbian couples in their sample managed these external contradictions at the border of the lesbian dyad, that is, between the couple as a dyad and larger social networks, social norms, and laws.

In a follow-up study, Suter and Daas (2007) examined how lesbian couples negotiate and/or challenge *heteronormativity*, which describes an ideology that assumes that heterosexual experience is the most morally acceptable and normal form of sexual expression (Suter et al., 2006; Yep, 2002). Again using relational dialectics theory, Suter and Daas (2007) found that lesbian couples communicatively negotiated the public–private tensions of their relationship, and thereby challenged heteronormativity, using *segmentation*, which involves moving from one dialectical pole to another dialectical pole. For instance, they found that lesbian couples wore rings and co-owned homes as a way of communicating nonverbally their commitment to each other. Some couples wore rings in obvious ways to reveal (or make public) their relationship, while others wore rings in discreet ways to conceal (or keep private) their relationship.

Although Suter et al.'s (2006; Suter & Daas, 2007) research demonstrates some of the ways in which lesbian couples challenge heteronormative views of romantic relationships, realistic fears about sexual prejudice and chronic daily stressors associated with being gay or lesbian may heighten an individual's susceptibility to psychological distress and adversely affect physical health (Lewis, Derlega, Berndt, Morris, & Rose, 2001). These challenges may become even more pronounced as gay and lesbian couples seek to have and raise children. Lesbians and gay men who want to become parents use a variety of approaches including adoption, artificial insemination for lesbians, and surrogate mothers for gay men (Buell, 2001). According to Black, Gates, Sanders, and Taylor (2000), approximately 22% of partnered lesbians and 5% of partnered gay men currently have children present in the home. Consequently, in addition to studying similarities and differences between same-sex and cross-sex couples, researchers have also devoted increased efforts toward understanding similarities and differences between same-sex and cross-sex parents.

Biblarz and Stacey (2010) recently summarized the empirical findings of 33 studies of two-parent families to examine the unique influence of gender on both parenting and child outcomes. In general, most of the empirical evidence yielded no significant differences in parenting behaviors and child outcomes for same-sex and cross-sex parents, though the majority of studies that included same-sex couples were studies of lesbian parents (91%). When differences did emerge, however, they typically favored same-sex couples. For instance, some researchers have found that lesbian couples are more likely to use competent and engaged parenting skills (Bos, van Balen, & van den Boom, 2007); to display warmth, affection, and attachment (Golombok et al., 2003; Golombok, Tasker, & Murray, 1997); and to spend time sharing interests and activities with children than are heterosexual parents (Golombok et al., 1997, 2003). Likewise, children from lesbian families are more likely to discuss

emotional issues with their parents (Vanfraussen, Ponjaert-Kristoffersen, & Brewaeys, 2003), less likely to experience behavioral problems (Gartrell, Deck, Rodas, Peyser, & Banks, 2005; Vanfraussen, Ponjaert-Kristoffersen, & Brewaeys, 2002), and less likely to self-report aggressiveness than children from heterosexual parents (Vanfraussen et al., 2002). Collectively, this body of research supports the general consensus that unmarried lesbian parents are raising children who develop at least as well as children being raised by married heterosexual parents (e.g., American Academy of Pediatrics, 2002; Tasker, 2005). It is important to note, however, that comparable research on intentional gay fatherhood has scarcely commenced (Biblarz & Stacey, 2010).

In general, then, empirical research on gay and lesbian families has focused primarily on comparing gay and lesbian couples with heterosexual couples and on comparing gay and lesbian parenting with heterosexual parenting in first-marriage families. Although scholars have rarely examined the intersections of gay and lesbian couplehood with gay and lesbian parenting, one notable exception is Bergen, Suter, and Daas's (2006) investigation of how lesbian couples symbolically construct a legitimate parental identity for nonbiological lesbian mothers. Using symbolic interactionism as their theoretical framework, Bergen et al. conducted in-depth interviews with 16 lesbian families that had conceived children through donor insemination. They identified three primary symbolic resources that lesbian couples used to construct a parental identity for the nonbiological partner: (1) address terms (e.g., "Mommy" and "Mama"), which functioned as a linguistic tool to communicate the nonbiological mother's parental status; (2) legal moves (e.g., second-parent adoption or joint custody), which attempted to redress the nonbiological mother's lack of legal rights; and (3) last names (e.g., incorporating the last name of the nonbiological mother into the child's name in some form), which functioned as both a linguistic tool and a legal move to connect the nonbiological mother to the child. Bergen et al.'s (2006) findings provide but one example of how lesbian couples use a variety of symbolic practices to legitimate their status as a family and to communicate their familial relationships to those outside the family.

## Adoptive Families

Communication scholars have given only scant attention to adoptive families, and scholars who do investigate adopted families do not usually focus on communication or other interpersonal processes (Galvin, 2003). Instead, the main focus of this research is child adjustment, comparing adopted with nonadopted children on dimensions of adjustment, such as internalizing and externalizing problems, attachment, and academic achievement (for reviews, see Bimmel, Juffer, van IJzendoorn, & Bakermans-Kranenburg, 2003; Lee, 2003; O'Brien & Zamostny, 2003; van IJzendoorn, Juffer, & Klein Poelhuis, 2005). Overall, the literature indicates that a large majority of adopted children and adolescents are well-adjusted. A small but notable group of children, however, experiences significant behavioral and/or mental health problems. This group of poorly adjusted adopted children probably accounts for the mean differences in adjustment that frequently are observed in studies comparing adopted with biological children (Bimmel et al., 2003; Brand & Brinich, 1999).

Many of the factors identified to affect child adjustment are unrelated to interpersonal processes and family communication, including age at adoption, early-childhood adversity, and prenatal exposure to alcohol (Haugaard & Hazan, 2003). There are some factors, however, that are very relevant to family communication, such as parent–child communication. Research has consistently found the communication of adoptive parents to be as positive as, or even more positive than, that of biological parents. Researchers investigating specific aspects of parent–child communication in adopted families, such as conflict or amount of verbal interaction (e.g., Lansford, Ceballo, Abby, & Stewart, 2001; Lanz, Ifrate, Rosnati, & Scabini, 1999; Rosnati &

Marta, 1997), also report few differences between families of adopted and biological children.

Another factor directly related to communication that has received increased attention lately is the openness of communication about the adoption itself (Brodzinsky, 2006; Wrobel, Kohler, Grotevant, & McRoy, 2003). Here, results are somewhat mixed. Whereas openness in communication generally is associated with better child outcomes, openness specifically regarding adoption status of the child is not uniformly associated with only positive child outcomes. For example, Grotevant et al. (2007) reported that although family members in open adoptions are generally more satisfied with the arrangement and more positive toward the birth mother than family members in closed adoptions, open-adoption families also report somewhat more negative affect than do family members who experienced a closed adoption. Ultimately, these authors conclude that given the dynamic nature of open adoptions, "one size does not fit all" (p. 97) in terms of how openness is arranged in different families, and families should be able to determine for themselves the level of openness they desire.

Most of the research reviewed above has been notable for the absence of theoretical explanations for the observed associations between communication behaviors and family outcomes. Thus, Rueter and Koerner's (2008) recent theoretical model is noteworthy because it posits that family communication, and specifically the sensemaking strategies associated with conversation orientation and conformity orientation, is central to the adjustment of adopted children. In their study, Rueter and Koerner compared the effects of conversation orientation and conformity orientation on child adjustment in three types of families: (1) those with all adopted children, (2) those with all biological children, and (3) those with both types of children. In families with low conversation orientation, adopted children were at three to five times higher risk for high externalization behaviors than biological children. Rueter and Koerner suggested that biologically related children have greater cognitive and therefore attitudinal similarities to their birth parents and thus may be more protected from the negative aspects of low conversation orientation than are adopted children, who perceive such parental communication as more hostile and punitive. Although this explanation has yet to be confirmed, it illustrates the potential of placing family communication theories center stage in the attempt to explicate the adjustment of adopted children.

## Conclusion

Family communication scholars have made tremendous progress since the first *Handbook of Interpersonal Communication*. Research on this topic has diversified in ways that now better reflect the complexity and diversity of family life. At one time, nearly all the research on family communication focused either on marriage or on parenting, but scholars have now turned their attention to a wider variety of family relationships and family forms. Scholarship on family communication also has become more sophisticated in many ways, including the assessment of physiological markers and statistical analyses that were not even imagined 25 years ago. Family communication has gone from an area studied primarily by people outside the discipline of communication to one in which communication scholars now play a central role. These are all positive developments.

Yet even as we laud these changes, family communication scholars must remain vigilant to ensure that they make a unique contribution. There are dangers in becoming enamored with the newest procedures and techniques. As we attempt to keep up with the tools that become prominent in other disciplines, we must not turn away from the distinctive perspective that communication scholars bring. It is common in other disciplines, for example, to use elaborate designs and statistics but measure communication in extremely simple ways, reducing communication into variables such as simple frequency of talk or into a construct that is definable along a single

dimension. Scholars in other disciplines also commonly equate interaction behaviors with communication, assuming that the meaning and purpose of behaviors in interaction are objective and therefore directly observable in a straightforward manner (for more detailed discussions of these issues, see Caughlin, 2010; Caughlin & Scott, 2010; Caughlin & Vangelisti, 2006). Yet as communication scholars, we should remind ourselves and others that the meaning of communication is more complex than that; for example, the same behavior can mean different things to two different family members. In such cases, there simply is no single objective and observable meaning of the behavior. For instance, sometimes when adolescents keep information from their parents, it is considered by the parents to be keeping a secret, whereas the adolescents consider the same withholding of information to be maintaining their privacy (Caughlin & Vangelisti, 2009). Attempting to observe such phenomena or trying to label one perspective as the more objectively correct one would miss the most interesting and important point of such phenomena: that the interpretations of communicative behaviors in families really do matter. They are not reporting error or bias; they are an inherent part of communication processes.

In our enthusiasm for adopting newer methods, we must not forget that the unique contributions we can make involve addressing the questions of perennial interest to communication scholars, such as what message features are indicative of sophisticated family communication or how does meaning making occur in families? Communication scholars will undoubtedly use a wide variety of theories and methods when addressing such questions, but it is our common attention to these sorts of questions that ought to give us our identity.

## References

Abe, J. A. A., & Izard, C. E. (1999). A longitudinal study of emotion expression and personality relations in early development. *Journal of Personality and Social Psychology, 77,* 566–577.

Afifi, T. D. (2003). "Feeling caught" in stepfamilies: Managing boundary turbulence through appropriate communication privacy rules. *Journal of Social and Personal Relationships, 20,* 729–755.

Afifi, T. D., Afifi, W. A., & Coho, A. (2009). Adolescents' physiological reactions to their parents' negative disclosures about the other parent in divorced and non-divorced families. *Journal of Divorce & Remarriage, 50,* 517–540.

Afifi, T. D., Hutchinson, S., & Krouse, S. (2006). Toward a theoretical model of communal coping in post-divorce families and other naturally occurring groups. *Communication Theory, 16,* 378–409.

Afifi, T. D., & McManus, T. (2006). Communal coping dilemmas in post-divorce families: Introducing meaning back into coping. In R. M. Dailey & B. A. LePoire (Eds.), *Applied interpersonal communication matters: Family, health, and community relations* (pp. 67–89). New York: Lang.

Afifi, T. D., & McManus, T. (2010). Divorce disclosures and adolescents' physical and mental health and parental relationship quality. *Journal of Divorce & Remarriage, 51,* 83–107.

Afifi, T. D., McManus, T., Hutchinson, S., & Baker, B. (2007). Inappropriate parental divorce disclosures, the factors that prompt them, and their impact on parents' and adolescents' well-being. *Communication Monographs, 74,* 78–102.

Afifi, T. D., & Schrodt, P. (2003a). "Feeling caught" as a mediator of adolescents' and young adults' avoidance and satisfaction with their parents in divorced and non-divorced households. *Communication Monographs, 70,* 142–173.

Afifi, T. D., & Schrodt, P. (2003b). Uncertainty and the avoidance of the state of one's family in stepfamilies, post-divorce single parent families, and first marriage families. *Human Communication Research, 29,* 516–532.

Ahrons, C. R. (1994). *The good divorce.* New York: Harper Collins.

Ahrons, C. R., & Rodgers, R. H. (1987). *Divorced families: A multidisciplinary developmental view.* New York: W. W. Norton.

Amato, P. R. (2000). The consequences of divorce for adults and children. *Journal of Marriage and the Family, 62,* 1269–1287.

Amato, P. R. (2001). Children of divorce in the 1990s: An update of the Amato and Keith (1991) meta-analysis. *Journal of Family Psychology, 15,* 355–370.

Amato, P. R. (2005). The impact of family formation change on the cognitive, social, and emotional well-being of the next generation. *Future of Children, 15,* 75–96.

Amato, P. R., & Afifi, T. D. (2006). Feeling caught between parents: Adult children's relations with parents and subjective well-being. *Journal of Marriage and Family, 68,* 222–235.

Amato, P. R., & Gilbreth, J. (1999). Nonresident fathers and children's well-being: A meta-analysis. *Journal of Marriage and the Family, 61,* 557–573.

Amato, P. R., & Keith, B. (1991). Parental divorce and the well-being of children: A meta-analysis. *Psychological Bulletin, 110,* 26–46.

Amato, P. R., & Sobolewski, J. M. (2004). The effects of divorce on fathers and children: Nonresidential fathers and stepfathers. In M. E. Lamb (Ed.), *The role of the father in child development* (4th ed., pp. 341–367). Hoboken, NJ: Wiley.

American Academy of Pediatrics. (2002). Coparent or second-parent adoption by same-sex parents. *Pediatrics, 109,* 339–344.

Badr, H., Carmack, C. L., Kashy, D. A., Cristofanilli, M., & Revenson, T. A. (2010). Dyadic coping in metastatic breast cancer. *Health Psychology, 29,* 169–180.

Baumrind, D. (1967). Child care practices anteceding three patterns of preschool behavior. *Genetic Psychology Monographs, 75,* 43–88.

Baumrind, D. (1971). Current patterns of parental authority. *Developmental Psychology, 4,* 1–103.

Baxter, L. A. (2011). *Voicing relationships: A dialogic approach.* Thousand Oaks, CA: Sage.

Baxter, L. A., & Braithwaite, D. O. (2010). Relational dialectics theory, applied. In S. W. Smith & S. R. Wilson (Eds.), *New directions in interpersonal communication* (pp. 48–66). Thousand Oaks, CA: Sage.

Baxter, L. A., Braithwaite, D. O., Bryant, L., & Wagner, A. (2004). Stepchildren's perceptions of the contradictions in communication with stepparents. *Journal of Social and Personal Relationships, 21,* 447–467.

Baxter, L. A., Braithwaite, D. O., & Nicholson, J. H. (1999). Turning points in the development of blended families. *Journal of Social and Personal Relationships, 16,* 291–313.

Baxter, L. A., & Clark, C. L. (1996). Perceptions of family communication patterns and the enactment of family rituals. *Western Journal of Communication, 60,* 254–268.

Baxter, L. A., & Montgomery, B. M. (1996). *Relating: Dialogues and dialectics.* New York: Guilford Press.

Beals, K. P., Impett, E. A., & Peplau, L. A. (2002). Lesbians in love: Why some relationships endure and others end. *Journal of Lesbian Studies, 6,* 53–64.

Bergen, K. M., Suter, E. A., & Daas, K. L. (2006). "About as solid as a fish net": Symbolic construction of a legitimate parental identity for nonbiological lesbian mothers. *Journal of Family Communication, 6,* 201–220.

Biblarz, T. J., & Stacey, J. (2010). How does the gender of parents matter? *Journal of Marriage and Family, 72,* 3–22.

Bimmel, N., Juffer, F., van IJzendoorn, M. H., & Bakermans-Kranenburg, M. J. (2003). Problem behavior of internationally adopted adolescents: A review and meta-analysis. *Harvard Review of Psychiatry, 11,* 64–77.

Black, D., Gates, G., Sanders, S., & Taylor, L. (2000). Demographics of the gay and lesbian population in the United States. *Demography, 37,* 139–154.

Bodenmann, G. (2005). Dyadic coping and its significance for marital functioning. In T. A. Revenson, K. Kayser, & G. Bodenmann (Eds.), *Couples coping with stress: Emerging perspectives on dyadic coping* (pp. 33–49). Washington, DC: American Psychological Association.

Bos, H. M. W., van Balen, F., & van den Boom, D. C. (2007). Child adjustment and parenting in planned lesbian-parent families. *American Journal of Orthopsychiatry, 77,* 38–48.

Braithwaite, D. O., & Baxter, L. A. (2006). "You're my parent but you're not": Dialectical tensions in stepchildren's perceptions about communicating with the nonresidential parent. *Journal of Applied Communication Research, 34,* 30–48.

Braithwaite, D. O., Baxter, L. A., & Harper, A. M. (1998). The role of rituals in the management of dialectical tensions of "old" and "new" in blended families. *Communication Studies, 48,* 101–120.

Braithwaite, D. O., McBride, M. C., & Schrodt, P. (2003). "Parent teams" and the everyday interactions of co-parenting in stepfamilies. *Communication Reports, 16,* 93–111.

Braithwaite, D. O., Toller, P., Daas, K., Durham, W., & Jones, A. (2008). Centered but not caught in the middle: Stepchildren's perceptions of dialectical contradictions in the communication of co-parents. *Journal of Applied Communication Research, 36,* 33–55.

Bramlett, M. D., & Mosher, W. D. (2001). *First marriage dissolution, divorce, and remarriage: United States* (CDC Advance Data No. 323). Hyattsville, MD: National Center for Health Statistics.

Brand, A. E., & Brinich, P. M. (1999). Behavior problems and mental health contacts in adopted, foster, and nonadopted children. *Journal of Child Psychology and Psychiatry, 40,* 1221–1229.

Brashers, D. (2001). Communication and uncertainty management. *Journal of Communication, 51,* 477–498.

Bray, J. H., & Hetherington, E. M. (1993). Development issues in blended families research project: Family relationships and parent-child interactions. *Journal of Family Psychology, 7,* 76–90.

Breivik, K., & Olweus, D. (2006). Adolescent's adjustment in four post-divorce family structures: Single mother, stepfather, joint physical custody and single father families. *Journal of Divorce and Remarriage, 44,* 99–124.

Breivik, K., Olweus, D., & Endresen, I. (2009). Does the quality of parent-child relationships mediate the increased risk for antisocial behavior and substance use among adolescents in single-mother and single-father families? *Journal of Divorce & Remarriage, 50,* 400–426.

Brodzinsky, D. M. (2006). Family structural openness and communication openness as predictors in the adjustment of adopted children. *Adoption Quarterly, 9,* 1–18.

Bruner, J. (1990). *Acts of meaning.* Cambridge, MA: Harvard University Press.

Buell, C. (2001). Legal issues affecting alternative families. *Journal of Gay and Lesbian Psychotherapy, 4,* 75–90.

Cahn, D. D. (1992). *Conflict in intimate relationships.* New York: Guilford Press.

Campbell, A., Converse, P. E., & Rodgers, W. L. (1976). *The quality of American life.* New York: Russell Sage Foundation.

Cardell, M., Finn, S., & Maracek, J. (1981). Sex-role identity, sex-role behavior, and satisfaction in heterosexual, lesbian, and gay male couples. *Psychology of Women Quarterly, 5,* 488–494.

Carlson, M. J., McLanahan, S. S., & Brooks-Gunn, J. (2008). Coparenting and nonresident fathers' involvement with young children after a nonmarital birth. *Demography, 45,* 461–488.

Caughlin, J. P. (2003). Family communication standards: What counts as excellent family communication and how are such standards associated with family satisfaction? *Human Communication Research, 29,* 5–40.

Caughlin, J. P. (2010). A multiple goals theory of personal relationships: Conceptual integration and program overview. *Journal of Social and Personal Relationships, 27,* 824–848.

Caughlin, J. P., & Huston, T. L. (2006). The affective structure of marriage. In A. Vangelisti & D. Perlmann (Eds.), *The Cambridge handbook of personal relationships* (pp. 131–155). New York: Cambridge University Press.

Caughlin, J. P., Huston, T. L., & Houts, R. M. (2000). How does personality matter in marriage? An examination of trait anxiety, interpersonal negativity, and marital satisfaction. *Journal of Personality and Social Psychology, 78,* 326–336.

Caughlin, J. P., & Malis, R. S. (2004). Demand/withdraw communication between parents and adolescents: Connections with self-esteem and substance use. *Journal of Social and Personal Relationships, 21,* 125–148.

Caughlin, J. P., & Ramey, M. E. (2005). The demand/withdraw pattern of communication in parent-adolescent dyads. *Personal Relationships, 12,* 337–356.

Caughlin, J. P., & Scott, A. M. (2010). Toward a communication theory of the demand/withdraw pattern of interaction in interpersonal relationships. In S. Smith & S. R. Wilson (Eds.), *New directions in interpersonal communication* (pp. 180–200). Thousand Oaks, CA: Sage.

Caughlin, J. P., & Vangelisti, A. L. (2006). Conflict in dating and marital relationships. In J. G. Oetzel & S. Ting-Toomey (Eds.), *Sage handbook of conflict communication: Integrating theory, research, and practice* (pp. 129–157). Thousand Oaks, CA: Sage.

Caughlin, J. P., & Vangelisti, A. L. (2009). Why people conceal or reveal secrets: A multiple goals perspective. In T. Afifi & W. Afifi (Eds.), *Uncertainty, information management, and disclosure decisions: Theories and applications* (pp. 279–299). New York: Routledge.

Chan, R. W., Brooks, R. C., Raboy, B., & Patterson, C. (1998). Division of labor among lesbian and heterosexual parents: Associations with children's adjustment. *Journal of Family Psychology, 12,* 402–419.

Clements, M. L., Cordova, A. D., Markman, H. J., & Laurenceau, J. (1997). The erosion of marital satisfaction over time and how to prevent it. In R. J. Sternberg & M. Hojjat (Eds.), *Satisfaction in close relationships* (pp. 335–355). New York: Guilford Press.

Cole, D. A., & McPherson, A. E. (1993). Relation of family subsystems to adolescent depression: Implementing a new family assessment strategy. *Journal of Family Psychology, 7,* 119–133.

Coleman, M., Ganong, L., & Fine, M. (2000). Reinvestigating remarriage: Another decade of progress. *Journal of Marriage and the Family, 62,* 1288–1307.

Collins, W. A., & Laursen, B. (2004). Parent-adolescent relationships and influences. In R. M. Lerner & L. Steinberg (Eds.), *Handbook of adolescent psychology* (2nd ed., pp. 331–361). Hoboken, NJ: Wiley.

Coontz, S. (2000a). Historical perspective on family studies. *Journal of Marriage and the Family, 62,* 283–297.

Coontz, S. (2000b). *The way we never were: American families and the nostalgia trap.* New York: Basic Books.

Cooper, S. M. (1999). Historical analysis of the family. In M. Sussman, S. K. Steinmetz, & G. W. Peterson (Eds.), *Handbook of marriage and the family* (2nd ed., pp. 13–37). New York: Plenum Press.

Cowan, P. A. (1993). The sky is falling, but Popenoe's analysis won't help us do anything about it. *Journal of Marriage and the Family, 55,* 548–553.

Crouter, A. C., Bumpus, M. F., Maguire, M. C., & McHale, S. M. (1999). Linking parents' work pressure and adolescents' well being: Insights into dynamics in dual earner families. *Developmental Psychology, 35,* 1453–1461.

Cummings, E. M., Ianotti, R. J., & Zahn-Waxler, C. (1985). The influence of conflict between adults on the emotion and aggression in young children. *Developmental Psychology, 21,* 495–507.

Darling, N., & Steinberg, L. (1993). Parenting style as context: An integrative model. *Psychological Bulletin, 113,* 487–496.

Dehle, C., Larsen, D., & Landers, J. E. (2001). Social support in marriage. *The American Journal of Family Therapy, 29,* 307–324.

DePaulo, B. M., & Morris, W. L. (2005). Singles in society and in science. *Psychological Inquiry, 16,* 57–83.

Deutsch, M. (1973). *The resolution of conflict: Constructive and destructive processes.* New Haven, CT: Yale University Press.

Donohue, W. A., & Kolt, R. (1992). *Managing interpersonal conflict.* Newbury Park, CA: Sage.

Dornbusch, S. M., Carlsmith, J. M., Bushwall, S. J., Ritter, P. L., Leiderman, H., Hastorf, A. H., et al. (1985). Single parents, extended households, and control of adolescents. *Child Development, 56,* 326–341.

Eitle, D. (2006). Parental gender, single parent families, and delinquency: Exploring the moderating influence of race/ethnicity. *Social Science Research, 35,* 727–748.

Eldridge, K. A., & Christensen, A. (2002). Demand-withdraw communication during couple conflict: A review and analysis. In P. Noller & J. A. Feeney (Eds.), *Understanding marriage: Developments in the study of couple interaction* (pp. 289–322). New York: Cambridge University Press.

England, P. (2001). Review of the book *The case for marriage: Why married people are happier, healthier, and better off financially. Contemporary Sociology, 30,* 564–565.

Federal Interagency Forum on Child and Family Statistics. (2009). *America's children: Key national indicators of well-being, 2009.* Washington, DC: Government Printing Office.

Fields, J. (2001). *Living arrangements of children: Fall 1996* (Current Population Reports, P70–74). Washington, DC: U.S. Census Bureau.

Fincham, F. D., Bradbury, T. N., & Grych, J. (1990). Conflict in close relationships: The role of intrapersonal factors. In S. Graham & V. Folkes (Eds.), *Attribution theory: Applications to achievement, mental health, and interpersonal conflict* (pp. 161–184). Hillsdale, NJ: Lawrence Erlbaum.

Fine, M. A., Coleman, M., & Ganong, L. H. (1998). Consistency in perceptions of the step-parent role among step-parents, parents, and stepchildren. *Journal of Social and Personal Relationships, 15,* 811–829.

Fisher, P. A., Fagor, B. I., & Leve, C. S. (1998). Assessment of family stress across low-, medium-, and high-risk samples using the family events checklist. *Family Relations, 47,* 215–219.

Fitzpatrick, M. A. (1988). *Between husbands and wives: Communication in marriage.* Newbury Park, CA: Sage.

Fitzpatrick, M. A. (2006). Epilogue: The future of family communication theory and research. In L. H. Turner & R. West (Eds.), *The family communication sourcebook* (pp. 491–495). Thousand Oaks, CA: Sage.

Fitzpatrick, M. A., & Badzinski, D. M. (1985). All in the family: Interpersonal communication in kin relationships. In M. L. Knapp & G. R. Miller (Eds.), *Handbook of interpersonal communication* (pp. 687–736). Beverly Hills, CA: Sage.

Fitzpatrick, M. A., & Koerner, A. F. (2005). Family communication schemata: Effects on children's resiliency. In S. Dunwoody, L. B. Becker, D. McLeod, & G. Kosicki (Eds.), *The evolution of key mass communication concepts: Honoring Jack M. McLeod* (pp. 113-136). Cresskill, NJ: Hampton Press.

Fitzpatrick, M. A., & Ritchie, L. D. (1994). Communication schemata within the family: Multiple perspectives on family interaction. *Human Communication Research, 20,* 275–301.

Floyd, K., Mikkelson, A. C., & Judd, J. (2006). Defining the family through relationships. In L. H. Turner & R. West (Eds.), *The family communication sourcebook* (pp. 21–39). Thousand Oaks, CA: Sage.

Gadlin, H. (1977). Private lives and public order: A critical view of the history of intimate relations in the United States. In G. Levinger & H. L. Raush (Eds.), *Close relationships: Perspectives on the meaning of intimacy* (pp. 33–72). Amherst: University of Massachusetts Press.

Galvin, K. (2003). International and transracial adoption: A communication research agenda. *Journal of Family Communication, 3,* 237–253.

Galvin, K. M. (2006). Diversity's impact on defining the family. In L. H. Turner & R. West (Eds.), *The family communication sourcebook* (pp. 3–19). Thousand Oaks, CA: Sage.

Ganong, L. H., & Coleman, M. (2004). *Stepfamily relationships: Development, dynamics, and interventions.* New York: Kluwer Academic/Plenum.

Ganong, L. H., Coleman, M., Fine, M., & Martin, P. (1999). Stepparents' affinity-seeking and affinity-maintaining strategies with stepchildren. *Journal of Family Issues, 20,* 299–327.

Gartrell, N., Deck, A., Rodas, C., Peyser, H., & Banks, A. (2005). The National Lesbian Family Study, 4: Interviews with the 10 year-old children. *American Journal of Orthopsychiatry, 75,* 518–524.

Goldsmith, D. J. (2004). *Communicating social support.* New York: Cambridge University Press.

Goldsmith, D. J. (2009). Uncertainty and communication in couples coping with serious illness. In T. D. Afifi & W. A. Afifi (Eds.), *Uncertainty, information management, and disclosure decisions: Theories and applications* (pp. 203–225). New York: Routledge.

Goldsmith, D. J., Lindholm, K. A., & Bute, J. J. (2006). Dilemmas of talk about lifestyle changes among couples coping with a cardiac event. *Social Science and Medicine, 63,* 2079–2090.

Golish, T. D. (2003). Stepfamily communication strengths: Understanding the ties that bind. *Human Communication Research, 29,* 41–80.

Golish, T. D., & Caughlin, J. P. (2002). "I'd rather not talk about it": Adolescents' and young adults' use of topic avoidance in stepfamilies. *Journal of Applied Communication Research, 30,* 78–106.

Golombok, S., Perry, B., Burtson, A., Murray, C., Mooney-Somers, J., Stevens, M., et al. (2003). Children with lesbian parents: A community study. *Developmental Psychology, 39,* 20–33.

Golombok, S., Tasker, F., & Murray, C. (1997). Children raised in fatherless families from infancy: Family relationships and the socioemotional development of children of lesbian and single heterosexual mothers. *Journal of Child Psychology and Psychiatry, 38,* 783–791.

Gordis, E. B., Margolin, G., & John, R. S. (2001). Parents' hostility in dyadic marital and triadic family settings and children's behavior problems. *Journal of Consulting and Clinical Psychology, 69,* 727–734.

Gordon, L. (1988). *Heroes of their own lives: The politics and history of family violence.* New York: Viking.

Gottman, J. M. (1993). The roles of conflict engagement, escalation, and avoidance in marital interaction: A longitudinal view of five types of couples. *Journal of Consulting and Clinical Psychology, 61,* 6–15.

Gottman, J. M. (1994). *What predicts divorce: The relationship between marital process and marital outcomes.* Hillsdale, NJ: Lawrence Erlbaum.

Graham, E. E. (2003). Dialectic contradictions in postmarital relationships. *Journal of Family Communication, 3,* 193–214.

Grotevant, H. D., Wrobel, G. M., Von Korff, L., Skinner, B., Newell, J., Friese, S., et al. (2007). Many faces of openness in adoption: Perspectives of adopted adolescents and their parents. *Adoption Quarterly, 10*(3/4), 79–101.

Grych, J. H., Fincham, F. D., Jouriles, E. N., & McDonald, R. (2000). Interparental conflict and child adjustment: Testing the mediational role of appraisals in the cognitive-contextual framework. *Child Development, 71,* 1648–1661.

Grych, J. H., Seid, M., & Fincham, F. D. (1992). Assessing marital conflict from the child's perspective: The children's perception of interparental conflict scale. *Child Development, 63,* 558–572.

Hagedoorn, M., Sanderman, R., Bolks, H. N., Tuinstra, J., & Coyne, J. C. (2008). Distress in couples coping with cancer: A meta-analysis and critical review of role and gender effects. *Psychological Bulletin, 134,* 1–30.

Hardesty, J. L., & Ganong, L. H. (2006). How women make custody decisions and manage coparenting with abusive former husbands. *Journal of Social and Personal Relationships, 23,* 543–563.

Hareven, T. K. (1980, April). *American families in transition: Historical perspectives in change.* Washington, DC: Research Forum on Family Issues, White House Conference on Families.

Haslam, N. (1994). Mental representation of social relationships: Dimensions, laws, or categories? *Journal of Personality and Social Psychology, 67,* 575–584.

Haugaard, J. J., & Hazan, C. (2003). Adoption as a natural experiment. *Development and Psychopathology, 15,* 909–926.

Hawkins, D. N., Amato, P. R., & King, V. (2006). Parent-adolescent involvement: The relative influence of parent gender and residence. *Journal of Marriage and Family, 68,* 125–136.

Hetherington, E. M. (1999). Family functioning and the adjustment of adolescent siblings in diverse types of families. *Monographs of the Society for Research in Child Development, 64,* 1–25.

Hilton, J. M., Desrochers, S., & Devall, E. L. (2001). Comparison of role demands, relationships, and child functioning in single-mother, single-father, and intact families. *Journal of Divorce and Remarriage, 35,* 29–56.

van IJzendoorn, M. H., Juffer, F., & Klein Poelhuis, C. W. (2005). Adoption and cognitive development: A meta-analytic comparison of adopted and non-adopted children's IQ and school performance. *Psychological Bulletin, 131,* 301–316.

Isaacs, A., & Koerner, A. F. (2008, May). *Linking familial typologies: An investigation of the relationship between parenting styles and family communication patterns.* Paper presented at the annual meeting of the International Communication Association, Montreal, Quebec, Canada.

Jenkins, J. (2000). Marital conflict and children's emotions: The development of an anger organization. *Journal of Marriage and the Family, 62,* 723–736.

Kantor, D., & Lehr, W. (1976). *Inside the family.* San Francisco: Jossey-Bass.

Karney, B. R., & Bradbury, T. N. (1995). The longitudinal course of marital quality and stability: A review of theory, method, and research. *Psychological Bulletin, 118,* 3–34.

Klein, R. C. A., & Johnson, M. P. (1997). Strategies of couple conflict. In S. Duck (Ed.), *Handbook of personal relationships* (2nd ed., pp. 469–486). New York: Wiley.

Koerner, A. F., & Fitzpatrick, M. A. (1997). Family type and conflict: The impact of conversation orientation and conformity orientation on conflict in the family. *Communication Studies, 48,* 59–75.

Koerner, A. F., & Fitzpatrick, M. A. (2002). You never leave your family in a fight: The impact of family of origin on conflict behavior in romantic relationships. *Communication Studies, 53,* 234–251.

Koerner, A. F., & Fitzpatrick, M. A. (2004). Communication in intact families. In A. L. Vangelisti (Ed.), *Handbook of family communication* (pp. 177–195). Mahwah, NJ: Lawrence Erlbaum.

Koerner, A. F., & Fitzpatrick, M. A. (2006). Family conflict communication. In J. Oetzel & S. Ting-Toomey (Eds.), *The SAGE handbook of conflict communication* (pp. 159–183). Thousand Oaks, CA: Sage.

Kurdek, L. A. (1993). The allocation of household labor in homosexual and heterosexual cohabiting couples. *Journal of Social Issues, 49,* 127–139.

Kurdek, L. A. (1994). The nature and correlates of relationship quality in gay, lesbian, and heterosexual cohabiting couples: A test of the contextual, investment, and discrepancy models. In B. Greene & G. M. Herek (Eds.), *Lesbian and gay psychology: Theory, research, and clinical applications* (pp. 133–155). Thousand Oaks, CA: Sage.

Kurdek, L. A. (1995). Lesbian and gay couples. In A. R. D'Augelli & C. J. Patterson (Eds.), *Lesbian, gay and bisexual identities over the lifespan: Psychological perspectives* (pp. 243–261). New York: Oxford University Press.

Kurdek, L. A., & Schmidt, J. P. (1986). Relationship quality of partners in heterosexual married, heterosexual cohabiting, and gay and lesbian relationships. *Journal of Personality and Social Psychology, 51,* 711–720.

Lansford, J. E., Ceballo, R., Abbey, A., & Stewart, A. J. (2001). Does family structure matter? A comparison of adoptive, two-parent biological, single-mother, stepfather, and stepmother households. *Journal of Marriage and Family, 63,* 840–851.

Lanz, M., Ifrate, R., Rosnati, R., & Scabini, E. (1999). Parent-child communication and adolescent self-esteem in separated, intercountry adopted, and intact non-adoptive families. *Journal of Adolescence, 22,* 785–794.

Laursen, B. (1993). Conflict management among close peers. In B. Laursen (Ed.), *Close friendship in adolescent: New directions for child development* (No. 60, pp. 39–54). San Francisco: Jossey-Bass.

Lawrence, A. R., & Schiller Schigelone, A. R. (2002). Reciprocity beyond dyadic relationships: Aging-related communal coping. *Research on Aging, 24,* 684–704.

Lee, R. M. (2003). The transracial adoption paradox: History, research, and counseling implications of cultural socialization. *The Counseling Psychologist, 31,* 711–744.

Lerner, R. M., & Spanier, G. B. (Eds.). (1978). *Child influences on marital interaction: A life-span perspective.* New York: Academic Press.

Lewis, R. J., Derlega, V. J., Berndt, A., Morris, L. M., & Rose, S. (2001). An empirical analysis of stressors for gay men and lesbians. *Journal of Homosexuality, 42,* 63–88.

Lyons, R. F., Mickelson, K. D., Sullivan, M. J. L., & Coyne, J. C. (1998). Coping as a communal process. *Journal of Social and Personal Relationships, 15,* 579–605.

Maccoby, E. E., & Martin, J. A. (1983). Socialization in the context of the family: Parent–child interaction. In P. H. Mussen & E. M. Hetherington (Eds.), *Handbook of child psychology: Socialization, personality, and social development* (Vol. 4, 4th ed., pp. 1–101). New York: Wiley.

Maccoby, E. E., & Mnookin, R. H. (1992). *Dividing the child: Social and legal dilemmas of custody.* Cambridge, MA: Harvard University Press.

Martin, J. A., Hamilton, B. E., Sutton, P. D., Ventura, S. J., Menacker, F., & Kirmeyer, S. (2006). *Births: Final data for 2004, 55*(1). Hyattsville, MD: Department of Health and Human Services, Centers for Disease Control and Prevention, National Center for Health Statistics.

Masheter, C. (1997a). Former spouses who are friends: Three case studies. *Journal of Social and Personal Relationships, 14,* 207–222.

Masheter, C. (1997b). Healthy and unhealthy friendship and hostility between ex-spouses. *Journal of Marriage and the Family, 59,* 463–475.

McLanahan, S. S., & Sandefur, G. (1994). *Growing up with a single parent.* Cambridge, MA: Harvard University Press.

McLeod, J. M., & Chaffee, S. H. (1972). The construction of social reality. In J. Tedeschi (Ed.), *The social influence processes* (pp. 50–99). Chicago: Aldine-Atherton.

Miller, L. E., & Caughlin, J. P. (2011). Cancer in the family. In M. J. Craft-Rosenberg & S. Pehler (Eds.), *Encyclopedia of family health* (Vol. 1, pp. 123–127). Thousand Oaks, CA: Sage.

Noller, P. (1995). Parent-adolescent relationships. In M. A. Fitzpatrick & A. L. Vangelisti (Eds.), *Explaining family interactions* (pp. 77–111). Thousand Oaks, CA: Sage.

Noller, P., & Feeney, J. A. (1998). Communication in early marriage: Responses to conflict, nonverbal accuracy, and conversational patterns. In T. N. Bradbury (Ed.), *The developmental course of marital dysfunction* (pp. 11–43). New York: Cambridge University Press.

O'Brien, K. M., & Zamastny, K. P. (2003). Understanding adoptive families: An integrative review of empirical research and future directions for counseling psychology. *The Counseling Psychologist, 31,* 679–710.

Olson, D. H. (1993). Circumplex model of marital and family systems. In F. Wals (Ed.), *Normal family processes* (2nd ed.). New York: Guilford Press.

Orbuch, T. L., Veroff, J., Hassan, H., & Horrocks, J. (2002). Who will divorce: A 14-year longitudinal study of black couples and white couples. *Journal of Social and Personal Relationships, 19,* 179–202.

Pasch, L. A., & Bradbury, T. N. (1998). Social support, conflict, and the development of marital dysfunction. *Journal of Consulting and Clinical Psychology, 66,* 219–230.

Pasch, L. A., Bradbury, T. N., & Davila, J. (1997). Gender, negative affectivity, and observed social support behavior in marital interaction. *Personal Relationships, 4,* 361–378.

Patterson, C. J. (2000). Family relationships of lesbians and gay men. *Journal of Marriage and the Family, 62,* 1052–1069.

Peplau, L. A., & Beals, K. P. (2004). The family lives of lesbians and gay men. In A. L. Vangelisti (Ed.), *Handbook of family communication* (pp. 233–248). Mahwah, NJ: Lawrence Erlbaum.

Peplau, L. A., & Spalding, L. R. (2000). The close relationships of lesbians, gay men and bisexuals. In C. Hendrick & S. S. Hendrick (Eds.), *Close relationships: A sourcebook* (pp. 111–124). Thousand Oaks, CA: Sage.

Petronio, S. (2002). *Boundaries of privacy: Dialectics of disclosure.* Albany: State University of New York Press.

Petronio, S., & Caughlin, J. P. (2006). Communication privacy management theory: Understanding families. In D. O. Braithwaite & L. A. Baxter (Eds.), *Engaging theories in family communication: Multiple perspectives* (pp. 35–49). Thousand Oaks, CA: Sage.

Popenoe, D. (1993). American family decline, 1960–1990: A review and appraisal. *Journal of Marriage and the Family, 55,* 527–542.

Popenoe, D. (1996). *Fatherless America.* New York: Free Press.

Ramey, M. E. (2010). *Turning points in the development of parent-adolescent relationships.* Unpublished doctoral dissertation, University of Illinois at Urbana–Champaign.

Reese-Weber, M., & Bertle-Haring, S. (1998). Conflict resolution styles in family subsystems and adolescent romantic relationships. *Journal of Youth and Adolescence, 27,* 735–752.

Reis, H. T., Clark, M. S., & Holmes, J. G. (2004). Perceived partner responsiveness as an organizing construct in the study of intimacy and closeness. In D. J. Mashek & A. Aron (Eds.), *Handbook of closeness and intimacy* (pp. 201–225). Mahwah, NJ: Lawrence Erlbaum.

Reiss, D. (1981). *The family's construction of reality.* Cambridge, MA: Harvard University Press.

Rinaldi, C. M., & Howe, N. (2003). Perceptions of constructive and destructive conflict within and across family subsystems. *Infant and Child Development, 12,* 441–459.

Rogers, L. E. (2006). Introduction: A reflective view on the development of family communication. In L. H. Turner & R. West (Eds.), *The family communication sourcebook* (pp. xv–xx). Thousand Oaks, CA: Sage.

Rogers, L. E., & Farace, V. (1975). Analysis of relational communication in dyads. *Human Communication Research, 1,* 229–239.

Rogers, S. J., & White, L. K. (1998). Satisfaction with parenting: The role of marital happiness, family structure, and parents' gender. *Journal of Marriage and the Family, 60,* 293–308.

Rosenfeld, L. B., Bowen, G. L., & Richman, J. M. (1995). Communication in three types of dual-career marriages. In M. A. Fitzpatrick & A. L. Vangelisti (Eds.), *Explaining family interaction* (pp. 257–289). Thousand Oaks, CA: Sage.

Rosnati, R., & Marta, E. (1997). Parent–child relationships as a protective factor in preventing adolescents' psychosocial risk in inter-racial adoptive and non-adoptive families. *Journal of Adolescence, 20,* 617–631.

Rueter, M. A., & Koerner, A. F. (2008). The effect of family communication patterns on adopted adolescent adjustment. *Journal of Marriage and Family, 70,* 715–727.

Salzinger, S., Feldman, R. S., Ng-Mak, D. S., Mojica, E., Stockhammer, T., & Rosario, M. (2002). Effects of partner violence and physical child abuse on child behavior: A study of abused and comparison children. *Journal of Family Violence, 17,* 23–52.

Sanford, K. (2003). Problem-solving conversations in marriage: Does it matter what topic couples discuss? *Personal Relationships, 10,* 97–112.

Sarason, I. G., & Sarason, B. R. (2009). Social support: Mapping the construct. *Journal of Social and Personal Relationships, 26,* 113–120.

Schaefer, E. S. (1959). A circumplex model for maternal behavior. *Journal of Abnormal and Social Psychology, 59,* 226–235.

Schrodt, P. (2006a). The Stepparent Relationship Index: Development, validation, and associations with stepchildren's reports of stepparent communication competence and closeness. *Personal Relationships, 13,* 167–182.

Schrodt, P. (2006b). A typological examination of communication competence and mental health in stepchildren. *Communication Monographs, 73,* 309–333.

Schrodt, P., & Afifi, T. D. (2007). Communication processes that predict young adults' feelings of being caught and their associations with mental health and family satisfaction. *Communication Monographs, 74,* 200–228.

Schrodt, P., Baxter, L. A., McBride, M. C., Braithwaite, D. O., & Fine, M. (2006). The divorce decree, communication, and the structuration of co-parenting relationships in stepfamilies. *Journal of Social and Personal Relationships, 23,* 741–759.

Schrodt, P., & Braithwaite, D. O. (2010). Dark clouds with silver linings: The (dys)functional ambivalence of stepfamily relationships. In W. R. Cupach & B. H. Spitzberg (Eds.), *The dark side of close relationships* (pp. 243–268). New York: Routledge.

Schrodt, P., Braithwaite, D. O., Soliz, J., Tye-Williams, S., Miller, A., Normand, E. L., et al. (2007). An examination of everyday talk in stepfamily systems. *Western Journal of Communication, 71,* 216–234.

Schrodt, P., & Ledbetter, A. M. (2007). Communication processes that mediate family communication patterns and mental well-being: A mean and covariance structures analysis of young adults from divorced and non-divorced families. *Human Communication Research, 33,* 330–356.

Schrodt, P., Ledbetter, A. M., & Ohrt, J. K. (2007). Parental confirmation and affection as mediators of family communication patterns and children's mental well-being. *Journal of Family Communication, 7,* 23–46.

Schrodt, P., Soliz, J., & Braithwaite, D. O. (2008). A social relations model of everyday talk and relational satisfaction in stepfamilies. *Communication Monographs, 75,* 190–217.

Seltzer, J. A., & Brandreth, Y. (1994). What fathers say about involvement with children after separation. *Journal of Family Issues, 15,* 49–77.

Shantz, C. U., & Hartup, W. W. (1992). *Conflict in child and adolescent development.* New York: Cambridge University Press.

Shantz, C. U., & Hobart, C. J. (1989). Social conflict and development: Peers and siblings. In T. J. Berndt & G. W. Ladd (Eds.), *Peer relationships and child development* (pp. 71–94). New York: Wiley.

Shelton, K. H., & Harold, G. T. (2008). Interparental conflict, negative parenting, and children's adjustment: Bridging links between parents' depression and children's psychological distress. *Journal of Family Psychology, 22,* 712–724.

Sillars, A., Canary, D. J., & Tafoya, M. (2004). Communication, conflict, and the quality of family relationships. In A. Vangelisti (Ed.), *The handbook of family communication* (pp. 413–446). Mahwah, NJ: Lawrence Erlbaum.

Sillars, A., Koerner, A. F., & Fitzpatrick, M. A. (2005). Communication and understanding in parent–adolescent relationships. *Human Communication Research, 31,* 103–128.

Simons, R. L., & Associates. (1996). *Understanding differences between divorced and intact families.* Thousand Oaks, CA: Sage.

Smetana, J. G. (1996). Adolescent-parent conflict: Implications for adaptive and maladaptive development. In D. Cicchetti & S. L. Toth (Eds.), *Rochester symposium on developmental psychopathology: Vol. 7. Adolescence: Opportunities and challenges* (pp. 1–46). Rochester, NJ: University of Rochester.

Smetana, J. G., & Asquith, P. (1994). Adolescents' and parents' conceptions of parental authority and personal autonomy. *Child Development, 65,* 1147–1162.

Smetana, J. G., Daddis, C., & Chuang, S. S. (2003). "Clean your room!" A longitudinal investigation of adolescent–parent conflict and conflict resolution in middle-class African American families. *Journal of Adolescent Research, 18,* 631–650.

Sobolewski, J. M., & King, V. (2005). The importance of the coparental relationship for nonresident fathers' ties to children. *Journal of Marriage and Family, 67,* 1196–1212.

Stacey, J. (1993). Good riddance to "the family": A response to David Popenoe. *Journal of Marriage and the Family, 55,* 545–547.

Stamp, G. (2004). Theories of family relationships and a family relationships theoretical model. In A. L. Vangelisti (Ed.), *Handbook of family communication* (pp. 1–30). Mahwah, NJ: Lawrence Erlbaum.

Stocker, C. M., Richmond, M. K., Low, S. M., Alexander, E. K., & Elias, N. M. (2003). Marital conflict and children's adjustment: Parental hostility and children's interpretations as mediators. *Social Development, 12,* 149–161.

Stone, A. M., Mikucki, S., Satterlee, K., Middleton, A. V., Brown, L., & Caughlin, J. P. (2010, April). *Communication and care among adult children of lung cancer patients.* Paper presented at the biennial Kentucky Conference on Health Communication, Lexington, KY.

Straus, M. A. (1990). Measuring intrafamily conflict and violence: The Conflict Tactics (CT) scales. In M. A. Straus & R. J. Gelles (Eds.), *Physical violence in American families: Risk factors and adaptations to violence in 8,145 families* (pp. 29–47). New Brunswick, NJ: Transaction Books.

Straus, M. A., & Gelles, R. J. (1990). How violent are American families? Estimates from the national family violence resurvey and other studies. In M. A. Straus & R. J. Gelles (Eds.), *Physical violence in American families: Risk factors and adaptations to violence in 8,145 families* (pp. 95–112). New Brunswick, NJ: Transaction Books.

Suter, E. A., Bergen, K. M., Daas, K. L., & Durham, W. T. (2006). Lesbian couples' management of public-private dialectical contradictions. *Journal of Social and Personal Relationships, 23,* 349–365.

Suter, E. A., & Daas, K. L. (2007). Negotiating heteronormativity dialectically: Lesbian couples' display of symbols in culture. *Western Journal of Communication, 71,* 177–195.

Symonds, P. (1939). *The psychology of parent–child relationships.* New York: Appleton-Century-Crofts.

Tang, S. T., Liu, T., Tsai, C., Wang, C., Chang, G., & Liu, L. (2008). Patient awareness of prognosis, patient-family caregiver congruence on the preferred place of death, and caregiving burden of families contribute to the quality of life for terminally ill cancer patients in Taiwan. *Psycho-Oncology, 17,* 1202–1209.

Tasker, F. (2005). Lesbian mothers, gay fathers, and their children: A review. *Developmental and Behavioral Pediatrics, 26,* 224–240.

Tejada-Vera, B., & Sutton, P. D. (2009). Births, marriages, divorces, and deaths: Provisional data for April 2009. *National Vital Statistics Reports, 58*(9). Hyattsville, MD: National Center for Health Statistics.

Tucker, C. J., McHale, S. M., & Crouter, A. C. (2003). Conflict resolution: Links with adolescents' family relationships and individual well being. *Journal of Family Issues, 24,* 715–736.

Turner, A. P., Larimer, M. E., & Sarason, I. G. (2000). Family risk factors for alcohol-related consequences and poor adjustment in fraternity and sorority members: Exploring the role of parent–child conflict. *Journal of Studies on Alcohol, 61,* 818–826.

Turner, L. H., & West, R. (Eds.). (2006). *The family communication sourcebook.* Thousand Oaks, CA: Sage.

U.S. Bureau of the Census. (2003). *Adopted children and stepchildren: 2000* (Census 2000 Special Reports: CENSR-6RV). Washington, DC: Government Printing Office.

Vanfraussen, K., Ponjaert-Kristoffersen, I., & Brewaeys, A. (2002). What does it mean for youngsters to grow up in a lesbian family created by means of donor insemination? *Journal of Reproductive and Infant Psychology, 20,* 237–252.

Vanfraussen, K., Ponjaert-Kristoffersen, I., & Brewaeys, A. (2003). Family functioning in lesbian families created by donor insemination. *American Journal of Orthopsychiatry, 73,* 78–90.

Vangelisti, A. L. (1993). Communication in the family: The influence of time, relational prototypes, and irrationality. *Communication Monographs, 60,* 42–54.

Vangelisti, A. L. (Ed.). (2004). *Handbook of family communication*. Mahwah, NJ: Lawrence Erlbaum.

Vangelisti, A. L. (2009). Challenges in conceptualizing social support. *Journal of Social and Personal Relationships, 26,* 39–51.

Van Lear, A., Koerner, A. F., & Allen, D. (2006). Relationship typologies. In A. Vangelisti & D. Perlmann (Eds.), *The Cambridge handbook of personal relationships* (pp. 91–111). New York: Cambridge University Press.

Veach, T. A., Nicholas, D. R., & Barton, M. A. (2002). *Cancer and the family life cycle: A practitioner's guide.* New York: Brunner-Routledge.

Vuchinich, S. (1999). *Problem solving in families: Research and practice.* Thousand Oaks, CA: Sage.

Vuchinich, S., & Angelelli, J. (1995). Family interaction during problem solving. In M. A. Fitzpatrick & A. L. Vangelisti (Eds.), *Explaining family interactions* (pp. 177–205). Thousand Oaks, CA: Sage.

Waite, L., & Gallagher, M. (2000). *The case for marriage: Why married people are happier, healthier, and better off financially.* New York: Doubleday.

Wamboldt, F., & Reiss, D. (1989). Task performance and the social construction of meaning: Juxtaposing normality with contemporary family research. In D. Offer & M. Sabshin (Eds.), *Normality: Context and theory* (pp. 2–40). New York: Basic Books.

Watzlawick, P., Beavin, J., & Jackson, D. D. (1967). *Pragmatics of human communication.* New York: W. W. Norton.

Whitchurch, G. G., & Dickson, F. C. (1999). Family communication. In M. Sussman, S. K. Steinmetz, & G. W. Peterson (Eds.), *Handbook of marriage and the family* (2nd ed., pp. 687–704). New York: Plenum Press.

Wrobel, G. M., Kohler, J. K., Grotevant, H. D., & McRoy, R. G. (2003). The family adoption communication model (FAC): Identifying pathways of adoption-related communication. *Adoption Quarterly, 7,* 53–84.

Xu, Y., & Burleson, B. R. (2004). The association of experienced spousal support with marital satisfaction: Evaluating the moderating effects of sex, ethnic culture, and type of support. *Journal of Family Communication, 4,* 123–145.

Yep, G. (2002). From homophobia and heterosexism to heteronormativity: Toward the development of a model of queer interventions in the university classroom. *Journal of Lesbian Studies, 6,* 163–176.

Zhou, Q., Eisenberg, N., Losoya, S. H., Fabes, R. A., Reiser, M., Guthrie, I. K., et al. (2002). The relations of parental warmth and positive expressiveness to children's empathy-related responding and social functioning: A longitudinal study. *Child Development, 73,* 893–915.

# CHAPTER 21

# Interpersonal Communication Across the Life Span

*Jon F. Nussbaum*

*Loretta L. Pecchioni*

*Kevin B. Wright*

ndividuals and their social relationships are not static but undergo change through developmental and experiential processes. Whether communication scholars are examining the skills that individuals bring to their interactions or the nature of social relationships, the life span communication perspective highlights not only how change occurs but also how changes affect and are revealed by the individual and the relationship. This chapter provides a brief overview of the life span communication perspective and its basic propositions; reviews its application through the examples of socio-emotional selectivity theory, family communication dynamics, and aggressive behavior and communication; and addresses the complexities of appropriate research design to capture these dynamic processes.

The significance of identifying and explaining behavioral change across time is a relatively new focus within the social sciences. Interpersonal communication scholars were initially introduced to the life span communication perspective with the writings of Knapp (1978) and Nussbaum (1989). Borrowing heavily from the sister disciplines of psychology, sociology, anthropology, and human development, interpersonal communication researchers have incorporated life span notions into empirical investigations, producing "an impressive literature that focuses upon not only differing interactive behaviors as we age, but also on the numerous changes in the communicative functions and meanings of our behaviors as we manage and negotiate our lives" (Nussbaum, Pecchioni, Baringer, & Kundrat, 2002, p. 368).

Paul Baltes's (1987) landmark theoretical writings in life span developmental psychology helped guide Pecchioni, Wright, and Nussbaum (2005) as they put forth several propositions concerning the communicative process as it develops across the life span. They proposed the following:

The nature of communication is fundamentally developmental.

A complete understanding of human communication is dependent upon multiple levels of knowledge that occur simultaneously (here we mean individual knowledge, dyadic knowledge, family knowledge, societal knowledge . . .).

Communication change can be qualitative as well as quantitative as well as rapid and continuous.

Life span communication scholars can incorporate all current theories of interpersonal communication into this perspective as long as the theories are testable, useful, and address change across the time.

Unique methodologies are required to capture communication change across the life span. (p. 10)

These five propositions place developmental change across time at the center of any discussion of interpersonal communication. In addition, beyond thinking developmentally and constructing theory that incorporates change across the life span, communication scholars must design their investigations to capture change as it occurs. While interpersonal communication theorists throughout the past 50 years have not been shy to incorporate the various notions of process (Nussbaum, 2007, has roughly equated "process" to "change") into theory, the end result of the majority of the empirical investigations meant to test theories of interpersonal communication do not come close to capturing or explaining process (change). The primary function of the life span perspective is to investigate and to document interpersonal change across the life span. The fundamental assumption of the life span perspective

within interpersonal communication—whether a scholar is interested in the ability of individuals to process, store, retrieve, or create messages; to communicate competently with others; or to understand the meaning of friendship or various familial relationships—is that an understanding of interpersonal change can enhance our ability to describe, explain, and predict communication behavior. The authors of this chapter would go even further and state that a complete understanding of interpersonal communication is impossible without knowledge of the changes that occur as we communicate interpersonally across the life span. To truly understand any communicative event, it is best to observe what transpires before, during, and after the event.

The remaining pages of this chapter are divided into several sections to highlight selected interpersonal communication scholarship across the life span. The first section highlights Laura Carstensen's socio-emotional selectivity theory as an excellent example of a life span theory with significant links to interpersonal communication scholarship (Carstensen, Isaacowitz, & Charles, 1999). Interpersonal communication research within the family will be discussed in the next section to highlight the changing nature of families across the life span. The third section focuses on aggressive communication and examines how interpersonal communication as an area of scholarship can be enhanced by incorporating a life span perspective in the research on aggression. The chapter concludes with a brief discussion of the methodological challenges of capturing interpersonal change within appropriate life span design and analyses.

## Socio-Emotional Selectivity Theory

Socio-emotional selectivity theory (Carstensen, 1995, 1998; Carstensen et al., 1999; Lockenhoff & Carstensen, 2004) asserts that individuals are guided by the same essential socio-emotional goals throughout life, but the priority of these goals changes as a function of perceived time left in life. According to Lockenhoff and Carstensen (2004), "perceived limitations on time lead to reorganizations of goal hierarchies such that goals related to deriving emotional meaning from life are prioritized over goals that maximize long-term payoffs in a nebulous future" (p. 1396). Changes in a person's time perspective (due to factors such as growing older or facing a terminal illness) often result in associated changes in social preferences that influence the composition of their social network partners. Socio-emotional selectivity theory posits that younger individuals and individuals who perceive themselves to be in good health tend to be future oriented when developing relationships and are interested in forming expanded and diverse social networks in an attempt to gain novel experiences, information, and new social contacts (Carstensen & Fredrickson, 1998; Lockenhoff & Carstensen, 2004). By contrast, older people or individuals at earlier points in the life span who are facing a terminal illness tend to prefer smaller social networks comprising familiar, emotionally close, and meaningful relational partners due to the perception that they have relatively limited time (Lockenhoff & Carstensen, 2004).

Goal reprioritization due to limited time perspective influences the composition of support networks, perceptions of social support, the ways in which people cope with stressful situations, and, for us, the structure and function of interpersonal communication. According to Lockenhoff and Carstensen (2004),

> When time in life is limited, younger people and older people alike pay more attention to the emotional aspects of situations, prioritize emotion-focused over problem-focused coping strategies, and prefer emotionally gratifying social contacts over contacts with novel social partners. As a result, greater emotional well-being is experienced. Also, satisfaction with social support networks is higher, which may

ultimately hold benefits for physical well-being as well. (p. 1396)

For individuals who have a strong future orientation, such as younger people or healthy individuals, "goals such as information gathering and personal development are best pursued in expanded social networks with an ample supply of novel social partners who can help the individual acquire knowledge and form useful new social contacts" (Lockenhoff & Carstensen, 2004, p. 1398). According to Lockenhoff and Carstensen (2004), when individuals perceive the future as relatively open-ended, they seek goals such as the acquisition of new information, goals that are aimed at personal development, and goals that are aimed at establishing new social contacts that could be beneficial sources of social capital in the future.

According to socio-emotional selectivity theory, individuals with a future time orientation should be more likely to have social networks that comprise a greater number of weak ties, while individuals with a limited (or present) time perspective should have a greater number of strong ties with their social network (Fredrickson & Carstensen, 1990; Lockenhoff & Carstensen, 2004). According to Lockenhoff and Carstensen (2004), "the familiar social partner choice represents an emotionally meaningful goal, whereas the novel social partner choice represents future-oriented goals related to information gathering and the development of new relationships, respectively" (p. 1399). Socio-emotional selectivity theory researchers have found that time perspective changes influence the composition of social networks in ways that typically lead to stronger ties when time is perceived as limited and a higher number of weak ties among people with a future-oriented time perspective (Lang & Carstensen, 1994; Levitt, Weber, & Guacci, 1993). Fisher (2008) and others have begun to use the fundamental assumptions of socio-emotional selectivity theory to guide their investigations of the changing nature of interpersonal communication as we age. Fisher found that conversations between individuals diagnosed with cancer change in predictable ways once a perceived "time limit" is placed within a relationship.

# Family Communication Across the Life Span

The life span (or life course) communication perspective is ideal for examining communication in families as it highlights the nature of change over time and families inherently experience growth, development, and reconfiguration (Pecchioni et al., 2005). Family development scholars often consider the family as a system that has a life course as the unit of analysis shifts from the individual to the social group. "Normative" family development occurs when individuals move from their family of origin to their family of orientation as they find a partner through marriage, cohabitation, or some other form of romantic linkage and begin a new family by having children (Pecchioni et al., 2005; Wrosch & Freund, 2001). The development of the children then drives the life course of the family, which is segmented into having young children, their growing up into adolescents, and the launching of children as they leave their family of origin to begin the cycle again. The couple who parented the children continue to change and develop as they move through their middle and later years. Thus, the configuration of the family changes as individuals enter and leave through marriage, birth, and death.

Of course, not all families follow this normative trajectory. When events occur "off time," different meanings may be assigned to these events. For example, the birth of a child that occurs following a marriage to a heterosexual couple in their 20s is "normative" and assigned particular meanings and often celebrated. The birth of a child to a teenage mother who does not marry the father is considered "nonnormative" and therefore assigned different meanings, both within the family and in the larger community. This interplay between normative and nonnormative points out the reality of diversity in family forms. As noted in the chapter on family

communication (Chapter 20, this volume), defining family is a complex process as individuals may define their family more or less broadly depending on the structural (i.e., legal and biological ties) and/or emotional (i.e., love, affection, interdependence) connections among the members of the family. The life span communication perspective helps us account for these multiple forms of family and how communication creates the sense of family through interaction patterns and how members of the social group make sense of their interrelationships as members of the family join or leave the family unit (Pecchioni et al., 2005).

Because the life span perspective focuses on capturing this change, we can examine how families' communication patterns change across time, how that communication creates the family, and how the family is reflected through its communicative practices. Most of the relevant research in the United States focuses on the nuclear family, consisting of two parents (a male and a female) and their biological offspring (Pecchioni et al., 2005). In addition, the research usually focuses on dyads within the family, particularly the marital dyad and parent–child relationships. Life span communication scholars, however, continue to expand on that research by examining a broader range of family types, exploring other family relationships, and moving beyond a focus on dyadic interactions because the perspective encourages accounting for the complexities of family changes.

Space limitations preclude a thorough examination of all the research examining family communication dynamics as they change over time, therefore a few key areas will serve to illustrate the benefit of applying the life span communication perspective to families. Specifically, we offer a brief review of interpersonal conflict between marital partners, the power dynamics between parents and children, and the relational closeness between grandparents and grandchildren.

*Interpersonal Conflict in the Marital Dyad.* Interpersonal conflict is inevitable in intimate relationships and reflects the differing opinions, goals, and approaches to making decisions that affect relational partners (see Chapter 13, this volume). Some of the first research conducted by scholars applying the life span communication perspective examined the nature of interpersonal conflict between heterosexual romantically involved and marital partners. As the relational partners move from two individuals who barely know each other to a couple, they experience an increase in the degree of interdependence and relational commitment (Hartup, 1992). Their connection to each other leads to a need to resolve any differences that arise; however, the frequency and intensity as well as the topics of conflict change over the course of the relationship.

Dating couples who are not yet "serious" generally experience relatively little conflict (Canary, Cupach, & Messman, 1995). As the couple's lives become more intimately intertwined and the consequences of each other's actions become more important, both the frequency and the intensity of conflict increase as they begin to discover more about each other and in the process discover their differences and struggle to find ways to resolve those differences. This process of discovering and resolving their differences may increase their mutual understanding and deepen their level of intimacy. Once a dating relationship has reached a certain level of commitment (although what that level is varies from couple to couple), the frequency and intensity of conflict remain relatively stable through the early years of their relationship.

For couples in long-term committed relationships, the changing dynamics of the relationship may lead to changes in the nature of the conflict that they experience (Zietlow & Sillars, 1988). As newly married couples negotiate the nature of their relationship with each other, they are often highly engaged and confrontational in their conflict styles. They invest time and energy into learning how they are going to live together and negotiate their responsibilities with each other and their new family. Over time, however, couples come to understand each other, so that they feel less of a need to engage in conflict because they know how to negotiate solutions together or

have identified issues on which they will not change each other's mind and so they agree to disagree. When these couples do engage in conflict, they are less engaged and confrontational, even when the topic of conflict is important to them. More details about these dynamics are reviewed in the section "Aggressive Communication Across the Life Span."

Reaching this level of understanding does not, however, mean that the couple do not engage in conflict (Pecchioni et al., 2005). New issues arise that require attention as the family ages. Child-rearing concerns change with the age(s) of the child(ren), work-related decisions may affect the family in a variety of ways and are likely to change across the career trajectory, and issues around retirement often require considerable negotiation before they are resolved. How each new conflict is managed depends on how earlier conflicts were resolved and whether the partners were and continue to be satisfied with those resolutions.

*Power Dynamics Between Parents and Children.* The parent–child relationship is one that inherently experiences a power differential because of the age difference that exists between the relational partners (Fingerman, 1995, 1996). This power differential is greatest when the child is young and the parent has the responsibility to regulate the child's behavior in socially appropriate ways (Maccoby & Martin, 1983; Osborne & Fincham, 1994). When the child is very young, the parent is more likely to regulate the child's behavior by providing prohibitions and directives because of the child's limited cognitive ability. Although a two-year-old may say "no" to her mother, she has limited power to change her mother's behavior, while the reverse is not as true. As children mature, they are more capable of understanding the consequences of their actions, and parents are more likely to begin explaining the nature of these consequences and to help children consider the perspective of others. Although directives and prohibitions continue, they are often couched in terms of trying to help children understand why these rules are in place.

The adolescent years are often characterized by power struggles between teens and their parents (Collins & Laursen, 1992; Kucynski, 2003). The adolescent is striving to achieve autonomy and develop self-reliance, while the parent is struggling to allow his or her child sufficient freedom while continuing to protect the child from harm. The resulting power struggles often become conflictual as the parent and child disagree on the child's behavior, dress, choice of friends, conduct around the house, and so on. Their communication may reflect high levels of conflict or avoidance of conflict through physical distance and/or silence. Parents often report struggling to find ways to reach their children during these years, when communication can seem so difficult.

Once the child reaches his or her early adulthood, the power distance between the adult child and his or her parents is reduced (Bugental, Olster, & Martorell, 2003). Some parent–child relationships become more like friendships as they share more of their adult lives together, especially after the children become parents themselves (Pecchioni et al., 2005). Some parent–child relationships, especially those marked by abuse or neglect during the child's early years, become nearly nonexistent, and thus, the parent has limited power over the child. Some parents continue to give unsolicited advice, which is generally not appreciated by the now adult child. However, adult children report turning to their parents for advice on a regular basis as they are considered to be not only older but also wiser. Communication between adult children and their parents then reflects the nature of their newly negotiated relationship based on a changed power dynamic.

For some parent–child relationships, a role reversal occurs in the parents' later years as they become incapable of taking care of themselves (Pecchioni et al., 2005; Williams & Nussbaum, 2001). The child now takes on the role of protecting the parent from harm. This transition can be difficult for all parties as they renegotiate the power dynamics of the relationship. Communicatively, raising concerns about a parent's ability to care

for himself or herself can be quite challenging. Some parents are grateful that their children are taking over decision making, while others resent the implication that they are no longer capable. In many situations, both of these conflicting dynamics exist as the parent remains capable in some realms of his or her life but is less capable in other areas.

*Relational Closeness Between Grandparents and Grandchildren.* Although most research on the grandparent–grandchild relationship has focused on the years when the grandchild is a minor, more attention is being given to the dynamics of this relationship as the grandchild transitions into young adulthood. Examining this transition is enlightening as it not only reveals how families define themselves as a family and transmit family rituals from generation to generation but also helps us track social change over time.

Both grandparents and grandchildren report that this relationship is an important one to them; however, grandparents are more likely to see this relationship as one that defines their place in the family (Harwood & Lin, 2000). During the grandchild's early years, the grandparent–grandchild relationship is often mediated by the middle generation (child to one generation and parent to the other). For example, women report being closer to their mothers than their husbands report feeling toward their mothers, and as a consequence, grandchildren are more likely to have frequent contact with their maternal grandmother and report feeling closest to her among their cohort of grandparents (Hagestad, 1985). In addition, grandparents and grandchildren who live geographically close visit each other face-to-face more frequently and report greater emotional closeness. The emotional closeness established during the grandchild's early years may also affect the effort they put into maintaining that relationship as they enter into adulthood (Pecchioni & Croghan, 2002).

An interesting transition in the grandparent–grandchild relationship occurs as the grandchild enters adulthood and takes on more responsibility for maintaining his or her relationship, even though parents may encourage them to do so. Although young adults, especially those in college, report being busy with their own lives, grandchildren continue to maintain contact with grandparents, especially with those with whom they feel close (Monserud, 2008; Pecchioni & Croghan, 2002; Soliz & Harwood, 2006). These efforts to maintain the relationship may be taken partly out of obligation, such as when a parent reminds the young adult child to call his or her grandparent, but these contacts are also made voluntarily because of the desire to maintain their closeness. Young adult grandchildren report contacting their grandparents just to chat, to ask for advice, to offer advice (e.g., regarding some information required by the grandparent), and to talk about family events (Lin, Harwood, & Bonnesen, 2002).

An interesting area of research is emerging on how the two generations are using technology to maintain contact and their emotional connection (Harwood, 2000). Although the grandchildren make frequent face-to-face visits, they also call, e-mail, or "virtually" visit (e.g., through Skype) their grandparents regularly. In fact, the current cohort of older grandparents report getting e-mail and other technological services so that they can maintain contact with their grandchildren. These frequent interactions help maintain their level of closeness even when they are geographically separated.

## Aggressive Communication Across the Life Span

Despite evidence that aggression and aggressive communication persist across time and across generations (Farrington, 1986; Huesmann, Eron, Lefkowitz, & Walder, 1984; Myers & Goodboy, 2006), relatively few studies of aggressive communication within the communication discipline have drawn on a life span perspective. There are numerous reasons for this, including the relative newness of life span communication

research in the communication discipline, the low number of communication scholars currently conducting research grounded in this perspective, and the widespread use of cross-sectional study designs employing undergraduate student samples in communication research (often ignoring individuals at earlier and later points in the life span). The majority of longitudinal studies of aggression in other disciplines have also been limited to a relatively short span of years, and those studies that have examined aggression for longer periods of time have been limited in terms of the types of questions they have asked (Tremblay, 2000).

Aggressive communication appears to demonstrate stability and can affect relationships throughout life. Such behaviors are ubiquitous as people encounter conflict in relationships with family members, peers, and coworkers throughout their lives. For example, Tangey et al. (1996) found that aggressive responses to anger remained relatively stable between middle childhood and adulthood. Several researchers have argued that aggression is as stable a trait as intelligence across the life span (Olweus, 1979; Parke & Slaby, 1983). In addition, researchers have identified a number of interesting patterns and variations in aggression and aggressive communication over time.

Examining aggressive behavior and aggressive communication from a life span perspective may provide important insights into the ways aggression and aggressive communication vary among individuals over time. Tremblay (2000) laments that in the past, "adult aggressive behaviors were studied without reference to childhood behaviors. Adolescent aggressive behaviors were studied as if they emerged during adolescence, and most specialists of the early development of aggressive behaviors concentrated on the school years" (p. 130). As early as in the 1960s, Lorenz (1966) argued, "A complete theory of aggression, whatever its orientation, must explain how aggressive patterns are developed" (p. 43).

The first studies of developmental trends in aggression can be traced back to the 1920s and

1930s. Over the years, aggressive communication has been conceptualized as a class of behaviors that serve the same function in social interaction: to hurt another person by doing harm to his or her self-concept or social standing (Galen & Underwood, 1997).

*Biological Influences on the Development of Aggressive Behavior.* There is some empirical evidence for innate forms of aggressive behavior, yet most life span aggression researchers acknowledge the contribution of genetic and environmental influences to aggressive behavior. In terms of empirical evidence for innate aggression, Lewis, Allesandri, and Sullivan (1990) found that four-month-old babies clearly expressed facial anger reactions to frustration, and these same reactions tend to become more pronounced in the following months as the child's motor skill development allows him or her to express anger in more complex ways (i.e., kicking and hitting). Tremblay et al. (1999) found that the onset of physical aggression appears to occur between 12 and 17 months after birth (and tends to peak around this time period); most children learn to inhibit physical aggression by the time they enter school.

Physical aggression clearly appears to be an ontogenetical antecedent to verbal aggression (Cynader & Frost, 1999). Researchers have found that children begin by displaying physical aggression in infancy, and they gradually shift to verbal aggression as their language skills develop (Choquet & Ledoux, 1994; Tremblay et al., 1999). Tremblay et al. (1996) found that aggression in children tends to become more indirect and verbal over time.

*Sex Differences.* Several developmental studies have found that boys generally tend to be more physically aggressive than girls (Campbell, 1993; Maccoby, 1990), although indirect aggression is often higher among girls (Cairns, Cairns, Neckerman, Ferguson, & Gariespy, 1989; Largerspetz, Bjorkqvist, & Peltonen, 1988). While boys are socialized to exhibit frustration and

anger in very physical, direct ways (Bjorkqvist, Lagerspetz, & Kaukianien, 1992; Bjorkqvist, Osterman, & Lagerspetz, 1994), girls tend to use more subtle and indirect forms of social aggression focused on relational and social characteristics (Cairns et al., 1989). Bjorkqvist et al. (1992) found that indirect aggressive strategies were common among girls as young as 11 years old. Girls have been found to rate social aggression as more hurtful than physical aggression, while just the opposite was found with boys (Galen & Underwood, 1997). Girls appear to be more likely to hurt others by damaging relationships with peers than boys (Crick & Grotpeter, 1995). However, Underwood (2003) proposes that understanding gender differences in aggression might not be as important as understanding the *meaning* of physical and social aggression for each gender.

In a longitudinal study, Cairns et al. (1989) found that physical aggression continued in male–male conflicts throughout childhood to early adolescence, while physical aggression in female–female conflicts decreased over the same time period. Feshbach (1969, 1971) tested sex differences in adolescent reactions to newcomers to a group and found that girls often acknowledged newcomers less frequently than boys, were less friendly, and sometimes chose not to speak to the group newcomer. In addition, reports of social alienation and ostracism increased more dramatically for girls than for boys as the participants entered adolescence.

*Childhood Aggression as a Predictor of Adult Aggression.* Some empirical evidence points to the stability of aggression that is already high in preschool years (Cummings, Iannotti, & Zahn-Waxler, 1989; Keenan & Shaw, 1994). Gustavsson, Weinryb, Goransson, Pederson, and Asberg (1997), in a nine-year longitudinal study of twins in Sweden (one subset of the sample was separated at birth and the other subset consisted of twins who grew up together) found the propensity to engage in verbal aggression to be a stable personality trait across time. In addition, higher verbal aggression scores were found to be predictive of lower family satisfaction and higher job stress.

Studies have produced conflicting results regarding the stability of aggressive behavior over time. Loeber (1982) found that aggression tends to decrease with age. Cairns and Cairns (1984) found that the mean frequency of physical aggression decreased from ages 10 to 18 years. In a rare 22-year longitudinal study, Huesmann et al. (1984) found that early aggressive behavior in life was predictive of later aggressive behavior. In addition, the male participants were found to exhibit more stability in aggressive behavior than female participants. However, Cairns et al. (1989) and Loeber and Hay (1997) found that physical aggression in children tends to increase systematically with age.

*Aggression and Aggressive Communication in Preadolescence and Adolescence.* Much of the developmental work on aggression in the past 30 years has focused on aggressive behavior during elementary school and adolescence. As we have seen, based on the results of a relatively large number of longitudinal studies, researchers have concluded that childhood aggression is one of the best predictors of adolescent and adult aggression (Coie & Dodge, 1988; Reiss & Ross, 1993). In terms of communication research, studies have largely focused on three contexts: (1) interactions with family members, (2) interactions with peers, and (3) the influence of the mass media on aggression.

Among adolescents, researchers have found that aggressive behavior with peers can lead to social rejection (Carlson, Lahey, Frame, Walker, & Hynd, 1987) and symptoms of depression (Hodgens & McCoy, 1989; Kovacs, Paulauskas, Gatsonis, & Richards, 1988). Research findings have pointed to developmental differences between aggressive children and their nonaggressive peers in terms of social, affective, and cognitive dimensions in laboratory and naturally occurring situations that elicit competition or the potential for aggressive reactions (see Lochman, Meyer, Rabiner, & White, 1991). Moreover, researchers

have found aggression among adolescents to be correlated with substance abuse (Farrington, 1994; Olweus, 1993). McCord (1983), in a 40-year longitudinal study, found that aggressive adolescents were more likely to be convicted of a crime as adults than nonaggressive adolescents.

Lindeman, Harakka, and Keltikangas-Jarvinen (1997), in a large-scale study of preadolescents and adolescents, found that aggression in preadolescence and adolescence developed in a curvilinear pattern. Specifically, aggression was found to be the least often used reaction during preadolescence, the most often used in midadolescence, and less frequently used in late adolescence (returning to preadolescence levels). These researchers argued that since cognitive abilities do not develop in a curvilinear fashion, these findings are most likely explained by changes in peer relationships, group norms, and developmental tasks. Mayeux and Cillessen (2008) argue that during adolescence, individuals may be engaging in relationally aggressive behaviors as a way to maintain popularity and/or gain social status. They found that adolescents who were popular and aware of their popularity scored highest on peer-nominated aggression. Continued focus on popularity and social status remains a viable avenue for research on aggression.

*Aggression in Young and Middle Adulthood.* In general, some aggressive behaviors established at an earlier point in the life span often persist into young and middle adulthood. Olweus (1993) found that individuals who were aggressive toward their peers in middle school and/or high school tended to be more likely to carry these behaviors into adulthood. In addition, Olweus found that adults tend to engage in more covert than overt aggression in the workplace. In a sample of adult employees (ages 21–50), researchers found that although women continued to use more covert forms of aggression than men, men did start to employ more indirect methods of aggressive expression in the workplace (Bjorkqvist et al., 1994).

Pulkkinen (1996), in a longitudinal study that measured aggression among participants at ages 8, 14, and 27, found that males who displayed proactive aggression in childhood were more likely to externalize problems and to be involved in criminal behavior in adulthood than participants who were less aggressive as children. In addition, Pulkkinen found that female participants who were proactively aggressive in childhood were more likely to internalize problems and display neuroticism in adulthood than their less aggressive peers.

Nakhaie (1998) found that younger adults were more likely to exhibit physical and verbal aggression in marriages than older adults. Suitor (1991) found that the frequency of verbal aggression during conflict situations between married couples tended to be significantly higher when children were in preschool and middle school than when the children were teenagers and adults, and the age of the child was a better predictor of engaging in verbal aggression than division of household labor.

Bookwala, Sobin, and Zdaniuk (2005) examined marital aggression from a life span perspective. Controlling for marriage duration and number of previous marriages, these authors found that younger and middle-aged couples were more likely to engage in verbal aggression than older married couples. Moreover, younger and middle-aged married couples reported more incidents of physical aggression than older married couples, and younger couples were more likely to throw things or hit one another than middle-aged or older couples. Younger couples were less likely to keep disagreements to themselves than middle-aged and older couples. These authors also found an age-by-gender interaction effect when examining the conflict resolution styles of each marital partner in the study. Specifically, older women were more likely to keep their disagreements to themselves during conflict situations, whereas younger women were the least likely to do so.

Sillars and Zietlow (1993) investigated married couples' (23–83 years of age) conflict behaviors. They found that young couples demonstrated more explicit conflict negotiation and more engaging and direct communication styles when discussing marital conflict. In contrast, midlife couples exhibited higher percentages of denial, equivocation, and noncommittal behaviors and lower frequencies of direct confrontation. Retired couples exhibited the highest frequency of noncommittal behaviors and the lowest frequency of direct confrontational behaviors. Sillars and Zietlow (1993) concluded that older couples may be more inclined than younger couples to choose their battles because they were more willing to engage in salient topics.

Bergstrom (1997) examined the self-reported conflict strategies of young, middle-aged, and older adults when in conflict with their mothers. He found a consistent linear increase in preference for solution-oriented styles of conflict and a corresponding decrease in preference for controlling styles as age increased. Bergstrom and Nussbaum (1996) contend that younger adults' more limited life experiences may be associated with their preferences for both competitive engagement tactics and avoidance tactics when conflict situations become more difficult to manage. Older adult preferences for more cooperative tactics as well as their being more selective in terms of the issues on which they are willing to engage in conflict may be the result of their greater life experience (including past experience with managing conflict over the course of their life).

*Aggressive Behaviors Among Adult Siblings.* Relatively few studies have examined sibling conflict following adolescence. Sibling relationships often contain the most frequent and intense conflict, with the most negative effects, especially during early childhood (Collins & Laursen, 1992; Vandell & Bailey, 1992). Martin, Anderson, and Rocca (2005) identified 10 types of aggressive messages siblings use with each other, including attacking the sibling's intelligence and threatening to get the sibling in trouble with the parents. Many of these aggressive messages appear to persist into adulthood. Sibling relationships are typically the longest relationships individuals have during their life span (Cicirelli, 1995; Mikkelson, 2005), and conflict patterns (including the use of verbal and physical aggression) between siblings often remain stable over long periods of time (although there is a tendency for less heated conflict in later stages of life). Variables such as birth order, control issues, and relational history may influence aggressive communication between siblings during conflict situations (Vandell & Bailey, 1992), although it is important to point out that aggression is unilateral whereas conflict requires mutual opposition.

Myers and Goodboy (2006) found that perceived sibling use of verbally aggressive messages decreases across the life span in that verbally aggressive messages are used more frequently in young adulthood than in either middle adulthood or late adulthood. As siblings enter old age, their relationships tend to become more egalitarian, which may partially account for the reduction in conflict. Myers and Goodboy (2006) also found that decreased affect between siblings due to decreases in liking, trust, and commitment may spur increases in aggressive behavior.

*Aggression and Aggressive Communication Among Older Adults.* As you might expect, relatively few studies have examined aggression among older adults. Similar to other areas of life span communication research, less is known about aggressive communication between older adults than between individuals at early points in the life span. However, most empirical studies have found evidence that aggressive behavior and confrontational conflict strategies tend to decrease with age (Archer, 2000; Bookwala & Jacobs, 2004; Myers & Goodboy, 2006). According to Bookwala et al. (2005), "as women and men grow older they tend to use fewer confrontational/maladaptive problem resolution techniques and they are less likely to engage in physical aggression during arguments" (p. 804). These authors contend that this pattern is part of a longitudinal trend they refer to as a "mellowing across the life span" when it comes to aggressive behavior in interpersonal

relationships. However, age cohort differences in terms of how people were socialized with regard to acceptance and tolerance for aggressive conflict in marriages may also explain the differences in aggression between individuals from different age groups.

In terms of verbal aggression, Straus and Sweet (1992) found that verbal aggression tended to decrease among married couples with age. Bergstrom and Nussbaum (1996), using a cross-sectional design, compared the conflict preference styles of younger and older adults. Younger adults reported using a controlling style more frequently than did older adults, whereas older adults reported using more solution-oriented conflict styles. These authors argued that their findings reflect important developmental processes during adulthood in that the frequent use of controlling behaviors among younger adults demonstrates that they have not fully developed the skills necessary for productive conflict management. By comparison, older individuals appear to have more highly developed skills (most likely due to greater life experience) for engaging in more productive conflict.

There is a tendency for older adults to engage in indirect rather than direct forms of aggressive behavior (Walker & Richardson, 1998; Walker, Richardson, & Green, 2000). Walker et al. (2000) also found that participants who rated themselves as more assertive and instrumental were more likely to report frequent use of indirect aggressive behaviors. These authors contend that this finding is likely related to the general trend among adults in general (young, middle-aged, and old) to use more indirect aggressive strategies, particularly in environments (e.g., the workplace, assisted living communities) where individuals often wish to avoid the negative social repercussions associated with more direct forms of aggressive behavior (Green, Richardson, & Lago, 1996). Bookwala et al. (2005) contend,

As people get older they orient themselves toward enhancing emotional closeness in their significant personal relationships. It is possible that one way people manage to achieve higher emotional benefits from their marriage is by avoiding confrontational or unpleasant interactions with their partner. (p. 803)

As addressed earlier, socio-emotional selectivity theory would support this contention by suggesting that as we age, we concentrate our energies on developing and maintaining more satisfying interpersonal relationships. The research on aggressive communication suggests that although early patterns may be well established, we can and do adapt our communicative behavior over time.

## Life Span Methodology

Hofer and Piccinin (2010) have recently noted that the study of age-related change "demands an integrative life span developmental approach, involving interdisciplinary collaborations and multiple methodological approaches . . . in both universal and idiosyncratic ways, over time" (p. 276). Nussbaum et al. (2002) have similarly noted that to conduct an empirical investigation that captures change across the life span is a rather complex task. As has been mentioned above, the great majority of life span research conducted in the social sciences, including research in the field of interpersonal communication, have investigated interindividual change with the use of various cross-sectional, age-comparative designs. Individual communication perceptions or behaviors are measured at one point in time and compared with different communication perceptions or behaviors in a different age cohort. Typically, the communicative behaviors of young adults (college-age students) are compared with those of middle-aged individuals (the parents) and, then, with those of older adults (the grandparents). These cross-sectional designs, while enabling the researcher to investigate interindividual differences and to make a statement regarding possible age/cohort differences, cannot assess change over time and

are very limited in their ability to reveal causal influences in causal processes (Alwin & Campbell, 2001). Keeping in mind that the "gold standard" for life span research is to observe, describe, explain, and predict intra-individual or intrarelationship change, the cross-sectional design is not appropriate. "The temptation to attribute true measurement of intra-individual change to the results of cross-sectional investigations that measure inter-individual change is often too much to overcome" (Nussbaum et al., 2002, p. 381). This misinterpretation of the data has consistently led to statements that reinforce the negative, deterioration myth of the aging process. For instance, conclusions based on cross-sectional studies of a long and continuous decline in the cognitive abilities of all individuals past the age of 30 is simply not true. Longitudinal research has shown that many cognitive abilities remain stable or increase as we age, well into our 70s (Birren & Schaie, 2006).

Schaie and Hofer (2001) and Hofer and Piccinin (2010) provide an excellent rationale for the use of longitudinal design and analysis as the most appropriate (and perhaps only) way to capture change across time. "Longitudinal designs permit separation of individual differences at the initiation of the study from within-individual change and provide a basis for obtaining valid inferences regarding change condition on study attrition and mortality" (Hofer & Piccinin, 2010, p. 270). In addition, longitudinal designs can capture different structured versions of change that occur in short bursts or in a rather long (aging), continuous process. Longitudinal designs also permit the cohort comparison or historical difference analysis that the traditional, and overused, cross-sectional designs have provided.

Nussbaum et al. (2002) and Nussbaum (2007) have discussed the use of longitudinal design and analysis in communication research. They note that numerous communicative processes may be much more difficult to capture than the physical or cognitive behaviors that are typically studied in longitudinal investigations. For instance, the role of context in longitudinal design has been recognized but has been overly simplified. Birth order is often considered as the only important contextual factor in psychological/sociological longitudinal designs. Interpersonal communication, on the other hand, is much more significantly affected by both micro and macro contextual factors. Variables such as the content of the conversation, the relational definition of the dyad (friends, cousins, mother–daughter, etc.), whether the interaction is intergenerational, whether this particular conversation will continue, and whether the interaction is taking place in a church, a dorm room, or a hospital lobby are only a few of the numerous contextual variables that must be considered. In addition, the cognitive state of the conversational partners may play a significant role in their ability to effectively communicate. Is there a maturation issue or an inability to capture the meaning of the changing nature of the relationship due to inadequacies in one of the individuals?

It is also important to note that longitudinal designs and analyses might move the communication scholar outside the realm of his or her comfort zone as far as statistical analysis and interdisciplinary team research are concerned. While traditional mean difference–based tests (t tests, multivariate analysis of variance, analysis of variance, and various nonparametric tests as well) are used in longitudinal designs, structural equation modeling, which involves the variances and covariances rather than mean structures, has been recognized as a much more valuable statistical tool for analyzing change within time-bound processes. Hofer and Piccinin (2010) have initiated the Integrative Analysis of Longitudinal Studies of Aging (IALSA). IALSA is an international network of more than 30 principal study investigators who are currently conducting large-scale longitudinal investigations of human behavior and hope to reinforce collaborative efforts to ultimately advance developmental theory and methodology. Interpersonal communication scholars who are rarely funded for large-scale longitudinal investigations can certainly take advantage of this collaborative effort to "data share" as a means to answer life span research questions in an appropriate manner.

## Summary

The study of interpersonal communication from a life span perspective spans a variety of academic disciplines. Communication scholars have played, and will continue to play, an important role in contributing to this important interdisciplinary body of work. In this chapter, we have attempted to provide a broad understanding of the life span perspective while also offering a more detailed look at interpersonal communication research in the areas of social support, family communication, and aggressive communication. Moreover, we discussed a variety of methodological challenges associated with interpersonal communication research from a life span perspective. Despite the advances that researchers have made in terms of understanding interpersonal communication over the past several decades from this perspective, there is much more work to be done in order to gain a sophisticated understanding of the development of interpersonal communication behaviors throughout the life course, especially as we work to incorporate this perspective into theories of interpersonal communication processes.

## References

Alwin, D. F., & Campbell, R. T. (2001). Quantitative approaches: Longitudinal methods in the study of development and aging. In R. H. Binstock & L. K. George (Eds.), *Handbook of aging and the social sciences* (pp. 22–43). San Diego, CA: Academic Press.

Archer, J. (2000). Sex differences in aggression between heterosexual partners: A meta-analytic review. *Psychological Bulletin, 126,* 651–680.

Baltes, P. B. (1987). Theoretical propositions of life-span developmental psychology: On the dynamics between growth and decline. *Developmental Psychology, 23,* 611–626.

Bergstrom, M. J. (1997, May). *Cooperative conflict behaviors of adults: A test of three life-span stages.* Paper presented at the annual meeting of the International Communication Association, Montreal, Quebec, Canada.

Bergstrom, M. J., & Nussbaum, J. F. (1996). Cohort differences in interpersonal conflict: Implications for the older patient–younger care provider interaction. *Health Communication, 8,* 233–248.

Birren, J. E., & Schaie, K. W. (2006). *Handbook of the psychology of aging* (6th ed.). San Diego, CA: Academic Press.

Bjorkqvist, K., Lagerspetz, K. M. J., & Kaukiainen, A. (1992). Do girls manipulate and boys fight? Developmental trends in regard to direct and indirect aggression. *Aggressive Behavior, 18,* 117–127.

Bjorkqvist, K., Osterman, K., & Lagerspetz, K. M. J. (1994). Sex differences in covert aggression among adults. *Aggressive Behavior, 20,* 27–33.

Bookwala, J., & Jacobs, J. (2004). Age, marital processes, and depressed affect. *The Gerentologist, 44,* 328–338.

Bookwala, J., Sobin, J., & Zdaniuk, B. (2005). Gender and aggression in marital relationships: A life-span perspective. *Sex Roles, 52,* 797–806.

Bugental, D. B., Olster, D. H., & Martorell, G. A. (2003). A developmental neuroscience perspective on the dynamics of parenting. In L. Kucynski (Ed.), *Handbook of dynamics in parent-child relations* (pp. 25–48). Thousand Oaks, CA: Sage.

Cairns, R. B., & Cairns, B. D. (1984). Predicting aggressive patterns in girls and boys: A developmental study. *Aggressive Behavior, 10,* 227–242.

Cairns, R. B., Cairns, B. D., Neckerman, H. J., Ferguson, L. L., & Gariespy, J. L. (1989). Growth and aggression: 1. Childhood to early adolescence. *Developmental Psychology, 25,* 320–330.

Campbell, A. (1993). *Men, women, and aggression.* New York: Wiley.

Canary, D. J., Cupach, W. R., & Messman, S. J. (1995). *Relationship conflict: Conflict in parent-child, friendship, and romantic relationships.* Thousand Oaks, CA: Sage.

Carlson, C. L., Lahey, B. B., Frame, C. L., Walker, J., & Hynd, G. W. (1987). Sociometric status of clinic-referred children with attention deficit disorders with and without hyperactivity. *Journal of Abnormal Child Psychology, 15,* 537–548.

Carstensen, L. L. (1995). Evidence for a life-span theory of socioemotional selectivity. *Current Directions in Psychological Science, 4,* 151–156.

Carstensen, L. L. (1998). A life-span approach to social motivation. In J. Heckhausen & C. S. Dweck (Eds.), *Motivation and self-regulation across the life span* (pp. 341–364). New York: Cambridge University Press.

Carstensen, L. L., & Fredrickson, B. L. (1998). Influence of HIV status and age on cognitive representations of others. *Health Psychology, 17,* 494–503.

Carstensen, L. L., Isaacowitz, D. M., & Charles, S. T. (1999). Taking time seriously: A theory of socioemotional selectivity. *American Psychologist, 54,* 165–181.

Choquet, M., & Ledoux, S. (1994). *Adolescents: Enquete Nationale.* Paris: INSERM.

Cicirelli, V. G. (1995). *Sibling relationships across the life span.* New York: Plenum Press.

Coie, J. D., & Dodge, K. A. (1998). Aggression and antisocial behavior. In W. Damon & N. Eisenberg (Eds.), *Handbook of child psychology: Social, emotional, and personality development* (Vol. 3, pp. 779–862). Toronto, Ontario, Canada: Wiley.

Collins, W. A., & Laursen, B. (1992). Conflict and relationships during adolescence. In C. U. Shantz & W. W. Hartup (Eds.), *Conflict in child and adolescent development* (pp. 216–241). Cambridge, UK: Cambridge University Press.

Crick, N. R., & Grotpeter, J. K. (1995). Relational aggression, gender and social-psychological adjustment. *Child Development, 66,* 710–722.

Cummings, E. M., Iannotti, R. J., & Zahn-Wexler, C. (1989). Aggression between peers in early childhood: Individual continuity and developmental change. *Child Development, 60,* 887–895.

Cynader, M., & Frost, B. (1999). Mechanisms of brain development: Neuronal sculpting by the physical and social environment. In D. Keating & C. Hertzman (Eds.), *Developmental health and the wealth of nations: Social, biological, and educational dynamics* (pp. 153–184). New York: Guilford Press.

Farrington, D. P. (1986). Stepping stones to adult criminal careers. In D. Olweus, J. Block, & M. R. Yarrow (Eds.), *Development of antisocial and prosocial behavior* (pp. 359–384). New York: Academic Press.

Farrington, D. P. (1994). Childhood, adolescence, and adult features in violent males. In L. R. Huesmann

(Ed.), *Aggressive behavior: Current perspectives* (pp. 215–240). New York: Plenum Press.

Feshbach, N. D. (1969). Sex differences in children's modes of aggressive responses toward outsiders. *Merrill-Palmer Quarterly, 15,* 249–258.

Feshbach, N. D. (1971). Sex differences in adolescent reactions toward newcomers. *Developmental Psychology, 4,* 381–386.

Fingerman, K. L. (1995). Aging mothers' and their adult daughters' perceptions of conflict behaviors. *Psychology and Aging, 10,* 639–649.

Fingerman, K. L. (1996). Sources of tension in the aging mother and adult daughter relationship. *Psychology and Aging, 11,* 591–606.

Fisher, C. L. (2008). *Adaptive communicative behavior of mothers and their adult daughters after a breast cancer diagnosis.* Unpublished doctoral dissertation, Penn State University, University Park.

Fredrickson, B. L., & Carstensen, L. L. (1990). Choosing social partners: How old age and anticipated endings make us more selective. *Psychology and Aging, 5,* 335–347.

Galen, B. R., & Underwood, M. K. (1997). A developmental investigation of social aggression among children. *Developmental Psychology, 33,* 589–600.

Green, L. R., Richardson, D. R., & Lago, T. (1996). How do friendships, indirect, and direct aggression relate? *Aggressive Behavior, 22,* 81–86.

Gustavsson, J. P., Weinryb, R. M., Goransson, N. L., Pederson, N. L., & Asberg, M. (1997). Stability and predictive ability of personality traits across 9 years. *Personality and Individual Differences, 22,* 783–791.

Hagestad, G. O. (1985). Continuity and connectedness. In V. L. Bengston & J. F. Robertson (Eds.), *Grandparenthood* (pp. 31–48). Beverly Hills, CA: Sage.

Hartup, W. W. (1992). Conflict and friendship relations. In C. U. Shantz & W. W. Hartup (Eds.), *Conflict in child and adolescent development* (pp. 186–215). Cambridge, UK: Cambridge University Press.

Harwood, J. (2000). Communication media use in the grandparent-grandchild relationship. *Journal of Communication, 50,* 56–68.

Harwood, J., & Lin, M. (2000). Affiliation, pride, exchange, and distance in grandparents' accounts of relationships with their college-aged grandchildren. *Journal of Communication, 50,* 31–47.

Hodgens, J. B., & McCoy, J. F. (1989). Distinctions among rejected children on the basis of peer-nominated aggression. *Journal of Clinical Childhood Psychology, 18,* 121–128.

Hofer, S. M., & Piccinin, A. M. (2010). Toward an integrative science of life-span development and aging. *Journals of Gerontology: Psychological Sciences, 65B*(3), 269–278.

Huesmann, L. R., Eron, L. D., Lefkowitz, M. M., & Walder, L. O. (1984). Stability of aggression over time and generations. *Developmental Psychology, 20,* 1120–1134.

Keenan, K., & Shaw, D. S. (1994). The development of aggression in toddlers: A study of low income families. *Journal of Abnormal Child Psychology, 22,* 53–77.

Knapp, M. L. (1978). *Social intercourse: From greetings to goodbye.* Boston: Allyn & Bacon.

Kovacs, M., Paulauskas, S., Gatsonis, C., & Richards, C. (1988). Depressive disorders in childhood: III. A longitudinal study of comorbidity and risk for conduct disorders. *Journal of Affective Disorders, 15,* 205–217.

Kucynski, L. (2003). Beyond bidirectionality: Bilateral conceptual frameworks for understanding dynamics. In L. Kucynski (Ed.), *Handbook of dynamics in parent-child relations* (pp. 3–24). Thousand Oaks, CA: Sage.

Lang, F. R., & Carstensen, L. L. (1994). Close emotional relationships in later life: Further support for proactive aging in the social domain. *Psychology and Aging, 9,* 315–324.

Largerspetz, K. M., Bjorkqvist, K., & Peltonen, T. (1988). Is indirect aggression typical of females: Gender differences in aggressiveness in 11- to 12-year-old children. *Aggressive Behavior, 14,* 403–414.

Levitt, M. J., Weber, R. A., & Guacci, N. (1993). Convoys of social support: An intergenerational analysis. *Psychology & Aging, 12,* 323–326.

Lewis, M., Allessandri, S. M., & Sullivan, M. W. (1990). Violation of expectancy, loss of control, and anger expressions in young infants. *Developmental Psychology, 26,* 745–751.

Lin, M., Harwood, J., & Bonnesen, J. (2002). Conversation topics and communication satisfaction in grandparent–grandchild relationships. *Journal of Language & Social Psychology, 21,* 302–323.

Lindeman, M., Harakka, T., & Keltikangas-Jarvinen, L. (1997). Age and gender differences in adolescents' reactions to conflict situations: Aggression, prosociality, and withdrawal. *Journal of Youth and Adolescence, 26,* 339–351.

Lochman, J. E., Meyer, B. L., Rabiner, D. L., & White, K. J. (1991). Parameters influencing social problem-solving of aggressive children. In R. J. Prinz (Ed.), *Advances in behavioral assessment of children and families* (Vol. 5, pp. 31–63). London: Jessica Kingsley.

Lockenhoff, C. E., & Carstensen, L. L. (2004). Socioemotional selectivity theory, aging, and health: The increasingly delicate balance between regulating emotions and making tough choices. *Journal of Personality, 72,* 1395–1423.

Loeber, R. (1982). The stability of antisocial and delinquent child behavior: A review. *Child Development, 53,* 1431–1446.

Loeber, R., & Hay, D. F. (1997). Key issues in the development of aggression and violence from childhood to early adulthood. *Annual Review of Psychology, 48,* 371–410.

Lorenz, K. (1966). *On aggression.* New York: Harcourt, Brace.

Maccoby, E. E. (1990). Gender and relationships: A developmental account. *American Psychologist, 45,* 513–520.

Maccoby, E. E., & Martin, J. A. (1983). Socialization in the context of the family: Parent-child interaction. In E. M. Hetherington (Ed.), *Handbook of child psychology: Vol. 4. Socialization, personality, and social development* (4th ed., pp. 26–47). New York: Wiley.

Martin, M. M., Anderson, C. M., & Rocca, K. A. (2005). Perceptions of the adult sibling relationship. *North American Journal of Psychology, 7,* 107–116.

Mayeux, L., & Cillessen, A. (2008). It's not just being popular, it's knowing it, too: The role of self-perceptions of status in the associations between peer status and aggression. *Social Development, 17,* 871–888.

McCord, J. (1983). A forty year perspective on effects of child abuse and neglect. *Child Abuse & Neglect, 7,* 265–270.

Mikkelson, A. C. (2005, February). *Communication in the adult sibling relationship.* Paper presented at the meeting of the Western States Communication Association, San Francisco.

Monserud, M. (2008). Intergenerational relationships and affectual solidarity between grandparents and young adults. *Journal of Marriage and Family, 70,* 182–195.

Myers, S. A., & Goodboy, A. K. (2006). Perceived sibling use of verbally aggressive messages across the lifespan. *Communication Research Reports, 23,* 1–11.

Nakhaie, M. R. (1998). Asymmetry and symmetry of conjugal violence. *Journal of Comparative Family Studies, 29,* 549–567.

Nussbaum, J. F. (1989*). Life-span communication: Normative processes.* Hillsdale, NJ: Lawrence Erlbaum.

Nussbaum, J. F. (2007). Life span communication and quality of life. *Journal of Communication, 57,* 1–7.

Nussbaum, J. F., Pecchioni, L., Baringer, D., & Kundrat, A. (2002). Lifespan communication. In W. B. Gudykunst (Ed.), *Communication yearbook 26* (pp. 366–389). Mahwah, NJ: Lawrence Erlbaum.

Olweus, D. (1979). Stability of aggressive reaction patterns in males: A review. *Psychological Bulletin, 85,* 852–875.

Olweus, D. (1993). *Bullying at school: What we know and what we can do.* Oxford, UK: Blackwell.

Osborne, L. N., & Fincham, F. D. (1994). Conflict between parents and their children. In D. D. Cahn (Ed.), *Conflict in personal relationships* (pp. 117–141). Hillsdale, NJ: Lawrence Erlbaum.

Parke, R. D., & Slaby, R. G. (1983). The development of aggression. In P. H. Mussen (Ed.), *Handbook of child psychology: Socialization, personality, and social development* (Vol. 4, pp. 547–641). New York: Wiley.

Pecchioni, L. L., & Croghan, J. M. (2002). Young adults' stereotypes of the elderly with their grandparents as the targets. *Journal of Communication, 52,* 715–730.

Pecchioni L. L., Wright, K., & Nussbaum, J. F. (2005). *Lifespan communication.* Mahwah, NJ: Lawrence Erlbaum.

Pulkkinen, L. (1996). Proactive and reactive aggression in early adolescence as precursors to anti- and prosocial behavior in young adults. *Aggressive Behavior, 22,* 241–257.

Reiss, A. J., & Roth, J. A. (Eds.). (1993). *Understanding and preventing violence.* Washington, DC: National Academy Press.

Schaie, K. W., & Hofer, S. M. (2001). Longitudinal studies in aging research. In J. E. Birren & K. W. Schaie (Eds.), *Handbbok of the psychology of aging* (5th ed., pp. 53–77). San Diego, CA: Academic Press.

Sillars, A. L., & Zietlow, P. H. (1993). Investigations of marital communication and lifespan development.

In N. Coupland & J. F. Nussbaum (Eds.), *Discourse and lifespan identity*. Newbury Park, CA: Sage.

Soliz, J., & Harwood, J. (2006). Shared family identity, age salience, and intergroup contact: Investigation of the grandparent–grandchild relationship. *Communication Monographs, 73*, 87–107.

Straus, M. A., & Sweet, S. (1992). Verbal/symbolic aggression in couples: Incident rates and relationships to personal characteristics. *Journal of Marriage and the Family, 54*, 346–357.

Suitor, J. J. (1991). Marital quality and satisfaction with the division of household labor across the family cycle. *Journal of Marriage and the Family, 53*, 221–230.

Tangey, J. P., Hill-Barlow, D., Wagner, P. E., Marschall, D. E., Borenstein, J. K., Sanftner, J., et al. (1996). Assessing individual differences in constructive versus destructive responses to anger across the lifespan. *Journal of Personality and Social Psychology, 70*, 780–796.

Tremblay, R. E. (2000). The development of aggressive behavior during childhood: What have we learned in the past century? *International Journal of Behavioral Development, 24*, 129–141.

Tremblay, R. E., Japel, C., Perusse, D., Boivin, M., Zoccolillo, M., Montplaisir, J., et al. (1999). The search for the age of "onset" of physical aggression: Rousseau and Bandura revisited. *Criminal Behavior and Mental Health, 9*, 8–23.

Tremblay, R. E., Masse, L. C., Pagani, L., & Vitaro, F. (1996). From childhood physical aggression to adolescent maladjustment: The Montreal Prevention Experiment. In R. D. Peters & R. J. McMahon (Eds.), *Preventing childhood disorders, substance abuse, and delinquency* (pp. 268–298). Thousand Oaks, CA: Sage.

Underwood, M. K. (2003). *Social aggression among girls*. New York: Guilford Press.

Vandell, D. L., & Bailey, M. D. (1992). Conflicts between siblings. In C. U. Shantz & W. W. Hartup (Eds.), *Conflict in child and adolescent development* (pp. 242–269). Cambridge, UK: Cambridge University Press.

Walker, S., & Richardson, D. R. (1998). Aggression strategies among older adults: Delivered but not seen. *Aggressive and Violent Behavior, 3*, 287–294.

Walker, S., Richardson, D. R., & Green, L. R. (2000). Aggression among older adults: The relationship of interaction networks and gender role to direct and indirect responses. *Aggressive Behaviors, 26*, 145–154.

Williams, A., & Nussbaum, J. F. (2001). *Intergenerational communication across the life span*. Mahwah, NJ: Lawrence Erlbaum.

Wrosch, C., & Freund, A. (2001). Self-regulation of normative and non-normative developmental challenges. *Human Development, 44*, 264–283.

Zietlow, P. H., & Sillars, A. L. (1988). Life-stage differences in communication during marital conflicts. *Journal of Social and Personal Relationships, 5*, 223–245.

# Author Index

# Subject Index

# About the Editors

**Mark L. Knapp** is the Jesse H. Jones Centennial Professor Emeritus in Communication and Distinguished Teaching Professor Emeritus at the University of Texas at Austin. Three of his books are *Nonverbal Communication in Human Interaction* (with J. A. Hall), *Interpersonal Communication and Human Relationships* (with A. L. Vangelisti), and *Lying and Deception in Human Interaction*. He is past president of the International Communication Association and the National Communication Association, a fellow of the International Communication Association, and a Distinguished Scholar in the National Communication Association. He served as editor of *Human Communication Research* and developed and edited the Sage Series in Interpersonal Communication. He received his PhD in 1966 from Penn State University.

**John A. Daly** is the Liddell Professor of Communication, TCB Professor of Management, and University Distinguished Teaching Professor at the University of Texas at Austin. He has served as President of the National Communication Association and on the Board of Directors of the International Communication Association and the International Customer Service Association. He is the author of more than 100 scholarly articles and book chapters, and he has served as editor of the journal *Communication Education* and as coeditor of the journal *Written Communication*. His most recent book is *Advocacy: Championing Innovations and Influencing Others* (2011). He received his PhD in 1977 from Purdue University.

# About the Contributors

**Tamara D. Afifi** is an associate professor in the Department of Communication, University of California, Santa Barbara. She is a former associate editor of the *Journal of Social and Personal Relationships* and a past winner of the Young Scholar Award from the International Communication Association. She has also been the recipient of the Distinguished Article Award from the Family Communication Division and the Franklin Knower Article Award from the Interpersonal Communication Division of the National Communication Association. Her research interests include information regulation (privacy, secrets, disclosure, avoidance) in parent–child and dating relationships, with particular emphasis on postdivorce families, and communication processes related to uncertainty, loss, stress, and coping in families. She obtained her PhD from the University of Nebraska at Lincoln.

**Charles R. Berger** is a professor in the Department of Communication, University of California, Davis. He is a former editor of *Human Communication Research* and former coeditor of *Communication Research*. He is a past president and fellow of the International Communication Association. His most recent book with Michael E. Roloff and David R. Roskos-Ewoldsen is titled *Handbook of Communication Science* (second edition, 2010). His research interests include the role cognitive processes play in message production and social interaction and the rational reappraisal of messages depicting hazards and threats. He received his PhD from Michigan State University.

**Dale E. Brashers** was a David L. Swanson Professorial Scholar, Professor of Communication and Medicine, and Head of the Department of Communication at the University of Illinois at Urbana–Champaign. His research focused on the management of uncertainty related to health and illness. He published more than 50 articles and book chapters, authored or edited two books, and worked as the principal investigator under numerous grants, including two major projects funded by the National Institutes of Health. He received his PhD in 1994 from the University of Arizona.

**Judee K. Burgoon** is Professor of Communication, Professor of Family Studies and Human Development, Director of Research for the Center for the Management of Information, and Site Director for the Center for Identification Technology Research at the University of Arizona. She holds an appointment as Distinguished Visiting Professor of Communication at the University of Oklahoma. She has also authored or edited 13 books, monographs, and special volumes and nearly 300 articles, chapters, and reviews related to nonverbal and relational communication, deception, dyadic interaction patterns, computer-mediated communication, and research methods. Her research has been supported by extramural grants from the National Science Foundation, Department of Defense, Department of Homeland Security, National Institutes of Mental Health, and Gannett Foundation, among others. Her awards and honors include the National Communication Association's Distinguished Scholar Award, the Mark L. Knapp Award for Career Contributions to Interpersonal Communication, the Golden Anniversary Monographs Award, and the Woolbert Research Award for Scholarship of Lasting Impact; the International Communication Association's (ICA's) Chaffee Career Productivity Award and Fisher Mentorship Award and election as an ICA Fellow; and election to the Society for Experimental Social Psychology. She earned her PhD in communication and educational psychology in 1974 from West Virginia University.

**Brant R. Burleson** was a professor in the Department of Communication at Purdue University until his death in December 2010. His more than 150 articles and book chapters centered on communication skill acquisition and development, the role of emotion in communication and relationships, the effects of communication skills on relationship outcomes, and supportive forms of communication such as comforting. He served as editor of *Communication Yearbook* and as coeditor of *Communication of Social Support: Messages, Interactions, Relationships, and Community* (1994). He was a National Communication Association Distinguished Scholar and a fellow of the International Communication Association, and he received the Berscheid-Hatfield Award for Distinguished Mid-Career Achievement from the International Network on Personal Relationships. He received his PhD from the University of Illinois, Urbana–Champaign, in 1982.

**John P. Caughlin** is a Conrad Humanities Scholar, an associate professor, and Associate Head of Communication at the University of Illinois at Urbana–Champaign. He has published articles recently in journals such as *Communication Monographs*, *Health Communication*, *Human Communication Research*, and *Journal of Social and Personal Relationships*. He is a winner of the Brommel Award from the National Communication Association for contributions to family communication, the Garrison Award for the Analysis of

Interpersonal Communication in Applied Settings, and the Miller Early Career Achievement Award from the International Association for Relationship Research. He earned his PhD from the University of Texas at Austin in 1997.

**Benjamin W. Chiles** is a doctoral candidate at Northwestern University. He has presented several research papers at the National Communication Association and at the Central States Communication Association conferences. His research interests include conflict, reconciliation, and family communication. He obtained his MA from Northwestern University in 2010.

**William R. Cupach** is a professor in the Department of Communication at Illinois State University. His research pertains to problematic interactions in interpersonal relationships, including contexts such as embarrassing predicaments, relational transgressions, and conflict. With Brian Spitzberg, he is coeditor and contributor to *The Dark Side of Interpersonal Communication* and *The Dark Side of Close Relationships* and coauthor of *Interpersonal Communication Competence*, *Handbook of Interpersonal Competence Research*, and *The Dark Side of Relationship Pursuit*. He has served as associate editor for the *Journal of Social and Personal Relationships* and is a past president of the International Association for Relationships Research. He earned his PhD from the University of Southern California in 1981.

**James Price Dillard** is Professor of Communication Arts and Director of the Center for Communication Research at the University of Wisconsin–Madison. His research interests revolve around the study of influence and persuasion, with a special emphasis on the role of emotion in persuasion. He is the editor of *Seeking Compliance: The Production of Interpersonal Influence Messages* (1990) and coeditor (with Michael Pfau) of *The Persuasion Handbook: Developments in Theory and Practice* (2002). In recognition of his research achievements, he received the Vilas Associate Award from the University of Wisconsin–Madison in 1994 and was appointed Liberal Arts Research Professor at Penn State University in 2010. He earned his PhD from Michigan State University in 1983.

**Bo Feng** is an assistant professor in the Department of Communication at the University of California, Davis. Her research interests focus on supportive communication in both traditional, face-to-face contexts and mediated contexts. She also studies cultural and gender differences in the mechanisms through which people seek, provide, and respond to support. Her research has appeared in *Human Communication Research*, *Communication Research*, *Journal of International and Intercultural Communication*, and *Health Communication*. She received her PhD from Purdue University in 2006.

**Mary Anne Fitzpatrick** is a Carolina Distinguished Professor of Psychology and founding dean of the College of Arts and Sciences at the University of South Carolina. Her publications include *Between Husbands and Wives: Communication in Marriage*, *Communication Theory and AIDS*, and *Explaining Family Interaction*. She is a fellow and past president of the International Communication Association and a recipient of the ICA Career Productivity Award. She earned her PhD from Temple University in 1976.

**Kory Floyd** is a professor and Associate Director of the Hugh Downs School of Human Communication at Arizona State University. He is a former editor of *Journal of Family Communication* and former chair of the family communication division of the National Communication Association. His research focuses on the communication of affection in personal relationships and on the interplay of affection, physiology, and health. His most recent book is *Communication Matters* (2011). He obtained his PhD from the University of Arizona.

**Howard Giles** is a professor in the Department of Communication, University of California,

Santa Barbara. He is a former editor of *Human Communication Research* and the current and founding editor of the *Journal of Language and Social Psychology* and the *Journal of Asian Pacific Communication*. He is a past president and fellow of the International Communication Association and past president of the International Association of Language and Social Psychology. His most recent (coedited) book is titled *The Dynamics of Intergroup Communication* (2010). His research interests include communication and aging across cultures, police–civilian encounters, and the roles of language in interpersonal and intergroup interactions. He received his PhD and DSc from the University of Bristol, United Kingdom.

**Laura K. Guerrero** is a professor in the Hugh Downs School of Human Communication at Arizona State University, where she specializes in relational, nonverbal, and emotional communication. She has authored more than 90 articles, chapters, and reviews on these topics, as well as several books, including *Close Encounters: Communicating in Relationships* (Guerrero, Andersen, & Afifi, 2011), *Nonverbal Communication* (Burgoon, Guerrero, & Floyd, 2010), and *Nonverbal Communication in Close Relationships* (Guerrero & Floyd, 2006). Her awards and honors include the Gerald R. Miller Early Career Achievement Award from the International Association for Relationship Research, the Dickens Research Award from the Western States Communication Association, and the Outstanding Doctoral Dissertation Award from the Interpersonal Communication Division of The International Communication Association. In 1994, she received her PhD from the University of Arizona.

**Leanne K. Knobloch** is an associate professor in the Department of Communication at the University of Illinois. Her research focuses on how communication shapes and reflects people's understandings of close relationships, particularly with respect to relationship development, relational uncertainty, and interdependence. In 2008, she received the Gerald R. Miller Award for

Early Career Achievement from the International Association for Relationship Research and the Early Career Award from the Interpersonal Communication Division of the National Communication Association. She earned her PhD from the University of Wisconsin–Madison in 2001.

**Ascan F. Koerner** is an associate professor of communication studies at the University of Minnesota–Twin Cities. His research focuses mainly on family communication patterns and the cognitive representations of relationships and their influence on interpersonal communication, including message production and message interpretations. His research has appeared in communication journals such as *Communication Monographs, Communication Theory, Human Communication Research, Journal of Marriage and Family, Journal of Social and Personal Relationships,* and a number of edited volumes. He earned his PhD from the University of Wisconsin–Madison in 1998.

**Timothy R. Levine** is a professor in the Department of Communication, Michigan State University. His research interests are diverse and include deception, communication and social relationships, persuasion, intercultural communication, and the history and philosophy of statistical inference. He has published extensively in communication journals such as *Human Communication Research* and *Communication Monographs.* He received his PhD in 1992 from Michigan State University.

**Erina L. MacGeorge** is an associate professor in Interpersonal and Health Communication in the Brian Lamb School of Communication at Purdue University. Her research, which has been published in journals including *Communication Monographs, Communication Research, Health Communication, Human Communication Research,* and *Sex Roles,* focuses on communication and coping processes, including advice giving, comforting, social support, and prayer. She has a particular interest in gender and culture as

influences on supportive interactions, and in the contribution of social support to the lives of women dealing with significant health issues, including miscarriage and breast cancer. She received her PhD in 1999 from the University of Illinois, Urbana–Champaign.

**Valerie Manusov** is a professor in the Department of Communication at the University of Washington. She was a cofounder of the nonverbal communication division in the National Communication Association and also served as that division's chair. She is the editor of *The Sourcebook of Nonverbal Measures: Going Beyond Words* and the coeditor of *The Sage Handbook of Nonverbal Communication,* among others. She works in the areas of nonverbal, interpersonal, and relational communication and has published more than 50 articles and chapters. Her particular research focus has been the interpretations made for ambiguous nonverbal cues in relationships and in politics.

**Matthew S. McGlone** is an associate professor in the Department of Communication Studies at the University of Texas at Austin. His research explores the linguistic devices people use to talk about abstract concepts (intelligence, justice, time, etc.) and the role of social stereotypes in interpersonal interaction. He has published articles in top journals in communication, cognitive science, discourse studies, psychology, and sociology. His research has been supported by extramural grants from the National Science Foundation and the U.S. Department of Education. He has served on the editorial board of *Psychological Science* and is currently on the boards of *Discourse Processes* and *Journal of Language and Social Psychology.* He recently edited a book with Mark L. Knapp on deceptive communication (*The Interplay of Truth and Deception,* 2009) and is writing a book with Joshua Aronson on stereotype threat. He received his PhD from Princeton University.

**Sandra Metts** is a professor in the School of Communication, Illinois State University. Her research interests include emotion in close relationships, sexual communication, relationship dissolution, and facework. Her books include *Facework* (with W. R. Cupach) and *Self-Disclosure* (with V. J. Derlega, S. Petronio, and S. T. Margulis). Her work has appeared in numerous edited volumes and journals such as *Communication Monographs*, *Human Communication Research*, *Western Journal of Communication*, *Communication Studies*, *Personal Relationships*, and *Journal of Social and Personal Relationships*. She is a past president of the Central States Communication Association, former editor of *Communication Reports*, and (currently) associate editor of the *Journal of Social and Personal Relationships*. She also conducts frequent training sessions for professional organizations and social groups on emotional competence. She received her PhD from the University of Iowa in 1982.

**Kristine (Fitch) Muñoz** is Professor of Communication Studies at the University of Iowa. She studies personal relationships and persuasion based on ethnographic fieldwork in Colombia, Spain, England, and the United States; her current work is a book that situates personal relationships within cultural codes of meaning. She has published or edited three books and 40 articles and book chapters in *Communication Monographs*, *Oralia*, *Communication Theory*, and other publications. She was the editor of *Research on Language and Social Interaction*. She received her PhD from the University of Washington.

**Karen K. Myers** is an assistant professor in the Department of Communication at the University of California, Santa Barbara. Her primary areas of research are membership negotiation, including organizational socialization and assimilation; vocational socialization; organizational identification; organizational knowledge; emotion management; and workplace relationships. Her work has appeared in publications such as *Human Communication Research*, *Communication Monographs*, *Communication Theory*, *Journal of Applied Communication Research*, *Management Communication*

*Quarterly*, and *Communication Yearbook*. She received her PhD from Arizona State University.

**Jon F. Nussbaum** is Professor of Communication Arts and Sciences and Human Development and Family Studies at Penn State University. He has published 13 books and more than 80 journal articles and book chapters. He studies communication behavior and patterns across the life span, including research on family, friendship, and professional relationships with well and frail older adults. His two recent books are *Brain Health and Optimal Engagement for Older Adults* and *Communication and Intimacy for Older Adults*. His current research centers on the relationship between communication behaviors and quality of life across the life span. He obtained his PhD from Purdue University in 1981.

**John G. Oetzel** is a professor in the Department of Management Communication at the University of Waikato, New Zealand. His research program centers on understanding and improving problematic interaction between and among people with different group identities (particularly cultural identities) within work and health settings. He is the author of *Intercultural Communication: A Layered Approach* (2009), coauthor (with Stella Ting-Toomey) of *Managing Intercultural Communication Effectively* (2001) and coeditor (with Stella Ting-Toomey) of *The SAGE Handbook of Conflict Communication* (2006). He has also authored more than 50 articles and book chapters in journals such as *Health Communication*, *Journal of Health Communication*, *Human Communication Research*, *Communication Monographs*, and *Communication Research*. He earned his PhD from the University of Iowa.

**Nicholas A. Palomares** is an associate professor in the Department of Communication, University of California, Davis. His research pertains to message production and processing, with specific foci on goal detection and gender-based language. His research has appeared in *Human Communication Research*, *Communication Research*,

*Journal of Language and Social Psychology, Communication Monographs,* and *Communication Yearbook.* He received his PhD from the University of California, Santa Barbara.

**Hee Sun Park** is an associate professor in the Department of Communication at Michigan State University. She teaches classes on organizational communication, cross-cultural communication, and research methods and applied statistics. Her current research projects examine multilevel aspects of group and organizational communication, cross-cultural differences in norms and interaction patterns, and health-related social influence processes and outcomes at workplaces. She received her PhD from the University of California, Santa Barbara.

**Malcolm R. Parks** is Professor of Communication at the University of Washington, where he also served as Associate Vice Provost for Research (1998–2006). He currently conducts research on interpersonal relationships, health communication, and social networks. Current projects include studies of impression formation and civic participation through online sites such as Facebook, research on what people know about others' social networks, and studies regarding how social networks might be used to promote health. His research and applied work has won numerous awards, including the Hammer Award for organizational innovation from the Office of the Vice President of the United States, the Woolbert Award from the National Communication Association, and, most recently, the Gerald R. Miller Book Award from the National Communication Association for his book *Personal Relationships and Personal Networks.* He is currently the editor of the *Journal of Communication.* In 1976, he received his PhD from Michigan State University.

**Loretta L. Pecchioni** is an associate professor in the Department of Communication Studies at Louisiana State University. Her research interests focus on interpersonal relationships across the life span, particularly in relation to family care giving. She is coauthor of *Communication and Aging* (2nd ed.) and *Life-Span Communication* and has published articles in *The Journal of Social and Personal Relationships, Health Communication, The Journal of Communication, Communication Reports, The Journal of Family Communication,* and *The Journal of Gerontology: Social Science.* She obtained her PhD from University of Oklahoma in 1998.

**Sally Planalp** is a professor in the Department of Communication Studies, The University of Texas–Austin. Her primary area of expertise is interpersonal communication with emphasis on face-to-face interaction, close relationships, emotion, and health communication. Her work has appeared in journals such as *Communication Monographs, Human Communication Research, Communication Theory, Journal of Social and Personal Relationships, Personal Relationships, Health Communication, American Journal of Hospice & Palliative Medicine,* and *Clinical Toxicology.* She has also contributed chapters to numerous edited volumes and is the author of *Communicating Emotion.* Her current major projects are collaborating on a communication training program for poison control centers and investigating the relationships between hospice volunteers and patients. In 1983, she received her PhD from the University of Wisconsin–Madison.

**Jeffrey D. Robinson** is an associate professor in the Department of Communication at Portland State University. His research foci include health communication, specifically provider–patient interaction, and the social organization of naturally occurring language. His research has appeared in communication journals such as *Human Communication Research, Journal of Communication, Communication Monographs,* and *Health Communication,* as well as medical journals such as *Journal of General Internal Medicine, Preventive Medicine, Social Science and Medicine,* and *Patient Education and Counseling.* He received his PhD in 1999 from the University of California at Los Angeles.

**Michael E. Roloff** is a professor of communication studies at Northwestern University. His research interests include bargaining and negotiation, conflict management, and persuasion. He wrote *Interpersonal Communication: The Social Exchange Approach* and coedited *Persuasion: New Directions in Theory and Research* (with Gerald R. Miller), *Interpersonal Processes: New Directions in Communication Research* (with Gerald R. Miller), *Social Cognition and Communication* (with Charles R. Berger), *Communication and Negotiation* (with Linda Putnam), and the second edition of *Handbook of Communication Sciences* (with Charles R. Berger and David Roskos-Ewoldsen). He has published in journals such as *Communication Monographs, Communication Research, Human Communication Research, International Journal of Conflict Management, Journal of Language and Social Psychology, Journal of Social and Personal Relationships,* and *Personal Relationships.* He is also Senior Associate Editor of *The International Journal of Conflict Management.* He served as editor of *Communication Yearbook* and currently is coeditor of *Communication Research.* He obtained his PhD from Michigan State University.

**Paul Schrodt** is the Philip J. & Cheryl C. Burguières Professor and an associate professor in the Department of Communication Studies at Texas Christian University. His research examines communication in stepfamily relationships, with a particular interest in behaviors that facilitate stepfamily functioning, stepparent–stepchild relationships, and mental well-being in family members. His research has appeared in journals such as *Human Communication Research, Communication Monographs, Personal Relationships,* and *Journal of Social and Personal Relationships.* He earned his PhD from the University of Nebraska–Lincoln in 2003.

**David R. Seibold** is a professor in the Department of Communication and Co-Director of the Graduate Program in Management Practice (College of Engineering), at the University of California, Santa Barbara. His research interests include interpersonal influence, group communication, organizational innovation and change, and theory–practice issues. He is a fellow of the International Communication Association and a Distinguished Scholar of the National Communication Association. He received his PhD from Michigan State University.

**Brian H. Spitzberg** is Senate Distinguished Professor in the School of Communication at San Diego State University. With William Cupach, he is coeditor and contributor to *The Dark Side of Interpersonal Communication* and *The Dark Side of Close Relationships* and coauthor of *Interpersonal Communication Competence, Handbook of Interpersonal Competence Research,* and *The Dark Side of Relationship Pursuit.* He is also author or coauthor of numerous scholarly publications on communication competence, communication assessment, conflict management, jealousy, and stalking. He currently serves on several editorial boards and as a member of the San Diego Stalking Strike Force and Association of Threat Assessment Professionals. He earned his PhD from the University of Southern California in 1981.

**Stella Ting-Toomey** is a professor of human communication studies at California State University (CSU), Fullerton. Her research interests have focused on fine-tuning the conflict face negotiation theory and the cultural/ethnic identity negotiation theory. She is the author and editor of 17 books. She has also published more than 90 journal articles and book chapters in journals such as *Communication Monographs, International Journal of Intercultural Relations,* and *International Journal of Conflict Management,* among others. She has delivered major keynote speeches on the theme of intercultural communication competencies in South Africa, Germany, Ireland, Norway, Portugal, China, Hong Kong, Japan, Canada, and different regions of the United States. She is the 2008 recipient of the 23-campus-wide CSU Wang Family Excellence Award and the 2007–2008 recipient of the CSU-Fullerton

Outstanding Professor Award. She earned her PhD from the University of Washington.

**Teresa L. Thompson** is a professor in the Department of Communication at the University of Dayton. She is the founding and current editor of the journal *Health Communication* and has published seven books and more than 75 articles on various aspects of health communication. Her work focuses on health care provider/patient interaction and communication and disability issues. She received her PhD in 1980 from Temple University.

**Karen Tracy** is Professor of Communication at the University of Colorado–Boulder. Her research investigates the problems, discourse strategies, and situated ideals of institutional interaction of different kinds, including emergency calls to the police, academic colloquia, education governance meetings, and, most recently, oral argument in appellate courts. She is a distinguished scholar in the National Communication Association, a past editor of *Research on Language and Social Interaction*, and the author of *Challenges of Ordinary Democracy: A Case Study in Deliberation and Dissent* (2010). Previous books include *Colloquium: Dilemmas of Academic Discourse* and *Everyday Talk: Building and Reflecting Identities*. She received her PhD from the University of Wisconsin.

**Anita L. Vangelisti** is the Jesse H. Jones Centennial Professor of Communication at the University of Texas at Austin. Her work focuses on the associations between communication and emotion in the context of close, personal relationships. She has published numerous articles and chapters and has edited or authored several books, including the *Handbook of Family Communication* and the *Handbook of Personal Relationships*. She is coeditor of the Cambridge University Press book series on Advances in Personal Relationships, was associate editor of *Personal Relationships*, and has served on the editorial boards of more than a dozen scholarly journals. She has received recognition for her research from the National Communication Association, the International Society for the Study of Personal Relationships, and the International Association for Relationship Research and has served as President of the International Association for Relationship Research. She received her PhD from the University of Texas at Austin.

**Joseph B. Walther** is Professor of Communication and Professor of Telecommunication, Information Studies & Media at Michigan State University. His research concerns the interplay of relational dynamics and computer-mediated communication systems, and his work has been influential in research on Web 2.0 environments, online dating, virtual groups and organizations, distributed education, and the mediation of interethnic relations. He has previously held positions at several universities in the United States and abroad and served as a division chair in the Academy of Management and the International Communication Association. He has twice been recognized with the National Communication Association's Woolbert Award for articles that have changed conceptualizations of communication phenomena and had an enduring impact on the field for more than 10 years. In 1990, he received his PhD from the University of Arizona.

**Kevin B. Wright** is a professor in the Department of Communication at the University of Oklahoma. His research focuses on life span communication, interpersonal communication, family communication, social support and health outcomes, and computer-mediated relationships. His work has appeared in more than 50 book chapters and journal articles, including *Journal of Communication*, *Communication Monographs*, *Journal of Social and Personal Relationships*, *Communication Quarterly*, *Journal of Applied Communication Research*, *Health Communication*, *Journal of Health Communication*, and *Journal of Computer-Mediated Communication*. He obtained his PhD from the University of Oklahoma in 1999.